Paris et le Rétabl[...]
[...]eux olympiques

[...]xactement le vendredi 25. La
[...]e Sorbonne : vaste rectangle
[...] lilas sale et orné de deux
— les nez augustes de deux
[...]et et Fénelon. En ce lieu
[...]it d'un de mes bachots et
[...]e l'„imagination créatrice,
[...]a Sorbonne en cette soirée de
[...] chose. Sur l'estrade ils
[...]lastron immaculé et l'habit
~~mondain~~ en vue des mon[...]
[...] de Tanzé dont j'avais fait
[...]l'Union des Sports Athlétiques
[...] pas seulement un mon[...]
[...]ond bon sens et une casac[...]
[...]t le recteur de l'Université
[...]ce Obolensky, maréchal de
[...]nie lequel avait accepté
[...]devait venir en personne.
[...] domaine distribuer des

Pierre de Coubertin

Selected Writings

Pierre de Coubertin

1863-1937

Olympism

Selected Writings

Editing Director:
Norbert Müller

International
Olympic
Committee

Lausanne 2000

Published by: International Olympic Committee
Château de Vidy, 1007 Lausanne, Switzerland

Translation: William H. Skinner, Washington, DC

Additional texts: John B.Dixon (CDI) and Translation Service of the IOC

Design and Cover: Dipl.Grafik Designerin Barbara Rau, Baden-Baden

Page design: T&T Communication, Le Mont-sur-Lausanne

Printed in Switzerland

ISBN 92-91490660

This oil painting, inspired by a photograph of Pierre de Coubertin at around 60 years of age, is the work of his nephew, Gaëtan de Navacelle, who knew him very well. The artist presented it as a gift to the President of the French Olympic Committee (CNOSF) at the time, Armand Massard. Today, the painting hangs in the Office of the President of the CNOSF in Paris.

Pierre de Coubertin

CONTENTS

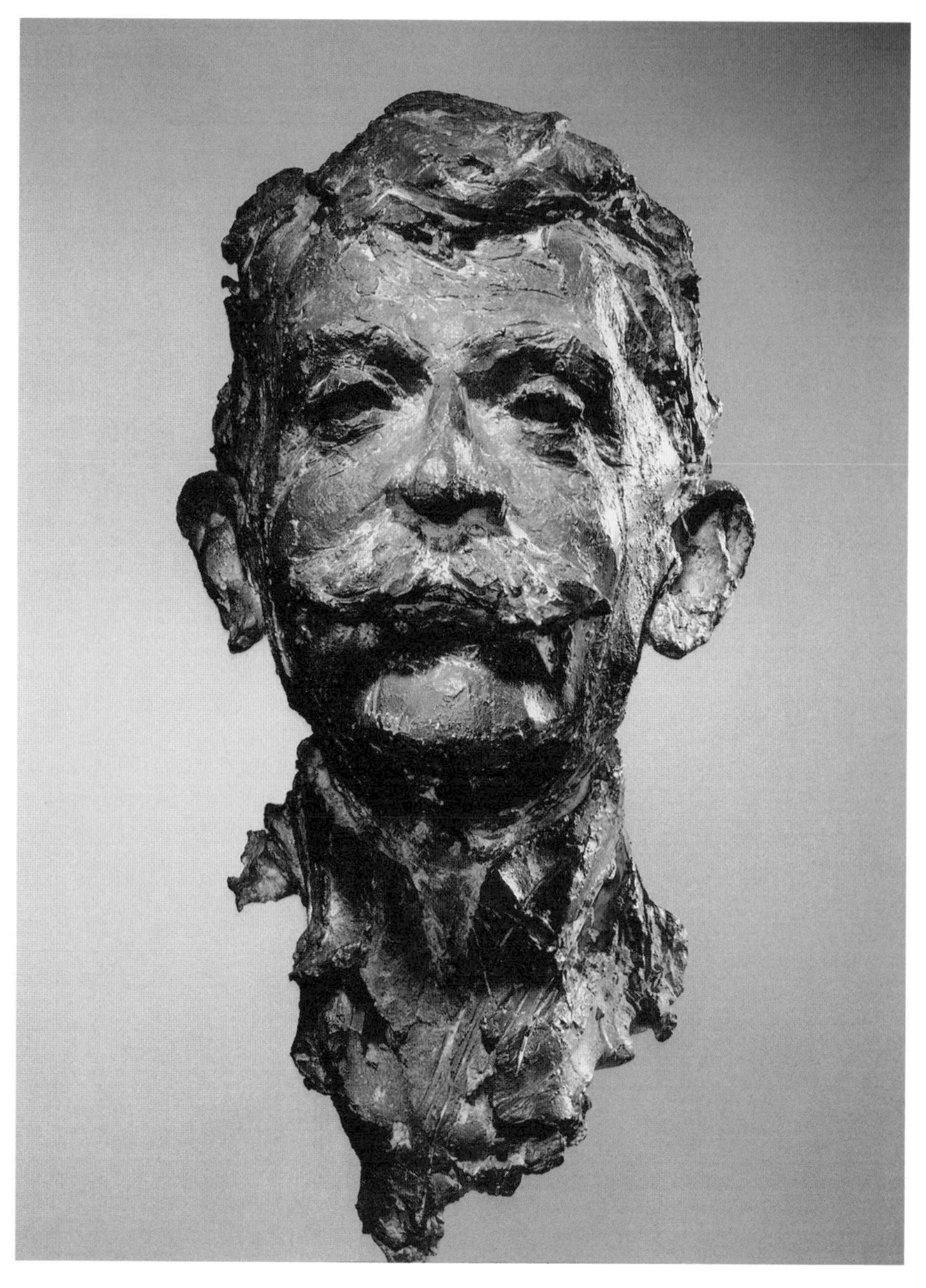

Pierre de Coubertin, cast in iron for the IOC by Karlheinz Oswald (GER) in 1999

PREFACE

by Juan Antonio Samaranch, IOC President

When I was elected President of the International Olympic Committee (IOC) in 1980, one of the items on my priority list was to promote Olympic education, as initiated by our founder Pierre de Coubertin. As a distinguished educator and talented writer, Coubertin devoted all his life to promoting physical education and Olympism, and to studying the history and culture of different countries and continents.

When Mr Geoffroy de Navacelle, great nephew of Pierre de Coubertin, dedicated to the cause of Olympism, came up with the idea of publishing the selected writings of our founder and renovator of the modern Olympic Games, it was enthusiastically accepted.

Dr Norbert Müller, the world-renowned 'Coubertin' researcher and professor at Johannes Gutenberg University in Mainz, Germany, was identified as the best choice to handle the editorial side of the project with the assistance of Mr de Navacelle and of Mr Raymond Gafner, Administrator delegate of the IOC. The three volume edition of the French version entitled "Textes Choisis Pierre de Coubertin" was finally published in 1986, and has since become a highly valued and widely-used reference book for the world at large. The work retrace the philosophical, educational, ethical and social aspects of Coubertin's rich literary legacy and led his renaissance in the academic world.

The necessity of promoting Olympic education and studies and propagating Coubertin's ideas in different languages, has led the IOC to publish an English edition of Coubertin's writings on Olympism, an initiative launched by Mr Geoffroy de Navacelle. Once again, Dr Norbert Müller was entrusted with the editorial tasks assisted by Mr de Navacelle. In contrast to the French edition, several new elements of Coubertin's writings, particularly on the early structure and organisation of the Olympic Movement, are included in this English edition.

This selection of Coubertin's writings, is a major contribution to Olympic education, and to strenghtening the role of the International Olympic Committee as the guardian of his legacy. "The best way of paying tribute to an illustrious past", wrote Coubertin, "is obviously to learn from its teachings in order to prepare for the future". The Olympism of today is faithful to Pierre de Coubertin's conception, building upon the foundations he laid down.

I am convinced that this first extensive English edition of Coubertin's writings, will undoubtedly be extremely useful, to all those interested by the Olympic ideal. I also hope that, the National Olympic Committees will make an effort, to produce it in their own languages in order to promote Olympic education.

In conclusion, I would like to pay tribute to Mr Geoffroy de Navacelle and Dr Norbert Müller, and express my sincere thanks to all those involved in one way or the aother in the production of the French and English editions. I recommend to all members of the Olympic Movement, and the public at large, to read this fascinating Olympic-related writings of Pierre de Coubertin.

Lausanne, April 2000

Juan Antonio Samaranch, IOC President

This manuscript by Pierre de Coubertin dates from 1889, i.e. three years before his first call at the Sorbonne to revive the Olympic Games. Aged 26, he had thus already developed some plans in the calm Normandy countryside. It is worth noting the humour with which he treats his own ideas and the pleasure he gets from thinking, imagining, inventing, devising... (Navacelle Collection)

À mes Idées

Mirville, 1er Septembre 1889

Mes Idées, je vous dédie mes Mémoires, en témoignage de reconnaissance pour les bons moments que vous m'avez procurés. Je ne suis pas sûr que vous soyez toutes, bien à moi, et qu'avant de venir habiter ma cervelle vous n'ayez pas résidé dans les cervelles d'autres personnes; néanmoins je vous sens bien à moi ce qui revient au même que si vous l'étiez réellement.

Nous ne nous sommes jamais beaucoup combattus. J'ai une tendance à vous accepter et à vous obéir, ayant confiance en votre rectitude et en votre justesse. Certaines d'entre vous ont déjà pris corps et se sont réalisées; cela donnera confiance aux autres, à la réalisation desquelles je n'ai pas eu le temps de travailler..... Elles attendront patiemment et ne me lâcheront pas

Oh! ne me lâchez pas! Vous êtes mon bonheur.
Penser, imaginer, inventer, combiner, quel plaisir.

Pierre de Coubertin

To my ideas

Mirville, 1st September 1889

To you, my ideas, I dedicate my memories as a mark of my gratitude for the happy times you gave me. I am not sure whether you are all mine, and that before you came to my mind you had not lived in other people's minds. Nevertheless, I feel you belong to me, which comes to the same thing as if you really did.
We never fought. I tend to accept you and obey you, and have faith in your soundness. Some of you have already taken shape and become reality. This gives confidence to other ideas, which I have not had time to work on. They will wait patiently and will not forsake me.
Oh! do not forsake me! You are my happiness.
To think, imagine, invent, devise: what pleasure.

FOREWORD

by Geoffroy de Navacelle de Coubertin

THE START OF A GREAT ADVENTURE

Known as the man who revived the Olympic Games, Pierre de Coubertin described himself as an educationalist, and explored all areas of human activity. As such, he deserves the worthy title of humanist, and even today his work is still amazingly topical.

This is shown by the many works published in the last 50 years by academics, historians and eminent researchers fascinated by this exceptional person. As a result, I felt that by publishing his writings and speeches I would be answering a need by making it easier for specialists and all those interested in human progress to gain access to them.

In 1981, I put this plan to the IOC President, Juan Antonio Samaranch, who agreed to the idea. Under his aegis, an international editorial committee was set up. This has pursued its work under the dynamic and expert leadership of Professor Norbert Müller, from the University of Mainz. For me this was the start of a thrilling experience.

The decision not to publish all of the known work, which runs to thousands of pages, just the part on Olympism and sports education could diminish the standing of Pierre de Coubertin, who wrote in one of his wills entitled "The Unfinished Symphony" that: "Olympism is only part of my life's work, approximately half in fact".

The late Professor Georges Rioux of the Sorbonne found an elegant solution by referring in his preliminary remarks to all the educational facets of Coubertin's work.

For him, it was a "Revelation" - the title he gave to the first of three volumes produced under the general title "Selected Writings by Pierre de Coubertin". These are supplemented by an extensive bibliography and an illustrated album on "his life through pictures".

It was obvious that world-wide distribution of the work would require an edition in English. Pierre de Coubertin, who was gifted at languages, had a good knowledge of English himself. He exercised his talents as a professional journalist by contributing to several publications in English, and his "Message to American Youth" marking the 40th anniversary of the revival of the Olympic Games shows the hope that he placed in such young people.

Attracted by the educational approach and sporting interest of the English-speaking world, which he knew well, he was inspired by the headmaster of Rugby School, Thomas Arnold; was a fellow pupil of the future British statesman, Austen Chamberlain, at the École des Sciences Politiques in Paris; and became friends with Professor William Sloane and American President Theodore Roosevelt.

The English edition was intended to appear in time for the Games in Atlanta, with the help of the chairman of the Pierre de Coubertin committee in America. This proved impossible, because of the long and painstaking work required to choose from the "Selected Works" those which would be of particular interest to an English-speaking readership. New texts were added for this purpose, which meant a considerable

The Chateau of Mirville, such as it is today, is close to the Paris - Le Havre railroad which allowed Pierre de Coubertin to come easily to Normandy, further more to sail for England and America. The lake was his favourite rowing place. (Navacelle Collection)

amount of work led by Norbert Müller. The translation was also checked in order to satisfy the largest possible number of readers.

In response to our request, the IOC provided its invaluable assistance, for which we express our grateful thanks.

In due course, I hope to see editions in other languages; but for now this is the one intended for the large number of English speakers around the world.

I hope that it will interest and give pleasure to those who read it.

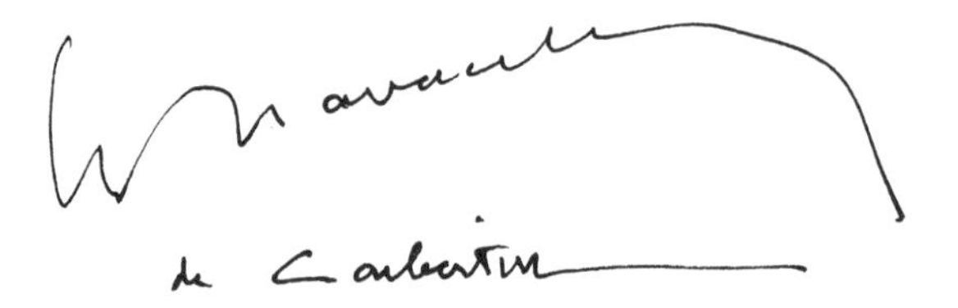

Geoffroy de Navacelle de Coubertin

EDITOR'S REMARKS

As part of its responsibility, set out in the Olympic Charter, to promote and develop Olympism throughout the world by means of Olympic education programmes, the IOC is clearly duty bound to publish the first comprehensive English edition of the Olympic-related writings of its founder Pierre de Coubertin. Such a collection ought to be available to the global market in time for the XXVIIth Olympic Games being held in Sydney in 2000. The need for an English version became clear throughout the Anglo-Saxon world, particularly after the IOC published, in French, three volumes of selected Coubertin writings in 1986[1] and following the publication in 1991 of a Bibliography of Coubertin Writings[2]. The only previous collection of Coubertin's writings in English, "The Olympic Idea", containing 64 Olympic-related texts and edited by the German Carl-Diem-Institute[3], had been out of print for a long time and, though its value was undisputed, it could no longer satisfy the demand from English-speaking countries for further Coubertin writings, particularly on the Olympic theme.

Interested readers of Coubertin's writings all over the world have had to deal not only with a general lack of suitable translations, but also with the fact that, even in France, the texts available in libraries, 95% of which are in French, are published as individual documents.

The debate on the future of the Olympic Movement and the validity of Olympic values, which has grown louder in the public domain as well as in sporting circles over the last twenty years, has inevitably re-awakened interest in the origins of the Movement and its foundation in Coubertin's work.

Coubertin and his writings are currently the subject of much academic discussion. The International Pierre de Coubertin Committee (CIPC) is particularly involved in the debate, in which the Coubertin conferences held in Lausanne (1986) and Le Havre (1997) were important milestones[4]. At its meetings in Olympia (Greece), the International Olympic Academy regularly discusses Coubertin's philosophies in great depth[5]. The English version of Coubertin's writings will be particularly helpful to the IOA.

1 IOC (ed.): *Textes choisis de Pierre de Coubertin.* Chief editor and research director: Norbert Müller. 3 volumes and 1 album. Zürich/Hildesheim/New York, Weidmann, 1986.
Volume I: Révélation [Revelation]. General introduction, selection and presentation of texts: Georges Rioux.
Volume II: Olympisme [Olympism]. Foreword, selection and presentation of texts: Norbert Müller.
Volume III: Pratique sportive [Sports Practice]. Foreword, selection and presentation of texts: Norbert Müller and Otto Schantz.
Album: Pierre de Coubertin – sa vie par l'image [his life in pictures], by Geoffroy de Navacelle.

2 See N. Müller, O. Schantz: *Bibliographie/Bibliography/Bibliografia: Pierre de Coubertin,* CIPC, Lausanne, 1991.

3 See Coubertin: *The Olympic Idea,* Discourses and Essays, edited by *Carl-Diem-Institut*, German Sports University, Cologne. Translated by John G.Dixon, Schorndorf, Hofmann, 1967. [=Coubertin: The Olympic Idea, Schorndorf 1967.]

4 See N. Müller (ed. dir.): *The Relevance of Pierre de Coubertin Today,* Report of the Symposium held at the University of Lausanne, 18-20 March 1986, edited by the International Pierre de Coubertin Committee, Niedernhausen, Schors, 1987.
See also N. Müller (ed. dir.): *Coubertin and Olympism. Questions for the Future.* Report of the Congress held at the University of Le Havre, 17-20 September 1997, edited by the International Pierre de Coubertin Committee, Niedernhausen/Strasbourg/Sydney, 1998.
See also J.J. MacAloon: *This Great Symbol. Pierre de Coubertin and the Origins of the Modern Olympic Games,* Chicago/London, Chicago University Press, 1981.
See also Y.P. Boulongne: *Pierre de Coubertin, humanisme et pédagogie: dix leçons sur l'Olympisme*, Lausanne, IOC, 1999.
See also J. Durry: *Pierre de Coubertin. The Visionary.* Paris, Comité Français Pierre de Coubertin, 1996.

5 See N. Müller: *The International Olympic Academy/IOA: Through its Lectures 1961-1998,* IOC, Lausanne, 1998.

Pierre de Coubertin's numerous publications amount to around 15,000 printed pages, the breadth and diversity of which can be seen in the appended bibliography[6]. His works comprise 30 books, 50 pamphlets, 1,300 articles and around thirty leaflets and posters.

The idea of publishing a selection of Coubertin's writings in English was mooted by Geoffroy de Navacelle de Coubertin, Honorary President of the International Pierre de Coubertin Committee (CIPC) and George Hirthler (Atlanta), an enthusiastic Coubertin protagonist in the United States, at the Centennial Olympic Games held in 1996. It was decided that the collection should comprise around 150 texts on the subject of Olympism and that basic texts on Coubertin's educational ideas ("Revelation") should be included as an introduction, but that this should be shorter than in the French edition.

The texts were selected on the basis of the following criteria:

- Originality of the text;
- Relationship to Olympism;
- Variation in order to show the dimensions of Olympism;
- Density of information concerning Olympism;
- Texts referring to North America, especially English articles, should be given special consideration;
- Texts on "sports practice" should relate to Olympic sports (because of the limited size of the publication).

3,200 pages were classified under the "Olympism" heading and carefully analysed so that any repetition could be omitted. The remaining books, pamphlets, magazine and newspaper articles were studied and listed.

Repetition, however, could not be avoided completely as some of Coubertin's key thoughts appear throughout his work. Some important texts could also have been included under a number of different headings.

Pierre de Coubertin's correspondence either as IOC President or as a private individual has not been included, as such material is very different in character and so extensive that extra volumes would be needed[7]. However, we have included a number of memoranda written by Coubertin when he was IOC President.

Some of the texts can't definitely be traced back to Coubertin, but contents and style, partly detailed knowledge only he could have had, speak for him as the author. Additionally, particular magazines show evidence of his work. Modern computer analysis of text structure and vocabulary will no doubt provide further evidence in the future. In same cases, the editor has found it necessary to correct obvious mistakes in the English versions of Coubertin's texts taken from previously published sources. This refers mainly to orthography, but also sometimes to grammar or meaning. These changes have not been indicated in the texts in order to provide maximum readability.

Many texts have been enriched by the addition of photographs, illustrations or further documentation in order to enhance the information provided in a vivid and attractive style. Some of the illustrations have only recently been discovered.

This collection, entitled "Olympic Dimensions", is designed to illustrate the variety and importance of Pierre de Coubertin's Olympic-related writings. In his "Unfinished symphony", the final item of the book, Coubertin himself writes that only around half of his work is connected to Olympism. In fact, just a third of his printed works are concerned with the subject. Of Coubertin's numerous historical, contemporary and political discourses, only the small proportion dealing with Olympic-related issues could be included in this collection.

The introduction was written by French pedagogue and psychologist Georges Rioux (Sorbonne), originally for the French collection published in 1986. Rioux[8] revealed to the experts a side of Coubertin on which very little light had previously been shed, ie the "revelation" of his ideas. His introduction is based on a historico-cultural view and interpretation of Coubertin's life and work. This is also mentioned a number of times in the notes on the texts contained in Part I. Rioux's observations have lost none of their meaning, although they had to be considerably shortened for the English version[9].

The first part of this edition, entitled "Revelation", explains how Coubertin developed his ideas, documenting the ever-prominent educational dimension of his work. This side of Coubertin, in both his youth and later life, is largely unknown.

A total of 46 documents are grouped together in chapters headed "The Search for a New Education", "Permanency of the Educational Battle" and "The String of Events". Although only a third of the texts included in the French volume entitled "Revelation"[10] appear in this English version, these essays nevertheless help to explain the philosophical and anthropological foundations of Coubertin's Olympism.

The second part of this collection, under the heading "Olympism", portrays the whole breadth of Coubertin's Olympic thinking, actions and feelings. 145 of his writings are presented under the following three main themes:

- Historical Perspectives on Olympism;
- The Philosophical and Educational Dimension of Olympism;
- The Olympic Movement.

We have not been able to include the history of the IOC[11] nor individual Olympic Games, although many of the texts deal with specific Olympic events. It is necessary to question the extent to which the essays reflect Coubertin's very personal views on the various events, for this is precisely what makes them so interesting.

Each chapter is set out in chronological order.

In order to help the reader, each chapter and most of the individual texts are introduced or commented upon by Norbert Müller. His observations are taken from identical texts in the French Coubertin collection, although he has added to some and written new ones for the 50 texts which did not appear in the earlier publication. The introductions and notes are designed to fill in chronological gaps, to explain why individual texts have been included in a particular chapter and to provide cross-references. However, they should not be considered a form of "critical apparatus".

If not indicated otherwise, footnotes referring to Coubertin's texts were written by Coubertin himself whereas those referring to the introductions were written by N. Müller.

6 Previous estimates of 60,000 printed pages are inaccurate: many texts have been published several times, often under different titles, which may have led to some confusion.

7 Two good examples of publications of Coubertin's correspondence are:
1) Carl-Diem-Institut (ed.): *Dokumente zur Frühgeschichte der Olympischen Spiele*, Cologne, Barz & Beienburg, 1970;
2) Czechoslovak Olympic Committee (ed.): Baron Pierre de Coubertin – Dr Jiri Guth-Jarkovsky, Prague, 1973.

8 Rioux, who died in 1991, was at school in Algiers with Albert Camus, who won the 1957 Nobel Prize for Literature. The character Dr Rieux in Camus' novel *La peste* was modelled on him.

9 Another reason for this is that many of the texts mentioned in the original introduction were excluded from the English version for space reasons. See Rioux, G.: *Propos liminaires* in *Textes choisis*, Vol.I: *Révélation*. Zürich, Hildesheim, New York, Weidmann, 1986, pp.1-34.

10 IOC (ed.): *Textes choisis de Pierre de Coubertin*. Editing Director: Norbert Müller. Volume I: Revelation. General introduction, selection of texts and presentation: Georges Rioux, Zürich, Hildesheim, New York, Weidmann, 1986.

11 See Gafner, R.(ed. dir.): *The IOC, One Hundred Years*. The Idea – The Presidents – The Achievements. 3 volumes. IOC, Lausanne, 1994-1996.

This edition provides information and help for many different interest groups. The following target groups have been identified:

The entire academic world (History, Philosophy, Pedagogy/Education, Sociology, Psychology, Comparative Studies and the various disciplines of Sports Science in particular);

the International Olympic Academy (IOA);

National Olympic Academies;

High Schools (teachers, students, libraries);

Journalists (press, radio, TV);

Individuals interested in Coubertin and Olympism;

Public and private libraries (especially university libraries);

Bid and Organising Committees for Olympic Games;

National and International Sports Federations;

National Olympic Committees;

the International Olympic Committee.

The following three indices have been compiled to help readers find references quickly and tap into the wide range of Coubertin's Olympic-related writings:

People,

Key words,

Cities, countries and continents.

Certain parts of this collection were compiled and structured through intensive collaboration over a number of years with my colleague, Dr Otto Schantz (University of Strasbourg II), who helped me produce the 1986 French version. I would like to take this opportunity to thank him for his contribution, which includes the appended bibliography.

William H. Skinner (Washington DC) took on the tricky job of translating the texts, rendering them in his own style, which is sometimes quite free but always very readable.

The IOC's Translation Service provided further translations, particularly Coubertin's "Olympic Memoirs" and the captions.

The Carl and Liselott Diem Research Archives (Director Dr Karl Lennartz), based at the German Sports University in Cologne, kindly allowed us to use 15 texts from the 1967 Coubertin collection "The Olympic Idea"*.

I would like to thank my colleagues, both staff and students, Dr Holger Preuss, Dr Heike Jüngst, Alexandra Pfirschke, Karin Theel and Ralf Tuttas, who have all been extremely helpful, as well as Mrs Barbara Rau for her design work.

I am also grateful to my wife Eva and my children Teresa, Andreas and Susanna for their patience.

The fact that the goal of publishing this collection worldwide in time for the Sydney Olympics and the new millennium was achieved in such a short period of time is due not least to the close and dependable co-operation of Mr Geoffroy de Navacelle de Coubertin, the translators and the IOC's Department of International Cooperation, particularly Mr Fékrou Kidane, Mrs Katia Mascagni Stivachtis and Ms Sylvie Espagnac. I would like to extend my heartfelt thanks to everybody involved.

Mainz, October 1, 1999

Dr Norbert Müller, Editing Director

Professor at the Johannes Gutenberg - Universität Mainz (Germany)

PIERRE DE COUBERTIN'S REVELATION

by Professeur Georges Rioux (†), Sorbonne

Tracing the origins and development of an extraordinary concept is not an easy task. It is impossible to account for such a concept by circumstances alone; it cannot be explained by cause and effect, nor can it be understood merely by listing a set of reasons.

Freedom involves the person as an individual, and character determines that person's actions. Ideas and achievements must not be dissociated from either the designs or the social atmosphere in which they were formed and fostered.

All this applies to the work of Pierre de Coubertin, who stands with one foot firmly planted in the closing days of the nineteenth century, the other in the earliest days of the twentieth.

BIOGRAPHICAL NOTES

Charles-Pierre, "son of Charles-Louis, Baron Fredy de Coubertin, age 40, and of Agathe-Marie-Marcelle Gigault de Crisenoy, age 38, his wife," was born on "January 1, 1863, at 5:00 P.M.[1]," at the small family residence at 20 rue Oudinot, in the Seventh Arrondissement of Paris.

Two brothers and a sister had been born long before him[2]. His father's ancestors, of long-standing noble lineage, most likely descend from an Italian family that emigrated to France. At the court of Louis XI, there was a king's chamberlain named Pierre de Fredy, Seigneur de la Motte, to whom a new French coat of arms was granted in 1477. A century later, in 1577, one of his grandsons, Jean Fredy, purchased the Seigneurie de Coubertin, located in the Chevreuse valley near Versailles. In 1720, another descendant built the chateau that is now home to the Fondation Coubertin[3].

His mother's family was of very ancient nobility, descendants of a companion of the Viking Rollo, first duke of Normandy. That family owns the beautiful Mirville property in the Caux region[4], with its sixteenth-century chateau built in a style typical of the region. The charm of these sites was to play an important role in the life of Pierre de Coubertin[5].

* The texts 3.3, 3.4,3.6 - 3.9, 3.17, 3.19, 3.20, 3.26, 4.1/4, 4.2.2/26, 4.2.2/41, 4.2.2/48 and 6.5.3 were translated by John B. Dixon.

1 The text in quotation marks is taken from Pierre de Coubertin's birth certificate, now in the Archives of the City of Paris.

2 Paul (1847), Albert (1848), and Marie (1855).

3 The Fondation Coubertin was established in 1968 by Yvonne de Coubertin, Pierre de Coubertin's niece, and by Jean Bernard, former president of the Association des Compagnons du Devoir du Tour de France, an organization of top workers. The purpose of this foundation is "to unite hand and mind" through the meeting of two worlds, one with a very ancient family, and intellectual and spiritual tradition, the other being the world of the aristocracy of labor.

4 The Caux region located on the north bank of the Seine, called "Upper Normandy".

5 Pierre de Coubertin's mother, Marie-Marcelle Gigault de Crisenoy, daughter of the Marquis de Mirville, inherited the entire estate located near Bolbec in Upper Normandy. Pierre spent most of his youth there.

His father, Charles-Louis de Coubertin, a painter[6], was a reserved man, even-tempered and generally serious in demeanor. His paintings reveal a sense of ordered harmony, in which sensitivity is subdued.

Madame de Coubertin was an elegant, well-educated musician, deeply drawn to any events that appealed to her emotional character. Yet she also knew how to exercise self-control. A pious and charitable woman, a Catholic as was her husband, she devoted her energies to the poor, and maintained deep friendships. She opened Pierre's mind, and began to educate him from a very early age.

Both parents were deeply attached to the past – he through taste, she through feeling –, and did not hide their faithfulness to royalist and legitimist ideas. They were profoundly patriotic, and were seriously troubled by the defeat in 1870 and the insurrection that followed[7]. Family life ebbed and flowed along with pleasures and joys, pains and shared hardships. The four Coubertin children remained profoundly marked by this national unhappiness.[8]

Influences and events play out according to the basic character of each individual. Very early on, Pierre de Coubertin got his first taste of life at Mirville, a rural setting that brought him to know himself[9]. There he found perfect harmony, along with the joy of activity performed in a context of freedom. Work, play, reading, music, drawing[10] – it all captivated Coubertin, leaving an indelible mark on him. The years passed. In Paris, his parents enrolled him at the Collège Saint-Ignace, a school run by the Jesuits on the Rue de Madrid. Father Jules Carron, who taught Humanities and Rhetoric, instilled in him a love of Greek antiquity, where body and soul were joined in a single effort of harmonious exaltation. In a world where ideas shape marble, art becomes a revelation of the simplicity of perfection, and sensation of the beautiful becomes the discovery of a truer world[11]. Pierre de Coubertin was already beginning his search for authentic humanity through world history.

A Bachelier ès Lettres and Bachelier ès Sciences at age 17, Coubertin achieved the balance that was so keenly sought. He participated in several sports, particularly fencing, horseback riding, boxing, and rowing.

At that point, Coubertin was faced with having to choose a career. His family's traditional principles and his own personal perspective clashed, since they were not proceeding on the same basic assumptions. In the end, in order not to disappoint his family, Coubertin studied law, but he preferred the courses at the École Supérieure des Sciences Politiques[12]. These courses appealed to his interest in the transformations in contemporary society, where everything, from social customs to scientific facts, and from moral practices to religious demands, was in flux. The times called for an ability to transform oneself and to progress, while also requiring a general education rooted in human universality.

In France, democracy had become entrenched. Pierre de Coubertin felt that he was a republican[13] at heart. For him, the duty of every individual was to save his humanity by taking responsibility for his own capacity to evolve. To accomplish this, the form of education then in force had to be changed. A fight had to be waged against didacticism and against discipline imposed from the outside. A form of education capable of fulfilling all of man's needs, at every level, had to be found.

While courageously shouldering on his duties as a family man[14], Pierre de Coubertin pursued his ideals unwaveringly. He believed that careful study of the past would serve as preparation for a better future; he hoped to be the educational guide to that future.

COUBERTIN'S WORK IN EDUCATION

Pierre de Coubertin's destiny was forged in the privacy of a schoolboy's dream. From that time on, he viewed the problem of education as the key to human happiness.

Each of Coubertin's written or spoken comments, which cover a very broad range of topics, provides an accurate view of his basic principles. The very essence of his philosophy was well established in the first decade of this century: the accelerated pace of change in the world calls for a new type of preparation through education.

As early as the end of the eighteenth century, civilization was undergoing a transformation. This evolution, picked up speed increasingly over the course of the nineteenth century. Machinery and the speed of modern means of communication meant

6 Charles de Coubertin, painter, studied with François-Edouard Picot, who in turn had studied with the painter David. He exhibited genre scenes and works depicting religious history at the Salon from 1846 through 1887. In 1896, he painted his famous allegorical painting entitled "The Restoration of the Olympic Games," which appeared on the cover of every issue of the *Revue Olympique* from 1906 through 1914.

7 During the Armistice, France had elected a National Assembly in February 1871, to decide on peace or the resumption of war. Meeting at Bordeaux, this Assembly appointed Thiers "head of the executive power of the Republic." Yet the exaltation produced by the siege of Paris, aggravated by the entry of German troops into the capital on March 1, the antagonism between the monarchists in the Assembly and the Parisian Republicans, and awkward financial measures, unleashed an insurrection that began with the uprising of March 18. Paris, left to its own devices, adopted a government called "the Commune." That government entered into war with the national government, which had withdrawn to Versailles. The week from May 20 to 28 was a bloody one, after the entry of regular troops into Paris. Violent street fights broke out all over the city, and the Hôtel de Ville, the Tuileries, and the Cour des Comptes were burned. Those in revolt shot their hostages (including the Bishop of Paris); they themselves were hunted down by the victors. In all, 20,000 were killed, 50,000 arrested, and 6,000 were sentenced to hard labor, deportation, and prison.

8 Ernest Renan captured well when he wrote, at the time: "We are living in the shadow of a shadow. What will they live on after us?" Ernest Renan (1823-1892), author of "L'Avenir de la Science" ["The Future of Science"] and of "Origines du Christianisme" ["The Origins of Christianity"]. On the subject of this quotation, see: Chaix-Ruy, Jules, "Le surhomme de Nietzsche à Teilhard de Chardin" ["Superman from Nietzsche to Teilhard de Chardin"], Paris, Centurion, 1965, p. 95.

9 The setting of the château de Mirville is particularly pleasant, inspiring a zest for life. The sale of the property toward the end of his life was a painful experience for Coubertin. Happily, Mr. Geoffroy de Navacelle, Coubertin's grand-nephew, repurchased the property, which thus remains in the family.

10 Pierre de Coubertin was quite a talented draftsman, a talent inherited from his father.

11 Esthetic harmony fosters spiritual growth. The universe is built around the individual who has become reconciled to himself: he rediscovers peace of mind.

12 Coubertin first rejected the idea of following in the footsteps of his brother Albert, who had pursued a career in the Army.

13 On May 4, 1903, in the *Indépendance Belge* (No. 52, p. 1), Coubertin wrote: "I have always belonged to the Republican party, and the Republic that I claim is the Republic espoused by Gambetta, by Jules Ferry, and by Carnot..."

14 On March 12, 1895 in Paris, he married Marie Rothan, a Protestant, the daughter of an Alsatian diplomat and a great collector. They had two children: Jacques, who died in 1950, and Renée, who died in 1975 (neither had any children). Gustave Rothan, Marie's father wrote *L'Affaire du Luxembourg* [The Luxembourg Affair](1884); *La politique française en 1866* [French Politics in 1866](1884); *L'Allemagne et l'Italie* [Germany and Italy] (1885); *L'Europe et l'avènement du Second Empire* [Europe and the Advent of the Second Empire] (1892); and *La France et sa politique extérieure* [France and its Foreign Policy] (1893), published by Calmann-Lévy in Paris.

increased production and more frequent contacts. The age of steam gave way to the age of electricity. Steam engines were replaced by internal combustion engines. At the close of the nineteenth century, the age of steel was about to begin. Mines and factories created cities. Advances in navigation caused port cities to expand. Urban life was changing. Popular culture was about to expand as a result of the invention of Linotype, which cut the cost of printing.

The late nineteenth century was content with empirical solutions temporarily applied to existing problems. Yet changes in the mode of existence stirred up new attitudes. At every level, individuals were attempting to express the meaning of what they felt; they no longer wished to be limited by the restrictive behavior of a bygone era. The desire for freedom was awakening; the rise of democracy was to become one of the hallmarks of the age.

An intellectual and social system ill-suited to historical circumstances gradually loses steam.

The general spirit of education became increasingly incompatible with the new conditions of scientific, industrial, and social life. While the issue of the freedom of education was one of the main concerns of governments discord was increasing between traditional education and the needs of a society in full transformation. Old educational principles were denounced for being overloaded with programs, using formal methods, and requiring a discipline imposed from the outside. These critiques were particularly applicable to secondary education, which was thenceforth indispensable in providing the framework of the democratic regime.

Education was to be a constant field of action for Coubertin. His analysis of the situation in his day was unfavorable. Why not engage, as early on as during secondary education, in the delicate apprenticeship of the democracy that is awaiting the citizen of tomorrow?

Coubertin felt that parents and teachers did not sufficiently understand what a student at a boarding institution feels behind the bars of prohibitions.

Everyone must discover the source of that essential energy in himself.

The young Coubertin had already become familiar with these values during his childhood at Mirville. Wherever he was, during his free time he broke away and participated in sports. The dynamics of sports brought him to take the initiative in the particular situations in which he was involved. Since the capacity to make decisions goes hand in hand with a need for balanced self-knowledge, Coubertin strove to master his situation. In this way, gradually he began to come to terms with the truth of his own life.

Although sports showed him inaccessible recesses hidden from reason, the stillness of reading opened up horizons of intellectual richness, moral effort, and esthetic spontaneity for him. The young Coubertin knew that it takes courage and intelligence to make all these opportunities real.

In his thirst for knowledge, he was quite taken by reading the works of Hippolyte Taine, a very influential author at the time[15]. One work in particular, *Notes sur l'Angleterre* [Notes on England], drew his attention. This 374-page work was published in 1872, and its chapter on education provided answers to Coubertin's primary educational concerns. Taine discusses the full value of the education provided to English students, as opposed to that given to French school children. According to Taine, two men were responsible for this fortunate transformation in English education: Canon Kingsley and the Rev. Thomas Arnold[16].

Coubertin could not resist the lure of England and set off in 1883, at age twenty. He was to return to England every year thereafter, in the spring or fall[17].

Taine's influence on the young Coubertin roused his spirit of criticism. The philosopher, taught him two approaches: first, to search for the governing faculty that, as Taine saw it, guides human action[18]. Then look for factors that influence this basic disposition[19].

Between his first trip across the English Channel to do research in comparative education and the publication of the results of that research from 1886 to 1889, Coubertin benefited from significant influences on the orientation of his thinking. Two professors at the École des Sciences Politiques, Albert Sorel and Anatole Leroy-Beaulieu, influenced Coubertin deeply, through the clarity and the rich content of their lectures alike.

In his lectures and publications, Albert Sorel was in tune with the natural curiosity of the young Coubertin, who was always after the deeper meaning of things.

Anatole Leroy-Beaulieu taught contemporary history. He stressed what was essential in the evolution of current events[20]. Working with him, Coubertin learned to describe situations and to seek out what is important in the daily life of ideas. The young Coubertin had long been interested in the great theoreticians.[21]

15 Hippolyte-Adolph Taine (1828-1893). French philosopher, historian, and critic. He attempted to apply the experimental methods of the natural sciences to the output of the human mind.

16 Thomas Arnold, born on the Isle of Wight in 1795, died in 1842. He entered holy orders in 1828. Appointed director of Rugby School that same year. The reforms he introduced in education affected all the schools in England. In 1841, one year before his death, he was appointed professor of modern history at Oxford. He wrote *a History of Rome*, produced an edition of *Thucydides*, and wrote *an Introduction to the Study of Modern History*. In 1875, the *Journal de la Jeunesse* printed the *Aventure de Tom Brown à Rugby* [*Adventures of Tom Brown at Rugby*], adapted from the work by Thomas Hughes entitled *Scenes in the Life of an English College*, written in English in 1857 and translated into French in 1875 (in 1861, the same author had published *Tom Brown at Oxford*). Pierre de Coubertin had been stirred by reading the *Journal de la Jeunesse*. Pierre de Coubertin's library included a work by Emena J. Worboise, *The Life of Dr. Arnold*, London 1885.

17 Pierre de Coubertin was impressed by the Victorian era (Queen Victoria, 1819-1901), a time when the British Empire was at its peak. When Coubertin left for England, the educational atmosphere in France was oppressive. In 1867, Victor de la Prade published a study provocatively entitled *L'Éducation homicide* [Homicidal Education]. The events of 1870-71 inspired Renan to publish his reflections on *La Réforme intellectuelle et morale* [Intellectual and Moral Reform], which came out in 1871. Michel Bréal published "a few words" on "Public Instruction," running to a mere 410 pages! (1872). Jules Simon published a 432-page book on *La Réforme de l'enseignement secondaire* [Reforming Secondary Education](1874). In 1882, Ferdinand Buisson began to head up the editing team of his *Dictionnaire de Pédagogie* [Dictionary of Education], which was published at first in fascicles.

18 Such as the faculty of poetry for La Fontaine, and the faculty of public oratory for Livy.

19 For Taine, this essentially meant "race" – with the philosophical definition of the period –, "time" and "milieu." Since man cannot escape from his origins, the interplay of these factors is found in all creation.

20 Anatole Leroy-Beaulieu published studies on French politics. In 1879*: Un empereur, un roi, un pape, une restauration* [One Emperor, One King, One Pope, One Restoration], *L'Église et le libéralisme de 1830 à nos jours* [The Church and Liberalism from 1830 to the Present], *L'Europe des Tsars et les Russes* [The Europe of the Czars and the Russians], etc.

21 He read Rabelais, Montaigne, Jean-Jacques Rousseau's *Émile ou de l'Éducation* [Emile, or On Education] in the 1824 edition, which he owned. He was familiar with the work by Dupanloup, *De l'Éducation* [On Education], published in 1851. Coubertin was also aware of the recent publication by Gabriel Compayré on *L'Éducation en France depuis le XVIe siècle* [Education in France Since the 16th Century], two volumes published in 1879.

Coubertin read John Locke's *Thoughts on Education*, published in 1643[22], Herbert Spencer's *Treatise on Intellectual, Moral and Physical Education*, published in 1861 and translated into French in 1878, James Mill and John Stuart Mill, and Alexander Bain's reflection on the *Sciences of Education*, published in 1879. His basic reading also included Darwin's *Origin of Species*. Darwin's transformationist system swept away all scientific theories, philosophies, and religious dogmas at a single blow.

Above all, Coubertin remained deeply marked by the harmonious Greek vision of philosophy, literature, the sciences and the arts to which the Jesuit Priest Jules Carron had introduced him.

With his passion for esthetics, Coubertin was well aware of the role of art. By linking the transitory to the eternal, art is capable of evoking everything that flows to and from man, in a manner that embraces all the rhythms of the soul[23].

Thus, over the course of his first few weeks in England, Pierre de Coubertin already knew that mere instruction must be transformed into general culture, and then flourish in a context of humanism.

Coubertin soon visited English and Irish schools and universities, observing them on several occasions. He questioned teachers and students alike, in an effort to understand fully educational changes that could not have been foreseen earlier in the nineteenth century[24].

The positions taken by such great writer-philosophers as Rabelais and Montaigne in France and Locke in England, who favored physical exercise as a guarantee of overall, healthy balance in man, did not lead to the desired changes. However, Canon Kingsley managed to persuade the young men in his entourage that the moral ideal could be served effectively only by strong, brave men. In learning to know himself, the athlete comes to master and effectively to associate the desire for strength with the desire for values. The "Christian athlete" movement inspired by Kingsley reached Oxford and Cambridge Universities[25].

When Coubertin reached England, education also bore the strong imprint of Thomas Arnold, a clergyman and director of Rugby College for fourteen years, starting in 1828[26]. By making sports a serious occupation, Arnold transformed the school into an institution. Taken together, initiative, the freedom to form a team that provides for the full development of the individual, and the taste for the fight gave each individual a style, the English style, that he would never lose[27].

Intellectual and physical culture can then accomplish their work unimpeded, never insisting on anything, but drawing strength from courage.

In Paris, some parents blamed all their children's failures on overwork. Others deemed the number of class hours excessive and leisure time too short. In general, they found that their children's education was overly intellectual.

For Coubertin, permanent and excessive fatigue derived essentially from physical weakness, intellectual dullness, and moral degradation. The key to the problem, therefore, lay in improving the human capacity of the physical education being dispensed at the time. Therefore, new principles of responsibility for games had to be introduced into French education. Following the example of England, the establishment of free associations among high school and college students to develop individual initiative should be encouraged. To engage freely in the athletic games one has chosen is to regain self-possession, disengaging from stereotypes imposed from the outside, becoming responsible and truly preparing oneself to be a man.

On July 1, 1888, the "Committee for the Propagation of Physical Exercise in Education" was founded, with Pierre de Coubertin as Secretary General. Jules Simon chaired the committee.[28]

That same summer Pascal Grousset[29], led a campaign against the "Anglomaniacs of sport," taking up the expression previously used by critics with regard to a racing event held in the Bois de Boulogne by the recently-founded Racing Club de France.

22 *Thoughts on Education* was translated into French twice, in 1695 and 1743. The work inspired Jean-Jacques Rousseau.

23 Specifically, Coubertin was familiar with allegorical works that render the full significance of education. A painting from Herculaneum shows the *Education of Achilles*. That same theme was taken up over the centuries by Primaticcio, Rubens, Philippe de Champaigne, Pompeo Batoni, Jean-Baptiste Regnault, and Eugène Delacroix (who died in 1863, the year of Pierre de Coubertin's birth). Poussin painted the *Education of Jupiter,* as well as the *Education of Bacchus*. Titian depicted the *Education of Eros*, while Murillo painted the *Education of the Virgin*. One of the main concerns of the age was expressed in 1875 by the sculptor De La Planche, in a marble group representing *Maternal Education*: a peasant woman helps her little daughter practice her spelling, while holding her near, tenderly.

24 Taine's book on England was preceded by a 664-page report presented in 1868 by Demogeot, Montucci, and Dr. Hillairet, entitled *L'Enseignement en Angleterre et en Écosse* [Education in England and Scotland]. Sent by the Ministry of Public Instruction under Victor Duruy, to inquire into the state of secondary education in Great Britain, they returned with a description that was anything but flattering. What a contrast between this image and the one given by Taine! What a fortunate change in school life!

25 The Stoic influence of Epictetus and Marcus Aurelius is clear here, as is the influence of Seneca, who states that one must be in complete possession of oneself in order to act morally in the various situations that life presents. All of this is covered by St. Augustine's dictum, "*Ab exterioribus ad interiora, ab inferioribus ad superiora.*" Body and soul lend life to one another in the balanced unity of the individual who is responsible for himself. In this view Coubertin found a specific illustration of one of his educational hypotheses.

26 Faced at the outset with the moral collapse of the institution, Arnold began the work of total and long-lasting educational transformation with clarity and generosity, courage and effectiveness. He did not seek to curtail the will of his students. Rather, he taught students to exercise their wills with full responsibility. For Arnold, morality was the work of the knowledge that each individual employs with respect to his own actions. Joy tells of a successful life. Existence assumes its full value and retains all of its rights.

27 As Catullus says, victory loves the effort, "*amat victoria curam*".

28 Among prominent committee members were Victor Duruy (1811-1894), former Minister of Public Instruction and historian, who was responsible for opening many primary schools and creating special courses for girls; Octave Gréard (1828-1904), from Normandy, Professor, Vice-Rector of the Academy of Paris in 1879, Member of the French Academy; main works: *Education et Instruction* [Education and Instruction] (3 volumes), *Madame de Maintenon*; Dr.Fernand Lagrange, physician who worked actively to promote sports in France, author of the following works: *Physiologie des exercices du corps* [Physiology of Physical Exercise] (1889), *L'exercice chez les enfants et les jeunes gens* [Exercise in Children and Youths] (1896), published articles in the *Revue des Deux Mondes* on "The Reform of Physical Education", among others.

29 Pascal Grousset (1845-1909) wrote under various pseudonyms. As Philippe Daryl, he wrote *La vie partout* [Life Everywhere], *Le Yacht* [The Yacht], *Jeux de balle et de ballon* [Ball Games], *La renaissance physique* [The Physical Renaissance], and *Sport de l'aviron* [The Sport of Rowing]. As André Laurie, he wrote *La vie de collège dans tous les pays* [High School Life in All Countries], *Le Capitaine Trafalgar* [Captain Trafalgar], *Mémoire d'un collégien* [A Schoolboy's Memoirs], etc. A journalist and politician, he worked with Stevenson in editing *Treasure Island* and with Jules Verne on *L'épave du Cynthia* [The Wreck of the Cynthia]. Founder of the *Ligue Nationale de l'Éducation Physique* [National League of Physical Education]. He was exiled to New Caledonia following the insurrection of 1871.

Grousset pleaded that school games be organized according to French tradition. In October 1888, he founded the Ligue Nationale de l'Éducation Physique [National League of Physical Education][30].

While the Committee chaired by Jules Simon and directed by Coubertin was focusing specifically on secondary education to usher in the new education that the Republic needed, from mastering the basics to the various fields of university-level specialization, the League recommended introducing physical exercises and games at all levels of education.

Staying true to the course he had set for himself, Coubertin pursued his work tirelessly. His ideas for the renewal of education were well received in some schools, particularly at the École Monge and the École Alsacienne.

On January 26, 1889, before the Association française pour l'avancement des Sciences [French Association for the Advancement of Science], Coubertin defined "Athletic Education" as an educational system with a specific objective, "to make men," and a specific method and laws. His educational theory touches on all of man's abilities. It creates a harmonious balance in man.

Since education across the English Channel was superior to French education, he argued, it was a good thing to "acclimate" it to France.

Early in 1889, Coubertin published a 206-page work entitled *L'Éducation anglaise en France* [English Education in France], with a preface by Jules Simon.

That same year, Coubertin held the "First Congress of Physical Exercises and School Competitions" at the World's Fair, with the consent of the government. On that occasion, he made official the results of a study that he had done in Anglo-Saxon countries, to determine whether Thomas Arnold's ideas had been applied there.

In July 1889, Minister Armand Fallières sent Coubertin to the United States and Canada, "to visit the Universities and colleges there, and to study the organization and operation of the Athletic Associations founded there by the youths of those countries."

Once he arrived, Coubertin traveled around, obtained information, made observations, and noted down his reflections. The Americans were preparing for their future in and around its universities. For the Americans, respect for the law remained compatible with civil and religious freedom. Athletic associations proliferated at the universities, and outside them. Athletes were chosen through extremely detailed anthropometric measurements[31].

During his travels, Coubertin was astonished at the discriminatory legislation then in effect in the Southern States. In his view, culture should bring men together, without requiring them to renounce their very selves; one can acknowledge differences without ceasing to be human. He was also surprised at the significant role that women occupied in American affairs. His visit to Canada provided Coubertin with proof of the superiority of English education over the overly narrow, existential model still employed by the French-Canadians.

In 1890, a report on his visit appeared in a 379-page book, entitled *Universités Transatlantiques* [Transatlantic Universities][32]. Starting at this point, Coubertin's philosophy of education took on its final form, resulting from an unwavering focus on lasting values and a direct answer to the educational questions of the day.

Since resistance to the educational renewal in France that had begun in the junior and senior high schools was growing increasingly obstinate, Coubertin broadened the scope of his original strategy[33]. "To shore up the frail edifice that I had just built, it seemed to me that restoration of the Olympic Games – this time as totally international games – was the only appropriate solution[34]."

By pitting his belief in the strength of his destiny against human weakness, Coubertin created new values and blazed previously unknown trails. He offered them to all comers, allowing every individual to discover greatness in himself. In his generosity to the future, Coubertin never short-changed the present. With his contagious enthusiasm, he brought his accomplishments into harmony with his dreams, thereby enabling the life-long athlete, at long last reaching the summits of Olympism, to hear "songs of joy rising from the cage of the Cosmos[35]."

For a man, true glory means vanishing into the radiance of an accomplishment that transcends the limits of time.

Such is the revelation of Pierre de Coubertin.

30 Members of the Committee of the National League of Physical Education included the learned chemist Marcelin Berthelot as honorary chairman; Berthelot was Minister of Public Instruction and Fine Arts in the Goblet Cabinet from December 1886 to May 1887, and Professor Étienne Marey as chairman. Other members included the sculptor Bartholdi, the architect Garnier, the novelist Jules Verne, education theorists Ferdinand Buisson and Gabriel Compayré, the politician Georges Clemenceau, etc.

31 Coubertin remarked, "It is reminiscent of a stable of race horses; there is the breeder who hands over the handsome beasts to the trainer" (p. 89); and again, "all this is not education, it is animal rearing" (p. 90). He added, "The impression they give is that of a distorted ideal, a down-to-earth education, unconscious but total materialism" (p. 120), in *Transatlantic Universities*, "New England."

32 This topic would be taken up again in various forms three years running. In 1895, he published *Le Monde américain* [The American World], in 1896 *Le mouvement universitaire aux États-Unis* [The University Movement in the United States], and in 1897, *L'Amérique universitaire* [University America]. His studies on "South American History" and "Idealism in the History of the United States" appeared much later, in 1916 and 1918.

33 Coubertin was to lead the battle head-on in French schools, and at the international level with the Olympic Games. He went beyond French schools, taking the battle for education to the international level with the establishment of the Union Pédagogique Universelle [Universal Educational Union] (1925).

34 Pierre de Coubertin, in his lecture entitled "Olympia," given March 6, 1929 at the festival hall of the Paris 16th Arrondissement City Hall. See text 5.1/14 in part II of this edition.

35 After Marcello Fabri (1889-1945) who, in his poem "Inconclusive arabesque," wrote: "The cage of the cosmos is lit with songs of joy." Cf. Émile Callot, *Introduction à un humanisme périmé* [Introduction to an Outdated Humanism], Gardet, Annecy 1958, p. 78.

Pierre de Coubertin here at the age of 31 as he appeared when succeeding in his proposal of renewing the Olympic Games. (Navacelle Collection)

COUBERTIN'S OLYMPISM

by Professor Norbert Müller, University of Mainz (Germany)

Pierre de Coubertin owes his international reputation to his success in reviving the Olympic Games in modern form. This overly simplistic view of Coubertin is a relatively recent phenomenon.

A specialist work published in Germany in 1908 presents Coubertin as "a remarkable French educational reformer", failing even to mention his work in restoring the Olympic Games. Until the 1930s, the name Coubertin appeared in the encyclopaedia books of many countries only on account of his contributions in the field of education.

Part I of this edition, "Revelation", demonstrated the many forms in which Coubertin expressed the ideals and educational aspects of athletics that inspired him. Here Olympism is situated within Coubertin's general concept of philosophy and education in their historical development. It is on this basis that the following Part II, "Olympic Dimensions", is especially significant within the framework of this edition. The mass of previously published studies, from which many divergent positions have emerged, calls for clarification based on incontrovertible documentation.

In this historical perspective, let us note that a similar process led to acknowledgment of the quadrennial Olympic Games as the pinnacle of the athletic world. This made it possible for the practice of sports, which originated in the particular context of England, to spread internationally over the course of the twentieth century.

This yearning for universality is one of the reasons that the Olympic Games have retained their strength and appeal down to our own day. Therefore the writings presented in the second section are also a reflection of international sports in the twentieth century.

Starting with Coubertin's own ideas on educational reform, and recalling the practical initiatives associated with them, this part will present the evolution of his conception of Olympism in its many forms. The focus will be on three different levels:

- the historical level,
- the philosophical and educational level and
- the level of structural organization.

Viewed in this way, it is only their Olympic perspective that distinguishes most of these writings from the educational texts on sports in Part I. They account for some thirty percent of all of Coubertin's writing. In this second part, we have put together ninety-eight articles that vary greatly in form and length. These items account for nearly thirty percent of Coubertin's "Olympic Writings", comprising newspaper and magazine articles, contributions to collective works, and selections from books. They include many speeches, which were often subsequently published[1].

In addition to printed works, this part includes major circular letters written by Coubertin, then President of the International Olympic Committee. The central questions of the Olympic Movement are raised in these letters. They expand and illustrate themes dealt with in his other writings. Despite their official nature, these

1 Most commonly, Coubertin had these publications printed and distributed at his own expense.

"circulars" are, in style and content, comparable to Coubertin's other publications. They are suitable for inclusion here, despite the small numbers of those to whom they were addressed.

68 articles deal with history, 49 with philosophy and education, 21 with structural organization, 3 with Lausanne as Olympic City and 6 are general retrospectives.

The reader today may find that Part II "Olympic Dimensions" is overly historical in tone. Yet we must recall that as President of the IOC, Coubertin often had to take sides on current issues involving the Olympic Games. Upon closer inspection, it often happens that we can look beyond the historical point of view, to shed light on issues that the Olympic Movement is still debating itself now. Some mistakes could certainly have been avoided if past experience had been taken into account.

Most of the descriptions of Olympic events are intertwined with stories drawn from contemporary history, suggestions for improving the Olympic effort, a critique of mistakes made, and appeals for greater cooperation. In most instances, these texts were written as reflections on the foundations of athletic education. Frequently the setting was conferences where Coubertin exercised his gift of public speaking to present his Olympic objectives to his many listeners convincingly, thereby urging them into action. The texts in the fourth chapter, "Historical Perspectives on Olympism", have been presented mainly in chronological order. They reflect the decades-long struggle that Coubertin engaged in for his ideas. His autobiographical writings on the period from 1887 to 1908 are rightly entitled: *Une campagne de vingt-et-un ans* [A Twenty-One Year Campaign] (Paris 1909). We have decided to include the *Mémoires Olympiques*[2] [Olympic Memoirs] in this volume because an autobiography produced late in his life will help fill in certain thematic breaks in our historical retrospective.

Part II "Olympic Dimensions" features focal points of primary interest around which the contents of the section are articulated. In this introduction, I will attempt to shed some light on the work as a whole, by describing Coubertin and his Olympic efforts from the perspective of their historical development. It is not always possible to distinguish between the historical and philosophical perspectives. In general, Coubertin wrote mostly on Olympism in the period prior to World War I. The reason was his need at the time to orient the Olympic Movement that he was in the midst of creating, right down to the smallest detail. Coubertin was managing director and editor of the International Olympic Committee's magazine, the *Revue Olympique*, which he used often to clarify his plans for Olympism[3].

In overseeing such a major magazine to get his movement off the ground, Coubertin showed not only his tireless will to work, once the course was laid out, but also his gifts as a publicist.

During and after World War I, issues regarding organization took a back seat to the basic matters of athletic education and Olympism. Coubertin's writings on the foundations of Olympism also date from this time. They are presented here in Chapter 5.1, "Olympism as a Spiritual Attitude". I will have occasion to refer to these writings again later in this introduction.

The issue of amateurism and the role of the arts in Olympism belong to the same group. Therefore, we have selected three areas that are essential to understanding Coubertin's concept of Olympism. The Olympic amateur has always been of capital importance within the Olympic Movement. Yet, as Coubertin perceived the Olympic ideal, the notion of the perfect amateur is only of secondary importance to him. By contrast, he set great store by harmony, which was to lead the athlete and the spectator alike to eurythmy in the reciprocal give and take of athletics and art.

Various topics in the history of the organization and the structure of Olympism have been grouped together in the sixth chapter, "The Olympic Movement". This chapter starts with texts on the structure of the IOC, and on the expansion of the Olympic Movement, an expansion involving both the form of the organization and its geographical extension. The texts are presented basically in chronological order, describing Olympic history on the basis of these elements of organization. They also complement Chapter 4.2.

The five texts in Chapter 6.3 shed light on Coubertin's overall concept of the various Olympic sports. Six of these articles are on specific Olympic sports. Our selection criteria were very strict, because Coubertin wrote many articles on the various sports. These articles are published together in Volume III of the French edition, which is about the practice of specific sports.

The present volume ends with two articles on the Olympic activities of the city of Lausanne.

Despite the enormous volume of writings that Coubertin left behind, he did not take a position on many issues that seem so critical to us today. The world political situation after World War II presented new problems, the complexity and entanglement of which Coubertin, who died in 1937, could only begin to sense. Some topics, such as the place of art in the context of the Olympic Games, appear frequently in his writings. It was his duty as an educator to refer back to his fundamental principles at all times, in hopes of being understood and followed.

COUBERTIN'S OLYMPIC VISION

Now let us trace out the Olympic stages in the life of Pierre de Coubertin. A look at his activities as an organizer, his continued efforts to have Olympism understood and to expand it, his countless appeals, plans and written texts all bear the stamp of an idealistic fighter and an inspired educator.

We have devoted ample room in this book to the historical perspectives of Olympism because these perspectives reflect the core of Coubertin's thought and writings. Far from contradicting the statements on the philosophical and educational dimensions of Coubertin's Olympism, (see Chapter 5 of this book), these perspectives are, in fact, a precondition for them.

2 The book was republished in English, French, and Spanish by the IOC in 1979, in order to make it available to all readers; cf. IOC (Ed.), *Olympic Memoirs*. Introduction by G. de Navacelle, Lausanne, IOC, 1979. New edition published in 1997.

3 Only a few articles were signed with his name. Yet we can say with confidence that Coubertin himself wrote the other articles that do not bear his signature. In some cases, authenticity has been established through subsequent signed reprints. In other cases, the style and content bear Coubertin's mark. There is one place in the Circular of January 1919 (see 6.5.3 in this volume), where he speaks of "articles that are always anonymous", which were sources of information and inspiration for the writers. By underscoring his actions in spreading the word in print in this indirect way, Coubertin confirms his responsibility as author.

Coubertin saw history as "the first of all the sciences in terms of significance and educational effectiveness[4]". History alone enables Coubertin to place his Olympism in a historical context, and thereby to ensure its success.

Coubertin's philhellenism was a product of his knowledge of history and his enthusiasm for youth. After specifying "respect for countries" as the first commandment of his faith, he added that to respect a country, one must know it and that, to know it, one must study its history[5].

This is not the proper place to assess Coubertin's historism, or to estimate all his historical works[6].

The next few texts show the depth of his knowledge of ancient and modern Greek history. For Coubertin, "nothing is comprehensible or explicable without history"[7].

What interested Coubertin most in history was the idea of the Olympic Games, an idea he owed to Father Carron, his humanities teacher at the Jesuit school in Paris. We do not know the precise date when Coubertin struck upon the project of restoring the Olympic Games for the internationalization of sports. In his speech of acknowledgment at the close of the 1894 Congress, he spoke of a hope that he had entertained for ten years[8].

Yet it was France, his own country, that Coubertin was thinking of in 1883, having just turned twenty, with regard to his plans for educational reform. When it came to finding an international model to popularize sports in France, however, his thoughts turned to Greece. The resurrection of Olympia, in the fields of politics, athletics, and religion became the foundation on which he based his actions.

Archaeological digs done between 1875 and 1881 at Olympia certainly had a great impact on Coubertin. He mentions them enthusiastically in his writings on Hellenism. In his first retrospective autobiography, *Une campagne de vingt-et-un ans* [A Twenty-One Year Campaign], he wrote "Germany had brought to light what remained of Olympia, why should not France succeed in rebuilding its splendors?[9]"

The archaeological discovery of Olympia, along with other spectacular digs in Greece and Asia Minor, seems to have profoundly influenced the thinking of the young Coubertin. What was known, around 1890, about Olympia and the ancient Olympic Games?

The Olympic festivals had ended in 393 AD, but the memory and meaning of the Games had not been lost[10]. As far back as the Middle Ages, many texts mention Olympia and its Games. The first extensive work exclusively on the Olympic Games appeared in Groningen in 1732 by Th. Antonides. Before 1723, the French Benedictine Bernard de Montfaucon drew up plans for excavating the city. In 1776, the Englishman Richard Chandler found the remains of a large Doric temple at Olympia, later identified as the famous Temple of Zeus. Yet, mainly for technical and financial reasons, systematic excavation was out of the question.

Early in the nineteenth century, on Easter Sunday 1821, the Greek war of independence broke out, in response to three hundred years of domination by the Turks. The war culminated in the annihilation of the Turkish fleet by the major European powers at Pylos in 1827. These events were obstacles for the Germans, who were planning to do the digs. In the footsteps of French peace-keeping troops, archaeologists landed on the coast of the Peloponnese in 1829 and began the initial digs. Their discoveries were sent to the Louvre, in Paris.

A quarter of a century passed before a historian of ancient Greece, the German Ernst Curtius, prompted resumption of the excavation, in a famous lecture on Olympia given in Berlin in January 1852[11].

Another twenty years passed, however, before an agreement was signed between Greece and Germany authorizing systematic excavation of Olympia by German archaeologists in 1875-1881. Enthusiasm ran high for these excavations, particularly in Germany. The Philhellenism found in architectural, literary, musical, and humanistic classicism had created close ties between the German mind and the Greek mind. Yet Philhellenism had swept through all of Europe, with same effect in France and England as in Germany. In France, a style inspired by antiquity had existed since the eighteenth century. It arose in the final decades of the Ancien Régime, and is commonly called the Louis XVI style. The classicism of the Revolution and of the Empire intensified these tendencies, which are proper to the nineteenth century. About a century later, Coubertin's Philhellenic feelings show the strength that these images had in cultivated circles[12].

Coubertin knew the prestige that Greek history, and consequently Ancient Olympia as well, enjoyed in the vast circles trained in the classical ideal of the nineteenth century. He noticed the attention given to the Panhellenic Games of Olympia and Delphi, which German and French digs were bringing to light. By orienting his movement toward the goals to which the ancient festivals had aspired, he was ensuring its prestige specifically among those still unfamiliar with sport. The appeal to antiquity touched a chord with the European countries and helped to unite them; it awakened the interest of the New World as well. In restoring life to the shared classical roots of western culture, Coubertin dispelled the suspicions that people in his time, when national feelings ran so high, might harbor about him as a Frenchman. Under other circumstances, he might have been accused of pursuing nationalist goals, had he chosen another approach.

The idea of "Olympic Games" had never disappeared entirely, strictly speaking, and Coubertin himself says as much in an article he wrote in 1896. He was thinking of the local tournaments that the Directoire had held on the Champ de Mars

4 Coubertin, *Histoire Universelle* [World History]. Vol. I: Foreword. Aix-en-Provence 1926, p. XIV.

5 Cf. Coubertin, "Erinnerungen" [Memoirs], Part 1, in: *Europäische Revue*, Vol. 12, Stuttgart 1936, no. 9, p. 708.

6 We refer the reader to two publications on Coubertin as historian: Y.-P. Boulongne, *Pierre de Coubertin et l'histoire* [Pierre de Coubertin and History], in *Stadion, Zeitschrift für Geschichte des Sports und der Körperkultur.* Volume VI, St. Augustin/Bonn, Richarz 1983, pp. 113-127; and B. Wirkus, *Der pragmatische Historismus Pierre de Coubertins* [The Pragmatic Historicism of Pierre de Coubertin], in G. Hecker (Ed.): Der Mensch im Sport [Man in Sports], Schorndorf, Hofmann 1976, pp. 32-45.

7 Coubertin, *Notre France* [Our France], Édition du Centenaire, Lausanne 1930, p. 206 [postface].

8 Cf. "Les Fêtes du Congrès" [The Festivities of the Congress], in *Bulletin du Comité International des Jeux Olympiques*, Vol. 1, Paris 1894, no. 1, p. 3.

9 Coubertin, *Une campagne de vingt-et-un ans* [A Twenty-One Year Campaign] (1887-1908), Paris 1909, p. 89.

10 On this topic, see the extensive documentation of Karl Lennartz, *Kenntnisse und Vorstellungen von Olympia und den Olympischen Spielen in der Zeit von 393 bis 1896* [Knowledge and Conceptions of Olympia and the Olympic Games from 393 to 1896], Schorndorf, Hofmann, 1974.

11 Ernst Curtius, *Olympia. Ein Vortrag im wissentschaftlichen Verein zu Berlin.* [Olympia. A Lecture at the Scientific Society in Berlin.], Berlin, Wilhelm Hertz, 1852.

12 See Rudolf Malter's treatment of this subject in *Der Olympismus Pierre de Coubertins. Beiträge zum Olympischen Gedanken.* [The Olympism of Pierre de Coubertin. Contributions on the Olympic Idea.] Vol. I. Published by the Carl Diem Institute, Cologne 1969, pp. 9-10.

in Paris, after the French Revolution, and of festivals that took place in certain Greek cities under that ancient name[13].

It is also possible that during a trip to America in 1889, his plan for the modern Olympic Games was encouraged following a meeting with historian William M. Sloane, a professor at Princeton University[14].

It was the local "Olympian Games" held at Much Wenlock, a small town in northern England, that came closest to Coubertin's plan for restoring the ancient Games. Coubertin had been corresponding with the physician and teacher Dr William Penny Brookes, founder of these games in 1850, and president of the local Olympian Society. Coubertin went to Much Wenlock in 1890, and has left an account of those games in an article reprinted in this volume[15]. Dr Brookes told Coubertin about the national athletic tournaments that took place in Athens under the name "Olympic Games" in 1859, 1870, 1875, and 1888/89. Brookes had established a prize for those tournaments, in the form of a silver cup[16].

In 1891 in the magazine *Greater Britain*, another Englishman, John Astley Cooper, proposed that a regular "Anglo-Saxon Olympiad" be organized in such varied fields as science, technology, art, and sports. It is possible that Coubertin was inspired by this proposal[17].

The timing was propitious, because the social and cultural internationalism of the end of the nineteenth century was making the internationalization of sports nearly a foregone conclusion. Discoveries and improvements in transportation and communications lent a decisive hand to the trend. The press had discovered sports as a topic of popular interest. World's fairs were encouraging comparisons between nations.

Therefore, in November 1892, Coubertin was in a position to propose the idea of restoring the Olympic Games, for the first time explicitly in a public forum, at the close of a lecture on modern sports at the Sorbonne. In expressing this thought, Coubertin was naturally pursuing ideological ends, not merely pragmatic ones. It implied restoring the ancient harmony between the body and the mind, which the educational system in the West had lost after the collapse of ancient culture. Coubertin appealed to history. Antiquity was to show the way, but only to the extent that the present demanded that it do so.

Coubertin's main priority at first was the idea of "peace among nations". In his early writings, he refers to international sporting encounters as "the free trade of the future" (p. 297), seeing the participating athletes as "ambassadors of peace", even though by his own admission he still had to take care, at the time of the founding of the IOC in 1894, not to say too much about this, not wanting – as he says in his unpublished memoirs – to ask too much of sportsmen or to frighten the pacifists. With his ideas of peace, however, Coubertin associated an ethical mission which, then as now, was central to the Olympic Movement and – if it were to succeed – had to lead to political education. On the threshold of the 20th century, Coubertin tried to bring about enlightened internationalism by cultivating a non-chauvinistic nationalism.[18]

COUBERTIN'S OLYMPIC "CAMPAIGN" (1894-1914)

This initial proposal to restore the Olympic Games met with incomprehension on the part of his listeners. Yet Coubertin did not give up, but clearly the public needed to be prepared for a new line of action. The opportunity came at an international congress organized by the Union of French Athletic Sports Associations

(U.S.F.S.A.). Its purpose was to standardize the norms of amateurism in athletic associations in France and abroad, in order to simplify international athletic relations[19]. As Secretary General of the U.S.F.S.A., Coubertin planned the agenda for this Congress so that athletic issues were at the forefront, leaving the matter of the restoration of the Olympic Games in the background, even though in Coubertin's mind this was essential. It was not until the final program was drawn up that he disclosed his real goal, by giving an entirely new name to the Congress: "International Congress at Paris for the Restoration of the Olympic Games[20]."

At the preparatory meetings held in New York in late 1893, and in London in early 1894, Coubertin had pleaded his case before national sports leaders. Despite this effort, even in 1894 many directors remained skeptical where Coubertin's Olympic plans were concerned. Nevertheless, seventy-eight delegates from thirty-seven athletic unions representing nine countries voted to restore the Olympic Games[21]. They reached an agreement on how to accomplish this goal and, at Coubertin's suggestion, they approved a list of members who would form an International Committee for the Olympic Games[22].

13 Cf. Coubertin, "The Modern Olympic Games", in *The Olympic Games in 1896*, Official report, part 2, Athens-London, Ch. Beck/H. Grevel, 1897, p. 4. See also text 4.2.1/8 in this volume.
Contests called "Olympic" games, Festivals, etc. were staged on local and national level in a number of countries. Some of them have been extensively studied others still need to be investigated.
However, it is evident that all these events show peculiarities and features concerning their programmes which were greatly influenced by local or national agonstic and popular traditions. Rühl lists the following "Olympic Games":

Robert Dover's Olympick Games	Cotswold (England) 1612-1999
Drehberg Olympic Games	Near Dessau (Germany)1776-99,1840-42,since 1989
Les Jeux olympiques au Rondeau	Grenoble (France) 1832 - 1954
Ramlösa Olympic Games	Sweden 1834, 1836
Montréal Olympic Games	Canada 1844
Much Wenlock Olympian Games	Much Wenlock (England) since 1850
New York Olympic Games	USA 1853
Shropshire Olympian Games	Shropshire (England) 1860-62, 1864
Evangelis Zappas' Olympic Games	Athens (Greece) 1859,1870,1875,1888/89
National Olympic Games	England 1866-68, 1874, 1877, 1883
Liverpool Grand Olympic Festivals	Liverpool (England) 1862-67
Morpeth Olympic Games	Northumberland (England) 1870 -1958
Lake Palic Olympic Games	Lake Palic (Yugoslavia) 1880 -1914

See J.K. Rühl, "The Olympian Games in Athens in the Year 1877,"in: *Journal of Olympic History* (The official publication of the International Society of Olympic Historians), Vol. 5, No 3, 1997, p. 27; see also R. Naul (ed.), *Contemporary Studies in the National Olympic Games Movement*, Frankfurt/M, Lang, 1997.

14 Regarding this visit, see Coubertin, *Universités transatlantiques* [Transatlantic Universities], Paris, Hachette 1890, p. 17. On William M. Sloane, see Coubertin, "Silhouettes disparues" [The Dear Departed], in *La Gazette de Lausanne*, December 20, 1928, p. 1.

15 See text 4.2.1/1 of this volume: "The Olympic Games at Much Wenlock." Another article on Dr. Brookes was written in English. Cf. Coubertin, "A Typical Englishman – Dr. W. P. Brookes of Wenlock in Shropshire." in: *American Review of Reviews*, January 1897, pp. 62-65.

16 Cf. Coubertin, *Une campagne de vingt-et-un ans* [A Twenty-One Year Campaign](1887-1908), Paris 1909, pp. 52-53. See also text 1.1/8 in Volume III of the French Coubertin edition.

17 Cf. J. A. Cooper, "Many Lands – one People". in: *Greater Britain*, London 1891, pp. 458-462.

18 Cf. D. Quanz, "Formative Power of the IOC-Founding: the Birth of the new Peace Movement", in: *Olympic Academy Report* 1994, pp. 121-133.

19 Cf. Coubertin, Conférence du Secrétaire Général à l´Assemblée générale de l´Union, in: *Les Sports athlétiques*, Vol. 4, 13 July 1894, pp. 2-4.

20 See documents 4.2.1/5 – 4.2.1/7 in this volume.

21 See text 4.2.1/9 in this volume.

22 This list appears in article 6.5.1: "The Work of the IOC".

Greece had no intention of allowing the honor of being the first country to host the new Olympic Games to be taken from them. That is why the delegates opted to hold the Olympic Games in Athens in 1896, not waiting for the Paris World's Fair of 1900. In keeping with the statutes, the Greek delegate, Dimitrios Bikelas, a philologist living in Paris, assumed the presidency of the newly-elected International Committee, in his capacity as representative of the host country. Coubertin, as Secretary General, was busy furthering his plans with tenacity and inspiration. This was essential, particularly because stubborn resistance to holding the Games was mounting in Greece, for financial reasons[23].

In the end, the undertaking was a success. The first Olympic Games of the modern era were held in Athens in 1896. They were such a great success that Greece, which viewed the Olympic Games as its own historical property, went so far as to demand that the Games be held on its soil permanently.

Hardly any attention was paid in Greece to what Coubertin had accomplished. National pride would not allow for a Frenchman to be the origin of so grandiose an event. For the first time since it regained independence in 1829, the Greek nation had been able to uphold its splendor at the Athens Games, and had affirmed that splendor before the eyes of the world. Yet Coubertin did not abandon his principles. The Games had to change location, as the members of the IOC meeting at Athens had once again confirmed. Several texts in this part relate details of this dispute[24].

So the first step in the renaissance of the Olympics had been taken. The next Olympic Games were set to take place in Paris in 1900. For Coubertin and the members of the IOC, the question was what to do in the interim. Should work come to a halt? Should the Committee be dissolved? This situation gave rise to a desire to call an Olympic Congress, which met at Le Havre in 1897. In his *Olympic Memoirs*, Coubertin provided the committee with its claim to legitimacy in the following terms: "At Athens", he said, "all efforts had been concentrated on the sporting side of the venture in an historical context; there had been no congress, no conference, no sign of any moral or educational purpose. To take that direction immediately after the Games was to remind people of the intellectual and philosophical character of my idea and to place the role of the IOC, right from the start, very much above that of a simple sports association[25]."

During these discussions, Coubertin was savvy enough to avoid issues of athletic technique and organization, such as the Olympic Games, to concentrate on issues of athletic education only.

The Dominican priest Henri Didon was Coubertin's paternal friend. The close relationship that Didon had with Coubertin, and his role as a model for Coubertin, are apparent throughout the 1890s. It was Fr. Didon who gave the key lecture on "the moral influence of athletic sports". The Congress at Le Havre also attempted to draw the attention of the French public to the work of the Olympic Committee, in view of the Games of the Second Olympiad, to be held in Paris in 1900.

Coubertin and his friends began preparing for those Games too late. The organizing committee was not formed until 1898. Of course, the committee worked relentlessly and sent a schedule of the Games to all countries, but it had not anticipated resistance on the part of the organizers of the World's Fair. Those organizers had planned an exhibition of sports-related equipment, and had scheduled athletic demonstrations in a schedule that ran throughout the year. That was supposed to allow all the attractive sports to be seen in their own right. These competitions were to be open to professionals and amateurs alike. The U.S.F.S.A. agreed to support the athletic program of the World's Fair, organized by the French government. Coubertin, who was offended by this move, withdrew from the work of the Union. It was not until 1899 that Coubertin realized that his attitude was getting him nowhere, and he came to an agreement with the organizers of the World's Fair. He had them include something called "Olympic Competitions" in the athletic program of the World's Fair. Coubertin and his colleagues on the IOC mounted a publicity campaign to promote participation in these events. He himself assumed responsibility for the track and field events. The only mention he ever made of the lack of success of the 1900 Games was in his two autobiographical works, *La Campagne de vingt-et-un ans* and *Mémoires Olympiques*. It is a miracle that the Olympic Movement survived this trial[26].

After a squabble between Chicago and St. Louis, the Third Olympic Games were held in St. Louis in 1904, once again within the context of a World's Fair. At St. Louis, too, it was difficult to draw a clear distinction between the program of athletic demonstrations and the Olympic Games per se. Yet a recent, systematic investigation of the sources[27] has shown that these Games were far less of a victim of the bedlam associated with World's Fairs than most historians of the Olympic Movement have claimed. European involvement was reduced to a bare minimum. Nevertheless, the decisions of the IOC were respected. The metric system was used in America for the first time. Coubertin did not go to St. Louis in person, but was represented there by his colleagues on the IOC, Kemény and Gebhardt. At that time, Coubertin was focusing his attention on an issue that concerned him as a writer and as an organizer: the establishment of a popular athletic movement in France, a topic covered in volume three of the French edition.

The 1904 IOC meeting in London marked the beginning of the series of annual meetings. The Games were awarded to Rome for 1908. Coubertin felt that this choice would result in an artistic display of particularly high quality. At the time, the Olympic Games had become a matter for the athletic associations of the host country. Where no international regulation had been established, national regulations were followed.

Coubertin, the "IOC personified", merely influenced the external form of the Games. Few sports had international athletic federations, so few conflicts regarding competence were to be expected on that front.

In 1901, the IOC had called an Olympic Congress for physical education in Brussels. That Congress did not meet until 1905. Rather than advocating unification of the Olympic program, as was its original purpose, this congress merely examined the opportunities provided by athletic exercises in the various domains of education

23 See text 4.2.1/10 in this volume.

24 See texts 4.2.2/6 and 4.2.2/7 in this volume.

25 *Olympic Memoirs*, Lausanne 1979, p. 27.

26 The physiological research that went hand in hand with the track and field competitions derived from the science of sports, as did a specialized congress on physical education in the demonstration program of the World's Fair, a congress in which Coubertin took part. He wrote a report on this topic in *L'Indépendance Belge* of January 22, 1900.

27 Undertaken by the Carl Diem Institute and by the author of this introduction, during his visit to St. Louis in summer, 1984.

and of life. From our perspective today, we must view the attention paid during these discussions to sports in houses of correction and in prisons as progress. Recommendations were also made regarding the long-term measures to be taken to further automobile sports. At the same time, there was talk in Italy of an Olympic automobile race from Rome to Milan during the 1908 Games, an idea that no one today would associate with the Olympic Games any more.

The scope of international participation in the Brussels Congress was surprising. Thus the IOC could justify its claim of being more than merely the organizer of the Olympic Games. The physical setting in which the Congress was so skillfully staged, with the support of the King of the Belgians, made a great impression. Coubertin needed this success, especially since the previous two Olympic Games had not received much coverage in Europe, and financial difficulties were beginning to come to light in Rome in terms of the 1908 Olympic Games[28].

Coubertin established an Olympic diploma, and used the Olympic Congress of Brussels to designate the President of the United States, Theodore Roosevelt, as the first recipient. According to Coubertin, Roosevelt set an example of ideal harmony in physical, intellectual, and moral accomplishment[29]. Coubertin thus underscored that his Committee's mission went beyond the Olympic Games.

In 1906, interim Olympic Games were held in Athens. The Greeks wanted to use the occasion to reassert their intention to hold interim Games in Greece two years after the main Games. Coubertin did not attend. He viewed these interim Games as detrimental to the four-year rhythm that had been set up. He may also have been held back because of the ingratitude that Greece had once shown him. The IOC itself supported these interim Games. Coubertin saw only one advantage to them: restoring contact between athletes and visitors and the spirit of Greece.

Yet Coubertin had a more serious motive for not going to Athens. In May 1906, he had held an advisory conference on art in Paris, at the request of the IOC. In the early years of his movement, Coubertin had intentionally left this aspect of his plan in the background, because he planned to move forward with his vast, long-term undertaking by stages[30].

The Congresses at Le Havre and Brussels had established a link between sports and science. They had failed to establish any link with art, however. As Coubertin saw it, the Olympic Games had to include elements that transcend international competitions and, by invoking the ancient model, should serve to underscore the true meaning of the Games.

In 1904, he wrote in *Le Figaro*, "The time has come to take the next step, and restore the Olympiad to its original beauty. At the time of the splendor of Olympia, literature and the arts, harmoniously linked with athletics, provided the grandeur of the Olympic Games. The same must hold true in the future[31]."

The advisory conference raised the issue of knowing "the extent to which, and in what form, the Arts and Literature could be involved in the celebration of modern Olympiads[32]". In a treatise on athletic Ruskinianism, Coubertin had written in 1911, "Sport, which must bring joy, can do so only when it wears festive clothing[33]". In this regard, English art critic John Ruskin (1819-1900) was Coubertin's main inspiration. Ruskin's theory, which held that beauty manifests the spirit of the universe, impressed Coubertin. The Olympic Games as a manifestation of youth renewing itself every four years, and as the expression of a new "cult of the human essence", needed a unique form. The opening and closing ceremonies, the proclamation of the victors, the Olympic rings, the flags, and later the Olympic oath and the Olympic flame, formed the framework of the festival. Such impressive creativity, from an esthetic perspective, assured the lasting value of the Games, because it echoed the significance that antiquity had accorded to the arts and to ceremonial festivals.

It is a small step from this to understanding Coubertin's taste for the music of Wagner, which brought him to the Bayreuth Festivals on many occasions. However, Coubertin's artistic work is not called "The Ring of the Nibelungen", it is entitled "The Olympic Games."

The 1906 Paris Conference voted to introduce five Olympic artistic competitions for architecture, sculpture, painting, literature, and music. The Conference drew up recommendations regarding the artistic form of athletic exhibitions of the widest possible variety.

Rome backed out of the 1908 Games, and London stepped in at the last minute. As a result, artistic competitions were not held until the Olympic Games of 1912 in Stockholm. Coubertin won the Olympic gold medal for literature at Stockholm, under the pseudonym Hohrod/Eschbach (Germany/France), with an "Ode to Sport[34]". He remained silent about his involvement and his victory, which is not mentioned anywhere in his posthumous literary work.

Artistic competitions continued to be part of the Olympic program until the Olympic Games in 1948. Since then, they have continued to be represented by the many artistic presentations of the Olympic festivals.

The 1906 Paris advisory conference had one other outcome: the international architecture competition for 1910, organized by the IOC. The suggested topic was a presentation of a model of a "modern Olympia". The Paris École Spéciale d'Architecture agreed to form the jury. Two architects from Lausanne won first prize for their model of an Olympic city along the shores of Lake Geneva[35]. The ties between Coubertin and Lausanne were thus solidly established.

The role of the arts in the Olympic Games and in everyday sports was quite significant for Coubertin, as amply shown in this volume.

Coubertin's Olympic project took on its final form at the London Games in 1908, and was enshrined at Stockholm in 1912. National athletic associations, and with them the athletes, accepted the Olympic Games as the pinnacle of world sports. The IOC had paved the way for this turn of events at the Olympic Congress of Paris in 1914, when each International Sports Federation (IF) was granted special technical responsibility within the Olympic Games.

28 Cf. *Olympic Memoirs,* Lausanne, IOC, 1979, pp. 45-48.

29 The diploma was also awarded to polar explorer Fridtjof Nansen and to the Brazilian Santos Dumont, a famous aviator at the time.

30 Cf. Coubertin, "Une Olympie moderne." [A Modern Olympia], in *Revue Olympique*, January 1910, p. 10 (text 4.1/3 in this volume).

31 Quote adapted from *Une campagne de vingt-et-un ans* [A Twenty-One Year Campaign], p. 12.

32 Circular of April 1906. See text 5.3/2 in this volume.

33 *Décoration, Pyrotechnie, Harmonies, Cortèges. Essai de Ruskinianisme sportif.* [Decoration, Pyrotechnics, Harmonies, Processions. Essay on Athletic Ruskinianism.], Paris 1912. See text 2.3/12 in the French edition. See also K. Clark (ed.), Ruskin today. London/New York, Penguin Books, 1991.

34 See text 5.3/10 in this volume.

35 Architects Monod and Laverrière also won the gold medal for architecture in 1912 for their model of an "Olympic stadium", an integral part of the "modern Olympia".

A year earlier, in May 1913, Coubertin had called a Pedagogical Olympic Congress in Lausanne, to examine the psychological and physiological influences of sports on the formation of character. The concept of "sports psychology" dates from this Congress, where Coubertin again underscored the varied educational responsibilities assumed by the IOC in the vast area spanned by his Olympic idea[36].

FROM "OLYMPIC IDEA" TO "OLYMPISM"

The philosophical and educational dimension of Olympism is highlighted in the fifth pivotal chapter of this volume. Coubertin wrote almost as copiously on this subject as on the historical dimension of Olympism. With one exception, these texts were all written after 1911. Therefore, we can infer that issues regarding the organization of the Olympic Games and of the Olympic Movement had become far less important to Coubertin by that time.

He focused all his energies on making his "Olympic idea" a reality, for which he had coined the new term "Olympism". For Coubertin, "Olympism" was not an institutional sort of system. Rather, it involved the moral attitude of an individual and, on that basis, the attitude of all humanity as well. To that end, Coubertin reintroduced the religious goals of the ancient Olympic Games into the modern version, essentially without changing the spiritual sense of the Games.

The texts on Olympism that we have selected are of primary importance in this Part, because in a many ways they reveal Coubertin's thinking about his "Olympic philosophy". An impassioned educator, Coubertin was convinced that the social and technical relationships in early twentieth-century civilization called for a new man and, consequently, for a new type of education. In Coubertin's view, Olympic education was based simultaneously "on the cult of effort and on the cult of eurythmy – and consequently of the love of excess combined with the love of moderation[37]."

Coubertin saw the true Olympic hero as an adult male individual[38]. This athlete was to be a symbolic image of the new generation being renewed at each Olympiad. As a result, Coubertin conceived of the Olympic Games as "the great quadrennial festival of the human springtime". He felt that participants and spectators alike should be suitably prepared for this festival. This preparation, in turn, could be achieved only through long-term athletic education for youth and for the populace as a whole.

In 1918, Coubertin answered the question, "What is Olympism?" as follows: "It is the religion of energy, the cultivation of intense will developed through the practice of manly sports, based on proper hygiene and public-spiritedness, surrounded with art and thought."[39] Coubertin seems not to have noticed that by imposing this syncretic direction, he was asking too much of his Olympic peers, of the athletes themselves, and ultimately, of his own movement. In forging the idea of a modern "*religio athletae*", he brought his movement beyond the educational goal that he had set for himself originally. The philosophical edifice that he was piecing together lost nearly all coherent meaning, especially since the transcendental reference that ancient man and athlete took as a basic assumption was lacking. To all evidence, Coubertin's vision of Hellenism and of the disorder in world politics had led him to this extreme.

World War I marked a decisive break in Coubertin's activities. The war put a sudden end to athletic internationalism which was in its first flush at the time. It meant canceling the Sixth Olympic Games in 1916. Coubertin's thoughts of Olympic peace inherited from the Ancients, and with it the ideal of eurythmy, collapsed.

To keep his movement, at least institutionally, beyond the reach of the war's caprices, he moved the IOC headquarters to Lausanne, in neutral Switzerland, in 1915. Coubertin had gotten to know and appreciate Lausanne through the 1910 architecture competition, and during the 1913 Olympic Congress. He may also have wanted to set up the IOC headquarters near the International Committee of the Red Cross, which also maintains its head office in Switzerland. Coubertin's writings about Lausanne and Switzerland are presented in Chapter 6.4 in this volume.

Coubertin's works on the history of the Olympic Movement often fail to point out that beginning in January 1916, and until the end of the war in 1918, Coubertin handed over his presidency of the IOC temporarily to Godefroy de Blonay, Swiss representative to the IOC. A patriot, Coubertin did his duty and entered the French army. At age 52, Coubertin was assigned to the task of advancing the civic instruction of French youth[40].

It would be an erroneous criticism to view these activities of Coubertin and his own Olympic idea as contradictory. He had put "respect for countries" as the first commandment of his faith. Should that commandment not be respected first and foremost when it is one's own native country that is at issue? He considered this form of nationalism unobjectionable, provided that it is tempered by true internationalism[41].

The disaster of World War I oriented Coubertin more than ever, after 1917, towards basic issues in athletic education. Sport, a common good shared by all social strata, specifically during the troubled period after 1918, should serve the cause of social peace and make the Olympic Movement a movement for peace throughout the whole world.

36 Cf. Coubertin, "Critique du Congrès de Lausanne." [Critique of the Lausanne Congress], in *Revue Olympique*, January 1914, pp. 10-12; February 1914, pp. 19-24; March 1914, pp. 42-45; April 1914, pp. 54-58. "La reprise des travaux du Congrès de Lausanne" [The Resumption of the Work of the Lausanne Congress] in *Bulletin du Bureau International de Pédagogie Sportive*, Lausanne [1929], no. 1, pp. 6-14.

37 Lettres Olympiques V, *in: Gazette de Lausanne*, November 28, 1918, no. 325, pp. 1-2. See text 3.17 in this volume.

38 See the debate, at the 1914 Paris Olympic Congress, regarding the admission of women to the Olympic Games, and regarding sports.

39 Coubertin, "Les Jardins de l'Effort" [The Gardens of Effort], in *Almanach olympique pour 1918* [Olympic Almanac for 1918], Lausanne [1917], p. 4.

40 On January 22, 1916, Coubertin was assigned to the position of interpreter in the army. Soon thereafter, he began a mission that he himself had outlined: to recruit volunteers among high school students through a campaign of lectures. Guided by the same desire, Coubertin had presented a "Report for the improvement and development of physical education" in educational institutions in France to the Minister of Public Instruction in 1915.

41 In Coubertin's most complete work on education, his book entitled *Notes sur l'éducation publique* [Notes on Public Education] (1901), major portions of which have been included in Volume I of the French edition, he wrote, "There are two ways of understanding internationalism. One is that of the socialists, the revolutionaries, and in general, of theoreticians and utopians.... The second is that of men who make observations without prejudice and take reality, rather than their favorite ideas, into account. For a long time now, these men have realized that national characteristics are an indispensable precondition for the life of a people and that, far from weakening them, contact with other people makes them sharper" (pp. 262-263).

When he said, "It is necessary to touch the crowd[42]", Coubertin described better than anyone else the program that he adopted after 1918. Clearly, the imperatives that the Olympic Games set down for the individual were not enough to make athletics an integral part of daily life. The Olympic education needed for that, Coubertin wrote in 1918, must have "permanent factories[43]". Yet he could not give anything more than recommendations and theoretical concepts. Time and time again, he called for the establishment of urban cultural centers along the lines of the "ancient gymnasium". He gave a practical example of such an institution by establishing the Olympic Institute at Lausanne. The work done there for Belgian and French soldiers interned in 1917-18 was exemplary. This was the first time Coubertin's desire to establish labor universities had been put into practice. His zeal in making appeals on this matter never flagged. Many examples of these efforts are included in Part I of this edition.

At the end of World War I, Coubertin entrusted an additional role to Olympism: "Face to face with a new world which needs to be ordered in accordance with principles which have hitherto been thought Utopian but are now ripe to be applied", he said, "humanity must draw upon forces in its past heritage which can be used to construct the future[44]."

Yet as they became increasingly popular, in Coubertin's view the Olympic Games had become farther and farther removed from their original purpose. Of course, in the midst of the war, he had managed to ensure that Antwerp would be the site of the 1920 Games, thereby ensuring the continuation of the ancient four-year cycle. But he was irritated to note that the Games had become a spectacle with an international reputation, even though the crowd "still only vaguely grasped their significance[45]". In vain, he hoped for some change in this respect, following the profound turmoil of World War I.

An idealist, Coubertin did not wish to sacrifice the lofty goals of his humanism to the technocrats who had become ensconced at the IOC, nor to the international athletic associations which had grown independent.

His colleagues at the IOC granted his wish to see Paris become the headquarters of the Olympic Games. After that crowning achievement, he wished to withdraw from the IOC.

In his farewell address to the 1925 Prague Olympic Congress, he revisited the subject of the conspicuous duty that every modern State has to ensure that everyone has a chance to engage in sports. In this way, the masses would not need to deify their athletic idols without engaging in sports themselves. He also announced initiatives on the educational front, outside the Olympic movement[46].

These initiatives resulted in the establishment of a "Union Pédagogique Universelle" [Universal Educational Union] (U.P.U.), founded in 1925 at Coubertin's recommendation. It proposed a universal program of education in 1930. His initiatives also resulted in publications by the Bureau International de Pédagogie Sportive [International Bureau of Sports Pedagogy] (B.I.P.S.), which he had founded in 1926, an organization that he directed.

It seems contradictory that Coubertin reproached members of the IOC for playing the role of "technical advisors" rather than that of "defenders" of the Olympic spirit[47], while at the same time speaking of the great success of the Olympic idea, and even of the "victory of Olympism[48]."

In his lecture entitled "Olympia", published in this volume, he made the following comment in 1929: "I handed over effective control of restored Olympism to my successor only when I judged the work of renewal to be complete down to its smallest details, adapted to present necessities[49]."

Having considered Olympism the ideal for a form of education that would accent the physical, mental, and moral faculties of the individual, how could Coubertin go on to articulate yet another line of thought clearly, once he left the IOC? Since Coubertin was well aware of his educational mission, he had to reject any sort of compromise, even when reality imposed its limits on him. No one could ask him to renounce his publicly-acknowledged share in the success of the Olympic Games. How could he have repudiated the work that formed the very fabric of his life?

Coubertin's high ideals for the Olympic Movement did not make it easy for his successor in the presidency of the IOC, the Belgian Baillet-Latour, or for any President of the IOC, to perform his duties. At the same time, this underscored the specific moral characteristics of the office.

The "Message to the Young Athletes of All Nations", sent from Olympia in 1927 and reprinted in this volume[50], the "Message to the Athletes and Participants in the Olympic Games of 1928 in Amsterdam[51]", and the "Message to American Youths[52]" on the occasion of the fortieth jubilee of the IOC in 1934 are important testimony to his attentive involvement in the on-going growth of the Olympic movement.

Coubertin had his share of family worries concerning the health of his two children. He himself suffered from premature ageing. Starting in the 1930s, the driving force needed to fuel the activities of an effective publicist had been broken. At first, he planned to write a five-volume memoir, only fragments of which were written. The first volume, published by the Bureau International de Pédagogie Sportive in 1932, Mémoires Olympiques [Olympic Memoirs], came out shortly thereafter in a German translation[53].

42 *XXVe Anniversaire des Jeux Olympiques.* Discours. [Twenty-Fifth Anniversary of the Proclamation of the Olympic Games. Speech.] Lausanne, April 1919. Special pamphlet. (IOC Archives). Reprinted in *The Olympic Idea,* Schorndorf 1967, p. 74. See text 5.1/9 in this volume.

43 Lettres Olympiques V, in: *Gazette de Lausanne,* November 28, 1918, no. 325, pp. 1-2. Reprinted in *The Olympic Idea,* Schorndorf 1967, p. 55. See text 3.17 in this volume.

44 XXVth "Anniversary of the Olympic Games." Speech, in: *The Olympic Idea,* Schorndorf, Hofmann, 1967, p. 74.

45 "L'apport de la VIIe Olympiade." [The Contribution of the VIIth Olympiad.] in: *La Revue Sportive Illustrée,* vol. 16, 1920, no. 3 (p. 10). See text 4.2.2/34 in this volume. Reprinted in *The Olympic Idea,* Schorndorf 1967, p. 86.

46 Cf. Coubertin, "Discours prononcé à l'ouverture des Congrès Olympiques." [Speech Given at the Opening of the Olympic Congresses]. See text 5.1/11 in this volume.

47 Cf. Coubertin, "Quarante années d'Olympisme." Allocution prononcée lors de la célébration du 40e Anniversaire. [Address Given on the Occasion of the Celebration of the 40th Anniversary]. See text 6.5.4 in this volume.

48 Coubertin, "La Victoire de l'Olympisme." [The Victory of Olympism], in *La Revue Sportive Illustrée,* Vol. 16, 1920, no. 2 (p. 2). See text 4.2.2/36 in this volume.

49 Coubertin, "Olympie. Conférence donnée à Paris le 10 mars 1929." [Olympia. Lecture Given at Paris on March 10, 1929], pp. 10-11. See text 5.1/14 in this volume. Reprinted in *The Olympic Idea,* Schorndorf, Hofmann, 1967, pp. 106-119, (quote, p. 118).

50 See text 5.1/12 in this volume.

51 See text 5.2/10 in this volume.

52 See text 5.1/15 in this volume.

53 Cf. Coubertin, *Mémoires Olympiques* [Olympic Memoirs]. Published by Bureau International de Pédagogie Sportive. Lausanne 1932. See also note 2 to this introduction.

54 Cf. Coubertin, "Aux Coureurs d'Olympie-Berlin." [Message to the Olympia-Berlin Runners]. See text 5.1/16 in this volume.

55 *Coubertin,* "Les Assises philosophiques de l'Olympisme moderne." Message radiodiffusé le 4 août 1935. [The Philosophic Foundation of Modern Olympism. Message Broadcast on August 4, 1935.] See text 5.1/17 in this volume.

56 Cf. C. Diem, "La Journée d'Olympie." [The Day at Olympia], in *Olympische Rundschau/Olympic Review,* Vol. 1, Berlin 1938, no. 2, p. 13.

Despite official invitations, Coubertin did not attend the 1928 Olympic Games in Amsterdam, or the 1932 Olympic Games in Los Angeles. Carl Diem's inspiration to hold an Olympic torch race for the 1936 Games was completely consistent with Coubertin's ideas. Coubertin's inspiring message to the runners carrying the Olympic torch to Berlin[54] is part of his Olympic testament.

Coubertin's most significant Olympic activity in his final years was a speech on the "philosophic foundation of modern Olympism[55]" broadcast on radio in 1935. In condensed form, once again he set forth the ideas that he had developed over the decades concerning modern Olympism. These ideas can be summarized in the following three sayings:

1. "To celebrate the Olympic Games is to appeal to history".
2. "Olympism is not a system, but a spiritual and moral attitude".
3. "My unshakable faith in youth and the future has been and remains the principle that gives life to my work".

From a distance, Coubertin followed the 1936 Olympic Games with great interest. The artistic aspects of those Games showed Coubertin's influence, in the performance of Beethoven's "Ode to Joy" on the opening night of the Games, for example.

Despite the violent debate raging at the time about the politicization of the Olympic Games and of sports, his hopes for the future of Olympism remained unshaken until his death in Geneva, on September 2, 1937. As requested in his will, Coubertin's heart was buried in Olympia on March 26, 1938, in the marble stele erected to commemorate the restoration of the Olympic Games, just steps from the ancient stadium. The International Olympic Academy (IOA), envisioned by Carl Diem at the ceremonies when the heart was placed there, was set up in the immediate vicinity[56]. The Academy was founded jointly by John Ketseas of Greece, and Carl Diem. It perpetuates the Olympic heritage of Pierre de Coubertin.

n soir de Novembre 1892... exacte
l amphithéatre de l'ancienne S
é, si j'ai bonne mémoire, de lil
es carrées d'où saillaient les
s qui devaient être Bossuet e
[illegible]
é quelque chose à dire sur l
les potaches présents à la Sor
pensaient à toute autre cl
mplaient, au centre, le plastr
spe impeccable du plus
es d'alors le vicomte Léon de
avant, un président de l'Unio
ut fort bien qu'il n'était pa
mais un homme de grand
sée. À ses côtés, se tenaient
Octave Gréard et le prince O
n du Grand Duc Wladimir
abonner à ce jubilé, et devai
ois de Boulogne le lendemain
à nos jeunes athlètes. Le f
tre était orné de drapeaux ru
drapeaux français; c'était l'

PART I

REVELATION

A young Pierre de Coubertin, dressed in sports kit, ca. 1885. (IOC Archives)

1. THE SEARCH FOR A NEW EDUCATION

1.1 EDUCATION IN ENGLAND: INTRODUCTION (1888)

Coubertin visited English and Irish schools and universities, observing them on several occasions. He questioned teachers and students alike, in an effort to understand fully educational changes that could not have been foreseen earlier in the nineteenth century. He contrasts the wonderful educational changes achieved by the two famous pioneers cited by Taine with what he had experienced himself during his secondary school years, and with what was still being done in the rut in which French education was stuck.

The 326-page work *Education en Angleterre* [Education in England] comprises an introduction and the following sixteen chapters: Through the Public Schools, Eton, Harrow, Rugby, Wellington, Winchester, Marlborough, Charterhouse, Cooper's Hill, Westminster, Christ's Hospital, General Comments and Conclusions, Catholic Schools, University Memories, Toynbee Hall, and Problems and Solutions.

Applying Le Play's method of observation, which was still new at the time, Coubertin was looking for the determining quality in English education that was so highly regarded then: helping the student discover his own human richness, and teaching him to live fully as a man, to become capable of integrating himself, later on, into a society that expects a great deal of its citizens.

I

Dear reader, what I am presenting to you in these pages is not a treatise on education; rather, these are impressions formed while visiting English public schools.

For a long time now, I have heard you complaining about the situation imposed on French children. You say that things have gone so far that their very right to be children has been taken from them.

They are being stuffed with knowledge.

They are being turned into walking dictionaries.

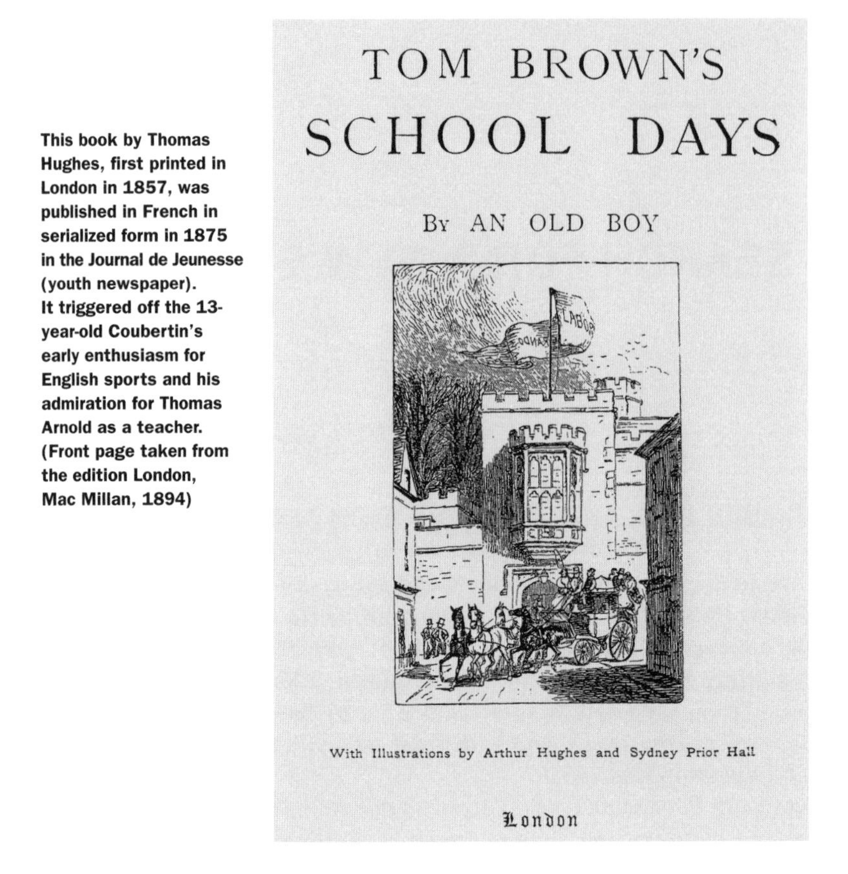

TOM BROWN'S
SCHOOL DAYS

By AN OLD BOY

With Illustrations by Arthur Hughes and Sydney Prior Hall

London

This book by Thomas Hughes, first printed in London in 1857, was published in French in serialized form in 1875 in the Journal de Jeunesse (youth newspaper). It triggered off the 13-year-old Coubertin's early enthusiasm for English sports and his admiration for Thomas Arnold as a teacher. (Front page taken from the edition London, Mac Millan, 1894)

They are being *overworked*; that is the hallowed term. Even as their intelligence is force fed the way geese are force fed, their physical strength is being sapped, their moral energy drained. That is your complaint, and you are right, absolutely right. Unfortunately, there is Saint Routine, patron saint of the University, and Saint Parchment, patron of the kingdom of France, who render your jeremiads futile. You are under their yoke. My God, what would become of your children if they did not have that diploma, so absolutely essential to any self-respecting Frenchman, or if, as their studies drew to a close, you could not present them with a menu of their future options, saying, like a waiter offering soups: "The military or the bench? Diplomacy or administration?" Just suppose one hardy soul among them should come up to you and say, "I want to create my own career". Just imagine the anxiety that that statement would cause you! You do not believe in self-made careers, because you are thinking of those first breaths of pure air that intoxicate high school students given their freedom, and you hasten to move your son from one harness to another.

Verba volant. Saint Routine and Saint Parchment must be stoned to death with deeds, not words. That is why, as I went around England, I collected as many deeds as possible, visiting the main educational institutions, and making inquiries of a large number of teachers and students. If I am not mistaken, this is called proceeding by observation, and that is how one acquires the certainty, a material certainty so to speak, that Le Play has shown to be superior to certainty arrived at by *a priori* reasoning and preconceived theories.

Cast an eye over these notes. You will see that, in a country as Christian and as civilized as our own, children are raised according to procedures that are diametrically opposed to those we use. At the very least, this proves that there are different paths for reaching the same goal. This education is free, as is fitting for an emancipated nation. It does not produce any drop in status, the scourge of our country and the cause of many a revolution. Doubtless it errs in other ways, since perfection is not of this world. Yet such advantages are worth looking at in detail. Of course, we must not rely on appearances alone. In this way more than in any other, the English, in whom the spirit of tradition and the spirit of novelty are intertwined, have grafted the present onto the past. Behind venerable facades devoutly preserved, they have built according to modern demands. The architecture of their public schools is Gothic. Their teaching is somewhat Gothic, too, but their education is not so at all.

Dear reader, this is what I hope to prove to you. I may succeed or I may not, but I beg you, please refrain from labeling me an "Anglomaniac". That is a term used as a shield by all and sundry, as though one cannot appreciate anything at all from the other side of the English Channel unless one's mind is distorted or one's viewpoint slanted.

Well then, we are agreed! We hate the English, and they hate us. But please, let us leave Ireland and the theories of Malthus alone, not to mention the countless clichés that speakers of English collect.

It is always useful to study one's neighbor, even if that neighbor is an adversary, for by imitating the good in him, one can correct it and do it even better. The less clearly forewarned, if they do not consider me an Anglomaniac, will say to me: "What is the use of studying them? We can draw no profit from such an exercise... *our characters are too different*". What a poor excuse! Education is first and foremost the art of making men. Are men not the same everywhere? Do they not all have bodies that must be strengthened, and characters that must be formed?

What I admire in our neighbors, too, is that they have remained true to their traditions. They understand them, and they are laying the groundwork for respect of those traditions by future generations. To the contrary, it is possible for a people, deceived, lost, blindly obeying some current of false ideas, to misunderstand its own nature, its destiny, its needs. They may raise their children in a manner that runs contrary to their character and to the qualities of their race. I believe that that is pretty much the case for us, and that French education is not the art of making Frenchmen. In any case, it is not the art of making men, for men do not consist solely of an intelligence, and we act as though that were the case.

The English have not fallen into that trap.

Merely instructing a child is not the same thing as raising the child. "There is a profound difference between instruction, which provides knowledge, endows the mind, and creates scholars, and education, which develops the faculties, raises the mind, and makes men". This quotation could pass for a truism, except that in our day, in France, deplorable confusion has been created between these two notions. It could be said in the past, and can be repeated with all the more reason today: instruction is everything, education, nothing.

The lines that I have just cited were written by Bishop Dupanloup. Guizot, who is equally worthy of quotation when it comes to education, said somewhere, "There is no freedom for these children if they are not left *alone* to some extent, and given over to themselves". Montaigne gave this precept: "To brace their minds, their muscles must be hardened". From Jean-Jacques Rousseau comes this axiom: "The weaker the body, the more demanding it becomes; the stronger it is, the more it obeys."

These four quotations from four French authors seem to me to summarize the spirit of English education perfectly, clearly, and completely.

Dear reader, I have ended up writing what almost amounts to a preface, and I apologize ... but the fault lies with you.

II

To beg your pardon, I will now present a second preface. The institutions I must discuss first are, in effect, prefaces to the secondary schools, a sort of transition that is easily handled, and that allows the child to enter the world of school gradually, to grow progressively more accustomed to it.

This school world in England is rather unusual, even bizarre in some ways. Traditions are maintained there with jealous care, so that reformers, unless they act with the greatest possible tact, run the risk of becoming extremely unpopular. The hierarchy there possesses considerable power. In a word, it is a true society with its own particular organization, its own customs, laws, and prejudices, as well. These young citizens are quite well aware of all this, as the proud statements one of them published in his school's magazine (*Rugby Magazine*) show: "We form a true social unit, a society within which we must not only learn, but act and live as well, – act and live not merely as children, but as children who will become men". The young writer was bragging a bit, in allotting this patent of importance to his fellow students, but in the end he was expressing well the thoughts of teachers and students alike. It is easily understandable that a child, suddenly transported into such surroundings, would feel particularly homesick and exposed, being in over his head before knowing how to swim. That is why there is a need for a transition.

The English have never been particularly hasty to be separated from their children. First, they find no financial advantage in it, because most often they have many children who are close to each other in age, which makes education easier and simpler. Collective lessons are always less costly than private lessons. What is more, in the public schools, board is expensive, so there are no savings to be realized in that regard. This perspective is important, even when considering classes that are comfortably well-off. A young couple deemed to be rather wealthy may well find itself, at some point, in a position where they have to count costs, even though they are not entirely penniless. This has to do with the organization of English society, where women most often marry without a dowry and where shares in an inheritance are not divided up under the watchful eye of the law, in an orderly fashion, likes slices of cake.

Throughout the world, there is no lack of people who consider secondary school the proper place for a child to spend childhood and adolescence. They feel that the earlier one leaves one's family, the better. Public opinion in England has not allowed itself to be drawn to such strangely paradoxical views. How can one think that society is what is least suitable for one's children, and what a sad compliment for those who think that way! To the contrary, the English, many of whom regard their secondary schools as a stopgap measure (what would they ever think of ours?), would like to extend the period during which parents and children live together in the same household for as long as possible. That is when family ties are formed, with such strength that they are capable of being sustained for a lifetime. Those who are united by such ties will be scattered all over, meeting up again only rarely. Yet buried in their memories they carry the deeply-engraved image of "home" with them. Have we not often noted the apparent contrast between this "home, sweet home", a name that comes so readily to British lips, and those far-off, nomadic, utterly independent lives that seem to suit people devoid of a native country, without home towns or families?

So parents want the period their children spend at home to be rather long, and long enough to set their memories deeply. When they do decide to separate from them, it is on the condition that three times a year, at Christmas, Easter, and during the summer, they will all be back together again for a good stretch of time, until the time comes when it is agreed that each one will follow his own destiny, entering active life.

One young mother who had just given birth to her firstborn said, "I will raise my child in the English manner. It's simple: you need a tub and lots of water". I realize that these conditions are necessary, but they are not unique, leading one to think that only people who live in England ever bathe.

In England, from a very early age, boys devote themselves to the charms of the out-of-doors, and lessons do not come along to trouble them too soon. Yet though they are less concerned with adorning their minds and setting their intelligence in motion early on, they think that it is never too soon to start forming their characters and developing their energies. No sooner has the young Englishman started to run by himself than he already knows he is a man, and that the tears his sister is allowed to shed are shameful for him. "Be a man", he is told over and over, all day long. Several times, I saw boys who were not yet learning to read, who already had enough self-control that they could choke back their tears when they had hurt themselves in a fall. Note that this first education is not at all Spartan. The nonsense of the late Lycurgus is quite absent. Mothers are very tender toward their children, fathers are indulgent, and the nursery system is not at all rude. Neither care nor delicate attention is neglected there. Thus they are seeking less to harden them to suffering itself than to keep them from giving it away by outward signs... a subtle distinction. I would like to discuss it in further detail, because it is a true distinction.

The results are obvious in their games. Boys do not make sand castles, they roll around on the grass, straddle fences, and climb trees. Their daring is proverbial.

Harrow football team, 1883 (taken from: Fifty Years of Sport at Oxford, Cambridge and the Great Public Schools, London, W. Southwood, 1922, p. 248)

Harrow football team in action (taken from: Fifty Years of Sport at Oxford, Cambridge and the Great Public Schools, London, W. Southwood, 1922, p. 243)

Everyone knows that charming scene depicted by Taine, in which a child astride his pony, entering a field near a bull with a menacing eye, calls back down the line of horses to his big sisters, saying, "Hey, girls, don't be afraid, I'll lead the way."

Such are the creatures that people English private schools. Those whose parents must be away for a while enroll them at a tender age, or those whose parents live in London and dread the climate, as well as those whose precocious intelligence is worthy of being pushed along. Students seeking merely to make the transition enter these schools late, often just to spend time there. As a general rule, public schools admit students no younger than twelve or thirteen, unless the institution also has a preparatory school. This is the case in Catholic schools, where students often enter for their first communion.

A teacher, usually a graduate from one of the universities, takes on some students at his home. This is the embryo of the private school. There are all kinds and sizes of them, and they are everywhere: by the ocean, in the country, near cities and far from them. The number of students varies considerably. Averages normally range from ten to twenty. Thirty is a lot. More than that would be too much, because then the teacher would have to share his authority. He would have to give up some of his functions, to have supervisors, *ushers*, what in France is known by the detested name of *pion*. That race of creatures is scarcely less execrable in England, it is just less widespread.

Ushers are not gentlemen.

Who will ever manage to give the word gentleman its true meaning? It is indefinable, yet it corresponds to a very clear idea: mothers who entrust their children to a gentleman know that their children will not lose their good manners while with him, that they will never hear an inappropriate word, and that they will not pick up any unseemly habits.

We must bear in mind that university education is a patent of distinction, and that a man who has been through Oxford or Cambridge never leaves them, whatever his background may be, without the polish that frequenting proper society provides. Yet that is insufficient to explain what was long a mystery for me: the ease with which the English become so distinguished or, if you will, their natural distinction. I would be drawn to search for an explanation in their extreme simplicity. With the exception of the London swells, simplicity increases in keeping with wealth and social position. There is no striking of postures among the men, nor any mincing ways among the women. Nothing is done for show. This may result in a little egotism and dryness in relationships, but the general tone is only the better for it.

In a private school, it is the teacher's wife who holds the reins of government within the house, the laundry, the infirmary, and the kitchen. She leaves her residence only to inspect and to give orders. It would never occur to an Englishwoman to imitate a certain keeper of a Paris "school", who brought her needlework into the study and had her students describe their mothers' and sisters' outfits to her. In England, there are two separate houses in practice, but the boys often go from one to the other; they are received in the salon. They even help out with showing guests around. When set up in this way, a private school is like an extended family...

This drawing by Pierre de Coubertin is of the little Château de Mirville in Normandy (France) in about 1840. The architectural style is typical of the residences of this region in the 16th century. A very artistic person, Pierre de Coubertin, who was also an excellent musician, inherited the gifts of his father who was a well-known painter in his day. (Navacelle Collection)

Are you having difficulty finding a private school? Then address your attention to one of the agencies listed in the *Times* or the *Standard*, which will provide you with a number of prospectuses free of charge. For a whole week, you will receive an avalanche of letters and little pamphlets. A circular has sent the teachers associated with the agency your name and address, and they are quick to tell you their terms, expressing their desire to merit your confidence.

Drawings or photographs of the house are often enclosed with the letter. The geological details of the soil and occasionally an analysis of the drinking water are also included. Before long they will be advertising that they have a Pasteur Filter, the way hotels now post signs at their entry reading: Elevator. Of course, everything is presented in the most favorable light, but I must say that, in general, the material setup is quite satisfactory.

Private schools are divided into several categories. Some are small preparatory schools, while others are truly secondary schools founded by a company of shareholders or by a group of teachers. Many hold middle ground between the two. Finally, others are "cramming" schools.

In the first category, I would list Bowden House school, located near Harrow. Children are admitted from the age of seven to eleven. The cost is 80 to 100 guineas per year (2,000 to 2,600 francs). Of course, it has all the facilities necessary for cricket and other games. That is listed on practically the first line of their prospectus.

Then I would cite Saint Edmund's College, Elgin Crescent, Notting Hill, W. This is the first of the day schools recently founded by an association of Cambridge University graduates. There, children are accepted from the age of six. They may commute, or be day boarders. Class hours are from 9:15 A.M. to 11:00 A.M., from 11:15 A.M. to 1:00 P.M., and in the afternoons, from 3:00 to 5:00 P.M., or from 2:00 to 4:00 P.M., depending on the season. Cost: 12 to 15 guineas per year (312 to 390 francs).

Appuldurcombe College, located on the Isle of Wight, is the former chateau of the counts of Yarborough. It is a splendid property, surrounded by a 700-acre park. It has been comfortably converted for its new use, yet it retains its grand appearance. It was the entire estate, not just the chateau, that was bought, including the hunting rights. For two pounds per year (50 francs), students age seventeen are permitted to kill the school's partridges. But the property is also used for more than mere entertainment. If the students are destined for life in the colonies, they are trained in agriculture, farming, and farm management. Among other modern languages, they are taught Hindustani.

Appuldurcombe can accommodate up to fifty students, a large number. Efforts to separate younger students from the older ones are made in vain; such separation is never quite fully achieved. All in all, the private school should never aim to replace the public school. It is suitable only for preparing young children for a change in their lives, to act as a vestibule for higher schooling.

As for the "cramming" institutions, they barely fall within the purview of this study, where it is my intention to discuss education rather than instruction. In these institutions, the goal is to stock up the student's memory in light of some critical examination. Happily, their role is not that significant in England, where examinations are such that regular and moderate work is nearly always enough to ensure success. Therefore, it is fruitless to tarry on this preliminary subject. Only a few explanations were needed. I am saving the detailed information for the public schools and the Universities. I may be reproached for having pushed this a bit far. But education, which is such a beautiful and grandiose work, has always seemed to me to comprise a multitude of small things, small details, small considerations that appear quite secondary. That is why my only purpose here has been to create a mosaic of facts, placing those that I was able to gather in person one next to the other.

First I will study the public schools in the United Kingdom: Eton, Harrow, Rugby, Wellington, Winchester, Marlborough, Charterhouse, Westminster, etc., then the major Catholic schools. Finally I will study the Universities, particularly Oxford and Cambridge. In conclusion, I will present considerations of the school-related problems we are facing in France and that the English system, modified and adapted for our race, might help in solving.

That, at least, is my hope.

Now all my prefaces are done, and we are about to embark for Eton. Here I would simply like to list the names of those who were particularly helpful to me in my efforts, and to whom I am happy to be able to address my thankful acknowledgment from afar. They are Messrs. Bowen (Harrow), Lee-Warner (Rugby), Cornish, Mitchel (Eton), du Boulay (Winchester), Thomas (Marlborough), Gunion Rutherford (Westminster), Croslegh (Cooper's Hill), R. Lee (Christ's Hospital), Norris (Edgbaston), Souter (Oscott), O'Hare (Beaumont), Liddon, Lane-Poole, Wilson-Lynch (Oxford), Sedley-Taylor, Waldstein (Cambridge), and Arnold (Dublin).

L'Éducation en Angleterre. Collèges et Universités. Introduction.
[Education in England. Secondary Schools and Universities. Introduction],
Paris, Librairie Hachette, 1888, pp. 1-23.

1.2 ENGLISH EDUCATION IN FRANCE (1889)

One can imitate only what one is already prepared to produce! Can English education – the best of what it has to offer – be adapted "to the character, aspirations, and nature" of the French? Coubertin attempted to do so in cooperation with the well-informed leaders of some institutions and university directors.

Early in 1889, Coubertin published a 206-page work entitled *L'Éducation anglaise en France* [English Education in France]. This book, written in the calm of Mirville and completed by September, 1888, summarizes the new situation that Coubertin was able to bring about in some Parisian schools, and shows "his plans and hopes" after five years of experience. The athletic association of the Lycée Lakanal, a government-run high school, joined the associations that had already been formed and were flourishing. But the constant effort to foster harmonious integration of humanized athletic activity within the overall situation of the various academic disciplines, and to effectively transform the atmosphere there, was thwarted at every turn by initiatives that were sometimes clumsily, and at other times deliberately directed against Coubertin's educational plans.

This book tells us of these efforts, and shares with us the author's educational critiques.

The work is divided into two parts. The first is entitled "At the École Monge", comprising four chapters: The Cure for Overworking, A Committee of Youths and of Rejuvenated People, The École Monge at Eton, and Sport, Freedom and Hierarchy. The second is entitled "Plans and Hopes", comprising eight chapters: The Question of Day Schools, In the Leafy Shade of Juilly, Our Students, Rowing, Our Strategic Plan, In the Distance!, The Choice of Careers, and A Speech by Paul Bert. The book ends with a ten-page appendix, which tells us of Coubertin's struggle to make his plans come to fruition: List of the Members of the Committee for the Propagation of Physical Exercise in Education, Letter to the Members of the Société d'Économie Sociale and of the Unions de la Paix Sociale, Letter to the Presidents of Rowing Societies in Paris and the Provinces, The National League of Physical Education. The books begins with a foreword by Jules Simon, Minister of Public Instruction from 1870 to 1879, which starts with these revealing words, "I have but one regret, and that is that I am not fifteen and I am not a student at the École Monge!" (p. V).

Coubertin wanted to teach the joy of living to everyone, a joy that was sensitive in its training and spiritual in its value. Sport becomes an essential means to that end, because motion is man's celebration.

The excerpts presented here provide an opportunity to get a sense of the quality of Coubertin's efforts in education, to make actions effective on the basis of a well-balanced personality.

1.2.1 THE CURE FOR OVERWORKING[1]

In 1887, the word "overwork" was on everyone's lips, and summed up the criticism which the French were levelling at their contemporary school system. Parents believed that their children had too many lessons and not enough free time, and that their education was too intellectual. On several occasions Coubertin addressed the issue of resolving this problem of overwork.

Coubertin is being ironic here. He shows that "routine" and "parchment" (i.e. a love of diplomas) are saints to which too many sacrifices are offered.

For Coubertin, permanent and excessive fatigue derived essentially from physical weakness, intellectual dullness, and moral degradation. Changes in programs do not mean physical or moral changes.

I

A few days ago, one witty hostess, an expert in the art of avoiding dead silences in the conversation, said in my presence, "Between the construction of the Eiffel Tower and the issue overworking, I always have something to get my guests talking". I do not know what the future holds for the Eiffel Tower, but I do know that the problem of overworking is heading toward a solution. This is a subject on which everyone has stated his own view, everyone has offered his own solution. One among all these new or repeated ideas has stood out. It is an idea that still has many opponents, yet I feel that all those who are looking for the key to the problem must rally around it. This key idea is to improve physical education.

The first people to cry *Overwork!* the way people cry *Fire!* certainly attacked existing programs, and they did so with a vengeance. They presented frightened parents with a list of everything that children have to learn, and a daunting list it is for those who take it literally. By putting one and one together, they concluded that since the sum of all this knowledge is far more than what a child is likely to accumulate between the ages of eight and seventeen, children taught in this style learn nothing, absolutely nothing. As the old saying goes, "He who grasps at too much loses everything". If we had listened to them, nothing of the existing programs would have been kept. Something completely new would have replaced them, based on other principles and other methods, striving toward a goal as yet ill-defined. I do not know how much disillusionment would have come from implementing so unwisely designed a plan. Yet the certainty that this great revolution did not achieve its goal would loom large. As before, overworking would remain a problem, or at least the physical weakness, intellectual dullness, and moral collapse apparently caused by overworking would. What surprises me, from my perspective, is not that children's schedules are overloaded, but that anyone is surprised at that fact. The great strides achieved in modern science have continually expanded the base of prior knowledge that each generation must use as a foundation to raise the monument that will mark its own passage. What is more, this same scientific progress has shortened distances, mixed up the ranks, destroyed the previous organization of society, and created fierce competition at the entry level of every profession. Yet people want students' schedules not to be overloaded during this period of the child's development, when no choices have yet been made regarding specialization in studies, when all these young travelers are entering active life with the same baggage!

1 This lecture was given on May 29, 1888 at the annual Congress of the Société d'Économie Sociale, under the title: "The Cure for Overworking and the Transformation of the Paris High Schools."

The Ecole Alsacienne playing rugby football in the Bois de Boulogne, Paris (taken from Une Campagne de vingt-et-un ans, p.27)

There is an injustice here, just as there is an injustice in failing to recognize systematically what has been done, perhaps rather timidly, to remedy this regrettable uniformity in the examinations. There is an injustice in not recognizing the sincere efforts and constant search by the leaders of the university army. Thank God they do not listen to their opponents, and that they do not resort to the revolutionary process, destroying in hatred what already exists, without gradually replacing outdated material! We must move forward by trial and error. My view of a plan to revise teaching programs from top to bottom would be no more positive than my opinion of the wild constitutional ravings that their authors present as a sure-fire way to ensure the happiness and tranquillity of the country for ever and ever. In both cases, it is pure reasoning and, frequently, the imagination that pay end up paying. No account whatever is taken of the impartial observations that Le Play has taught us to view as a necessary basis for making any progress at all.

Once they have finished with programs, they attack health conditions. Some people head right for their target, writing draft legislation that is remarkable for the fact that it never has more than one or two articles. Some such citizen would gladly submit legislation in which Article 1 would read: "No school may be opened in a city". Article 2 would say: "All schools now in existence must be relocated to the countryside". Period. No objections, please... now off to the country with you, and hurry up about it.

In America, houses are moved on rollers when the site where they were built loses favor. But if we were to plan to relocate our schools that way, they would fall apart. These old buildings can no longer handle such modern treatment. In all seriousness, I could speak to you at length of the many difficulties that arise with regard to founding high schools in the countryside, at least these days. Aside from the fact that many of these difficulties are quite obvious, there is another important point that relates more immediately to my topic. Such relocation would do nothing to solve the problem of overwork. A high school in the countryside is not a myth. There are some. This very morning, several of you admired the magnificent buildings and the beautiful gardens of the Lycée Lakanal. A plethora of precautions has been taken there in terms of health conditions. Far be it from me ever to think of speaking ill of proper hygiene. Two days ago in this very place, Dr. Rochard eloquently recalled the wonderful results that can be achieved by observing his rules. But frankly, when I see a discussion starting on the question of unilateral or bilateral lighting in classrooms and study halls, I feel a twinge of regret that our children are in such sorry state that we find ourselves musing over such details on their behalf.

Day schools are a third hobby horse, a third panacea, the only remedy for overworking in the eyes of those who support them. As I see it, the day school is the best type of education from many points of view, and we must work to make them more widespread. But with regard specifically to overworking, such schools cannot be considered a remedy. They do not even make it easier to implement a remedy – far from it. Parents are not always free to be at the service of their children on holidays. So, what do they do when they are not at school? They take them to stores or on visits. Older children too often manage to run off God knows where.

Gentlemen, I said before that the current system engenders physical weakening and intellectual dullness, as well, and always moral collapse. So you can well imagine what I think of plans to militarize education, and to provide a counterweight against the fatigue caused by study through military exercises. You might well create more solid muscles that way, but you will also assuredly create minds that are even less open, and characters that are even more colorless. We have enough sheep of that kind in our poor country – we do not need any more like them. That is exactly what would happen if two utterly dissimilar disciplines, military discipline and scholastic discipline, were mixed up, or if two utterly dissimilar creatures, the soldier and the child, were brought together.

So do not jostle these programs around. Change them wisely and gradually – that is the most preferable approach. Do not spend a fortune to move schools to the countryside, because that would not solve your problem. Do not introduce militarism into education, because that would complicate matters even more. Do not use any large-scale remedies that are less effective than smaller-scale ones. I would ask you to be convinced of just one thing: that your children have to play. They do not play because they do not know *how* to play. Teach them to play! This expression may seem paradoxical, but that is because we do not agree on the meaning of the word *play*. The director of one institution was showing me around an airy yard, planted with a dozen trees. About thirty children were engaged in tiny, Lilliputian motions, playing a thousand pranks there. Four or five were in detention in the corner. Several were walking about with a serious air. Others were squatting down, playing a game of marbles. A few others were having fun just sticking out their tongues and making faces. Their well-intentioned master, rubbing his hands together, said to me, "You see how they play about!" In fact, when you let children out telling them to play, these are the very kinds of games they play. These games have nothing at all to do with the ones we want to introduce into education, which

The rugby football team of the Ecole Monge, Paris (taken from Une Campagne de vingt-et-un ans, p.46)

require different efforts altogether. The first time one touches an oar, it plunges several feet down into the water, then shoots up into the air, spraying water all over everyone. The novice fencer is amazed at seeing his foil go astray all the time, despite his best efforts. In lawn tennis, the ball hits the beginner's head more often than his racket, just as in horseback riding, all it takes is a barely perceptible movement on the part of the horse for the rider to go tumbling off. Regardless of how easy it may seem, do you really think that you would manage to kick a big ball with your foot on your very first try? Just try it and see.

All this requires teaching and training. Many people understand that, but until now few have dared to say so, and no one has dared to do it.

II

That honor was reserved for a man whom I was unwise enough to invite here tonight. His presence here makes it embarrassing for me to tell you all the good things I think of him. At any rate, I will be sure not to tell you his name... Well, his name is Mr. Godart, director of the École Monge.

The École Monge was founded in 1869 by a group of alumni from the École Polytechnique. Today, the school occupies a large site located between the Boulevard Malesherbes and the Avenue de Villiers. Thus it is situated in one of those new, airy, and sumptuous neighborhoods with straight avenues and white stonework that contrasts so sharply with the twisted streets and darkened walls of the Latin Quarter. The difference is even more perceptible between the schools built on the Left Bank and the institution I am speaking about.

A covered, 80 x 30-meter courtyard stands at the center. Picture the hall of a fabulously rich financial company minus all the counters and clerks. The ground is covered in asphalt, and the roof is glazed. There is a gallery at the second-story level, onto which open a long series of doors and windows. At the two ends, there are gymnastics crossbars and stands completely covered with equipment. When you are there, you understand that this school is unlike any other. You sense that it is a compilation of school-related experiences, that routine is looked at askance, and that novel approaches are appealing. In the past, innovation focused on teaching. Along with its younger sister school, the École Alsacienne, the École Monge forged a path that the University soon followed. Prospects for the future are even more encouraging: from now on, efforts will be focused on education.

The report that Mr. Godart submitted to the last General Meeting of stockholders gave some indication of major reforms. The issue of overworking was addressed masterfully in that report. It omitted the useless recriminations that I opposed so vehemently a few moments ago. It did contain a very clear overview of the situation as it stands, and of potential remedies. Despite all that, however, I would scarcely have believed that it could have been implemented so quickly. One gets some idea of the intelligence and sheer force of will required to perform this task so successfully when one considers that the school has 850 students, and that the task was to have those students take a step forward into the unknown – and not just the students, but their parents as well. Their objections had to be foreseen and resolved ahead of time; the enthusiasm of some would have to be bridled, while the ardor of others needed kindling. All the while, no error could be committed, no disorder created, and the studies themselves could not be slowed down in the slightest. I would like to be able to recount for you in detail certain things that happened during this transformation, but I must move right along and explain what that transformation was. Then I will come to the heart of my address, namely how to obtain the benefits of a similar regimen in our high schools.

At the École Monge, Sundays are holidays, and Thursdays are set aside for outings. As they were insistent that these outings not be eliminated, the new forms of recreation were spread out over the other days of the week: Tuesdays and Fridays for the older students, Mondays, Wednesdays, and Saturdays for the younger ones. Those who are preparing to enter the advanced government schools are following a different schedule for the moment, because the main focus is not to place their next round of examinations in jeopardy. So if you happen to pass by the École Monge at about two o'clock in the afternoon on one of the days I just mentioned, you will see an enormous carriage headed up by a team of four horses, followed by a number of omnibuses full of children. They are all heading to the Bois de Boulogne. The carriage drops all the young horseback riders off in front of the riding school at the Jardin d'Acclimatation. Some of the omnibuses head for the Pré Catalan, others for the lake. At the Pré Catalan, a cycling instructor is available for those interested in learning his art. Elsewhere, there are groups of all sorts. Out on the lake, some are rowing around in those heavy boats designed for dowagers, that the guards rent to the public. Soon, however, the handsome skiffs with their moveable benches that the school has ordered will replace them. Then, on one of the great lawns in the woods, some students are even playing cricket, if you please. You might object that all this must cost the families a pretty penny, that it is exorbitant. The cost of the transportation, the entrance fee for the Jardin d'Acclimatation, and the rental of the Pré Catalan: ten centimes per student per day, or a total of three francs a month. Riding lessons cost one franc, and the horseback rides in the woods under the watchful eye of a riding master are two francs an hour. Let me assure you that no pressure is brought to bear on the parents, and that students not participating in these outings do supervised work at the school. I must say, however, that there are few such students, and that there will be fewer and fewer of them as time goes on.

III

Gentlemen, you will easily see what is keeping other schools from simply following the example set by the École Monge. For high schools, in particular, this model is inconceivable: they are located far from the Bois de Boulogne, with the single exception of the Lycée Janson de Sailly. These schools house a large number of students. A general regimen must be found that is applicable for them all. Finally, they do not have the financial resources necessary in such instances. Not all of these schools has its own special board, so the schools do not benefit from the generosity of board members, should they choose to contribute. By contrast, though, the high schools do host outings on Thursdays, yet I am not at all in favor of them. At the École Monge, the Thursday outings are held in the country, thanks to the omnibuses that transport the students there. The decision was made to retain this practice; case closed. Nearly everywhere else, these outings take place clear across Paris. It would be a great pleasure for me to see these outings eliminated, for reasons that would take too long to present here. What is more, there is an easy reform that could be implemented. It would consist of this: instead of giving Thursdays from noon until the evening as free time, five hours off would be given twice a week. We must not believe that, even with the programs already in place, the length of working hours cannot be reduced. Just the opposite has been proven over and over, and I must say that if these hours have not been cut back, it is basically because no one knows what to put in their place.

You might ask what I would put in there place, myself. I will tell you.

If you picture exactly where the major secondary schools (the only ones I am addressing here) are located on a map of Paris, you will see that they fall roughly into three groups. The schools in one group have easy access to, or are located directly on, the Bois de Boulogne. This is true for the Lycée Janson de Sailly and the École Gerson, located on the rue de la Pompe in Passy, and for the École Monge. This is also applicable for the Lycée Concordet and its subordinate institutions, the Collège Chaptal, and the day school in the rue de Madrid, via the St. Lazare train station.

The two other groups are on the Left Bank. There, you have a high school under construction on the Boulevard de Vaugirard, and the Jesuits' secondary school. At the gates of Paris, there is the Lycée de Vanves. On the Sceaux railway line, there is Lakanal, Arcueil, and Sainte-Barbe de Champs. At the departure platform of that railway line, though granted it bears only the vaguest resemblance to a railroad, there is the École Alsacienne. Finally, there is another group of schools that comprises the Lycée Saint-Louis, the Lycée Henri IV, the Lycée Louis-le-Grand and the

Students in The Ecole Alsacienne gymnasium in Paris at the end of the 19th Century (IOC Archives)

Lycée Sainte-Barbe de Paris, which are nearly equidistant from the Orléans, Sceaux, and Montparnasse railway lines. The Lycée Charlemagne, isolated at the far end of the Rue de Rivoli, is not very far from the Orléans train station.

In these three directions, our secondary students must find what they are missing in Paris: fields of play and organized sports. Therefore, the important thing is to create school parks consisting of vast fields divided and maintained according to the needs of those sports, along with a shed, a covered playground, and changing areas. Students from the various schools would go there by turns to spend the afternoon. There, out in the country, the widest possible variety of activities could be provided for them: walking, running, chases, cricket, tennis, etc.

You see, gentlemen, that this is a modest project, one that is specific, limited, and yet difficult to implement. I would be forced to abandon it were it not for the warm, unanimous support that makes me confident that it will be implemented soon. A committee is going to take up this task, for truly it is a task, if I do say so. This committee will be chaired by an eminent man whose eloquent voice touched us all last year, Mr. Jules Simon. The committee also includes Mr. Gréard and Mr. Morel, the Director of Secondary Education, representing the University; Mr. Picot, representing the Institute; General Thomassin, for the Army; Mr. Patinot for the press; Dr. Rochard, Dr. Brouardel and Dr. Labbé, representing the Medical School, which has led the fight against overworking. There will also be the directors of the École Monge, the École Alsacienne and École Gerson, and the superior of Juilly, where physical exercise is highly valued. Finally, there will be the presidents of the Association for the Encouragement of Fencing, of the Association of Water Sports, of the Union of Rowing Associations, and of the Racing Club de France.

These are the names, most of which are well known and held in high esteem, under the auspices of which we will make our appeal to subscribers. But the creation of parks is not the only goal. To make sports more popular, there must be powerful inducements, competitions, and prizes. This means that a whole organization must be set up. In the beginning, we will encounter considerable ill will among the students themselves. It is only after persistent effort that we will overcome their apathy. But we will triumph, of that I have no doubt.

Gentlemen, you came here to listen to the discussion of the transformation of the high schools of Paris. No doubt, you expected loftier considerations and overviews. You may think that the "plan" I have just outlined is a bit on the scanty side to be worthy of the title "transformation". Regardless of the significance that I attach to and for sport itself, I now avow that I view it mainly as a means to an end. In keeping with all English schoolmasters and more than a handful of French schoolmasters, too, I expect three things of it. First, I expect sport to re-establish among our younger generations the balance between body and mind that has been completely lacking for so long. I expect sport to give them not some fleeting form of strength, but long-lasting good health and an extension of youth that allows the individual to leave behind a solid and complete body of work. Second, I expect sport to rid youth of temptations, at a critical age, against which *nothing* in our current regimen effectively militates. I expect sport to provide a field of enthusiasm, to produce a healthy sense of fatigue, and to appease the senses and the imagination.

Yet, gentlemen, I expect a third thing of sport, as well.

For a hundred years, the attention of our schoolmasters has focused entirely on issues of teaching, which some have confused, and sometimes pretended to confuse, with education. Education today is still what the Empire, grafted onto the Ancien régime, made of it. The child is a number. Anything that could exercise the child's initiative is removed, and all responsibility on the child's part is denied. The purpose seems to be to create twenty-one-year-old children. Sport will destroy all that, slowly but surely. In fact, sport presupposes voluntary grouping, and produces a spirit of good conduct, good sense, and character. It stratifies and advances individuals who become auxiliaries to the schoolmasters. It makes children more like human beings.

We may well hope that, once sport has brought about this transformation of the current system, which is a mix of the barracks and the convent, there will be other things among the masses of this country than socialists and followers of General Boulanger.

Gentlemen, I cannot tell whether there are many among you who wear the red carnation, but that is not a matter of great concern to me. We are gathered here under the auspices of a man[2] for whom knowledge of the greatness and decadence of peoples no longer held any secrets, a man who condemned those governments of chance that sprang forth from a single day of tumultuous disorder. And so I have the right to say, and to repeat, that we expect this transformed education to produce citizens who will no longer need to have recourse to such procedures, active and determined citizens who will adopt as their own the motto of the minister of whom I spoke earlier: citizens who will love God, country, and freedom.

"Le remède au surmenage" in:
L'Éducation Anglaise en France [English Education in France],
Paris, Librairie Hachette, 1889, pp. 3-20 (Chapter I).

1.2.2 OUR STUDENTS

In this chapter Coubertin describes from personal experience the dismal situation in French high schools (lycées). He wonders whether the students are in a position to realize what a wretched situation they are in, that they are locked up in a cage and must accept rules of behavior which have nothing to do with free thinking. Sport should help here, but are schoolchildren in a position to appreciate its value? He calls on his colleagues on the Committee for the Propagation of Physical Exercise in Education to tear down the barriers in the high schools with the aid of sport.

I did not keep a tally of the students I saw over the course of last winter, but the list would be long. Indeed, this unusual inquiry, which at first held no particular charm, became quite captivating in the end. Besides, one perfects one's skills as an observer by actually making observations. Details that go unseen at first soon draw one's attention, guiding one's way of thinking. Rather than paying attention to the group as a whole, one focuses on individuals. One learns to identify groups, to perceive what is really there, and to form conclusions. This is how modern novelists work in their thirst for the depiction of reality. All they want in their novels are things that have been *truly lived;* as a result, they must *document* such things thoroughly before putting them into their writing.

"Cross the sidewalk when the day students are leaving school", said one man whose advice was quite sound, "and keep your eyes and ears open". I was diligent in my efforts. I also followed along on their walks, noting their gestures, their facial expressions, their smiles. I tried to grasp isolated words or snippets of conversation, and even managed to do so at times. Then I would make my official visit. I would produce the handwritten letter kindly provided by Mr. Gréard, as a result of which cellars and attics alike would be flung open for me if I so desired. A slight, politely concealed expression of astonishment would pass across the principals' faces, accustomed as they are to seeing inspectors with their eyeglasses and their great frock coats come and go. I would be informed immediately about what I wanted to know, a prospectus in my hand and a ring of keys ready to provide access throughout the establishment. These institutions are all alike: the refectories, with their rows of tables and their unique, stale and damp odor; the dormitories, with their rows of numbered beds and a dais that seems meant for a teacher to instruct students in the art of sleeping. Often, through the windows, one could see students at recreation, walking up and down with the seriousness of thinkers who have reached the great heights of the human spirit. Of course, my guides never forgot to point out the gymnasium, always empty – not of equipment, but of youth to use it. The Principal and the Bursar could not help but congratulate themselves on this state of affairs... the students were a constant source of satisfaction, etc. It is true that these men, these devoted and upright men who are so poorly compensated but so rightly honored, do work for the best. It is not the worker, but the tool that is worthless... So they say that they are happy. The Chaplains certainly seemed on the verge of bemoaning their lot, but they

2 Le Play.

refrained, since they did not want to compromise themselves to no avail... Surely, whatever value there may have been in these house visits, the real study, the instructive and fascinating study, was out in the street.

The roof and walls of a house do not hide the inside from the gaze of passersby any more than the tunic of a student hides what it covers. At first sight, neither the face nor the turns of phrase provide the slightest hint of a personality, which, in point of fact, is often lacking. The student's tunic has a gift for yellowing the skin, rendering the gaze lifeless, the smile dazed, and for making the student's gait utterly awkward. In replacing the tunic, no tailor could ever achieve so completely negative a result. The tunic will remain a masterpiece of the grotesque. As it is also the most illogical and inconvenient invention ever, there is no reason to be surprised that it has lasted so long. These various qualities have ensured its survival. Prudence alone might dictate imposing this garment on all French children from twelve to eighteen, to avoid jealousy. Then private schools would be forbidden to design jackets made of fancy soft, elegant material that have all the advantages of a uniform with none of the inconveniences. These innovations are an affront to equality, and make foreigners think that pupils in government schools are less hardy, less bright, and less graceful than the others... And everyone knows that just the opposite is true.

Despite the universal similarity that the tunic and the kepi give our students, they are quickly categorized, depending on which categories they fit into. Quickly it becomes clear that there are three fundamental types of student. There is the tall, thin, slightly hunched student who walks as though overwhelmed by the weight of a brutal destiny; he is a *flop*. He gives an impression of doleful resignation, of one who has given up the fight. In those heads, there must be desires for freedom, vague impulses toward flight that they are too weak and too undecided to achieve. Other students fit into the category of the *anxious type*: his look is agitated, restless, never settling anywhere. One would almost say that he always feels at fault, and that he is trying to avoid the schoolmaster's gaze. Finally, there is a third type: self-important, clever, exuberant, a little slovenly, a loud talker with quite common looks, an ill-behaved rascal. You would recognize him readily as the type of student who, with a grimace, chokes down the smoke from a big cigar. You have probably heard one on the train, speaking of "raw materials" as though speaking of one of his girlfriends. All three categories have been marked for life. Certainly there are decent, honest individuals among them, students who are active, dedicated, and intelligent. But something of the schoolchild will always remain in them. The boastful ones will design revolutions; the anxious will carry out those revolutions, and the flops will endure them.

What do they talk about on their walks? About their exams and their classes to a certain extent, but mostly about what they see as they walk. Should a lady of the evening pass by, the whole group turns around with grin and pointed comments. Then they all start telling stories about things they have never done, old tales told many a time before but always with some new feature added. In short, the old unhealthy idea always comes back; there is the real recreation. It is mixed in with mathematics, Latin, and all the other work. But this idea has real consequences, and oversight can put a stop to them. Clearly, they commit very serious acts, over and over. These acts stem from boredom, and they are repeated through weakness. I had always readily thought that, through prejudice, students in public schools were systematically put down. I did not believe that they were any worse than students at private schools, from the point of view of morals, but they are. This distinction does not provide the grounds for anyone else to be particularly proud, with some rare exceptions. Boredom and weakness are widespread, as are their disastrous consequences. In the case of public secondary schools, however, there is also the matter of a lack of moral teaching. Church-based teachers often mix too much religion into their instruction; most lay teachers do not mix in enough moral instruction. Justifiably preoccupied with the scientific aspect of their mission, to which they devote all their attention, lay-school teachers are uninterested in the conduct of their students. They feel that students' behavior is none of their business, that it is not their area... The burden of this delicate and important task falls squarely on the shoulders of the master of studies – which is to say that the task is not done at all. The master of studies in a public high school is concerned with one thing only, namely whether the student does or does not have respect for him, a respect to which the master attaches all the more importance the less worthy of it he is.

So, here we have a strange situation: the convent or the barracks. In the first, my son receives a narrow education; in the second, none at all. In the one, he is not allowed to blink without the opinion of his teachers; in the other, once his homework is done and his lessons have been learned, they wash their hands of him entirely! There has been talk of codifying moral instruction... Outside of religion, there is no moral instruction to teach to children. There certainly is such instruction for grown adults, which is merely religion with the label removed. Without that label, however, children scarcely understand it and they do not learn it. I do not know where we will be in a hundred years, but today, it is clear that there is no education without religion, i.e. without the idea of God and without the notion of the life to come. I find the circumlocutions of some teachers deplorable and quite ridiculous in their efforts to reword their sentences to avoid having to pronounce the word God, or implying that a second life will follow this one. One can make an accomplished mind out of a child raised in absolute atheism; but if you manage to make that person an honest man, it comes about through no fault of your own. Whether one is Catholic or Lutheran, Calvinist or Orthodox, religion is not a lesson to be learned, it is an atmosphere to be breathed. That is why government institutions, which necessarily welcome children from different religions, must be day schools and not boarding schools. Other lay, Catholic, Protestant, or even free-thinking institutions should be set up around them. Why not? There must be freedom for all. It's just that one would quickly see the difference between one group and the other.

And so, boredom and weakness, those purveyors of immorality, hold sway pretty much from top to bottom in French education. In the public high schools, add to that the absence of moral instruction and the poor utilization of holidays, and you have the formula for creating a high school student. I return to this unfortunate issue of holidays because it is essential. In religious institutions, boarding students go out once or twice a month, whereas many public high school students

At the Ecole Monge and the Ecole Alsacienne the first school sports clubs were established after 1887 on Coubertin's initiative. Here: students starting a race from their school in Paris. (IOC Archives)

are free every Sunday. Many of these students return to strange settings, a home that is askew, fragmented families. Sometimes they return to a father, an uncle, or a tutor who is so overloaded with work that he cannot take care of the student. So there they are, left to their own devices in the streets of Paris where their best safeguard is to be ugly and dirty. Everyone knows that that is a scant safeguard at best. Shyness need be overcome only once, and there is always a well-intentioned pal ready to help with that initial defeat. I have seen the sailors, Pierre Loti describes, on a spree in the streets of Brest. They are so funny, they sing so loudly, and despite it all they still have such open expressions that one finds oneself starting to laugh, thinking indulgently of the coarse life they have led. One easily excuses this uproar on shore leave. In the streets of London, I have also encountered properly dressed gentlemen staggering from one street lamp to the next, and even more often dead-drunk women carried away by policemen. It is a revolting and disheartening sight. But there is worse yet: there is that atrocious, distressing sight, a schoolchild on a spree. You see them in the bars in the Latin Quarter and in the little mezzanines in the Europe district of Paris, not to mention the ones who let themselves be picked up on the sidewalks in a swoon, with an intense desire to "know what it's like". In the Rue de Moscou and the Rue de Turin, on Sundays in the winter, groups gather around a table with a few bottles of beer, two or three women, a schoolchild, a couple of students from the École Polytechnique... What a nice switch for these youths, hunched over as they are all week, poring over their math! They feel great, but what is there to do? They hang out for a while, chewing the fat, asking each other's opinions. A fine rain begins to fall, gradually forcing them, almost without a thought, close to their girlfriends from the previous Sunday. The group welcomes the schoolchild because he is so young; his naiveté is amusing for a while, just for now... He leaves late, a bit dizzy, feeling that he has "become a man". Poor lad! You will live to regret it.

Such a premature fall from grace is so easy to avoid! Once again, I do not believe in the dangers of the street. Send children across Paris by themselves, toward something they want, something that amuses and captivates them... and nothing will steer them from their path. But if they have the whole day free, bad companions, and a little unhealthy precociousness, then they are lost.

"Ours is not a robust generation", confesses one chronicler *(Journal des Débats*, June 8), "and yet we did plenty of gymnastics in our childhood: twice a week a retired fireman came to the high school. As soon as lunch was done, we would go down to the older students' courtyard. That frightful man was waiting there, standing between the two martinets he called his assistants. He used to make us get in line, addressing us with the brutality of a soldier who never learned Latin and who consoles himself for that fact by boasting of his ignorance. He was the harshest of our teachers, because he feared that we would view him as our inferior. In fact, the students did hold him in some disdain, particularly after eighth grade. They pretended to treat him as the ancient Stoics treated Fate: submitting to it, without attempting to reason with it. Unfortunately, he had considerable, material means for making us feel his authority. He could not have cared less for our disdain. He carried on regardless, and we tired before he did, as if he had truly been Fate. Squatting down, standing up, stretching our arms, stamping our feet in place, all this on command, then working out with dumb-bells, with weights, and finally climbing up onto the gymnastics equipment, not like squirrels, but rather like mechanical puppets, it was always the same program, and the acrobatics were the worst of it". Given this experience, is it any wonder that the author of these lines feels "great coldness with regard to feats of strength and other patriotic distractions"? This is one of the curious and characteristic traits of the generation before us: showing children the brutal and terrifying side of all virile things. It seems that for a long time, the focus has been on turning children away from physical exercise, to make such exercise as unattractive as possible in children's eyes. Children, young and old alike, need to be encouraged to become involved in exercise. Some are gifted with enough boldness to start out on their own, but these children are the exceptions. The others view horses, fencing masks, and bicycles with a mixture of longing and fear. Their desire remains hidden unless one helps them to show it... and time keeps passing. One must also exercise great caution, because children are discouraged by inappropriate jests, harsh words, and failure to succeed for reasons that they cannot perceive; they go astray. If children do not have a certain degree of spontaneity or taste for exercise, in other words if they are *forced*, they will surely have bad memories of the experience, a feeling of rancor and a dislike for the very sport that one would like them to enjoy.

For they must like *one* more than the others. Novelists who want to make their hero seductive always make him slender, fit, *ready for any exercise of which the body is capable*. This is all well and good in books; in practice, it is meaningless. It is true that there are some adroit people who seem to be in command of their bodies and who are always successful right from the start with the movements they want to perform. But this very ease makes it impossible for physical exercises to produce beneficial effects for such people. Because they engage in all sports, they do not work hard at any one of them in particular. In general, and as a rule, "an easy sport has no effect". Don't tell me that the more one practices a sport, the easier it becomes. On the contrary: muscular perfection is practically limitless. One is always striving toward its limits, without ever reaching them.

How will we win over our students? Do they like sports? Are they at least open to liking them? Certainly all our students have certain pretensions. When they walk by a horse being put through its paces, they look it over with what they hope will seem a practiced eye. When pressed, they talk of Mérignac and Vigeant with the disinterest of fine connoisseurs. Though they have never set foot on a bicycle, they will explain that it is rather easy to stay nearly immobile, just by balancing a bit on the pedal... But there is quite a gulf – or, rather, quite a wall to be knocked down – between all this posturing and getting them to the point where they would mount a horse, assume a stance, foil in hand, or learn to handle a bicycle on their own and for their own enjoyment. We shall knock that wall down, my fellow Committee members, shall we not? Yes! We will rain blows on it until there is nothing left of it at all.

In these three chapters, we have taken a short trip through day schools, religious boarding schools, and public high schools. I have attempted to show that physical exercise is indispensable for day schools, and that their success and development come at this cost: that a voluntary and powerful athletic program, organized by the students, involving the vast majority of them and exercising its influence throughout the school, would make the problems in the system disappear. Most religious boarding schools will resist reforms that contradict deeply-rooted ideas and an immutable rule taken as the point of departure and as the center. This, at least, is my conviction. Finally, opposition in the public schools will come instead from the students themselves, rather than from the teachers. A dogged and unflagging fight will ultimately overcome their ill will... So be it.

Nos lycées, in:
L'Éducation Anglaise en France [English Education in France],
Paris, Librairie Hachette, 1889,
pp. 108-120 (Chapter VII).

1.2.3 LETTER TO THE MEMBERS OF THE SOCIÉTÉ D'ÉCONOMIE SOCIALE AND OF THE UNIONS DE LA PAIX SOCIALE

On August 1,1888, on behalf of the Committee, Coubertin sent a letter to the members of the Société d'Économie Sociale and of the Unions de la Paix Sociale to ask for their help in a crusade to be undertaken "against a system of education that is so ill-suited to the needs of the age".

The "Société d'Économie Sociale" was founded by Le Play in 1856. In 1872, the first "Unions de la Paix Sociale" sister societies were founded. Starting in 1886, the two groups jointly published the Société's report La Réforme sociale, to which Coubertin contributed several articles. The primary goal of the Société d'Economie Sociale was social and moral developement. Coubertin became a member of the "Unions de la Paix Sociale" in 1883. He was introduced by the Comte de Damas. In the list of members for 1888, he appears as a member of the "Société d'Économie Sociale" as well as of the "Unions de la Paix Sociale". Coubertin acted as secretary at the meeting on May 25, 1887.

Dear Sirs, Paris, August 1, 1888

The Committee that has just been established to propagate physical exercise in the schools, and thereby to bring about the transformation of French education, has been placed under the patronage of Mr. Jules Simon, the illustrious speaker at your congress in 1887. Three of the Committee's vice presidents, Mr. Picot, Dr. Rochard, and Gen. Thomassin, belong to the Unions. The secretary of the Committee is also honored to be counted among your ranks.

Other ties of even greater significance unite the Committee with the Unions, the goal that it aims to achieve being first and foremost among them. Many a time, Frédéric Le Play dwelt on the deplorable tendencies of our current academic regimen, and on the need for immediate reform. We are going to try to achieve one of the points in his program. Were he still alive, we would certainly enjoy his support and assistance. In our view, improved use of recreation time and the spread of sports among school children are but means to an end. We have set our aim higher. The reason we are using these means is that observation and experience have shown that they are effective in giving young people the precious qualities of energy, perseverance, judgment and initiative that, among us, are the prerogative of only a few. Much can be expected of a generation brought up in this way.

At times I have wondered – and certainly I am not the only one who has asked this question – how it is that the doctrines that form the overall social reform program have not had any clear impact on French society so far. These doctrines were proclaimed by an illustrious man whose name is familiar to everyone. They have been supported by societies whose simple, ingenious machinery makes it easy to propagate them. Now, these doctrines are defended by devoted citizens thoroughly persuaded of their value. What is missing from these doctrines that keeps them from gaining the upper hand and revitalizing the country? The reason is that the doctrines of Frédéric Le Play are eminently reasonable, and that they are addressed, when all is said and done, to a people that is not. To adhere to these

Pierre de Coubertin himself practised various sports, especially swimming, riding, rowing, tennis, boxing and here in the photo (on the right) he can be seen fencing. (O.Schantz Collection)

conclusions and to this program of reform, one need not be a great genius, have special skills, an eagle eye or infinitely broad knowledge. All one needs is common sense, a little moderation in one's thinking, a little tolerance in judgment, and not too many preconceived ideas. These qualities are exceptional among the French, who even go so far as to despise them as being too bourgeois. I ask you, is it the done thing to join a Society that agrees to debate with its adversaries, is not contemplating widespread upheaval, and has not yet even thought of choosing a rallying symbol? Oh, if the Unions de la Paix had chosen some flower as their emblem, their success would have been quite different! But this is not the case, and those who have rallied under banners of the Unions de la Paix are few in number. The number is growing, but too slowly.

Social reform must be achieved through education. Our efforts must focus not on adults, but on children, in order to ensure our success. We must give those children qualities of mind that will make them capable of understanding, and qualities of character that will render them capable of performing the transformation in which your illustrious founder saw France's salvation.

It was in this light that I believed I could call for your support, glad to join a work whose fortunes look bright. I seek the support of the Unions that form an elite in the reflective and active part of the population. Your support does not mean merely gifts that some of you may wish to make, to help create our school parks and to set up the organization of our athletic competitions. Above all else, your gift is moral support, which is such a great source of strength. Talk about us, and get people to know who we are. Take an interest in all our innovations. There is one more thing you can do. In Paris, aside from a few substantial facilities, we face countless problems. Distances are great. In order to have playing fields, we must either go far off to find them, or pay dearly. From another perspective, the freedom that we are demanding for the children here presents dangers that are far less substantial in provincial cities. Many among you, gentlemen, live full time in the provinces, or you spend much of the year there. It is you whom I address now, asking you to look around you, and to study the situation of the high school that are nearby. You can bring about considerable and beneficial reform where you live, by introducing the new discipline that is now producing such satisfying results at the École Monge. Support the establishment of sports associations in your area. Foster individual initiatives. If you want to form groups of like-minded people to accomplish this task, forming local committees on our model, we will be available to you at all times to help and support you in your task. This is a limited task, but quite a useful one in its way, even if your only focus is to relieve the problem of overwork, providing physical exercise as a counterweight to intellectual fatigue. A much broader task would be, like us, to introduce new principles of discipline and responsibility into education by means of games. In this case, we cannot recommend highly enough English-style games, which are wonderfully well-suited to engendering and maintaining these principles. Puerile and poorly understood patriotism must not prevent these games from being adopted.

The editors of the *Revue* are pleased to present a list of Committee members in the attachment to this letter. Among the notable individuals on the list, death has created a void, taking from us Mr. Allou, a renowned and valiant defender of all freedoms. You will note that we have recruited our membership from far and wide. In effect, our work is shielded from any political quarrels. It is purely social, and that is one more consideration for you. We are confident that you will assist us in the crusade that we have undertaken, against a system of education that is so ill suited to the needs of the present day, and that has proven incapable of producing the true citizens that France needs.

Pierre de Coubertin

Secretary General of the Committee
Member of the Société d'Économie Sociale

Lettre aux membres de la Société d'Économie Sociale et des Unions de la Paix Sociale, in:
La Réforme sociale [Social Reform] (September 1, 1888)
Vol. 8, series 2, part VI, pp. 249-252. Reprinted in:
L'Éducation Anglaise en France [English Education in France],
Paris, Librairie Hachette,1889,
pp. 199-202 (Appendix II).

1.3 TRANSATLANTIC UNIVERSITIES (1890)

1.3.1 - 1.3.6 INTRODUCTION[1]

In July 1889, the French Minister of Public Instruction Armand Fallières sent Coubertin to the United States and Canada, "to visit the universities and colleges there, and to study the organization and operation of the Athletic Associations founded there by the youths of those countries[2]". Coubertin set out in late September. In the interim, he prepared for his trip by re-reading Tocqueville's Democracy in America[3]. Coubertin, too, saw America for the first time at a young age: he was only twenty-six.[4] Like Tocqueville, Coubertin was to come to understand in situ the conditions that a democracy must fulfill to properly perform its role in education, for, although France had rejected the aristocratic order, it had not been able to establish a stable democracy, and its educational concepts remained reactionary.

Once he arrived, Coubertin traveled around, obtained information, made observations, and noted down his reflections. The Americans were preparing for their future in and around their universities. Their efforts did not always seem well coordinated, but the resulting progress was creating a fruitful spirit of rivalry. That spirit benefited from the dominant Anglo-Saxon character, from an abundance of scholars and researchers, and from the vastness of the continent.

For the Americans, respect for the law remained compatible with civil and religious freedom. To be honest, to be charitable, and to take risks to realize profits remained the basis for conduct.

Athletic associations proliferated at the universities, and outside them. In Coubertin's view, two systems of education stood in contrast to each other: one, based on free games, came from England; the other came from Germanic gymnastics. Athletes were chosen through extremely detailed anthropometric measurements[5].

Coubertin found that the United States of the day, with their wealth of institutions of higher learning, nevertheless had only a very small number of secondary schools, and that their main concern was to prepare students for the university entrance examinations. Organizing education in this way results in a relatively shaky intellectual and moral foundation at the very moment when students are entering the most important period of their lives in the formation of the man and the citizen. To compensate for that shortcoming, new schools had been founded inspired by Arnold's teaching. In them, athleticism produced "strong wills and right hearts, at the same time as robust bodies". In these institutions, freedom was "wisely regulated". Nevertheless, Coubertin viewed freedom as excessive in most of the universities, while readily agreeing that "this excess of independence does not produce bad results".

Starting at this point, Coubertin's philosophy of education took on its final form, resulting from an unwavering focus on lasting values and a direct answer to the educational questions of the day.

During his travels, Coubertin was astonished at the discriminatory legislation then in effect in the Southern States. In his view, culture should bring men together, without requiring them to renounce their very selves; one can acknowledge differences

without ceasing to be human. He was also surprised at the significant role that women occupied in American affairs. In terms of athletics, women had gymnasiums with appropriate equipment, but he felt that open air and natural exercises would be far more suitable for them. His visit to Canada provided Coubertin with proof of the superiority of English education over the overly narrow, existential model still employed by the French-Canadians.

Not everything was negative, as Coubertin saw it; rather to the contrary. During his first three-month stay across the Atlantic, he saw other styles of behavior and new dimensions to life. He witnessed a great, creative spirit, articulated around nature and training, according to various modalities. He noted that in a brand-new, vast country, most of what is taken for granted was being transformed: intellectual, physical, and moral standards, as well as the rules of society and religion. This crucible of various civilizations showed him that man is essentially made for the future, and that through education, he can hope for more freedom, more justice, and more happiness.

During his visit to Princeton University, Coubertin met Professor William Sloane. Theirs was to be a long and fruitful friendship, one that well served the restored Olympic Games, a project that Coubertin already had in mind. His thoughts constantly moved to the universal. In 1890, a report on his visit appeared in a 379-page book, entitled Universités Transatlantiques [Transatlantic Universities][6].

His report focused on nine main topics: At Sea – Around New York – New England – English Canada and French Canada[7] – From North to South – Louisiana, Florida, and Virginia – Washington and Baltimore – One Book, One Congress, and One Ship, and – Conclusions. These topics are addressed in sections that vary greatly in length, depending on the particular subject.

1 See G. Rioux: "Pierre de Coubertin éducateur." in: *Textes choisis,* Vol. I, Révélation, pp. 15-16.

2 For Coubertin's notes on Canada, see de Bouthillier-Chavigny, *Justice aux Canadiens-Français!* à M. le Baron Pierre de Coubertin ["Justice for French-Canadians!" To Baron Pierre de Coubertin]; Montréal, Cadieux et Derome, 1890.

3 Published in 1834 when the author had just turned twenty-nine.

4 Coubertin was quite familiar with Tocqueville. He had quoted him in London, in his lecture on Le Play.

5 Coubertin remarked, "It is reminiscent of a stable of race horses; there is the breeder who hands over the handsome beasts to the trainer" (p. 89); and again, "all this is not education, it is animal rearing" (p. 90). He added, "The impression they give is that of a distorted ideal, a down-to-earth education, unconscious but total materialism" (p. 120), in *Transatlantic Universities,* "New England."

6 This topic would be taken up again in various forms three years running. In 1895, he published Le Monde américain [The American World], in 1896 Le mouvement universitaire aux États-Unis [The University Movement in the United States], and in 1897, L'Amérique universitaire [University America]. His studies on "South American History" and "Idealism in the History of the United States" appeared much later, in 1916 and 1918.

7 His statements concerning Canada arouse contradiction immediately after the book appeared, that the Franco-Canadian Vicomte de Bouthillier-Chavigny presented a reply in bookform under the title "Justice aux Canadiens-Français". The one-hundredth return of Coubertin's first book was celebrated, at the Laval University in Quebec, with an important Congress concerning the "History and Future of Olympism" under the leadership of Professor Fernand Landry. See F. Landry, M. Landry, M. Yerlès (eds.), Sport... The Third Millenium. Procedings of the International Symposium, Quebec City, May 21-25, 1990. Sainte-Foy, Laval Univ. Press, 1991.

Map showing the places in the US and Canada Coubertin visited during his 1889/90 trip to North America.

1.3.1 AROUND NEW YORK

The first thing that strikes one is the four years of study, the eating clubs, the dormitories, the countless athletic, literary, and other associations – the excessive independence of the young people. This is a phenomenon one encounters pretty much everywhere, from North to South, and from East to West. American universities are often, and improperly, called "colleges". What the French call "*collèges*" are known as "schools". "Public schools", the term used in England to designate the leading "*collèges*" of that country, are called "primary schools" in America. Primary education in America is well known. It has been studied extensively in Europe in recent years, and I shall not address that topic here. The mission entrusted to me by the Minister of Public Instruction concerned secondary and higher education only, which is less widely known even though it may well deserve to be. Yet there is a link between primary schools and the universities: the high schools, which I shall discuss below. These high schools may be compared to the less advanced German Gymnasiums. In fact, they are higher-level primary schools of a particular type. But when one considers how important this period of education between the ages of eleven and seventeen is, one deplores, along with most American educators, the fact that the United States is so rich in universities and yet, by contrast, has so few *collège*-type schools. High schools are boarding schools and, moreover, the main preoccupation is to prepare students for the examination for entrance into the universities. This cannot provide truly complete results, or a solid basis, from either the moral or the intellectual perspective.

And yet some *collège*-type schools do exist. Others are being founded, and we may look forward to a time when this lacuna will be filled. The allaying of the ancient Anglo-American hatreds plays a certain role in this, as well as in the rapid and nearly excessive development of English games. It is certain that, following the Civil War the United States, having survived a terrible fratricidal fight intact, took confidence in themselves. They realized that they formed a solid nation, and the fear of allowing themselves to be weakened by adopting foreign ideas or customs gradually disappeared. So football, rowing and, in general, all outdoor exercises have made their way into the New World. At the same time, educators have turned their gaze toward Great Britain to draw on principles of reorganization from there, principles that would have produced even greater results if German ideas had not come in, causing disorder and sowing bad seed. American education is a battlefield where German pedagogy and English pedagogy are at each other's throats. This is so, not only because the Germans are a powerful party within the Union, but especially because for the past thirty years, the elite youth has gone off to complete its education at German universities.

The few *collège*-type schools that do exist here and there, and those that are now being founded, have escaped from German influence, and the sound educational ideas expressed by the great Arnold are firmly in place there. Princeton has the good fortune of having nearby, under its wing, the Lawrenceville School, which will prepare strong generations of students for Princeton, and will assure the university enormous superiority over other rival universities.

Autour de New York, in:
Universités Transatlantiques [Transatlantic Universities], Paris, Librairie Hachette, 1890, pp. 27-30
(Paragraph IV, Chapter II: "Around New York").

1.3.2 NEW ENGLAND

1. Here's the man who is taking charge of showing me Cambridge. No one has had time to explain to him what I am doing in America, but there he stands with his hat on, and with a schedule ready for me. It's all set! We are going to see the library, the playing fields, the laboratories, the collections... and we will end up at the gymnasium. Meanwhile, we will pay a visit to the famous tree where Washington took charge of the army in 1775!

We did see plenty of young people that day playing football, tennis, or training for foot races. We also saw antediluvian carcasses and countless shells. Washington's tree looked quite venerable, befitting its age, with tin patches on the trunk and the meticulous tidiness of elderly men who take good care of themselves. A rather picturesque spectacle awaited us at the gymnasium.

It is called the Hemenway Gymnasium, named for an alumnus who gave 500,000 francs for its construction. The interior is chock full of ropes and gymnastic equipment. Daylight was fading, but the electric lighting was not yet casting its glare from the ceiling. In this half-light, one could see young people wearing sleeveless jerseys engaging in inexplicable contortions where they stood. At the same time, the screeching of pulleys, and the noises of inadequately lubricated metal and pulleys came from all corners. In the middle, a handful of jumpers were working at leaping over a bar gradually raised higher and higher. But what were the others doing? Impossible to say at first glance. Eventually I realized what it was. They were moving clearly marked weights that slid in grooves, pulling with their arms or legs, lifting with their heads or shoulders, pushing with their knees or their... well, name whatever body part you like. It was the triumph of *localized gymnastics*. One of them had been told to work on a deformation of his left hip, another had learned the night before that the diameter of the little finger on his right hand was one half of one millimeter larger than that of the little finger on his left hand, and a third had received disastrous revelations about the size of his forearm. So they were working conscientiously, the first at overcoming his hip, the second at re-establishing the balance between his little fingers, and the third at making his forearm larger! All of this, to what end? Simply to end up looking like a *standard man*. So I asked to see a standard man, and we took a small circular staircase that led to the offices of Dr. Sargent.

I felt as though I were at the draft board. A magnificent working office opened before me, full of ancient statuettes, engravings, photographs, books and papers. On the threshold of the door, three or four utterly naked young men were waiting until their names were called. Dr. Sargent rose from behind his desk, and graciously extended his hand to us. One of his assistants was engaged in an examination. He interrupted him, and had him start over to give me an accurate idea of his method and his principles. The student first tested his strength on a sort of dynamometer. Then the strength of his breathing was determined using a spirometer. Finally a small round instrument was placed over his heart, with a rubber tube running up into the doctor's ear. Fifty-eight measurements were then taken on him, from the soles of his feet to the top of his head, and the fifty-eight figures, called out loud and repeated by a scribe – just like being at the tailor's – were entered into fifty-eight little squares on a printed sheet that I was given as a souvenir. That was not the end of it. The individual being examined was asked about his father and his mother, his grandfathers and his grandmothers, what diseases they had died of, and which of them he looked like most. Information about his heartbeat, the size of his liver, and his breathing rate were written down. He was asked if he caught colds easily, and if he had nosebleeds. Then he got dressed and, before leaving, paid the "examination fee."

The doctor then showed me the large registers where the beginnings of a new science, anthropometry, are contained. I thought of the joys of antiquarians in the year 2000 searching through these little books. Family portraits will be replaced by anthropometric sheets on one's ancestors. People will have their friends pause before a yellowed tablet, covered with figures and framed in gold: "Here is my great grand uncle", they will say... "See how strong his biceps were!" Dr. Sargent has reconstructed the *standard man*, a bit by chance, of course; using a graphic outline, he traces the curve of your deformations, i.e.

The 1879 Princeton-Yale football match was one of the first championship games played under Intercollegiate Football Association rules (taken from: Don Oberdorfer, Princeton University: The first 250 years, Princeton 1995, p.82)

where you stand in relation to the standard man. We can see quite famous *curves* there! Those of Hanlan the rower, Sullivan the famous boxer... Just moments before, on the body of the student being examined, we noted a "depression caused by the student's desk."

After another visit to the gymnasium, where an employee moved the equipment while the doctor explained the mechanism to me, we entered the trophy room, overflowing with banners, cups, and medals won at various schools. There were also portraits of athletes, with the dates of their victories! How regimented all this is! These games are in the hands of *directors* who organize them like despots... It is reminiscent of a stable of race horses; there is the breeder, who hands the handsome beasts over to the trainer.

From the first moment Americans turned to English games, they brought along the excessive zeal that characterizes Americans. Exaggeration was soon to follow. For a team of players who are supposed to fight against an other team on a particular date, before a huge, enthusiastic crowd, no sacrifice is too great. Everything is organized around the training of these men, on whom people in New York, Albany, Boston, etc., are going to wager enormous sums. Other students are left outside. They are sent off to the football field, or they are sent to the boat house. Such students would get in the way of the champions. That was when the gymnasiums were developed. They were built as a sort of compensation for students who could never defend their university's honor in athletic tournaments. At the same time, gymnasiums were used systematically to strengthen and to shape the bodies of the champions in a manner above suspicion. This gymnastic work and these periodic examinations are not yet mandatory at this school, but they required at many other universities.

As we left the Hemenway Gymnasium that evening, my thoughts were quite confused. Certainly I had seen curious, interesting things. I had also seen other utterly ridiculous things. But I could not formulate my basic impression, balancing out the sum of all my good and bad impressions.

At this point, I know quite well what to think of it, and my judgment is clear and precise. This whole approach is not education, it is animal husbandry!

La Nouvelle-Angleterre, in:
Universités Transatlantiques [Transatlantic Universities],
Paris, Librairie Hachette, 1890, pp. 84-90
(Chapter III, Section III: "New England").

2. When I have two or three otherwise unoccupied hours before me, I take the electric trolley that goes to Cambridge, to observe the students and engage in conversation with those whom I know, observing their behavior and their interactions. When you are dealing with children fourteen, fifteen, and even sixteen years old, if you want to know how they have been raised, it is quite simple. Just watch them play, listen to them talk to their teachers, and find out how they wash themselves. This threefold criterion is still the best one I know. It is never wrong. But for men this age, you need more details and broader observation.

American students practise hurdling (taken from Sport im Bild, no.40, 1908, p.1217)

The shady Yard is the center of university life. From it, one can see nearly all the dormitories. The sounds of martyred pianos float out from the open windows, and my thoughts turn to the quadrangles of Oxford and Cambridge. How much greater is the freedom here! When night comes, no surly porters will be lying in wait for stragglers, and heavy gates will not shut the students in until morning. Who worries about them? Hardly anyone knows them. They barely know each other, from one group to another.

Yesterday I dined at an eating club. The guests, few in number, did not resemble one another. There were those with blond hair and those with brown; those with dry personalities and those who were quite polished, the elegant and the sloppy. One of those seated by me dreamed of a life of hard work and hubbub, another of tranquillity, enormous trees, and a rocking chair. In other words, the first wanted to climb stairs, the second wanted to lounge about on the landings...

One of my friends, who finished at Harvard two years ago already, revealed to me the amounts of money that he had spent while there. He belonged to that very small group of aristocrats who do not quite know what to base their pretensions to nobility on, and assert their pretensions through ferocious exclusivity. If you cannot trace your lineage back to some English peer or hang some sort of escutcheon on your automobile, at least throw money out the window. Otherwise, don't plan on becoming part of their circle. But their circle really is not that interesting, in any event! They do a thousand eccentric things, a thousand foolish things to impose themselves somehow on a society that has no aristocracy, and that scarcely grasps the meaning of the word. In Boston, there is still an aristocracy to a certain extent. Beyond that, however, the situation is hopeless. Eventually these young men must yield to public opinion, at which point they become attorneys for the fun of it, to gain some standing in the world.

Harvard seems chaotic to me, a confused and rather awkward imitation of the English universities. It is not truly American in atmosphere or trends. Some quick wits get lost in this churning mass, where no particular current is established. In short, the University is a likeness of New England. It is a region that bears some comparison to France early in the reign of Louis XVI. It is the end of an era, with its uncertainties, its inconsistencies, and its insipidity... Such conditions can be overcome, particularly in America; often these periods are merely transitory. But anyone looking for the United States in New England today runs the risk of returning to Europe without having understood anything!

After the meal, we went to write our names in the register at the Hasty Pudding Club. This club draws its odd name from a dense pudding that is meant to be eaten very quickly. The club puts on shows; they practice the art of caricature with plenty of spirit and no small measure of talent. Then we met the delightful Professor Cohn, who teaches French literature and manages to get students to like it. I overwhelmed him with questions of all kinds, and he answered with exceptional kindness. He drew my attention to the absence of a *basis* in American studies. The students know quite a lot, and they are eager to learn, but there are no *humanities* to shore up the structure. Those here in France who go attack the humanities with such hatred and sarcasm should come here and see the void that they leave behind... Schools founded on the Lawrenceville plan will remedy this state of affairs.

La Nouvelle-Angleterre, in:
Universités Transatlantiques [Transatlantic Universities],
Paris, Librairie Hachette 1890, pp. 94-98
(Chapter III, Section VI: "New England").

3. I have just spent twenty hours in Lenox, Massachusetts, a fashionable spot some four hours West of Boston. It is located amid picturesque mountains, with plenty of handsome esplanades. Wealthy people have summer homes there. The tiniest bit of property sells at a steep price, and that is not all you need if you wish to settle here. One has to be *admitted*. The good American people here enjoy the small pleasure of playing at aristocratic customs. They inquire seriously about the lineage of those newly arrived, and gossip about whether or not it is seemly to receive them. These pretensions are so utterly out of keeping in America that one cannot help but laugh. In fact, even in the best families one finds nearly total ignorance where family origins are concerned. People know who their parents are, they know more or less who their grandparents were, but all the rest is shrouded in mist. Never mind that the people of Lenox take themselves seriously. How many travelers judge America according to Lenox, or England according to the House of Peers!

From there, I went on to the small town of Amherst, where the father of academic anthropometry, the venerable Dr. Hitchcock, resides. Amherst College was

Sport at American universities: tennis courts at Harvard around 1900 (taken from Sport im Bild, no.37, 1905, p.888)

founded in 1821, and forty-seven students were there when it opened its doors. Now there are three hundred sixty students. The board of directors has ten lay members and seven ecclesiastics. The right to fill vacancies created by death or resignation belongs to the alumni. This involvement of alumni in university governance is not the least of the peculiarities of the American system. For my part, I see a number of advantages to it. In this way, universities are solidly supported and defended. Routine cannot take hold, and the competitive spirit is maintained. Finally, from the social perspective, how great are the gains in belonging to a group whose members go through life providing mutual support! Amherst has gone even further in that direction, by involving the students themselves in school governance. The Faculty shares power with a Senate comprising four seniors, three juniors, two sophomores, and one freshman, all elected by their respective classes. Any questions involving "good order and decorum" are brought before these young senators. They rule as they see fit, and the signature of the president renders their decisions enforceable. This system has fully satisfied its inventors since it was put in place.

Nearly all of these three hundred sixty students come from Massachusetts and surrounding states. Some come from the West, five are foreign. The South is represented by just two Virginians. I learned these facts while rolling down in a minuscule car along an incredibly steep path that goes down to the plain, as Amherst is situated on a hill crowned in a most ravishing way by its graceful buildings. Today there is an athletic festival, with running, jumping, and prizes to be awarded. It is

Harvard v Yale football match, 1905, played in front of 40,000 spectators in Cambridge, Mass. (taken from Sport im Bild, no.51, 1905, p.1225)

the Fall Meeting. But clearly the good Dr. Hitchcock has a great deal less sympathy for these sports than for the lovely arm and leg exercises done four times a week in his gymnasium, to the sound of the piano... for he is one of those who *believe* in music. In the United States, gymnastics instructors either believe or do not believe in music. Those who do delight in seeing their students undulate like jumping jacks to the melody, and to hear, at the last chord, the *clack* of all the heels hitting the ground together. Dr. Hitchcock is good humor and good health incarnate. His deep faith in his system is the finishing touch in making him a likable man. Now he is an old man; he has reached his goals: he has persuaded many a student that a man's body is "built" just as a house is built, that the universal remedy for all illness is well thought-out and regimented gymnastics, and that one must be measured every two weeks to "know oneself". One cannot say that he is unaware of it the moral role of athletics. He has not the slightest doubt of what that role is. Hence what a materialist scent rises from the booklets he has published! The name of God pops up in them here and there, to no avail. The impression these booklets gives is of a distorted ideal, down-to-earth education, unconscious but total materialism.

The schedule of courses here is not unusual. On the one hand, literature, on the other the sciences, with a hyphen in between, so that those who are strong on

When travelling Pierre de Coubertin had no camera with him but frequently made drawings in his note-book of the various sites he was visiting. Here the banks of the Hudson river when in the USA in the year 1907 (Navacelle Collection)

writing at least know how to do addition, and the scientific types do not mistake the name Regulus for some civil engineering firm. These programs are rather complete, well planned, and the students at Amherst seem to be hard workers. They have few distractions. The town is small, and its streets, which have scarcely been laid out, soon fade into countryside.

At the hotel, we were served at table by women of the type that Max O'Rell has so wittily called "duchesses", with the one exception that nowhere in the world are there to be found any duchesses that are so haughty, so dishonest, and so completely intolerable. Their brusqueness, their disgusted air, their insolent looks, and their endless mockery make these American waitresses a real nightmare for the traveler when, upon leaving the major cities, he ventures out into such small towns as this. With all his might, he longs for the day when modern science will make it possible to replace these duchesses with a silent and obedient sort of fluid.

La Nouvelle-Angleterre, in:
Universités Transatlantiques [Transatlantic Universities],
Paris, Librairie Hachette 1890, pp. 117-121
(Chapter III, Section XIII: "New England").

A book by a French Canadian (a Coubertin's relative) criticizing Coubertin's reports on the education system in Canada (O.Schantz Collection)

Vte DE BOUTHILLIER-CHAVIGNY

JUSTICE

AUX

CANADIENS-FRANÇAIS !

a

M[r] le Baron Pierre de Coubertin

MONTRÉAL
CADIEUX & DEROME, LIBRAIRES-ÉDITEURS
1603, RUE NOTRE-DAME, 1603

1890

1.3.3 BRITISH CANADA AND FRENCH CANADA

Their good sense and their perseverance – two prime qualities among these people – once served to defend them against the invader. When one compares their numbers today with what population statistics just after the transfer of Canada to England, when one recalls how they were treated, the cruelties inflicted on them, the injustices they had to suffer, one cannot help but admire the results they have achieved after a struggle consisting of skill, patience and stubbornness. They were able to make marvelous use of even the slightest of concessions, profiting from the most insignificant circumstances, and gaining territory by any means possible. Twice, in bad times, the United States came to them, to conquer and liberate them; and twice, they joined forces with their persecutors to repulse that emancipation, which they considered dangerous, attractive as it may have been. One would look in vain for another example of such remarkable political spirit in the history of the world. Now they enjoy total freedom. The federal government, infinitely better understood and better constituted than it is in the United States, lavishes its benefits on them. Helped by the extreme fecundity of their race, and by the wise counsel of a man who undertook the work of colonization – the famous Father Labelle –, they are spreading to the north and west, into territories believed uninhabitable, which are quickly growing fertile under their hands. Their future seems assuredly prosperous. All would be for the best, were they not in a position of notorious inferiority with respect to the most important thing in the lives of modern peoples: education.

One must not conclude from this that instruction has been neglected in the schools. Trade schools, in particular, are well organized, and the care exercised in these schools to teach the students English guarantees them superiority over their British rivals in the future, rivals who cannot – or will not – learn a word of French. But their ideas are forcibly twisted in a certain direction, which stunts their subsequent growth. Their minds are made to move within a restricted sphere from which nothing great or original can come. Above all else, it is education that is lacking. Physical exercises, cleanliness, the formation of the character, the exercise of freedom – for the Canadians, all that is nonsense. Next to them, the young English play at manly games, entering active life with initiative and will... The result is that all the benefits go to them, all business happens around them, their ideas dominate, and thus they regain what their numerical inferiority would cause them to lose otherwise, even in Montreal itself. The French Canadian, with his robust health, clears the land, toils hard, and sows the seed laboriously. The English Canadian reaps. Never, perhaps, has the superiority of English education been seen in any clearer or less uncertain way than in the presence of this race, with its strong qualities, that possesses everything... except initiative and independence of character. In the race for the dollar, for which the French Canadians have acquired a taste as I mentioned above, they are not the ones who are coming in first.

Canada britannique et Canada français, in:
Universités Transatlantiques [Transatlantic Universities],
Paris, Librairie Hachette 1890, pp. 133-136
(Chapter IV, Section II: "British Canada and French Canada").

Lesson for girls at the Chicago Normal School for Physical Education (taken from C.Diem, Sport in Amerika. Berlin, Weidmann, 1930, p. 35)

1.3.4 FROM NORTH TO SOUTH

1. The waters of Lake Michigan break against the wooden jetties that hold the sandy beaches in place; the swells fill the horizon. In the distance, the only thing visible is a chimney that marks the entrance to the underwater tunnel that Chicago built so that it could have clean water, because this liquid mass that the storm is shaking is fresh water. These huge waves are not ocean swells at all. It is a difficult concept to grasp, and one wonders if the Queen of the Prairies has not suddenly been transported to the ocean's edge.

It is no longer as easily transportable as when it was swept by fire. When I was eight, they told me, "Chicago has burned down, there is nothing left, nothing at all!" I held onto a vague recollection of that fantastic, superhuman catastrophe. Well, Chicago does not look in the slightest like a city that burned to the ground nineteen years ago. Its immense streets are bordered with elegant buildings that have powerful facades and marble pilasters. Everything there has such a strong, solid, and definitive feel that one creates a past and historic memories for it. For a moment, one might feel moved to ask how to get to the royal palace. There is such a palace, too, where His Royal Highness, Money, reigns as undisputed sovereign: the Chicago Board of Trade. We had been heartily encouraged to visit it, to see the "commotion". It is true that an infernal racket goes on there, and that the spectacle is impressive. Yet pretty much the same thing goes on in all great centers of business, although nowhere else is the setting so grandiose. The Board of Trade, with its cyclopean columns and its tall stained-glass windows, does look somewhat like a church, an exotic palace, and one finds oneself looking for the eyes of the idol, the great high lama, the throne...

Surrounding the sovereign there is the court, with its mandatory cortege of favorites and courtesans, whose slightest gesture is of interest to the public, whose least little utterance is repeated, and whose least thoughts are tapped. An American newspaper always captures the attention of its readership by speaking of the current happy few, particularly by giving them statistics about their income. The millionaire is the very type, the ideal. For young people, the millionaire constitutes what Roland was to the Middle Ages, or Lauzun under Louis XIV. The millionaire is granted a sort of mysterious power, and when fate crushes him, there is a sort of general disbelief. That is what a reporter recently recounted, by headlining the story of a catastrophe with these strangely philosophical words: "Millionaire burned alive! All his millions unable to save him!"

By what moral degeneracy, what rot would a society in which money exercises such influence not be marked, according to European logic? Well, this is not the case! Chicago society loves beautiful things; it is stirred by noble sentiments and pursues its moral perfection even as it pursues wealth. In a word, it is rising. Read De Varigny's book, *Les Grandes fortunes aux États-Unis* [Great Fortunes in the United States]. In it, he presents the major millionaires of the century. He describes their humble beginnings, their stubbornness, their tumultuous lives. When he reaches the moment of triumph, when the man makes his fortune, the character is always the same: a bit of a skeptic, rather authoritarian, a little gruff perhaps, but generous in his giving, in aiding the unfortunate, and in founding schools, hospitals, or museums. That is what an American millionaire is like.

There is one who lives quite close to Chicago, whose name is known universally. He is Pullman, the builder and, I believe, inventor of the famous sleeping cars that bear his name: Pullman cars. Making a colossal fortune and employing 5,000 workers in his workshops was not enough for him. Everything that the wisest and most tactful philanthropy suggested that he could possibly do to improve their lot, he did. The patronage that he provides resembles the patronage that a great industrialist inspired by the same principles would provide in France, with the following exception: nothing is asked of the worker in return for what has been done for him, and the worker is treated as an equal, as is the customs among American citizens. This beehive of workers is located three quarters of an hour by rail from the city center. To get there, one crosses vast, uninhabited spaces. No matter, it is all still Chicago! By using this rather ridiculous subterfuge, they have managed to tally up nearly 1,500,000 inhabitants in the city. In reality, there are over 900,000, which is still not bad for such a young city!

Once we arrived at our destination, we toured the various workshops, the foundries with their furnaces, the incandescent metal and the noise of the heavy drop hammers, the woodworking shops where the cars take shape little by little as they slide along the rails, from one worker to the next. We visited the cabinet-making shops, and the painting, carpeting, and linen shops. Everything is done here, and when the cars leave the factory, all that's left to do is climb aboard. Then we visited the bank, the schools, the theater, the library, and the churches of the various religious sects. Residential housing was available in all sizes and price ranges. The workers never own them, a setup far preferable to one in which the worker gradually becomes a homeowner. The problems with that arrangement have been fully demonstrated in Europe. Rents are lowered every five years, I believe, and whenever a child is born. This is the bonus for morality and stability. Mr. Pullman has also founded an athletic association whose medals are highly prized. Many of the workers belong to it... In England, too, workers form athletic associations, rowing and playing cricket. So this proves that even the most strenuous manual labor does not replace sports. Those who see nothing but physical movement in sport can thus see that a whole side of the matter is escaping them.

Du Nord au Sud, in:
Universités Transatlantiques [Transatlantic Universities],
Paris, Librairie Hachette 1890, pp. 222-227
(Chapter V, Section XI: "From North to South").

2. The lights of Chicago are coming on; blue or yellow electricity glows all around. In the hotels there is music at dinner, and the theaters are opening their doors. It is time to relax for the busy man, whom interviews, meetings, and business have kept shut up inside a wall of facts all day long. He has calculated, computed, and reasoned, and here he is now, leaving behind the cloud of dust he has been living in. He casts one last glance at the piles of paper, sends one last visitor on his way, listens to one final complaint and, joyfully noting that he has completed his work day, he heads off to relax at a luxurious table, at some lighthearted show, or at a dazzling party. His wife, too, has spent her day dealing with *practical* and *immediate* matters. She has been busy with the children, the house, and her work. To any visitors who may have come calling, she sends a response consisting of quite a simple sentence, but one that, for us, would appear so impolite: *Mrs. X begs to be excused*. She begs to be excused, she does not have the time to chat with you. She is not free. If she does have a bit of leisure time, she will use it to read magazines and newspapers, keeping up to date with events and discoveries. She rejoices in this life that she loves. Fortune is smiling on her, though perhaps tomorrow will bring utter ruin. She knows this, but does not worry about it. The woman who does her cleaning is her equal. She has no doubt of that fact, and is not in the least surprised by it. Rarely, in her prayers, does she ask anything of God. She honors God because she believes in him, but the idea never enters her mind of having God become interested in her happiness. Her husband, for his part, shares this rather platonic belief. He knows that he has a *mission* to accomplish in this world, and he will define this mission for you in three terms: to be honest, to be charitable, and to do business. In return for that, God will be happy.

After all, this is an ideal! It's just that we Europeans have difficulty in understanding it. The Greeks sought the perfection of the individual through the harmony of his various faculties. The Middle Ages preached asceticism, i.e. the soul subjugating the body, its supposed enemy. Then came the military ideal, and now it is activity that predominates. When all is said and done, whether one fights against things, people, events or oneself, it always comes down to the struggle, and the struggle is noble[1].

Du Nord au Sud, in:
Universités Transatlantiques [Transatlantic Universities],
Paris, Librairie Hachette 1890, pp. 231-233
(Chapter V, Section XIII: "From North to South").

1.3.5 LOUISIANA, FLORIDA, AND VIRGINIA

1. In the paperwork documenting his donation, Paul Tulane stipulated that he had the education of Whites in mind. That hardly needed to be said. Young Negroes bold enough to enroll would have had a bad time of it. In the North, Blacks and Whites are on the same footing. One even sees many mixed-race schools, and racial prejudice continues to decline. But here, it persists in all its strength. The Negroes have their own cafes, cars reserved for them on the trains, and their own place at the theater. They must yield to the Whites everywhere, even in church! They are in the majority and could, if they wanted, put an end to these shameful distinctions. But they are happy-go-lucky, divided, and very timid. Slavery has left them subject to their former masters, and doubtless it will take time for feelings of equality to come to one group and the other.

However this may be, the *Negro question* is justly worrisome to American statesmen, and from time to time it gives them the opportunity to set up eccentric projects. One senator has proposed returning them all to Africa. "It is their native country", he said, "What a glorious mission for them to bring the civilization they have gotten from us to their brothers who remained barbarians!" I hope someone somewhere laughs in the face of that mischievous senator. In any event, the Negroes laughed uncomfortably at the prospect of that "glorious mission". With regard to Blacks, Whites believe that they can do anything they want. They cheat at election time when the ballots are counted, and they are not afraid to boast out loud about

1 In one American city where I spent two weeks, I was shown around for the first few days by a Frenchman who had settled in the country by marriage. "We will dine at the Union Club", he told me one morning, by way of setting out the schedule, "and then my friend Williams will show us his racehorses, which are at the Hunting Grounds outside the city". Before eating at the Union Club, we went to pick up his friend Williams. He sold calico fabric in a small street full of shops, advertisements, and commotion. The store front looked like all store fronts, with name Williams and Co. spelled out in gold letters. The interior was vast, in the form of a gallery with very long counters, lots of employees, a few buyers, and astonishing heaps of all the calico fabrics that exist the world over. The cashier's desk is to the right as you enter. Seated on a very high moveable chair, a young man, about thirty, elegantly dressed and with a distinguished air, was issuing receipts. He raised his eyes, greeted us with a smile and continued on with his work, saying to my companion, between signatures, "Great day yesterday! My horse jumped beautifully". The image of a prize horse jumping over those counters and piles of calico fabric stayed in my mind for quite a long time.

it. In a dispute, the Black man is always wrong. People speak to him as they would to a dog, and everyone does his best to give him a clear idea of his inferiority. Yet that inferiority is far from proven. After so many years of servitude, it is not surprising that the intelligence is slow to open up. In the schools, the little Negroes learn wonderfully, and show great aptitude for work. Then it all comes to a sudden stop. They never get past a certain limit, but that limit is gradually being pushed back. In Europe, moreover, we have plenty of examples in our schools of Negro students winning first prizes and passing their examinations brilliantly. I would also add that, most often, these students are well loved by their classmates, and have become the most popular because of their likable character and their liveliness. The point is that they are likable, more likable than the grubby, drunk creatures sometimes seated next to me in American trains, and to whom I would much prefer nicely turned out Negroes as neighbors.

Louisiane, Floride et Virginie, in:
Universités Transatlantiques [Transatlantic Universities],
Paris, Librairie Hachette 1890, pp. 257-259
(Chapter VI, Section IV: "Louisiana, Florida, and Virginia").

2. In the train car bringing us back to Jacksonville, there was a woman of about forty, elegantly dressed. Her face was very lightly colored, so lightly that I did not notice it at first. But as the train was about to depart, the conductor whispered in her ear. She made a gesture to say no; he persisted, raising his voice. Soon everyone knew what the argument was about. The woman had a little Negro blood in her veins. Her wealth and her distinction did not place her beyond the reach of the law. She had to move to the Negro car, which was also the smoking car, dirty and uncomfortable. She protested. Then the conductor called his coworker and, without further ado, they took her by the arms and, since she was heavy, dragged her into the other car. Faced with this ignoble scene, some of the Americans present cackled rudely. If the Southern states are stupid enough to uphold this brilliant legislation much longer, one must believe that they will pay for it dearly in the end, unless the federal government decides to get involved and whip them into shape like naughty children.

Louisiane, Floride et Virginie, in:
Universités Transatlantiques [Transatlantic Universities],
Paris, Librairie Hachette 1890, pp. 266-267
(Chapter VI, Section VIII: "Louisiana, Florida, and Virginia").

1.3.6 WASHINGTON AND BALTIMORE

One would gladly travel many miles around the world to have the pleasure of meeting Bishop Keane. Everyone who knows him is unanimous in boasting of the charm of his words and his manners. Yet his modernism would strike terror in the minds of many Catholics in Europe. He respects the past, he loves the present, and believes in the future; he is wise. He respects the past because it is very wise. He knows all about studying each era through the right lens... and God knows, the lenses have changed often enough! He loves the present because every day he notes with joy the good that is being done around him. He has faith in the future because he is an American to his fingertips, and nothing frightens him. My God! Life these days is like a hunt. Those who do not know how to ride a horse very well are obsessed with falling off. Speed makes them uneasy and obstacles rattle them badly, making them go astray. The others, solidly seated on their mounts and totally self-confident, overcome the same obstacles as easily as you please! Catholics in the United States seem to belong to this second group. They are good horsemen, afraid of nothing. They are being talked about a great deal these days. The have just celebrated the one hundredth anniversary of the official establishment of Catholicism, and of the installation of Bishop Carroll, who was a friend of Washington. At the time, they numbered 40,000. Now there are ten million of them. The celebrations of this religious centennial coincided with the inauguration of the Catholic University of America in Washington. A sort of "lay council" met at Baltimore to discuss various questions relating to the press and to spreading the faith.

The idea of founding a great Catholic university in this country is an old one. National councils[1] have discussed the matter on several occasions. The council held in 1884 adopted the plan. Miss Mary Gwendoline Caldwell, whose grandfather was a theater director and whose father was a gas manufacturer in New Orleans, gave $300,000 (1,500,000 francs). In short order, thanks to other contributions, they managed to collect a total of $4 million. A vast piece of property was purchased, and the first stone was formally laid on May 24, 1888, in the presence of Cardinal Gibbons, the President of the United States, and an enormous crowd. Bishop Spalding of Peoria gave the most magnificent, and at the same time the most daring, speech that has ever come from the lips of a Catholic priest. Let me quote a few passages from it here:

> "*Let us congratulate ourselves*", declaimed the bishop in an outburst of patriotism, "*let us congratulate ourselves for having proved by deeds that respect of the law is compatible with civil and religious freedom; that a free people can prosper and grow without a sovereign and without war; that Church and State can act separately for the public good; that the government of the majority, when men have faith in God and in science, is, after all, the most just and the wisest form of government. This experience assures us the place of honor among the nations that aspire to a life that is more and more free, that is more and more noble.*"

1 These councils consisted of all the Catholic bishops of the United States; there have been three such councils in this century.

Later on, in presenting what amounted to a program for the future, he said,

> *"Let us now propose to prepare the advent of a social organization that will assure everyone shelter, food, and clothing; let us conform to the divine word: 'Oh Israel, you shall not suffer there to be a single beggar, a single poor man within your borders!' We have the right to aspire to that happy time when no man will be condemned to thankless, fruitless labor; to a time when no distinctions shall exist between individuals".* Further on, he added, *"Science has enabled us to prolong life, to fight against disease, to ease pain, to fertilize the soil, to illuminate our cities, and to improve our living conditions. At the same time, it has opened up for us the heights of the firmament, and the mysterious details of creation have been revealed to us gradually. We know the history of the world, we have uncovered the secrets of lost civilizations, and our discoveries increase daily. All this is but a prelude, a preface to a new age. For pretending that our progress is material only is to lack good faith. Everything points to the exact opposite. Other eras have seen more arresting characters than those we see today, but the world has never been governed with so much wisdom and justice."*

There are not many over there that speak like Bishop Spalding! But there are many who think like him.

Washington et Baltimore, in:
Universités Transatlantiques [Transatlantic Universities],
Paris, Librairie Hachette 1890, pp. 307-311
(Chapter VII, Section VI: "Washington and Baltimore").

1.3.7 TRANSATLANTIC UNIVERSITIES: CONCLUSIONS

The report on his mission in Canada and the USA which Coubertin prepared for the French Minister of Public Instruction in a comprised form gives his impressions and conclusions concerning France.

To His Excellency
The Minister of Public Instruction

Dear Sir,

Paris, March 1, 1890

In an order dated July 17, 1889, you entrusted me with a mission to the United States and Canada, to visit the universities and colleges there and to study the organization and operation of the athletic associations founded by the young people of those two countries.

The information that I collected and the observations that I made during my trip have brought certain reflections to mind, which I would like to submit to you. These reflections will conclude this unusual report, which comprises merely supporting documentation; its unorthodox style stands in sharp contrast to the customary seriousness of documents on education. I thought that my sketches would gain in faithfulness in this way, and that I could thus give a clearer, more vibrant impression of these transatlantic universities, to which we Europeans have so infrequently turned our attention. Yet these universities are worthy of capturing our attention. It is around them, even within them, that the Americans, who are as desirous of knowledge as they are of wealth, are preparing our future rivals. Their efforts are not always well thought out. In their zeal, they are mixing the wheat with the chaff, but perseverance and hard work overcome all difficulties, and their progress must prove a stimulus for fruitful competition on our part.

I

At a time when concern for placing due importance on physical education is being expressed so vigorously in France, it is interesting to take a look at a country where the two most opposite extremes in terms of systems of physical education coexist: free games from England, and scientific gymnastics from Germany. In the preceding pages, I have dwelt long enough on the nature of each of these methods, and there is no need to revisit the matter here. Yet it is important to note that these free games, by the very fact that freedom guides their organization, are well suited for getting students to engage in gymnastics. There are gymnasiums in England, and students use them gladly. By contrast, intolerance lies at the base of Germanic gymnastics. It allows only group movements, rigid discipline, and perpetual regulation. Dr. Lagrange has refuted its exorbitant claims with regard to health. Others have taken on the task of establishing its worthlessness from an educational perspective. In the United States, a reaction against it is underway, and one can look forward to a time when university presidents will take the incredible power granted to gymnasium directors away from them. These directors have a controlling hand not only on the bizarre apparatus that they have invented–or sometimes believe they have invented, but also on the games themselves. Since they are unable to make these games disappear immediately, they take them over for their own benefit, choosing the strongest and most agile of their students, to whose training they devote themselves entirely. The result is that during peak season, university teams go from competition to competition. Crowds gather to watch them go at it. Gamblers wager enormous sums and, while the champions are engaged in this exaggerated athleticism, their classmates are kept out of the way so as not to impede their training. They are beginning to show some concern about this deplorable state of affairs, and one must hope that reform will be swift. In any case, this stands as a warning to us not to allow physical education to take on the scientific and authoritarian character espoused by some theorists, friends of the rational and ignorant of educational theory, who are more concerned with principles than with their implementation.

To fill a void that exists within the range of instructional institutions in America, and which corresponds exactly to the most significant period in a child's formation, schools are being established based on the immortal doctrine of the great Arnold. The honorable Mr. Marion drew inspiration from Arnold when preparing the report that he submitted to the committee that you had instructed, Mr. Minister, to study reforms to be introduced in our public high school system. Arnold's program is reproduced in that report nearly in its entirety. In fact, he was the first to use athletics to produce strong wills and upright hearts at the same time as robust bodies. It was he who, through freedom and the hierarchy of merit, was able to prepare children for their roles as citizens of a free country. It was also he who gathered teachers about him, and made them his collaborators. It was he who pursued the lie, and who proclaimed the need above all to create honest men. It was he who said, "Education is a game of chess."

Freedom in these new schools is wisely regulated, as in the schools in England. By contrast, it is excessive in most universities, yet this excess of independence does not yield bad results. Even the Jesuits are happy with this state of affairs, and nothing better proves that freedom is as fruitful among children as it is among adults. Restrictions are sometimes useful, but freedom must be at the base of all educational institutions. Young Americans have a special need for independence, and thus what I reported above concerning the trends in physical education must be considered accidental and temporary. These trends are due to an infatuation with things German which cannot have very deep roots, for it runs contrary to the genius of the country.

Debating Societies are widespread. They must not be viewed as similar to the academies of former times which, in fact, were devoid of freedom of thought. In America as in England, the teacher takes care not to prompt his student. The teacher is unconcerned with having the student shine in a public session, in some role of Greek tragedy or in a recitation of Latin verse. The teacher focuses on having the student hold forth all on his own on "grown up" topics, so that he grows accustomed to finding the right words–and especially to finding his own ideas, which is even more difficult. I cannot recommend strongly enough that similar conferences be instituted in our public high schools. Our older students would gradually lose that deplorable timidity that too often paralyzes them at examinations, and stays with them throughout their careers. My advice would be to forbid discussions of religious topics or domestic politics, but frankly to encourage discussion of anything that concerns foreign policy. The scholastic press is also useful. The few efforts that have been made in France have succeeded, but most teachers still have doubts about the role that a well-edited monthly or bimonthly newspaper can play in a secondary school. If they could only imagine how much easier their task would be, they would not hesitate to push their students in this direction. There are school papers everywhere in America. I receive many of them, and even more from England. I have been reading them attentively for several years now, but I have never seen an ill placed word in them. Most of them are not monitored. I am well aware that all these means are rather modern, but it is my view that we must educate men for the twentieth century, not the seventeenth.

II

Outside of universities and colleges, athletic associations are numerous and prosperous. Some are simply formed among young people in order to play certain sports, such as cycling or lawn tennis. Most often, however, these associations own buildings where real clubs are set up. One can write, dine, and play billiards there. A large gymnasium in the upstairs area, and bowling, showers, and sometimes a swimming pool in the basement allow members to engage in energetic and healthful exercise throughout the winter. For summer. these associations also have playing fields and boat houses outside the towns where they are located.

Membership dues are generally not very high, either thanks to the generosity of the founders, or because of the large number of honorary members who share in the costs without incurring any new ones. Athletic sporting competitions held by these associations, in their gymnasiums during winter and on their playing fields in summer, are well attended. Straight races and obstacle courses, high jumps and long jumps, and pole vaulting are all on the program. Fencing has a few adherents, and boxing is widespread. The gymnasiums always have polished wooden floors and stuffed mats replace the sawdust that we use. Sawdust has its inconvenient aspects: it produces dust that fills the air and makes it unbreathable. Among the improvements to be introduced in France, I would note the creation of rubber tracks for running. They surround the gymnasiums, and are most often supported on a gallery that runs at the mezzanine level. The most popular sports are baseball and football. Cricket is not as popular as it is in England. Baseball is extremely simple in terms of its rules, but it is quite difficult to play. Our school children are not yet persevering enough to take pleasure in an exercise in which they will not succeed from the start. By contrast, football has been wildly popular with them since it was introduced, and its success is well established. It amuses the newest players; in addition, the muscular development and the improvement in the skill of its players are unlimited.

Winter sports, tobogganing, snow shoe races, and especially ice yachting, can be listed here only as providing youths in North America with delightful recreation. These pleasures will never be within our grasp, unless there is a general upheaval in global weather patterns! Horseback riding is not taught in the schools. In the cities, there are riding schools where riding is frequently practiced. Associations have been formed for this, as well. They meet one or two evenings each week and sometimes, to liven up the meeting, a band is set up on the stage and they gallop to the music, as at the racetrack. On other occasions, members organize cavalcades, carrousels, or excursions that take an entire day, or even longer. These riding schools have changing rooms, reading rooms, and resting areas. It is desirable for our French riding schools to be organized along the same model. Yet the effort in France seems to focus on making horseback riding as unappealing as possible.

After any rather taxing exercise, Americans young and old take a "shower bath". This is not quite the same thing as a shower. Perhaps we do not agree on the usefulness of a shower for everyone without exception, but it is hard to argue that washing after exercise that has caused heavy perspiration is unhealthful. A shower bath is installed with the greatest possible ease, and all one needs is some good will and a little money to make it available to our students. This improvement is absolutely necessary. Since, in passing, I am touching on a topic of such significance, let me point out to you, Mr. Minister, the danger that leaving things as they are would present a state of affairs that is contrary at all points to the laws of hygiene. For a year now, I have seen a great many students playing sports in their dress clothes, after simply removing their tunics. That is fine for a recess that lasts just a few minutes. But once the exercise takes an athletic turn, such clothing practices must not be tolerated. Wool jerseys do not cost an arm and a leg. They are useful for *all* exercises, and can be worn for a very long time. No other article of clothing is more useful.

III

English education has been criticized for being too expensive, and this accusation has been repeated by all the enemies of progress and school reform. Fanciful writers have cited figures whose enormity is equaled only by their inaccuracy and, with a certain amount of bad faith, British school children have been depicted as lazy and stagnant beings. This is not the time to reassert the truth and to debunk these false allegations. Suffice it to note that the exaggerated costs in some schools derive merely from the useless luxury with which parents surround their children. Far from adding to those costs, games are actually an opportunity for savings, even as they prevent the establishment of *clans*, those groups of students that are so contrary to the spirit of equality and democracy. What I saw in the United States has absolutely confirmed this opinion of mine.

IV

The degree of civilization achieved by this great country, with its short but glorious past, and with a future that seems to brilliant, and particularly the role that France played in its emancipation, will not allow us to keep the story of the events that have played out there from the teaching of history for much longer. In that study, young French students will find both strong interest and profound lessons in patriotism, as well as admirable examples of virtue and energy. This will make a deep impression on them, and will stir their most ardent feelings of generosity.

In concluding this list of wishes, Mr. Minister, let me thank you most sincerely for the confidence you have shown in me. I have done my best to merit that confidence, in a manner worthy of France and of the Government of the Republic. It is my hope that this trip will not have been made in vain, since I return with the impression that we are not taking the wrong path in following the direction that the study of English educational institutions has opened for us. Therefore let us pursue our reforms, strengthened by the example of England and America. Let us attempt to implement the program summed up in these words: sports and freedom.

Most respectfully yours,

Pierre de Coubertin

Conclusions in:
Universités Transatlantiques [Transatlantic Universities],
Paris, Librairie Hachette 1890, pp. 361-379
(Chapter IX, Sections I-IV: "Conclusions").

Pierre de Coubertin thirty years old, as a young fighter for educational reforms in France (Navacelle Collection)

2. PERMANENCY OF THE EDUCATIONAL BATTLE

Under this heading, we have placed major texts by Coubertin that clearly underscore his determination to achieve the primary goal that he had set for himself early on, as well as the quality of the arguments that he advanced to succeed in his undertaking.

In the first selection, dating from 1887, Coubertin began his arguments in favor of English education, which he then held up as a model. The other two texts list the essential characteristics of good educational practice.

2.1 ENGLISH EDUCATION

When Coubertin reached England, education also bore the strong imprint of the work of Thomas Arnold, a clergyman and director of Rugby College for fourteen years, starting in 1828[1]. By making sports a serious occupation, Arnold transformed the school into an institution. Taken together, initiative, the freedom to form a team that provides for the full development of the individual, and the taste for the fight gave each individual a style, the English style, that he would never lose.

Gradually the educational qualities that Arnold was able to foster became clear to Coubertin. Arnold espoused a psychological education that is capable of discovering hearts of flesh, making each individual responsible for his own power of invention; a moral education that gives full value to decision-making; and a physical education that entrusts the discovery of the secrets of wisdom to sport, making it an essential part of proper preparation for life.

The following speech held in Paris on April 18, 1887, to the members of the Société d'Économie Sociale was followed by a discussion of Coubertin's arguments. Coubertin re-used the important parts of this talk in his book *L'Education en Angleterre.*

1 Faced at the outset with the moral collapse of the institution, Arnold began the work of total and long-lasting educational transformation with clarity and generosity, courage and effectiveness. He did not seek to curtail the will of his students. Rather, he taught students to exercise their wills with full responsibility. For Arnold, morality was the work of the knowledge that each individual employs with respect to his own actions. Joy tells of a successful life. Existence assumes its full value and retains all of its rights.

Ladies and gentlemen,

In approaching the subject of this talk, my primary duty is to define one area, in so broad a field, that I propose to study in particular. In fact, my scope must extend beyond England alone. In England as elsewhere, education assumes various forms. There is elementary and secondary education, private and public, general and professional. It is true that these distinctions are less significant in England than in other countries, like France, for example. There are general principles, identical tendencies that affect the way any Englishman, rich or poor, raises his children. That is why the term 'English education,' as vague as it may seem, does have a special meaning, and corresponds to a clearly defined system.

This evening, I would like to speak to you about general, secondary, public education. However I will not push that classification any further, and I will not follow Bishop Dupanloup's fourfold division of the field into religious, intellectual, disciplinary, and physical education. Nothing could be further from the spirit of English education. Religion plays a large, but separate, part in it. Discipline is understood there as consisting of certain in-house rules of order, no more. What the eminent Bishop of Orleans finds so essential to French secondary schools, the English dismiss as dangerous and contrary to nature. They reject the regulation of every moment which demands nothing more than obedience – a virtue that, as virtues go, they never seem to have made much of a fuss about, or even to have understood its nature. Specifically, they reject preventative discipline, which their instincts exclude almost absolutely from permitting in government, not to mention in secondary schools.

As for physical development, not only does it occupy a very important place in their system, but it influences the system as a whole, playing a very effective moral role. One final preliminary remark: the schools whose educational plan I am about to outline, and details of which I will provide glimpses of in passing, are "public schools", Harrow, Rugby, Eton, Winchester, etc. There is the category of Catholic schools, as well, the organization of which is rather perceptibly different. Finally, there are the smaller schools, "*boîtes*" as we would call them, where one or two teachers, always out in the countryside somewhere, gather together fifteen or more young children whose parents find themselves needing to separate from before the children are old enough to enter the "public schools."

I

To instruct is not to educate. There is a fundamental difference between "instruction, which provides knowledge, endows the mind, and creates scholars, and education, which develops the faculties, raises the mind, and makes men[2]". This quotation could pass for a truism, except that in our day, in France, deplorable confusion has been created between these two notions. It could be said in the past, and can be repeated with all the more reason today: "Instruction is everything, education, nothing."

The ultimate goal of teachers in England is to make men and to get them to teach themselves thereafter. Character and good method: that is their goal. Yet it would be erroneous to believe that this principle causes them to neglect hard work. The extreme difference that they recognize between instruction and education means that one is separate from the other, that they do not go hand in hand, and above all that they are not evenly distributed over the various stages of life. Clearly, as early as very young childhood, little English children engage in the delights of the out-of-doors. Their daring is proverbial. Everyone knows that charming scene depicted by Taine, in which a child astride his pony, entering a field near a bull with a menacing eye, calls back down the line of horses to his big sisters, saying, "Hey, girls, don't be afraid, I'll lead the way". To the greatest possible extent, children are raised in the countryside, and in any event their natural taste for physical exercise is encouraged. But between the ages of eight and twelve, they work a great deal. In another context[3] , I have commented on how serious the entrance examinations for the "public schools" are (the usual age ranges from twelve to thirteen) and, in addition, if one compares these programs to those presented six or seven years later to university candidates, one is struck by how few things the students are supposed to have learned in the interval. The point is that after an initial period of instruction, during which one is to profit from the open, relaxed mind of the child to inculcate the basic notions of all knowledge, and to give the child good work habits, there follows a period of education which is quite significant in another way, because it is decisive, its results will be definitive, and above all because it includes that *crisis* that we call the awkward age, but for which we take fewer pains – I do not know why – than our neighbors.

So there the child is, in a "public school". What is he doing there? Thomas Arnold will tell us. This great man, who died in 1842, the headmaster of Rugby, a school that he headed for fourteen years, can be considered the father of modern English education. He was the first to adopt and to apply the principles that are its foundation. I have taken the following quotes from the collection of this correspondence, quotes that say more that any development of them could. He said, "I wish to form Christian Gentlemen; my goal is to teach children to govern themselves, which is far better than governing them myself". A profound statement, worthy of reflection on the part of those who wish to govern schools as autocrats, with an iron hand. This Dupanloup of England recalls for them that they are wrong regarding the nature of their mission, which is not to form slaves, but masters! Sovereign masters at that, who, far earlier than the law recognizes, are free to use and to abuse what is subject to them. To hope to withdraw this sovereignty from them, and to try to do so, is a dangerous thing. Here below, man must feel isolated, feel alone with himself, know his strength, and as early as possible, be placed in the presence of the heavy responsibility that is the counterbalance to all power.

That is what Arnold thought. One day, when problems had arisen requiring that several students be expelled, showing discontent in the ranks, before the whole school Arnold spoke these words, which have remained famous and which sum up his whole approach: "It is not necessary that there be 300, 100, or even 50 students here; but it is necessary that there be nothing but Christian Gentlemen". This passage deals with an error in public opinion, then as widespread in England as it is today in France. The public held that secondary schools were institutions intended to correct bad character,

2 Bishop Dupanloup.
3 See Coubertin: Les Collèges Anglais, Harrow School. In: *Réforme sociale,* November 1, 1886.

a detestable notion that can only serve to make a school into a correctional institution and consequently, a rotten place for the honest children who happen to be there. This feeling was so widespread that unless capital offenses were committed, parents acknowledged that their children had a sort of *right* not to be expelled from school. That was not how Thomas Arnold saw things, who wrote somewhere that "the first, the second, and the third duty of any school director is to get rid of unpromising characters". His expressions are worthy of comment. The term is not "to expel", but "to get rid of", and the adjective "unpromising" does not limit this measure from being applied to those guilty of something, but to all those who are not making the most of their time at the school because, if they are not making the most of it, they are preventing others from doing so, as well. So it is not always a punishment, it is often a simple warning, a petition to the parents to take the child back. This corresponds to a very British idea, that of selection. In the physical order, as in the moral order, it is always the elite that is targeted, because a superior phalanx, though few in number, yields infinitely more than very widespread mediocrity. Thus everything tends to be given to those who already have something, as in the Gospel.

In the eyes of the English, school life is acceptable only if it is a continuation of family life. To take a child and to put that child in close quarters with other children, to sever the child from all communication with its relations and the outside world, is a monstrosity for them. Students must be surrounded by every possible comfort; care must be given that they do not lose any of the habits of good society, and that they do not neglect any measures of hygiene, and even the elegant touches that encircled their childhood. In the "public schools", and this is the main point of difference from religious schools, students are spread out among the homes of the teachers, each of whom houses between ten and thirty students. If there are too many students for the teacher to dine with every day, he invites them to tea, at the least. I have had the opportunity to be at table on these occasions. The service is flawless, the food simple but excellent. They do not file in by rows, and they do not stare dumbfounded at guests because they are accustomed to seeing them. They know how to be polite and how to show guests around graciously. At Eton, in one of these residences called "boarding houses", I recall having gone to knock at the door of a boy I knew, accompanied on my way there by the daughter of the teacher. She went in with me, and carried on a bit of polite conversation. My young host had returned from playing cricket. He had had the astonishing idea of washing his hands, and the nerve to ask for hot water, as well! How effeminate, wouldn't you say? What do you expect? It's just that the English have realized that if you don't give children hot water, they won't wash!

II

Two things dominate in the English system, two things that are also means for achieving their ends: freedom and sports.

The route taken by a French child on his way toward freedom is lined with walls, the insides of which look like a prison. Then, all of a sudden, the walls are removed. By contrast, the English take pains to remove all constraints. Then, just at the developmental stage when an adolescent becomes a man, a small barrier indicates points

Thomas Arnold (1795-1842), Headmaster of Rugby School, 1828-1842 (Photo: Rugby School Archives)

out the dangers of the abyss to him. It is a fact that among the English, although school children are more free, older students are less free than in France. But it is important not to hide the world from children. Indeed, to hide evil is to underscore it, just as placing a curtain across a painting of a nude entices your sons to lift the curtain. It gives them the notion that it is forbidden.

I repeat, education must be a preface to life. The man will be free; the child must be so also. The point is to teach the child to use his freedom and to understand its significance. Anyone who has visited English schools, set up in the middle of the countryside as well as in very small towns where they are the center of things, is struck by a curious sight – that of all these younger and older children, passing in groups, crossing streets, going into stores, or running in the fields. They never wear uniforms that smack of military camps. Yet they are all dressed alike, which shows how little attention they pay to the relative degree of elegance of their clothing.

A quick overview of their school day will give a better idea of the freedom they are allowed, and how they make the best use of it. Rising time is the time of the first class. They can get up earlier to study or go for a walk. In summer, the young students never fail to imitate the sun, running about in the countryside at the crack of dawn. In any event, there is no bell to wake them up suddenly, nor is there that vile quarter hour set aside for washing up in the morning, usually consisting of dipping fingertips into a little saucer.

The English do not like dormitories, not merely for reasons of hygiene, but because they find that solitude and cleanliness are two powerful means of education. The constant community of companions imposed on children under this false pretext that that's life – while nothing could be further from the truth – weighs more heavily on them than one can say. Wherever the group can generate a spirit of healthy rivalry, students are grouped together to great advantage, in classes and games. In the study or in the dormitory, competition holds no further meaning. That is why young English students have their own rooms most of the time, or at least a little place apart where they work. In this model, dormitories consist of separate compartments which provide the illusion of solitude, at least to a certain extent. At the secondary schools, boys live surrounded by small objects that remind them of their home and family. They take pleasure in decorating their little rooms. On the walls, one sees portraits of their parents, of their friends, and engravings of the hunt. Often there are flowers, nice little books, displays of arms... That is where they do their homework when they see fit to do so. The homework must be completed by the assigned date, that is all. This sanctuary is nearly inviolable. The teacher crosses its threshold as infrequently as possible, more as a visitor than as a monitor.

Classes are held at set times. It is up to the students to arrive there on time. They do not file into class in rows, and at the sound of a bell.

Is there any need to talk about freedom in their games? It is total. Cricket, lawn tennis and football have never been imposed. British students have never been forced to make that strange comment recorded by Bishop Dupanloup: "Sir, if you only realized how much it bothers us to amuse ourselves in this way". I cannot go into much detail listing all the types of recreation they have to choose from, which would be rather uninteresting in and of itself. But everywhere, in addition to outdoor games, I saw heated swimming pools, gymnasiums, boxing rings and tennis courts, as well as workshops where they can be initiated in the mysteries of woodworking and other manual work. None of these activities is regulated with respect to hours. Let me add that the gates are always open, and walks in the countryside are always possible. In the evening, when they return to their rooms to enjoy some well-deserved rest, a student is not forbidden to sit at his desk to review a lesson, or to write a letter by *his own* candle's light, which he is not required to extinguish at one particular time rather than another.

This freedom has two essential corollaries: responsibility, and hierarchy, or the monitoring of students by the students themselves. By responsibility, I mean the inevitable chastisement or the inevitable cost incurred by those who commit a misdeed. Repentance or change of attitude on their part changes nothing with respect to this outcome. The chastisement may consist of an assignment, but if the misdeed is the slightest bit serious, the punishment is physical. To help you understand just how popular canes are, need I mention the case in which students revolted at one time because there was a question of banishing the practice from their midst? Far from being considered ignominious, canings are deemed a competition in courage, the one undergoing the caning often having to fight hard to hold back his tears or his cries. In some religious schools, this traditional means of repression has been replaced by rulers, rather violent strokes given on the fingers or the back of the hand. This is more convenient for the one administering the punishment, but the invention is unfortunate. It is not the hands, which are always easy to maim, that should be chosen... I will not dwell on this point, but there is another kind of punishment: just as the prizes given out at a competition sometimes are accompanied by small amounts of money, the system of fines is widely practiced, especially when it is a matter of damage that can be repaired through payment. If a student were to become indebted to a certain extent, and his parents refused to get him out of this situation, there is no doubt that he would be required to sell off his little books and engravings to raise the required sum. The child thus learns how to behave. He acts at his own risk, and must calculate the results of his actions ahead of time. Well-intentioned counsel is available to him, provided that he goes and seeks it out. There is someone nearby who is watching out for him, but with his back turned. He will answer when called upon, but will not provide advice unless asked.

It seems that, in a school, it is not so much the error in and of itself that is disturbing (Saints preserve us from faultless children, as Fenelon said), but rather the high regard with which it may be viewed by classmates. To keep resistance against authority from becoming a source of glory, the English have decided that the best method to use is to have authority, or at least some authority, reside in the very milieu from which resistance may come. It is one of their favorite principles that stability is achieved only by involving the greatest number of individuals in the work of maintaining the status quo. To shift the application of such a maxim onto a society of children was, without doubt, a bold move. Arnold did not hesitate to do so, nor did any of the others. Arnold assessed the measure in these terms: "I cannot accept, in theory or in practice, the current system in our "public schools", which tends to grant children so much independence, unless the students in the upper class can act as intermediaries between the teachers and the rest of the school, and thus transmit to the others, through their example and influence,

The sixth form room at Rugby School in the 1880s (taken from A.P. Stanley, Life and Correspondence of Thomas Arnold, D.D., London 1904, p. 105)

principles of right conduct, rather than the very imperfect principles that generally reign in a society of children left free to determine good and bad for themselves". For Arnold, student in the Sixth Form (the oldest class), and particularly the *praepostors* and the *monitors*, i.e. the top fifteen students in whom power is invested, were like "officers in the army and navy". He added, "When I have confidence in them, there is no position in England that I would prefer to this one; but if they do not support me, I must withdraw". Does this not sound like the head of a constitutional state speaking of his ministers? The authority of the monitors has undergone some changes. Much has been done to put a stop to abuses of *fagging*, a sort of slavery that had derived from this system initially. Today, the older students understand their duties better, and abuse their power relatively infrequently. A teacher at Harrow recently wrote to me, saying that "their authority is frankly popular, and our boys are proud to be governed by the eldest among them, rather than by us". This was true even when they had to perform certain domestic services, for which they received a certain number of clouts in passing.

Here I have touched on an important point: the power of public opinion. This is a force that teachers use, and that they do not attempt to restrain in any way, but only to direct, so that it makes their own task easier. These English schools are true societies, with their own laws, prejudices, and characteristic traits. I would even say that this society has its own code of honor, which the students refrain from breaking. The young English usually settle their disputes – their serious disputes – by fist fights, disputes that require a black eye or a bloody nose for honor to be satisfied. In addition, the combatants have the joy of being punished, since these duels are forbidden. But at least they fought it out before the eyes of their classmates and, through the good offices of their witnesses, they have not missed out on any of the time-honored practices for such circumstances.

So far I have spoken only from the physical, material perspective. There is also the intellectual and religious perspective. Beside the freedom to come and go, there is freedom to think and freedom to pray. I do not wish to enter into detail on a topic that I have voluntarily set aside, and I will limit my remarks to a few words on the main characteristics of instruction, the method of teaching. It is not, as in France, like a ladder on which a student advances one rung each year. One needs a certain number of points to advance from one class to the next, and the examinations, which are given two or three times a year, define and regulate this passage, so that an intelligent, hardworking boy may advance more quickly than the others. This is the opposite of the system here in France, in which one cannot be ahead on one point and behind one another. To take one example, there is no special history program for the seventh grade that differs from that for the sixth. History is dealt with as a whole, and children of different ages find themselves taking the same course.

Nearly everywhere now, studies are divided so that preponderance is given either to the classical course, or to the scientific course. Classes are more like conferences. Homework is assigned for a period of time that allows them to work on it in greater depth, and to give the work a personal touch. Finally, teachers like to have their students present reports on books that they are required to read, and about which they must form an opinion. The intelligence is treated like character, like their bodies, with respect and a degree of seriousness.

Debating Societies are certainly one of the more unusual aspects of this system. As you know, these are assemblies where parliamentary procedure is followed scrupulously, and where students practice public speaking. Such societies are found throughout the entire United Kingdom, even in the smallest of towns. They exist in the colonies, as well, and Mr. de Hubner mentions a Hindu school where he found students engaged in debating, under the tutelage of their English teachers... do you know what topic? You'll never guess... If it would not be preferable for India to shake off the yoke of England! One must hear these debates to have some idea of the freedom of opinion that is tolerated in them. Arnold himself established a magazine at Rugby, a review in which the articles were written by the students at the school, and sometimes by first-year undergraduate students who have just left the school. This example was imitated everywhere. There is not a single school without its own weekly or bimonthly publication. Can you picture our high school juniors being allowed to print their wild imaginings in a newspaper? In England this seems quite a simple thing, and, in fact, it is so. Censorship is not often required. Such freedom of opinion would be found shocking in France, because it would produce divergent opinions within families. In England, such divergence does not disturb the peacefulness of the home. Even the most conservative father does not grow indignant at hearing his son make a radical confession of faith upon leaving the school benches. "My son is a home-ruler", one Irishman said to me, "He adores Gladstone. I hate him, myself."

Aside from political opinions, religious beliefs also benefit from this great tolerance. But this fact is due especially, we must note, to the nature of the Protestant religion, a very elastic religion that accommodates the most diverse attitudes. Every child is not necessarily led to first communion, or to the act corresponding to it. So here, there is a conquest for the minister to achieve, what Arnold called "a chess game against Satan". Religious instruction is given every Sunday before the students, whose attention and respectful behavior is required, at least. In general, dissenters do not show a desire to have their children not attend these sessions. But when they do, their wishes are faithfully respected. Catholics do not attend these schools, not because they would find any serious impediment to the exercise of their religion there (only in small towns where there is often no Catholic chapel); rather, it is mostly because they fear the influence of the Protestant spirit that necessarily holds sway there.

III

Gentlemen, I now come to what seems to me the most noteworthy aspect of English education: I mean the role that sports plays in that education. This role is physical, moral, and social, all at the same time. We have a two-fold reason to consider it here, because I believe that, although we may hope for certain reforms in our system, it is only through sports that they can be introduced. It even seems to me that a trend is developing in this direction that we might use quite advantageously.

Sports means movement, and the influence of movement on bodies is something that has been evident from time immemorial. Strength and agility have been deeply appreciated among savage and civilized peoples alike. Both are achieved through exercise and practice: happy balance in the moral order, *mens sana in corpore sano*, as the ancients used to say.

But I must steer clear of generalities, and limit myself exclusively to the English territory that I have chosen. Nothing, in my opinion, can give a better idea of what public feeling is on this issue than this passage from a novel that has enjoyed great popularity, one in which the world of the schools is extremely well depicted. I am opening a parenthesis to quote from it; I have worked hard to translate it as accurately as possible, but this was extremely difficult because the author's thoughts find scarcely any corresponding notions in our minds. The chapter is entitled *Muscular Christianity.* The author writes:

> *"In the course of the studies that I have undertaken to inform myself about muscular Christianity, the goals and the means used by its members, I was led to acknowledge that alongside this society, there was another, whose members deserve the simple name of athletes, the point of contact between the two being that, on both sides, it is considered a great advantage to have strong and agile bodies; but the one group does not seem to harbor any doubt as to why they have a body, and they parade it from one end of the world to the other in the service of their interests, or the satisfaction of their whims, whereas the others have inherited the old chivalrous maxim that a man's body must be well trained and developed by its master in order then to serve for the protection of the weak, the advancement of all just causes, and the conquest of the world."*

Addressing his hero, the author says the following succinct and meaningful thing:

> *"Young man, you belong to an army whose rallying cry is to fear God and to do 400 kilometers in 400 hours."*

Here, surely, is an association of ideas in which sports is treated with honor, because it is ranked equally with the fear of God. To put solid fists to use in God's service is a condition for serving him well. To create vigorous health for oneself is a necessity in order to have a full existence, for one loses time by being sick, and time is money. The Gospel admonition to offer your left cheek when they strike you on the right is little practiced. It is replaced by advice of the motto of the United Kingdom: "If you strike, I strike". To me, these seem to be the current ideas on the role of physical strength and sports in this world, and although these maxims are not always formulated so clearly, they slumber at the back of the mind of every good Englishman, who knows how to find them there when he needs to. But let us return our attention to education.

Thomas Arnold, and I beg your leave to have him come back on stage yet again, asked himself the following question: "Can one hasten the transformation that makes a man of the child, without in so doing running the risk of crushing his physical and intellectual faculties?" This is a question that tormented Arnold for a long time. He sensed that every boy must pass through a critical phase, and he was convinced that the "public schools" had the advantage of causing this phase to occur earlier. In his view, there is nothing worse than a mind galloping ahead of the body. As it develops, the intelligence must find a wide envelope that is strong enough to contain it, and to resist its expansion. The child must still be a child, even though he already possesses a man's body. In a word, one must hurry to create a man, morally and physically, of this child who has bad instincts and passions whose assault he will suffer; he must be given *premature* muscles and will, what Arnold called "true manliness". Initiative, daring, decisiveness, the habit of self-reliance and of taking responsibility for one's own failures... all these are qualities for which one cannot make up for lost time. It is far more important to cultivate them from early childhood than to strive to inculcate scientific notions in young minds, notions that vanish all too quickly for the very reason that they were placed there too late.

What is the effect of this concern? How does one put such principles into action? Above all, what is the end result? Any agglomeration of men constitutes an ensemble of vice and corruption, and children are the seeds of men. In our boarding schools, we hear complaints that the work is too hard, the air is not pure enough, and aspects of proper hygiene are too often neglected. These are regrettable failings, indeed, but that is not all; there is far worse. There is the constant danger posed by life in common. Gentlemen, it may seem to you that this danger is scarcely conjured up by the English system that I have presented to you. You might say that it is quite true that the pure air of the countryside, prudent moderation in the division of work, and the strict observance of the laws of proper hygiene place children in excellent material, physical conditions. But lack of oversight and excessive independence must increase the drawbacks of their frequent contact. If this is not the case, if these drawbacks are, rather, more rare and their impact less serious, it is for a general and powerful reason that it is important to know. There is a fact that must be noted here. The practice of the current system of education, already long established, has yielded only good results. It is the "public schools" that have populated the universities of Oxford and Cambridge with those young men of virtue to whom Taine renders homage, which is one form of proof already. But the main proof lies in the testimony of the men whose position in the schools and long experience puts in a position to assess the morality of the students better than anyone else. Well, all those whom I have questioned on this topic have been unanimous in their answers. They have all praised the state of morals, and they state quite clearly that sports is the reason for this, that the role of sports is to pacify the senses and to put imaginations to rest, to stop corruption in its tracks by isolating it, preventing it from spreading, and, finally, by arming nature for the fight.

Minds, like bodies, are constantly occupied by that *passion* which carries them away and subjugates them. This is, I repeat, encouraged as much as possible. The English believe in the need for enthusiasm at this age. But they think, too, that it is not easy, even if it is a good thing, to engender in children such enthusiasm for Alexander or Caesar. They must have something more alive, more real. The dust of Olympia is still what stirs their healthy competitive spirit the most, and the most naturally. They gladly pursue honors for which they see grown men proud to compete. Is all this harmful to work, not merely in terms of the time it takes, but also through the preoccupation, the constant thinking that results from the very tournament nature of these games? It has been said that the life of the thinker and that of the athlete are utterly opposed. For my part, I have often seen that those who were the leaders in physical exercises were also leaders in their studies. Their excellence in one area gives them a desire to be first in everything. There is nothing like the habit of victory to assure success. Finally, if it were true, many Englishmen would simply say "Too bad", feeling as they do that one can remake oneself intellectually, but not morally, and that in consequence instruction must yield before morals. That is not the view held by some "moderns", who are calling for an increase in the standing of studies, to the detriment of sports.

Sports – to conclude our consideration of their influence on the moral order – also stimulates courage. One must realize that youth do not always remain in that beneficial and delicious state of fatigue experienced by dilettantes in the field. Tedious training, real suffering, and even danger are met with a singular lack of concern and sang-froid. It is stiff, unrelenting competition. Nothing forges souls more strongly, too strongly perhaps, because energy can, at times, degenerate into hardness and brutality. That is the flip side of the coin.

Games also provide the perfect terrain for social education. The students, who form their own athletic associations, are fully responsible for organizing the games. They band together, elect their own leaders, and then obey them with remarkable discipline.

The mission of a club president is to oversee the matches and to propose toasts. The secretary calls meetings and the treasurer renders his accounts to the general meeting... a whole society in miniature. Not only do they have to purchase and maintain new equipment for the games, but they build elegant pavilions with

Thomas Arnold Memorial in the Rugby School chapel. Arnold is buried in the chancel of this chapel. (Photo: N.Müller)

meeting rooms and changing areas. All this is taken most seriously, and the way associations function shows the good sense and reason of their organizers, a feat of which our secondary students would be incapable. The college review published by the students contains all the sports news, providing details of the glorious battles fought with the representatives of rival establishments.

IV

Gentlemen, when I began this talk, I attempted to spell out for you the goal that English schoolmasters seek. Turning next to the means used to achieve that goal, I discussed two of its principles: freedom and sports. You have seen that these two small words sum up the whole system. Now, I must fill in the blanks as far as the results obtained are concerned, the good and the bad alike.

First, I must point out the absence of any reaction on the part of the students when it is over. You have all often observed the exuberant outbursts we French engage in upon completing secondary school. One would think school was a sort of prison. Those escapees who do not head right to government schools throw aside

The Rugby School headmaster's house, where Arnold lived (Rugby School Archives)

their books at the first opportunity, the better to savor their freedom. No more constant constraints, no more incessant communal living with classmates... at long last, they breathe free. How many of them become drunk on those first mouthfuls of fresh air! Aside from those who fall by the wayside, how many good students, on whom so many hopes were founded, lapse into a sort of *dolce farniente* from which nothing can rescue them. They are *failures*, useless men. Although some do eventually return to their books, this happens only after fairly long interval, which means that a great deal of time has been lost, and things forgotten.

This scenario is so true, Gentlemen, that you rush to push your children into the first career that comes along. If they respond by saying, "I want to create my own career", you grow worried because you fear the outcome. You do not believe in self-made careers because in France, well-intentioned people tend to stop in mid-course for lack of motivation. In England, however, that is the rule. The army, the navy, the diplomatic corps, and the courts take in only a very small number of children raised in the "public schools". The others, once out of the schools they leave with tears in their eyes, enter the work force in increasing numbers. The good times, the times for playing sports to excess, are over. Now it is time for steady effort; they must succeed. Some of them search for their path for a long time, but in the end, they find it. Then there are the colonies, that career of expatriation so well suited to the English, who bring their "old England" with them wherever they go. Whether they are "squatters" in New Zealand or planters in America, they are better off for having received such a strong physical and moral education in their schools. Muscles and character are objects of urgent necessity in such circumstances. Although the main cause for our own colonial impotence lies with our deplorable system of succession, it seems to me that education also plays its part.

The young Englishman leaving school is generally gifted with plenty of common sense. He is familiar with the great laws of society in this world, which he has seen in miniature, in the microcosm surrounding him. Theories glide right over him without wearing him down. He is possessed of self-control, a good method for learning what he does not already know, and a great deal of innocence and freshness in mind. Yet his practical sense often makes him an egotist, though this defect is more attributable to the race than to education. It is just that the type of individual I am sketching for you at the moment is an elite sort of person. If you are familiar with the English, you know that life is untenable for the timid, the weak, and the lazy. In the tumult of existence, such persons are driven back, overwhelmed, and stepped on. They are tossed aside, seen merely as impediments. Nowhere is selection more pitiless. There are two distinct races: the race of men with frank expressions and strong muscles, with a self-assured stride, and the race of weaklings with resigned and humble faces, a vanquished air. Well, what holds true in the world holds true in the schools as well! The weak are tossed aside. The benefits of this education apply only to the strong.

Another criticism can be leveled at this type of education: that it is very expensive. Taine estimates the average cost for a schoolchild at 5,000 francs; that figure is exaggerated. Mandatory costs at Harrow are 3,500 francs. In the first year, an additional 500 francs in expenses must be expected. Rugby is less expensive (about fifteen pounds less). The cost of religiously-affiliated schools comes nowhere near these figures. Even when one adds up costs in these schools quite lavishly, the total comes to no more than 2,500 at the Jesuit school at Beaumont. This is close to what our own schools cost and, frankly, the spread is well worth the difference between the two systems. Then again, comparison is only fair if one mentions the length of stay in both cases. Students spend two or three years in the "public schools", four at the most.

This is already quite to the liking of the English. One must not lose sight of the fact that among them, school is a last resort. If they could do without it, they would, and without hesitation. They tolerate it only provided that there are long vacations that allow children to come home for Christmas, Easter and summer, to be re-immersed in family life. As you know, home is like a cult with them. They leave home with such apparent ease because they know that that is the way things work in this world. They feel that the home is the best school to attend. Children leave it as late as possible, and return periodically. Where else could they be better off until their education is complete?

Here, then, are a great number of principles that clash with our own. Open any of our treatises on education and you will see that the older children become, the harder they must work; that in school, the only way to maintain their innocence is never to let them out of sight, not even for a moment, and to live by the famous dictum *nunquam duo – raro unus – semper tres;* that regulations must resemble a railway timetable, that everything must be foreseen in them, leaving no place for the slightest indecision; that letters must always be opened and usually read before being given to the students who, for their part, cannot carry on unfettered correspondence. Try to find a single one of our schools where censors, principals, prefects of studies, etc., have not increased in number, where students do not need a pass to do anything, ever. Then take a look at a neighboring country, just as Christian and as civilized as our own. There, the older the children get, the more they play. Not only are they left to themselves a great deal, but this is deemed necessary for their physical and moral education. Their motto is: the less regulation the better. Their letters are not scrutinized, and they are permitted to subscribe to illustrated papers and magazines. Solitude is viewed as essential, and the whole system operates with a few schoolmaster who teach and direct at the same time. Is any greater contrast possible? Can one imagine anything more dissimilar?

No rows, no bells, no notes, no fixed study hours, little silence... and no crowds! Gentlemen, if your children were to hear me give this list of negatives, they would applaud beyond all measure. They would make you promise to send them across the Channel. Yet I am convinced that their enthusiasm would dissipate quickly. They would find themselves left to their own devices; they would feel the void surrounding them. Perpetual responsibility would weigh heavily on them, and to withstand it they would have to expend twice the energy as their fellow classmates. On occasion, the "public schools" have accepted and kept French students whose moral fiber made them suitable candidates. They have left those schools without losing any of the incomparable qualities that are the privilege of their race, and from the English they have learned the initiative, decisiveness, daring, and common sense that we envy. These French students had what it takes to work hard to catch up to their former classmates, who had outpaced them in terms of instruction.

In approaching Dover, a rolling valley comes into view, in the middle of which rises the religious capital of the United Kingdom. It is there that those whom our government wished deprive of the honor of teaching the worship of God and the service of France found asylum, under the protection of a country that is truly free. We have sometimes felt regret that this exile does not better serve the children that live with it. It takes persecution for a French secondary school to be founded abroad. Can we not put this circumstance to good use, to widen the circle of ideas and customs a little?

In any event, although the students at Canterbury do not enjoy the benefits of English education, their eyes do gaze on England's trees and fields, their lungs breathe in its bracing air. That is quite something in itself. But there are trees and fields and pure air in France. Will we never see schools built in the countryside in France? Will we never see an end to those huge stone boxes that are the Mazas of education?

L'Éducation Anglaise, in:
La Réforme Sociale [Social Reform],
Vol. 7, Series 2, No. III, June 1, 1887,
pp. 633-648.

2.2 ATHLETIC EDUCATION

The following talk was published in the 1889 report by the "Association française pour l'avancement des Sciences". In the talk, dated January 26, 1889, Coubertin spoke in his capacity as secretary of the Association pour la réforme de l'éducation scolaire en France [Association for Educational Reform at School Level in France]. He defined "Athletic Education" as an educational system with a specific objective, "to make men", and a specific method with its own laws. It is, he said, a science. To treat it as nothing more than an attractive practice of games of relaxation, as some do, is to skew its basic meaning, and to negate its true value. He contrasted French education, based on authority, obedience, and boredom, to English education, which is designed as a suitable aid for the physical, intellectual, and moral strengths of each individual. Sports are practiced enthusiastically and with high spirits, spilling out into the general atmosphere of studies and the results of those studies. In France, public opinion distorts proper education. Many people are fooling themselves when they engage in simple healthful exercises, believing that they are "involved in sports". Sports, when properly understood, leads to the triumph of the will and to the human ideal.

That same year, Coubertin held the "Congress for the Propagation of Physical Exercises in Education" at the World's Fair, with the consent of the government. On that occasion, he made official the results of a study that he had done in Anglo-Saxon countries, to determine whether Thomas Arnold's ideas had been applied there. In most of those countries, "Athletic Education" became the standard basis for all education. In Coubertin's view, this was a point scored against his detractors.

Coubertin is referring here to the annual congress of the "Société d'Économie Sociale" where the foundation of the "Comité pour la propagation des exercices physiques dans l'éducation" was announced on May 29, 1888. On July 15, the athletics association of the Alsace School was created. In the same month, using the pseudonym of Philippe Daryl, Pascal Grousset began publishing a series of articles on school games, where he called for physical education to be oriented towards French traditions.[1]

In October 1888, a rival to the Comité was created. This was the "Ligue nationale de l'éducation physique", led by Grousset. Its foundation led to tensions for a while between the members of the Comité.[2]

Gentlemen,

I am well aware of the great honor you have shown me in allowing me to stand on this stage, previously graced by so many distinguished speakers. Yet I must also note how well suited my topic is for this particular audience, and this gives me confidence in your indulgence.

I will speak about a science, one of the most useful and surely one of the greatest of all sciences, since its purpose is to make men. What is more, as far as France is concerned, this science has just taken a major step forward. Some might be disposed to think that it has stepped backward, but I will strive to prove just the

1 Cf. Ph. Daryl, *La Renaissance physique*, Paris, 1888.

2 See also Coubertin's description in *Une Campagne de vingt et un ans*, Paris 1909, chapters IV-VI, pp. 23-53.

opposite, to show that it has, in fact, advanced. In any case, you have founded this Association to study developments in the sciences, and everything that is new – or renewed if we allow that there is nothing new under the sun – everything that interests and affects you. That is why I have chosen a broad title that may seem a bit pretentious. I have not come here to speak to you only of school games, which have been much discussed for the past six months, but of the entire educational system to which school games are only a preface. I shall speak about the combination of precepts and maxims that constitute *Athletic Education.*

I

Anyone involved in education has read Bishop Dupanloup's book summarizing his reflections drawn from his long experience in educating youth. At the beginning of chapter one, he writes, "When I tried to ascertain what the two fundamentals of education are, after a great deal of study and hard experience, I found that they are *authority* and *respect*". Among the most recent arrivals in English libraries is a small book by Dr. Thring, director of the school at Uppingham for many years. At his recent passing, his fellow citizens poured forth testimonials of admiration. Thring defined education as "a labor of *attentiveness*, *hard work*, and *love*". At first glance, these two definitions seem quite compatible. They complement each other. Attentiveness, hard work, and love are the three elements that constitute a teacher. Authority and respect are their effect on the student. In reality, however, Bishop Dupanloup and Dr. Thring have found formulas for two systems so deeply opposed, I would go so far as to say mutually hostile, as is possible to conceive.

For centuries, education in France has been a labor of authority. In this respect, the facts are so obvious that no further proof need be adduced. In certain periods, the form of authority has soften a little, but its substance has always remained the same. The Jesuits have handed down their traditions to the University. Now, as before, education is like a surgeon operating on the child entrusted to its care, destroying what is deemed harmful in the child. The child leaves the education process shaped, made manageable, formed in the image of the society in which he is to live, a society whose errors and contradictions he already bears. If the teacher has been capable of fulfilling the severe and majestic role incumbent upon him, he will have inspired in his student the habit of obedience, and above all of respect for authority. Being subject to his own superiors, the teacher will have made the child a dependent creature, accustomed to the requirements of hierarchy, no longer willing even to discuss the advantages and drawbacks of that hierarchy. This is what goes on in state-run schools and church schools alike, and Bishop Dupanloup has expressed the characteristics of this system in the two words that best summarize it: authority and respect.

The watchwords of education in England are freedom and independence. There, the teacher is an overseer, under whose watchful eye the child is placed so that, through his word, his example, and his teaching, he helps develop the goodness and honesty that the child already has within. To reach this goal, the teacher does not believe that he is entitled to use violent means. He appeals only to reason and

The french School Games following the English example **(taken from Le Petit Parisien, no. 70, June 8, 1890, p. 1)**

feeling. He breaks nothing, he frustrates as little as possible. Yet since this is, at one and the same time, a work of great delicacy and exceptional boldness, he surrounds himself with everything that might work in tandem with his own discrete direction. He makes of his school a microcosm of the outside world. He brings into it the air that is breathed there, the advantages and the permitted pleasures enjoyed there, the awkward situations one is faced with, and even some of the obstacles that one must overcome. His art consists of adapting all this to the child's physical, intellectual, and moral strengths. What work, gentlemen, and what acute observation is required at all times to achieve these results! Furthermore, if you could only imagine how thrilling this hunt for minds can be, this pursuit of immaterial game that often slips away, then you would understand why one of the most illustrious contemporary English teachers has defined his task as a labor of attentiveness, hard work, and love.

Let us note in passing a singular paradox: for a long time now, corporal punishment has vanished from our schools, while it continues to exist, albeit in a rather limited way, in English schools. Yet it is the French that I am accusing here of being authoritarian. The matter of chastisement (physical or other) is secondary; the paradox is only superficial. In France, we do not whip the flesh, but the mind; and we whip the mind until it is subdued, bleeding on the inside. Like the body, the mind must wear a uniform, whereas among our neighbors, both wear whatever clothing suits them best. The details matter little, provided that the fabric is of high quality and the cut is good.

I had no concept whatever of these things when, almost unconsciously and moved by a strange instinct, I summoned the entire French educational system as a witness before my childhood bench. As soon as I finished secondary school, of which I retained only what are customarily called *good memories*, I set about trying to discover why we were educating our children in that way, and whether foreigners were doing the same. I have retained very vivid impressions of that time, not so very long ago. Let me tell you briefly what I have observed in France and England since then. We are in scientific surroundings here, and I am allowed to use the experimental method that illustrious scholars have advocated even in the field of social activity.

There is a widespread feeling floating about in our schools, one that I would readily identify as the source of all ills: boredom. The children are bored, and so are the teachers. These living beings suffer from inhabiting a place where life has been brought to a standstill, replaced by a sort of artificial movement consisting of regularity, obedience, and reasoning. They would find anything but this inertia of mind and body more suitable. The work is not terribly hard, perhaps, but there is no respite from it; teachers and students alike lead miserable lives. Some students seem to have an air of resignation, of assuming their assigned role. They delve deeply into their studies, their books becoming their companions. A precocious passion for science, ambition, or even natural energy push them along this path. Then the teachers, at long last finding an interesting subject in the midst of all these dully uniform children, grow attached to such students, showing them great favor. At the same time, their classmates grow distant from them, regarding them with distrust. The masses cannot allow an individual to go over to the enemy, and the teacher is the enemy!

Unless I am mistaken, that is the formula for what is called the *troublemaker*. The expression is common, but a poor choice of words. "Trouble making", strictly speaking, describes a tendency in the human mind that causes it to reject all constraints, and to despise all forms of authority. With few exceptions, this tendency is very weak in children or, more specifically, in adolescents. Until quite far along in his development, the child follows the opposite impulse, seeking a mainstay or guide. The child comes to you, he consults you... provided that he feels you are his friend. What is known as the trouble-making spirit comes from another source. It is hostility directed not against authority as such, but against the individual who exercises it, who causes suffering with his candy-coated words, who is suspicious, who spies and imprisons, and who merely says to the rebellious school child, "This is for your own good". Indeed it is for his own good! He comes to believe it, if it is repeated often enough. But the future affects him less than the present and, almost despite himself, he struggles to break his chains. The teacher is disguised as the enemy, and as long as the teacher fails to cast aside that disguise, he will be detested.

So the hard working students, the eggheads who go over to the teacher's side, lose the friendship of their classmates. They are viewed askance, teased and bullied, and they find solace for their misery in redoubling their intellectual efforts, making brilliant plans for the future. However, if there is a young knave at the school whose fists are strong, whose words are biting, and who is exceptionally bold, he is the one who becomes the ideal, the model, even the hero! The other students flock to his moral barricade. His revolts against authority are applauded, and if they had a shield, they would use it to carry him about the courtyard in triumph. Yet no one holds him in high esteem. Among the youngsters who form his retinue, not one would confide a secret to him, speak to him openly, or seek his advice on an honorable and delicate matter. In case of danger or illness, no one would want him at their side. What they see in him is a champion of independence, an embodiment of all their desires and hatreds! Revenge! What a strange system of education produces these results!

So the secret code that school children obey is directed entirely toward the fight against teachers, and the means at their disposal are varied. There is one means in particular that is rather dangerous to use because, like morphine, it glides into the veins and poisons the blood: lying. Gentlemen, you know as well as I that once a child has acquired to habit of defending himself against his parents or teachers by lying, some of that practice always stays with him. Frankness returns to him only with a great deal of effort, and he is never again thoroughly honest. Yet in French schools, I note with regret, but also with certainty, that children lie terribly, and what is even more incomprehensible, many teachers attach only secondary importance to this phenomenon. They are more interested in a well-told story or a well-done problem than in the value of a clear conscience.

Let us continue our psychological examination. There is yet another category of student of whom I have not spoken. There are the *weak*, those whom education should strengthen but too often merely makes fearful or brutish. I am speaking of the pale, sickly child who, suddenly transported into school surroundings, was totally dazed at first, but is now starting to recover and look around. He soon understands the situation. He can go join the little group of students who hang around the teachers, acting as their emissaries and spies, and become a victim of the other students for that very reason. To offset that ill treatment, he will take unsavory satisfaction in causing the guilty to be punished from time to time. Otherwise, he can join the majority and learn the art of being hard and mean, of persecuting and victimizing. That is the alternative. In the first case, the child becomes fearful. In the second, the child is a brute. Where is the moral gymnasium where they can test their strength little by little, growing a bit stronger and climbing a bit higher every day? Where is it? If it does not exist, how can character be formed?

There is one last, painful, and more terrible point. Boredom, laziness, weakness, and brutality all have one and the same outcome: immorality. Yes, immorality has invaded our schools. It is there in word, in thought, and in deed. This evil has been pointed out before, and not just in recent times. I would like to read for you a report by Mr. Sainte-Claire Deville, dated twenty years ago and calling the attention of the Academy of Moral and Political Science to this serious topic. In his report, the author points out the constant danger of large gatherings of children. He explains it scientifically, and speaks of the precautions that must be taken to drive out the gangrene. He speaks of how one must cut, carve, and cauterize constantly. But people do not want to delve deeply into this issue with him because it is frightening, and because they sense from the outset its unappealable condemnation of our system. Yet what is gained by delaying the solution of an obvious problem, one that no one can escape? It is far better to address the problem head on. Some assume a lofty attitude, acknowledging that truly "something must be done along these lines"; others with a more distant stance declare that the evil is not as great as people say. In that case, why this nervous, constant surveillance? Why is every effort made not to lose sight of the students for a single instant, if the only danger they face is thumbing their noses at the teachers behind their backs? Far from it! All teachers readily acknowledge the true danger, and that is why they watch over them so carefully. Their concern in this matter is expressed by the jealous care with which they pursue and break up budding friendships. The friendship of two boys is forbidden at school. There seems to be no notion that a healthy friendship is one of the most powerful means of education. Even if some do concur, they do not change their approach as a result, because they are frightened of their responsibility. They fear any danger in the face of which they feel helpless since only the weakest and worst of all means of defense, surveillance, is at their disposal.

The educational system and the organization of schools are not the only guilty parties, however. Public opinion plays a role, as well. If any shred of the thinking in the outside world makes its way into the schools, all it does is introduce into the schools the stupid ideas held on this matter on the outside. From earliest childhood, your children are well aware that you consider as indispensable to the flourishing of manly faculties that sort of social baptism which is, in reality, a baptism of mud. In their highly visual language, students call it "the wedding". Well, at school they engage in this 'wedding' in their own fashion, since they make no distinction between one that is unacceptable and one for which you hold a treasure-trove of indulgence in reserve. Not that indulgence should be withheld regarding isolated mistakes that are all the more readily excusable as they occur at a certain age and under circumstances of nearly irresistible temptation. But it is profoundly shameful to see such mistakes elevated to the status of glamorous deeds, and to hear those who commit them talk about them with proud satisfaction which they take no pains to hide. What we in France call "living it up" is not merely engaging in blameful acts, but being particularly proud of it. While biding their time until they are able to engage in such activities themselves, your children, gentlemen, hold obscene conversations. Their thoughts are turned toward unhealthy subjects, and a certain number are the prey of abject vices...

To prove to me that I am exaggerating, you might say that if our schools were really in such a pitiful state, those who went to them would retain so terrible a memory of them throughout their lives that they would flee from these abhorrent places, and that there would be no associations to bring them together with their former classmates from time to time, as is the case nearly everywhere. My answer is simple. Routine has spread its mantle over all of this. Yet I am convinced that this mantle covers a multitude of grudges that will all burst forth at the same time, in an immense outburst of anger. What bitter feelings will be expressed then. How many people will repeat these words of Mr. Maxime du Camp! Listen to them carefully: "I have never felt any nostalgia for my school days. Even now, I cannot look at a passing group of students without being overwhelmed by sadness. When I happen to dream that I have return to school, I awake with my heart pounding."

It is quite another thing to go back to school for a moment, to delight in seeing the darks walls, the gloomy corridors, and the crowded courtyards once again. That is a very human feeling. Man collects memories of his sufferings more eagerly than he does the memories of his joys, and the people who shared in those sufferings always remain more or less his friends. Form an association of ex-convicts, and let that association hold its annual dinner in the prison itself. Partygoers will come from all over. Then, of course, distance lends enchantment. From the top of a mountain, look at the deeply furrowed plain, covered with the ruts over which you have just climbed, and the ground will appear solid. Ravines and ruts disappear. Likewise, when the bad days are not too numerous in a child's life, the impression they produce grows steadily weaker. As it wanes, youth helps attenuate the bitterness of such times. We feel such deep sorrow at its passing that no pain can stand up to its charms, charms that make us forget all the rest. Finally, for us French, there is one last palliative. Boarding schools, as they stand, are not new here; in fact, they have been somewhat improved in recent times. As a result, boarding schools enjoy the respect that we, a changing people, have for unchanging things. Children go off to a school because their fathers went there. It is a necessary step... and in saying such things to your heirs, gentlemen, you feel vague stirrings of pride. You are almost happy to have worn a very heavy harness, and still to be standing. Nevertheless, let me return to what I was saying before. Many citizens curse their weakness of character, their pessimism, and their rheumatism. Were they to discover that education is responsible for these ills, they would pick up their axes that very moment to lay waste this latter-day Bastille. They would expose it and they would destroy it. Wisdom, therefore, instructs us to prepare something to put in its place.

II

I confess that I did not believe I would find the bases for this reconstruction in England. The steamer that brought me there for the first time, nearly six years ago, was carrying an knee-jerk Anglophobe, for whom I claim the benefit of extenuating circumstances, given my extreme youth and inexperience. Besides, this Anglophobia was rather useful from the point of view of the research I did, and whose results I am now presenting to you. As I came to know a school world that completely contradicted everything I had been accustomed to consider here as constituting the very foundations of education, my incredulity forced me to look for the tiniest flaw. I rooted about everywhere looking for it, hoping to be successful in the attempt, while doubting that I ever would be. I never did find that flaw.

As bored as our schoolchildren seem, British schoolchildren seem to be having fun. That is the first striking thing. At first, one thinks that their cheerfulness is due largely to the good air that they breathe. When a Frenchman goes to England, he visits *one* school, and never fails to wax ecstatic about it. But it is always one of those superb establishments of ancient origin, majestic in appearance, located in the countryside, surrounded by greenery and open space. Yet I must tell you that there are schools within the cities, as well, in the very heart of London, and that in those schools as elsewhere, in the fog of the big city with no greenery and not much space, the children seem happy. Large or small, rich or poor, aristocratic or democratic, these schools are all the same. Everywhere there is happiness, and everywhere there is confidence, as well. Nothing military, nothing authoritarian, but something indefinable that makes one perplexed and jealous. That is the initial impression... and then one comes up against the prodigious, incomprehensible impact of sports. The purpose of these athletic games, as they are called there, at first seemed to be to entertain the children while improving their strength. Ensuring cheerfulness and health within the school is already an enormous advantage. Yet here is something quite different: if you wish to find the cause of the exceptional social hierarchy among children, you will discover that sports has made it possible, by providing them the *material on which to base their enthusiasm*, which is lacking among our students. If you want to know what the powerful counterweight to this total and quite astonishing freedom is, you will find that it is sport that prevents abuse of their freedom. If you wish to delve into the issue of morality, which you might assume such an arrangement would endanger, you find that here, sports is the great moralizer.

These results are so astonishing that it takes a long time to accept them. Physical activity is obvious and very natural. Social activity calls for many observations and detailed studies. But moral activity is quite difficult to grasp. What makes the study of it all the more complicated is the deplorable habit in English schools of denigrating one another. At Winchester, they have nothing at all good to say about Eton. You have just arrived from there quite filled with wonder, so you hurriedly return there, hoping to find the famous tiny flaw. You do not, but they advise you to go on to look for it at Harrow, where it is not to be found, either. Thus you make your trip around England several times. It gives you an opportunity to note once more the significant fact that those who are most active in sports are at the same time the most well instructed and the most advanced. You ask to meet the boating captain. He turns out to be the same individual just introduced to you as the president of the Literary Club. Paul Bourget, in a recent book, expressed this quite eloquently. He wrote, “If only you knew how fruitful the marriage of vigorous physical exercise and intellectual culture is in terms of virile splendors!”

It remains for me to tell you, Gentleman, what sport is. I have finished with England. I have rendered it homage. Now let us consider France and the form of education that is appropriate for it, as though the system we are proposing for it were not borrowed from any foreign people. However, let us not lose sight of the fact that this system has proven itself among our neighbors. Let us not forget that it is the result of a reform that they undertook fifty years ago, and that what they have done, we, too, can accomplish.

III

The word I just used, intentionally, to give it its true meaning here, is as poorly understood as it is frequently used. Picture an elegant individual going for a short horseback ride in the woods every day. Picture a regular at Gastinne-Renette taking up pistol shooting. Picture Parisians on summer vacation bathing in the sea for twelve minutes every morning, and then playing lawn tennis for an hour or two. You might think that all these people are engaged in sports. Well, they are not. They are engaging in healthful exercise that cannot fail to have some salutary effect on their constitutions, but that is not what I am talking about. Aside from these trivial exercises, there are those that the young English are engaging in now, and that the Greeks and Romans did before. Athens, Rome, and London seem to have been the three great centers of sport. Perhaps one day someone will discover, in some Egyptian mummy, a treatise on the proper development of physical strength. There is nothing to indicate that, outside these three empires, sport has not been cultivated with a passion. Yet these are the only ones that can be cited with certainty; it is appropriate to note, too, that they are the only ones to have exercised the most powerful and long-lasting action on the world. If we cast our gaze around us, aside from the so-called sports enthusiasts whom I disparaged a moment ago, we will see others who are more serious, for whom elegance and style do not count, who are engaged in one kind of exercise and practice it throughout their lives with enthusiasm. But curiously enough, most of these people work; they are employees. Among the lazy whom fortune dispenses from working – or whom their nobility prevents from working –, they have scarcely any imitators.

In the Bois de Boulogne, there are two gatherings of young people. One group is having fun shooting pigeons and skating in winter, in a rather small space, while the others are engaged in running, like those athletes of Antiquity of whom Greece was so proud. No need for me to tell you which ones are engaged in sport, and which ones are not. Have you watched those rare teams of rowers training for a regatta passing along on our rivers? Have you observed their passive obedience to the captain, whom they have voluntarily accepted? Have you admired their determination in the face of fatigue, and the expression of daring that passes across their faces that are contorted by exertion? If you have noticed all this, you must have understood that there was some pleasure in it. It is a harsh sort of pleasure to be sure, and one certainly cannot taste its delight right off the bat. Yet that delight is far superior to all those offered by insipid pleasures, trivial recreational activities, and relaxing exercises. Understood in this way, sport leads directly to that human ideal: the victory of the will. It is in this way that sport is great and philosophical, bringing us back to Stoic teachings where posterity has revealed many errors and exaggerations, but whose nobility and purity have never been challenged. Gentlemen, the *Manual* of Epictetus is a manual of sport. The *Meditations* of Marcus Aurelius are the thoughts of a sportsman, i.e. those of a fighter. The moral fight is independent of the physical fight, I do not deny it. Some elite souls have not needed the second to triumph in the first, but that is the exception to the rule. In fact, one must be endowed with an exceptional character to reach the will directly, without first acting on the envelope that contains it, whereas it is possible for everyone to strengthen the one by the other.

Here sport is defined by its outcome. It is free effort, it is the fight, it is hardening, the muscular culture of the body and the character. I would be negligent if I did not speak of its impact on the mind, all the more so since that impact, according to so many people, is harmful. Here again, there is confusion between sport per se, and exercises that are ordinarily classified under that name. I have said that they were

Pierre de Coubertin ◯ during a visit to Oxford in 1894 with the Racing Club de France rugby football team (Navacelle Collection)

hardly unpleasant. They are amusing, and that is all. Therefore, from the intellectual perspective, they are debilitating. They lull the mind to sleep, they provide the subject matter for insignificant conversations, and if one adds to this list the fact that those who practice them are generally idle dandies, one readily understands why public opinion judges them unfavorably. The effect of exercises in which effort plays a preponderant role is quite different. In those exercises, decisions often must be made quickly, and there are even dangers to be faced. They call for equal measures of quick reflexes and sang-froid in execution. To comprehend this difference fully, I would ask that you consider not merely the adolescent, but the child and the man, as well. Those daring youngsters who climb walls and leap across streams are engaging in sports after their own fashion, are they not? The fall or the dunking that lie in wait for them are considered just another attractive feature. Often, their older siblings accomplish a great deed of the same type, or maintain extreme effort right to the end because there is someone there to whom they want to show off their strength. Yet children are not bothered if no one is watching them. They take great delight in overcoming a natural difficulty, and the greater the obstacle, the greater, too, is their satisfaction at having overcome it. This is somewhat the same feeling that, at the other end of the spectrum, guides rescuers, explorers, and missionaries, all those who love the attack, the fray, the physical contact. The stakes may be human or divine, the motive material or moral; glory or money may be the issue. It matters little! All this is sport. So tell me, are these sportsmen not intelligent?

Transported to the field of education, the athleticism whose principles I have just outlined in broad strokes elicits two objections. The first is that it is not suitable for all characters, and the second is that it causes brutality. In fact, there are some sickly children for whom athletic education is worthless. But those children do not have to attend school. If one wishes to sour their characters, give a bitter after-taste to an entire existence, to make *failures* of them, there is no method more certain than to mix them in with other children. So I will not concern myself with those children here. Then there are those individuals who are a bit weak, rather timid, for whom moderate and well-understood training can have an excellent effect. In the end, one does not have to be very strong to like the fight, and children can be quite easily moved in that direction if they are not rushed, if they are allowed to go forward at their own pace, and if suitable encouragement is provided when needed. What is more, as self-esteem becomes involved, the child will exercise secretly, to catch up to his more agile and skillful classmates, and will not stop until he has done so. Many secondary considerations operate in the same way. The soldier is proud of his uniform, and the desire to wear a saber or an epaulette is such a common thing that there is no point on dwelling on the example. There is nothing surprising in the fact that jerseys and white flannels stir children's competitive spirits and, once they wear those uniforms, they become as soldiers, they insist on honoring the uniform... From the little imp who climbs a tree to the citizen who rescues someone at his own peril, there is a gradual series of efforts proportional to the means of every individual. This elasticity of sport is the very reason why it is appropriate for everyone.

The second objection is more serious. Very clearly, the practice of athletic exercises must be accompanied by moral intervention on the part of the educator. The result of simply introducing athletics wholesale into our schools would be to increase the amount of hazing and ill treatment. To give children strength only to turn around and forbid them to use it would be a terrible mistake. It is essential that an outlet be found. This is where the teacher enters the picture. When he entrusts an important mission to a young man, the young man immediately conceives a loftier idea of his dignity. He has become a protector rather than the protected individual that he was before. This lifts him up in his own estimation. It also disarms him: he could use his strength without consideration, but it would be for a good cause, at least. Otherwise, he would not run the risk of losing the trust to which he attaches such importance. He will not soon grow weary of the pleasure of being treated as a man. From that point on, his fists are at the service of authority and good order. He supports the government because he is part of it, and his password is "gentleness and calm". He brings as much gentleness and calm as he can to the performance of his task. I can do no more than mention this topic, which would require lengthy development. What I am presenting is merely the framework of the system. But you can readily see what the role of the teacher is, the tact, skill, and subtlety he must have, as well as the amount of hard work, attentiveness, and love. Any act on his part that is excessively authoritarian would compromise the situation, disorienting his young lieutenants who are so full of good intentions but so lacking in experience.

There is one more objection that has been raised many times. People say that athletic education is not applicable to the French race. I refuse to discuss this matter, mainly because one would have to admit the inferiority of our race, not from such and such a special perspective, but from the general perspective of character and will. One would have to say that we are suited only to resignation, to being the governed, and that daring, energy, and initiative cannot develop in us. I am astonished that Frenchmen could possibly think along such lines, and I am indignant that they dare to say so.

IV

My work would be incomplete if, after defining athletic education, I did not tell you who can provide it. Is it the University? Religiously-affiliated education? I do hope that the University will provide such education one day, but it is not at that level that we must start. To accomplish this task requires an independence that its teachers do not have; nor do the members of religious congregations. University professors are functionaries responsible for carrying out the letter of the law. Circulars tell them of the spirit of the laws. Financial management is handled entirely apart from them. Given the system of education that France has practiced until now, this state of affairs has been understandable and excusable, but it is in total disagreement with the principles that I have just outlined for you. Let there be no mistake: the evil resides in the things, not in the people. Some people, taking into consideration the honor of those who are part of the University, their selflessness, their skills, and their zeal for work, are surprised that any education given by such men can be criticized. The point is precisely that these good workers have imperfect tools at their disposal, so the results do not correspond to what their rare and precious qualities promise.

We must be concerned with more than removing obstacles and breaking down the hindrances that the old system raises against the new. We must improve the situation of teachers and educators. This situation is absolutely unworthy of the glorious work they do. There is no role more noble than that of forming men, citizens, and in my view the moral strength of a nation is measured by the respect that it shows to the teachers of its youth. Therefore, we have occasion to free both teachers and students in France, because both suffer from the narrow constraints imposed on them. Who would agree that a well-chosen principal, commendable for his virtues and his knowledge, does not know more about the government of his school than the commissioner of education to whom he reports, who cannot know everything, understand everything, and foresee everything – or the minister who enjoys the strange satisfaction of having the same composition done at the same time throughout all of France? The man who boasted of that great feat was merely pushing a pernicious principle to its extreme. You may think that an organization that would confer absolute power over their staff to principals is no less pernicious, and I would agree. Is this not the very heart of the matter? If the principal knows his school better than the commissioner of education, the teacher knows his class better than the principal. Why are all those involved in this magnificent work, who place their stamp on the being that they help in forming, not also invited to bear their share of the burden of governing the school? Why does the director not surround himself with their counsel, drawing inspiration from their ideas? Besides, what could be more natural than to summon principals and school directors to educational councils, at times for one or two provinces, and at other times for all of France?

That is what the University cannot achieve, unless private initiative opens the way for it. It is up to non-governmental education to begin the reform for the time being, by improving the situation of teachers morally and financially, called as they are to a new role, a broader and more individualized one; morally, by linking them to the administration of schools, and financially, by expanding the tutoring system. This non-governmental education must also be lay, not in the irreligious sense erroneously associated with the word (those who separate religion from education in boarding schools are creating grand illusions for themselves, and they are condemning themselves to educational mediocrity from which they will never escape), but in the sense that religious congregations held within the narrow confines of an immutable rule suffer from exactly the same evil as the University: centralization.

Before it is implemented, the tutoring system must be defined. People have used the term "tutoring system" to designate something that cannot be described as such in any way, shape, or form because the main thing is missing: the tutor. There is a great deal of confusion about this word, and everyone attributes his own meaning to it. This state of affairs must stop. For my part, I will do my best in this regard at an upcoming conference.

So it is up to private lay education to implement this reform. It has already started, and those who drew up the plans for the reform have already decided to implement it come what may, without undue haste, but with a determination that no setback can overcome. The association founded for this purpose insists on stating loud and clear that it has no ulterior motives, that it is not planning any attack, and that it is a league of peace and harmony. But if you think that young Frenchmen do not leave existing schools with muscles that are hard enough and a character that is solidly forged; if you believe that those who educate them do not occupy the position in the State that their merits and the sublime purpose of their mission deserve; and above all, if you believe that it is through education that a people is hardened, that their field of action is extended and that their destiny is assured, join us, and rest assured that our sole concern will always be to love and to serve the great nation of which providence has made us citizens.

L'Éducation Athlétique, in
Association pour l'Avancement des Sciences [Association for the Advancement of Sciences] (Ed.):
Compte rendu de la 18e session [Report on the 18th Session],
Paris, Masson 1889, pp. 15-25.
Special Pamphlet, Paris 1889, 23 pp.

Samedi. 12 Avril 1895 — Vingt-deuxième année—N° 12 — Samedi 25 Avril 1896

RÉDACTION
RUE D'HERMÈS
N° 5

ADMINISTRATION
RUE D'HERMÈS
N° 5

LE MESSAGER D'ATHÈNES

Journal international paraîssant tous les mercredis

ABONNEMENTS
GRÈCE un an 35 fr. | ÉTRANGER, un an 40 fr.
» six mois 20 fr. | » six mois 25 fr.

A. Z. STÉPHANOPOLI
PROPRIÉTAIRE-RÉDACTEUR EN CHEF

ANNONCES
Annonces ordinaires 50 centimes la ligne ou son espace
Réclames, 2 francs la ligne.—Faits divers, 3 fr. la ligne.

Les abonnements et annonces pour la Grèce et pour l'Étranger sont reçus : A Athènes, aux *Bureax du Journal*, — Pour Paris et le reste de la France, *chez MM. Havas, Laffitte et Cie* 8, Place de la Bourse et chez *MM. John F. Jones et Cie*, Compagnie générale de publicité étrangère, 31 bis, rue du Faubourg Montmartre. — Pour la France et l'Allemagne, chez *M. Ammel*, à Strasbourg, 5, rue Brûlée. — Pour la Suisse, chez *MM. Haasenstein et Vogler* à Genève.

SOMMAIRE

Fêtes de la paix.— Obsèques de M. Tricoupis. — La France et M. Tricoupis.—Les princes.—La situation en Crète.—L'amiral Canaris et le système actuel.—Le parti tricoupiste.—Le grève du Laurium.—Le schisme bulgare.— Nouvelles et renseignements. — Jean Moréas. — Accord avec la Russie et l'Allemagne.—Télégrammes.—Les scandales de Berlin.

FÊTES DE LA PAIX

C'est du levant, d'où nos pères l'ont reçue, que nous revient aujourd'hui la lumière. Les regards, les pensées de tous les peuples aryens, de la race des « Purs », sont en ce moment tournés vers l'Hellade. Dans notre ère de paix relative, propice au culte des souvenirs et au rétablissement des liens fraternels, les Jeux olympiques restaurés,—sur l'initiative de M. de Coubertin, un bon Français dont nous sommes fiers, —ont vu accourir sur les voies sacrées de l'Attique et de la Phocide, se presser dans l'enceinte du Stade, des représentants de nations diverses : Français, Belges, Helvètes, Germains, Scandinaves, Anglo-Saxous de la Grande Bretagne et de l'Amérique. Ces fils diversifiés de l'antique Europe (encore un nom emprunté aux légendes et mythes helléniques !) se sont rencontrés et unis pour revivre ensemble les émotions des lointains ancêtres de notre civilisation et ressusciter les anciennes fêtes amphictyoniques.

L'écho nous en revient, à nous qui n'avons pu nous y rendre, par les correspondances des journaux ; et les lecteurs du *Signal* en particulier apprécieront la bonne fortune d'avoir, de première main, les impressions d'un témoin oculaire, notre collaborateur Hauterive, que son goût pour les voyages et pour les exercices du sport, joint à son admiration éclairée pour la Grèce et à sa compétence dans les questions étrangères, qualifiaient si bien pour le compte-rendu de ces fêtes.

* *
*

Fêtes de l'humanité et de la civilisation, fêtes vraiment pacifiques et fraternelles ! Tels furent les Jeux d'autrefois, notamment ceux qu'inaugura, il y a 2, 672 ans de cela, le triomphe de l'Eléen Koroebos, le coureur aux pieds légers, ouvrant, sans s'en douter, l'ère des Olympiades. Tels promettent d'être ces Jeux Olympiques renouvelés, agrandis, où ne concourront plus seulement les athlètes et les coureurs, les archers et les discoboles des cités grecques ; mais, venant de tous les points du monde, les champions de tous les exercices physiques, tous les habiles dans les *sports* ou, comme disaient nos aïeux, dans les «desports» de l'adresse et de la force.

Après Athènes, Paris, dans quatre ans, à l'occasion de son Exposition de la fin du siècle ; quatre ans plus tard, New-York, ou telle autre cité du Nouveau-Monde ; puis Londres, Rome, etc. seront tour à tour la scène des Jeux et des championnats futurs. Les qualités physiques de nos races modernes y trouveront l'occasion de s'affirmer et de se disputer la palme ou le «record» dans de pacifiques tournois. Et les vainqueurs, à défaut de Pindares pour célébrer leurs louanges en odes lyriques immortelles, auront la gloire éphémère que distribuent les journaux de toute langue et de tout pays.

C'est à ces Jeux fraterels, Olympiques, Isthmiques, Pythiques, etc, que la Grèce de jadis, divisée par les contreforts de ses montagnes, morcelée en autant de républiques que de vallons dut de garder, à travers ses querelles et ses dialectes, à travers ses querelles et ses guerres intestines, la conscience de son unité de race, le sentiment de solidarité qui devait l'unir dans les grands périls, comme celui de l'invasion de Xerxès, sa confiance dans la valeur des bras et des cœurs de ses citoyens, et enfin sa foi dans ses destinées immortelles.

Ne pouvons-nous espérer que les mêmes causes produiront les mêmes effets? Rapprochés à périodiques époques dans ces grands concours d'hommes, où les applaudissements qu'on donne aux vainqueurs seront tour à tour pour des Hellènes ou des Italiotes, pour des Germains, pour des Anglo-Saxons ou des Slaves, comment nos peuples modernes n'apprendraient-ils pas—ce que l'ethnologie et la linguistique confirment, d'après les données de la Bible, — que nous procédons d'une même parenté originelle, et que nos tribus et nations diverses ne sont, après tout, comme celles de la Grèce antique, que des lignées ou «phratries» se rattachant à une même «patrie». Et, s'il faut à ces «phratries» — séparées aujourd'hui comme alors, mais appelées à se rapprocher toujours plus à mesure que se développera le sentiment supérieur de la fraternité et de la solidarité humaines, — s'il leur faut absolument des rivalités et des luttes, pourquoi ces luttes ne se borneraient-elles pas aux iréniques combats des nouveaux Cirques d'Olympie ? Pourquoi ces rivalités ne se satisferaient-elles pas de l'émulation qui précède et dela gloire qui suit, pour les vainqueurs et pour leurs «cités», ces pacifiques combats?

* *
*

Il est d'ailleurs un autre élément de concorde et d'union qui, comme il contribuait au rapprochement des anciens Hellènes, se retrouve dans notre civilisation moderne et doit agir de plus en plus sur les peuples qui s'en réclament. Nous voulons parler du lien religieux. La foi aux mêmes sacrifices étaient comme le génie planant au-dessus des dissensions des Grecs. Delphes, en son haut vallon dominé par les cimes du Parnasse, où présidait sur le chœur des Muses, Phoibos-Apollon, dieu de l'harmonie et de la lumière ; Delphes, au pied des roches Phœdriades, où la source jaillissante de Castalie purifiait les pèlerins venus pour consulter l'oracle Pythien ; Delphes était le sactuaire, le centre du culte national de toute la Grèce. L'assemblée amphictyonique qui avait là son siège groupait douze peuples, douze cités indépentantes, dans l'union d'une fraternité religieuse. C'était cette assemblée qui avait établi les trêves religieuses, en vertu desquelles toutes les hostilités étaient suspendues en Grèce pendant la durée des Jeux Olympiques et rendait inviolable le territoire de l'Elide ou de l'Isthme, en traitant comme un sacrilège le fait d'y pénétrer en armes.

Or, si la religion des Grecs, qui n'était, après tout, qu'une mythologie naturaliste si confuse, a pu produire de tels fruits de rapprochement et de paix, combien plus la religion du Christ, du «Prince de la Paix»—dont le sommaire est: amour, fraternité divine, -- devra-t-elle, mieux comprisse, produire, au sein de la

The first Modern Olympic Games immediately became known as a "Festival of Peace". (N. Müller Collection)

2.3 THE EDUCATION FOR PEACE

In 1889, Coubertin used the Congrès de la Ligue de la Paix, chaired by his paternal friend Jules Simon in the Sorbonne in connection with the World's Fair, as an opportunity to look at international peace as a product of education at grassroots level, i.e. in schools.

Self-government by schoolchildren, e.g. in settling disputes, is cited as a model of this education for peace. But in Coubertin's view, school sport can also make a very useful contribution, and he uses an example from boxing to illustrate this.

Are you one of those skeptics that, since you do not believe in the improvement of international relations and the "softening" of the human race, greets the various declarations by members of the League of Peace with a shrug and a sneer? If you are, then I pity you, because these statements are an endless source of constant hope for the future. Although some men once dreamed, and perhaps still do, of the total disappearance of war, that scourge that is not without its usefulness – such people are rare, and their dreams harmless. That is not the goal sought by the eminent citizens who are passionately involved in the great issue of arbitration.

They are not seeking to transform the world into the sheepfold in some painting by Watteau. They do not curse the noble actions accomplished in the course of struggles that are often unjust and criminal, but whose actors remain heroes nonetheless. What horrifies them, and clearly they are right, is seeing nations immobilized in the perpetual expectation of war, seeing all the genius, the work and the attention of times of peace turned toward perfected destruction and the manufacturing of engines of death, seeing billions swallowed up in ruinous budgets and life brought to a halt at the word of a despot. This spectacle is sad and shameful enough for us to agree to examine the proposals of those who are groping along, seeking to rid Europe of this cancer.

One of the ways they have found to spread the habit of arbitration in ordinary practice involves education. The following resolution was issued quite recently by the Congress of the League of Peace: "All States will implement a method in universities, gymnasiums, and junior and senior high schools through which all questions and disputes that arise between students are regularly submitted to an arbitration panel comprising students freely elected by their classmates". This idea has already begun to flourish in a country in free America. It is ingenious and in keeping with a great principle that is too often ignored: the only way to change the man is to change the child. Yet several objections may be raised. First, schoolchildren must accept arbitration voluntarily. If it is forced on them, the goal will never be reached. Well, it is to be feared that only those who are afraid to exchange a few punches or kicks will accept such arbitration. The arbitration panel will become the refuge of "cowards", and will soon be discredited.

Note, however, that hand-to-hand fighting and punches – especially punches – are not without a certain usefulness in high schools. Teachers must never approve such actions, but if they are clever, they will know when to ignore them in certain cases. This way of fighting has nothing in common with ruinous armaments, machine guns, and torpedoes. To the contrary, it makes peace more long-lasting and more solid. The English call boxing gloves "the keepers of the peace". Boys are allowed to practice with their gloves on, apparently because at some point they will have occasion to fight with them off.

Where is the harm in all this? The harm is not so great if one is careful. How else do you recommend developing courage in a child, teaching him respect for others, and helping the child grasp the great law of "every man for himself?" It is charitable and just to try to amend that law, but its basis will never change. Then again, in truth, do these fights in school really have so great an impact on society? Do they really contribute to thoughts of war? I do not believe so. Once again, it is not a question of causing fighting to disappear, but rather the parade of folly that accompanies modern war.

A thousand times more regrettable than punches thrown by youth are the sword thrusts of men. It is there that arbitration would be precious as part of customary practices. Since we do not admit what seems so simple to our neighbors, namely that relief for injuries should be sought through the courts, and that compensation for them is possible, why should an honorable jury comprising men known for gallantry not have the right to deal in affairs of honor, to determine whether bloodshed is necessary? At the risk of seeming overly frank, let me add that if bloodshed is unnecessary, the custom of punches would be infinitely preferable. But as Dr. Lagrange has said, how many men who have no fear of losing their lives still "fear for their hides?"

Thus the procedures recommended by the Congress of Peace will either fail, or triumph to excess. In the first instance, arbitration will be despised by schoolchildren. In the second, they will use it to the detriment of any virile resolution or energetic action. The result will be to create men who are inimical to any arbitration, or effeminate men. Yet I repeat, the project is significant enough for us to follow up on it.

English education provides a pre-appointed arbiter: the *captain*, a student who, because of his age, his history, his popularity, his strength and his skill at games, has been found worthy to become his classmates' leader. His intervention is frequent, his words carry great weight, and his authority is beyond dispute. More often than one might believe, the captain settles quarrels and intervenes in disputes. When a battle is necessary, he directs it with a wisdom that would appear surprising to many people. Rarely, I believe, is his arbitration challenged. When the captain judges that punches are superfluous, the students give in and obey him. That is the state of mind that is desirable among schoolchildren. More pacific tendencies would be signs of weakness.

Furthermore, I believe that demonstrations like those that took place at the opening of the Sorbonne are singularly well-suited for propagating the ideas of international peace and harmony. Young students came from all over, wearing the insignia of their universities and bearing the "traits of the great human races" on their faces. Banners of former enemies stood there side by side, bowing to science. At the banquet in Meudon, in his splendid address to France's guests, Mr. Lavisse said these beautiful words: "Everywhere that men agree to live together, under the same laws, with the same feelings and the same passions, this collective existence is legitimate, it is august, it is sacred, and it is inviolable. Young people, you will form the opinions of tomorrow. To a world wavering between old and new ideas, where phenomena of ancient barbarism strangely enough rub elbows with the marvelous advances of civilization, give this doctrine: the greatest of all crimes against humanity is to kill or disfigure a nation". Mr. Lavisse's audience will hand down that doctrine to the world through the universal federation of students that they founded. Their organization is not based on utopian principles of the fusion of peoples, but rather on the infinitely just principle of respect for nations. They will keep up to date on their respective work; they will exchange ideas and discoveries; they will gather to celebrate great anniversaries, and I believe that in this way, they will work fruitfully at the task of peace.

Finally, along another line of thought, I would like the teaching of history not to consist of a dry enumeration of battles. Take one of the rare candidates who comes to the baccalaureate examination fully prepared to answer any history question that may be asked. He will give you an accurate and complete list of all the battles fought in the Thirty Years' War. Ask him what the population of Europe was under Louis XIV and he will say nothing, except perhaps to hazard a guess that it was 36 million. How can we expect that, once he is a man, he will understand the social question if he does not comprehend the problem of the increase in population which lies at its foundation? He has no idea of the status of industry and trade in the various periods of our history. For him, the emancipation of the towns is a meaningless expression. The great days of Auvergne, in his mind, evoke the image of a cattle market. Richelieu set up intendants, but he is not quite sure why. From time immemorial, peace treaties have been negotiated only to be broken. This last impression is complicated by the idea that peace is an abnormal state, that war is periodic and always will be. In this way, a child's mind is skewed by this mania for making him learn the names of battles, but nothing more. In reality, most of these battles are historical facts of the fifth or sixth order of importance. We must believe that, if only from the perspective with which we are now concerned (not to mention the other serious consequences that can result from it), the teaching of history must be revised from top to bottom.

L'Éducation de la Paix, in:
La Réforme Sociale [Social Reform],
Series 2, No. VII, September 16, 1889,
pp. 361-363.

2.4 ATHLETICS AND GYMNASTICS

As representative of the French Minister of Public Instruction at the Physical Training Congress in Boston in late 1889, Coubertin became acquainted with North America for the first time. His impressions concerning this continent should accompany him throughout his life. His lecture in Boston gives a short survey of the situation of Physical Education in Europe. However, Coubertin lays the emphasis on the person and the work of Thomas Arnold, whom he deeply respects. Coubertin further reports about the Physical Education Congress in 1889 which took place in the course of the World's Fair in the same year in Paris. The following text is of special importance to the reader because it presents Coubertin's own English and therefore gives an insight into Coubertin's gift of the English language.

Mr. President, Ladies and Gentlemen,

I thank you for the hearty welcome you have given me by your applause; I do not take it as granted to my unknown self, but to my country, your sister republic. Dr. Harris kindly said that you would be interested in what I have to tell you. I do not agree with him, and I firmly believe that the result of my boldness in answering the call will be to give you rather a poor idea of the way we Frenchmen speak English. It may also give an unfair idea of the way we fulfil our duties. Being commissioned by the French Government to visit the universities and colleges of this country, not only with reference to the subject of physical training, but with reference to other branches, my duty is to present my report previous to any public statement on the subject. But I understand, from inquiries I have made, that the French Minister of Public Instruction is not here today, and I trust you will be kind enough not to let him know what I have been doing in Boston!

I was asked the other day what, in my opinion, American education was like. I answered that in some respects it looked like a battle-field where English and German ideas were fighting. While I fully acknowledge that from the physical point of view nothing can be said against the German system, I believe, on the other hand, that from the moral and social point of view no system, if it can be called so, stands higher than the English athletic sport system as understood and explained by the greatest of modern teachers, Thomas Arnold of Rugby. His principles are the ones on which the French Educational Reform Association was founded last year. I wish I could give you a detailed account of the work our Association is engaged in carrying out; it is nothing less than a general reform of secondary education. We leave aside the primary school question which our government has lately settled, as I believe, in the best way. In such schools a systematic course of physical training is needed, and the experiments that have been tried in France have proved so successful that there is no reason why we should try anything else. The German methods have now only to be developed in all our primary schools and made the general rule. We also leave aside higher education, for the simple reason that if we want to have well-trained men, who will enjoy manly games and sports, the best and quickest way to realize that wish is to train the boys who are to become the men, and to develop a strong taste for manly games among them.

Relay swimmers training at the New York Athletics Club (taken from Sport im Bild, vol.1 no.25, 1906, p.638)

We believe that the most important period in a boy's education is the one extending from his twelfth to his nineteenth year. During that period not only his brain, not only his body, but above all his will can be trained. His qualities as a citizen depend almost entirely on the lessons he receives at the early time of his life. I must state what kind of a citizen we need in France; I do not know if our ideal type is the same as yours, though I am inclined to think that the difference is not very great. We want free-minded self-governing men, who will not look upon the State as a baby looks on his mother, who will not be afraid of having to make their own way through life. Such is the work that our Association has pointed out to French teachers as being the most important part of their duty. It involves practically what I call the training for freedom.

Now, where is the ground on which such a training can take place? What is the freedom a boy of fifteen can enjoy? Is it intellectual freedom? How can this be fulfilled? I believe if a boy were left to his own impulses in that way , he would learn nothing at all. He would set aside Latin, Greek, History, and Mathematics, and be content with reading novels on rainy days. Is it moral freedom? I need not say what would come of that. His play is the only part of his life where he can enjoy freedom. Let him have the management of his own games, and as a result you will produce a man perfectly suited for social life, that is, as long as you consider society as a gathering of free men: some do not, and it is quite natural that they should have another aim in education. We do, and this is our aim.

Now, can the English system of free athletic sports be carried on together with a systematic course of gymnastics? I believe that to a certain extent it can, as long as you do not make that course compulsory, and it does not interfere with the management of the athletic clubs and societies.

I must draw your attention once more to the fact that I am not speaking of the public schools or the universities. I need not say that I have been very much interested in what I have seen in this country, at Amherst, Harvard, Cornell, and other places. The work done there must be good. Its usefulness is proved by the fact that such men as Dr. Hitchcock of Amherst, Dr. Sargent of Harvard, and Dr. Hartwell of the John

Hopkins believe in it and carry it out themselves. I am only speaking of the schools where boys from twelve to nineteen are taught. They are the same as our French lyceums, colleges in England, and some recently founded schools in this country, for instance, Groton School, Lawrenceville, the Berkeley, and others, where Arnold's precepts are followed. Any one who has read Stanley's "Life and Correspondence of Arnold", or that charming book "Tom Brown's School-days", knows what kind of good Arnold has done for his country. But I did not realize how great the change had been until last year when Mr. Gladstone told me about the state of things when he himself had been an Eton boy, sixty-five years ago. The moral standard was very low then. The boys had sport, but they turned it into brutality, hazing, fagging, and mischief of all kinds went on every day. Masters and pupils looked on one another as strangers, if not as enemies. Then came Arnold; in five years' Rugby was completely transformed, and the reform spread throughout England. That was some fifty years ago; and if you closely study the political, social, and moral events in England for the last fifty years, you will find, as I did with no little bewilderment, that the change was sudden and general in politics as well as in society. I wish I could give you more details; – I am writing a book on the subject, – but the only thing I will say is, that the educational reform carried out by Arnold and his followers has been one of the most important events in the life of the English people, and that it prepared the way for the bright period called the Victorian era, the chief characteristic being the wonderful influence of athletic sports on the moral and social qualities of boys.

In connection with the Exhibition we had a great number of congresses in Paris this summer, so many indeed that the "Figaro" proposed to give a prize to the man who should not be a member of any congress, if such a man could be found. Among others we had one on Education, of which I had the honor to be the secretary. Early in January we issued a circular and sent it to the head-masters of English colleges all over the world. Six thousand copies were sent, and we got a great many answers – from the Cape Colony, from Australia, from America, from English settlements in China, and from Canada –, to the following questions: What are the games played in your school or university? If there are local games, give the chief rules. How many hours do the boys play? A day? A week? What about riding horseback, fencing, military drill, rowing? Are they allowed to form athletic associations? Have they debating societies? Do you believe in athletics improving companionship? Morality? Work? Temper? I added that detailed accounts, books, pamphlets, and school reports and papers would be accepted with gratitude, and we got so many that we were obliged to open a library to put them in.

This inquiry has shown us that all over the world Englishmen, who perhaps knew very little about Arnold himself, still believe his views and ideas to be the best. We are now trying to introduce a reform of the same kind in France, according to the perhaps unchristian, but very practical principle: when you find your neighbour has something good, take it.

Athletics and Gymnastics. Lecture of the Physical Training Congress in Boston, in:
Barrows, Isabel (Ed.): *Physical Training. A Full Report of the Papers and Discussions of the Conference Held in Boston, in November 1889.*
Boston, Press of George H. Ellis, 1890, pp. 112-115.

2.5 – 2.7 INTRODUCTION

The following three texts on Sports Psychology (2.5), Social Education (2.6) and Art in Education (2.7) are taken from the Coubertin anthology *Notes sur l'éducation publique* [Notes on Public Education]. In the preface to this, Coubertin writes that the observations made should be seen as the result of the journeys he had undertaken in many different countries in Europe and North America. Everywhere there were major trends favouring educational reform in spite of national characteristics.[1] For Coubertin and the suggestions he makes here, it can be seen that this part of his educational reform is aimed at adolescents.

The three chapters selected here are indicative of Coubertin's thinking. His pedagogy is aimed at the psyche of the person, their moral qualities. Thus he speaks, in a very avant-garde way, of "sports psychology". Coubertin's vision is social education. This means more than physical, mental and moral training. He regards social education as essential to modern democracy. As a new, modern science, sociology helps with this. His text on "Art in education", a wish that he is presenting here for the first time in such detail and with such forcefulness, seeks to bring art into schools not as a technique, but as an individual feeling, thereby laying the foundation for a lifelong appreciation of art.

2.5 SPORTS PSYCHOLOGY

IN THE MODERN WORLD, WHO ENGAGES IN SPORTS, AND WHY?

To get a better grasp of the question, it is a good idea to disregard old memories, and simply to look about us. The sporting instinct that I mentioned before does not slumber in each of us, only to be awakened at our first call. It may even be impossible to engender this instinct if the seed of it is not already present in the individual. Do not consider athletics an extension of the need to move about, the tendency to exert oneself that is innate in children. It appears only at adolescence, and sometimes not until the onset of manhood. It is neither proof of good health nor a manifestation of an excessively strong constitution. In many circumstances, I have observed young children systematically accustomed to practicing different sports, either adolescents who had been influenced by the example of persuasive classmates, or who had experienced a desire to shine in competitions and to earn applause at them – and at other times vigorous, agile, well-built youth who showed up to partake of the forced training of the regiment. Neither group had acquired the sporting instinct they lacked in this way. As soon as the external, artificial action stopped – the persuasion or the constraint to which they were responding – they stopped exercising. Although the exercise was not unpleasant, it did not correspond to any need or irresistible impulse within them. This need, this impulse is often found among individuals from utterly divergent backgrounds, i.e. those who have had no contact with sport either through education or camaraderie, and even among individuals not endowed with exceptional physical potential.

1 *Notes sur l'éducation publique* [Notes on Public Education], Paris, Hachette, 1901, p.7.

Another observation that I will not hesitate to mention, though it contradicts a widely held opinion, is that most athletes are people who work. I do not mean intellectuals or men who are mentally superior to others. That would be absurd. When Bourget wrote that the marriage of high culture and vigorous exercise was "fruitful in virile splendors", he was speaking of the character, and not of the intelligence. Doubtless physical exercise does enlighten the mind by providing a useful counterbalance to intellectual work, but why and how would it do any more than that? Putting muscles back in the human equation, in a role too long ignored, does not mean that they become the equal of the mind, whose humble servants they must remain. In response to the exaggerated concerns of the adman who once fretted over "paying highest honors to the muscles", it may not be a bad thing to recall, in passing, that highest honors are due to the mind alone.

But merely observing the fact that athletes are most often working people does not get us very far afield. These are employees, men with careers, a profession, sometimes even engaged in manual labor; such men are hardly unenthusiastic. In England, soldiers gladly spend their recreation time playing sports. Many workers, miners and others, do likewise. One cannot claim that all these people compelled to engage in sports because of the kind of lives they lead; their lives are neither sedentary not lacking in muscular fatigue. Furthermore, it is not an issue of race because the same observations can be made in the United States, where society is quite mixed in terms of race. Finally, it seems that in this regard, continental Europe confirms rather than denies Anglo-Saxon experience. In France, Belgium, and Germany the evidence points in this direction. It would be appropriate to conclude, therefore, that sport is a form of *activity*, a quality that does not depend on the intelligence or the state of health. It is far from universal, but modern civilization serves as a stimulus for it, providing many outlets for its expression.

Yet to determine more precisely the nature of the allure that influences this type of active individual, we should review the various forms of sport, and try to draw psychological distinctions. Too often, we forget that the general term "sports" covers a broad range of dissimilar exercises, and that the expression has been expanded to include loving sports with a completely platonic sort of love. Those who own racehorse stables or who are familiar with horses, for example, are known as "sportsmen" even though they themselves do not engage in riding at all. Psychologically, sports fall into two main groups: some are sports of *balance*, others sports of *combat*. The word balance here is understood in the sense of understanding and harmony. Rowing, skating, horseback riding, bicycling, tennis, and gymnastics are sports of balance, whereas fencing, boxing, wrestling, swimming, mountain climbing, football, automobile racing and air navigation are sports of combat. A quick analysis will substantiate this classification, which may come as quite a surprise.

Let us consider rowing. The novice rower, in his fixed-seat yawl, may experience satisfaction at conquering the twofold challenge that the water and his own awkwardness pose. Yet once he has acquired enough experience to be able to switch to a racing boat with its mobile seats, his impressions will change. His physiological state has then changed. The muscles have been classified in some way. The muscles that have a specific role to play remain active. The others are useless; in their initial, inexperienced eagerness they merely got in the way. Now they return to a resting state. The resistance of the water decreases gradually and training soon reduces it to a minimum. What, then, is the rower's "state of mind?" What is the origin of the pleasure that he experiences? This pleasure resides almost exclusively in the mechanical harmony between him and his boat, in the rhythm that governs his stroke, in the absolute regularity of the effort, in the happy proportionality of the expenditure of force and the effect achieved. The man becomes a machine, but a machine that continues to think and to desire, and that feels the strength that arises in it, becomes concentrated and escapes with the same mathematical accuracy as steam or electricity. There is certainly a healthy sensation in this, and extraordinary power. At times, it can be intoxicating. Every rower has felt this, and recalls, like rude awakenings, the little glitches that broke his rhythm, throwing off the harmony of his race: an oar caught in weeds, inopportune jostling from a distracted fellow rower, a wrong move on the part of the coxswain. The craft does not come to a halt for so trivial a thing, but the individual in it suddenly losses the sense of equilibrium that held him in its charms.

The same unconscious search for balance occurs in horseback riding. Obviously the man often enters into a struggle with the horse. It is a struggle interests him, all the more so since both the intelligence and strength are involved. Inferior as it may be in the chain of being, the animal still has ideas of its own, and intends to see those ideas prevail. Yet if the struggle continues, the rider grows weary and categorizes his mount as "restive". Very often, that means the horse is untamable. A "restive" horse loses its value in more than a merely practical sense. It also loses its value from the perspective of sport. It may be a pleasure for bold youth, spurred on by danger, to match wits with it, like cowboys taming wild horses on ranches in America. Yet no one will think that this battle is the ultimate in horseback riding, nor the greatest pleasure riding has to offer. One Yankee writer praised the horse in the following bizarre terms: "It makes a man feel like he has four legs". Certainly Buffon would not have put it like that. But the idea is right and expresses, in a new way, something quite ancient. Ancient imaginations created a four-legged man, the centaur, symbolizing the highest degree of perfection in equestrian sports – to the point that the horse's muscles appear as an extension of man's, so harmonious and complementary is their interaction. Modern civilization has not changed this equestrian ideal. It has remained unchanged. Although beginners may sometimes be amused by the sharp responses that threaten to unseat them, the accomplished horseman is delighted not feel them at all. He takes delight in using his skills to diminish, to the point of complete elimination, any hint of "discontinuity" between him and his mount.

There is little need to dwell on this matter with regard to skating, since a skater is an acrobat par excellence. Yet it is noteworthy that the material balance constantly created and broken by the skater is not enough to satisfy him. He wants to be in harmony with the ice, and to realize, in this way, the sort of rhythmic perfection that makes skating, in the words of one charming expression, "melody in motion". I dare say that it takes even more than that. To be complete, his happiness requires intimate harmony with the countryside. The vast, bare woods, the snow flecked with blue, the red sun in the mist, the silence of slumbering nature become necessary for him. But these are northern subtleties that Parisians accustomed to the "Ice Palace" or the "North Pole" may never have felt, hypnotized as they are by a desire to carve their initials or their signature into the smooth surface of the ice. Races in the snow must be grouped with skating, feet armed with the broad racquets the Canadians call snow shoes, or with skis, the long wooden skates so dear to the Scandinavians. Besides, Canada and Scandinavia no longer hold a monopoly. "Ice sports" are expanding and being perfected all the time. They now have headquarters in Saint-Moritz in the Engadine. They are making conquests as far away as Transylvania.

Once again, balance lies at the heart of cycling. In this sport, there are infinite gradations of balance, from the sturdy bicycle a paunchy good townsman straddles, head down, all the way to the unicycle that only a clown knows how to handle. Like his brother the skater, the cyclist unconsciously imitates birds. His ideal is to overcome gravity. To do that, he must no longer feel the friction of the machine, nor the displacement of his own center of gravity. Modern industry provides him with such perfect equipment that each device has its own personality, its own temperament, in a sense. It is up to the cyclist using the machine and his own skill to achieve the greatest amount of balance he can. In the gymnasium, a good number of exercises call for the same psychological elements. There is intimate harmony between a man and the flying trapeze, as well.

Sports of combat are completely different – not just wrestling and fencing, or boxing, which are forms of combat, but swimming, too, where the adversary is an object. People say that someone "swims like a fish", but nothing could be further from the truth. A fish moves about in the water as a matter of course, as a human being does on dry land. Swimming is not normal. It is a combat with a hostile element which is stronger, and will have the final say if one does not manage to escape its embrace in good time. The force of the waves certainly makes the spectacle more moving, but the gentlest, calmest wave does not eliminate this combative aspect of the sport, which is its essence and its charm.

The battle that the swimmer does with the water is the same battle that a mountain climber fights with the mountain. One realizes this if only by observing the look that the climber casts on the mountain from below before beginning to ascend its slopes. Under its impassive mask, the mountain will defend itself against him like a living adversary, causing him to stray from his course, puzzling him, raising a disconcerting series of obstacles: huge rocks to climb, endless snowy slopes to cross. And this is just the beginning. To do him in, the mountain holds in reserve thick fog to envelop him, deep crevasses that with yawn at his feet, and heavy avalanches that will try to sweep him away along their thundering course. The mountain will try to flatten him through dizziness, the cold, dry north wind, and the chill. The climber will be victorious only through a virile combination of well-husbanded energy, intentional self-mastery, and solid prudence. Of course, this is indeed a battle, and a battle of the most modern type, a battle won by strategy, not impetuosity.

Let me draw your attention, too, to the combative instinct in certain sports, sports that share a special feature: man seems to remain more or less passive in the face of the strength he has expended, and of which he sometimes ceases to be master. Take, for example, sailing, tobogganing, ice yachting, air navigation and, at least for the time being, automobile racing. The toboggan is a sled used by

American Indians to pile up the fruits of the hunt, a device they dragged along behind them through the forests of the New World. The "Palefaces" turned it into an instrument of dizzying locomotion, the sides of snowy hills decked out with long, icy trails for the purpose. It goes without saying that nothing in the world can stop a toboggan once it has started down the trail. An ice yacht, which would be more accurately called a "sail skate", consists of two wooden cross-pieces set at right angles. Two metal blades at the ends of the crosspiece bite down into the ice. At the back end of the other piece, there is a third blade that can be directed as desired, acting as a rudder. Near the intersection of the two pieces stands the mast that carries the sails. Passengers hold fast as best they can to the mast; the sail is raised, and the machine starts to move. It is so lightweight that the speed increases until it becomes a mad, unbelievable race full of zigzags and fantastic leaps, during which, of course, all control of the rudder is lost. Almost all of these sports involve a fight against nature, a challenge. One can scarcely speak of air navigation, still full of unknowns and dangers. What Horace said of the earliest navigators, "*Aes triplex circa pectus erat*", applies to the first aviators, as well. Yet it is possible that in the future, new discoveries will make it possible to move about *by air* easily and safely. Then balloons will become a means of locomotion like the automobile, the sporting character of which is quite temporary. A gas-powered tricycle gives new sensations to someone who gets on one today: the power and response of his mount please him, the speed intoxicates, and handling the machine amuses him. Future generations will fail to perceive them as such, so physically and morally accustomed to them will they be. By contrast, the foil, the trapeze and the oar will always be instruments of sport.

Games also present contrasts. As a rule, games that involve a ball are categorized as games of balance, first because of the positions themselves, as so well expressed by the advice a tennis player gave his student: "Lean on the ball", he said, and because of the rapid, unplanned succession of movements. It is not a matter of repeating the same gesture, but of remaining at the ready to perform the appropriate movement, and to be able to execute it accurately, and thus with self-control[1]. Football, by contrast, is a sport of combat. In football, the battle is a collective effort, which explains why the Americans have managed to apply principles of Napoleonic strategy to this admirable game. It also explains why an English general once told me that in every good football captain there are the makings of a future army leader. In fact, his enthusiasm has led him astray, as recent events will certainly help him see. Polo, which is played on horseback, hockey, which is often played on ice, and water polo, which is a sort of aquatic handball, all partake of those characteristics that I have attributed to horseback riding, skating,

1 In my view, it is this "self-control" that often leads to fatigue in ball sports that is out of all proportion to the muscular force expended, because it involves a rather significant expenditure of nervous force. The effect is all the more pronounced in fencing matches in which the foil is used. My learned friend, Dr. Fernand Lagrange, has attributed the nervous, mental depression that he has observed following matches in many fencers, and in himself, to the role played by the brain in the combination of blows. Since then, I believe I have noticed that this depression, which is already less pronounced when using the sword, is nearly non-existent with the saber, the fist (boxing), or the baton. Of all weapons, it is the foil that demands the greatest "self-control" in the arms, the hands, and even the legs.

Compulsory indoor fitness training for American students (taken from Sport im Bild, no.8, 1906, p.107)

and swimming. In hunting, one must draw a distinction between shooting, which is a matter of balance, and the pursuit of the game, which is a battle. In any case, I do not want to give greater meaning to this analysis than is due, merely by drawing it out endlessly. I have focused on this psychological classification of sports because I believe that it makes a subject that has been little studied to date more interesting and more understandable. I have focused on it as well because it eliminates the pompous and nonsensical distinction between strength and agility, a point usually made in the speeches given at awards ceremonies. "Young students" are encouraged to cultivate both. In fact, there is not a single exercise in which strength and agility are not combined and, at times, in equal measure, all appearances to the contrary notwithstanding. Most of the time, agility consists in properly distributing strength, which is why the public sees nothing but strength at times, while they do not see it at all at other times. In working with weights, for example, the spectator cannot perceive the moment when the "knack" kicks in, no more than it realizes, in wrestling, the ingenious applications that wrestlers make of the laws of mechanics. Every good boxer possesses great agility, just as every good skater possesses great strength. Strength and agility are, in the end, merely appearances. Balance and combat are instincts.

Now I would like to point out what are, to my mind, the psychological effects of sports on those who engage in them. These days, the physiological effects of sports are studied in great detail. Curious experiments are being conducted that will fully elucidate the matter. But the psychological side has remained in the shadows. Far be it from me to shed bright light on so sensitive a subject. I shall limit myself to outlining the results of my personal observation, for documentary purposes.

First of all, we must remember that physiology and psychology share common, imperfectly delineated borders. One of the main physiological effects of sport is to discipline and classify the muscles. The beginner uses a great many muscles that have nothing to do with the maneuver required. In their awkward zeal, these muscles get in the way of the action, causing it to fail. Gradually these muscles are persuaded to remain at rest. In terms of physical exercise, eight times out of ten awkwardness is due to an excess, not a lack, of muscular activity. This awkwardness disappears as the education of the muscles progresses. Then movements become more sure, gestures confident, and the vision grows accustomed to precise, rapid assessments of distance. A bit of this confidence, and a bit of the perseverance, too, find their way into the mind. I believe that, in general, sports give their adepts, all other things being equal, a certain clarity of judgment, and somewhat more tenacity in their actions. But does it really strengthen character and develop what we might call the moral musculature of the man? That is certainly the fundamental question.

Initially, one is tempted to make distinctions, answering "Yes, in some cases, and no in others". Is it possible, for example, to compare, in moral terms, a mountain climber with a tennis player, or a boxer with a skater? Some sports brush up against danger at all times, such as horseback riding and swimming. Then there are sports like boxing that place not one's life, but one's skin at risk, and as Dr. Lagrange has so witty said, how many men who are not the least bit afraid to lose their lives nevertheless fear for their hides! Finally, there are other sports, like fencing, that suggest danger. The weapon that threatens you may well have been made harmless through capping, but in vain! You strike it aside with as much alacrity as the real tip that it imitates. Such exercises seem made to act on the morals, with an intensity that is quite different from those sports in which one can engage without running the slightest risk, and even without having the slightest notion that there might be any risk at all.

These sports certainly do require courage and sang-froid, but *circumstantial* courage and sang-froid. This point of reflection is hardly surprising; is this not true of most manual work? A Parisian roofer displays remarkable sang-froid in the exercise of his profession and, to carry his heavy loads, a coal carrier needs plenty of courage. Does this mean that these qualities will continue to be present in these individuals after the roofer comes down from his rooftop or the coal carrier puts down his sack? That claim cannot be made. Life is full of similar examples. With relative ease, we acquire the characteristics we need to accomplish a given task. Duty or the imagination generate them, and habit makes them commonplace. But in a way, these characteristics remain localized, or rather, specialized. They come to the fore in given circumstances, for a given purpose – always the same circumstances and purpose. The difficult thing is to extend them to all circumstances, and to all purposes. For this, one must replace habit with will.

Will! That is what makes sport fruitful, transforming it into a marvelous instrument for "virilization". In the professions that I have just mentioned, and in others of the same kind, the limits of *useful* effort are soon reached. It is unnecessary, and perhaps even unwise, to strive beyond that point. To what end? An intelligent worker aims at providing the most work in the least possible amount of time, and with the least fatigue possible. The sportsman remains a stranger to utilitarian concerns. The task that he accomplishes is one that he has set for himself. Since he does not need to return to his task the very next day to earn his living, there is no reason for him to conserve his energy. In this way he is able to cultivate effort for effort's sake, to seek out obstacles, to place a few obstacles in his own path, and always to aim a little higher than the level he must achieve. It is this idea that is so well expressed by the motto chosen by Fr. Didon for his students at Arcueil, who had formed an athletic association. At their first meeting, he told them, "Here is your watchword: *citius, altius, fortius*! Faster, higher, stronger!"

Here we are moving beyond sport, as it were, and entering the realm of philosophy. This language is not new. It is the language of Stoics in every age. Greek gymnasiums doubtless rang out often with similar words, spoken by obscure students of the great thinkers, and repeated by simple gymnastics instructors who did not believe that this recipe for virility could ever be lost among civilized peoples.

Antiquity made abundant use of it, that is sure. But do we rely on it in our own time? Is it even applicable to our current civilization with its feverish haste and harsh competition? Has not the very nature of these sports that have come down to us from so long ago, after so long and so total an eclipse, changed completely? Does sport not tend to become confused with the use of more and more highly-perfected instruments of locomotion? Is this the same athleticism whose moral influence was constantly proclaimed, and that Fr. Didon's watchword sums up?

Time will give the ultimate answer to these questions, but it is already clear that although the forms are new, to some extent, the spirit has remained the same. The sporting instinct is always unevenly distributed; not everyone who wants it has it. Among those who do have it, not all reach the limits of what they can achieve. Not all seek out fear in order to overcome it, fatigue to triumph over it, and difficulty to master it. Yet there seem to be more of these individuals than one might think, at first glance. As a result, one can draw this conclusion: today, as in times past, the tendency of sport is toward excess. It aims at more speed, greater height, more strength... always more.

That is its drawback, in terms of human balance, but so be it! That is also its nobility – and its poetry.

La psychologie du sport, in:
Notes sur l'Éducation publique [Notes on Public Education],
Paris, Librairie Hachette 1901,
pp. 152-173 (Chapter X).

2.6 SOCIAL EDUCATION

Physical, intellectual, and moral education are not enough for democracy: it will also require social education. By this, I do not mean that it calls for teaching sociology in its schools. As in political economics, there are certain basic ideas in sociology, certain characteristic facts, that help us understand the world and humanity (such as the essential traits, for example, that distinguish shepherding peoples from farming or hunting peoples), but these ideas find their rightful place in general instruction. Establishing a special course of instruction, accordingly, would be insane. Sociology, a science barely out of its infancy, will fit into higher education once it has made sufficient progress. Moreover, it will always have the vacillating, uncertain nature of sciences governed by laws constantly refuted by exceptions, laws that circumstances always keep from being enforced. We must take care not to introduce so imprecise an order of knowledge into secondary education.

But there is a type of sociology with which adolescents must be made familiar, because the habits that it will cause the adolescent to acquire, the ideas that it will instill in him, will contribute greatly to the good of the group to which he belongs, at the same time that they improve and simplify his own life. The two bases of this new branch of democratic education are proper hygiene and cooperation.

The importance of proper hygiene is acknowledged by everyone, but only in a purely theoretical way. We have made of hygiene a kind of remote divinity, served by priests whose mission is to impose this religion. Of course, these priests never succeed and never will. In order for the kingdom of proper hygiene to come, every person must become his or her own hygienist. This is not a utopia. In Gutenberg's time, if someone had predicted that the day would come when the poorest of the poor would learn to read from a printed book, they would have laughed in the face of any man mad enough to express such a view. Upon reflection, it is far less unlikely to think that the day will come when every person will know what care must be given to his or her body or home in terms of cleanliness, and by what means one can avoid certain diseases and unhealthy atmospheres. If an epidemic should then occur, or if some other circumstance should arise that causes public authorities to issue a temporary order for special measures, they will find the intelligent and eager assistance they need, not the obstinate resistance of a population with retrograde tendencies.

This desirable outcome can be achieved only through systematic instruction. Yet it is obvious that such instruction must come from the top, not from the bottom. As long as it is not seriously organized in the upper schools, it will be pointless to implement it at the secondary level. How will you ever get the son of a peasant or a manual laborer to accept the need for practices that the son of the wealthy planter or the shop foreman neglect? Not only are the middle and upper classes insufficiently concerned with the healthiness of their residences, and show evidence of a deplorable ignorance of the laws of proper hygiene, but bodily cleanliness, the easiest and most important to follow of all these laws, is making only gradual headway among them. Aside from the Anglo-Saxons and the Scandinavians, one cannot say that daily washing has become the habit of any people. Among the Scandinavians and the Anglo-Saxons themselves, as among even the most apparently refined aristocracies of Europe, many still rebel against the healthful influence of hydrotherapy. Instruction in hygiene alone will overcome this apathy and indifference.

Analysis of the human body would be appropriate here. In the plan of studies outlined in the previous chapters, zoology was almost completely eliminated. While so many essential topics have a hard time making it into the program of secondary education, can we afford to keep such topics as the circulation of the lizard and the snail, the respiratory tract of reptiles, and the visual mechanism of birds? Studying man in his place among the members of the animal kingdom, and analyzing the structure and arrangement of his organs, may well be quite scientific and logical. But studying man by looking at oneself in the mirror, studying man as *oneself*, from the perspective of consolidating one's health and maintaining one's strength, now there is something far more interesting and practical.

Of course, there is one field of experience that can render great service as a complement to such instruction: physical exercise. If exercises are done in the form of games or sports, certain rules of hygiene must be observed both to promote the healthy effects of such activity, and to counteract its drawbacks. If teenagers are placed under the direct supervision of their parents or teachers, it is the parents and teachers who must ensure that proper sleep and nourishment are obtained, but it will be difficult for them to do any more than that. Matters become quite impossible to regulate if young people enjoying a limited amount of freedom are involved. Who will keep a boy from rowing in a cotton jersey without having a sweater to throw on his shoulders as soon as he stops, or from standing still after running a race, watching the next race without putting on a piece of warm clothing? Who will break him of the habit of wearing that absurd thing known as a gymnastics belt, or of sucking lemons during the rest break in a football match? Who will prevent him from taking a cold shower after the perspiration dries on him, from drinking cold drinks while swimming, or from running a bicycle race as soon as he gets up from the dinner table? He alone can protect himself against the dangers of such practices by not engaging in them, but these dangers will become real in his eyes only if they are explained to him scientifically. If they are presented as recommendations or commands, he will ignore them completely, viewing them merely as one more expression of overly attentive concern. Yet once he understands the function of the skin, the digestive process, and the effect of exertion on the muscles, once he understands that he can control his own training, for example that simple examination of the urine passed after exercise shows whether his exertions exceeded his fitness level, once he knows why the disturbance of the body through vigorous exercise after a meal can bring on appendicitis and perityphlitis, he will perceive the *immediate* interest of these things. They will become part of his life, and will take on substance in his eyes.

Although understanding and observing the laws of proper hygiene are necessary in a modern democracy, the habit of cooperation is even more so. In a democratic society, the source of all practical strength and the basis for all meaningful efforts is the fact that citizens band together to form resistance or to join forces, to rein in the group or to urge it forward. In electing leaders, defending interests, studying problems, or bringing about reform – it is always to this basic fact that the members of society must return. It alone can provide effective aid. The *vae soli* of Scripture could be carved onto the pediments of our buildings, so well does that saying apply to the conditions of life in our day.

Are cooperation and association instinctive tendencies in man? The issue has been debated at length. Yet these theoretical discussions, interesting as they may well be, are only of relative importance, because one capital fact dominates them. Whether man is drawn to cooperation or not, at first he exhibits obvious awkwardness and clumsiness in the effort. Whether this principle is foreign to man's nature, or whether man has grown unaccustomed to it through heredity, the effect is the same. We see plenty of examples of this all around us. We can safely say that the main characteristic of the 19th century has been the launching of democracies. The variety of their accouterments and the differences in their appearance were distracting. To see an emperor, sword in hand, leading the people in one place, and a powerful aristocracy in another, put us off the scent. If we take a good close look, it is truly democracies that are on the march. In general, their gait is cumbersome and irregular, as though they were missing a limb or suffered from a damaged organ. If you will pardon the expression, they move about a bit like legless cripples.

People say that what is lacking is freedom. Yet the most agile people are not the most free. The proof that freedom is not enough is that in some cases, public authorities, not satisfied with merely authorizing citizens to do so, have actively encouraged citizens to form associations. Therefore, we must acknowledge the need for an apprenticeship. At that point, the issue is to determine whether the apprenticeship should begin as early as secondary education. If only the external mechanics of association building were at stake, there would be no advantage to starting early. Voting, the authority of elected officials, the orderly holding of meetings, budgets and minutes – the whole mechanism can be learned easily by a man with an open mind, even if he possesses only rudimentary education. Yet the fuel that will drive the mechanism must be introduced. No association, regardless of its purpose, can function unless it is fed by a mixture of personal activity, mutual tolerance, and a proper understanding of common interests. Not only do these qualities not arise spontaneously, they are slow to take root in grown adults. The earlier one gets to work on them, the better one's chances of instilling them deeply in the character.

Thus the most useful citizen in a democracy is not the one who has been made to study sociology, to whom the theory of solidarity and mutual responsibility has been explained, but the one who enters active life already prepared for the group effort, unconsciously trained in the movements, the rhythm, and the restraint that this effort demands. Such an individual cannot be trained by theories, but only through practice.

This idea was not entirely novel when Arnold took it as his own. Traces of it, granted that they are slight, can be found in the work of few educators in the last century. Yet it is doubtful that Arnold, the Headmaster of Rugby, who had not engaged in any special studies and who did not profess any great esteem for the eighteenth century, drew upon any such source. He looked around, immediately understood the new needs, and perfected the rudimentary institutions that he found at arm's reach to meet those needs. Some traditional groupings among English schoolchildren had been maintained, and they became the seeds of regular associations. They learned to govern themselves with wisdom and moderation. This social life even became so familiar to them that people outside them began to believe that it (and the athletic life) had always existed among them, that it was the fruit of a racial penchant, an irresistible atavistic tendency. Of course, the vagaries of their domestic history did especially prepare the English people for self-government, but it is clear that they became much more expert and skillful at it after the principle of cooperation was introduced into their educational institutions. In addition, there is no reason to think that other races are, by nature, rebels against this principle and that similar experiments are doomed to fail in other places. Furthermore, it goes without saying that these experiments will assume a form in Germany that is quite a different from the form in England, and in Italy from what it is in Sweden. Each people will shape associations according to its own genius, its particular ideas and customs. The question must be addressed at a higher level. Whatever the government of a democracy, its political institutions, its aspirations or its social features, it needs cooperation to live and to prosper. It matters little whether that cooperation is fully free or is directed and supervised by the State. Cooperation must be *learned*, and there are advantages to learning it from earliest childhood. This truth will impose itself on democracy, and democracy will have to introduce cooperation into school life in order to prepare its future citizens for active life. How can this preparation be brought about?

It is hardly worth mentioning here certain bizarre things, word of which has come from across the English Channel or from the other side of the Atlantic. Once, in England, there was a School-Republic whose students governed themselves. I believe that they even governed their teachers. I was assured that the rules were not at all unreasonable, and that they did not change all that often. In my past research, I did not have time to verify this story, something I do not regret in the slightest. In any event, that was an educational fantasy, one which could not be applied in any general manner. The same must be said of the "School-City" that, apparently, has just been established somewhere in America. It bears all the markings of a well-ordered town. The mayor, his deputies, and the town councilors are all students. They share the administrative tasks of the school as though each task were a sort of public service department. The reporter who discovered this little marvel sings its praises and recommends it as a model for educators in the Old World as well as the New. Educators, for their part, are entitled to look upon such establishments with a degree of irony, or absent-mindedly. But they would be committing a serious error if they assimilate these exaggerated efforts with the reasonable applications in other places of the underlying principle that inspires such efforts.

The new associations formed by students can be grouped into five main categories. In general, they involve games and sports, literature or the sciences, the arts, public speaking, and charity. For now, the first type is probably the most common and the least subject to debate. This comes as no surprise, since if there is any government to which young people have an undisputed right, it is that of games. Yet this right was denied to them for a long time, under the pretext that exercise was incompatible with good order and discipline. Nowadays, even when the point is conceded in theory, there are still efforts to suppress it in practice. This is certainly the case in France. Harsh rivalry, resulting from the splitting of secondary education between the state institutions and religious congregations, makes any improvement in this area difficult. Any freedom established in one camp is immediately denounced as an excessive liberty by the other, which rushes to decry abuses of that freedom, even if such abuses are imaginary. Despite this unfavorable situation, sports associations have increased in number in French schools. The first were founded in 1888 and 1889. Today there are about one hundred of them, with some 4,000 members. The interesting feature of this movement is that the initiative came from the outside, and that the school administration greeted it with ill humor, if not outright hostility. Thus any results that have been achieved are due almost entirely to the students themselves. Those who initiated the idea could not do much to help them, and as a rule, teachers did not want to get involved in any way.

I cannot go into the details of the French experience in this forum. I refer the reader to specific documentation on this issue[1]. Yet without dwelling at length on the issue, I can point to the main results that it produced. The associations have seemed useful for the proper functioning of games, even indispensable for organizing some skillful and complicated sports, such as football. The associations have not resulted in any disorder, and the expenses they have occasioned their members have been quite small. Finally, although it is doubtful that they have exercised any positive influence on work, it is clear that they have not done any harm in that respect. The significant thing, however, is to determine what their social impact has been. That impact is extensive, indeed. An in-depth study done some years ago under the auspices of the eminent Henri Marion, late professor of education at the Sorbonne, showed how positive its effects have been. Thus, despite the impromptu, unplanned nature of these small associations, their fragile framework has worked well. If, in keeping with a widespread view that I do not wish to debate here, one believes that French soil is ill-suited for self-government, one must admit that the success of these associations is simply all the more convincing.

With the exception of English *public schools* and institutions in the United States and the British colonies inspired by them, there are few school groups that are specifically literary or scientific in nature. The Jesuits have maintained the institution of the "academies", and use them to great advantage. Yet even though the young members of these academies in general enjoy great latitude in the choice of subjects for papers and debates, the teacher remains present to intervene in the discussion, if need be, specifically to direct the recruitment of the Assembly and to restrict it to *good* students. Moreover, there are no dues, which means there is no budget to prepare or finances to manage. Social education is reduced to a minimum. About all they learn from the experience is how to remain courteous among colleagues, and how to choose leaders well. That is something, to be sure, but it is not enough. It is easy to picture truly free literary associations, particularly in conjunction with a secondary education system transformed along the lines of the principles expressed above. The purpose of these associations would be to provide some additional education, such as detailed study of foreign literature (ancient or modern). The sciences will be able to form similar groups. Why should chemists,

1 Two reports have been published on the organization and operation of the athletic associations in French junior and senior high schools. The first, written by me, appeared in the *Revue Universitaire* of May 15, 1892. The second, written by Mr. Maneuvrier, appeared in the *Revue Internationale de l'Enseignement* of December 15, 1894.

botanists, and nature photographers not have the free use of a small laboratory and a little museum where their vocation could be confirmed and deepened? Cooperation – which is essential to make these new ideas viable – would not be the only thing to find its place in such groups. Understanding and morals would find a home there, too.

Later on I will speak about the role of art in education. There is hardly any need to dwell on public speaking, and the need to have future citizens practice it early on. Past a certain age, useful skills cannot be acquired unless the individual is naturally predisposed for them. These skills are of two types. To express oneself well, if not on stage then at least at a meeting of any sort, one must first order one's thoughts quickly and clearly. Then, those thoughts must be expressed in words appropriate to the circumstances and to the effect that one wishes to produce. Boileau claimed that all one needed in order to "speak clearly" was "to understand well". Yet democracy has helped us put our finger on the inaccuracy of this precept. Democratic speech, obviously, is quite the opposite of declamation, and dramatic presentations cannot replace the training acquired in a debating society. In fact, these shows present so many difficulties, specifically the fact that they are expensive and take a long time to put on, that there is no reason to regret their passing or to hope for their return to fashion. From the perspective of cooperation, in any event, they are ineffective. Usually, English debating societies focus on the great questions of the day, repeating what is said in the House of Commons. This topicality may be displeasing, but aside from politics, so many problems of the greatest interest are likely to elicit the attention of young people that one cannot use them as an argument against the institution itself.

Finally, there is charity. Once again, it is England that provides us with the right approach. As attractive as the idea may be of organizing little St. Vincent de Paul societies in schools, this notion presents more problems than advantages. Nothing could be worse than placing youth in contact with those who choose to be poor, if I may use that cruel expression, with that half-disguised poverty, clothed in hypocrisy, that gathers at the doorstep of charitable organizations in the cities. Yet can contact with true poverty, the poverty that rubs elbows with vice, be achieved without exposure to danger? From the perspective of hygiene alone, should such poverty not be kept as far from students as possible? British ideas have been expressed along another order of ideas entirely. What a beautiful task, what a profoundly healthy and admirably educational undertaking it is for boys of fifteen to collect as much money as possible from their classmates and teachers in order to secure a vast field near the sea or a river from a generous town, rent camping equipment, reach an agreement with railways for reduced-price fares, and run a camp for a week or two at the start of the vacation for children from the poorest and most deserving of the school population. Understood in this way, charity – or rather, solidarity – can give rise to associations of an extremely high educational value.

Thus, from a variety of perspectives, the markers are already in place for the social education in which democracy will find fulfillment of a legitimate instinct.

L'Éducation Sociale, in:
Notes sur l'Éducation Publique [Notes on Public Education],
Paris, Librairie Hachette 1901, pp. 217-235 (Chapter XII).

2.7 ART IN EDUCATION

If one had to define art from the sole perspective of its role in education, I would say that art is first and foremost the sense of beauty. That is how Ruskin understood it. But the application that he made of his doctrine was so British in character that he rendered it nearly incomprehensible to other peoples. Nonetheless, it is correct and applicable to all. To awaken the sense of beauty in young minds is to work at beautifying the life of the individual and at perfecting the life of society. But how should one go about it? The question must be a thorny one, because I have noticed that most of the solutions offered are awkward and ineffective. In any event, it is not the most artistic of nations that seem the most inspired in this regard. Greece and Italy have done next to nothing. In Germany and France some awkward efforts have been made. The most satisfactory initiatives are probably those undertaken in America – private initiatives, of course, and sometimes difficult to track down. I remember visiting a small school of fine arts in St. Louis, Missouri ten years ago, which I had chanced upon. I was deeply impressed by the genial simplicity of the method of instruction. There were some old canvases there, a few marble groups – art objects of secondary importance, but showing judicious selection on the part of the teacher. They were objects well-suited to awaken in the students an understanding of line, relief and color. Their quick sketches, showing clear traces of their inexperience, stood right alongside these paintings and statues. One of the two rooms served as an atelier. The other, at first glance, seemed to be an odd shambles. There was a huge medieval mantelpiece, a monumental Renaissance door; there were polychrome frescoes on the wall, a table and very handsome Louis XVI chairs, flamboyant glasswork, and a wrought-iron center light. At first, I failed to see the point of the collection. Then I was thunderstruck to learn that, with the exception of a tapestry that decorated the back of the room, everything in it had been made by the students. In a word, the professor explained his method to me: "This is our laboratory", he said. This man, no distinguished artist himself, had approached the study of art very simply, without concern for the routine, conventional approaches that get in our way, we from the Old World. With his tight budget, he could not afford to purchase valuable objects on his frequent trips overseas; but he took notes and made sketches, and acquired photographs and reproductions of all sorts. Throughout the museums of Europe, history book in hand, he went looking for what typifies an era and evokes its deepest hopes when they were in full flower. Upon his return, his students got down to reproducing that distant beauty whose image he brought back to them, under his direction, and with clear, passionate concern.

As regards art in education, particularly in secondary education, this example provides not so much a basis to be copied as useful clues to be followed. Yet such procedures apply to only one of the four categories that must be distinguished from the perspective of artistic culture. In the first and highest category there are *those who are active*, i.e. those who create, imitate, or interpret works of art. In the second, there are those who have a *feeling* for artistic beauty, even though they themselves can neither produce nor reproduce it. In the third, there are those who *understand* art through knowledge and reasoning, but who do not possess the gift of feeling it. Finally, in the fourth category there are those rare individuals who are absolutely unamenable to any concept of things artistic. It seems to me that, in general, insufficient account is taken of these essential differences, specifically of the difference between feeling and knowledge, both of which provide access to the pleasures of the arts, but to pleasures of a far more intense and higher order in the first instance as compared to the second. If these differences are taken into consideration at all, that consideration comes too late, at a point when the classification has already long since happened. At what age does this classification occur, and to what extent can the tendencies of this classification be rectified? This is a very important point to clarify. Unfortunately, there is no clear-cut answer. Individuality, though it may be but little advanced, plays a role here, an obscure role that is almost subterranean in nature. The seeds of art are mysterious, full of caprice and oddity. They experience sudden growth spurts and long periods of dormancy, superficial speed and fruitful delays. Yet without attempting to foresee what will come of them, one can work along with them, preparing for the classification and helping it along. The elementary school period is suitable for this task. By teaching children to use a crayon and brush, to understand perspective and to evaluate distances, to learn to read music, to sing and to perform solfege, one makes available to their potential capacities the instruments that they will need in order to grow, no matter what. If some individuals show absolutely no evidence of artistic skills, time used in this way is still not wasted. Education of the eyes, the ears, and the fingers is never wasted on anyone. By contrast, if there is any sense of a present or future artistic impulse, it can no longer be ignored. Any interior impulses will be guided on the outside by the gestures learned. The adolescent will not possess a complete mechanism, but an alphabet, a key: he will have the embryonic instruments of artistic creation or interpretation.

The outline and method of secondary education must change. Apprenticeship of the mechanics ceases to be a rule applicable to everyone. This is where music and drawing lessons applied without discernment could result in wasted time and effort. To the contrary, secondary education is a time when room should be made for art theory. History is certainly one way in which that theory is the most accessible to young minds. If you point out the role that art should play in the life of a people in general, your students might retain what you say, but they will not understand it. Because they still do not know what art is, they cannot conceive of the need for it. However, if you tell them what role art did play in the life of a particular people, a people that they can picture chronologically and on the world map, then the issue becomes specific for them. The link between the genius of a people and its art will become comprehensible to them. Of course, this will result in general enlightenment, as well. As we have already said, Greece can be explained by its monuments, its sculptures, its music and its theater, as well as by the political institutions of its States or the intestine quarrels of its citizens. It is so easy and so obviously useful to include art in the study of history that it is surprising that one must still make the case for doing so.

This approach to teaching is applicable across the board. Even those sentenced to the cruel fate of remaining unmoved before Praxiteles' Hermes or Rembrandt's "Night Watchman", before St. Peter's in Rome or Notre Dame in Paris, must still

Rhythmic gymnastics as a form of artistic expression in education (taken from E.Jaques-Dalcroze, Rhythmus, Musik und Erziehung, Ed.Schwab, Basel, 1921, p.80)

know why the world was moved by them. Yet the educational system must also take into consideration those fortunate students who can feel art. The educational system must try to make art understood by all. It must give some the opportunity to feel it, and it must also encourage the halting efforts of those who act, of those who are already trying to express what they feel. The word 'privileged' points out where these intentions run into trouble. Among every people that has intentionally invited democracy to take its place among them, rather than noticing suddenly that democracy had taken hold without their knowledge, the concept of equality has become a cornerstone of public life, specifically of education. Yet as early as secondary education, one must concede that there are privileges instituted by nature, even if one rejects those instituted by men. Just because one adolescent struggles just to draw an eye or to read the music to a simple nursery rhyme, this is no reason to prevent a fellow classmate who fills the margins of his dictionary with quick, witty silhouettes, or who plays fragments of a Beethoven symphony by ear, from following his instincts! In failing to take these facts into account, not only are you gratuitously slowing his artistic development, but you appear, at least, to be blocking his overall growth. Art is not some decoration to be superimposed on a finished object. It is part of the very essence of the individual who feels its impulse. It can guide him well in all his future growth.

The conclusion is that we must establish in secondary education the artistic laboratory so ingeniously devised by that professor in St. Louis, Missouri. It is a good thing to make sure that, in the schools, new construction should have fine outlines and harmonious colors, and that handsome facades should be embellished with terra cotta or majolica ornaments, and that there should be some decorative fresco in the entry, some eloquent marble piece in the formal courtyard. On festival days, it is a fine idea, a happy inspiration, for concerts by distinguished artists to be organized by the administration. But one problem with all these things is that they are very expensive; secondly, and more seriously, they are not enough. The eye of a man, and to a greater extent that of an adolescent, wanders aimlessly when looking at familiar objects. What school boy ever notices the things that surround him day in and day out? By dint of seeing them, he no longer knows whether there is any depth to the painting, or any grace in the gesture of the statue. As for musical showers poured over him unforeseen, their effects are minimal and fleeting at best, unless there is something to keep them going. Visits to monuments and museums are usually handled in the same naively perfunctory way. These esthetic pleasures should be reserved for those who can gain some benefit from them, making them more desirable in the eyes of the others – the only way to make them more attentive to the value of art. Among teachers, one can certainly find the wherewithal to form a small arts commission that, depending on the case, would take the initiative on desirable measures, or would exercise oversight over the students' undertakings. I would like students to have choral and instrumental clubs, and an open atelier for drawing, watercoloring and sculpting – and I would like to see regular musical performances and an annual exhibition provide the necessary encouragement for these clubs. But, you might say, this all appeals to vanity. Well, of course! What makes you think that education is possible without appealing to vanity?

This is how secondary students can most reliably be initiated into art, becoming baptized in it. Will Beauty, revealed in this way, be a powerful aid for him in his ascent toward Goodness? One must not rely too heavily on such an outcome. This issue of the moral value of art has been debated for a long time. It would be easier to come to some decision if one first took pains to define what kind of morals one is considering in framing the issue. Art enlightens the intelligence, captivates thought, and incites ambition. These are precious enough moral results, but morals per se scarcely benefit in the process. The character is not strengthened, the conscience does not grow any more resolute, nor does resistance to evil become more frequent. Goodness, Beauty, and Truth are a lay trinity that the modern world tends too often to compare to the theological trinity, the three persons of which form one God. Here, unity is a fiction. Each of the terms does not necessarily encompass the other two. The concept of Beauty, in particular, can be quite independent from the concepts of Goodness and Truth. Beauty, as created and contemplated by humanity, is not always good or true. It is just that at a time when man is pushed by society's demands to twist the truth more and more, and when the turmoil of his young mind blurs the outlines of Goodness, it is quite natural for us to rely readily on Beauty. Clever and nearly excessively liberal eclecticism is spreading further every day. Its influence is spreading out into all areas, and many uncertainties and doubts find refuge in it. This is the origin of the tendency to believe that art is a moralizing force, in the most absolute, most complete sense of the term. The educator must not accept this notion. Yet this is no reason to neglect art, as educators have done so far, no doubt through fear of playing host to an eccentric and extravagant guest within its rigid walls. Earlier on, I agreed with Ruskin that the sense of beauty embellishes the life of the individual and perfects the life of society. Is this not sufficient reason to legitimize any effort whose purpose is to engender and to foster that sense?

Since I have mentioned Ruskin once again, let me also mention the charming sort of artistic propaganda he sowed throughout Anglo-Saxon society. Before he came along, did anyone try to give a smart look to even the plainest room, the humblest little space? Special artisans used to decorate rooms set aside for that purpose because of their size, or because of the wealth of their inhabitants, but no one had thought of becoming his own decorator and upholsterer in order to provide a note of meticulousness and elegance in his own home. I am unaware that this meticulousness and elegance in English workers' houses, a phenomenon so widely observed these days, has done any harm in terms of work or foresight. In boarding schools, I have not noticed that adolescents who decorate their rooms or their "cubicles[1]" are any less masculine or, in the universities, that the handsomest rooms belonged to students who were any less industrious or more well-off. On many occasions, I found just the opposite to be true. So there is nothing in all this that is unworthy of a boy. Yet it is clear that this is first and foremost the domain of girls. It is the bridge by which art is introduced into the domestic economy. Perhaps a course on the history of furniture could advantageously replace lessons spent naming various acids or certain Pharaohs.

In conclusion, it is appropriate to fling the doors of secondary education wide open to art, and not to ask of it, from an educational perspective, any more than it can give, yet not to distrust it either. If caution need be exercised with respect to art at any point in the educational curriculum, I would prefer to say that higher education is that time. That is an age when young imaginations already find at their service steady pencils and brushes skilled enough to create, at times, shameless works of fancy of no benefit to morals, taste, or studies. Although art can sometimes compromise an examination or cause a vocation to go astray, the focus must remain on the student.

L'Art dans l'Éducation, in:
Notes sur l'Éducation Publique [Notes on Public Education],
Paris, Librairie Hachette 1901,
pp. 297-310 (Chapter XVIII).

1 Small, three-sided rooms, open on the fourth side, located in the dormitories.

2.8 PHYSICAL EDUCATION IN THE 20TH CENTURY: RECORDS

In the leading article of the Figaro in January 1903, Coubertin refers to the latest development of sport, the striving for records. For him this is the logical quintessence of effort. Modern sport exceeds its limits as he would later describe it. Decisive for the sportsman, as Coubertin views it, is that the sportsman stays in control of himself. In contrast to this, Coubertin sees the personal record, the constant improvement of one's own performance. The Swedish sports badge is the best example for it.[1] From the point of view from today's sport-scientists, Coubertin's opinion on concerning the importance of anthropometry expressed in the final clause seems worth reading.

More foreign words! What can you expect? As absurd as it seems to me to say "referee" when one can just as easily say "*arbitre*" in French, or to speak of a "scrimmage" and a "try" when these terms can be translated simply as "*mêlée*" and "*essai*", I still find our nationalistic pride that shrinks in fright from using words that have no such substitutes quite puerile. The English word "record" seems to have no equivalent in any other language, since that is the term used throughout the world. The best evidence that this word is now a naturalized citizen of the world is that I do not need to resort to any sort of paraphrase to explain it. Everyone knows what it means.

Not everyone, however, appreciates the educational value of the expression, and bringing these two ideas – education and records – together will certainly seem a daring move. A record, you see, is considered the quintessence of effort. Therefore it is viewed as extraordinarily harmful in a time when our quest for the average tends to gain the upper hand over our thirst for perfection. This is a mistake. Records can be put to excessive use, but taken by themselves, they are less prone to exaggeration than is competition. The reason is simple. Competition places you into a struggle, making you another living being's competitor. A record faces you up against an inanimate fact, a figure, a measure of space or of time. Strictly speaking, you are fighting only with yourself.

Your ambition and will are your only driving force. You can lose your control over them momentarily, and they can manage to get the better of you, only in a rapid sort of intoxication that is hardly enough to cancel out your body's warning signals. In short, you are on your own. Imagine how different your state of mind would be if in front, behind, and beside you, other sets of muscles and other brains were working away, their very presence upsetting and overtaxing your nerves. Your analysis, your measurements of their strength, and your knowledge of their habits, advantages and weaknesses will be all for naught; you remain at their mercy. The race that you enter into, then, is inspired and directed in large measure not by your muscles and brain, but by the muscles and brains of the competitors whose victory threatens your own.

You must have exceptional natural poise and plenty of experience to remain in complete control of yourself under such circumstances. That is where the risk of "forcing" yourself, an eloquent popular term, comes in. To force yourself does not mean making yourself do something. It means unconsciously going beyond the limits of what you can achieve without risk.

Victory and new records as features of modern sport (taken from Les sports modernes illustrés, Larousse, Paris, 1908, p.106)

I must stress this point because the use of excessive competition in the physical education program I advocated in my earlier articles in *Le Figaro* would be quite problematic. The purpose of that program is to make a young man resourceful and ready for the life of initiative, of the unforeseen, and of endurance that our time offers him, by helping him grow accustomed to the basic practice of every lifesaving, self-defense, and locomotion exercise in use in the modern world. This cannot be accomplished through competition. Though I do approve of the "Three Sports" race that our friend Mr. de Lafreté is organizing, as an interesting and useful experiment, I do hope that such initiatives will remain the exception, not the rule. One would run the risk of unfortunate accidents by putting that system into general practice.

Another experiment that has been debated at some length in England and in America – six hours of various sports within eight hours by the clock – could not have been brought to a successful conclusion under the agreed conditions, i.e. leaving no *significant* signs of fatigue, if those sports had been a series of competitions. During the experiment I was able to go all out, giving it my best shot at all times in terms of strength and speed. If I had had competitors on my back for six hours, I could not have come through unscathed. What matters (as anyone who has followed my thinking on this topic will agree), is not that a young man be capable of winning trophies in all sports, but that he be in shape to practice them all and to make use of his strength without distinction, as the occasion may require.

In this apprenticeship, can we dispense with all forms of competition? In general, should we hope that human beings will one day be so sensible, so careful of their self-interest, health, proper mental balance, and physical condition that they will have no further need for a competitive spirit? No, not at all! That would be a utopia! This is the fundamental utopia that doctors and physiologists have

1 Concerning the Swedish sports badge see Coubertin, "La chevalerie du sport," in: *Almanach olympique pour 1919,* Lausanne, Impr. Réunies, 1918, pp. 20-24.

introduced into physical education. We must fight it ceaselessly, because although it is presented attractively, in reality it is nothing more than a bonus for inertia and routine. It is absolutely essential for us to measure ourselves against someone or something else. If we have no rivals at our heels, at the very least we should keep a record in front of us, to urge us forward.

Which record? The Swedes, who are not as narrow-minded as their disciples on the continent – far from it – reply: "Your own. Measure yourself against your own performance, trying to gain an inch or a second more every day. Make progress step by step. Pay attention to the recommendations of science, and forget what your neighbor is up to". This is excellent advice, but I do not think that it can be applied over long periods of time except by professionals, given the degree of daily resolve and tenacity that it requires. For non-professionals, "what the neighbors are up to" is, in fact, a powerful stimulus. I cannot see how amateurs could do without it. However, one should be familiar with those eloquent achievements, the "world records" held by great champions. But I would also like to see what I would call average records, results that a man of average strength and training can achieve, printed in a small paperback format right next to the statistics records of the great champions. You must understand that I am using the word "record" in the broadest sense of the term here, including the ascents of mountain climbers and the distance covered by a balloon in twenty-four hours, as well as the number of kilometers run on the open road. All types of sporting life, all forms of exercise should have a place in this little book, which would be like an examination of muscular conscience. You would fill in your own statistics on blank pages, recording what you manage to accomplish. What a great record book that would be! Try it yourselves. You will no longer be tempted to speak ill of a record.

PS – One kind correspondent asked me about anthropometry. "Where does it fit in your system?" he asked, adding that I would be wrong to dismiss it. I do not dismiss it at all, provided that it is accompanied by the proper general hygiene on which it depends. It is quite useful to take one's measurements. It is part of the thorough, varied checks that we should make of ourselves. It is quite easy to do without the involvement of a doctor. In the process, you are making your doctor's occasional work all the easier. But when anthropometry is turned into a sort of oracle, as it is at some universities in the United States, my estimation of it drops considerably. The notion that there exists an absolutely *standard* man, whose inner and outer measurements can be determined so that, by taking your height as a starting point, you can find out the exact size that each of your organs should be, as well as all the proportional ratios that you must attain – seems an unreasonable idea to me. The applications of anthropometry that I have seen abroad have proven to me that it opens the door to a sort of bogus gymnastics that is as excessive as it is ineffective.

L'Education Physique au XXe siècle: Le record, in:
Le Figaro, Vol. 49, January 10, 1903, pp. 1-2.

2.9 PHILOSOPHY OF PHYSICAL CULTURE

In this article, Coubertin gives us his interpretation of a philosophy of physical culture, which he defines partly with psychology. This is based chiefly on the ancient saying: "Know thyself". The moral and intellectual forces which vie to improve the human body are extremely varied, and the social forces are irreplaceable, he says. This contribution is one of a long series of articles which appeared in the Olympic Review ahead of the Olympic Congress on Sports Psychology and Physiology in 1913.[1]

A few months ago, I promised – perhaps a bit rashly – that I would outline the basic principles of what I call the "philosophy of physical culture". That promise was unwise, since the topic is so vast and so important that I am truly ashamed to address it like this in passing, in the inadequate context of a newspaper article. However, my critique of the various systems that I take to task specifically for their ignorance of and disdain for psychology would be meaningless unless I followed it up with some positive suggestions. People have long used the expression, "Everyone's a critic". No one has the right to tear something down unless he also provides the outlines for a way to build something in its place.

KNOW THYSELF

In some ways, this ancient precept is the be-all and end-all of physical culture, summarizing its requirements and objectives. Man himself is the main artisan of improvements in the human body. To work effectively toward improving himself, a man must, first and foremost, know himself. It goes without saying that we are not talking about the initial stages of childhood education. Although teachers may use certain psychological and physiological facts, the fruits of experience and observation, to great advantage during that phase, the child's cooperation in the effort can be only unwitting at best. Soon, however, conscience awakens in the child. In any event, the admonition to "know thyself" takes on its full meaning as an underlying tenet in adolescence.

AMBITIONS, STRENGTHS AND WEAKNESSES

The next task is to focus the individual's ambitions, to list his strengths and weaknesses so that all of the one can be used to offset the effects of the other, to the extent possible. This is the general program of physical culture. Ambitions? Nothing can be done without them. Ambitions need not focus on the loftiest goals. Not everyone is destined to be honored as a champion. It is hardly desirable for everyone to entertain such aspirations. But to aim for the middle is still ambitious. I do not hesitate to say that without ambition, nothing will be gained in physical culture despite the counsel and direction of even the most highly qualified, most devoted instructor. Such ambition may be instinctive, or it may come from some external

1 Later also in the collection *Essais de Psychologie Sportive.* Lausanne/Paris, Payot, 1913.

Boat race between Oxford University rowing clubs (taken from Sport im Bild, no.9, 1905, p.206)

factor. It may result from heredity, personal taste, a particular predisposition, self-interested calculation or a healthy sort of envy. The origin of ambition is of secondary importance here. What counts is that it exists, and that it is translated into action. Some vague desires and intentions remain off in the distance, never becoming reality. I am talking only about desires and intentions that are likely to produce tangible results, with enough energy to trigger the necessary movements.

Once ambition is in place, we must find out how best to satisfy it. The law of "least resistance" operates here, as elsewhere. Culture of the body produces three categories of strength: physical strength, obviously the primary, key strength; followed by moral strength and social strength. We hardly need to be reminded that muscles are not the only factor to take into consideration in terms of physical strength. We must also consider the nervous, respiratory, and digestive systems, etc. This has been very well expressed by Dr. P. Tissié, who said that the dynamism of the muscle, supported by its elasticity, its tone, and its contractility, results simultaneously "from the nervous system through neural input, from respiration through the oxygenation of the blood, from the circulation through the contributions of blood plasma, from the digestion through the contributions of nitrogenous or hydrocarbon nutritive substances or fuels, and finally from the joints and bones, through the fulcrums of the joints and through the bony rigidity of the arms themselves acting as levers". All these are different but interconnected sides of the same issue. But we shall not dwell any further on that here. This point of view is beginning to be accepted fairly generally. It is not the physiological, but rather the psychological, aspects that tend to be neglected in terms of the culture of the body.

Many moral and intellectual forces work in harmony to improve the human body. Reflection and observation play a role almost as important as the will, daring, and perseverance. Doubtless, the will and its adjuncts, daring and perseverance, form a trinity that is unequaled in its power to generate improvement. Yet we can make significant progress as well by observing, in ourselves and in others, the effects of physical exercise, and by knowing how to reflect on those effects methodically and productively. Applying the intellectual faculties to the culture of the body in this way does not just come about as the result of some innate sense of rapport. We must learn to do it, and we must strive to practice it.

Certain social strengths are unquestionably useful: comparative analysis, a taste for the struggle, a spirit of reconciliation, solidarity, esprit de corps... Of all the forms of camaraderie to which man is inclined, perhaps none acts more forcefully and more effectively on him than the camaraderie of sports. The shared threat of some danger, or at least of risk, frequent mutual assistance, physical exhilaration, and the impact of a virile, healthy undertaking all work together to make the social aspects of physical exercise pleasant and efficacious. The habit of making comparisons, which elicits admiration and at times a little advantageous twinge of envy, as I said before, are natural outcomes of this process. The effort involved in the struggle and the victory are another consequence. In the end, a group is formed, giving rise to feelings of solidarity and esprit de corps.

So much for strengths. There are three types of weakness, as well: physical, moral, and social. The weakness of a particular organ, general muscular sluggishness, and nervous excitability are all hereditary or acquired physical flaws. Hesitation, fearful movement, and all forms of feebleness are moral weaknesses. Social weaknesses include paralyzing shyness caused by the presence of others, raging irascibility, and that combination of faults that cause a player to be labeled a bad character, for example. Clearly the psychological makeup of each individual, which is determined by these criteria, will vary enormously from person to person. But as for this data,

WHAT USE SHOULD WE MAKE OF IT?

Well, once noted and monitored carefully, either by the individual more or less on his own if we are talking about a savvy, astute adult, or under the direction of a teacher if the individual is incapable of doing so on his own, the data should be recorded on a card. This practice is beginning to gain favor these days at various institutions for physical education, but only insofar as physiological data is concerned. Cards drawn up in this way would become the fundamental guiding principle for student and teacher alike. Would you think, then, that the physical development of irascible people, sluggards, resolute people, hesitant people, bold people, timid people, big bluffers, or reserved people could ever be guided in precisely the same way? Forcing so many dissimilar, even diametrically opposed personalities through the same mold seems absurd; yet because of our old habits, we now consider this approach the most normal thing in the world.

There, briefly put, is what I understand by the philosophy of physical culture. Rather than say more about this topic here, I will await your objections and criticisms, ready to respond. That approach will help shed light on the subject as a whole more effectively than if I were to provide further explanations at this juncture.

"La philosophie de la culture physique."
in: *Revue Olympique*, May 1909, pp. 73-76.
Reprinted in: *Essais de Psychologie sportive* [Essays on Sports Psychology].
Lausanne/Paris, Librairie Payot 1913, pp. 94-102.

The ancient athlete as victor, a symbol of physical and spiritual harmony. Marble votive relief (ca. 460 BC) of an athlete crowning himself (National Archaeological Museum, Athens)

2.10 SPORTS AND ETHICS

Ethical considerations have received only occasional and involuntary support from physical exercise. In conclusion, sport is merely an indirect stimulus for ethics. In order for it to become a direct stimulus, we must make the purpose of sport the creation of a sense of solidarity, which will cause sport to reach beyond itself. This is the sine qua non for cooperation between sport and ethics.

At awards ceremonies and congresses, speechmakers have exercised their talents at length on this subject, which lends itself to lofty pronouncements. Nevertheless, data to back them up remains quite vague. So we owe a debt of thanks to Lieutenant Hébert, a French naval officer, who wrote an interesting brochure on masculine education and "physical duties" in which he defined those duties in great detail.

According to Hébert, these duties are summed up in two basic rules: *use all means necessary to develop your physical abilities, and maintain those abilities by abstaining from anything that could debase them.* Surely never has a more direct bridge been built from one side of the river to other, from sport to ethics. To abstain from "anything that could debase physical abilities", is to abstain from excess of any kind. This is a law of pure ethics, apparently, at least, for later we shall see the limitations implicit in this wording.

No law of this kind has ever been enforced. It would be futile to turn to Hellenic civilization to find any traces of it. The level attained by the Greeks in this regard was not very high. A remarkable sense of social balance often replaced ethical rules. Moreover, our own civilization would do well to return to the Ancient Greeks' approach to this issue. Our civilization would draw principles of desirable elasticity from them, but not of higher ethical standards. The culture of sports in Greece, moreover, was never as widespread as we have believed. If we read them closely, many authors convey widespread notions of long-standing hostility on the part of public opinion with regard to physical exercises. Besides, those who engaged in exercise were not at all seen as models of virtue and continence. In our days, in England, the country most active in sports, it would probably be going too far to say that sportsmen are more virtuous, in the strictest sense of the word, than other citizens. Thus, although men have sometimes practiced the first of the "physical duties" I listed above, generally men have not gone so far as to submit to the constraints required by the second set of duties. Here and there, some have "used all necessary means to develop [their] physical abilities". But to maintain those abilities, men have not "abstained from anything that could debase them". Ethical consideration have received only occasional and involuntary support from physical exercise. It is evident that by calming the senses and occupying the imagination and leisure time of youth, physical exercises have been useful in serving the cause of virtue. But aside from a short period of training or the obligations imposed by professional interest, we have yet to see men voluntarily abstain, through the simple desire to perfect their bodies, from any act that might affect and diminish that perfection.

Since we have not seen such behavior, must we conclude that it cannot be? Is it even desirable in the first place? This is the question we must answer first.

Constraint presumes some sort of leverage. What is the leverage in this situation? There may be several: utilitarianism, for example, or altruism, or even self-interest. We can easily imagine a man "using all necessary means to develop his physical abilities" motivated by a sense of the advantages he may gain, and the superiority that such advantages will give him over his peers. This is a legitimate and efficient point of view. We can also imagine that he might aim for that goal through a noble desire to be useful, and to serve the interests of the group. Yet in both cases, in order to maintain the abilities he acquires, a man would not necessarily abstain from every excess. The go-getter and the devoted individual will engage in excesses because they will wear themselves out in their efforts – excessive mental exertion, or even excessive solidarity and fraternal zeal. The only one who will not commit these excesses is an individual for whom self-concern is strong enough to tame the passions if need be, or to suppress any unwise fervor. But would this person not be a monster? He would be Nietzsche's Superman, in the domain of physical culture. Adoring his own body, which has become his idol, he would gradually subordinate everything to his concern for establishing and maintaining bodily perfection. One shudders to think of the infinite, refined ferocity, and indeed of the potential barbarism that human nature, influenced in this way, would harbor. Just a few such persons in the crowd would have a powerful impact, making a significant imprint on the society of their day.

As I said before, it is entirely possible for such a creature to exist. Although no such individual has existed in any clear-cut way in the past, there have been notable precursors. Current circumstances tend to favor its definitive arrival. Scientific progress gives today's man in-depth knowledge of his body, and gives him a wide range of appealing approaches to physical culture. Furthermore, uncertainty and an apologetic approach to religion means that there is now room for new religions or new approaches to religion. When man turns away from God, is it not the most natural thing for him to turn to self-worship?

Those who believe in "the goodness of nature", the followers of Jean-Jacques Rousseau, dismiss such fears. They confuse physical education with moral education, harboring the illusion that although the second does not engender the first, the first implies the second. As they see it, a physically educated man is unfailingly won over to virtue. For him, worship of the body is devoid of danger, since that religion contains its own countermeasures.

All this is based on the confusion of character and virtue. The qualities of the character are not based on ethics. They are not part of the domain of the conscience. These qualities are courage, energy, will, perseverance, and endurance. Great criminals and even avowed scoundrels have all possessed them. They can be used to do ill just as well as good. That is why the doctrine of *direct* moral development through physical development is false and troubling. It derives from belief in a "standard" man, the dangers of which I have already noted and challenged. Man is a composite made up of elements that react one against the other; yet those elements cannot be substituted for one another. Muscular perfection, in and of itself, ensures neither mental perfection nor moral perfection.

That is why this expression of physical duties that I am discussing is incomplete, and must be modified. "Use all necessary means to develop your physical abilities *to use them for the common good* – maintain those abilities by abstaining from anything that could debase them *pointlessly*", that is how the sentence should read. These simple words added to the original text put everything back into the proper place, chaining the deplorable "superman" in his crib. The altruistic principle proclaimed in this way may seem platonic, and it is to a certain extent, but it remains key. As public opinion grows to consider this corrective measure part of the individual law of physical culture, it will tend to disapprove of individuals who transgress that law too openly, rejecting altruism of any kind in favor of self-promotion. The word "pointlessly" underscores the dependent stance that the muscles must always keep with respect to thoughts and feeling, and with respect to social utility.

To conclude, sport is merely an indirect stimulus for ethics. In order for it to become a direct stimulus, we must make the purpose of sport the creation of a sense of solidarity, which will cause sport to reach beyond itself. This is the *sine qua non* for cooperation between sport and ethics.

One final word: you will note that in the course of this study, I have used the terms "sports" and "physical culture" almost interchangeably. The reason is that in my view, the only difference between these terms is theoretical. In theory, physical culture is distinct from sport. In practice, there will never be any voluntary physical culture (*intensive* physical culture, of course, the only form under consideration here, the one Lt. Hébert meant), that does not involve the sports aspect.

Le Sport et la Morale, in:
Revue Olympique, February 1910, pp. 20-22.
Reprinted in: *Essais de Psychologie Sportive* [Essays in Sports Psychology].
Lausanne/Paris, Librairie Payot 1913, pp. 129-137.

Pierre de Coubertin cycling in Nice in or about 1905. (Navacelle Collection)
He constantly praised the benefits of cycling:

"Lausanne, May 1937 (Year II, XI Olympiad)
Is mankind really aware of everything it owes to the bicycle, – not only concerning the technique, but also, I would even say, above all concerning its physical upward trend? Is mankind aware of the incredible extent of dexterity, balance, self-confidence, physical well-being, muscular strength that this wonderful invention has brought the human race?...
This alone is reason enough for cycling to be represented in the Olympic games program, as a kind of thank you homage towards mankind."

Pierre de Coubertin[1]

3. THE STRING OF EVENTS

In looking closely at the details of Coubertin's activities, we are struck by the diversity and complexity of the factors that enter into play. We see the commitment of a man totally engaged in his work, and a society in transition, though still deeply attached to a bygone era. All this plays out under material and moral conditions that limit the chances of success for the projects he hoped to implement. Ultimately, the effectiveness of his efforts stemmed from Coubertin's character. Patiently, he cultivated the art of hope, never losing sight of his objectives. It is this struggle that we will now illustrate through some of his writings which are strikingly modern and wide-ranging, yet reveal the fundamental individuality of the man who penned them.

3.1 – 3.2 INTRODUCTION

These are two rare articles in which Coubertin looks at sport in universities. Against the background of the victorious American soldiers in World War I, he sees obligatory sport at American universities as the foundation for a superior generation of young men. However, there would also be other acceptable models between the total neglect of physical training by European students and the professional system in the United States.

In Letter XI, Coubertin stresses that academic youths have a greater responsibility for ensuring social peace among their people than the broad majority.[2] Once again, he attacks the alcohol problem as an evil afflicting young people, and offers sport as a remedy.

In this text, Coubertin announces for the first time that he wants to make pedagogical sports reform a personal priority for everyone in the future.

1 French original text: "Lausanne, Mai 1937 (An II de la XIe Olympiade)
L'Humanité se rend-elle bien compte de tout ce qu'elle doit à la Bicyclette – et non pas seulement au point de vue technique, mais aussi – et je disai même surtout – au point de vue de l'amélioration corporelle? Reconnaît-elle la dose incroyable d'adresse, d'équilibre, de confiance en soi, de "gaité physique", de puissance musculaire que cette invention merveilleuse a portée dans la race? ...Ne fut-ce que pour cela, le cyclisme doit figurer au programme des Jeux olympiques, comme en une sorte d'hommage de gratitude humaine. Pierre de Coubertin."
(Carl & Liselott Diem Archives)

2 See text 2.6 "Social Education" in this volume.

3.1 OLYMPIC LETTER X: SPORT IN THE UNIVERSITIES

The other day, in the Vaudois Academic Club, I ventured to do some preventive weather-forecasting in order to show the University of Lausanne that it is in course of committing an imprudence. I am not the only one, moreover, to give warning of the vast wave of Americanism which is crossing the Ocean and is about to break on Europe. The phenomenon is expected; it is in the natural order of things. But it is not only language, lavatories, railways, and banks which are going to be Americanized; it is going to happen to the universities too, for let us not forget that the universities of the United States played the leading part in the preparation and the launching of the war – as in its conduct. Their power, already enormous, will be increased tenfold as a result. Their formula for training the individual will be at premium on all the intellectual markets. This formula allots a very considerable part to sporting culture, and the remark of N. Webster, "A fencing room is no less necessary in a university than a chair of mathematics", is more apposite than ever. I do not share this excessive view. For me the university is first and foremost the temple of the Spirit. But between the American conception which embodies physical exercises in the study program, makes them obligatory, makes the award of the diploma to some extent conditional upon them – between this extremist conception and the contemptuous indifference to athletics in which the greater part of the universities of the old world continue to bask, there are various gradations. If we Europeans wish to maintain due proportion in this respect, we can do so only on condition of not neglecting such an important aspect of pedagogic science. The student must be left free to organize his sporting life, but he must be encouraged in it by the provision of material, technical and financial facilities and by the creation of a favorable atmosphere about him. But how can such an atmosphere be created if professors know nothing and care nothing about the matter? The time is at hand when it will no longer be possible to pooh-pooh it. It will rise up suddenly. Then watch out for panic action, botched improvisations and ill-considered solutions.

Lettre Olympique X,
in: *La Gazette de Lausanne*, no.4, January 5, 1919, p.1.

3.2 OLYMPIC LETTER XI: THE SPORTING SPIRIT OF STUDENTS

There is another aspect to the "sporting spirit" of the student. For his own sake, for the development of his gumption in life, and for the clarity of his thought it is useful to him to like these violent exercises whose marriage with high intellectual culture is in Paul Bourget's words so "fruitful in manly splendors". But it is also useful to him in carrying out the social task which will lie ahead of him in the new society. Formerly the practice of sport was the occasional pastime of rich and idle youth. I have labored for thirty years to make it the habitual pleasure of the lower middle class. It is now necessary for this pleasure to enter the lives of the adolescent proletariat. It is necessary because this pleasure is the least costly, the most egalitarian, the most anti-alcoholic, and the

The annual association football match between Oxford and Cambridge Universities (taken from Sport im Bild, no.9, 1905, p.217)

most productive of contained and controlled energy. All forms of sport for everyone; that is no doubt a formula which is going to be criticized as madly utopian. I do not care. I have weighed and examined it for a long time; I know it is accurate and possible. The years and the strength which remain to me will be employed to ensure its triumph; it will be my contribution to those social reforms whose principle was the basis of the pact of sacred union during this long war and whose achievement will have to be honest and swift if we do not want civilization to blow up like a boiler without a valve.

University students, messengers of knowledge and imagination, will constitute the most active battalions in this great task; let us say if you wish that they will have to be its aviators. Now I have said, and I repeat, that sport by reason of its potent physical and moral effects will be an inestimable instrument in their hands for the establishment of social peace. They must therefore know how to handle it with tact and how to derive the maximum effect from it. Popular Olympism is about to be born; let the students prepare to serve it.

Lettre Olympique XI,
in: *La Gazette de Lausanne*, no.12, January 13, 1919, p.1.

Theodore Roosevelt: supporter of the Olympic Movement in the United States as Honorary President of the 1904 St Louis Olympics. As an active sportsman, he was a model for Olympism as a philosophy of life. Here, the American President is seen canoeing during a hunting trip to Canada in 1908 (taken from Sport im Bild, no.42, 1908, p.1296)

3.3 OLYMPIC LETTER XII: THEODORE ROOSEVELT

This is Coubertin's personal obituary for the former American president Theodore Roosevelt, with whom he had a close intellectual and personal relationship. Roosevelt was connected with the Olympic Movement not just as the honorary president of the 1904 Games in St. Louis, but also in the way that Coubertin regarded him as the prototype of the all-round educated and sporting Olympic man of the 20th century. The two maintained a lively correspondence and, as a token of his admiration, Coubertin dedicated to him the first part of his trilogy "Éducation des adolescents au XXe siècle: La Gymnastique utilitaire"[1]. For the Olympic Congress in 1913, Roosevelt sent an autobiographical contribution[2], to which Coubertin referred in particular in the following Olympic Letter.

The great man who has just died, and before whose tomb universal respect has been expressed, remained a devotee of athletics up to the end of his virile existence. But contrary to what is imagined, this cult in Theodore Roosevelt was the outcome neither of heredity nor of temperament. Reread the message which he sent to the Congress on the Psychology of Sport held here in 1913, the text of which is given in extenso in the volume containing the record of the work and discussions of the Congress. You will find there a Roosevelt singularly different from the man whom photographs and descriptions have popularized. This man whose name today symbolizes every form of energy was a delicate and timid youth, even sickly, lacking decisiveness and endurance. How vivid is the story of the incident while travelling, in which his weakness was revealed to him through his inability to stand up to ragging, and the consequent birth of a resolve deliberately to toughen himself so as to be able to face the buffets of life. This operation began in a modest boxing hall and finished on the ranches of the Far West among the cowboys whose fatigues and dangers he loved to share. Chroniclers like to depict the

The Outlook
287 Fourth Avenue
New York

Office of
Theodore Roosevelt

April 16th 1913.

My dear M. de Coubertin:

I thank you for your letter and appreciate it. I wish I could have been present at the Congress of Lausanne. I take the liberty of sending you herewith an article I have just written on "The Vigor of Life", which possibly may be of interest to you. It is a physical impossibility for me to prepare a special article now. Just at this time I am worked to the very limit.

With regret and good wishes,

Sincerely yours,

Theodore Roosevelt

Baron Pierre de Coubertin,
20 rue Oudinot, Paris.

Theodore Roosevelt's letter, enclosed with his contribution to the 1913 Congress (IOC Archives)

famous ranch man surrounded by the "roughriders" whom he later made his companions in war. What is generally not known is that after entire days spent in the hardest equestrian sport Roosevelt would plunge into the reading of the classics and strengthen his mind after strengthening his muscles. Thus, when the circumstances of his political career had brought him to the forefront the world was astonished to see in his person a combination of elements of physical and mental strength which were no longer thought compatible. There was much talk about the oddity of this overburdened Head of State who took time off to ride a horse every day and to wrestle. It took some years to find out that this eccentric was a great philosopher. And the crowds began to listen to his voice.

Indeed, if an epitaph at once laconic and complete were required for a tombstone, I should propose to apply to this faithful friend of our task the words which serve as a motto for the Olympic Institute of Lausanne – "Mens fervida in corpore lacertoso" – an ardent mind in a trained body ... And this would have been the epitaph which he would have preferred above all others.

Lettre Olympique XII,
in: *La Gazette de Lausanne*, no.25, January 26, 1919, p.1.

1 Cf. *La Gymnastique utilitaire,* Paris, Alcan, 1905.

2 See Th. Roosevelt: "Ma philosophie." In: *Congrès International de Psychologie et Physiologie sportives.* Rapport. Lausanne, IOC, 1913, p.37-38. See Th. Roosevelt: "The Vigor of Life." in: Theodore Roosevelt. *An Autobiography.* New York, Scribner's 1926, pp. 30-56

3.4 – 3.5 INTRODUCTION

Coubertin attributed great educational value to fencing, and especially boxing, for their virilizing effect. He was keenly disappointed at the 1912 Games in Stockholm to see boxing dropped from the program for legal reasons. He greatly enjoyed both sports, which he practiced personally, and it is no surprise that he published many articles on them. In the following two Olympic letters, Coubertin recalls the educational importance of self-defense sports for young people. He also stresses the cathartic function of boxing. Theodore Roosevelt showed the effectiveness of this by opening boxing clubs in the poor quarters of New York.

3.4 OLYMPIC LETTER XIV: THE VALUE OF BOXING (I)

I was describing the other day how Theodore Roosevelt had used boxing as the first stage in the deliberate build-up of his manhood. Now boxing is not in favor with Lausanne opinion. Parents do not like their children to take part in it; in this they are very wrong. Boxing, in their eyes, is only the art of biffing – an art which comes quite naturally in case of need to the ends of a strong and well-muscled man's arms. This is completely mistaken. Boxing is not at all instinctive. Try, if you have never had a lesson, to deliver a straight punch or kick. You will discover not only your clumsiness but the complete ineffectiveness of your effort, which will glance off or become deadened of its own accord. The gesture which nature teaches a man threatened by an attack is to grab any handy weapon – or else to seize the opponent and try to throw him down, which is a way of risking everything. The boxer's attitude is much more calculated. He begins by covering up by means of a skilful stance, behind which he prepares to fight, sees blows come, decides to slip or parry them, chooses the place for his attack or counter, and hurls his full strength forward at the crucial moment; a complete tactics and strategy in miniature which call for a large number of psycho-physiological qualities. The boxer needs sangfroid and calm, quickness of eye and decision, remarkable speed and above all a continuous fount of courage playing steadily throughout the combat with no weakening of any kind.

Add to this other merits. Boxing is a sport for men in a hurry, giving the maximum of exercise in the minimum of time. It requires little equipment. What is needed? A pair of padded gloves, bathing trunks, and soft-soled heel-less shoes – that is all. Nothing is healthier, incidentally, than such a costume, or more correctly such a lack of costume. Lastly boxing brings into play the various groups of muscles almost as harmoniously as rowing, and like rowing has the advantage of ruling out one source of nervous fatigue – holding back. The boxer exerts the whole of his strength each moment without hesitation or reserve. It is perhaps the physical satisfaction due to this massive expenditure of energy which results in such a combative sport having such a pacifying influence.

Lettre Olympique XIV,
in: *La Gazette de Lausanne*, no.41, February 11, 1919, p.1.

Boxing lessons were part of the Lausanne Olympic Institute's training programme, 1917/18 (IOC Archives)

3.5 OLYMPIC LETTER XV: THE VALUE OF BOXING (II)

It is not so paradoxical to call boxing a "pacifying sport". In English public schools the masters used to nickname boxing gloves "Keepers of the peace". And in fact they fulfilled this function to the general satisfaction. In New York a police chief opened boxing halls in the districts of ill repute, and there was an immediate drop in the statistics of bloody affrays and lethal assaults. This is not surprising. In both youth and man there exists a fighting instinct which is not only excusable but normal, and which can only be appeased by affording it some outlet. That is why a boy's education is not complete without some contact with "combat sports".

"Combat sport?" may be divided into armed combat and unarmed combat. The first includes exercise with the sword, the saber and the single stick. The second is divided into boxing and wrestling. For many reasons, which I cannot go into in these short Letters, the single stick and boxing seem to me to be particularly suitable in youth. Courses in boxing and single stick are cheap and easily organized, and can be introduced into the program of gymnastic clubs and even into the school curriculum.

There are two single stick methods – the ordinary method and the method of Professor Vigny of Geneva, which is original and active. Both lead up to the saber, which is a magnificent form of fencing, at present too much neglected. In the same way there are two methods of boxing – the so-called English or Anglo-American method which uses only the punch, and the French method which mingles kicks and punches. The presence in Lausanne of an interned officer, Lieutenant Desruelles, a champion and famous instructor in French boxing, has made it possible to introduce this very complete form of exercise here. The gymnasts who have made acquaintance with it have immediately taken to it, incidentally furnishing proof of the excellent gymnastic preparation which they had enjoyed in their clubs. English boxing is taught in several halls in this city in a fitting manner, that is to say without neglecting an essential courtesy. Much harm has been done to boxing by the occasional organization of spectacles in which, in order to appeal to a special public, an attempt seemed to be made to accentuate the apparent brutality of the sport. We may entrust it without misgiving to boys; it will make men of them and not louts.

Lettre Olympique XV,
in: *La Gazette de Lausanne,* no.52, February 22, 1919, p.1.

3.6 OLYMPIC LETTER XVI: HORSE-RIDING

Horse riding was one of Coubertin's favorite sports, as he had practiced it since his childhood and was a skilful horseman. In his view, this sport allows the rider to experience a perfect and intense joy. He even saw the origin of sport in the contact between man and horse. Coubertin strove to extend this "noble" sport to all levels of the population. To achieve this, he believed it necessary to alter the way in which horse riding was taught. In several articles, he spoke out in favor of this "popular riding"[1].

The most noble conquest ever made by the horse was man. It goes a long way back. I even see in it the origin of sport. For sport, let us not forget, is not at all natural to man. Effort for the sake of effort is not an animal datum. None of our "cousins" – whether monkey, cat or pony – consciously tries to train or harden itself. Now I do not think that it was contact with weapons which led man to conceive of sport but rather contact with the horse. The horse doubled our stature, our strength and our speed. It is he who initiated us into the heady delights of the chase, giving us, in the amusing phrase of an American writer "the sensation of having four legs", instructing us in the charming complexities of equilibrium, inspiring us with that "pride of life" which is the basis of the sporting instinct.

The friendship thus sealed has never been denied, but the greater part of youth remains stranger to it. An equestrian aristocracy, with stiff-necked manners, has succeeding in erecting barriers between those whose means permit them to possess a horse and those who cannot aspire to this privilege. A bizarre idea! Ought only those who own their own boat learn to row, and does one need to buy a bicycle before learning to ride it? Every healthy boy must feel a keen desire to mount a horse and even if this only happens to him two or three times he will have discovered and felt something at once new and ancestral, which will make him grow, if one may dare to put it in this way, both muscularly and even mentally. Jules Simon used to say to me, "How can one let a youngster grow his moustaches before he has flung a leg across a horse?"

There are also people who still claim that popular horse-riding could not coexist with skilled horse-riding without harming it. Yet in many countries – England or California for example – this coexistence is a fact and no one objects to it. It is true that the spread of popular horse-riding would call for methods and procedures which have not yet been perfected. Well then! Let's go to work on them.

Lettre Olympique XVI,
in: *La Gazette de Lausanne*, no.61, March 3, 1919, p.1.

3.7 OLYMPIC LETTER XVII: PHYSICAL EXERCISE AND CONSTRAINT

In the following Olympic Letter, Coubertin states his view on a 1918 campaign in France to make sport obligatory from the age of six. He argues vehemently from an educational conviction that sport cannot be practiced through coercion if it is to achieve its lifelong effect. What is more, such compulsory sport is impossible to implement.

It is said that a French group wants to bring to the vote a law whose first article would run as follows: "Every French citizen will undergo physical culture from the age of six years". If this text is correct, it evinces a fine naivete. How often throughout history similar edicts have been promulgated on this field or that, and everyone knows that a common fate has made them null and void within a short time, if not on the day they were drawn up. It is the same with any measure which demands an external or internal constraint in order to remain in force. But it cannot be too frequently repeated that physical effort is unnatural to the human being, who only forces himself to it under the stress of immediate necessity or because of the drive of a passionate desire transformed into a need. In this instance, what will be the type of constraint and who will impose it? Do you really imagine that the family will assume the task? Under the impact of present events and the exhortations of the press it may perhaps do so for a few years, after which the newspapers will think of something else, and the parents too. Will a sort of muscle-police then be created with inspectors responsible for making house-checks to see that every small child not yet at school is conscientiously performing exercises under the vigilant eye of its progenitors? ... How many months do you give such a system before they show the inspectors to the door? "And it will be right" as the ancient formulae used to have it.

Constraint, in this matter, can achieve nothing, absolutely nothing. There remains the need born of habit. That can achieve everything. It is because it existed in England, in the United States, in Bohemia ... that they were able to improvise astonishing armies; it is because it was beginning to be born in France that the endurance of this country surpassed all expectations. The Germans were busy developing it there on the eve of the war – too late. Let us ponder these facts. They have the savor of practicality. Let us sprinkle this salt on the sugared faith of the theoreticians.

Lettre Olympique XVII,
in: *La Gazette de Lausanne*, no. 64, March 6, 1919, p.1.

1 See Coubertin, "L'équitation populaire" in: *Revue Olympique,* February 1906, p.20-22. Reprinted in Coubertin, *Textes choisis,* Vol.I, pp.194-196. See Coubertin, "L'équitation populaire: but, conditions, moyens." in: *Revue Olympique,* November 1912, pp.170-173; December 1912, pp.181-184; January 1913, pp.8-11.Reprinted in: Coubertin, *Textes choisis,* Vol.I, pp.197-205.

3.8 OLYMPIC LETTER XVIII: APPARATUS

In this Olympic Letter, Coubertin voices his opposition to a campaign in France to abolish gymnastic apparatus. He tries to explain to readers how mastery of such equipment represents a learning process that has a powerful effect on the mind, and a high intrinsic value.

I should like to say a word about four unfortunate persons who have been expelled from their home and persecuted in all sorts of ways. Yet they were honorably known for having worked for the muscular improvement of youth at a time when this task was particularly meritorious, because its champions lacked the support of public opinion. The persons in question are our old pieces of gymnastic apparatus the fixed bar, the trapeze, the horse and the parallel bars. It is amusing to observe the indignation felt about them by people who have never met them and have no idea how pleasant and healthful their acquaintance was. Pedantic and scholarly memoranda – more pedantic than scholarly – have drawn up lists of imaginary misdeeds on the part of these appliances. Formerly they used to have uncompromising adepts, so true is it that even in the field of physical exercise the sectarian spirit of insufficiently-instructed man will find an outlet. Now the tables of fashion are turned and it is thought very modern to have a gymnasium with no ropes and a parquet gleaming like a ballroom and simply dotted with little mats like those which serve to call the faithful of Islam to prayer.

This is all part of the fundamental error which leads specialists to see nothing but the physiological side of sporting activity and to seek obstinately for "rational methods" in an order of things which is primarily passionate. The most "scientific" method is worth nothing unless fertilized by the psychic power of the instructor who uses it.

Lettre Olympique XVIII,
in: *La Gazette de Lausanne*, no.76, March 20, 1919, p.1.

3.9 OLYMPIC LETTER XIX: SPORTING PLEASURE

In this letter, Coubertin refers to the discussions about sports psychology at the 1913 Olympic Congress in Lausanne. The sporting instinct, which Coubertin describes in his book *La gymnastique utilitaire*[1] (Useful lifetime sports), must be coupled with "sporting pleasure". Only thus does sport retain its character.

Some people are surprised that on two occasions recently I have spoken of the passionate character of the sporting instinct. Yet it is the right term. Exercise ceases to be sporting when it ceases to be passionate. But try to make anyone understand that who has never experienced the intensity of muscular joy. And not everybody experiences it. There are many natures who merely missed being initiated at the right time. But there are others who remained absolutely rebellious to such joys. This question of "sporting pleasure" was discussed formerly at the 1913 Congress at Lausanne. I

Coubertin loved ice-skating and saw it as an exemplary life-time sport. Here: Ice-skating in the Bois de Boulogne, Paris (taken from Les sports modernes illustrés, Larousse, Paris, 1908, p.285)

remember that one of the most cultivated and distinguished of French gymnastic teachers, Paul Christmann, brought the valuable reinforcement of a conviction based on long experience to the thesis which more than one of us was supporting. "The body", he said, "needs a certain dose of pleasure, and pleasure is not well-being, it is intense physical pleasure. Now sport affords pleasure, i. e. intense physical pleasure. That is why a young man called upon to choose between a pleasure which will lay him low and a pleasure which will lift him up will come to prefer the second to the former. Thus the intoxication of the muscles pacifies the senses not only through fatigue but through satisfaction. It does not merely neutralize them, it contents them". The pedagogue who "did not like children" was unable to grasp such an idea, but the kind of man who is tending to replace him is much more inclined to accept it.

This is one of the aspects through which athletics is closely united with morality. Yes! Athletics touches everything – morality, art, social organization ... You have not heard the last of its claims; one day I shall take up an idea which Marcel Prévost developed at the Brussels Olympic Congress in 1905, and shall explain to you how it even touches literature. D'Annunzio will not contradict me.

Lettre Olympique XIX,
in: *La Gazette de Lausanne*, no.104, April 17, 1919, p.1.

1 L'éducation physique. Part I: La gymnastique utilitaire. Paris, Alcan, 1905.

Pierre de Coubertin rowing his boat "Yale" on Lake Leman the age of 72. Rowing was his favourite sport and he considered it one of the best all-round disciplines (Navacelle Collection)

3.10 OLYMPIC LETTER XX: WHY THE CITIZENS OF LAUSANNE SHOULD ROW

When asked in 1922 which sport he thought was the ideal sport, Coubertin decides on rowing.[1] He loved and practised rowing even when he got older, and also published numerous articles on this subject.[2] This Olympic Letter is adressed at the citizens of Lausanne and the young people living in the Canton de Vaud, urging them to use the ideal conditions Lac Léman provides for rowing.

The marionettes, dear readers, often make three little turns and then go off. Allow me to do the opposite and make "one big turn and then come back". Olympism is not taking final leave of you, but it is taking leave for some months. We will meet again, God willing, in the autumn. And now comes in the sweet of the year – an opportunity for you to follow my advice not only in your children's persons but in your own. You have sunny days ahead of you and a peerless stretch of water. Take advantage of them. Remember that with boxing, rowing is the most perfect sport in existence and that for a Lausannois it is a crime not to make use of his admirable lake. The Ouchy fleet of boats is not bad, far from it, and if you encouraged it more it would be still better. There are some well-balanced canoes with which you will be able to sketch the desirable mechanical figure. Don't be surprised at this language. The boat, the rower and the oars form three parts of a machine and the perfection and pleasure of the movement depend upon the relationships which are established between them. It is the rower's pleasure to feel himself a thinking machine, to experience at each stroke how strength wells up within him, spreads out and flows away. Rhythmed like music and happening in the heart of nature between air and water, this deliberately disciplined motion is the most satisfying and fortifying in existence. This coming summer, on his incomparable Thames, the Englishman will again take his pleasure in this fine sport. And I should be very surprised if on the banks of the Spree and the Alster, where luxurious rowing-clubs have been built in recent years, the German were not to return to garner energy and hope on the water. May Vaudois youth, which is so favored from a nautical standpoint, not fail to haunt one of these factories of manly strength in which, according to the old adage, the strength of the city is forged. Civium vires hodie, cras civitatis vis. The strength which your sons acquire today will be their country's strength tomorrow.

Lettre Olympique XX,
in: *La Gazette de Lausanne,* no.116, April 29, 1919, p.1.

1 See Coubertin, "Le sport et l'intelligence." in: *La Revue Mondiale,* no.22, November 15, 1922, p.146-148.

2 See Coubertin, "L'aviron." in: *Revue Olympique,* April 1908, p.60-63.Reprinted in: Coubertin: *Textes choisis,* Vol.III, p.222-224.See Coubertin, "La cure d'aviron." in: *Revue Suisse de Médicine,* July 3, 1928, pp.1-2. Reprinted in: Coubertin: *Textes choisis,* Vol.III, pp.226-231.

3.11 EDUCATIONAL USE OF ATHLETIC ACTIVITY

The Bureau International de Pédagogie Sportive [International Bureau of Sports Pedagogy] started work at a meeting followed by a reception at the Palace, held in November 1928 at the aula of the University of Lausanne under the auspices of that city. Coubertin, who had agreed to head up the organization, gave a speech on the educational use of athletic activity in honor of the occasion. Most of his speech, which carries the weight of a real manifesto, is republished here.

As reported by *Sport Suisse,* Coubertin began with an exhortation in the literary style, comparing the grumpy father-figure of Jean de Pierrefeu with the graceful image of Jacques Peyronny, describing the little football captain Montherlant described as "a stocky fourteen-year-old with the authority of a team leader, concerned about athletic hygiene, a dutiful student, healthy, normal, yet disturbing in his unspoken egotism". Coubertin then stated the limited extent to which he agreed there is room to improve the situation. After limiting the problem in geographical terms, he said, "Must we include gymnasts and fencers, swimmers and rowers among those that Mr. Grumpy condemns? Are all these individuals corrupt? Once exceptions have been made for the right people, if the only ones left are football and tennis players or runners, you must admit that this shows remarkable narrowing of the field, in any event". To what extent are these individuals responsible? Hasn't great deal been done to corrupt them, starting with the increased number of stadiums?

The following article combines Coubertin's speech with remarks by the journalist author.

TOO MANY STADIUMS

"Stadiums are being built unwisely all over the place. Those curious enough to leaf through the nine volumes of the *Revue Olympique* during the years when it was a monthly publication, the official publication of the International Olympic Committee, would find warnings against athletics as a show, and the eventual consequences of that approach-articles written eighteen, twenty, and twenty-two years ago. At the time I said that once seats for forty thousand spectators are built, you have to fill them, and that means drawing a crowd. To draw that crowd, you will need a publicity campaign, and to justify the publicity campaign you will have to draw sensational numbers... Yes, I said these things over and over, but no one listened to me. Almost all the stadiums built in recent years are the result of local and, too often, commercial interests, not Olympic interests at all. Now that the consequences I predicted concerning this state of affairs are becoming more widespread, people are on the attack against the athletes, accusing them of the corruption that has been forced on them for the past twenty years. Yes, I admire the fact that athletes are not a hundred times more corrupt than they actually are. In my view, these oversized showcases are the source of corruption at the root of the evil. Get rid of them, and everything else will clear up of its own accord. Gate money will return to normal, betting will falls off, and advertising will fades. Federations will be less subject to unhealthy temptations, and the occasions of evil will grow distant; their

Too many stadiums! Coubertin did not want spectators, but active sportsmen. Here: the stadium in Amherst, Mass. (taken from C.Diem, Sport in Amerika, Berlin, Weidmann, 1930, p. 3)

power and the occasions to abuse that power will diminish. The athlete will be protected from himself. No one will need to insist that athletes live by such high – though not superhuman – standards of virtue that many of those outraged at their failure to live up to those standards would be unable to do so themselves, under similar circumstances". Yet Mr. Coubertin sees this merely as a negative sort of remedy. He said, "We have the right to hope for a much more significant, positive result. Not only do we make it easy for outside influences to corrupt the athlete, we fail to foster the athlete's inner strength to resist. We fail to provide a support for the individual athlete to lean on in his moral development."

THE FAULT LIES WITH EDUCATORS

"If there has been failure – and I have just set forth the very narrow sense in which I accept the usage of that expression – , it is educators who are responsible. There are three kinds of educators: parents, teachers, and journalists, whom modern civilization has invested with a delicate role, whether they want it or not. In the hands of these people, to varying degrees and in very different ways, athletic education is a powerful tool for human development. They have not known how to use it. Teachers are the guiltiest party, because it was up to them to influence parents and the press. They did so, in the beginning. They once did so in England, where they were inspired by the teachings of the great Thomas Arnold. They did so in France forty years ago, when high school students, rising up at my call against a sad, depressing existence, broke down the doors of their jails to let in the fresh air (in the words of Frantz Reichel, who was typical of the group). Then a series of wise principals and teachers, the likes of Fringnet, Morlet, and Adam, conspired with this youthful hurricane and courageously set about harnessing its strength. Despite a certain commissioner of education who insisted that sports are an "amusement", these educators used sports to create a moral culture. One of their students who became director in his own right, Louis Dedet, now director of the Collège de Normandie, has always led his students as once he led his football teammates. Because my friend Marshal Lyautey said so first, I am emboldened to claim that this is the first generation to win a war not by giving our nation a sort of courage it did not need, but by providing the physical and psychological stamina the country lacked fifty years before.

Now is not the time to list how and why, through a series of different moves in France and England, educators let slip from their hands the tool that had produced such wonderful stirrings of the national soul. Besides, would I be understood? Are historians, who are only now beginning to make room among their battles and timelines for questions of economics, ready to admit the influence of major educational trends on the events that they are relating?" After a few words about the revamping of educational programs toward which the Union Pédagogique Universelle, also headed by Mr. Coubertin, is working, he then set about defining the moral use of athletics.

FROM THE ATHLETIC TO THE MORAL DOMAIN

"Four years ago I had the following inscription, which is concise in the way that Latin can be, engraved on a medal for the fostering of sports in Africa, a movement that I started: *Athletae proprium est se ipsum noscere, ducere et vincere*. It is up to the athlete to know, to govern and to conquer himself. This text may come across as pretentious, since it reflects both Socrates and St. Paul. In any event, it certainly cannot be found lacking in truth. The athlete who, through perseverance in training, hopes to win a prize that his own lack of exceptional natural ability fails to guarantee him is drawn to this threefold obligation of knowing himself, governing himself, and conquering himself. Must we conclude that all athletes are destined for moral perfection? Not at all, for these qualities remain locked up within the narrow confines of a limited form of ambition. It is up to the educator to draw them out, to extend them to the whole personality. It is up to him to transpose them, in a way, from the merely technical level to the general level. To do that, it is not absolutely essential that the teacher engage in any particular sport himself. Of course, that would be preferable. In so doing, he would acquire considerable prestige. Forty years ago, I watched as students at one of the leading *public schools* in England, Clifton, near Bristol, rejoiced at the news that the headmaster whom the trustees had just appointed had, when a student, performed a six-foot jump. The fact that he held a record back then increased his professional authority in a singular way.

The French educators to whom I just referred were not at that level, but they did keep abreast of athletic technique. They maintained an interest in their students' successes, mingling with them and presiding at their meetings. On many occasions – the example of my illustrious friend Fr. Didon at the school in Arcueil comes to mind – I have heard them discussing the familiar but important topic of transferring athletic characteristics from the domain of sports to that of morals. They praised that robustness of mind that Arnold and Kingsley had espoused so valiantly in England forty years before. They were well aware that although a Latin translation assignment improves the mind (an activity that is becoming much too foreign to us), it is sport, with all its violent contact, its options and its opportunities, that prepares (excuse me! that can prepare) the body and the character for the battles of

Athletic progress has no boundaries, for men as well as for women. Here, the start of the 100 metres women's freestyle final at the 1928 Olympics in Amsterdam (taken from the Official Report of the Games of the IX Olympiad, Amsterdam 1928, Ed. J.H. de Bussy, 1931, p.772)

life. They sensed that sport combines the only two things that, taken together, ensure peace among societies: mutual assistance and competition. They sensed that it is in sports that the combination of confidence and wariness, daring and prudence, enthusiasm and self-control so necessary for success is achieved. These are, as it were, the foundations of proper human balance.

This athletic conception of education must be restored, Gentlemen, in those places where it has existed, and it must be created where it has not. To do this, we must earnestly desire the reforms this approach calls for, namely autonomy for school and university sports, their independence from existing sports federations. (The organization of those federations is precarious. I believe it will collapse as corporate structures expand.) We must forbid high school students from participating in public competitions where entrance fees are collected. We must forbid university students from participating in such events without the university's approval. The incessant travel associated with championships and sub-championships must be stopped. Such travel interrupt studies. It is very expensive, and is the worst way to see the country. These "blinkered" trips create much more prejudice than they dispel. In my view, every school should have a school sports association that serves not just one or two students, but as many as possible in all sports (you know that I believe gymnastic sports come first in this). The competitive spirit should be maintained in these associations through regional interscholastic meets only, from school to school. The associations should be run by the students, under the supervision of teachers, chaired by the director of the institution. A small sports newspaper, excluding advertising and written in part by the students themselves, will keep them abreast of what that they should know, presenting world events and the major developments in contemporary life."

Wariness of feminism was no longer appropriate in the 20th century, although Coubertin thought it should be encouraged (Photo taken from E.Jaques-Dalcroze, Rhythmus, Musik und Erziehung, Ed.Schwab, Basel, 1921, p.80)

WARINESS OF FEMINISM

"Schools must be supported in these efforts by the public authorities, but especially by parents. Will parents pitch in? I urge them to get involved, but I will not stoop to flattery to try to ensure success. On the contrary, I go so far as to tell many of them that their current spinelessness is pitiful. How are they raising their sons, and especially their daughters? In many countries today, it is the girl who corrupts the boy, but parents encourage boys at a young age to show that they are flirts, wise and crafty. Parents find this amusing and take delight in it. This is creating not just a generation of neurotics, but a generation of indifferent individuals, the worst lot in the world. This society is growing lax. Let it beware of neighboring countries, youthful Asia, the new Africa. Let it beware, too, of the working population everywhere which is most numerous and vigorous. Lacking the education they have unwisely been denied, these people are beginning to take up sports, showing an educational interest in them that is quite noteworthy.

Can the young women I have mentioned before, with justified cruelty, acquire a moral sense through sports, too? I do not believe so. Physical education, athletic physical culture, yes. That is excellent for young girls, for women. But the ruggedness of male exertion, the basis of athletic education when prudently but resolutely applied, is much to be dreaded when it comes to the female. That ruggedness is achieved physically only when nerves are stretched beyond their normal capacity, and morally only when the most precious feminine characteristics are nullified. Female heroism is no phantom. I would even say, more directly, that it is just as common and perhaps even more admirable than male heroism. But there was no need for Edith Cavell or Gabrielle Petit, revered by the Belgians, to be athletes. At the risk of disappointing those literary types who will take this tack, I would also say that in my opinion, Joan of Arc was not an athlete either.

Although I would like competitions among boys to be more infrequent, I emphatically insist that the tradition continue. This form of athletic competitiveness is vital in athletic education, with all its risks and consequences. Add a female element, and the event becomes monstrous. The experience of Amsterdam seems to have justified my opposition to allowing women into the Olympic Games. On the whole, reaction so far has been hostile to repeating the spectacle that the women's events provided during the Ninth Olympiad. If some women want to play football or box, let them, provided that the event takes place without spectators, because the spectators who flock to such competitions are not there to watch a sport."

"HIGH TIDE"

"Yet the special feature of athletic education is that it continues past adolescence, overflowing into adulthood. Its purpose is to hone the young man, and to keep honing him as an adult. But there is a lower cut-off point for athletic education: it has no place in childhood. We are making a terrible mistake these days by involving children in organized sports at such a young age. Athletic education loses its edge as an incomparable instrument if used too soon. As a result, precocious development is rewarded. This is a general flaw in education these days. Our contemporaries seem to want to hurry the growing season. By nearly eliminating springtime, they think they can prolong summer, i.e. the period of full production. Nature scorns such schemes, and soon claims her rights. Beware the early fall and winter. By forcing the flower, you may merely make the leaves drop all the sooner.

The wear and tear of age are the only upper limit on athletic education. This is the second error we are committing these days. Sports are basically considered a thing for the young (and thus fleeting in nature), and something to be done in groups. To have an effective impact on the city, the nation, and the race, sports must be engaged in individually and for an extended period of time, insofar as possible. A great army leader once said that there was no source of energy as consistent as a twenty-eight to thirty-year-old soldier. Likewise, nothing is as resplendent in civilian life as what I would call "*high tide.*"

One must have lived by a seashore where the tides are strong to appreciate the power and majesty of the expression "high tide". It describes the moment when the water has reached its greatest height; it appears to hesitate for a moment before it begins to recede. Sometimes the wind seems to abate, as well. One might even think that the earth itself joins in the relaxation of the other elements. Flames rising from a country fire, reminiscent of primitive religions, forego their customary spirals, rising straight to the heavens.

Such a moment exists in human life. It is a time when the mental and muscular tide has reached its peak, and when the individual may be lucky enough to be aware of that it is so. Not everyone has such good fortune. Any number of circumstances may prevent it: health problems, inadequate educational opportunities, crushing burdens...for fate is unequal and unjust in its ways. Yet so many people let that magnificent moment pass them by simply because they are not paying attention, even though they could have lived it with a passion. For so many others, earlier efforts at the right time would have guaranteed them precious mastery.

Man can do much to possess the joys of high tide. The difficulty is that to be successful, he must extend the youth of his muscles and hasten the maturity of his brain, in order to bring the body and the mind to harmonious completeness. It is my fervent hope that the work of the Educational Union, once completed and assimilated, will provide timely assistance as far as people's minds are concerned. As for their muscles, until the ancient gymnasium is reestablished – ancient in principle, of course, but updated in form – and until every city builds one or two such gymnasiums instead of the stadiums I denounced a moment ago, how can you expect individual adults to keep themselves in good athletic condition? Where would they go for exercise in the few, fleeting moments they might carve out for it in their busy professional schedules?

You may be surprised that I am bringing the individual adult into this field of athletic education. Some of you might think I am showing exaggerated solicitude toward the individual, but as things now stand in society, I must continue to view him as the most interesting of beings. People may think that this individual escapes the control of the educator, however. Not at all. If he has been well guided during his education, the individual will be his own teacher. As far as adults are concerned, there are two issues I pointed out a long time ago, but these issues have not managed adequately to focus the attention of educators so far."

SATISFYING THE PASSIONS

"The body must enjoy a certain measure of sensual enjoyment. Sensual enjoyment is not well-being, it is intense physical pleasure. This need is not felt at every age, because it is not animal in essence. Given this fact, times when spiritual or ascetic considerations predominate can dull its impetus for a while. But when a human being passes through a phase of "bodily freedom", if I may put it that way, a measure of intense physical enjoyment once again becomes essential to the proper, vital functioning of the individual. Sport produces physical enjoyment, i.e. intense physical pleasure. Many sportsmen will attest that under certain circumstances, this pleasure takes on the imperative and disturbing character of sensual passion. Clearly, not everyone experiences this. It requires certain a sense of equanimity, and the ardor and absence of cares or self-control issues at the heart of any sensual exhilaration. But some swimmers, riders, fencers, and gymnasts will tell you that they know that exhilaration well. The intoxication of the wave, the gallop, the struggle, or the trapeze is just as strong as conventional drunkenness. It is both real and definite, and it is superior to the "other" form in that it is never artificially provoked by the imagination, and rarely disappointed through satiety. It calms the senses not only through fatigue, but through satisfaction, as well. It does more than just neutralize the senses; it satisfies them.

Adult males have another passion that must be calmed through satisfaction of some sort, though to a considerably lesser extent. That passion is anger. The term, no pun intended, is too acrimonious. In French, the word "colère" ["anger"] evokes the onset of uncontrolled violence, wrongly excluding cold or watered-down forms of anger. These are much more destructive feelings for those who experience them and give in to them. Moralists answer that we merely need to control ourselves. That is all well and good, but it is far too simplistic. The simplicity derives from on-going confusion between character and virtue. The qualities of the character are not based on moral considerations. They are not subject to the conscience. These qualities are courage, will, perseverance, poise, and stamina.

Three-fourths of them are physical. Tell me, wouldn't a man who breaks a chair or smashes a glass to calm his anger be better off picking up a piece of sports equipment and using that instead, however brutally? Do you think this is a utopian view? On the contrary: it is practical, common sense, as experience has shown. I have told this story about Theodore Roosevelt many times before. Once, when he was in charge of the New York police and was concerned about the bloody fist fights that kept breaking out in an area known as "downtown", he opened several free boxing gymnasiums in those neighborhoods of ill repute. Right away, the number of street fights decreased at an astonishing rate."

Mr. Coubertin then mentioned the 1913 Congress on Sports Psychology, held in the same university aula. A number of famous people participated in the Congress, including the historian Ferrero who gave the opening address. President Roosevelt himself sent a most compelling autobiographical contribution, "on the role that sports has played in his life, and the way he had used boxing, of which he was afraid, to go from being a fragile, anxious, timid adolescent to a bold and robust man". After reviewing the agenda arranged for those attending the conference, Coubertin acknowledged that Lausanne was justified in claiming that the 1913 Congress gave them pride of place in the field of athletic education. Those claims are further supported by the actions of the Olympic Institute during the war years, when it operated for the benefit of French and Belgian internees. Then Coubertin related how the International Bureau of Sports Pedagogy [B.I.P.S.] had come about in response to public opinion which, though exaggerating present excesses, was calling for intervention and corrective action.

THE FOUNDING AND ACTIVITY OF THE INTERNATIONAL BUREAU OF SPORTS PEDAGOGY [B.I.P.S.]

"We pitched in. We took a chance. Our initiative met with general satisfaction, a good sign. I did not expect such satisfaction to be so widespread or complete. The Office's first move was to canvass a broad spectrum of opinions. I joined others in the organization in interviewing a great number of competent people, or people considered to be so, such as educators, journalists, and athletic directors. I was quite surprised to find they agreed nearly unanimously on one essential point. Their views are summarized in the following argument. The present is lost. We cannot expect much from this generation, and it is beyond our means to reform it (I am not so sure about that myself). We must work on tomorrow, on the next generation that is about to enter the schools. The master of the hour is the school teacher, the professor. The place for improvement is at the graduate level of teacher training. Young teachers must pay attention to the educational uses of athletics. The time for non-didactic, but quite fruitful, instruction is before youngsters engage in sports, while they are still reciting the muscular alphabet, so to speak, particularly once they begin to approach sports as they grow older. A whole philosophy of youth must be introduced, one that will form the basis of manly philosophy later on: one does not cheat. Success achieved in games through twisting the truth does not count. It is like trying to eat by ingesting poison. The unfortunate thing is not failing, but failing to try. When a classmate fares better, at times with the help of a bit of luck that you yourself did not have, it is understandable that you will feel vexation, but nonetheless, don't show it, repress it. You must endure physical and moral scrapes without complaining, and especially without boasting. Bluffing is useless in sports, because athletic results are written in statistics or in deeds. They do not let you lie to others or to yourself. Training overcomes a great deal, though not everything. Training is a daily resolve, a step-by-step climb, interrupted by pauses and set-backs but propped up on a solid support called the will.

It is the task of our International Bureau of Sports Pedagogy [B.I.P.S.] to spread this gospel, but it would appear that other duties have devolved upon it, as well. The agenda of the Brussels Congress of 1905 was recently placed before our colleagues once again. It seems to them that many issues on that agenda were insufficiently appreciated at the time, and that in any event, those issues remain unresolved. It would be most advantageous to study these issues once again, in greater detail, drawing on the cumulative experience of the past twenty-five years. Let me cite some of them for you. In New York State in the late nineteenth century, athletic exercises were already being used for the moral re-education of inmates at the enormous penitentiary at Elmira. Remarkable results were reported. Recently I wondered what had become of those methods, unknown here in the Old World. Over there, far from abandoning them, athletic exercises have been expanded considerably. They sent me an enormous book on penitentiary operations there in the past year, and sports play a tremendous, unheard-of role. What they are doing at Elmira is going on elsewhere, as well. It would be useful and interesting to gather information and study how sport works in such surroundings. We can already imagine how the story is going, to some extent. We know that sport reintroduces in the guilty person, in the degenerate, a sort of human pride that carries with it a penchant for devotion to honor. These are nuances, subtle and ephemeral nuances that we must seize upon and hold firmly in place. More than that, it is worth opening up this field of psychology, which is apt to become quite fertile.

Pride gives rise to confidence, too, and confidence is what the modern malady known as depression (modern especially in terms of how widespread it is these days) most easily overcomes. The February 1912 issue of the *Revue Olympique* presented the view that athletic remedies are suitable for many sufferers of depression. Today, several distinguished specialists readily concur. One can always think and talk about it while waiting to take action. Finally, the common ground of sports and military service has not been established, or at least not very clearly. Action and reaction on this topic has been endless. Neither the great leaders nor the officers of lesser rank who are in direct contact with the troops have been able to see eye to eye on appropriate limits for steps to be taken. Finally, let me venture into the infamous hornet's nest of the issue of amateurism. In some respects, the arguments over this issue include a whole series of subtle, complex psychological considerations, which places it squarely within the reach of what an institution like the International Bureau of Sports Pedagogy [B.I.P.S.] should be looking into.

Gentlemen, you can readily see that the B.I.P.S. is not afraid of taking on work. Frankly, the prospect frightens me a bit – there will be far too much to do. Who is going to direct all this? I am just an old retired staff general now. I will gladly do what I can to provide discerning support and impartial advice. Yet something more is needed. The representatives that several governments have already assigned to join in on our work from a distance (an honor as well as an incentive) will demand more. You must find me some enthusiastic, deeply persuaded coworkers, individuals oriented toward the global perspective (if all that were at stake were minor excesses in this country, there would be no point in going on the attack). These people must always keep a lookout on the mountain top where I have set him. Our observations must not gradually sink to the level ground of statistics. The great utopia of our day is to make contacts, to exchange opinions, and to accumulate statistics. This utopian vision can mask countless cobwebs of routine and illusion. Beware of that danger. The real point of any international organization, whatever its specific purpose, is to act like the weather bureau. It must test the atmosphere and announce changes in the weather as far in advance as possible. In this way, public opinion can be advised of looming dangers (dangers that are often its own fault) and can figure out what to do to counteract their effects in due time. The people who run these organizations have no need to spend their time on inquiries or counter-inquiries, looking for some inspirational genius at the back of a filing drawer. They must be vigilant, at all times, so that their sharp eye can pierce the mist that surrounds reality."

FROM GAMES TO HEROIC ACTS

"Gentlemen, memories of the 1913 Congress are still quite vivid for me as I stand in this place. I recall what Professor Millioud, who followed the debates at the Congress with great interest, said: "Ultimately, sport is a kind of activity that ranges from games to heroic acts, covering all the stages in between."

When I began, I brought up the image of a little football captain standing at the threshold of life, at the dawn of his adult days. Now, my thoughts turn to the valley that runs along behind these snowy peaks. There stands a monument to a young athlete whose image should hover over schools when young men are receiving manly instruction. Bear with me as I conclude by recalling briefly what constituted the greatness of Chavez' adventure. Crossing the Alps by airplane in his day was considered a nearly superhuman feat. Given equipment design and aviator training then available, that opinion was quite accurate. Chavez trained in all sports, but he gave them all up for flying, and had already flown to great heights. He began flying in February 1910, and six months later he had ascended to 2,587 meters. Like his peers, Chavez took great pleasure in these flights. But on one occasion, the young Peruvian encountered something unfamiliar to him: fear. Testing himself in on that terrible transalpine route, he returned to Brig gasping for breath. The great Turenne shouted, "You're trembling, old thing, but you'd be trembling even more if you knew where I'm going to take you tomorrow". So on September 23, 1910, fortified by valor and drunk with desire, Chavez, convinced that he would court death but preferring anything to retreat, entered the gorges of the Alps. There, he saw things passing below him that had never before been seen by man. Caught in terrible updrafts, frozen with cold, and fighting with his rebellious engine and the elements, he swooped down at Domodossola, broken, overwhelmed, but having accomplished his long-desired feat.

Conquering the air: the American Wilbur Wright successfully demonstrating his flying skills outside Paris (taken from *Sport im Bild*, no.35, 1908, p.1085)

As it landed, his aircraft was twisted, dismantled, and falling apart, just like Chavez himself. His nerves, tensed to the breaking point through obedience to his all-powerful will, had taken their revenge on his organs. After terrible suffering, Chavez died, having voluntarily sacrificed his robust and joyful twenty-three years for the love of glory. The eternal struggle claimed one more victim. The sublime example of mind over body shone forth once again for humanity."

This is nearly the entire text of the address Coubertin gave on November 7, a speech that amounted essentially to a manifesto, as we mentioned earlier. It contains statements that must be taken into serious consideration, statements sure to touch off explosions on several issues. He presents athletes not as being guilty for the upsurge in corruption that is now alarming friends of sports. The builders of stadiums, amoral parents, and careless educators are at fault, and Mr. Coubertin takes them sharply to task. Moreover, he has called for the "independence of school and university athletics", and for "forbidding high school students from participating in public competitions where an entrance fee is charged". These measures will turn the most problematic areas of current arrangements upside down. He let it be known that in his view, athletic federations are becoming deplorably decadent, and that perhaps some day they will be reorganized along the corporate model. Furthermore, he is among those who consider athletic sports "gymnastic sports", and has often said that the "boundaries are poorly drawn" between these two areas. Finally, as we know, Mr. Coubertin considers current amateur regulations "ludicrous obstacles". The battle front that he has outlined is admittedly quite vast. All this, of course, will lend itself to lengthy and bitter debate, but athletic life will gain strength from it. In the end, athletic life will be cleaned up, in keeping with the hopes of all those who believe that indeed "athletic activity is a magnificent tool for human progress."

L'utilisation pédagogique de l'activité sportive,
in: *Le Sport Suisse*,
November 21, 1928, no. 1074, p. 1 (I)
November 28, 1928, no. 1075, p. 1 (II)
Special pamphlet, Geneva, *Sport Suisse*, 1928, 8 pages.

3.12 THE ORIGINS AND LIMITS OF ATHLETIC PROGRESS

In June 1936, shortly before the Olympic Games in Berlin, this essay appeared in four instalments in the Berlin newspaper *BZ am Mittag.* Two years later, after Coubertin's death, the original French version was published in the *Olympic Review.* The article is a kind of sporting legacy. In it Coubertin summarizes once more many of his views on modern sport. He makes a distinction between developing the human body, mental properties, psychological sources of development and the conditions under which each sport is played. Coubertin compares these efforts with his Utilitarian Gymnastics first presented in 1902. The question of the mobilization of the muscles is no less significant. In the third part, Coubertin looks at the influence of the spectator, where the element of sports psychology comes into play. In the fourth section, he explores the question of whether there are limits to the athlete's potential for improvement. Here he sees the difference in personal or collective improvement, posing the question of whether the individual or the race plays a more important role. As in ancient times, sport was still an important element of modern progress in 1936.

I

Athletic progress in adolescence and young adulthood can arise from three sources. First, the body's muscles can be developed. The body can, in fact, be significantly improved. It can be strengthened, made supple, more hardy, more skillful, and better balanced. This result can be achieved through perseverance in exercise and through well understood training, especially if propitious circumstances contribute to the process.

Yet in developing the human body for purposes of athletic success, mental properties play a major role, at times even a preponderant one. Remember that the modern Olympic cycle began with the triumph of a Greek peasant in the marathon. He was naturally robust, but he had not undergone any scientific preparation. Far from it. He prepared by fasting and praying before the Holy Icons in keeping with his religion. Let me add that at every Olympiad since then, I have always seen how strength of will and poise have "forced" a success, in some way. Sometimes the most physically gifted athletes are eliminated by others who, though less well off in that regard, used greater energy and force of will to achieve their victories.

This, then, is a second, psychological source of development. One can train one's will and perseverance just as well as one's muscular capacity. Finally, there is a third source. The first two are concentrated within the individual. The third source lies outside the individual. It consists of the developments in athletic equipment, or in the conditions under which each sport is played. This might mean new equipment, or merely that such equipment is updated thanks to some discovery or a better adaptation of the items used. For example, consider the modern rower. Not only has his boat become astonishingly light weight, but the mobility of the seat, now placed on rollers, and the extension of the oars beyond the fulcrum point provide him with enormous mechanical assistance. Compare him to the rower of yesteryear, handling his heavy craft with oars that were too short. Truly there is not a single exercise that has undergone a more complete transformation thanks to human inventiveness. Rowing is now well established as the most perfect gymnastic exercise there is.

What can we say about the bicycle, the result of a brilliant idea in applied mechanics, using a toothed gear wheel and a transmission chain connecting it to the pedals? In fencing, the heavy, awkward gear of fifty years ago has been replaced by lighter outfits and masks, and with weapons that are smooth to use. Not only has the fencer's game been made easier, but his tactics have been transformed, even more so than those of boxers, following the improvements in boxing glove design. In this regard, muscular development seems directly related to improvements in equipment, and to changes in men's movements and attitudes that have been the result. The benefits reaped by the runner or the gymnast as a result of the cinder track or new pieces of gymnastics equipment are less evident, but they are of the same order. By contrast, the situations of climbers and discus or javelin throwers have not changed much with respect to their ancient counterparts.

II

For a long time, it appeared that specialized training would most likely guarantee limitless athletic development. People expected marvelous things from it, according only secondary importance to general training. Each specialist trained almost exclusively in the movements considered essential for the sport in which he hoped to excel. He considered any movement or set of movements that appeared to be part of the gymnastic grammar of another sport not only as useless, but as harmful. It is obvious that one cannot hope to be completely successful in any sport without engaging in specialized training, but theories based on an alleged incompatibility of one sport with another have already been discredited. Although football does not train the individual for horseback riding, it is not at all harmful to engage in that pursuit, no more than running and jumping do harm to a boxer. I recall that forty-seven years ago, I saw a young Canadian take second place in trick riding the first time he mounted a horse. He was a football player. A little later, at the games of the First Olympiad in Athens, an American student placed in the discus, a sport that he had never practiced previously. Such incidents convinced me of the value of athletic eclecticism, a theory that serves as the basis for the "Utilitarian Gymnastics" system that I have outlined, specifically in the *Revue des Deux Mondes* in February, 1902.

Today, specialized training is used in a well thought-out and efficient way. But that is not the case – at least not to the same extent – for general training, even though that should be a fundamental and prerequisite stage. The reason, it seems to me, is that two interrelated issues have been neglected: internal equilibrium and the mechanical structure of the individual. If one observes an athlete in action closely, one quickly notices that for the athlete, everything depends on internal equilibrium, on the way in which that equilibrium is created, modified, controlled, and broken. It all depends on the way the muscles move at the urging of the will which

Masculin strenght as athletic progress. Olympic Games Antwerp 1920: United States Navy representatives practising their specialities on board U.S.S. Frederick. (taken from Spalding's Athletics Library no. 94R: Olympic Games Hanolbook, New York, ASP, 1922, p. 144)

demands some particular motion of them, and on the structure that the individual's bones, shown in x-ray images, determine how the body's leverage mechanism responds. Until now, all this has been neglected. For a long time, instructors have merely set up programs for "strength and agility training", rather a simplistic approach, one must admit. Japanese instructors conceive of their task differently. Hence they spend a great deal of time and much care in training the athlete (particularly for jujitsu fighters). The reason is that they attribute great significance to the development of bodily equilibrium. One of their renowned teachers once told me that one must work to bring the student to a point where, even in the dark, the slightest contact with an adversary, a mere touch of the hand perhaps, will make it possible to assess the adversary's state of equilibrium, and to determine where the adversary's center of gravity is located at that exact moment. It is almost like a new "sense" that must be created and developed in this way. One can well imagine that such a task would require a very long and very consistent effort. Without going quite so far down that path as the Japanese, it would be opportune for European methods to draw inspiration from their example, and to make more room for "equilibrium" than is now the case in physical education.

The issue of "mobilization" of the muscles is no less significant. It is doubly so, as it were, in a positive and negative way. The success of an athletic movement depends not only on the precise and rapid action of the muscles, which have a role to play in it, but also, and especially, on the inaction of those muscles that are not involved and that, were they to become so, would merely obstruct the action. Picture the bridge of a ship, where the actions that have been ordered are to be carried out when the whistle blows. Each man must know what that signal means for him. If everyone were to rush forward at the same time because they have not been properly instructed beforehand, the result will be disorder, which always means inefficiency. The same is true for the movements of the muscles. So often, I have observed in myself and in others the harmful action that occurs when learning a new sport through the obstruction of the muscles. Some muscles are essential for the movement, while others should remain still, but create confusion and awkwardness by moving inappropriately. This training of the muscles can be achieved only through repetition, and most often remains incomplete. Can we not study this matter scientifically, and thereby determine the best methods for accomplishing this goal quickly and completely?

Finally, there is the issue of the structure of the body. As the application of x-rays for the observation of the human body is perfected, we will certainly be able to obtain data that is useful for athletics. For a long time, it has seemed to me that in fencing and in equestrian events, for example, although morphological type does not play the primary role that people have tried to attribute to it, the body's skeletal type does play exactly such a role. Consequently, it is important to know what that type is. X-ray processes are there to achieve this. This knowledge is useful for the instructor, as well as for the student.

"Know thyself". This famous saying should be essential to athletic development. That is why I have advocated filming exercises, and why I have recommended to a major movie studio that they should develop small cameras that are easy to use and inexpensive. These cameras could provide a clear view of the athlete in motion – clear enough for the athlete to realize, in watching himself, the awkward movements he is making, thus making it possible for him to correct them. The instructor can critique the position of his students until he is blue in the face, but nothing will be as powerful for them as the irrefutable testimony of the movie. This applies not only to the rider, the fencer, and the rower, but more or less to all sports.

III

Let us move on to another order of idea, or rather to that indirect agent of development: the spectator. The spectator has always played this role, and does so now more than ever before because there are so many of them and because the sites where they gather are becoming increasingly large. Only the artist, a dramatic or comedic actor, a virtuoso singer or violinist, can say how strong the bond is that unites him to his public. There is a strange and troubling attachment that flows back and forth between them, sometimes rattling the most solid of nerves on the performer's part. It can stir the viewer or listener to approval or disapproval far beyond the bounds of fairness. This situation happens on the field and in other sports arenas, as well. One need only think about it – it comes as no surprise. One must also admit that it can be a source of progress or of potential reduction in capacity. At football matches, for example, we often see discouragement overwhelm a player on whom the public had placed great hopes. When we see this discouragement enter the player's body and run, as it were, throughout his limbs, we say "He is tired". That may well be true, but quite often it is the public, in fact, that feels disappointed and disillusioned. This collective feeling is sensed immediately, you can be sure, by the person who caused it. Certainly this is not a reason for his athletic development to be stunted. Yet all it takes is for this experience to happen several times in a row, and his progress will grind to a halt, perhaps even shift into reverse.

Here, then, are several points of view that one can use to assess the origins of athletic development. This topic could be amplified at considerable length if this paper were anything but a rapid overview, intended to provide a simple overall analysis, a quick survey.

What are the limits of this development? Will these sources of development that we have examined dry up or run their course? Everything changes, especially these days given our general haste, our taste for speed, and the means available to satisfy our desires. "Fashion", which is essentially a combination of the spirit of imitation and the spirit of novelty, has played a considerable role in athletic development. From the very beginning, over forty years ago, I have held that the renewed Olympism is big enough to encompass the whole world. The reason is that I saw Olympism as a sort of guarantee or insurance against any lack of constraint, or any hostility that may suddenly come into vogue. Once a trend has spanned the globe, it becomes more difficult to get rid of it. As time goes on, in fact, fashion is becoming a less significant element in athletic development, because sports tend to become a habit, then a need, in the individual.

But there is still more to the issue of spectators. It has been shown that the absence of spectators discourages athletes, even diminishing their abilities. This is almost a general rule. One of the troubling issues today, however, is that quite often nearly half the spectators, a good third of them in any case, do not understand much about the athletic event they are witnessing. Often it is these very spectators who show the greatest enthusiasm and cheer the loudest. A few years back, an Australian minister told me that one should only allow those who have played the sport themselves to enter a football stadium as spectators. This is an appealing witticism at first glance, but it is unfair. Football would gain in moral value in the process, but it would certainly also lose its appeal and attractiveness. It is also true that although spectators are necessary for athletic development, they may also be harmful to it in other ways or under certain circumstances. Moreover, various sports are popular with the public to differing degrees. Why does a crowd gather for one particular match, while it remains quite sparse at the most beautiful performances of a team of gymnasts on the apparatus?

For my part, I think it goes without saying that spectators are essential for maintaining the high level that sports have achieved in our day, for example. But since spectators are a mobile component, one might well inquire as to the boundaries within which that component is likely to grow. Is it absolutely essential that there be a crowd of spectators? No, it is not. There are thousands of examples to prove that very often athletes have performed just as well on days when the throng was less than expected. A certain level of discouragement may ensue when crowds are thinner than expected time after time. What is more, athletes are somewhat like actors in this regard. I remember seeing the leading artists of the Comédie Française perform admirably before a half-empty house in Chicago forty-three years ago. The famous Coquelin headed the cast. I do not know what happened, perhaps an English theater company was in town at the same time, and was preferred by the public. After the play, as I was talking with Coquelin about this incident, he told me, "We played as well as if the house had been full, did we not? That is because we played for ourselves. A real artist can forego the public, if he must. What he cannot stand, without suffering, is feeling less than perfect with regard to himself". This is a bit of a paradox, but it is nonetheless quite true. One can say the same for a top athlete, as well. He will always suffer if he feels he is unrecognized, but he will suffer even more if he holds himself in low esteem.

So as far as spectators go, it does not appear that either an increase or slight decrease in their numbers will have much of an impact on athletes. Perhaps, as the competence of spectators spreads and increases, athletes will appreciate that competence even more than they appreciate the sheer number of spectators.

IV

What about improvements in equipment? Are there any limits to it? In theory, no. Yet we must note that there are limits beyond which the equipment might, in a sense, replace man by making his efforts so easy. This would cross a line that might well be the very frontiers of sport. Let us consider a specific example. Ancient runners ran in the sand in order to increase the level of difficulty, and thus increase their own merit, as well. Modern runners are driven by the opposite concern. They want to make the race easier, in order to increase their speed. This has produced cinder tracks and shoes with cleats. But suppose we could imagine shoes, or even tracks, with springs that would somehow throw the runner forward with each step. In this case, it is not just the movement that is being made easier, but some of the athletic effort would then be done by the equipment the athlete is using. The speed achieved in this way will not be entirely his own.

No doubt, ingenious inventions may come along that we do not expect. Yet it is quite unlikely that these developments will ultimately be capable of greatly increasing athletic development. If this is so, the limits we are attempting to define here will be reached only through improvements in the human body. Obviously these improvements have limits, and cannot even be expanded considerably, though they can be made in significant proportions.

Individual improvement or collective improvement?

Will the individual or the race be at issue?

That is the question now posed by the rise of political institutions, an issue whose significance, I imagine, has not been fully appreciated by many people. In closing, I would like to say something about it.

If someone were to ask me what we need now to make a handsome athletic race, I would say: less nerve and more mental preparation, in an atmosphere of calm and proper proportion. That is what I meant when I tried to define modern Olympism

Winter training at the Thames Rowing Club, London 1906 (taken from Sport im Bild, no.48, 1906, p.1304)

when I created it. For a very long time, I was misunderstood. Finally, people did understand. Better late than never. Thousands of journalists and even athletics instructors have exercised their talents on this topic. The journalists did so without reflecting sufficiently on the matter, and instructors did so without the experimental athletic data necessary to support their reasoning. That is why progress has been so slow.

The idea that over-stimulation of the nerves in obedience to the will plays an effective role in athletic success has become widespread. One often speaks of an athlete who becomes victorious "sustained by his nerves". The expression is inappropriate, and such cases are, indeed, rare. The victorious athlete reaches his goal sustained by his body under the command of his will. In this arrangement, the nervous system is merely a subordinate, a servant. Yet it is a servant that has an unfailing tendency to set itself up as a master, and to exercise a most dangerous despotism over man, particularly over civilized man. The nervous system has a way of getting up on a pedestal and shouting: "I'm the genius here!" By dint of proclaiming this anti-truth, by dint of repetition, it has managed to take root in people minds generally. The nervous system, I repeat, is merely a servant, fractious by nature but very precious, provided that it is tamed from earliest youth and trained to obey at all times.

This is true of sports and in all other areas.

There remain many subconscious traits of the old belief in the basic incompatibility between the training of the muscles and the training of the mind. This is madness. This attitude can be explained historically, but it is a state of affairs that must no longer be tolerated. It is time to wipe this viewpoint out. Those who have participated in or run athletic programs know that intelligence rules in those programs as a matter of course. I would go so far as to say that intelligence rules them even more than it rules other activities. For me, intelligence means understanding; it does not mean knowledge, at least not knowledge in and of itself. But the use of knowledge is part of intelligence. I do not believe that knowledge, as specialized as it has become in our time, greatly develops a human being. In any case, the manner in which men are educated is inadequate and mediocre. Civilization consists of a mass of wealth on the one hand, and a mass of thought on the other. One cannot say that wealth is very wisely or reasonably distributed. We do not even have an accurate inventory of our riches yet. But ideas are not treated much better. Intellectual culture remains the prerogative of too restricted a number of individuals. It must be spread around, dispersed, popularized. A broadly intellectual atmosphere is required for athletics to flourish properly. A long time ago, a French novelist and friend of mine, Paul Bourget, said, "If only you knew how fruitful the marriage of vigorous physical exercise and intellectual culture is in terms of virile splendors!" The world is only barely beginning to realize this, if at all. And yet, the future is here.

I just said that in order for a handsome athletic race to flourish, an atmosphere of calm and proper proportion had to be prepared for it. Social calm does not mean some bourgeois tranquillity, it means order. Order can rule under widely differing political systems, but it will rule in institutions only if it rules first in people's minds. That is why modern progress is essentially educational, first and foremost.

Proper proportion is the sister of order. They are siblings, intended to grow up together. I use the term 'proportion,' but that is not the word I want. The term that springs to mind "eurythmia". In this regard, however, we, the French and the Germans, do not see eye to eye very well. The Germans believe that the concept of rhythm predominates in this Greek term. In French, we focus more attention on the first syllable. It evokes the idea of the beautiful, the perfect. Everything that is properly proportioned is eurythmic. It was Hellenism, above all else, that advocated measure and proper proportion, co-creators of beauty, grace, and strength. We must return to these Greek concepts to offset the appalling ugliness of the industrial age through which we have just lived.

Hellenism again! We used to believe that Hellenism was a thing of the past, a dead notion, impossible to revive and inapplicable to current conditions. This is wrong. Hellenism is part of the future. Its philosophy of life is suitable for and adaptable to modern existence. That is why sport is such an essential element in modern progress.

Les sources et les limites du progrès sportif [The origins and limits of athletic progress].
In: *Olympische Rundschau* (*Revue Olympique/Olympic Review*), Vol. 1, Berlin 1938, no. 2, pp. 1-2 (I); no. 3, pp. 1-2 (II),; no. 4, pp. 1-2 (III); no. 5, pp. 1-2 (end).

3.13 BETWEEN TWO BATTLES. FROM OLYMPISM TO THE POPULAR UNIVERSITY

Swept along by its desire for efficiency, the technology of the day, produced by a society undergoing a complete industrial transformation, did not take into consideration which means it used in bringing that transformation about. Ultimately, it was leaving out the essentially human element.

Intelligence and courage are essential in upholding the absolute value of man, regardless of an individual's status in the particular social order of the day.

The times called for an ethic of education and educational reform that would enable each individual to reach his full potential freely, in his essential truth. Pierre de Coubertin had understood this from the beginning of his educational efforts. As early as 1890 he developed this plan and started to look for allies.[1]

At Toynbee Hall, a private educational institution free of charge for the laborers in the very poor neighborhood of Whitechapel in London, Coubertin observed the work done to improve the lot of those whose pathetic fate centered on bitterness and regret at no longer being able to hope. Despite the material, moral, and physical poverty of the students, the education provided devotedly and regularly – by university student volunteers who lived among them – made it possible to discover the human richness of each worker, and to make that richness fruitful by awakening the creative spirit. Intellectual and physical culture can then accomplish their work unimpeded, never insisting on anything, but drawing strength from courage. By acting freely, each person takes possession of himself once again, and the present becomes a promise of the future. These results confirmed Coubertin's belief that in order for any city to be worthy of the name, it must, first and foremost, be a community of autonomous men acting in the service of higher values. A humanist does not dissociate man from society.[2]

Throughout his life, he worked passionately to establish a Popular University that would be able to facilitate the advancement of all individuals.[3]

My friends seem surprised that since I managed to win the Olympic battle on a broader scale than they had generally predicted, I was not content merely to work, from then on, to consolidate the results as they stood. They were surprised that I went ahead to engage in another battle on uncertain ground, with a small number of troops, and in the disturbing clarity of the dawn of social upheaval.

My initiative was not at all unpremeditated or hasty. Rather, it was an action readied long ago; recent events merely hastened its appearance, accentuating the need for it.

Sports began to be introduced into French schools thirty-five years ago. That, and the restoration of the international Olympic Games seven years later, put me in touch with school and university life in my native France as well as in other countries. I was in a position to note that, in fact, "the level of studies was declining".

1 Cf. Coubertin, "Appel pour la création d'un enseignement universitaire ouvrier [1890]." In: *Anthologie,* Aix-en-Provence, Impr. P. Roubaud, 1933, pp. 165-166.

2 See Coubertin, "Toynbee Hall. Le patronage social à Londres et les étudiants anglais." In: *La Réforme Sociale,* 2e série, tome III, 1er sept. 1887, pp. 227-233.

3 See Coubertin, *Mémoire concernant l'instruction supérieure des travailleurs manuels et l'organisation des universités ouvrières,* pamphlet, s.l. 1923 (11 pages).

That was being whispered about then in informed circles. Today it is spoken of aloud, pretty much everywhere. But today, as before, no serious work is being done to find a solution to the problem.

What is more, we would first have to agree on the cause of the problem. As I see things, the cause is easily identified. The implementation of "athletic education" gave me a chance to assess the mental status of students and teachers alike. I realized that one could not find fault either with the intelligence and good will of the students, nor the zeal and talent of the teachers. The methods? The methods have scarcely changed at all, despite many minor alterations in detail, not all of which have been for the better. These are the same methods that, in another age, produced clarity in young minds. Why do they not do so any more?

The reason is that the time foreseen by Berthelot has come, when, as he wrote many years ago:

> *"It will become impossible to assimilate all the discoveries of the age. Since the human mind can no longer absorb the vast majority of established facts, it will no longer be able to generalize, i.e. to expand and develop". This is a disturbing statement, and appears to have no way out. How can we get around this unavoidable consequence of scientific progress? Leibniz gives us the answer. He, too, prophesied when he said, in his Discourse on the Method of Certainty and the Art of Invention: "One may say that the sciences grow shorter as they increase, for the more truths one discovers, the more ready one is to recognize a regulated order in them, and to make propositions that are more and more universal, and of which other propositions are merely examples or corollaries, such that it is possible that a great many of those that have preceded us will be reduced over time to two or three general theses."*

These two ideas, brilliantly expressed by two great men in striking terms, have continuously guided my efforts as though they were the two great luminous orbs that the timeless figure drawn by Puvis de Chavannes holds aloft in his outstretched hands.

The central problem lay with what is called secondary education. That is where the remedy had to be applied. It is the task to primary school to lay the technical foundations of education. The advanced schools and universities are responsible for teaching practical or scientific specialties. Between these two schools, secondary education must be "a time of general ideas". That was the basic principle of the reform. It presupposed that synthesis would be replaced by analysis as the method of instruction. In fact, what has secondary education been until now, not only in France, but in most other countries as well? A broad effort at synthesis, carried out in the mind of the adolescent through various elements called physics, chemistry, literature, history, botany, etc. In the end, this was supposed to give the student a homogeneous concept of the world and of life. This synthesis no longer happens. The elements that once brought it about have become too numerous, and some essentials had to be discarded. Other are no longer used except in forms that are difficult to assimilate. Pointlessly advanced in some subjects while totally ignorant of others, the adolescent is disoriented by this artificial scattering of his knowledge, an overabundance of formulas and ready-made notions, and his inability to draw any practical conclusions from what he has learned.

Yet all of human existence is dominated by two realities: man depends on the planet on which he lives, on its movement, and on the laws of mechanics, physics, and chemistry that rule it. By the same token, man has sixty centuries of recorded history behind him, a time during which the heritage "that he inherits and for which he is responsible" was created. So let us take these two realities that govern our lives, and let us analyze them by going from the general to the particular, from general principles to details, from the overall scheme of things to more details explanations, depending on the time available. This will create a "time for general ideas" that, sandwiched between primary school and the university, will form the new style of secondary education, and will provide all students with an initial, beneficial insight.

These ideas, outlined for the first time in 1900[4], were not understood, and failed to excite public opinion. Explained in a more detailed manner seven years later[5], they were accused of utopianism, and aroused anger in some quarters. Yet a small core of supporters came together around these ideas. With the valuable support of my late friend Gabriel Lippmann, I set up detailed programs, one for sciences, the other for "humanities". Lippmann, an illustrious physician, was not the slightest bit hesitant in agreeing to "sabotage" physics and chemistry as independent parts of secondary education. He fully adhered to the idea that this independence did not need to be maintained to the detriment of other fields of knowledge. He also agreed that there is no educational or social interest at stake in having students learn which particular process of trial and error, or which experiments, gave rise to a particular law or a particular finding. We said that as far as the student was concerned, there is no such thing as physics or chemistry, strictly speaking, nor is there astronomy or geology. There are merely phenomena that are physical, chemical, astronomical, or geological in nature, etc. The student encounters these phenomena, and they must be explained to him during his "planetary excursion". His "historical excursion", for its part, must bring him step by step through all the centuries and across all the continents. Cutting history up into pieces like a cake, by period or by country, was excusable only at a time when historians had not yet "come full circle" in the ages, like geographers working on the oceans or elevations. Today, bridges have been built over the ignorance of yesteryear. Leibniz' comment takes on its full meaning. Let us take advantage of this fact to establish, deep in young minds, firm foundations on which the structure of the special knowledge needed for the proper functioning of modern societies can be built with absolute certainty.

An *Association for Educational Reform* was established, ultimately, to help spread these ideas and to establish our programs more widely. The title of the association was unfortunate. It said too much, or not enough. What is more, the association did not prosper. At the very first meeting of its board, at the Sorbonne, in the chambers of the Academic Council, a split formed that placed those who wanted secondary education to be completely revamped against those who wanted to limit

4 Notes sur l'Éducation Publique, Paris, Hachette 1901.
5 L'Analyse universelle Paris, Alcan, 1912.

actions to the post-secondary school level. After giving me grounds to hope that they would joint the first group, many went over to the side of the second. By questioning its very principles, these differences of opinion compromised and delayed our action. We resolved to wait, and to take advantage of the delay to continue to perfect our programs, by reviewing them for the third time, point by point.

Were these programs really capable of practical application? Some admirers continued to harbor doubts. War was to give us the opportunity to put them to the test. When internees began to flood into Switzerland, people who were by definition out of work and often disoriented by the peculiarity of their status, an effort was made to provide them with physical and mental activities. The Olympic Institute, plans for which I had drawn up in Lausanne back in 1913 but which was not yet functioning, appeared to be well suited for this purpose. It was suggested that I devote the Institute to the good of the French and Belgian internees. That is what happened. In addition to a wide variety of sports, those who were enrolled, including non-commissioned officers and even some officers, studied science and history according to the program of the defunct association. With the support of associates from time to time, two interned officers, Messrs. Trystram and Callandreau, joined me in shouldering the main effort. Through this experience, the "sciences" program was consolidated over time, and the "humanities" program, which used history as the guideline, was completely transformed.

I had traced out the canvas of world history in forty chapters, which left scarcely any time unaccounted for between them. The order in which they were arranged no longer pleased me, however. They needed a simpler, more striking, in a word more educational, organization. The division I ultimately adopted grouped the annals of man into four parts:

I. The Empires of Asia.
II. The Mediterranean Drama.
III. The Celts, the Germans, and the Slavs.
IV. The Formation and Development of Modern Democracies.

I did not stop to consider that in this classification, the first two titles were geographical in nature, the third ethnic, and the fourth political. What mattered was that all the events of history could fit into this framework, and that it could be used like an accordion (please pardon the pedestrian image). In other words, it could be used either for rapid overviews or for in-depth study. Successive audiences in Lausanne, Luxembourg, Mulhouse, and elsewhere, have shown that this framework is indeed elastic. They have convinced me to make this arrangement permanent, since it accomplishes what I set out to achieve.

The ancient chronicles tell of how, on the night of December 31 in the year 406 AD, the Barbarians crossed the Rhine and, overwhelming those who were guarding the river, spread throughout the Gauls.

This comparison has often come to mind when I think back to the closing days of 1916, when it seemed that the nations were crossing a painful crest, thereafter to spill out into the night over the unknown plains beyond the peaks. Then the nature of the fight changed. Great social spasms shook Russia to its foundations, raising equally passionate hopes and fears on all sides. Economic dangers appeared,

SOCIÉTÉ DES SPORTS POPULAIRES

Une équipe de football dans chaque commune — Un gymnase et un terrain de jeu municipaux avec bains-douches dans chaque bourg — Une piscine de natation dans chaque ville — Des rameurs sur toutes les rivières — De l'équitation et de la boxe individuelles chaque fois que l'occasion se présente — Une section chorale dans chaque société de gymnastique — Le moins possible de règlements, de hiérarchie et d'insignes — Pas de politique, pas de paris, pas de "dirigeants" étrangers au sport.

Cher M. Depaquiat
Avez vous mes livres en vente?
Prévenez moi dès que vous les aurez
Car cette affaire m'inquiète
à vous
P.C.

Coubertin liked using letters and postcards bearing the mottoes of his initiatives. After 1905, he very often used this postcard with mottoes from the popular sport campaign. Translation: "Association of Popular Sport
• A football team in every village.
• A gymnasium and a playfield in every small town.
• An outdoor swimming pool in every town.
• Rowing on every river.
• Horse-riding and boxing for everyone wherever it is possible.
• A department for singing in every sports club.
• No more rules, superiors, and rewards than absolutely necessary.
• No politics, political parties and no outside influences on sport." (taken from J.Durry (ed.dir.), Sport et Démocratie, Catalogue, Paris, Assemblée Nationale, 1998, p.3H)

against which no one had yet taken any defensive action. There was a confused sense that this war was not going to be like any other, and that, dominated by a new element – the unity of the world – , this war was creating unexpected opportunities. Once it was over, accumulated rancor and cramped appetites would clash in a gigantic battle for the conquest of power. Merely pushing the working class back into its previous status was not an option. The only choices open to discussion were to join forces with it or to submit to it.

Various opinions are in the process of being formed about these alternatives. Some, in light of the flaws in and the breakdown of society, its inability to reform itself, are attached to the idea of a new, more just society – and thereby a more Christian society. Others think that we have what it takes to rebuild, and that it is just a matter of time until that is apparent. But in the near future, whether the working class is in full control of power or merely involved in the exercise of that power, the issue of preparing that class is just as essential. Yet there is no such preparation. Some of us were already concerned about this situation years ago. Recently, I came across the text of an invitation I sent out in 1890 to about twenty qualified individuals, for the purpose of studying ways to prepare "the fourth estate" (in those days, the term "the fourth estate" was used to designate the proletariat) for the governmental mission that the expansion of democracy seemed to be reserving for them. The meeting never took place. No one was interested in it, except for the Rector, Mr. Gréard, who had assured me of the Sorbonne's hospitality (the old Sorbonne, this time). Perhaps he was perhaps motivated by his interest in seeing me leave the field of physical education, where my efforts were annoying him a bit.

Time has passed. The problem has become severe, so severe that some, believing that it is too late to take any practical steps, are now resigned to what they call the collapse of culture, and the return to a primitive barbarian condition. I am not such a person. I expect a great deal of the working class. It is possessed of splendid strengths, and seems to me to be capable of great things. Moreover, are we not deluding ourselves a bit as far as that culture, of which we are so proud, is concerned? There is so much dross mixed in with the pure metal, so much incoherence, insipidness, hollow vanity, and thinly disguised pornography!

Whatever the case may be, here is how the issue stands, as I see it. There is no way to link the working class suddenly with high culture *as the previous age understood it*. The working class must prepare its own inventory of high culture, so that if the temple that contains the accumulated wealth of civilization should be entrusted to its care in the future, that temple will be respected and maintained.

From this viewpoint, a plan for labor universities was devised. In writing it up, the work and experiments that I have just discussed were extremely helpful to me, even though this plan differs in some respects. These are intermittent universities. The plan calls for two three-month sessions a year, with the administration entirely in the hands of the workers. The teaching is divided into eighty-four lessons per session, twenty-four of which are devoted to the study of world history, thirty-six to the general structure of science, eight to philosophy, six to criticism and eurythmia, and ten to exercises in language and style.

All this is novel. One must agree that it would be impossible for me, in the space of these few pages, to give even a brief overview. The project is already familiar to those interested in it. It is up to them to assess it and to use it as they see fit. In any event, manuals must be prepared for them, the "text books" needed for this different concept of education, according to which the educated man will no longer be only an individual who has honed his style and his thought through contact with certain masterpieces, but above all, a man for whom what we might call the five basic notions remain clear and present: the idea of astronomy, the immeasurable universe within which the heavenly body that carries us moves; the idea of the earth, and of the laws that govern that heavenly body; the idea of history, of the accomplishments of preceding generations; the idea of proper hygiene, of the human machine, of its potential output and the means to watch over it; and the idea of philosophy, of the thirst for the ideal, for justice, for light, and for the beyond that has always tormented man, and always will torment him, forever differentiating him from the animals.

"What?" you may say, "you want to teach all that to manual laborers? What foolishness! They have neither the time nor the taste for such studies."

I know; I am familiar this disdain and these ironies. When I planned to re-establish the Olympic Games, people took me for a madman, too.

Yet the Games were re-established, and the principle of the Games has now been accepted by all nations. The rhythm of the Olympiads has entered the fabric of international life, and is now a regular factor in that life. The Eighth Olympiad is to be celebrated in Paris in 1924, along with the thirtieth anniversary of the restoration of the Games. Amsterdam is already beginning to prepare for the Games of the Ninth Olympiad in 1928. In faraway countries, youths are training in the muscular exertions that will earn them the honor of appearing in the stadium on the walls of which, through a recent decision of the International Olympic Committee, the names of the victors shall be carved from now on. This Committee, which I have had the honor of chairing from the start, and on which sit representatives of forty-two countries in Europe, America, Asia and Africa is, as was said last year on the rostrum in Geneva, a miniature League of Nations. Through over twenty-seven years of operation, it has faced many conflicts but it has never failed in its task. It has moved on at a steady pace, along a path of progressive internationalism.

It is that very internationalism which, these days, is the best, or rather the only guarantee of the survival of the movement for athletic renewal that is so necessary for the health of modern societies. Let us make no mistake, *sports are not natural for man*, and the athleticism of a people is an artificial and delicate plant. Without the religion, the spectacle, the hubbub, and the advertising that prolonged its existence, Ancient Olympia would never have thrived for so many centuries. The athleticism of the Middle Ages, so little known by so well worth knowing, was unable to sustain itself for very long, despite all the elements that made it so lively. The modern movement is in no way the result of spontaneous actions. It came about only through the stubborn initiative of a few individuals, Jahn in Germany, and Arnold and Kingsley in England, who succeeded where Amoros had failed. In 1886, when my colleagues and I undertook to "toughen France up again" through sports by forcing open the doors of the secondary schools, France was anything but well disposed to our plan. A friendly writer once related the story of our efforts[6]. But the cause has not yet been won. Let us beware. Periods of athleticism in History have been short-lived and rare. In this field, as in others, England is flagging quickly. In France, a sumptuous facade is being built. Behind it, there are plenty of holes. Even now, nowhere is the future of sports assured. At least the Olympic torch is running from city to city around the world. Its course extends even to the Far East. Should the runners grow weary, some young nation will come forth to take the torch from the unconcerned hands that were ready to let it fall.

Thus the athletic flame will be kept from being extinguished. That is why I re-established the Olympic Games, and not for the vainglory of restoring lost architecture.

Entre deux batailles. De l'Olympisme à l'Université ouvrière.
In: *La Revue de la Semaine*, Vol. 3, January 20, 1922, no. 1, pp. 299-310.

6 "Le Néo-Olympisme et la Guerre" [Neo-Olympism and the War],in: *Revue Hebdomadaire,* May 10, 1917.

3.14 FATHER DIDON

This is an obituary on Coubertin's fatherly friend, the Dominican priest Henri Didon, who died on March 13, 1900[1]. It is well known that the Olympic motto "citius, altius, fortius" came from him, and in the presence of Coubertin he made an impression on his pupils with this motto at the start of a sports festival at the school in Arcueil, on March 17, 1891. In 1894, Coubertin made this into the Olympic motto. But the article is not about this; rather it is to praise the all-round achievements of a great man as preacher, pedagogue and proud Frenchman. Coubertin praises his free spirit and critical thinking within the French church[2].

Just after a statue of Lavigerie, the great cardinal who was both a great patriot and a vigorous pioneer of civilization, was dedicated on the shores of Africa, death came too soon for a monk who was to become, in France, the Lavigerie of education.

Anyone who had contact with Father Didon saw his soul, for it was always on the front lines, on the hill top, looking straight ahead, taking special care to be in plain sight at all times. The struggle was his greatest passion; he sought it out even in the pulpit. One day he said to me, "It's funny, when a congregation doesn't resist me, I feel paralyzed. That's why, sometimes, I deliberately go beyond the bounds of my own thought, to force them into revolt."

Work was his second passion, and modernism the third. I recall a speech he once gave at an awards ceremony. Before my spellbound students and their uneasy parents, with unparalleled boldness he launched a frontal assault on the bête noire of the day, anti-Semitism, calling it by its real name: laziness. His irony was biting as he took on a spiritless society that complained of being dominated and manipulated by a bunch of Jews.

In broad outline, he pointed out productive careers in trade, industry, finance, and the colonies, and manly and noble occupations, as well as the military, to his young French audience. Of course, he loved the national armed forces, and the last speech he gave in honor of the services was accused of amounting to flattery of the officers present. The newspapers reported summaries of it. I, at least, saw the speech merely as a grandiose philosophical view of the role of force in the world, though that view may have been a bit overstated.

Unity in the life of such a man is expressed not through his words, but through his deeds. Everything that Fr. Didon ever did was directed toward the same goal: to be a man of his time. For him, there was no retreat from, not any regret for, the past – nor was there fear or reticence with regard to the future.

He felt that he was doing what he was meant to do when young men were entrusted to him for their education. As a preacher, his bold use of language was more charming than disturbing. As an educator, he set a powerful example. In all his varied activities, he sowed love and true liberalism all around him. He was always looking for ways to get his students involved with students in public secondary schools. He himself was also looking to meet people whose way of thinking differed from his own.

In the context of these brief letters, I cannot relate all the beauty and moral strength that my close friendship with him these past ten years has shown me in him. Perhaps I will do so at another time.

The Dominican priest Henri Didon (1840-1900) (N.Müller Collection)

Now that he is gone, who can fill the place he carved out for himself? There is no education in France. We know only how to prepare syrupy little sacristans or shriveled little logicians. Truly I admire the reserves of strength and intelligence that enable our race to withstand the inept distortion to which it has been subjected for so long.

Le Père Didon. Lettre d'un indépendant, N° XVI [Letter from an Independent, No. 16], in: *L'Indépendance Belge*,Vol. 71, April 11, 1900, p. 1.

1 Cf. S. Hoffmane, *La carrière du Père Didon, dominicain (1840-1900).* PhD Thesis, Paris-Sorbonne IV, 1981.

2 See also text 5.2/4 "New Mottoes" in this volume.
See also N. Müller, "Henri Didon - Der Urheber der Olympischen Devise", in: N. Müller, M. Messing (eds.): *Auf der Suche nach der Olympischen Idee.* Kassel, Agon, 1996, pp. 49-62.
See also A. Arvin-Bérod, *Les Enfants d'Olympe.* Paris, CERF, 1996.
See also M. Lochmann: "Les fondements pédagogiques de la devise olympique "citius, altius, fortius". "In: N. Müller (ed. dir.): *Coubertin and Olympism.* Questions for the Future. Report of the Congress 17th to 20 th September 1997 at the University of Le Havre. Sydney, Walla Walla Press, 1998, pp. 92-101.

3.15 MENS FERVIDA IN CORPORE LACERTOSO (1911)

Modern sport goes to excess, Coubertin wrote elsewhere. This requires a motto which corresponds to the bodily effort of the athlete and the shaping of his character. The much-quoted Latin phrase by the writer Juvenal "mens sana in corpore sano" is completely unsuitable to be applied to modern athletics, as it covers only the hygienic aspect of sport, says Coubertin, and as such belongs in the Museum for Ancient History. The phrase "mens fervida in corpore lacertoso" coined by the latinist Merlet corresponds perfectly to Coubertin's understanding of sport.[1]

All things shall pass. Revolutions overturn not only governments, but systems as well. The poor old *mens sana* which had served as a speaking topic for so many orators has been relegated to the Museum of Ancient History. No longer will anyone dare comment on it when handing out awards, nor seek an indisputable system of wisdom in those five words. New words will replace the old. Our active age suddenly realized that it was advocating a prescription for mediocrity and inertia. To be healthy: so what! Do you conquer the world with negative characteristics? Yet let us make a few distinctions. Healthy bodies are not yet the general rule, and alas, healthy minds are at least as rare, or even rarer. To wish this twofold good on one's neighbor is not to express some superfluous wish. It is a very helpful call to individual effort, to achieve (to the extent possible) that priceless "sanity", the source of equilibrium and comfort or, one might even say, happiness. Yet this ideal remains a little too clinical to apply to the ambitions of sportsmen. The saying *Mens sana in corpore sano* is excellent in terms of proper hygiene, but not at all in terms of athletics. That bothered Mr. Coubertin. Even something truly athletic was not enough for him. He wanted something Olympic. He had decided that the mind had to be impassioned, and the body well trained. Tell us more! This is the kind of young people you need to hold wonderful "Sorbonne festivals", where young people act on stage in a most erudite manner, handily throwing in a "reverse waist lock" worthy of the best wrestler in mid-dialogue. He called upon Mr. Morlet, that exquisite Latinist and former principal of the Lycée Michelet, to assist him. Morlet, a scholarly friend of sport, quickly came up with the most suitable words to translate this new thinking into the language of Cicero. They found the words they had been looking for. The new motto was presented at Budapest for the first time, where it met immediately with the approval of those who heard it. It so happens that, as the motto reads, the typical Hungarian is rather "*fervidus*", and willingly "*lacertosus*". The applause was thunderous. This expression is now on its way around the globe. It has been carved in bronze in commemoration of the most recent Olympic Games. It is most appropriate, indeed. The gentlemen concerned with proper hygiene still have their *Mens sana* on their hands, and their *corpore sano*; they know how to go about it, and they will gain great profit from it. The athletes, for their part, will have to maintain quite a delicate balance between the exuberant zeal of the mind and the daring suppleness of the body. Their effort will be a bit like flying in airplanes. Sometimes people fall out of them and die, but it is a glorious end. On such wings, however, those who remain aboard have a shot, at least, at reaching the highest peaks of pure Olympism.

Mens fervida in corpore lacertoso, in:
Revue Olympique, July 1911, pp. 99-100.

"Mens fervida in corpore lacertoso" – "a fervent spirit in a well-trained body" perfectly reflects Coubertin's understanding of sport. Coubertin drew the title page with this motto himself (Navacelle Collection)

1 About this motto see also texts 5.1/10 and 5.2/4 in this volume.

3.16 SPORT AND THE SOCIAL ISSUE

The Olympic Congress on Sports Psychology and Physiology in 1913 in Lausanne was heavily criticized in a left-wing socialist Swiss newspaper. Coubertin feels obliged to emphasize the social importance of sport. He stresses the equality of all athletes in the stadium. Two concepts underlie every sports event: mutual assistance and competition. These are also the basis of modern democracy, he argues. As such, the social issue in sport is part of every human struggle for justice. Without saying that he is the author, Coubertin quotes in German the corresponding verse of the "Ode to Sport" with which he won the Olympic gold medal in the 1912 literature contest in Stockholm.[1]

The violence unleashed against the Congress of Lausanne in one Swiss socialist revolutionary tract would not have been worthy of attention except for the fact that, at nearly the same moment, efforts were also underway to organize socialist athletic groups. This correlation is in keeping with two trends that are apparent in these circles, regarding the social role that sports can play in our time. That role is considerable, but it is clearly a pacifying role. That is exactly why the progress of sports is of interest to some socialists, while it irritates others. The progress of sports irritates those who support class warfare, and draws the sympathetic interest of those who place their hopes in gentler means to bring about the changes that they desire in the organization of society.

The practice of athletic exercise does not iron out inequalities in social conditions, but it does place relationships on an equal footing. In this respect, form is likely more important than content. After all, who would dare guarantee that equal conditions will produce social peace? Nothing could be more uncertain. Things are quite different, however, with regard to the egalitarianism of relationships. It is easy to say that this is the most useful type of egalitarianism to implement in a democracy. The example of America, though too brief to draw definitive sociological conclusions yet, provides intriguing evidence of what I am advocating here. There are few countries where conditions are more unequal, yet relationships more egalitarian. So far, however, social peace has reigned there more completely and more solidly than elsewhere.

Egalitarianism – no doubt easier to establish in a new country – does not arise and is not sustained on its own anywhere but on the playing field. There, it is truly imposed first of all through attire. The athletic uniform has never been very complicated, but it is becoming simpler every day as the habit spreads of exercising in the nude. Soon elegance in clothing will no longer be an issue, except with regard to the shape of the body and the quality of the skin. Social distinctions have nothing to do with inequalities based on such features. After dress come actions. Who will be the strongest, the fastest, the toughest? This is truly the proper occasion to repeat the words written by authors of the *Ode to Sport* heard in Stockholm:

O Sport, du bist die Gerechtigkeit!
Vergeblich ringt der Mensch nach Billigkeit und Recht
In allen sozialen Einrichtungen;
Er findet beide nur bei Dir.

The social aspects of sport were particularly important after the First World War. Swimming was popular with everyone, young or old. The primitive facilities at this swimming pool in Bingen am Rhein in 1922 fail to spoil the swimmers' enjoyment (N.Müller Collection)

Um keinen Zoll vermag der Springer seinen Sprung zu höhen.
Nicht um Minuten die Dauer seines Laufs.
Die Kraft des Leibes und des Willens Spannung ganz allein
Bestimmen die Grenzen seiner Leistung.[2]

Yet egalitarianism is not engendered by the athletic act alone, but by the details that surround it, that prepare for it, and that follow after it, as well. More often than not, this all calls for a good dose of manual labor. Once a fellow worker lends you a hand, you must return the favor when necessary, without the slightest concern for social rank between the parties. The consideration to which both of you are entitled in the field is not measured by the quality of your ancestors or the number of thousand-franc notes you have. It is measured by the strength of your muscles, your physical energy, and the strength of your effort.

In this brief analysis, we have touched on two points that we should consider at greater length, because they allow us to raise the question to a slightly higher level. We have just seen two characteristics of sports, the bases needed for any

1 "Ode to Sport." See text 5.3/10 in this volume.

2 Oh Sport, you are Justice! The perfect fairness which men seek in vain in their social institutions rises around you of its own accord. No man can surpass by one centimetre the height he can jump or the time for which he can run. His combined strength of body and mind alone set the bounds to his success.

athletic group that wants to prosper. These characteristics are *mutual assistance* and *competition*. At first glance, these may seem to be of unequal value. Theoretically that is true, but in practice one must acknowledge that one is as important as the other. Competition by itself does not create an athletic spirit, without which the group is bound to collapse, if it ever manages to get together in the first place. Sport calls for an intense spirit of competition and solid camaraderie. Anyone who has had any experience of this will corroborate what we are saying. Thus, sport is based on mutual assistance and competition.

These same principles serve as the foundations of modern democracy. The ethnic, economic, industrial, and scientific conditions in which nations develop and evolve today impose harsh and constant individual competition on them. Nothing points to relaxation of this arrangement any time soon. Mutual assistance is essential in alleviating these conditions. Without it, one might well imagine a return not to the barbarian ways of old, but to a kind of barbarian existence that might not be much better than the old one. Happily, mutual assistance pops up everywhere. It is like a herb that grows all by itself, right next to the poison for which it is the antidote. A feeling of solidarity is spreading throughout society, which sees it as a key precondition for proper balance and health. It is unplanned, and widespread.

Sport would seem an excellent preparatory school for our lives these days, and an excellent peacemaker, too. Note that these principles of competition and mutual assistance are linked closely to the egalitarianism we were discussing earlier – an equality not of conditions, but of relationships; one might say an equality not of "resources", but of "manners". So it all fits together, and one can readily understand how sport acts counter to everything that might tend to encourage class warfare. It destroys envy because of the absolute, nearly mathematical justice of which it boasts. It drives away ill will, replacing it with a zest for life. It reduces social distance, at times eliminating it altogether, at times going so far as to overturn the social hourglass by placing a humble craftsman higher than a prince. It quickens the spirit of the struggle, of effort, and of risk, yet the innate solidarity it engenders counteracts any woefully brutal or wild excesses that the taste for the struggle, the effort, and the risk might stir up. What other factor can we find that is capable of influencing social relations this way? It cannot be said too often: the only effect of this influence is to ease social tensions. Some socialists fear this result because the mediocre plans they have devised, plans that remain more or less unacknowledged, would be upset or compromised. Other socialists who are really seeking only the public good , as they see it, are ready to take advantage of the unanticipated and potent support, which everyone finds acceptable, that sports offer.[1]

Le Sport et la question sociale, in:
Revue Olympique, August 1913, pp. 120-123.

3.17 OLYMPIC LETTER V: OLYMPIC PEDAGOGY

In this important article for readers of the *Gazette de Lausanne,* Coubertin coins the term "Olympic Pedagogy", which needs "permanent factories". By this, Coubertin means the individual freedom of each person to practice sport, developing equality and fraternity from this practice, and becoming involved in building new democratic forms of the state following the chaos of World War I. Coubertin demands that Olympism be involved in the realization of human rights. In this way, he is anticipating modern developments in an almost prophetic way. Olympic pedagogy is, thus, a principle of life founded on the practice of sport.

This Olympic pedagogy which I recently said was based at once on the cult of effort and on the cult of eurythmy – and consequently on the love of excess combined with the love of moderation – is not sufficiently served by being glorified before the world once every four years in the Olympic Games. It needs permanent factories. The Olympic factory of the ancient world was the gymnasium. The Olympiads have been renewed, but the gymnasium of antiquity has not – as yet. It must be.

It must be for the particular reason that municipal institutions are going to play the foremost part in the world to come. The State, whether we like it or not, is in process of collapsing. The huge idol still receives the adoration of the faithful, and they even seem more numerous than ever, but no oracle will fall henceforth from its closed lips. In the wings the priestly college is in confusion; it feels the fatal and imminent discomfiture approach.

Both those who wish to preserve the former social scaffolding while repairing it and those who wish to replace it by a new scaffolding have an equal interest in making the city the basic cell of their activity. From all sides it will be approached and asked to solve the most varied problems. The era of wide dominions has ended. A striking disaggregation is about to begin everywhere. The movement, which for two hundred years has carried Europe towards the agglomeration of its peoples and towards administrative unification, is giving way to the aim of achieving social equality. This aim will be pursued locally. Satisfaction with enlarged boundaries and the beauties of bureaucratic uniformity will no longer move the masses.

In the modern city that is about to be born – as in its illustrious predecessor, the Greek city – the gymnasium is destined to hold an eminent and essential place. Let us therefore draw up a plan of its main porticos.

Lettre Olympique V, in:
La Gazette de Lausanne, no.325, November 28, 1918, pp.1-2.

1 See also text 2.6 "Social Education" in this volume.

3.18 OLYMPISM AT SCHOOL: IT MUST BE ENCOURAGED!

When he wrote this article, Coubertin was planning an on-going series of courses on Olympism at the Centre Universitaire Méditerranéen in Nice.

When the series began, given his advanced age, he was able to give a series of only three courses. He was unable to assume the duties and responsibilities of a "chair of Olympic studies." Therefore, the existence of such a chair at Nice was short-lived.[1]

The establishment of a "Chair of Olympic Studies" at the Centre Universitaire Méditerranéen in Nice breaks down a door that, despite appearances, was not yet open even a crack. Of course, the alleged opposition between the muscles and the mind, though is continues to haunt many brains that are unconsciously reactionary, is no longer so widely professed. A youthful audience would laugh at the idea. But there was a gulf separating that notion from the idea that a fruitful alliance of the two could official enter the educational playing field. That gulf was more than a mere step; it was a big leap. Mr. de Monzie must be thanked for having helped make it possible. Mr. de Monzie likes new things, especially when they are wearing classical tunics. That was the case, here. In addition, the principle involved is essentially Mediterranean. But how far? Olympism did not come to the world spontaneously in Rome, or Egypt, or Carthage, of course, nor among the Ligurians nor, certainly, among the Cretans. But it is Hellenic, beyond all question, and even excessively so. There is a whole historical preamble that must be taken into account. And then, what does Asia make of all this? What do the Hindus (outside of Alexander), the Japanese, or the Chinese have to say? And the Scandinavians and the Germans – and the Quechua or the Maya? It can easily be shown that among a great many people – not all – the athletic instinct is present, even right from their very origins. Is this Olympism? Not at all. In order for Olympism to become manifest, the athletic instinct must be surrounded by esthetic and moral concerns, as well. It must invite philosophy to arbitrate its competitions, and in some way the national religion, whether a lay religion or not, must act as a backdrop.

It is remarkable that all this was present in embryonic form in the unintended Olympism that nearly took root during the Middle Ages. It was quick to take shape because it was full of vigor, but it faded just as fast for various reasons, but mainly because it was never a matter of state or a matter of education, as ancient Olympism had been. Chivalry became scattered and dissipated. Yet a few bits of the ideal, twice blessed by the prestige of success, continued to shine in the thought of Ling de Jahn and of Thomas Arnold. There were a few traces of it, too, in the tentative work of Amoros, work that collapsed as soon as it began.

All this is not merely history, but biology seen from the perspective of the psyche, so long and so obstinately ignored as a viewpoint. Simply by attempting to draw up even the most summary of lists, Olympic education reveals its wealth and diversity.

During the "intellectual" period of the life of the International Olympic Committee, when the *Revue Olympique* served as its publication and primarily during the first fifteen years of this century, from the Congress of Le Havre (1897) to the war, more or less, such subjects were pointed out, and the ground work laid for future efforts. Recently, the Bureau International de Pédagogie

Coubertin is awarded a special "Chair of Olympic Studies" at the Centre Universitaire Méditerranéen in Nice, 1931. (Photo: N.Müller)

Sportive has taken up where that work left off. It is clear that an initiative such as the one mentioned at the beginning of this article is well positioned to enable them to direct public opinion soon, an opinion that has so far been content to remain distracted and distant. In this way, athletic education will be called upon definitively to take its proper place on account of its objective, as the Congress of Lausanne defined it twenty years ago.

L'Olympisme à l'école. Il faut l'encourager,
in: *La Revue Sportive Illustrée*, Vol. 30,
1934, special issue, [p. 36].

1 About the topic of "Olympic Education" in schools at the beginning of the 21th Century, see N. Müller, Olympische Erziehung [Olympic Education], in: O. Grupe / D. Mieth (eds.), *Lexikon der Ethik im Sport,* Schorndorf, Hofmann, ^{2}1999, pp. 385-395. See also the introduction of chapter 5 in this volume.

3.19 OLYMPIC LETTER VI: PANEM ET CIRCENSES

The sixth Olympic Letter for the readers of the *Gazette de Lausanne* looks at the fundamental question of what value sports activity has for the ordinary person. For Coubertin, because of the decline of the monarchies and the new world order after the disaster of World War I, the answer lies in the regular practice of sport. Sport will provide people with a durable form of social cohesion, and give back to young people in all countries their belief in the future.

The human race has always asked its rulers for amusement as well as a livelihood. "Panem et circenses" – bread and the circus – cried the Roman world. Today's formula is no more educative, and more vulgar. "Potatoes and the cinema", demands the crowd. We already have official departments for potatoes and we are in danger of some day having ministries of the cinema. Could nothing better be found?

Let us look around us and see what are the general needs of the age. It seems that the primary effort is towards a more just distribution and remuneration of labor, then towards a better delimitation between the area of public services and that of private initiative, whose frontiers are drawn in a frequently vague and sometimes absurd fashion, and lastly towards an education within the range of all and no longer the monopoly of a small number. But all these reforms risk remaining sterile unless we succeed in creating a center for popular spectacles and enjoyments in which a simple, clear and tangible idea can draw together not only people of all ages and all professions, but of all opinions and all situations. Do not imagine that a democracy can live healthily if its citizens have nothing to hold them together but legal texts and electoral summons. Formerly there were the public solemnities of the Church and the splendid pomp of the monarchy. How are you going to replace them? By unveiling statues and making speeches in frock coats? Go on!

There is only one cult that is capable of engendering a permanent kind of civic unity today, and that is the cult which will develop around youthful exercise, symbol of the endurance of the race and the hopes of the nation.

And into the bargain this cult will kill that of the bottle.

Lettre Olympique VI,
in: *La Gazette de Lausanne*, no.331, December 4, 1918, p.3.

3.20 OLYMPIC LETTER VIII: THE FORMATION OF CHARACTER

Physical exercise for organic balance or to gain physical strength? In the following text, Coubertin tries to explain these two different functions to the readers of the *Gazette de Lausanne.*

The alpha and omega of everything we have said hitherto is the distinction that must be repeatedly stressed between physical exercise as a mere agent of organic compensation and physical exercise as a creator of moral force and national force. In the first case it simply supplies the counterpoise of moderate and well-dosed movement to an adolescent or man whose existence is too sedentary or too cerebral; it then plays the same part with regard to the individual's health as the policeman plays with regard to public safety. In the second case physical exercise – if conceived and applied in a certain way – can help to forge character, reburnish a community, and even, in democratic times, to provide a link between different social classes. It then escapes from its narrow physiological frontiers, establishes itself at the center of education between psychology on the one hand and art on the other, and becomes a main factor in general progress. Such it was in ancient Greece; such it nearly became in the middle ages; as such it has arisen again in the modern world, at first unconsciously among the Anglo-Saxons at the time of Kingsley and Thomas Arnold, and then in a world-wide and definite manner after the revival of the Olympic Games as proclaimed in Paris in 1894.

The error consists in thinking that these two conceptions of physical exercise are parallel and must be governed by common rules. In reality they are divergent, both in aims and methods. The one exalts effort, while the other is scared of it; the one seeks out danger while the other proscribes it. This explains the diversity of their functions. Physical exercise is always suitable for bringing equilibrium to an organism. If men neglect to bear this in mind, it will be to the detriment of the health of the next generation, if not of their own. But on the other hand it is only at certain historical epochs that physical exercise is called upon by general consent to accomplish a task of renewal, of restoration, of general rigor. We are living in such an epoch.

Lettre Olympique VIII,
in: *La Gazette de Lausanne*, no.341, December 14, 1918, pp.1-2.

3.21 ADDRESS DELIVERED AT ANTWERP CITY HALL IN AUGUST, 1920: SPORT IS KING.

In 1920, Coubertin uses the opening of the 19th IOC Session in Antwerp, in the presence of the King of Belgium, to justify giving priority to sport under the motto "Sport is King".

This consists of three elements: progressive work; unfaltering devotion to a disinterested ideal; and daily adoption of service to all.

According to Coubertin, sport establishes the principles that form all democratic order. For this reason, he also uses this speech to call for young people from the proletariat to be given free access to sport.

Your Highness, Your Honor the Burgomaster, Gentlemen:
Sport is King.

Can we harbor any lingering doubt as to its royalty now that we hear so much outstanding testimony to that effect every day, primarily the fact that after an anguished period of unbelievable violence and scope, the course of the modern Olympiads is resuming with a dependability unmatched in antiquity? Clearly Belgium has been key to this success. Belgium has expressed its wish to add to the national honor it won in 1914 the honor it is winning in 1920, the honor of organizing the Games intelligently and rapidly, or, if I may use an expression that is more candid than scholarly, the honor of its resourcefulness. Belgium has won that record, as well. Under the circumstances, Belgium's honor advances rather than diminishes the athletic strength of which the Olympic Games are both a symbol and an expression.

Royalty of any kind runs risks. The future of sport, crowned though it may be with the favor of the people and the enthusiasm of youth, is no exception. We who are, in a way, its worldwide chancery must ensure, to the extent possible, the endurance of its power, working to make that power ever more effective and prestigious. What factors make for the true stability of a throne? Such a question is most appropriate in this country. The answers lie close at hand – all we need do is look around us.

Three things make the future of sovereignty certain: progressive work done with judicious boldness, an ever-vigilant concern for ideals and selflessness, and finally, daily adaptation to the common good, to the service of all. Armed with this precious information, we can set about drawing up plans for a wise athletic policy.

I

The progress of sports, technical progress in particular, has gone uninterrupted since it resumed its rightful place in education. However, let us take care that the technical perspective not harm the educational point of view, which requires that things happen fairly discretely. Education is ill suited to fanfares and festive facades. Progress would not be served – far from it! – if we mistook preparatory physical education for athletic education (itself still full of untapped resources), and introduced more bureaucracy in the form of a class of mandarins, with all the attendant promotions and permanent inspectors, into the machinery of State. Nor would progress be served if, under the pretext of publicity, the press waged an intensive campaign to stir up the tide of disapproval that inevitably follows the impact of a trend foisted on public opinion. Finally, progress would not be served if scientific affectation invaded the field, or if athletic instructors, busy as they are searching for the ideal way to train muscles, became devotees of physiological Jacobinism, just as carried away by discipline and uniformity as political Jacobins can be.

Sport needs freedom. It requires respect for individuality, the chance for each individual to adapt the good or bad aspects of his own nature to exercise, both those that lend him an advantage and those that present a handicap. What, then, will athletic progress be? What path should we take to encounter it? The answer is simple. Let us work toward making the daily practice of sports easier, toward increasing the number of auspicious occasions that call upon the individual to break down useless barriers, to simplify complex regulations. Let us make athletic equipment available everywhere, and let us continue to perfect that equipment even as we seek to make it less expensive to manufacture. Let us try to draw the various sports closer together, to combine them, and to ennoble them by delighting in their divergence and in the harmony of their similarity. This is the direction in which we must head, the path along with we should direct our steps with every confidence.

II

Yet we would accomplish nothing if these material improvements did not go hand in hand with moral improvement, which is essential.

Commercialism has been a threat to sports since long before the terrifying boost provided by recent events. The two great athletic movements in history, Greek athleticism and the chivalry of the Middle Ages, had to withstand attacks in their own right. Although eventually they succumbed to those attacks, it was only after long and valiant resistance against them. No sooner had the modern movement begun to take shape than corruption tried to find its way in. Corruption means more than profit, the thirst for money that directly or indirectly tempts the athlete, the champion, in a thousand clever ways, but also distracts him and soon defeats his chivalrous spirit. Once the athlete stops placing delight in his own efforts above all else, and the intoxication of physical strength and balance that result from them, once he allows himself to be dominated by considerations of vanity or self-interest, his ideals become tainted. His value as an educational example, if one can use that expression, is irretrievably diminished.

The thirst for gold is the root of many evils in our day. After bringing about its loathsome holocaust, it goes on to compromise the very freedom won through the valor and heroism of its victims. So in these times, when conscience sometimes seems to be losing its privileges, when respect for promises made seems to be weakening, it is absolutely essential that a practical school of chivalry be opened for young people, a school where youth will learn that success is achieved only through the will and perseverance. Success is affirmed only through uprightness and loyalty. That school will be sports.

Antwerp City Hall, venue of the 19th IOC Session in 1920. The Antwerp Games represented a turning point and new

departure in Olympic history. During the IOC Session at the City Hall, Pierre de Coubertin himself raised the issue of working class participation. After the 1920 Olympics, sportswomen created a new international force with the formation, in 1921, of the Fédération Sportive Féminine Internationale (International Women's Sports Federation), which prompted the conservative IOC to make an effort to retain control over female sport (Text taken from R.Renson, The VII Olympiad: Antwerp 1920. The Games Reborn. Antwerp/Ghent, Pandora/Snoeck-Ducaju, 1996, p.91. Picture: postcard)

While not denying the value of regulations, one must admit that they will always remain inadequate instruments for athletic purification. A law is only as sound as the men who enforce it. Here, too, it is the men that one must keep in mind. Management of athletic associations is too often left in the hands of professional administrators or politicians, individuals, in any event, who are personally unaccustomed to any athletic activity. The dangers of this situation have been condemned many times. An Australian minister once said that it would be appropriate to declare that anyone who has never played football cannot enter a stadium to attend a major match. This was merely a witticism, of course, but one that aptly underscores the direction in which athletes should be heading. How greatly boxing, that wonderful, manly sport, would benefit from getting rid of and being kept away from the public, which has acquired a habit of congregating around it. The public compromises the sport because its presence leads to scandalous exploitation of the muscles of its top champions!

Perhaps other remedies will work, but this is certainly the most practical and the most readily available: athletic associations should be resolute in keeping their distance from anyone offering to manage them but who is really thinking only of using other people's muscles to build up his own political fortune, or to cause his own personal affairs to prosper.

III

Now we come to the third factor that guarantees the stability of athletic sovereignty. I am referring to the conquest of the masses that athletic organizations, as they have existed so far, have been unable to reach. How could they have? We are dealing with the self-baptized, the proletariat, in the pejorative sense of a social have-not. The hour of proletarian revenge has sounded for, we must acknowledge, nothing can be done from now on without it. It is the horde, and a horde overwhelms an elite that has not always remained worthy of its privileges. Yet the proletariat is not ready for its task at all. It has not been instructed. No one has ever bothered to show it all the riches housed in the intellectual temple, a temple that now depends, in part, on that same proletariat for its very preservation. Above all, no one has done anything to dispel the bitterness – no, let us speak frankly, let us use the words that are fitting – to soothe the intense anger, the accumulated hatred that form the disturbing substrate of the new foundations now being laid.

Sport has an enormous calming ability. An exasperated man who smashes a chair does calm down right away, but at the cost of destroyed furniture and of his diminished dignity. Let him turn instead to intense exercise. The effect will be the same, but nothing will be destroyed. On the contrary, valuable strength will have been produced and stored. My illustrious friend Theodore Roosevelt knew this well. Early in his political career, he was in charge of the New York police force. He took the bold step of opening free boxing gymnasiums in a neighborhood with a bad reputation. There was an immediate and considerable reduction in bloody street fights, which had been daily fare in that section of the enormous city. Let us bear this incident in mind – it opens up a whole world of unexpected opportunities for us.

Now we must address a subject that is still uncommon, so I mean you no insult, Gentlemen, when I say that until now, you have not had much occasion to think about it. The entire philosophical aspect of the issue rests on the fact that sports are based on a curious and fruitful combination of equality and inequality. An athletic record is a limit that a man reaches by working with the strengths nature gave him, and the strengths that the strength of his character have developed within it. His social position or the name and fortune he inherits from his parents have nothing to do with it. The fact that he may be a prince or a craftsman will not help him jump any farther, or add a hair to the distance that a runner, swimmer, or rower can cover in a given amount of time. Nature has distributed these strengths very unevenly among men, and the life's chances further increase the inequality of that distribution. Thus the elimination of man-made social distinctions and the affirmation of nature's aristocratic caprices go hand in hand. The seeds of the principles that form the basis and point of departure for any rational form of democracy are found in the practice of athletics.

What must we do to take advantage of these conditions, conditions so favorable for the education of democracy, and yet so useful as shock absorbers for overly-sudden social upheavals? Just this: learning and maintaining athletic activity must be made available to proletarian youth for free, or close to it.

Who will do that? The State, the cities, the labor unions? Certainly, each of them will have a role to play, a role in organizing, drumming up interest, and providing financial support. But the existing athletic federations and the associations must also get involved in this great social undertaking. Setting aside some of their antiquated regulations, and breaking away from the narrow trade unionism that is beginning to invade them, these associations must hold classes in all sports, at no cost. Unless they do so, their usefulness will remain limited. They will become of real public utility when they do become involved in such work.

Your Highness, Gentlemen, please forgive me for having spoken too long – but not for long enough, in a way. I wanted to give you a pilot's view of a very broad area. Your Majesty, who is accustomed to this fast, daring form of locomotion, will pardon me. The Seventh Olympiad is being celebrated at the crest of peaks that separate dissimilar worlds. It calls on the past that it claims to continue, but the gaze of those participating in the Olympiad is focused on a future fraught with great danger but unlimited hope.

Let us strive to eliminate those dangers while fulfilling those hopes.

Le sport est Roi. Discours. Speech by Baron de Coubertin,
Address delivered at the Opening Meeting of the XVIIIth Plenary Session of the I.O.C.,
held at Antwerp City Hall in August, 1920.
Special pamphlet. Reprinted in: *The Olympic Idea,* Schorndorf 1967, pp. 82-85.

3.22 ON THE TRANSFORMATION AND SPREAD OF HISTORICAL STUDIES: THEIR CHARACTER AND CONSEQUENCES

At this conference at the Academy of Athens in 1927, Coubertin stressed the need to study world history using the following approach: "First we must take a prismatic view of men and of things; second, we must replace the concept of 'cause' with the concept of 'function." In the second part of the speech, Coubertin talked about the political effect of taking an interest in history: "History would safeguard international peace... History can do more still for social peace". With this, Coubertin showed just how much he had learned from his teachers Albert Sorel and Paul Leroy-Beaulieu at the École des Sciences Politiques.

Mr. President and Members of the Academy,

It is indeed a great honor to speak in these illustrious surroundings, an honor made even greater by your warm welcome. Yesterday, Athens honored me by reviving one of the most highly regarded tokens of esteem that the ancient city possessed[1]. Today, as in those Olympic times whose spirit I have attempted to restore, it is my singular good fortune to present to you a purely intellectual work[2], conceived and written during the free time that my work as General Ephor of the Games has left me. To make everything that surrounds me as Greek as possible, I must now critique my own work, in application of Socrates' famous precept which, as we have been saying these days at the University, remains the foundation of all philosophy, for it is both the leaven and the safeguard of human reason.

I

Gentlemen, I first proposed to write a world history, taking advantage of every opportunity to complete the task. The fact that things turned out quite differently until recently may seem an inaccurate assertion. Yet, if you follow closely, an examination of the facts will confirm what I have said. In order to be fruitful, the study of world history requires the possession, in space and time, of accurate and complete data to which the mind can refer at all times, effortlessly and without strain. Only recently have these conditions been fulfilled. While fruitless conflicts were brewing among nations, one event occurred the significance of which has passed unnoticed. Is not the most consequential event very often the one least noticed? The gaps that persisted in geography and in history, in the chain of knowledge, have been filled – certainly not in terms of details, where much remains to be discovered, but in the overall view, in the tracing of boundaries that are now interrelated. I suppose the younger

1 The dedication of a marble seat at the stadium, engraved with the name of the honoree, a practice that had been abandoned since antiquity.

2 L'Histoire universelle, presented to the Academy by the author.

generation has a difficult time grasping this idea. Men of my age cannot forget the doubt in which they were raised concerning polar land masses, the regions of central Africa and Asia, and many of the special features of the earth's structure. Our doubts were even greater with regard to the ethnic and political past of many peoples whose names were barely known, or about whom we were reduced to conjecture. The science of geography and the science of history have now "come full circle". Man possesses the essential secrets of his home, his architecture, and his habitat. This is a great novelty, Gentlemen! Will this mean, as one Parisian wit has claimed to fear, that because the planet has lost its mystery, its children will also lose interest in living on it and, since they cannot go beyond it, that they will turn in on themselves, becoming disillusioned and melancholy in the process? I think that, on the contrary, interest in life will be greatly enhanced by the hope of ultimately establishing a human organization on a substructure based on solid realities, an organization that may well be less picturesque, but more admirable and more stable, too.

Yet even this will not be achieved spontaneously. To stay within the limits of the subject at hand, it does not follow that world history has become easy to assimilate merely because it has become possible to write. The right setting must still be created for it. In ourselves, we must create a state of mind that makes us capable of grasping its true proportions, of enjoying it, and of sticking with it. Proportion, balance, and measure are the basic needs of our nervous age. These are incomparable qualities. All we see of them is what appears through art. We remain unconcerned with the other aspects that concern social or economic perspectives, and public and private life. The technical progress of which we are so proud threatens to founder in the void, or even in hell, unless we manage through strength of will to place on them that divine harness forged long ago here in Greece: eurythmy.

With regard to the uses of world history, a desire for proportion is indispensable, but that desire will be effective only if it is aided simultaneously by the activity of the mind. I will point out two activities of the mind that, I believe, we must make habitual.

First we must take a prismatic view of men and of things; second, we must replace the concept of 'cause' with the concept of 'function.'

Truth does not exist in some sort of well from which it must be drawn, according to the fable. Truth resides at the center of the prism. Men believe that they are wise even though, in dealing with ideas and facts as though they were flat planes, they see only the front or back of them or, as the saying goes, the pro and the con. In reality, we must take a prismatic view. This perspective is possible only by moving about on all sides of the thing that one wishes to judge. We must fill in the information our vision fails to provide through our efforts of independent reflection.

When the notion of empires succeeding each other by special decree of Providence, a stance that produced Bossuet's admirable discourse, faltered among men, science was called upon to administer an area whose scope and resources were not yet fully known to it. Science established the principle of causality, making causality its quartermaster. Everyone was required to turn to causality under all circumstances. In fact, it did have an answer for every question, in a system of individual reports where facts were recorded according to strict rules of historical compatibility. At the very least, this doctrine established

The Academy of Athens, venue of Coubertin's lecture on 14th April 1927 (Drawn by A.Castaigne, taken from The Century Illustrated Monthly Magazine, 1897, p.387)

the habit of detailed investigation and of conscientious oversight, but, if I dare say so, it is fundamentally anti-universalistic. Its very nature condemns it to near-sightedness, and to increasing that near-sightedness as it goes along. The concept of 'function,' rooted in mathematics, works quite differently. This concept is powerful enough to pervade everything – and to render everything fruitful. In the natural order, phenomena appear increasingly as functions of each another. It is not surprising that the same is true for history. What is missing, however, are the advantages of using impartial notation and graphics. Function throughout history cannot be followed easily. It can be interrupted and concealed. We must dig it up like some archaeological artifact. Yet it provides insights and controls. Function confirms the parallelism and interdependence of events. We have no need to distinguish "primary" from "secondary" causes. That is a fixation whose rigidity and absolutism are as ill suited to the collective life of peoples as they are to the agitation of the oceans. Human actions do resemble waves, after all. They are distinct yet connected; they have no clear beginning or end.

II

In the study of history, the divisions we have adopted act like Ariadne's thread. Such divisions are nearly impossible to do without. Those who react against excessive division and subdivision, which is sometimes pushed to extremes of pedantry, claim that they are approaching their subject as their thoughts direct them. Yet very often they are merely concealing the old classification they rely upon, as though they were not using it at all. Once we turn to world history, however, this approach becomes useless. Through the adventures of a novelist who recently wandered about in this terrain, we have had the opportunity to see how easy it is to lapse into the kind of fantasy presented in motion pictures. The point is that as far as world history is concerned, divisions are useful for more than merely distinguishing the main events of an era more clearly, or for better enumerating the stages of the evolution of a group. Before we attempt to instruct others, we must first find our own way through six thousand years of history, cut up as it is into dead ends and intersections, rich in drama and anecdote, bathed in uneven light and deceptive shadow. Balance and awareness are the keys! The slightest exaggeration in favor a specialist's knowledge or an ethnic passion, or even a form of belief, will result in considerable errors. What is more, the more vast the area to be divided up, the greater the need for clear, concise divisions. Such divisions must be few in number, capable of encompassing the whole topic without being overwhelmed by it. Yet one cannot avoid having to retrace one's steps at times, covering terrain previously visited. Marking divisions by the century or half century would mean treating all time as perfectly equal. Establishing divisions by race or nation would result in endless repetition, a parade lacking color and dimension. These are the main difficulties, among many others, that must be overcome. I make no claim to have succeeded in this matter. Yet warm support for the plan that I adopted has encouraged me to believe that the progress has been real. This plan comprises four parts, into which the sixty duly recorded centuries that are our immediate heritage can fit indisputably, though justifiably:

- the Empires of Asia,
- the Mediterranean Drama,
- the Celts, the Germans and the Slavs, and
- the Formation and Development of Modern Democracies.

Only the fragmented spirit that still subconsciously dominates our attitudes can explain why Asia has been held apart from traditional historical study for so long. Europe is now paying dearly for its obstinate indifference on this point. Posterity will marvel at the fact that kingdoms like those of Tai Zong or Akbar the Great, facts like the odyssey of Buddhism, adventures like those of Babar or Hideyoshi – and a hundred other things of such captivating interest and profound import – were relegated to a sort of dark and stuffy annex, whereas the minds of schoolchildren and their teachers labored to recall the names of birds and insignificant stories. The history of Asia is bursting with events whose consequences influence us strongly. We are tardy in coming to unravel the complex framework that they form.

There is yet another area where the geographical configuration has guided and dominated history at every turn. That is the Mediterranean world, where everything comes together, unlike Asia where everything spreads out from the center of the continent towards the periphery. Of course, the Mediterranean is not neglected in education. Yet its historical autonomy is not held in the esteem it deserves. The mere fact that educational programs are at a loss as to where the Norman period should be placed underscores the shortcomings of the texts being used.

Then there is a third group, remarkable for the opposite characteristic. Here, so to speak, the absence of any particular geography complicated and slowed human advancement. Europe came to exist through the combined or adverse actions of three great races; until that happened, Europe lacked internal contours, and had no clearly-defined mind set. These general aspects are easily grasped, but the realities that they encompass can be examined endlessly. It is like a work of art accessible to all in outline, but detailed analysis of which lies in the hands of the critic or artist.

We must turn to the early sixteenth century, when printing had just given the world the wherewithal for the popular spread of ideas, to find the origins of modern democracies. The fight that these democracies have waged against the endlessly new and varied forms of imperialism is far from over. America has played a leading role in this regard. At its command, all sorts of activity have gotten under way. The American continent has, in turn, assumed a significant position in world history. Like ancient Asia, no room has been made for it. Asia was deemed to be slumbering away in its opium-induced dream, and America was thought to be too busy counting its dollars. The misunderstandings that have arisen from this second scenario have been particularly fraught with undesirable consequences. The fact that we long believed that solidly built urban communities would be content with this ideal, as they continued to grow, shows a lack of historical sense on our part. This raises doubts about the methods on which we in Europe have prided ourselves, claiming that we knew how to promote that ideal.

Let us face facts: the world is unified. Let us accept a situation that was bound to come about. We had grown accustomed to measuring things and people by means of a sort of fourth dimension: the European dimension. We must abandon this practice, and we must learn to use those measures that are shared by all men, from now on.

III

So even as it was becoming possible to write a world history, it was becoming absolutely essential to teach it. Two things stood in opposition to this approach: the fascination with modernism, fed by our truly outstanding technical achievements, and the naive pride of the younger generations in light of those achievements. Detached as they are from the past, the younger generations choose to regard it merely as a subject for academic research. They recoil at the thought of seeking a wealth of beneficial experience in it that could be a source of inspiration for the present. Their scientific enthusiasm is backed up by the calculations of the wealthy. A sort of pact links these two groups at the foot of a monument to production, the goddess of the moment. The faithful see civilization's ultimate goal as an indefinite expansion of the worship of production. This is a rather flimsy, short-sighted ideal for a society that believes it is innovative. In a way, it is innovative, because it seems to be searching for the dawn by looking west. Yet society has had no dearth of warnings. The predictions of its leaders are met time and again with rebuttals, and the framework of their calculations is constantly shaking.

Let us note that history is wreaking this revenge because, ironically, it is just as we were on the verge of paring back its dominance in education, its political significance has increased dramatically. History lies at the heart of all contemporary upheavals. The wars in our recent past were steeped in historic origins. The wars that threaten our future are even more so. These wars erupt as the result of a protracted failure of countries to understand each other, the very same lack of understanding that has caused, or at least facilitated, so many catastrophes in the past. The Chinese and the Mexican dramas are being played out on two sides of the Pacific where ancient historical passions are doing battle in the guise of economics. In the future, the fate of White Africa will be determined by the past of Black Africa. We still have a hard time believing that it had a past before we arrived there. So is this the right time to reject history, to diminish its role and to weaken its prestige, and to keep it cut up in regional and national slices? On the contrary, we should entrust to it the most important function there is, managing the political weather map. It should be up to history to test the atmosphere, to signal the formation of hurricanes and to track their potential course among men. In this way, history would safeguard international peace, to a great extent.

History can do more still for social peace. From the psychological perspective (something that is more widely discussed than reflected on in our day), teaching falls into two categories, depending on whether it does or does not promote modesty. Some forms of teaching which, by their very nature, are isolated within airtight walls; light falls upon them from the ceiling. These approaches pose a threat to democracy, because more than any other form of government, democracy demands fresh air and clear horizons. Democracy needs more than a compass on the table to give it direction. In these laboratories, specialization soon results in innocuous vanities; only minds strong enough to stand up to themselves can ever escape.

The fresh-air approach to teaching clearly includes astronomy, the science of the heavens. In a way, astronomy makes the infinite, an incomprehensible thing, tangible for us. It forces us to recognize the limits of our own intelligence. Yet the modesty born of the appalling vastness of space is tempered by justifiable pride in our ability to count the billions of stars, to calculate their distance, to detect their movements, and to penetrate many of the secrets of the matter of which they are made, through spectral analysis.

The modesty born of the study of world history is different. This study shows us how slow and uncertain progress is. It shows us that the only guarantee of progress is effort made over the long term. Anyone who studies history as a whole must conclude, first, that humanity is taking small steps toward a better world; second, that what it achieves is extremely fragile and may break down at any moment; and third, that the continuity and coordination of the efforts of one generation with those of the next are the only things capable of integrating what has been accomplished. Was it always so? Have such continuity and coordination always been the express preconditions of progress? No such claim can be made. Clashes, disturbances, and destruction were bound to occur, less as a result of the imperfection of individuals than of the inferior situation they occupied with respect to the planet that ruled over them, a planet that they are now in a position to rule in their own right. And so I faced what I have already characterized as the essential phenomenon of our day: the historical and geographical unification of our knowledge. Clearly, the free circulation of thought will be added to these two. This discovery holds the greatest possible potential for transforming society.

I will not dwell any further on these topics. It is clear that one cannot even sketch their outlines in so brief an address. I shall be happy if I have succeeded in convincing you of the truth of the axiom printed at the front of each of these volumes, because it summarizes their spirit and points to its practical implications:

> *"Any fragmentary teaching of history is made useless by the absence of a preliminary understanding of the annals of humanity as a whole; this introduces principles of disproportion in time and space into the mind, causing scholar and politician alike to go astray."*

IV

Before concluding, I must salute our hosts. Yet will I not be showing disrespect to Minerva and her illustrious majordomo, Pericles, by expressing my gratitude to others? Those whose custom it is to go to pray atop the Acropolis abstain from doing otherwise. Often I, too, have taken part in that sacred tradition. Yet I have quite another image in mind just now, faded and forgotten, but a very appealing image nonetheless. It is one of those images that, though kept in the background of history, remains among the most prestigious because of its expressiveness, because of the fragrance of life that they cast about them. Gentlemen, I am thinking of that simple Athenian girl whose studious adolescence was spent alongside her father, a simple teacher, in close contact with Literature, the Sciences, and Philosophy. One day, her radiant beauty brought her to the highest ranks. I am thinking of the Empress Eudoxia, wife of Theodosius II. It is not in the palace at Byzantium that I see her, doing battle with her authoritarian sister-in-law who, having governed in her brother's name, claimed that that was how it had been, to the bitter end. Nor do I see her in the dramatic episodes of the incident that destroyed the peace of her conjugal home. You know the story. You recall how the marvelous fruit sent by the emperor went from hand to hand over the course of a morning, returning to the one who gave it. This aroused his distrust, making him suspect that there would soon be betrayal where in fact there had merely been innocent flirtation at most. He grew distant from his wife. What a wonderful movie could be made from the details of this trivial adventure that so quickly became a dramatic event! The adventure was to come to an end much later, in the dark setting of Jerusalem where Eudoxia, abandoned and disillusioned, had withdrawn to grow old and die. Doubtless she was seeking the consolations of religion there. Yet she did not renounce the consolations that came from cultivating the mind. Among other works, she left a sort of heavy and disordered poem, reflecting her agitated state of mind. That work contains brilliant moments that have been compared to certain passages in Dante and Shakespeare. None of these settings is what I have in mind. The scene I am recalling dates from the year 438. At the time, the empress, in the prime of her reign, was traveling through her States. Solemnly received at Antioch, she gave an impassioned address before the Senate of that city, extolling the glories of Hellenism. So there she is, close to us, and suddenly in touch with our contemporary activities! Perhaps she spoke in a setting much like this. Certainly, among her listeners more than one of the old senators, upon hearing her begin to speak, condemned the impulsive sovereign who broke with custom in two ways: by infringing on imperial hieratism, and on the traditions of the gyneceum. Yet I imagine that quickly her warm, inspiring voice silenced their concerns, and made the senators at first attentive, and then enthusiastic. Was this not the living symbol of Hellenism that stood before them?

For us, Eudoxia speaking to the Senate at Antioch embodies the Greek trinity, one person in three: classical, Byzantine, modern. Was I not right in wishing to salute, in this beautiful and multifaceted princess, that imperishable Hellenism whose merits she extolled? Fifteen centuries have gone by, and yet that Hellenism remains youthful, ready for new adventures.

In this book, the chapter I devoted to ancient Greece ends with these lines, which I will read to you because I think they echo, in some respects, the speech given so long ago that I have just mentioned:

> *"In truth, in the Mediterranean world from which Greece was to disappear for several centuries, everything was Hellenic, for the Greek genius had touched everything and had invented or shaped everything. In all areas, from metal-working to farming, government to education, medicine to the arts, and literature to law, it was the Hellenes who had perfected, innovated, and directed. Pythagoras believed that the sphere is the most perfect shape. One might say that Hellenism has progressed spherically, as though in concentric waves, toward all horizons at the same time, and always with the same combined rhythms of momentum and measure, knowledge and intuition."*

Gentlemen, let us unite around this divine sphere, in order to maintain and protect it, for the world still needs it.

De la transformation et de la diffusion des études historiques: Caractère et conséquences.
Communication faite à l'Académie d'Athènes à la séance du jeudi 14 avril 1927.
Off-print, Lausanne 1927.

3.23 THE TRUTH ABOUT SPORT. THE IDEAS OF PIERRE DE COUBERTIN. An Open Letter to Frantz-Reichel

After leaving the IOC, Coubertin devoted himself exclusively to his reform initiatives in education. Here, he is concerned particularly with adult education, which was gaining importance in other European countries as well, for example, in the adult evening class movement in the 1920s. As he was under no illusion about putting this plan into practice, he tried here, too, to ask his former brothers-at-arms for support. In France, these included Frantz-Reichel, who had organized the 1924 Olympic Games as secretary general. He asks Reichel to support him in implementing the idea of communal sports gymnasiums in France, so that workers would at last have access to sport in the sense of physical fitness and well-being.

My dear Friend,

I do not know whether, when you relive our common memories as pioneers of sports education in France – forty years for me and soon as much for you – you are satisfied with the results obtained. Personally I am far from it. The brilliance of the Olympic Games does not blind me in the least. They, of course, aim only at an elite, for their purpose is to honor and exalt those athletes whose exceptional prowess kindles the ambition and emulation necessary for the maintenance of sports activity in general. However, opposite the elite there is the crowd – all those who engage in sports without pretending to excel in them. Among these there has been a big advance in technical skill but very little in numerical strength. The percentage of real sportsmen in the population remains slight. Bluff and publicity conceal the true situation. The racket of the press and the deluge of championships mislead popular opinion. A country is not truly sporting until the day when the greater part of its citizens feel a personal need for sport. Judged by this criterion I do not know if even America is a sporting country. If all those who talk about sport were forced to be silent tomorrow, then those who engage in sport would look like a decimated phalanx.

The reason for this state of affairs, to speak only of France, is that we have shown far too much favor to collective and juvenile sports, to the detriment of what is of primary interest from the racial standpoint, I mean the adult individual. What would become of hygiene if we only provided ablution facilities for children and if men had to form teams in order to obtain them? It is the same with sport. The collective character makes it difficult to practice and surrounds it with obstacles. In addition, by thrusting the very young into intensive sport we prematurely exhaust sport's power of attraction and neutralize its benefits. Basically, youth in its prime is least in need of this persuasion. Its exuberance will always find a muscular outlet. It is enough to supply the means. There is no point in so much incitement. And it is for the adult overtaxed and exhausted by modern life that sport constitutes an essential counterbalance, an almost infallible means of recovery, a discipline that nothing can replace. Now what facilities do our organizations provide for him in this respect? However backward we are in the matter of hydrotherapy we may foresee a day when there will be plenty of shower baths available to the public. But where is the urban agglomeration in which a man with an unexpected free hour can employ it in sport? What gymnasium – free or almost free – is open to him? Public parks provided with apparatus exist in Chicago, Denmark, Germany ... I don't know of any in France. Even these are open-air installations, insufficient and imperfect.

That is the reason why I wish to see a revival in an extended and modernized form of the municipal gymnasium of antiquity. I should like a place where petitions and records are forbidden, but where any adult at any convenient moment, and without risk of being spied upon and criticized, may practice the simplest forms of exercise – running, jumping, throwing, and gymnastics ... and for a moderate charge engage in boxing, take a fencing lesson, gallop in a riding ring or swim in a pool. That is the establishment that alone will make a sporting nation of our France – as of any other nation for that matter. It can't be done by creating ministries of sport, or multiplying monitors and playing fields, or mingling boy-scouts in all the national and international parades, even less by appealing to the League of Nations which already has enough officials as it is. And let the "bourgeois" look out, for the establishment of which I am speaking could well be built one day at their expense by the proletariat, which is already organizing Workers' Olympic Games in which the sporting spirit is superior to theirs.

As for me, I shall never lose my interest in Olympism and sport, but my sixty-five years are at grips with a new task which calls for all their strength – the transformation of the very foundations of educational methods – and I cannot therefore give myself as I should to this work of re-establishment which is necessary for the prosperity of sport. That is why I appeal to you, my old comrade-at-arms. Moreover you can do what I cannot do in France, since although you have sometimes been opposed, it has never been with the enduring jealousy and the deceitfulness from which I have had much to suffer. I have kept no bitterness on this score, incidentally. As the proverb says "No man is a prophet in his own country", and Greece, by engraving my name in marble in the most illustrious places in the world – Olympia and Athens – has compensated me for ever for all disappointments past or future.

Therefore, my dear friend, I put my hopes in you for this urgent crusade. Believe me always

Your affectionate and devoted

Pierre de Coubertin

La verité sportive. Les idées de Pierre de Coubertin, in: *Le Figaro*, Vol. 73, July 8, 1927, p.3.
English version in: Coubertin, *The Olympic Idea*. Schorndorf, 1967, pp. 100-102.

3.24 THE CHARTER FOR SPORTS REFORM

On September 13, 1930, as an official member of the Greek government delegation Coubertin addressed the Société des Nations in Geneva to present and explain his Charter of Sports Reform.

He was supported in this by his Greek friend Joannis Chryssafis, director of physical education in the Greek Culture Ministry and one of the few active members of the Bureau for Sports Education and the Union Pédagogique Universelle initiated by Coubertin in 1926.

Coubertin described this day as a decisive moment in the history of sport. To disseminate the Charter all over the world, a special edition was published in German, English, French, Spanish and Italian. It was also publicized in poster form, e.g. at the Bern federal exhibition a short time afterwards.

The objections brought against Sport may be classed under three headings:

That it strains and overtaxes the body.
That it assists in dulling the intellect.
That it spreads a commercial spirit and breeds a love of money.

It is impossible to deny the existence of these evils, but the Sports themselves are not responsible for them. The guilty parties are: – Parents, Schoolmasters, Public Authorities, the Directors of the Federations, and the Press.

The following counter-measures are indicated:

The establishment of a clear distinction between Physical Culture and Sporting Education on the one hand, and Sporting Education and actual competition on the other.

The creation of an "Athletic Degree" according to the Swedish formula, with tests varying in difficulty with age and sex.

International Championships only every second year, that is to say the 1st and 3rd of each Olympiad.

The suppression of all Sports meetings organised by Casinos and Hotels and of all those meetings occasioned by Exhibitions and Public holidays.

The suppression of all world-wide Games which are merely useless repetitions of the Olympic Games and which have an Ethnical, Political or Religious character.

The suppression of Boxing Matches with purses.

The introduction of Individual Gymnastics on a footing of perfect equality with other individual games.

The amalgamation of Gymnastic and Athletic Associations.

Agreement that there is a difference between a Teacher of Games and a Professional – the first to be considered an amateur in all Sports which he does not teach.

The introduction of an oath, given in writing by all – such oath to enumerate the various ways in which profit could be made.

Refusual to allow women to take part at the same meetings as men.

à propos de la Charte de la Réforme Sportive

On s'est sans doute un peu trop pressé de commenter la « charte de la réforme sportive ». Il est dans les habitudes du jour de traiter en vitesse aussi bien les idées que les kilomètres. C'est pourquoi les commentateurs de la première heure en différents pays, ont négligé d'apercevoir l'angle primordial sous lequel il convient d'envisager ce document. Ce n'est ni l'angle d'une région déterminée ni celui d'une date précise. Ceux qui, depuis longtemps, ont cru devoir faire appel à moi pour que je leur donne un programme de « redressement », savaient bien que je ne le formulerais pas, ce programme en promenant mes regards autour de mon clocher natal ni en les tenant fixés sur le calendrier. Le mouvement sportif est un mouvement mondial et si l'on veut en apprécier les caractéristiques profondes aussi bien que les orientations probables ou les besoins prochains, il faut avant tout tenir compte de l'espace et du temps, tout comme s'il s'agissait de juger sainement des événements de l'histoire universelle. C'est du reste parce que, dès le premier jour, ~~je lui ai appliqué~~ cette norme lui fut appliquée que l'olympisme rénové a vécu et prospéré. Appuyé sur la seule France il fut mort au berceau. Confié aux soins de la seule Europe, il eut expiré dans l'adolescence. Appréciant en 1924 dans la Revue de Genève les Jeux de Paris, j'écrivais ceci : "la critique européenne est intéressante tout juste au point de vue documentaire. Bien plus essentielle à noter est l'idée qu'on se fait de l'olympisme à Manille, à Tokyo, dans l'Inde ou bien dans les cités australiennes ou sud-américaines.

Page written by Coubertin at the turn of the year 1930/31 concerning the Charter for Sports Reform, in which he defends the reasoning behind and benefits of the Charter and describes the criticism as unfounded.[1] (IOC Archives)

All cities to renounce the construction of Super-Stadiums intended for the sole purpose of staging spectacular Athletic meetings, and to substitute in their place buildings after the style of modernised Ancient Greek Gymnasiums.

All juniors under sixteen years of age to be forbidden to take part in competitions in front of spectators.

The forming of Scholastic Sports Associations under whose colours alone scholars will be allowed to take part.

The enrolment age for Boy Scouts to be raised.

Development of Medicine for Sport based on the "state of health" instead of the "unusual case" and paying much more attention to the examination of the Psychic characteristics of the individual.

Encouraging by every means physical exercice for adults in oppositions to youths, who on the contrary could be restrained a little.

Intellectualisation of Scouting by means of general astronomy and universal history and geography.

Raising the tone of the Sporting Press by the introduction of articles dealing with Foreign affairs and events of world-wide interest.

La Charte de la Reforme sportive.
English version in: *Bulletin du Bureau International de Pédagogie Sportive.* [International Bureau of Sports Pedagogy]. No 3, Lausanne 1930, pp. 8-9.

1 A propos de la Charte de la Réforme Sportive
On s'est sans doute un peu trop pressé de commenter la "Charte de la réforme sportive". Il est dans les habitudes du Jour de traiter en vitesse aussi bien les idées que les kilomètres. C'est pourquoi les commentaires de la première heure en différents pays, ont négligé d'apercevoir l'angle primordial sans lequel il convient d'envisager ce document. Ce n'est ni l'angle d'une région déterminée ni celui d'une date précise. Ceux qui, depuis longtemps, ont cru devoir faire appel à moi pour que je leur donne un programme de "redressement" savaient bien que je ne le formulerais pas le programme en promenant mes regards autour de mon clocher natal ni en les tenant fixés sur le calendrier.
Le mouvement sportif est un mouvement mondial et si l'on veut en apprécier les caractéristiques profondes aussi bien que les orientations probables au besoin prochains, il faut avant tout tenir compte de l'espace et du temps, tout comme s'il s'agissait de juger sainement des événements de l'histoire universelle. C'est du reste parce que, dès le premier jour, cette norme lui fut appliquée que l'Olympisme rénové a vécu et prospéré.
Appuyé sur la seule France il fut mort au berceau. Confié aux soins de la seule Europe il eut expiré dans l'adolescence. Appréciant en 1926 dans la *Revue de Genève* les Jeux de Paris j'écrivais ceci: la critique européenne est intéressante tout juste au point de vue documentaire. Bien plus essentielle à noter est l'idée qu'on se fait de l'Olympisme à Manille, à Tokyo, dans l'Inde ou bien dans les cités australienne ou sud-américaines.

English translation:
Concerning the Charter for Sports Reform
People have probably been rather too hasty with their comments on the Charter for Sports Reform. It is currently fashionable to deal with ideas as quickly as we cover kilometres. This is why the first remarks in various countries have neglected to see the main point of view without which this document should not be considered...
It is neither that of a certain region nor of a precise date. Those who, for a long time, believed that they should appeal to me for a recovery programme knew full well that I would not draw it up by looking to my home town nor by keeping to a deadline.
The sports movements is a global movement, and if we wish to appreciate its underlying characteristics as well as possible adjustments to future needs, it is above all nessessary to be aware of space and time, just as if one were sensibly judging the events of universal history. It is also because this rule was applied to it from the very beginning that restored Olympism has lived and prospered.
Supported by France alone it would have died in the cradle. Left to the care of Europe it would have expired in its adolescence. Whilst commenting on the Games in Paris for the *Revue de Genève,* I wrote the following: European criticism is interesting only from a documentary point of view. Far more essential to note is the idea which exists of Olympism in Manila, Tokyo, India or even in Australian and South American cities.

3.25 SPORT IS A PEACEMAKER

At a difficult time in terms of world politics, Coubertin wrote a commentary on this topical issue at the request of the Belgian sports paper *La Revue Sportive Illustrée.* In the United States, there were heated discussions about a boycott of the Olympic Games in Berlin over the issue of the participation of German Jews. Coubertin does not make any specific reference to this, but interprets the question from an anthropological angle in the style of his *Éssais de Psychologie Sportive*[1]. Muscles and discipline are the two parameters that control the athlete in the fight for war and peace.

The *Revue Sportive Illustrée*, an old and faithful friend, has asked me for "a few lines" for its first issue in 1935. How could I turn them down? Yet many readers are well aware that it is far more difficult to make sense and to phrase things appropriately in "a few lines" than in a pamphlet – and that sometimes it is easier to be clear in a small book than in a pamphlet.

So of all the athletic topics now in the news (there are few at the moment), any one that I might choose would require lengthy explanation. At the same time, however, it is important to respond immediately to alarms being raised about the use of athletic strength in the service of war and revolution. "Bellicose nations", on the one hand, and the "Third International" on the other, are daily accused of plotting the worst possible things, gathering under their auspices cohorts of athletes inflamed by a passion for bloody revenge or rankling social hatred.

The issue involves two things: muscles and discipline. Of course those who engage in energetic, even violent sports love strength and cultivate it. It does not follow, however, that they love and cultivate blind discipline. To the contrary. Eight times out of ten, the vigorous athlete is an independent person, capable of imposing limitations on himself, for example in order to gain victory for his team or for the colors of his club, limitations that may even include self-denial. All this is subject to the condition that he remain master of his own person, and that he sacrifice to the group only that which he pleases, on its behalf. So if nationalist youth or revolutionary youth is training ardently and constantly, it is clear that these groups will benefit from their efforts by virtue of the old saying *civium vires, civitatis vis*. This does not mean that they themselves will become more intransigent, more exclusive, or above all more obedient or cruel in the process; not at all. The athlete is often quieter than his non-athletic classmates...and happily so. Yet he remains observant and critical. He does not take kindly to being "brainwashed."

These and other distinctions must be taken into consideration. Because they are individualists, athletes tend to be interested in and to appreciate the performances of their rivals. When they are political or social adversaries, even on guard on the barricades or in the trenches, you will always see them paying close attention not only the records that have been broken, but also to unsuccessful attempts to beat them, provided that those attempts were made with guts, to the maximum extent possible.

In a German copy of his Olympic Memoirs, Coubertin underlines the pacifist message of Olympism even towards the end of his life with the inscription "May Olympic peace and joy be with you". (N.Müller Collection)

So believe me when I say that you should stop raising these alarms. Manly sports are good for everyone and under all circumstances. Sports will not make angels of brutes, but there is a great possibility that they will temper that brutality, giving the individual a bit of self-control. That, at least, is something!

Le Sport est pacificateur, in:
La Revue Sportive illustrée,
Vol. 31, 1935, special issue (p. 44).

1 Coubertin, *Essais de Psychologie sportive* [Essais on Sports Psychology], Lausanne/Paris, Ed. Payot, 1913.

3.26 ADDRESS BY BARON DE COUBERTIN DELIVERED AT THE CEREMONY OF HIS 70TH ANNIVERSARY

In the hall of the University of Lausanne, Coubertin thanks his friends, especially Francis Messerli, for the ceremony which was held in honour of him. He remembers the 1913 Olympic Congress which was held at the same place and other meetings. However, he does not want to speak of the past, but he conjures up the future and again delivers a message to the youth, the new generation.

Ladies and Gentlemen,

At the moment I must present a startling picture – one which circumstances have made increasingly rare – that of a man overburdened with riches and not knowing how to distribute them. Everything that has just been said would call for a sort of recitation of the "Litanies of gratitude" on my part; even then my feeling of all that I owe you in the way of thanks would be far from satisfied. But you will be spared the monotony of such a performance, since happily this meeting is being so to speak prolonged by other manifestations, and it will therefore be possible for me to offer my thanks in series. In a short while, Mr. State Counsellor and Mr. Mayor, we shall be beside the lake around one of these agapes which Lausanne tradition is skilled in making extremely sumptuous while yet retaining their charming and cordial intimacy. I shall then have an opportunity to express the nature and strength of the feelings which bind me to the city of Lausanne and the Vaudois country. Tomorrow, the day is devoted to sports. I shall then be able to address myself to you, my dear presidents and friends, and to talk to you about the sports matters which we have at heart, and to profit from the occasion to thank the great moving spirit behind everything which is happening on my birthday, namely Francis Messerli. At this moment, since we are assembled in this University which is the temple of youth, it is to its head and guide that I wish first of all to reply.

The setting in which our assembly is being held awakens far-off and potent memories within me. It is here that there met nineteen years ago the International Congress which founded the psychology of sport and with which are still linked the names of two famous participants, Roosevelt and Ferrero. Next door is the room where five-and-a-half years later, as we were emerging from the terrible war, I dared to mark the neglected fifty-year anniversary of the French Republic (1870-1920) – which elsewhere was still unjustly refused admission to the galleries of history by setting out its achievements in six lectures. It is here too that I first communicated to the public the principles for a reform of secondary and post-school education drawn up by my collaborators and me, as they are summarised on the placard which someone has tactfully placed behind me pendent to the Charter for Sports Reform. All this was done under the auspices of three rector friends, Messrs. de Felice, Lugeon and Chavan, whose names I could not forget to mention at the same time as that of Rector Arnold Reymond, to whom I am attached by bonds of the liveliest sympathy and admiration.

But these memories I evoke are of the past. Youth likes to be told about the future, and how right it is! One must not omit to do this if one has the chance to speak to youth. Particularly as the voices which issue from the twilight, whether of age or of suffering, have a right to be doubly heard when they speak of faith. And that is the word I wish to utter.

A passage from Goethe, transposed into a little-known English verse, contains a piece of advice which runs something like this: "Keep firm in the saddle, boys, and strike boldly through the mist!" The mist ... is thus a fleeting darkness, and on the other side we will find sun and blue sky again. We must believe this. Certainly the mist which is about to rise on your path, my dear young friends, is singularly opaque, dark and menacing ... Far be it from me to ignore its disturbing form and even its very real dangers. But never mind, plunge through the mist, and I tell you again, you will find fresh sunlit life on the other side. Courage, therefore, and hope! Indomitable courage and tenacious hope.

To sustain and guide you, nourish a triple will: the will to the physical joy which results from intense muscular effort – even excessive and violent effort- next the will to honest, complete and unremitting altruism ... for mark well, the coming society will be altruistic or will be nothing: choose between that and chaos; – lastly the will to understand things as a whole. Lift up those eyes, threatened with myopia by the slavery of specialisation: do not be afraid of becoming long-sighted. Look towards the far horizons of nature and history. From these heights man draws his strength and motive-power.

Such are my wishes for all, for this favoured city, for the coming generations, for all those who have responded to our appeal and asked sport to burnish both their muscles and their will, for the nations in whose hearts I have found all along my life a happy welcome, for the cities of light and for those which are still in darkness.

"Keep firm in the saddle, boys; strike boldly through the mist" and have no fear. The future is with you.

Discours de Monsieur le Baron de Coubertin prononcé au cours de la cérémonie en l'honneur de Monsieur le Baron de Coubertin à l'occasion de son 70e anniversaire.
In: *70e Anniversaire de Pierre de Coubertin.* Publication du Comité Olympique Suisse et du Bureau International de Pédagogie Sportive, Lausanne 1932. English version in: Coubertin, *The Olympic Idea,* Schorndorf, 1967, pp. 122-123.

PART II

OLYMPIC DIMENSIONS

...e soir de Novembre 1892... exacte...
...amphithéâtre de l'ancienne S...
...si j'ai bonne mémoire, de lil...
...es carrés d'où saillaient le...
...s qui devaient être Bossuet e...
[illegible] l'écrit a...
...a quelque chose à dire sur l...
[illegible] la Sor...
pensaient à toute autre che...
...mplaient, au centre, le plastr...
...pe impeccable du plus [illegible]
...s d'alors le vicomte Léon de...
...avant un président de l'Unio...
...ent fort bien qu'il n'était pa...
...mais un homme de grand...
...ée. À ses côtés, je tenaient...
...ctave Gréard et le prince O...
...n du Grand Duc Wladimir
...abonnées a jubilé, et devan...
...ois de Boulogne le surlendem...
à nos jeunes athlètes. La fê...
...te était orné de drapeaux ru...
...rapeaux français; c'était l'...

Allegorical painting dated 1896, commemorating the revival of the Olympic Games, by Charles de Coubertin, father of Pierre, a well-known artist at the time. This painting, currently housed at the Olympic Museum, featured on the cover page of the Olympic Review from 1906 to 1914. (Olympic Museum, Lausanne)

4. HISTORICAL PERSPECTIVES ON OLYMPISM

This chapter contains a total of 68 texts related to the history of Olympism. Coubertin's reference to history has already been discussed in the introduction to this volume. His interest in Olympia and in the Olympic Games is the very reason that led to the writing of his history of the Olympics. We have limited our choice of texts to shorter summaries.

In chapter 4.1, "Hellenism and Philhellenism", we have included texts on history or the history of athletics that make it easier to understand the subject[1].

By contrast, when Coubertin wrote the history of the Olympics, he was speaking from experience and thus provides an authentic source. That is why we have given as much exposure as possible to the major Olympic events, to the extent that materials available allow. We have previously discussed the existence of some interruptions. To respect historical coherence, particularly in chapter 4.2.2 "Specific Olympic Events" introductions, at times quite lengthy ones, have been necessary. Chapter 4, "Historical Perspectives of Olympism" contains a complete account of Olympic history until Coubertin's death in 1937. The texts are presented mostly in chronological order and show Coubertin fighting indefatigably for his Olympic mission.

1 For Coubertin's qualities as a historian, please refer to the introduction to this volume. This is not the place to judge Coubertin as a historian, placing him in the overall context of his work, even though one third of his books are purely historical in content, and his four-volume World History describes him as a "professor of history". Of a total of nearly 1,250 articles, approximately 300, are purely historical in nature.
More than half of the volumes in Coubertin's library were works on history. Twenty-nine books dealt with Greek and Roman history, twelve with the history of art, and thirty with partially historical biographies. He had no books on the history of sport per se. Such writings were quite rare at the time. Coubertin was enthusiastic about historical form, even when romanticized. This shows his taste for history, including literature of a historical nature.
See N. Müller, "Coubertin und die Antike." in: *Nikephoros*, Vol.10, 1997, Hildesheim, Weidmann 1998, pp. 289-302.
See B. Wirkus, "Der pragmatische Historismus Pierre de Coubertins." in: G. Hecker et al. (eds): *Der Mensch im Sport.* Festschrift zum 70. Geburtstag von Liselott Diem , Schorndorf, Hofmann, 1976, pp. 32-45.
See B. Wirkus, "Werden wie die Griechen". Implikationen, Intentionen und Widersprüche im Olympismus Pierre de Coubertins, in: *Stadion,* Vol. 16/1, 1990, pp. 108-116.
See Y.-P. Boulongne, "Pierre de Coubertin et l'Histoire." in: *Stadion,* Vol 6, 1980, pp. 113-127.

4.1 HELLENISM AND PHILHELLENISM, COUBERTIN'S VIEW OF THEIR INFLUENCE ON OLYMPISM

4.1/1 – 4.1/6 INTRODUCTION

In this special edition of the *Revue Olympique* dated April 1906, on the occasion of the intermediate Olympic Games of 1906 in Athens, Coubertin introduces us to his ideas on Hellenism. He did this to open the eyes of his readers, especially those traveling to Athens, to the real meaning of these Games. In a rapid overview of all of Greek history, Coubertin attempted to define Hellenism, offering thoughts on the meaning of Greek art and the true pleasure that it provides. He described the special value of the ancient Olympic Games, and made recommendations for site visits. His reflections concluded with the appeal "The Philhellenic Duty" to visit the site, to acknowledge Hellenism as a principle of culture, and, following his own example, to count oneself among the "Philhellenes".[1]

In the following chapter "Olympia", there is a short description of what Greek athletics as a whole meant in terms of his "Pédagogie Sportive" (1921), in the part dedicated to the history of sports, and a somewhat more detailed work (1906) on the Olympic Games[2]. This is in addition to the collection of articles from 1906, printed together here, with the exception of the recommendations concerning site visits and reading materials. His comments end with an appeal, along with suggestions, that these sites should be visited to better understand them.

Coubertin revealed the relationship of the 1910 architecture competition to the Olympic Games, the topic of which, suggested by the IOC, was "A Modern Olympia". In it, he developed the idea of a permanent Olympic site, based on arguments inspired by his philosophical vision, and his comments on how they could be organized[3].

Throughout his life, Coubertin considered himself a Philhellene. Living in Lausanne, he took active part in the work of the Association of Liberal Hellenes, which then became the Greco-Swiss Friendship Association of Lausanne, the chairman of which, Francis Messerli, was Coubertin's closest friend and advisor in Lausanne[4]. In front of this society he extensively explained his thoughts regarding the topic "What we Can Now Ask of Sport" concerning the situation of the world at the end of World War I on February 24, 1918.

Greece paid belated tribute to Coubertin by erecting a commemorative stele in Olympia in 1927, but also by including him in the Greek delegation to the League of Nations in Geneva. He was invited to participate as a guest of the Greek State in the fortieth jubilee of the Olympic movement in 1934 in Athens. His state of health prevented him from accepting, so he sent a message expressing once again his deep respect for the Hellenic spirit and for the Greek people.

The Open Letter by Coubertin on his understanding of Philhellenism in 1934 published here shows that, throughout his life, he never stopped drawing nourishment from Greek culture. In the conclusion of his last major work on education, on "The Origins and Limits of Athletic Progress" (1936), he once again invoked the essence of the Greek spirit embodied in the concept of eurythmy[5].

A true bibliophile, Pierre de Coubertin would stick his own personalized bookplate on the inside cover of his books, to mark his property. Devised and drawn by Coubertin himself, it features the motto which is wholly characteristic of the man: "Voir loin, Parler franc, Agir ferme" (See afar, speak frankly, act firmly). The coat of arms is that of the Coubertin family, with nine shells on a dark blue background. The Greek-looking monument is in fact in Alsace, not far from the home of Coubertin's wife's family. (Navacelle Collection)

1 The recommended readings mentioned in this special pamphlet for those traveling to Greece give us some indication of the literature that Coubertin used as a basis for his remarks. In part, it mirrors the catalogue of his private library, made in 1944. This bibliography included his own book, published in 1897, *Souvenirs d'Amérique et de Grèce* [Souvenirs of America and of Greece], where he had recorded his first impressions of Athens and of the Olympic Games of 1896. See also texts 4.2.2/1-4.2.2/3 in this volume.

2 It appeared in the monthly political and literary magazine, *Revue pour les Français*, published by Coubertin in cooperation with Gaston Bordat from 1906 to 1913, following in the tradition of the *Revue du Pays de Caux*, published in 1902 and 1903.

3 Other texts on this competition are reproduced in chapters 5.3, "The Contribution of the Arts", and 6.4, "Lausanne, Olympic City."

4 He had also appointed him executor of his estate. After Coubertin's death in 1937, Dr. Francis Messerli was the last person to direct the International Bureau of Sports Pedagogy. He organized two major congresses on sports pedagogy in Lausanne, in 1944 and 1948.

5 See text 3.12 in this volume.

The valley of Olympia seen from the East prior to the 1870-75 excavations (N.Müller Collection)

4.1/1 THE PHILHELLENE'S DUTY

If you are not yet a "Philhellene", and should you resolve to become one as you stand at the foot of the Acropolis, let me tell you what your task would be. These days, the commandments of a good Philhellene are summed up in a single one: work hard to ensure that Europe no longer stands in the way of the advance of Hellenism. As we have often said in the past, Europe has done just that for the past eighty years. It is impossible to cast an impartial glance over the history of this period without noting that the military, diplomatic, and financial "assistance" provided to Greece were necessitated by events in which European responsibility was directly involved. Hellenism has proven its strength by advancing – and with prodigious speed – despite these endless roadblocks. From now on, let us let Hellenism do as it pleases. It has numbers, the prestige of history, and the excellence of biology on its side. No other Eastern people has such prerogatives to the world's confidence.

May your Philhellenism focus on *tomorrow*, not on *yesterday*. May it consist not of tender pity for the feeble heirs of a noble race, but of enduring sympathy for soldiers working toward a great future. Then, wholeheartedly, you will be able to join in the rallying cry that will certainly greet the closing of the Games: *Zito Hellas!* Long live Greece!

Le devoir d'un phillhellène, in: *Revue Olympique,* April 1906, p. 64.

The editor has determined that this text, though unsigned, was written by Coubertin.

4.1/2 OLYMPIA

In the central Peleponnese, at the foot of Mt. Kronion where the Alpheus and the Kladeos flow together, the ruins of Olympia, holy city of ancient athletics, lie in their glorious decay. At this moment when the restored Olympiads are drawing crowds of competitors and spectators to Athens once again, it seems fitting to recall in a few short pages what we should know about so curious and so original a chapter in Greek history[1].

The existence of Olympia spans a period of 1,170 years, from 776 BC to 394 AD. For eleven centuries, Olympia grew constantly in beauty, though not in size. In fact, it was not a city. During the interval between Olympic Games, which took place every four years, only those on pilgrimage or traveling went there. On certain dates, women from the neighboring countryside and regions met there to celebrate the so-called rites of Hera (we know that women were not admitted to the Games). Yet no one lived there but the staff assigned to keeping watch over the buildings, and to maintain the sanctuaries. The high-level administration of the Games was the task of the city of Elis. To that end, Elis appointed ten magistrates who began their duties ten months prior to the Games. Nevertheless, the center of that administration remained in Elis. That is where assurances were given (in order to compete, athletes had to be free and of pure race; they could not have committed any crime or impious act – and those who signed up had to complete the thirty-day training period imposed on them). Then, while "messengers of Zeus" ran throughout the Greek world proclaiming the sacred truce, judges, athletes, chariots, and horses that had gathered at Elis went in formal procession along the sacred way to Olympia, making their solemn entrance there.

Temperatures must have been hot, because the Games were celebrated at the full moon following the summer solstice (in late June or early July). No one feared this date so late in the year. Delegations from the Greek cities soon began arriving – distinguished guests and their entourages, artists, men of letters, merchants seeking lucrative orders or advantageous deals, and of course the "see and be seen" crowd. A huge throng settled on the banks of the Alpheus, but outside the Altis, or enclosure. In this way, Olympia proper retained its serene beauty and its tranquil majesty during the festivals.

In the beginning, the Games lasted only one day, but the number of competitors was increasing all the time. It came to pass that in 472 BC, the Games could not be concluded until very late in the night. From then on, the standard length was five days. The first day was spent in ceremonies and sacrifices. Rich offerings were presented at all the altars. A lottery was held, too, to determine the order of the competitions; the athletes swore an oath before the statue of Zeus. Foot races (distance and speed) were held on the second and third days, as well as wrestling, boxing, fighting, and the pankration. Youths competed first, followed by adults. To avoid the heat, competition began at dawn. Long before sunrise, the stadium of Olympia, measuring 211 meters by 32 meters, and with a capacity of 40,000, was

1 Those readers interested in learning more should read Mr. C. Diehl's remarkable book entitled *Excursions archéologiques en Grèce* [Archaeological Tours in Greece], Paris, A. Colin, 1890.

Model of ancient Olympia (Archaeological Museum Olympia, Photo: N.Müller)

full. As soon as the sun's first rays, breaking over the peaks of the mountains of Arcadia, cast their light upon the plain, fanfares rang out and the official procession (the judges in purple), the ambassadors, and the guests took their places on the steps. The competitors' names were called immediately. The first part of the fourth day was devoted to equestrian events, naturally the most elegant. The wealthy pretended to hold the other competitions in disdain, proud of the fact that their fortunes enabled them to bring horses and chariots, the transportation of which was extremely expensive. From the hippodrome, people moved back to the stadium to attend the Pentathlon (a prize awarded for a combined event that included jumping, discus and javelin throwing, running and wrestling); finally, there was the race in armor, which brought the competitions to a close. Prizes were awarded on the fifth day. Before the temple of Zeus, a branch of wild olive taken from the sacred tree planted by Hercules was placed on a table of gold and ivory along with a palm branch, symbol of strength and immortality. Each athlete was given these items while the herald called out his name and place of origin. We know that such selflessness was merely a facade. A winner, whose trip to Olympia often was paid for by his home town, received all sorts of honors and advantages upon his return. It was not uncommon for an athlete to receive a life annuity, or to be exempt from taxation. After receiving their symbolic awards, the winners went to the Prytaneum where a formal banquet was held, attended by all individuals of renown, whether official representatives or not. These were individuals that current slang would refer to irreverently as "the big cheeses", and, in all likelihood, many a toast was proposed... How odd this arrangement of Olympic festivities seems to us, does it not, so remote, yet so similar to what happens in our own day, minus the sacrifices and with more band music?

Phidias' famous statue of Zeus was brought to Constantinople after the imperial edict of Theodosius outlawed the holding of the Games, but the buildings themselves remained. They survived the invasion of Alaric, as well. It was Theodosius II

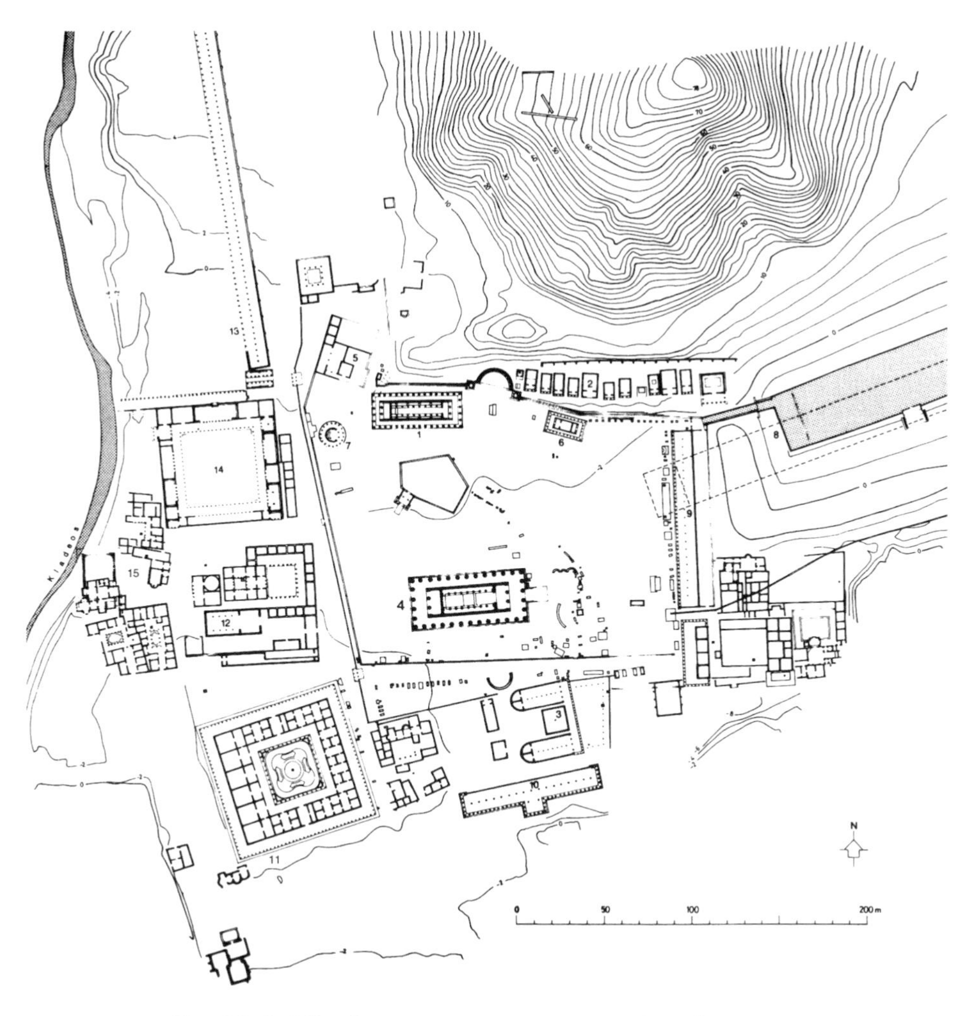

Plan of Ancient Olympia

The ruins of Olympia, buried underneath the alluvial sands of River Kladeos since the middle ages, were only rediscovered in 1766 by Richard Chandler of Oxford. French explorers were digging in 1829 at the Temple of Zeus and in the church. From 1875 to 1881, German archeologists under the direction of E.Curtius and F.Adler excavated the sanctuary. (Plan by L.Demeyer taken from IOC (ed.), Olympism in Antiquity. Lausanne, Olympic Museum, 1993, p.30)

Legends:

1 Heraion
2 Terrace of treasuries
3 Bouleuterion
4 Temple of Zeus
5 Prytaneion
6 Metroon
7 Philippeion
8 Stadium
9 Echo colonnade
10 Southern colonnade
11 Leonidaion
12 Workshop of Pheidias
13 Gymnasium/Training race track
14 Palaistra
15 Bathing facilities

who had them burned to the ground in a fit of foolhardy rage. Earthquakes in 522 and 551 completed the destruction. Slavic invaders, French feudalism, the Venetians and the Turks succeeded one another on that unlucky soil. Soon the ruins were buried, so deeply that it took five or six meters of digging to uncover them.

The idea of excavating Olympia haunted many a mind, from the scholarly Benedictine Montfaucon in 1723 to Lord Spencer Stanhope in 1824, and Winckelmann and Richard Chandler in between. It was a Frenchman, Fauvel, who, entrusted with the mission by the Marquis de Choiseul-Gouffier, first identified the location of the great temple. It was another Frenchman, Abel Blouet, who began to excavate it in 1829 during the Morée expedition. Later Curtius, who had become the preceptor of the future Emperor Frederick III, won his pupil over to the idea of a glorious archaeological expedition. The work begun by virtue of an agreement reached in 1874 between Germany and Greece lasted six years and cost more than a million: 130 statutes or bas-reliefs, 13,000 bronzes, 6,000 coins, 400 inscriptions, 1,000 terra-cotta works, and 40 monuments were uncovered. All these things remain in Greece. All Germany got was the bill...and the honor. Yet that honor is great, and the civilized universe owes Germany a great debt of gratitude.

Today Olympia is visited by many tourists. The railroad that runs there from Patras stops right in a side valley. Even the inns and the museum stand at a respectful distance from the ruins, so that nothing disturbs the impressive and grandiose solitude of the site. Not a building, or even a part of a building, remains standing, but enough of the foundations are still intact for the tourist to make out the floor plan and outside appearance of them all, guidebook in hand. Before entering the Altis (the sacred enclosure) through the south gate – through which the formal processions once entered – , there stands the Leonidaion, a vast caravansary where distinguished guests, and the Roman governor of Achaea in later times, were housed. To the left stands a site claimed to be the "workshop of Phidias", and the Theokoleion, the residence of the priests involved in serving the sanctuaries. Further to the right, behind the Leonidaion, there is the Bouleuterion where the directing magistrates during the Games held forth, forming a sort of Olympic senate. As soon as you enter the enclosure, you are standing before the temple of Zeus. The building was 64 meters long (Greek temples were never large). Six columns adorned its facade. The temple housed the gold and ivory statue of Zeus whose removal and disappearance were mentioned above.

Before the temple lay the agora, a broad space that had gradually been cluttered with many monuments and statues erected as tokens of the athletes' gratitude or of the piety of the cities. There is no apparent order in the clutter of the ruined pedestals, yet one can sense that there must have been artistic viewpoints among these art objets. Certainly greenery played a role in the over-all impression. Olympia was filled with giant plane trees, olive trees, and silver poplars that greatly increased the beauty of the place. The agora was enclosed by a vast portico that separated the hippodrome from the stadium. The hippodrome has vanished. Not a trace of it is visible today. Since it stood near the banks of the Alpheus, it must have been washed away by the flooding of the capricious river. The stadium, nestled at the foot of the mountain, was separated from the agora by a vaulted passage way nearly two hundred meters long. At the center of the agora stood the altar of Zeus, an elliptical, two-story structure where the ashes of sacrificed animals were left, so that the inside floor grew higher with each passing Olympiad. Nearby there stood the tomb of Pelops; an ancient sanctuary called the Heraion where the precious table used in the distribution of prizes was kept; the Philippeion, a rotunda built by Philip of Macedonia after the battle of Chaeronea; and finally, hard against Mount Kronion, the thirteen *treasuries* built by the cities of Sycion, Syracuse, Megara, etc., as places to put their offerings; and the *Zanes*, series of images of Zeus built with the money received in fines levied against athletes for errors they committed during the Games. There were also the monument of the conquerors of Plataea, the monument erected by the Eleans in memory of their campaign in Arcadia, and a group of thirty-five bronze children offered by the city of Messina. Later, the magnificent exedra of Herod Atticus dominated all the rest. In fact, there was no water in the Altis, and Herod Atticus, an extremely wealthy patron, rerouted a tributary of the Alpheus which then cascaded into a semicircular basin surrounded by twenty-one statutes. A bit further along stood the Prytaneum where the closing banquet was held. Then outside the enclosure, protected by massive dikes against the flooding of the Kladeos, there stood the great gymnasium surrounded by porticos 200 meters long, and the palaestra. That is where the competitors completed their training on the eve of the opening of the Games.

Such was Olympia. The beauty of the surrounding countryside, the wealth of art objects, the astonishing jumble of buildings, the high standing of the institution, the nobility and harmony of the pageants, the intensity of patriotic rivalries – all worked together to make Olympia one of the most moving and grandiose centers of ancient civilization.

Olympie,
in: *Revue pour les Français,*
April 1906, p. 135-139.

The editor has determined that this text, though unsigned, was written by Coubertin.

4.1/3 A MODERN OLYMPIA

The following articles appeared in the *Revue Olympique*. It is understood that neither the Olympic Committee nor the competitors are bound by them, but if need be, competitors may find some facts and information in them that can shed light on their task, making their work easier. The subject dealt with here is, in fact, of a new sort. When Olympia was being excavated, a great deal of effort was spent "restoring" it. Ingenious and conscientious talent was tapped. Yet now we are talking about something quite different. The new Olympia should take the Ancient Olympia into account only to the extent that the demands of the present coincide with the customs of the past. Other than instances of such happy coincidence, useful and deliberate innovation is the order of the day. Not all young architects are experienced athletes or versatile sportsmen. Therefore, we hope to do them a service by providing desirable information. The author of *A Modern Olympia* has examined the following topics, in this order: the setting; administration; qualified individuals; the schedule of the Games; the spectators; and finally, ceremonies. He has stated his personal ideas on all of these topics which, we repeat, are binding on no one but the author. Competitors should seek only general information in these texts, not prescriptive formulas. Clearly, several of these ideas will be open to debate, and of unequal merit. These ideas do not come from the International Committee and will have no influence on the decision it will reach. Let each person weigh them, adopting or rejecting them in total independence.

I. THE SETTING

Ancient Olympia was a city of athletics, art, and prayer. The order of these three terms has at times been wrongly reversed. The sacred nature and the esthetic nature of Olympia were consequences of its athletic role. The city of athletics was an intermittent thing. The city of art and prayer were permanent. The same will hold true for the modern Olympia. Its *raison d'être* will be the celebration of the Games. In the period between Games, secondary, local, and special competitions will be held there. Yet art and religion will remain there continuously. By this, we do not mean that a church or religious space, or even one of those temples that express an indeterminate deism, should be built there. If God should be invoked at the opening or closing of the Olympiads, which would correspond to the feelings of the Germanes, the Anglo-Saxons, and the Slavs and could, consequently, be imposed by them on the Latins, clearly that ceremony would be held outdoors. It should be short and simple. Only under these circumstances would the ceremony achieve the desirable sense of majesty. In no case should any provision be made for a building devoted to performing religious rituals. We have used the term "religious" in another sense. Olympia did not deserve that adjective solely because it had temples, altars, and priests. The city drew its holiness from the feeling of patriotic piety that imbued the place, that saturated its atmosphere and enveloped its monuments. Any Olympia worthy of the name and of its goals must give the same impression. A sort of seriousness, not necessarily austere, but one that allows for joy, must surround it so that, in the silence between competitions, it draws visitors as a place of pilgrimage, inspiring in them a respect for places devoted to noble memories and profound hopes.

Architecture must produce this effect with the aid of sculpture, painting, and the other decorative arts. One can readily understand that a group of buildings in the form of an army camp, a train station, or a grain market would not be up to the task of forming the ideal city. From another perspective, the site selected will necessarily influence the architectural design. Lake Geneva or San Francisco Bay, the banks of the Thames or of the Danube, the Lombardy plain or the Puszta vary greatly in line and color. Each landscape will inspire different plans, and this is a good thing, because the close collaboration of man and nature is one of the essential elements of eurythmia in such matters.

Nevertheless we can point out certain general principles. One of the most fortunate characteristics of the modern era is that we have returned to the idea of great spaces, to an understanding of their beauty and of their possible uses. In general, previous generations have not managed to do that. In China and in Heliopolis, there are some traces of isolated monuments, but nearly everywhere else we find a jumble, and that jumble seems to have been progressive. It existed first in India and in Egypt. Greece accentuated it, and the Roman Forum brought it to an unprecedented level. In using our minds to reconstruct the buildings whose ruins lie at our feet, we come up with an improbable chaos. Any notion of gaining perspective from a distance seems to have been eliminated systematically. The Altis at Olympia was chaotic, as well, and it is difficult for us to believe that eurythmia would not have been greatly enhanced if a little "air" had been given to so many disparate monuments jammed together so strangely.

There is nothing worth imitating in this arrangement of things. It was impractical and bothersome, as well as subject to criticism from the artistic perspective. Nevertheless this type of architectural agoraphobia that affected out ancestors must not incite us to delve wildly into contrasting agoraphilia. The modern Olympia must necessarily include a number of buildings, as will be seen from an analysis of its organization, as presented below. In many cases, these building must stand close together, given their uses. It would be quite inconvenient to have them separated by any great distance. In addition to that practical inconvenience, beauty, too, would suffer as a result of the fact that the entire city could not be taken in at a glance. The great artist Bartholdi used to say that the shape of a monument should be enough to indicate its purpose from a distance. That was his way of putting it, but it is clear that the modern Olympia should not be comprised of buildings scattered in a park alongside a casino.

There is yet another danger to be avoided. In our day, the science of horticulture has created a type of garden that is pretty in and of itself, but so insipid that it becomes displeasing. This is the style of the stereotypical casino park. One by one, all the spas have adopted this style, as well – rolling lawns, a variety of trees arranged with scientific regularity, flowering baskets scattered along the sandy lanes, every one of which is crooked. This style used to be called the English garden, as opposed to the French style, the mathematical regularity of which went so far as to trim the trees to exact uniformity. There is room for harmonious versatility somewhere in between these extremes. The casino look is not the only threat. Long, straight walkways quickly begin to look like a cemetery. Yet they are necessary, because nothing else is more conducive for formal processions. Watch out for the hospital style, too. All it would take is a few covered walkways connecting various building to make the modern Olympia look like a model sanitarium.

Clearly the answers are not easy to come by! For fifty years we have built, and have seen built, great numbers of casinos and hospitals, but neither our generation nor any of those immediately before it has ever seen anything that bears the remotest resemblance to an Olympia. As arduous as this makes our task, it also makes it all the more interesting.

To conclude, first the Olympic city must be visible to the visitor if not in its entirety, we believe (the layout of the terrain may not lend itself to this), then at least as a grandiose and dignified ensemble. Second, it is desirable for this first view of the city to be related to its role, i.e. to the extent possible, its look should underscore its twofold nature, athletic and artistic. Third, the shape of the city must clearly attempt to fit into the surrounding countryside, and to take advantage of it. Fourth, it would be a mistake to imitate the crowding of the ancient site. It would also be a mistake to take the opposite approach, spreading the site out too much. It seems to us that these are general principles regarding the setting of the city. After that, let us not stand in the way of a potential masterpiece of design that might draw its inspiration from a completely different ideal, offering a sort of Olympic Mecca enclosed behind its jealous walls, hiding its marvels behind a discreet screen, as it were. Sometimes genius comes up with strange ideas, and genius must be encouraged, above all.

One final word. When one speaks of Ancient Olympia, it is understood that the site consisted of two distinct sections. The Altis, or sacred enclosure, was Olympia proper. Outside and across from it stood the secular city, the city of the hotel keepers and merchants. This type of arrangement should be retained. At the very least, it would be appropriate to draw inspiration from it, ensuring that the residences of the athletes, the restaurants, and all sorts of auxiliary facilities are kept along the outskirts, somewhat disguised, and far from the "Court of Honor", if there is one, without any direct connection to what must be the heart and center of the city, i.e. the athletic, musical, theater, and library venues.

That is what we have to say regarding the setting. Will the buildings all be of the same style? Will they borrow the best elements from various known styles? Or will a new style emerge, one worthy of the name 'Olympic?' As great as such an ambition may seem, is it not appropriate to tempt young, talented individuals, eager for legitimate glory and respectable fame?

II. ADMINISTRATION

Administration of the new Olympic city should not differ greatly from that in Ancient Olympia, since by definition the needs of the institution require that its administration be both intermittent and permanent, a twofold characteristic that is contradictory in appearance only. Ancient Olympia did not go dormant from one Olympiad to the next. At best one could say that it grew sleepy at times. It is clear

The whole world of the Olympics 1924 on one floor (1200 square meters, 7 telephone lines): floor plan of the Organizing Committee of the Paris Olympics of 1924 (taken from French Olympic Committee (ed.), Rapport officiel.Jeux de la VIIIe Olympiade. Paris, Libr. de France, 1924, p.781)

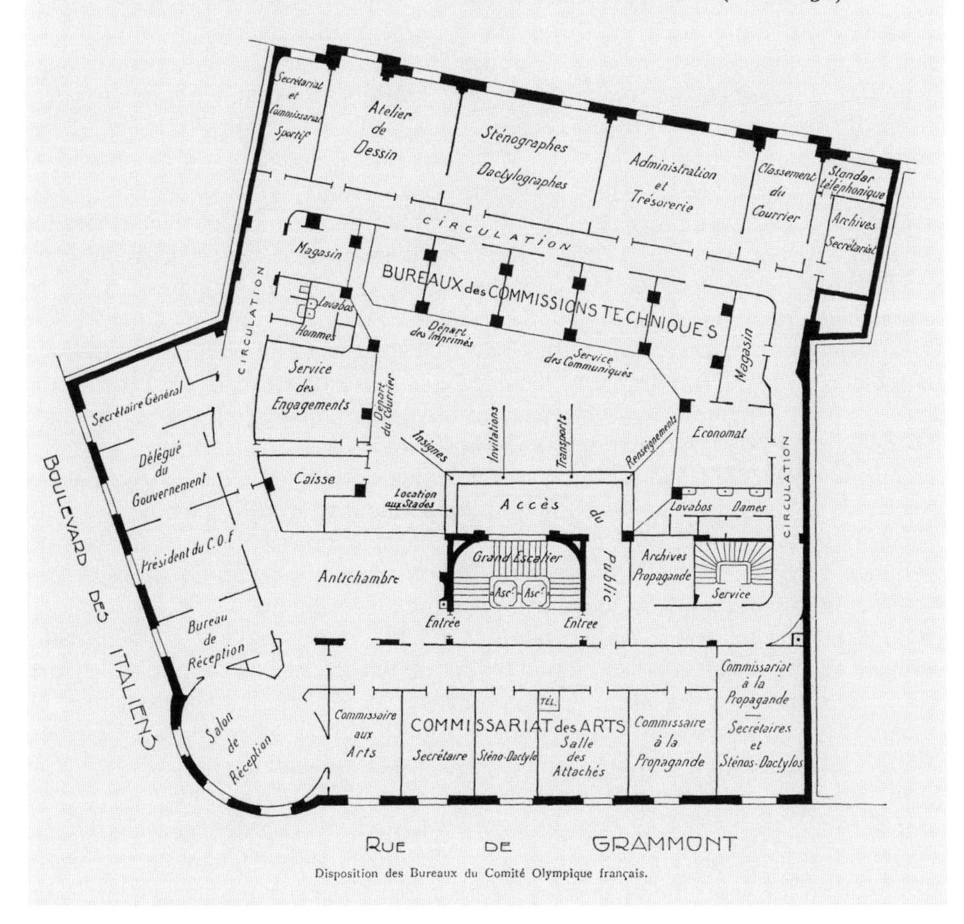

that competitions, festivals, and pilgrimages brought life to it often. Besides, preparatory work for the Games began at least a year in advance, and it would take at least six months for total calm to be restored after the Games were over. Thus the period of inactivity between Olympiads should, strictly speaking, amount to only two years. Not to use some of the facilities during that time would mean depriving the city of considerable budgetary resources, a point which cannot be overlooked. In the competition that this study addresses, no limits on cost are imposed on the imaginations of the architects, but this no reason to ignore a significant source of potential profit. Moreover, even if the Olympic city remained in a state of complete nirvana for this two-year period, there would still have to be a small administrative core to oversee it, and to see to its timely upkeep.

From the administrative perspective, then, four types of organizational machinery must be distinguished. The first, absolutely permanent type concerns the upkeep of the buildings and fields. The second, which is more or less permanent, deals with the potential use of these buildings and fields between Games. The third, periodic type involves the organization of each particular Olympiad. The fourth type, which is also permanent, provides for Olympic business services and all that goes with them.

One can go about satisfying these desired elements in a great many ways, so the plan we are suggesting contains no absolutes. In our view, this is a generic plan open to modification, of course, and certainly to improvement, by all. First, we suggest a Board of Directors and an Olympic Senate, the two permanent institutions in the city from an administrative perspective. A Curator, who would be on the Board of Directors and would reside within or nearby the enclosure, and a General Secretary, a member of the Olympic Senate, would centralize the business of their respective departments. The first would handle all material issues: repairs, landscaping, water and electricity supplies, etc. The other would maintain correspondence with the national Olympic Committees and the athletic federations and associations. The Curator would be accountable to the Board of Directors, the General Secretary to the Olympic Senate. In effect, an Olympic Senate already exists in the form of the International Committee, which has always intentionally refused to become involved in the organizational details of the Olympiads. It has reaffirmed its determination to represent the institution by remaining outside and above internal competitions and quarrels. The selection and replacement of members of the Board of Directors, which would probably be the financial entity created to run the city, would be subject to standard legislation for this type of corporation. The Senate would continue to recruit its members along the lines adopted by the International Committee, and under the same conditions. Finally, there would be a Commission comprising nine members (four appointed by the Board, five by the Senate), which would be responsible for authorizing the artistic or athletic festivals that may be organized by groups outside the Olympic institution in the period between Games, and for determining the conditions under which such festivals could take place. The permanent library department would be handled by this Commission.

If the plan we have just suggested were adopted, provision would have to be made for a *Senate building*, consisting of a large reception hall and a meeting room for about fifty people, and an *administrative building* consisting of a meeting room for the Board of Directors, a meeting room for the joint Commission, the residence of the curator, the offices of the maintenance departments (six employees)[1], and the offices of the General Secretary (two employees)[2]. These two buildings would be located within the enclosure, the Altis. In addition, provision would have to be made for the residence of the chief gardener and the residence of the grounds keeper, both of whom could also act as concierges at the entrances. What remains, then, has to do with the intermittent administrative machinery, i.e. the space needed by the Organizing Committee for the Olympiad (sports, art competitions, festivals and presentations, finances and dispute resolution, etc.). These premises should be built on the outskirts of the enclosure, in architectural annexes to the city, so that the appearance of the city is not marred, yet the distance between these buildings and the city is not impractical and bothersome.

In the same area there should be an expandable sort of hotel, one designed so that it remains open at all times, but so that during the Olympic periods it can accommodate a considerable number of residents. Let us note that providing lodging for the public, the spectators, is not at all what we are talking about. This hotel would be built for those who, because of their roles as delegates or participants in any form whatsoever in the organization of the festivals or competitions, must have a temporary residence, generally for a fairly long period. These would be men at the peak of vital activity. They need comfort but would be willing to put up with a certain degree of simplicity and uniformity in food and lodging. The architecture and layout of the institution, of course, would take their cue from these special conditions. Around it, space would have to be provided for setting up a camp, and also some sort of barrack buildings to house the athletes during the Games. Since these structures can be used only in fair weather and for very brief periods, special procedures would have to be implemented in selecting the materials and plans for building them. In subsequent chapters, we will analyze approximately how many athletes will have to be accommodated at each Olympiad, as well as the number of "officials", members of juries, etc. Members of the Organizing Committee should not number more than fifty or so.

Side buildings would be linked to the hotel, specifically including stables for about sixty horses, and lodging for staff in transit, numbering perhaps fifty men. There is no need to provide repair workshops, electric power plants, or similar facilities. There is no reason to think that the modern Olympia would be built in a desert, far from a city that could provide the power, water, and light it needs. More and more, power, water, and light will become available throughout the countryside, serving even the smallest of settlements.

We do not claim to have provided for every contingency in this scenario, and as we said before, the administrative formula proposed here might be replaced by something else. Nevertheless, we feel that we have covered the essential administrative machinery needed in a modern Olympic city, and thus that we have been of effective help to competitors in the international architecture competition.

1 Water and electricity, buildings, gardens, finances.
2 Correspondence and archives.

III. THE PROGRAM OF THE GAMES

When the Olympic Games were restored in 1894, it was stipulated that to the extent possible, they would include all the forms of exercise in use throughout the modern world. This hope was fully realized at the Fourth Olympiad, held in London in 1908. The program of the London Games will certainly never be surpassed in terms of the number of competitions held. It is probable that this number will not always be equaled. Whatever the case may be, we will use the London Games as a basis for drawing up a list of sports that the modern Olympia must accommodate, while taking into account certain wishes expressed, or certain decisions made, since those Games by the International Committee, such as the elimination of track cycling. This decision eliminates the velodrome from the list of buildings to be provided.

Five major divisions stand out to which architectural concern must be given: athletic and gymnastic sports, sports of combat, water sports, equestrian sports, and finally, games as such.

Athletic and gymnastic sports include individual and group gymnastic exercises, foot races, jumping, and throwing (shot, discus, and javelin). For these sports to function at their ease, they require a *broad field and tracks*. Of course, the tendency has been to build oval tracks with the field at the center and spectator stands on the sides. With a stadium like the one in Athens, or an arena as in London, the general appearances are esthetically equally displeasing. What a difference between these boring ellipses and the track at the Racing Club of Paris, for example, so artfully designed across shaded lawns! The fields at Hurlingham in London and Travers Island in New York are other noteworthy examples. They prove that one can achieve technical excellence without sacrificing the beauty of the facility.

Sports of combat include fencing per se (epée, saber, single stick, and baton), boxing, wrestling and shooting. Long hidden away in hermetically sealed rooms, places that were necessarily unhealthful, fencing finally came to the realization that it could easily become an outdoor sport – and everyone has benefited. Fencing, it would seem, is the one sport that is best suited for the *spaces surrounded by porticos* of which architects of yesteryear were so fond. Boxing and wrestling would also be appropriate for such spaces. Given the need to ensure safety, only *shooting ranges* are suitable for shooting. The practice is common today, but the ugly side walls of these ranges can be transformed into green embankments. In addition, if skeet shooting is included in the program as it was in London, a fan-shaped *field* with a horizon broad enough to eliminate any possible danger must be provided.

The water sports are swimming and the related game of water polo, rowing, and yachting. We will say up front that a yachting venue cannot be created artificially. If the new Olympia is located along or built at a seashore or on a lake such as Lake Geneva, or if, like Berlin or Madison, the site is near a true network of lakes, yachting races can be organized there. The architect's role in such instances is limited to designing a *sheltering harbor* and a few piers or landing stages. Nevertheless, a small navigable river, though inadequate for yachting, will do for rowing. A *pool*, either outdoor or indoor, should be provided for swimming. If an indoor pool is built, complete thermal baths should be included in the structure since hydrotherapy is a necessary adjunct to any athletic activity. The opportunity to build them is tempting, since modern man has not yet begun to rival his great Latin ancestors in this regard.

Obviously, equestrian sports are the most cumbersome and expensive. That is why they have not always appeared in complete form in the Olympic Games so far. Yet the London Games did include polo, as well as an international horse competition which, although it was held outside the Olympiad, complemented it well. Equestrian events in the Olympic Games should not include either horse races or horse competitions, in the usual sense of the terms, i.e. competitions where the improvement of the equestrian race, and questions related to it, are taken into consideration as seriously as the talents of the rider, if not more. In addition to polo, exercises that exhibit the skill, energy, suppleness, and knowledge of the competitor should be included, specifically routines and obstacle courses, rings, pig-sticking, etc. In the future, one can also expect to see more of a wonderful sport, fencing on horseback, along with its companion sport, wrestling on horseback, which is scarcely practiced at all in England these days. So a *field of play* for polo, and an *arena* for the equestrian events are essential for this portion of the Olympic Games. The arena may be indoors or outdoors, its shaped determined according to each competitor's fancy.

Only two games internationally recognized through their universal practice can be classified under the heading of games as such. Cricket has practically no appeal for those who are not British, and at least so far, it seems that one must be an American to have a taste for baseball. Lacrosse is almost exclusively a Canadian game. Lawn tennis and football are another matter as, to a certain extent, are closed-court tennis and field hockey. Football and field hockey require a *field* of the proper dimensions, that is all. Eight *tennis courts* are more than enough for even the largest tournaments. Closed-court tennis is played in rooms; the art of architecture can hardly modify the necessarily ungraceful aspects of such spaces.

Modern industry has managed to create artificial ice, but it is hardly reasonable to expect that the time will come when a perfected form of chemistry will be able to place durable, long-lasting snow on hillsides. Thus skating is the only one of the three great winter sports that might be included within the Olympic enclosure, if necessary. It would be better to adopt a solution in which these special sports are grouped together in winter, under the title "Northern Games."

By contrast, an *airfield* should be provided, with the equipment needed for airplanes and for filling free-standing balloons, since dirigibles cannot be considered athletic equipment. One final sport, mountain climbing, can be included in the program of the Games only by awarding a prize to the individual who accomplished the climb judged to be the most meritorious among all those done in the previous four years. It may be called to our attention that we have not mentioned the automobile. The same thing that applies for cycling applies for automobiles: it is only accepted by the IOC on the road, as a *cross-country* event.

So much for the athletic part of the program of the modern Games. Now we must turn to the literary and artistic portion.

As you will recall, the purpose of the advisory conference which met at the Comédie-Française in Paris in May, 1906 at the invitation of the International Olympic Committee was "to study the extent to which, and the form in which the Arts and Literature could be involved in the celebration of the modern Olympiads and, in general, be associated with the practice of sports to benefit from them and to ennoble them". We will not go into the many resolutions issued by that conference, nor the very fruitful discussions that were held on the various items on the agenda offered for the deliberation of the conference. One agenda item dealt with holding artistic and literary competitions that would be associated with the Olympic Games from that point on. This was, in fact, a return to ancient tradition, with some additional clarification. Yet as the restorer of the Olympiads, Mr. Pierre de Coubertin, has written, first the Games had to be restored; then they could be refined. Now that three Olympiads have been held, we can turn our thoughts to surrounding them with refinement and beauty. Before now such efforts would have been premature. The plan to establish five competitions for architecture, sculpture, painting, literature, and music were approved unanimously. From now on they will be part of each Olympiad, on par with the athletic competitions. The only requirement is that the topics selected must be inspired by the idea of sports, or must deal directly with athletic topics. Provided that the judges' decisions are made in time, winning works may be exhibited, performed, or staged during the Games, depending on whether paintings, statues, symphonic poems, or dramatic works are involved. In any event, winners of these competitions will take part in the general distribution of prizes along with the victorious athletes.

In keeping with this resolution, to which the International Committee plans to give the force of law as soon as possible, the English organizers of the Fourth Olympiad published a program for 1908 drawn up with the help of the Royal Academy of Arts. They selected the subjects for the competition: a procession of ancient athletes, a football match, a group of discus throwers, a swimming facility with a pool, sports club, and ancillary facilities, respectively the subjects for painting, sculpture, and architecture. But the program was not finalized until October 1907, and could not be implemented for lack of time. It will be taken up again at future Olympiads, certainly with some modifications; the choice of subject will probably be left up to the competitors. However things may turn out, from the point of view that we are dealing with here, the modern Olympia must include an *enclosure* for musical concerts or theatrical productions, and exhibition *galleries*. We use the term "enclosure" purposefully. It is to be an enclosure, not a concert hall or theater – not that that solution must necessarily be ruled out. In any case, it is largely a matter of weather conditions. But now that a taste for the outdoors is being revived, this is not the time to see only one side of the issue. Besides, can we not find some new solution like the one devised for the People's Theater at Bussang, where the outdoors and the building can work together in a thoroughly Olympic way? It is up to the architects to strive toward this goal. In any event, they have been forewarned: the modern Olympia will have paintings, sketches, and statues to exhibit, as well as musical events and theatrical presentations to stage.

IV. QUALIFIED INDIVIDUALS

How many athletes will take part in the Games in this modern Olympia? This issue is of great interest to those participating in the architecture competition. The numbers of athletes and spectators are two key pieces of information. The size of the new city depends on them. For the athletes, there is the preliminary problem of qualification. Clearly, the Olympic Games cannot be open to all comers at a time when such hospitality, given the universal popularity enjoyed by sports, would easily lead to more than ten thousand registrations, requiring endless elimination rounds. But what procedure can be used to determine the number and quality of those allowed to compete?

Qualification has technical, ethnic, social, and moral aspects. The Greeks included another: certain religious requirements were the rule. Today, of course, discussion of such a requirement would be pointless. Similarly, any attempt at establishing privileges for certain social classes to the detriment of others would be repugnant to the public conscience. Modern sports can admit of no other aristocracy than the aristocracy of the muscles, one that is not the prerogative of any single category of individuals. So much for social qualification. In a way, ethnic qualification is already covered in the charter of the restored Olympiads. The charter states that no country may be represented by anyone but its own nationals: those who are citizens by birth, or those who have been duly naturalized. Residency, even lifetime residency, is not enough. One must be able to draw inspiration from the flag under whose colors one is doing battle.

Moral qualification existed in antiquity, and was related to the regulations dealing with religion. We believe that this qualification should be reinstated in our day. As the solemnity of the Olympiads increases, greater tribute will be paid to them, so to speak, through the purification of the participants and through the creation of a true elite worthy such exceptional circumstances. But regulation of technical qualifications is needed most urgently. As we said before, one can readily understand that competitions at the Olympic Games must be restricted to potential champions. If just anybody could register, elimination rounds would fill the entire Olympic schedule with uninspiring competitions. It would be both expensive and difficult to hold such competitions. Until now the National Olympic Committees set up in every country to prepare for the Games have held the elimination rounds. In other instances, the National Olympic Committees have simply chosen those athletes worthy of representing their country, athletes able to place honorably if not to win the gold, from among those available to make the trip. This approach has had its share of problems. In some cases, elimination rounds were not held under desirable conditions of accuracy and excellence. In other cases, the direct selection of athletes has been marred by arbitrary decisions. So it would seem fitting for winners of national competitions held in the various sports over the previous four years to qualify automatically, for example. Then the National Olympic Committees would simply have to draw up a list of "recognized" championships, i.e. those that have the necessary guarantees in place. This would greatly simply the issue of qualification. Here again, however, certain problems might arise because real national championships – competitions in which representatives of

The very first Modern Olympic Games attracted unexpectedly large crowds of spectators. (taken from La Revue Sportive Illustrée, April 1906, p.6)

the various regions of the country face off against each other – do not yet exist in all countries. Take a country as vast as Venezuela, for example. Clearly it will be some time before the spread of athletics justifies any such competition. Yet this is no reason for a Venezuelan athlete to be denied the chance to compete in the Games. In such countries, the direct-selection method, handled by an ad hoc committee, will still be used for a long time to come.

Whatever the methods used ultimately with regard to technical qualification, the number of competitors must continue to be limited by general Olympic regulations to a given number of athletes per country and per branch of sport. The maximum number established in this way will certainly rarely be attained because although countries with considerable human and financial resources are able to take advantage of all the opportunities they are given, less fortunate countries will generally send just a few competitors who have a real shot at winning. Furthermore, it would scarcely seem possible to treat each nationality on a different footing since athletic geography does not coincide with political geography. Currently Sweden has no trouble coming up with a full list of competitors, while Russia does.

All in all, the average number of athletes participating in the four categories of sports on the Olympic program will range from 800 to 1,200. Those four categories are athletic and gymnastic sports, sports of combat, water sports, and equestrian sports. The numbers can be further broken down roughly as follows: athletic and gymnastic sports: 500 to 600 competitors; sports of combat: from 180 to 250 competitors; water sports: from 60 to 100 competitors; and equestrian sports: from 60 to 100, for a total of 800 to 1,200. Then there are the team sports, which implies a rather considerable increase in numbers: let us say 200 to 500. These figures seem reasonable for a model Olympiad, on the basis of which those competing in the architecture competition should draw up the dimensions for the city they are designing. It hardly seems likely that the numbers of artists and men of letters who will present works at the Olympic Games will ever require elimination rounds. If such rounds were to become necessary, they would be easy to handle: a national jury in each country would allow only the best works to pass.

V. THE SPECTATORS

As we said before, the number of spectators, like the number of athletes, is a key factor in calculating the requisite size of the Olympic city. At first glance, it would seem that as much space as possible should to be provided to accommodate the largest possible crowds. We have grown accustomed to judging the success of a festival by the number of those in attendance. The more the merrier, as they say. To apply this coarse principle in a permanent and long-lasting way to the Olympic Games would be to commit a very serious error. We say "in a permanent and long-lasting way" because in the beginning, the crowd does play a role, the role of consecration. The thousands and thousands of spectators who came to Athens, St. Louis, and London to applaud the victors in the first Olympiads conferred on the institution its global and international character. Moreover, when it comes to Olympiads that are always held in one country after another by turns, one can always count on drawing a crowd because the spectators are always changing with the country. The project we are discussing here, the establishment of a new Olympia, does not allow for that consideration. The way things go, one can foresee a time when people will have had enough as far as athletic events are concerned. Fashions will change, and the sentiment of non-athletes will grow indifferent. At that point, appeals to the crowd through posters and advertisements, etc., may no longer work. Certainly the modern Olympia, through the beauty of its setting and the involvement of the arts, will always draw a fair number. Yet it would be futile to count on the faithfulness of the crowd.

We must hasten to add that such faithfulness would not necessarily be desirable, from either the technical or the artistic perspective. Too large a crowd, where non-athletes are present in greater numbers, is harmful in terms of the technical aspects of the sport. In principle, the ideal sports spectator is a sportsman on holiday, taking a break in his own exercise routine to follow the exploits of a more skillful or better trained friend. Of course we cannot stand on principle alone, but we must strive towards it. From the artistic perspective, not only is the shape and color of the modern crowd ugly, but it is difficult to provide everything that the crowd needs to control it: bleachers, enclosures, barriers, ticket windows, etc.

From one perspective, it is difficult to recommend an invitation-only system which would fully satisfy demands for the dignity and decorum of the Olympic institution, because it completely eliminates the possibility of income. A mixed system could be implemented in which a certain number of tickets would be sold at a price, while other tickets would be distributed judiciously and wisely among those who cannot pay. This is a rather modern and democratic approach. There is a whole category of people who show more interest in an event the more it costs to attend. Such people existed in ancient Athens, and they are still to be found today wherever civilization is somewhat advanced.

Yet in addressing this topic issue, we are straying from the topic at hand. The issue of "profit and loss" does not lie within the purview of the architects, who are asked to imagine a setting for the modern Olympiads that is worthy of the past and of the future. Besides, all this resulted from trying to determine the approximate number of spectators. Well, we will suggest an average of ten thousand. That is the figure one should reckon on. We are far from the 70,000 or 80,000 spectators jammed into the stadiums in Athens or London. At the very least, however, we can rely the devotion of these ten thousand, and what is more, they will not ruin the esthetic appeal of the setting.

They will not ruin the setting as long as they are well distributed within it. To accomplish this even distribution, care must be taken to avoid the unfortunate style of bleacher where everyone is crowded together. When all is said and done, such designs are heavy, consisting of geometrical ridges that are displeasing to the eye, guaranteed to detract from everything around them. You can try to embellish a set of bleachers in all kinds of ways, place them in the loveliest landscape. Once filled with spectators, however, they will almost always look like a hideous, hulking mass. The problem can be avoided by using lawns and terraces, where spectators are free to move around. If they do form groups, they do so only temporarily. Although the appearance of these groupings may be ugly, at least they are transitory. That is something, at least. Of course, the use of lawns and terraces requires a great deal more open space. It also requires no small measure of art and taste. It requires irregularity, imagination, and order – all at the same time. Above all, technical requirements must be respected; one area cannot dominate another, and one cannot block the view of the other.

Une Olympie moderne,
in: *Revue Olympique,*
October 1909, pp. 153-156 (I. Le Cadre), [I. The Setting]
November 1909, pp. 167-170 (II. L'Administration), [II. Admintistration]
December 1909, pp. 184-187 (III. Le Programme des Jeux), [III. The Program fo the Games]
January 1910, pp. 9-13 (IV. Les Qualifiés), [IV. Qualified Individuals]
February 1910, pp. 26-28 (V. Les Spectateurs), [V. The Spectators].
Special pamphlet issued by the *Revue Olympique* to those participating
in the International Architecture Competition, Paris 1910.

4.1/4 WHAT WE CAN NOW ASK OF SPORT...ADDRESS GIVEN TO THE GREEK LIBERAL CLUB OF LAUSANNE, FEBRUARY 24, 1918

Ladies and Gentlemen,

In accepting your gracious invitation and agreeing to give the first of your series of addresses I am not only obeying the dictates of an unshakeable philhellenism but reviving within myself a precious and far-off memory. More than twenty-three years ago now, on an evening in November 1894, I was invited to speak to members of your celebrated Athenian club "Parnassus". I described to them what was to be expected from the propagation of sport. Some months earlier the restoration of the Olympic Games had been proclaimed in the great amphitheater of the Sorbonne Palace at Paris; this initiative had set the seal on the task to which I had devoted myself since 1886, and ensured its final success. I had thus come to bring greetings to the Greeks in the name of Neo-Olympism and to persuade them to consecrate its existence by permitting the Games of the first of the modern Olympiads to be celebrated under their auspices at the foot of the Acropolis. Enthusiasms were born and grew around this idea – and also violent antagonisms. I have forgotten neither the one nor the other.

Today, when more than a quarter of a century has passed since these events, it is easier to see their significance and scope. We knew already with certitude, before general war was let loose, that the sporting renaissance created national strength through the cultivation of individual energies. The present great tragedy has proved it in an unanswerable and bloody fashion. Now sport can do something more for us; if we know how to let it, it will be able tomorrow to safeguard the essential good without which no durable reconstruction will be possible – social peace.

I rejoice that I have been given the opportunity to begin preaching the second part of the Gospel of Sport among a Hellenic community, as I did the first in times past, and that I thus have the opportunity once more to place my endeavor under the patronage of that civilizing force whose past merits every honor and whose future deserves every confidence – Hellenism.

I

The idea of invigorating and perfecting military preparation by means of physical exercise is very old. In Chaldea as in Egypt and also in the Far East, governments of a warlike and conquering tendency made use of such a system, and it is probable that they helped things along by appealing to the sporting instinct when they encountered it – incidentally it was rare and undeveloped. The sporting instinct is not an animal instinct. Neither the idea of progress nor the idea of risk which are so to speak its two poles appear accessible to animals. The cat and the polo pony – the most sporting in appearance – seek nothing beyond the game; their muscles amuse themselves, that is all. Now the sporting instinct is something very different. It is above all a power instinct; I personally have reached the conclusion that it was born of man's contact not with the weapon but with the horse. The armed man was not necessarily a sportsman; the man on a horse had to become one, willy-nilly. I would like to quote in this connection a suggestive passage from Herodotus which unfortunately I do not have to hand.

Thus the remotest antiquity knew and practiced military preparation through physical exercise; but civic preparation was invented by you, the Greeks. The former could be ensured by the sole action of authority; the latter necessarily called for the voluntary cooperation of the individual. The sporting instinct was for the one only an occasional reinforcement, but for the other a vital condition. Thus you became the fathers of sport. You organized and codified it, you made it a permanent institution, a factory of collective strength.

Olympism was to some degree both the crown and the emblem of this organization. At fixed periods all the other manifestations of national life grouped themselves around a considered athleticism. The athlete collaborated with the artist and the philosopher for the glory of their native land. At the same time he embodied its potential strength, since his training enabled him to become its defender at short notice. Thus when the Persian peril threatened Hellenism between 500 and 449 B.C. unexpected armies and navies barred the way to the ambitions of Darius and Xerxes and the greed of their advisers. There had been hesitation before the massive forces of the adversary; more than one city was inclined to submit to the ultimatum. Athens rose up. Victory proved it right. Now if many centuries later – for history has eloquent turnings and sometimes repeats itself strangely – an English general was able to say that the battle of Wateloo had been won on the playing-fields of Eton, how much more accurate still is it to proclaim that the glory of Marathon and Salamis was forged in the precincts of the Greek Gymnasium.

The Greek gymnasium! Of all the institutions of the ancient world the least known, the least studied and perhaps the most fruitful; the institution which best explains the greatness of classical times, since it formed the basis of a superior civilization. When Antiochus the Great wanted to Hellenize Jerusalem, his first act was to open a gymnasium there. He knew that everything else would follow from that.

The Greek gymnasium – to which we will shortly return in order to examine it for ideas suitable to our present needs – was scattered throughout the Greek interior and the Mediterranean coasts and islands. Hellas bequeathed it to Rome, which allowed it to decay. This happened very slowly of course. From Egyptian Alexandria to Sybaris the tradition endured, and was effaced only slowly by the impact of Roman influences, which drew the masses to the Games at the Circus and the sophisticates to the delights of the Thermae. A passage in Seneca gives us a vivid glimpse of this athletic decline, to which Christianity was shortly to give the deathblow. For it is remarkable to observe the severity shown to physical culture by the Church, which was relatively indulgent towards the products of pagan genius (and we must be grateful to it for this); it attacked physical culture as the source of that "pride of life" which the Scriptures had anathematized. We need not become indignant. In the eyes of History its action is justified; the world of that time had need of asceticism; luxury and plutocracy were threatening it with death. In our day, on the other hand, we were bearing the over-heavy burden of that over-long period of ascetic philosophy, and it was necessary to return towards physical education even at the risk of later going too far in that direction. For humanity is like a pendulum which seeks equilibrium but achieves it only transiently on its ineluctable flight from one excess to another.

Even after the Emperor Theodosius' edict suppressing the antique Olympiads had broken the thread of athletic tradition, there remained here and there modest gymnasia where obstinate amateurs lingered; but they were no longer lit by the gleams of artistic beauty and intellectual effort, for mind had become divorced from muscle. This obscure epoch deserves research. I should have liked to lead the way myself; I shall not be able, and hope that others may share this ambition. Who knows whether such research might not help us better to grasp the character and scope of those outbursts of energy of which the Greek empire time and again provides a fascinating and mysterious spectacle throughout the thousand years of its stormy history?

Better known to us, although insufficiently studied, are the manifestations of the sporting spirit in the Middle Ages. For in its efforts to regulate Chivalry the Church had for a while to depart from its anti-sporting severity and even to tolerate tournaments. Now it would be a mistake to suppose that tournaments were always the exclusive privilege of the nobility. As proof of this I will only mention the amusing challenge sent by the burgers of Paris to those of the province in 1330 with the permission of King Philip VI. The provincials, who came for the most part from Amiens, St. Quentin, Rheims, and Compiègne, were beaten by the Parisians. There were more than 70 of them all told. A paymaster from the capital and a burger of Compiègne shared the prizes for valor, which were presented to them by a young Parisienne, daughter of a draper. Incidentally one of these jousters had broken a leg and the other had not escaped without a severe buffeting. Here, without a doubt, was the love of risk, which is one of the essential elements of sport. However, it was a rudimentary sport, without training and without organization. The same characteristics were observable in the Homeric matches of 'soule' – the ancestor of football – which the Sire of Gouberville used to organize around his estate at Cotentin, and which are described in his private journal with picturesque simplicity. The governments of those days do not seem to have approved of these customs. Edward III of England forbade his people any exercise save archery and Charles V of France, himself a great lover of tennis, proscribed it for his subjects. It is certain that the sporting spirit could easily have developed in Europe in the Middle Ages. But feudalism repressed it, and as soon as the Church became detached from Chivalry it returned to its distrust of physical culture, in which it appeared to descry a dangerous forerunner of free thought.

From Rabelais to Rousseau there were apologists for physical education. Basedow and Pestalozzi even made meritorious attempts to pass from theory to practice. Then the great German patriot Ludwig Jahn and the Swede Ling sought to spread their gymnastic doctrines in their respective countries. But Jahn's one idea was to create a military force capable of achieving German unity, and Ling's aim was to promote health through scientifically regulated physical activity.

It was left to the great Englishman Thomas Arnold to take up the Greek work at the point where a hostile fate had interrupted it, and to clothe it in an educational form adapted to modern conditions. The world had forgotten how organized sport can create moral and social strength, and thereby play a direct part in a nation's destinies; had so far forgotten it that the spread of Arnold's doctrines and example first in England and then throughout the British Empire was an almost unconscious process. Rugby School may thus be truly considered as the starting-point of the British revival. The United States at first remained indifferent to this movement. Noah Webster's assertion that "a fencing hall is as necessary to a college as a chair of mathematics" found no echo, and on the eve of the Civil War American youth was steeped in the excesses of an unbalanced intellectualism. The fearful shock gave it a rude awakening. Gymnasia were built; they were very different from the institutions that had borne that name in antiquity, and they sometimes pushed scientific pretensions to the point of pedantry, but within their walls sport gradually gained a victory. It was the true descendant of Hellenic sport, but thanks to modern inventions and progress it possessed ingenious appliances and new resources. Its technical range was considerably extended and its formula more precise. It was "the habitual and voluntary cult of intensive muscular effort based on the desire for progress, and capable of going to the point of risk". That is its definition: it includes the ideas of will, continuity, intensity, improvement, and possible danger; these five elements are the ingredients of sport. It is thus a function of strength and links up with the Stoic philosophy, towards which it may lead its adepts. This is the kind of sport which I had in mind thirty years ago when I made a pact with Jules Simon for the reinvigoration of France. The conviction of the septuagenarian philosopher was no less ardent than my own, and events have fulfilled our hopes. A manlier and broader education soon begot results as fruitful as those whose benefits the England of Thomas Arnold had reaped some time before. In vain did Frenchmen blinded by party spirit undertake the sorry task of portraying to the outside world a decadence which existed only within themselves. History will delineate the rising curve which enabled the Republic to write in forty years the most admirable of colonial epics and to guide youth through the dangers of pacifism and freedom pushed to extreme limits right up to that 1914 mobilization which will remain one of the finest spectacles which Democracy has given the world.

The part played by sport in this revival has been noted across the Ocean and probably better appreciated there than in Europe itself. But France is only one more example of the virtue of Greek formulae perfected by Anglo-Saxon civilization. There are others. In the last fifteen years almost every nation has been paying increasing attention to this long forgotten branch of manly education. None has had cause to regret it. Whatever the methods employed – state intervention or private initiative – the cultivation of individual energies by means of sport has blossomed everywhere into a national force. Sweden and Germany recognize it, as do Belgium and Switzerland. Well then, have we nothing more or nothing of a different kind to ask of sport? Can it do nothing to satisfy the one need which tomorrow is going to dominate all others, since the task of reconstruction hinges upon it? Can sport not help us to establish social peace?

II

It is readily agreed that the best foundation for social peace within a democratic society would be the establishment of a happy equilibrium between the inequality introduced by nature among men and the equality which legislation seeks to impose. But where are the bases and bounds of such an equilibrium?

The thing which makes inequality hard to bear for those who are adversely affected by it is its tendency to perpetuate injustice. People revolt against it because it usually has the twofold characteristic of being permanent and unjustified. If it were transient and justified it would no longer arouse enmity. Now we may note that while in other fields it is almost impossible to create such conditions, in the republic of sport they arise of themselves.

What is a sporting result? It is a figure or a fact. You have a maximum height above which you cannot jump, a minimum time below which you cannot sprint a hundred meters. The weight that you lift and the rope that you climb also express in kilos or in meters the value of your effort. If a rock-climber, you are capable of climbing this mountain and not that; if a rider, of mastering this horse but not that other. On all sides you encounter restrictions of a more or less mathematical severity. But you could not see them when you began. Nobody knows his exact limitations in advance. Only one road leads there – training and hard work. And when one has reached the goal, when one has set up one's own record, i. e. the best result one can reach, effort is still required to stay there. No insurance guarantees you the permanent possession of this record. Only persistent work can safeguard it. There, incidentally – if you will allow me this parenthesis – is the whole secret of sporting education. Sport plants in the body seeds of physio-psychological qualities such as coolness, confidence, decision etc... These qualities may remain localized around the exercise that brought them into being; this often happens – it even happens most often. How many daredevil cyclists there are who once they leave their machines are hesitant at every crossroads of existence, how many swimmers who are brave in the water but frightened by the waves of human existence, how many fencers who cannot apply to life's battles the quick eye and nice timing which they show on the boards! The educator's task is to make the seed bear fruit throughout the organism, to transpose it from a particular circumstance to a whole array of circumstances, from a special category of activities to all the individual's actions. That is what Thomas Arnold did, and what British educators learned from him. But let us come back to our social standpoint. Inequality in sport is based on justice, because the individual owes what success he obtains only to his natural qualities multiplied by his will-power; it is moreover a very unstable inequality, because this ephemeral form of success exacts continuous effort if it is to endure even for a little. These are interesting data for Democracy. It is not surprising if in sporting circles we see an easy blending of authority and freedom, and above all of mutual help and rivalry. Now Democracy needs to be able to blend these ingredients, but naturally finds a thousand difficulties in doing so. Sporting authority is inevitably due to merit recognized and accepted. Choose a football or rowing captain for any other reason than his technical worth, and the team's success is compromised. Furthermore, if a badly understood restriction

Since 1936 the Olympic Flame is lighted by the sun in the antique Olympia before the torch runners take it. This symbolically connects the antique Olympic Games with the modern Olympic Games. (taken from P.Wolff, Was ich bei den Olympischen Spielen sah. Berlin, Specht, 1936, no.1)

chafes any member of a team and interferes too far with his individual freedom, his teammates feel the ill effects. Thus the sportsman has before his own eyes a permanently-valid lesson in the necessity of command, control and unity, while the very nature of the comradeship around him obliges him to see in his comrades both collaborators and rivals – which from the philosophic angle seems to be the ideal principle of any democratic society.

If we add to this that the practice of sport creates an atmosphere of absolute frankness, since it is impossible to falsify results which are more or less numerical and whose only value lies in being open to general scrutiny (even with himself a sportsman cannot cheat successfully), we shall reach the conclusion that the little republic of sport is a sort of miniature of the model democratic state.

Is there a way of attaching the one to the other, as the cell to the organism? There is an absorbing problem for our times! In the same way that individual sporting education consists in extending to all the individual's actions the manly qualities engendered around sporting activity, there would then be a social sporting education the aim of which would be to employ the modest mechanisms of organized sporting activity in the apprenticeship to public life. We find this already in the ingenious conception of the Arnoldian public school; but this time there would no longer be any question of a selected class of scholars, but of an operation upon the whole social body. Is it possible?

Let us now return to the Greek gymnasium and observe it from this angle. We find that its principle is a triple cooperation, the importance of which might perhaps have escaped us. In the first place there is a cooperation of subjects; sport, hygiene, science and art are found mingling together. In the second place there is a cooperation of ages; three generations are present – the adolescent, the adult, and the old. And in the third place there is professional cooperation; the practician and the theorist, the man of science and the man of letters, the politician and the private individual, the guild member and the independent, rub elbows in a sort of beneficent promiscuity. How could this fail to foster qualities of understanding, reconciliation, and appeasement? The young man and the older man, the artist or philosopher and the athlete, do not differ so widely in their ideas, interests and passions that they cannot clasp hands. When they do not know one another it is because they have been kept apart, have been prevented from becoming acquainted and learning to esteem one another. Let us not forget however to note one essential point: it is not around the idea of the public weal that all these forms of cooperation can gather, but around that of "muscular joy". That is the great lesson of the Greek gymnasium. To try to reconstitute it on any other basis would be like seeking once again a Utopia in which there are no debit accounts. Sport was the master of the household in the Greek gymnasium; it welcomed Mind and bowed before it as though before a distinguished guest. In order to act upon youth it is necessary to understand its ardent desire to live, and in order to understand this, it is necessary to profess the cult oneself to the utmost. A failure to understand this higher principle would make any attempt to restore the ancient gymnasium barren.

For this is the theme on which I wish to end, far though I am from having exhausted the subject. We must restore the municipal gymnasium of ancient Greece and it will give us social peace. We have facilities for this task that the ancient world never knew. Let me enumerate some of them for you. First of all the technical developments which I mentioned just now, and which a beneficent industry has produced lavishly in the field of sport. What joy the splendid youth of Hellas would have felt in far-off times had it possessed the foil, that docile weapon, the supple and firm boxing glove, the coaxing bicycle, and above all the outrigger, that marvelous craft the very feel of which lends the rower wings! What an intoxication for the bygone athlete had our numerous gymnastic appliances been to hand! Indeed, never has sporting pleasure been made more attractive than in our days, nor its opportunities for exercising its fascination more numerous. Running tracks, facilities for jumping, climbing and throwing, premises or terraces for combat sports, an open-air riding school, a boathouse on the neighboring river if nature or man have made it navigable – these are capital outlays with a hundred per cent return for any municipality intelligent enough to make them. A similar improvement is taking place in the field of hygiene. While air-therapy and sun-therapy have not needed to make much progress, water-therapy has found at once its most ingenious and least aristocratic because at once inexpensive and exquisite formula – the shower bath. When one knows at what a trifling cost shower-baths can be installed and maintained, it seems incredible – and unflattering to the public authorities that they are not in operation in every town of any size. It will come. And what could be more natural than to situate shower baths near sports grounds and sports buildings?

So here we are with an embryo of a modernized classical gymnasium. In what form can we invite art to enter it, apart from the architecture that is to form its setting? In the classical gymnasium there was no doubt dancing, there was certainly singing, and think what choral song might become today with the repertoire which the centuries have stored for it! Byzantine hymns, war songs and love songs from Poland and Russia, from England and Scandinavia, from France and Spain, from Germany and Italy ... there is a profusion of them, forming a polyphonic treasure of incomparable richness. A vocal quartet is not very difficult to form and little by little it will turn into a massed choir. Add to this if you will the open-air theatre; art will then be fittingly lodged in the new gymnasium.

But this is not all. Formerly there used also to be philosophy. The master taught under the porticos a few paces away from the athletes. He was a more accessible person in those days, less distant from the ordinary run of mortals in his ideas and more down-to-earth in his language. It would be idle to seek to call him back and his cooperation might well prove a great disappointment. But history is there to take his place, history whose teachings we today realize were so tragically lacking in contemporary society at the moment when it drew near the abyss, history whose broad lines and long vistas – intelligible to all – have been disappearing under the meticulous search for the isolated detail, under lists of useless dates and a dry desert of documentation, history, the sole instructor of the coming democracies, the sole sure guide for the masses along the paths of wisdom.

I am well aware that explanations are necessary and that one cannot introduce so in a few words this novelty of a sort of popular university based on scientifically vulgarized history teaching. I am ready to welcome objections and to reply to them. Here I must be content with simple exposition.

The four bases of the Greek gymnasium are thus within our grasp and its task remains the same, but increased by two circumstances which require mention. Firstly, that canker of ancient societies which slowed down their progress and sterilized their efforts – slavery – has vanished. Secondly, there has arisen the scourge of modern times – alcoholism – whose haunt, the public house, will be destroyed only by replacing it. I must confess that the indifference of anti-alcoholic societies in this respect has always been a matter of regret to me. In thirty years they have given us no support in our sports propaganda campaign. They have remained deaf to the appeals that we have addressed to them with a view to effective collaboration, and have always preferred to keep to direct warfare and try to kill the public house in the sole names of virtue or of science. They must know, however – for it has been proved – that alcoholism has no more powerful antidote than athletics and that there is a sort of physical incompatibility between alcohol and training; moreover, isn't the "unwinding" which the manual laborer seeks in the pub a social necessity? Isn't it the same "unwinding" which the business-man seeks in his club, and if so what right has he to ask of the manual laborer an abstinence which he does not practice himself? Grave hours are at hand for democracy. Insatiable plutocratic appetites and the lust for power pushed to madness on the one hand, and the revolt against too long-suffered injustice on the other, combine to keep civilization under the threat of an aftermath of war which could be worse than the war itself. Henceforward it will no longer be possible for any caste to govern the world, to order it to move or to stop – or even to slow it down for a moment. The City of the Future can be built strongly and durably only through the collaboration of all its citizens. Let us apply the motor forces of this collaboration at the points where it is reasonable to harness and group them. Let us not fall into the Utopia of complete communism. Equality must stop at the threshold of the family hearth, for men will never give it access to their homes or allow it to interfere in family affairs. Intimate social relationships are governed by heredity, tradition, and everyday habits. They are expressed in minute but persistent differences of language and modes of life. And it is logical that it should be so. But it is no less logical that public life should cease to be influenced by this sort of particularism. And why should song and gymnastics not be greedily sought occasions for meeting and contacts between young people regardless of class or means? May the Greek gymnasium therefore be restored in the modern community; may it open to new generations the way to an intelligent and pure civic sense, and to fraternal and joyful cooperation.

Ce que nous pouvons maintenant demander au Sport...
Conférence faite à l'Association des Hellènes Libéraux de Lausanne, le 24 février 1918.
Lausanne, Edition de l'Association des Hellènes Libéraux de Lausanne, 1918 (22 pages).
English version in: Coubertin, *The Olympic Idea,* Schorndorf, 1967, pp. 43-51.

4.1/5 TO MY HELLENIC FRIENDS. AN OPEN LETTER DATED APRIL, 1934

Dear Friends, April, 1934

I am deeply moved by your invitation to participate as a "Guest of the Nation" in the celebration of the Fortieth Anniversary of the Restoration of the Olympic Games. I am even more deeply moved, if that is possible, by the honor shown to me by the President of the Republic and the Chairman of the Council, who wrote personally to invite me.

Although adverse circumstances prevent me from coming to Athens, please know that I will be there among you in spirit during this ceremony, which is being held at the location selected long ago, at my urging, by the International Olympic Committee. It is important for its current members to gather in their turn at the foot of the eternal mountain, to honor the work we have done together so far. It is particularly important for them to have an opportunity to pay solemn tribute to the memory of the great ancestors whose efforts long ago laid the foundations of culture.

This is an act of gratitude, but an act of hope, as well. After overcoming its modernist agitation, and fully accepting the good and useful things provided by scientific progress, by the very force of ideas and things modern society will return to the Hellenic ideal, the most sensible and the most profound of all the ideas that men have striven to put into practice.

My faith in Hellenism, in its future, and in its continued fruitfulness has grown ever more firm over the past forty years. At the eventide of my journey, I see clearly – for evenings are known for their final, brief, but intense clarity – that above and beyond all forms of government, economic organizations, and diplomatic understandings – above all else, one might say – must reign that threefold harmony first outlined in Hellenism.

In attempting to strike a balance among morality, the city, and the individual, Hellenism based that balance on conscience, solidarity, and personal instinct. In their approaches to life, most peoples have neglected one or another of these three factors. "Only Hellenism could understand that balance had to be created on three levels, laboring to bring them into harmony by placing the intimate and mysterious call of the conscience on one level, the imperatives of communal duty on another, and the prolific freedom of individual instinct on the third."

I would change nothing in these lines that I wrote twenty years ago. Today, as then, I would add this piece of advice: "You foreigners who gather at the foot of the Acropolis, after completing at the sacred rock the traditional pilgrimage that humanity owes to the illustrious dead who left an unparalleled legacy to humanity, remember the living. In the white streets of Athens, bow with respect before the Orthodox priest and the merchant, whose obstinate patriotism during centuries of slavery and poverty fed the sacred flame of the Hellenism that the world needs, in their humble sanctuaries and modest stalls."

ZITO ELLAS! [Long Live Greece!]

Pierre de Coubertin

A mes amis hellènes,
in: *Textes choisis*, Vol. II, p. 73.
Special printing (Archives of the IOC)

4.1/6 THE NEW PANATHENEAN GAMES

During his visit to Greece in 1927, Coubertin spoke to the minister of culture about reviving the heritage of Ancient Greece through the holding of regular events. One such event was the reintroduction of the Panathenian Games, but these were actually held just once, in 1930[1]. In the following article, Coubertin explains the significance of the Panathenian Games.

It must be acknowledged that there was something lacking about the celebration of modern Olympiads. Vainly had I endeavoured to preserve the particular stamp of antiquity about that institution while adapting it to the requirements of modern times. But the Athens stadium had been steeped too long in the silence of death. Now the glorious monument seemed to have come back to life only to lose it again. Celebrate there again the restored Olympic Games, would not be possible before a long time; moreover it would be with the risks of a very imperfect installation, for, as one knows the curving of the track is too short for our modern runners. Their speed is so great that they require much wider and easier curves. As things are, they feel constrained and even run the risk of coming to harm. The vexation felt on realizing this gave birth in Athens to a somewhat barbarous scheme. There was a talk in certain sporting circles of raising the level of the stadium so as to give sufficient width to the track... Of course, the Athenian common sense rebelled against such a treatment of the sacred spot twice consecrated to eternal youth. And yet, Greeks were alarmed at feeling that their participation in the celebration of the renewed Olympiads, was not what it should be. Now that peace was restored and regular work, made possible, that feelings became keener. A solution was found, and I am glad I contributed to it in that same spirit of ancestral piety and of due regard to present needs which has guided me for the past thirty-three years and is still guiding my friend and successor, Count de Baillet-Latour. This solution consists in the restoration of the famous "Panathenaea", in their amplification and transformation. It is the mayor of Athens who in the course of an official reception given to me at the Town Hall on the 7th of April last, expressed, while (mentioning) that celebrated name, the wishes of the city. Plans to that effect were immediately elaborated, with the consent of the Government, by the Hellenic Olympic Committee. Celebrated for the first time in 1930, they will be known as the "Panathenaeas of the 9th Olympiad" and will be held in future once every fourth year. They will consist of three parts: athletic contests in the stadium, an historical procession from the stadium to the foot of the Acropolis, and finally a music festival in the theatre of Herod Atticus. As regards the last point, I proposed and obtained that a "Cycle of Gluck" should be taken up. The divine strains that bring back to us, as it were, the melodious presence of the soul of

1 The secretary present during the meeting was the young Jean Ketseas, who, with Carl Diem, put forward the idea of an Olympic Academy in 1938. That is why various publications mistakenly claim the founding of the Academy to be a result of this meeting.
Cf. N. Müller: IOA. *30 years of IOA as mirrored by its lectures 1961-1990.* Lausanne, IOC, 1991, pp. III-VI.

antiquity, do not receive nowadays the honour due to them. The numerous admirers of Gluck have often expressed the wish that a cycle of his great works should be performed; as far as I am concerned, the proposal was not a new one. But where could one find a more perfectly appropriated frame, a more favourable atmosphere, surroundings better adapted?

The athletic contest will not last more than two or three days at most, for they will be strictly limited to the ancient trials of strength and skill: races on classical distances, jumping, throwing of weights and wrestling, – all according to the ancient methods which differ widely from ours. They differ chiefly on a point of capital importance. For the present-day athlete, every thing is made smooth and easy. Highly perfected, elastic tracks are set for him, every detail being calculated in order to help his effort and enable him to increase his records. But such are not the "courses of life". So that good care was taken in ancient times to make things as difficult as possible to him so as to increase his merit in victory and his endurance in the trial. Here are two philosophies of sport opposed to one another and almost contradictory. Each has its own adepts, but those of the latter discuss the former only in theory. Henceforth they will have living arguments before them and it will be possible to make interesting comparisons. Of course, the majority will remain staunch followers of the modernist point of view, but there are already some countries where the ancient conception has been taken up again and a legion of athletes will be formed whose performances will be followed with no little interest.

It is the duty of all to hail with goodwill the homage thus rendered to ancient athletism and immortal Hellas. Besides, the Olympic unity will be hereby strengthened. It has been sought in vain to destroy or at least to weaken it. It answers a deep feeling based on powerful realities. That is why it has always emerged from the subtle attacks levelled against it. It will never be beaten.

Les nouvelles Panathénées, in:
Bulletin Officiel du CIO, September 1927, pp. 5-6.
English version in: Coubertin, *The Olympic Idea,* Schorndorf, 1967, pp. 104-105.

4.2 THE SIGNIFICANT STAGES IN THE DEVELOPMENT OF THE OLYMPIC MOVEMENT

4.2.1 THE EARLY HISTORY OF THE OLYMPIC MOVEMENT

The first section of the "early history of the Olympic Movement" describes the "Olympic Games of Much Wenlock". For Coubertin, aside from the excavation at Olympia, this was the event that contributed most toward shaping and inspiring his understanding of the "international" Olympic Games[1].

In the following article Coubertin mentions that he visited the site of the Much Wenlock Olympic Games in late October 1890, and that he contacted their founder, William Penny Brookes. For this occasion Brookes organized a kind of Olympic sports meeting entirely for Coubertin. In memory of the Olympic movement he also planted an oak tree, a large tree today, in the field of the Wenlock Olympic Games.

Elsewhere Coubertin notes that as far as he was concerned, the only possible name to be used was "the Olympic Games: it was even possible to invent another one[2]".

4.2.1/1 THE OLYMPIC GAMES AT MUCH WENLOCK – A PAGE FROM THE HISTORY OF ATHLETICS

WHAT DO YOU MAKE OF MUCH WENLOCK?

I can just imagine your confusion at the connection of this barbaric name and these ancient memories. Much Wenlock is a town in Shropshire, a county located along the border of Wales. The fact that the Olympic Games, which modern Greece has been unable to restore, are being revived today is due not to a Hellene, but to Dr. W. P. Brookes. He is the one who began them forty years ago. At age 82, still alert and vigorous, he is still organizing and running them.

Athleticism is widely but incorrectly held always to have been the natural pastime of the Anglo-Saxons, even though it is neither a pastime, nor natural, nor ancient. Forty years ago, athleticism had few enthusiasts as deeply supportive as W. P. Brookes. Those who knew him were astonished at the significance he attached to the matter of physical education, still poorly understood at the time. Certainly they must have wondered what influence the promotional activities that this stubborn man engaged in would have outside the area where he practiced medicine. I can just

1 In Germanic or Scandinavian Europe, as far back as the late 18th century, at the time of the philanthropists, there were also a great many local "Olympic Games". Obviously, Coubertin was unaware of this fact. On this topic see K. Lennartz, *Kenntnisse und Vorstellungen von Olympia und den Olympischen Spielen in der Zeit von 393-1896* [Understandings and Representations of Olympia and the Olympic Games from 393 to 1896], Schorndorf, Hofmann 1974.

2 Coubertin, "The Modern Olympic Games," in: *Official Report*, Part 2, Athens/London 1897, p. 4.

imagine that some of his fellow citizens did as the residents of Limoges once did. When they saw my friend Lagrange engaging in athletic experiments, which were to give rise to his work entitled *Physiologie des exercices du corps* [The Physiology of Physical Exercises], they said to each other, with a look of pity, "Poor Lagrange! He's off his rocker!" In fact he did take off, but only to move to Paris where the laurels of the Institut de France awaited him. For his part, Dr. Brookes never left Much Wenlock, but he held the number one position there which, as Caesar said, is better than being number two in London.

The story of the physical renaissance in England is a curious tale to tell. Whatever the taste and zeal of the English in a former age for manly sports, there is no denying that the 18th century had made a clean sweep of it. The only places frequented by students were taverns and dives where they played cards. At Eton, some exercises did attract a few adepts, and Wellington was able to claim that the battle of Waterloo had been won "on the playing fields of Eton". But that was nothing more than an isolated incident. Besides, can one really compare these coarse amusements, marked by such brutality, with modern athleticism which is – you will forgive me for going, once more, against the grain of deep-rooted prejudices – , a school of savoir-faire and of social refinement? Look in Dr. Johnston's dictionary. Under the word *Athletic*, you will find a definition that shows that the very meaning of the culture of physical strength through exercise had been lost. Historians will put Canon Kingsley, and his group of "Christian athletes" who professed and put into practice the adage *mens sana in corpore sano,* in the forefront of those who rediscovered this meaning. At the same time, the great Arnold appealed to athleticism, making it his most powerful moral ally at the restored Rugby. A few years later, the first athletic club was established at Exeter College, Oxford (1850). Five years after that, St. John's College, Cambridge, stepped to the fore in its own right. In 1857, Cambridge had an athletic federation, and its students organized competitions. In 1864, the first of the famous interscholastic meets took place, the results of which are now telegraphed from one end of the world to the other. The *Times* published just two scant lines on the results in an remote corner of the paper, which was otherwise filled with the somber details of war between Denmark and Germany.

How times have changed! "From the furthest ends of Australian pastures to the ranches of Texas, from the Pampas of South America to the plateaus of the Himalayas, around the Kraals of southern Africa and in the marketplaces of China and Japan, groups gather to hear the story of the battles of strength and endurance that take place on the Isis and the Cam, with much greater interest than in the battles of the Old World for the supremacy of power. On the island where athleticism was born, and in the countries of its adoption, no news is so anxiously awaited, gathered more regularly, disseminated more quickly, or commented upon more universally than the results of the eight-man intercollegiate rowing competition, the athletic sports meets at the Queen's Club, or, indeed, of baseball games in New York and Chicago[1]. "Oh, there was no lack of opponents, no attack was spared". People have cried out, cursed, and fought against this spread of athleticism, but the nay-sayers have been drowned out by the rising tide. I believe that this tide is healthy and fruitful. I will do *anything* to increase its strength, to help it overcome the obstacles that are thrown in its path in France today, as in England before.

Prize-giving ceremony at the Much Wenlock Games in the 1880s. Brookes, the founder of the Games, standing on the right of the lady who is presenting the prize. (Wenlock Olympian Society Collection)

But when you go looking for the origins of this vast movement, in order to see what those origins really were, merely tracking down the main factors will not be enough. From time to time ideas move around the world, spreading like an epidemic. It is very difficult to credit them all to a single individual. Generally one finds that, without coming to an explicit understanding or reaching an agreement among themselves, several men were working on the same task at the same time, in different places.

That is what happened in England. Isolated efforts were made here and there, and the episode that I will recount for you is one of the most curious in the annals of athletics. It is a story enveloped by a veil of poetry, fragrant with the scent of antiquity. Dr. Brookes studied medicine in Paris under the Restoration. Evidently he had felt the mysterious influence that the Greek civilization has continuously exerted over humanity throughout the ages more strongly than anyone else. The ideal – so pure and so practical, so divine and yet so human – that was the keystone of the Greek system was perfectly designed to captivate the English when they began to link great destinies in the beyond to the clear, simple meaning of life. This is not a rare occurrence with them, this twofold perspective, eyes cast down on the ground yet lost in the heavens, this double current that causes them to seek rest from their business activities in reading Plutarch and Homer.

This is why Dr. Brookes wrote words that sum up his entire program at the top of the statutes of the Olympian Society: "The purpose of the Society is to contribute to the development of the physical, moral, and intellectual qualities of the residents of

1 C. Turner, *The Progress of Athletism.*

Wenlock, through the encouragement of outdoor exercises, and through the annual competition for prizes and medals intended to reward the best literary and artistic productions, as well as the most remarkable feats of strength and skill". This program is summed up in the wonderful saying *Civium vires civitatis vis*, the strength of the citizens is the strength of the city – interpreted in the Athenian, not the Spartan sense. Yet in some ways antiquity was not enough for Dr. Brookes. It did not know of gallantry. So he drew on some chivalrous customs of the Middle Ages. He had the winner of the tournament bend his knee to receive the symbolic laurel from the hands of a lady.

On festival days, long processions wound through the streets of the small town. School children sang hymns and strew flowers. Banners were carried aloft. Green garlands adorned the houses. At the head of the procession the herald strode in full regalia. At the end of the procession, riding on horseback, came the tilters who competed for rings, a very popular exercise at Wenlock. For the most part, the athletes were young farmers from the neighboring area, people who did not always have the most delicate touch, but solid, fearless riders nonetheless. Wenlock is located at the bottom of a valley. The railroad from Wellington to Craven Arms crosses the valley; the houses surround the grandiose ruins of an abbey founded by the Benedictines of La Charité-sur-Loire. Pastures and hills dotted with woods lie all around. The playing field of the *Olympian Society* includes a track for foot races, areas for cricket and lawn tennis, a track for equestrian exercises, great stands for the spectators, a pool used in good weather, and finally, a carefully manicured lawn where open-air dances are held. But what contributes most to the beauty of the site are the skillful plantings that surround the place with a wreath of green. An exceptional variety of precious species is represented there. All these trees commemorate some significant event, a victory, or a visit. For the jubilee of Queen Victoria, they planted an oak to which a poet addressed inspired verses, the tree's roots watered with champagne, according to custom. Other trees bear the names of the King of Greece, the Empress of Germany, the Prince of Wales, Lord Charles Beresford, Lord Wolseley, Herbert Gladstone, etc. As you can see, my tree is keeping fair company. It has golden yellow leaves and a great desire to grow. Since it will fly the three colors of France during ceremonies there, I hope it will grow very tall, too.

France's colors were flying everywhere last October 22, and despite the stubborn, raging rains that fell, the procession was as solemn as any self-respecting procession should be. A triumphal arch decorated the entrance to the field. It was made of flowers, and bore a great banner wishing me welcome, and wishing prosperity for my country. Then we proceeded to plant the tree, and from a great silver goblet, the foam of the champagne was poured onto the shrub. Then the goblet was passed around, in the English manner, each one putting his lips to it while Dr. Brookes addressed friendly words to me, words that modesty prevents me from repeating. I would like to single out just one thing from his remarks: Dr. Brookes knows France, he understands it, and he loves it.

I will not say anything about the foot races and the other exercises that have now become widely accepted here in France. The equestrian portion of the competition, however, merits description. Tilting consists of picking up a metal ring with a pointed wooden lance while at full gallop. At Wenlock, the lance is very long and the ring very narrow. Moreover, to increase the difficulty a hedge is placed across the track just past the stand where the ring hangs. So the rider's task is difficult, and he is owed a great deal of credit. Every year, the person crowned champion the year before must defend his title. The herald solemnly proclaims the challenge, and the champion throws his glove to the ground. All those who accept the challenge come one by one to pick up the glove, and the battle ensues. I have already mentioned how the winner receives his award from the hands of a lady, who places a richly embroidered shoulder belt over his shoulders, and places a crown of laurel on his head.

The "Yeomanry", or regional cavalry of the County, which participated in the last tournament, engaged in tent-pegging, another quite fascinating sport. People in the Indies are mad over this sport. It consists of driving pieces of wood into the ground such that a flat surface approximately 30 centimeters on a side is created above the lawn. The rider, this time armed with a heavier, stronger lance, arrives at a full gallop, drives the point of his lance into the wood and, with an appropriate flick of the wrist, wrenches the wood from the ground. One difficulty, which is easily surmounted, however, consists of hitting the center of the target with enough force to penetrate it with the iron. But as soon as one feels the resistance, without losing a fraction of a second since the horse is still galloping, one must overcome the real problem: lifting the recalcitrant piece of wood from the ground.

To conclude these personal reminiscences, I would like to mention that the festival ends with a banquet for about 60 individuals, followed by a ball which could not be held outdoors because of the weather. During the banquet there were a number of toasts accompanied by singing. In England when they want to honor a guest, they sing a song telling him he is "a jolly good fellow". Mr. Gladstone himself accepted that honor, and the day before that, if memory serves, the electors of Mr. John Morley had granted him what they call "the musical honors". The ball was held in the great reading room attached to the public library. This, too, is part of the domain of the Olympian Society, which is concerned with the brain as well as the muscles, you will recall. In truth, Wenlock is a happy place. I do not know whether there is any other town that is so well provisioned with everything that a progressive and generous municipality can make available to its citizens. The moment one sets foot there, one senses the privileged nature of the place. The train station is a delightful cottage surrounded by flowers and banks of greenery. The City Hall houses a collection of curiosities found in the area, and few athletic Associations have, I believe, a more beautiful field of play than the one used by the Olympian Society.

All this material and moral progress, all this physical and intellectual culture took a rather long period of time, during which athleticism spread throughout England, overflowed to America, Australia, and the Indies, and has taken hold in Holland, Belgium, France, Italy, South America, and so on. It has not taken on the form that Dr. Brookes gave it at Wenlock. It is based on the principles of the past, which are as true and as noble today as they once were in the gymnasiums of Athens, yet their form is modern. This means cricket, football, rowing, gymnastics, fencing – in a word, exercise that is appropriate for our customs and habits in 1890. An effort was made about 1866 to expand and generalize the Olympic Games. A festival was held at the Crystal palace that year, one that was repeated the following year in Birmingham and then in Shrewsbury, if memory serves. This movement served a purpose. It gave supporters of athleticism an opportunity to get together and get a count of themselves. Soon, though, enthusiasm for these physical exercises spread with irresistible power. There was no need to invoke memories of Greece or to seek encouragement from the past. People like sports for sports' sake.

An even more daring effort took place in Greece. Dr. Brookes, whose activity and energy are equaled only by the clarity of his vision and the uprightness of his approach, the Dr. Brookes who had maintained a voluminous correspondence with all those whom he felt were favorable to his cause, wrote to the King of the Greeks. In response to Dr. Brookes' efforts, the king donated a magnificent cup for the competitions at Wenlock, and supported the restoration of the Olympic Games at Athens. But patronage is not everything. The Greeks took part in one competition, and then rested. In the annals of Wenlock, I have seen the results of this competition, and the names of the winners. Since then, there has been nary a word about Olympic Games at Athens.

Dr. Brookes acted extensively and under all sorts of circumstances, but he also spoke a great deal. He spoke with that simple and intelligent eloquence that, when placed at the service of a fixed, authoritative idea, is irresistible to his listeners. In 1866, at the festival that I mentioned a little earlier, at the end of an address he spoke these memorable words, which must be meditated upon religiously: "If the time should ever come when the youth of this country once again abandons the fortifying exercises of the gymnasium, the manly games, the outdoor sports that give health and life, in favor of effeminate and pacific amusements, know that that will mean the end of freedom, influence, strength, and prosperity for the whole empire". I say that these words are memorable because they were prophetic. The reason for England's expansion, its prodigious progress over the past forty years, is none other than its children's love for "the fortifying exercises of the gymnasium, the manly games, the outdoor sports that give health and life."

Les Jeux Olympiques à Much Wenlock,
in: *La Revue Athlétique,*
Vol. 1, December 25, 1890, no. 12, pp. 705-713.

4.2.1/2 PHYSICAL EXERCISES IN THE MODERN WORLD. LECTURE GIVEN AT THE SORBONNE (NOVEMBER 1892)

This document is tremendously important in Olympic history. Here, for the first time, Coubertin went public with his idea of reviving the Olympic Games in modern conditions. Forty years later, in his Olympic Memoirs, he describes this moment in a very narrative form[1].

To the astonishment of the experts, the manuscript long believed to have been lost was published in 1994 by François d'Amat as "The Olympic Manifesto" through the Lausanne-based "Les Editions du Grand Pont", in a facsimile of the French original and as a transcript, but also with an English translation. The IOC supported this project. The first part is almost identical to Coubertin's article "Le Rétablissement des Jeux Olympiques"[2] which appeared in the American Popular Magazine *The Chautauquan*[3] under the title "The Re-establishment of the Olympic Games" in September 1894. The second and third paragraphs contained around 30% of the same material.

Coubertin had already included, word for word, the final section with the suggestion of reviving the Olympic Games in his first autobiography "Une Campagne de vingt-et-un ans"[4], in a reference to his speech in 1892, so this was already known.[5]

Physical exercises count in the modern world three cities which serve them as a metropolis: Berlin, Stockholm and London – from where three systems have subsequently spread to other regions, each based on ideas well known to the ancient world, incompletely or unconsciously accepted by the middle ages and renaissance and which can be summarized in three words: war, hygiene and sport. I would very quickly like to describe the characteristic features of each, indicate their progress through the present age and finally describe France's part in this great movement that has so aptly been called the physical renaissance.

I

The century which began so tragically and which is coming to an end in troubled and uncertain peace follows one of great intellectual activity and veritable physical inertia. There might perhaps be grounds for seeking in this over-subtle contrast the initial causes of some of the imbalances from which we are suffering today. But that is not our field. Let us note merely that everywhere at the end of the 18th century violent exercise and virile games had gone out of fashion, and men went in search of amusement and pleasure elsewhere. In this respect, even

1 See text 4.2.1/9 of this volume.
2 See *Revue de Paris* June 15, 1894, pp. 170-184.
3 Vol. 19, pp. 696-700.
4 Paris 1909, p. 90.
5 Coubertin had published a short summary of his 1892 speech in the "Compte Rendu des Fêtes du Jubilé de l'Union". In: *Annuaire 1892-1893 de l'U.S.F.S.A.*, Paris 1893, p. 64.

the England of the day was in a most surprising condition. It was no longer the England of the Tudors living in the open air and enjoying all the associated pleasures, nor was it the England of Thomas Arnold and the creators of athletic education. It was an irresolute people among whom native brutality was mixed with a kind of weakening of purpose, which could have heralded decadence had Napoleon not arrived to strengthen Great Britain, as the north wind halts a thaw. In France, the tennis courts were deserted; they were the place for exchanging oaths, but nobody played there. Long gone were the days when Sire de Gouberville used to push his ball around on the beaches of Cotentin on Sunday afternoons surrounded by the valiant youth from the neighbouring villages; when those Homeric combats which Mr. Siméon Luce finds recounted in the parchments he consults were contested from parish to parish; and when the clergy of Avranches themselves, at certain festivals of the liturgical year, went down in procession to the river bank to indulge in a joyful game of hockey. All that was dead, and when the Directoire, steeped in memories of Ancient Greece, wanted to set up on the Champ de Mars in Paris something akin to the Olympic Games, one indispensable element was missing: competitors. There were doubtless boys who came, as boys do at fairs, to try climbing the greasy pole and win the traditional leg of mutton or bottle of Benedictine. But that is not enough to supply athletics meetings and, lacking a Racing Club and a Stade Francais to organize and maintain them, the Directoire competitions quickly faded and died like roses.

It is true that, at the same time, on our borders, beyond our borders and far away, at the foot of the Pyramids, on the Danube, in Spain, beneath the walls of the Moscow Kremlin, for the twenty years of a mad and sublime epic the soldiers of France gave the world one of the most athletic spectacles it had ever witnessed. In that short space of time, they exhausted the strength which the nation had accumulated over several centuries. The blood that they spilled was that of the tennis players and the Sires de Gouberville, it was the blood of France, tainted in the towns, still intact in the country ... and not that of the weaklings and libertines of the Regency. And then, Gentlemen, you know how our soldiers are. When they have no more strength left, they invent it!

Oh! the great need to rest that France had after this long outburst of courage, and great heavens! how well one understands that France should go and play dominoes instead of exercising its tired muscles. Sated with victory, France gradually fell asleep while, beside its black, total, horrible defeat had awakened energies which laboured grimly at the undertaking that you know: the German empire. It was thus that military athletics was born in Berlin.

It has often been said in France that on the battlefields of 1866 and 1870, the real winner was the schoolmaster; if it is to this belief that we owe the sight of schools opening across our country and popular education spreading so rapidly, then thank heaven for it. But I think that, in believing this, we are giving the teacher more than his due and rather forgetting his colleague, the gymnastics master.

German gymnastics, Gentlemen, that which immediately after Jena found ardent and convinced apostles to preach its gospel, then numerous, docile disciples to follow its precepts, is energetic in its movements, based on strict discipline and, in a word, military in its essence. Everywhere in Germany, right up until yesterday,

The main auditorium in the old Sorbonne. Here, on November 25, 1892, Coubertin for the first time publicly expressed his idea of international Olympic Games. (Source: Bibliothèque de la Sorbonne)

reigned hierarchy, obedience and precision. From childhood, the little schoolboy took his seat in the row and looked up at a superior to await orders from him. As an older pupil, he continued to make his muscles and will supple, to be able to mobilize them as soon as the call came. For that is the goal of German gymnastics, and it is easy to distinguish the qualities and imperfections that such an ideal brings with it. As a student, his greatest pleasure was to fight with his companions, and the scars that resulted on his face were like marks of nobility. There was uniformity in the smallest details of his existence, and the regulation of them seemed to procure within him a joy which the English and French are incapable of grasping. Even today, one has merely to visit a German university, to attend one of the students' meetings where glasses are emptied upon command, to understand the disciplinary frenzy that has worked on this great people. In the constitution of their revolutionary party, the socialists themselves have included something of the militarism which has impregnated the whole of Germany during the present century.

Fêtes du Cinquième Anniversaire de la fondation de l'Union des Sociétés Françaises de Sports Athlétiques.

Commission d'organisation.

Président : M. le Vicomte Léon de Janzé.
Vice-Président : M. M. Gondinet.
Secrétaire Général : M. le Bon Pierre de Coubertin.
Secrétaire : M. Jules Marcadet.
Trésorier : M. L. P. Reichel.
Membres : MM. Georges Bourdon - Paul Champ - Paul Dedet - Ch. Delagrave - Lucien Faure Dujarric - C. Heywood - R. Jung - Ad. de Pallissaux - le Cte Jacques de Pourtalès - G. Raymond - Ch. Richefeu - E. Saint-Chaffray - R. Schmitten - G. Waroquet.

Programme.

Dimanche 20 Novembre (Après-midi). - Excursion à Ville d'Avray. Punch.

Lundi 21 Novembre (Soir). - Assaut d'inauguration du "Club House" du Stade Français.

Jeudi 24 Novembre (Après-midi). - Cross-Country Interscolaire à Bellevue.

Vendredi 25 Novembre (Soir). - Séance solennelle dans l'Amphithéâtre de la Sorbonne.

Dimanche 27 Novembre (Matin). - Réunion Interclubs au Bois de Boulogne.
(Soir). - Banquet

Toutes les Sociétés de l'Union participeront à ces fêtes. Des fêtes locales seront organisées par les Sociétés de province que leur éloignement empêcherait d'y prendre part.

Les prix du Cross-Country et de la Réunion Interclubs consisteront en objets d'art. Les membres de l'Union désireux d'offrir un prix ou de participer aux dépenses occasionnées par ces fêtes sont priés d'adresser leur offrande à M. L. P. Reichel, Trésorier, 9 Rue Royer-Collard. Paris. Toutes les autres communications doivent être adressées à Mr de Coubertin, 20 Rue Oudinot. Paris.

IMP. MESNEL, 128, RUE DU BAC. PARIS.

Programme of festivities for the fifth anniversary of the founding of the Union des Sociétés Françaises des Sports Athlétiques (USFSA – Union of French Sports Associations) in 1892. Coubertin first mentioned the idea of international Olympic Games at the formal Session held on 25th November 1892. (IOC Archives)

I said that German gymnastics was energetic in its movements. On that condition alone, it is effective. Now, for this energy to be maintained, gymnasts must perpetually be under a warlike influence. The idea of war must never cease to inspire them. If Germany frees itself from that idea, its innumerable gymnastic clubs will rapidly change. Already in some parts of its territory, sport has made its appearance: the result of twenty years of peace at home and abroad . The young athlete is beginning to think about physical effort for itself, and not its more-orless longer term consequences. If he wants to jump a hedge, he will make himself as light as possible in order to clear it as high as possible. Now, in the country, one does not have bare arms or legs or a thin jersey as the only clothing on one's body. For his part, the gymnast is less concerned about achieving athletic prowess than moving nimbly with arms and baggage. In the same way, if they are no longer inspired by the prospect of military service, ensemble movements become tedious, gestures become weak; they are barely sketched out; there is no soul in them. Likewise, group runs break up; the runners regain their individuality; they no longer worry whether they go well together, in step; it is who goes fastest, who arrives first.

From a physical point of view, German gymnastics is artificial; it is made up of exercises which have no raison d'etre in themselves, which are not in nature and which can be obtained from men only by offering them as a goal something grand and noble which can fascinate and train them. This, Gentlemen is what has made it successful, and it is this which will undoubtedly cause its decline in the future.

But it has had offshoots. In America and Australia, not to mention France, which we shall come back to presently, numerous clubs have been created. Wherever they go in the world, the English take a tennis racquet and a bible with them, and are never parted from them. When they go abroad, the Germans take sauerkraut and gymnastics. You know how large the German colony is in the United States. Certain recent facts have drawn attention to what I, were I a citizen of the United States, would consider a national danger. Now, the Germans in America profess great admiration for European Germany. Well-established in their land of freedom, with an ocean between them and their former homeland, they ceaselessly praise the yoke that they were unable to bear, proudly say the name of the Emperor and dream of Germanizing through language and customs a large part of the new world where they are established without the slightest intention of returning. Thus they have founded gymnastic clubs for their children based on those in the old country and which constitute a totally separate and homogeneous organization in that chaos of systems that they refer to over there as Physical Education.

You will tell me that this gymnastics lacks what I referred to earlier as the essential condition for its success: the military idea and prospect of the battlefield. Do not believe it, Gentlemen. You are led to see only merchants, traders and businessmen in these 69 million inhabitants. There is a thinking America, a scientific America and there is also a military America. While, materially, the traces of the War of Secession have disappeared, the moral traces are still visible: the shock produced in American hearts by this Herculean struggle has been passed right down to today, and I declare that the patriotism of the United States citizen is one of the strongest and most formidable that I know; one can expect anything from it.

While at West Point, where French military traditions are still honoured, an elite corps is trained, that of the officers of the federal army, each state now possesses a militia which one would be most mistaken to regard as a worthless national guard. I lack the time and competence to study the operation of it but I can draw your attention to three facts: the number of men enrolled, the perfection of their arms and equipment and finally the remarkable mobilization experiment which has just been conducted in Pennsylvania, when the occasion was far from favourable. The call was unexpected and it was not a question of fighting enemies from outside but of maintaining order in the midst of a bloody strike. Within 24 hours, these traders and businessmen left everything; the 25th hour found them armed and at the designated location.

For the most part, these militias are commanded and organized in German style. They present a singular mixture of those civic virtues which have produced the English volunteers and that spirit of discipline which distinguishes the German soldier. When the United States has rebuilt its navy, which it is working on, its spirit of enterprise could well become the spirit of conquest. I am one of those people who believe that, in the future, the Washington government will be trigger-happy. For these different reasons, it might be that military gymnastics escapes from the banks of the Spree where its decline seems imminent, to find pontiffs and worshippers on the banks of the Mississippi. In all cases, it will always have a chance of sprouting where there are great ambitions to be satisfied, revenge to be taken or slavery to be broken.

In Australia, the German colony is so small that it is barely worth mentioning. But some clubs have nevertheless sprung up, and although less widespread or aggressive than in the United States, militarism does play a role in the concerns of the public. Need I remind you of the agitation caused in the Australian cities by the incidents over the Samoa islands and the New Hebrides, the desire clearly expressed by public opinion to seize New Caledonia later or the sending by New South dales of a militia contingent to support the English in the Sudan?

In all this, I appear to be abandoning sport to study diplomatic issues. In reality, I am merely insisting on that important social law, namely that a close correlation between frame of mind, ambitions, the tendencies of a people and the way in which they understand and organize physical exercise in their country exists there.

II

That is true of Germany, Gentlemen, and that is true of Sweden. To move from German gymnastics to Swedish gymnastics is to hear a pastoral symphony after a heroic symphony. The Swedes are a happy people with little history for the last hundred years who devote themselves peacefully to a national and beneficent sport, skating, and to a singular and at first sight anodyne gymnastics called, after the name of its inventor, the Ling system.

I would hasten to say that between Ling and skating, it is definitely skating which would be the more entitled to receive the gratitude of the Swedes, their good health, the smooth balance of mind and body that distinguishes them. That tranquil temperament, the regular breath of life which sustains them, are, they believe, thanks to the learned inventor, but I have no hesitation in attributing these, on their behalf, to the wild races on the smooth northern ice, in the frozen air, to the healthy joys of the Scandinavian winter.

This does not mean that this Swedish gymnastics, which is even timidly starting to establish some colonies in Germany, London and New York, is devoid of merit. Our friend, I could say our illustrious friend, Dr. Lagrange, a member of the Board of our Union, went to study it in its native surroundings, and readers of the "Revue des Deux Mondes" know the impression that the Stockholm Institutes made upon him. "Swedish gymnastics", he said, "is the gymnastics of the weak". Precisely, and that is why we do not want it. Through the moderation of its movements it is suitable for delicate children and the aged alike. Through its scientific character, it is applicable to the sick. It was the medical side which chiefly interested and captivated Lagrange. "The French doctor who goes to study in Stockholm", he writes, "finds himself in the presence of things which are so new to him that he initially has difficulty in finding his bearings amidst such varied movements as he sees performed in the public or private 'Institutes'. But gradually the light dawns in his mind and he ends up classifying all these ingenious procedures and seeing that they are seeking, in short, two results: measuring out exercise and localizing it". To give you an idea of the boldness of this medical gymnastics based on a particularly thorough study into the muscular system, I shall tell you that through exercises and the different massages which are the corollaries of this, it treats even diseases of the heart. The results seem excellent, and for more than half a century, the Swedes have not tired of going to the Institutes in search of health. That alone makes it worth attending to, but lovers of physical exercise are not generally recruited from among the sick. It is the sound of body that we are dealing with. It is good that Swedish gymnastics should look after young children, particularly at an age when they are at risk of deviations and deformities; that the sick should be brought to it; and that it should offer the old exercises in keeping with what remains of their strength. But it should not seek to exercise power in the empire of the young; they need precisely what it repudiates: effort and emulation. Effort is obtained from it only by amplitude, never by energy of movement; it is reached slowly, never brusquely. And as for emulation, it is a dogma for this gymnastics that men must not measure themselves against each other, only against themselves.

To get our young athletes to give up effort and emulation, we should first have to remove all the blood from their veins. While a drop of blood is left, they will not give it up, that I guarantee. Truly, to give them such precepts would be to make fun of them, and that is too much like the caricature by Cham where the mother says to her little girl in the Tuileries Gardens: "Go and enjoy yourself, dear, but be careful not to catch a cold or get too hot, or crease your dress or get your boots dirty, mess up your hair or undo your cravat".

In Sweden itself, there has been a party of reformers working on making Swedish gymnastics more masculine, if I may put it like that; they are viewed with that indignation mixed with interest that revolutionaries everywhere always attract; they will gain the upper hand ... for a little while. When Swedish gymnastics ceases to make claims other than to the sick and the weak I see nothing that will prevent it from spreading all over the world, and for my part, I would have no objection helping it.

III

Gentlemen, we have already seen at the start of this discussion, how mistaken those were who believe that the taste for physical exercise is so deeply anchored in the English that it can never be eclipsed. These people cheerfully imagine that what they see has always existed; an England without sport is a nonsense to them. Now, this nonsense marked the whole of the end of the last century and the beginning of our own. Popular games had fallen into disuse; the monopolization of the right to hunt resulting from the creation of large properties had deprived the petty bourgeoisie of the country of their favourite pastime, and if boxers were to be seen killing each other here and there, or a rowing competition was held on the Thames, it was between professionals to give spectators the pleasure of losing their money on exaggeratedly high bets. There was nothing sporting or athletic about it. The England of those days knew only two distractions: doing business more or less honestly and getting drunk more or less completely. Colleges were a miniature version of society: no spirit of solidarity; indifference among the masters; the law of the jungle among the pupils. When studying this vulgar and shapeless organism, one cannot foresee all that the genius of an educator will bring out in the way of refinement and delicacy. For, – and here I am going against a common prejudice in France – in the whole world, there is not a system more refined, more delicate or more tender towards youth than the current English system; appearances are deceptive.

English athletics, Gentlemen, only recently began, and it is already taking over the world . The history of this great movement has not yet been written, but we know the main events. The names of Canon Kingsley and his followers do not yet belong to the distant past: sixty years have sufficed for this prodigious transformation. The first workers were less worried about going to school than obtaining some healthy pastimes. They were far-sighted, however. A certain philosophical glow surrounded them: reminders of Greece, respect for the stoic traditions and a fairly clear idea of the services that athletics could render the modern world were not slow in drawing attention to them. They were mocked, but ridicule did not discourage them. When the movement gained ground, they were furiously and angrily attacked . But their work was already under the protection of youth. The universities of Oxford and Cambridge had started to associate themselves with it. There they must have found the seed of magnificent recovery, a very necessary purification. At the same time, that great citizen, Thomas Arnold, the leader and classic model of English educators, gave the precise formula for the role of athletics in education. The cause was quickly understood and won. Playing fields sprang up all over England. The number of clubs grew. You have no idea of their number. London has a whole collection, not in the aristocratic quarters, but in the poor and popular areas. Every village has one or two, with the result that, while English law does not provide for the physical education of children, private initiative largely replaces it. Then, when they left their native land, the sons of Albion took the precious recipe with them, and athletics flowed into the two hemispheres in the most varied of climates.

In the United States precisely after the age of Romanticism, we wished to know what had become of it there, and taking advantage of the numerous congresses grouped around the Centennial Exhibition in 1889, we distributed throughout all the British and English-speaking colonies 7,000 copies of a questionnaire on games, their influence on education and their progress. This progress is constant, and the replies were of a unanimity that proved to us that the upward movement of athletics would attain gigantic proportions and that the experience of fifty years had merely confirmed everywhere the doctrines of Arnold and Kingsley. In the United States, to cite this country of statistics, Dr. Sargent, (an authority on the subject) estimates that between 1860 and 1870, 1 million dollars, from 1870 to 1880, 2.5 million dollars, and from 1880 to 1890, 25 million dollars were spent on setting up playing fields and exercise halls or manufacturing apparatus, making it a total of 28.5 million dollars.

In Australia, the Cape, Jamaica, Hong Kong or the Indies, the club yearbooks and rules for athletics meetings gave the impression of a veritable rising tide which I estimate today – and I would say that my calculations are based on very imperfect data – at around six million individuals, counting only adults registered as active members on the books of properly constituted clubs. In my calculations, I am including neither Belgium nor Holland where every day sport is making major strides, nor the countries where there might be isolated groups of amateurs.

A special press has been set up to cover the interests of the athletic world. Countless newspapers have appeared. The results of a baseball match played in Chicago or a rowing competition on the Paramatta travel around the world and find a place in the Times which, forty years ago, timidly devoted a small corner to announce the first foot races between Oxford and Cambridge. On the days of major meetings business stops, offices are empty, and there is a truce like in Ancient Greece to applaud the young people as they pass.

They pass, Gentlemen, with the merit of seeking in effort only the effort itself, of imposing upon themselves constraints to which no-one is pushing them, of submitting themselves to a discipline which is doubly effective because freely consented to. It is very noble and fine to think of war; it is laudable to think of hygiene; but it is more perfectly human to worship effort in a disinterested way and love difficult things simply because they are difficult.

That is the philosophy of sport in general and of our union in particular.

IV

In 1886, Gentlemen, France was not so badly endowed in terms of physical exercises as some people seem to believe. I shall not mention the brave Colonel Amoros who was certainly a convert, but had composed a collection of religious and moral songs which his pupils would sing as they stamped their feet, which means that the Salvation Army has as much right to regard him as an ancestor as gymnastics does.

I shall limit myself in passing to salute the gymnastics clubs, the result of defeat... and springboard to victory, let us hope. Whatever may have been said by some who sometimes confuse them with that childish masquerade that has been called school battallions, they have rendered great and noble services, and the mere feeling which inspired their creation must make them sacred to all Frenchmen. The Club Alpine also deserves being mentioned for having reminded our compatriots that on their borders there are summits where one can breathe air which has never been used and where one stores up health of the body and of the soul. Finally, how could one forget fencing? Is it not our national sport, in which only Italy can rival us for supremacy, the one which allows us to savour honourably the joy of fighting, the greatest after the joy of living?

In 1886, however, a wing was missing from the edifice of physical education. I do not know if many architects had noticed, but none, to my knowledge, had presented a precise plan of the intended construction. One appeared in the newspaper Le Francais on 23rd August (1887) and although I do not wish to bring personal issues into this discussion, I insist on this date out of a feeling whose legitimacy could not be contested . At that time, the Academy of Medicine was rising up strongly against mental fatigue. It seemed to the author of the plan in question that an exit was being sought where there was only a wall. The Academy of Medicine stubbornly insisted on wanting a revision of the programmes as much to reduce the amount of mental work as to make room for Games. We have no time to play, it said. This was a serious mistake: there was time, there was sufficient time, and we were not wanting to be given more, but we made poor use of it. As for public opinion, it was getting lost in another direction. Why does nobody play at your institution: it said to the University. Go on, get going. Play and get people to play. That was easy to say and impracticable to do. The thing had to come from outside, a private initiative; it was necessary for a club with a base on each of the banks to undertake to throw a bridge across this river. The Sorbonne was one such base; the Racing Club and the Stade Francais could be the other – these two clubs, the one founded in 1882, the other in 1883 had ignored each other for some time. A man who has done more than any other for Athletic Sports, Mr G. de Saint Clair, brought them together on 18th January 1887. After a rally that day in the woods of Ville d'Avray, the Union des Sports Athlétiques was decided upon; it was definitively established and received its first statutes on the following 29th November. The first months of 1888 passed in discussions and steps leading to the constitution of a Committee for the Propagation of Physical Exercises. Mr Jules Simon and Mr Gréard were the first to enrol . Meetings were held on the following 31st May and 5th July; an inter-school cross-country race took place just outside Paris. You know the rest: the founding of the Physical Education League, the Gironde League which groups together the lycées of the Bordeaux Academy, the holding of competitions all over France, sometimes with too much noise and not enough competence, in short this great movement which for us, in five years has led to the result that you know, Gentlemen, and with which you are satisfied: your presence here confirms it.

V

SO MUCH FOR THE PAST; WHAT ABOUT THE FUTURE?

I shall not tell you, because the role of prophet is one full of danger, and also because it is high time I concluded this brief survey of universal history that has been presented to you tonight. The Union has great duties to perform towards both, the University and its own members; it will not fail in these.

Cela suffit pour encourager votre serviteur à songer maintenant à la seconde partie de son programme. il espère que vous l'y aiderez comme vous l'y avez aidé jusqu'ici et qu'avec vous, il pourra poursuivre et réaliser ~~grâce à vous, une œuvre grandiose et bienfaisante.~~ sur une base conforme aux conditions de la vie moderne, cette œuvre grandiose et bienfaisante: le rétablissement des Jeux Olympiques

Final paragraph of the manuscript of Coubertin's speech. For the first time, Coubertin mentions his idea to revive the Olympic Games. **(taken from Fr. d'Amat (ed.): Le Manifeste Olympique. Lausanne, Les Editions du Grand Pont, 1994, p.41)**

As for athletics in general, I do not know what its fate will be, but I wish to draw your attention to the important fact that it presents two new features, this time in the series of these secular transformations. It is democratic and international. The first of these characteristics will guarantee its future: anything that is not democratic is no longer viable today. As for the second, it opens unexpected prospects to us. There are people whom you call utopians when they talk to you about the disappearance of war, and you are not altogether wrong; but there are others who believe in the progressive reduction in the chances of war, and I see no utopia in this. It is clear that the telegraph, railways, the telephone, the passionate research in science, congresses and exhibitions have done more for peace than any treaty or diplomatic convention. Well, I hope that athletics will do even more. Those who have seen 30,000 people running through the rain to attend a football match will not think that I am exaggerating. Let us export rowers, runners and fencers; there is the free trade of the future, and on the day when it is introduced within the walls of old Europe the cause of peace will have received a new and mighty stay.

This is enough to encourage your servant to dream now about the second part of this programme; he hopes that you will help him as you help him hitherto, and that with you he will able to continue and complete, on a basis suited to the conditions of modern life, this grandiose and salutary task, the restoration of the Olympic Games.

Conférence faite à la Sorbonne au Jubilé de l'U.S.F.S.A., le 25 novembre 1892.
In: Pierre de Coubertin: *Le Manifeste Olympique*, édité par François d'Amat.
Lausanne, Les Editions du Grand Pont, 1994, pp.66-79.
Revised by N. Müller & H. Skinner.

4.2.1/3 – 4.2.1/8 INTRODUCTION

The following five documents differ from the other writings of Coubertin presented in this volume. These are official documents involving the holding of the International Congress of 1894, which was to reach the decision to restore the Olympic Games. The historic value of these documents justifies their inclusion here, even though they are not signed by Coubertin.

The first document "An Appeal" refers to a meeting in 1893 when Coubertin, as secretary general, spoke of the need to call the International Congress of 1894. He addressed the issue of distinctions drawn between amateurs and professionals in antiquity and in modern times. The U.S.F.S.A. was to become the precursor of a "purified" athletic movement, and was to use the Congress called for 1894 to that end. The restoration of the Olympic Games was not mentioned explicitly, but allusion was made to values proper to the ancient Olympic Games. Clearly Coubertin was attempting to avoid irritating his audience with specific proposals that were too novel.

On January 15, 1894, a circular letter was sent along with the "Preliminary Program" to all the known athletic associations abroad.

On November 27, 1893 in New York, and on February 7, 1894 in London, Coubertin had held preparatory meetings with the local representatives of athletics. In this way, he hoped to prepare peoples' minds, and ensure the greatest possible chances of success for his project.

Another significant document that we also reproduce here is the official program of the Congress of Paris, printed in May, 1894. From then on, the "Olympic Games" were as important as the "issue of amateurism". The program included more than the proposal to restore the Games; it already began to deal with the practical matter of potential athletic disciplines, qualification to participate in the Games, and how the Games were to be organized. In addition, it was proposed that an International Committee be established to prepare the first modern Olympic Games.

As additional sources, we have reprinted the agenda of the Congress and related exhibitions. In the Official Report of 1896, Coubertin describes how he got his ideas and the past history of the Games of Athens.

4.2.1/3 THE CONGRESS OF PARIS

This Congress has been called by decision of the Board of the Union des Sociétés françaises des Sports athlétiques in the spring of 1893, at the request of Mr. A. de Pallissaux and Mr. Coubertin. Three committee members were placed in charge of organizing the congress: Baron Pierre de Coubertin, secretary general of the Union, for continental Europe; C. Herbert, secretary of the Amateur Athletic Association, for England and its colonies; and W. M. Sloane, Professor at Princeton University (United States) for the American continent.

A preliminary meeting was held at the University Club in New York on November 27, 1893. A second meeting was held at the Sports Club in London on February 7, 1894. In the meantime, the program of the Congress was sent with the following appeal to the athletic and sports associations throughout the world. The appeal read, "It is our honor to inform you of the enclosed program for the International Congress, which will meet in Paris next June 17 under the auspices of the Union des Sociétés françaises des Sports athlétiques. The purpose of this Congress is twofold. We must uphold the noble and chivalrous character of athleticism, which has distinguished it in the past, so that it may continue effectively to play the admirable role in the education of modern peoples that was attributed to it by the Greek masters. Human imperfection always tends to transform the Olympic athlete into a circus gladiator. A choice must be made between these two incompatible approaches to athletics. To defend against the spirit of gain and professionalism that threatens to invade them, amateurs in most countries have established complex legislation that is replete with compromise and contradiction. In other places, too often the letter of the law is shown greater respect than the spirit.

Reform is necessary, but before it is implemented that reform must be discussed. The issues placed on the agenda of the Congress deal with the compromises and contradictions that persist in amateur regulations. The project mentioned in the last paragraph, should it come to fruition, would mean appropriately sanctioning the international understanding for which we hope to pave the way. The time for its implementation has not yet come. The restoration of the Olympic Games, on foundations and under conditions that are in keeping with the needs of modern life, would bring together representatives of the nations of the world every four years. It may be hoped that these peaceful, courteous confrontations are the best form of internationalism.

In taking this initiative that may have such significant results, the Union is not attempting to usurp the primacy that does not belong to any one country or society in the republic of the muscles. The Union merely believes that the clarity of its principles and attitude, as well as the high-level friendships it is honored to have made in France and abroad, puts it in a position to give the signal for the reform movement, the need for which is felt more and more every day. Therefore the Union is acting in the general interest, without any ulterior motives of blind ambition."

Le Congrès de Paris,
in: Bulletin du Comité International des Jeux Olympiques
[Bulletin of the International Committee of the Olympic Games],
July 1894, no. 1, p. 1.

Paris, 20, Rue Oudinot,
le 15 Janvier 1894.

Monsieur,

J'ai l'honneur de vous communiquer le programme du Congrès International qui se réunira à Paris le 17 Juin prochain, sous les auspices de l'Union des Sociétés françaises de Sports Athlétiques.

L'objet en est double.

Il importe, avant tout, de conserver à l'athlétisme le caractère noble et chevaleresque qui l'a distingué dans le passé, afin qu'il puisse continuer de jouer efficacement dans l'éducation des peuples modernes le rôle admirable que lui attribuèrent les maitres Grecs. L'imperfection humaine tend toujours à transformer l'athlète d'Olympie en un gladiateur de cirque. Il faut choisir entre deux formules athlétiques qui ne sont pas compatibles. Pour se défendre contre l'esprit de lucre et de professionalisme qui menace de les envahir, les Amateurs, dans la plupart des pays, ont établi une législation compliquée pleine de compromis et de contradictions; trop souvent d'ailleurs, on en respecte la lettre plus que l'esprit.

Une réforme s'impose et avant que de l'entreprendre, il faut la discuter. Les questions qui ont été mises à l'ordre du jour du congrès ont trait à ces compromis et à ces contradictions qui subsistent dans les règlements amateuristes. Le projet que mentionne le dernier paragraphe serait l'heureuse sanction de l'entente internationale que nous cherchons non point encore à réaliser, mais seulement à préparer. Le rétablissement des Jeux Olympiques, sur des bases et dans des conditions conformes aux nécessités de la vie moderne, mettrait en présence, tous les quatre ans, les représentants des nations du monde et il est permis de croire que ces luttes pacifiques et courtoises constituent le meilleur des Internationalismes.

L'Union des Sociétés Françaises de Sports Athlétiques, en prenant une initiative dont les résultats peuvent être si considérables, n'a pas cherché à usurper une préséance qui, dans la république des muscles, n'appartient à aucun pays et à aucune société. Elle a seulement pensé que la netteté de ses principes et de son attitude ainsi que les hautes amitiés dont elle s'honore, tant en France qu'à l'étranger, l'autorisaient a donner le signal d'un mouvement de réforme dont la nécessité se fait sentir chaque jour davantage. Elle agit ainsi dans l'intérêt général et sans aucune arrière pensée de mesquine ambition.

Le Congrès s'ouvrira à Paris, le Dimanche 17 Juin et durera huit jours.

Les *mémoires écrits en Français seront reçus au Secrétariat général jusqu'au 10 Juin. Les mémoires écrits en langues étrangères, jusqu'au 1er Juin seulement. Ils seront classsés en deux catégories selon qu'ils émaneront de personnalités individuelles ou de Sociétés.* L'envoi de mémoires ou de communications est libre : nulle condition n'est exigée, mais les sociétés devront, en tous les cas, joindre à leurs envois le texte des règlements qui les régissent. Tout mémoire qui ne traiterait pas de l'une des questions inscrites au programme ci-joint, sera rigoureusement écarté.

Des cartes donnant entrée dans la salle des séances seront à la disposition des personnes qui en feront la demande avant le 10 Juin en justifiant de leur désir de prendre part au Congrès. Les Sociétés d'amateurs pourront se faire représenter par des Délégués. Elles devront en ce cas, en donner avis avant le 10 Juin.

Nous vous demandons de vouloir bien publier et faire connaître autour de vous la présente lettre ainsi que le programme qui l'accompagne.

Veuillez agréer, Monsieur, l'expression de mes sentiments les plus distingués.

Bon Pierre de COUBERTIN,
Secrétaire général.

Circular from Pierre de Coubertin, Secretary General of the USFSA, announcing the International Athletic Congress (J.Kössl Collection)

4.2.1/4 CIRCULAR LETTER, JANUARY 15, 1894

I have the honour to communicate to you the programme of the International Congress which will be held in Paris on 17th June next, under the auspices of the Union des Sociétés françaises de Sports Athlétiques.

Its purpose is twofold.

First and foremost, it is vital that athletics retain the noble and chivalrous quality which distinguished it in the past, so that it can effectively continue to play within the education of modern peoples the admirable role which the Greek masters attributed to it. Human imperfection tends always to transform the Olympian athlete into a circus gladiator. One must choose between two athletic methods which are not compatible. To defend oneself against the spirit of lucre and professionalism which threatens to invade them, the Amateurs, in the majority of countries, have created complicated legislation full of compromises and contradictions; what is more, too often the letter rather than the spirit of this legislation is respected.

Reform is needed, and before this is undertaken it must be discussed. The issues included on the agenda of the congress relate to these compromises and contradictions which exist within the amateur rules. The project referred to in the last paragraph would be the pleasing sanction of international harmony that we are, as yet, in no way seeking to achieve, merely to prepare for. The re-establishment of the Olympic Games, on a basis and in the conditions in keeping with the needs of modern life, would bring together, every four years, representatives of the nations of the world, and one is permitted to think that these peaceful, courteous contests constitute the best form of internationalism.

By taking an initiative, the results of which may be so considerable, the Union des Sociétés françaises de Sports Athlétiques has not sought to usurp a precedence which, in the republic of muscle, belongs to no country and no society. It thought merely that the clarity of its principles and its attitude, and the great friendships of which it is proud, both in France and abroad, authorized it to give the starting signal for a reform, the need for which is felt more strongly with each passing day. It is therefore acting in the general interest, and with no ulterior motive of petty-minded ambition.

The Congress will open in Paris on Sunday 17th June, and will last eight days.

Texts written in French should reach the General Secretariat by 10th June, and texts written in other languages no later than 1st June. They will be divided into two categories, according to whether they are from individuals or from Clubs. Anyone is free to send texts or speeches; no conditions are set, but clubs must in all cases include with their papers the text of the rules which govern them. Any text which does not relate to one of the points on the attached programme will be rigorously excluded.

Cards giving access to the meeting room will be available to anyone who requests one before 10th June, giving justification for their wish to take part in the Congress. Amateur Societies may be represented by Delegates, in which case they must give notification accordingly before 10th June.

Please be kind enough to publish and make known to others the present letter and accompanying programme.

Yours etc.

Circulaire annonçant le Congrès International Athlétique. Paris, 15 janvier 1894. Off-print.

4.2.1/5 PRELIMINARY PROGRAM (1894)

UNION DES SOCIÉTÉS FRANÇAISES DE SPORTS ATHLÉTIQUES
INTERNATIONAL CONGRESS AT PARIS June 1894

For the study and extension of the principles of amateurism.

COMMITTEE MEMBERS

FRANCE AND CONTINENTAL EUROPE: Baron Pierre de Coubertin, Secretary General of the Union des Sports athlétiques, 20, rue Oudinot, *Paris.*

ENGLAND AND ITS COLONIES: C. Herbert, Hon.-Secretary, Amateur Athletic Association, 10 John St. (Adelphi), *London.*

AMERICAN CONTINENT: W. M. Sloane, Professor at Princeton University, Stanworth, Princeton (N. J.), *United States.*

PRELIMINARY PROGRAM

I. Definition of the amateur; basis for that definition. – Possibility and usefulness of an international definition.
II. Suspension, disqualification, and requalification. – The facts that motivate them, and means of verifying them.
III. Is it proper to maintain a distinction among the various sports from the perspective of amateurism, particularly for horse racing (gentlemen) and pigeon shooting? – Can one be a professional in one sport, and an amateur in another?
IV. On the value of art objects given as prizes. – Is it necessary to limit that value? – What steps can be taken against someone who sells the art object that he has won?
V. The legitimacy of assets derived from charging admissions to the field of play. Can this money be shared among the associations or the competitors? Can it be used to defray the costs of travel? To what extent can teams be reimbursed either by the opposing team, or by their own association?
VI. Can the general definition of the amateur be applied equally to all sports? – Does it include special restrictions for cycling, rowing, athletic sports, etc.?
VII. On betting. – Is it compatible with amateurism? – Ways to prevent it from spreading.
VIII. On the possibility of restoring the Olympic Games. – Under what circumstances could they be restored?

The Unions and Associations that participate in this Congress will not be bound by the resolutions adopted. The purpose of the Congress is to state opinions on the various issues that are submitted for its consideration and to prepare, but not to enact, international legislation.

The order of the Sessions and the schedule of festivals that will be held in Paris on the occasion of the Congress will be determined at a later date.

Programme préparatoire.
Special printing, January 1894 (Archives of the IOC).

4.2.1/6 THE PARIS CONGRESS 1894: PRESS RELEASE

As you know, the International Congress is to meet at the Sorbonne under the presidency of Senator Baron de Courcel, to work towards establishing modernized Olympic Games that would take place every four year like their "great ancestors", and in which every sport would be represented.

Sixry-one French and foreign delegates have already registered as participants in the Congress, including Count Lucchesi-Palli for Italy; Professors Posada and Aniceto Sela of the University of Oviedo, for Spain; Lieutenants Bergh and S. de Drakenberg for Sweden; Messrs Todd, Clark and Britten for the "National Cyclist's Union"; Dr Bikelas for Greece; Mr Alexis Lebedeff for Russia; Ireland and Belgium are also represented. The Athletics Societies of Mebourne sent some important reports.

The Paris Polo Club designated as its representatives Vicomte de la Rochefoucauld and Mr René Raoul-Duval; the French Equestrian Society, Baron de Carayon la Tour and Baron du Teil du Havelt; the Alpine Club, one of its Vice-Presidents, Mr Durier; the Society for the Encouragement of Fencing Mr de Villeneuve and Colonel Derué, etc.

The Congress has the patronage of the King of the Belgians, the Prince of Wales, the Prince Royal of Sweden, the Prince Royal of Greece and Grand Duke Vladimir of Russia. The Duke of Aumale is also a patron.

The opening will take place on 16th June in the vast amphitheatre of the Sorbonne: Mr Jean Aicard is to speak on "Strenght and the Law" and the famous Hymn to Apollo will be executed, for the first time, by twelve choristers from the Opera.

Throughout the Congress (16th to 24th June) there will be a session in the morning at the Sorbonne. The afternoon and evening will be devoted to various duties and receptions. The first will take place at the Luxembourg on Sunday 17th June, with a Jeu de Paume competition. The second will be an evening party at the Racing Club on Thursday 21st; the programme includes torch races and fencing bouts on the superb lawns of the Croix-Catelan, lit up as bright as day; choirs will be heard, alternating with the ring of trumpets. The fête will be presided over by the President of the Municipal Council of Paris: the profit from entrance fees will be given to the poor.

The Congress will end on the evening of Saturday 28th June with a grand banquet given at the Palais d'Hiver du Jardin d'Acclimatation, hosted by Baron de Courcel.

Le Congrès de Paris: Note pour la presse,
May/June 1894. (Off-print, 1 page.)

4.2.1/7 PROGRAM OF THE IOC FOUNDING CONGRESS (1894)

Cover of the final Program of the IOC Founding Congress (June 1894)

CONGRÈS INTERNATIONAL DE PARIS

POUR LE RÉTABLISSEMENT DES JEUX OLYMPIQUES

Samedi 16 Juin, à 4 heures

SÉANCE SOLENNELLE D'OUVERTURE, A LA SORBONNE

Discours de M. le Baron DE COURCEL, *Sénateur*, Président du Congrès.
Causerie de M. JEAN AICARD, Président de la Société des Gens de Lettres.
« **Hymne à Apollon** » (1re audition, avec chœurs).
Le Solo sera chanté par Madame JEANNE RÉMACLE,

Dimanche 17 Juin, à 9 heures 1/2

CHAMPIONNATS VÉLOCIPÉDIQUES DE L'UNION DES SPORTS ATHLÉTIQUES

AU VÉLODROME DE LA SEINE, A LEVALLOIS

Chemin de fer: Gare Saint-Lazare pour Clichy-Levallois

A 2 heures 1/2

CHAMPIONNAT DE LONGUE-PAUME AU JARDIN DU LUXEMBOURG

Lundi 18 Juin, à 9 heures 1/4

1ère SÉANCE DU CONGRÈS à la Sorbonne

(AMPHITHÉATRE B)

Entrée par la Rue Saint-Jacques, n. 46

Messieurs les Délégués seront seuls admis à cette Séance

A 4 heures

M. LE PRÉSIDENT DU CONSEIL MUNICIPAL DE PARIS

Recevra les Délégués au Congrès, à l'Hôtel-de-Ville

(Rendez-vous à l'Hôtel-de-Ville à 4 heures moins le quart très-précises)

Mardi 19 Juin, à 9 heures 1/4

2ème SÉANCE DU CONGRÈS à la Sorbonne

(AMPHITHÉATRE A)

A 3 heures

Excursion sur la Marne : Goûter au Garage de la *Société d'Encouragement au Sport nautique* à Nogent-sur-Marne.

Mercredi 20 Juin, à 9 heures 1/4

3ème SÉANCE DU CONGRÈS à la Sorbonne

(AMPHITHÉATRE A)

Jeudi 21 Juin, à 9 heures 1/4

4ème SÉANCE DU CONGRÈS à la Sorbonne

(AMPHITHÉATRE A)

A 8 heures 1/2

FÊTE DE NUIT

Organisée par le *Racing-Club de France* en l'honneur des Délégués au Congrès, et sous la Présidence de M. CHAMPOUDRY Président du Conseil Municipal de Paris.

sur la Pelouse de la CROIX-CATELAN (Bois de Boulogne)

Illuminations et feu d'artifice.— Courses à pied aux flambeaux (150 m. — 500 m. — 2000 m. Steeple). Assauts d'Escrime (Sabre, Epée, Fleuret). — Chœurs sans accompagnement. — Sonneries de trompe.

PRIX DU BILLET (au profit des Pauvres), 5 francs pris avant, 10 francs sur le terrain

Vendredi 22 Juin à 9 heures 1/4

5ème SÉANCE DU CONGRÈS à la Sorbonne

(AMPHITHÉATRE A)

A 4 heures

Goûter à la *Société de Sport de l'Ile de Puteaux* (Quai de Seine, Neuilly-St-James)

Samedi, 23 Juin à 9 heures 1/4

6ème SÉANCE DU CONGRÈS à la Sorbonne

(AMPHITHÉATRE A)

A 7 heures

BANQUET AU PALAIS D'HIVER DU JARDIN D'ACCLIMATATION

Sous la Présidence de M. le Baron de COURCEL

Page 2 of the final Program of the IOC Founding Congress

MEMBRES HONORAIRES

S. M. le Roi des Belges.
S. A. R. le Prince de Galles.
S. A. R. le Prince royal de Suède et Norwège.
S. A. R. le Prince royal des Héllènes.
S. A. I. le Grand Duc Wladimir de Russie.
S. E. le Ministre de l'Instruction publique d'Autriche.
M. le Président du Conseil municipal de Paris.

Mgr le Duc d'Aumale.
M. le Comte Czaki, Ministre de l'Instruction publique de Hongrie.
Lord Aberdare.
M. Hodgson Pratt, Président de l'Alliance Universitaire Internationale.
M. Ernest Lavisse, de l'Académie Française.
M. Joseph Reinach, Député.
M. Frédéric Passy, Membre de l'Institut.
M. R. Bonghi, Membre du Parlement Italien.
M. R. Feldhaus, Membre du Parlement Allemand.
M. le Général de Boutowski, Attaché à la direction des écoles militaires russes.
M. le Dr Harris, Commissaire de l'Éducation des Etats-Unis.
M. Frédéric Bajer, Membre du Parlement Danois
M. Balfour, Membre du Parlement Anglais.
M. le comte Fisogni, Membre du Parlement Italien.
M. H. Lafontaine, membre du Parlement Belge.
M. Alexandre Hegedius, Membre du Parlement Hongrois.
M. Elie Ducommun, Président du Bureau international de la Paix.
M. G. de Saint-Clair.
M. le Vicomte Léon de Janzé, Président de l'Union des Sports Athlétiques.
M. Eug. Spuller, Député, ancien Ministre.
M. Marion, Professeur à la Faculté des Lettres.
Sir John Astley, Président du Sports-Club de Londres.
M. le Capitaine Balck, Président de l'Union Gymnastique de Stockolm.
M. Franz Kémény, Directeur de l'Ecole Royale d'Eger.
M. Jules Simon, de l'Académie Française.
M. Janssen, Membre de l'Institut.
M. le Comte Hoyos, Ambassadeur d'Autriche-Hongrie, à Paris.
M. le Dr Gilman, Président de l'Université Johns Hopkins (Baltimore).
M. l'Amiral baron Lagé, Président de l'Union des Yachts Français.
M. Jean Phokianos, Président de la Société Panhéllénique de Gymnastique.
M. le Comte de Juigné, Député, Président de la Société Hippique française.
M. le Baron de Suttner.
M. le Dr Jiri Guth, Professeur au lycée de Klatovy (Bohême).
M. Capuccio, Président du Rowing-Club Italien.
M. Parmentier, Président de l'Union des Sociétés de Gymnastique de France.
M. le Dr W. P. Brookes.
M. C. Waldstein, Directeur de l'Ecole Américaine d'Athènes.
Lord Dufferin, Ambassadeur d'Angleterre.
M. G. A. Adée, Président du New-York Athlétic-Club.
M. G. Strehly, Professeur au Lycée Montaigne.
M. le Dr Zubiaur, Recteur du Collège national de l'Uruguay.
M. L. A. Cuff, Secrétaire de la New-Zealand Amateur Athlétic Association.
M. de Méléniewski, Député de la Noblesse de Kiew.

PRÉSIDENT DU CONGRÈS

M, le Baron de Courcel, Sénateur, Ancien Ambassadeur.

COMMISSAIRES

MM. le Baron Pierre de Coubertin, Commissaire général, 20, rue Oudinot.
E. Callot, 160, Boulevard Malesherbes.
A. de la Frémoire, 7, place Malesherbes.
Ar. Masson, 5, place Péreire.
le Vicomte de Madec, 83, boulevard de Courcelles.
Fernand d'Orval, 14 avenue de l'Alma.
le Comte Jacques de Pourtalès, 7, rue Tronchet.
Théodore Stanton, 9, rue Bassano.
le Comte de Villers, 19, avenue Victor Hugo.

COMMISSAIRE, CHARGÉ DU SERVICE DE LA PRESSE

M. Franz Reichel, 9 rue Royer-Collard.

DÉLÉGUÉS

1 **Association des Instituteurs pour l'Education Physique de la Jeunesse.**
MM. Moulin, Instituteur, 17, avenue Parmentier. — Picart, Professeur de jeux scolaires, 109, boulevard Soult.

2 **Union Vélocipédique de France.**
MM. Roussel. — Pagis. — le Dr Minart. — Duval. — Mousset, 68, avenue de la Grande-Armée.

3 **Racing Club de France.**
MM. Michel Gondinet, 8, rue d'Argenteuil. — P. Lejeune, 32, rue Drouot.

4 **Société de Sport de l'Ile de Puteaux.**
MM. André Toutain, 20, place Vendôme. — Jusserand, Ministre plénipotentiaire, 90 bis, rue de Varennes.

5 **Polo Club de Paris.**
MM. le Vicomte de La Rochefoucauld, 47, rue de Varennes. — René Raoul-Duval, 53, rue François Ier.

6 **Société d'Encouragement de l'Escrime.**
MM. H. de Villeneuve, 41 bis, boulevard de Latour-Maubourg — Le colonel Dérué, 79, rue d'Amsterdam. Ad. Corthey, 41, rue Lepic.

7 **Société Panhellénique de Gymnastique d'Athènes.**
M. D. Bikélas, 4, rue de Babylone.

8 **Union des Yachts Français.**
MM. Morel-Fatio, 3, rue du Général Foy. — Gaston Fournier, 54, rue Notre-Dame-de-Lorette. — de Boulongne, 63 rue de Miromesnil. — Deha, 26, rue de la Trémoille. — Loste, 45, rue Boissy-d'Anglas. — Le Vicomte de Rochechouart, 100, rue de l'Université.

Page 3 of the final Program of the IOC Founding Congress

9 **Société de Gymnastique de Saint-Pétersbourg.**
M. ALEXEI LEBEDEW.

10 **Federazione Gimnastica Italiana.**
M. le Comte LUCCHESI-PALLI, 4, rue Vezelay.

11 **Société Hippique Française.**
MM. le Baron DU TEIL DU HAVELT, 14 rue de Berri. — Le Baron DE CARAYON LA TOUR, 9, rue de Berri.

12 **Nederlandsche Voetbal en Athletiek Bond.**

13 **Stade Français.**
MM. GARCET DE VAURESMONT, 14, rue George-Sand (Auteuil). — L. H. SANDFORD, 7, rue Dumont d'Urville.

14 **Union Chrétienne de Jeunes Gens.**
MM. RIDEOUT. — ADRION, 14, rue de Trévise.

15 **Union Nationale des Sociétés de Tir.**
MM. MÉRILLON, 30, avenue d'Iéna. — LERMUSIAUX, 6, rue de Parme. — LEFÈVRE, 22, rue des Batignolles. — LECŒUVRE, 56, boulevard Beaumarchais. — CHAPRON, 6, rue Paradis.

16 **Association des Sociétés de Gymnastique de la Seine.**
M. H. DEROSSELLE, 3 rue des Prouvaires.

17 **Union des Sociétés de Gymnastique de France.**
MM. LOUTIL, 20, avenue Bel-Air. — SANSBŒUF, 91, boulevard Malesherbes.

18 **Amateur Athletic Association (Londres).**
Victorian Amateur Athletic Association (Melbourne).
M. C. HERBERT, 10, John St (Adelphi) Londres.

19 **National Cyclist's Union.**
MM. N. L. CLARK. — R. TODD. — J. BRITTEN, 57, Basinghall St. Londres.

20 **Irish Amateur Athletic Association (Dublin).**
MM. D. D. BULGER. — J. T. MAGEE.

21 **Club Alpin Français.**
MM. CHARLES DURIER, 7, rue Greffulhe. — PIERRE PUISEUX, 15, rue Soufflot.

22 **Amiens-Cycle.**
MM. CHENU. — LAMY.

23 **Svenska Gymnastik-forbundet (Stockholm).**
MM. FRÉDÉRIC BERGH, 73, avenue d'Antin. — STEN DE DRAKENBERG, École de gymnastique, Joinville-le-Pont.

24 **Ligue Vélocipédique Belge.**
MM. CARROEN. — J. HANSER.

25 **Association Vélocipédique d'Amateurs.**
MM. L.-P. REICHEL, 9, rue Royer-Collard. — RENÉ LACROIX, 108, boulevard Richard-Lenoir.
G. DE LAFRETÉ, 62, rue Boissière.

26 **Decimal L. T. & B. Society.**
MM. GASKETT JAMES, 48, rue de Chaillot. — J.-H. LE COCQ, 78, avenue Kléber.

27 **Université d'Oviedo (Espagne).**
MM. le Professeur ADOLPHO GONZALÈS POSADA. – Le Professeur ANICETO SELA.

28 **Athletic and Running Club (Bruxelles).**
M. ADOLPHE ZIANE, 39, rue de l'Ecuyer, Bruxelles.

29 **New-York Athletic Club.**
M. le Professeur W.-M. SLOANE, Hôtel d'Orient, rue Daunou.

30 **La « Jeune Epée ».**
MM. JOSEPH RENAUD, 29, rue de la Victoire. — SAUTON, 1, rue d'Edimbourg.

31 **Stade Bordelais.**
M. A. MANGEOT, 3. rue du 29 Juillet.

32 **Union sportive des Etudiants de Caen.**
M. FRANZ REICHEL, 9, rue Royer Collard.

33 **Fédération Belge des Sociétés de Courses à pied.**
MM. KETELS, Palais du Roi, Bruxelles. — CHARLES DEREINE, 49, rue du Marché, Bruxelles.

34 **Association vélocipédique Internationale.**
MM. J. SLOAN. — O. SLOAN, 43, rue Vivienne.

35 **Wenlock Olympian Society.**

36 **Académie d'Armes.**
MM. ROULEAU, 350, rue Saint-Honoré. — Robert, 28, rue Serpente.

37 **Polytechnic-Club (Londres).**
M. le Comte O'CONNELL, 68, avenue du Bois de Boulogne.

38 **Société d'Encouragement au Sport Nautique.**
MM. CH. FENWICK, 21, rue Martel. — F. BOUDIN, 5, rue Baillif.

39 **Union Athlétique du 1er Arrondissement.**
MM. LÉON GUILLEBONT, 194, rue de Rivoli. — LÉCUYER.

6-94 Paris — Imp. PELLUARD, rue Saint-Jacques, 212

Page 4 of the final Program of the IOC Founding Congress

Le Congrès International de Paris (1894).
Special printing, June 1894. (Archives of the IOC)

4.2.1/8 THE MODERN OLYMPIC GAMES

Whenever a new idea has sprung up, assumed a practical form and become a reality, it is not always easy to explain why this particular idea, more than any other, has emerged from the stream of other thoughts, which are as yet awaiting their realization. This however is, not the case with the reinstitution of the Olympic Games: Their revival is not owing to a spontaneous dream, but it is the logical consequence of the great cosmopolitan tendencies of our times. The XIXth Century has seen the awakening of a taste for athletics everywhere; at its dawn in Germany and Sweden, at its meridian in England, at its decline in France and America. At the same time the great inventions of the age, railroads and telegraphs, have brought into communication people of all nationalities. An easier intercourse between men of all languages has naturally opened a wider sphere for common interests. Men have begun to lead less isolated existences, different races have learnt to know, to understand each other better, and by comparing their powers and achievements in the fields of art, industry and science, a noble rivalry has sprung up amongst them, urging them on to greater accomplishments. Universal Exhibitions have collected together at one spot of the globe, the products of its remotest corners. In the domain of science and literature, assemblies and conferences have united the most distinguished intellectual labourers of all nations. Could it be otherwise, but that also sportsmen of diverse nationalities should have begun to meet each other on common ground. Is not emulation the mainspring of all exertions, whether mental or physical? Switzerland took the lead by inviting foreign marksmen to take part in its own federal shooting matches; Bicycle races have been run on every track in Europe; England and America have challenged each other by sea; and by land; the ablest fencers of Rome and Paris have crossed swords with each other. Gradually sport has become more international, exciting the interests and widening the sphere of action. The revival of the Olympic Games became possible, nay I may say, even necessary.

For a great many years I had studied the school-life of English and American youth. Although we may criticise on many points the teaching, which public schools afford in England; there can be no reasonable doubt about their effecting a strong and vigorous education of body and character. To the merits of this education we may ascribe a large share in the prodigious and powerful extension of the British Empire in Queen Victoria's reign. It is worthy to note that the beginning of this marvellous progress and development dates from the same time which saw the schoolreforms of the United Kingdom in 1840. In these reforms physical games and sports hold, we may say, the most prominent place: The muscles are made to do the work of a moral educationer. It is the application according to modern requirements of one of the most characteristic principles of Grecian civilisation: To make the muscles be chief factor in the work of moral education.

In France, on the contrary, physical inertion was considered till recent times an indispensable assistant to the perfectionning of intellectual powers. Games were supposed to destroy study. Regarding the development of the character of the youth, the axiom, that a close connection exists between the force of will and the strength of the body never entered anybody's mind.

As a general rule, most of the great national questions reduce themselves to questions on education, particularly so in democratic constitutions. We have only to search the schools and universities of a democracy for the secrets of its greatness or its decay. The ameliorations introduced into them spread most widely and most strongly. So one, convinced of the truth of that statement, was naturally led to consider how well it would be for France, were we to introduce into our schoolsystem some of that physical vitality, some of that animal spirit; from which our neighbours have derived such incontestable benefits.

The work, to do so, thus undertaken in 1888, has thriven rapidly. "L'Union des Sports Athletiques" whose commencements were most modest, included already in 1892 a considerable number of sporting societies, established in schools, formed and governed by the pupils themselves. The necessity of studying the achievements in other countries in order to be able to work more efficaciously at home at the success of the enterprise have brought me, whilst travelling in foreign parts, into contact with men, who had likewise given a large share of their attention to physical education. At the Universal Exhibition in 1889, by the invitation of the French Government, international conferences, treating on all sorts of questions, met in Paris, amongst them one on physical education. Having been intrusted with its organization, I had sent everywhere a letter in form of an interrogatory to find out the way in which physical exercises were dealt with in different schools and universities abroad.

To this purpose I established a monthly paper: "La Revue Athletique", hoping to raise the interests in manly sports in France, by comparing our results with those arrived at in different places. The mission on which the ministry of Public Instruction sent me in 1889, and which afforded me the opportunity of visiting the large establishments for Public Instruction in North America had enabled me likewise to add some new documents to my International book of investigations. All my researches convinced me however; that at the close of the Century, that had seen its rise, Athletism run already great dangers to degenerate, and to be stopped in its progress, if some strong and energetic influence were not brought to bear upon it. Everywhere I found discord, civil war raging between the partisans and adversaries of one particular kind of sport. This state of affairs seemed to me to be caused by a tendency to excessive specialisation. Those who went in for jumping, despised rowing, fencers were against cyclists, marksmen looked down on lawn-tennis players, even amongst the adepts in one and the same sport there existed no more harmony. The admirers of German gymnastics denied all merits to the Swedish method, and American football-rules seemed to the English player devoid of all common sense. Moreover a mercantile spirit threatened to invade sporting sense. Moreover a mercantile spirit threatened to invade sporting circles. Men did not race and fight openly for money, but nevertheless a tendency to a regrettable compromise had crept in. The desire to win was often prompted by one not inspired by mere ambition for honourable distinction. If we did not wish to see Athletism degenerate and die out a second time, it had to be purified and united.

Of all measures tending to this desired end, only one seemed to me at all practicable, namely the establishment of a periodical contest, to which sporting societies of all nationalities would be invited to send their representatives, and to place these meetings under the only patronage which could throw over them a hallow of greatness and glory: "The patronage of Classical Antiquity" ! To do that, was to re-establish the "Olympic Games". That name forced itself upon us, it was not even possible to invent another one.

We have to admit that this name had never entirely fallen into disuse. It was sometimes applied, either to describe local sports like those for example, which the "Directoire" tried to establish at the Champs de Mars in Paris, or those which are even now held in certain villages in Greece; or to designate some premature and unskilful reinstitution attempted in Athens in King Otho's reign . It was however no longer the name which was required it was the thing itself. It was not to be a local and fleeting creation, but a universal and lasting one. I had the idea of convoking in Paris an Athletic International Congress, but very soon I found out that this was not to be done without some preliminary labour, and I put myself therefore in harness at once. To unite the great French Sporting Clubs, and to enter into communication with like Societies of other countries was of the first importance in order not to give to strangers the edifying spectacle of national discord on one hand, and to obtain from abroad numerous adherents to this cause, on the other.

The "Union des Sports Athlétiques" had raised by its establishment and its rapid progress, the defiance and jealousy of other periodicals. All my efforts tended to improve the relations between "L'Union Vélocipédique de France, L'Union Nationale des Sociétés de Tir, L'Union des Sociétés de Gymnastique, La Société d'Encouragement de L'Escrime, L'Union des Sociétés d'Aviron, L'Union des Yachts Français". I only half succeeded in my endeavours, it was possible however to clear up more than one misunderstanding and even to trace a plan for a friendly collaboration on certain points.

Abroad the task was apparently still more difficult, in reality however much easier and less ungrateful. Soon some connection was formed between our clubs in Paris and those in Belgium. A cordial agreement with England was brought about less rapidly. The presence of Mr Herbert at the head of the Amateur Athletic Association facilitated many things; he knew our efforts and encouraged them. The National Cyclist Union resisted a long time, it could not see the advantage of a treaty uniting it to a foreign federation. Ten months of negotiation and even the intervention of our ambassador in London M. Waddington, were required to obtain for our rowing men from the "Amateur Rowing Association" the right to take part in the famous Henley Regattas, which are held according to its rules.

In the Spring of 1893,, the Situation was so far improved that a congress could be convoked. We were on good terms with Belgium, England and America, an invitation therefore was addressed to all Sporting Societies in the world asking them to send delegates to Paris, during the month of June 1894.

I called to my assistance such personal friends as Professor Sloane of Princeton University, or gentlemen with whom I had been corresponding on that subject for a long time, like M. Kemeny from Hungary, General Boutowski from Russia; Mr Herbert from England, Commander Balk from Sweden.

The Programme for the Congress was drawn up in such a way as to disguise its main object: "the revival of the Olympic Games"; it merely put forward questions on sport in general. I carefully refrained from mentioning such an ambitious project; afraid it might raise such a storm of contempt and scorn as to discourage beforehand those, favourably disposed towards it. For whenever I had alluded to my plan at meetings in Oxford and New York etc. I had always been sadly conscious that my audience considered it utopian and impracticable.

To show however that something more important than an ordinary sporting conference was intended to be held, I insisted on our meetings taking place in the Halls of the Sorbonne. M. Greard, rector of the University of Paris, most graciously accorded us permission to do so. It seemed to me that under the venerable roof of the Sorbonne the words "Olympic Games" would resound more impressively and more persuasively on the audience. I wrote to Their Majesties the Kings of Greece and Belgium; to Their Royal Highnesses the Crown-prince of Greece, the Prince of Wales, the Crown-prince of Sweden and to H. I. H. the Grand Duke Wladimir requesting them to accept the Hon. Membership of the Congress. Baron de Courcel, member of the Senate, our former ambassador at Berlin, consented to become president. I soon saw myself surrounded by friends who all took a keen interest in the success of the work. We projected a series of festivities to make their stay agreeable and attractive to the foreign delegates. But would those delegates really come ! At the beginning of Spring it was still doubtful; we nearly gave up hope. Germany, Switzerland and Holland did not respond at all, in other countries they began to make excuses. Again and again we had to return to the onset, invite, insist, – the amount of letter writing we had to go through vas most appalling. Success came at the last moment, English, American, Swedish, Spanish, Italian, Belgic, Russian delegates arrived in numbers. The Greek representative, M. Vikelas, a habitual resident in Paris, had shared our hopes and fears from the beginning. We found even adherents where we had least expected them; Australia sent us her warmest wishes for success. The opening meeting on Sat. June l6th had an audience of 2000 people. At its conclusion the Delphic Hymn to Apollo was sung. The Congress, opened under such happy auspices brought forward its most characteristic project. The idea of the revival of the Olympic Games came triumphantly to the front.

Their reestablishment was unanimously decided upon. We proposed to fix the year 1900 for their first celebration, but it was thought advisable to advance that date to 1896 and at the proposition of M. Vikelas, Athens was chosen as the place for their inauguration. Their next celebration is to be in Paris in 1900, and then they are to be held after each interval of 4 years in every large capital of the world in turn. An International Committee of 14 members was formed to carry out the decisions of the Congress.

Thus was begun an undertaking, which seems to be destined to bring about great results. It has often been criticised since then, yea even violently attacked by some. Everybody does not comprehend it, many speak of it without knowing anything about its origin and its purpose. As for myself I hereby assert once more my claims for being sole author of the whole project: I take the opportunity to thank most warmly those, who have assisted me in carrying out successfully this work and those, who join, with me in hoping that the revival of the Olympic Games will bring Athletism to a high state of perfection, and that they will infuse new elements of ambition in the lives of the rising generation: a love for concord and a respect for life!

Athens April 7/19[1], 1896

Pierre de Coubertin

The Modern Olympic Games. In: *The Olympic Games B.C. 776. – A.D. 1896.* Official Report.
Second Part: The Olympic Games in 1896. Introduction. Athens/London, Ch. Beck/H. Grevel, 1897, pp. 1-8.

1 The date show the difference between the Greek and Gregorian Calendars.

The main auditorium of the new Sorbonne with the famous painting of the French artist Puvis de Chavannes "The sacred wood". Here the re-estblishment of the modern Olympic Games and the institution of the IOC were decided on June 23, 1894. (taken from H.-P.Nénot (ed.), La Monographie de la Nouvelle Sorbonne. Paris, Impr. Nat., 1903, pl. XVII)

4.2.1/9 THE PARIS CONGRESS AND THE REVIVAL OF THE OLYMPIC GAMES

In his Olympic Memoirs, 37 years later, Coubertin describes the founding congress in 1894, the first stage in reviving the Olympic Games, in a very personal way. In retrospect, his preparatory trip to the USA in the autumn of 1893 appears rightly sisgnificant. But his distance towards the amateur issue is also striking, yet this must have been influenced essentially by his later negative experiences in connection with the problem.

It was an evening in November 1892... Friday the 25th to be precise. The scene: the main auditorium in the old Sorbonne, a huge rectangle tinged, if I remember rightly, a dirty lilac shade and decorated with two square niches out of which jutted the august noses of two prelates, Bossuet and Fénelon. In this gloomy hall I had taken one of the written papers for my "bachot" exam, and searched desperately for something to say on "Creative Imagination". However, the students crowded into the Sorbonne that autumn evening in 1892 were thinking of quite different matters. They were gazing in admiration at the platform, at the immaculate shirt front and dress coat of impeccable cut of the most prominent man about town of the time, Viscount Léon de Janzé, whom I had shortly before made President of the Union des Sports Athlétiques, being well aware that he was not only a leading figure of society but a man of great intelligence and reliable character. On either side of him were seated the Rector of the University, Mr. Octave Gréard, and Prince Obolensky, Marshal at the court of the Grand-Duke Vladimir. De Janzé had agreed to act as patron for this "jubilee" and was to come in person to the Bois de Boulogne two days later to present the prizes to our young athletes in whose honor the amphitheater was decked with Russian flags alternating with French flags; it was the Alliance some ten months ahead of time.

The jubilee of what? We were supposedly celebrating the fifth anniversary of the Union des Sports Athlétiques with a series of festivities: a meeting at Ville d'Avray, a fencing match, a cross-country race at Meudon, the whole ending in a magnificent tea given and presided over by the famous astronomer Janssen... for at that time we had a number of helpers well placed in the worlds of letters, science, and politics: Victor Duruy, Jules Simon, Georges Picot, and a host of others who had been the first, in 1888, to lend their support to my initial campaign. So was it the fifth anniversary of the USFSA that we were celebrating? Not at all. The baby had been surreptitiously switched. It is true that on the same date, five years earlier, at the end of a frugal luncheon two small Paris clubs had joined forces to form the Union des Sociétés Françaises de Courses à pied (Union of French Running Clubs). And this in itself was a very fine, very daring gesture on the part of Georges de Saint-Clair, for members of the Stade Français were only grudgingly permitted to run on the terrace of the Orangerie in the Tuileries on Sunday mornings, and the Racing-Club's lease at the Croix-Catelan could not have been more precarious. A little later, I had to intervene with the municipal authorities at city hall in order to try and regularize the situation. You can imagine our surprise, Saint-Clair's and mine, when we received a letter one day informing us that the club would be allowed to lay down running tracks in these lovely grounds, but that "immediately on request, the club was to be ready to roll them up and take them away". Such were the bureaucrats of the day. For them, the members of the Institute who patronized our activities must obviously have been slightly out of their minds.

It was in this way, using an amended birth certificate – for a copy of which an unfriendly journalist kept maliciously pestering me – that we seized the opportunity of holding these festivities with the sumptuousness permitted by budgets that were still extremely meager. The meeting at the Sorbonne, which constituted the intellectual part of the celebrations, comprised, together with the Marseillaise, the Russian national anthem, and an ode written for the occasion, a three-part lecture on the history of physical exercise: Georges Bourdon spoke on Antiquity; J. J. Jusserand, future Ambassador for France in Washington, on the Middle Ages, and I on modern times.

Now I had decided to end my talk in sensational fashion with the announcement of the resolution to bring about an early revival of the Olympic Games. The time had come to take the plunge!

Naturally, I had foreseen every eventuality except what actually happened. Opposition? Objections, irony? Or even indifference? Not at all. Everyone applauded, everyone approved, everyone wished me great success, but no one had really understood. It was a period of total, absolute lack of comprehension that was about to start.

And it was to last a long time.

Four years later, in Athens, on the occasion of the Games of the first Olympiad, I well remember an American lady who, after congratulating me, said, smiling: "I have already watched Olympic Games". "Really!" I said, "and where was that?" "In San Francisco". Seeing my bewilderment, she added: "They were very beautiful. Caesar was there". A reconstitution, a pageant, a show of the kind the Hippodrome in the Avenue de 1'Alma, or London's Olympia were in the habit of putting on in those far off days, these were what were to stand obstinately between me and my audience in 1892. Full of good will – but no understanding – they were unable to comprehend my idea, to interpret this forgotten thing: Olympism, and to separate the soul, the essence, the principle... from the ancient forms that had enveloped it and which, during the last fifteen hundred years, had fallen into oblivion.

This placed me in a lonely position, very difficult to endure. If I had been a multimillionaire, I would have been able to find a way out, but how, with the modest resources of my youthful income, which up until then had been just sufficient to give a little help to the school sports associations which were being formed in French high schools, or to allow me to travel here and there to organize various necessary meetings, could I be expected to carry out the international activities now required? And without sufficient means how were these activities to be carried out at all?

One other source of misunderstanding existed among sportsmen themselves: their inability to collaborate between one sport and another. The present generation – come to think about it, the lack of understanding between sports is hard to explain since they all rest on the same foundation of physical well being and preliminary physical training. Their psycho-physiological base is identical. But in the 19th century sportsmen were firmly convinced that as the practice of one sport differed from that of another, the two were mutually harmful. A fencer would deteriorate if he were to box. An oarsman should beware of taking up the horizontal bar. As for the horseman of the day, the mere idea of running or playing football would have been extremely distasteful to him. There was only tennis, still in its infancy, and swimming that did not arouse any mistrust: the first of these sports was only an elegant pastime, and the second a useful accomplishment recommended for reasons of health and safety in case of accident or lifesaving.

The representatives of the different sports had never, as far as I know, met together for a joint purpose before I invited them to meet for the foundation of the Committee for the Propagation of School Sport; one year later, the Committee for the Organization of the Contests at the 1889 Congress, the list of whose members I had drawn up, brought them together officially, this time at the Ministry of Public Education. It was amusing to see how they eyed one another with suspicion. But they were all mainly students, for at that time we were dealing with educational circles exclusively. The situation was quite different where the Olympic Games were concerned. Here we were dealing with adults...

The winter of 1892-93 went by without the idea causing any stir among the general public. Whenever any allusion was made to it, it was always the notion of a hippodrome-type spectacle that was uppermost in the person's mind. The great joke among "cultured" people was to inquire whether women would be allowed to attend the new Games as spectators and whether, as in certain periods of antiquity, general nudity would be enforced on the athletes in order more effectively to bar the weaker sex from the precincts of the competitions.

My plans, before the meeting in November 1892, had been based on the idea that the repercussions stirred up by the project would be great enough to ensure the success of an international congress, in which I rather naively imagined that governments and universities would take part with official delegations. I soon realized I had been too optimistic. What was to be done then? Very quickly, I decided to keep the idea of a Congress, but to use a little deception. In the files of the USFSA (for no sooner had it seen the light of day, than it acquired files like any bona fide modern organization) there lay a project for an International Congress to settle the question of amateurism, proposed by A. de Pallissaux, one of the most loyal and enthusiastic pioneers of the early days. With what fond memories I look back on the friendly collaborators of the time, without forgetting the storm clouds that sometimes passed between us.

Amateurism, an admirable mummy that could be presented at the museum of Boulak as a specimen of the modern art of embalming! Half a century has gone by without it seeming to have suffered in any way from the unceasing manipulations to which it has been submitted. It seems intact. Not one of us expected it to last so long. In tackling this problem we felt sure that we should succeed in less than five years. But for me, the planned Congress had, above all, the importance of providing me with an invaluable screen. I therefore drew up a preliminary program and had it approved by the Congress of the USFSA, which had been transformed at the beginning of 1890. Henceforth it had a Board and a Committee, each merging into the other and separating with equal ease. In this way, it was a sort of Janus with one face looking at the Jockey-Club, from the ranks of which we recruited our honorary members at twenty francs a year, and the other at the middle classes, a fraction of whom, full of drive and initiative, provided us with the enthusiastic assistants we needed and gladly entrusted us with the muscles of their sons. This fusion of the classes, not always easy to maintain, or even to bring about, amused me.

I have the program of the 1894 Congress here before me as I write, in two distinct versions between which lies a space of some ten months. At the head, an immovable trinity composed of three members: C. Herbert, Secretary of the Amateur Athletic Association (London), for Great Britain and the British Empire; W. M. Sloane, professor at Princeton University, for the American continent; and myself, for France and continental Europe. This unusual geography was intended to simplify propaganda for me. My two colleagues had accepted mainly in order to please me.

Herbert, who was quite taciturn but much more understanding than he appeared at first sight, had at his disposal, as administrative head of the AAA, a whole propaganda network already organized on a wide footing. Sloane, owing to his position and his already great reputation, had access to the transatlantic university circles that I had already noticed in 1889 as dominating American athletics and without which nothing could be done.

After the names of the three members of the Board came the following eight Articles which, I believe, have never been reproduced since:

I. – Definition of an amateur: bases of this definition. – Possibility and utility of an international definition.

II. – Suspension, disqualification, and re-qualification. – Facts motivating such actions, and means of checking them.

III. – Is it right to preserve a distinction between different sports from the point of view of amateurism, especially with regard to horse-racing (gentlemen) and pigeon shooting? Can one be a professional in one sport and an amateur in another?

IV. – Regarding the value of the objects of art given as prizes. – Should a limit be placed on their value? – What steps should be taken against anyone selling the art object awarded to him as a prize?

V. – Legitimacy of the funds produced by admissions to sports grounds. – May this money be shared among the clubs or among the competitors? May it be used as compensation for traveling expenses? – To what extent may members of the teams receive compensation from the rival club or their own club?

VI. – Can the general definition of an amateur be applied to all sports? – Does it comprise special restrictions with regard to cycling, rowing, athletics, etc.?

VII. – Betting. – Is it compatible with amateurism? – Means of stopping it from spreading.

VIII. – Of the possibility of reviving the Olympic Games. – Under what conditions could they be revived?

The final program published at the beginning of 1894 was more fully developed and more precise. It contained dates: June 16-24, 1894, the announcement that the sessions would be held at the Sorbonne and that the opening ceremony on June 16 would be presided over by Baron de Courcel, a Senator and former Ambassador to Berlin (as a matter of fact, it was Mr. Casimir-Perier, Minister of Foreign Affairs at the time, who had first accepted this post and then declined, recommending me to get in touch with Mr. de Courcel). In addition, there were eight honorary Vice-Presidents, including an Englishman, an American, a Belgian, a Swede, and a Hungarian; a few assistant officials, including Frantz-Reichel, "for the press", and the announcement of a number of still somewhat vague festivities. The program had had two new paragraphs added. Above all, it was now divided into two parts: the first headed "Amateurism and professionalism" comprised the first seven Articles reproduced above; the second, under the heading "Olympic Games", consisted of the 8th Article above and the two new Articles that follow

IX. – Conditions governing competitors. – Sports represented. – Organization, frequency, etc.

X. – Nomination of an International Committee responsible for preparing the revival.

Finally, regulations were laid down, while preserving as far as possible the elasticity I wished to confer on it, in particular by specifying that "the Unions and Clubs taking part would not be bound by the resolutions adopted". In this way the document assumed an appearance of assurance, of certainty far removed from the reality. In fact, I was embarked on an adventure about whose immediate success I was far from feeling reassured.

In the autumn of 1893, I had returned to the United States for four months. I had spent a long time visiting the Chicago Exhibition, stayed in California, and returned to Washington and New York via Texas and Louisiana. In Chicago, I had stayed in the luxurious Athletics Club and visited the Olympic Club in San Francisco, with its prophetic name. In all the universities I was visiting for the first time or had already visited in 1889, I had been met with a warm welcome, in spite of the fact that my book Universités Transatlantiques, published in 1890, was not at all well received by the professors, who found the form somewhat light and the contents not sufficiently complimentary. In any case, nowhere did the idea for the revival of the Olympic Games meet with the enthusiasm it deserved. My kind friend William Sloane alone was wildly enthusiastic about the project. The day before I left New York to return to Europe, he gave a dinner at the University Club in New York, and the guests he had chosen with great care and thought were among the most receptive to the ideas of both sport and history. Very warm conversation, sincere interest, but an obvious feeling of inevitable failure. The same impression, only stronger, in London in February 1894. Sir John Astley invited a number of friends to the Sports Club to talk about my plans but the number of those who accepted gradually diminished to a mere handful of somewhat inert guests. Meanwhile, spring was advancing without bringing any encouraging promises. I never thought of giving up however. It would have been difficult anyhow, for applications to join, without being numerous enough or firm enough, were coming in from all over the world, from New Zealand and Jamaica, as well as from Amiens and Bordeaux.

There were two sources of anxiety however: the universities were not showing any real interest. I had counted a great deal on their participation to add body to the "classical" character of the scheme. And then Germany was not reacting as it should either. At the time, I had no connections in that country but I considered the support of the Germans indispensable alongside that of the British and the "Latins", an expression that I still used, only later coming to recognize how artificial and inaccurate it was. Armed with some sort of an introduction, I visited the German military attaché in Paris, of the famous Colonel Dreyfus case. On his advice, I wrote twice to a Prussian Minister, Mr. de Podbielski, who had been described to me as the big white chief of sport, but I never received any reply.

This inclusion of Germany in the affair risked causing the French gymnastics associations to withdraw their support, which had been given, moreover, without the least enthusiasm. On May 15, 1894, Mr. Cuperus refused in virulent terms to allow the Belgian gymnastics associations to join: "My federation", he said, "has always believed and still believes that gymnastics and sport are diametrically opposed activities and it has always fought against the latter as incompatible with its principles". My own mind was made up on this matter. I considered such a doctrine absurd, but what could I do? The Union des Sociétés Françaises de Gymnastique had joined. Mr. Sansboeuf had advised me however that his members would resign if the Germans were to join. I found this not only annoying, but humiliating. This perpetual "protestation" against the victors of 1870 exasperated me. In fact, what could have been less French, less chivalrous, less in the spirit of "Fontenoy" than raising one's fist in rage and anger, while remaining seated? Is this the way our fathers understood "the interval between battles"? I could not start to say to what extent, during my adolescence, I had suffered from this attitude, which a false, mean conception of patriotism imposed on my generation. Although I had grown up in the shadow of Sedan, I never felt in myself the soul of the vanquished. The awakening of 1878 inspired me and the magnificent turning-point of 1889 liberated me by giving me an idea of the capacities of the nation and faith in a future differing from the past but not unworthy of it.

As the date for the Congress approached, everything remained, as it were, streaked with light on a gray background. It was as if I had collected around me a small orchestra that, with its eyes fixed on my stand, was awaiting the signal to start, without knowing exactly what tune it was going to play. I concentrated all my efforts on the opening session and the first choral performance of the Hymn to Apollo discovered in the ruins of Delphi. Gabriel Fauré lent a hand with good grace.

Suddenly the name of the Congress changed. The words "Congress for the Revival of the Olympic Games" appeared on the letters of invitation, one of which can still be seen in the Olympic Museum in Lausanne. In the marvelous setting of the main amphitheater in the Sorbonne (the new Sorbonne this time), graced with Puvis de Chavannes' "Sacred copse", after an academic speech by Baron de Courcel and between a fine ode by Jean Aicard and a clever commentary by Theodore Reinach, the playing of this sacred piece of music created the desired atmosphere

THE EASTERN TELEGRAPH COMPANY, LIMITED. ATHENS STATION. ΤΗΛΕΓΡΑΦΕΙΟΝ ΑΘΗΝΩΝ

Greek Received Form).

Fokianos president Syllogue gymnastique Athenes. Congres exprima voeu pour celebration a athenes des premiers jeux olympiques internationaux 1896

Bikelas

Telegram sent from Paris by Vikélas, announcing the choice of Athens as the site for the inaugural Modern Olympic Games to Fokianos, President of the Athens Gymnastics Association (PGS Archives, Athens)

among the huge audience. A subtle feeling of emotion spread through the auditorium as if the ancient eurhythmy were coming to us from the distant past. In this way, Hellenism infiltrated into the whole vast hall. From this moment, the Congress was destined to succeed. I knew that now, whether consciously or not, no one would vote against the revival of the Olympic Games.

It was, in fact, unanimously proclaimed at the last session on June 23. The Congress members had performed an honorable task. Divided into two commissions, one for amateurism, the other for Olympism, they were presided over on the one hand by Michel Gondinet, President of the Racing Club de France, and on the other by D. Bikelas, member of the Pan-Hellenic Gymnastics Society. The Vice Presidents were Professor W. M. Sloane and R. Todd, member of the National Cyclist's Union, for the first group, and Baron de Carayon la Tour, member of the Société Hippique Française, for the other.

The sessions went very well. There were a number of interesting discussions on technical matters and on the question of amateurism, which the Rector of the University came down from his apartment to attend on several occasions.

As far as the Olympic Games were concerned, everyone accepted my proposals almost without discussion. The meeting voted one after the other the various fundamental principles I had previously decided on in my own mind: the interval of four years, the exclusively modern character of the events, the exclusion of school sports (Bikelas and the Swede Bergh would have liked to include competitions for children, which I considered impractical and dangerous), and finally the appointment of an International Committee – permanent in its principle and stable in its composition – whose members would be the representatives of Olympism in their respective countries.

As to the choice of Athens and the date of 1896, this did not fit in at all with my original plan for the reason that, underestimating like most of my contemporaries the youthful strength of the recently resuscitated Greece, I did not think she was capable of coping with the inauguration of world sports championships.

At one time I had thought of inaugurating the Games in Paris in the first year of the 20th century, as I explained in the Revue de Paris dated June 15, 1894, doing everything possible to "steep in Hellenism" the celebration of the Games. A number of conversations with D. Bikelas, whose friendship had charmed me right from the start, led me to change my opinion. For his part, he wanted them to be held in Greece but at the same time hesitated before the responsibility of involving his country in such an adventure. We encouraged each other and Athens was selected to the accompaniment of wild applause.

The idea of holding the Games in different countries was accepted without too many objections being raised. It was essential in fact. Otherwise no country would have been willing to accept the expense of such an undertaking. Greece, at any rate, would have been out of the question from both the technical and the financial points of view.

I was allowed a free hand in the choice of members of the IOC. Those proposed were elected without amendment; the list comprised: Bikelas for Greece; Callot and myself for France; General de Boutovsky for Russia; Colonel Balck for Sweden; Professor Sloane for the United States; Jiri Guth (Bohemia); F. Kémény (Hungary); C. Herbert and Lord Ampthill for England; Professor Zubiaur for Argentina and L. A. Cuff for New Zealand; finally Count Lucchesi Palli accepted provisionally for Italy and soon afterwards Count Max de Bousies for Belgium. Nobody seemed to have noticed that I had chosen almost exclusively absentee members. As their names figured on the long list of "honorary members of the Congress", people were accustomed to seeing their names and readily assumed that they were staunch members always at their tasks. I needed elbow room at the start, for many conflicts were bound to arise. Some at any rate would want to seize the helm, either to benefit from the success of the venture or to modify the direction. Such is human nature.

Olympic Memoirs, Chap.1, Lausanne, IOC, 1997, pp.12-24.

4.2.1/10 – 4.2.1/11 INTRODUCTION

How difficult it was for Coubertin to win Greece over to holding the first Olympic Games can be seen in the next two chapters of his Olympic Memoirs.Recent sports historical research[1] offers a whole new interpretation, on the basis of the Vikelas estate but also of books of minutes and correspondence by the 1896 organizing committee subsequently discovered by K. Georgiadis. This shows that, understandably, being far away in Paris, Coubertin could not be the driving force; rather it was Vikelas and Crown Prince Constantine on the spot in Athens. Coubertin got married in 1895 in Paris, and according to evidence in K. Georgiadis's source work, was difficult to reach during the decisive phase. In his historical reminiscence in the following two texts, he exaggerates his actual contribution. His achievement as the man who had the ideas and got things going is not affected. It has taken 100 years for research to give the figure of Vikelas, the first president of the IOC founded in 1894, his rightful place.

4.2.1/10 THE CONQUEST OF GREECE

A few days after the Congress came to an end, Sloane, Callot and I joined Mr. Bikelas for a meeting in the small apartment he kept in the Rue de Babylone, in Paris. It was there that the edifice of the IOC was consolidated.

Bikelas was reluctant to accept the presidency. I favored the idea of a mobile presidency belonging by right to the nationality of the next Olympiad. Everything that might help to strengthen the international character of the cycle that was about to start seemed to me of paramount importance. Bikelas would only have to occupy the post until the end of the year 1896 and I would then take over for the next four-year period. Meanwhile I would occupy the post of "Secretary General", a position of greater interest than most presidencies, for a Secretary General is the kingpin of an active administration.

This was the way I had acted with the USFSA in order to transform it and make it a cornerstone of the "muscular" revival in France. I appointed Ernest Callot as Treasurer, one of the elders, who combined a love of Letters with a love of Sport and shared our ambitions and hopes; then I explained my plan, which was to complete without undue haste, but without any delay either, the facade of the IOC and to endow its members with the armor of complete independence by refusing admittance to any "representative" of anybody or anything as well as any "subsidy" from any source whatsoever. "The poor man's armor" murmured Bikelas. But they all understood perfectly the need to act in this way if we wished to ensure the future of an institution bearing an illustrious name, but lacking

1 See K. Georgiadis, *Die ideengeschichtliche Grundlage der Erneuerung der Olympischen Spiele im 19. Jahrhundert in Griechenland und ihre Umsetzung 1896 in Athen.* Dissertation, Sports Faculty of the Johannes Gutenberg University, Mainz 1998. Published by Agon, Kassel 2000.
A. Morbach, *Dimítrios Vikélas. Patriotischer Literat und Kosmopolit.* Leben und Wirken des ersten Präsidenten des Internationalen Olympischen Komitees. Würzburg, Ergon, 1998.
D. C. Young, *The Modern Olympics. A Struggle for Revival.* Baltimore/London, The John Hopkins University Press, 1996.

practical foundations and still largely misunderstood by the general public. In the audience of two thousand who heard the *Hymn to Apollo,* there were more artists than sportsmen and the end of the Congress fizzled out in the general excitement caused by the assassination of President Carnot.

We also reached agreement concerning the principle of the equality of sports. Already during the Congress, at the meetings on June 19 and 22, I had had to intervene in order to prevent the so-called "minor sports" from being treated simply as appendages of "athletics", as was to re-occur so often subsequently and for a long time to come.

Some idea of these important decisions is given in No. 2 of the quarterly bulletin I immediately began to publish. The following passages are taken from its pages "We have been asked to clarify the nature of our undertaking. Here, in a few lines, is our reply... Our intention, in reviving an institution that has lain forgotten for so many centuries, is as follows: Athletics are assuming growing importance every year. The part they play appears to be as important and as lasting in the modern world as it was in antiquity; they reappear moreover with new characteristics; they are international and democratic, suited therefore to the ideas and needs of the present day. But today, as in times gone by, their effect will be beneficial or harmful depending on the use made of them and the direction they are made to take. Athletics can bring into play both the noblest and the basest passions; they can develop the qualities of unselfishness and honor just as much as the love of gain; they can be chivalrous or corrupt, virile or bestial; finally, they can be used to strengthen peace or to prepare for war. Now, nobility of sentiments, high regard for the virtues of unselfishness and honor, a spirit of chivalry, virile energy and peace are the prime needs of modern democracies, whether republican or monarchic..."

About the middle of the summer, the IOC was finally constituted by the acceptances of those who had been appointed without my having been able to sound them out beforehand. On September 4, Mr. Cuff's acceptance arrived from Christchurch and on the 15th, the Duke of Andria's from Naples. Twelve nationalities were thus represented at the start, and one of the tasks of the Committee was to complete its numbers. It was a "self-recruiting body", like the organizing body of the Henley Regattas. But it had already become what it was to remain for the next thirty years, and what it still is today – a committee composed of three concentric circles: a small *nucleus* of dedicated active members; a *nursery* of willing members capable of being educated along the right lines; and finally, *a facade* of people of varying degrees of usefulness, whose presence would serve to satisfy national pretensions while lending prestige to the whole.

In the autumn, Mr. Bikelas left for Athens, preceded by a quantity of personal letters accompanying the first numbers of the *Bulletin.* On October 4, he wrote to me on arrival: "All the way from Brindisi, my compatriots have spoken to me with enthusiasm and delight about the Olympic Games". This sentiment was echoed by the correspondent of *Le Temps* in Greece. The following day, a second letter. Mr. Bikelas had seen the Prime Minister, Mr. Tricoupis, and found him "well disposed", in spite of the fact that he would have been happier if the whole affair had never arisen. Bikelas proposed convening a meeting of the Commission of the Zappeion, which has under its jurisdiction not only the monument of the same name but also the ruins of the Stadium close by.

Meanwhile, I was amassing documents with a view to the early drawing up of a detailed program. On July 26, Mr. G. Strehly, a teacher at the Lycée Montaigne in Paris, and a famous gymnast, had sent me his suggestions concerning individual "gymnic" sports (the only ones worth considering). This expression "gymnic" sports referred to the horizontal bar and all other apparatus. It is the right word. Today, thirty-five years later, I am still doing everything in my power to have it accepted. Then Herbert in London sent the distances to be adopted for the footraces.

Next came the proposals of the Executive Committee of the UVF for cycling. These were simply a two-kilometer sprint, without pace-makers, and a 100 kilometer race with pace-makers. Less reasonably, the National Cyclist's Union of Great Britain asked, in addition to a mile, a 10 km and a 100 km race, for "a time race, say twelve hours". Finally the Société d'Encouragement de l'Escrime (Club for the Encouragement of Fencing) had drafted, at my request, a project comprising contests for amateurs and teachers (foils only, with heats by pools).

With these documents stuffed into my trunk, I took the express to Marseilles and embarked on the *Ortegal* bound for Piraeus, both anxious and joyful – but more joyful than anxious – as I had always been on the eve of battle. While I was at sea, I examined the long, ominous letter in which Mr. Stephen Dragoumis, a Member of Parliament and President of the Zappeion Commission, explained to me, after the departure of Bikelas who had had to leave Athens, the discouraging conclusions to which he and his colleagues had come. In fact, he was very politely suggesting I should not come and inviting me to give up my Olympic project.

Our arrival at Piraeus in the dark, the sacred vigil on the deck in the majestic silence of the night, the landing at dawn, welcomed by a number of youthful enthusiasts, who immediately became good friends, the pilgrimage to the Stadium, almost unrecognizable as such: a huge mound stripped of its marble, in the background a few ruins and the famous passageway through which the athletes used to enter the stadium... Unforgettable, enchanting hours. Scarcely had I moved into my room at the hotel than I received the visit of the French chargé d'affaires, Mr. Maurouard, and while he was there, that of the head of the government, Mr. Tricoupis, who, putting aside all protocol, seemed in a hurry to establish contact and perhaps gauge my powers of resistance to his pressure, for as I learned afterwards he was determined to do everything possible to put a stop to the idea. He pretended to object purely from the financial point of view, although in my opinion this was not his only reason.

It was a fact that Greece at the time was in rather a difficult situation. The Prime Minister was afraid that the powers to which Greece was indebted might object to "lavish expenditure" by Greece when only the strictest economy would enable her to honor her outstanding debts. I objected that the expenditure involved was comparatively small. "Look around you, examine the matter", said Mr. Tricoupis as he left. "I am sure that you will come to see that Greece does not have sufficient funds to accept the mission you wish to entrust to her."

It was not until several days had passed that I found time to walk up to the Acropolis, or to see anything of Athens. I had become a sort of ball thrown back and forth between two political teams. The opposition, led by Mr. T. Delyannis, had opted enthusiastically for the idea of the Olympic Games. The press was divided into two camps and introduced a violent note into the dispute. I spent my days visiting politicians and journalists, under the guidance of my new friends, Georges Melas, son of the Mayor of Athens, and Alexander Mercati, son of the Director of the Bank and a childhood friend of the Crown Prince.

The coachman driving the landau got down from his seat and said to Georges Melas with the charming familiarity of those days: "Young Master George, I am going to tell you what your friend must do to persuade Mr. Tricoupis". I was annoyed that the Greek I had learned at school was of no use to me, especially as a result of the pronunciation we had been taught. But, on the other hand, everyone spoke French. I was particularly surprised to find a Greece that was so alive, that had remained so true to herself, at the same time both very old and very modern. Henceforth I had confidence in her future. I would continue to have great faith in the renewed destiny awaiting her.

However, I was unable to meet the one person I needed, the kingpin of the whole affair. During his stay, Bikelas had used all his charm and enthusiasm, but he had left me the task of erecting the scaffolding... As the King was in Russia, the Crown Prince was acting as regent and this made him a little more timid in his dealings with a hostile cabinet. However, in the course of two long conversations with him, I had acquired the firm conviction that he was definitely on our side. After inquiring into the sports resources of Athens, the grounds, and the manpower available, I drafted a project for a budget, which although modest seemed sufficient to me. From memory, no longer having the figures before me, I believe it must have been somewhere in the neighborhood of 250,000 Drachmas. In the Stadium, of course, provision had been made only for wooden tiers.

I then called on Mr. Tricoupis again to tell him of my favorable impression. He had been prepared for this. He raised no objections but refused any participation on the part of the government. I asked him if I could count on a "benevolent neutrality". He promised me I could... but not without mental reservations, I imagine. I then requested the use of a hall in the Zappeion, which they could hardly refuse.

With my friends, whose numbers were swelling, I drew up letters of invitation to a meeting, which was held on November 12 and was attended by a large audience. Fortunately, I was already used to this sort of vague gathering which has to be flattered, lulled to sleep, and shaken up in turn. A Committee was set up, under the patronage of the Crown Prince – his prior acceptance to act as patron had effectively silenced any opposition to the principle. Colonel Mano, Mr. E. Scouloudis, a Member of Parliament and former Minister, Commander Soutzo, in command of a cavalry squadron, and Mr. Retzinas, Mayor of Piraeus, were elected Vice-Presidents; Mr. Paul Skouses, Treasurer; Mr. A. Mercati and Mr. G. Melas, Secretaries. The date of the Games was fixed from April 5-15, 1896. That year, we would be lucky enough to see the dates of Easter of both the Greek and the western church coincide. The program I had brought with me from Paris was adopted.

Four days later, on November 16, I gave a lecture to the great literary society of Athens, the Parnassus. The hall was crowded. If Mr. Tricoupis' party would not yield neither would the opposition. I still have, in a number of *Romos,* the witty satirical journal written in verse, an amusing caricature showing Mr. Tricoupis and Mr. Delyannis, their hands lost in big boxing gloves, fighting over the Olympic Games. It was not without a certain anxiety that after a month's stay I had to leave

Athens, by land this time. The Panachaic Gymnastics Club gave me a rousing welcome at Patras. One of its committee members had been appointed to accompany me to Olympia. It was late in the evening when we arrived there. I had to wait till dawn to see for the first time the sacred landscape, which I had so often seen in my dreams. I spent the whole morning wandering round the ruins. I was not to see Olympia again for thirty-one years, on the occasion of the official commemoration of the revival of the Games. From Patras, after a brief halt at Corfu, I reached Brindisi and then Naples where, welcomed by my new colleague the Duke of Andria, I gave a lecture on December 7 at the Philological Circle, presided over by a famous Member of Parliament, Mr. Borghi – a lecture which left me with the impression of having completely wasted by breath. Far from the strains of the Hymn to Apollo and the reassuring silhouette of the Parthenon, any evocation of the Olympic Games naturally lacked conviction.

Olympic Memoirs, Chap.2, Lausanne, IOC, 1997, pp. 26-33.

4.2.1/11 THE FIRST OLYMPIAD (ATHENS 1896)

As soon as I had left Greece, Mr. Scouloudis did everything he could to destroy the foundations that had been laid. He invited the other three Vice-Presidents to come and see him, persuaded them that the budget I had made out was unrealistic, that the expenses would be enormous and the profits nil... Having sufficiently shattered their confidence, he announced to the rest of the Committee that the whole affair should be shelved and that they should put the matter to His Royal Highness, leaving the final decision to him.

He felt quite sure what this decision would be, but things turned out quite differently to what he had expected. The Crown Prince received the delegation, put the report down on his table, saying that he would study it, and after a little polite conversation sent the gentlemen on their way. I do not think he had a moment's hesitation. His mind was already made up. Although kept secretly informed of everything that was going on, I do not know the exact details of what happened between the Prince and the King, on the latter's return, but certainly the King must have appreciated the fact that the heir to the throne was at the head of a scheme of the most pure and generous Hellenism, for six months later when I called on him in Paris, where he was on a short visit, the King spoke to me with evident pride of the qualities the Crown Prince had shown in the organization of the Games.

These qualities were very real ones. I admired the intelligence and tact with which he succeeded in maneuvering and keeping his balance in a delicate situation; but, even so, the situation could not last. Mr. Tricoupis could not get over having had his formal wishes disregarded like this. He seized on the pretext of an incident that occurred during a strike to place the King in the position of having to "choose" between his son and his Minister. Calmly but firmly, the King expressed his regrets at the resignation Tricoupis handed in to him. Tricoupis withdrew, furious. The Olympic Games continued to rankle with him, to such an extent in fact that, as they drew near, he left for Nice. There he was to meet with a sudden and unexpected

Jeux Olympiques
—1896—
Athènes

M.

Le Congrès International Athlétique réuni au Palais de la Sorbonne, à Paris, le 16 Juin 1894, sous la Présidence de Mr le baron de Courcel, Sénateur de la République Française, a décidé le rétablissement des Jeux Olympiques et leur première célébration en 1896 à Athènes.

A la suite de cette décision, acceptée par la Grèce avec empressement, le Comité Hellène, institué à Athènes, sous la Présidence de Son Altesse Royale Monseigneur le Prince Royal de Grèce a l'honneur de vous inviter à participer aux Jeux Olympiques de 1896, qui seront célébrés à Athènes du 5 au 15 Avril 1896, et dont vous trouverez ci-joint le programme et les conditions.

Nous vous prions de vouloir bien répondre à cette invitation, faite après entente préalable avec le Comité International des Jeux Olympiques siégeant à Paris.

Veuillez agréer, Monsieur, l'assurance de ma considération la plus distinguée.

Athènes le 30 Decembre 1895.

Le Secrétaire Général
du Comité Hellène des Jeux Olympiques

Timoléon J. Philémon

Official invitation to participate in the 1896 Olympic Games in Athens, dated 30th December 1895 (Hellenic Olympic Committee Archives)

death, news of which reached Athens during the Games, one evening of great festivities, amid the splendor of the bright lights and the music. Without waiting for the denouement of the situation, the Crown Prince immediately reorganized the Committee originally formed on November 12, modifying the provisional organization as little as possible. He added a number of new collaborators, among them Mr. Delyannis, who in the meantime had become Prime Minister, and Mr. Zaimis, the present President of the Republic. He kept the two Secretaries but also took on Constantin Mano and George Streit, who was subsequently to have a brilliant political career. He placed his brothers at the head of technical commissions. Finally, he appointed Mr. T. Philemon, former Mayor of Athens, to be Secretary General and sent him right away to Alexandria to visit Mr. Averoff and obtain from him the funds needed for the reconstruction of the Stadium in marble, as in the days of Pericles. Time was running out. Since June 23, 1894, months had been wasted as a result of opposition to the project. The spring of 1895 was drawing near. There was scarcely a year left to complete everything.

Very few sportsmen today know the actual program of the 1896 Games. It is not surprising, after thirty-seven years! Here it is, as published at the beginning of the IOC's quarterly Bulletin:

A. – *Athletic sports:* Footraces: 100 m., 400 m., 800 m. and 1,500 m.; 110 m. hurdles (Regulations of the Union Française des Sports Athlétiques).
Field events: long jump, high jump, pole vault; putting the weight and throwing the discus (Regulations of the British A.A.A.).
Marathon

B. – *Gymnastics:* individual: rope climbing, hand over hand; horizontal bar; rings; parallel bars; horse vault; weightlifting.
Group movements (teams of ten).

C. – *Fencing:* foil, saber, and rapier for amateurs and teachers (special Regulations of the Société d'Encouragement de 1'Escrime, Paris).
Wrestling: Roman and Greek.

D. – *Shooting* with military weapons, rifle, and pistol (Regulations in the process of being drafted).

E. – *Yachting*: Steam yachts over 10 miles (Regulations of the Cercle de la Voile, Paris). Sailing (Ratings and Regulations of the Yacht Racing Association of Great Britain) for boats of three, ten, and twenty tons maximum and over twenty tons. Distances: 5 and 10 miles.
Rowing: single sculls, 2,000 m. without turn; skiff: double sculls without turn, gig and outrigger; fours (single oar) without turn, gigs (Regulations of the Rowing Club Italiano). *Swimming:* sprint: 100 m.; long distance and sprint 500 m.; long distance 1,000 m.; water polo.

F. – *Cycling:* Sprint: 2,000 m., track, without pace-makers; 10,000 m., track, with pacemakers; Long distance: 100 km., track, with pace-makers (Regulations of the International Cyclist's Association).

G. – *Riding:* manège, steeplechase, trick-riding, haute école.

H. – *Athletic games:* Lawn tennis, singles and doubles (Regulations of the All England L.T. Association and the Marylebone Cricket Club).

I have made a point of reproducing this text in full. Everyone can see now how much truth there is in the often repeated legend that the modern competitions consisted, at the start, purely of athletics, to which were later added various other sports. How much truth there is in it?... Not a single word.

This program which, even after the reorganization of the Committee, still kept the original date of November 12, 1894 (the date of the meeting in the Zappeion), presents the different categories of sport listed as compulsory in the charter, all on an equal footing: athletics, gymnastics, nautical and combat sports, riding... If I now add that most of the protocol for the opening and closing ceremonies, the hoisting of the winner's national flag at the prize giving ceremony after each event...date from the same period, everyone will have to agree that the new Olympism asserted itself right from the start just as it was to continue. This is the movement against which a violent opposition – the result mainly of a failure to understand, and to a lesser extent of disappointed ambitions and jealousy – raged for over twenty years, continually renewing its attacks from all quarters, but succeeding only once, in 1900, in its evil designs and even then not sufficiently to defeat us.

The program reproduced above was published with the approval of the Board of the IOC, that is to say Mr. Bikelas, Mr. Callot and me. Bikelas was quite terrified at having to countersign a document "emanating from his future sovereign". I insisted however. It was a decisive turning point and I was determined not to miss any opportunity of asserting the predominance of the IOC, however frail and unprepossessing it might still be.

During the months of January and February 1895, Bikelas, who had returned to Athens, wrote to me on an average three times a week. His enthusiasm was unbounded and he was unstinting in his efforts. He acted as a sort of liaison officer. One day he sent me the translation of an inaugural speech the Prince was to make. "Kindly read it, pen in hand". Another day he informed me of the first big subscriptions. Then those at the helm, still rather uncertain of themselves, needed reassurance regarding plans for the cycle-racing track, the arrangement of the seats in the Stadium, the invitation card, advice on the running track...

In the meantime, the blocks of marble were piling up in the venerable precincts, and all over the world the propaganda was starting up. Committees were formed. In Hungary, despite the fact that everyone was feverishly preparing the millennial celebrations of the Magyar State for the same year, 1896, Olympism was not neglected. Count Czaky had Kémény sound me out when everything seemed to be going wrong in Athens. Why not inaugurate the Olympic Games in Budapest during the millennial festivities? I took good care not to repulse these offers, but contented myself with using them to spur on the Greeks.

Balck wrote from Stockholm that he had "done some good work", that the Crown Prince (the present King) was interested. "We are a little anxious, but we will do everything in our power". At the same time, from Russia, General de Boutovsky sent in an account of his efforts. He was meeting with "a great deal of indifference". "Our press", he wrote, (February 2, 1895), "finds the question of Physical Training unworthy of mention in a newspaper of a certain standing."

From England, the news was encouraging. Mr. Romances, Greece's chargé d'affaires at the time, and Mr. Constantin Mano, an undergraduate at Oxford, were stirring up interest and collecting funds among the Greek colony. There was hardly a country with which some form of correspondence was not going on, often timid or misguided, but leaving room for hope. All this, as a general rule, came my way before being forwarded to Athens, which infuriated Mr. Philemon. He was an active man, shrewd, a good administrator I believe, but with a jealous and proud character. He felt inadequate and that annoyed him. Consequently he welcomed with ill-concealed satisfaction the troubles I was experiencing in France and especially the storm that blew, for a while, from the banks of the Spree.

In Paris, of course, the government ignored the movement although it had approved it the year before. A subsidy to help French athletes go to Athens! What nerve! We had to form the French Committee ourselves, with Mr. de Courcel as President, and Mr. Fabens as Acting Secretary. After agreeing to join, Mr. Merillon, President of the *Union des Sociétés de Tir* (Union of Shooting Clubs), solemnly withdrew, "the Union having decided there was no reason to participate in the organization". What is astonishing is the indignation shown in his letters on the subject. "It is almost incredible", he wrote to me on February 14, 1895, "that the organizers of the Olympic Games should have imagined that the *Union Nationale de France* would agree to become an *appendage of their committee* and that shooting would be 'a mere branch incorporated and *fitted into a whole series of sports*'". I quote these words for they show the strange mistrust that still prevailed regarding the principle of cooperation between sports, even in circles that were supposedly enlightened. However, common sense finally prevailed and France's athletes joined the others at the foot of the Acropolis, where their absence would have been a scandal.

They knew that they would have to compete against the Germans but no longer let it worry them. A group created in Berlin by Dr. W. Gebhardt, with whom I corresponded regularly, sought to rouse the interest of the Germans and seemed to be succeeding until, about the end of the year (1895), a letter was received in Athens from a big gymnastic club in Germany declining the invitation originally accepted. The refusal was based on a completely false interview that had been published in a French newspaper and had escaped my notice. The words attributed to me were so misplaced that the German protest seemed moderate in the extreme and completely justified in every way. As soon as I was told about it, I got in touch with Gebhardt, but at the very same moment the *National Zeitung* reproduced the letter from the gymnasts. There was immediately a public outcry in the German press. Right away, I sent off a denial with a copy to Mr. Rangabe, the Minister for Greece in Berlin, who thanked me and informed me of the steps he had taken to give *"the widest possible publicity"* to this denial. He said he had managed to "have a copy given to the Chancellor, who would bring it to the notice of the Emperor", all very necessary steps "for anger in Germany had reached alarming proportions... Only yesterday", he added "I received some fifty articles from all over the Empire" This anger quickly died down however, and Gebhardt who had acted with firmness summoned a meeting in Berlin which, after hearing his explanation, asked him unanimously to assure me by telegram of "its wholehearted support and its wishes for the success of the joint enterprise". He was kind enough to send a copy of this message to the French Ambassador, Mr. Jules Herbette.

This took place on January 16 (1895). In Greece, although Asty had received my denial on January 1 and had published it, Mr. Philemon behaved as if he believed in the authenticity of the interview. I heard later from Gebhardt that he had even taken advantage of the incident to try and do away with the IOC, "a temporary organization that no longer has any reason to exist". The reporter for *Le Temps,* in his letter from Greece on January 12, tells of the excitement caused all over Greece by the incident. Let down by German public opinion, Philemon had to abandon his evil designs. However, it was not until February 7 that, reprimanded by me, he decided to send me a telegram to the effect that the Greek Committee "had never believed" the words attributed to me. It was a little late for me to find this assertion really convincing.

The great day finally arrived when the crowd was admitted to the stadium, which had been restored to all its pristine glory, and when King George officially proclaimed the revival of the Olympic Games, pronouncing the ritual words: "I declare the Games of the First Olympiad of the modern era open". The cannon salvoes immediately resounded, followed by the release of pigeons, which wheeled joyously over the stadium; choirs sang the beautiful cantata composed by the Greek musician Samara, and the contests began. The idea had become reality and was now part of history. "All this is your doing", said Gebhardt to me (we always spoke English together). The group formed by the IOC on either side of the Crown Prince represented the perennial nature of the enterprise and the international character I was determined to preserve at all costs. All around us resounded the nationalistic fervor of the Greeks intoxicated by the idea of seeing Athens become the permanent home of the Games, acting as host every four years to this flattering and profitable influx of visitors.

Elsewhere I have described the pomp and ceremony of these first Games, the difficulties and technical disappointments, the enthusiasm of the spectators, the underhand intrigues, the discouragement of some of my colleagues, and finally the royal initiative claiming for Greece the monopoly of revived Olympism... And I, too, would willingly have given in if I had not realized with absolute certainty the impractical nature of such a plan, which could only be doomed to failure. No one could seriously believe for a moment that Athens would be able to go on indefinitely every four years making the supreme effort required for the periodic renewal of the organization and the financing. But try and make a nation gone wild with excitement see reason, a whole people suddenly confronted with a living vision of its most glorious past. The whole Greek world had thrilled in unison at this spectacle. A sort of moral mobilization took place. Even the monks on Mount Athos, at that time separated from the mother country by an unwelcome frontier, sent donations for the celebration of the Games. And while, to the rest of the world, the revival of the Olympiads was still no more than a brilliant, picturesque item of news, on Greek minds it was having the effect of the most potent elixir. So much so, in fact, that when a year later war broke out between Greece and Turkey for the liberation of Crete, the Olympic Games were blamed for being largely responsible and having served as a screen for the preparation of this bellicose enterprise by enabling delegations from the Greek colonies overseas to gather in Athens for warlike discussions. There was very little truth in these allegations. At most, it might be said that

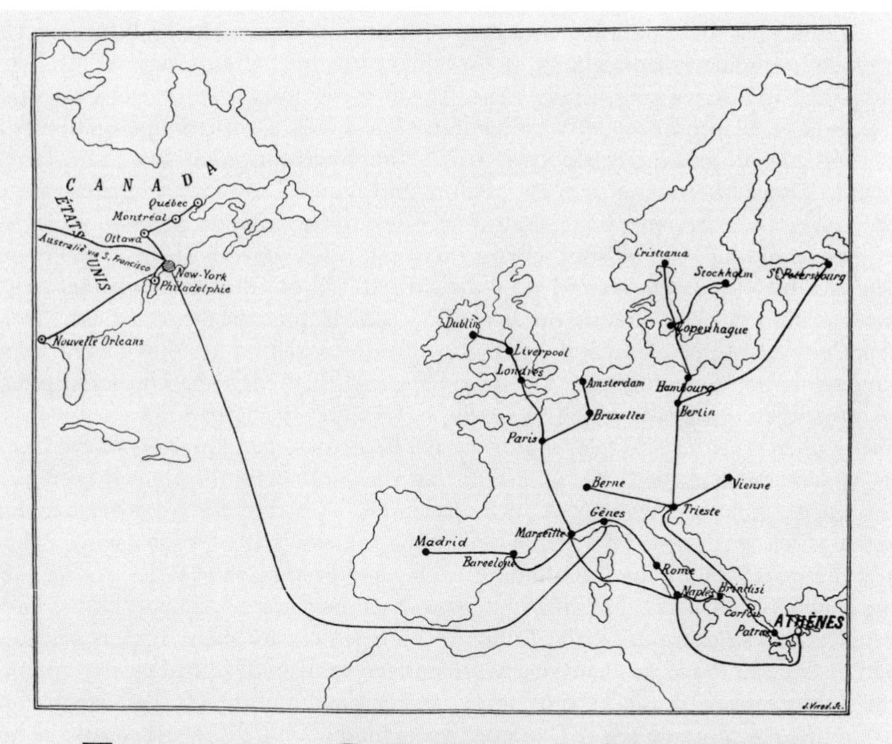

Jeux Olympiques

ATHÈNES

5-15 Avril 1896

L'Agence Th. Cook et Son, de Londres, s'est mise en communication avec les différentes Compagnies de Chemins de fer et de Paquebots dans le but d'obtenir des réductions de prix en faveur tant des concurrents que des simples curieux qui, de toutes les parties du Monde, se rendront en Grèce à l'occasion des Jeux Olympiques.

Advertisement by travel agent Thomas Cook and Son for group travel to the 1st Olympic Games in Athens (taken from Bulletin du Comité International des Jeux Olympiques, no.4, 1895, p.4)

the festivities had tended to speed up a movement that had already been preparing beforehand by the force of circumstances. It was not the first time that the Cretans had taken up arms in order to gain their freedom. And their cause had all the power conferred on it by right and justice since, in spite of the overwhelming defeat suffered by the Greek forces, it led in the long run to an improvement in the situation in Crete and the setting up of a regime preparatory to complete autonomy and the future return of the island to Greece.

At any rate, these political considerations did not tend to make European government particularly favorable to the revival of Olympism. Nor was the IOC's role simplified in any way: especially mine. The auspices for the second Olympiad did not look at all promising. My collaborators at a loss, Greek public opinion supporting a man resolutely opposed to the implementation of my "circulating" plan..., I was more alone than ever before and reduced, to an even greater degree than when I was preparing the 1894 congresses, to counting on nobody but myself.

Above all I had to hold out against the King, whose speech at the final banquet attended by all the athletes had faced me with the famous dilemma: whether to give in or to resign. I had already decided to do neither. But, on the other hand, resistance on such an occasion was hardly possible. I decided to act as if I were stupid, pretending not to understand. I decided to ignore the King's speech on the pretext of an ambiguity; speaking half in Greek, half in French, he had not used identical terms when repeating his proposal to fix the permanent headquarters of the Games in Athens. I also ignored the statement that the American athletes had been made to sign, backing the sovereign's idea. The press built the whole matter up, but I acted as if I was unaware of what was going on, the part of a man who will not and therefore cannot hear anything. And the very evening the Games closed, I sent the King a public letter thanking him, as well as the town of Athens and the Greek people, for the energy and the brilliance with which, by their support and their action, the call made on them in 1894 had been answered. In it, I clearly specified the continuation of the scheme and the perennial nature of the International Committee by alluding to the Games of the second Olympiad, which would be held in Paris... The letter was short and to the point. The German and English versions appearing at the same time as the French, it became of little importance whether the Greek version was published or not. The outward form was, of course, perfectly polite and courteous, in accordance with the demands of protocol, but the deed itself was nonetheless of a rare insolence. The members of the Committee, who were for the most part staunchly monarchist, showed considerable alarm, for I had not consulted my colleagues or submitted anything in advance. Philemon hid his face in distress. What was to become of him?... I was not very reassured myself. However nothing happened. The IOC survived the test without resignations or even any cracks in its structure. The Crown Prince, who moreover perfectly understood the impossibility of trying to monopolize the Games on behalf of Athens, did not back up the King, whom Philemon had, in fact, caused to take a rash, thoughtless step. Thus the crisis blew over and the Second Olympiad, in Paris, began to loom on the horizon. Unfortunately, if there was one place in the world where everyone was completely indifferent to the whole idea, it was Paris...

From the technical point of view, these first Olympic Games had nothing sensational about them. The performances had, obviously, beaten no records nor exceeded any hopes. All that was accomplished, a great innovation for the time, was cooperation among different sports, but this was a tremendous step forward, laying the foundations for a whole new future. When I say that nothing really sensational had occurred, exception must be made of the Marathon. The idea of an illustrious member of the Institut de France, Mr. Michel Breal – who, in his enthusiasm, had written to me immediately after the revival of the Olympiads to say that he would give a Cup for this race, the Marathon – was wildly ambitious for the day. It was an enormous distance – between 42 and 44 kilometers – and likely to be considered exaggerated even by the technicians. We had been reluctant to create such a race even though it had been so generously endowed even before its birth, but it was hardly possible, once word had got about, to avoid doing so. The Greeks had few runners. None of us imagined that the winner would be one of them and especially an "untried" competitor. Spiridon Louis was a magnificent peasant dressed in the popular kilt and quite unfamiliar with the finer points of scientific training or in fact the modern notion of training at all. He prepared himself for the event by fasting and prayer, and it was said, spent the night before the race praying by the light of candles in front of icons. His victory was magnificent in its brilliance and simplicity. At the entrance to the stadium, filled with over sixty thousand spectators, he arrived without any signs of exhaustion, and when Prince Constantine and Prince George, in a spontaneous gesture, seized him in their arms to carry him to the King standing before his marble throne, it was as if the spirit of Ancient Greece had entered with him into the arena. Wild applause greeted his victory. It was one of the most extraordinary sights I have ever seen. I shall never forget the scene and it left me convinced that psychic forces play a much more active role in sport than is generally believed; other experiences I met with after 1896 have confirmed this conviction but even with the help of medical science the truth remains obscure and the practical consequences have not yet been divined.

This does not mean that the scientific side of training should be neglected, and in Athens, too, proof of this was given by a second incident. Princeton University in America, where my friend W. Sloane taught, had sent five outstanding athletes. One of them, Robert Garrett, who had never thrown a discus in his life, grew interested in this sport and succeeded so well right from the start that he told me he would like to enter for the Olympic event. He was afraid however that it might be considered "pretentious and ridiculous" of him. I encouraged him, and he did so well that he even won a prize! He owed this to the perfection of his general physical preparation. A few years before, I had seen a young Canadian, who was not a horseman, become in similar fashion one of the winners of the trick-riding competition. Thus, in addition to the importance of the mind, we have evidence of the value of general methodical training: fruitful data destined to light the way to the future.

However, throughout the provinces of Greece and on all Greek islands, small boys, as they ran out of school, amused themselves "playing at the Olympic Games". After having run, jumped and thrown a few stones just for the fun of it, they formed up into a procession, and the biggest of them, suddenly becoming serious, would hand the others an olive branch. This symbolic gesture made in Athens again, after so many centuries had elapsed, gave them an unconscious contact with their great past that they vaguely sensed. This symbolic game, full of poetry, in the divine countryside of Corfu was my last vision of the first Olympiad. Now I had to set to work to ensure its succession.

Olympic Memoirs, Chap. 3, Lausanne, IOC, 1997, pp.36-49.

4.2.2 SPECIFIC OLYMPIC EVENTS

4.2.2/1 – 4.2.2/3 INTRODUCTION

Coubertin could not deny his journalistic passion. He made use of his stay on the occasion of the first Olympic Games in Athens by reporting for the French newspaper *Journal des Débats.* The French press was supplied with first-hand natural impression from the new big event of sport by dispatch.

In Coubertins anthology *Souvenirs d'Amerique et de Grèce*[1] (America and Greek souvenirs) the letters from Athens were published again, with minor editorial corrections and additions.

In 1897, the Olympic Letters I, III and IV also appeared in the English translation of the original texts from the Journal des Débats in the *Report of the Commissioner of Education for the year 1895 - 96*[2].

Animated by the big success of the US-College students, the US-Commissioner of Education had obviously qualified the Olympic Games of Athens in 1896 of being so important that he included these Coubertin-articles in his report. Sport historically they are significant because they give a very personal and authentic account of his judgement. The Olympic Letter II which has not been translated tells us about the ecclesiastical Easter ceremony in Athens, Letter V about the closing ceremonies and Coubertins mixed feelings at the end of the Olympic days of Athens. This Letter from April 15, 1896 ends with the rigorous assessment Coubertins: The last Olympic Letter, Letter VI from April 24, 1896, melancholically describes Coubertins continuing journey to Patras and his yearning for Olympia.

4.2.2./1 OLYMPIC LETTER FROM ATHENS (MARCH 26, 1896)

The Athenians enjoy a twofold spring this year; at the same time it warms the illuminated atmosphere and the popular spirit; it gives life to the small, fragrant flowers that force their way between the marble slabs of the Parthenon and imparts a smile of satisfaction on the lips of the proud 'Palakares' (champions of the people). The sun shines and the Olympic games are at the hand. Nothing remains of the irony and fears of the last year. The skeptics are silent and the Olympic games have no more enemies. French, Russian, American, German, Swedish, and English flags are for sale on every hand. The Attic breeze joyously raises its lights folds, and the men in 'fustanellas,' who lounge before the picturesque show windows of the rue d'Hennes, rejoice at the spectacle. They know that the whole world is coming (l'univers va venir) and approve of the preparations made for their appropriate reception. These preparations are manifold. Everywhere the marbles are scraped, new plaster and fresh paints are put on, the paves are at work, and people are busy cleaning and decorating. The street of the stadium is a fine sight, with its triumphal arch and Venetion masts. Its usual whiteness is exaggerated to a dazzling brilliancy. But it is no longer the favorite promenade. The interest is centered elsewhere upon the banks of the formerly disdained Illissus. Every evening, toward 5 o'clock, the citizens pass in long procession, observing the work on the stadium with the eye of connoisseurs. The Illissus has no water, as usual; but no one notices this anymore. A monumental bridge now spans the celebrated river and gives access to the level plain upon which the restored stadium opens. Tomorrow, Easter Monday, April 6, King George will proclaim the re-establishment of the Olympic games there, which fifteen hundred and two years ago the Emperor Theodosius declared suppressed forever.

The inclosure of the stadium produces an intense impression, which becomes even more vivid in reflection. Behold the spectacle that the ancient have so often contemplated! It rises again before your eyes. Up to this time we have not been accustomed to such a plan, and the unfamiliar lines at the first sight surprise and confuse us. The silhouette of the Greek temple has never been lost; the porticos and the colonnades have known twenty renaissances. But the stadia died at the same time as the athletic games. Their architectural features were known, but they have never been restored. A living stadium (stade vivant) has not been seen for centuries. Yet a few hours, and this one will be alive with the collective life imparted to the monuments by the crowds that throng them. A crowd will ascend the staircases, fill the benches that rise one above another, and mass themselves in the passages. A very different crowd, no doubt, from that which last entered a similar stadium, animated, however, by like sentiments, by the same sympathy for youth, and by the same desire for human harmony.

There will be room for about 50,000 spectators. Part of the benches are of wood, time having failed for hewing a sufficient number of marble blocks and putting them in place. After the games, the construction will be finished, thanks to the inexhaustible liberality of M. Averoff. Bronze chariots, statues, and columns will break the somewhat severe monotony, and this generous citizen will have endowed his fatherland with a monument worthy of it. The central rink is not dusty as formerly; the track has been made of cinders by an English workman, and according to the latest rules of modern art.

Everything tends to show that henceforth the stadium will be jealously maintained by the Greeks, for- and this is an interesting fact- in this country where bodily exercises count no more adepts, where fencing and gymnastic societies of recent formation have had much trouble in recruiting a few members, the mentioning of Olympic games has sufficed to create athletes. The young people have suddenly become conscious of the vigor and suppleness stored away in the race; their ardor has been so great, their enthusiasm so persistent, that foreign competitors will here meet improvised rivals as formidable as veterans.

The Hungarians have already arrived under the leadership of our amiable representative in Hungary – M. Kemény, director of the Royal School of Budapest. They have met with an enthusiastic reception; speeches have been interchanged; the band has played. Within a few days the Russians are expected; after them the Americans, the Swedes, etc. The news that the municipal council of Paris has voted an appropriation to the French delegates reached us during a session of the

1 Paris, Hachette, 1897.
2 Washington, D.C. 1897, Vol.1, pp. 1329-1334.

committee on games at the palace of the Royal Prince. The Prince was delighted to know that the participation of France was henceforth assured. Our representatives do not yet pronounce Greek in the modern way; M. Combes[1] has come too late. But they will learn many things during their short sojourn at the foot of the Acropolis. How amazed they will be the first day in the presence of the reality of those places associated in their memories with the idea of antiquity, but which they will find so young and full of life. How they will wonder at the easy freedom with which resuscitated Athens surrounds the Parthenon without being dwarfed by the majestic beauty of the monument and without diminishing in the least its tranquil serenity. Then suddenly a double revelation will come to their minds. They will recognize that antique Greece has been deformed by unskillful teaching and that there exists a modern Greece of which they know nothing. They will perceive that the one is connected with the other by the closest bonds of resemblance and heredity. And the history of the world will take, in their eyes, a new sense and different coloring, because henceforth they will know that a nation may be walled in a tomb and yet not be dead.

Au Jour Le Jour. Lettre Olympique,
in: *Journal des Débats, Politiques et Litteraires*. Paris, April 6, 1896, p.1.
English version based on the translation taken from: Report of the Commissioner of Education for the Year 1895-96, Washington D.C. 1897, Vol. 1, pp.1329-1331.

4.2.2/2 OLYMPIC LETTER FROM ATHENS (MARCH 31, 1896)

The program of the 'Great Week' has definitely been arranged. At this moment it is set and will appear tomorrow. Easter Monday, April 6, is the day announced for the inauguration of the Stadium, the beginning of the Olympian games. The King will preside, surrounded by his ministers, members of the Greek Parliament, and the diplomatic corps. Foot races will begin on that day and continue during the several days following. The city is to be illuminated in the evening. On Tuesday, the 7th, there will be fencing at the palace of the Zappeion, and at nightfall the Acropolis will be illuminated. On Wednesday, the 8th, the shooting 'stand' and the 'Velodrome' will be officially opened. The stand is constructed at Calitthera, on the road from Athens to Phalerum. The committee on shooting, presided over by His Royal Highness Prince Nicolas, desired to do a great thing. They have erected a magnificent building that will also remain after the games. It contains vast halls, luxurious dressing rooms, and a terrace which serves as a gallery, from which the view extends beyond Salamis to the step shores of the Peleponnesus. The Velodrome is erected in the plain of New Phalerum; it has been copied from that of Copenhagen and seems to satisfy the requirements of the cyclists. The Athenian Society has already tried it, and the royal family on this occasion occupied a pretty gallery reserved for them. This is a raised platform, surrounded by a balustrade and ornamented with mosaic flooring. From this the Parnassus, the Pentelicus, and the Hymettus can be seen. The Acropolis appears above the villas of the Phalerum, and in the midst of this classic scene, surrounded by classical decoration, the most modern (fin de siècle) of sports takes the first place. A striking contrast in truth – the bicycle at the foot of the Parthenon!

How many times have these words been thrown at me with a scornful accent as a supreme argument against the modernisation of the Olympic games! Very well; today it shocks no one. To play lawn tennis before the Colosseum or to ride a bicycle under the Arch of Titus would indeed cause a disagreeable impression. The Roman monuments are dated; they belong to an age. The Parthenon has none; it belongs to all times; no manifestations of popular life can disfigure it. On Easter Thursday the competition between gymnasts will take place at the Stadium; Swedes, Germans, Greeks, and the Englishmen will take part. The violent opposition of the president of the Belgian Federation to the admission of gymnasts to the Olympian games has not been successful; what little opposition remains will no doubt vanish before the hour strikes for the second Olympiad. Friday will witness a race at Marathon and celebrations at night in the harbor of the Piraeus.

Saturday is given to swimming competition. It will take place in the charming little Bay of Zea, toward whose shores descend the closely built houses of modern Piraeus, adorned with balconies and terraces covered with fruitful vines. Rustic seats surround the shore, the lowest reaching to the blue waters of the beautiful bay. Never had swimmers for the displays of their strength a more charming inclosure. The last two days, Sunday, the 12th, and Monday, the 13th, are devoted to other nautical sports – yachting and rowing. A pavilion has been constructed in the Bay of Naunichie to shelter the boats and give to the rowers the comfort of an English club. The pavilion is elegant. It is built of different colored wood, and near it are the ruins of an antique temple, which behind the hill can yet be seen, half buried in the sand, some remains of the long walls which connect Athens with Piraeus. Upon a promontory rises the villa 'Coumoundouros', the favorite residence of the great minister. Thus is repeated in epitome on the shores of this bay the wonderful history of the Greek nation in spite of opposition; here athletics become historic; but here the past is so intimately interwoven with the present that only strangers are surprised by the relation.

The international committee will hold a session on Saturday. Six of its members have arrived – M. Bikelas, Greek delegate; General Boutowski, Russian delegate; Dr. Gebhardt, German; Messrs. Kemény and Jiri Guth, Hungarian and Czech representatives; Commandant Balck, Swedish representative, and your obedient servant. This international committee represents the permanency of the institution. To this committee falls the difficult task of making the various national committees cooperate in this unique work. There are some rivalries existing among them; some misunderstandings; some opposed tendencies. The presidency of the committee belongs to the nation in which the games will be celebrated. M. Bikelas has presided until now. For four years it will pass into French hands. Tuesday, the 14th, the close of the Olympian games for 1896 will take place in the stadium. The King will distribute prizes to the victors, which consist of a diploma and a medal, the work of a Chaplain. This celebrated artist has engraved upon one side the silhouette of the rock of the Acropolis, with the Propyleae and the Parthenon; on the other side the head of Jupiter Olympus. It is no more the symbolic branch of antiquity, but neither is it the 'venal prize' which is so dearly beloved by modern sportsmen. It is a simple souvenir associating art with athleticism, and thus maintaining traditions of

1 Minister of public instruction at the time these letters were written.

the disinterestedness which ought to be the very base of sports. Amateurism will never have had a grander manifestation in its favor. Even those who are used to accept without embarrassment gold pieces earned by their endurance or their agility would blush to even touch the coin here. In this unrivaled scene, in the presence of overwhelming glories, a money prize would seem unbearable. This sentiment proves better than anything else that the principle is itself wrong.

Lettre Olympique, Athènes, le 31 mars,
in: *Journal des Débats, Politiques et Litteraires,* April 8, 1896, p.3.
English version based on the translation taken from: Report of the Commissioner of education for the Year 1895-1896, Washington D.C., Vol.1, pp. 1331-1332.

4.2.2/3 OLYMPIC LETTER FROM ATHENS (APRIL 12, 1896)

The triumph of the 'barbarians' in the Olympic competition has in general been very gracefully accepted by the audience. At the entrance of the stadium, in full view of the audience, there is a mast, at the foot of which, after each test, the 'order number' of the conqueror is fastened, while at the peak of the mast the flag of his country is displayed. This is an ingenious device for announcing the victors to the audience and for distinguishing the international character of the games. From this place of honor have been seen, waving by turns, the colors of the great European nations; but the flag that has been seen most frequently is the Star-Spangled Banner of the United States. This was just, as Americans were the first to become interested in our work, and the only people who have never doubted our success. The two teams that were equipped and sent out by the Americans have shown from the beginning their athletic valor and surpassing enthusiasm. Already the astonished Athenians proclaim them professional; they can not believe that these handsome young men, with such flexible muscles, are students in a hurry to return to their studies, but modestly satisfied to have in this manner increased the prestige of their universities.

Whenever the American flag unfolds on the stadium, it excites wild enthusiasm. High up, crowded together on the last tiers, some sailors rise, swinging their caps and uttering loud hurrahs. It is the crew of the Federal cruiser *San Francisco*, at this time anchored in the harbor of the Piraeus. Below, near the famous subterranean passage from which today, as formerly, the athletes enter and go out, there is a group standing, from which frantic acclamations arise. They are those entered as competitors and their friends from the American School of Athens, who salute the champion with the rallying cry of his club or college. Each transatlantic association has a distinct yell, in most cases formed of the syllables of the name, or of the initials which one utters in pronouncing them. Sailors and students, agitated by the same patriotism, answer each other with growing enthusiasm, over the heads of the crowd. The audience commences by laughing. Then they applaud, because they feel the sincerity of the joy manifested; the juvenile ardor animating these inharmonious manifestations.

The Olympic games are not by no means the first contact between America and Greece; other ties exist between them other than 'Cook's tickets', other interests than those of tourists from widely separated countries. The educated American, perhaps more than the European, considers a pilgrimage to the Acropolis a supreme

The Parade of the Winners at the Closing of the Athens Olympics 1896. Drawn by A.Castaigne (taken from The Century Illustrated Monthly Magazine, Nov.1896, p.51)

satisfaction that every enlightened mind should secure to himself as the greatest source of mental culture. He is not, as we are, imprisoned under the ruins of the Roman Empire, that is so heavy and complicated; he understands more readily the ethereal organization of this antique democracy, with which his own has more than one resemblance. It is this feeling that has prompted Americans to found a school of archaeology at Athens. This fact is little known outside of Athens. Even here people do not appreciate its importance, which is, however, considerable. This American colony, established on the slopes of Lycabettus, supported by the voluntary contributions of citizens, solely devoted to the culture of science, opens up to the future of the United States an endless perspective.

The Greeks, who love the Americans, and know that the love is returned, have therefore heartily applauded their success; they have even smiled at that student of Princeton, a self – made (improvisé) discobolus, who won a prize which they believed to be theirs by hereditary rights. But their chagrin would have been intense had the cup offered by M. Michel Bréal to the 'Marathon runner' escaped them. They were not compelled to undergo that strain. It was a Greek who first entered the stadium, having accomplished in two hours and fifty minutes those 42 kilometer which separate Athens from Marathon. His arrival created great excitement. The stadium was completely filled. The picturesque hill that overhangs it from the side of the sea was covered with people; there were at least 60,000 spectators. In the hemicycle were the King of Greece, the King of Serbia, the Grand Duke George, the Grand Duchess Theresa, the prince royal of Greece, the Grecian ministers, and the diplomatic corps. In a moment, as the approach of the victor was signaled, the whole multitude arose as if moved by an electric current. The thunder of applause rolled across the plain toward the foot of Parnassus, as if to awaken in their subterranean abodes the manes of their ancestors; it was, in fact, not simply the accomplished act which provoked these transports, but rather the pent-up remembrance of the whole glorious past manifested, in that runner, the vision of the Greek. Then, in order to withdraw him from the dangerous effusion of a delirious crowd, the prince royal and his brother, Prince George, carried him away in their arms to the dressing room, and then the enthusiasm arose anew, like an irresistible wave, before that superb picture, which placed side by side, in so graphic a manner, the past and the future.

It was long before quiet was restored. Just beside me I saw a lady unfasten her watch and send it as a present to the young hero of the day. A patriotic landlord of a hotel signed an order for 365 good repasts, and one of the bootblacks at the corner of a street offered to take care of his boots in future gratuitously. There is a comic touch in this, but it is impressive if one considers the sentiment that prompted these offerings. All those seen by me on that eventful evening. Even the greatest sneerers, had participated in the general emotion, and our distinguished countryman, M. Charles Maurras, who had opposed me formerly for wanting to internationalize the games, declared himself converted. He said to me: "I see" – and this is profoundly just – "I see that this internationalism will not destroy the fatherlands, but will fortify them."

Lettre Olympique, Athènes, le 12 avril,
in: *Journal des Débats, Politiques et Litteraires*, Paris, April 22, 1896, p.3.
Englsh version based on the translation taken from: *Report of the Commissioner for the Year 1895-1896,* Washington D.C., Vol.1, pp. 1332-1334.

Humorous depiction of the 1st Olympic Games: Headline: Olympic Games; 1st line: 10 km cycle race; 2nd line: lawn tennis; 3rd line: centaur racing; 4th line: football match; Legend: relief paintings recently found during excavation in New Olympia (taken from Lustige Blätter, vol. XI, no.19, 1896)

4.2.2/4 – 4.2.2/6 INTRODUCTION

The whole Greek nation was enthusiastic about the Games, and the press echoed their feelings. Those echoes were substantial for the time, particularly in countries which had won medals at Athens.

Coubertins "Olympic Letters from Athens" cannot claim to give a full account of the Games, but the style of reporting is noteworthy. It makes for a pleasant contrast with the *Campagne de vingt-et-un ans* [Twenty-One Year Campaign], which focused so much on behind-the-scenes details. The Greek Organizing Committee published an official report in 1896-97, in a Greek-French and German-English edition, which provides us with a full account of the sequence of athletic events, now recorded in the Olympic statistics. But who today speaks of the modest performances of the winners, influenced by the cooler temperatures at Easter, 1896? The Athens Games showed, right from the start, that it is not the performances but the names of the winners – among them the name of the marathon winner, Spyridon Louis, in particular – that make Olympic history.

A good overview is given by Coubertin's following article "The Olympic Games of 1896" which was exclusively published in English in the American Magazine *The Century Illustrated Monthly Magazine* in 1896.

Three hundred eleven competitors were counted, including eighty-one foreigners from twelve countries. The number of actual participants was smaller as some of them signed up for several disciplines. International participation remained quite limited. Travel to Greece was difficult then, because there were few ship companies and no links by rail. A Paris and London travel agency that planned to organize "group travel for fans" did not attract sufficient numbers, even though the foreign visitors who did participate in the trip were not particularly upset by that fact. Aside from the Greeks, the Americans and the Germans had the largest contingents in attendance.

At the opening ceremonies, the German member of the IOC, Dr. Willibald Gebhardt, at the sight of the splendor of the festival and the enthusiasm of nearly one hundred thousand spectators, said to Coubertin: "All this is your work!" Many more said as much to Coubertin later on, as well.

In all, winners were proclaimed in forty-three competitions in nine sports. On the final day, all the winners received their awards, including the silver cup for the winner of the marathon, a prize offered by Coubertin's friend, the French classical philologist Bréal, who had conceived the idea in 1894. The press made Louis the hero of Greece. His performance provided an opportunity to praise this liberated people and their glorious past.

Coubertin had stayed in the background throughout these celebrations. In his *Campagne de vingt-et-un ans,* he wrote: "The efforts that the Greeks made to "suppress" me at every opportunity hurt, though they came as no surprise[1]". At the close of the Athens Games, the Greeks demanded that the Games be held in Greece on a permanent basis. Coubertin energetically opposed this idea, and was able to win over the members of the IOC who were there in Athens, as evidenced by the "minutes" of their meeting held in Athens. He also held firmly to this position in the face of opposition from the crown prince, being unwilling to sacrifice a universal idea to the nationalist enthusiasm of the moment. It was also at Athens that Coubertin succeeded Dimitrios Bikelas as president of the IOC since, in keeping with the regulations, the

chairmanship passed to the country that would host the next Olympic Games. Moreover he denied a report in the New York Times which announced an alleged agreement to hold the Olympic Games in Greece permanently. The basis of the report was a spectacular signature-gathering campaign by American athletes in favor of Athens as the permanent site of the Games. The only criticism came from an Athenian newspaper, The *Messager d'Athènes* [Athens Herald], which expressed regret that "we have expressed thanks and congratulations for the success of the Olympic Games to everyone except the individual who promoted them in the first place".[1]

4.2.2/4 THE FIRST OLYMPIAD

Almost everything that went well at Athens from then on was the result of the personal efforts of the crown prince. He persevered in his task, and his support was unfailing. Unfortunately, the individual working most closely with him was not up to the task, though it is only fair to say that nothing in his background had prepared him to handle it. Mr. Philemon was a veritable Olympic ministry. It is impossible to believe the amount of bureaucratic machinery in which he was enmeshed. That machinery produced copious and unproductive loads of paperwork, and enormous waste. The overall work over which the prince presided was excellent. The detailed efforts that he could not oversee got lost in the administrative maze that had been unwisely set up. Once the Games were assured of support from the public authorities, anyone who managed to pull it off could get a piece of the action and become involved in the organizing effort. Everyone wanted to be part of the "Philemon Ministry". In addition, people were a bit intoxicated by the financial success that happened immediately. As early as February 19, 1895, Mr. Philemon told me that subscriptions had already been received in the amount of 130,000 drachmas. I had urgently asked Mr. Syngros, a very wealthy Athenian, to start off the subscriptions, but he was beaten to the punch by Mr. Schilizzi from Constantinople, who gave ten thousand drachmas. Mr. Syngros wrote the next day that he would give the same amount. Gifts increased in number, and very quickly. Greek expatriate communities in Marseilles, Alexandria, and London insisted, as I had thought, on having the honor of showing their patriotism on such an occasion. The Greek government was temporarily in the hands of Mr. N. Delyanni, former and future ambassador to Paris. Then it was headed by Mr. T. Delyanni, head of one of the major political parties. The government indicated that it was disposed to authorize issuance of special "Olympic" postage stamps, with proceeds from those sales going to the treasury of the Games. From all points of view, this was preferable to the lottery that the Tricoupis cabinet had rejected.

At this juncture, Mr. Averof of the Alexandria colony announced that he would give a million to rebuild the Stadium. The crown prince had skillfully elicited this gift. This meant savings of thirty-two thousand drachmas in the budget of the Games, a figure that had been included at the last minute to cover work needed on the Stadium. In the original plan that I had had to put together, the royal box was

1 Coubertin, *Une Campagne de vingt-et-un ans* [A Twenty-One Year Campaign], Paris 1909, p. 126.

The Greek satirical magazine Romos describes the debate of summer 1895 for and against holding the 1896 Olympic Games in Athens: on the left, Greek Prime Minister Theodor Delyannis, who was in favour of the idea, and on the right, opposition leader Charilaos Tricoupis, who was against. (IOC Archives)

placed on one side, with a grandstand for honored guests across from it, the semi-circles between them being reserved for the non-paying public. On January 24, Mr. Bikelas told me that an engineer that he knew was confident that he could realize savings of several thousand drachmas over my estimates by placing a single stand at the back, surrounding the royal box. He asked me for my view of this plan, but I felt I could add nothing more, since I had merely sketched and drawn up the initial plans and estimates catch as catch can, in the absence of anyone else to do so. When they learned of the Mr. Averof's princely gift, their enthusiasm knew no bounds.

Then I had to deal with the velodrome. I was urgently pressed for plans and an estimate, work that lay far beyond my area of competence. I wrote here and there, but the only responses I received were unclear and inadequate, so I decided to undertake an on-site study of the velodrome at Arcachon where I happened to be at the time. With its builders as my guides, I was able to send an initial draft plan to Athens, where it would have to be worked out in detail. In the meantime, however, the cycling committee had decided to copy the velodrome at Copenhagen. When I returned to Paris, I went to visit the two great artists, Chaplain and Puvis de Chavannes, on behalf of His Royal Highness, to ask the first to design a medal, and the second to design the diploma to be given to the winners at the Games from then on. Chaplain agreed immediately, and engraved that handsome composition, one of the best he has ever done, showing the head of Olympian Zeus on one side, and the Acropolis on the other. Puvis de Chavannes hesitated for a long time. He came to my home to look at the photographs and drawings I had brought back from Greece. He asked me questions that left me astonished at his ignorance of "Greek lines", lines whose purity he had so thoroughly understood and depicted. In the end, with regret he refused to design a diploma. He wrote to say that although he would have liked to design it, he found it impossible to make it

Hellenic enough! So the diploma was designed by a Greek artist – who was afraid of lapsing into a classical style, and went ahead with a bizarre kind of modernism.

Another request came from Athens, this time for the text of the invitations and especially for a list of the associations, federations, groups, etc., to which they should be sent. I updated the lists from the Congress of Paris, making additions as best I could in the absence of an international telephone book, which still does not exist even now. Here is the text I suggested, which was the one they used: "The International Athletic Congress meeting at the Palais de la Sorbonne in Paris on June 16, 1894, under the chairmanship of Baron de Courcel, Senator of the French Republic, voted to restore the Olympic Games, to be held first at Athens in 1896. In accordance with this decision, which was readily approved by Greece, the Greek Committee meeting at Athens under the direction of His Royal Highness, the Crown Prince of Greece, has the honor of inviting you to participate in the 1896 Olympic Games, to be held at Athens from April 5 to 15, 1896. Enclosed please find the schedule and conditions. The courtesy of a response to this invitation is requested. This invitation has been sent upon prior agreement with the International Committee of the Olympic Games, which is based in Paris". The invitations were signed by the secretary general of the Greek Committee, Mr. Philemon. Enclosed was the schedule for the Games, which I had written up and had approved by those attending the meeting at the Zappeion, except for the equestrian competition which had been eliminated, though I have never known why.

Since they were constantly aware of the great effort that they were making, the Greeks imagined that the whole world had to be aware of it, as well. In fact, this is a fairly normal feeling – and they were astonished that I was unable to provide an approximate figure regarding the number of potential competitors and spectators. As early as February 28, 1895, Mr. Baltazzi, chairman of the cycling committee, wanted to be assured of "the arrival of no less than about thirty runners". On March 17, Mr. Damala, secretary of the Committee of Water Sports, asked me to write back, telling him "what countries and clubs have already indicated that they will participate". This was still fourteen months before the opening of the Games! All I could do was urge the members of the International Committee on, so that they would form the groups needed. I set the example for them myself in France. In fall 1894, I had formed a French Olympic Committee. Félix Faure, President of the Republic, agreed to be its honorary chairman. Mr. de Courcel, Mr. Spuller, Mr. Gréard, Michel Bréal, Mr. Mézières, Paul Bourget, Paul Lebaudy, and Mr. D'Estournelles were members of the committee, as well as the vice-presidents of the Union Vélocipédique and representatives of the fencing, athletic sports, polo, yachting, and rowing associations, and finally the chairman of the Union des Sociétés de Tir, Mr. Mérillon. Mr. Mérillon soon withdrew, after having had his Union pass a resolution to the effect that it would refuse to participate in the Olympic Games – the same strategy that would be used again twelve years later. Mr. Mérillon wrote a letter presenting his apologies, in which he said, "It is apparent from the schedule and the methods of operation made available to the (Greek) Committee that shooting would become a branch incorporated and embedded into other sports". He expressed his great indignation that "the creators of the Olympic Games" would ever have imagined that the French Union Nationale des Sociétés de Tir would agree to become "an annex of their Committee!" We had no such dark designs, and the objection has gained neither clarity nor accuracy over time. The secretary of the French Committee was Mr. Raoul Fabens, who devoted himself to its work with great zeal and intelligence. The Committee met at the Sorbonne.

In early 1896, I had a prospectus printed, which we sent out not only within France, but throughout neighboring countries as well. Along with a review of the organization of the Olympic Games, it contained the terms arranged for the trip. Thanks to the energetic activity of Mr. Noblemaire and Mr. Lefèvre-Pontalis, we had managed to arrange an exceptionally low price: three hundred francs in first class from Paris to the Piraeus, via Marseilles, round trip. In addition, the Compagnie des Messageries Maritimes agreed to add an additional departure on March 31, if there were two hundred passengers to book passage, and a cruise on the steamship the *Sénégal* had been arranged from March 29 to April 13. The cruise did take place and met with great success, thanks, if I am not mistaken, to the *Revue générale des Sciences,* which replaced the Compagnie. An agreement stipulated that the Cook company would make its agencies and representatives available in all countries and in a special manner to any individual who wished to go to Greece. Despite our efforts, a small number of French citizens decided to take part. The competitors themselves needed to be subsidized to get them to make a go of this first trip. We had a great deal of difficulty in attracting them. It was Mr. Fabens who managed to do so in the end, through force of will and perseverance. He placed himself at the head of the French team, to bring it to Athens. Things went quite smoothly in Sweden and Hungary. Our colleagues Kemény and Balck pulled off great successes. Likewise, Professor Sloane managed to bring two strong teams from America. In Belgium, the campaign waged against us by the Fédération de Gymnastique had paid off, and the Count de Bousies wrote to me that he was encountering hostility from some, and getting the cold shoulder from others. Only a few Belgian cyclists had announced that they would participate. The actions of our English colleagues, supported by the work of Mr. Mano who was then staying at Oxford, did not produce much result. For my part, I had written urgent letters to the major British newspapers, appealing for the participation of the major English associations. In general, the newspapers accompanied publication of my letter with sympathetic commentaries, yet tinged with a note of irony. They did not believe in the Olympic Games. By contrast, they advocated periodic Pan-British games, and recommended that they be held immediately. In my heart of hearts, I believed that about a hundred competitors and a few thousand spectators from abroad would attend. I felt that this would be a fair achievement for the beginnings of international athleticism, but I did not dare say anything about this to my Greek friends, seeing that the ambitions of the Athenians were growing daily, and had long since lost all touch with reality.

The strangest incident occurred with regard to Germany. Since it had not taken part in the 1894 congress, it did not have a representative on the International Committee, but since the crown prince was the brother-in-law of Emperor Wilhelm, no one at Athens had thought that it would be difficult to get the major German associations to participate. Mr. Rangabé, Greece's ambassador to Berlin, had formed a committee to this end, under the chairmanship of Prince Philip von Hohenlohe, eldest son of the chancellor, with Dr. Gebhardt as secretary. Then, late in 1895, a vehement protest movement arose in Germany after the *National-Zeitung* had reproduced and commented favorably on the response from the *Central-Ausschuss zur Förderung der Jugend und Volksspiele* to the invitation that had been sent to him from Athens. This response was a categorical refusal, based on an alleged interview in which, six months earlier, I was said to have done my best to prevent the Germans from participating in the 1894 congress, and hoped sincerely that the Germans would not come to Athens. This assertion was ridiculous. And really, was it worth it to claim that I had deprived myself of the involvement of French gymnasts by demanding that the Germans be invited, so that in the aftermath I could be held responsible for their not attending? The movement spread in a flash. In Germany, there was a chorus of curses, picked up with great enthusiasm by the Greek press. On January 4, the *Times* correspondent in Athens wrote, "The words attributed to Mr. Coubertin have caused a veritable storm in Greece and Germany". I wrote immediately to the Crown Prince, to Dr. Gebhardt, to Mr. Rangabé, and above all to the *National-Zeitung*. Baron von Reiffenstein, who had attended the congress of Paris in a private capacity and who had been very well treated there, came loyally to the rescue, as did the director of *Spiel und Sport*, which had received and published all the communiqués relating to the congress. On January 5, Mr. Rangabé wrote to me from Berlin, saying "This refutation is absolutely critical, because irritation in Germany has taken on unsettling proportions, and has even reached Greece. Just yesterday, I received some fifty articles from all over the kingdom, all in the same vein, but there is nothing unusual in this, since once news of this sort is printed in the major papers, it is always commented upon by other press publications. Therefore, I hope that thanks to your effective steps, emotions will be calmed, and soon. First, you are aware that the *National-Zeitung* published your response, which was excellent in all respects. To be sure, the paper did print some disagreeable commentaries along with it, but trifling enough and intended to provide cover for their retreat. Then, in keeping with your wishes, I took steps to ensure that the letter which you were kind enough to send me received very wide attention. To that end, I sent out a translation of your letter with a request that it be printed in the major newspapers. I also asked Dr. Gebhardt to seek an audience with the chancellor, to give him a copy, and to provide him with all the necessary information. I think that in this way, the Prince von Hohenlohe will certainly bring your letter to the attention of the Emperor, and everyone knows that His Majesty wishes to maintain excellent relations with France". Shortly thereafter, the German Committee called a general meeting, following which the Committee wired me their "unanimous sympathy and their best wishes for the success of the joint effort". Still, I had heard nothing from Greece. It was not until February 7, 1896 that Mr. Philemon decided to telegraph me: "Greek Committee never believed words attributed to you initiator renaissance Olympic Games". He followed this telegram a little later on with a cordial letter.

This was the final display of recognition from Athens. They had no further need of me. They were sure of their success. I was no longer anything more than an intruder reminding them by my very presence of the fact that this was a foreign initiative. From then on, not only was my name never again mentioned, but everyone seemed to make a special effort to erase any memory of the part that France played in restoring the Olympiads. Most of the people I had brought together a year before around this nascent effort avoided meeting me, or pretended not to know me. The first letter sent to the *Times* by Mr. Larroumet, in which that eminent author, whom I did not know in fact, spoke of the great success achieved by "the Olympic Games that one of our compatriots, Mr. Coubertin, has just restored", struck an emotional chord in me. I must also mention the courageous intervention of Mr. Stephanopoli, who wrote in *The Athens Herald* at the end of the Games, "One thing surprised us in this country, where we pride ourselves on having hearts that remember, and that is that we have expressed thanks and congratulations for the success of the Olympic Games to everyone except the individual who promoted them in the first place". Finally, I will never forget the tactful gesture in which the Crown Prince, at a dinner given by Mr. Bikelas, had a toast presented to me by the Minister of Foreign Affairs, Mr. Skouses, a toast in which, meaningfully, he hastened to join.

The efforts that the Greeks made to "suppress" me at every occasion hurt, though they came as no surprise. The changes that were occurring in their minds made their attitude understandable, sincere, even excusable. They were preparing to lay claim to the exclusive possession of the Olympic Games, and the idea of having such crowds show up every four years at the renovated stadium overwhelmed them with hope and joy. Given the sort of mental solitude in which I had been left, I had plenty of opportunity to examine the basis for these aspirations. To me, they seemed utterly unreasonable, from the point of view of the institution itself and of the goal that I had sought in restoring the Games. In this vast assembly, it was, ultimately, the Greek element that was not just in the majority, but actually dominated things in overwhelming proportions. Greeks had come from all over. Foreigners, by contrast, were few and far between. Many countries were represented, but by only a very small number of individuals. I calculated the money spent by those foreigners, the length of their absence heightened by the fact that there were no railroad links between Athens and the rest of Europe, and the fact that few steamships came to call at the Piraeus. I attempted to assess the profit, in hard numbers, that the celebration of each Olympiad would bring to Greece, and the sums that it would have to spend on them. Finally, I considered the political problems that might arise between Olympiads, and that might prevent them from being held on a regular basis. I was quickly convinced that locating the seat of Olympism permanently and exclusively in Greece meant suicide for my work. Therefore, I resolved to fight with all my strength against the obstacles that had sprung up in its path, in the space of just a few days.

The Athenian press labored to link the restoration of the Olympic Games to the Zappas brothers' foundation, and called for Parliament to pass a law ensuring that the Games would be celebrated at regular intervals in the future. The most delicate aspect was that, in the toast raised at the end of the luncheon for four hundred offered by the king in the great hall of his palace, His Majesty made a direct reference to the possibility of selecting Athens as the "stable and permanent site" of future competitions. This royal statement had disconcerted the members of the International Committee. At the same time, a sort of petition was making the rounds, signed by the members of the American teams, which was supporting the same goal. What could be said? Many of my colleagues were asking themselves if we had any other choice than to give our assent and disband. They were afraid that if we did not act, and act immediately, we would be forced to do just that given the weight of universal public opinion. Yet public opinion was not paying the slightest bit of attention to what was happening in Athens. The brilliance of the Games, enhanced by the presence of the King of Serbia, Grand Duke George, and Archduke Charles-Louis masked the relative lack of attention paid elsewhere to these events. It was viewed as a dazzling one-time curiosity, but not as an institution whose future conditions were worth discussing. Of all the fears I felt about going forward, this one, the fear of hostility and of the pressure of universal public opinion, was the strongest. I decided to disregard it, and I did well to do so.

As soon as Mr. Bikelas passed the presidency of the International Committee to me at the end of the Games[1], I sent the following letter to His Majesty, which I then sent to all the newspapers:

"Sir,

In assuming the presidency of the International Committee of the Olympic Games, my first act must be to thank all of Greece, in the person of its august sovereign. Through the efforts of its sons, led by the most noble one among them, the work that I had made so bold as to entrust to them came to fruition.

Two years ago, when the Congress of Paris began, Your Majesty deigned to send me a telegram of encouragement. I now permit myself to remind Your Majesty today that my wishes have been fulfilled, and that the Olympic Games have been restored. In presiding over this restoration, Your Majesty has given us, my colleagues and myself, the right to continue to count on your benevolence in the future.

Sir, please accept this expression of my deepest respect, and my unwavering gratitude."

I sent a letter of correction to the *Times*, which had published an incorrect report implying that the International Committee had opted not to continue its work. Finally, in a long meeting with His Royal Highness the Crown Prince, I spelled out my reasons for persevering. I suggested that Pan-Hellenic Games be established that would be interleaved with the series of international Olympiads. The prince had already had that idea, and he was quite partial to such a solution. It also seemed to please His Majesty, who received me most warmly when I went to take my leave of him, and to thank him at the same time for showing me the honor of conferring upon me the rank of Commander in the Order of the Savior.

By contrast, the Athenian press and some of the public took my boldness quite badly. I received insulting letters, in which I was termed a "thief, trying to rob Greece of one of its historic jewels". None of this kept me from thoroughly enjoying a blissful rest at Corfu on my way back to France, without a trace of remorse to bother my Philhellene's conscience.

La première Olympiade, in:
Une Campagne de vingt-et-un ans [A Twenty-One Year Campaign] (1887-1908).
Paris 1909, pp. 118-128 (Chapter XIII).

1 The regulations of the International Committee, which I myself had recommended in 1894, assigned the presidency to the country where the next Games were to be held. In keeping with this rule, Mr. Bikelas held the chairmanship from 1894 to 1896. I held it from 1896 to 1900. Later on, I will discuss how the rule came to be changed.

4.2.2/5 THE OLYMPIC GAMES OF 1896

The Olympic games which recently took place in Athens were modern in character, not only because of their programs, which substituted bicycle for chariot races and fencing for the brutalities of pugilism, but because in their origin and regulations they were international and universal, and consequently adapted to the conditions in which athletics have developed to the present day. The ancient games had an exclusively Hellenic character; they were always held in the same place, and Greek blood was a necessary condition of admission to them. It is true that strangers were, in time, tolerated; but their presence at Olympia was more a tribute paid to the superiority of Greek civilization than a right exercised in the name of racial equality. With the modern games it is quite different. Their creation is the work of "barbarians". It is due to the delegates of the athletic associations of all countries who assembled in congress at Paris in 1894. There it was agreed that every country should celebrate the Olympic Games in turn. The right of the first belonged to Greece, as decided by unanimous vote; and in order to emphasize the permanence of the institution, its wide bearings, and its essentially cosmopolitan character, an international committee was appointed. The European and American members were to represent the various nations where athletics were held in honor. The presidency of this committee falls to the country in which the next games are to be held. A Greek, Mr. Bikelas, has presided for the last two years. A Frenchman now presides, and will continue to do so until 1900, since the next games are to take place in Paris during the Exposition. Where will the Games of 1904 take place? Perhaps in New York, perhaps in Berlin, or in Stockholm. The question will soon be decided.

It was in the course of these resolutions, passed during the Paris Congress in 1894, that the recent festivals were organized. Their successful issue is largely due to the active and energetic co-operation of the Greek crown prince Constantine. The Athenians lost courage when they realized what was expected of them. They felt that the city's resources were not equal to the demands that would be made upon them; nor would the government (Mr. Tricoupis then being prime minister) consent to increase facilities. Mr. Tricoupis did not believe in the success of the games. He argued that the Athenians knew nothing about athletics; that they had neither the adequate grounds for the contests, nor athletes of their own to bring into line; and that, moreover, the financial situation of Greece forbade the country from inviting the world to an event which would entail such large expenditures for preparations. These objections were substantiated; but on the one hand, the prime minister greatly exaggerated the importance of the expenditures, and on the other hand, it was not necessary that the government should directly bear the burden of them. Modern Athens, which recalls the Athens of ancient days in so many ways, has inherited the privilege of being beautified and enriched by its children. In those times no more than in the present the public treasury was not always well filled, but wealthy citizens who had made fortunes abroad liked to crown their commercial career by some act of liberality to the mother-country. They endowed the land with superb edifices of general utility – theaters, gymnasia, and temples. The modern city is full of monuments that it owes to such generosity. It was easy to obtain what the state could not give from private individuals. The Olympic

Games had burned with so bright a luster in the past of the Greeks that they could not but have their revival at heart. Furthermore, the moral benefits would largely compensate for all pecuniary sacrifice.

The crown prince apprehended this at once, and decided to lend his authority to the organizing of the first. He appointed a commission, with headquarters in his own palace; made Mr. Philemon, ex-mayor of Athens and a man of great zeal and enthusiasm, secretary-general; and appealed to the nation to subscribe the necessary funds. Subscriptions began to come in from Greece, but particularly from London, Marseilles, and Constantinople, where there are wealthy and influential Greek colonies. The chief gift came from Alexandria. It was this gift that made it possible to restore the Stadium's condition in the time of Atticus Herodes. Right from the beginning the intention had been to hold the contests in this justly celebrated spot. No one, however, had dreamed that it would be possible to restore the marble seats that, it is said, could accommodate forty thousand persons to their former splendor. The great enclosure would have been utilized, and provisional wooden seats placed on the grassy slopes which surround it. Thanks to the generosity of Mr. Averoff, Greece is now the richer by a unique monument.

Two years ago the Stadium resembled a deep gash, made by some fabled giant, in the side of the hill which rises abruptly by the Ilissus, and opposite Lycabettus and the Acropolis, in a retired, picturesque quarter of Athens. All that was then visible were the two high earth embankments that faced each other on opposite sides of the long, narrow racecourse. They met at the end in an imposing hemicycle. Grass grew between the cobblestones. For centuries the spectators of ancient days had sat on the ground on these embankments. Then, one day, an army of workmen, taking possession of the Stadium, had covered it with stone and marble. This is the work that has now been repeated. The first covering served as a quarry during the Turkish domination; not a trace of it was left. With its innumerable rows of seats, and the flights of steps that divide it into sections and lead to the upper tiers, the Stadium no longer looks like being cut out of the hill. It is the hill that seems to have been placed there by the hand of man to support this enormous pile of masonry. Only one detail is modern. One does not notice it at first. The dusty track is now a cinder-path, prepared, according to the latest rules of modern athletics, by an expert brought over from London for this purpose. In the center a sort of esplanade has been erected for the gymnastic exhibitions. At the end, on each side of the turning, antiquity is represented by two large boundary-stones, forming two human figures, and excavated while the foundations were being dug. These were the only finds; they add but little to archaeological data. Work on the Stadium is far from being completed, eighteen months being quite insufficient for the undertaking. Where marble could not be placed, painted wood was hastily made to do the duty. That clever architect Mr. Metaxas cherishes the hope, however, of seeing all the antique decorations, restored statues, columns, bronze quadrigae, and, at the entrance, majestic propylaea.

When this has been done, Athens will truly possess the temple of athletic sports. Yet it is doubtful whether such a sanctuary is the one best suited to the worship of human vigor and beauty in these modern days. The Anglo-Saxons, to whom we owe the revival of athletics, frame their contests delightfully in grass and verdure. Nothing could differ more from the Athenian Stadion than Travers Island, the summer home of the New York Athletic Club, where the championship games are decided. In this green enclosure, where nature is left to have its way, the spectators sit under the trees on the sloping declivities, a few feet away from the Sound, which murmurs against the rocks. One finds something similar in Paris, and in San Francisco, under those Californian skies which reminds one of the skies of Greece, at the foot of those mountains that have the pure outlines and the iridescent reflections of Hymettus. If the ancient amphitheater was more grandiose and more solemn, the modern picture would be more intimate and pleasing. The music floating under the trees makes a softer accompaniment to the exercises; the spectators move about at friendly ease, whereas the ancients, packed together in rigid lines on their marble benches, sat broiling in the sun or chilled in the shade.

The Stadium is not the only enduring token that will be a reminder to Athens of its inauguration of the new Olympiads; it is also a velodrome and a shooting-stand. The former is in the plain of the modern Phalerum, along the railway connecting Athens with Piraeus. It is copied after the model of that in Copenhagen, where the crown prince of Greece and his brothers had an opportunity of appreciating its advantages during a visit to the King of Denmark, their grandfather. The cyclists, it is true, have complained that the track is not long enough, and that the turnings are too abrupt; but when were bicyclists ever content? The tennis courts are in the center of the velodrome. The shooting-stand makes a good appearance, with its manor-like medieval crenelations. The contestants are comfortably situated under monumental arches. There are also large pavilions for the rowers, built of wood, but prettily decorated, with boathouses and dressing rooms.

While the Hellenic Committee thus labored over the scenic requirements, the international committee and the national committees were occupied in recruiting competitors. The matter was not as easy as one might think. Not only had indifference and distrust to be overcome, but the revival of the Olympic Games had aroused a certain hostility. Although the Paris Congress had been careful to decree that every form of physical exercise practiced in the world should have its place on the program, the gymnasts took offense. They complained that they had not been given sufficient prominence. The greater part of the gymnastic associations of Germany, France, and Belgium are animated by a rigorously exclusive spirit; they are not inclined to tolerate the presence of those forms of athletics which they themselves do not practice. What they disdainfully designated as “English sports” have become especially odious to them. These associations were not satisfied in declining the invitation sent them to return to Athens. The Belgian federation wrote to the other federations, suggesting a concerted stand against the work of the Paris Congress. These incidents confirmed the opinions of the pessimists who had been foretelling the failure of the fêtes, or their probable postponement. Athens is far away, the journey is expensive, and the Easter vacations are short. The contestants were not willing to undertake the voyage unless they could be sure that the occasion would be worth the effort. The different associations were not willing to send representatives unless they could be informed of the amount of interest that the contests would create. An unfortunate occurrence took place almost at the last moment. The German press, commenting on an article which had appeared in a Paris newspaper, declared that it was an exclusive Franco-Greek affair; that attempts were being made to shut out other nations; and furthermore, that the German associations had been intentionally kept aloof from the Paris Congress of 1894. The assertion was acknowledged to be incorrect, and was powerless to check the efforts of the German committee under Dr. Gebhardt. Mr. Kéméy in Hungary, Major Balck in Sweden, General de Boutowski in Russia, Professor W. M. Sloane in the United States, Lord Amphtill in England, Dr. Jiri Guth in Bohemia, in the meantime, were doing their best to awaken interest in the event, and to reassure the doubts. They did not always succeed. Many people took a sarcastic view, and the newspapers delightfully indulged on the subject of the Olympic Games.

Easter Monday, April 6, the streets of Athens had a look of extraordinary animation. All the public buildings were draped in bunting; multicolored streamers floated in the wind; green wreaths decked the house fronts. The two letters "O.A.", the Greek initials of the Olympic Games, and the two dates, 776 BC, 1896 AD, indicating their ancient past and their present renascence were everywhere. At two o'clock in the afternoon the crowd began to throng into the Stadium and to take possession of the seats. It was a joyous and motley concourse. The skirts and braided jackets of the palikars contrasted with the somber and ugly European garments. The women used large paper fans to shield themselves from the sun, parasols, which would have obstructed the view, being prohibited. The king and the queen drove up a little before three o'clock, followed by Princess Marie, their daughter, and her fiancé, Grand Duke George of Russia. They were received by the crown prince and his brothers, by Mr. Delyannis, president of the Council of Ministers, and by the members of the Hellenic Committee and the international committee. Flowers were presented to the queen and princess, and the cortège made its way into the hemicycle to the strains of the Greek national anthem and the cheers of the crowd. Within, the court ladies and functionaries, the diplomatic corps, and the deputies awaited the sovereigns, for whom two marble armchairs were ready waiting. The crown prince, taking his stand in the arena, facing the king, then made a short speech, in which he touched on the origin of the enterprise, and the obstacles that had to be surmounted to bring it to fruition. Addressing the king, he asked him to proclaim the opening of the Olympic Games, and the king, rising, declared them opened. It was a thrilling moment. Fifteen hundred and two years before, the Emperor Theodosius had suppressed the Olympic Games, thinking that in abolishing this hated survival of paganism he was furthering the cause of progress; and here was a Christian monarch, amid the applause of an assemblage almost exclusively composed of Christians, announcing the formal annulment of the imperial decree; while a few feet away the archbishop of Athens, and Père Didon, the celebrated Dominican preacher stood. In his Easter sermon in the Catholic cathedral the day before, Didon had paid an eloquent tribute to pagan Greece. When the king had resumed his seat, the Olympic ode, written for this occasion by the Greek composer Samara, was sung by a chorus of one hundred and fifty voices. Once before, music had been associated with the revival of the Olympic Games. The first session of the Paris Congress had been held on June 16, 1894, in the great amphitheater of the Sorbonne, decorated by Puvis de Chavannes; and after the address of the president of the Congress, Baron de Coubertin, the large audience had listened to that fragment of the music of antiquity, the hymn to Apollo, discovered in the ruins of Delphi. But this time the connection between art and athletics was more direct. The games began with the sounds of the last chords of the Olympic ode. That first day established the success of the games beyond all doubt. The ensuing days confirmed the fact in spite of the bad weather. The royal family was assiduous in its attendance. In the shooting contest the queen fired the first shot with a flower-wreathed rifle. The fencing-competitions were held in the marble rotunda of the Exposition Palace, given by the Messrs. Zappas, and known as the Zappeion. After that the crowd made its way back to the Stadium for the footraces, shot putting, discuss-throwing, high and long jumps, pole-vaulting, and gymnastic exhibitions. A Princeton student, Robert Garrett, scored highest in throwing the discus. His victory was unexpected. He had asked me the day before if I thought it would be ridiculous should he enter for an event for which he had trained so little! The stars and stripes seemed destined to carry off all the laurels. When they ran up the "victor's mast", the sailors of the San Francisco, who stood in a group at the top of the Stadium, waved their caps, and the members of the Boston Athletic Association below frantically broke out, ''B.A.A., rah! rah! rah!" These cries greatly amused the Greeks. They applauded the triumph of the Americans, showing that there is a warm feeling of goodwill between these two nations.

The Greeks are novices in the matter of athletic sports, and had not looked for much success for their own country. Only one event seemed likely to be theirs from its very nature – the long-distance run from Marathon, a prize that had been newly founded by Mr. Michel Bréal, a member of the French Institute, in commemoration of that soldier of antiquity who ran all the way to Athens to tell his fellow-citizens of the happy issue of the battle. The distance from Marathon to Athens is 42 kilometers. The road is rough and stony. The Greeks had trained for this run for the past year. Even in the remote districts of Thessaly young peasants prepared to enter as contestants. In three cases it is said that the enthusiasm and the inexperience of these young fellows cost them their lives, so exaggerated were their preparatory efforts. As the great day approached, women offered up prayers and votive tapers in the churches, that the winner might be a Greek!

The wish was fulfilled. A young peasant named Loues, from the village of Marousi, was the winner in two hours and fifty-five minutes. He reached the goal fresh and in fine form. He was followed by two other Greeks. The excellent Australian sprinter Flack, and the Frenchman Lermusiaux, who had been in the lead the first 35 kilometers, had dropped out by the way. When Loues came into the Stadion, the crowd, which numbered sixty thousand persons, rose to its feet like one man, swayed by extraordinary excitement. The King of Serbia, who was present, will probably not forget the sight he saw that day. A flight of white pigeons was let loose, women waved fans and handkerchiefs, and some of the spectators who were nearest to Loues left their seats, and tried to reach him and carry him in triumph. He would have been suffocated if the crown prince and Prince George had not bodily led him away. A lady who stood next to me unfastened her watch, a gold one set with pearls, and sent it to him; an innkeeper presented him with an order good for three hundred and sixty-five free meals; and a wealthy citizen had to be dissuaded from signing a check for ten thousand francs to his credit. Loues himself, however, when he was told of this generous offer, refused it. The sense of honor, which is very strong in the Greek peasant, thus saved the non-professional spirit from a very great danger.

136 Supplément illustré du Petit Journal

JEUX OLYMPIQUES A ATHÈNES
Notre compatriote Masson, vainqueur de la course vélocipédique

A lithograph printed in the French magazine Le Petit Journal on 26th April 1896, entitled "Olympic Games in Athens. Our countryman Masson, winner in the cycle race". Paul Masson won three gold medals on the Neo Phaleron cycle track: the 333 m time trial, 2,000 m sprint and 10,000 m track race. (N. Müller Collection)

Needless to say that the various contests were held under amateur regulations. An exception was made for the fencing competitions, since in several countries professors of military fencing hold the rank of officers. A special contest was arranged for them. To all other branches of the athletic sports only amateurs were admitted. It is impossible to conceive the Olympic games with money prizes. But these rules, which seem simple enough, are more complicated in their practical application by the fact that definitions of what constitutes an amateur differ from one country to another, sometimes even from one club to another. Several definitions are current in England; the Italians and the Dutch admit one that appears too rigid at one point, too loose at another. How can these divergent or contradictory utterances be conciliated? The Paris Congress made an attempt in that direction, but its decisions are not accepted everywhere as law, nor is its definition of amateurship everywhere adopted as the best. The rules and regulations have no uniformity any more. This and that is forbidden in one country, authorized in another. All that can be done until an Olympic code is formulated in accordance with the ideas and practices of the majority of athletes is to choose among the existing codes. Therefore, it was decided that the foot races should be under the rules of the Union Francaise des Sports Athlétiques; jumping, putting the shot, etc., under those of the Amateur Athletic Association of England; the bicycle-races under those of the International Cyclists' Association, etc. This had appeared to us to be the best way out of the problem, but we would have had many disputes if the judges, (to whom the Greek name of ephors had been given) had not been headed by Prince George, who acted as final referee. His presence gave weight and authority to the decisions of the ephors, who were composed of representatives of different countries. The prince took his duties seriously, and fulfilled them conscientiously. He was always on the track, personally supervising every detail, a recognizable figure, owing to his height and athletic build. It will be remembered that Prince George, while traveling in Japan with his cousin, the czarevitch (now Emperor Nicholas II), felled the ruffian who had tried to assassinate the latter with his fist. During the weightlifting in the Stadium, Prince George lifted an enormous dumb-bell with ease, and tossed it out of the way. The audience broke into applause, as if it would have liked to make him the winner of the event.

Every night while the games were in progress the streets of Athens were illuminated. There were torchlight processions, bands played the different national anthems, and the students of the university got up ovations under the windows of the foreign athletic crews and harangued them in the noble tongue of Demosthenes. Perhaps this tongue was somewhat abused. That Americans might not be compelled to understand French, nor Hungarians forced to speak German, the daily programs of the games, and even invitations to luncheon, were written in Greek. On receipt of these cards, covered with mysterious formulae where even the date was not clear (the Greek calendar is twelve days behind ours) every man carried them to his hotel porter for elucidation.

Many banquets were given. The mayor of Athens gave one at Cephissisa, a little shaded village at the foot of Pentelicus. Mr. Bikelas, the retiring president of the international committee, gave another at Phalerum. The king himself entertained all the competitors, and the members of the committees, three hundred guests in all, at luncheon in the ballroom of the palace. The outside of this edifice, which was built by King Otho, is heavy and graceless; but the center of the interior is occupied by a suite of large rooms with very high ceilings, opening one into another through colonnades. The decorations are simple and imposing. The tables were set in the largest of these rooms. At the table of honor sat the king, the princes, and the ministers sat at the table of honor, and the members of the committees also were there. The competitors were seated at other tables according to their nationality. At dessert the king thanked and congratulated his guests, first in French, afterward in Greek. The Americans cried ''Hurrah!'', the Germans ''Hoch!'', the Hungarians ''Eljen!'', the Greeks "Zito!", the French "Vive le Roi!" After the repast the king and his sons chatted long and amicably with the athletes. It was a really charming scene, the republican simplicity of which was a matter of wonderment particularly to the Austrians and the Russians, little used as they are to the spectacle of monarchy thus meeting democracy on an equal footing.

Then there were nocturnal festivities on the Acropolis, where the Parthenon was illuminated with colored lights, and at the Piraeus, where the vessels were hung with Japanese lanterns. Unluckily, the weather changed, and the sea was so high on the day appointed for the boat races, which should have taken place in the roadstead of Phalerum, that the project was abandoned. The distribution of prizes was likewise postponed for twenty-four hours. In the Stadium, on the morning of April 15, it occurred with much solemnity. The sun was shining again, and sparkled on the officers' uniforms.

When the roll of the victors was called, it became evident, after all, that the international character of the institution was well guarded by the results of the contests. America had won nine prizes exclusively for athletic sports (flat races for 100 and 400 meters; 110 meter hurdle-race; high jump; broad jump; pole vault; hop, step, and jump; putting the shot; throwing the discus), and two prizes for shooting (revolver, 25 and 30 meters). But France had the prizes for foil fencing and for four bicycle-races; England scored highest in the one-handed weightlifting contest, and in single lawn-tennis; Greece won the run from Marathon, two gymnastic contests (rings, climbing the smooth rope), three prizes for shooting (carbine, 200 and 300 meters; pistol, 25 meters), a prize for fencing with sabers, and a bicycle race; Germany won in wrestling, in gymnastics (parallel bars, fixed bar, horse vaulting), and in double lawn tennis; Australia, the 800-meter and 1,500-meter foot-races on the flat; Hungary, swimming-competitions of 100 and 1200 meters; Austria, the 500-meter swimming-competition and the 12-hour bicycle race; Switzerland, a gymnastic prize; and Denmark, the two-handed weightlifting contest. The prizes were an olive-branch from the very spot, at Olympia, where the ancient Altis stood, a diploma drawn by a Greek artist, and a silver medal chiseled by the celebrated French engraver Chaplain. On one side of the medal the Acropolis, the Parthenon and the Propylaea can be seen; on the other a colossal head of the Olympian Zeus, after the type created by Phidias. The head of the god is blurred, as if by distance and the lapse of centuries, while in the foreground, in clear relief, the Victory which Zeus holds in his hand can be seen. It is a striking and original conception. After the distribution of the prizes, the athletes took their places for the traditional procession around the Stadium. Loues, the winner of the Marathon, came first, bearing the Greek flag; then the

Marathon winner Spiridon Louis arrives in the Athens stadium, 1896 (taken from The Olympic Games in 1896. Official Report. Athens/ London, C.Beck/ H.Grevel, 1897, p.77)

Americans, the Hungarians, the French, the Germans. The ceremony was made more memorable by a charming incident. One of the contestants, Mr. Robertson, an Oxford student, recited an ode that he had composed in ancient Greek and in the Pindaric mode, in honor of the games. Music had opened them, and Poetry was present at their close; and thus the bond was once more renewed which in the past united the Muses with feats of physical strength, the mind with the well-trained body. The king announced that the first Olympiad was at an end and left the Stadium, the band playing the Greek national anthem, and the crowd cheering. A few days later the guests had left Athens. Torn wreaths littered the public squares; the banners that had merrily floated in the streets disappeared; the sun and the wind held sole possession of the marble sidewalks of Stadium street.

It is interesting to ask oneself what the results of the Olympic games of 1896 are likely to be, regarding both Greece and the rest of the world. In the case of Greece, the games will be found to have had a double effect, one athletic, the other political. It is a well-known fact that the Greeks had completely lost the taste for physical sports during their centuries of oppression. There were good walkers among the mountaineers, and good swimmers in the scattered villages along the coast. It was a matter of pride with the young palikar to wrestle and to dance well, but that was because bravery and a gallant bearing were admired by those around him. Greek dances are far from athletic, and the wrestling competitions of peasants have none of the characteristics of true sports. The men of the towns knew no diversion beyond reading the newspapers, and violently discussing politics at the tables of the cafes. The Greek race, however, is free from the natural indolence of the Oriental, and it was manifested that the athletic habit, if the opportunity be offered, would easily take root again among its men. Indeed, several gymnastic associations had been formed in recent years at Athens and Patras, and a rowing-club at Piraeus, and the public was showing a growing interest in their feats. It was therefore a favorable moment to speak the words "Olympic games". No sooner had it been made clear that Athens was to aid in the revival of the Olympiads than a perfect fever of muscular activity broke out all over the kingdom. And this was nothing compared to what followed the games. I have seen small boys, scarcely out of long clothes, throwing big stones, or jumping improvised hurdles in little villages far from the capital, and two urchins never met in the streets of Athens without running races. Nothing could exceed the enthusiasm with which the winners in the contests were received, on their return to their native towns, by their fellow citizens. They were met by the mayor and municipal authorities, and cheered by a crowd bearing branches of wild olive and laurel. In ancient times the winner entered the city through a breach made expressly in its walls. The Greek cities are no longer surrounded by walls, but one may say that athletics have made a breach in the heart of the nation. When one realizes the influence that the practice of physical exercises may have on the future of a country, and on the force of a whole race, one is tempted to wonder whether Greece is not likely to date a new era from the year 1896. It would be curious indeed if athletics were to become one of the factors in the Eastern question! Who can tell whether it may not hasten the solution of this thorny problem by bringing a notable increase of vigor to the inhabitants of the country? These are hypotheses, and circumstances show such calculations at long range. But a local and immediate consequence of the games may already be found in the internal politics of Greece. I have spoken of the active part taken by the crown prince and his brothers, Prince George and Prince Nicholas, in the labors of the organizing committee. It was the first time that the heir apparent had an opportunity of thus coming into contact with his future subjects. They knew him to be patriotic and high-minded, but they did not know his other admirable and solid qualities. Prince Constantine inherits his fine blue eyes and fair coloring from his Danish ancestors, and his frank, open manner, his self-poise, and his mental lucidity come from the same source; but Greece has given him enthusiasm and ardor, and this happy combination of prudence and high spirit makes him especially adapted to govern the Hellenes. The authority, mingled with perfect liberality, with which he managed the committee, his exactness in detail, and more particularly his quiet perseverance when those about him were inclined to hesitate and to lose courage, make it clear that his reign will be one of fruitful labor, which can only strengthen and enrich his country. The Greek people have a better idea now of the value of their future sovereign: they have seen him at work, and have gained respect and confidence in him.

So much for Greece. On the world at large the Olympic games have, of course, exerted no influence as yet; but I am profoundly convinced that they will do so. May I be permitted to say that this was my reason for founding them? Modern athletics need to be unified and purified. Those who have followed the renaissance of physical sports in this century know that discord reigns supreme from one end of them to the other. Every country has its own rules; it is not even possible to come to an agreement as to who is an amateur, and who is not. All over the world there is one perpetual dispute, which is fed further by innumerable weekly, and even daily newspapers. In this deplorable state of things professionalism tends to grow apace. Men give up their whole existence to one particular sport, grow rich by practicing it, and thus, deprive it of all nobility, and destroy the just equilibrium of man by making the muscles preponderate over the mind. It is my belief that no education, particularly in democratic times, can be good and complete without the aid of athletics; but athletics, in order to play their proper educational role, must be based on perfect disinterestedness and the sentiment of honor.

If we are to guard them against these threatening evils, we must put an end to the quarrels of amateurs, that they may be united among themselves, and willing to measure their skill in frequent international encounters. But what country is to impose its rules and its habits on the others? The Swedes will not yield to the Germans, nor the French to the English. Nothing better than the international Olympic games could therefore be devised. Each country will take its turn in organizing them. When they come to meet every four years in these contests, further ennobled by the memories of the past, athletes all over the world will learn to know one another better, to make mutual concessions, and to seek no other reward in the competition than the honor of the victory. One may be filled with desire to see the colors of one's club or college triumph in a national meeting, but how much stronger is the feeling when the colors of one's country are at stake! I am well assured that the winners in the Stadium at Athens wished for no other recompense when they heard the people cheer the flag of their country in honor of their achievement.

It was with these thoughts in mind that I sought to revive the Olympic games. I have succeeded after many efforts. Should the institution prosper, – as I am persuaded, all civilized nations aiding, that it will, – it may be a potent, if indirect, factor in securing universal peace. Wars break out because nations misunderstand each other. We shall not have peace until the prejudices that now separate the different races are outlived. To attain this end, what better means is there than to bring the youth of all countries periodically together for amicable trials of muscular strength and agility? The Olympic games, with the ancients, controlled athletics and promoted peace. It is not a vision to look at them for similar benefactions in the future.

The Century Illustrated Monthly Magazine,
Vol. LIII, New Series, Vol. XXXI, November
1896 to April 1897, pp. 39-53.

Session of IOC members in Athens, from left to right (standing): Willibald Gebhardt (Germany), Jiri Guth (Bohemia), Francis Kemény (Hungary), Viktor Balck (Sweden); (seated): Pierre de Coubertin (France, Secretary General), Demetrius Vikelas (Greece, President), Alexis de Butovski (Russia) (Photo: A.Meyer, IOC Archives)

4.2.2/6 MINUTES FROM ATHENS (APRIL 12, 1896)

The minutes from the first IOC Session, held during the Olympics in Athens, were signed by Coubertin in his capacity as IOC Secretary General, a post to which he was elected at the founding congress in 1894. They contain little regarding Coubertin's personal opinions, however they do contain important information on the history of the Olympic Movement, which is of great interest. The principle of alternating the place where the Olympic Games are held and the IOC rules of procedure are recorded in the minutes of the sixth meeting, which was held on April 12, 1896.[1]

1 Meetings were held on April 4, 6, 7, 9, 10, 12 and 14. Minutes of all decisions see "The 2nd IOC Session in Athens", in: *Olympic Review*, no. XXV-8, April-May 1996, pp.22-24.

Considering that the resolution adopted by the Paris Congress, which states that the Olympic Games must be held successively in all the world's capitals, constitutes the very basis of the work for which it is responsible, the International Committee has decided, in accordance with the requests received, to put *New York, Berlin* and *Stockholm* to a vote by its members for the celebration of the 1904 Olympic Games. The Committee has taken note of the proposal made by Mr Kemény to hold a subsequent edition of the Olympic Games in Budapest.

Dr Gebhardt is responsible for compiling the general report on the 1896 Olympic Games.

The seat of the International Committee shall, henceforth, be in the city where the forthcoming Olympic Games are to be celebrated. The Bulletin will be published there, and wherever possible will be in three languages: French, English and German. The presidency of the Committee still belongs, as decided by the Paris Congress, to the country in which the Olympic Games are to take place.

The president of the Committee will have complete freedom to organize the Secretariat: he may choose secretaries from outside the Committee itself, but these will stay in office only for the duration of his presidency.

Those members of the International Committee who have not submitted at least one annual report to the president, or who have neglected, without a valid excuse, to attend or be represented at the Olympic Games, will be assumed to have resigned. The Committee appoints its own members and replaces those members who cease to be a part of it. It has the right to exercise control over general decisions taken by the National Committees which affect the institution.

Each member of the International Committee endeavours to meet, on his part, the expenses incurred by publication of the Bulletin and the Committee documents, by seeking advertising and grouping together the societies.

The president may call a meeting of the International Committee when he deems it possible or desirable to do so.

Athens, 31/12-3-1896

The Secretary General
Pierre de Coubertin

The President
D. Bikélas

Comité International des Jeux Olympiques. Session d'avril 1896 à Athènes.
Protocole des décisions adoptées par le Comité.
In: *Les Jeux Olympiques. Supplément du Messager d'Athènes.*
6/18 avril 1896, no 15, p.69.
The date show the 12 days difference between the Greek and Gregorian Calendars.

employment in the neighbourhood), that I authorize you to make this proposal on my behalf.
"Believe me, very truly yours,
"LONDONDERRY."

THE OLYMPIC GAMES.

TO THE EDITOR OF THE TIMES.

Monsieur le Directeur,—Une dépêche lancée d'Athènes et rédigée sans doute par un philhellène enthousiaste a porté à la connaissance de la presse Européenne la nouvelle que les Jeux Olympiques étaient désormais fixés en Grèce. Il n'en est rien. Les Jeux Olympiques circuleront à travers le monde comme l'a décidé le congrès international réuni à la Sorbonne, il y a deux ans. Ceux de 1900 auront lieu à Paris. Pour 1904, le comité aura à choisir entre New York, Berlin, et Stockholm. Il est tout naturel que l'éclatant succès que notre entreprise vient de remporter ait inspiré aux Hellènes le désir de la monopoliser à leur profit. Mais nous ne pouvons souscrire à un semblable projet. Pour ma part, ayant voulu les Jeux d'Athènes alors que les Athéniens eux-mêmes n'y voyaient point et les repoussaient, j'estime que le moment n'est pas venu de renoncer à une œuvre qui vient d'être inaugurée si brillamment.

Recevez, Monsieur le Directeur, l'expression de mes sentiments les plus distingués.

Bon. PIERRE de COUBERTIN, Président du Comité International des Jeux Olympiques, Paris, 31, Rue de Lubeck.

Athènes, 23 Avril.

THE LONDON BUILDING STRIKE.—Affairs in the London building trade have come to a crisis, and to-day all the men, with the exception of the bricklayers, will

In this letter to the New York Times, Coubertin protests about the false report that all future Olympic Games would be held in Greece.

4.2.2/7 TO THE EDITOR OF THE TIMES

Dear Sir,

An article datelined Athens, no doubt written by an enthusiastic Philhellene, informed the European press that a decision has been made to hold the Olympic Games in Greece from now on. Nothing could be further from the truth. The Olympic Games will move about the globe, as was decided at the international congress held at the Sorbonne two years ago. The 1900 Games will be in Paris. In 1904, the committee will choose between New York, Berlin, and Stockholm. It is perfectly understandable that the brilliant success of our undertaking recently inspired the Greeks to desire to monopolize it to their advantage. But we cannot sanction such a plan. I am the one who hoped for the Athens Games even when the Athenians themselves did not believe in them at all and rejected the notion. I do not feel that the time has come to put a stop to this undertaking, which has just begun so brilliantly.

Sincerely,

Baron Pierre de Coubertin

Chairman of the International Committee
of the Olympic Games
31, Rue de Lubeck, Paris.

New York Times,
April 30, 1896, p. 12.

4.2.2/8 THE CONGRESS OF LE HAVRE

The Olympic Congress of Le Havre in 1897 was the next step in the Olympic movement. It is the focus of the following excerpt from Coubertin's "Une Campagne de vingt-et-un ans". Aside from a report in the Olympic Memoirs, and occasional general references, Coubertin's writings include no analysis of the work accomplished at this Congress. Coubertin merely provided the following summary: the debate, he said, was based on the ideas of his great educational model, Thomas Arnold, but it did not produce any specific results. Clearly, one result of the small turnout from abroad – thirteen delegates from ten countries – as well as the majority French participation, meant that debate centered largely around sports in French schools, with the foreign participation simply showing the international nature of the Congress. It is easy to understand why Balck, a Swede, criticized the deliberations as being out of keeping with the work of the IOC, and reproached Coubertin for attributing excessive interest to educational theories[1].

Yet Coubertin remained convinced that this was exactly the opening that the IOC needed to increase its strength, and that as a result it would withstand attacks better. In this instance, he had a heavy-hitting ally in the person of the English delegate, Courcy-Laffan. Coubertin soon called him to the IOC; Courcy-Laffan was to be one of its most highly visible members for many decades[2].

At Le Havre, Coubertin avoided any renewed discussion of issues of the organization of the Olympic Games. First, the Games had to take on a certain consistent aspect.

Coubertin felt that the IOC was not yet "sufficiently ready" for that task. With limited manpower, a lack of material resources, and above all an organization in delicate balance (making it impossible to rely on regularly constituted or recognized administrative or technical support), Coubertin was unable to make so unwise a move[3].

The fact that this Congress was held at all marked a turning point. The activity that it stirred up, in fact, stabilized the Olympic movement.

The Congress of Le Havre was followed by other Olympic Congresses over the course of Olympic history. We will discuss the significance of these Congresses in other parts of this volume[4].

The idea of convening a Congress was the only approach I could think of. There was no other effective and practical way to get the International Committee to realize its own importance, and at the same time to give it the opportunity to show the rest of the world what it does. Four years were going to pass before the next Olympic Games were celebrated. It would have been quite unwise to put things off until that solemn occasion began to draw closer. What is more, it fell within the attributes of the Committee, according to its own statutes, to "convene and to organize any display and, in general, to undertake any and all measures appropriate to orienting modern athleticism in desirable directions". Thus the Committee was remaining faithful to its mission by calling a congress.

But what would that Congress turn out to be? Shortly after I left Athens, a draft law had been filed by the prime minister, Mr. Delyanni, for the purposes of ensuring the growth of athleticism in Greece, and to regulate the celebration of the Olympic Games in the stadium at Athens. This draft law did not take the origins of the restoration of the Games into account at all, nor did it consider the conditions in which that restoration had taken place. In the toast I mentioned above, King George had addressed the athletes from the world over who were gathered around him, suggesting to them the possibility of "indicating" Athens as the appropriate place to hold future Olympiads. This was a very tactful nuance. In addition, the crown prince, as chairman of the Greek Committee, in the final meeting that I had the honor of having with him before my departure, had limited himself to the idea of Pan-Hellenic Olympiads. Such Games would be much more advantageous to Greece because they would be far less expensive to put on, and more likely to enhance the development of physical culture among the sons of Greece. But the Greek government is extremely constitutional, and Mr. Delyanni did not believe that he needed to become entangled in all that. Without even consulting the prince, as I learned in a letter from Colonel Sapountzakis, and, with all the more reason, without bothering to warn me of his intentions, he had rushed to do homage to public feelings, adopting the most radical solution, i.e. ignoring proper conventions and agreements.

Our colleague, Mr. Bikelas, immediately sent a circular letter to all the members of the International Committee, calling for the meeting of a second congress which "would complete the work of the Congress of Paris" by recording the creation of the Greek Olympiads, attributing to them the same character and the same privileges as to the international Olympiads. The Greek Olympiads would be celebrated in the intervals between the international ones, so that from then on there would be Olympic Games every two years. Most of the members of the Committee consulted me before stating their positions. I did not want to oppose Mr. Bikelas's wishes at all, even though I considered the plan premature. Olympic Games every two years seemed to me to be something for the future, and too frequent for the time being. In any event, the calling of the Congress suited me only on two conditions:

1.that this congress would not call into question the work done in 1894, specifically the constitution of the International Committee; and

2.that it would extend its activity beyond technical matters, debating theoretical and educational issues, as well.

From the start, I had made a fair number of sacrifices on behalf of the International Committee. I was not about to let a mechanism be destroyed that could, in the end, be extremely useful, nor allow it to fall into something of a vassal relationship to the Greek organization. As for the Congress itself, it was essential that it be given a solid foundation. By limiting its program to revising the Olympic regulations, we would have run the risk of making its work uninteresting, resulting in a total fiasco. This was all the more true in that the political horizon in the east was growing dark, and who knew if Greece, a year later, would still be talking about holding games in the future at all?

1 Cf. Coubertin, *Olympic Memoirs*, Lausanne, IOC, 1997, p. 54.
2 Cf. Coubertin, "Silhouettes disparues: Rev. De Courcy-Laffan." in *Gazette de Lausanne,* December 20, 1928, p.2.
3 Cf. *Olympic Memoirs*, Lausanne, IOC, 1979, p. 27.
4 See N. Müller, *One Hundred Years of Olympic Congresses 1894-1994,* Lausanne, IOC, 1994.

Of course, I was far from sure about the events that were in the offing, and I did not think that the claims concerning Crete could lead to war so quickly. It is said, by the way, that the 1896 Olympic Games had helped push the Greeks to this extreme, and that the Games had enabled the leaders of Pan-Hellenism to meet in Athens under the cloak of sports, where they made their preliminary moves. I have never placed any faith in this assertion, and I am unaware that any real proof was ever produced to support it. To the contrary, it seems to me that the movement in favor of Crete was rather spontaneous. Yet I think there is no doubt that the success of the Games went to the head of public opinion, to a certain extent, giving the Greeks dangerous confidence both in their own strength and in the good will of foreign countries. Whatever the case may be, war broke out, and very quickly turned into a quasi disaster. Public sentiment in Europe was generally hostile to Greece. The French, above all, were harsh in their judgments of Greece's unwise initiative. This was something new. From the time of Navarin, France had remained true to Greece and I deplored this exhibition of feelings that ran counter to tradition. With a few Philhellenes, and at the request of the Association of Greek Students in Paris, I recall organizing a conference held early in 1897 in the great hall of the Learned Societies' Building. The conference was rather stormy, because it was interrupted by expressions of Ottoman sympathies on the part of some of those in attendance. Nevertheless, the meeting ended with the passing of a warm resolution in support of the Hellad. My friend, Mr. d'Estournelles, chaired that meeting along with Mr. Michel Bréal, who had responded to our invitation by writing to me as follows: "What you are doing is truly good, because our good Greek friends seem to me to have forgotten everything they owed you". As I said, this all took place in early 1897, and when the Congress opened, there was, in fact, no longer any question of holding the Games in Athens. In the wake of such dearly-won peace and amid the sadness of national mourning, it would have been impossible decently even to discuss the possibility. I was very glad to have written up the program for the Congress in such a way that it would remain unaffected by the repercussions of outside events.

Among other items, the agenda included the study of issues of hygiene and education related to physical exercises; the physiology of sports and their moral impact on adolescents; the effects of exertion on the formation of the character and the development of the personality; the teaching of sports hygiene; the practice of hydrotherapy, and so on. These issues were debated primarily by three notable speakers, Fr. Didon, Gabriel Bonvalot, and the Rev. de Courcy-Laffan, then headmaster at the Cheltenham school and the delegate to the Congress from the English Association of Headmasters. On that day, the great festival hall at the Le Havre City Hall rang out, as you can well imagine, with enthusiastic applause. Everyone was most astonished, after the admirable speech by Fr. Didon, to hear the British delegate improvise a talk in perfectly styled French.

Why Le Havre? The choice may seem surprising. There had been talk of Berlin, Stockholm, and even Paris. No one, of course, had suggested this city in Normandy, but then again no one objected when I expressed my clear desires in this regard. Ultimately, it was a matter of holding an out-of-place event, one that was useful but unnecessary. There was no real reason for it to take place; it had no inexorable reason to be held. Therefore, its success remained rather problematic, and getting it

Le Havre town hall, venue of the 1897 Olympic Congress (Archives of the City of Le Havre)

underway presented some serious obstacles. I absolutely insisted on having my Congress in hand, in a city where I was guaranteed to see it come off as a big success, no matter how many foreign delegates came. At the time, Félix Faure was President of the French Republic, and Le Havre had become the "presidential city", since the head of State maintained his private residence there, and spent most of his summers there. That made it possible for me to obtain Mr. Faure's immediate acceptance of the honorary chairmanship of the Congress.

In July 1896, a resolution of the City Council had placed the City Hall at the disposal of the International Committee, so that it could set up its offices and hold the sessions of the Congress in it. The organizers were Messrs. W. Langstaff, Dr. Robert Sorel, Maurice Taconet, C. Jacquemin, Henrotin, and Georges Lafaurie, all Le Havre natives. The first three, in particular, went to great pains to ensure that the budget of the treasurer, Mr. Lafaurie, was paid up in full through subscriptions. Even though vast sums were not involved, for a time interest seemed to flag, to the point that we had to plan for the possibility of a postponement. What would have happened in another city? They left the decision up to me. At the time, I was in Luchon. My confident side won out, and I telegraphed back that they should forge ahead. No sooner had I returned to Normandy than I fell ill. I left my sickbed just in time to preside over the sessions, an effort that was to cause serious problems in my convalescence. The sessions lasted for six days. I was unable to attend any of the festivities that I had taken such delight in planning. I was aware that they were a great success. The gymnastics festival held by torch light on the beautiful Place Gambetta, located between the theater and the Bassin du Commerce, and particularly the illumination of the cliffs of La Hève were blessed with good weather and very warmly received. The delegates met in Rouen, and arrived in Le Havre by boat along the Seine. On July 30 they made a trip to Étretat, and on August 1, they attended the Le Havre regattas. The opening session took place on July 26, and the closing dinner was given on July 31, at the Hôtel Frascati, with the government authorities in attendance. All in all, particularly thanks to the astute and enthusiastic devotion of Mr. Langstaff, everything went very well.

The President of the Republic welcomed the members of the Congress to his villa on the coast in two groups. First, I presented to him the many French delegates, then the foreign delegates. Only Russia and Hungary alone had sent official representatives of the Ministers of Public Instruction. Yet there were also Swedes, Americans, Englishmen, Italians, and Germans representing either universities or major athletics associations. The debates were interesting and eagerly followed. The rector of the Académie de Caen took part, as did the subprefect of Le Havre, who even joined with Fr. Didon in presenting one of the resolutions that the Congress passed.

As I said, the Congress did not touch the issue of the Olympic Games. Everything stayed as it was. Most of those in attendance were education theorists and hygienists, few were technical experts. Moreover, once political events had stripped the main issue of any currency, namely the modus vivendi to be established between the International Committee and the Greek Committee, there was no longer any reason to change anything that had been started by the Congress of Paris. As for the results that I had hoped to achieve, I was completely successful. The members of the International Committee had gathered in the right conditions to give them a feeling for their stability and usefulness, at the same time. The French head of state had sponsored their meeting, and had given evidence of his personal interest in it. Once again, their course was laid out for them, and none of them hesitated to set off along it. From then on, there was never any question among us of dissolving our undertaking and handing over its work to others. However, another crisis was to arise, one that would last longer and be more difficult to overcome than the last.

The year 1897 should also have provided an opportunity for an interesting commemoration on the part of the Union des Sports Athlétiques. It had just reached its tenth anniversary, yet no one gave any thought to it. The Union had fallen into a relative slump, and Mr. de Janzé intended to withdraw from it, as did I. As no successors were to be found to replace us, we let our names continue to be used, even though the use of our names was no longer connected with any reality. Although I was unable to convince the Union to celebrate its tenth anniversary at the appropriate time, I did at least arrange for it to celebrate the anniversary in spring 1898, at the same time as the anniversary of the Comité pour la Propagation des Exercices Physiques [Committee for the Propagation of Physical Exercise]. The anniversary was celebrated at a joyous banquet, followed by a theatrical presentation organized by Count Albert de Bertier, for which he had written a most witty piece that was performed by outstanding artists.

Le Congrès du Havre, in:
Une Campagne de vingt-et-un ans [A Twenty-One Year Campaign] (1887-1908).
Paris 1909, pp. 129-135 (Chapter XIV).

4.2.2/9 THE OLYMPIC CONGRESS AT LE HAVRE (1897)

In his Olympic Memoirs, 34 years later, the Le Havre Congress looks very different to Coubertin. It was a chance to make known the young institution, and doubtless also Coubertin himself, in his native Normandy. The jubilee congress organized in Le Havre by the International Pierre de Coubertin Committee in 1997 looked at the importance of this congress in the course of Olympic history, and accorded it an important place.[1]

Why Le Havre? People could not get over it. What on earth did this large Normandy port have to do with Olympism?

On his return from Athens, Dr. Gebhardt had expressed the wish that the next meeting of the IOC should be held in Berlin. Messrs. Bikelas, Kémény and Guth had agreed, he said. But I took good care not to consult them, and before the summer I approached the Le Havre municipal authorities. Nothing would have been more foolish at this point than to call a meeting of the IOC, all on its own, in broad daylight, in a big capital. I well remember the reply of a young girl, today the wife of a well-known writer, when asked whether "she had danced much this season". With a charming moue she replied: "My parents do not feel that I am quite ready yet. They refuse to *let me come out* until next year". I considered the IOC in exactly the same way. I felt it was not ready to *come out* yet. Its small size, its lack of material resources, and especially its lack of solid foundations, making it unable as yet to rely either on a permanent administration or on regularly constituted and recognized technical forces made me reject the idea of such an unwise step. On the other hand, I considered it more important than ever to preserve its absolute independence by taking care to avoid owing allegiance to any protective power. It was important not to undermine the victory won in Athens, nor on the other hand to exaggerate its importance.

Until then, I had always spent a good part of the year in Normandy: relations, home, any political interests I had, everything, in fact, made me love this birthplace of my family. It was easier for me therefore to find support there than anywhere else. The French President, elected the previous year after the unexpected resignation of Casimir-Perier, was a native of Le Havre and had kept a summer residence in his home town. I was sure that I could interest him in the idea.

In Athens, all efforts had been concentrated on the sporting side of the venture in an historical context; there had been no congress, no conference, no sign of any moral or educational purpose. To take that direction immediately after the Games was to remind people of the intellectual and philosophical character of my idea and to place the role of the IOC, right from the start, very much above that of a simple sports association. Without listening therefore to any of

1 See N. Müller: "The 1897 Congress of Le Havre after a century of Olympism." in: *Coubertin and Olympism. Questions for the Future.* Report of the Congress, 17th to 20th September 1997 at the University of Le Havre. Niedernhausen / Strasbourg / Sydney, Schors, 1998, pp. 44-53. See Y.-P. Boulongne: Pierre de Coubertin, his roots and the Congress of Le Havre 1897, in: *Coubertin and Olympism. Questions for the Future.* Report of the Congress, 17th to 20th September 1997 at the University of Le Havre. Niedernhausen/Strasbourg/Sydney, Schors, 1998, pp. 34-43.

Le Comité International des Jeux Olympiques

prie S. E. Monsieur le Ministre de l'Instruction Publique de Bavière

de lui faire l'honneur de vouloir bien participer

au Congrès Olympique du Havre par l'envoi de délégués

This typical invitation was completed by hand by Pierre de Coubertin himself, as he had no secretary. Invitation sent to the Bavarian Ministry of Culture (Bayrisches Hauptstaatsarchiv Munich)

the objections raised, I persisted in my Le Havre project and made sure first of all that we could use the Town Hall and then that we could count on the cooperation of two close friends: Father Didon, Prior of Arcueil College, and Gabriel Bonvalot, famous for his journey through central Asia. They were two of the most popular speakers of the day. A flexible program was drawn up, leaving us free to deal with any problems we liked, to take them up and drop them at will. Here is the program:

EDUCATION

The psychology of physical exercise: characteristics of each type.

The distinction between free games and compulsory exercise; advantages and disadvantages of each.

The moral effect of physical exercise on children, adolescents; influence of effort on the formation of character and the development of personality.

The organization of physical training in high schools and colleges; can the pupils organize and run this themselves, and how? Consequences of leaving pupils free to do as they choose. The role of authority.

HYGIENE

The physiology of physical training; rules peculiar to each form of exercise. Teaching hygiene in high schools and colleges; program of such teaching. Clothing.

Hydrotherapy considered as a complement to physical exercise; under what form it should be used.

SPORT

The question of cash prizes and the definition of an amateur.

The organization of international competitions; frequency and general conditions. The creation of a universal Olympic Union and a "Universal Olympic Bulletin".

The revival and development of physical training during the 19th century; history of this movement in different countries throughout the world.

The sports part of the program was hardly touched on at all; it was there just for the form. The creation of a Universal Olympic Union and a Bulletin in several languages had been included in order to please our Hungarian colleague, F. Kémény, who had a tendency to be rather ambitious in his ideas. The participation of the Rector of Caen Academy, the Prefect of the department of Seine-Inférieure, the Sub-Prefect of Le Havre, and a fairly large number of foreign dignitaries enhanced the prestige of the discussions. On two days at his villa by the sea the Head of State received members of the Congress, in whose honor a number of quite successful festivities were arranged.

It was during one of the public sessions, while Father Didon, in the main assembly room in the Town Hall, was whipping up the enthusiasm of a large audience with one of those rousing speeches at which he was so expert, that I was handed the card of a delegate who had arrived late, the Reverend Courcy Laffan, Headmaster of Cheltenham College and the representative of the Conference of British Headmasters. After greeting him, I invited him to come and sit in the front row facing me. He was still in the prime of life, of slender build and with remarkably fine features. He gave an impression of perfect balance between intelligence, strength, and sensitivity. He had just landed from Southampton. When Father Didon brought his speech to a close, too soon for the liking of the audience, the discussion was declared open, but nobody seemed anxious to speak after him. So I thought that a short speech in English would break the ice and, apologizing for my indiscretion, I asked the Headmaster of Cheltenham to say a few words. Unhurriedly, almost without a moment's hesitation, both modest and at the same time self-assured, Mr. Laffan stood up and in a French of the greatest purity, with a measure and choice of expression that were quite unexpected, he expounded his ideas on the moral value of sport. His ideas coincided with Father Didon's, but the way in which he put them was so very different, revealing a quiet but at the same time refined elegance, that the contrast drew forth a fresh burst of enthusiasm from the audience and made this session a real festival of French eloquence. For my part, I was convinced that a new collaborator with the most invaluable qualities had fallen from the skies to

A rare written document of how Coubertin totally used his personal possession, also his huge inheritance from his father, for the spreading of his reform ideas, his travels and the organization of the Olympic Movement.
Here: Memorandum of Coubertin's gurantee to cover festival costs of the Olympic Congress 1897. (Archives of the City of Le Havre)

Copie.

MEMORANDUM

LANGSTAFF, EHRENBERG & POLLAK

Havre, le 3 Juillet 1897

à Monsieur Jacquemin Fils

J'ai vu Mr de Coubertin Jeudi, il m'a dit qu'il fallait garantir les fr 1100 environ aux Gymnastes, prière donc de faire le nécessaire.

etc etc

Salutations empressées

H. R. Langstaff

help us. Laffan, whose fundamental Celticism inherited from his Irish ancestors gave him a certain tendency towards mysticism, told me afterwards that, on this very first day, he had felt himself "called" to serve the Olympic cause with all his power. In fact, he was to remain true to it to the end of his days, and the friendship between us remained close and steady.

The Le Havre Congress had to do without any help from Greece. The Greeks were fighting for the independence of Crete and the restoration of the legitimate frontiers, but fate proved hostile. Friends and enemies fighting in the service of their country had no time to turn their eyes towards Normandy. Therefore, the Hellenism that had permeated the atmosphere of the first Congress in 1894 started to fade before the influence of England, which was closer. It was to Arnold that we turned, more or less consciously, for inspiration. In fact, for the last ten years I had been trying to implant his doctrines in France; in the principle on which they were based I discovered such clarity and such strength that I was surprised to find the modern world so slow to understand. Even now there did not seem to be any great progress on this point, in spite of the threefold support of Father Didon, Laffan, and Bonvalot. Even within the Committee itself, not everybody was satisfied. Balck felt that we were wasting our time and that the subjects discussed had "nothing to do with our world". For a moment, he even considered resigning. This was the only temporary faltering in his loyalty. Others felt, like him, that by endeavoring to see to everything, we risked dispersing our forces. I thought exactly the opposite and that by imitating a chameleon, the IOC would make itself more effective and more elusive, and consequently less vulnerable to attack. Now there was no escaping the fact that a battle was imminent, and I felt it would be more dangerous than the last, more unexpected in its maneuvers and even more uncertain in its outcome.

Olympic Memoirs, Chap.4, Lausanne, IOC, 1997, pp.50-54.

4.2.2/10 – 4.2.2/12 INTRODUCTION

The next articles relate to the Second Olympic Games, held in Paris in 1900. In the introduction to this volume, we noted that the term "Olympic Games" should be taken with a grain of salt with respect to these games, lost as they were in the tumult of the World's Fair. We must assume that Coubertin had hoped for too much from the U.S.F.S.A., even though that organization was fully supported by him, and that he realized too late that he was alone. The first excerpt from *Une Campagne de vingt-et-un ans* addresses organizational problems, and gives a brief overview of how the Games went. The second excerpt from the *North American Review* in June 1900 exists only in the English language and can be seen as an excerpt to attract the North Americans to participate at the Olympic Games in Paris in 1900. He uses the opportunity to show the situation of sports in the most important European countries like Germany, Sweden, England, Austria and Russia. The third excerpt is taken from *Olympic Memoirs* 1932, which is similar to 4.2.2/11. The last paragraph gives a very short and reserved estimation of the Olympic Games from 1900, which according to Coubertin did not have much to do with his Olympic Idea.

Coubertin bore some responsibility for the debacle that these Games were. In 1894, he was part of the Preparatory Committee for the athletic competitions during the 1900 World's Fair. He was well aware of the events that could have been foreseen.

Coubertin the publicist was very active in the period around 1900. He devoted his time particularly to vast studies of the political future of Europe. This topic had even taken such hold of him when he was thirty-five that his concern for the Olympics was pushed into the background. Many articles written in English attest to his special interest in foreign policy at this time. He wanted to work in the United States in support of culture and friendly relations with France[1].

He was also caught up in a domestic political conflict, when, in 1898, a move was made to appoint him as the Republican candidate to the National Assembly for the Le Havre district[2].

The series of basic articles that he sent in 1900 and 1903 to the major newspaper *L'Indépendence Belge* is also remarkable for the political history of the period.

His most complete work on education, *Notes sur l'éducation publique* [Notes on Public Education], was published in 1901, and won him respect abroad, as well[3].

1 To this end, he established prizes at some American universities, and from 1901 to 1907 published La *Chronique de France*, a literary and political magazine sent free of charge to major foreign libraries. The purpose of the publication was to make France better known abroad.

2 In a public letter in March, 1898, he justified his rejection of this mandate, which he felt was an honor. See *Lettre aux Électeurs de l'Arrondissement du Havre* [Letter to the Voters of the Le Havre District], Le Havre, March 1898.

3 See the reference in the introduction to this volume (to W. Münch, *Zukunftspädagogik. Berichte und Kritiken, Betrachtungen und Vorschläge* [Future Education. Reports and Critiques, Considerations and Recommendations], Berlin, Springer, 2nd Ed., 1908, p. 49-59).

4.2.2/10 PREPARATIONS FOR THE SECOND OLYMPIAD

Since physical exercises had been part of the 1889 World's Fair, it was simple enough to give them greater exposure at the 1900 Fair. This was accepted in principle from the start. I remember talking about it with Mr. Georges Berger, almost the day after the first of these World's Fairs closed. He was one of the commissioners of the World's Fair, and a member of the Institute. All indications were that he would be appointed to oversee the operations of the next fair, but Mr. Alfred Picard was appointed instead. Mr. Picard had no other claim to preeminence over Mr. Berger than his great confidence in his own omniscience.

On January 30, 1894, Mr. Alfred Picard, who had only recently begun his work, received Mr. Strehly and me at the Conseil d'État. Mr. Strehly, the eminent professor, had placed his signature next to mine on the document that we submitted to the commissioner general, a copy of which I kept. The plan was to hold an Athletic Fair inside as accurate a reproduction as possible of the Altis at Olympia. The Fair was to have three sections: the ancient period, Egypt, India, Greece and Rome; the Middle Ages: chivalry and popular games; and the modern era: German and Swedish gymnastics, the athletic renaissance in England, and athleticism in the New and Old Worlds. Fencing, hunting, and ice sports formed an additional section. Outside the Altis, Roman baths and an American athletic club (the one in Chicago) were to be reproduced. The plan called for holding races, games, and wrestling in the ancient style, in the gymnasium and in the stadium. It was quite clear that cafes, shops, and shows where an admission fee would be charged were to be forbidden within this area, that no concessions would be allowed there, and that the Olympia of 1900 would be distinctly educational in character. I cannot go into the details of the plan here, but these were the basic outlines. I took this opportunity to tell Mr. Picard about the International Congress that was to meet at the Sorbonne in June, 1894, and about the eventual restoration of the Olympic Games (the modern ones) that would be the likely result. I told him that we would suggest 1900 as the starting date for the modern Games, and that the first Olympiad would thus coincide with the World's Fair[1].

Mr. Picard listened to my explanations, and those that Mr. Strehly offered, without expressing any opinion whatsoever. He told us that he was going to "file" the plan, and that he would call us in due course, which, by the way, he never did. Neither Mr. Strehly nor I ever heard anything more about it. As for the Olympic Games, Mr. Picard took absolutely no notice of them, because on the following September 2 (the Sorbonne Congress had taken place in the meanwhile, and the Olympic Games had been restored), the Minister of Trade, at the suggestion of Mr. Picard, appointed an eighty-member committee to study the possibility of a "program of competitions relating to physical exercise" that could be organized "in the Vincennes area during the 1900 World's Fair". The arrangement was not very fortunate. The composition of the committee, chaired by General Baillod, was a bit more so. I was unable to take part in the work of that committee, because I was in Greece busy with preparations for the 1896 Games when it met. When I returned to Paris, the report was nearly ready to be submitted. Moreover, 1896 was the focus of all our efforts. We would have to see about 1900 at a later date.

When the Congress of Le Havre (1897) was over, the time had come for us to think about the Second Olympiad. But what was the status of the World's Fair competitions? What were the commissioner general's plans? That was what we had to know first and foremost. The committee I just mentioned had not met for over two years, and no one was talking about reconvening it. There was vague agreement that there would be "physical exercises at Vincennes". Yet at the time, Vincennes had a very bad reputation. The annex that would be set up there was commonly called the "dumping grounds of the World's Fair". People said that the office of the commissioner general assigned any project that he did not find interesting to Vincennes, as well as those projects that might be abandoned at the last minute if circumstances demanded. In addition, the general classification of exhibits at the Fair, which had been slow in coming, had caused great disappointment for future athletic exhibitors. Several sent their condolences to me, expressing their fervent wish that sports objects and equipment be placed in a single category. Although I was sure that their wishes were no longer likely to be granted, I sent a letter to the Minister of Trade, Mr. Henry Boucher. Several newspapers printed it and supported my position. Here is the relevant passage: "The public will certainly be rather surprised to note that, in the general classification, physical exercises are scattered about in the strangest manner. The words "gymnastics", "fencing", and "school games" humbly end a long list of objects included in Class 2, under the title "secondary education". Bicycles are grouped with automobiles. Class 33, "commercial navigation equipment", will cover everything that has to do with swimming and rowing. I suppose skating falls under cutlery. In any event, "athletic associations" are mentioned in class 107; you have done me the honor of appointing me to be a member of this category, which is supposed to deal with "institutions for the intellectual and moral advancement of laborers". As things stand, if visitors to the Fair want to admire the plans of the handsome gymnasium of the Chicago Athletic Club, for example, which is a club for adults, they will have to go find them among the equipment for junior and senior high schools. If the athletic association of the island of Puteaux or of the Polo Club of Paris wants to exhibit, they will take their place among institutions for laborers". After expressing my regret that nothing had been attempted from a retrospective point of view to show the progress that had been achieved in athletics, I closed by asking the minister what had become of the famous committee and the competitions at Vincennes. Mr. Boucher's reply, as I well imagined, did not provide any satisfaction concerning classification, or any formal assurance with regard to the competitions. The minister did announce "a series of competitions to be held near Lake Daumesnil in the Bois de Vincennes", but he thought it "premature" to form "special committees" responsible for organizing them.

After one final effort by Mr. Ribot, who approached Mr. Picard to see if he might possibly be disposed to hold the Olympic Games within the enclosure of the Fair, an effort that resulted in a blunt refusal from the commissioner general, I felt quite free of any scruples. I approached the Viscount de La Rochefoucauld regarding the task of overseeing the organization of the 1900 Olympic Games. Even today,

1 As I mentioned above, 1900 seemed too far off for the 1894 Congress, and we ended up recommending 1896 and Athens for the inauguration of the new Olympiads.

though several of our fellow workers bitterly criticized me for making that choice, I think that it was a fully justified. I believe that if we had to do it all over again, I would do exactly the same thing. Charles de La Rochefoucauld was a childhood friend of mine, and a high school classmate. I had always admired his energy which, it is true, at times bordered on brutality. Yet his high social position made up for that little problem. He was fully capable of obstinate perseverance, as he had demonstrated in establishing his Polo Club de Bagatelle. A passionate sportsman, he was particularly interested in athletic exhibitions, without being held captive by any of those "little cliques" whose influence I feared. Moreover, no one else had the means in hand to preside over the French Olympiad in a more princely fashion. A simple banquet given by him a few years before, on the occasion of an international polo match, had taken on the feeling of a sumptuous feast, given the setting in which it was held. With its main courtyard, its marble staircase, its two galleries, its rows of salons, and the green vistas of its gardens, his residence in the rue de Varennes needed no other special adornment to enchant the gaze of the guests. A festival held there would be a spectacle in itself, and it was not within the power of any World's Fair commissioner general to equal it. All we would have to do is add a garden party at the Chateau de Bonnétable, admirably restored and close enough to Paris that one could go spend the day there, and the Second Olympiad would immediately take on a special, truly French feeling. Old France, opening its most aristocratic residences in this way to young athletes on the occasion of the most democratic of international events – was this not both intriguing and tantalizing?

Charles de La Rochefoucauld shared my outlook fully and enthusiastically. Together, we immediately formed the organizing committee for the 1900 Olympic Games. As secretary general, we selected none other than Robert Fournier-Sarlovèze, now mayor of Compiègne, then a brilliant retired cavalry officer and dedicated sportsman. Fournier-Sarlovèze, as energetic as La Rochefoucauld, also had a calculating mind and good administrative sense. He would keep his eye on everything, and would make his operation tick. These two men were perfect complements to each other. The "athletic commissioners" were selected with respect both to their competence and their independence. These commissioners were: Mr. Hébrard de Villeneuve and Count Potocki for fencing, Count de Guébriant and P. de Boulongne for yachting, Messrs. Dubonnet and E. Caillat for rowing, G. Strehly for gymnastics, Georges Bourdon for athletics, Pierre Giffard for swimming, Baron Jean de Bellet for lawn tennis, Bruneau de Laborie for boxing, Baron Lejeune for polo, O'Connor for close tennis, C. Richefeu for open-air tennis, Count Jacques de Pourtalès for golf, Count de Bertier for archery, and Count F. De Maillé for bicycling. Other commissioners were to be appointed or added to these later on. The committee also included Count Philippe d'Alsace, Messrs. Baugrand, Boussod, the Duke de Brissac, Mr. Cambrefort, Baron de Carayon La Tour, Count Chandon de Briailles, the Marquis de Chasseloup-Laubat, Mr. Dupuytrem, Count d'Esterno, Baron André de Fleury, Mr. Alfred Gallard, Gordon Bennett, Jusserand, Count de Lorge, Frédéric Mallet, and André Toutain. For the most part, I allowed La Rochefoucauld complete freedom in making his selection, but in general his choices met with my approval, in any event. I believe that it would have been impossible to form a committee of men who were at the same time as devoted to sports, as imbued with the spirit of athletics, and as personally disinterested as were these.

The first meeting was held on May 29, 1898 at La Rochefoucauld's private residence, where the official headquarters of the Committee were located. The preliminary program that we submitted was approved and sent to the newspapers immediately. The day after that meeting, I received a letter from Henri Desgrange, who was eager to make his velodrome in the Parc des Princes available to us. He wrote, "I have a lawn measuring 26,000 square meters, a 666-meter track, and everything you need for foot races, tennis, cycling, etc. The only thing I can't give you is the Seine". At the same time, Mr. Pierre Lafitte offered us his newspaper, *La Vie au grand air* [Outdoor Life], as an official publication, and Mr. Pierre Giffard thanked us profusely for entrusting organization of the swimming events to the *Vélo*, of which he was director. Promises of cooperation came flooding in from abroad. The Amateur Athletic Associations of England, Ireland, and Scotland, the Dansk Idraets Forbund, and the University of Philadelphia were the first to sign on. In addition, a Russian committee formed by General de Boutovsky, a member of the International Committee, and by Mr. Lebedeff, delegate to the Congress of Le Havre, had formed. Finally, the "powerful team" that all of Australasia planned to put together to represent it in Europe that year had received orders at the last minute not to set out. Its visit was postponed for eighteen months in order to coincide with the Paris Olympic Games. Our Australian colleague, Mr. Cuff, informed me of this on September 18.

I have not yet presented the program for the Games. In athletic sports, it included the traditional 100, 400, 800, and 1,500 meter races, and the 110 meter hurdles, the various jumps and throws, and a general championship given the bizarre name of pentathlon, bizarre in that it consisted of only four events. Gymnastics included the climbing rope, various pull-ups on the horizontal bar, ring exercises, parallel bars, the pommel horse, and weights. Fencing featured the foil, saber, and epée for amateurs and (by way of exception because of Sweden), for instructors. There were also English and French-style boxing, single stick and baton fencing, and Swiss and Roman-style wrestling. Water sports included sailing races, river races for yachts less than five tons, and sea races for twenty-ton yachts. There were rowing competitions for one, two, four, and eight-man teams. Swimming events included the 100, 500, and 1,000 meters, with diving, life-saving, and water polo competitions. Cycling featured a 2,000-meter speed race without coaches, a 100-kilometer long distance race with coaches, and a tandem race, 3,000 meters on a track, without coaches. The cycling events were those that the Union Vélocipédique de France had chosen for Athens in 1896, at my request. The gymnastics portion was put together by Mr. Strehly.

How could we pull this program off? The plan was very simple. Circumstances obliged us to deal with the second Olympiad quite differently from the first. It was absolutely essential to *scatter* the competitions around, in terms of location and date alike. There was no point in trying to group sports and festivals together to create a "Two-Week Olympic Event", the brilliance of which would always be overshadowed by the neighboring World's Fair. Earlier on, we had not considered the problematic side, from this particular perspective, of choosing the year 1900. At the very least, there was one bright side: the scattering of the events made them much less expensive and much easier to organize. Yachting was to take place at Le Havre and at Meulan, through the auspices of the Union des Yachts Français and the Cercle de la Voile de Paris. Rowing would also take place on the Seine. The *Vélo* was responsible for swimming. The island of Puteaux was to be the site of lawn tennis competition. Golf and archery were to go to Compiègne, open-air tennis to the Luxembourg palace, and polo to Bagatelle. The championships in sword, saber, and foil would be entrusted to the Société d'Encouragement de l'Escrime. The velodrome at the Parc des Princes would do nicely for the cycling championships, not to mention the velodrome at Buffalo which was also available. Several of our colleagues who liked Henri Desgrange's proposal were thinking of concentrating other competitions at his site, such as athletics and football, for example. I was opposed to this plan because as a token of acknowledgment, for which I was to be singularly well compensated, I had reserved the athletics competitions for the Racing-Club and the football competitions for the Stade Français. These were founding clubs in the Union des Sports Athlétiques, or "senior members" as they were known. Since they had gone to great lengths, it seemed only fair to me that they should have a place of honor.

What was our financial plan? It, too, was quite simple. As had been my custom before, I assumed responsibility for all the advertising, telegrams, correspondence, etc. In approaching each of the associations whose assistance we were soliciting, we used the following terms: "Every year, you organize a major athletic event. In 1900, would you simply give that event an international character, with greater solemnity than usual. In return, we will exempt you from having to provide the prizes to be awarded, which means significant savings for you". The issue of prizes was, in turn, solved in the following manner: we sought and obtained the gracious cooperation of three artists whom we had selected from among the most renowned in France. One of them sculpted a statuette for us, the second fashioned a medal. The third designed a diploma. The molds and plates were to be broken once the number of copies needed had been made. Thanks to this combination of arrangements, it took only a few thousand francs to cover all the expenses of the Second Olympiad, and we were already practically assured of receiving twice that amount. As I have already implied, there were not to be any festivals in the usual sense of the term. The real festival would be the spectacle of the World's Fair itself, every evening. It would have been absurd to try to compete with such an attraction. The receptions hosted by Charles de La Rochefoucauld in the sumptuous settings at his disposal would be the only festivals held by the Olympic organization.

Nearly all the associations in question had already been sounded out and had warmly welcomed our activities when an obstacle arose in an area that took me quite by surprise. There had already been an unusual cry of alarm from America. Some of the "leaders" of the Amateur Athletic Union had schemed to get control of the Games. One of them, in particular, with the assistance of the American commissioner to the World's Fair, had advanced plans for a gigantic club that he sought to build within the grounds of the Fair. He planned to surround it with playing fields where various competitions would be held under the control of the Amateur Athletic Union. Despite quasi-official support from his government, the ingenious promoter was obliged to withdraw his plans, which had met with disapproval on the part of some of his fellow countrymen. Caspar Whitney, then a member of the International Committee for the United States and whose opinions in athletic matters carried a great deal of weight, wrote to me on June 29, 1898, to alert me to the need to be wary of this individual. A little later, he wrote, "Above all, have nothing whatsoever to do with the Amateur Athletic Union and the crowd that runs it. That federation does nothing for the good of sports, and its directors think of nothing but promoting themselves. They are a kind of politician, etc". He gave free rein to his indignation on this point, at great length. For a while, the idea persisted of organizing competitions among Americans only at the Paris World's Fair, under the pretext of "showing the French how to train to succeed in sports". In time, that idea faded away on its own.

Then the real obstacle arose. It was very skillfully arranged in the name of the Union des Sports Athlétiques. Ardent speakers addressed the committees of the Racing-Club and the Stade Français, managing to get them to reject our proposals. From the start, I had noticed a certain reticence on their part, but I could not determine the reason for it. Their reticence was explained and clarified when the governing board of the Union approved and disclosed an agenda one evening in November, 1898, in which the Union stated in advance that it would reserve its support exclusively for whatever organizing efforts were made in 1900 by the city of Paris or by the government of France.

Why *exclusively*? The reason was that at the time, the U.S.F.S.A., which was angling for a government subsidy, was trying to rid itself dramatically "of the counts and marquis" by whom it was, apparently, encumbered. One member wrote to me the day after this memorable meeting, adding these provocative and nasty words: "Your inferiority is that you have no ribbons to hand out". Best of all was the fact that for the previous two years, against my better judgment, my name continued to appear on the lists of the U.S.F.S.A. as secretary general. At that point, I said that I had had enough. Mr. de Janzé, reminding me that he "was not in the least attached to the honor of being president of the Union, and had remained as such only at my insistent urging", decided to leave the organization, as well.

The agenda approved by the Union, being merely a maneuvering tactic, was not very significant in and of itself. In the letter I quoted above, Mr. de Janzé declared it unenforceable. The hostility to the Fair that they had banked on did not exist. In organizing the 1900 Olympic Games, as was our right, we remained firmly resolved not to stand in the way of any official initiatives abroad, should they arise, though that possibility that seemed to be growing less and less likely. But many petty, personal and unfulfilled ambitions and much trifling, aggravated envy were stirred to action on the basis of this incident. Ringleaders tried to blow the affair out of proportion. A vast intrigue developed that, in the end, affected the Organizing Committee of the Games. Charles de La Rochefoucauld grew fearful, and in a moment of panic that he regretted afterwards, he resigned in the early months of 1899. I allowed myself to be influenced by my disillusionment at what had just happened. In addition, I was harassed "in the name of patriotism" so that French athleticism could be presented in 1900 "united and without divisions". I gave in, and I was wrong.

Les apprêts de la deuxième Olympiade, in:
Une Campagne de vingt-et-un ans (1887-1908).
Paris 1909, pp. 136-145 (Chap. XV).

4.2.2/11 THE MEETING OF THE OLYMPIC GAMES (PARIS 1900)[1]

The Olympic Games of ancient times brought the Greek world together every four years in the beautiful valley of Olympia, to contemplate a spectacle, the uniformity of which seems to have constituted an additional charm in the eyes of the spectators.

From the start, they knew almost exactly what they were going to see, and they were delighted in knowing it. In this respect, the inclination of the modern world is entirely different: our contemporaries take pleasure in variety and novelty, for two reasons – first, because the facility and rapidity of our means of transport have intensified their curiosity; and, second, because, as the duration of their existence has not been prolonged in proportion to the number of objects soliciting their attention, they have not the leisure to see the same things twice.

When, nearly ten years ago, I conceived the plan of reviving the Olympic Games in a modern form, it was necessary for me to observe this tendency and take it into account. Today, as in former times, the Olympic Games respond to a natural and healthy inclination of humanity in all times and in all countries. If young men are active and in good health, they will be fond of manly games and competitions in which they display their strength and agility, and, incited by the instinct of emulation, they will desire to contend, in the name of their country, against young men of other countries. But, as regards the arrangement of these periodical festivals, the situation has changed, and the sole means of insuring their success and of rendering them as splendid and brilliant as possible, consists in giving them a great variety of aspect.

This is the reason why the International Congress which met in Paris in June, 1894, decided, at my request, that each of the new Olympiads should be celebrated in a different city of the world, and why Athens was chosen as the scene of the first Olympic meeting in 1896. Paris was to be the second, four years later. Personally, I cannot repress a strong desire that the third Olympic Games, those of 1904, should take place at New York. By choosing New York the distinctly cosmopolitan character of my enterprise will be clearly shown.

Where variety is concerned, I have good reason to rejoice; for nothing will resemble the festivals at Athens in 1896 less than those at Paris in 1900. We have not been drawn into the error of constructing a cardboard Stadium to reproduce that of Pericles, with the hill of Montmartre in the background to replace the Acropolis on its rock. This would have been ridiculous and paltry. We began by considering with good reason that there was no need to trouble ourselves with the preparation of amusements and special festivities, because the Exposition in itself would constitute a permanent festival full of attractions, and hence the organizing committee need only be engaged with the technical part of the sport in question. It appeared that at Athens this point had been rather neglected, because the committee was also engaged with the interests of the spectators, and had to take measures for their amusement, for the decoration of the sights and monuments, and for the preparation of attractions of all kinds, in order to bring the largest numbers of spectators and to detain them. The same anxiety does not exist now and the interests of the athletes predominate above everything else.

I

The Olympic organization founded by the Congress of 1894 is very simple. It consists of an International Committee, of which I have the honor to be President, which numbers about twenty members belonging to the chief nationalities of Europe and America. These include, for example, Prince Serge Beliosselsky for Russia, Lord Ampthill for England, Count Brunetta d'Usseaux for Italy, Commandant Balck for Sweden, Baron de Tuyll for Holland, Professor William M. Sloane, of the University of Columbia, for the United States, etc. The whole business of the International Committee consists in promoting the celebration of the Games, and in deciding in what country they shall take place. This being done, the International Committee leaves the immediate preparations for the Games to the sub-committee appointed for that purpose, contenting itself with seconding this subcommittee and supporting it abroad with all its influence. The committee which organized the Olympic Games at Athens in 1896 was not nominated by the government, but by the Crown Prince, who presided over it. That of 1900 has been appointed by the French Government, and is placed under the direction of a Delegate General, M. Merillon, a former deputy, now a magistrate, a most distinguished, agreeable and competent man. A statement of the plans for the preparation of the different competitions may interest my readers.

There are ten sections. The first comprises Athletic Sports and Games; the second, Gymnastics; the third, Fencing; the fourth, Shooting; the fifth, Equestrian Sports; the sixth, Cycling; the seventh, Motor Car Racing; the eighth, Aquatic Sports; the ninth Firemen's Drill; the tenth, Ballooning. It might be objected to this classification that it includes neither Alpine Climbing nor Skating; that, on the other hand, Firemen's Drill is not a sport, and that balloons and the art of guiding them is still in its infancy. But it is impossible to obtain a faultless classification, or to contrive that all kinds of sport without exception should be seen at the same meeting. If, as has been suggested, Sweden should some day organize Olympic Winter Games in ice and snow, they will include Tobogganing, Snow-shoes and Skis, but they will be forced to exclude Cricket, Football and Foot Races. It is an amusing paradox to consider that, in order to completely render the Olympic Games, one would have to go to St. Moritz in the Swiss Engadine, where sun and snow are abundant all winter that men skate in flannel slippers, and women open their parasols when going for a sleigh-ride. There, indeed, one might, if forced to do so, combine summer sports with those of winter.

Meanwhile, there is the question of spring in Paris, and the restrictions imposed by the place and climate must not be forgotten. On the other hand, the current programme is sufficiently complete to provide most interesting competitions. Thus, the first section comprises athletic sports, foot races, jumping, etc., and games. The distances of the foot races are those of the French championships, in which the best English runners have taken part on several occasions

1 In the original text the word "Olympian" was used. In order to prevent any confusion among the reader it was changed into "Olympic".It is not clear if Coubertin himself or somebody else translated the text into English. The amount of orthographical mistakes shows that the writer definitely did not speak English as his mother tongue.

SEUL PROGRAMME OFFICIEL — Prix : 20 CENTIMES

République Française

EXPOSITION UNIVERSELLE DE 1900

Réunion Internationale

COURSES A PIED & CONCOURS ATHLÉTIQUES

AMATEURS

ORGANISÉS LE

JEUDI 19 JUILLET

à DEUX Heures

SUR LE TERRAIN DU **RACING-CLUB de FRANCE** (PELOUSE DE LA CROIX-CATELAN, AU BOIS DE BOULOGNE)

PAR

l'Union des Sociétés Françaises de Sports Athlétiques

Président d'honneur : MONSIEUR LE MINISTRE DU COMMERCE.

Vice-Président d'honneur : M. **RABIER**, Directeur de l'Enseignement Secondaire au Ministère de l'Instruction Publique.

Président: M. le Baron **Pierre de COUBERTIN**, Président du Comité International des Jeux Olympiques.

The official programme of the Athletics Championships held in Paris in 1900 does not state that these were in fact the Olympic Games. Nevertheless, Coubertin is not only referred to as president of this event, but also as president of the IOC. (Archives of the City of Paris)

within the last ten years. That is to say, the distances are nearly the same. If the "100 yards" has become 100 metres, and the "one mile" 1,500 metres (instead of 1609, the exact equivalent of the mile), the hurdle race corresponds exactly to the English distance; the hurdles are of the same height, and they are arranged in the same manner. As to the running competitions, the long and high jumps, pole-vaulting, and putting the weight, are performed in the same fashion. The games entered as international are Football (Rugby and Association), Hockey, Cricket, Lawn Tennis, Croquet and Golf; there will also be a match at Bowls. All these games are played in France. There are others, such as Baseball, La Crosse, etc., of which only exhibitions can be given, as they are not played in France. For example, if the American residents in Paris succeed in forming a baseball team to play another team from America, this contest will receive the patronage and support of the Committee of the Exposition, which might give a prize; but it will necessarily retain an American-that is to say, a purely national – character.

Gymnastics are only open to foreign gymnasts as individuals. Gymnastic societies will not be invited to compete in groups, but to send their best gymnasts to take part in the international championship, which will be individual.

Several gymnastic festivals reserved for French societies will only take place during the course of the Exposition. This is a prudent decision; in adhering to it, no attempt has been made to exclude certain nations whilst admitting others, but the aim has been to avoid trouble and dispute. Gymnastic societies, to whatever country they belong, always behave in a more or less martial fashion; they march in military order, preceded by their national flag. After the troubled circumstances of late years, it would be a delicate affair to unite the flags of recent opponents upon the field of contest.

Fencing of course includes matches with foils, with sabres, and with swords. One can foresee a fine contest, in which the French and Italian schools will be opposed, and will establish their respective merits in a sensational manner. Boxing will, of course, be subdivided into English and French boxing. It is impossible to combine the two methods, which has been sufficiently proved by the recent match which took place in Paris between Charlemont, our best French boxing champion, and Driscoll, a second-rate English boxer. No doubt, the contest will give rise to some difficulty with regard to the rules to be observed, for these are not yet drawn up with all the desirable clearness.

Then the Equestrian and Aquatic sports follow, i. e., polo, and rowing, sailing and swimming matches. There had been some debate about having an equestrian competition in the real sense of the term, but the difficulties of transporting valuable horses, especially during Exposition time, are so great that the idea has been abandoned. There will be target-shooting, pigeon-shooting, archery, and shooting with the cross-bow and with firearms. There will be a whole week of track-racing, preceded by a sensational twenty-four hours' race for cyclists. Finally, the seventh, ninth and tenth sections will include motor-car races, competitions of sappers and firemen, free balloon races, and trials of carrier-pigeons. All this is doubtless interesting; but it is not pure sport, and for that reason I shall pass it over in this paper.

II

To judge by the series of letters I have received for many months American athletes appear to be desirous of participating in large numbers in the Olympic Games on the banks of the Seine and, as the opportunity of imparting information is afforded me by the *NORTH AMERICAN REVIEW*, I wish to take advantage of it by replying, as far as possible, to all the questions that I have been asked. These questions are generally the following: What will the competitions consist of ? Who will organize them ? When and where will they take place ? Will they be reserved for amateurs ? As to the first question I have already given an explanation. On the second, there is only one word to add -the business of preparing the competitions of 1900 has been assigned to the most competent individuals and societies. For some time the directors of the Exposition appeared to be wanting in interest for sport. Thereupon, a private committee was formed with the object of organizing the Olympic Games, since the Exposition seemed on the point of renouncing them. Last spring, or rather later, the point was reconsidered, and it was decided that sporting competitions should in some way or another form part of the Exposition.

But the Directors, not having the necessary competence, appealed to the societies. This appeal was answered, and with striking unanimity offers were made to assist the Official Organizing Committee presided over by M. Merillon. Thus, the Paris Polo Club, presided over by Vicomte de la Rochefoucauld, has undertaken the preparation of polo matches; the Society for the Encouragement of Fencing, of which M. de Villeneuve is the devoted director, is empowered to arrange the fencing contests; athletic sports are entrusted to the care of the French Athletic Union, which is not only the most important in France, but also is connected by treaty with the celebrated Amateur Athletic Association of England. Lawn Tennis is directed by the Société de l'Ile de Puteaux, founded by M. de Janzé. These suffices show that, in all branches of sport, care has been taken to enlist competent aid, and this is certainly not an insignificant detail. In how many circumstances have these very athletic competitions failed, for lack of competence in those by whom they were arranged ?

At the request of my American friends, I made it a special point that the athletic sports should take place toward the middle of July. In this way the athletes of the American universities, on their arrival in Europe, can take part in the English championships, which take place on the first Saturday in July, and thence travel to the Continent to take part in those of Paris. The gymnastic championship will also be held in July. For fencing, the period chosen is from May 15th to June 15th. The polo matches will take place in succession from June 1st to June 20th. The cycling will take place in September, about the 8th; the rowing matches in June, the swimming in July. Generally speaking, the competitions, with the exception of football, which is a winter game, will be held between May 15th and September 15th. This is, doubtless, too long a period; it would have been better for the whole to have taken place in the period of six weeks, but the Commissary-General of the Exposition insisted on the duration being prolonged as long as possible, and his desire was acceded.

Just as the competitions will not all take place at the same time, they will not all be held at the same place. Vincennes had been first chosen as capable of uniting them all; but although possessing a wood which almost rivals that of Boulogne situated on the other side of Paris, just at the other extremity, Vincennes does not offer the indispensable conditions to certain sports. It is perfectly adapted for athletic sports, gymnastics, cycling and lawn tennis; a cycling track of fine dimensions is already in course of construction; there will be tracks for the foot races and good tennis grounds. But it lacks the space for golf, shooting and polo; as for the lakes, there can be no question of having the rowing, still less the sailing, competitions upon them. It is therefore almost decided that the shooting will take place at Satory, near Versailles, on the ordinary exercising ground of the troops garrisoned in Paris; that the polo matches will he played on the Polo Club ground in the Bois de Boulogne; that the rowing competitions will take place at Courbevoie, and the sailing competitions at Meulan, two pretty spots in the neighborhood of Paris, where the Seine is wide and straight. As for the golf matches, in order to find good links one will have to go to Compiègne, an hour's railway journey from Paris. The Society of Sport at Compiègne has made links which would satisfy the wishes of the most exacting players.

The most important question-that of amateurism still remains. As different countries have not the same definition of an amateur, one can imagine the difficulties that arise when it is proposed to include representatives of all nations in the same competition. With regard to this point, the conditions are not the same for all branches of sport. The gentlemen who shoot pigeons or who take part in a yacht race look forward to gaining cash prizes, and are not disqualified on that account. In fencing, there are no professionals, strictly speaking, but, on the other hand, professors fence with amateurs; and only recently all the competitions have shown both to be in equal numbers, and no prizes of any kind were ever given-they fought for honor alone. Personally, convinced as I am that amateurism is one of the first conditions of the progress and prosperity of sport, I have never ceased to work for it; and when in 1894 I proposed to revive the Olympic Games, it was with the idea that they would always be reserved for amateurs only. This time, however, a slightly different theory has prevailed. It was decided that if it was necessary to reserve the first rank for pure amateurs, and in all cases to guard against any person suspected of the slightest taint of professionalism slipping in amongst them, it would be right to have classes for professionals too. Therefore, there will be special competitions, but the line of demarcation between amateurs and professionals will be strictly laid down and closely adhered to.

The motive which, perhaps, has chiefly influenced this decision is as follows: We are at the beginning of a new century, and the Paris Exposition is certainly a unique, almost an exceptional, occasion for attracting and bringing together representatives of foreign nations of all classes. Therefore, it is a matter of importance to establish records which will be a sort of athletic starting-point for the twentieth century. The amateurs and professionals, without intermingling in the least, will be able to see each other at work, and comparisons which will be of advantage for sport will be the result. I do not say that I am a convert to this way of thinking; it is not my own, and I shall do everything in my power that the following Olympic Games may revert to the true theory of amateurism, which declares the uselessness of the professional and desires his disappearance. But I am now explaining another view of the question, which is not without interest, and which may be accepted, because by maintaining an absolute separation between amateurs and professionals, it prevents the former from losing their quality as amateurs by co-mingling with the latter. The direct and personal interests of amateurs will thus be protected and safeguarded in 1900, and that is the important point.

III

I hope I have sufficiently characterized the competitions of the Exposition of 1900 by giving these details, it may be seen that above all it will be a sporting manifestation of great interest. The fact of the coincidence of the Exposition has the advantage of relieving the organizers of all other anxiety. It is certain that there will be no lack of spectators, and it is also certain that foreign athletes will not find their stay in Paris tedious, and that they will carry away a pleasant remembrance of it. Perhaps on this account it may be as well to remark that the exaggerated statements of the expenses visitors will incur are without foundation. Paris is one of those cities which possess the greatest number of hotels, even in proportion to the enormous number of foreigners who visit it on this kind of occasion; they are of all descriptions; there are many of those modest, picturesque and comfortable hotels which are never seen in the New World; in view of the Exposition others will be added to those which already exist. All this constitutes a guarantee that competition will prevent the prices from being raised beyond reasonable limits. But I could not too strongly recommend the teams who wish to take part in the athletic competitions to intrust the care of preparing and engaging lodgings and making the necessary arrangements for food, etc., only to managers who speak French well, and are accustomed to life in Paris or French life in general. Not only, by acting like this, the team gain great saving of expenses, but they will have the chance of being more comfortably lodged and much better served. It is unnecessary to mention that the sporting societies, and especially the French Athletic Union, which has its offices in Paris, at 229 rue St. Honoré, will take pleasure in assisting foreigners coming from all over the world the best they can.

They are coming in very large numbers. In the course of last summer I visited several European towns, in order to make arrangements with the members of our International Olympic Committee, and I found a strong desire everywhere to persuade representatives of all kinds of sport to compete in Paris. What struck me during this journey was the astonishing progress made by sport in the last ten years. Anglo-Saxons have some trouble in getting used to the idea that other nations can successfully devote themselves to athleticism. I can understand this and the feeling can certainly be excused, for they are the ones who, especially for the last fifty years, have best understood and practiced bodily exercises. But if this honor is incontestably theirs, it does not mean that young men of other races, with blood and muscles like their own, should not be worthy of walking in their footsteps.

The countries that surprised me the most in this rapid advance were Germany and Sweden. Berlin is really on the way of becoming a great sporting centre. I visited the rowing clubs which succeed each other along the banks of the Spree, at the gates of the capital with interest; they are rich and prosperous. It has to be noted that the Emperor takes great interest in rowing; from his private purse he has built a club for the students at the Berlin colleges, and he has founded imperial regattas, which he gives important prizes every year, and which he often presides over in person. After what I have seen I should be very surprised, if Germany had not a very fine sporting future to come. It already builds and manufactures boats and all kinds of sporting articles, and this industry seems very prosperous, a proof that a market exists.

Neither the English nor the French purchase sporting implements from Germany. As for Sweden, the progress of sport was impeded for a long time by the rather exorbitant pretensions of the famous Swedish Gymnastics, who, having cured numbers of invalids and strengthened countless children, laid claim to suffice also for young men, and to supply the place of manly games and exercises of strength for them. This is, of course, not the case, and the fact that, by the action of the Crown Prince and representatives of gymnastics, with Major Balck at their head, all kinds of sport are practiced more and more, clearly indicates that no system of gymnastics, however complete and scientific it may be, can supply the place of their beneficent action. There are notably two establishments at Stockholm, Tattersall and Idrottspacken, which include all kinds of sport, from riding to skating, in conditions absolutely worthy of the finest American clubs of New York, Chicago or Boston.

At Vienna, in Austria, an athletic club has recently been opened in the celebrated Prater; the building, which is very elegant, is surrounded by football and lawn tennis grounds and tracks for cycling and foot-races. Finally, even at St. Petersburg, where they are behind in this respect, a movement in favor of physical exercises is noticeable. It is thus clear that sport is gradually spreading over the whole world, and taking the place of unhealthy amusements and evil pleasures in the lives of young men. This fact will please all true friends of youth and progress. Doubtless, one can discern and regret certain abuses. These may be found in everything; but when one compares the abuses which sport causes with those to which it puts an end, one cannot refrain from singing its praises and laboring for its propagation.

It is for this very purpose that I have revived the Olympic Games, and everything I have said here encourages me in this task. It has enemies, like every other free and living work, but it also has stanch friends who are of great assistance. It is to these that I appeal to prepare from this time onwards the celebration in America of the Olympic Games of 1904, in the belief that they will be a great success, and that they will draw qualified representatives of all the sporting societies of the world across the ocean, for a manifestation which will be worthy of the noble and ancient Olympic past and of the glorious future of the great American Republic.

In: The North American Review, Vol. CLXX, June 1900, pp. 802-811.

4.2.2/12 THE SECOND OLYMPIAD (PARIS 1900)

Eleven years earlier, I had met with such immediate understanding, practical good sense, and encouragement from the three directors of the 1889 Universal Exhibition, particularly Mr. Georges Berger and Mr. Alphand, that I had naively counted on the same support in 1900. Having agreed to the new idea of encouraging school sport in France, how could anyone, in 1900, refuse when it came to an undertaking like the revival of Olympism after its success in Athens and the interest it had met with in the press? But a dictatorship of one had replaced the flexible triumvirate, and like a great many remarkable men, the General Commissioner in 1900, Mr. Alfred Picard, was averse to "taking over" somebody else's idea. Our one and only conversation dated back many years, to January 30, 1894 in fact, several days before the revival of the Olympic Games. Right from the start, he disliked the idea of including the *second* Olympiad within the Paris Universal Exhibition; nor was he any more enthusiastic about the related idea of having a separate sports section – both modern and retrospective – which I had put to him the same day in the form of a project signed by myself and Mr. G. Strehly, a teacher at the Lycée Montaigne and a famous Hellenist and gymnast. The project comprised building within the precincts of the Exhibition or its immediate surroundings a reproduction

Women competed in the Olympics for the first time in Paris in 1900, in golf (taken from La Vie au Grand Air, no.109, 1900, p.727)

of the Altis of Olympia. Inside the monuments were to be grouped all the objects and documentation concerning sport, from Antiquity and the Middle Ages to the modern era. While assuring us of his friendly interest, Mr. Picard had obviously "filed away" the scheme in the back of his mind and was only waiting for the opportunity of consigning it to some dusty archive. We never received the promised summons, and when, three years later, the official catalogue of the Exhibition appeared, sportsmen were horrified to see that skating had been put in the cutlery section, rowing in lifesaving, sports associations in social welfare, etc. I had realized long before that as far as the Olympic Games were concerned there was nothing to be expected from Mr. Alfred Picard, who had even been approached by Mr. A. Ribot, a former Prime Minister, but to no avail.

This being so, I determined to organize the 1900 Games free of any outside interference by means of a private committee, of which the Vicomte de La Rochefoucauld had agreed not only to act as President but also to allow its offices to be installed in the La Rochefoucauld mansion, in the rue de Varennes in Paris. The plan seemed exceedingly daring at first sight; in actual fact, it was far less so. My reasoning was as follows: the organizers of the Exhibition were planning, according to the admirable pleonasm a zealous civil servant had invented, to hold a number of "Physical training and sports competitions". The whole idea was doomed from the start and; in any case, in view of the site chosen (Vincennes), the multitude of committees and sub-committees, and the enormity of the program (they were planning to include billiards, fishing and chess), would be nothing more than a vulgar glorified fair: exactly the opposite of what we wanted the Olympic Games to be. For the athletes, in fact, we wanted to provide what they would not be able to find elsewhere. In Athens they had come in contact with antiquity in its purest form. Paris should show them the Old France with all its traditions and finest settings. The crowds would have the competitions and the festivities of the Exhibition, while we would organize Games for the elite – the elite among athletes, who would be few in number but composed of the greatest champions in the world; the elite among spectators, men and women in society, diplomats, professors, generals, and members of the Institute. For these, what could be more delightful, more charming than a garden party at Dampierre, a reception at the rue de Varennes, excursions to Esclimont or Bonnelles?

Our ideas did not stop here however. We needed a General Commissioner to be the kingpin of the whole affair. I had succeeded in persuading Robert Fournier Sarloveze to accept the job, counting on his energy and his flexible and practical intelligence. With him came the Compiègne Sports Club, its fine playing fields, its pleiad of keen, friendly members. Athletic sports, footraces, and competitions would be left to the Racing Club to organize as a token of gratitude for the support it had given in the promotion of school sport. For the same reason, football would be the prerogative of the Stade Français. In this way, the two founding clubs of the USFSA would be fittingly honored for all their pains. The Société d'Encouragement de l'Escrime promised its support; others too offered theirs...

To fully understand the ambitiousness of such a plan, the reader must make an effort of imagination and try to visualize the state of affairs thirty years ago. In those days, nothing could be more difficult than trying to persuade a number of spectators to attend a sports meeting. Such meetings roused little interest. Only cycle-racing tracks sometimes succeeded in drawing the crowds. When, a few years earlier, the Racing Club had been visited by the fine team of the Manhattan Athletic Club of New York, admissions barely covered two-thirds of the cost. The following year, the first Anglo-French football match to be played in France had ended in a sizeable deficit in spite of the fact that it was presided over by the new Ambassador to France, Lord Dufferin. And when, shortly afterwards, the first eights rowing match held at Andresy against the London Rowing Club ended in a French victory, to the polite but nevertheless great surprise of our guests, public opinion attached very little importance to the event. How could you expect otherwise? Sport, according to a university professor, was a mere "recreation" and should not be expected to be anything else. Public opinion was still in the same rut...

The first meeting of the Organizing Committee of the 1900 Olympic Games was held in the La Rochefoucauld mansion. It was a great success. The Committee consisted of about forty members, eighteen of whom were appointed as stewards and placed in this capacity in charge of different sports. They included Marius Dubonnet and E. Caillat for rowing, Bruneau de Laborie for boxing, Hebrard de Villeneuve and Count Potocki for fencing, Jacques de Pourtalès for golf, Jean de Bellet for tennis, etc. The program was the same as in Athens, only restored to its original form, that is to say with the addition of boxing and polo, and slightly amplified in certain details for other sports. Shooting was left out, while archery was added. A Mountaineering Prize was offered for the most remarkable climb made anywhere in the world since the 1896 Games.

The press – especially of the right, but also of the left – gave the idea a warm reception. Individual sportsmen seemed satisfied. On June 16, 1898 Henri Desgrange placed the Parc des Princes Velodrome at our disposal; then Giffard took over the organization of the swimming contests and Pierre Laffite offered us the use of his *Vie au Grand Air* as official publication. Mr. Molier spoke of a gala performance at his famous circus and Count Potocki of a gymkhana to be given by the Etrier Riding Club. Abroad, people had been waiting a long time to hear the official plans. Confidence was immediately restored. Everyone set to work with a will. Letters from Mr. de Bousies and General de Boutovski announced the creation of committees in Belgium and Russia; and from Australia, L. A. Cuff promised – to use his own words – "a powerful team".

We were about to start arranging the athletes' accommodation mainly by building well-equipped, well-situated camps (athletes were not so particular in those days), when everything seemed to go wrong. I must have been very naive not to have expected it. I had stupidly thought that the federations, whose regulations we would be applying and to whom we would leave the formation of the juries and the running of the contests, would find these responsibilities sufficient reward to interest them in the project. And the decorations? Good heavens, I had forgotten the decorations! In France, what madness on my part! Unless we were to create our own "International Order" we would not have a single green, yellow, or purple ribbon to pin on anybody. Impossible, moreover, to count on any Olympic "honors" in the rewards handed out by the Exhibition.

Tension grew. E. Caillat had already warned me that "the French Rowing Federation was making a tremendous fuss". At the Town Hall, they were denouncing the gathering of "counts and marquesses" who were meeting at the rue de Varennes. On November 9, 1898, the USFSA passed a motion to break off from us, in spite of the efforts of our colleague in the IOC, Ernest Callot, who had warned us the day before of the growing unrest. The USFSA was going through an internal crisis caused by certain ambitions, which it is not my business to judge here. The repercussions of this move however were quite small. The official organization of the Exhibition's competitions was not progressing and nobody had any confidence in the General Commissariat in this respect. Our difficulties had increased, but they had not become insoluble. Abroad, the Committee was known as the "La Rochefoucauld Committee". A complication arose as a result of a most unexpected American move. Colonel H... had arrived in Paris, bearing a plan for the organization of a Sports Exhibition coming under the United States Commission; there would be playing fields, competitions... so as to "teach other countries what real sport was like". Nothing could have been more misplaced than such a move. Unfortunately the American Commission seemed to encourage the idea and Mr. Picard (unexpectedly) appeared favorable. I took care not to show any hostility. I even maintained very courteous relations with the Colonel for nearly a year. I was convinced that his project was not practicable. There was no need to oppose it therefore, but it did add to the general confusion. As far as the Exhibition was concerned, there seemed to be no progress. "All other powers are suspect", I had been told confidentially, "and, in *his* eyes (the eyes of the General Commissioner), only the scribes of the Commissariat possess the qualities required to organize the sports

Première Année. — N° 35. Huit pages : CINQ centimes Dimanche 6 Octobre 1889.

Le Petit Parisien

TOUS LES SAMEDIS
SUPPLÉMENT LITTÉRAIRE
5 CENTIMES

SUPPLÉMENT LITTÉRAIRE ILLUSTRÉ

TOUS LES JOURS
Le Petit Parisien
5 CENTIMES

DISTRIBUTION DES RÉCOMPENSES DE L'EXPOSITION AU PALAIS-DE-L'INDUSTRIE

Le Défilé devant la Tribune du Président de la République.

Prize-giving ceremony at the World Exhibition held at the Palais de l'Industrie in Paris in 1900. Parade in front of the President of France. A comparison with the Olympic Games Closing Ceremony springs to mind. Olympic medals were also presented at the end of the Games until 1932. They were presented by the respective Head of State in 1896, 1912, 1920 and 1928. (N.Müller Collection)

events properly". Finally, on February 19, 1899, Daniel Merillon was appointed Director General of these competitions. He was not exactly the man needed, but it meant that there was at least "someone". The slight conflicts referred to above did not lessen the cordiality of our relations. It seemed to me that we could come to an agreement with him and, without actually merging the two groups, form some sort of association in order to achieve a decent celebration of the Second Olympiad. Mr. Ribot approached Mr. Alfred Picard again but once more came up against his stubborn opposition to the Olympic Games, which he dismissed as an "anachronism".

Meanwhile, Charles de La Rochefoucauld became the subject of subversive attacks, which I never tried to get to the bottom of because I was afraid I might discover the work of a friend who would be diminished in my eyes as a result. Certain social rivalries are sometimes excusable although far from glorious. Anyhow, on April 22 the session suddenly became exceedingly stormy and ended abruptly with a sensational resignation. We managed to find another President; there was one at hand. As for our General Secretary, Fournier-Sarloveze, he was not one to be easily put aside. But I measured the hazards that were suddenly looming, the little time that was left, the disadvantage of appearing divided nationally in an international context. We should have consulted the IOC, but time was running short. I therefore allowed the Organizing Committee to vote its own dissolution. It authorized me to write to Mr. Merillon as I thought fit. I informed the latter privately and he immediately thanked me in a very warm reply. We then agreed on the terms of an official letter that I sent him on May 15. Several months had passed since his appointment, but this seemed to be the whole extent of the Commissariat's work. Merillon, however, did not remain inactive. He had proposed a certain number of measures that were considered indispensable, but no reply had been given. I have a letter from him in which he informs me of his annoyance and says that he had threatened to resign if his proposals were not immediately put into effect – then another, joyful, exultant "Everything is signed. We are *at last* going to be able to set to work". At last! In fact, it was already too late.

On June 5, 1899, Mr. Bikelas, Count Brunetta d'Usseaux who had joined the IOC the year before, and I met at Merillon's house. Our host was mainly worried about the other countries, whose committees set up for the Exhibition could be of no help and in which he felt that it was only our colleagues that could save the day. He had asked me to send them a circular, which I did immediately. I even suggested taking advantage of a proposed journey to central and northern Europe to speed up the efforts of members of the IOC. The purpose of this journey was to collect information with a view to writing a series of reports on "The Future of Europe", which I had promised for *"L'Indépendance Belge"*, and which in fact came out in the autumn. Merillon would have liked me to extend my journey to include as many countries as possible, with a view to helping to the maximum the undertaking for which he was responsible, but Mr. Picard refused to grant him the necessary funds. I assured Merillon that wherever I went I would serve his cause all the more fervently as it was also my own, owing to the fact that we were having to make do with "the Competitions of the Exhibition" instead of the Olympic Games: a poor and clumsy title we had had to accept for the time being for want of something more elegant and appropriate.

My first stop was Berlin. During my fairly long visit, I was able, without detracting from the main study I was carrying out, to observe the state of mind of sports officials. It was not exactly excellent. The Imperial Government, however, showed a great deal of interest in the Paris Exhibition and had given tangible proof of it. As a matter of fact, the following year the German section was to be one of the chief attractions of this Exhibition on the Champ de Mars and make a big contribution towards improving relations between the two countries. In 1899, such an eventuality seemed a long way off. A meeting was held in the Palast, arranged by the German General Commissioner, who invited me to lunch afterwards. The meeting having been somewhat strained, the lunch was rather "cold". Not that there was any deliberate ill will, but fears had been expressed regarding the moral security of the German athletes who would be coming to Paris and "might risk being insulted". These were the words used by a German in Paris in a letter to one of the delegates at the meeting, who made the mistake of reading it out loud. Prince Aribert of Anhalt was in the chair and made the even greater blunder of failing to intervene. I naturally protested. Nobody, however, suggested a German withdrawal, but it was obvious that their participation would lack enthusiasm. When one looks back and compares the attitude in those days with that of the Franco-German meetings of more recent years – even though no farther removed from equally tragic and bloody events – one can measure the remarkable progress made in sporting spirit.

In 1900, it was still only among real sportsmen that this spirit existed instinctively. The general public had no idea of it at all and, as may well be imagined, the Civil Service even less. In addition, while these gentlemen responsible for the Champ de Mars were totally lacking in sporting spirit, they were equally deficient in efficiency. Vague circulars were sent off from time to time, devoid of any useful information. By a curious paradox, it was the defunct committee, the La Rochefoucauld Committee, that continued to be regarded with confidence in other countries; and, never receiving any reply – and with good reason – it was to the President of the IOC that people turned. Complaints kept coming in. On October 11 – six months before the opening date – Caspar Whitney expressed the Americans' dissatisfaction. On the 23rd, Jiri Guth announced that everyone in Prague was completely discouraged, not knowing what was going on or what to do. Shortly afterwards came the same reproaches from Copenhagen. On all sides were heard expressions of mistrust regarding the Games "organized by that band of incompetents in Paris", as Sloane put it. Every time, I was requested to intervene. Whitney naively asked his embassy in Paris to persuade the Exhibition to give up the official plan and simply hand over "the money and the freedom to act" to those chosen by the IOC. And on April 14, 1900, Count Thun Valsessina, Franz Joseph's Chamberlain, demanded that there should be an Austrian member of the IOC "for the Paris Games"; the Canadians made the same demand.

Meanwhile the days continued to pass. Nothing concrete was being achieved... not even the acquisition of any offices except those of the new sub-committees, and of course the issuing of endless regulations. Vincennes was abandoned; no money, no stadium, no grounds. Just as members of the IOC were being asked to make up juries, the clubs were being asked as a last resort to give direct support and lend us their grounds, in particular the Racing Club for the athletic sports day. And to think that in 1898 my plan had been rejected out of hand as being "mean and unworthy of the nation".

The foot races, jumping and throwing events... were held therefore in the Bois de Boulogne on July 19, 1900, under my presidency and the honorary presidency of the Minister of Trade, Mr. Alexandre Millerand, who spent the afternoon with us and showed great interest in the exploits of the athletes; I refrained, however, from informing him of the real state of affairs, as he seemed to be so completely unaware of the whole matter. Most politicians of the time shared the opinion of the university professor I quoted above; for them, sport was something quite unimportant, only to be appreciated to a minor degree like any other healthy amusement. In this respect, bowling did not seem to them to differ in any way from football. As for Olympism, they considered it a totally superfluous, eccentric neologism. Six years later, at a banquet, the word "Olympism" still brought an incredulous, disdainful smile to the lips of the minister...who must, however, have changed his mind since.

Of the other events in 1900, I have nothing to say here. A great deal of goodwill was shown. The athletes did their best. Interesting results were achieved, but with nothing Olympic about them. According to the words of one of our colleagues, "our idea had been used, but it had been torn to shreds in the process". What he said was very true. It typifies what happened in 1900. It proved, at any rate, that we should be careful never to allow the Games to become dependent on or be taken over by a big fair where their philosophical value vanishes into thin air, and their educational merit becomes nil. Unfortunately the alliance we had concluded was more indissoluble than we thought. On two other occasions, in 1904 and 1908, for budgetary reasons, we were unable to sever our relations with exhibitions. It was not until 1912 that the break was finally completed, in Sweden. However, in this "unholy union", Olympism would at least enjoy an increasingly independent position and would no longer be reduced to the role of humiliated vassal to which it had been subjected in Paris.

Olympic Memoirs, Chap.5, Lausanne, IOC, 1997, pp.58-69.

4.2.2/13 – 4.2.2/15 INTRODUCTION

The period between the 1900 Olympic Games in Paris and the Olympic Games held in America in 1904 was, once again, not a time of great Olympic activity. For the second time since 1896, the IOC met in Paris in 1901 to assess the events that had taken place, particularly the 1900 Games, and to decide on where to award the Games for 1904. The 1904 Games were actually awarded to Chicago, but soon a dispute arose with St. Louis, which wanted to add the jewel of the Olympic Games to its 1904 World's Fair. The following selection from Coubertin's *Une Campagne de vingt-et-un ans* describes preparations for the 1904 Games from the European perspective, as well as the problems that faced Coubertin.

By awarding the Games to an American city, the president of the IOC, in keeping with the statutes of the organization, had to give up his position in favor of an American representative for four years. Yet Professor Sloane insisted that Coubertin continue directing the IOC. In addition, it was decided in Paris to call an Olympic Congress in Brussels to settle questions relating to the unification of the program of competitions and the regulations. Nevertheless, this Congress did not take place until 1905. Rather than dealing with it, Coubertin was already wrestling with the issue of the site for the Fourth Olympic Games in 1908. Since St. Louis was too far away to have the IOC meet there, he called its third Session to order in London, in 1904. That is where the Games were set to be awarded to Rome for 1908. After "three silent years during which the IOC scarcely met, and when copious correspondence was exchanged", Coubertin thought that "the time had now come for it to "come out"; it was at last ready to be shown to the world[1]". Thus the meeting at London was held with great ceremony.

It is hard to understand why Coubertin did not want to underscore his love for America by visiting the St. Louis Games. We must imagine that this was to show his irritation over a counter-movement to the Olympics, called the "International Union", guided by J. E. Sullivan, director of the Olympic competitions within the context of the World's Fair. Coubertin did not write a single article about the 1904 Games in St. Louis.

4.2.2/13 NEWS FROM CHICAGO

We have received excellent news from overseas concerning preparations in Chicago for the upcoming Olympiad. Our American friends have lost no time in getting down to work. As soon as word was out of the International Committee's decision that the 1904 Olympic Games would be held in Chicago, the local committee, formed on a temporary basis in 1900 to get the project off the ground and to attract preliminary support was transformed into a permanent association. You will recall that this committee included the best known and most influential citizens in the city. If Chicago were to be selected, they had agreed to take the necessary steps to make sure that the 1904 Games would be

1 *Olympic Memoirs*, Lausanne, IOC, 1997, p. 76.

celebrated under conditions that would make their success guaranteed. By the end of the first meeting, held last June 5, five commissioners had been appointed: Mr. H. J. Furber, Dr. W. Harper, President of the University of Chicago, Volney Foster, President of the Union League Club, J. B. Payne, a former justice of the Supreme Court of the United States, and E. A. Potter, President of the *American Trust and Saving Bank Co.*

These commissioners met on July 5, and decided to seek incorporation immediately, i.e. formal government recognition of the association formed under the name *The International Olympian Games Association.* The initial capital of the corporation was $200,000; it was incorporated for a term of ten years. Its purpose was to organize the 1904 Olympic Games. In conformity with this decision, the usual formalities were completed with the Secretary of State in Springfield, and a general meeting gave the five commissioners full authority to take the legal steps needed to establish the corporation. In addition, the general meeting decided that a certain number of sub-committees would be formed, and would begin operations immediately. Here is an outline of the general organization already in place. You will see that it is quite thorough.

ORGANIZATION OF THE OLYMPIAN GAMES ASSOCIATION
PRESIDENT. – VICE-PRESIDENT. – SECRETARY. – TREASURER.

COMMITTEES
GENERAL COMMITTEE

1. Legal
2. Finance
3. Publicity
4. Auditing
5. Administration
6. Athletic
7. Program
8. Concessions
9. Music
10. Spectacular display
11. Decoration and Illuminations
12. Prizes
13. Public order
14. Invitations
15. Transportation
16. Ceremonial
17. Reception
18. Banquets
19. Site
20. Preliminary athletics
21. Construction

Commissions
National – Interstate – International – Intercollegiate

The first two sub-committees to be formed were Finance and Publicity. Mr. B. G. Rosenthal chaired the first of these. Mr. H. W. Hingbothen, who presided over the organization of the 1893 World's Fair, and Mr. C. L. Hutchinson, director of the Art Institute and treasurer of the University, were both members of that sub-committee. The sub-committee on Publicity was chaired by Mr. Adisson C. Thomas, general manager of the Western Press Association who, of course, brought the valuable support of that powerful organization to the table.

Public opinion continues to be won over to this effort, and warmly supports those who are engaged in it. If there is anything that can increase sympathy for, and rouse the passions of, the inhabitants of Chicago, it would certainly be disagreeable attacks such as those published in the Greek press. Certain newspapers (not those most highly regarded, to be sure) have recently spoken of the Chicago Olympic Games in disdainful terms, going so far as to suggest that an understanding has been reached among European athletic associations to ensure that the Games fail. These attacks have been scorned. If they were repeated, clearly their effects would be the opposite of what was intended. But we are confident that the Greek newspapers will come around to a more sound point of view, particularly because, in the final analysis, Hellenic civilization can only benefit from the celebration in foreign countries of Olympiads that recall an institution from its glorious past, of which the Greek people are justly proud. Whatever the attitude of other countries may be in this matter, one would truly have to misunderstand Americans to think that they could be put off from their plans by the specter of opposition from old lady Europe.

As for the success of the Games, the recent change at the helm of the Republic will have no repercussions. It is quite clear that President Roosevelt, one of the most daring and avid sportsmen in the whole world, will pay special attention to the preparation and implementation of the 1904 program. Newspapers are full of tales of the athletic prowess of the new head of state, whose exploits have long since made him quite popular.

Mr. Henry Bréal, who spent part of the summer in Chicago, was warmly welcomed there. He saw for himself that the undertaking for which he had acted as a skillful advocate at the meeting of the International Committee in Paris last May is already guaranteed the greatest and most brilliant possible success.

Courrier de Chicago,
in: *Revue Olympique*, 1901,
no. 4, pp. 55-57.

4.2.2/14 MOVING THE 1904 OLYMPIC GAMES (CIRCULAR LETTER TO THE MEMBERS OF THE IOC)

Dear Colleague,

The moving of the 1904 Olympic Games from Chicago to St. Louis has been welcomed most enthusiastically in the United States, and we have reason to believe that the American Olympiad will be celebrated with all the excellence desired. President Francis has promised me that the management of the World's Fair will be prompt in setting the dates and conditions for the competitions. In addition, I have asked the Committee of the Amateur Athletic Union, the most powerful athletic association in the United States, to see to it that this is done.

Moreover, the opening of the Third Olympiad, which will coincide with the tenth anniversary of the 1894 congress, will provide an occasion for a celebration in Paris, the date and program for which will be determined at a later date. At that celebration, a model will be on display of the monument that the famous sculptor Bartholdi has agreed to create in commemoration of the restoration of the Olympic Games. Starting today, we are opening a subscription to build this monument, which will be placed in the vicinity of Paris. We hope that you will participate. Subscriptions should be sent to me, and will be paid into the Crédit Lyonnais.

Sincerely yours,

Pierre de Coubertin

Circular letter from the President of the IOC, April 30, 1903 (Archives of the IOC)

4.2.2/15 CHICAGO OR SAINT LOUIS

The International Olympic Committee met in Paris on Tuesday, May 22, 1901 and the days that followed. The city of Prague had kindly invited us to meet within its walls and, of course, we would have accepted their hospitality, but the personal preferences of many of our colleagues obliged us to opt for Paris. The meeting was held at the Automobile Club de France, under the patronage of the head of state – Mr. Loubet, at the time – who received us most warmly at the Elysée Palace at the end of our meetings. I continued to hold the position of president of the Committee, though that is not how things should have been. I have already recalled the provision adopted at my request in 1894, according to which the presidency of the Committee is supposed to pass for four years to a representative of the country where the next Olympic Games are to be held. At that time, we were already thinking of holding the Third Olympiad in the United States, but the incidents that took place in 1900 had not allowed us to transform this intention into a definitive resolution. In addition, when the time came, Professor W. M. Sloane energetically opposed replacing me. He said that the International Committee should continue to be presided over by its founder, for otherwise the whole undertaking might be compromised. He went so far as to make acceptance of this proposal a *sine qua non* for his subsequent support. The well-founded nature of many of his arguments was undeniable. Successive managements would not produce the desired unity and coherence. But I did not want a presidency for life at any cost; I proposed a term of ten years, and the regulation was modified to reflect this change. It was under these conditions that the 1901 meeting began. The main purpose of the meeting was to decide on the location of the 1904 Olympic Games.

On February 13, 1901, a banquet presided over by Dr. W. Harper was held at one of Chicago's leading clubs. Following that banquet, a committee was formed to win the honor of hosting the Third Olympiad for the city of Chicago. Of course, this movement had not come about spontaneously. I no longer recall its origins, but the first document I have is a clipping from the *New York Sun*, dated November 13, 1900, alluding to a dispatch from Paris indicating that Chicago was likely to be selected for 1904. That dispatch had given rise to a protest in the United States by Mr. James Sullivan, secretary of the Amateur Athletic Union. In a vehement interview, Mr. Sullivan made most surprising and unexpected statements. In that interview, I learned, first, that the International Olympic Committee no longer existed; second, that I no longer had anything to do with matters related to athletics; third, that an "International Union" had been founded in 1900 in Paris by Mr. Sullivan, representing the United States, and by Mr. Saint-Clair and Pierre Roy in the name of France, Lieutenant Bergh on behalf of Sweden, etc.; fourth, that the Olympic Games would take place in 1901 in Buffalo, at the same time as the Pan-American Exhibition, of which Mr. Sullivan was commissioner of athletics; fifth, that after that we would all wait and see... This interview caused no small amount of hilarity in the United States. One New York newspaper, which published a list of the members of the International Committee, followed the list with these nasty lines: "The freezing horror of the situation can only be fully appreciated when it is seen that Mr. J. E. Sullivan is *not* on the committee". Mr. Sloane and I looked into the matter. On December 12, 1900, Mr. Sloane wrote to me: "It seems quite certain that work was done to set up an international commission to organize Games at Buffalo for next year, but I have been unable to learn any more than that, because those who know the facts are keeping a tactful silence, or are quite reticent to speak."

As for the International Union that I was hearing about for the first time, they had tried to establish it without our knowledge during the Paris World's Fair, with the idea of monopolizing future Olympic Games to their own ends, but the plan had failed. Mr. Sullivan's interview was the final blow. Mr. Bergh told a reporter for the *Chicago Record* that not only had he not taken part in any foundation of this kind, but that in fact he disapproved of any effort aimed against the International Committee. Other disavowals followed. Mr. Sullivan was rather taken aback in the face of these developments, and the reaction to all this in Chicago was what you might expect. Once some New York hostility was perceived, local patriotism latched onto the project, which was then taken to heart. Besides, in 1904 Chicago was going to celebrate its centennial, the centennial of a few huts laid out on its soil at the initiative of a few bold trappers. What better way to draw the world's attention to this anniversary than to hold the Olympic Games in the same location? The group that formed immediately was broadly representative of Yankee energy. It included the heads of the three major banks in Chicago, the president of the Art Institute, the president of the University, a qualified representative of the press, and five or six "prominent" citizens. As I said, this happened on February 13. On May 10, I had in my hands a very complete file to submit to my colleagues on the International Committee.

The file included the official petition, signed by fourteen members of the Chicago Committee, a letter from their chairman, Mr. H. J. Furber, a statement by the president of the University of Chicago, Dr. Harper, stipulating that the University's playing fields would be offered at no cost for the celebration of the Third Olympiad, and finally, a letter from the French Minister of Foreign Affairs, who sent copies of these documents duly authenticated by the French Consul in Chicago[1] to the International Committee. Other, less official documents set forth the financial plans (two hundred thousand francs had already been subscribed in advance), and a tentative schedule for the Games, congresses, and artistic exhibitions that Chicago would host in 1904. The schedule was remarkably well done, and it was to be quite useful for the future. But the Chicagoans' efforts did not stop there. To improve their chances, they had hired an attorney. Mr. Henry Bréal had been given the responsibility of advocating their cause. This he did skilfully and with enthusiasm in equal measure. What is more, our American colleagues were supportive of the idea. Mr. Stanton recommended Chicago highly, and Professor Sloane and Mr. Whitney, who had been unable to attend, rallied to the cause without reserve. There was only one problem that might arise. There was already talk of delaying the World's Fair scheduled to be held in St. Louis in 1903 until 1904. Clearly, it is the lot of American world's fairs to be late. Rather than being celebrated in 1892, Christopher Columbus had to wait until 1893. The same was to prove true for the centennial of the Louisiana Purchase. We received word from St. Louis of the visit of a delegate who was to ask us, in light of this delay, to choose St. Louis, if possible. But no documentation was there to support this request. The envoy did not appear in person; all he did was write. When pressed, he told me that at the last minute in St. Louis, "they were not yet in a position to make an official proposal". Given the enormous lead that Chicago had, and the doubts that continued to arise regarding the definitive date of the World's Fair, how could we hesitate? After all, there would still be time to approve moving the Games if events dictated. In the meantime, the excellent example set by Chicago, where a competent and powerful committee had formed in due time, with all the guarantees desirable, deserved encouragement.

The vote went to Chicago, and the news, cabled immediately to Chicago, was received enthusiastically there. Two thousand students at the University, who had been joined by groups from all the schools and institutions in the city, formed a huge parade that wound its way to Marshall Field. There, in the presence of five or six thousand spectators, a "mammoth bonfire" was lit. In its glow, eloquent speeches were given, and messages of support sent by the students in neighboring cities were read. As of the day after that event, those who had initiated the project got down to work in earnest. Their first act was to transform their embryonic organization into a permanent association which was then incorporated, i.e. legally recognized. It was incorporated for a period of ten years, with initial capital of $200,000. Its officers were Messrs. Furber, Dr. Harper, J. B. Payne, a former justice of the Supreme Court of the United States, Volney Foster, president of the Union

League Club, and E. A. Posser, president of the American Trust and Saving Bank Co. Competent committees were appointed and began operations. Of course, the press bluffed its way along, creating Olympics columns, filling them with sensational stories. They even announced as a certainty that the King of Greece would come to Chicago. It is true that the Greek Consul, a certain Mr. Salopoulo, had contributed to this notion, suggesting to the organizers, in a letter made public, that the presidency of the Games should be offered to the monarch. This untimely excess of zeal elicited vigorous protest, as public opinion would not allow for a foreign sovereign to be called upon to exercise such a function. The role rightfully belonged to the president of the United States. Mr. McKinley, to whom I had written on May 28, 1901, seemed likely to accept. After the assassination of the president, the attitude of his successor, Mr. Roosevelt, left no room for doubt. This most athletic of heads of state was, of course, entirely supportive of the Olympic Games. Thus Mr. Furber found a most favorable welcome when he went to Washington. In addition to substantial local resources, they could now count on a hefty subsidy from the federal government. On May 28, Mr. Roosevelt agreed to open the American Olympiad in person, and to have the Army and Navy participate, as well[2]. So everything was going along as planned. But when Mr. Furber, who was going all out and was making a trip around Europe to raise support for the Games, came to see me in Alsace, I noticed that he had some concerns in the back of his mind. So I was not so surprised when I received a long official letter from him on November 26, accompanying an equally long letter of explanation.

Here is what had happened. For some time already, the rescheduling of the St. Louis World's Fair to 1904 was a done deal. The enormous delay gave rise to doubts that it might not be ready even for 1904. At the same time, "athletic ambitions" were taking root in the minds of the organizers. It was believed that they intended to reach an agreement with the Chicago Committee to bring the competitors and the spectators of the Olympic Games to visit St. Louis. But clearly, they had greater ambitions. They wanted the Games. Thus, the managers of the World's Fair were waiting for Mr. Furber upon his arrival, to ask him to have Chicago withdraw. They let it be understood that St. Louis would compete with Chicago, if need be, and that it would offer a whole series of competitions with enormous prizes. This approach was far from sporting, but a fairly Yankee procedure all the same. Mr. Furber responded, as one might expect, that it all depended on the International Committee, but that the Chicago Committee did not rule out the possibility of holding amicable discussions first. This response was wise, because Mr. Furber, who had spent several months in Europe, did not know whether the opinions of his own fellow citizens had changed. He wondered, in particular, whether the new directors of the Amateur Athletic Union, whose officers are elected every year, would be in favor of Chicago or St. Louis. Then the president of the World's Fair, Mr. D. R. Francis, accompanied by his most eminent colleagues, went to Chicago to confer with the Games Committee. At the same time, he had urgent steps taken with regard to me through the French Commissariat, then under the direction of Mr. Michel Lagrave.

1 The text of this document was published in the Revue Olympique of July 1901, so I will not include it here.
2 The Revue Olympique of July 1902 published the President's letter.

It soon became clear that the Chicago Committee was a bit rattled by the vehemence with which St. Louis was making its claims. In addition, moving the Games seemed to be a humiliation. The newspapers thundered on, and on December 5, a colossal meeting of students, along with their teachers, approved a pressing appeal to the International Committee urging it not to give in. The elections at the A.A.U. had gone in Chicago's favor. Mr. Furber advocated a solution that could be supported by St. Louis. The two cities would ask the president of the United States to request of the International Committee that the Games be delayed until 1905, when they would be held in Chicago. Nevertheless, loyal to the end, the members of the Chicago Committee persevered in implementing their original plan despite the hostility of St. Louis, even though the International Committee did not require them to do so.

The issue was now quite clear. Personally, I was in favor of moving the Games despite my repugnance at allowing the Games to be attached to a World's Fair again. Moreover, I took precautions with the authorities at the St. Louis World's Fair and the directors of the Amateur Athletic Union to ensure the autonomy of the Games, and to prevent incidents like those that occurred in 1900 from recurring. Once I received all the guarantees I wanted in this regard, I proposed to the members of the International Committee that it approve moving the Games once the opinion of President Roosevelt had been unofficially sounded out. Here is how the vote went. Twenty-one votes out of a possible twenty-six were cast. There were fourteen votes in favor of the move and two opposed, with five abstentions. I telegraphed the results to Mr. Furber on February 10, 1903, and confirmed them the next day in a joint letter sent to the members of his Committee. Immediately thereafter, I asked the president of the Amateur Athletic Union of the United States, at the time Mr. Walter H. Liginger, and his colleagues on its board, to reach an agreement directly with the management of the St. Louis World's Fair with regard to the new program for the Games. The simplest thing would have been, surely, to implement the admirable program drawn up by the Chicago Committee as it stood. But to ask the people in St. Louis to appear to accept the tutelage of the people in Chicago would have been a daring move indeed! In these circumstances, calling on the Amateur Athletic Union seemed to me to be the surest and fastest way of proceeding. On August 10-12, 1903, a delegation from the A.A.U. met in St. Louis with the new director of the "Physical Culture Department" of the World's Fair, who was none other than Mr. James E. Sullivan. Now he was quite enthusiastic about our Games, and in a great hurry to work toward the success of the Third Olympiad.

I must say right away that his task was enormous, and the success he achieved was considerable. Unfortunately, a relatively small number of European athletes crossed the ocean to participate. The high cost of the trip and of their room and board meant that large teams could not be counted on, in any event. But it is clear that the Chicago-St. Louis quarrel, and the hesitation that resulted from it, kept the number of athletes volunteering to attend even lower.

The St. Louis Games did feature some original approaches. The "star attraction", so to speak, was incontestably what the Americans called, in their picturesque language, the "anthropological day", a day that lasted forty-eight hours, in fact. In the course of these singular athletic meets, competitions were held in the Stadium pitting the Sioux against the Patagonians, the Cocopa of Mexico and the

Moro of the Philippines, the Ainu of Japan, the Pygmies of Africa, the Syrians, and the Turks – the latter flattered, no doubt, at being included in such company. All these men competed in the usual civilized contests, foot races, rope climbing, shot put and javelin throwing, jumping, and archery. Nowhere else but in America would anyone have dared to put such thing in the program of an Olympiad. But for the Americans, all is permitted. Their youthful enthusiasm certainly enjoyed the indulgence of the shades of the great Greek ancestors, if, by chance, they happened to be wandering by at that moment among the amused throng.

Chicago ou Saint Louis,
in: *Une Campagne de vingt-et-un ans (1887-1908).*
Paris 1909, pp. 153-161 (Chapter XVII).

4.2.2/16 THE THIRD OLYMPIAD IN THE UNITED STATES AND THE IOC MEETING IN LONDON

The following chapter from Coubertin's Olympic Memoirs comments on Olympic activities in 1904. In addition to the 1904 Olympic Games in St Louis, already described in the preceding texts, it is the 1904 IOC Session in London that is meant, at which the 1908 Olympic Games were awarded to Rome.

Fortunately, the IOC was not harmed in any way by the 1900 adventure. The three concentric circles referred to earlier: nucleus-nursery-facade, had been strengthened by a number of new recruits: Godefroy de Blonay (Switzerland), Colonel Holbeck (Denmark), Clarence de Rosen (Sweden) and Sir Howard Vincent (Great Britain) were already firm partisans. Prince Georges Bibesco (Rumania), Messrs. Reyntiens (Belgium), de Beistegui (Mexico), de Ribeaupierre (Russia) and Hebrard de Villeneuve (France) were favorably inclined but nothing more. Finally, Prince Salm-Horstmar (Germany) and Prince Serge Beliosselsky (Russia) formed the "icing on the cake". The Olympic idea had gained rather than lost ground, because before the year 1900 was out people were discussing where the Third Olympiad should take place. Actually, in 1894, it had already been tacitly agreed that it should be held in the United States. Greece, France, the United States, the original trinity chosen to emphasize the world character of the institution and establish it on a firm footing. Chicago immediately came forward as candidate. The President of the University, Dr. Harper, was all in favor of the idea and the few enthusiastic citizens grouped round him found a keen champion of their cause in the person of the French Consul, Mr. Merou. The latter sent us Henry Breal, son of the enthusiastic, learned professor to whom I remained closely attached by ties of gratitude. Chicago! I remembered very vividly my conversations in 1889 with Pullman, the philanthropic multimillionaire whose career was so typical of the America of those days, and with the above-mentioned Dr. Harper, as he explained with cold emphasis that the superiority of his university was due to the fact that "it was run like a railway company". But on top of this first impression of a noisy, smoke-ridden city of slaughterhouses was superimposed another, quite different, almost beautiful. Impressed with the grandeur and real beauty of the World Fair in 1893, I had felt myself filled with admiration at the sudden rising of this vigorous sap.

3rd Olympic Games, 1904: Athletics Week at the end of August 1904 was the focus of interest. Famous American athletes were heralded in the St Louis dailies. (taken from the St Louis Post Dispatch, 14th August 1904)

The idea of holding the Games in Chicago appealed to me. It was beginning to receive a favorable press in the United States when a furious letter written by James E. Sullivan was published. In it, he said that the question was far from settled, in view of the fact that the Olympic Committee and its President had been abandoned in favor of an "international union", recently founded in Paris; and he mentioned among the "founders", Count Brunetta d'Usseaux for Italy, Professor Bergh-Petre for Sweden, Messrs. G. de Saint-Clair and Pierre Roy for France, and himself for the United States. Brunetta, who was becoming increasingly enthusiastic about the IOC every day, and Professor Bergh immediately sent off a strong letter of denial. Pierre Roy decided to do the same. After a first sharp reply, Sullivan wrote a second, more conciliatory letter on March 21, 1901 to acknowledge it, in any case not everyone in the United States shared his views. At the end of 1900, the *Morning Telegraph* had written that "all this was a campaign against Chicago", concluding with the barbed words: "*The freezing horror of the situation can only be fully appreciated when it is seen that James Sullivan is not the American member of the IOC*". The fight was on! Fine! Nothing is better for firmly establishing a committee than having the candidates come to blows. It reminded me of Jules Simon's bantering words when several people each claimed the honor of initiating the scheme in favor of school sport in France: "The success of an idea is to be judged by the number of people who claim credit for it."

On May 21, 1901, at a meeting in the Automobile Club premises in Paris, the IOC unanimously accepted Chicago as the venue for the 1904 Games; on receiving the cable announcing the result of this vote, the students celebrated the news with a mammoth bonfire. I had just written to the President of the United States explaining, after a short history of the revival of the Games, how necessary it was for him to act as patron to the Games and to proclaim them open himself, when President McKinley was assassinated. This crime automatically led to the succession of the Vice-President, Theodore Roosevelt. He was a firm partisan, an invaluable friend to our cause, and with his accession to the presidency the prospects of the Third Olympiad improved immeasurably.

Everything got off to a good start. A program was drawn up which, in addition to sport, provided for literary and artistic events. Luxurious editions were brought out in English, French, and German. During the summer of 1901, Mr. Furber, President of the Organizing Committee, stayed with me at my home in the country and we came to an agreement on a quantity of details. However, towards the end of the year, I noticed a certain disquiet and a slight reserve in his letters. The reason soon became apparent. The centenary of the handing over of Louisiana by the First Consul Bonaparte to the Republic of the United States was to be celebrated in St. Louis, Missouri, in 1903, with a gigantic exhibition. But just as eleven years earlier the exhibition that Chicago, in the name of the whole of the United States, was organizing to commemorate the fourth centenary of the discovery of America by Christopher Columbus had had to be postponed, so the St. Louis exhibition would not be ready in time either. It would be held therefore in 1904. One could be forgiven for thinking that this could only add to the success of the Chicago Games, by bringing with it an increased influx of spectators. Unfortunately, a long-standing, keen rivalry existed between the two towns. St. Louis insisted on being allowed to hold the Games. If necessary, the town would organize its own. During the course of 1902, this threat, which was at first ignored, gradually assumed menacing proportions. A mass meeting was held in Chicago to protest against any such transfer, but a certain wavering began to be noticed among the organizers. The President of the University, Harper, wrote that they would leave the decision to us and that if we decided in their favor they would "carry it through to a successful conclusion". A certain anxiety could be detected in his letter. Before I had even received it, I had already written to the President, who was in a better position than anyone to appreciate the situation properly. On December 23, 1902, after receiving the mainly favorable messages from my colleagues (14 in favor, 2 against, 5 abstentions), I wrote unofficially to ask President Roosevelt to decide the matter. As I had expected, he opted in favor of the transfer. There was a fast and furious exchange of telegrams. Chicago resigned itself to the inevitable and Mr. David R. Francis, President of the St. Louis Exhibition, cabled us his heartfelt thanks. As for Sullivan, who had now rallied to our cause and was carried away by enthusiasm, he said that it was going to be "the most splendid series of sporting feats the world had ever seen."

But was the world interested? Not yet. That summer, transported by the thrilling strains of Wagner in Bayreuth, I had an opportunity of sorting out my impressions and examining the Olympic horizons in peace. Music and sport have always been my most perfect means of solace and escape, the most fruitful aids to reflection and clearer vision, as well as powerful stimuli, like "massage of the mind", encouraging me to persevere. In fact, after a period of difficulties and perils, all immediate worries were suddenly removed. The Third Olympiad would be celebrated with all due pomp and ceremony. An experienced team had been put in charge of the arrangements. They would undoubtedly make a great many mistakes, but there was no fear of any of the mishaps experienced by their predecessors in 1900. The Olympic seal, the presence of the President, the authority of the IOC, whose daily program would be headed by the names of its members... all this could be counted on. The only black spot on the horizon was that the Americans imagined they had far greater drawing power than, in fact, they had. In particular, they expected great things of the "princes" (there were three of them at the time) as well as of the lesser nobles belonging to the IOC. They offered us a fine hall for our sessions. I had firmly decided, without letting them suspect it, of course, to decline the invitation. There would have been six or seven of us round a table prepared for thirty. And people would have said, "What? So that's the famous IOC that makes so much fuss and trouble!" However, the IOC did meet in 1904, for the time had now come for it to "come out". It was at last ready to be shown to the world, but this was to be in London, in the Lord Mayor's traditional residence, Mansion House, under the patronage of King Edward VII, with as much as possible of the incomparable prestige bestowed by Old England on the youthful institutions that appeal to it for support, to add luster to our sessions. And while in London, the IOC was to entrust to the Eternal City, to Rome-the-glorious, the responsibility for staging the Games of the Fourth Olympiad four years later.

Everything went according to plan. The session was a great success from every point of view, except that I would have liked to have found a way of associating the Universities of Oxford and Cambridge in our work, as well as the famous old public school of Rugby, that Mecca of sports education. But my dear friends, R. S. Laffan and Sir Howard Vincent, had arranged matters so well that apart from our meetings, a whole week was taken up, from June 19-27, with various festivities: luncheon at Mansion House, dinners at Westminster and with the famous, wealthy Guild of Fishmongers, excursions to Windsor and Hurlingham, etc. And then, not all my colleagues seemed to understand my persistent wish to involve the university world in the Olympic revival. In America where, as I have already said, the universities dominated athletics at the time, this association had already been achieved. In Europe this was nowhere the case. I have no intention here of criticizing the students or rather their mentality and that of their professors. A digression of this nature would be out of place here, but it is unfortunately only too true that, between 1890 and 1930, cooperation on the part of the universities was constantly and regrettably lacking in a great many fields (Olympism being only one of them). The few attempts they did make to participate in non-academic affairs tended to be dispersed and only too often lost in the by-ways or dead ends of sterile discussion, almost never showing any continuity or great determination to follow the great world lines of communication. When, much later, students took up sport, they wanted to have special Olympic Games just for themselves. The workers, in their turn, wanted the same and I have been criticized for adopting a contradictory attitude in the two cases. I will explain my reasons in due course.

On March 24, 1903 Senator Todaro, in his capacity as President of the Federazione Ginnastica Italiana, officially announced to me the unanimous decision made a few days earlier by representatives of Italian gymnastics clubs to request that Rome should be chosen to stage the Fourth Olympiad. Three years had

The first Olympics in the "New World", St Louis 1904. Harry L.Hillman winning the 200 m hurdle race; the first black Olympic medallist, George C.Poage finished third as well as in the 400 m hurdles. His performance marked the beginning of a long record of brilliance displayed by black Americans in the Olympics. (taken from Spalding Official Athletic Almanac for 1905. Official Report 1904. New York, A.S.P., 1905, p.240)

As part of the 1904 Olympics accompanying programme, various competitions were held for the natives of different continents, under the title "Anthropology Days". Coubertin condemned this abuse of the Olympic name as "inhuman". (Photo taken from M.Bennitt/ F.Stockbridge, History of the Louisiana Purchase Exposition, St Louis, World's Fair, 1905, p.573)

elapsed discreetly and almost in silence, with hardly any IOC meetings, but filled with a copious, detailed correspondence destined to consolidate the ties between its members and their position towards the different sports groups and countries. The London meeting focused the limelight on the successful result of our efforts.

Rome's candidature, which had been abandoned temporarily by President Todaro, had found a determined champion in the Secretary of the Italian federation, Mr. F. Ballerini. At my request, Count Brunetta d'Usseaux made public his enthusiastic support. The only difficulty was the tendency towards regionalism, which was much stronger at that time than now. Rome's supremacy was by no means obvious to all. Milan considered herself the only sports metropolis in the whole peninsula. Turin, too, put forward her claim. But Olympic Games in Milan or Turin would be very ordinary events and would not help in any way to further our cause. I wanted Rome because there alone, after its excursion to utilitarian America, would Olympism be able to don the sumptuous toga, woven with skill and much thought, in which I had wanted to clothe it from the beginning.

We surrounded the voting with a sort of solemnity, as a result of which my German colleagues withdrew their proposal to choose Berlin. I had taken care to present the vote as an international tribute to Ancient Rome. This would also help subsequently to offer effective resistance to any tendency to lessen the impact of the Games by sharing them between several cities. So far there had never been any misunderstanding on this point. Athens, Paris, Chicago, and St. Louis had each put forward their candidature as single centers. This time, a number of newspapers and committees speaking of the award of the 1908 Games to *Italy*, revealed the subconscious wish to share the contests among several Italian towns. This was a grave threat that had to be avoided at all costs. That is why we made such a point of always speaking of Rome and only of Rome. Immediately the voting was over, the result was taken to the Italian Embassy. The Ambassador cabled it, together with our respects, to the Sovereign as well as to the Mayor of Rome, Prince Colonna. Earlier, on February 27, the Communal Council, meeting in the Capitol, had discussed the matter and decided to act as patrons should the opportunity be given them. Prince Colonna's reply was enthusiastic. The Master of the King's Household cabled no less explicitly to say that the King had commanded him to send his sincere thanks to the International Committee which, "by proclaiming Rome the venue for the Fourth Olympiad" had given Italy "such a striking token of cordial esteem".

Shortly afterwards, our colleagues Gebhart and Kémény embarked for the United States, discreet bearers of our best wishes to the organizers of the Games. Now that it had just strengthened its position in Europe, the IOC wanted to draw as little attention as possible to the weaknesses of the American organization. The essential points had been gained. It would have been unwise to expect more. "Patience" remained our motto.

So the St. Louis Games were completely lacking in attraction. Personally, I had no wish to attend them. I harbored great resentment against the town for the disillusionment caused by my first sight of the junction of the Missouri and the Mississippi rivers. After reading Fenimore Cooper, what had I not been led to expect of the setting where these rivers with their strange resounding names actually met! But there was no beauty, no originality. I had a sort of presentiment that the Olympiad would match the mediocrity of the town. As far as originality was concerned, the only original feature offered by the program was a particularly embarrassing one. I mean the "Anthropological Days", whose events were reserved for Negroes, Indians, Filipinos and Ainus, with the Turks and Syrians thrown in for good measure! That was twenty-six years ago! Now tell me that the word has not advanced since then and that no progress has been made in sporting spirit...

Olympic Memoirs, Chap.6, Lausanne, IOC, 1997, pp.72-79.

4.2.2/17 A SUCCESSFUL CONGRESS AND A FEW REAL ACHIEVEMENTS (1905)

The main focus for 1905 was the Olympic Congress in Brussels, which was preceded by an IOC Session about which Olympic research knows almost nothing.[1]

The original topic to be discussed at the congress, the standardisation of the rules of sport for the Olympic Games had been forgotten since the convention in the year 1901. Coubertin made use of this opportunity and replaced the original topic by an analysis of the situation of the position of physical education in the different areas of life and in the different countries.[2] The Congress passed 63 recommendations.[3]

The inclusion of games in the physical education of schools and the equality of the competing gymnastic movement were underlined in those days. The building of sport grounds and halls, the instruction of trainers, the promotion of skiing and syndicates for sport clubs was demanded.

For Coubertin the fact was even more important that for the first time in Brussels it had come to the co-operation of several groups of people, who up to then had not been involved with sport.

The second focus on 1905 is equally informative, as it provides a detailed description of Coubertin's activities during what was an important year for the Olympic Movement. These include his first visit to a pope, on this occasion Pius X, in the Vatican.[4]

In the panorama of "Olympic years" unfolding my mind, the year 1905 strikes me not necessarily as the most brilliant but certainly as one of the most useful and productive.

For me, it began with a fairly long stay in Rome, where the purpose of my visit was twofold: to ensure the Roman celebration of the Fourth Olympiad, which fell in 1908, and to persuade the Vatican to raise the sort of interdict laid on sports education in many clerical circles. The first point was not achieved; the second was, and fully.

1 A few details are known to us from the correspondence of Jiri Guth, made available by the Prague-based Olympic researcher Jiri Kössl. These include the decision about giving a name to the 1906 intermediate Olympic Games in Athens.

2 In the official announcement of the programme, written by Coubertin, detailed descriptions of each issue were given. Cf. Revue Olympique, 1905, no. 1, pp. 9-15.
Apart from the consultation committee six main seminar papers were presented, which are given in the report Coubertin often referred to, especially the preparation of "Gymnastics in the Antique" from G. Strehly.

3 See IOC (ed.): *Congrès International de Sport et d'Education physique.* Auxerre, Lanier, 1905.
See N. Müller, One Hundred Years of Olympic Congresses 1894-1994. Lausanne, IOC, 1994, pp.56-67.

4 The German sports historian Willi Schwank recently presented a study on this which created quite a stir. See W. Schwank, "Pius X. und Pierre de Coubertin. Eine Begenung im Zeichen Olympias." In: Wissentschaftliche Kommission Kirche und Sport (ed.): *Forum Kirche und Sport.* Vol.2, Düsseldorf 1996, pp. 29-56.

Everything seemed to conspire towards the success of the next Games. Rome had all the resources which, at the beginning, had been lacking in Athens; everyone seemed favorably inclined, from the King down to the humblest official. Actually, this favorable attitude was not exactly accompanied by any wild enthusiasm, but this was perhaps not necessary for *continuing the work* even though Hellenic fervor had been essential for founding it. But we still needed an Organizing Committee. The one that Count Brunetta d'Usseaux had formed the year before was without a head. No one could be found for the post and, consequently, the regionalist tendencies to which I have already alluded could not be halted. When I speak of regionalism, I am not suggesting that Italy was not united at the time; there was no longer, of course, any of the secessionist inclinations of earlier days among Piedmontesi, Venetians, Romans, Neapolitans, or Sicilians. But their character, temperament, way of seeing and doing things remained so different that, apart from questions of truly national interest, cooperation was difficult and misunderstandings frequent and lasting. Obviously I do not intend here to go into details of the innumerable negotiations and conflicting ambitions. I have already touched on some of them in a book of recollections published in 1908. As had been the case in Athens eleven years earlier, I had had to set to work myself to make up for the deficiencies of others and draft the plans and estimates for the Games myself. The King and Queen were kind enough to suggest the "Piazza di Siena" in the Villa Borghese, a natural stadium of perfect beauty that was, in fact, ideally suited to athletic sports. I chose the Piazza dei Armi for the gymnastic events and the Baths of Caracalla for the combat sports. What wonderful settings and how simple to prepare! The Tor di Quinto was available for equestrian sports and games; the River Tiber, between Ponte Molle and Ponte Margherita, for rowing and swimming; the Capitol for the ceremonies and receptions... The initial estimate based on all the details compiled was divided into twelve sections. The total amounted to 303,000 liras. Happy days! Admittedly, as in 1896 and in 1900, the 1908 Games seemed designed mainly for an elite: five hundred competitors and approximately fifteen to twenty thousand spectators. The estimate included the prizes – statuettes and medals – which would increase considerably in value as I had decided to have the moulds broken as soon as the Games were over (I always demanded that this should be done after each Olympiad – but to no avail) and the salary of a Director General, to which post I planned to appoint the General Secretary of the Racing Club de France, Mr. Gaston Raymond, subject of course to the club's agreement.

Negotiations with the Vatican were much less difficult. Unlike most heads of religious establishments, Pope Pius X, who regularly gave prizes for the famous regattas held in Venice, and Cardinal Merry del Val, Secretary of State who had been educated at Eton, were not at all prejudiced against sport (I am talking here of real sport and sports contests and not the tame, purely *recreational* games allowed up till then in such establishments). His Holiness, interested in the idea of a Roman Olympiad, spoke very favorably of it and at the same time promised early, tangible proof of his sentiments. The following season a festival of gymnastics was held during a pilgrimage of French, Belgian, and other Catholic guilds, which the Pope presided over in the famous courtyard of St. Damase; a very sympathetic spectacle, the photographs of which have always been a great success on occasions when slides and photographs depicting the early days of Olympism have been shown.

Some of the participants in the 1905 Olympic Congress in Brussels (taken from L'éducation physique, 1905, p.317): from left to right, seated: Mssrs Dudok de Wit, Cap. H.Angell, G.Demeny, Ms Lefebure, Ms Kritchevsky, Col. Derué, Baron Pierre de Coubertin, Col. Victor Balck, Baron F.W.C. van Tuyll, Count A.Mercati, W.H.Grenfell, Count Brunetta d'Usseaux, Racine. Standing: Mssrs Bonamour, Jourdain, Cap. Holbek, Dr Tissié, ?, E.Vestine, Ed.Etling, A.Fringnet, Rev. de Courcy Laffan, Dr Demoor, A.Fosseprez, F.Zièrer, Dedet, ?, L.Kiel, Ch. Simon, Beltram, Ch. Lefebure, General de Butovsky, Cap. Hutton, E.Rouzier-Dorcières, J.Dalbanne, T.Vienne, E.Briotet, Prof. van Aken.

When the IOC met in Paris in the spring of 1901, it had to discuss three converging proposals concerning the convening of an International Congress for the Standardization of Sports Regulations. One was made by our German colleagues, the other by various Swedish groups, and the third by the Amateur Athletic Union of the United States. The first proposed drawing up a sports code which would be made compulsory for all future contests. It was much too dictatorial, and besides why should the IOC feel entitled to institute such peremptory legislation without consulting the federations and technically competent clubs? Here, we had a glimpse of the confusion that was to prevail between the Olympic Games and ordinary international championships for such a long time to come. The members of the IOC were "trustees of the Olympic idea" and were responsible for ensuring that the four-yearly contests were held according to this spirit; this did not make them fit to take the place of the technicians in the actual running of these contests. People outside the Committee found it difficult to understand this and even – sometimes – those on the Committee.

The second proposal, as I have said, was made by Sweden; it was inspired by that rather over-simplified and infuriatingly logical way of viewing questions which, combined with certain unexpected complexities, often makes the Scandinavian mentality so difficult to understand, even by those foreigners who are the most enthusiastic about everything Scandinavian. To their mind, since we were reviving the Olympic Games, we should do it faithfully, rigorously cutting everything modern out of the program and limiting it strictly to the events held in ancient times. I have no need to point out the negative, impractical and, finally, destructive character of such a proposal.

The third proposal was the only one worth retaining. Mr. L. P. Sheldon, sent by the American Athletic Union for the purpose, was allowed to put it to the IOC himself. He did so with talent and moderation. It was suggested that we should encourage an exchange of views among all those interested in the question of drawing up regulations for sports contests and give the backing of our authority to any agreements reached. Why not? Especially as it lay completely within the spirit and possibilities of the IOC.

This brings us to the Brussels Congress. In December of the same year, 1901, I took advantage of a visit to Paris by King Leopold of the Belgians to ask for an audience with a view to obtaining his patronage. Leopold II was probably the most intimidating of all reigning monarchs. A sort of ankylosis had made him accustomed to remain standing up, leaning on his stick, and he was in the habit of receiving visitors in this fashion even if, interested by the conversation, he allowed it to go on a long time. His great height, his always slightly mocking gaze, and his trenchant remarks made him quite formidable. If he took a dislike to his visitor, he could turn quite nasty. Did he like sport or, rather, had he liked it earlier? I am not very sure, but as a means of training men to be strong and fit he realized its great value and the contribution it could make to his colonial aims. Some years later, he asked me to produce plans, regulations, and programs for a "college for colonial preparation" which I took the greatest pleasure in drawing up for him in considerable detail. Naturally, sports training played a great role. The project came to nothing; I had made it secular and the King approved it this way, but the clerical influences at work in the country thwarted it.

The Congress planned for 1904 was adjourned until 1905. We were joined by an invaluable new member for Belgium, Count Henry de Baillet-Latour who, before taking over from me twenty years later as head of the IOC, was to play a leading role among us and render the Olympic cause outstanding service. His predecessor, alarmed at the responsibility of organizing the Congress, had suddenly withdrawn – so suddenly in fact that his conduct brought us within a hair's breadth of disaster, from which we were saved by the spontaneous intervention of a French diplomat favorably disposed towards the IOC.

On October 7, 1904, Count Smet, the Belgian Prime Minister, whom I knew personally, informed me that the Foreign Minister had agreed to allow the invitations to be sent out by the Belgian legations. This was an important point. He deeply regretted moreover that the Burgomaster of Brussels, Mr. de Max, had refused us the use of his famous Town Hall. But Count de Baillet arranged for us to have the Palais des Académies, which was in fact more conveniently situated and better suited to our purpose.

The official opening ceremony of the Congress, which was held in June 1905, was honored with a speech by Marcel Prevost, President of the Literary Society, who had come specially from Paris to speak on *"The Mind in the School of Sport":* a charming contribution to the sessions which, apart from this speech, were dedicated wholly to technical matters. It was the turn of the latter, as at Le Havre it had been the turn of education. The program was very ambitious. It was pretentious enough to attempt to cover all aspects of the question; it filled five or six octavo pages and formed a complete list. Naturally it was impossible to go into all this in full detail; it was more of a manifesto. One point of discussion that it is interesting to recall was the role of sport in the army. The French representatives began to show themselves in favor. The German representatives, and all their followers, declared themselves against the idea. According to them, it was purely a waste of time for soldiers, and an occasion for troublesome breaches of discipline. Everyone will remember how, ten years later, this reluctance on their part was swept away by the force of the evidence and how the value of sports training suddenly took on the greatest importance.

The IOC's Session, held during the Congress, produced a great number of concrete results. The German Committee had *appointed* its new President, General Count von der Asseburg, to replace Prince Salm-Horstmar, who wished to retire. This was contrary to the very essence of the IOC. There was no question of giving in. However, when the General contacted my colleagues individually, as a delegate to the Congress, he said that it was his Committee that had made a mistake and that he wished to apply for election. Naturally we then elected him with the greatest pleasure. He was a charming man on whom one could always count. Olympism had caught his enthusiasm right away. He helped a great deal in Brussels to maintain a pleasant atmosphere. The circumstances were actually quite difficult. Delcasse had just resigned as a result of the Kaiser's landing at Tangiers and the ensuing events. People were talking of the possibility of war. The Belgians were suspicious. The Scandinavians for their part were on edge, for the sudden separation from Sweden demanded by the Norwegians had not been accomplished without friction. But all this was forgotten in the excellent sporting atmosphere. This meeting of over two hundred members, sometimes divided into commissions, sometimes grouped in plenary session, carried on its discussions in an excellent spirit inspired solely by a desire for the public good.

Naturally, all that was actually accomplished boiled down to a pious expression of wishes. But in those days, when congresses had not yet been overdone, "wishes" still had a certain value. Above all, the very size of the meeting had done great honor to the IOC. The recent creation of the British Olympic Association, which helped to counterbalance the Deutscher Reichsausschuss für Olympische Spiele, gave us two powerful wings. London and Berlin now possessed permanent Olympic centers working with us and under us to a certain extent. This placed us in a much stronger position with regard to Athens. Our colleague Mercati had taken immediate advantage of the fact to establish closer relations, which the Crown Prince moreover had continued to favor as much as he could. Additional Games were to be held in Greece in 1906. It was understood that the IOC would give its support as well as secure that of the bodies already set up in different countries by its members. Thus, even though the Brussels Congress had taken place during the most dangerous period of political tension experienced by Western Europe since 1887, it had succeeded in achieving the maximum of Olympic peace that we had ever obtained. This did not mean, however, that we had heard the last of our enemies.

Olympic Memoirs, Chap.,7, Lausanne, IOC, 1997, pp.80-87.

4.2.2/18 – 4.2.2/20 INTRODUCTION

When the Olympic Games were awarded to Rome in 1908, hopes ran very high. The city of Rome, with its treasures of ancient art, was supposed to ennoble the Olympic movement and give athletic internationalism a decisive impetus. In Coubertin's absence, the fifth Session of the IOC at Athens on the occasion of the 1906 Intermediate Games decided to transfer the 1908 Games to London. The printed "Circular Letter" officially informed the members of the IOC of this decision.

With the exception of the special issue of the Revue Olympique in 1906 on Hellenism, Coubertin did not comment on the Intermediate Games of 1906 in Athens. In the following chapter of his Olympic Memoirs, he acknowledges that these Games were organized with greater polish and success than the previous ones, but he deplored the lack of a guiding principle. He was alluding to the strict principle of holding the Games every four years, even though in 1896, by way of compromise, he himself had suggested that Pan-Hellenic Games be held every two years after the Olympic Games took place.

Preparations for the Fourth Olympic Games in London in 1908 went ahead auspiciously. The short time available for such preparations, and the overly-narrow choice of themes means that the Olympic art competitions planned for 1908 were cut. Some political complications arose regarding the right of the British crown colonies (the Dominions) to participate. For the first time, the IOC advanced a supra-national policy and created its own sporting geography, since the Dominions were allowed to participate autonomously if they so desired. The groundwork was thus laid for conflict in 1912.

The decision to adopt the decimal system was another problem. It had been accepted without opposition in St. Louis in 1904. In England, it met with lively resistance.

The track and field competitions turned into a pitched battle between the English and the Americans. Protests regarding the advantages given to English athletes rained in. Press campaigns in the United States and denials in England cast a shadow over these Games.

Coubertin describes these problems in the chapter "The Fourth Olympiad – London 1908" of his *Olympic Memoirs* which is the third following text. Details about the actual holding of the 1908 Games, especially particular incidents and events, can be found in the article "The Chronicle of the 1908 Games".

Of course these Games were not set in the context of a World's Fair, but they did take place on the site of a French-British Exhibition, and in connection with it. These Games did feature some firsts. In October 1908, under the name "winter sports", separate competitions in boxing, artistic skating, soccer, and field-hockey were held. These were the precursors of the Winter Olympic Games, an event to which we shall return in chapter 4.2.3.

**"Rebuilding of the past allied to new forms of locomotion."
Vision of Dresden painter Max Schaberschul (1875-1940) in the run-up to the Intermediate Olympic Games held in Athens in 1906 (taken from La Revue Sportive Illustrée, no.7, October 1906, p.14)**

4.2.2/18 CIRCULAR LETTER TO THE IOC MEMBERS (DECEMBER 1906)

Dear Colleague,

It is my honor to recommend to you that Captain Grut be admitted to our Committee as the representative for Denmark, to replace Colonel Holbeck who is retiring. Captain Grut, former aide-de-camp to His Majesty King Christian IX, is currently Chief of Staff of the Corps of Engineers, and in him we will have a competent and amiable colleague.

Secondly, pursuant to the wishes of our British colleagues I propose that the Olympic Cup for 1907 be awarded to the "Henley Royal Regatta Committee", in witness to the long and valuable services that this Committee has rendered in the cause of Sports. You awarded the Olympic Cup, which I had the pleasure of instituting last year and a reproduction of which appears on the facing page, to the Touring Club de France for 1906.

Our next meeting will take place this spring in The Hague rather than in Berlin, at the request of our German colleagues. In keeping with the agreements reached in Athens, we will work out the competition regulations requested for future Olympiads at that meeting.

Given the particular difficulties that have arisen in Rome, and which we have had to keep secret, the International Committee, at its meeting in Athens, invited the "British Olympic Association" to organize the 1908 Games. This invitation has been accepted, and the success of the Fourth Olympiad seems assured.

Sincerely yours,

The President of the International Olympic Committee

Circular Letter from the President of the IOC (Archives of the IOC).

4.2.2/19 THE CHRONICLE OF THE 1908 GAMES

INCIDENTS AND CRITICISMS; THE MARATHON; THE TRACK AND THE JURY; DECEPTIVE PLACEMENTS; A TRULY INTERNATIONAL OLYMPIAD; AMATEURISM, ONCE AGAIN.

Now that the London Olympic Games are nearly over (we still have football, hockey, skating, etc.), the colossalism of these Games is quite apparent. Please excuse this neologism; it alone expresses the overall impression that the Fourth Olympiad leaves behind, with its enormous crowd of athletes who came from all over to participate. Against this backdrop, the few incidents that arose during the festivities grow dim, and in particular the disproportion of the incidents themselves to the noise made about them becomes apparent. It is true that the outcome was deliberate and intentional. Everyone now knows that plots had been hatched in various places to cause these Games to fail, or at the very least to boycott the success of the Games if it could not be prevented in the first place. This was a naive

The Danish team in London, 1908, led by lady gymnasts involved in demonstrations as part of the accompanying programme (taken from Sport im Bild, 1908, p.923)

effort that left behind hardly a trace, except perhaps for the observation that it is not within the power of any national group, regardless of how powerful it is or believes itself to be, to thwart the combined actions of others for no reason at all.

Among the incidents that were exploited, some are not open to debate. The matter of the time limit imposed on the cyclists is one example. At its Congress in Leipzig just a few days later, the Union Cycliste Internationale hastened to suppress this rule. It was a hasty decision made in particular circumstances, one that may have to be reviewed soon and that, in any event, is only of secondary significance. The disqualification of Dorando Pietri, winner of the marathon, infuriated popular opinion. No one can dispute the fact that Dorando was the moral winner of the competition, or that, technically, he could be disqualified. He made it to the Stadium; he did not reach the finish line. He was supported because he was falling down. Whatever the cause of his repeated fainting – a problem with his food intake or the emotions caused by the welcome of the crowd – it deprived him of the means to forge on ahead to the finish line on his own. The thing is, who can deny that in a race of over forty kilometers, failing at the finish line is nearly the equivalent of victory? That is how the English saw it, and the exquisite gesture of their gracious sovereign merely spoke for the unanimous sentiment of the nation. The suitability of "marathons" can be debated ad infinitum. There are plenty of good arguments to support the view that there is no excuse for a marathon except in Greece, as a historical reminder, and that in and of itself, a marathon is hardly a reasonable challenge. But once the principle of the thing has been accepted, we do not believe that a similar race could be organized in a more remarkable way than it was in 1908. From Windsor, where Her Royal Highness the Princess of Wales oversaw the start, to the Stadium, everything had been foreseen: automobiles, doctors, baggage transportation, possible stopping areas, and the refreshments that might be desirable. The rules that were adopted, which are as sporting as they are wise, will remain a model of the type.

At the finish line, the track was somewhat overrun. In fact, complaints were made that this was the case every day, a well-founded criticism. Far too many people had access to the track. However, it must be noted that all foreigners clamored to be allowed in, and that more than one raised a fuss when efforts were made to close the gate on him. It does not matter. It was a serious mistake to permit such heavy traffic. The esthetics of the situation suffered even more than the technical aspects. At times, one would have thought that encampments were actually taking place on the central lawn.

The experience of the national jury, even tempered by the existence of an "Honor Committee" of foreign delegates, was not to everyone's liking. That, perhaps, would have been quite a difficult result to achieve. Whatever the case may be, it is clear that the principle of an international jury, which had already been tried and about which there had already been some complaint, is defensible despite its shortcomings. There does not seem to be a definitive choice between these two systems, for the moment. Besides, any decision made in this respect applies only to the current Olympiad, and is not at all binding on the next.

One widespread and apparently quite appropriate criticism concerns the number of points scored so far by the United Kingdom. At first glance, it appears that the English have taken a lead in the competition that is discouraging for other nations. They already have an enormous overall score. But one must not forget that the coefficients used to calculate the totals are out of touch with reality. At the very least, they correspond to reality only if one accepts that the value of the different groups of sports is unequal. The Congress of Paris placed them all on the same footing, and Olympic tradition is in keeping with common sense in demanding that it be so. Fencing and water sports are just as "Olympic" as foot races. Yet in London, the coefficient for fencing was four, because there were four competitions, while the coefficient for foot races, with a larger number of competitions, was three times greater. This is a special item that the International Committee must consider at its next meeting. Until then, it is appropriate to note that the ridiculous supremacy foot races were claiming is already under heavy attack. Swimming, wrestling, and gymnastics have made their way into the Stadium, not to mention cycling. This lesson will be most profitable in terms of public opinion, which specialists in foot races had led astray. Although equality has been restored in moral terms, it has not yet done so numerically.

First place finishes in the individual gymnastics competitions (the famous pentathlon that is so worthy of admiration and which we hope will be continued) were distributed as follows: one Italian, one Englishman, one Frenchman, and two Germans. Results of team competitions were as follows: Sweden: 438 points; Norway: 425; Finland: 405; Denmark: 378; France: 319; Italy: 316; Holland: 297; England: 196. The absence of a German team was regretted, detained as they were by the Frankfurt festivals. Similarly, the bad luck of the parade team was much regretted; unfortunately, they performed their exercises at too late an hour for them to be appreciated as they should have been. France and Hungary shared the laurels in fencing, beating out the English, the Belgians, the Italians, and the Dutch. In shooting, Belgium, Sweden, Norway, and Canada shared the victory with the United States and England. The diving competitions were won by a German and a Swede. The wrestling competition was quite remarkable. In the Greco-Roman style, no fewer than sixty-eight competitors in four categories, from ten different countries, took part. Hungary, Finland, Sweden, and Italy won the prizes, while in freestyle wrestling, England and the United States carried the day. These details show that the Fourth Olympiad was not only international in its participants, but even more so in its results.

Was it "pure" in the amateur sense of the term? We hope so, with all our hearts. Yet the fact that some doubt remains regarding a few participating athletes is enough to justify an inquiry. Like Caesar's wife, the Olympic athletes should be above all suspicion. In truth, it is not individual personalities that are involved, but rather a "system" that some bad athletic practices seem to be in the process of making common in certain settings. In this case, the real culprit is public opinion. In its thirst for national victories, it has let itself take a nefarious path in some countries; now opinion can no longer distinguish between amateurs and professionals. For a long time, people have said that amateurs may well be harboring more than one avowed professional among their ranks and, on the contrary, that there are some true amateurs among professionals. Although amateurs among professionals cannot be allowed to qualify, we must be ruthless in disqualifying professionals among amateurs. To do that, we must begin by unmasking them. It seems that this issue has entered an acute phase. Perhaps one of the benefits of the Fourth Olympiad will be that it has put the matter into such sharp focus it is now difficult to avoid it.

La Chronique des Jeux de 1908,
in: *Revue Olympique,*
August 1908, pp. 115-118.

The editor has determined that this text, though unsigned, was written by Coubertin.

4.2.2/20 THE FOURTH OLYMPIAD (LONDON 1908)

One would look in vain in the same number of the *Olympic Review* for any mention of the transfer of the Olympic Games from Rome to London. This new difficulty reminded us of others, which made us decide to be prudent and keep a discreet silence. Consequently the decisions reached once the British Olympic Association had become sure of success were not officially reported to any newspaper. Discreetly, the curtain fell on the setting of the Tiber and opened immediately on that of the Thames. All the preparations had been carried out during the Athens Games which, although more brilliant and better organized than the first, had nevertheless left an impression of uncertainty and confusion because they were without stable foundations. This uncertainty and confusion had infiltrated even into the ranks of the IOC. The nine or ten members who had gone to Athens momentarily lost their heads at one of their meetings and Brunetta d'Usseaux had been powerless to stop them. They had voted a sort of resolution advocating an early reorganization of the IOC and had even offered the honorary presidency to the Crown Prince. The latter had been somewhat embarrassed by the offer. An absurd gesture on their part for, by Hellenizing the committee in this way, they were depriving it of all international independence. Furthermore, except for the last resolution, all this remained subject to the President's approval. The President naturally rejected it all, including the honorary title offered to the Crown Prince. Shortly afterwards, the Prince and I had a long talk in Paris about the matter. It was not very agreeable, either for him or for me, but the situation was so ridiculous that we both ended up laughing. I had decided to speak completely freely and frankly and our talk followed this pattern right till the end. Therefore, the "session" in Athens, in which neither Laffan, Baillet Latour, Blonay, nor Sloane had taken part, could not be considered properly representative of Olympic doctrine.

But there was an "observer" there, who was later to play a prominent role. I am referring to W. H. Grenfell, since raised to the peerage as Lord Desborough, who, having already been in close touch with the IOC for a year, had been fired up with enthusiasm for Olympism. Laffan and he (he shortly afterwards succeeded Herbert, who had retired on account of illness) formed, together with Sir Howard Vincent, a wonderful trinity of practicality, virile determination, and enthusiasm. Left to the care of such men, the Fourth Olympiad could not fail to be a brilliant success. There was also an Exhibition, but its only role was to provide the necessary funds. A pleasant change from earlier experiences.

In fact, when the Franco-British Exhibition was inaugurated in London, on November 26, 1906, Lord Desborough immediately made it clear what a unique and predominant place the Olympic Games were to occupy.

Lord Desborough, whose prestige as a leader had been enhanced by the legends surrounding his name as a result of his sporting feats – in particular his crossing of Niagara Falls – had said in a manifesto to the British press: "Now that the Olympic Games are to be held in England, which has given birth to so many different kinds of sport, it is essential that they should be organized and celebrated in a fashion worthy of this country's sporting fame."

And this is what happened, in almost every respect. How is it possible then to imagine outrageous statements like the one written below immediately after the Games by a French journalist, F. Frank-Puaux, otherwise known for his sporting spirit, and reproduced eagerly and with favorable comments in other countries "The Games have dealt a final blow to England's reputation for sportsmanship; the English have clearly shown, now that they are faced with serious rivals from other countries, that they no longer possess the same broadmindedness, impartiality, and independence that they had persuaded the world was their prerogative". And if I were to look into my files, I could easily pick out a number of American documents, private letters, brochures, articles, etc., in which the accusations were even more virulent.

What had given rise to all this bitterness, then? There was absolutely no real foundation for it; it was just that the very magnitude of the event had suddenly projected renascent Olympism into the full glare of reality like a beam of suppressed life force in which up till then people had only believed *archaeologically speaking* and that, consequently, sports passions – and this was a very modern phenomenon – became heightened and raised to a pitch never reached before. We have witnessed many similar grandiose spectacles since then. But our memories of the stadium in London have never been surpassed. The huge amphitheater, sometimes black with people gone wild with enthusiasm, gave off a feeling of organic power which I, for my part, have never come across since and which I had never experienced with other crowds, whether in Europe or across the Atlantic. On this occasion, there seemed to be a direct confrontation between the two Anglo-Saxon nations creating, within the Games, a sort of muscular duel between their champions. Finally, as soon as the success of the Games appeared assured, there was a series of protests from the French federations aimed at disturbing the smooth running of the Olympic machine, discrediting the International Olympic Committee and denying it its privileges. All these circumstances caused a considerable stir, which gradually calmed down but not without having given rise to a few short sharp clashes. Even so, the Games do not seem to have suffered. On the contrary, these sudden bursts of violence seem to have given them added interest.

In the spring of 1907, the International Olympic Committee, meeting at The Hague, had already received the most satisfactory reports from the British organizers. The work they had accomplished in less than six months was truly remarkable. The foundations of the whole edifice had been laid in the various sectors, even in those – untried as yet – of Art and Literature. The program had been submitted beforehand for examination by three committees formed of members of the IOC, which made it possible to finish the work very quickly. Certain concessions had to be made however. It was the first time that Swedish and German gymnastics doctrines had been brought face to face in the same precincts, and that international rowing regattas on the Thames were to be made accessible to all countries. In Athens, complaints had been made about the international juries. For the 1908 Games everyone was inclined to try the idea of wholly British judges, with a number of foreign "stewards" appointed to help them if necessary: a poor solution ill-suited to simplifying the running of the events. On the other hand, there were none of those diplomatic and ethnic difficulties with which the following Olympiad was to be plagued. Even so, the status of the Dominions was not exactly

London 1908: Shortly after the start of the marathon at Windsor Castle. Below right: the Italian Pietro Dorando, subsequently disqualified following an American protest, crosses the finishing line in the stadium, with the judges' help (taken from Sport im Bild, no. 1908, p.999)

No. 32 SPORT IM BILD 999

Moment kurz nach dem Start des Marathon-Laufes bei Schloß Windsor. — Unten: Der Italiener Dorando, der später auf einen Protest der Amerikaner hin disqualifizierte Sieger des Marathon-Laufes, passiert, von Bahnfunktionären unterstützt, das Ziel im Stadion.

sie infolge der gewaltigen Hitze so unerwartet wenig geleistet hätten. Die Ueberzeugung der Engländer, die besten Distanzläufer der Welt zu haben, hat durch den diesjährigen Marathonlauf jedenfalls einen schweren Stoß erlitten. Einer der frischesten Läufer war der Schwede Svanberg, der als Achter eintraf und im Stadion noch einen veritablen Spurt zum besten gab. Im ganzen erreichten von 59 Gestarteten 28 Läufer das Ziel, einschließlich Dorandos. Der Italiener tritt übrigens augenblicklich in einem Londoner Varieté auf, wo er sich zu wohltätigen Zwecken mit dem Pokal der Königin dem begeisterten Publikum zeigt. Kdy.

straightforward. From the very beginning, as soon as the Games were revived, Australasia (as it was called in those days) had had a representative on the IOC and because of the tremendous distances involved no one was in the least surprised. But both Canada and South Africa were also part of the British Empire, and it was obvious that in London their teams would want to be considered as such, but at the same time as separate nations in their own right and with their own teams. Hence the need to define territorial jurisdictions for Olympic purposes – irrespective of international law but without contradicting its principles too much and taking into account above all the sporting realities. The problem was an extremely complex one. And it was not settled all at once. Rough and ready compromises had to be made. Some idea of its complexity can be gained from the following: What would be the status, for example, of a Canadian living in England? Would he be free to choose to join either the Canadian or the British team as he liked? What decision was to be made concerning the so-called "natives", who were British subjects in one of Britain's colonies? And once a rule had been adopted for England, how would it apply in the case of Germany, for example, if Bavaria or Saxony suddenly decided to demand a team of their own? When I founded the IOC, I automatically invited a Hungarian and a Czech to be members, in view of the sporting importance and autonomy of these countries. But Hungary was a country with distinct prerogatives, Bohemia not. The storm was to break in 1912. In 1908, there was just a little grumbling in Vienna. As far as Germany was concerned, I had consulted General von der Asseburg in confidence. I believe he spoke to the Emperor about it, at any rate to the Chancellor. The reply was that the Reich preferred by far the idea of a single, joint team from the Olympic point of view but that they understood that the very special constitution of the British Empire required separate teams. No difficulty, therefore, from the Germans. The United States' attitude however was quite different; Sullivan and his very powerful group were quite indignant at Britain's "privileges".

Another thorny problem – the metric system, which was absolutely vital. And even though changing the 100 yard race into the 100 meters (which made it 109.3 yards) was not a catastrophe for Britain's athletes technically speaking, many of them felt it a sort of national humiliation. All this had been gone into beforehand by both the British Olympic Association and the IOC, thus greatly simplifying and speeding up the examinations and discussions at The Hague. The session was a delightful one. Placed under the patronage of the Prince Consort and inaugurated by the Foreign Minister, it was held in the beautiful, peaceful setting of the Hall of Treve, one of the most "historic" in the Binnenhof. There we saw, for the last time, one of our most popular colleagues, Sir Howard Vincent, who died suddenly just before the Games, and – for the first time – a future Hungarian colleague, Mr. Jules de Muzsa, who was much appreciated subsequently, but had to wait a whole year before being admitted as a member because his government had sent him to The Hague, "appointing" him as successor to F. Kémény, who wished to retire. It was impossible for us to accept this. The day the IOC ceased to be a "self-recruiting body", it would lose its main strength: total independence. All my colleagues were now convinced of this and considered this privilege of free election the cornerstone of our constitution. The Games of the Fourth Olympiad were opened amid great pomp and ceremony on July 13, 1908. King Edward VII and his Queen, the Princes and Princesses of Sweden and Greece, and the diplomatic corps all attended the ceremony, which was most impressive. For the first time, the march past of fifteen hundred athletes grouped behind their nineteen flags fulfilled one of the wishes expressed at the Conference in the Comédie Française; they had almost all (except the Americans) agreed to wear their sports outfits and the whole appearance of the parade was transformed. "But", as pointed out in the *Olympic Review* for July 1908, "how much more perfect the whole effect would have been if, instead of the popular tunes played by military bands, there had been one of those massed choirs which excel in England performing the incomparable cantatas of Handel". Unfortunately, this had not been possible to arrange. I am continually astonished at the lack of interest shown for so many years in the idea of combining sports meetings and open-air choral performances. That sculptors and painters should hesitate to cross a forgotten threshold is understandable, but that the public should be so reluctant to try a combination whose individual beauties complete each other so well passes all understanding. There is, however, an explanation in the distortion of taste and the growing familiarity with virtuosity which means that, nowadays, the general eurythmic sense is weakened and that the development of virtuosity has made us grow used to the separation of sensorial impressions. The artistic education of the people needs to be taken in hand and started all over again. I shall be returning to this point and to my Olympic efforts in this respect.

From the artistic point of view, there were to be other disappointments in London. The art contests that the Royal Academy had agreed to organize finally fell through. Instead of allowing competitors to choose their own subjects, it was thought best to have set themes. To which were added the real difficulties inherent in the transport and display of the models for the sculpture. And it was in fact the sculptors who this first time seemed the most inclined to answer the call.

Another disappointment was the absence of equestrian events.

All this, however, was to be set right four years later in Stockholm. On the other hand, we met with satisfaction on many points. The grouping of sports had never been more apparent. The swimming pool had been dug in the stadium itself and the wrestling rings built there too. The swimming pool, surrounded by beautiful stonework reminiscent of the fountains at Versailles, possessed an ingenious mechanical device for raising the metal diving board and lowering it again between races in order not to interfere with the spectators' view of the running events.

In London, gymnastics were given a place of honor and were extremely popular with the spectators. For many, they were a revelation. The Scandinavian gymnasts were greeted with loud applause. "Birds, they are like birds!" everyone said. The fencing matches were held right next to the stadium, in huge marquees that were beautifully decorated and very well designed from the technical point of view. In all these contests, the results emphasized the international character of the Games. The individual prizes for the gymnastics events were won by an Englishman, a Frenchman, and two Germans. The four Scandinavian countries won the collective gymnastics prize. France and Hungary shared the laurels for fencing. The wrestlers, of whom there were sixty-eight, represented ten nationalities. The prize-winners were a Hungarian, a Finn, a Swede, and an Italian.

It was in the field of athletics that the Anglo-American battle was concentrated and both teams showed so much keenness and determination to win that one might have thought that all their historic rivalries had been roused and that their national honor was definitely at stake. Except for the javelin event won by the Swede Lemming, the British and American champions completely swept the board. Mention should just be made, however, of a South African and a Canadian among the medal winners. The division of medals was flattering enough to satisfy national pride, but this is not how it turned out in fact. When passions are roused to such a pitch, incidents are bound to arise. Each side accused the other of lacking fair play. A minor incident speaks volumes concerning the state of mind that prevailed. On their return home, when the transatlantic victors were solemnly received in the New York City Hall, they paraded on a leash...the British lion in chains! This almost caused a diplomatic scandal. From the very first day, King Edward had taken exception to the American athletes because of their behavior and their barbaric shouts that resounded through the stadium. I just could not understand Sullivan's attitude here. He shared his team's frenzy and did nothing to try and calm them down. This was followed on his return by a new betrayal; he persuaded the Amateur Athletic Union to appoint a commission for the purpose of forming a new International Olympic Committee and drawing up the statutes of future Games. But this time, nobody listened to him or followed him in his attempt to make a distinction between the "Olympic Games proper" and "other sports". The first category was to consist exclusively of foot races, jumping and throwing events.

The IOC no longer had any need to fear such maneuvers. Its constitution was now impregnable. At the banquet given by the British Government and presided over by Sir Edward Grey, I had been able to give a full account of its policy, its plans and the limits within which we intended to restrict our own powers and ambitions. Everything was quite clear and the success of the next Games assured.

There were a large number of parties in London. For the athletes in particular, there were six banquets with 250 and 300 guests, a big ball, and receptions everywhere. At the beginning of the Games, a religious service was held in St. Paul's, during which the Bishop of Pennsylvania gave a highly philosophical sermon.

The Games had an appendage this time under the name of "Winter Sports". These were held in October and included boxing, skating on an artificial rink, football, hockey... It was far from an ideal solution but the strong feelings prevailing in Great Britain regarding sports seasons had made it necessary. As for the Nautical Olympiad (yachting and rowing), this had been celebrated at the Isle of Wight and Henley. The regatta at Henley had been somewhat lacking in technical interest but offered the loveliest show imaginable. No matter; these small "mutilations" of the general program would simply have to be avoided in the future.

Olympic Memoirs, Chap.9, Lausanne, IOC, 1997, pp.96-105.

4.2.2/21 – 4.2.2/25 INTRODUCTION

The subject of this report is the 1912 Olympic Games in Stockholm. No previous Games had ever been so successful. After the 1908 Games in London, the IOC, and particularly its President, Pierre de Coubertin, had to resolve issues about the future athletic program of the Olympic Games, redefine the regulations that governed amateurism and that had remained unchanged since 1894, settle jurisdictional conflicts with the international athletic associations, and deal with political influences on the Games.

The meetings of the IOC in Berlin (1909), Luxembourg (1910), and Budapest (1911) were very significant for the future course of the Olympic movement. At the same time, the responsibilities of the various members of the IOC were increasing. In 1911, the IOC had forty-five members from thirty-one different countries.

Both of the published chapters of the Olympic Memoirs show the multifarious IOC-activities of these years. Even though they were written in retrospective in 1930 the authenticity of the contents has been checked.

Coubertin noted regarding the 1912 Olympic Games: "No previous Olympiad had been planned with more seriousness, attention and care".[1] In this published chapter "The Fifth Olympiad Stockholm (1912)" he discusses the first proper involvements of the modern Olympic Games with international politics in great detail. There he writes many interesting side effects of the Games.

In Sweden, organizing efforts were in the hands of Victor Balck, a member of the IOC since 1894. According to Coubertin, the Olympic Games at Stockholm were essentially Balck's triumph. While the previous Games in 1908 had, once again, been lost in the noise of the metropolis that was London, this time all Stockholm lived under the spell of the Olympics[2].

Before Stockholm, certain thorny problems regarding nationality arose, problems that were to remain unsolved as far as the Olympic movement was concerned. The Austrian Empire protested against the presence of an autonomous delegation from Bohemia. Russia lodged a similar protest with respect to Finland.

Coubertin passionately defended the idea of a specifically "athletic geography", which he wanted to see clearly distinguished from the realities of governmental politics. He was thinking particularly of the services rendered by Jiri Guth, a founding member of the IOC. Long before the Austrians got into the act, Guth had founded a Czech Olympic movement. Under pressure from Vienna, Guth had had to agree to allow the Czech delegation to be designated only by the addition of his name after them of the Austrian State. With regard to flags, it was decided that in case of victory, a standard of nationality would be raised above the flag of State, which was also important for Finland as a Grand Duchy of the Russian Empire in those days, since the Finns won nine victories in Stockholm.

The first Olympic artistic competitions were held in Stockholm, as well. We will return to this point in chapter 5.3 in this volume.

Among the athletic disciplines, the new "modern pentathlon" was introduced. This was one of Coubertin's personal wishes, long opposed by members of the IOC. The pentathlon was closely associated with the useful lifetime sports ["Gymnastique utilitaire"] that Coubertin had advocated since the early years of this century.

4.2.2/21 THE IOC IN BERLIN (1909)

The time had now come for the long awaited Session of the IOC to be held in Berlin. Soon after the London Games, where the Germans had been so well received, and some time before the Stockholm Games, for whose success they were willing to do everything possible, the occasion could not have been more favorable. The German delegation, consisting of General Count von der Asseburg, Count C. Wartensleben, and Dr. W. Gebhardt, was more "Olympic" than it had ever been. The General in particular, who was much liked by his colleagues on the IOC, enjoyed a reputation in Berlin that enabled him to ensure the maximum prestige for the meeting. A number of new members had joined the International Olympic Committee in December 1908. In the same ballot, we had elected: for the United States – replacing James Hyde who had acted only in a temporary capacity – Allison V. Armour, a famous yachtsman who was a familiar figure at the Kiel regattas and a personal friend of Kaiser William; for Romania, George A. Plagino; and for Turkey, Selim Sirry Bey, a fine athlete and a great Francophile, who had, however, served under the orders of German instructors. These newcomers would all be very pleased to have the 1909 meeting held in the capital of the German Empire. Finally, for once the agenda of our sessions contained nothing the least bit political. The program for the 1912 Games in Stockholm, on the one hand, and the examination of amateurism on the other, gave it an almost exclusively technical character. Everything was in its favor. By the end of 1908, the Session looked most promising: the sovereign's patronage, the Crown Prince's personal participation, the holding of the meetings in the Upper House, everything augured complete success.

This success, however, was nearly compromised by the death of General von der Asseburg, who died suddenly on March 31 after two days' illness. His sudden and completely unexpected demise as the result of a stroke left me at a loss for several days. It took a certain courage on the part of Wartensleben, who was still very young and not even a Berliner, not to ask us to cancel the meeting. Nevertheless, he bravely placed himself at his colleagues' service, and I was delighted. It was, after all, the best solution. He handled the arrangements superbly. Everything was left just as prepared by the General, and Wartensleben replaced him as host. From May 27 to June 2, work sessions and receptions followed in quick succession. The Crown Prince, Chancellor Bethmann-Hollweg, and the Foreign Minister, von Schoen, lavished their attentions on the Committee, who were even received by the Emperor on the last day. This stay in Berlin, under rather special circumstances, gave me an opportunity of seeing some very interesting things indeed, but it would be out of place for me to recount them in these "Olympic" memoirs. It is far more appropriate that I should keep them for my "personal" memoirs and limit myself here to an account of the main technical results of the meeting. In the course of six very busy sessions, we voted unanimously in favor of Stockholm and began to study the program for the 1912 Games. Actually, the choice of the Swedish capital had been practically decided on in London the previous year. Our German

1 *Olympic Memoirs*, Lausanne, IOC, 1997, p. 110.
2 Cf. ibid, p. 139.

colleagues withdrew the candidature of Berlin, as we knew they would, postponing it unofficially until 1916. The Swedes, who are averse to improvising and do not like to be caught unawares, had prepared and submitted a fairly complete preliminary draft, inviting discussion, however, on several important points.

Perhaps it would be a good idea here to explain how, in what form and by what methods the program of the Olympic Games was prepared in those days, for many sportsmen have no idea of this at all and a great many faulty ideas have been published on the subject.

The fundamental charter of the Olympic Games laid no absolute obligations either on the organizers or on the International Olympic Committee, except as regards the compulsory sports categories. This charter had been drawn up by the IOC in accordance with the instructions laid down by the Sorbonne Congress in 1894. The categories referred to above were as follows: athletics, gymnastics, combat sports, nautical sports, and equestrian sports. However, nothing was laid down as to distances or even the subdivisions of each category. I had always considered that later there would have to be a fixed program, always the same, whose details would be drawn up by a congress at which the National Olympic Committees would be represented. Nevertheless, in 1909 the National Committees were still in the process of formation; not every country had one. Hungary, Sweden, Germany, Bohemia, and England were, if I remember rightly, the only countries to have properly organized committees. In a large number of other countries, Olympic Committees did exist, but either because their existence was still precarious or because they lacked authority, they could not as yet be counted on. As for the federations, the international ones were still very few in number, all coming up against financial difficulties and, for the most part, having great trouble in exerting their authority. The others – the national ones – were as a general rule anti-Olympic, feeling – quite wrongly – that the National Olympic Committees were rival organizations, and wanting to deal directly with the Organizing Committee of the Games without realizing what chaos this would lead to. The Olympic Games comprised a collection of all sports, and if it had not been for the National Olympic Committees the organizers would have had to contact not only each country, but each sports group in each country.

The question of National Committees was a very complex one. They were free to form themselves more or less as they wished. At one time, we had an American Committee with a hundred members and a Japanese Committee with only four. We interfered neither in their formation nor in their running. We even had to be prepared for the appearance of several opposing or conflicting committees in the same country. This had already happened in South America. How, in such cases, were we to recognize the right one? In order to avoid incidents of this kind, I had a very dictatorial text voted which I hoped we should never have to use but which could, if necessary, be referred to by the organizers of the Games to get them out of a difficult situation. According to this text, "recognition" of a National Committee was up to the member or members of the IOC for the country in question. Their decision was final. Armed with this draconian power, we avoided as far as possible being forced to use it, resorting in preference first of all to diplomatic persuasion. Very often the situation seemed

12th IOC Session, Berlin 1909: IOC members and guests at the opening ceremony (IOC Archives)

inextricable, but as the time for the Games approached, it would unravel itself owing to the desire of the selected competitors not to miss the Games and the pressure they brought to bear on their officials to make them listen to reason.

All this explains why, contrary to my original idea, the IOC was obliged to play an active role in the technical preparation of the Games. During the whole of this period, extending from 1896 to 1914, we encouraged the Organizing Committees to submit their programs (inspired by us in 1896 and 1900, and drawn up entirely by themselves in 1904, 1908, and 1912) for discussion and subsequent amendment by mutual agreement. This generally took from eighteen months to two years and it must not be thought that we disregarded the opinions of the federations and other competent groups. Even though indirectly, the latter were nevertheless duly consulted and had many opportunities of letting us know their opinion, which was always taken into account wherever possible, provided they used the proper channels to give voice to their ideas and did not try to revolutionize the sacrosanct principle of the institution.

This was how, in Berlin in 1909 and in Luxembourg in 1910, the program for the Games of Fifth Olympiad was prepared down to the smallest detail. We put the finishing touches to it at Budapest in 1911. No previous Olympiad had been planned with more seriousness, attention, and care... For London, even though the time had been short, these same qualities had been evident in the preparation. For the Stockholm Games, however, they really came into their own. Naturally, certain compromises had to be made here and there. It should not be forgotten that we were still very much in the position of someone saying to another: "You have some lovely reception rooms. Please let us use them for a wonderful party, at your expense". This humorous way of putting it, which I often laughingly repeated, remained and will continue to remain true. It will be seen further on that it was still true in 1920 and in 1924. For the Fifth Olympiad, it compelled us to accept the temporary suppression of boxing. Not only was Swedish public opinion against this sport but boxing matches were even prohibited by law in Sweden. Although boxing was never noted for its moderation, in my "educational" plan I continued to attach great importance to it in spite of its present imperfections. But in this instance we had to give in. Sweden, for her part, agreed to a number of tremendous concessions, in the field of gymnastics in particular. When I visited that country in 1899 for the first time, I would never have believed it possible that the intransigence of Ling's disciples would weaken twelve years later to the extent of tolerating the glorification of all sports in the heart of Stockholm and the setting up of the detested apparatus right in the middle of the stadium. Fortunately, in those twelve years the evolution in Sweden's attitude to sport, which had started some time before, began to speed up thanks to the encouragement of the King and Princes and above all of our popular and enthusiastic colleague Balck.

The Swedish Committee asked that in addition to boxing, cycling, too, should be suppressed; their request was granted only in part, in so far as the track races were concerned – which I was quite pleased to see excluded – but not the road races. The principle of the marathon was raised once again, but everyone recognized the inadvisability of suppressing it. Equestrian sports and art contests took the place allotted them by protocol, but which unfortunately had been denied them in London. The bulk of the sessions was taken up with discussions on amateurism, which I shall go into in the next chapter.

Shortly after the Berlin meeting, Dr. W. Gebhardt, who had waited till it was over to retire, handed in his resignation and we elected in his stead Baron von Venningen, a brilliant all-round athlete who was very soon to become one of our most popular members. Gebhardt, who had been elected in 1895, had been with us for fourteen years and had accomplished much. The chief founder of the German Olympic Committee, he had been head of the German teams in 1896 and 1900 and, with F. Kémény, had represented the IOC at St. Louis. Shortly afterwards, a second member was elected for Italy: State Councilor Attilio Brunialti, a Member of Parliament and Vice-President of the Physical Training Institute. He was an invaluable addition to our ranks. The two newcomers made their debut at the next meeting in the spring of 1910. It should have been held in Budapest, but I readily accepted our Hungarian colleagues' request to postpone it until 1911 for reasons beyond their control. I knew that the Budapest meeting would be a very fashionable affair accompanied by a great many social events and I wanted to slip in a work session between Berlin and Budapest, in a more neutral town. Luxembourg had already been sounded out. The government of the Grand Duchy and the town council agreed to have us. The Grand Duchess Regent, who unfortunately could not attend herself, gave us a very fine banquet in her name. A party given by Mr. and Mrs. Pescatore, at the Chateau de Septfontaines, was the occasion for us to acquire a new member, for soon afterwards we elected as member in Luxembourg

Mr. Maurice Pescatore, at the time a Member of Parliament, and the most sporting and charming of colleagues. We were to lose him nineteen years later when this indefatigable horseman and hunter died suddenly and prematurely, just after renewing his hunting and exploratory exploits a last time by crossing Africa from East to West. I was surprised and delighted to hear Minister of State Eyschen, head of the Luxembourg Government, in his speech of welcome praise the constitution of the IOC. Until then, we had heard nothing but criticism from the heads of the federations whose ambitions it disturbed.

But after glancing at the few articles composing the constitution, Mr. Eyschen, whose political sense was highly regarded in Europe, had noticed and appreciated the originality of its mechanism, so well designed to ensure the complete independence of the Committee and the defense of modern Olympism against everyone and everything. For me, this was invaluable encouragement to resist certain tendencies towards faint-hearted timidity that sometimes appeared in our ranks.

Olympic Memoirs, Chap. 10, Lausanne, IOC, 1997, pp. 106-113.

4.2.2/22 BUDAPEST (1911)

Like 1905, 1911 was one of our most profitable years. The Budapest meeting filled the center of the stage but the work we accomplished, whether it concerned matters there or elsewhere, covered a great many fields. In passing, I should like to pay tribute to Hungary for having, right from the start, shown herself to be particularly understanding of the spirit of Olympism and for having remained one of its most loyal adherents right up to the present day. To me, Hungary was a friend. Poland, with its youthful camaraderie, had influenced my childhood. Hungary was the country of my adolescence and youth, just as England and the United States were the countries of my early manhood, and later Greece and Switzerland, the countries of lasting attachment. I owe so much to so many cosmopolitan friendships. They never in any way detracted from my love of my own country. But, just as much as I believe in the value of this kind of cosmopolitanism, I feel equally strongly that one must be wary of the brand of cosmopolitanism born of mere travel, with its risk of dangerous misunderstanding and illusion.

Budapest welcomed us, in the month of May 1911, with a display of the most lavish hospitality. Halls had been prepared for us in the Palace of the Academy of Sciences. It was here that the Archduke Joseph, standing in for the sovereign who was absent, made his speech of welcome after that of the Prime Minister, Count Khuen-Hedervary. A reception at Court, banquets given by the government and the town, and a host of festivities of all kinds mingle in my memory together with the strains of the gypsy orchestras that filled our ears throughout our stay with their haunting music that was a mixture of deep melancholy and frenzied abandon.

At that time, the Committee was composed of forty-three members belonging to thirty-one different nations. It had assumed its definitive form at last, having been considerably strengthened by the election of eminent figures like Baron von Venningen and Count Sierstorpff in Germany, the State Councilor Brunialti (Italy), Professor, and later

Senator, Jigoro Kano, the reviver of jiu-jitsu (Japan), Baron Willebrand (Finland), General Sir Hanbury Williams (Canada), Messrs. Sverre (Norway), Bolanachi (Egypt), and Evert J. Wendell (United States), who were soon to be joined by Prince Otto von Windischgraetz and Count Rudolf Colloredo in Austria. All, or almost all of them, were sportsmen in the real sense of the word, in keeping with the idea I had formed from the very beginning, that is to say men competent enough to be able to get to the bottom of any particular question, but far enough removed from any exclusive specialization ever to become its slaves, men international enough not to be blinded in any international question by their strictly national prejudices, men – finally – capable of holding their own with technical groups and who could be counted on to be completely free of any material dependence upon the latter. Among all these men, now accustomed to meeting and, in fact, taking great pleasure in their annual reunion, real bonds of friendship had grown. All the rest of the year, I corresponded regularly with them.

It has been believed and said – it was an easy way to cast aspersions on us – that they had all been "appointed" by me. Nothing was further from the truth. Only one of all those I have mentioned had been my personal candidate. Elections have always been held regularly, but the actual choice was always preceded by long investigations, sometimes by direct correspondence with the person involved, but always with his sponsor or sponsors.

People have also wondered a great deal about the IOC's budget. Obviously it was quite different from any other. This did not make it any more mysterious however. When people were told that a member's annual subscription amounted to no more than twenty-five francs, they would not believe it. It was however the truth, pure and simple. And the amount was not increased until the war. Of these twenty-five francs, twenty went to the Olympic Review and five to the IOC's funds. The Olympic Review – subscriptions to which played a very minor role – was sent to clubs or individuals whose backing was deemed important, and its budget was completed by the revenue from advertising. The IOC's office expenses, although "world-wide", were comparatively small. I had made them my personal responsibility. Every member naturally paid his own annual expenses and the exceptional expenses involved whenever a Session was held in his country. Such terms cooled the ardor of many more or less undesirable candidates. Not one penny in the way of subsidies ever came our way. What a lot one can do with even limited resources when one deliberately rejects the absurd and heavy mantle of administrative routine, red tape, superfluous documents, and the tyranny of the typewriter.

The Budapest meeting was outstanding not only for its fashionable brilliance. Its eight work sessions were copiously filled. We put the finishing touches to the program for Stockholm and if, for the reasons I have already mentioned, we had to give up for the moment the idea of including boxing, three technical successes were achieved which it had not been possible to carry through before. First of all, regarding equestrian sports. These had been included from the beginning. Pure force of circumstances had caused them to be omitted at the last moment from the second program in Athens owing to the material impossibility of obtaining the horses in time. Neither Paris nor St. Louis had been ready for the addition of riding to the other sports. In London, in spite of the organizers' manifest goodwill, the time available had been too short and certain prejudices had raised obstacles. Nothing of the kind however occurred in the case of Stockholm. Even so a determined and prolonged effort had to be made. Our second Swedish colleague, Count Clarence von Rosen, did everything that was needed with an enthusiasm and a zeal that never flagged for an instant. On a propaganda tour all over Europe, he won over to his cause both governments and armies. As a result, these first "Equestrian Games" had an exclusively military character about them, and this was to remain so in the following Olympiads. But this could not be helped, at any rate at the beginning.

Another innovation was the creation of the "modern pentathlon". I had already submitted the idea to the IOC on two previous occasions, and my proposal had always been greeted with a lack of understanding and almost hostility. I had not insisted. This time however the grace of the Holy Sporting Ghost enlightened my colleagues and they accepted an event to which I attached great importance: a veritable consecration of the complete athlete, the modern pentathlon was to comprise a footrace, a horse race, a swimming race, a fencing match and, finally, a shooting contest, which I would prefer to have had replaced by a rowing race, but this would have added greatly to the difficulties of organization, which was already quite complicated enough. The modern pentathlon has met with growing success ever since, without my real intentions ever being carried out: courses unknown to the competitors, events following each other in quick succession, almost non-stop, horses provided by the organizing country and drawn for by lots at the last moment – this is what I had thought would give the whole a first-rate educational character.

Opposition based on class was perpetually raised against this conception of the event and culminated in causing the present organizers to forget completely the principles laid down by the creator of the pentathlon.

The third of the achievements I wish to mention was the institution of a hunting and a mountain climbing prize for the finest climb and the best hunting feat accomplished since the celebration of the previous Olympiad. The idea had been put forward at the initial Congress in 1894 and had been transmitted to us by this assembly in the form of a recommendation. I imagined it being completed later by a third Olympic prize of the same kind for aviation. All this was in the spirit of "all games, all nations". It was, moreover, easy to organize, and the cost was minimal... However, in all three cases, complete indifference and sometimes even positive ill-will without discernible cause were manifest; one minute people would be in favor, the next minute against, revealing obvious caprice and lack of purpose. I hope that we shall come back one day to the above-mentioned idea. It is a good one.

Art competitions were also held finally, five years after the program had been drawn up by the Paris Conference. Very simple rules and regulations were published in English, French, and German (Olympic Review of September 1911), but not without a certain reluctance on the part of the Swedish Committee to which the IOC Executive Board had to promise its direct assistance for the sending out of invitations. I heard afterwards that Swedish artists and writers had shown violent opposition to the idea and I shall have an opportunity later of describing the strange situation to which this led us.

In order to encourage future competitors and, if possible, create a movement in favor of the idea, we made great efforts at the IOC during 1911. Most of my colleagues, I must confess, had some little difficulty in getting really interested in this part of the scheme. I found myself doing most of the work and bearing most of the expenses. First of all, a special architecture competition was arranged in Paris and I managed to persuade President Fallières to act as patron. The subject of the competition was the establishment of plans for a "Modern Olympia". All competitors were admitted without distinction as to nationality or anything else. The subject had been explained and commented on previously in a series of articles in the Olympic Review from October 1909 to March 1910. It certainly offered enough technical problems and varied prospects to attract young architects. The correspondence however bore witness to a great deal of hesitation and indifference on the part of the latter. In addition to these articles, collected in a brochure for propaganda purposes, the Review published a second series entitled "Decoration, Pyrotechnics, Harmonies, Processions". The text was sent to art clubs, schools, and groups as well as to the small "intellectual" circles likely to be interested.

When the jury of the "Modern Olympia" competition, presided over by Mr. T. Homolle, former head of the School of Athens and now head of France's national museums, awarded the prize to the very fine project of two Vaudois (Swiss) architects, Mr. Eugène Monod and Mr. A. Laverrière, the IOC gave a party in honor of the two prize-winners; an original festivity and, I would like to add, the most beautiful I have ever seen from the eurhythmic point of view. It was held by night, in the courtyard of the Sorbonne filled, in spite of the threatening weather, by an appreciative audience of some two thousand guests. Behind the artificial groves were concealed an orchestra and choirs. The courtyard was plunged in darkness. Very clever lighting effects were used to illuminate the peristyle and vary its aspect in a multitude of different ways and colors. The program of music, the motions performed by one hundred gymnasts bearing torches and palms, who acted as extras, and the sixteen ephebes, whose silent exercises occupied the esplanade along the front of the Richelieu Chapel, all helped to create a perfect harmony of sound, light, silence and silhouettes. The architectural beauty of the setting helped enormously. The interlude of medieval and modern fencing, the small procession of hurdy-gurdies and bagpipes accompanying Saint-Saens' "King John's Ceremonial March", the Greek women's dances, and finally the performance of Maurice Pottecher's charming play "The Philosopher and the Athletes", which included a real wrestling match, all these followed each other in quick succession until the brilliant close when, after the fireworks had been let off from the top of the monument at the foot of the dome, the choral works of Rameau and Palestrina poured forth their majestic tones over an attentive, enthusiastic audience. All this required merely the participation of a gymnastics club, a fencing school, and the musical associations of one district of Paris. For me, it was not only the fulfillment of a wonderful dream, but the acquisition of a certainty concerning popular art. In this respect, civilization had strayed from the right path and the "revival of eurhythmics" alone would set it back in the right direction again: eurhythmics, a lost art, about which people talk a great deal without really knowing what it was like in the olden days!

The number of the Olympic Review which contains an account of the festivities held on May 16, 1911, and at the same time the report on the Budapest Session (which started a week later), also contains the preliminary program for the Sports Psychology Congress, due to take place in Lausanne in 1913, and announces for the spring of 1914 big celebrations to be held in Paris for the purpose of commemorating the twentieth anniversary of the revival of the Olympic Games, at the same time as a Congress of members of National Committees for drawing up the definitive technical conditions governing future Games. Thus, Budapest symbolizes for us the soundness of the foundations on which we had built the IOC and the greatness of the hopes we entertained for the completion of the edifice: all of which I tried to express by having inscribed on a new medal the motto which I hoped to see replace the eternal Mens sana in corpore sano, whose "eminently hygienic" ideal remained "a little too medical to be proposed to the ambitions of the young". Mens fervida in corpore lacertoso originated here. "Athletes", joked a newspaper, "will have a hard time trying to strike a balance between the irrepressible ardor of the mind and the daring suppleness of the body. It will be almost like flying an airplane: one can fall from it, one can even kill oneself, but the end is a glorious one, and on the wings of the biplane in question those who do not fall have a chance perhaps of attaining the heights of perfect Olympism."

To bring the year 1911 to a close, I must mention my visit to Holland. After stopping off in Brussels and Antwerp, with a slightly longer stay at The Hague and the University of Leyden, I attended a meeting in Amsterdam of the Presidents of Dutch sports associations, and at the end of a dinner given by our dear colleague van der Tuyll I had taken, in agreement with him, the first tentative steps towards the future celebration of the Olympic Games in Holland. I felt that this would be a very worthwhile and profitable experience. The big cities of the world were not particularly suited to such events. The Hague and Amsterdam were both more appropriate. But the Dutch seemed both anxious to see their towns chosen and at the same time intimidated by the responsibilities involved. The matter was discussed in a short article published in Dutch in our Review. From then on the possibility remained on the horizon, and to help us keep it there we were lucky enough to have in F.W. van der Tuyll the most firmly convinced and the most convincing of champions. Eighteen years later, the possibility was to become fact. Unfortunately, he was no longer there to enjoy it.

Olympic Memoirs, Chap. 10, Lausanne, IOC, 1997, pp. 122-130.

4.2.2/23 THE FIFTH OLYMPIAD (STOCKHOLM 1912)

Very little was left now of the attempts to supplant the IOC by the creation of a new international organization. Sloane had written on February 27, 1911 to tell me that Sullivan had not only come to see the futility of such an undertaking but that, on being invited to join a band of die-hards who still dreamed of it, he had refused and had even done his best to discourage them. The federations, on the other hand, were rather more reluctant to face the facts. In 1909, the International Cycling Union had proclaimed its determination to refuse any form of participation in the "International Committee's Olympic Games", reserving itself the possibility however of taking part in "those scheduled to be held in Athens". But the Greek committee, which had hoped to celebrate intermediate Games at the foot of the Acropolis in 1910 – to which we would have extended our help as loyally as in 1906 – was obliged to give up the idea, for lack of money, an economic crisis. From

Athens we received an unofficial proposal to include the Athenian series in our own cycle: the Games would be celebrated every eight years in Greece, and every other eight years in another country. It was impossible to agree to this proposal. It would have meant torpedoing our own work without any real benefit to anyone. International politics were far too uncertain for the choice of the venue for the Games to be fixed such a long time in advance. It was vital for the IOC to preserve complete freedom of action in this respect too.

After the cyclists, it was the turn of the oarsmen to attempt a somewhat underhanded maneuver against the IOC at a Congress held in Lucerne towards the end of 1908. This, too, was doomed to failure. While the federations were forced to recognize the ineffectiveness of their attacks, the National Olympic Committees were consolidating their power. Mr. Bolanachi and Count Gautier-Vignal had formed committees in Egypt and Monaco, with the Khedive and the Monegasque sovereign agreeing to act as Honorary Presidents. The British and German committees were now firmly established. The same was true of Hungary. The American committee, under the presidency of Colonel Thompson, with Sullivan as Secretary, was gradually taking its definitive form. The Belgian, Danish, and Spanish committees (the last of these three had quite recently been formed by our colleague the Marquess of Villamejor, brother of the Count of Romanones) were all working well. Colonel S.W. Djoukitch had just created one in Serbia. There were committees in Australia, Canada, Holland, Italy, Japan, Norway, Portugal, and Romania. Only the French and the Swiss seemed to be having a little trouble in sorting themselves out. However they gradually succeeded in finding solutions without offending the feelings of the local federations in the case of the former, and those of the independent cantons in that of the latter.

But there was also a Czech committee and a Finnish committee. The first was one of the oldest, in fact. Conceived in 1899, it had been formed in 1903. Doctor Jiri Guth-Jarkovsky had brought to its constitution all the perseverance and tenacity of which his Czech patriotism was capable. He had succeeded in persuading not only Mr. Srb, the Mayor of Prague, to be its Honorary President but also Prince Lobkovitz to be its patron. As for Finland, although not so old its committee was no less attached to the cause of national independence and in 1908 we had elected a Finnish member, Baron von Willebrand. Now things were moving fast. The Olympic Games were becoming an affair of State. Royal families were becoming involved and governments too..., so much so that in both St. Petersburg and Vienna storms were brewing.

Luckily matters could be settled without too much difficulty in Austria. Instead of attacking the Czechs alone, the Austrians had turned on the Hungarians too. A mere question of alphabetical order. So as not to be accused of favoring English or German over French, the Swedes had made a point of using the Swedish language – which nobody except themselves understood – far more than was reasonable. Thus, well beforehand, the newspapers discussed the alphabetical order in which the athletes would march past on the opening day. The Austrian Minister in Stockholm, having thus been made prematurely aware of this minor matter, pointed out to Vienna that in order to do things properly the Austrian athletes and the Hungarians should form a single contingent for the march past. The Imperial

Chancellery agreed with him, and informed Stockholm that this was what should be done. Now the Hungarians took exception to this interference in their Olympic rights and, on January 19, 1912, Mr. von Muzsa notified Sweden, on behalf of the national committee, that their team would withdraw from the Games if this order were maintained. Great excitement, much exchange of diplomatic notes. Finally, a tacit surrender on the part of the Chancellery.

By then, the Austrian footballers had for several months been demanding the exclusion of the Czech teams and trying to involve the Germans in their quarrel. What made the situation particularly tricky was that our new colleague, Prince von Windischgraetz, had, by his marriage to the Archduchess Elisabeth, become the grandson of the Emperor Franz-Joseph, and that whatever his own views and conciliatory tendencies he could not, under the circumstances, oppose his Chancellery, which demanded the removal of the name of Bohemia from the list of Olympic countries. On top of all this, I received a letter from the Russian Ambassador in Paris, Mr. Isvolsky, likewise demanding the removal of Finland on behalf of the "Imperial Ministry of Foreign Affairs".

There were three sides to the affair. The composition of the International Olympic Committee was involved to a certain extent, then the formation and order of march of the contingents taking part in the Games, and finally the color of the flag to be raised in case of the victory of a Czech or a Finnish athlete. On receipt of the first protests, the Swedish committee had replied very loyally that it was up to the IOC to decide, and that its decision would be respected. My colleagues would never have allowed two of their number to be forced to resign, but it had not yet come to this. Neither Dr. Jiri Guth nor Baron von Willebrand was in danger of having to take such a step. All that was being requested was that, opposite their names on the IOC's list, the word Austria should be printed instead of Bohemia, and Russia instead of Finland. Everyone therefore was waiting for the IOC's decision, and members of the IOC were waiting for that of their President.

I was in a quandary because, on the one hand, there was an undeniable political fact and, on the other, a just cause and the gratitude we owed the countries that had backed us so faithfully. My personal sentiments however had to take second place to those dictated by my function. Had I been free to do so, I would have given a place of their own not only to Bohemia and Finland but also to Poland and Ireland. Having spontaneously, before the expected letter arrived from the Russians, put Finland on the list after Russia and placed Bohemia between Austria and Belgium, I started on a long exchange of correspondence that was as diplomatic as I could make it. I called attention to this concession, pointing out that the Czar bore among other titles that of Grand Duke of Finland, and the Austrian Emperor that of King of Bohemia, and that as a consequence these two countries enjoyed a status differing from that of other territories of lesser autonomy; above all, I kept returning to the undeniable existence of a "sports geography", quite distinct from a political geography; I contrasted the way in which we had been led to decide in favor of Bohemia and Finland with the refusal we had given to the Croatian Sokols' request which had been made last year and which we did not consider to be based on any firm grounds... My whole aim at this point was to play for time, and to this end I deliberately confused the issue by writing one time to St. Petersburg or Vienna

In 1912 an ample array of equestrian contests was on the program of the Olympics, although they had been listed as Olympic sports as early as 1894. Coubertin felt much obliged to Sweden for their admission. Here: E.-H. Deloch (GER) in the Prize Jumping. (Photo taken from E.Petersen/S.Hermlin, Dem Femte Olympiaden. Olympiska Spelen I Stockholm 1912 I bild och ord. Gotehburg, Ahlen & Akerlund, 1912, p.297)

Coubertin had a special partiality for football, especially for rugby with the players' physical input and emotional concentration; later also for English soccer. Here the Olympic final 1912 between Great Britain and Denmark (4:2). (Photo taken from E.Petersen/S.Hermlin, ibidem, p.57)

As a classical contest Coubertin admired wrestling also in the modern Olympic Games. Here in Stockholm 1912: J.K.Salila (FIN) turning R.Fogelmark (SWE) in the Middle Weight B. In the Middle Weight A a wrestling contest lasted no less than 11 hours. (Photo taken from E. Petersen/ S.Hermlin, ibidem, p.151)

directly, another time to Stockholm, and on yet another occasion to the national committees. I soon saw that all this was causing considerable annoyance not only to Mr. Isvolsky but also to the Russian Ministry, and in fact St. Petersburg ended up by leaving us alone. With Vienna, which was more stubborn, we finally had to give in, in agreement with the Czech committee itself, whose initials (COT) alone continued to appear on the list as a reminder and a hope. The question of flags was solved as follows: in case of victory, a standard with the Czech or Finnish colors would be raised above the Austrian or Russian flags. And this is how the Russian flag came to be hoisted in celebration of victory! A remark I gave myself the pleasure of making to General Woyeikof at the end of the Games. For this famous General of the Court, whose role at the beginning of the revolution was to be so debatable, was present. He had sailed in a warship to attend the Games, at the head of an enormous delegation of young officers, and even accompanied by a balalaika orchestra – to the great joy of the Grand Duchess Maria, wife (later divorced) of Prince William of Sweden, who had remained Russian in her heart.

These details, which I will refrain from prolonging, show clearly enough that the Fifth Olympiad, like the loveliest roses, also had its thorny side! In fact, what an intricate web of diplomatic difficulties, of petty personal intrigues, of feelings to be spared, of wounded vanity, of underhanded tricks. One had to be constantly on the alert and be able to see incidents coming long before they actually happened in order to prevent them from growing. These were the thorns. But how can I describe the roses? What a fine show of blooms! Never had a Swedish summer been more glorious. For five whole weeks, nature was resplendent, the sun perpetually shining, with light sea breezes, radiant nights, the joyful atmosphere of gaily-decked streets, flowers everywhere, and illuminations dimmed only by the brilliance of a light that never paled. In the wonderful setting of the city, the general gaiety of the young knew no bounds. There was little time for sleep, but nobody wanted to sleep anyway. Festivities succeeded festivities without visible adverse effect on muscular feats. The Gothic stadium, with its pointed arches and towers, its technical perfection, its well-planned and methodical regulations, seemed a model of its kind. Depending on the need, it acted as a banqueting hall, a concert hall, or a ballroom and was always ready again the next morning for another series of athletic events. In one evening we saw it covered with squares of grass laid side by side, strewn with obstacles and decorated with banks of flowers for the equestrian games. Everything was done silently, quickly, without error. Whereas in London the life of the huge metropolis had not been influenced by the invasion of Olympism, the whole of Stockholm was impregnated with it. The whole city took part in the effort in honor of the foreigners and we caught a glimpse of what the atmosphere of Olympia must have been like in ancient times – although on a larger scale, embellished and enhanced by the presence of all the modern facilities and amenities, without any of the ugliness they so often bring in their wake, so that Hellenism and progress seemed to have joined forces to act as hosts together.

The Crown Prince was everywhere, indefatigable, lucid, practical, always smiling, and his committee resembled him. Balck dominated the scene with his popular silhouette. No detail was too petty for him to ignore. This Olympiad was his triumph, the culmination of his past efforts to persuade his country to go in for sport of all kinds without in any way rejecting traditional gymnastics. And even if there were still a few unrelenting advocates of this exclusive cult who, it was said, had fled Stockholm in order not to see the apparatus of this wider cult set up there, public opinion was none the less with Balck.

Looking at the Olympic Review for 1912, now in the seventh year of its existence and dedicated more and more to its educational role, I see that the whole of the June number is devoted to Sweden, with a resume of its past history and a glance at its present situation, completed by well-chosen excerpts from the delightful book just published by Andre Bellesort. The same number also contained an account of Swedish sports organization. Sweden was sparing no expense or effort to receive the youth of the two worlds. And it was only fitting for youth in its turn to benefit from the lesson learned in Sweden... This point of view was developed at the beginning of the following number in English, under the title "Pax olimpica", a delightfully inspired sermon written by Laffan, that was eminently classical and at the same time called attention to the great precepts of tolerance and mutual respect bequeathed to us by the Olympism of the ancients: a sermon whose influence will be far-reaching, for never before had such harmony reigned among so many athletes. This was followed by the report on the artistic and literary contests. The results were not particularly brilliant and were weakened still further by the Swedish artists' insistence on being treated separately and holding a second competition of their own, a demand to which we made the mistake of acceding even though its impropriety and unsuitability should have made us refuse it right away. However the first competitions were actually held, prizes awarded, and the prize-winning works exhibited. It was a first step in the right direction, that was the main thing.

The August issue contained the minutes of the IOC Session that started on July 4, in the Senate Hall of the Riksdag Palace, in the presence of the Crown Prince and Princess together with other members of the royal family: a very well-attended Session; our English, American, German, Italian and Austro-Hungarian colleagues were all there. Our Japanese colleague took part for the first time. The Sixth Olympiad was to be celebrated in Berlin; the Chancellor of the German Reich sent the Kaiser's greetings. Everything looked promising. By then the Paris Congress would have drawn up a program and the final regulations.

The July issue published the results of the Games. The United States had won 26 first prizes, Sweden 23, Britain 10, Finland 9, France 7, Germany 5. Then came Italy, Hungary, Norway, South Africa, Canada, Belgium, Greece, Holland, etc.

There were two pentathlons: the "modern" – mine – which had got off to a very good start, and the "classical", the winner of which ran the 200 meters in 22.9 seconds, and the 1,500 meters in 4 min. 44 sec., jumped 7.70 m, threw the discus 35.57 m and the javelin 46.71 m. The figures recorded by the winners of the separate events were: 21.7 sec., 3 min. 56 sec., 7.60 m, 45 meters and 60 meters. An interesting comparison of the feats of an all-rounder with those of the specialists.

The American team had been brought over on a big liner, which managed to steam right into Stockholm, where it served as their hotel: a liner set up as a permanent training center with running tracks on the deck, stationary bicycles, a canvas swimming pool in which the swimmers were attached by a rope and pulled back after each stroke, discuses and javelins secured by cords so that they could fall into the sea and be pulled back on board again! Technical achievements of this kind, accompanied by iron discipline, deserved their reward and received it. Sullivan, who was whole-heartedly dedicated to the cause again, led his team with absolute maestria and exemplary conscientiousness, while Colonel Thompson, who presided over it from his yacht, increased by the cordiality of his hospitality the favorable impression created by his young compatriots.

Britain, in spite of the keenness of her officials, was ill prepared and almost lost heart at the sight of her long list of failures, but Finland, without financial resources, without proper sports grounds, handicapped by its extremely severe winters, carried off an astonishing number of victories, simply because its athletes were determined to do their country honor.

A record. A Swedish woman, Mrs. Wersall, had all six of her sons taking part in the Games in one way or another, the youngest as boy scouts enrolled to help in maintaining order and carrying messages. How true to ancient ideals! The IOC awarded her the Olympic medal.

Two innovations. In London, there had been St. Paul's. In Stockholm, there was no cathedral worthy of the name. So a short religious service was held in the stadium at the beginning of the opening ceremony: a simple psalm, a prayer in Swedish given by the Archbishop of Uppsala, then another in English composed and spoken by the Rev. Laffan: ten minutes in all. And in the midst of the great silence of these thousands of spectators and athletes, the occasion seemed to reach the sublime. But I had a feeling we were exceeding our rights...

To avoid the intrigues usually accompanying the award of decorations, the King had created a new one especially for the occasion: a silver medal with a blue and pale yellow ribbon, which was to be handed out fairly freely. It was a perfect solution, but the seekers after distinctions operated behind the scenes, so that, by the end of the Games, we had once again the usual unsavory situation, titles to be weighed, "exchanges" to be made between the orders of the host country and those of visiting countries, the flagrant bargaining, the hierarchies to be respected...

The press? It was not yet what it should have been, especially with regard to critical faculties and impartiality. Progress over London however. Rather spitefully, the foreign press announced that the "deficit would be in the neighborhood of 400,000 marks" and said that "it would always be this way". I immediately asked Balck to send me the accounts as quickly as possible so that I could publish them. Expenses amounted to 776,000 crowns; receipts to 822,767 crowns. A fine surplus. As for the construction of the stadium which, in its completed state, would cost in the neighborhood of a million, it was a permanent building to be helped by subsidies from the State and the town. Stockholm stood to gain whichever way you looked at it.

The splendor of the Equestrian Games was the last act. Rosen had wanted them to be magnificent and had done everything possible to ensure that they would be-and they were! The curtain fell on this Grand Finale. Then came the departures. The time had come to leave and, while the fleeting northern summer was drawing to a close and the rays of the sun became more oblique, the last visitor went off full of gratitude towards his Scandinavian friends and full of hope for the future of Olympism...

Olympic Memoirs, Chap. 10, Lausanne, IOC, 1997, pp. 134-143.

4.2.2/24 A BIRD'S EYE VIEW OF AN OLYMPIAD

Glorious weather, enthusiastic crowds, and the unified coordination of effort and will are three terms that summarize the essence of the Fifth Olympiad. These terms will serve as praise for organizers and participants alike, but they are inadequate for the critical task before us. From the start, this *Revue* has espoused the resolution of the International Committee, as expressed in the famous dictum: *citius, altius, fortius.* No matter how successful any Olympiad may be, one can and one must set one's sights even higher. This may be a difficult task to accomplish at times, and through men's errors or particular circumstances, some Games may take a step backward from the achievements of previous ones. In preparing for the next Games after that, one must simply get back onto the track that leads upward, that is all. This time, nothing of the sort happened – just the opposite. But simply by mentioning this possibility, we underscore the spirit in which we approach this study of the recent Olympiad.

This Olympiad holds the record for the number of participants. It is an enormous figure, and resulted in some awkward situations which the Swedish Committee handled as skillfully as possible. It is true that parade teams are included in this number. However, the spectators, particularly those who came from outside, account for a total that is not quite proportionate to the number of those participating. It is clear that many spur-of-the-moment decisions to make the trip were reversed by the ridiculous increase in prices that occurred at one point. Prices were then lowered and kept within generally reasonable limits, but the effects could not be overcome. Local commerce would have greatly increased its profits, which were considerable enough in any case, if it had wisely contained early ambitions. This lesson will be reflected upon profitably by other capitals. It is important not to view the Olympic Games as the goose that laid the golden egg. Our readers should not be surprised to see us dealing with the commercial issue this way. It would be quite immature to believe that the Ancients were unconcerned with the prosperity engendered by the Games, or that the business stirring around Olympia was of no interest to them!

The administrative machinery of the organizers was absolutely perfect. Nearly every detail had been foreseen, and always in the simplest, most practical way. Extraordinary ingeniousness, and admirable order and method governed the functioning of the offices. A minimum of workers produced a maximum of work, a result that many a government and many a public administration could have come to study on site. A great patriotic feeling buoyed everyone. The watchword in every heart was "Make Sweden proud". A committee of remarkable men, presided over by such powerful individuals as Colonel Balck and Mr. J. S. Edström, also had the valuable support of the presence of the heir to the throne as head of the committee. The active interest taken by His Royal Highness the Crown Prince in the work of the committee did not waver or fade for an instant. The understanding between them remained steadfast, and once again one could see in these circumstances the extent to which "Union makes for strength."

The athletic spirit seemed to increase on the part of the participants, if not on the part of the crowd. The crowd – consisting primarily of Swedes – allowed its patriotism to burst out in the most naively anti-sporting manner. It was not uncommon in the Stadium for a dazzling victory by a foreigner to be received with scattered bravos, while the vanquished, if they were Swedes, received lengthy ovations.

Of course, no one took serious offense at these displays, which were poorly controlled but not badly intentioned. Sweden has never before hosted an international athletic event, and it is quite natural for the patriotic perspective to win out over the sporting perspective on this occasion. Moreover, continental gymnasts who have seen their uneven and parallel bars boycotted thoroughly until now by exclusive practitioners of the Swedish method must admit that they were greeted with extreme tolerance. The sporting spirit of the various athletic groups was clearly better than in 1908. Apparently in these crowded and overheated surroundings, no one can expect a disqualification to pass without objections and polemics. Nor can we expect disappointment and jealousy never to result in raucous outbursts. Ancient athletes, we must continue to repeat, were no more angelic in this regard than athletes today. If they had been angelic, they would not have been athletes! It is sufficiently pleasing to note that disagreeable incidents were few and far between, and that the appeal expressed in this magazine[1] seems to have been heard and borne its fruits. The *Pax Olympica* did not reign unchallenged, but it did reign, and that means a great deal.

They say that when the architect of the Berlin stadium visited the stadium in Stockholm, he tipped his hat, saying, "I salute my Swedish colleague. One can do no better than this". This was flattering praise indeed from a man whose own project has been justly admired. Mr. Torben Grut deserves this praise in every respect. His work was appreciated by everyone. Though he is a great artist, Mr. Grut is a modest man. He praised the French master Viollet le Duc, and attributed his own triumph to that famous man. But the originality of his design and the skill with which it was implemented stand. When the appropriate sculptures are added to decorate the Stadium, which will alleviate its still-unpolished look, this monument will create a great impression indeed. The layout of the Stadium is perfect. Corridors, locker rooms, showers, press area, telegraph and telephone set-ups, bleachers, open area – everything has been combined in the most practical way. During the Games, the Stadium underwent prodigious transformations. In succession, it served as a concert hall for four thousand singers, a restaurant for three thousand guests, and the next day, it was ready for the competitions. The lawn could be replaced by a hard court surface, and vice versa. On the evening of July 15, football was played there. The next day at dawn, twenty obstacles had arisen, and equestrian paths separated by two long banks of hydrangeas crisscrossed the space. These rapid changes were made possible through clever preparation of the subsoil, and the installation of a flawless mosaic of large squares of turf, cut in a checkerboard pattern.

For the first time since the restoration of the Games, death cast its shadow over the celebrations. The Portuguese runner Lazaro fell victim to sunstroke while running the marathon, and died the next day. One death in sixteen years out of so many thousands of athletes is very little, to be sure, and there is no better proof that the Olympic program in no way overtaxes the strength of those for whom it is held. Although the marathon was run during the warmest hours of the day for reasons unrelated to the sport, the outdoor temperature cannot be held responsible. The

1 See "Pax Olimpica", in: *Revue Olympique,* July, 1912, pp. 99-102.

victim must have found the mild heat of Sweden easier to take than the climate of his native country. It is more likely that this incident was due to intestinal causes. In any event, from now on either the marathon will have to be held in the morning, or strict measures will have to be taken to prevent competitors from ingesting harmful foods along the way. Lazaro left behind a widow who had recently had a child. In a gesture of universal sympathy an athletic benefit was held at the Stadium after the Games, which raised a considerable sum on her behalf.

The Fifth Olympiad saw a number of innovations. Some were athletic innovations and we will address them in our next issue, which will contain technical comments on the 1912 Games along with a general table of results. Other innovations were more general. There are two that draw our attention in particular. The first was the establishment by His Majesty King Gustav V of a special decoration called the medal of the Fifth Olympiad. This medal, with the royal crown at the top and attached by a pale blue ribbon striped with yellow, bears the likeness of His Majesty, with the three crowns of Sweden interlaced with palms and laurels on the back, and the words: Femte Olympiaden, Stockholm 1912. In keeping with custom, the king reserved the exclusive right to award the medal.

The second innovation was the religious ceremony that opened the period of the Games in the Stadium. A prayer was said in Swedish; the crowd stood to join in singing a religious song; and finally the following prayer, composed and recited by the Rev. de Courcy Laffan, gave this unique moment infinite grandeur. Here is the text of the invocation:

O Lord, God of all the nations of the earth in Whom we live and move and have our being, our Father!

Thou hast called Thy children hither from all quarters of the Earth, from the East and from the West, from the North and from the South to show forth in frank and chivalrous contests Thy sacred gifts of manly prowess and to teach and learn by turns the secrets of manly strength and manly endurance.

Pour out, o Lord, the fullness of Thy Holy Spirit on all who take part in these Olympic Games.

Fill them with the spirit of friendship, the spirit of brotherhood, the spirit of International unity and concord.

Set far from us all misunderstanding, all bitterness, all jealousy, all ill will.

Give to those who conquer the temper of generous sympathy, give to those who are conquered by the temper of generous admiration.

And so bless this gathering of the chosen youth of all nations that our Olympiad may be an instrument in Thy Hand for the peace of the world, for the goodwill of all peoples, for the building of Thy kingdom on Earth as it is in Heaven.

For thine, o Father, is the kingdom, the Power and the Glory for ever and ever. Amen.

Une Olympiade à vol d'oiseau,
in: *Revue Olympique*,
August 1912, pp. 115-119.

The editor has determined that this text, though unsigned, was written by Coubertin.

4.2.2/25 THE ORIGINS OF THE MODERN PENTATHLON

One of the most interesting innovations at the 1912 Olympic Games was the institution of the modern pentathlon. This innovation will be long-lasting not so much because of the trophy that Sweden managed to win on this occasion, but because it has met with universal support. There was, of course, a possibility that such a novel thing would not be readily accepted right away, particularly because many objections were raised when Baron Pierre de Coubertin, who devised the event, outlined its particulars four years ago. Since then, however, the movement in favor of "all-round athleticism" has gained strength, to the point that the final announcement regarding the new Pentathlon was immediately welcomed by many. Forty-two entries from twelve different countries were registered. There were thirty-two at the start, Danish, French, American, Dutch, Norwegian, Russian, English, Swedish, German, and Austrian. Of those thirty-two, nine withdrew during the trials, leaving twenty-three who made it to the end. This, it must be noted, is a magnificent result, particularly since the events taken together amounted to an extremely difficult effort, and since they took place without any pomp and circumstance, far from the bleachers and the applause. From a purely athletic perspective, the modern pentathlon marked the highest peak of the Olympiad. Nowhere else was muscular effort as intense, nor the selflessness of the athletes as great.

For the record, let us review the schedule of events. The shooting competition was held on Sunday, July 7. This was a duel shoot at 25 meters, twenty shots to be fired in four series of five at seven-meter targets, visible for three seconds at ten-second intervals. On Monday, July 8, there was a 300-meter freestyle swimming competition. The same evening, competitors were shown the equestrian course, and they were given a map of the terrain. At the same time, lots were drawn and those athletes who did not have horses had an opportunity to try out those made available to them. On Tuesday, July 9 and Wednesday, July 10, there was fencing with epées. The winner was the first athlete to score three hits against his opponent. On Thursday, July 11, there was the equestrian competition (a four-and-a-half kilometer course, with many obstacles). Finally, on Friday, July 12, there was a cross-country race of approximately 4,000 meters.

The order of these events is open to criticism. The exhaustion of the nerves and muscles is not taken into consideration. It is not a good idea to end the pentathlon with the two most exhausting competitions, namely the equestrian event and the foot race. We would suggest the following order: shooting, foot race, fencing, swimming, equestrian event. The fencing competition, perhaps, might not be limited to a single weapon, with a choice possible between the epée and the saber. What must be changed, in any event, is the regulation concerning the equestrian event, as well as the manner in which the points are counted.

There is only one truly logical and fair way to hold the equestrian event, and that is to provide all the competitors with horses that they have not had an opportunity to ride until that time, and to send them out onto terrain with which they are unfamiliar. But this last condition is not always easy to fulfill. Suitable sites near a large city are not so numerous that, even if the secret has not been divulged, it would be impossible to figure out which one has been selected. Therefore, riders from the country where the Olympiad is to be held have a major advantage. What is unacceptable in any case is that some competitors should be entitled to ride their own horses, while others can try out the mounts offered to them only once, and superficially at that. The best solution would be to set the obstacles in place at the last minute, and to assign the horses by drawing lots.

The rankings achieved in the five events were used as the basis for totaling up the points. First place finishers received one point, second place two points, and so on. But the number of competitors varied from event to event because of the withdrawal of some athletes, which became a source of relative unfairness. In addition, in the equestrian event each competitor received one hundred points at the start, from which points were subtracted, two for the first refusal or shying away, five for each subsequent refusal or shying away, five if the horse falls, ten for each time the rider falls, two for each five-second period beyond the maximum set time. These may well have been pointless complications in the calculation.

Despite these minor flaws, overall the pentathlon was run in a way that satisfied those who advocate it. A perfect athletic spirit reigned among all the competitors. Winners and losers showed the same enthusiasm for this superb institution, a veritable benchmark of virility and perfect athleticism.

This enthusiasm has been reflected overseas, as well. Mr. V. Skiff, who played such a significant role in running the Third Olympiad in his capacity as Director of the great St. Louis World's Fair, and who will assume similar responsibilities in San Francisco in 1915, has just given a very valuable art object to Mr. Coubertin, in the name of the Trustees of the San Francisco World's Fair, to commemorate the establishment of the modern pentathlon. It has been mutually agreed that the use of this art object will follow in the footsteps of the trophy that Mr. Coubertin himself created for the pentathlon. The trophy is a large solid gold plaque, decorated with bas-relief figures designed by the well-known Swedish carver Lindberg, with the following inscription on the back: *Donné par la Panama Pacific International Exposition à Pierre de Coubertin, rénovateur des Olympiades, à l'occasion du Pentathlon moderne, pour être remis par lui à chaque Olympiade au vainqueur de l'épreuve qui en aura la garde jusqu'à l'Olympiade suivante* [Given by the Panama Pacific International Exposition to Pierre de Coubertin, restorer of the Olympiads, on the occasion of the establishment of the modern pentathlon, to be given by him at each Olympiad to the winner of that competition, who shall keep it until the next Olympiad]. A second copy of this plaque will be kept by the president of the International Committee.

With these two trophies, the modern pentathlon begins life with every assurance of long-term, considerable success. We should expect to see "modern pentathlons" spring up all over the place, like "marathons". The distinction is, however, that running a modern pentathlon is more difficult and more expensive...but the outcome is more interesting and more impressive.

Les débuts du Penthatlon moderne,
in: *Revue Olympique*,
October 1912, pp. 151-154.

The editor has determined that this text, though unsigned, was written by Coubertin.

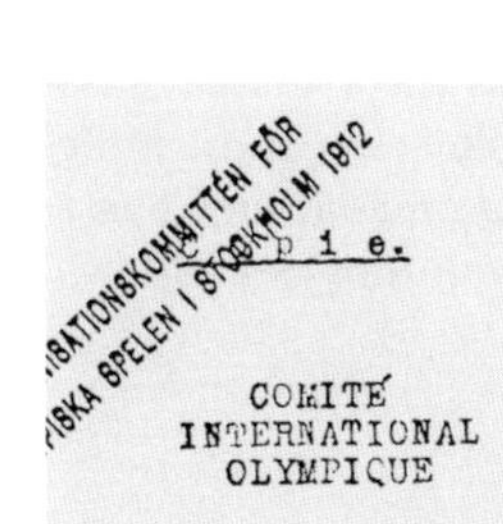

p i e.

COMITÉ
INTERNATIONAL
OLYMPIQUE

Modern
Femkamp

20, Rue Oudinot.

Dear Mr. Hellström,

I enclose the draft of the Challenge Cups form. I think it necessary to alter slightly the text as indicated. The one I suggest is safer for various reasons.

As to the Modern Pentathlon I am personnally opposed to the admittance of ladies as competitors in the Olympic Games. But as they are this time admitted as tennis players, swimmers etc. I do not see on what ground we should stand to refuse them in the Pentathlon. However I repeat that I greatly regret the fact. Therefore I leave it to you to decide and if you refuse or accept the engagement, I shall agree with you.

Yours truly,

P.C.

It is my intention to arrive early in June.
I hope nothing will stop me from so doing.

Participation of women in the modern pentathlon, Stockholm 1912 (National Archives, Stockholm)

4.2.2/26 CLOSING WORDS (STOCKHOLM 1912)

This text is Coubertin's "Paroles de clôture" at the closing banquet of Stockholm from June 26, 1912. In this he hints at the possibility of Berlin hosting the VI Olympic Games which were sacrificed because of World War I, as the symbolic passing on of the Olympic torch from Sweden to Germany. The Olympic torch of the antiquity leads to the symbol of the indelible Olympic idea including present day, like it experienced its most conscious markedness in the Olympic Torch Run in 1936.

Your Royal Highnesses,
Ladies and gentlemen,

The hour has struck for the closing of this splendid festival which will make such a deep mark in Olympic history. In another few moments the celebration of the Vth Olympiad will have ended.

It leaves us sunny memories, not only because Swedish earth and water have decked themselves out for us with all the enchantments of a radiant summer, hut because the art of the spectacle and the concern for technical perfection have been combined by you, Gentlemen of the Swedish Committee, in the most brilliant and successful way.

Power and money are far from enough to make an Olympiad; perseverance, patience and tolerance are necessary. Above all one must have a high and serene conception of the twofold role to which sport can and must aspire within the great modern democracies – the role of agent of human equilibrium inherited from the athletics of antiquity and the role of social educator inherited from medieval Chivalry. We must look not only towards the Olympic gymnasium, Gentlemen, but also towards those much-neglected and much-misunderstood tournaments of the middle ages, whose only fault was sometimes to push beyond reason the elegant cult of honor, stoicism and generosity.

I can pay no greater homage to the Swedish nation, Your Grace, than to say to those who represent it here that on many occasions in history it has been seen with admiration to draw its inspiration from this twofold ideal.

And now, Gentlemen, through our mediation a great people has received the torch of the Olympiads from your hands, and has thereby undertaken to preserve and if possible to quicken its precious flame.

A custom has arisen that the last word spoken on the evening of the Olympic Games shall be to salute the dawn of the Games to follow. I am therefore going to ask you, in the name of the International Olympic Committee, supreme and steadfast guardian of the restored institution, to raise your glasses in honor of the VIth Olympiad.

May it contribute like its illustrious predecessors to the general welfare and to the betterment of humanity! May it be prepared in the fruitful labor of peaceful times. May it be celebrated, when the day comes, by all the peoples of the world in gladness and concord!

Paroles de clôture, in: *Revue Olympique*,
September 1912, pp.142-143.
English version in: Coubertin, *The Olympic Idea,* Schorndorf 1967, pp.38-39.

4.2.2/27 – 4.2.2/33 INTRODUCTION

The IOC held an Olympic Congress in Lausanne in 1913, and another one a year later in Paris, on technical aspects of sports. In an article entitled "Les Congrès Olympiques" ["The Olympic Congresses"] (1913), Coubertin stated his position on the role of Olympic Congresses within the Olympic movement. In his comments on these congresses in his *Olympic Memoirs*[1], Coubertin describes the high value that he saw in them.

It is difficult to determine exactly which Congresses can be called Olympic Congresses. There had been no clear separation in either 1897 or 1905 between the Olympic Congresses and the meetings of the IOC, which at first had been called "meetings", and then "Sessions". One can even presume that as the movement became more and more successful over the years, Coubertin could afford the luxury of determining and shaping responsibilities and procedures gradually.

After World War I, the term "Olympic Congress" was used to describe only the form of the technical Olympic Congresses in a format that had been used since 1914, a distinction that Coubertin introduced in his "Pédagogie Sportive" ["Athletic Education"] (p. 57).

The Lausanne Congress came at a time when the Olympic movement, with the Stockholm Games, had reached its first high point. But it was precisely this comparison of international performances, the essence of the Olympism, that had given rise to a large number of new problems[2].

In the criticism leveled by the medical community on the exaggerated forms of training, Coubertin saw a threat to modern athletics as a whole. That is why he tried to draw the attention of medicine to the psychological issues posed by physical exercises. The Congress of Le Havre in 1897 had already focused on this goal.

The Lausanne program that is presented in the following text uses the concept of "sports psychology" for the first time, but he did not use the term in the way we understand it today. As his description of the program makes clear, the term dealt with issues regarding Pédagogie Sportive, a topic Coubertin had addressed in previous years in the Revue Olympique, and that he had presented in preparation for the Congress of Lausanne in a book of collected essays entitled *Essais de Psychologie sportive* ["Essays on Sports Psychology"][3].

Coubertin describes the work of this Congress in detail in chapter XIV "The Sports Psychology Congress" of his *Olympic Memoirs.* In addition, all the contributions to the debate were grouped together in a book of reports published by the IOC. Coubertin provided a critical analysis of the topics discussed, in a four-part series published in the *Revue Olympique* in 1914 under the title "Critique du Congrès de Lausanne" ["Critique of the Congress of Lausanne"].

1 Of its twenty-four chapters, eight deal with the Olympic Games, eight with the Olympic Congresses, and eight others with other Olympic topics.

2 Coubertin acknowledged as much in 1900, and described it in his article entitled "La Psychologie du Sport" ["Sports Psychology"]. See text 2.5 in this volume.

3 Some texts taken from that book are printed in part I of this, others in volume III of the French edition.

Unquestionably the level of technicality of this Congress was higher than at Le Havre and Brussels congresses. Because of World War I, the subjects they debated were dropped for a long time. It was not until 1928 that Coubertin was able to continue his study, thanks to the recently established International Bureau of Sport Pedagogy (B.I.P.S.)[4].

An Olympic Congress was held in Paris the next year, in 1914, on the occasion of the twentieth anniversary of the IOC. The thirty-two Olympic Committees then in existence attended. The jubilee was particularly solemn, as was only fitting for a movement that had become famous worldwide. At the same time, the congress was a quiet triumph for Pierre de Coubertin, who continued to go unacclaimed in his native France.

At this Congress the IOC, in association with the representatives of the National Olympic Committees (N.O.C.s), shaped the long-awaited unified program for future Olympic Games. The "Olympic maturity" of each athletic discipline was assessed. Even then, however, they could not agree on cuts.

Coubertin had never questioned the fact that the Olympic Games were to remain a matter of individual, male competitors, and the IOC was loyal in its support of that view. That is why the Congress rejected a resolution to allow women to compete in the athletics category. Women were granted access to swimming and tennis only. By contrast, a majority of the IOC supported team sports.

Overall the Congress of Paris was a success since many issues were settled, some of which had been pending since 1896. The respective areas of competence of the IOC, the N.O.C.s, and the specialized International Federations were determined amicably, and the authority of the IOC remained intact in the final analysis. Coubertin stated his position on matters relating to the internal structure of the Olympic movement in many publications, which are summarized in chapter 3.1.

Coubertin analyzed the Congress of Paris in greater depth only in chapter XV "The 20th anniversary of the Olympic Games" of his *Olympic Memoirs.* It is abundantly clear that technical, organizational issues no longer held his attention.

The Congress of Paris had scarcely concluded when World War I broke out. For years, the work of the Olympics was hampered, and made nearly impossible. The Olympic concept of athletic internationalism as a messenger of peace was swept aside by political reality, and the Olympic Games in Berlin 1916, for which the Congress of Paris had established the rules in principle, were canceled.

There is only a single report written by Coubertin concerning the four war years, namely the printed chapter "The Four War Years" in his *Olympic Memoirs.* In order not to cause problems for the IOC, given his enlistment in the French army, Coubertin resigned his office as president for a three-year period. The circular letter printed here as text 4.2.2/30 is the letter Coubertin sent to the members of the IOC to tell them of his decision.

4.2.2/27 THE OLYMPIC CONGRESSES

The Olympic Games are held every four years. Every year, the International Committee holds a solemn Session, occasions on which festivals are held. The Sessions at The Hague in 1907, Berlin in 1909, Luxembourg in 1910, and Budapest in 1911, to mention only those, were outstanding. These meetings were sometimes, and most inappropriately, called Congresses; yet the only individuals allowed to attend were the members of the International Committee. The term Congress, therefore, cannot be used in these circumstances.

The International Committee has, of course, organized congresses, not at regularly scheduled dates, but only when there were serious grounds to justify such initiatives. According to the statutes, the Committee is "1. To hold Olympic games on a regular basis; 2. To make the celebration of those Games increasingly perfect, worthy of their glorious past and in keeping with the high ideals of those who restored them; and 3. To hold or organize any and all exhibitions and, in general, to take any appropriate steps to orient modern athleticism in desirable directions."

These are the reasons why the Congresses of 1897, 1905, 1906, and 1913 were held. The first, which was held at the City Hall of Le Havre under the honorary presidency of the President of the French Republic, Félix Faure, proclaimed the close relationship of sports and moral standards. This was a very new topic at the time, and no one was accustomed to discussing it in public. Such speakers as the explorer Bonvalot and the illustrious Dominican preacher, Father Didon, leant their eloquence in support of this fruitful topic.

The second Congress met at the Palais des Académies in Brussels, under the honorary presidency of His Majesty King Leopold II. The program dealt with the whole subject of technique in physical exercises, and the book that tells of the discussions and work of this Congress, which was attended by a wide range of indisputable authorities in the field, is exceptionally valuable. Whatever one's particular perspective may be, this encyclopedia covers it. The chart of athletic difficulties included in it remains the clearest and best ever attempted.

The next year in Paris, at the famous Foyer of the Comédie Française, a kind of Congress was held that brought together artists concerned with renewing art and sportsmen eager to ennoble sports, under the aegis of renascent Olympism. From that meeting came the great movement that expands day by day, and that will bring back the happy reign of ancient eurythmy.

The Congress of Lausanne has been called in order to christen a new science, or to speak in more precise terms a new branch of science, by making it more widely known: sports psychology. The part played by our *Revue* in this initiative is well known. The famous French weekly *L'Opinion* paid us a most flattering compliment in this regard recently, in the words of one of its most sensible editors. He wrote that everyone now knows "that the restoration of the ancient Games was anything but the isolated and fortuitous fantasy of an amateur, but rather the result of

4 Cf. Coubertin, *La reprise des travaux du Congrès de Lausanne* [Resuming the work of the Congress of Lausanne], in: Bulletin du B.I.P.S. (1929), no.1, pp. 6-14.

lengthy contemplation: the mooring post, if you will, the dazzling symbol, the publicity necessary in the eyes of the public for a whole system of physical, intellectual, moral, and esthetic education... This philosophy of sports, which we hope to see emerge little by little from technical facts and brutish figures, and this new orientation toward effort sustained by poise and rhythm, are already found in articles printed in the *Revue Olympique*". Our great colleague congratulates us for having "sown this good seed". The Congress of Lausanne will, in a sense, hallow the longstanding efforts of the *Revue Olympique* to make of this new Olympism "a whole system of physical, intellectual, moral, and esthetic education". In so doing, it will continue and complete the work of the previous Congresses.

Les Congrès Olympiques,
in: *Revue Olympique,*
February 1913, p. 19-20.

The editor has determined that this text, though unsigned, was written by Coubertin.

4.2.2/28 PROGRAM OF THE LAUSANNE OLYMPIC CONGRESS OF 1913

INTERNATIONAL OLYMPIC COMMITTEE

–

CONGRESS OF LAUSANNE
(Psychology and Physiology of Sports)
MAY 1913
under the patronage of the Federal Council of the Swiss Confederation

Mens fervida in corpore lacertoso
MCMXIII

ORGANIZING COMMITTEE
Honorary President: Mr. Decoppet, Senior Member of the Council of State, Director of the Department of Public Instruction of the Canton of Vaud

President: Dr. Morax, Director of the Health Department, Canton of Vaud

Members: Mr. Godefroy de Blonay, Dr. Centurier, Prof. Larguier des Bancels, Prof. Millioud, Dr. De Montet, Dr. Reinbold

Commissioners: (French language) Dr. De Montet, Villa Alexandra, **Vevey.** – (German language) Dr. Mallwitz, 33, Kessel Strasse, **Berlin**, Dr. Hans Reber, **Gstaad** (Canton of Bern). – (English language) Mr. Arthur Ireland, 45, avenue d'Ouchy, **Lausanne**, and Grove House, **Raunds**, Northamptonshire, England.

Congress on Sports Psychology and Physiology.

–

Lausanne 1913.

PROGRAMS

ORIGIN OF ACTIVITY IN THE SPHERE OF SPORT.

Natural individual aptitudes: general aptitudes (suppleness, dexterity, strength, endurance); special aptitudes (inborn disposition to certain form of exercises). – What part does **atavism** play in sport and what is its influence? Observations and conclusions to be drawn therefrom. – Do natural aptitudes suffice to simulate the individual, or does this require the presence of the **sporting instinct**? Nature and action of this instinct. Can the spirit of **imitation** or the effort of the **will** produce it or act as a substitute for it?

PERSEVERANCE AND FORMS.

Perseverance which alone makes the true sportsman can only be assured when the sense of the **need** of sport has been brought into existence. Cannot this desire be brought into existence physically by the habit which results either from the **automatic** action fom the muscles or from the **desire for fresh air** engendered by violent exercise – or morally by **ambition**, whether resulting from the vulgar thirst for applause, or having as its aim a nobler ideal, such as the pursuit of beauty, health or bodily power?

The physiological and psychological **characteristics** of each class or species of exercise: the **intellectual** and **moral** qualities which each sport develops or utilizes. – The different conditions under which sports are practiced: **solitude** and **companionship; independence** and **cooperation; initiative** and **discipline**; formation and training of a team.

RESULTS.

Of the strictly accurate character of results in the sphere of sports. – **Training**; fundamental rules: how it differs from ordinary course of life. – Overtraining: **fatigue.** – Normal training may be purely physical and result only in **resistance** to fatigue, but it may also contribute to **moral progress** by the development of the will, of courage and of **self-confidence**, and doubtless also to intellectual progress by the producing of **self-possession** and **mental sanity**. Under what conditions is it possible to expect this progress? – **Records**; state of mind of the recordmaker.

In conclusion, does not activity in the sphere of sport contain within itself the germ of a practical **philosophy** of life?

Special pamphlet, Lausanne 1912, 4 p. (Archives of the IOC).
Reprinted in *Revue Olympique*, April, 1912, pp. 54-55.

4.2.2/29 THE SPORTS PSYCHOLOGY CONGRESS (LAUSANNE 1913)

At the end of the 19th century, Switzerland was not at all what one would have called a sporting country, even though certain sports were practiced there. She was sporting only after the fashion of Toepffer, which was not bad in itself but tended to be insular and not at all international. Switzerland had her gymnasts, her Alpine wrestlers, and that was the whole extent of it. She had no aspirations towards external laurels and used her mountains solely for walking and not yet for winter sports. Politically she was very canton-minded and particularly mistrustful of her federal powers. Consequently Switzerland took no interest in the revival of the Olympic Games and her indifference had not really bothered me, because I did not know the country very well as yet. The way it appeared to me from a distance was the way I felt it should remain. None of the tourists passing through had any inkling of an internal evolution; neither had I. Led by chance, in 1903, to study its institutions and brought into contact with its new military system by one of its most famous officers, Colonel de Loys, I immediately realized that here, in the center of Europe, was a small country which had not only played an important part in the past but had a great future ahead of it and which was quietly acting as a testing ground for the civilized nations of the world. From then on, Switzerland became of infinite interest to me.

From the sporting point of view, she appeared so favored by nature as well as atavistic and other circumstances that it was hard to understand how she could be so slow to take advantage of them. "Switzerland, queen of sports" is the title of an article published in the Olympic Review for November 1906 and which, in retrospect, takes on a rather prophetic tone although the prophecy has not yet been completely fulfilled.

Such a country was predestined to play a very important Olympic role, but it had to be convinced of the fact. And it is no criticism of its inhabitants to remind them that nothing is ever easily got out of them unless they are already prepared in their own minds to make the necessary concession. Our Swiss colleague Godefroy de Blonay came to realize this more and more as he slowly and painstakingly tried to form a National Olympic Committee in spite of strong cantonal opposition to this sort of undertaking.

But I am not writing an article on Switzerland here. In my Histoire Universelle, I was able to express in all sincerity my great admiration for this country. Here, I only want to recall how, wishing to win Switzerland over to our cause, I had begun with Lausanne and why, in trying to woo Lausanne, I had resorted to the stratagem of a scientific congress.

Lausanne's international role, which started long ago, the day the Pope came to place the Imperial crown on the head of Rudolph of Habsburg, had been somewhat neglected at the beginning of the 20th century. People came to consult famous doctors, others took pleasure in stopping there on their way through, some even lingered happily on, but it had no clearly defined role to play. Its university, which had recently moved into grand new premises whose rather unusual architecture had at least the freshness and sparkle of youth, occupied a very honorable position in the academic world without playing any leading role. Spreading delightfully along the lake, under its crown of forests, and offering every imaginable opportunity for sport, it was (either within its walls or in the immediate neighborhood) the ideal spot for setting up the administrative headquarters of Olympism. But for this to come about, we had first of all to be accepted.

Lausanne 1913: the opening of the Olympic Congress, presided over by Coubertin, in the centre of the rostrum (IOC Archives)

I wanted to see medicine, which to my mind was fast becoming too predominantly physiological, take greater interest in psychology. Having had a great many doctors as friends, starting with the sportsman Fernand Lagrange, the charming author, of the Physiologie des Exercices du Corps, I may be allowed to speak bluntly. And not so long ago in Praxis, the bilingual journal of the Swiss medical profession, I explained my point of view on the "morbid case" which, instead of being considered the exception, as it should, was tending more and more to be taken for normal in a variety of fields and in particular that of sport. This is not the place to try and give even a summary of such a difficult question. But what I said on that occasion was sufficient to give birth to the Lausanne Congress. I had spoken with my colleagues about the matter as early as 1909 and, two years later at the Budapest meeting, had given them a sort of manifesto which they welcomed enthusiastically and which was shortly afterwards published in English, French, German and Italian. It is quite short; and I feel it worthwhile reproducing the text here in its entirety.

ORIGINS OF SPORTING ACTIVITY

Natural aptitudes of the individual; general aptitudes (suppleness, skill, strength, endurance); especial aptitudes (innate facility for a particular form of exercise). – Role and influence of sports *atavism;* observations and conclusions to be drawn. – Are natural aptitudes enough to encourage the individual or does he also need *a sporting instinct?* Nature and action of this instinct. – Can it be produced or replaced by the spirit of *imitation* and the effect of *will?*

CONTINUITY AND METHODS

The continuity vital for the creation of a real sportsman is obtained only when the *need* is created. Is it possible for the sporting need to be created physically by the habit resulting either from muscular *automatism,* or from the desire for fresh air produced by intensive exercise and also morally from ambition, whether this ambition is the result of the desire for applause, or aims at a nobler object, such as striving after beauty, health or power. *Psychological particularities* of each category of exercise: *intellectual* and *moral* qualities developed or used by each sport. – Different conditions governing the practice of sport *solitude* and *comradeship; team spirit* and *rivalry; initiative* and *discipline;* formation and development of a team.

RESULTS

The strictly accurate character of sports results. – Training: differences from the state of *inurement.* – Normal training can be purely physical and lead only to the building up of *resistance,* but it can also contribute to *moral progress:* by the development of the will, courage and *self-confidence* and undoubtedly also to intellectual progress by the creation of *calm* and *mental order.* Under what conditions?

Finally, does not sports activity contain the seeds of a practical *philosophy* of *life?*

This program, if I may say so, had to be defended against the medical profession and, on the other hand, put over convincingly to the philosophers and teachers to win them to our cause; and we had at the same time to start to arouse the interest of sportsmen themselves. It was – paradoxically enough – a doctor who helped me, an old friend of my parents-in-law, Dr. Morax, at that time head of the Health Service in the Canton de Vaud. His three sons made names for themselves in the arts, literature, and science. At Morges, where he lived, he led a patriarchal existence, keenly interested in everything that was going on in the world. Nothing happened in Europe or farther afield that did not awaken a shrewd, thoughtful, sympathetic echo in this lively old man always surrounded by young people and ever a champion of the boldest schemes. He immediately took a very keen interest in the Congress, grasping right away my half-voiced thoughts and the profound reasons for its Olympic, and even Swiss, opportuneness. Through him I gained the cooperation of a University professor, Mr. Millioud – whose courses had been attended by Benito Mussolini, at that time an obscure student struggling courageously against an adverse fate -, the cooperation of the Rector, Mr. de Felice, and of the head of a famous private school, Mr. Auckenthaler. This is how the first group came to be formed. I persuaded a distinguished historian and philosopher, Guglielmo Ferrero, to make the opening address, as well as Theodore Roosevelt to write a message of encouragement. After that I had few illusions as to the discussions that were about to start. The subjects indicated were too unusual, they were still too unfamiliar to most of the Congress members for the whole project not to be doomed to failure. But the program would live on, the prestige of certain names too, and the originality of the attempt would finally capture the attention of those who mattered.

The Congress opened on the morning of Thursday, May 8, 1913. On the two previous days, the IOC Session was held in the University Senate House; three new members were admitted: the Duke of Somerset for Great Britain, Count Penha-Garcia for Portugal, and Baron de Laveleye for Belgium. The opening session took place in the Auditorium. The town was bedecked with flags. A troop of small boy scouts formed a guard of honor on the steps. The fine choirs of the Choral Union and the Men's Choir of Lausanne were loudly applauded and Federal Councillor Decoppet made a speech on behalf of the Supreme Council of the Confederation. In my reply, I had the sad duty to pronounce a funeral speech in memory of Dr. Morax, who had recently died. Ferrero then made an original speech full of deep philosophical significance. After which the Congress asked me to preside over its work and chose as Vice-Presidents the representatives of the Belgian and Austrian Governments, as well as Professor Millioud and Mr. Auckenthaler. A book was subsequently published containing the various memoranda presented there; many are interesting but bear witness, as I mentioned above, to a certain difficulty in keeping strictly to the subject. Roosevelt's autobiography was a striking example for all, as was the profound study by Louis Dedet, a former athlete, at that time head of the famous Normandy College, on the subject of teams, their formation, their organic life, their dissociation, etc.

The Municipal Council of Lausanne and the Mayor, Mr. P. Maillefer, had inaugurated the series of festivities on May 7. The next evening, the famous terrace of the *Abbaye de l'Arc,* through whose centuries-old trees the whole panorama of the Lake of Geneva could be admired, was the scene of a party which could not have been held anywhere else in the world. On the lawns, twenty-two of the finest wrestlers cheered on by their fellow cowherds and shepherds in their picturesque costumes competed in the light of resin torches. From behind the trees and shrubs could be heard the songs of the choirs. Finally, the stirring tones of the "Ranz des Vaches" rang out, while the torches went out one by one and the wrestling came to an end by the light of the moon. On the third evening, an amusing revue, specially prepared for the Congress, was given in the Casino. The witty songs and dances were a great success and there were many encores. There was also a Venetian Fete at Ouchy, a ball given by Baron and Baroness Grandson Castle, and finally, to bring the Congress to a close, a luncheon given by the State Council of the Canton of Vaud in the historic halls of Chillon Castle set off with beautifully reproduced decorations and costumes.

The IOC had no practical consequences to draw from this Congress. Its role had been limited to serving as sponsor to a new order of subjects of scientific study and it was pleased to be able to note the very satisfactory conditions in which the baptism had been celebrated. During its Session, after settling a whole pile of "current affairs" – the traditional expression used to denote those that had in fact remained in abeyance for some time – and after discussing and approving the programs and regulations of the Paris Congress scheduled for the following year, the IOC found itself faced with the Thorpe affair.

Hardly were the Games of the Fifth Olympiad over than James Thorpe, the winner of the classical pentathlon and the decathlon, was accused of disguised professionalism. The dossier had been forwarded by the Swedish Committee and the American Committee to the IOC, which was called on for the first time to decide a matter of this kind and in such a sensational case. The dossier consisted of four parts: a letter from James Thorpe to Sullivan, a letter from the head of Carlisle College in Pennsylvania also to Sullivan, a note from Sullivan to the President of the IOC, and finally a statement by the President and Secretary of the Amateur Athletic Union of the United States and of the Olympic Committee, who after a thorough examination of the case had given their opinions together with their reasons. Now twenty years later, on reading these documents again, I feel the same impression of perfect dignity and loyalty I had felt at the time; a feeling shared by all my colleagues too. Thus, at the suggestion of the British members present in 1913, the Duke of Somerset and Reverend Laffan, the IOC, once it had reached its decision, sent its congratulations to the American officials for their "outstanding sporting" attitude on this occasion. There were of course a number of people who maintained that Thorpe was an American citizen of Red Indian origin and that it was because of this that he had been so easily "sacrificed" as a scapegoat. This is not true. This so-called "sacrifice" resulted in the United States falling several places lower on the honors board for 1912, and this was quite a blow to their national pride. Concerning the facts of which Thorpe was accused I have nothing to say. At the time, in the United States, there were a great many needy students good at sport who in the summer played for professional baseball teams, often under borrowed names. In 1909 and 1910, Thorpe had done exactly the same thing under his own name, but without realizing the consequences of his action. Nobody had known anything about it and on his return to Carlisle College he had continued to be considered as an amateur. On reading his very frank letter and the sincerely moving one from the head of his college, how could I not help thinking of certain tennis players who had done as much or even more without being troubled in any way?... But even so there was no cause for hesitation and Thorpe, disqualified, had to give back the prizes he had won in Stockholm.

Olympic Memoirs, Chap.14, Lausanne, IOC, 1997, pp.144-153.

4.2.2/30 THE 20TH ANNIVERSARY OF THE OLYMPIC GAMES (PARIS 1914)

About the year 1910, I was shown at the Ministry for Foreign Affairs one day a document whose contents I cannot remember but which, after circulation to another department, had been returned to the Quai d'Orsay marked right across in a big angry scrawl with the words: "The French Government does not recognize the Olympic Games". It would not have been very difficult for me to find out the name of the ill-tempered high official who had thus given full vent to his exasperation. But while his identity left me indifferent, the form of his statement annoyed me intensely. "Oh!" I said to myself, "just wait! You'll soon see whether the French Government recognizes the Olympic Games or not! "From that moment on, I was determined to make the celebration of the 20th anniversary of their revival in June 1914 so remarkable that the cream of officialdom and fashionable Paris society would be unanimous in its homage to the revived institution.

There was only one real obstacle – and right at the start. We would have to force the Government's hand and practically compel it to accept the patronage of the celebrations rather than ask it, as would have been more usual – which would only have resulted in inquiries, counter-inquiries, interminable investigations, and the whole mass of red tape for which our sacrosanct civil service was renowned. The IOC was to meet in Budapest (May 1911). The President of the Council, Mr. Monis, Minister of the Interior, was bed-ridden as the result of an accident. I took myself off to Place Beauvais and had my card taken up to his principal or assistant secretary who, if I am not mistaken, bore the same name as himself and must have been a relation of his. I was received by an elegant young man, very much a man of the world, who immediately understood the situation. "Look", I said to him, "this is what is going to happen. A committee comprising four French members among forty foreigners from thirty different countries are going to vote. This committee would undoubtedly vote to hold the celebrations of the 20th anniversary of the revival of the Olympic Games in Paris, in June 1914 and would honor the French Republic with the patronage of these celebrations. What a bad impression it would make if this honor were not accepted right away and if the reply were only to come a long time afterwards, after being discussed right, left, and center. On the other hand, I know perfectly well that our administrative and political customs impose these tortuous proceedings. Here is the text of the letter that I shall send, as soon as the voting is over, to the President of the Council. What do you think of a reply couched somewhat as follows?"... And I read out my letter and the reply, the text of which is contained in the *Olympic Review* for July 1911: "You were kind enough to inform me of the result of the voting by which the IOC meeting in Budapest, etc. (here followed the necessary particulars). I beg to thank you for this interesting communication and I would ask you to convey the sentiments of friendly gratitude on the part of the French Government to members of the IOC."

This is exactly how things came to pass. The decision was taken by unanimous show of hands on May 25. Less than four weeks later, I was in possession of the Minister's letter, written in the terms previously agreed on. I then decided to share the work in preparation for the big Congress of National Committees with a special commission, elected by the IOC, and to keep for myself alone the organization of the festivities, a large part of the expenses for which fell to my lot anyway. The commission, of which I was President, was composed of Messrs. Brunetta d'Usseaux, de Blonay, Callot, Laffan, Sloane, van Tuyll, and von Venningen. Its main purpose was to prepare the numerical representation of the National Olympic Committees at the Congress and then to study the possible bases of a standard program for future Olympiads. The commission met eight months later, on March 27-28, 1912, in Basle, to hear the reports of Professor Sloane on the first question, and of Reverend Laffan on the second. Various National Committee Presidents, in particular Messrs. Duvignau de Lanneau (France) and de Laveleye (Belgium), had come to explain their colleagues' views. The European Gymnastics Federations and the International Shooting, Swimming, and Rowing Federations had been invited to give their opinion. At the Session in Stockholm, four months later, the IOC approved with a few minor amendments the commission's proposals and empowered it to carry on with its work. The commission, in fact, took advantage of the presence in Sweden of the Presidents or representatives of the German, American, Belgian, Russian, Italian, Austrian, Danish, Australian, French, Greek, Dutch, Hungarian, Japanese, Luxembourg, Norwegian and Finnish National Committees to talk with them, as well as with the athletes from these various countries. This resulted in copious documentation on the aims and opinions of technical circles. At the same time, I handed to all Committees the official invitation to the Paris celebrations. The commission met again in Lausanne on the eve of the Congress in 1913. As a result of the final approval given to its proposals by the IOC, the program and regulations of the Paris Congress were published in English, French, and German in the *Olympic Review* for June 1913.

The Committees recognized by the IOC were entitled to the following maximum number of delegates: Germany, Britain, France, the United States, Italy, and Russia, 10; Austria, Belgium, Spain, Greece, Holland, Hungary, and Sweden, 6; all other countries, 5; except for Finland, Luxembourg, Monaco, and Czechoslovakia, which would be restricted to 2. As members of the IOC were entitled to vote as such, they could not be delegates of their National Committee. Countries without National Committees could send three delegates appointed by their Minister for Foreign Affairs, but their vote would be consultative only. Next came the proposals concerning the verification of powers, the Congress office, the debates and discussions; the languages authorized (English, French and German), then the questions raised (qualification: sex, age, nationality, amateur status of competitors in the Games – number of events for each sport – list of compulsory events, optional sports – technical regulations – juries and prizes). I am only quoting the chapter headings. It was all very detailed and, as we have seen, the result of discussions which had gone on for nearly two years and were backed by very thorough research.

Before starting to arrange the program of the festivities I had waited till President Fallières' seven-year term of office came to an end; of all French Heads of State since the resignation of Jules Grévy, he was assuredly the least "Olympic". As soon as his successor had been elected, I would inform him of our intentions, but a certain number of "social" steps had already been taken. Early in the spring of 1913, I went to Paris and received from the new President, Mr. Raymond Poincaré, a most cordial reception. At the same time I went to visit the Minister for Foreign Affairs, Mr. S. Pichon, whom I had known when he was Resident General in Tunis, and President of the Municipal Council of Paris. Everything was quickly settled. Shortly after the Congress and the Session in Lausanne, I returned to Paris bringing with me for the Head of State a detailed program which extended over a fortnight and comprised no fewer than seventeen ceremonies or festivities. He himself was to appear on three occasions: at the Sorbonne, the Trocadéro and...the Elysée. The President started to laugh. There was exactly one year to go. "Is it definite?" he asked. "Absolutely", I answered. "Then I shall note it down", he said simply. He jotted down the dates that concerned him in a notebook. As I started to explain the character I had sought to give to the event: "Oh! I understand", he interrupted. "*The whole of France!*" And a satisfied smile showed that his patriotism fully approved.

Some words are a reward in themselves. And, as a matter of fact, in the program that the President had just approved, a party at the Hotel de La Rochefoucauld, given by the Duke and Duchess of Doudeauville, a garden party at the Chateau de Maintenon, belonging to the Duke and Duchess of Noailles, and a costumed riding display organized by Count Potocki fitted in between the receptions given at the Elysée, the Ministry of Foreign Affairs, and the City Hall. There was also to be a fencing match at the Cercle Hoche, organized by its President, Duke Decazes, a nocturnal fete in the Bois de Boulogne and a rowing demonstration on the Seine, given by our French colleagues Count de Bertier and Mr. Albert Glandaz, a party at the German Embassy... to which were later added a party given by Count Brunetta and an original banquet at the Ambassadeurs Restaurant, the host being Colonel Thompson, President of the American Committee.

The whole of France... A performance at the Comédie Française, which formed part of the personal receptions given by Madame de Coubertin and me, comprised three stages of French dramatic art, from the medieval farce "Franc Archer de Bagnolet", to Flers and Cavaillet. All the programs and menus were engraved by Stern, in the styles of the different periods. The *Olympic Review* devoted a number to anecdotes concerning the Parisian sights and monuments past which Congress members would be driven from the Bois de Boulogne to the Sorbonne, including Sainte-Clotilde, the Pantheon, the Elysée, the Trocadéro, private homes, City Hall, etc. Finally, a luxuriously presented booklet entitled *Notes on Contemporary France* was handed to each Congress member. Messrs. A. Ribot, Léon Bourgeois, E. Perrier, etc., a dozen well-known authorities had cooperated in its production. People were wondering what I was up to. At that time, I did not feel that war was imminent or even inevitable. Perhaps one day I shall have an opportunity of explaining my reasons for this opinion; but I considered that nothing was more likely to lead to war than the passion for self-disparagement which had reached such absurd proportions among my compatriots. And I had even less difficulty in combating this passion as I considered it completely unjustified by any concrete reality. Two years beforehand, talking in Stockholm with a German officer of the High Command, beneath whose outer veneer of courtesy could be detected an imperceptible disdain for Republican France, I had told him that, in my opinion, at no other period of her contemporary history had France possessed such a wealth of latent and scattered forces, which it would only take an upheaval to turn into an invincible block. I remember the stupor that appeared on his face at the expression of this opinion by the head of an ultra-aristocratic group. He realized that I was firmly convinced of what I said. In June 1914 therefore, I had no difficulty in shaping my acts according to the feelings expressed in all sincerity in 1912.

But as fate is often ironical, it brought forth just at the wrong moment another typically French phenomenon – a double ministerial crisis beating all previous records for political instability. On their arrival in Paris, Congress members witnessed, the very day after its constitution, the fall of Ribot's cabinet, in which Mr. Léon Bourgeois held the post of Minister for Foreign Affairs. The reception at the Quai d'Orsay was scheduled to take place two days later. "Naturally, it won't be held?" queried several, rather amused without wishing to appear so. "And why

20th anniversary of the revival of the Olympic Games. Official poster created by the Swiss painter Edouard Elzingre (IOC Archives)

not?" "There is no Minister". "There will be one". And in fact, Mr. and Mrs. Viviani, who had moved in that very morning, were ready at the appointed hour at the entrance to the reception rooms, friendly and relaxed as if they themselves had made all the arrangements for the party down to the last detail. In this large international gathering formed by members of the Congress (nigh on one hundred and forty), there were men of culture, with a rich experience of life, who had occupied important positions. And more than one was surprised to see how undisturbed the French seemed to be by their ministerial troubles.

A highlight of the commemorative ceremony at the Sorbonne, presided over by the Head of State, surrounded by ambassadors, and during which were read over one hundred addresses or telegrams from sovereigns, crown princes, governments, universities and societies, was a performance given by the famous Swedish singers who had come to Paris for the festivities. This was the first public appearance of the Olympic flag, a great many of which had been made, and it was a tremendous success. All white with the five interlaced rings: blue, yellow, black, green and red, it symbolized the five parts of the world united by Olympism and reproduced the colors of all countries.

The festival at the Trocadéro did not come fully up to expectations. The scenario had been based on a plan of rhythmic gradation. After a prelude performed by a septet of harps in a bluish obscurity, the "Echos of the Past", a number of ancient and Byzantine hymns, had been sung by the Greek Church choir. Then, while the lights gradually came on, the "Voices of the North", those of the Swedish singers, evoked the hopes of the Olympic revival, the finale celebrating the resurrection, with the accompaniment of the serried ranks of the Choir School, all interspersed with stirring organ music and stanzas expressing the main idea up to the final apotheosis: a procession of girls, in ancient costume, coming to honor the flags of the countries that had organized the first five Olympiads: Greece, France, the United States, Britain, and Sweden. The famous *Marseillaise,* arranged by Gossec and accompanied by the sound of bells, then rang out. The harmonies were perfect but the light effects very poorly regulated and the procession somewhat disorganized.

In order not to disturb the eurhythmics, the President had agreed to make his entry silently and in the dark, much to the horror of protocol!

These 1914 festivities, ending at Rheims in a splendid entertainment given by the Marquis de Polignac at the Athletes College, in no way interfered with the work of the Congress. Apart from the day of the excursion to Maintenon, two sessions had been held every day, one in the morning and one in the afternoon, from 2 to 4; fifteen sessions in all. A considerable amount of work was consequently accomplished. The delegates showed infinite goodwill, and were unsparing in their efforts. I presided over all the sessions, except for one, and never had any trouble. The speeches were always restrained; summaries in French or English rather than translations enabled all to understand rapidly. I tried above all to ensure that the discussions were varied and lively while at the same time keeping them as short as possible. We succeeded in going over the whole program, in spite of its size. Nobody thought for a moment that the minutes of the Congress would never be published. In order to avoid any mistakes, a commission had been appointed to compare the texts that had been drawn up in three languages. This commission was to meet during the month of August and publication to take place in the autumn. However it was not until November 1919, five years later, that the IOC was able to print the decisions concerning the events decided on, the juries, the special regulations, the entries and the qualifications, etc. These had all been drafted with a view to the Games of the Sixth Olympiad for which Berlin was already preparing with the manifest desire to outdo anything that had ever been done before. That is why the entries had been arranged in considerable numbers and almost all sports were included in the general program for the 1916 Games, which a world tragedy was suddenly to cancel.

Olympic Memoirs, Chap. 15, Lausanne, IOC, 1997, pp.154-163.

4.2.2/31 THE FOUR WAR YEARS (1914-1918)

The war which had flared up between Germany, Britain, the Austro-Hungarian Empire, Belgium, France, Russia, and Serbia created a state of affairs which could have threatened the very existence of the Olympic institution and whose first effect had been to put an end to any intentions on the part of its President to retire.

It had, in fact, been my wish to give up the functions I had been exercising *de facto* for twenty years and, although no decision had been reached, I had discussed the possibility with several of my colleagues. In the present circumstances, however, it was quite out of the question for me to retire before the end of my ten-year period of office in 1917. A captain does not leave the bridge of his ship during a storm.

Two problems immediately arose, one concerning the next Games and the other the actual composition of the IOC.

Regarding the first point, barely two weeks had passed since the invasion of Belgium when I received proposals for "transferring" the Games – at first somewhat vague plans but soon made more precise by a favorable move on the part of Sullivan, who had been one of the pillars of the recent Congress and whose loyalty now proved unshakable. He asked for "instructions". We could not hesitate. An Olympiad may fail to be celebrated; its number remains. This is the ancient tradition. The Germans, who at that time believed in a rapid war and a sure victory, did not ask to be relieved of the Olympic mandate. To make a move in favor of the United States or Scandinavia would have been to take a step whose outcome would have been difficult to foresee and to risk subsequent cracks in Olympic unity, without any advantage for anyone. I therefore rejected any kind of action of this sort.

The question of the composition of the Committee would not have come up if British public opinion, which for the first time showed itself lacking in moderation and level-headedness, had not pressed certain international academic or scientific associations to expel their German members. France, Belgium, and Russia did not seem prepared to do this. Here too, such action would have been tantamount to sowing bad grain in unknown soil. The situation could have been embarrassing if there had been a German or an Austrian on the Board of the IOC, but fortunately this was not the case. The Board could therefore continue as it was and merely suspend its sessions. Later on, we would see how things turned out. To anticipate the future with hasty decisions would only have made matters worse. With the approval of my Belgian and French colleagues, I therefore rejected the demand of Mr. Thomas A. Cook, who then handed in his resignation.

Once these two points had been settled, two more arose concerning which, on the other hand, I considered that prompt action was called for. It was not very clear where the headquarters of the IOC were actually located. Some thought they were in Paris because that was where I had my principal residence at that time. But in those days we followed a custom dating back to the very beginning of the modern Games, according to which the registered office was transferred every four years to the country where the next Olympiad was to be held: a privilege which was very seldom claimed but which could in fact be claimed by Berlin if it wished. Consequently, in the present state of Europe, administrative stability had become indispensable to Olympism.

We had already spoken of the matter at the IOC and my colleagues had not seemed very enthusiastic about my intentions. In view of the seriousness of the circumstances I decided, after informing those who were still accessible, to override the objections and, on April 10, 1915 in the Assembly Room of the Lausanne City Hall, we signed the document establishing Lausanne as the world administrative center and the repository of the archives of modern Olympism. Mr. de Blonay, the member in Switzerland, accompanied me. The Mayor, Mr. Maillefer, and the members of the Town Council received the document on behalf of the town. The State Council of the Canton of Vaud was also a party to this important act in which Mr. Motta, then as today President of the Confederation, took part by sending an encouraging telegram from the Federal Council.

My second move concerned the future celebration of the Games of the Seventh Olympiad (1920). The IOC Session that had been held in Paris in June 1914 had already been called on to examine the matter. Budapest and Antwerp had both applied to stage the Games. Antwerp had been represented by a delegation that had presented us with an eloquent address magnificently printed and bound. It had been too soon then to make a decision. A sort of preliminary ballot had divided the votes almost equally, although with a slight advance for Budapest.

Meanwhile, in the month of October 1914, when the mission which had been entrusted to me by the French Government, as soon as it had moved to Bordeaux, caused me to travel all over France, I had passed through Lyons on several occasions. There, Mr. Herriot had shown me the magnificent stadium he had started to construct. Consulted by him as to the opportuneness of a candidature on the part of Lyons for 1920 or 1924, I had been careful not to discourage him. During the following year I arranged the signing of an important document in which Lyons, while applying to stage the Games of the Seventh Olympiad (1920), stated that it agreed to withdraw its application in favor of Antwerp, should the latter maintain its application for that date, and to postpone its own candidature until 1924. The document was signed by the Mayor of Lyons and, for Belgium, by the Comte d'Assche. Shortly afterwards, an eloquent letter from the Comte de Baillet-Latour confirmed the agreement on behalf of the Belgian Olympic Committee. Thus, just as I was determined to prevent any transfer for 1916. I felt equally strongly that it was preferable to pave the way for 1920, and even for 1924, on different soils. That is why, not content with considering Antwerp and Lyons, I listened a little later to proposals emanating from America.

But not from the United States; Sullivan had just died suddenly: astounding offers nevertheless continued to be made. The prestige of the IOC had been enhanced over there by an *International Olympic Committee Day,* set aside by the San Francisco Exhibition to do it special honor. American exhibitions have the custom of dedicating special days in this way to countries or institutions. One of the organizers, who was in Stockholm in 1912, had been very much struck by Olympism there. The modern pentathlon in particular had roused his enthusiasm. It being impossible to celebrate the Olympic Games in San Francisco in 1915, he had nevertheless asked the IOC at least to patronize a pentathlon event. Our colleague Allison Armour had been delegated to represent us. On March 18, 1915, therefore, the Olympic flag had flown over the exhibition and, in the main courtyard, a grandiloquent speech had been made by the President of the exhibition, accompanied by an exchange of medals.

Shortly afterwards, Cuba entered upon the scene. By now we had grown accustomed to the idea of the Sixth Olympiad coming and going without being celebrated but continuing to count on the list, as in ancient times. It was on the year 1920 that all aspirations were focused. Atlanta, Cleveland, and Philadelphia had all three promised the earth. The committee that had been set up in Havana was less lavish in its promises, more aware of the difficulties, but at the same time assured of the support of the government, including the head of the Republic, President Menocal.

Whether the project would later succeed or be withdrawn, it nevertheless helped us to conquer South America, for which the propaganda departments with which I was then associated gave me invaluable help. In this part of the world, we had had many disappointments: a series of Argentinean members who had been of no help at all, and either complete lack of understanding or attempts at independence that were carried to the extreme and were exceedingly annoying for us. At one point, the Chilean clubs had made life very difficult for our colleague, Professor Garcia, even though he had been elected on the recommendation of their government, and the least I can say of the Chilean military delegation to the Games in Stockholm is that it acted very incorrectly towards the IOC; after that, an attempt had been made in Buenos Aires to hold an independent "Olympiad".

In Brazil sport was slow in developing, but in Mr. de Rio Branco, a former football captain, and now Minister in Bern, we had a reliable and devoted colleague. In 1916, I was able to set up in Paris an interim Committee, whose kingpin was Mr. de Matheu, Consul General of El Salvador, and which thanks to him carried out the most active propaganda. An illustrated brochure entitled "Que es el olimpismo?" was widely distributed in South American countries, superimposing its action on that of the Spanish Committee, into which the enthusiasm and generosity of the Marquis de Villamejor had breathed new life. Madrid, too, where in 1916 I had an opportunity of presiding over a meeting of this Committee, produced excellent propaganda in the form of a booklet on Olympism.

Too old to fight in 1914, Pierre de Coubertin nevertheless enlisted and was assigned to the national propaganda service. Coubertin decided that for the duration of his service Baron G. de Blonay should serve as interim president of the IOC. (Navacelle Collection)

The tremendous homage paid to the IOC in San Francisco had even more direct repercussions in the Philippines where the Americans, from the beginning of their occupation, had taken pains to encourage sport. Before the war even, I had got in touch with the Far Eastern Athletic Association, whose headquarters were in Manila, and whose President in 1915 was Doctor Wu Ting Fang of Shanghai, aided by excellent American advisers. With the enlightened backing of YMCA officials, they did some remarkable work and, now that the prestige of the IOC had reached their shores, showed themselves quite eager to place their "Far Eastern Games" under its wing. They felt called on to regenerate China, Japan, and Siam and took delight in adding the population figures. Without agreeing entirely with the strict mathematical accuracy of the American estimates for the future, we were nevertheless ready to trust them. "They had", they wrote to me, "created an *Olympic Kindergarten*". This was encouraging. What we lost on one side, we therefore recuperated on the other and I had been right when I wrote in one of the last numbers of the *Olympic Review* that if the war were one day to prevent an Olympiad from being celebrated in Europe, the following would be staged there, and that if the youth of this continent were temporarily forced to relinquish the Olympic flame, there would be another youth on the other side of the world ready to take over.

The Olympic Review was one of the first victims of the holocaust. Its last issue had appeared in July 1914. It was impossible to continue it. In fact, I had already decided to discontinue it after December and I had invited my colleagues to replace it with a bulletin of a more technical nature in three languages. I considered, on the eve of the recent cataclysm, that it had completed its mission and I wished to have more time for my own historical research. But from July to December it would publish and explain the documents and minutes of the Congress. Fate decided otherwise. It was printed at Ghent and in the upheavals of war many of the collections placed on one side were destroyed.

During the war several members died: Count Brunetta d'Usseaux, Baron de Venningen, killed on the front during the first weeks, and Evert Wendell. In addition, the place vacated by Mr. A. Ballif, who had resigned, was taken by the Marquis de Polignac. In 1918, shortly before the Armistice, three new members were elected from North and South America, Messrs. Bartow Weeks, Dorn y de Alsua, and P. J. de Matheu. Finally, in 1917, my own mandate had expired and been renewed through the intermediary of Mr. de Blonay, who had been kind enough, as of January 1, 1916, to agree to take over my official functions for me, which were very much reduced anyway owing to the fact that neither a plenary nor a partial meeting could be held until peace was signed. At least everything was kept going ready for the day we could start again.

Olympic Memoirs, Chap.16, Lausanne, IOC, 1997, pp.166-173.

4.2.2/32 GODEFROY DE BLONAY – INTERIM PRESIDENT. CIRCULAR LETTER TO THE IOC MEMBERS (JANUARY 1916)

My Dear Colleague,

You will not be surprised that, since the war is going on, I could not but agree to take part in it, in spite of my age. You will also understand that, having become involved, I do not think it right that our Committee should be led by a soldier. I have therefore asked our colleague and friend, Baron Godefroy de Blonay, to perform the functions of president *ad interim*. It is equally logical that the leadership of the Committee, whose seat is in Lausanne, should be in his hands for as long as hostilities continue. You are well aware of his competence and devotion. I ask you to give your confidence and support both to him and to our dear secretary, Count Brunetta d'Usseaux.

It was a great comfort to me to see that the majority fully agree with me about the Olympic future. We have restored an ancient, not a short-lived tradition. However terrible the present upheavals may be, the course of history cannot be interrupted and Olympism has gone down in history.

I fully expect that, with or without me, you will continue to lead the development of Olympism, and I take this opportunity to express to all of you, with my loyal attachment, my profound gratitude for the 20 years that we have devoted to a shared effort.

Yours affectionately,

Pierre de Coubertin

Circular Letter of the IOC-President,
[January 1916], (Archives of the IOC).
French original in: *Textes choisis,* Vol. II, p. 261.

N° 80. — 14 Août 1920.

26e ANNÉE

	France et Colonies	Étranger
Trois mois...	7.50	8.50
Six mois.....	14. »	16. »
Un an........	27. »	30. »

Les abonnements partent du 1er de chaque mois.

Le Rire

JOURNAL HUMORISTIQUE PARAISSANT LE SAMEDI

60 Centimes

F. JUVEN, éditeur
1, rue de Choiseul, 1
PARIS

Tout changement d'adresse doit être accompagné de 50 centimes.

Copyright 1920 by LE RIRE, Paris

LES OLYMPIADES D'ANVERS

PLUS DE LUTTES DE CLASSES... VIVE LA LUTTE CLASSIQUE!

Dessin de NOB.

Cover of the French satirical journal "Le Rire", stating that the true and unique "International" is not the Moscow one, but the one from Antwerp. Caption underneath: "Plus de luttes de classes... Vive la lutte classique!" ("No more class struggles... Here's to classical wrestling!") (taken from Le Rire, no.80, 1920)

4.2.2/33 – 4.2.2/36 INTRODUCTION

The following four excerpts concern the Seventh Olympic Games, held at Antwerp in 1920. In these texts, Coubertin does not simply describe the preparations for and progress of these Games, but the state of the Olympic Movement at the end of World War I, as well.

In the first text, a chapter taken from his Olympic Memoirs, Coubertin first of all outlines the political situation in the IOC after World War I. Regarding the description of the Olympic Games of Antwerp, in particular Coubertin's statements concerning the neutrality of the cultic development deserve attention.

In the second text, entitled "The Contribution of the Seventh Olympiad", he calls the Antwerp Games "in a way, the Olympiad of the resurrection". It was practically a miracle that the city of Antwerp felt bound by the offer it had made before the war to host the 1920 Games, despite the enormous destruction Belgium suffered during the war[1]. It was not until November 30, 1918 that Coubertin made the request of the Belgian government, proposing a program adapted to suit the post-war circumstances. He had refused to postpone the Games until 1921[2].

In the third text which is known to us in English and French, Coubertin very broadly and thoroughly mentions the difficulties in organising the Games so shortly after World War I. He explains the conditions of the different sports[3].

After the Games, Coubertin related his impressions of them, and in particular the individual sports and supporting program, in a 24-page brochure that today provides a valuable account of the holding of the Seventh Olympic Games. The specially printed brochure was certainly intended to make the Olympic new beginning widely known to the outside world.

The title of the fourth text reproduced here, "The Victory of Olympism", expresses the pride that Coubertin felt in having managed to keep the Olympic Games going on their four-year cycle, and to prove the Olympic Movement's ability to endure despite the failure marked by the cancellation of the Berlin Games of 1916. Here he compares the Olympic Games of 1920 to all the previous ones and sees in them the final victory of Olympism.

4.2.2/33 THE SEVENTH OLYMPIAD (ANTWERP 1920)

As soon as the armistice was signed, I began getting in touch with those of my colleagues who were nearest at hand. It was important for this Session to be held in Lausanne, which had in the meantime become the permanent administrative center of Olympism and needed to have its newfound status confirmed in this way. In the spring of 1919, it would be twenty-five years since the Games had been revived.

1 In June 1914, the Belgian government had given its consent to the request made by Antwerp for 1920. The competing city, Lyons, withdrew on September 6, 1915 in an agreement officially reached with the city of Antwerp in its favor.

2 See N. Müller/S. Gieseler, "Olympische Spiele im Schatten des 1. Weltkrieges." [Olympic Games in the shadow of World War I], in: N.Müller/M. Messing, *Auf der Suche nach der Olympischen Idee,* Kassel, Agon 1996, pp.135-156.

3 See Coubertin, "Autour de la VIIme Olympiade." Special print, Lausanne, La Concorde, 1920. Reprinted in *Textes choisis,* Vol. II, pp. 268-276. Coubertin provided it for the Official Report of the USOC, which appeared in late 1920, making only some minor changes to the text in the third-to-last section.

Without giving it more importance than the circumstances justified, this coincidence could nevertheless be used to add color and interest to the Session. The Swiss public authorities were of the same opinion. Mr. Gustave Ador, who had recently been elected President of the Confederation, a post which had been thrust upon him because of the universal respect in which he was held and the gratitude of the belligerents for his efforts to bandage their wounds, immediately agreed to preside over the ceremony which was held with all due solemnity, and was a great success in spite of the rigors of a winter that lingered on. Our Lausanne friends, led by the indefatigable and devoted Dr. Messerli, arranged a brilliant and varied setting for our Session. The discussions were peaceful as was only to be expected among friends happy to meet again and to witness the soundness of the Olympic fabric. It was outside the conference rooms that agitation was rife. Paris was the center of the trouble. Unbelievably, a peevish, disloyal opposition had sprung up and was directed against the choice of Antwerp. If ever a gesture were called for, at such a moment, what could have been better than the choice we were making of Antwerp as the venue for the Seventh Olympiad? What other candidature could equal it? I am sure that, duly informed, the conscience of the world would have manifested with enthusiasm in Antwerp's favor. In Belgium, at any rate, great interest was taken in our meeting and the government, aware of the responsibility represented by the award of the Games, declared itself ready to accept it.

The Count de Baillet-Latour had not been content merely to discuss the matter with King Albert and the ministers. With his realistic idealism, he had examined all the possibilities and was determined to go ahead and make a success of the Games. Although serious attempts had been made to discourage him, he gave Antwerp's promise – encouraged somewhat by the assurances brought to him from Britain by the Reverend Laffan – that everything would be ready at the appointed time. And so, in fact, it was.

Cuba had gradually faded from the scene. In view of Belgium's candidature, none of the others could hope to succeed. However, a big problem arose: the participation of the "central empires", as they were still called. It was only a few months since the last German soldier had left Belgian soil and since the last cannon shot had been heard on the battlefield. Common sense suggested that it would hardly be wise for a German team to appear in the Olympic stadium before 1924. On the other hand, to ostracize any member country, even right after the conflict that had torn Europe asunder, would create a rift in the Olympic constitution which had been so strong until then; and it might become a dangerous precedent. The solution however was very simple. At each Olympiad, according to the custom introduced in 1896, it is the Organizing Committee that sends out the invitations. In this way, the Organizing Committee is in control of distribution, without the fundamental principle of universality having to suffer any direct infringement. The IOC had therefore no new decision to make. Nevertheless, despite the opinion of several of us, a middle way was chosen which consisted in enumerating the countries that would be invited, with the excuse that the others were not represented on the IOC. This was a double mistake, for while death in Germany and resignations elsewhere had left several empty spaces in our ranks, there remained the Hungarians who were neither dead nor on the point of resigning.

During the 1919 Session, fourteen French military planes landed in Lausanne from Nancy, at the invitation of the Lausanne School of Civil Aviation. A letter from the President of the Cabinet, the War Minister, informed me that by sending this squadron, with the authorization of the Federal Government and "on the occasion of the 25th anniversary of the revival of the Olympic Games", Mr. Clemenceau wished to mark the "high esteem" in which he held the IOC and its work. In this way, the discontented were invited to keep quiet but even so they continued for a long time to grumble and show their ill will in many ways. What exactly did they want? Nothing very precise. Pressed finally to make known their complaints, the newspapers that backed them fell silent and France's participation, in its turn, began to take shape.

In Antwerp, the directorial – and sometimes even dictatorial – activity of our colleague worked wonders. Everything had to be created from scratch, and everything was – admittedly not on the lavish scale and with the sumptuousness provided for in the original drafts presented to the IOC before the war when the city's candidature had been submitted for the first time, but in a perfectly orderly way and with as much moderation and tact as elegance and brilliance. Concerning the number and quality of the entries, we were quickly reassured. One of the most common anxieties related to the brutal disappearance of so many athletes and the lack of training of those that remained. In this connection, the Interallied Games, held in Paris in the spring of 1919 under the aegis of General Pershing, who had a stadium built for the purpose near Vincennes and which still bears his name, were extremely useful. They had been arranged with a view to providing a healthful and enjoyable means of occupying the enforced leisure of the troops of the different armies, whose immediate demobilization and return home had, for many reasons, not been considered practicable and large numbers of whom were thus held on French soil with very little to do. Naturally, attempts had been made in certain circles to mislead the public by talking of a "Military Olympiad" and suggesting that it should take the place of the regular Olympiad a year ahead of time. Once again the question of the numbering of the Games and the four-yearly interval! I have before me a letter from J. J. Jusserand, giving me an account of the steps he was taking (President Wilson was in Paris at the time) and assuring me that the Americans would never allow use to be made of the terms "Olympic" or "Olympiad" for such a purpose. The Interallied Games, as might have been expected, showed moreover that muscular value and sporting enthusiasm were not on the decline.

The Games of the Seventh Olympiad opened brilliantly on August 14, 1920, in the presence of the King and Queen of the Belgians, accompanied by the Duke of Brabant, Prince Charles and Princess Marie-José. The parade, the opening address, the choirs, the release of the pigeons, the salvoes, the whole splendid ceremonial, the educational value of which had begun to be realized in Stockholm, showed just how strong Olympism still was, even so soon after the war, and to what extent its laurels continued to be prized above all other sporting honors by the youth of the world. In the evening, the King and Queen gave a banquet in the Palace in exclusive honor of the International Olympic Committee; this was followed by a very large reception, at the end of which the sovereigns departed for Brussels.

Cardinal Mercier, who was there, had officiated in the Cathedral that morning at a religious service, conceived this time according to a different plan than the one that took place in 1912.

Regarding this point I have not yet had an opportunity of giving an explanation. By holding a public service in the stadium itself, as in Stockholm, before the start of the competitions, we would be forcing the athletes, already grown men, to take part in a religious ceremony that might be displeasing to some. By inviting them, quite outside the Games, to a ceremony in a church, we were only associating religion like any other great moral force of mankind with the celebration of the Olympic Games. Then again, it was important that the ceremony should be sufficiently neutral in character to rise above all differences in doctrine. No mass, no priestly address at the altar: the *De Profundis,* a hymn to the memory of the dead of the previous four years, and the *Te Deum,* a hymn of success and hope; lay hymns, they might be called, and ideally suited to beautiful musical interpretations. To which could be added a speech, provided that it was couched in liberal terms. This unusual program appealed to Cardinal Mercier. The ceremony had a special grandeur about it this time owing to the tragic fact that the list of Olympic dead was terribly long. And all those present came away, I believe, deeply impressed by the words spoken in the Cathedral by the famous prelate in a moving service accompanied by the magnificent music of the choirs and organ.

During the Games, all the political, civil and military authorities of the city, the province and the country showed continual keen interest in their success. None more so than the Governor of Antwerp, Baron Gaston de Schilde, who was very popular with all who met him. Antwerp had been brilliantly decorated. From the city center to the stadium, the route was lined with Olympic flags. Everywhere the five multicolored rings and the motto: *Citius, Altius, Fortius* were prominently displayed. The festivities were numerous and highly successful, and pipers from a Scottish regiment often added a picturesque note.

The oldest members of the IOC, General Balck, Professor Sloane, the Reverend Laffan, Doctor Guth-Jarkovsky, Baron G. de Blonay, Baron van Tuyll, and Count von Rosen found themselves, once again, united in the same ideal and, around them, a large number of others formed the growing squadron of those who would eventually take over and to whom they would hand over the flame. Distant colleagues were there too: Japanese, Indians, South Africans, Brazilians, potential colleagues from recently emancipated nations – Ireland, Poland – who submitted their candidatures, a representative of the city of Los Angeles, entrusted with the mission of securing the future Games for this city, representatives of the YMCA, now very much attracted by the powerful influence of Olympism, which they had often ignored in the past. Among the last-named, an enthusiast, Elwood Brown, was to become, during the following years, the keen advocate and champion of Olympism throughout the Near and Far East.

Where would the 1924 Games be held? The question was on everyone's mind. In fact, there was complete lack of agreement among sports officials. They all wanted a great deal, but did not know what: reforms, innovations, transformations. In the speech that I made before the King the day he honored the opening meeting of the IOC Session with his presence, I indicated that our hopes for the

High Olympic Society (from left to right): Baron Pierre de Coubertin, American Scoutmaster Welsh, King Albert I of Belgium and Count Henri de Baillet-Latour enter the Olympic Stadium for the Opening Ceremony on 14th August 1920. (taken from R.Renson, The VII Olympiad: Antwerp 1920. The Games Reborn. Antwerp/Ghent, Pandora/Snoeck-Ducaju, 1996, p.31)

The turning point, half way through the marathon during the 1920 Antwerp Olympics. For the first time, the Olympic flag with its five rings was displayed in all the Olympic venues. (Photo: C.F.Du Houx, Antwerp 1920, taken from R.Renson, The VII Olympiad: Antwerp 1920. The Games Reborn. Antwerp/Ghent, Pandora/Snoeck-Ducaju, 1996, p.91)

future lay in democratic expansion. The sovereign was one of those in whose presence one feels free to express one's thoughts. But no sure trend could be discerned as yet; it was wisest to wait and see. I advised postponing the decision and at the same time proposed convening, in Lausanne in 1921, a Congress which would revise, in so far as the new situation required, the technical decisions reached in Paris in 1914, and to which this time were invited the delegates of the International Federations as well as those of the National Olympic Committees. In addition to this Congress, I planned another, of an educational and social character, for the purpose of studying the measures to be taken to organize sport for the masses. This was the movement that I had sought to start in France in 1906, and which this time would be on the world scale under the wing of the IOC.

The IOC gave its agreement. The atmosphere of our meetings revealed some uncertainty and hesitation concerning the direction to be taken. I felt a vague desire on the part of members to have no decisions to make and to leave everything to me. It became obvious that the choice of venue for the following Games would have to be postponed, but if this were the case then Paris could never hope to see its candidature accepted. Persistent ill humor prevailed among the French, their teams made themselves far from popular, even in the equestrian events. Within the IOC itself, the opinion of the "neutrals" tended to predominate and to them Paris seemed a choice that would only perpetuate the memories of the war. On the other hand, the French federations demanded to be awarded the Games, saying out loud that "we would then see how the Olympic Games should be organized", and quite a few foreign federations lent a willing ear to these words. The press acrimoniously backed up these demands. I was not at all convinced of the feasibility of the plan, but I felt that it was not at all a bad idea to give them a chance. I therefore drew up in my mind the details of a rather unusual maneuver and waited quietly for the right moment to put it into effect.

Olympic Memoirs, Chap. 17, Lausanne, IOC, 1997, pp.176-183.

4.2.2/34 THE CONTRIBUTION OF THE SEVENTH OLYMPIAD

Even though here and there a competitor, embittered by his lack of success, a crotchety journalist, or just a professional spoilsport disputed the evidence, the success of the Olympic Games at Antwerp surpassed all expectations. From August 14 to September 12, despite equally unfavorable political, economic, and atmospheric conditions, the Seventh Olympiad was held with a mastery, a perfection and a dignity matched by the strenuous and persevering efforts of its organizers.

What will the outcome of this success be? Each of the preceding Olympiads was characterized by an overall result that, in sequence, summarizes the history of neo-Olympism. When the Olympic Games were restored in Athens two years after it was declared that they would soon be re-established, the institution received its baptism of tradition at the foot of the Acropolis, its connection to an illustrious past. It was essential that this baptism take place at a site without peer. The halo was placed on the head of Olympism, a sign of the aspirations of its founders and the destiny they sought. The Second Olympiad (1900), held in Paris under seriously deficient conditions, established the modern nature of the undertaking, because though it laid claim to antiquity, neo-Olympism also means responding fully to the needs of the present age. The Third Olympiad (St. Louis, 1904) showed the universalistic tendencies of the movement which, in order to prosper, had to escape from the Mediterranean world, from Europe as well, and conquer the New World. With the Fourth Olympiad (London, 1908), the resolve grew to encompass not only all nations, but all sports as well. All games, all nations. That had been the initial intent, but the full scope of it could be realized only gradually. The London Games made it possible to make such a claim. The Stockholm Games confirmed and justified this outlook. The Fifth Olympiad, held in Stockholm in 1912, became a real "matter of State". Sovereigns, the government, and public authorities did everything necessary to do honor to the name of Sweden. Little by little, the Olympic Games of the modern era began to rival their ancient predecessors in size and splendor. Then came a test. A bloody cross marks the place of the Sixth Olympiad, for which Berlin was already preparing with great generosity. War spread and lingered. 1916 came and went. Where would Olympism stand in the aftermath of this turmoil? The only ones who could be confident were those who knew of the historical power of the underlying principle of Olympism, and the potential impact of its educational action. But there was still only a handful of such individuals. The crowds had seen five successive Olympiads held with increasing pomp and circumstance, and yet we felt that they still had only a vague grasp of the meaning and import of the Games.

That is what the Seventh Olympiad gave us: the understanding of all, the certainty of being understood by everyone from then on. At long last, the primordial nature of these festivals was understood – festivals that are above all, at a time of dangerous specialization and regrettable "compartmentalization", festivals of human unity. The effort of the muscles and of the mind, mutual assistance and competition, exalted patriotism and intelligent cosmopolism, the personal interest of the champion and the self-denial of the team member – all are bundled together in an incomparable synthesis to perform a common human task. All sports are linked together, saluted by flags, encouraged by the Church, and honored by Literature and the Arts. Youth as a whole, whether patrician or plebeian, is called upon to choose the fastest, the strongest, the most daring.

This arrangement for which I have worked these twenty-five years, that I have sculpted slowly, so to speak, has now been welcomed by public opinion. In perceiving its beauty, its reason for being, and its appropriateness, public opinion will be ready to uphold it, as well.

That is the contribution of the Seventh Olympiad. It has shown the universe, in radiant relief, the educational, moral, and social dynamism that restored and modernized Olympism harbors.

L'apport de la VIIe Olympiade,
in: *La Revue Sportive Illustrée,*
Vol. 16, 1920, no. 3 (p. 10).

4.2.2/35 THE SEVENTH OLYMPIC GAMES[1]

The athletes have made good progress and the public is becoming more enlightened: a twofold statement summing up my impression of the Olympic Games of 1920.

The second point is to be especially noted. For the first time upon taking up my pen the day after such an event, I do not feel the necessity of explaining, in the form of an introduction, what neo-Olympism is, why and how the Games came to be reorganized and what the special features of their quadriennial celebration are. In spite of the efforts of a certain press serving personal interest, first to discredit this organization (the Olympiad) by its silence and then to break the silence with a series of lies – the Olympiad has succeeded through repeated successes and growing importance in implanting itself in the very heart of international life.

The program of the Olympic Games which is still unsettled as to the details was first discussed at the Paris Congress of 1914, and will be practically decided by the Congress at Lausanne in 1921. It is now classified under five different divisions: athletic sports, gymnastic sports, defensive sports, equestrian sports, and nautical sports: to which the combined sports (old and modern pentathlons), cycling and other games; and finally, competitions in the art field must be added. Such is the plan.

Athletic games (racing, jumping, hurling of the discus, of the javelin) have this characteristic – that the players consider themselves as kings of the Olympic arena and the sole inheritors of the classical period. However, even when the British championship was generally recognized in the world of sports, the oar and the cricket shared popular favor with racing. When the Olympic Games were reorganized they were done so on the understanding that each of the five kinds of sports was of equal importance. In France, particularly, the parties interested have never ceased to rebel against this "equality". Something of this spirit is always present in the relations between the "athletes" and their comrades in gymnastics, fencing, boxing, or rowing. One feels that they are always on the alert to consider themselves wronged individuals and to form groups among themselves, in the various countries, to defend themselves against imaginary persecution.

Nevertheless the games held during the Seventh 0lympiad went off brilliantly. Feats were accomplished, in some cases records beaten. Special mention is due of the famous marathon race. This race which covers the historical distance between Marathon and Athens, about 42 kilometres, was, in fact, re-invented by a member of the Institute of France. As soon as he heard of my plan to reorganize the Olympic Games, Monsieur Michel Breal, full of enthusiasm, informed me that he would donate a silver cup as a reward to the runner able to repeat the classical feat – without dying as a result of it!

Everyone knows how the first race from Marathon to Athens was run, in 1896, and how the winner, a shepherd named Spiridon Louis, had insisted upon fasting for two days and spending the night in prayer before holy pictures. Since that time we have never seen such fresh, enthusiastic young men enter an 0lympic Stadium for the races as those who competed on August 22, 1920. The first one was from Finland, the second from Esthonia; and thus the two young republics carried off envied laurels. The third runner, an Italian, after reaching the goal, turned around, faced the astounded onlookers, and made a double somersault to prove to the spectators that his feet were still in good condition; he was followed by a Belgian who made an extra-round carrying a kind of shield with the national colors. Both of these clever stunts were enthusiastically hailed.

On the whole, it seems to have been feared that there would be a noticable falling off in performances, at least on the part of those from the belligerent countries, which had suffered most from the war and its resulting miseries. This was not evident, except perhaps in the bearing of the competitors filing past on the day when the official opening took place. Here and there a person whose gait was less elastic than usual, whose face looked older could be noticed; but the power of endurance remained great.

Indeed, it is evident that such failures that took place were not due to this "falling off"; but in certain groups, in 1920 as in 1912, to a lack of unity of action, to careless preparation and especially to the refusal to sacrifice a spirit of rivalry and personal antipathies in favor of the general good and success of the Games.

These very necessary qualities are more common among the gymnasts. In the 0lympic Games, gymnastics are divided into three different classes: those performed by an individual, those performed by groups, and those exercises in which use is made of dumb-bells and weights. The exercises contained in the first and third divisions do not receive the credit they deserve because of the fact that they no longer enjoy public favor. This is not the moment to discuss their merits or demerits. In spite of the indifference of the crowd, the athletes proved themselves worthy of their traditions. Their feats, displaying suppleness of body, wonderful control of nerve and muscle, rejoiced all who witnessed them. When the performances of these young men once more win popularity, and their right to a place in the world of sports is recognized, then the people will realize that they have been depriving themselves, for a long time, through snobbishness, of a sight most pleasing in its physical strength and beauty. The contests in groups were held, according to custom, in two divisions:

(1) those played according to "Swedish method";

(2) those played according to "European method" – an unwise division, not only because of its geographical inexactness, but because it gives greater importance to the method. What difference does it make how an athlete is trained; one must see what he can do and how he does it. Indeed, the task of the jury is a hard one, but it is always so wherever personal interests enter.

Fencing with foils – to go on to the defensive sports – was a sad surprise to its devotees. It is evidently dying out. For my part, I do not hesitate in placing the blame for this on the rules in vogue. The International Federation of Fencing would render the cause a great service in bringing about a complete reform in the established regulations. To restore fencing with foils to the place it deserves, by right and tradition, would emancipate at the same time fencing with sword and rapier. Each manner of fencing loses in trying to resemble one another. On the contrary, their differences ought to be accentuated more strongly. This does not mean that the

1 The editor did not feel justified in making corrections to style or expressions, even if these seem necessary today. The English version was forgotten for decades. The editor thanks Anthony Bijkerk for this information.

Olympic Games did not bring out wonderful fencers, among them is the Italian champion Nedo Nadi, who occupied the first place, and who is the incarnation of gracefulness and strength combined.

For the fencers, those using both sword and rapier, a field out-of-doors had been prepared, but they were unable to take advantage of it because of the inclement weather. Though it is very agreeable to assemble enthusiastic crowds in the open air, it would seem far better, nevertheless, that provision be made to conduct games, as important as the Olympic Games, in a sheltered place.

Boxing had undoubtedly greater success in the Seventh Olympiad than ever before. It took years of hard struggling to introduce this sport and then to keep it in favor. In Sweden, the public authorities insisted upon it being given up. Though the International Committee yielded in the matter, it declared, that in the future, it would refuse any concession whatever on important matters relative to the Olympic program.

This time the public agreed with it. The people came in great numbers, full of enthusiasm, and at Antwerp, boxing received its papers of Olympic naturalization. Its champions proved themselves worthy of public esteem. In general, their spirit of being "good sports" was very pleasing. Here were found working in harmony, physical strength and courtesy, scorn of blows and prudence, opposite virtues which, when combined, make for true manliness, and boxing, when properly taught and well conducted, can become a most instructive sport. Some people regretted that French boxing was not on the program. Although it is now but little practiced, its true lovers still remain who seek to popularize it again, so that we may hope once more to see this fine practice restored to its place in the world of sports.

The contest in wrestling (Graeco-Roman and catch-as-catch can) which I could not follow, and about which I know little, seems to have pleased its large circle of friends. Wrestling is an important feature of the Olympic Games and could not be separated from the other defensive sports. There is one sport, ignored like French boxing, i.e., the cane, which it seems to me might very usefully be restored to its old popularity. At present, it is not sufficiently practiced to be added to the Olympic contests.

As usual the equestrian sports consisted of cross country riding, steeple-chasing, and epreuves de dressage, but besides this there was a contest in vaulting (act of leaping on a horse). No longer could a sport uniting such rare qualities, which too often are unappreciated, be ignored – and which is one of the finest exercises. Polo, in spite of the present difficulties in its organization did take place. Henceforth, fencing on horseback is the only sport missing, and a practical solution in this case has not been found. Then the equestrian games would be complete.

Swimming, for which a magnificent pool had been installed on the order of a "nautical stadium", in some respects a model of its kind, carried off the usual laurels before its numerous admirers. Women are allowed to compete. They excelled in it, breaking all former records. Water polo brought out groups of young people, rivalling in skill and endurance.

The contests in rowing were held on a canal in Brussels, having as a setting the worst landscape possible; walls of factories, reservoirs, gasometers – so very horrid, that all attempt to hide its ugliness was abandoned. Splendid teams met in this anti-Olympic setting. The finale of the race, with eight rowers, disputed between the Leander Club (England) and a team from the Naval Academy of the

United States was won by the latter, though the victory was a very close one. This incident brought up the question of "amateurism", a hard matter to unravel; for, in all fairness, how is it possible to have two teams compete, one of which is made up of men with military training, alike in strength, who may have been urged on and trained according to the good pleasure of those in authority – and the other team, of individual origin, composed of volunteers who could give but brief and irregular moments to its practice.

The classical pentathlon and the decathlon are not, properly speaking, "combined sports", for they borrow most of their numbers from the class of athletic sports. It is quite different with the modern pentathlon which includes shooting matches, fencing, swimming, running and riding. This contest which I had great difficulty in bringing about, because it so upset established customs, assembled numerous competitors from the different nations, but Sweden maintained its superiority, established in 1912. The first four winners were Swedes.

The Swedes were much feared; it was said that their neutrality was in their favor, and so too in the case of the Americans, they were believed to have the advantage, because the best of everything was at their disposal. True, both won many laurels, but Finland, on the whole, bore off the palm. This country, swept over by war and revolution, but yesterday uncertain of the morrow, attained an unheard of record. There were barely sixty athletes in the contingent from Finland for the various games, but they won about fifteen first prizes, not to mention the second and third places which went to them. Who was it who said that only the big nations could think of having their representatives victorious, that there was nothing for inexperienced men to hope for, that success was in proportion to the money spent?

No, the victory of Spain in football, the qualifications of the Swiss and Egyptian candidates, of the Portuguese fencers, of the Brazilian oarsmen, all were a credit and honor to their nations, which heretofore were too timid to come forward and take part in the Games. And what about the Italian contingent? The Italians asserted themselves firmly on every field by their energy, their determined spirit, their bearing, their discipline, their national spirit, in spite of the fact that they received but little financial assistance, that they came from afar, and had neither traditions nor experience in the Olympic Games. They were wonderful.

Thus it is proved once more that the secret of success does not lie merely in the technical preparation given but above all in the mental attitude of the men, together with the firm moral resolution which inspires them. In 1908, this point was emphasized by the Bishop of Pennsylvania, in St. Paul's Cathedral, London, when addressing the athletes of the Fourth Olympiad. The point was brought out again strongly by Cardinal Mercier, at the inaugural service in the imposing Cathedral of Antwerp, where the De Profundis for the deceased athletes was sung, together with the usual Te Deum, sung with great pomp.

This never-to-be forgotten ceremony naturally deeply impressed the congregation which filled this cathedral made famous by Rubens. In the afternoon of the same day the program for the Opening of the Games in the Stadium was held according to established custom: the defile of the athletes, grouped according to country; the address to the King; the Sovereign's reply, pronouncing the Games to be officially opened, which was received with the sounding of trumpets, salutes of

Aileen Riggin (USA, 1st in Springboard Diving) and Nick Skoglund (SWE), two youngest competitors at the Antwerp Olympics 1920 (taken from Spalding's Athletic Library no.94R: Olympic Games Handbook, New York, ASP, 1922, p.156)

cannon and the flying away of pigeons which bore about their necks the colors of the nations represented. This time, there were two innovations; first the pledges taken by the athletes, spoken aloud by one of them (a Belgian holding the flag of his country) in the name of all, as follows: "We swear that we are taking part in the Olympic Games as loyal competitors, observing the rules governing the Games, and anxious to show a spirit of chivalry, for the honor of our countries and for the glory of the sport". Thus modern Games go back, little by little, to their illustrious ancestors by the successive restoration of both the ceremonies and the symbolic acts which gave to the former so great and deep a meaning.

The second innovation was the appearance of the Olympic flag, with its five entwined rings, multicolors on a white background, evoking the five parts of the world united by Olympism, and at the same time reproducing the colors of every nation. This flag was inaugurated in Paris, June, 1914, during the celebration of the 20th "anniversary of the reorganisation of the Olympic Games", but it had never yet appeared at an Olympiad gathering. At Antwerp, its glorious colors were displayed everywhere, and its popularity was great, so great that a group of athletes, one fine night, in the town, carried off everything so as to bring home with them this tangible souvenir of the Seventh Olympiad. Unfortunately, the Police were on guard: arrests, trials, consular interventions, followed.

Of course, this was not the only trouble which happened, there were a great many other disturbances. But does anyone suppose that formerly, in Olympus, there were never disputes or squabbles? How could one bring together hundreds and hundreds of young people, belonging to every nation, who but yesterday looked askance at one another, to live happy healthy lives, without expecting to hear now and then a hasty word spoken or a quick gesture made ?

According to the testimony of Mr. Verdyck, the tireless and loyal secretary-general of the Committee on Organization, the Games of 1920, in this respect offered the minimum number of unpleasant incidents, and their pacifying influence is shown further in the fact that two teams, one Dutch and one Belgian were able to face each other in the Stadium, to the great astonishment of several politicians, without any other display of feeling but that of the finest sportsmanship.

This international comradeship was intensified fortunately by the manner in which the athletes were lodged. Schools – in general luxurious and well-equipped, provided with plenty of room and lovely gardens – had been put at the disposal of the various countries represented in which to lodge their men. And so there sprang up the Italian house, the English house, the French house, the American, etc. Only the very small groups had to live in the hotels.

Each house displayed its national emblem and between its occupants friendly rivalry arose. They visited each other, entertained each other, even gave concerts and plays among themselves. The good manners and courtesy found at these gatherings were remarkable, and here was a splendid opportunity to fight against a certain free unrestrained "I don't care" feeling – which sometimes betrayed itself in the Stadium in careless attire and uncared for appearance.

I have not spoken of the art contests. They are not yet equal to it, although far in advance of 1912. The writers seem to be intimidated by subjects on sports; musicians have nothing to do with them; architects walk around their "Palace of Sports" of which they are seeking the eternal silhouette, a monument already out of use before having existed. As for the sculptors, a rather humorous incident happened regarding them. Having no knowledge of technique, the jury put aside the reproduction of bodily movements in all exactness and perfection, because such movements were not considered sufficienly ''artistic". Let us hope that the contests of the Eighth Olympiad will be the final dedication of the value of inspiration offered by the Games, and will tempt young talents to combine artistic taste with physical hardness.

Antwerp is just the city where the combination of these qualities may be found, and that is the reason it served as a far more appropriate place in which to hold the Games of 1920 than was generally realized. Too often is it considered as merely a commercial center, with here and there museums recalling past glory. But the wonderful harmony which is revealed there in both the construction of the city and in its buildings, its harbor, its public squares and parks, its institutions, the element of life itself – all this seems to contain such strength and equilibrium, energy and beauty, that the visitor, however little time he may have for observation, returns filled with a spirit of admiration and confidence. It was in this harmonious setting that the Games were held. As to the details, the committee in charge accomplished wonders. Count Henry de Baillet-Latour may be proud of the work he supervised, and which, placed on a firm financial basis, never ceased for an instant in bringing perfection in technique, together with a lofty pedagogical ideal.

It was in the City Hall of Antwerp, a splendid example of municipal art, which is presided over by the most courteous 'Burgomaster', that the Olympic International Committee held its meetings. King Albert favored us by opening the session himself. Thirty members, belonging to twenty-three nations, took part in it – the "Olympic Senate", assembled again, on the morrow of the long and terrible war, as staunch and as united as it was six years ago. Neither did it feel the need of making any defensive moves against the new attack directed against it. It simply ignored it. The International Committee contrary to the opinion of its adversaries, does not look upon its authority as an exclusive right; it would gladly share it, were it not for the conviction that it would be seriously endangering the future of a progressive institution by giving any part over to those who eagerly covet it.

At present there are critical conditions throughout the world. Between now and the close of the year, events will follow a more marked course and then we can scrutinize the horizon better. This horizon is over-cast. However, the general public, indifferent and amused, does not seem to worry about it. I admit experiencing during the whole period of the Games, a painful surprise in noting among so many different peoples, a kind of outlook unconscious of approaching dangers. We fear the improbable recurrence of yesterday's peril; no one seriously considers the danger which is growing greater day by day, not in the distance, but under our very feet. Nevertheless, it was with great confidence upon pronouncing the Games of the Seventh Olympiad over, that we, according to custom, extended the invitation to all to partake in the Games of the Eighth Olympiad.

This ceremony took place with all due pomp on September 12. Heretofore, the official close of the Games had been announced at a final banquet. But the solemn words lacked somewhat of their grandeur there. This time, with a background of a setting sun, the Stadium crowded with spectators, the formula was invested with its old time significance. The equestrian games were just over; in the midst of the great silence the crowd suddenly became attentive and the glorious words resounded calling together the Games of 1924: "May joy and good-fellowship reign, and in this manner, may the Olympic Torch pursue its way through the ages, for the good of a humanity always more enthusiastic, more courageous and more pure. So may it be! (Amen.)"

Then, as on August 14, the trumpets resounded and the cannon boomed while the Olympic banner was slowly lowered and the first sounds of a cantata were heard, sung and played by 1.200 voices and instrumentalists, a work by the celebrated Peter Benoit, beloved of the people of Antwerp, his countrymen. And so ended the Olympic Games of 1920, in the city of Rubens.

Autour de la VII[me] Olympiade. Special print, Lausanne, La Concorde, 1920.
Reprinted in *Textes choisis*, Vol. II, pp. 268-276.
English version with modifications in the last paragraph in: American Olympic Committee (Ed.): *Report of the American Olympic Committee. Seventh Olympic Games Antwerp*. Belgium 1920, Greenwich/Con. 1921, pp. 47-58.

4.2.2/36 THE VICTORY OF OLYMPISM

Olympism is a great, quiet piece of machinery. Its gears do not screech and its movement never stops, despite the handfuls of sand that certain individuals throw on it in a persistent but unsuccessful attempt to impede its operation. When the time comes for the International Committee to make a decision, it does so without concern for anything but the good of the institution whose destiny has been entrusted in it. Events have proved the Committee right, and have shown that it choose the best possible approach. This is how the various stages in the restoration of the Olympics have been reached, and how the modern world has come to be invited to these solemnities every four years. As time goes on, these occasions evoke the ancient Greek ideal more and more. The program of the Games has been complex: the Arts, Literature, imposing ceremonies, connection with religion, increasingly ardent appeals to the noble, chivalrous spirit as the basis for any durable and pure athletic activity, and finally educational exhibitions intended to show increasingly the tremendous educational role that intense physical exercise can play. These are the peaks that Olympism has reached since its restoration twenty-six years ago. Among those who responded to my appeal and voted to restore the Olympic Games on June 23, 1894, there is not a single one, I believe, who imagined a more eminent role in the modern world for the work that they were supporting.

That same world has been shaken by a major cataclysm, and the Sixth Olympiad (1916), which was not held, will remain a bloody mark in the annals of world history. But as soon as peace was on the verge of being restored, youth has again resumed its interrupted dream, and is preparing for the next Games. What more astonishing proof could we possibly want of the vitality of the movement?

Public opinion has registered its surprise...surprise that Belgium dared to suggest, and that the International Committee dared to agree, that it host the Seventh Olympiad, that all the material and political difficulties were able to be overcome, that everything was ready in time, a magnificent stadium built, an organization zealous about every last detail put in place...

In our day, when too little is done and too much said, one might almost say that Olympism is setting a new record in this regard!

That is how things are. We are grateful for it and proud of it. We are grateful to the Belgian people. They have given humanity a striking example of what indomitable hearts can achieve, hearts that, to use the beautiful expression of Thomas Aquinas, are "always ready to fight after every storm". We are also proud of our organization, which made this prodigious work possible and facilitated it.

In 1910, in his speech welcoming the International Olympic Committee to the Palais Municipal of Luxembourg, Mr. Eyscher, Senior Minister of the Grand Duchy, said that having looked over our statutes, he regretted that they had not been applied to politics, because he had never seen statutes so simple and so fruitful. If the various specialized departments on which the moral and material advancement of States depend were modeled on Olympism, they would gain in economy, speed, and efficiency alike.

This was high praise indeed coming from so well-regarded a government official. In fact, why should the principle that is the source of our strength not be put into more general practice? It was once applied at Elis. It is applied in our time at Henley. There is nothing exclusively athletic about it. Moreover, this would not be the first time that economists and administrators would do well to have recourse to the practices of the athlete.

Let us hope that this will come to pass. In any event, the fact is that our present victory combines three elements on which that victory is based: first, the excellence of the Olympic organization which, once again, has shown its superiority after a quarter century of varied experiences; second, the outstanding characteristics of the Belgians as revealed in the Peace, characteristics that the 1914 war profiled tragically and unforgettably; and finally, the lifeblood of youth, changeless, always energetic, always ready to rise, ardent, joyous. It was the same for the athletes at Olympia. Now, three thousand years later, that lifeblood is still striving among the youth gathered in Antwerp to establish balance in humanity.

La victoire de l'Olympisme,
in: *La Revue Sportive Illustrée,*
Vol. 16, 1920, no. 2 [p. 2].

4.2.2/37 – 4.2.2/39 INTRODUCTION

The year 1921, which is described in the following chapter of Coubertin's *Olympic Memoirs* in "The 1921 Manoeuvre", was in fact a very turbulent one with regard to Olympic history.

Not only the holding of a technical Olympic Congress in Lausanne in 1921, which was supposed to conclude the work of the 1914 Congress, but also important decisions such as awarding the 1924 Olympic Games to Paris, combined with the decision for Amsterdam in 1928, were unique and justify the choice of title for this contribution. To safeguard the future Olympic programme in technical terms, experts in various sports such as riding, winter sports and mountaineering also met in Lausanne in 1921. France was authorized to stage the "1st Olympic Winter Sports Week" in 1924, which later became the Olympic Winter Games. The IOC had to defend itself against the ambition of the International Federations to set up their own world federation in competition with the IOC. And there was also the first revolution against Coubertin's autocratic style with the constitution of an Executive Board chaired by Godefroy de Blonay, Coubertin's interim representative from 1916 to 1918.

In the second text entitled "Six Government Departments for One Stadium" Coubertin describes the chaotic situation within the French administration regarding the organizational preparation of the 1924 Olympic Games in Paris. But the last section is also important, as Coubertin states why he had already held the post of IOC President for 25 years.

The third text, "The Capitol in Rome" relates to the 22nd IOC Session in Rome, in 1923, which was important in the history of the IOC. In his opening speech, Coubertin talked about the conflict between capital and work. All those who worked for the purity of sport, whether workers or students, were equal as "serviteurs de l'idée olympique" (servants of the Olympic ideal). The IOC members were received by Pius XI at the Vatican.

Many details concerning the next Games were gone into, but the main questions dealt with were those concerning German and Russian participation, regional Games, propaganda in South America through the YMCA and the sports conquest of Africa. The "loss of earnings" issue was to present the IOC with new, difficult problems in relation to the Olympic amateur.

4.2.2/37 THE 1921 MANEUVER

The situation called above all for a declaration of unity, and that is why the pilot at the helm felt that everyone was looking to him to steer a steady course. The danger was not so much that some other body might succeed in taking over Olympism. A French politician and a French journalist were waging a fruitless campaign to hand over the Games to the League of Nations, which had only just come into being and had not yet found its feet. Such proposals had very little chance of being accepted and it was as easy to fight against them as against the attacks of certain federations, eager to see their delegates sitting at the table of the

IOC. The real danger lay in the frittering away of the Olympic idea, which risked being brought about by the proliferation of regional games that were the result of the general impatience that seemed to prevail. They were being created here, there and everywhere, or at least we were continually being bombarded with plans, programs, and announcements of the formation of committees and sub-committees.

During the last two years of the war, the threat of secession had hung over Olympism. By indirect and unofficial action I had always succeeded in thwarting any such attempts. The "League of Neutrals", which had for a while been mooted, had never been more than a project without any real substance. The "League of Belligerents" of the German group had been nothing more than a vague idea and even if they were to try and carry it through now, it would surely be only very short-lived; Hungary and Turkey would probably be very reluctant to join in. On the other hand, if all these "Games" which were to be organized in Ireland, Poland, Catalonia, the Balkans, India, and the Near East were allowed to take root, it might lead to cracks in the Olympic structure. Admittedly all these undertakings looked to us for blessing and depended on our patronage. But largely ignorant of Olympic matters and unfamiliar with the spirit of the IOC, those who conceived them and sought to organize them harbored ulterior motives of a nationalistic or a religious character which would only upset the whole movement in the end.

I let the year 1920 come to a close and the petty arguments left over from the Games in Antwerp die down: settling of accounts, technical disputes, etc. The overall impression left by these Games was not affected. During this period I had set in motion the preparations for the Congress in Lausanne. The Government of the Swiss Confederation had agreed that the invitations should be issued in each country by the Swiss legations and consulates.

It was important that they should arrive well in advance; especially as this time the situation was much more complicated than in June 1914. In Paris we had only had to invite the delegates of the National Committees for the purpose of drawing up the list of the various events in each sport and the technical conditions governing them. In 1921, we had the same problem but many others had arisen in the meantime, which it was not feasible to put all together for discussion by a single assembly.

The table of "Congresses and Olympic Conferences" gives a good idea of the extent of the problem. In fact, there was a whole series of conferences spaced out from May 26 to June 12, 1921: first of all a Consultative Conference on Winter Sports (May 26-27), then a Conference on Mountaineering (May 28), followed by a Conference on Equestrian Sports (May 29-30). Next came a Congress of the International Federations organized by Mr. Paul Rousseau who was planning the creation of a sort of super-federation or inter-federal council: a solution that would be either a help or a hindrance depending on the state of mind prevailing at the time, but to which, in principle, I was in no way opposed, as some seemed to believe. The Olympic Congress itself would take place from June 2-7. Finally, plans had been made to hold a Consultative Conference on Literature and Art, and a Conference of "Municipalities", intended simply to clear the ground with a view to the subsequent organization of sport for the masses and the "restoration of the ancient gymnasium", of which I had spoken for the first time in Paris, in November 1912, and which remained – as it still does – a wish dear to my heart.

Once this copious program had been approved by the IOC, I drafted a circular letter to my colleagues, sent it to them and at the same time issued the text to the press. It was dated March 17, 1921. The announcement of my decision to hand in my resignation after the 1924 Games preceded the following passages:

> *The choice of city for staging them (the next Games) is of particular importance this time, owing to the fact that the Eighth Olympiad will coincide with the thirtieth anniversary of their revival. Many gratifying candidatures have been received. If we consider the merits of the rival cities, the name of Amsterdam seems to prevail... But, on the other hand, at this moment when the reviver of the Olympic Games judges his personal task to be nearly at an end, no one will deny that he is entitled to ask that a special gesture should be made in favor of his native city, Paris, where the modern revival of the Olympiads was prepared by him and officially proclaimed on June 23, 1894. 1 wish therefore, in all fairness, to let you know, my dear colleagues, that at our next meeting I shall appeal to you on this great occasion to sacrifice your preferences and your national interests and agree to award the Ninth Olympiad to Amsterdam and proclaim Paris the venue for the Eighth.*

It was a masterly coup d'état! A double one, in fact, since it decided the future for two Olympiads, a decision that nothing prevented the IOC from making but which had never been done before. There was a certain confusion and surprise in Paris, elsewhere too. Nobody had expected such a radical and sudden presidential intervention. It was morally impossible to refuse what I was asking. That is why, once the first hesitations were over, French sporting circles en masse deserted the opposition they had been building up against us almost automatically and, suddenly, the clouds that had been piling up cleared away and the sun shone in a clear sky.

The series of "Olympic Congresses and Conferences" opened in an atmosphere of goodwill and understanding, which promised well for their results. This atmosphere continued right through the meetings, in spite of some tricky questions that were raised and the heated discussions that were bound to follow. First among these was the problem of the "Winter Games". The Scandinavians did not want them at any price. In 1894, skating had been included in the list of desirable events. London, which possessed an "ice palace", had been able in 1908 to organize satisfactory events. But in 1912, Stockholm eagerly seized on the argument that it had no suitable premises, in order to rid itself of the burden of organizing this event. However, in the last twenty-five years, winter sports had not only developed in a number of other countries but they were so truly amateur, so frank and so pure in their sporting dignity, that their complete exclusion from the Olympic program deprived it of much force and value. On the other hand, how were they to be organized? In addition to the Scandinavian resistance, there was the twofold concern that they could not take place at the same time or in the same place as the Summer Games. It is possible to manufacture artificial ice, but not snow, and even less mountain peaks.

Would the Dutch be expected, in 1928, to erect a chain of mountains bought second hand or made especially for the occasion? To set up a sort of autonomous cycle, nevertheless related to its big brother, was obviously the only solution, even though full of drawbacks. For this reason, I had attempted to interrupt the discussion with a first meeting between specialists. Mr. A. Megroz' report, on behalf of the Consultative Conference, somewhat lessened the shock and finally it was bruited abroad that France – if it were selected (which was not the case as yet) – would be entitled to organize, in Chamonix in 1924, a week of winter sports on which the IOC would bestow its patronage, but which "would not be an actual part of the Games". This last clause was later cancelled. The "Winter Games" were finally founded in spite of the Scandinavians who ended by abandoning their objection and realizing that, in view of the roles of Switzerland and Canada in particular, they could no longer lay claim to the practical monopoly they had exercised for so long.

The report of the Conference on Mountaineering was drawn up by a famous climber, Dr. Jacot-Guillarmod, well known for his expeditions to the Himalayas. Few Alpine clubs were represented even though they had agreed in principle to take part but without much enthusiasm. Admittedly, it is quite difficult to measure the comparative merits of exploits of this kind but, as nothing prevented each Olympiad either from declaring that there were no grounds for awarding a prize or from proclaiming two prize winners *ex aequo,* the proposal to invite each Alpine club to put forward the claims of its candidates was not at all impracticable. In Chamonix in 1924, there was no doubt in anyone's mind that the Mount Everest expedition far exceeded the rest of the field in endurance and courage, but in 1928 we were obliged to give up this mountaineering prize and, as I have already said, in doing so we committed in my opinion a very serious mistake.

The Conference on Equestrian Sports was recruited by special invitation addressed to the Ministers of War. It must not be forgotten that all these conferences were purely consultative ones, organized for the purpose of clearing the ground for members of either the IOC or the Congress, depending on which assembly was concerned by the questions raised. I have already mentioned how brilliant the Equestrian Games were at the Fifth Olympiad (Stockholm 1912), thanks to Count von Rosen's competent zeal, but that the whole context had been exclusively military. It was undoubtedly inevitable because, apart from hunting and polo-sports that are too expensive to be practiced by any other than a restricted circle of millionaires – civil equitation always tends to be eclipsed by the military.

Outside certain horse breeding countries, colonial regions where horses are used for transport, or territories like California where they have been kept out of tradition, riding has always been handicapped by organizational difficulties, which could of course have been overcome by enlightened and ingenious action on the part of governments. But such action never materialized in the fashion and to the extent needed. It is impossible for me to attempt to examine this question here; it would take far too long. For over twenty-five years I have never ceased bringing the matter up in articles or in schemes of various kinds, but always with the same goal: to spread equestrian sport among the "unmounted", that is to say those who cannot afford to keep a horse of their own. I obtained many assurances of approval from people as varied as the "rough rider" Theodore Roosevelt and the distinguished horseman Count Maurice de Cosse-Brissac, but when it came to implementing the measures, I came up against an insurmountable barrier, as if it were a question of giving up a class privilege, or surrendering a precious feudal right. I can still hear the bursts of applause that greeted certain speeches at the Equestrian Games' banquet in Stockholm in 1912... and those present included a galaxy of Princes, Grand-Dukes, heads of missions, and all the officers taking part in the competitions. Everyone seemed to be in wholehearted agreement. But this was not actually so. The knights of the Middle Ages were far less exclusively aristocratic in their ideas on riding than their successors today. At the Conference in 1921, which was attended among others by the Italian General Bellotti and the Belgian General Joostens, I could only have my ideas adopted as a remote possibility and I had to content myself with attaching a summary of them to the minutes. The Olympic equestrian program remained as it was, at least provisionally, but provisional solutions of this kind have a way of lasting indefinitely.

Paul Rousseau did not succeed any better either in creating his super-federation. He had to be content with the maintenance of an "Office of International Federations" which was only very reluctantly granted the minimum rights of intervention and the bare means of existence. I do not know whether this new body would have come up to its promoter's expectations, but from the Olympic point of view it would certainly have helped the IOC by freeing it of a technical role that was too extensive and the responsibilities which I had always hoped it might be able to throw off one day. At any rate, the Congress of the International Federations, both at the first meeting which I was asked to open and at the final banquet, showed that between them and the IOC the era of misunderstandings had come to an end.

The Olympic Congress itself, to which I had appointed, as was my right, our Swedish colleague J. S. Edström as President, was quite lively, and at times positively stormy. Edström presided with his usual devotion, intelligence, and brilliance... and a show of authority that made me smile when I thought of how often I had been accused of authoritarianism. The atmosphere was very different from that of the 1914 Congress, in spite of the calming influence of the Vaudois setting. The effects of the war years that were only just over were still making themselves felt. Nationalistic feelings were aroused for the least little thing and, while in 1914 we had met for the purpose of establishing a permanent Olympic legislation, this time instability and uncertainty prevailed. Right from the start, delegates considered the possibility of a new Congress in 1925, which could be convened to revise what was decided in 1921: obviously a regrettable state of mind, which circumstances however excused to a certain extent. As soon as it met therefore the Congress agreed, as had been hoped, on the venue for the next two Games. At the very first session held on June 2 in the evening, the IOC accepted my request and awarded the celebration of the Eighth and Ninth Olympiads to Paris and Amsterdam.

The motion had been proposed by Mr. Guth-Jarkovsky, and seconded by Messrs. de Baillet-Latour and de Polignac. An objection having been raised for vice of form, the motion was put to a second vote, which gave the same majority in favor of the double award. I had abstained, wishing less than ever to interfere with the liberty of vote, but it would have been really regrettable to see Amsterdam – which had shown great sporting spirit and international goodwill in withdrawing in favor of Antwerp and was doing the same again in 1921 in favor of Paris, subject to the conditions already mentioned – deprived of a satisfaction so long awaited and so legitimately claimed. With regard to Paris, everybody was in agreement. It would have been the same for Amsterdam except for the fact that, as the Congress approached, a bout of bad temper had broken out in Italy and an attack of impatience in America. Rome had suddenly realized that it could have obtained the 1924 Games or at any rate those of 1928, and Los Angeles, seeing her chances postponed until 1932 at the earliest, had considered the wait too long for transatlantic opinion, accustomed as it was to prompt action. On both sides of the Atlantic the press had reacted, fortunately without the effects being felt until some time after the publication of my letter on March 17. The Italian excitement had reached such a peak within the space of a few days that Mr. Gaston Vidal, Under-Secretary of State for Technical Education, had considered it best to have himself replaced at the last moment as representative of the French Olympic Committee at the Lausanne Congress. Our colleague Montu became very embarrassed and decided to withdraw after the vote. As for the American delegates, they seemed to harbor a grudge but did not know exactly how to express it as there was no valid reason for it.

Since the events of 1901 and 1905 (the transfer of the 1904 and 1908 Games from Chicago to St. Louis and from Rome to London), the IOC had decided to consider only applications that were backed by an already soundly prepared organization and by serious financial guarantees. Such had been the case with Stockholm, Berlin, and Antwerp; and would be for Amsterdam too. Rome, on the contrary, no longer offered any guarantee; no committee had been formed, nor were there any funds to fall back on. In these troubled times after the war and as I had definitely decided to retire, there was also, on top of all the arguments already mentioned, the wish on my part to arrange matters for the near future so that the ensuing stability might help my successor, whoever he was, in the first days of his tenure of office.

With the same end in view and under the pretext of a long journey which I had planned at the time, I persuaded the IOC to approve the creation of an Executive Board which was none other than an enlarged "bureau": a consecration in law of an already well-established state of affairs. The Board, which was to take over on October 1, 1921, comprised Messrs. de Blonay, Guth-Jarkovsky, de Baillet-Latour, Edström, and de Polignac.

Many foundations had been laid in Lausanne with the minimum of upset, but somewhat incoherently. The actual organization had been excellent, thanks to the local powers that be and also to the enthusiasm of the General Commissioner, my friend Eugene Monod, who had won the architecture competition in 1911. We now had three years ahead of us to make the Games of the Eighth Olympiad the "finest and most perfect that had ever been celebrated". This was the ambition of the organizers and they hoped in good faith to succeed completely in their aim.

Olympic Memoirs, Chap. 18, Lausanne, IOC, 1997, pp. 184-192.

4.2.2/38 SIX GOVERNMENT DEPARTMENTS FOR ONE STADIUM

Their hopes were disappointed at first. The above heading of a humorous article by Mr. Robert de Jouvenel, published in L'Oeuvre, gives an account of what happened. Within a very short time in fact the Olympic Games fell prey to an administrative hydra with six heads. The Departments of the Interior, Foreign Affairs, War, and Public Education were automatically involved in the affair, as well as the Paris Municipal Council. An agreement with the Department of Agriculture regarding the site on which the French Olympic Committee wanted to build its stadium brought the number of Departments up to six. On June 27, 1921, shortly after the Lausanne Congress was over, Count Jean de Castellane presented to the Municipal Council, of which he was a member, a proposal preceded by a short, perfectly clear report. It should have been possible to start from there without any ulterior motives regarding personal advantages or the interests of different districts; the Games could then have been prepared along the lines desired. Such, unfortunately, was not the case. If one compares this initial document which I have just quoted with the report of the Council's session of March 11, 1922, as published in the "official Municipal Bulletin" of March 12, one realizes the terrible rumpus that had grown in the short space of eight months round a very simple question, complicated unfortunately by another which was not so simple. As Mr. de Castellane said, they would have to make arrangements for a stadium capable of holding about 80,000 spectators, a site for the nautical sports, and one for the combat sports with about 15,000 seats. In addition they would have to arrange proper access and transport, and finally estimate the total credits required. After which, all they would have to do would be to place the funds at the disposal of the French Olympic Committee, subject to the control of a supervisory commission representing the State and the City associated by reason of the joint voting of the necessary credits. The French Parliament was ready to vote on the matter. The Council would have been too, if it had not been more concerned with taking advantage of the situation to create something permanent. Anyone who knows Paris, its districts, its administrative ramifications, the spirit of its officialdom and the position of its suburbs, will readily understand the very different influences exerted by any building projects, depending on whether these projects are of a temporary or a permanent character. In the latter case, interests, not to say appetites, clash with such violence that those concerned lose all sight of the starting point or the goal to be achieved.

This is what happened on the present occasion. From December 1921 until April 1922, the confusion gradually grew worse and by mid-March things were so bad that the French Olympic Committee was compelled for a moment to consider the possibility of abandoning the project. At the IOC, we were prepared against just such an eventuality; not that I ever thought for a moment that the conflict would reach such a pitch, but I knew only too well the city of my birth, where I had lived for over sixty years, for me not to be on my guard. Therefore I had come to a tacit agreement with Los Angeles of which, as it happened, one of our new American colleagues, W. M. Garland, was a very influential citizen. Over there, the huge stadium, work on which had begun as soon as the hope had been held out that an Olympiad might one day be staged there, was nearly completed. A pre-Olympic meeting was already planned there for 1923 and nothing would be simpler, if it were to prove necessary, than to postpone the meeting until 1924 and turn it into the real Olympic Games instead. Knowing this enabled me to watch what was going on in Paris with seeming serenity and to speak confidently, as if unconcerned by these events, to journalists and interviewers who were becoming increasingly numerous. Count Clary, President of the French Olympic Committee, and Frantz-Reichel, who was its devoted Secretary General, kept me constantly informed throughout the crisis of the slightest incidents. Their letters are instructive. One day, the Prefect of the Seine read out to the Municipal Council an excerpt from a confidential letter that I had sent to Mr. Poincaré, at that time Minister of Foreign Affairs, a letter whose odyssey from the Quai d'Orsay to the City Hall, unknown to the addressee, has never been completely elucidated. The Municipal Council was getting more and more confused. One of the councilors even suggested that they should invite the "Sokols to come; this would be one of the main attractions of the Olympic Games"!

It was the government that prevented the vessel from foundering. The President of the Republic, Mr. Millerand, showed great interest in the Games and refused to countenance any tendency on the part of the French capital to give up after he himself had encouraged the French Olympic Committee to put in its candidature. The President of the Council, Mr. Poincaré, was unfortunately too taken up with political worries to pay much attention to the question. A word from him, however, would have been sufficient to show the importance he attached to the affair being started. Fortunately, it finally got under way, although somewhat haltingly, and it was decided to build the stadium... at Colombes.

If I had had my say, none of the sites considered would have had my approval. There was one right in the heart of Paris that offered far greater advantages. In front of the Military Academy, on the Champ de Mars, the disappearance of the famous "Machine Gallery" built in 1889 had left free a huge esplanade whose fate was undoubtedly settled and on which no permanent building would ever be built in order not to spoil one of Paris's most beautiful prospects. But to use it for the brief period of the Olympic Games would not affect it at all. At that moment the Military Academy, with its huge buildings, its open spaces and its courtyards, was almost unoccupied. I had been to look at it again in order to check the layout and the dimensions. What wonderful "athletes' quarters" it would have made! Expenditure would have been reduced considerably, quite apart from the fact that nowhere else in the city would transport present less of a problem: tramways, metro, boats, everything was within easy reach. Whichever way one looked at it, this solution was far better than any of the others, but it was not up to the IOC to interfere or try and sway public opinion. I tried to recommend it unofficially, but to no avail.

In the spring of 1922, the IOC was to meet in Paris. When we met, the crisis was almost over. It had been agreed that this time it would be a business meeting without the usual social events. There was in fact only one dinner party given by the French Committee, a small reception at the Elysée and an original luncheon at the invitation of our colleague Glandaz on "Marshal Joffre's famous barge" which, now moored near the Concorde Bridge, had become one of the capital's most fashionable restaurants with a well-deserved gastronomic reputation. The IOC had just welcomed a number of new members: General Sherrill in the United States; Mr. de Alvear in the Argentine Republic, of which he was shortly to become Head of State and pay us the rare honor of nevertheless remaining one of us; Colonel Kentish in Great Britain; Baron de Guell in Spain; J. J. Keane in Ireland; Prince Lubomirski in Poland, and Dr. Ghigliani in Uruguay. The IOC now had 54 members belonging to forty-two countries.

The main work accomplished at the 1922 Session consisted in adapting the new bodies and adding the few necessary modifications to the essential texts. The Executive Board had met prior to the sessions of the Committee and its powers and proceedings had been suitably defined. Apart from the creation of the Executive Board at the registered headquarters (Lausanne), the modifications made in the Statutes of the IOC related to the official language (French), to the secretariat, and above all to the duration of the presidential powers which were reduced from ten to eight years. I believe that I have not yet mentioned the way in which, about the year 1901, these powers had been the object of a complete modification. On January 1 of that year, they should have passed into the hands of our American colleague, W. M. Sloane. The regulations that I had had accepted in 1894 provided for this four-yearly transfer of powers, but this presupposed that the venue for the celebration of the following Games was already fixed at the time. It was universally agreed at that time that the next Olympiad would be held in America, but Chicago's project was barely outlined as yet. No official application had been sent in and, consequently, no voting had taken place. Sloane had not been content to stress this particularity of the circumstances prevailing. He had generalized the question and, without even mentioning the matter to me beforehand, had submitted a proposal to the IOC for modifying the Statutes, stating that in his opinion a stable and long presidency of ten years was the only way to make Olympism strong and fruitful and that as a consequence he refused to take over from me. The unanimous agreement of our colleagues would have compelled me to give in even if, in those difficult times, I had not felt the truth and strength of the arguments put forward. This is how the "Olympic monarchy", as some called it, came to be established. It is amusing that it was the result of the action of a citizen of the most democratic of all republics. My term of office was therefore prolonged until 1907. Re-elected then, and again in 1917, my term of office would not come to an end until 1927. But as I had notified my intention of retiring after the 1924 Games, my colleagues decided that my successor would be elected for the period of two Olympiads, that is to say for eight years, his term of office starting from the date of his taking over. 1925 would be a favorable date, one year after the Games, and three years before the following Games; that is why I agreed to remain at my post until that year.

Olympic Memoirs, Chap. 19, Lausanne, IOC, 1997, pp.194-199.

4.2.2/39 THE CAPITOL IN ROME (1923)

In Rome too, the chance lost in 1906 had to be made up for. Of the few wisps of cloud that had loomed on the horizon at Lausanne in 1921, none were left. I was therefore very keen for the 1923 Session to be particularly brilliant. Our colleagues, Colonel Montu and the Marchese di Guglielmi, spared no efforts in their determination to make a success of it and they succeeded magnificently. The Session held under the patronage of the King and Queen of Italy opened in the main hall of the Capitol on April 7, 1923, in the presence of the sovereign accompanied by the Presidents of the Chamber and the Senate, the Secretaries of State for Foreign Affairs and for Fine Arts, the Prefect of Rome, and a great many guests. It was closed on April 12. Members of the IOC took away with them a vivid and lasting memory of the royal reception in the Quirinal, and the party given at the Palazzo Rospigliosi by the Marchese and Marchesa di Guglielmi, as well as of the dinner at Aventino by Col. Montu, during which guests were able to admire the wonderful spectacle of the ruins of the Palace of the Caesars lit up specially for the occasion. They visited the Vatican where, in the course of a long preliminary audience, their President received further assurances from Pope Pius XI of his friendly interest in Olympism. They were also entertained by the National Tourist Office and the Italian Olympic Committee. Finally, they enjoyed the satisfaction of having accomplished a considerable amount of work in the course of their numerous meetings.

Many details concerning the next Games were gone into, but the main questions dealt with were those concerning the German and Russian participation, "regional" Games, propaganda in South America, and finally the sports conquest of Africa. The German question should have been very simple to solve since, on the one hand, no break had ever occurred and, on the other hand, the German members of the IOC had disappeared. The Secretary General appointed for the organization of the Sixth Olympiad (Berlin 1916), who, in this capacity, had played an active role in the discussions of June 1914 in Paris, had been invited to go to Rome to reach an agreement with the IOC concerning the election of new members but, owing to a misunderstanding, he failed to appear and it was not until the following season that Secretary of State Lewald and Mr. O. Ruperti were elected. Our Bulgarian, Turkish, and Hungarian colleagues had already taken their seats: they were Messrs. Stancioff, Selim Sirry Bey, Count Geza Andrassy, and J. de Muzsa. There was still the Austrian vacancy to be filled, no candidate having been put forward. The IOC agreed this time to approve the solution that it had made the mistake of rejecting at Lausanne in 1921 and which was based on the twofold principle of the integral and permanent maintenance of universalism on the one hand, and on the other, of its having nothing to do with the sending out of invitations, this task being entirely up to the authorities of the country organizing the Games.

After Germany, Russia. It was not without emotion that we heard our colleague Prince Leon Ouroussoff, a former diplomat, describe the lot of his compatriots divided into two groups which, with complete liberalism, he asked to be given equal rights to take part in the Games in Paris; both the Soviet teams and the teams of the émigré sports clubs were to be admitted on the same footing. I always regretted the way in which his proposal was received and rejected for "administrative" reasons. Nobody realized better than I the practical difficulties involved nor the perhaps insoluble problems its application would raise, but I think that the IOC would have brought honor on itself had it given the proposal a different welcome and forwarded it at the right moment to the French Government, backed by encouraging comments.

The situation with regard to the Armenians, who also had a club of young émigrés demanding admission, was quite different. For the time being, Armenia existed only as a hope and a memory in the hearts of its loyal subjects and it could hardly, like Bohemia or Finland before it, lay claim to a leading role in "sports geography". The other national questions were settled. For the second time the Irish Free State was represented at the Session. Its documents in Celtic accompanied by the English version had a delightfully archaic look. The creation of the Kingdom of Yugoslavia had ipso facto solved the Croatian question, and the American Government had very liberally agreed to the desire of the Philippines to be allowed to march in a group behind their own flag at the Olympic parade. On the eve of the Games in Paris, the IOC would number 62 members and 45 countries. The "small, older brother" of Lausanne would for the moment exceed in numbers the big, younger sister in Geneva.

Of the host of projects produced right after the war and aimed at the creation of "regional" Games, there remained practically nothing. I was pleased because I had seen no real future in the movement but had thought it best to leave it to wear itself out. Only the Far Eastern Games, now placed under our patronage, survived. They answered a real need. The only other plans I was interested in were those for the African Games, about which I shall speak in a moment, and the South American Games which Brazil had introduced by inaugurating them the previous year (1922) on the occasion of the centenary celebration of its independence. Not only had they been placed under the patronage of the IOC, but the Brazilian Government had sent me an invitation to come and preside over them. Circumstances unfortunately prevented me from leaving in time, but Count de Baillet-Latour was able to replace me. In the course of a journey through most of the South American continent, the delegate of the IOC had not only received the most flattering welcome for the work he represented but had used his time most profitably for the "Olympization", to coin a neologism, of these new countries full of as yet unsatisfied sporting ambitions. He had been able, in the meantime, to smooth out difficulties, put an end to conflicts, and resolve tricky questions. Whether the Games at Rio were to become a truly stable, regular institution or not, it was worthwhile seeing them renewed in the near future for the benefit of other cities further apart from each other – as a result of inadequate transport rather than actual distance – than was the case in Europe. We needed a choice of centers like Mexico, Havana, Santiago, Montevideo, and Buenos Aires, where athletes from nearby countries would have an opportunity of competing against each other either in Central America or in South America. This would also be an excellent "Olympic kindergarten", according to the term used in Manila.

The Count de Baillet gave the IOC an account of his long voyage and all the work accomplished on its behalf; his report was received with unanimous applause. Obliged to cut short his travels, he had not been able to come back via California

Opening of the 22nd IOC Session in Rome, 1923, in the Hall of the Capitol, attended by King Victor Emmanuel III of Italy. Coubertin enthused, "Today we shall trace out the initial move of the final battle to be waged if we are to complete the sporting conquest of the world". (IOC Archives)

and Japan where he was to have presided over the Far Eastern Games, which were being held in Osaka. Los Angeles, where the stadium was almost completed, had looked forward eagerly to his visit in the hope of obtaining assurances from him regarding the 1932 Games since those of the Eighth and Ninth Olympiads had already been awarded. But I was determined, obdurate as I was, to renew the gesture made at Lausanne two years earlier and to commit the future even beyond the present horizons. In addition to the keenness and the enthusiasm of its advocate (our colleague W. M. Garland), Los Angeles held three powerful trumps. First of all, the state of progress of its Olympic preparations, which represented an invaluable pledge of success; then its privileged situation, from the point of view of political and social events, far removed from the trouble that I felt brewing – I discussed the threat in this same year, 1923, in a series of articles published in a Swiss paper under the general title: "Where is Europe going?" Finally, the time had really come to show some gratitude to the sporting youth of the United States for the efforts made since Athens and for its always brilliant and plentiful participation in past Games. These three reasons decided members of the IOC to vote unanimously in favor of awarding the celebration of the Tenth Olympiad to Los Angeles.

Our meetings were marked by many interesting discussions, which I cannot go into here. Since the Olympic Review had ceased to be published, the minutes of the annual Session were generously published in full in a brochure at the expense of our colleague Albert Glandaz, and consequently the text is available for all to see. The problem of "loss of earnings" gave rise to the first skirmishes, which were to be repeated and even become quite heated without ever degenerating into real clashes;

for it is worth mentioning, much to the credit of its members, that on no occasion since its creation had the IOC ever experienced any of those disputes that are quite pointless but nevertheless introduce a certain bitterness into the proceedings. I shall not go any further into this new aspect of the problem of amateurism. I have already discussed it at considerable length in an earlier chapter. "Loss of earnings" crystallized the fatal conflict between the modernist trends of progressive circles and the diehard conservatism of the old English idea of sport. No one was more attached to the doctrine of "pure" sport than the Reverend Laffan and yet this great Englishman, who possessed a profound sense of history, was himself looking on this occasion for ways of coming to terms with a social evolution that he clearly felt the futility of opposing simply with the ineffective, traditional non possumus.

It remains for me to speak of the "conquest of Africa" on which, on the threshold of my Olympic career, I had been so keen and which in fact raised one of the most topical aspects of the colonial question.

The speech addressed to King Victor Emmanuel at the inaugural meeting of the IOC Session in the Capitol included this passage:

> "*And perhaps it may appear premature to introduce the principle of sports competitions into a continent that is behind the times and among peoples still without elementary culture – and particularly presumptuous to expect this expansion to lead to a speeding up of the march of civilization in these countries. Let us think however, for a moment, of what is troubling the African soul. Untapped forces – individual laziness and a sort of collective need for action – a thousand resentments, and a thousand jealousies of the white man and yet, at the same time, the wish to imitate him and thus share his privileges – the conflict between wishing to submit to discipline and to escape from it – and, in the midst of an innocent gentleness that is not without its charm, the sudden outburst of ancestral violence...these are just some features of these races to which the younger generation, which has in fact derived great benefit from sport, is turning its attention. Sport has hardened them. It has given them a healthy taste for muscular relaxation and a little of that reasonable fatalism possessed by energetic beings, once their efforts have been accomplished. But while sport builds up, it also calms down. Provided it remains accessory and does not become a goal in itself, it helps create order and clarify thought. Let us not hesitate therefore to help Africa join in. Delegates of the competent authorities have come here to discuss the matter with us...* "

In fact, in addition to the Session of the IOC, there were meetings of a consultative commission which comprised, together with a representative of the Italian Minister for the Colonies, delegates from Algeria, Morocco, the Regency of Tunis, and Colonel See, bearing a special message from Marshal Lyautey, at that time Resident General. Our Portuguese colleague, Count Penha-Garcia, had been delegated to represent his country. I shall not go into details concerning the discussions, but I will say right away, once and for all, what became of the project, so as not to have to return to it later: what became of it for the moment at least, for I am quite sure the plan will be taken up again. It comprised the holding of "African Games" every other year, with a very simple program to start with and which, naturally, would have been almost exclusively regional in character. I would like to have seen these Games reserved for the natives alone. It was preferred, however, to include competitions for colonials who had been in the country for at least two years. Admittedly, this point of view was quite understandable, but it complicated the proceedings at the start. The cities recognized capable of holding the first Games were Tunis, Rabat, Casablanca, and Dakar for French Africa, Tripoli, Benghazi, and Asmara for the Italian possessions, Libreville in the Belgian Congo, Luanda and Sumac for Portuguese Africa, Cape Town and Nairobi for South Africa. The mistake I made was to consider (and to reveal this idea to the IOC) the possibility of a more solemn, more magnificent inauguration to be held in Algiers in 1925. To start with, this decision was greeted favorably in Algeria and Mr. T. Steeg, who was Governor General at the time, also showed his interest. However, it very soon met with opposition that was all the more formidable as it lacked both direction and a center. Those against it tried above all to waste time, to blunt good intentions. It was a question of perhaps personal, but at any rate administrative, rivalries. Eventually the inauguration had to be postponed until 1929, and Alexandria was substituted for Algiers. The preparations at the time were considerable; a very fine stadium was built. Our colleague in Egypt, A. C. Bolanaki, threw himself into this scheme with a keenness and a generosity made even more effective by his competence which was recognized by all... At the *last moment,* an English political maneuver, in which France joined, rendered ineffective all the work done and King Fouad was left to inaugurate the fine stadium at Alexandria discreetly and on a purely local scale. I am unable to explain this rather annoying matter since, when it broke out, I had already ceased to be President of the IOC. But at the back of it all, there was the basic conflict, the struggle of the colonial spirit against the tendency to emancipate the natives, a tendency full of perils as far as the general staffs of the mother country were concerned. The arguments used would not have been without value...earlier on; but they belonged to a past that was completely dead. It was a long time since they were applicable. The *Olympic Review* had dealt with the fine subject of "The role of sport in colonization" in the issue for January 1912. Twenty years later, I thought that opinion had evolved sufficiently to allow the idea to be put into effect! It appeared that the time was not yet ripe. It must be getting nearer now and I remain convinced that before long, in spite of everything, sport will be organized throughout Africa but perhaps less well than if Europe had been clever enough to take over the running of the movement at the right moment.

At any rate there still remained the "African medal" placed annually at the disposal of heads of posts and missions... for the encouragement of sport. It would do for the moment – for want of anything better. It shows a black man throwing a javelin and, on the other side, legible through some bamboo, a Latin inscription, since Africa is polyglot for the colonials as well as for the natives: *Athletae proprium est se ipsum noscere, ducere et vincere.* To know, to govern, and to master oneself – the eternal beauty of sport – is the fundamental aspiration of the true sportsman and the prerequisite for his success.

Olympic Memoirs, Chap. 20, Lausanne, IOC, 1997, pp. 200-207.

4.2.2/40 – 4.2.2/41 INTRODUCTION

The following two texts refer to the Games of the VIII Olympiad in 1924 in Paris. In the chapter "The Eighth Olympiad (Paris 1924)" of his *Olympic Memoirs,* Coubertin takes a positive approach in his description of the Games in Paris in 1924. In the last paragraph, he talks about leaving the IOC, which he had scheduled for 1925, and his last activities. His suggestion to create a Technical Committee for the Olympic Games, composed of three IOC members, six representatives of the NOCs and six of the IFs, was adopted by the Executive Board in November 1924 in Lausanne.

The second text is Coubertin's speech of thanks given to the mayor and prefects at City Hall in Paris, on 24th June 1924. In this, Coubertin includes his native city of Paris in the compass of western history. The organizational problems are forgotten; gratitude comes to the forefront.

4.2.2/40 THE EIGHTH OLYMPIAD (PARIS 1924)

The Games of the Eighth Olympiad were inaugurated at Chamonix in February 1924 and this snowy prelude was a great success from every point of view, helping to calm the ill feeling and weaken the prejudices of the Scandinavians, whose champions naturally distinguished themselves. The thaw (which will always be the great drawback of these Winter Games; even St. Moritz had one four years later) was fortunately followed, the day before the opening, by a period of intense cold and fine weather. There were a number of memorable moments, such as the ice hockey match between the teams of Canada and the United States. There was also the moving occasion when, at the foot of Mont Blanc, the medal for mountaineering was awarded to one of the leaders of the famous Mount Everest expedition, a courageous Englishman who, defeated but not discouraged, swore to leave it next time at the top of the highest summit in the Himalayas. In short, this first week augured well for the destiny of the Winter Games, as for France's Olympic organizing ability.

Unfortunately in Paris, four months later, things went less well. It was inevitable that the events of 1922 should have had prolonged and, in certain cases, irreparable repercussions. Administrative red tape and lack of understanding were worse than usual. Luckily the patience and perseverance of the organizers overcame all difficulties. One cannot be too grateful to them. Nor to the foreigners whose keenness took on the character of an enthusiastic homage to France. The government was completely oblivious of all this and failed to take advantage of it. A very junior civil servant modestly confided to me: "Personally, I can only judge as a man in the street, but even so I cannot help feeling that the government has failed to take advantage of all the opportunities offered by this Olympiad". How right he was and how well his criticism summed up the mistakes that had been made! This is not the place to go into and discuss all the details of the situation, for that would involve a detailed study of the state of mind of members of the government and public opinion in France after what I call "the headless victory" in a chapter of my as yet unpublished "other" memoirs. What a unique opportunity for addressing the youth of the world assembled together in Paris and proffering them the palm of peace ringed round by the glory of their recent triumphs! What a start for the new era which was of such concern to all peoples! However, there is no point now in dwelling on sterile regrets. Better simply to give an account of the positive aspects of this Parisian Olympic period.

First of all, there was the universal good humor of the athletes, over which seemed to preside from on high two eminent figures: President Doumergue and the Prince of Wales, whose smiles have in fact become legendary. Since it is sport we are concerned with, I shall start with the athletes. Those who describe them at every moment as difficult to please are just showing their own ignorance as well as their unawareness of the athletes' continual state of excitement and effervescence due on such a solemn occasion to the bringing together in one place of several thousands of young people for whom the Olympic laurels constitute the supreme sporting ambition. Add to this the restrictions imposed by training, the obstacles to be overcome, the physical disorientation, the fatal difference between the expectation and reality, the bad luck, the nervousness produced by the imminence of their event... What do you, the average man in the street, whose superficial and peremptory opinions are mass-produced by a hastily written and often unfair report (for sports journalists, whose job also has its difficulties, are not always perfectly fair), what do you know of all the determination, sang-froid, self-control and generous mutual assistance called for in the athletes' quarters? At least have the decency to pay tribute to the strength of the sporting spirit capable of resisting the exaggerated behavior of those spectators – of whom you were perhaps one – who so often tend to glory not so much in healthy, loyal rivalry but in animosity and bitter jealousy. A few bored spectators watching superb gymnastic or nautical feats that had the misfortune to be "unfashionable"; avid crowds of excitable and excited spectators as soon as a football or a boxing match promised scenes of violence... Compared with these, how balanced and how virile in the serenity of their practical philosophy do the actual athletes appear. There are obviously exceptions, many of them! But the overall impression remains; from Stockholm to Antwerp, from Antwerp to Paris, its encouraging action continued. In Paris, more than ever, it was strengthened. President Doumergue had only been in the Elysée a week when, accompanied by his escort, he drove in state to the Sorbonne to attend the celebration of the 30th anniversary of the revival of the Olympic Games. He was presented with a case containing two medals, one the medal struck thirty years earlier, on which was written: "The International Congress in Paris proclaims the revival of the Olympic Games, June 23, 1894" – and by its side another, with an identical design, inscribed with the words: "The nations assembled here celebrate the thirtieth anniversary of the revival of Olympism, June 23, 1924". As my colleagues and I welcomed the Head of State, a host of thoughts crowded through my mind, above all the memory of the ceremony in June 1914 on the eve of the cataclysm during which, for four long years, so many young lives born to savor the joys of sport were to be sacrificed on the altar of Armageddon: a ceremony very similar to the present one, with its choirs, hunting horns, Olympic flags, speeches...very similar and yet one felt that the wheel of history had turned and that a sort of unstable egalitarianism had taken the place of the quiet social certainties of a period that had gone for ever.

In the evening, at the Elysée, the President gave his first banquet in honor of members of the IOC, who had been joined by the Mayor of Lausanne, invited to the Sorbonne to represent the headquarters of the new Olympism. The next day, in the afternoon, a big reception was held in the festival hall of the Hotel de Ville, accompanied by a theatrical performance. The Session of the IOC opened on June 25 at the Palais du Louvre, in the sumptuous gala apartments of the Ministry of Finance. We met there on June 25-28, then the Session was interrupted to allow the Executive Board, now in regular office, to prepare various reports. The Session started again on July 7 and continued until July 13, ten meetings in all attended by a number of new members: Lord Cadogan (Great Britain), Dr. Kishi (Japan), Mr. Benavides (Peru), and Mr. Aldao (Argentina).

On July 5, the Games were solemnly opened in the stadium accompanied by the usual pomp. In addition to the President of the Republic the guests of note included the Prince of Wales, the Crown Prince and Princess of Romania, the Prince Regent of Ethiopia, Prince Henry of England, Prince Gustav-Adolf of Sweden, members of the government and representatives of the city of Paris. Pigeons were released, the canon fired, and songs were sung while the huge Olympic flag was hoisted to fly over the stadium until the closing of the Games. In the morning a ceremony similar to the one in Antwerp was held in Notre Dame, and its austere "neutrality", in this unique setting, took on an impressive majesty.

The Ras Taffari with his cone-shaped coat and huge hat could not visit the athletes in the changing rooms of the stadium, but the young princes took the opportunity to mingle with them. The Prince of Wales enjoyed talking with the champions and soon set everyone at ease. One afternoon, standing talking to me on the grass of the stadium, he looked at his watch and asked anxiously: "Is there an Englishman competing in any of the next events? I would very much like to go and play polo in the Bois de Boulogne. I have in fact promised to do so, but if there is an Englishman due to compete, I cannot go". I went to inquire. "Yes, your Highness, there is one", and the Prince gave up his game of polo without a moment's hesitation or the slightest sign of annoyance. At the big banquet for two hundred guests given by the British Olympic Association, over which he presided, he was seen, in the presence of ambassadors, ministers, and even Marshal Foch... to rise to his feet and hand a glass of champagne to each of the twelve pipers who were sitting in a row behind him after marching twice round the hall playing their bagpipes. When the time came for toasts, he proposed the first to his father, to the head of the French State, and the heads of state of the other countries taking part. On sitting down, he said to me: "Phew! Well, that's the first hurdle behind me..". And shortly afterwards, rising again, he made a rousing speech in praise of Olympism.

The simplicity shown by Prince Carol of Romania was scarcely less. He drove to the stadium every day in an open car, usually accompanied. One afternoon, he came alone. A police sergeant came running up to the presidential grandstand to look for me: "Sir", he said, "there's a man who says he is the Crown Prince of Romania, but he must be an imposter. He is all alone in his car and driving it himself. He is being taken to the police station for infringing the regulations". I hurried over. The Prince looked delighted. "Why did you come?" he said. "They were going to carry me off to the police station, it would have been great fun!" The men on duty did not feel the same way about it, and looked very shamefaced!

While the fencing, boxing and wrestling matches were being held with differing fortunes, and in the stadium the finals of the footraces, the jumping and throwing events were taking place to the cheers of the public, and in other settings swimmers, oarsmen and modern pentathlon competitors were vying with one another for victory, a silent watchful team in the offices of the Rue de Grammont was working hard to keep the whole machinery working. To all those who composed this team, I wish to express here my grateful admiration for their labors so sportingly accepted and undertaken. At the same time I wish to praise the invaluable activity of Count Clary, President of the Committee, who was unsparing in his efforts, and especially the work of the keystone of the whole edifice, the indefatigable and ever youthful Franz Reichel, to whom members of the IOC presented an address signed by every single one of them.

The Marquis de Polignac had specialized in the organization of art contests which, thanks to his efforts, were at last worthy of Olympism. But not content with this, he also succeeded in organizing at the Champs Elysées Theatre an "Eighth Olympiad Season of Art". It gave Parisians the opportunity in particular of hearing the Ninth Symphony – the one that was always for me the ideal Olympic symphony performed by the Dutch orchestra and choir of the famous Mengelberg Company of Amsterdam. This was not the only reference to the next Olympiad, for which Amsterdam was to be the venue. The Dutch Ambassador, at a brilliant reception in the Legation, made a skilful allusion to "carrying on the torch" as referred to in the words pronounced at the closing of the Games. When the time finally came to pronounce them, three flags were hoisted in the stadium: those of Greece, France, and Holland, and the three national anthems were played in their honor. This ceremonial will be continued in order to pay tribute to the immortality of Hellenism as well as to the Games that have just drawn to a close and to those that are to be held next. With this addition, the protocol of the Olympic ceremonial was finally completed; I had constructed it little by little and in stages, so as not to take by surprise spectators and actors who might be ill-prepared or unreceptive. Even today many people still cannot understand its educational value and consider the symbolism outdated. Nevertheless they have grown used to the ceremonial, and it is very unlikely that any changes will be made.

Thus my preparations for retirement were gradually being completed. There still remained two important points however. On several occasions I had persuaded the IOC to approve the decision to engrave the names of winners, after the celebration of each Olympiad, on marble plaques fixed to the walls of the stadium in order to perpetuate their great feats. It will be objected that Olympic stadiums are not all assured of longevity but, in case of demolition, would it not be possible, for example, to transport the triumphal steles to the City Hall? Because the ambition to win in these quadrennial tournaments is the highest experienced by the sporting youth of the world, it seems to me important to ensure for them the kind of civic reward that had been conceived and awarded in ancient times. The retrospective promises made to me concerning this point with regard to the Games in Stockholm and Antwerp had not been kept and neither Paris nor Amsterdam looked as though they were going to do anything about it either. This was a big mistake, although easy to remedy with the help of a modicum of good will, perseverance, and money.

In addition, the time seemed to have come to give the International Federations, now consolidated and more reasonable in their relationship with Olympism, a fairer share in the technical organization of the Games. But I thought I had better leave the advantage of accomplishing this project to my successor, as yet unknown. The Executive Board met in Lausanne every autumn, for three whole days, in order to examine current affairs and prepare the next Session of the IOC. At the meeting on November 15, therefore, I presented to my colleagues, to do with as they pleased, a project which was subsequently replaced by other arrangements and which, consequently, was never made public. It provided for the creation of a Technical Committee of fifteen members, whose powers were to last for a period of three years, from January 1 of year II of each Olympiad until December 31 of year IV. This Committee would be composed of three members of the IOC, six representatives of the National Olympic Committees, and six delegates from the International Federations. This Committee would be responsible, during the period of preparation of the Games, for supervising this preparation from the technical point of view, for obtaining and transmitting the wishes of the Federations and the Committees, seeing to the correct interpretation and application of the regulations and, during the period of celebration, to examine any complaints, consider any relevant action to be taken, and carry out any investigations into the eligibility of competitors, the working of juries, etc. The purpose of setting up this Committee, which never in fact saw the light of day, was to restore to the IOC its full senatorial role and at the same time to associate the technical bodies more closely in the joint operation by allotting them a fair share of power and responsibility.

Olympic Memoirs, Chap. 21, Lausanne, IOC, 1997, pp. 210-217.

4.2.2/41 ADDRESS BY BARON PIERRE DE COUBERTIN (PARIS 1924)

MR. PRESIDENT OF THE CITY COUNCIL,
MR. PREFECT OF THE SEINE,

The City of Paris is entertaining us with such good grace and such warmth that I should be inclined to confusion in expressing our thanks, did it not occur to me that in honouring us she is in a way honouring herself; for in our baggage, which does not contain merely the documents which we are going to use during our meeting, we are restoring to France and Paris some forgotten pages of their history.

When King Henry IV entered Paris long ago, he spent the second day of his stay here and of his effective reign, so the chronicle says, in playing furiously at tennis. An alert Englishman, who was then a guest in our capital and noted daily incidents with much humour, described in his tablets his anguish at seeing a reign open in such a futile manner. It boded no good, he said, and went on to reproach the French for spreading a taste for sport in England; according to him our nation was unreasonably addicted to it.

Well, you know what this reign was like; it was full of excellent things, the most celebrated being the fowl in the pot and the Edict of Nantes.

This is simply in order to say that Paris has already been a sporting capital. Then things turned about, and it was England which became so sporting that 35 years ago there were people who became rather annoyed with me because I in turn had borrowed the habit and taste for sporting exercises from the English and was introducing them into this country, where I was in danger, they said, of lowering the level of studies. Thus the ocean of sport seems to have its ups and downs just like the salt ocean.

Sporting mutualism, if I may use the expression, is at the beginning of its career, and has much ado to control such a current. The modern world is better placed in this respect than the ancient world, because sport has become completely international and we may therefore hope that this the movement will not stop, since if it were to weaken at one point it would revive at another.

Mr. President and Mr. Prefect, in the name of our colleagues I again proffer all our thanks. In this illustrious and brilliant Town Hall we are happy and charmed to be able to offer you the homage of the International Committee and, forgetting for a moment that Paris is my native town, and knowing with certainty that I am complying with the intimate wishes of all my colleagues from the other countries, I ask your permission to cry "Long live Paris!"

Discours de Monsieur le Baron Pierre de Coubertin (à l'Hôtel de Ville de Paris, le 24 Juin 1924), in: *Rapport officiel. VIIIe Olympiade*. Paris, Librairie de France, 1924, p. 637.

4.2.2/42 PRAGUE (1925)

Coubertin describes here the last stage of his Olympic work as IOC President, the 24th IOC Session and the holding of the technical and pedagogical Olympic Congresses at the end of May 1925 in Prague. The topic which dominated was the amateur question, but not in Coubertin's mind. His Olympic Manifesto, the speech at the opening, appears under 5.1/10.

In fact, two congresses met at Prague: the IOC, the twenty-four NOCs, and seventeen international sport federations held discussions about the Ninth Olympic Games to be held in Amsterdam in 1928, on a large number of individual issues of organizations. These included redefining the amateur, a topic that drew particular attention. The Olympic Congress on education dealt with matters of special interest to Coubertin at the time. At the end of his presidency, he wanted to see such issues as the participation of adolescents and women in sports, sports for all, and the proper conduct of the athlete dealt with once again at the Olympic level. Coubertin was one of the most active participants. He spoke often during the discussions, and offered a number of solutions.

The invitation to hold the congress as well as the IOC Session in Prague in 1925 had reached us in Rome two years earlier and had immediately been accepted. It was signed by the Foreign Minister, Mr. Benes. That same year I visited President Masaryk during his stay in Montreux and was pleased to note the interest he showed in modern Olympism. It was only right anyway to render homage to the splendid town of Prague, certainly one of the most beautiful in the world, one of the most interesting

Pierre de Coubertin, accompanied by Jiri Guth-Jarkowsky (left) and his wife at the Olympic Congress held in Prague in 1925, where he resigned as IOC President. Baroness de Coubertin supported him with her intelligence and affection. (IOC Archives)

too from the point of view of history with its rich accumulation of dramatic and profoundly human ups and downs. For me, who right from the start had always associated Bohemia with the Olympic movement and had never ceased to stand up for its rights, it was particularly pleasing to end my presidential career there. And it was also a means of showing my gratitude and affection to my faithful collaborator and friend Guth-Jarkovsky, the only representative left of the original team.

The IOC Session opened in the Town Hall on May 26, 1925. The newcomers included among others Count Bonacossa (Italy), Baron Schimmelpenninck (Holland), the Secretary of the State Lewald (Germany), Mr. Ivar Nyholm (Denmark), and Dr. Haudeck (Austria). At the first meeting, Captain Scharroo announced satisfactory news from Amsterdam. In fact, thanks to him and his assistants, everything ran smoothly even though for a short while the Ninth Olympiad had been in serious danger because the Pietists, who had risen up in arms against the "heathen" nature of this revival, had succeeded in blocking the voting of credits. It looked at one time therefore as though this Olympiad was going to break a record before it had even got properly started – a record for stupidity. But public opinion rebelled against the hesitations of those in power, and a public subscription had clearly shown the latter that they were on the wrong path. Order was restored. Even so, to think such things could happen in the 20th century! What a lesson for those who believe they have seen the last of the manifold aspects of obscurantism and have "laid low the hydra of ignorance". On the contrary, what never ceased to worry me was the growth and aggravation of intellectual insufficiency. Because knowledge is nothing without understanding; and specialized knowledge, which nowadays one imagines is capable of enabling man to grasp problems in their entirety, only serves on the contrary to distort them, for him. Having for a quarter of a century now studied this problem, its probable consequences, and its possible solution, I was impatient to be able to devote myself to it entirely and that is why I was perhaps occasionally a little inattentive and absent-minded during the Olympic discussions in Prague. In this respect I felt that my role was over. I was aware of leaving my successor a privileged and unassailable situation.

After matters regarding Holland, we examined those regarding California, which was still a long way off but even so more advanced than had ever previously been the case. The future of our conquest of Africa, compromised by the defection of Algeria, had become more promising since Alexandria had agreed to accept the inheritance and since A. C. Bolanachi was devoting himself to the task so wholeheartedly. The Winter Games met with no resistance. Our Scandinavian colleagues, who were now convinced and converted, had rallied to the idea without any reservations. I was very pleased, having always wanted to see this winter appendage duly legalized, but I blame myself for having allowed a text that could later cause trouble to become part of our Rules and Regulations under the title, "Charter of the Winter Games". On the contrary, we should have prohibited all separate numbering and given these competitions the same number as the current Olympiad.

Finally, we opened the cupboard where the skeletons were stored and took out, to study once again, the problem of amateurism, with all that that involved: loss of earnings, pocket money, distinction between instructors and professionals, consequences of contacts between amateurs and professionals, etc. All this was to be discussed once again by the congress, which was not likely to be stormy because of its agenda but liable, rather, to incidents caused by certain troublemakers. On the other hand, completely unexpected outside interference came to trouble the election of the new President of the IOC. It was aimed at preventing the presidency from passing into other than French hands and attempted to persuade me to agree to stay on until the following year, which would give the maneuvering time to succeed. It would have been completely wrong of me to agree to such proceedings. The members of the Executive Committee who were consulted – together with the Reverend Laffan – were quite categorical in their protests. At the banquet followed by a reception given in the famous "white room" of Hradschin Palace by Mr. and Mrs. Benes on May 27, the minister told me that he had been asked to bring his influence to bear but had refused considering that it would have been incorrect on his part to meddle in any way with the independence of the IOC.

The election was held the next day, May 28. The number of voters being 40, the majority required was 21. In the first ballot some votes were still wasted on my name, against my wish, as a token of esteem: in the second ballot, Count de Baillet-Latour was elected. Calm and satisfaction greeted this election, which bore witness to the strength of the Olympic organization and gave everyone a feeling of security. The session finished on this note the day before the congress opened. Very brilliant parties had been held almost daily: presidential garden party, gala performance at the Opera, matinee in the famous Wallenstein Palace, dinners given by Councilor and Mrs. Guth-Jarkovsky, by the Minister of Health, the Mayor of Prague, the Automobile Club, and the Czechoslovak Olympic Committee, etc. For the opening of the congress, a number of magnificent choral works were heard, whose solemn tones in this historic spot roused memories of Jan Huss and King George of Podiebrad.

It had been decided that I should hand over my powers in Lausanne and that my successor's authority should date from September 1. Consequently, I was still President in office and empowered to act as such during the congress. On the proposal of General Sherrill, my colleagues had appointed me "Honorary Life President of the Olympic Games" specifying that this honor should never be conferred on any one else after me. But, as I had already done in 1921, I appointed

J. S. Edström to chair the meeting. This choice was popular with the federations too, Edström being both a member of the IOC and President of the International Athletics Federation. To this delicate role he devoted admirable zeal and conscientiousness, accompanied by a certain directness tempered, however, with a sense of justice and kindness to which no one took offence. This time, however, he found the assembly difficult to manage and, during the first few days, felt slightly discouraged. In my opinion this was due rather to the almost insoluble nature of the problem we were again facing than to the state of mind of the majority of congress members. They sincerely wished to further the good of sports institutions, but felt themselves invested with often contradictory mandates depending on their nationality and the particular sport they represented. Nationalist passions had been so exacerbated by the war that many points of view were distorted by them while, on the other hand, there was a growing tendency, inspired by the general atmosphere and also by a sort of secret instinct of social preservation, to pay lip service to internationalism in the most varied fields; a strange contradiction of the day, to which many of our contemporaries have already had occasion to call attention.

Another congress was held in Prague in conjunction with the technical congress. It was educational in nature and we had organized it in cooperation with the Czechoslovak Government, taking care to specify that "neither the principle nor the methods of physical education were in doubt" and that the meeting would "in no way have the task of looking for or adapting better methods", but simply of studying the course to be followed in order to improve various aspects of sports organization without weakening or modifying its fundamental character". These special aspects were as follows: excess of exhibitions, boxing matches, restrictions during adolescence, participation of women, revival of the "ancient gymnasium", promotion of fair play and the spirit of chivalry, cooperation of universities, sports cures, and fighting against false sportsmen. It was, as one can see, a series of questions which, although seemingly having nothing in common, were all connected by the strong yet tenuous thread of a common concern of a psycho-physiological nature. Each question was accompanied by an explanatory paragraph set out in terms designed to exclude the possibility of straying from the subject as defined. The Educational Congress, however, drifted fairly quickly into one of the usual ruts of contemporary speech-making, i.e. the inability to deal with an objective and practical subject without being led astray by the wish to emphasize an opinion or promote a special interest. As a general rule this leads to eloquence without substance, and without useful impact. However the subjects entered on the agenda were particularly dear to me and it was at my wish that they had been included; fortunately I had an opportunity of returning to them subsequently under more favorable circumstances.

In accordance with the decision reached, Count de Baillet-Latour took office on September 1. Shortly afterwards he paid his official visit to the Vaudois Council of State and the Municipality of Lausanne. The President of the Council of State and the Mayor of the town gave a dinner in his honor. We later went to Bern, where the President of the Confederation, Mr. Musy, entertained us to lunch after our visit to the Federal Palace and the exchange of the customary compliments.

Olympic Memoirs, Chap. 22, Lausanne, IOC, 1997, pp. 218-223.

COMITÉ
INTERNATIONAL
OLYMPIQUE

Lausanne, Juillet 1925
(An II de la VIIIe Olympiade)

MON CHER COLLÈGUE,

Le Jeudi 28 Mai, à l'issue de notre session de 1925, tenue à l'Hôtel de Ville de Prague, le comte Henry de Baillet-Latour a été élu président du Comité International Olympique pour la période 1925-1933. Il a été convenu que son entrée en fonctions aurait lieu le 1er Septembre. A partir de cette date, je vous prierai donc de vouloir bien lui adresser vos communications.

Pendant plus de trente années, votre amitié fidèle et votre dévouement à notre œuvre m'ont rendu la tâche aisée. Je vous en remercie encore une fois. Je n'ai pas besoin d'exprimer ma confiance qu'il en sera de même pour mon successeur dont vous connaissez de longue date la compétence et l'activité. Vous pouvez envisager l'avenir en toute sécurité. L'institution mondiale que nous avons édifiée est en état de faire face à toutes les éventualités.

Croyez, je vous en prie, à mes sentiments de gratitude et d'affection.

Pierre de Coubertin

Farewell letter from IOC President Pierre de Coubertin to all IOC members, in which he announces the handing over of his official duties to his successor, Henri de Baillet-Latour, on 1st September 1925. (IOC Archives)

4.2.2/43 CIRCULAR LETTER OF FAREWELL (1925)

The following circular letter from Coubertin was his last official word as president of the IOC.

Lausanne, July 1925
(Year 2 of the Eighth Olympiad)

Dear Colleague,

On Thursday, May 28, at the conclusion of our 1925 Session held at the City Hall of Prague, Count Henry de Baillet-Latour was elected president of the International Olympic Committee for the period 1925-1933. It was agreed that he would take up his office on September 1. As of that date, please send your correspondence to his attention.

For more than thirty years, your faithful friendship and your devotion to our work has made my own work easier, and I thank you once again for it. I need not express my confidence that you will do the same for my successor, whose competence and energy you have known for a long time. You can look forward to the future with complete assurance. The worldwide institution that we have built is ready to meet any and all challenges.

Very sincerely yours,

Pierre de Coubertin

Archives of the IOC

4.2.2/44 OLYMPIA (1927)

Coubertin visits Greece and his beloved Olympia again after an absence of 31 years. In his *Olympic Memoirs,* he describes quite unsentimentally his feelings and departure. At Olympia, a pillar is erected in his honour at the entrance to the Altis, in which his heart would be placed in 1938. Around this, the International Olympic Academy has been located since 1961, bringing together the youth of the world for Olympic studies. At Olympia, Coubertin makes a moving appeal to the youth of the world, which appears under 5.1/12. In Athens, Coubertin has discussions with the Minister of Culture on the future of Olympism. The idea of the new Panathenean is mooted, and this is realized in 1930.

On April 16, 1927, a special train left Athens for Olympia carrying a whole inaugural procession led by the Minister of Public Education, Mr. Argyros, and composed of the Rector of the University, the President of the French School of Archaeology, the presidents of a large number of sports associations, and a number of professors as well as various foreign guests. The journey is a long one. The railway skirts the bay of Eleusis, follows the coast facing Salamine, crosses the Corinth Canal and hugs the gulf as far as Patras, then turns south to Pyrgos and finally reaches Olympia, in the valley through which the river Cladeos flows. The ruins are quite near, at the foot of Mount Kronion, almost at the junction of the Alphaeus and the Cladeos. The village and small railway station situated nearby have been discreet enough to conceal their modernism so that nothing disturbs the grandeur of the sacred precincts and the pious reveries of the pilgrims who visit them.

I had already made the same pilgrimage thirty-three years previously, in a solitude conducive to thought, accompanied only by a member of the Panachaic Society of Patras who had been kindly appointed for the purpose. One evening in November 1894, I had arrived from Athens, on my way home to France via Italy, aware both of the results already obtained and the terrible difficulties that awaited me in the future. I remember the path that wound up towards the small hill on which the museum and the hotel are situated. Cool, pure air, fragrant with the scent of the fields, wafted from the banks of the Alphaeus. For a moment, the moon lit up a vaporous landscape, then the starry night fell on the two thousand years I had come to recapture. The next day I rose early and sat at my window waiting for the sun to rise, and as soon as its first rays brushed the valley, I hastened alone towards the ruins. I was neither surprised nor disappointed at their smallness, which is due on the one hand to the restricted proportions of the buildings and on the other, to being crowded so close together (this absence of open spaces so characteristic of Greek and Roman civilizations represents a striking contrast to Persian architectural planning). Greek architecture, which I had yet to get to know, is a moral form of architecture that magnifies all dimensions. My meditation lasted all morning and only the sound of the bells of the herds on their way to Arcadia broke the silence.

Memories of that earlier scene came crowding back to me on that evening of April 16, 1927. Many houses had been built round the station, but in the neighborhood of the hotel and museum nothing had changed. We passed near a sort of obelisk covered with tarpaulins. It was the white marble monument erected by the Greek government and on which I knew that my name was engraved in both Greek and French letters. There was a big banquet at the hotel, a sort of popular feast with local dishes that savored of ancient times. And once again I repeated the gestures and movements of my earlier visit; the vigil at the window watching the light of a fugitive moon sliding over the meadows of the Alphaeus and, at dawn, wandering through the ruins in pursuit of the grandiose scenes of another age.

The inauguration ceremony was held at ten in the morning on April 17. We gathered together, surrounded by many spectators who had flocked in from the neighboring villages, at the foot of the monument draped in a Greek and a French flag. Three priests, decked in their robes, sang psalms and intoned prayers in quavering voices that seemed to rise up out of a Byzantine past, heir to Christianized Hellenism. Then the Minister made a speech, to which I replied briefly. Next the Swiss chargé d'affaires associated his country and the town of Lausanne in the ceremony that had just been performed: a ceremony imbued with a simplicity in perfect keeping with the grandeur of the place. The special train left again at 12:45 to bring us back to Athens as night fell.

I wish to reproduce here the text of the message that was sent by wireless that same day to "The sporting youth of all nations". This text has not always been faithfully reproduced and certain translations have misinterpreted one passage.

"Olympia, April 17, 1927
(Year IV of the Eighth Olympiad).

Today, amidst the glorious ruins of Olympia, has been inaugurated the monument commemorating the reestablishment of the Olympic Games thirty-three years ago. Thanks to the generosity of the Hellenic Government, the initiative it was good enough to honor has now materialised into an event of historic importance. It is for you now to keep the flag flying. My friends and I have not laboured to restore the Olympic Games to you in order to make them a fitting object for a museum or a cinema; nor is it our wish that mercantile or electoral interests should seize upon them. Our object in reviving an institution twenty-five centuries old, was that you should become new adepts of the religion of sports, as our great ancestors conceived it. In this modern world, so full of powerful possibilities, and yet threatened by so many risks of degeneration, Olympism may be a school of moral nobility and purity as well as of physical endurance and energy; but only on condition that you continually raise your conceptions of honour and sporting disinterestedness to the height of your muscular strength. The future depends on you."

Various events had been organized in Athens mainly as a result of the efforts of J. E. Chryssafis, Director of Physical Education. He had for years devoted himself unsparingly, with enthusiasm and great effectiveness, in the service of the public good. He and the new member of the IOC for Greece, Mr. George Averoff, who died prematurely two years ago, seemed to me to be doing everything in their power to erase from my memory any recollection of the unfortunate episodes of the first Games. But in fact nothing remained. That my ideas should have met with objections at the time, even arousing excessively chauvinistic feelings, was only natural. Everyone now understood that by conceiving the new Games on a completely international level and by wishing to situate them on a world scale, I had not only chosen the only practical means of ensuring their continued survival but at the same time had served the best interests of Hellenism. I have never for a moment ceased serving it in other ways too, always by seeking to exteriorize it, to present it not as a relic of the past worthy of respect and reflection but as a thing of the future worthy of faith and devotion. At the bottom of the crucible in which the fate of future society is prepared, there is a sort of latent eliminatory conflict between the principle of the Roman state and that of the Greek city. In vain, futurist pride strives to create something new. We are doomed to reconstructing on one of these two foundations. Appearances seem to favor the Roman state. As for me, I believe in the Greek city.

I hope my readers will forgive me for these thoughts which might seem unrelated to Olympism. But during my extended stay on Greek soil, I was particularly pleased to see that my philhellenism was now understood and appreciated by all my good Greek friends. That is why, among the tributes with which they honored me, there was perhaps none by which I was more touched than the revival of a custom that had been neglected since ancient times: the dedication of a marble seat in the stadium with the name of the beneficiary engraved in gold letters on the back. I occupied my seat only once. It was to watch an athletics meeting held on the occasion of the visit of an English university team: cinder tracks, spiked shoes, the stadium restored. But today's athletes entered the stadium through the old underground passage used by their forerunners twenty centuries before: and their souls were the same and their youth ringed round by the same youthful surge of muscular joy.

When, after the races, we had an opportunity of talking together, it was to discuss the question of the stadium and its curves. Everyone is familiar with the insoluble nature of the problem. The curves are too short for present-day speeds and the runners are handicapped and even risk injuring themselves. The modern tendency to simplify the athlete's attempts to set ever higher, more amazing records by giving him every possible material aid, is exactly the opposite of the ancient conception which aimed at making his efforts more praiseworthy by surrounding them with obstacles to be overcome. Thus the track of soft sand and the springy cinder track represent the two extremes of the idea of sport. But was the problem really insoluble? I was mistaken.

A number of out-and-out modernists had found a solution. It consisted in enlarging the stadium by a third by doing away with two rows of seats, thus increasing the usable area. The idea of mutilating Pericles' stadium in this way! It must have been a "barbarian" who proposed such a sacrilegious idea. The students from the north, brought up in the wholesome traditions of the classics and history, protested indignantly against such utilitarianism, already rejected, it should be added, by the people of Greece. At one moment, I saw one of them raise his eyes to the divine Acropolis still bathed in the last rays of the setting sun while the shadows spread fast around us. The stadium was gradually emptying. The marbled whiteness was taking over again. The student, full of the joy of living, his body suffused with the voluptuous glow that comes only from the healthy tiredness induced by sport, and fired with youthful hope and ambition, seemed, with his fixed stare, to be imploring Minerva and paying her homage. He was like a sculpture representing neo-Olympism, the symbol of the future victories awaiting Hellenism-still so very much alive, and eternally adapted to human circumstances.

Olympic Memoirs, Chap.23, Lausanne, IOC, 1997, pp. 224-229.

Pierre de Coubertin in Olympia in 1927, accompanied by his daughter Renée. A highly intelligent woman, she helped her father with his work. (Navacelle Collection)

4.2.2/45 MODERN CHIVALRY

In the introduction to this book, we discussed the educational initiatives that Coubertin had undertaken after resigning from the IOC. At the same time, his commentaries on Olympic events became even rarer. The following short text makes an appeal for the "modern chivalry" that he hoped to see illustrated by participants in the 1928 Games. He speaks directly to the participants in Amsterdam, and exhorts them, as though moved by a premonition of his own death, to respect the principles of the Games.

The April, 1911 issue of the Revue Olympique contains a document that happened to cross my desk the other day. It is a speech given in Amsterdam on March 29, 1911 at the end of a banquet held in my honor, under the presidency of our dear, late friend F. W. De Tuyll, by the representatives of the Athletic Federations and Associations of Holland. At the end of the speech, I mentioned the future of the Olympics in Holland, and I dwelt at length on this point even though there were some skeptical smiles around me. As of then, Baron de Tuyll and I knew well that one day the Olympic Games of the modern era would be held in Amsterdam.

Seventeen years have passed, and now that day has come. It would have come even sooner, had the athletes of Holland not been so gracious four years ago in allowing my wish to be granted, that the Eighth Olympiad be held in Paris, my home town. That Olympiad coincided with the Thirtieth Anniversary of the restoration of the Olympic Games, announced at the Sorbonne on June 23, 1893. May my Dutch friends find here, once again, an expression of my gratitude for their self-denial. May they find their reward in the success which, I am convinced, will crown their efforts.

Yet the completeness of this success does not depend on them, but on their guests. It will be achieved only if the degree of "sportsmanship" among the competitors attests to progress in the order of moral values. Technical values are not at issue here. They exist already, and they are considerable. Moral values also exist, and they are much greater than anyone believes. The only proof of this I need is the 1924 Games, when, for three weeks, I saw with my own eyes, and on too many occasions to count, athletes, runners, boxers and others reaching down into themselves to find the strength to resist the negative passions that the exacerbated spectators hurled at them, as did some of their own unworthy coaches. Those who are "laymen" in the world of sports have scarcely made any progress yet, and I do not expect them to do so as long as the majority of them is not made up of ex-athletes. Therefore, it is essential for today's Olympic competitors to know that they must count on themselves alone in their quest for the spirit of chivalry, the culminating point and the supreme goal of athletic activity.

In truth, the only chivalrous knights left were isolated here and there, with no common code, no fraternal organization, without the occasion or the means to help one another. Then, a century ago in England, there appeared those "muscular Christians" in whom one finds in embryo all the qualities of the chivalry of former times, its high ideals, its healthy roughness, its generous zeal. All that was brought up to date, separated from war and from blood, and oriented toward the less picturesque but broader horizons that are the new democracies. Now man, by perfecting his own self, serves the cause of the long-forgotten common good more directly than in the past.

A demonstration of modern chivalry at the 1928 Olympics: Swede Inga Gentzel, runner-up in the 800 m, congratulates the winner, Lina Radke (Germany). (taken from J.Waitzer/W.Dörr, Welt-Olympia 1928 in Wort und Bild, Berlin/Zürich, Conzett & Huber, 1928, p.97)

At Easter, in 1927, among the age-old ruins of Olympia, the Greek Minister of Public Instruction removed the sheeting that covered a monument commemorating the restoration of the Olympic Games. As he honored me by recalling past events, my thoughts turned to Kingsley and Arnold, and to the chapel at Rugby where the great clergyman rests who was, as I see it, one of the founders of athletic chivalry. I regretted the absence of another Englishman, a man dear to my heart, the most faithful and devoted of my colleagues, the Reverend de Courcy Laffan, who died so young.

Now, on these vague shores of the North Sea where everything you see was conquered, used, rebuilt, and transformed by human labor, the singular grandeur of the Dutch landscape, young knights are going to hold their quadrennial meeting amid grandiose solemnity, in a stadium filled with a cosmopolitan crowd. They will take an oath, every word of which commits them, binds them in the name of honor. Then they will give it their all, I am sure. Yet as in any human, and therefore imperfect, undertaking, there will be errors, faults, and failings. But on the last day, if nearly each one in this vast field of these athletes can swear that he strove with complete loyalty, without wavering for an instant, then the moral profits will have been made and the Ninth Olympiad will stand as another noble and happy step along the path of chivalry's advancement. May this be so. This is my wish and my hope.

La chevalerie moderne,
in: *Officieel Feestnummer*. Olympische Spelen te Amsterdam 1928.
Textes recueillis par J. Feith/J. Hoven/W.J.M. Linden. Gouda 1928, [p. 8].

4.2.2/46 – 4.2.2/47 INTRODUCTION

The following two articles relate to the Tenth Olympic Games in Los Angeles, in 1932. The first, "Aarau, Prague, Los Angeles", dwells on the elevated status of these Games and their contribution to the educational unification of the world. In the second, Coubertin calls the Tenth Olympic Games an "Apotheosis of Olympism". The Los Angeles Games were characterized by the outstanding performance of the Japanese team. Coubertin believed that this opened the way for Olympism to spread throughout Asia. In 1934, he sent a "Message to American Youth", to whom, above all others, he entrusted the realization of his educational plans[1].

4.2.2/46 AARAU, PRAGUE, LOS ANGELES

The Games of the "Tenth Olympiad of the modern era", according to the correct expression which is not always used, sometimes through inadvertence and other times through cantankerousness, took place among great pomp and circumstance, with nature playing right along. Southern California is often a bit trying for Europeans at this time of year. In fact, the opening of the Games was preceded by a "heat wave" that abated, courteously enough, for the arrival of the athletes. They seem to have greatly appreciated the various comforts that surrounded them. Their numbers were considerable, attesting to the fact that throughout the world, the Olympic laurel remains the most sought after, the one for which they are willing to make great efforts and enormous sacrifices. This does nothing much to assuage the managers of federations who feel that their annual championships have been attacked, even diminished in stature because of this preference on the part of athletes. That is why at times they try to destroy the Olympic Games, while at other times, since they fail in their attempts to ruin them, they try to take over management of the Games. That is a subject to which we will have to return, because it is of great significance from the educational perspective.

The crowds that attended the opening of the Games came mostly from across the Atlantic, and they had never before seen such a spectacle. They seem to have been greatly impressed by it, and the organizers, for their part, seem to have achieved the maximum of the desirable Olympic eurythmia on this solemn occasion[2]. All the symbolic beauty of the parade, the ancient formula, the flag and the flame constantly crowning the stadium...the oath, the flight of pigeons in the colors of the participating countries, nothing of what had been prescribed in old Europe from the beginning of the restoration was left undone over there. The choral groups were more powerful and more appropriate than ever before. The current president of the International Committee was fully justified in declaring that the Olympics had reached full pitch. Their founder wrote, "The Olympic Games are not merely world championships, but the quadrennial festival of universal youth, of the human springtime, the festival of passionate efforts, multiple ambitions, and of all the forms of youthful activity of each generation as it stands at the threshold of life. It was no mere happenstance that brought together writers and artists at Olympia long ago, gathering them around sports in antiquity. This incomparable assembly achieved the prestige that the institution enjoyed for so long. Since I wished to restore not so much the form as the principle of this age-old institution, because I saw in it an educational orientation that had once again become essential for my country and for humanity, I had to try to restore the powerful supporting structures that had once shored it up: the intellectual support, the moral support, and to a certain extent, the religious support – to which the modern world added two new forces: technical improvements and democratic internationalism."

The celebration of the Tenth Olympiad made this point of view tangible, in a way, to a whole segment of the world, and its consequences will be long-lasting. The enormous participation by Japan, and the extension of Asian understanding, coinciding with impeccable preparation on the large scale as well as in the details – that is the first assessment of the 1932 Games. Of course, there will be other lessons to draw from them. As of now, it seems that the educational unification of the universe has taken another step forward. This is a crucial thing. But in light of this, what is the value of quarrels and eulogies about the disqualification of a particular athlete or the presence of a particular undesirable individual?

Aarau, Prague, Los Angeles,
in: *Bulletin of the Bureau International de Pédagogie Sportive,*
No. 9, Lausanne [1933], pp. 6-7.

4.2.2/47 THE APOTHEOSIS OF OLYMPISM

The Revue Sportive Illustrée has been too faithful a friend for me to turn down its request for an opinion about the recent Olympic Games and how the recently-concluded Games went on the other side of the world. The Los Angeles Games are the last for which I, as president of the International Committee, proposed the site and called the vote on awarding the Games to that host city. The voting took place at the Capitoline Hill in Rome, during our 1923 Session. Nine years ahead of time! If the proposed site had been a city in Europe, I would not have agreed to any decision made so far in advance, because of the obvious imprudence of such a move. But absent some seismic catastrophe, California was not subject to any of the threats looming even then in the eyes of observant Europeans. I would not have wanted to end my third ten-year period as president of the IOC without underscoring, in a gesture of this kind, the ambition I had expressed from the start concerning the new form of Olympism: that it should encircle the globe, and thus not be subject to the chance events in a particular region or to narrow, nationalist views. My colleagues shared my understanding of how valuable this outlook is.

Events have fully justified our expectations. Despite adverse economic conditions and a banking crisis of unexpected scope, despite a press campaign with a bitterness of tone and an unfairness of intent equaled only by the self-interested calculation that inspired it, the Games of the Tenth Olympiad became a glorious apotheosis on the shores of the Pacific Ocean. As soon as Count de Baillet-Latour

1 See text 5.1/15 of this volume.
2 See the article entitled "La valeur pédagogique du cérémonial olympique" ["The educational value of the Olympic ceremonies"] in no. 7 of the *Bulletin*, text 5.2/9 in this volume.

arrived in Los Angeles, he was kind enough to telegraph me to express his satisfaction at finding "so perfectly Olympic an organization and spirit" there. He himself was responsible for that in no small measure, since he had been particularly attentive and shrewd in his efforts to support our common cause throughout this year. I say this without any intention whatsoever of detracting from the credit due to the directors and organizers of the Games.

Of course, Olympism was already quite familiar and deeply appreciated in the Los Angeles area. Proof of this comes from the eagerness they showed in bidding for the Games. Besides, the Americans had their first taste of hosting the Games during the Third Olympiad (St. Louis, 1904), which some people today conveniently malign and denigrate in retrospect, to suit the ambitions of certain individuals. Of course the Americans have always participated in the Games held in Europe, as well. This time, however, it was Asia that experienced the full effects of our restoration efforts – for which they had prepared by periodically holding Far East Games, a sort of "Olympic kindergarten."

The consequences will be enormous, and are already being felt by those who contemplate the Olympic Games and international championships in general from the vantage point of their own interests, for we are seeing the emergence of new moves. In all likelihood, the Games of the Ninth Olympiad in 1936 will probably not yet provide the means to allow these new moves to develop profitably.

In this area as in so many others, power changes hands, principles change form, and centers of gravity shift. A structure comprising independent, interrelated segments is gradually replacing the tutorship system from which Europe has benefited for so long. Europe itself has hastened this demise through its tactlessness in using the system.

The power that Olympism retains in the face of the lizards proclaiming its imminent or more gradual collapse derives from its most deeply human, and therefore universal, aspects (as is the case for most institutions rooted in Hellenism). Served by a college of unselfish priests who are haunted by neither ordinary concerns for profits nor a need to rise above their own merits, Olympism withstands the attack of any assailant and emerge unscathed.

These are the thoughts that come to mind following the recent Games, provided that ordinary prejudices are set aside to assess them. As it happens, these Games, with their far-reaching consequences, took place on the blessed soil of California. There, nature's splendors provided a backdrop for the exquisite efforts of the people of that state, whose instinct for art and beauty has long since drawn them onward and upward to greater destinies.

... California, o glorious land of labor, art and song! ...

Pierre de Coubertin

Founder and Honorary President
of the Olympic Games

L'apothéose de l'Olympisme,
in: *La Revue Sportive Illustrée,*
Vol. 28, 1932, no. 3 [p. 26].

4.2.2/48 – 4.2.2/49 INTRODUCTION

From his home in Lausanne, Coubertin played an active role in the preparations for the Eleventh Olympic Games of 1936, in Berlin.

He was in close contact with Carl Diem, the "spiritus rector" of the Olympic movement in Germany. These two men were brought together by their shared intentions concerning athletic education and their shared understanding of the artistic and solemn form that the Games should assume. Their association began in 1913, during preparations for the Games planned for 1916 in Berlin.

The Berlin Olympic Games provided a remarkable opportunity for artistic growth, but the IOC underestimated the dangers resulting from the combination of athletics and politics[1]!

Coubertin neither disowned the 1936 Olympic Games, nor that "strange figure"[2] Adolf Hitler. He thanked "the German people and their leader for what they have just accomplished" in the following message at the close of the Berlin Games. Also Carl Diem, since 1912 his "genial and enthusiastic friend" in Germany, misinterpreting the Nazi intentions at that time, was not able to inform Coubertin objectively of the political circumstances.

The French Coubertin researcher Professor Yves Pierre Boulongne[3] evaluates Coubertin's position at that time under the following aspect: "We should not forget that [the ageing] Coubertin, in a way a prisoner of his own utopia, believed that the more "the epidemic of sport" would spread in the world, the greater the chance for peace would be. From this single point of view, Germany was indeed a nation of sport. Obviously a false syllogism!"[4]

French newspapers proclaimed that Coubertin's Olympism would die out after the 1936 Berlin Games and the Games planned for Tokyo in 1940. Coubertin stated his position on this matter in the Parisian daily, *Le Journal.*

4.2.2/48 MESSAGE AT THE CLOSE OF THE BERLIN GAMES

Take care to maintain the sacred flame!

Soon the Games of the Eleventh Olympiad will be no more than a memory, but what powerful and diverse Games they were!

Those memories will be of beauty, first and foremost. Since the time I called the Conference on Arts, Literature, and Sports thirty years ago in Paris to establish a permanent connection between the restored Olympics and expressions of the mind, bold efforts from Stockholm to Los Angeles have helped make this ideal a reality.

1 The IOC did issue a statement demanding that the German government recognize the racial equality of the athletes.

2 See "The Unfinshed Symphony" as appendix of this volume.

3 Yves-Pierre Boulongne, member of the French Resistance against Hitler since 1939 and prisoner in Buchenwald (1943-45).

4 Comment of Yves Pierre Boulongne in his letter on November 29, 1999 to the editor. (N.Müller Collection). See Y.-P. Boulongne, *La vie et l'œuvre pédagogique de Pierre de Coubertin* (1863-1937). Ottawa, Leméac, 1975. See also Y.-P.Boulongne, *Pierre de Coubertin. Humanisme et pédagogie.* Dix leçons sur l'Olympisme. Lausanne, IOC, 1999.In order to assess Coubertin's understanding of National Socialism see also J.Durry, *Pierre de Coubertin. The Visionary.* His Life – His Work – His Key Texts. Paris, Comité Français Pierre de Coubertin, 1996, p.77.

Now, Berlin has made this link a permanent feature of the Games, through such gallant and utterly successful initiatives as the Race of the Sacred Torch from Olympia, and the magnificent Festival held in the monumental Stadium on the opening night of the Games. Both events were instituted by my genial and enthusiastic friend, Carl Diem.

Our memories will also be of courage, because it took courage to deal with the difficulties to which the Führer had already responded with the by-word of his will, Wir wollen bauen, and to stand up to the unfair and subversive attacks through which sporadic efforts were made to dismantle construction works in progress...

Finally, we will have memories of hope, because under the aegis of the Olympic flag with its five symbolic rings, athletic understandings were reached that are stronger even than death...

Freude, schöner Götterfunken

Tochter aus...

The choices and struggles of history will carry on, but gradually understanding will replace dreadful ignorance; mutual understanding will soothe impulsive hatreds. In this way, what I have worked toward for half a century will be strengthened.

I thank the German people and their leader for what they have just accomplished. And you, athletes, remember the Flame lit by the ardor of the sun, that came to you from Olympia to shed light on us and to warm our age. Guard it jealously deep within you, so that it still burns bright on the other side of the world when you gather to celebrate the Twelfth Olympiad in four years, on the far-off shores of the great Pacific Ocean!

English version in: Coubertin, *The Olympic Idea*,
Schorndorf 1967, pp. 135-136.
Manuscript in the Archives of the IOC.

4.2.2/49 THE GAMES IN TOKYO IN 1940? COMMENTS BY MR. PIERRE DE COUBERTIN, RECORDED BY ANDRÉ LANG

On the last day of the Berlin Games, Jacques Goddet, our outstanding colleague and editor-in-chief of Auto, published a passionate concluding article, a sort of "J'accuse!" denouncing those responsible for perverting and disfiguring the Olympic idea.

The intent of his charge was to show that Mr. Coubertin's ideal is now a dead letter; that the Games now serve merely as a showcase for the most cynical highest bidder; and that Tokyo in 1940 will see the triumph of Japanese racial propaganda, just as Californian propaganda triumphed in Los Angeles in 1932 and Hitler's political propaganda did in Berlin in 1936.

Most French sports journalists, without going to such extremes, have expressed similar fears. Though marveling at the spectacle, they deplore the fact that human effort is now merely a pretext for a putting on a show. They fear that the Olympic idea will soon be killed off, buried beneath their trappings of the Games.

So I wanted to find out what the one man to whom the world owes the restoration of the Games after fifteen centuries feels about this.

Pierre de Coubertin is a legendary man. He carries his seventy-four years with such ease that one could easily believe he dyes his mustache and hair, both snow white, to look a little older.

From the start Mr. Coubertin rose in revolt against my characterization, but quite decorously, a smile never far from his lips:

Coubertin: “What? The Games “disfigured?” The Olympic idea sacrificed to propaganda? That is utterly wrong! The wonderful success of the Berlin Games has served the Olympic ideal magnificently. The French are the only ones, or practically the only ones, playing Cassandra. They are making a great mistake in failing to understand this. The Olympic idea must be allowed to spread freely, without fear of the passions or the excesses that produce the excitement and enthusiasm that have to be there. Trying to force athletics to fit into the confines of mandatory moderation is a utopian pursuit. As for the dispute about amateurism and the indignation some feel regarding the Olympic Oath, pardon me while I laugh! First, there is not and never has been any such thing as amateurism. Second, there is not a single word in the Oath, which I wrote very carefully, that refers to amateurism. These are childish disputes. Only the Olympic spirit matters. All the rest is of trifling importance.

Lang: Doesn’t it bother you that athleticism, the only real Olympic sport, is a bit overwhelmed at every Olympiad?

Coubertin: Why should that bother me? The only true Olympic hero, as I have always said, is the individual male adult. Therefore no women, no sports teams. But how can women, sports teams, and all the other games not be allowed in during the Olympiad? At Olympia there was a sacred enclosure, the Altis, set aside exclusively for the consecrated athlete. A vast communal life surged around this enclosure. With the natural changes that modern life imposes on us, that is what happened at Berlin. In the name of what rigid moral standards can this be condemned?

Lang: Don’t you find the selection of Tokyo and the desire of the Japanese to astound the world in 1940 fraught with rather dangerous consequences?

Coubertin: Not at all. I am glad of it. I wanted it. I consider the arrival of the Games in Asia a great victory. In terms of Olympism, the only thing international rivalries can be is fruitful. It is good for every country in the world to have the honor of hosting the Games and to celebrate them in their own way, according to the imagination and means of its people. In France, people are worried that the 1936 Games showcased Hitler’s strength and discipline. How could it have been otherwise? On the contrary, it is greatly to be desired that the Games should gladly wear the clothing that each country weaves during the four years of preparation for them. So many things can happen! Perhaps the expansion of the Workers’ Games will profoundly change the nature of the Thirteenth Olympiad. So much the better, so much the better! The Games must embrace the life of the world and not remain prisoners of utterly arbitrary regulations.

Lang: So you think that if France did not go to Tokyo...

Coubertin: ...it would be committing a serious error? Yes! It is already committing one by protesting the decision of the International Committee.

Lang: What can be done to win an honorable place in the Twelfth Olympiad?

Coubertin: Work. The example of Germany is there to show to us what can be achieved if you make it your business to focus on working. If I were training the competitors, I assure you they would show up at the stadium in good shape!

Lang: Why, in fact, are you not in charge of at least managing the training?

Coubertin: Why?

For a moment, Mr. Coubertin was amused by my naiveté.

Coubertin: Because I never asked for anything. Because no one ever offered me anything. Because I insist on nothing except my independence. When I turned 70, I received wonderful expressions of esteem and friendship from the four corners of the earth. Only France forgot me.

In a gesture of quiet pride, Mr. Coubertin concluded: "Well, I am not the one who is most embarrassed by that omission."

But what will French sports journalists, disowned by the founder of the Games, make of it?

Les Jeux à Tokio en 1940?...
Déclarations de M. Pierre de Coubertin recueillies par André Lang,
in: *Le Journal,*
Paris, August 27, 1936, no. 16019, p. 1.

4.2.3 HISTORICAL ASPECTS OF THE WINTER OLYMPIC GAMES

The following two texts by Coubertin relate to winter sports, and are more or less directly connected to the Olympic Games.

Coubertin's vision of the future, his "Modern Olympia" of 1909, also provided for winter Olympic competitions. Since the cost of building a skating rink, which would have made it possible to hold artistic skating competitions in London in 1908, was too high, Coubertin made a fall-back suggestion: "It would be better to adopt a solution in which these special sports are grouped together in winter, under the title "Nordic Games".[1]

Fifteen years later, in 1924, an Olympic winter sports week was held in Chamonix as a prelude to the Paris Olympic Games. In 1925, the IOC decided to introduce Winter Games, due to pressure from certain countries in Central Europe and from Canada. In 1926, at the 22nd IOC Session in Lisbon, the IOC recognized that week-long event in hindsight as the "1st Olympic Winter Games". The closing speech that Coubertin gave for that week of winter sports is included here. There is also a letter to the editor of the French sports newspaper *L'Auto,* in which Coubertin spelled out the purpose of the Winter Olympic Games in relation to the Olympic Games. For twenty years the IOC had refrained from instituting Winter Games as such, since there were the Nordic Games. It was not until 1908 and 1912 that it held skating competitions and, in 1920, ice hockey events. This was done essentially to honor Victor Balck, founding member of the IOC. But when the International Ski Federation (FIS) held the FIS International Competitions at Lahti (Finland) in 1926, the appeal of the Nordic Games fell considerably. Political tensions between Sweden and Norway also contributed to the decline in popularity of the Nordic Games.[2] The last of them were held in 1930. Coubertin was not particularly fond of the idea of Olympic Winter Games, which explains the small number of articles that he wrote on the topic.

Winner's certificate from the 1924 Olympic Winter Sports Week in Chamonix, designed by the French artist Yves Plumerau (IOC Archives)

4.2.3/1 SPEECH AT THE CLOSING CEREMONY OF THE WINTER GAMES (CHAMONIX, FEBRUARY 5, 1924)

Mr. Mayor, Ladies and Gentlemen,

I think that many of us would not rest easy if I failed to take this opportunity to express the admiration and gratitude that the efforts made to assure the greatest degree of technical perfection at this first Olympic tournament of Winter Sports inspire in us.

One of the most highly qualified Scandinavian coaches said yesterday that in many respects what we have seen can serve as a model, even for the highly regarded organization of the Nordic Games. That, dear Colleagues of the French Committee, is something that should make up for certain acerbic and unfair national criticisms.

Among the many spectators who attended the competitions over the past few days, there are many who have seen for the first time exercises whose beauty they did not even begin to imagine. Perhaps they are surprised to find them so rough and violent. The reason is that we live with a two-fold error. The first

1 "Une Olympie moderne [A Modern Olympia]. III. – Le programme des Jeux [The Program of the Games]." In: *Revue Olympique*, December 1909, pp. 186-187.

2 See also J. Lindroth: "The Nordic Games, Swedish-Norwegians relations and politics," in: M. Goksøyr (ed.), *Winter Games - Warm Traditions*. Oslo, ISHPES, 1996, pp. 293-301.

French warrant officer C.Mandrillon, surrounded by the national delegation flag-bearers, swears the Olympic Oath at the 1924 Winter Games in Chamonix. (IOC Archives)

is the error of the hygienists and the educators who fail to distinguish physical education and sports. Physical education is a thing that is good for everyone. It must be scientific and moderate. It is the government's role to ensure that it proceeds in a regular way. Sports are something more. Sports are a school for daring, energy, and persevering will. By their very nature, they tend toward excess. They need championships and records; it is the beautiful and loyal brutality of sports that make people strong and healthy. The other error is our own, that of athletes who tends to think that sports sustain themselves on their own, and spread because of their very nature. On the contrary, sports are delicate plants requiring a great deal of care to keep them from withering and rotting. Winter Sports are among the purest, and that is why I was so eager to see them take their place in a definitive way among the Olympic events. They will help us to keep a watchful eye on the athletic ideal, to keep it from all evil. In practice, there are, of course, great difficulties in carrying out this plan, but an initial experience like the one we have just had is a precious advantage.

Our thanks go out to all those who helped to make this great success possible.

Discours prononcé au Stade de glace de Chamonix
avant la clôture des Jeux,
mardi 5 février 1924,
in: French Olympic Committee (Ed.):
VIIIe Olympiade 1924. Rapport officiel [The Eighth Olympiad, 1924. Official report], p. 721.

Pierre de Coubertin loved trekking in the French and Swiss Alps. He also tried to ski. Here he appears in his familiar attitude. (Navacelle Collection)

4.2.3/2 FRANCE AND THE 1928 WINTER OLYMPIC GAMES. Letter from Baron Pierre de Coubertin to the editor of *L'Auto*

DEAR SIR,

I have read a notice in various newspapers that begins as follows: "Since 1921, winter sports have been part of the Olympic Games. The IOC acknowledged that if the country hosting an Olympiad was unable to organize winter sports events, then that portion of the program could be entrusted by it to another country."

Not a word of these assertions is correct. The International Committee has never accepted such an infraction of the basic rules of Olympism. An Olympiad is awarded to a city, not to a country, and it cannot be "shared" under any pretext. Therefore the current agitation is utterly unfounded, particularly since its origin is an alleged move on the part of the Dutch Committee – and I have received formal assurances that such a move *never took place.*

Skating and ice hockey have always been part of the program of the Games, circumstances allowing. But the 1924 Winter Sports Week held at Chamonix *on the occasion of* the Eighth Olympiad was not part of the program, at the express request of the Scandinavians.

Sincerely,

Pierre de Coubertin

La France et les "Jeux" d'hiver en 1928,
in: *L'Auto*, January 16, 1925, p. 1.

Pierre de Coubertin at the age of about sixty years old when he gave up the presidency of the IOC and from then on exclusively concentrated on his educational aims. (Photo: Carl & Liselott Diem Archives, Cologne)

5. THE PHILOSOPHICAL AND EDUCATIONAL DIMENSION OF OLYMPISM

This chapter on Olympism is extraordinarily important. It contains 49 texts in which Coubertin explains his Olympism, with which we are already familiar from information given on the history of Olympism. In the introduction to this volume, we provided a detailed analysis of the philosophical components of the Olympic restoration advocated by Coubertin.

Discussions today are often based on a certain prejudice about Olympism. It is widely believed that the "Olympism" exists as a global phenomenon. The chronological order of the texts in this chapter has been preserved as much as possible, which reveals a process of evolution. It was not until the speech broadcast on radio in 1935 about "The Philosophical Foundations for Modern Olympism" that we see Coubertin bringing all these elements together.

The German philosopher and 1960 Olympic champion Hans Lenk wrote a detailed study in 1964 "on the values, aims, and reality of Modern Olympic Games".[1] He came to the following conclusion: Olympism represents "the present action" of partial values. This is not an abstract form. Lenk has analyzed the most significant texts written by Coubertin and other Olympic leaders on this issue, drawing from them an overall sketch of Coubertin's "Olympism". It was not until twenty-five years after Coubertin's death that such statements became possible. The selected texts reveal technical aspects of the evolution in Coubertin's Olympic philosophy. They make it quite clear that it was not until the end of his life that Coubertin's ideas formed a complete unit, in a series of "integrating Olympic values" (in Lenk's terms). Those values will make it easier for us to approach this chapter:

- the cultural and religious celebration,
- artistic and spiritual training,
- the idea of the elite and of equal chances,
- competition and contest,

1 H. Lenk, *Werte, Ziele, Wirklichkeit der modernen Olympischen Spiele.* Schorndorf, Hofmann, 2nd Ed. 1972.

– sportsmanship: fair play, and the spirit of chivalry,
– the regular holding of the Games, tradition, and armistice,
– internationalism and nationalism ("understanding people" and cultural pluralism),
– the community of all the athletic disciplines,
– the notion of amateurism,
– Olympic independence, and
– the ancient model and the modern form.

It is surprising to see how this educational program has survived over so many years despite widespread incomprehension of its fundamental ideas. It is surprising, too, to see the various ways and forms in which this commitment finds expression in the beginning of the second Olympic century in so many countries and continents, in line with the Olympic traditions and the current status of sport education. The IOA which has steadily developed at Olympia since 1961 as the University of Olympism, professes a comprehensive commitment to Coubertin's mandate. The National Olympic Academies (NOAs) which have sprung up since 1966 to about 100 in 2000 have in various ways given a new emphasis to the Olympic concept in schools and universities and among the sports and Olympic organizations.

The Olympic Charter, in force in December 1999, refers on several occasions to the content and form of Olympism and Olympic education:

Definition of Olympism in Article 2 of the Fundamental Principles: "Olympism is a philosophy of life, exalting and combining in a balanced whole the qualities of body, will and mind. Blending sport with culture and education, Olympism seeks to create a way of life based on the joy found in effort, the educational value of good example and respect for universal fundamental ethical principles."

The Olympic Charter obliges the NOCs to promote Olympism in all areas of education. Prompted by the successful efforts of the IOA, the NOCs recognized the need to begin "Olympic education" at the grass roots. The Olympic Movement is an educational mission which is becoming increasingly topical as a result of media coverage. The fact that its values may seem unattainable does not mean that the idea is obsolete or misguided. Olympism contains visions which offer an ever-changing field of opportunity to athletes and everyone else concerned. Coubertin's much-quoted philosophical retrospective of 1935 "The Philosophic Foundation of Modern Olympism"[2] can only be understood by picturing this value structure of Olympism as the end product of a process that continued over forty years. If we are to answer the Question of what Olympism can mean in educational terms and what an "Olympic education" can contain, we must seek a starting point, once again, in Coubertin, since nothing has been done since his time to revise its content. Even the Olympic Charter adopted Coubertin's principles to that effect.

Under this heading we can group the following five pedagogical features of an "Olympic education":

– The concept of a harmonious development of the whole human being;

– The idea of striving for human perfection through high performance;

– Sporting activity voluntarily linked to ethical principles such as fair play and equality of opportunity, and the determination to fulfil those obligations;

– The concept of peace and goodwill between nations, reflected by respect and tolerance in relations between individuals;

– The promotion of moves towards emancipation in and through sport.[3]

Concerning the following chapter the first section (5.1), with eighteen texts, relates to Olympism as a spiritual attitude. These fundamental ideas, dating from after World War I, clearly show that it took a long period of maturation.

The second section (5.2), with ten texts, deals with the individual principles of Olympism, without without trying to force them into a system of values.

Throughout his life, Coubertin oriented his principles as a function of the demands of society and politics. He refined his idea of what constitutes Olympism incessantly. It seemed extremely important to him that the Olympic Games should have a cultural and religious form that was capable of guaranteeing the value of the Games by itself. That is why this section includes texts in which he analyzes the introduction and meaning of several Olympic symbols.

There is a close relationship between these texts and the ones in which Coubertin speaks of the involvement of the arts in the Games, as well as in local athletic events (5.3).

The twelve texts regarding the arts express, in part, Coubertin's hopes of causing a strong esthetic sensation in athletes and spectators alike, a sensation that he called the ideal of eurythmy, by linking athletics and art.

The fourth section (5.4) comprises nine texts on amateurism. Coubertin attributed less significance to amateurism than is generally thought. This issue was of ongoing concern to him and to the IOC. It remained a constant source of conflict. In the final analysis, this debate reflected the standing that high-level athletic competition and the Olympic Games enjoyed throughout the world.[4]

2 See text 5.1/17 in this volume.

3 See O.Grupe, "Die Olympische Idee ist pädagogisch. Zu Fragen und Problemen einer olympischen Erziehung", in: N.Müller/M.Messing (eds.): *Auf der Suche nach der Olympischen Idee*, Kassel, Agon, 1996, pp.23-38. See N.Müller, "Olympische Erziehung", in: O.Gruppe/D.Mieth (eds.): *Lexikon der Ethik im Sport*, Schorndorf, Hofmann, 1998, pp.385-395.

4 See also L. Ferry, "Olympisme, Humanisme et Démocratie" in: N. Müller (ed. dir.): *Coubertin and Olympism.* Questions for the Future. Report of the Congress 17th to 20th September 1997 at the University of Le Havre. Niedernhausen / Strasbourg / Sydney, Schors, 1998, pp. 169-179.
See L. Da Costa, *Olympism and the Equilibrum of Man,* ibidem, pp. 188-199.
See N. Nissiotis, "Olympisme, Sport and Aesthetics with Reference to the work of Pierre de Coubertin", in IOA (ed.): *Report of the 26th Session of the IOA.* Lausanne, IOC, 1987, pp. 83-90.
See N. Müller, "Olympische Erziehung [Olympic Education]", in: O. Grupe, D. Mieth (eds.): *Lexikon der Ethik im Sport.* Schondorf, Hofmann, 2nd Ed. 1999, pp. 385-395.

The entrance to the ancient Stadium at Olympia with a view of the sanctuary (Photo: H.Kaebernick)

5.1 OLYMPISM AS A SPIRITUAL ATTITUDE

5.1/1- 5.1/2 INTRODUCTION

This is a speech of acknowledgment that Coubertin gave at a dinner at the end of the founding Congress in 1894. The speech shows that Coubertin was not thinking merely of restoring the quadrennial Olympic Games, but that he was also planning to reintroduce sports in general to modern life, in keeping with the ancient Greek ideal of harmony.

Coubertin was not toasting the "Olympic Games", but the "Olympic idea... (as a) gleam of joyful hope[1]."

Coubertin give his second speech on November 16, 1894 in Athens, before the large audience of the "Parnassus" literary society. In it, he sought to adapt his Olympic ideas to the perspectives of his Athenian listeners, in order to draw them toward an attitude with respect to the 1896 Games in Athens that would be more favorable than the rather reserved attitude of the Greek government.

He expressed his regret at the lack of a philosophical basis in modern sports, and spoke of the moral counterweight that should prevent its collapse.

5.1/1 SPEECH AT THE CLOSING BANQUET OF THE CONGRESS OF PARIS (1894)

Gentlemen, gratitude is among the virtues most easily practiced. It is also a feeling most easily expressed. At the close of this congress that has fulfilled the hopes of the first ten years of my adult life, as I look around to find those to whom I must express my thanks, I have the impression that my speech would turn into a litany. Therefore I hope, Gentlemen, that you will excuse me if I mention no one by name, and if, after expressing my profound thanks to all those who have helped and supported me, I ask you to look toward those *things* that dominate men in this world, and to reflect for a moment on a profoundly and strangely philosophical sight.

In this year, 1894, we have had the opportunity to meet in this great city of Paris, a city whose joys and worries are shared by the whole world, so much so that some have called it the nerve center of the world. We have had the opportunity to bring together representatives of international athletics and in a unanimous vote, so lacking in controversy is the principle, they decided to restore an idea that date backs some two thousand years, an idea that stirs men's hearts today as in days past, an idea that satisfies one of the most vital instincts and, regardless of what some may have said, one of the most noble. These same delegates, assembled in the temple of science, heard a two thousand-year-old melody with their own ears, a melody reconstructed through scholarly archaeology resulting from the successive labors of several generations. At the close of the Congress, electricity spread the news everywhere that Greek Olympism had come back into the world after an absence of several centuries.

1 "Les Fêtes du Congrès. [The Celebrations of the Congress]." In: *Bulletin du Comité International des Jeux Olympiques*, Paris, July 1894, no. 1, p. 3.

The Greek heritage is so vast, Gentlemen, that all those in the modern world who have conceived of physical exercise in one of its many aspects have legitimately been able to lay claim to Greece, which embraced them all. Some viewed training as a form of national defense, others as the search for physical beauty and health through a delicate balance between mind and body, yet others as that healthy drunkenness of the blood that has been called joie de vivre, and that exists nowhere else as intensely and as exquisitely as in exercising the body.

In Olympia, Gentlemen, there was all this, but there was also something more that we have not dared to put into so many words because, since the Middle Ages, the qualities of the body have been rather discredited, and they have been dissociated from the qualities of the mind. In recent times, bodily characteristics have been allowed to serve the mind, but they are still treated as slaves. Every day, they are made to feel their dependence and inferiority.

This has been an enormous mistake, the scientific and social consequences of which are, so to speak, impossible to calculate. In the end, Gentlemen, man is not made up of two parts, the body and the mind. There are three: body, mind, and character. Character is not formed by the mind, it is formed above all by the body. That is what the ancients knew, and that is what we are relearning, painfully.

Those of the old school have groaned at seeing us hold our Sessions in the midst of the Sorbonne. They realized that we were in revolt, and that we would end up destroying the edifice of their worm-eaten philosophy. This is true, Gentlemen. We are rebels, and that is why the press, which has always supported beneficial revolutions, has understood and helped us. In passing, let me thank the press wholeheartedly for this support.

Gentlemen, I am surprised at the language I have used, and that I have carried you up to such lofty heights. Please excuse me. If I were to go on, this joyful champagne would go flat with boredom, so let me hasten to give it center stage. I raise my glass to the Olympic idea, which has crossed the mists of time like a ray from the all-powerful sun and is returning to shine on the gateway to the twentieth century with the gleam of joyful hope.

Excerpt from the article: Les Fêtes du Congrès [The Celebrations of the Congress].
In: *Bulletin du Comité International des Jeux Olympiques,*
Paris, July 1894, no. 1, p. 3.

5.1/2 THE NEO-OLYMPISM. APPEAL TO THE PEOPLE OF ATHENS (NOVEMBER 16, 1894) LECTURE GIVEN TO THE PARNASSUS LITERARY SOCIETY AT ATHENS

LADIES AND GENTLEMEN,

You are all familiar, at least by reputation, with the Sorbonne building in Paris. It is the seat of our famous University whose history has, for so long now, been closely intertwined with events in the life of our country. The famous names associated with it and the learned works produced there all contribute to making that ancient house a respectable one, a house whose traditions have been preserved to this day in new and sumptuous walls. An immense amphitheater has been placed at the center of the new Sorbonne. One of our most skillful artists, Puvis de Chavannes, has placed a vivid fresco in it. It was there, in spring 1889, that the banners of all the world's universities were brought together for an international festival. It was also there, more recently, that universal science acclaimed the name of Pasteur on that illustrious scientist's seventieth birthday.

Finally, it was also there on last June 16 that Baron de Courcel, a senator, and now Ambassador of France to the Court of St. James, opened the International Congress for the restoration of the Olympic Games. Nearly two thousand people filled the hall. The government, the Academy, and the university were well represented. After the president of the Congress gave a remarkably erudite speech on the role of athletics in the world, the poet Jean Aicard struck a moving and vibrant note, singing the moral grandeur of the fight and of physical strength. Then in a sacred hush, for the first time in two thousand years choirs sang the hymn to Apollo unearthed at Delphi. The effect was deeply moving. In one of those mysterious glimpses that music sometimes gives us of lost worlds, for a few seconds those gathered at Paris perceived Greek antiquity in all its splendor.

From that moment on, Gentlemen, the Greek genius was among us, transforming a modest congress on athletic sports into a quest for moral betterment and social peace. My goal had been achieved.

I

At first I feared sarcastic comments, or at least the sort of ironic benevolence with which, in a time of skepticism, workers who do not seem to be adequate to their task are received. Just a year before, in the United States, I called a meeting of representatives of American athletics. Later in London, I met with top-level sportsmen. Having prepared the terrain in this way, I thought the Congress of Paris had some chance of success, though it still stood a great chance of failing. Gentlemen, such is the prestige of antiquity, particularly the part of antiquity you represent, that public opinion immediately supported this project, even though its scope was astonishingly broad and could have left the public disbelieving. Nor was there any smiling or scorn among those who misunderstood the plan, who believed that we were trying to revive not the fundamental idea of the Olympic institution but merely its external form. Yet would this total restitution of the past not be ridiculous and torturous? Just imagine a procession of Panathenians all dressed up in costume, ascending an artificial rock to a cardboard Propylaea, fake incense burning in painted wooden tripods while ancient hymns are sung to dead gods, their worship now replaced by a more austere, more divine, and more pure religion. Such an event would be a twofold blasphemy.

The thought that guided me was quite different. To explain better it to you, allow me to look to the past, and to retrace the history of athletics for you in broad outline.

Today we know that Egypt was unfamiliar with athletics. The silence of the hieroglyphs, so rich in details about all the circumstances of life on the banks of the Nile, has instructed us on this point. It is true that the Egyptian army was well trained. The locations of certain way-stations and information about the time needed to cover the distances between them allow us to compare the Pharaohs' soldiers with those in the modern infantry, in terms of the distance and pace of military marches. The comparison does the ancients proud. Wrestling was taught in the camps, as well, and curiously the rules are pretty much the same today. The winner had to overturn his opponent so that both shoulders touched the ground, forcing the opponent to admit defeat.

This was a shortened form of battle that was quite natural for man, whose instincts have always been warlike. Yet this is not the practice of sports, strictly speaking. All the less reason to go looking for traces of it in the Far East, in regions where the Buddha with his fixed smile dozes seated on a lotus, the very picture of physical inertia and indifference to the muscles.

Homer is a bit vague on the topic, and it was not truly until Lycurgus that sports came onto the world stage. Sports were brought onto that stage by education, and it was under the same aegis that they were to return to the stage a second time, in the early nineteenth century.

Of course, it is absolutely noble and beautiful to engage in manly exercises with the intention of defending one's country better and fulfilling one's duties as a citizen better. But there is another thing that is more perfectly human, if one dare speak in such terms. That is to seek in athletics a marvelous solidification of the human machine, a delicate balance of mind and body, the joy of a fresher and more intense life, the harmony of the faculties, calm and happy strength. Athletics can best serve the interests of a nation and enrich its destiny when viewed in this light. My Athenian friends, the honor for showing the world this particular approach belongs to you.

I need not retrace the manly splendors that it produced – you are more familiar with them than I. The life of the gymnasium was an admirable compromise between the two types of strength over which men fight, and that it is so difficult to bring back into balance once the equilibrium has been upset. Muscles and ideas rubbed shoulders congenially in this system. It seems that this harmony was perfect, to the point of uniting youth and old age, as well. As a rule, your ancestors were unfamiliar with the extravagances of the adolescent and the glumness of the old man. The science of living was at its height then, and the science of dying derived from it quite naturally. People knew how to live without fear and to die without regret for an immutable city and an undisputed religion – something, alas, that we no longer know how to do.

Then a seed of decadence slipped into this healthy existence. It is the same seed that, unless we are careful, will ruin our nascent hopes: money. Without doubt, the athlete of Olympia was protected, to a certain point, by the sacred nature of the exercises in which he engaged, and the crown of wild olive placed on the victor's head remained a symbol of selflessness and the chivalrous spirit. But his home town, overjoyed at his victory, enriched him beyond all measure, surrounding him in the prime of life with unreasonable luxury. What we call professionalism today is an old story, as you see. Certainly we are justified in believing that many citizens deplored these tendencies. But either they did not know how, or were simply unable, to put a stop to them. From year to year, the philosophy of athletics grew dimmer and dimmer. Eventually, it died out completely. As the centuries passed, athletics perished lamentably in the bestial drunkenness of the Roman circus.

Christianity fought it, both because it was pagan and because it was becoming cruel. A great wind from on high had overtaken ancient civilization, and had scattered its delicate ruins. A new law, one made of equality and solidarity, a harsh and grandiose law, was proclaimed to the universe. I have often thought of the look of indignant horror that the sublime words of the Sermon on the Mount would have produced in a pagan from the Golden Age. The most violent form of anarchy would not seem any more execrable or insane to a capitalist in our own day.

Yet there is no incompatibility whatsoever between Christian hopes and the cultivation of the body's abilities. The Middle Ages made a gross error in treating the human body as a pile of rags, and in teaching man to despise life. Yet sportsmen did exist even during that period so deeply marked by such sincere and naive absolutism. Chivalry was a vast athletic confraternity.

It may seem surprising that absolutism, upheld by the accomplishments of a small number of men, did not participate in the great movement known as the Renaissance. Humanity, at long last understanding the riches of which it had voluntarily deprived itself, retraced its steps to gather up those riches. It found only some of them, though it did put them to good use. Yet the others remained buried in the earth, like the wall panels, statues, columns, and mosaics that archaeology is bringing to the light of day for our enlightenment and instruction.

Gentlemen, even a most cursory study of the history of this century is surprising for the kind of moral disorder that the discoveries of industrial science seem to cause. Life has been turned upside down. People feel the earth on which they stand trembling at regular intervals beneath their feet. They no longer know what to hold on to, because everything around them is moving and changing. In their disarray, as though attempting to create a counterweight to the material forces that are piling up into cyclopean walls, they look for all the bits of moral force scattered throughout the world. I believe that this was the origin of the philosophical movement of the physical renaissance that was so pronounced in the fourteenth century.

Note that in most countries, some sort of upheaval brought this movement about. Prussia rallied after Iena, just as France did after Sedan. For both countries, the disaster for the national armed forces marked the beginning of a manly era when everything was directed toward recovery. In that task, gymnastics immediately assumed a preponderant role. Similarly in America, the taste for exercise began to grow following the terrible Civil War that shook the Republic of the United States to its very foundations. Until then, American society had pretended to disdain such exercise, and to hold that physical strength and intellectual culture were incompatible.

You see how history repeats itself. Although there is no modern-day Lycurgus to write an athletic code, the reflection of Sparta is quite evident. Alongside it Athens is being reborn along the foggy banks of the Thames. The two systems, the two theories, coexist once again: physical exercise for war, and athletics for the individual.

The Athenian idea is coming to light timidly, or at least much more modestly. The famed Kingsley and a number of his friends began to engage in sports. That was sixty years ago, and it was a novelty. England, which fate seems to have marked as the native country of sports, had never known them, in fact. It is not because a few lords with rather brutal customs rode at the hunt all day, nor because a few peasants played ball or practiced archery, that England can be considered the land of sports. Its youth was apathetic, and its pleasures were not lofty in the least. Thus Kingsley's exhibition was received with scornful disdain. The irony became all the more biting when his followers grew in number. Irony turned into anger – creatures of habit complained. Since then, we in France have learned the price of such outcries.

Then came Thomas Arnold, the greatest educator of modern times who, more than any other Englishman, is responsible for the current prosperity and prodigious expansion of his country. With Arnold, athletics made its way into a great school and transformed it. From the day the first generation, trained under his guidance, was released on the world, the affairs of the British Empire made an about face. There may not be any more striking example of the old truth that a handful of good workers can transform a whole society.

You all know what became of English athletics. Not only does athletics reign over education, where it provides the teacher with an extremely powerful yet very delicate instrument for moral education, but it has also invaded the territory of the entire Empire. Today, it is everywhere. In France, Germany, and Belgium it is rubbing elbows with traditional gymnastics, and is settling in alongside gymnastics as a highly ambitious younger brother. In Italy, Hungary, and in South America, and even in Russia and Spain, athletics is raising its flag. It is even here in Greece: your gymnastics associations, the Piraeus Rowers' Association, the Fencing Circle, and cycling clubs compare favorably with many associations already established in western Europe.

This movement is universal and fast moving. This is where we must remember the lessons of Antiquity. Let us avoid the pitfalls that the experience of your ancestors has shown us.

Modern sports has something more, and something less, than ancient sports. It has improved equipment: swimming, wrestling, and various forms of gymnastics are the only sports that have remained unchanged. Rowers row in skiffs or outriggers built to be exceptionally light. Cyclists move about on that wild creation, the bicycle, which is now advancing from one success to another. We have racquets, balls, skates, and foils that meet every demand.

What we lack, however, is the philosophical foundation, the loftiness of the goals, the whole patriotic and religious apparatus that surrounded the festivals of youth. Prior to the competitions, the athlete went through a sort of purification that was to make him worthy of appearing in them, and any defect in his life was an insurmountable obstacle. Today, it is impossible for us to imagine a cyclist being required to go to city hall for a certificate of good conduct in order to be allowed into the velodrome, or a fencer engaging in a knightly vigil at a church, like the knights of the Middle Ages. Yet we know that athletics is exposed to serious dangers, that it can decline into commercialism and into the mud, and we know that we must protect it from such a fate at all costs. If we fail to maintain its nobility, the hopes based upon it will be dashed. It will play no role at all in schools, and will have no effect on the life of the community. On the contrary, it will contribute to corruption by adding another element to it.

Is it impossible, then, to find the moral counterweight that is so urgently necessary, in a new order of ideas appropriate for the needs of the time?

Gentlemen, there are two trends in modern athletics to which I would like to draw your attention. It is becoming democratic and international. Its social revolution which has now been achieved among men – and which might be achieved in terms of things as well – explains the first of these characteristics; the speed of transportation and the frequency of communications explain the second.

I will not argue the merits or defects of democracy in this setting. I would like to use the words of Fr. Didon. One day, when someone in his presence was lamenting the rise of the democratic tide, the eloquent Dominican responded, "I never worry when people talk of what the weather is doing outside, for the simple reason that it is not within my power to change it". That is a wise thing, indeed. I might say the same regarding internationalism, understood of course as respect for, not destruction of, native countries. It is a trend that grew out of the deep need for peace and fraternity arising from the depths of the human heart. Peace has become a sort of religion, its altars surrounded day after day by an increasing number of faithful. How can we not mention this religion at a time when one of its leading pontiffs, the great Emperor, whose power was so gentle and whose authority so salutary, has entered into eternal rest amid the respect and grief of the whole world? Since I have mentioned this event which is particularly moving for you and for us, I must also mention the beloved and venerated leader of the French Republic, that just, upright, and good man in whose honor flags bore the band of mourning five months ago. One could write the words of Scripture on these two coffins as a glorious epitaph: Blessed are the Peacemakers!

Gentlemen, this is the order of ideas from which I intend to draw the elements of moral strength that must guide and protect the renaissance of athletics. Healthy democracy and wise and peaceful internationalism will make their way into the new stadium. There they will glorify the honor and selflessness that will enable athletics to carry out its task of moral betterment and social peace, as well as physical development.

That is why every four years the restored Olympic Games must provide a happy and fraternal meeting place for the youth of the world, a place where, gradually, the ignorance of each other in which people live will disappear. This ignorance perpetuates ancient hatreds, increases misunderstandings, and precipitates such barbaric events as fights to the finish.

II

What must these Olympic Games be in order to succeed and to measure up to what we expect of them? Your interest in asking us this question is all the greater because you will soon have the honor of hosting the first Games.

First I would like to focus on a point of singular importance, because it may lead to some confusion. Certainly we all agree that this celebration should be absolutely as dazzling as possible. But adding festivities of a different nature to the Games, such as fairs, industrial competitions, and popular exhibits, means compromising the success of the Games. The nature of these Games entails a certain sobriety of form that will make them all the more solemn. Do not be afraid that by making the program rather austere, you will be harming the overall outlook, or that you will drive visitors away. The honor of engaging in the struggle and the hope of being crowned victor at Athens, at the foot of the Acropolis, the joy of seeing this pure atmosphere, of seeing these horizons that nature and history have made doubly majestic, of visiting these plains and valleys from which science has managed to draw out secrets by unearthing buried cities, all this, believe me, is equal to any attraction that your ingeniousness could devise. The great celebration is to come to Athens. What other festival could be worth that?

The program for the 1896 Games, and please excuse me for using a few technical expressions here, the program of the Games as I recommend it to you on behalf of the International Committee that I represent, includes the following competitions, which can be divided into three groups.

Group one: Athletic sports, foot races, jumping, shot put.

Gymnastics, individual exercises, pull-ups, group movements, etc.

These events would be held in the Stadium.

The setting for the second group would be the bay and the plain of Phaleron.

Water sports, sailing races, rowing and swimming competitions would be held in the bay.

Cycling and other games, cricket, and lawn tennis, would take place on the plain.

The third group would include fencing, boxing, and wrestling, which would take place in the magnificent rotunda of the Zappeion. Shooting, for which you have a range, and the equestrian competition, finally, would take place at the handsome gymnasium of the Equestrian School. Having studied the issue, I do not think it is possible to hold a polo championship. Horse races have been excluded from the general program by the Congress of Paris, on the grounds that this is a sport in which emphasis is on the improvement of the animal, rather than that of the rider.

Please understand that this program has not been slapped together on the spur of the moment. This is not the place, however, to explain the harmony of the program to you. I can merely give you a rapid overview. The Games are set to run for thirty days.

The objections, for there are objections, can be summarized in the following points:

1. The Games will be very expensive. This is incorrect. The only rather considerable expenses are the preparation of the grounds and the construction of temporary bleachers in the Stadium, and the installation of a cycling track in the Phaleron.

In any event, the bicyclists of Athens are beginning to find that there is a need for one anyway. I would also mention the prices, except that Mr. Michel Bréal, a member of the Institut de France, and Mr. Alexander, Ambassador of the United States, have already begun a list of generous donors which leads me to believe that expenses will be considerably reduced on this account. Long ago, I had come up with an estimated total of some 200,000 francs. Today, now that I have a better idea of the facilities that the country has, I would reduce that figure to 150,000 francs, and there is no reason to believe that further economies may not be realized. I believe that the 150,000 francs will be recovered quickly, plus interest.

2. The second objection is based on your alleged athletic inferiority. This inferiority is absolutely relative and theoretical. I would not bet two drachmas that your athletes will fail to win any laurels at the Olympic Games. And then, Gentlemen, did your forefathers weigh and re-weigh their chances before rising against the Turks? Had they done so, you would not be free now. These are things that do not bear discussion, they are unworthy of you!

When we began to play football with the English, we expected to lose. In our seventh meeting, we beat them, and we started up again not two weeks ago! In this context, the dishonor lies not in being beaten, but in not fighting in the first place.

III

Now I come to a concern of a more delicate nature, one which has come to light a bit late, but which is nonetheless worthy of consideration. People have asked whether it is appropriate to have an international competition held in Athens at a time when Greece is in a rather anomalous position with respect to certain European powers.

Gentlemen, modesty is a beautiful thing, but as the song says, you can have too much of a good thing, excess is all things is a flaw! I am well aware that yours is a small country, a fact that people point out to you over and over. But of what importance is that to me if, at the same time, you are a great race? Is the influence that nations have exercised throughout the ages ever measured by the size of their geographical borders? Has the Hebrew people, never outstanding in either the perfection or the size of its national organization, not shaken the foundations of the world? As divided as they were, did your ancestors not invent the cult of the ideal beauty that is art?

But therein lies the problem. Your magnificent past is such a heavy burden that it is crushing the present. In other countries, some people are in the habit of considering you as mere sentinels guarding a treasure. God forgive me, I believe that even here, some Greeks have been persuaded that their modern mission must be limited to that function alone. A whole form of literature has expanded on this idea in various ways, from the scholar Fallmerayer and his paradoxical conclusions to the sad About, whose pamphlet seems to have been written in a concierge's lodge by some retired theater worker – acerbic, witty, and short-sighted.

I can readily understand that once one has ascended to the Parthenon, which is, in a way, the basic pilgrimage of all humanity, one is more readily accompanied by the shades of Phidias and Pericles. But when one goes back down into Athens, into the modern Athens that is so lively, so robust, and so full of zeal and gusto, and particularly when one reflects on the fact that sixty years ago there was nothing here but a few tumble-down houses, and that all this is the product of barely two generations, the names Ypsilanti, Capo d'Istria, and Colocotronis come to the lips. One bows with respect to their memory, before the immense suffering, labor, and longing – hopes always dashed but never extinguished – that was your history in the dark days of captivity.

Here, Europe is intervening once again to seek your gratitude. It seems that Europe has done everything, and truly when one recalls how late its cooperation was and with what poor grace it provided that cooperation, Europe's claims seem a bit ridiculous in retrospect. I am well aware that you have a Lord Byron, a Santa-Rosa, and a Fabvrier to console you for the ingratitude and indifference of governments. Thanks to them, you can forgive the Austrians for having provided supplies to the Turks, the Lord Commissioners of the Seven Islands for having persecuted your Ionian brothers. You can forget the disdain of Mr. de Villèle and the grotesque considerations of Mr. de Salab on the "legitimacy" of the Ottoman yoke.

Gentlemen, in the long series of events that have astonished the nineteenth century, from the brilliant era that marked its beginnings to the great social upheaval that is troubling its waning years, there have been three events to which the adjective "marvelous" can be applied. We have seen Germany and Italy become unified, we have seen the Republic of the United States grow in a colossal way, and we have seen the light of civilization shine on the vast continent of Africa. In terms of science, we have seen a series of extraordinary discoveries that have nearly changed the basic conditions of human life. But all that has been nothing more than a logical outcome in keeping with the laws of universal development. It required a fair amount of perspicacity to foresee these results, yet there was nothing in them that ran counter to the nature of things. The situation is quite different for the three events that I would like to discuss. Those events are: France after 1870, and the radical transformation of the Empire of Japan. In terms of Greece, a race that has been subject to every conceivable torture, which has suffered the longest and most formidable form of enslavement, has risen to freedom on its own, through a simple demonstration of invincible will and energy. In terms of France, an exhausted country worn out by revolution and rendered skeptical through the collapse of its successive governments, obtained wealth, stability, and calm after an unspeakable disaster, by seeking them in the extreme opposite of its previous situation. In terms of Japan, a great people believed frozen in the depths of an ancient civilization has suddenly been rejuvenated, and has entered lock, stock and barrel, so to speak, into the complicated existence of the western world. All this is illogical, as illogical as an earthquake or volcanic eruption, the causes of which exist, but so hidden and so internalized that we can no longer discern them.

Gentlemen, whatever the case may be, and to return to the matter at hand, you have achieved one of the greatest feats of the century. Your perseverance has raised the spirits of all captives. You have achieved the victory of justice, you have forced the hand of fate. Now you can look forward with confidence, recalling the immortal words of Gambetta: "Great reparations may come from right, and we or our children may hope for them, for the future is open to everyone."

Therefore, always look to eternal Greece through the passing vicissitudes of your national life. Do not refuse the honor that a friend has been long in preparing for you, an honor given to you under the vaulted ceilings of the Sorbonne with enthusiastic unanimity, and with a quiver of gratitude and emotion.

There exists among you a form of patriotism that I have not seen developed to such an extent anywhere else but in the United States. For a good citizen who has lived and grown rich far from his native country, patriotism consists of designating the country as an heir of some of his goods. In this way Athens has seen many of its most handsome buildings built, and a number of its most useful institutions created. I mention the name Zappas here, because the men who bore it seem to have been particularly inspired, recalling that commercial activity and athletics were the great strengths of your past. Across from the monument decorated with their statues, the old Stadium awaits universal youth. It is there that the modern Olympic Games should be inaugurated on the Tuesday after Easter, 1896.

In conclusion, I would like to recall this truly typical incident, culled from one of the last chapters in the history of the people of Israel. In his incomparable prose style, Renan tells us of the curious attempt by Antiochus the Great to Hellenize Jerusalem. To achieve his objectives, the first thing Antiochus built was...a gymnasium.

Gentlemen, I leave you with that thought. The passing centuries have not decreed a divorce between athletics and Hellenism. Their union was so close that no such divorce will ever be decreed. As you toil on behalf of sport, rest assured that you are working on behalf of your native country!

Le Néo-olympisme. Appel à l'opinion athénienne.
In: *Le Messager d'Athènes*, Athens, 1894,
no. 39, pp. 287-288 (I); no. 42, pp. 306-309 (II).

5.1/3 WHY I REVIVED THE OLYMPIC GAMES.

In this article from 1908, which survived only in this Engllsh version, Coubertin tries a location requirement of the Olympic movement with regard to the forthcoming Olympic Games in London in 1908. In a similar though much shorter way, as in his essay "Une Olympie moderne" Coubertin refers to the example of the antique Olympic Games for the modern time and from this derives the main difference to world championships. Typical for Coubertin's creative powers in those days is the further development of the sense of the Games, from the fair play, the beauty of the fight and national representation to a total philosophical idea, Olympism. He mentions "humanity in general" as the greatest fundamental element. The relation to the white race in the final sentence of this article can only be interpreted from the point of view of 1908. Special notice is given to the contribution of arts.

This contribution which is merely preserved in the English translation can be regarded as the most detailed early presentation of Olympism from Coubertin's hand.

If, in reviving the Olympic Games I had merely sought to restore one of the noblest and most interesting of ancient institutions, I do not think I should have needed an excuse, for such an ambition would certainly have been both comprehensible and legitimate. It might, however, have been reasonably characterised as a fanciful and superfluous undertaking. There is so much work to be done to supply the myriad needs of our day that we ought not to waste ourselves in unnecessary efforts. I have in mind a statement by the great Dr Arnold about the cultivation of some rare plants. "How interesting", he said, "to give oneself up to this if only one's life could be twice as long as it really is !" But the Olympic Games are in no way comparable to the cultivation of rare plants. It is my profound conviction that they are one of the cornerstones of progress and health for the youth of our day. Let it be understood that if among the readers of this article there are any who despise athletic Sports, and see in them nothing but expensive and puerile amusements, I do not address myself to them, for we have no common ground of argument. But I do not expect to encounter such a point of view, it would be quite out of date. Certainly there have been abuses, particularly in England and the United States, and it is always right to combat abuses; but this does not affect the value of the fundamental principle underlying the practice of athletic sports-that there is nothing else with which young men can employ their strength in their hours of recreation and liberty with such advantage both moral and physical. It is not the moment when the whole civilised world, from Petersburg to Madrid and from Tokyo to Punta Arenas, is adopting Anglo-Saxon ideas on this point, that Anglo-Saxons themselves are likely to renounce them.

Well, then, the athletic life of modern youth demands the revival of the Olympic Games; and fully convinced I called for their revival, not merely thinking of France or England, Greece or Italy, but of humanity in general. But, I may be asked, what difference do you make between the Olympic Games and what are nowadays called world-championships? Were the games of antiquity anything else than our competitions for world-championships, on their own lines, and taking into account the meaning of the word "world"? I do not deny that, and I agree that world-championships do form part of the Olympic Games; nevertheless, the Olympic Games are "something else" as well, and it is just this, "something else" that matters, as it is not to be found in any other variety of athletic competition.

There are two ways of regarding athletic sport: first, the individual point of view, which is, let me hasten to say, the best and the most desirable. On the day when a nation exists in which each young man possesses sufficient taste for physical exercises to make him practise them regularly , either alone or with his comrades, seeking in wholesome sports an admirable means to perfect his health and increase his strength, then on that day humanity-or a section of it, at least-will have realised perfection. But we are not there yet, and hence we are constrained to regard athletic sport from a second and quite different point of view-that of organised competition. Athletics for the sake of winning something: this directly is the potent incentive and the dangerous canker with which we have to reckon. Potent incentive, we cannot deny; the most potent of all, in fact. Human society works by the principle of competition; it has always been so, and will remain so. Competition is becoming more and more intense, bringing greater and greater dangers of corruption. Unbridled competition entails grave risks to the Spirit of fair play, gives occasions of blameworthy acts to the commission, engenders a lamentable atmosphere of jealousy, envy, vanity , and mistrust. This can be seen in all branches of activity, and athletic life cannot escape from it. Certainly athletic organisations, societies, and federations lead no placid and peaceful existence; they are torn by violent quarrels, and too often seek to injure one another, to steal away each other's champions. This state of things will continue, being, indeed almost inevitable. I am forced to acknowledge that the individual practice of athletic sports, regularly and perseveringly undertaken for the sake of health, beauty, and harmony, is a chimera. A few individuals may be capable of this, but the rank and file will never be.

We must therefore fall back upon the system of organised competition, and allow it to dominate athletic sport. But we can give it a counterpoise, a regulator, as those ancient Greeks did who, we find out, had to grapple with most of the problems that perplex us. Their regulator was Olympia. At Olympia vulgar competition was transformed, and in a sense sanctified, by contact with national sentiment superbly excited.

Over-excited, I might even say; for it was excess that in the end ruined and corrupted ancient athleticism. But the end came very slowly. For centuries athleticism, its home in Olympia, remained pure and magnificent. There states and cities met in the person of their young men, who, imbued with a sense of the moral grandeur of the Games, went to them in a spirit of almost religious reverence. Men of letters and of the arts, ready to celebrate the victories of their energy and muscle assembled around them; and these incomparable spectacles were also the delight of the populace. No doubt, low ambitions and mean passions were present; there is no human assembly without them, no human institution which they do not infest. But despite them the whole result was something grandiose and strong, which dominated Hellenic civilisation, happily and gloriously influencing the youth of the country, and through them the entire nation.

Such were the Olympic Games of ancient times; such should be those of our own day. I have clearly perceived the danger run by athleticism in an atmosphere of advertisement and bluff, such as our modern atmosphere is apt to be in a society where effort is generally applied to the quest for material gain, where athletic sports are likely to be commercially exploited by the organisers of public exhibitions. I

Opening bars of the Olympic Anthem with a dedication by composer Spiridon Samara. It was performed at the 1896 Opening Ceremony and became the official IOC Anthem in 1958. The text was written by Kostas Palama. (Georgios Dolianitis Collection)

saw the necessity for re-establishing the Olympic Games as a supreme consecration of the cult of athletics practised in the purest spirit of true sport, proudly, joyfully, and loyally. But to reach a realisation of the idea many stages had to be achieved, and naturally this took time. First of all, the new Games have to be exclusively modern in form; to revive chariot-races, for instance, would only have been possible by instituting a hippodrome devoid of interest for the mass of young men, and to make mere actors of the participants; an overloaded programme would be the result because modern sports are very numerous. Secondly, the new Games must be international; that is to say, the competitors must be the best representatives of civilised nations. In ancient times they were already international in the sense that there was as much difference between the citizens of the various cities of Greece, Italy, and Egypt as there could be now between an Englishman, a Spaniard, and an Italian. Those cities readily went to war with one another, and even in times of peace their rivalries were acute. But in our days, despite the rapidity and number of means of transport, it is not easy to periodically unite representatives of all countries, because of the difficulties they encounter in leaving their daily occupations, and in finding, either wholly or in part, the necessary contingent expenses.

It was done, however, in 1896, 1900, and 1904, not to speak of the Athenian series of games inaugurated in 1906. We may,therefore, consider that one stage has been accomplished, and that the Olympic Games of London are going to consummate definitive success. Our English friends have brought a truly admirable zeal and intelligence to the preparation of the Fourth Olympiad. Lord Desborough has been a matchless president, and how can I say enough about the moving and working spirit of the organisation, the Rev. R. S. de Courcy Laffan, who gives us a spectacle of antique virtue revived in devoting to the cause of athletic sport, a mind of the highest culture, accustomed to interest itself in the great concerns of morals and philosophy ? Surely, during the twelve years they have been celebrated with an ever-increasing brilliancy of success, the Olympic Games have given proof of sufficient vitality to assure their future, and we no longer need to fear any break in the continuity of our revived Olympiads.

Will the achievement then have reached the culminating point for which I have been aiming? Far from it; and I do not even hesitate to say that in my eyes only the pedestal of the structure is complete. Anyone who studies the ancient Games will perceive that their deep significance was due to two principal elements: beauty and reverence. If the modern Games are to exercise the influence I desire for them they must in their turn show beauty and inspire reverence-a beauty and a reverence infinitely surpassing anything hitherto realised in the most important athletic contests of our day. The grandeur and dignity of processions and attitudes, the impressive splendour of ceremonies, the concurrence of all the arts, popular emotion and generous sentiment, must all in some sort collaborate together. This cannot be achieved by a single Olympiad, nor even by three or four; it will need at least a quarter of a century. But, then, when one aspires to create or recreate institutions of this magnitude, the first condition is not to be in a hurry.

Here again we must be resolutely modern. Let us have no clumsy and tactless restitutions. But it is possible to draw inspiration from the past without copying it. To take one example from many: at Olympia the competitors-and it was certainly not one of the least impressive episodes of the Games-assembled before the statue of Jupiter and took solemn oath that they would compete fairly and loyally, swearing also that they were without reproach and worthy to meet their adversaries. Jupiter does not exist any more, and we have lost faith in statues. But I see the athletes of the future taking the oath before the Games, each upon the flag of their own country, and in the presence of the flags of other lands solemnly affirming that they have always been loyal and honourable in sport, and that it is in a spirit of loyalty and honour they approach the Olympic contests. Would not this provide a scene of dignified beauty fit to inspire actors and spectators alike with the most noble and generous emotions? And similarly, if for vulgar choruses and bands performing selections from operettas we were to substitute an interpretation by great massed choirs of masterpieces by a Handel or a Gluck, should we not be confirming in the completest manner the marriage of Arts and Sports-that is to say, of muscular strength and creative imagination, those two poles of human life?

In this order of ideals all is yet to be done; but much has been prepared in the path of progress. The International Olympic Committee, in summoning a conference which met at the Comédie Française in Paris in 1906, and henceforward discussed the best means for drawing together Sports, Arts, and Letters, gave the signal for a movement of high importance in this line. Henceforth, the scattered efforts of artists can be directed towards a definite aim. Sculptors and musicians have already grasped the possibility of seeking new inspiration in athleticism. At this moment the whole of Brussels is admiring the splendid group, “Lutteurs à Cheval,” from the chisel of the great Belgian sculptor, Jacques de Lalaing; Paris has been hearing with emotion Augusta Holmès's fine oratorio, entitled “Ludus pro Patria“; and the ears of Athenians still ring with the harmonies of the “Olympic Hymn”. composed by the Greek musician Samara. Meanwhile Architects have attempted to evolve plans for gymnasiums modelled on antique ideals. When he died, Bartholdi, the celebrated sculptor, left the International Olympic Committee the designs for a "Monument des Sports", which was to be one of the finest works of art that the world had seen. On the other side, dramatic art is by degrees accustoming itself once more to the open air, and in many different countries performances recalling the theatre of antiquity take place. Finally, in Switzerland the well-known musician Jaques-Dalcroze is striving with admirable zeal to reform choreographic art, degraded as it has been by the vulgarity and stupidity of our modern dances.

Thus, on all sides individual efforts are ready to converge towards an ideal of general harmony. The arts are drawing together, sound, line, colour, and form seem to be preparing to associate once more in movement, which is living beauty, and thus to constitute the spectacular element of the modern Olympiad. With their aid a worthy setting for the Games may be framed -a setting in which athletes shall move well prepared to assist in the great festival, and shall be conscious of the special glory it confers upon them. It is the rule now that no one can take part in the Olympic Games other than as a representative of his own country. This is a first step, for previously the nationality of competitors had not always been taken into account, but merely their technical qualities. A fundamental article of the general regulations drawn up in 1894 reserves the right of the organising committees to reject any candidate whose character or previous record of conduct might reflect injuriously upon the dignity of the institution. We must establish the tradition that each competitor shall in his bearing and conduct as a man of honour and a gentleman endeavour to prove in what respect he holds the Games and what an honour he feels to participate in them. Then we should revive, as I have said, the ceremony of the oath; and we should seek the means to conclude the Olympiad with a distribution of prizes commensurate with the dignity of the occasion. At present this prize-giving takes place in a wretchedly undignified fashion. The victors, hastily clothed, listen to some dull little speech, and then carry their prizes off under their arm in the midst of the rough cheers of their comrades. The question of costume is a somewhat delicate one. Modern dress, for men at least, is not a thing of beauty. But the costume of his sport is to the athlete what his uniform is to the soldier, and it is in that garb he ought to appear at the final ceremony. The procession of victors-ridiculous in the clothes of town-life -would at once gain charm if fencers carried their weapons and tennis players their racquets, if cyclists led their machines and polo-players held their sticks, all wearing the costumes of their respective sport.

Such is my view of the development which ought to take place in the institution of the modern Olympic Games. I myself am determined to work for this, and I feel assured of the concurrence of all my loyal collaborators, among whom I count-and in the first rank-Father Time himself, because without him nothing lasting can be achieved in such undertakings. The work must be lasting, to exercise over the sports of the future that necessary and beneficent influence for which I look-an influence which shall make them the means of bringing to perfection the strong and hopeful youth of our white race, thus again helping towards the perfection of all human society.

Translated by Helen Chisholm.
In: *Fortnightly Review,* vol. LXXXIV, New Series, July 1908, pp.110-115.

5.1/4 – 5.1/8 INTRODUCTION

In late 1918 and early 1919, Coubertin published twenty-one "Olympic Letters" in the Lausanne newspaper, *La Gazette.* The purpose of these letters was to rouse the sympathies of the readers in support of Olympism and of the work done in Lausanne by the Olympic movement, such as the Olympic Institute. Five of these letters dealing with major topics in Olympism are included here.

In his "Olympic Letter III" dated October 26, 1918, Coubertin expressed his concern regarding general principles of education that take into consideration the mind only, or the body only. The perspectives of Olympism, on the contrary, are broad and open.

The "Olympic Letter IV" dated November 2, 1918, contains a significant definition of Olympism as "a state of mind".

The "Olympic Letter VII" dated December 11, 1918, raises questions about the "recipe" for "becoming Olympic". The answer is astonishingly simple.

Letter XIII underlines the life force of Olympism, in spite or precisely because of the bitter experiences of World War I. In this text, Coubertin rejects the YMCA's plans to move the Olympic Games forward to 1919 in Paris. Only the four-year rhythm can safeguard the future of the Olympic Movement. With this, Coubertin is also reacting to the wish of US General Pershing to hold the planned Inter-Allied Games in 1919 in Paris as a "War Olympics".

In his Olympic Letter XXI, Coubertin returns to this issue with even greater plain speaking. As a man of principle, Coubertin does not want to bow to political pressure.

5.1/4 OLYMPIC LETTER III: OLYMPISM AND EDUCATION

Somewhere, Montaigne wrote that one should imagine the body and the soul as two horses yoked to the same shaft. He hitches them up two at a time. I prefer to hitch them up four at a time, and to distinguish not only the body and the mind, which is too simplistic, but rather the muscles, the understanding, the character, and the conscience. This corresponds to the four-fold duty of the educator. But both cases involve hitching things up, and the major flaw in modern education is that it is no longer conversant with the art of hitching up, i.e. of associating the action of divergent forces into a harmonious convergence. It has allowed itself to be carried away by extreme compartmentalization, by which it was then swept away. Each strength works in isolation, without any link or contact with its neighbor. If the topic is muscles, the only thing they want to see is animal function. The brain is furnished as though it were made up of tiny, air-tight compartments. Conscience is the exclusive territory of religious training. As for character – no one wants to take responsibility for that. In a short time, the educated man will end up looking like those primitive mosaics in which little pieces formed larger, crude and stiff pictures. What a decline in comparison to Greek education, which was so lucid, its outline so clear!

Let us not try to hide the fact that Olympism is a reaction against these unfortunate tendencies. Olympism refuses to make physical education a purely physiological thing, and to make each type of sport an independent, separate exercise. It refuses to catalogue the knowledge of the mind, and to classify it into mutually isolated categories. Olympism refuses to accept the existence of a deluxe education reserved for the wealthy classes, no shred of which should be handed out to the working classes. It refuses to condense art into pills that everyone will take at set hours and to establish timetables of thought along the lines of railways schedules. Olympism is a destroyer of dividing walls. It calls for air and light for all. It advocates a broad-based athletic education accessible to all, trimmed with manly courage and the spirit of chivalry, blended with esthetic and literary demonstrations, and serving as an engine for national life and as a basis for civic life. That is its ideal program. Now can it be achieved?

Lettre olympique III,
in: *La Gazette de Lausanne,* no. 294, October 26, 1918, p. 1.

5.1/5 OLYMPIC LETTER IV: OLYMPISM AS A STATE OF MIND

Did I present modern Olympism last time as being imbued with the revolutionary spirit, when I said that its purpose was to tear down the dividing walls in education? Yet knocking down walls means transforming the layout of a building, not destroying the supporting walls or even altering the look of the architecture. I do not want to incur this reproach, being among those who consider revolutions violent and almost always fruitless. Most revolutions kick in doors that were in the process of opening, and the sudden brusqueness of the gesture causes the door to fall back on itself and close once again. What is more, the only true revolutions are those movements that intend to put ready-made institutions into place suddenly, each detail of which has been worked out in advance. This has nothing at all to do with Olympic education. Olympism is not a system, it is a state of mind. The most widely divergent approaches can be accommodated in it, and no race or time can hold an exclusive monopoly on it.

Olympism is a state of mind that derives from a twofold doctrine: that of effort, and that of eurythmy. Notice how much the association of these two elements, the taste for excess and the taste for due measure, is in keeping with human nature. Though apparently contradictory, they are the basis for any total virility. Is there any man, in the full sense of the word, who is constantly worried about being sparing in his strength, limiting his initiatives, and who takes no pleasure whatsoever in going beyond what is expected of him? At the same time, however, is there any man in the full sense of the word who is displeased at seeing his intense zeal crowned with joyful tranquillity and self-control, surrounded by order, balance, and harmony?

Neither the tendency toward effort nor the habit of eurythmy develop spontaneously in us. They require apprenticeship and training. Don't count on the hypotenuse of the square, even backed up by the fables of La Fontaine, to take their place. These virtues become part of our nature, taking root in us through practice. That is what makes organized athletic activity superior, the fact that it imposes both measure and excess on anyone engaging in it.

Lettre olympique IV,
in: *La Gazette de Lausanne*, no. 319, November 22, 1918, p. 1.

"The Joy of Effort", bronze medallion produced for the Olympic arts competition by Professor R. Tait McKenzie, USA, 1912. A bronze cast was made and given by the USOC to Sweden to remember the Fifth Olympic Games. It was placed in a wall beside the Olympic Stadium entrance at Pierre de Coubertin's request (taken from E.Petersen/ S.Hermlin, Dem Femte Olympiaden. Olympiska Spelen i Stockholm 1912 i bild och ord, Gothenburg, Ahlen & Akerlund, 1912, p.358)

5.1/6 OLYMPIC LETTER VII: THE RECIPE FOR "BECOMING OLYMPIC"

If someone were to ask for the recipe for "becoming Olympic", I would say that the first prerequisite is to be joyful. No doubt, my answer seems surprising. The term "Olympic" incorrectly evokes an idea of tranquil balance, of forces in perfect counterbalance, a scale in perfect equilibrium. *Mens sana...* the old saying that pops up in speeches when prizes are awarded. But come now! This is hardly human, or at the very least, hardly youthful! It is an ideal for old fossils! In life, balance is a result, not a goal, a reward rather than something to be sought out. It is not achieved by taking every possible precaution, but by alternating one's efforts.

Well I ask you, what feeds effort but joy? As Jules Simon once said, "When one climbs up to the mountain tops, one must see joyful humanity... Let us be joyful!" That was how he ended his opening speech at the Congress on Physical Education held in 1889, a congress that did so much good in guiding French opinion, particularly that of young people in the schools, into new directions. His hand rested on my arm, punctuating his original speech with an energetic gesture. He preached by example, the dear man. He had known disappointments and difficulties. Life's problems had never spared him, and well-deserved victories had escaped him. To see him view life from such an obstinately joyful angle proves that in this business, physical health is not everything, and that the joy in question is not exclusively animal in nature.

Of course, athletes know the price of good muscular humor and the strength of the contentment that it provides, but it is not enough to create the total joy in which another element plays a part: altruism.

Now we have gone from Olympism to the Gospel. "Love your neighbor as yourself", commands the Good Book, in teaching the paths of salvation. Rejoice in humanity that is constantly being reborn, advises Olympism. Have faith in it, pour out your energy on it, mix your hopes with its. Egotistical joy is not an intermittent sun. Altruistic joy is a perpetual dawn.

Lettre olympique VII,
in: *La Gazette de Lausanne,* no. 388, December 11, 1918, p. 1.

5.1/7 OLYMPIC LETTER XIII: THE PERIODICITY OF THE OLYMPIC GAMES

In Paris, people fuss, they fuss intensely. That could be the refrain of an appropriate song, the verses of which would go on and on. Rather than list the things that people in Paris do fuss about, it would be quicker to list what they don't.

They are also fussing about the Olympic Games. When they learned that the new municipality of Strasbourg was having a stadium built bear the Kehl bridge in order to give the unemployed something to do, the Parisians wanted to hold world championships there in 1920. In addition, the committee of the YMCA, an organization that gets involved in lots of things because of the great services that it has rendered in many areas, is talking about a "Super-Olympiad" to be held this spring in the Paris area. What on earth is a "Super-Olympiad?" When he entered Babylon, not even the victorious Alexander, as eager as he was to Hellenize the East, came up with such a thing.

Our friends are growing alarmed at this disorder, which threatens the Olympic calendar. They are growing alarmed at all these conflicting plans. They should rest assured. Recently a generous initiative presented the Olympic flag, inaugurated in 1914, to the universities of the New World. The flag features five multicolored rings blazing against a snow white background. Now the Greek government is going to join in the Twenty-Fifth Anniversary of the Restoration of the Games by erecting a marble stele in the ruins of Olympia to commemorate the importance of the event.

All this goes to show that the Olympic idea is coming out of the crucible of war even more alive than when it went in. We should expect that the Seventh Olympiad (which occurs in 1920, not 1919) will suffer somewhat from the excitement that its very approach is arousing. That is hardly what matters. When I restored the Olympiads, I did not look to what was nearby, I looked to the far-off future. I wanted to give the world, in an enduring way, an ancient institution whose guiding principle was becoming necessary for its health.

It is this same principle, and the many applications that contemporary civilization authorizes of it, that I am trying to analyze in the course of these Letters, which my readers in the Canton of Vaud are welcoming with great support... and now I will get back to my subject.

Lettre olympique XIII,
in: *La Gazette de Lausanne*, no. 31, February 1, 1919, p. 1.

5.1/8 OLYMPIC LETTER XXI: THE PERSHING OLYMPIAD

I am obliged, after briefly taking leave of my *Gazette* readers, to add a short post-script to my Letters, at the risk of competing with the comments by Mr. Philippe Godet on the daily outrages to which the French language is subjected. Here is one that closely concerns Olympism, and to which recent abuses require us to draw the public's attention. A French newspaper, which is at times not afraid to massacre grammar – as is true, alas, of so many others like it -, describes the inter-allied military contests led by the head of the American army as the "Pershing Olympiad". This is the result of both historical and technical ignorance. An Olympiad is a date on the calendar established, based on fixed and equal intervals of four years. It is therefore absurd to speak of organizing an Olympiad. As the Olympiads were re-established, starting from 1896, nothing can prevent the seventh from starting in 1920, the eight in 1924, the ninth in 1928, and so on. The only issue that arises is that of celebrating these Olympiads with Games. The sixth (1916) could not be celebrated in Berlin as had been intended. The seventh (1920) is expected to be celebrated in Antwerp. Olympiads can, therefore, in no case be likened to the Games with which they are customarily celebrated. For their part, these Games have a program that is summarized succinctly in the words: all games, all nations. The very essence of the Olympic Games is that they are international and include different types of sports: gymnastic and athletic sports, combat sports, water sports, equestrian sports, etc. The term Olympic is constantly used to describe local or technically limited competitions. This is a mistake. It was necessary to point this out, and explain once more the value of terms that are becoming commonly used.

Lettre olympique XXI,
in: *La Gazette de Lausanne,* no.134, May 17, 1919, p.1.

5.1/9 THE TWENTY-FIFTH ANNIVERSARY OF THE PROCLAMATION OF THE OLYMPIC GAMES

The speech that Coubertin gave at the celebration of the twenty-fifth anniversary of the proclamation of the Olympic Games, in Lausanne in 1919, makes a clear distinction between Olympism and plain athletics.

Global political upheavals, particularly the October Revolution in Russia, finally brought Coubertin to proclaim the opening of Olympism to the masses of all countries, before a meeting of all the members of the IOC[1]

It has been five years since representatives from all countries came to Paris to celebrate the twentieth anniversary of the restoration of the Olympic Games, an event that took place in Paris in 1894. Five years have passed, and in the interim a world has collapsed. Olympism is not a victim of the catastrophe. It has weathered the storm without fear and without reproach. Horizons have suddenly grown wide before it, bearing witness to the importance of the new role ahead.

1 A famous event took place during the festivities of the twenty-fifth anniversary. The President of the French Council, Georges Clemenceau, with the consent of the Swiss government, sent a flying honor guard to show the high esteem in which he held Coubertin's work.

Olympism is the veneration of peaceful and confident youth. Day by day, peacefulness and confidence became increasingly useful tools for the old civilization of yesteryear, given its occasional lack of strength. Peacefulness and confidence are essential foundations for the youthful civilization of tomorrow, which will be born amidst raging storms. Yet they are not natural companions. From the cradle on, human beings grow alarmed. Throughout life, fear lies in wait. As the grave draws near, fear tries to overwhelm them. Man has been able to fight this enemy, which so skillfully troubles his work and rest, through his courage, a noble virtue that some attributed only to the ancestors in the belief that the present generation has allowed its flower to fade in their hands. Now we know what to say about all this.

But courage is a virtue of war, giving rise to temporary heroes. As I once said in a treatise on education, the real antidote, the permanent antidote to fear is not courage but confidence, and confidence does not work without its sister, peacefulness. So we return to what I was pointing out earlier as the essence of Olympism, and how Olympism differs from the simple athletics that it encompasses and surpasses.

Let me make this distinction clear. The athlete enjoys his effort. He likes the constraint that he imposes on his muscles and nerves, through which he comes close to victory even if he does not manage to achieve it. This enjoyment remains internal, egotistical in a way. Imagine if it were to expand outward, becoming intertwined with the joy of nature and the flights of art. Picture it radiant with sunlight, exalted by music, framed in the architecture of porticoes. It was thus that the glittering dream of ancient Olympism was born on the banks of the Alphaeus, the vision of which dominated ancient society for so many centuries.

We stood at one of those turning points in history when the human spirit, eager for progress but often derailed by exaggerating a good idea, was on the verge of throwing adolescence off kilter. Adolescence was about to shoulder the burden of drab, complicated educational theory, a moral code that alternated between awkward indulgence and unwise severity, and a hesitant and mean-spirited philosophy. That is why we believed that the time had come to reopen the Olympic era, and through that act to give fruitful sanction to the athletic renewal that was in its infancy. We did so by bringing together the athletic utilitarianism of the Anglo-Saxons and the prestigious and resonant approaches bequeathed by Ancient Greece. After weighing the practical chances for the undertaking in New York and London, I asked immortal Greece for the dose of idealism required for this remarkable synthesis. Gentlemen, that work has now been solidified by a quarter century of success. You have just paid tribute to this effort in terms that would have embarrassed me, if the words were meant for the worker. This worker is not aware of deserving such praise, because all he did was obey an instinct that was stronger than his own will. But he accepts joyfully these expressions of praise for the Idea, of which he was but the first servant.

Earlier I mentioned the festivities of June, 1914. At the time, we thought we were celebrating the total success of this idea. Yet today I have the impression that I am seeing its rebirth. The reason is that now, nothing is accomplished when only limited numbers are involved. That may have been sufficient before, but not now. The masses must be touched. In truth, in the name of what can the masses be excluded from Olympism? By virtue of what aristocratic decrees does there exist some link between physical beauty and the muscular power of a young man, between his perseverance in training and his desire to win, on the one hand, and, on the other hand, the list of his forefathers or the contents of his wallet? Such contradictions in terms, which are unfounded in law, lived on after the social organization that created them. It is morally right that it was an autocratic gesture based on an outburst of barbarous militarism that dealt them the death blow.

Faced with a new world that must be ordered according to principles thought to be utopian until now, and that can now be applied, humanity must find all the strength it can in the heritage of the past in order to build its future. Olympism is one of those strengths. To guarantee social peace, it will not be enough to distribute the effort of production and the ease of consumption of the objects needed for material life more equitably among men. Nor will it be enough to give adolescents free access to intellectual development in keeping with their mental capacities, rather than in keeping with the social position of their parents. The pleasure of the muscles, that source of joy, energy, calm, and purity, must also be placed within the grasp of the most humble, in the many forms that the improvements of modern industry have made possible. That is the integral and democratic Olympism of which we are laying the cornerstone today.

This opening ceremony could not have taken place under any happier auspices. The High Council of the ancient Swiss Confederation and its revered leader, the highly-qualified representatives of this region of the Canton of Vaud so beloved of the gods and of men, the directors of a city outstanding among all others for its grace and hospitality, singers whose renown has spread beyond the borders of their native land, and an elite group of alert and vigorous gymnasts surround this event with the five-fold prestige conferred by history, civic activity, nature, youth, and art.

May Fortune, which loves boldness, smile on the magnificent gesture just made by Belgium in seeking the privilege of hosting the Seventh Olympiad of the modern era next year.

Times are still hard. The dawn now breaking is the dawn of a day following the storm. Toward noon, however, the sky will brighten and the rosy ears of corn once again will fill the arms of the harvesters.

XXVe Anniversaire des Jeux Olympiques.
Discours prononcé, par le Président du C.I.O. á la
Cérémonie commémorative. Lausanne, April 1919.
Special brochure (Archives of the IOC)

5.1/10 MENS FERVIDA IN CORPORE LACERTOSO (1924)

In this note accompanying the "Official Report of the Games of the Eighth Olympiad" (Paris, 1924), Coubertin underscores the specific nature of the Olympic Games with respect to simple world championships. In this matter, the significance of the intellectual aspect must be stressed. The Olympic Games, and therefore Olympism, ultimately must remain in the service of the Spirit, a principle that Coubertin repeated often but which, in this instance, reads as an accusation.

MENS FERVIDA IN CORPORE LACERTOSO

Eight Olympiads, thirty-two years... a long time for an individual, but so short a time in light of history! It is enough, however, to give us confidence in the capacity of an institution to endure, even though that institution has claimed that it was in constant progress throughout the period.

That is the case here.

No one better than its founder can present the panorama of the modern Olympic Games from the day the series began in the Stadium at Athens. The successive celebration of the Games attests to a slow but steady ascent. The only thing that matters is that a sense of the flaws to be corrected should go hand in hand with legitimate satisfaction at their success. In saying this, I am not thinking of potential improvements in technical matters. There is no end to such improvements. In undertakings of such magnitude, certain details will always go wrong. There will always be something to change. People will always want to "do better", and that effort will be made. I am speaking, rather, of the fundamental characteristics of Olympism.

After the Games of the Seventh Olympiad (Antwerp, 1920), I recall that I expressed the desire to see even greater, more complete universality. After the Games of the Eighth Olympiad, it is intellectualism that garners my concern.

Despite the handsome and meritorious effort made to clothe the recent Games in art and thought, they remained too much like a "World Championship". Of course, that is what they must be. Athletes coming from all four corners of the earth have a right to insist on as perfect an organization as possible. But there must be something else, too. National geniuses must take part, the muses must be involved. Beauty must be honored. The whole system of powerful symbolism embodied by the Olympic Games in the past must flourish, a symbolism that the Games must continue to represent today. Those who follow after us must strive to choose suitable approaches. Our task has been to show the way.

This is how the Olympic Games will become what they must be, and only that: the quadrennial celebration of the human springtime, an ordered, rhythmical springtime in which the rising sap remains in the service of the Spirit.

Pierre de Coubertin

Mens fervida in corpore lacertoso,
in: French Olympic Committee (ed.): *Rapport officiel. Jeux de la VIIIe Olympiade*
[Official Report. Eighth Olympiad]. Paris, Librairie de France, 1924, p. 4.

5.1/11 SPEECH GIVEN AT THE OPENING OF THE OLYMPIC CONGRESSES AT THE CITY HALL OF PRAGUE, MAY 29, 1925

This speech is particularly meaningful. In the presence of sport leaders from all over the world, meeting in Prague, Coubertin took leave of his office as President of the IOC. The IOC Session held just before this speech had elected the Belgian Henri de Baillet-Latour as the new President. Coubertin took the opportunity to offer a reflection on the basic educational values of sports and of Olympism. For Coubertin, the point was to set the younger generation on a path whose educational meaning was more clearly defined. It was also necessary for this path to culture to be open to the weak, and that the authentic use of cultural values become comprehensible to the privileged, once again.

This speech also deals with the matter of Olympic amateurism, hotly debated at the time, and the role of the IOC with respect to other athletic organizations.

In Prague, Coubertin participated only in the deliberations of the Olympic Congress on education. Visibly, he wanted to avoid taking part in the debates of the Olympic Congress on technical issues, which was responsible for drawing up the general rules on amateurism in the charter of the IOC, and to become involved in the entanglements regarding competence related to that debate. There may also have been some lassitude on his part. Later, he acknowledged that he found circumstances more favorable for reflecting on the educational issues raised in Prague. This fact shows how low his confidence was in the educational strength of the IOC.

This was why he called the Olympic Congresses on education in 1897, 1905, and 1913. The fact that, once again, at the end of his labors, he was able to take part in a congress bears witness to his attachment to the institution.

As he had announced, Coubertin subsequently devoted his time to "the advent of an educational philosophy that produces mental clarity and critical calm". A few weeks after Prague, he founded the Union Pédagogique Universelle (U.P.U.), and in 1926, he founded the Bureau International de Pédagogie Sportive (B.I.P.S.). In the speech reproduced in this volume (text 6.5.4) that he gave on the occasion of the fortieth anniversary of the Olympic movement, he goes into greater detail in his analysis of the functions of these institutions.

Later on, the IOC honored Coubertin's educational legacy by publishing his educational explanations in its Bulletin, and by including the issue of "Olympic education" in the agenda of every Session of the IOC.

Your Excellency, Gentlemen,

On his last day, the person who is about to leave the fertile land where he has lived for many years, that he has cultivated with his own hands, and that the flowering of success and friendship have made beautiful for him, would like to climb to the heights from where there is a clear view to the horizon. There, thinking of the future, he will fret about the work left undone, the improvements to be made, and the measures to be advocated against potential dangers. None of you will be surprised that this is my state of mind at this moment. Because the field is broad and the time short, you will, I am sure, excuse me for skipping vain compliments and sticking to the heart of the matter. In place of an ornate speech, please accept this personal, clear, and frank report.

My first concern relates to certain utopias that I have been unable to overcome so far. The first utopia consists of believing that sports, as a permanent part of our habits, runs no risk of ever going out of style. This is a serious mistake. Sports are a bodily discipline maintained by the passionate expenditure of inordinate effort. Therefore, it is not natural for man who always tends to obey the law of least resistance. For now, sports are upheld by fashion, an irresistible power, but one that is soon depleted. One would have to be completely ignorant of history to believe that the current infatuation of the crowd will continue indefinitely. This infatuation, which my friends and I worked so hard to create forty years ago because it would provide useful leverage for us, will disappear the same way it came: satiation will kill it. What will be left then? Does the *need* for athletics exist in the individual? No. The noise made around some champions is powerless to create such a need. The need will arise only when the champion himself stops being concerned about whether people are watching him or not. The true athlete is the individual for whom the spectator exists only in a state of contingency. Using this method of calculation, how many athletes are there in Europe? Very few.

So this is one direction in which we must work. Less publicity, less advertising, fewer restrictive organizations, intolerant syndicates, and burdensome hierarchies. But the various forms of sport, of *all* sports, including equestrian events, placed as free of cost as possible at the disposal of *all* citizens – will be one of the duties of the modern municipal system. That is why I have called for the restoration of the municipal Gymnasium of antiquity, made accessible to all without distinction according to opinion, belief, or social status, placed under the immediate and sole authority of the city. In this way, and only in this way, will a generation that is healthily and completely athletic be created.

Another utopia consists of believing that, in the name of science, athletics can be linked to moderation, and can be made to coexist with it. That would be a monstrous marriage, indeed. Sports cannot be made fearful and prudent without compromising its vitality. It needs the freedom of excess. That is its essence, its reason for being, the secret of its moral value. It is fine to teach people to be bold and reflective; but to teach them to be afraid of daring is folly. Daring for daring's sake in the absence of real need – that is when our body overcomes its own animal nature.

This is not to say that scientific control should be rejected, but it must play the role of adviser, not despot. It, too, is susceptible to reform because it leaves out a whole part of its domain by insisting solely on physiology to the detriment of psychology. Scientists measure a man, noting down his various index values. In passing, let me note that one very important value is not observed: man's mechanical shape. Radiography may be called upon to supply this need. This would be a significant advantage for technical improvement. But again, this is a physiological element, and I repeat, the data provided by physiology will remain imperfect so long as it is not completed with data relating to the psyche. In nearly all sports, sudden decisions, on the one hand, and hesitation, on the other hand, prevent progress and lay the groundwork for defeat. Fear is the cause...and where does fear hide in the body? It takes on different forms depending on whether it is located in the nerves, the brain, or is simply in the muscles, because the memory of a previous failure in the muscles is often enough to call it forth. We see this time and time again in horses. Why do we fail to observe it in man? For a long time now, I have pointed out these problems in hopes that specialists would plan on delving into them. They are not doing so. Thus notion that anatomy is sufficient for everything takes hold, that anatomy in physical education should play the role of a managing director with unlimited powers. This is the third utopia that I wish to discuss with you.

Gentlemen, no doubt you would be surprised if I passed over the infamous issue of amateurism in silence. This matter is not as insoluble as it is believed. Before the war, a little good will on both sides would have been sufficient to solve the dispute. Today, the matter is complicated because the cost of living has transformed the elements of the debate. Public opinion is not about to let athletics become the pastime of the rich. It is not my impression that we should expect of this congress a single definition of the amateur that would be applicable to all sports. What we must strive toward, however, is for current regulations to be applied in all honesty in every Federation. That is not what now happens. There is no use denying the evidence. There is plenty of cheating and lying. This is the repercussion in the world of athletics of a decline in morality. Sports have developed within a society whose love for money threatens to cause that society to rot right to the marrow. Now it is up to the athletic associations to set a good example of the return to believe in honor and sincerity, by driving lying and hypocrisy from their midst. Before trying to write a perfect definition of the amateur, let them start by imposing absolute respect for the imperfect definitions now in force, which people have become accustomed to disobeying shamelessly. Let them be ruthless in disqualifying those pseudo-amateurs who rake in enormous profits more or less directly from their participation in public competitions, people who are generally less athletic and, in any event, much less respectable than many a professional. An individual oath required of all athletes will be the best way to place athletic competitions back under the control of the honor system. For nineteen years now I have been advocating such a step, and I am glad to see that public opinion has, at long last, come around.

The restored Olympism will be the most effective artisan in this effort at purification provided that people stop wanting to make the Olympic Games into world championships. It is because they are imbued with this idea that some technical experts are always seeking to destroy the Olympic constitution, to gain power that they believe they are prepared to wield in its entirety. Once again, I have insisted on placing my colleagues on the International Olympic Committee on their guard against making any concessions in this matter. If modern Olympism has prospered, it is because there was, at its head, an absolutely independent board that has never been subsidized by anyone. Since it was self-recruiting, it avoided any semblance of electoral chaos and does not allow itself to be influenced either by nationalist passions or by the weight of corporate interests. With a managing board comprising delegates from the National Committees or from the International Federations, Olympism would have died out within a few years. Even now, if this essential condition for its survival were renounced, the future of Olympism would be compromised. The task of the International Committee is to select the site of the next

Olympiad, and to ensure that the principles and traditions that are at the foundation of that celebration are respected. Thanks to the method used to recruit its membership, it alone is sure to succeed in this task. It is the duty of the National Committees to regulate the participation of each country in the quadrennial Games. As for the International Federations, it is their perfectly legitimate right to handle the technical aspects of the competitions in complete freedom. Let there be harmony among the three powers: the International Committee, the National Olympic Committees, and the International Federations. This will be the best way to keep the Olympic Games at the desirable level of excellence.

Is there any need to recall that the Games are not the property of any country or of any particular race, and that they cannot be monopolized by any group whatsoever? They are global. All people must be allowed in, without debate, just as all sports must be treated on equal footing, without concern for the fluctuations or caprices of public opinion. The wonderful name of athlete, moreover, applies equally to the gymnast who works with the horizontal bars, to the boxer, the equestrian, the rower, and the fencer, as well as to the runner and the javelin thrower. There is no scale of relative worth to be drawn up among these exercises, on the pretext that the public favors one or another of them for the time being. In contrast, it would be pointless to try to increase the number of group events. The Games were established for the glorification of the individual champion, whose exploits are needed to maintain general eagerness and ambition. The circumstances are poorly suited to including too many team sports, because in general the need has been recognized to limit the length of the Games, and thus also to limit the expenses occasioned by the Games. Yet I do not believe that these two issues are directly connected. Great savings will be realized when an Olympiad is held if that celebration is planned far enough in advance, and with great method, discipline, and disinterest. But in this area as in so many others, wasteful habits have reigned, formed through bad policy based on the idea that unrestrained luxury will necessarily result in common ease and prosperity. The issue of luxury must be reflect upon. Its vulgarity makes it sterile. It merely tends to crush moderating forces, making social contrasts a source of even greater irritation.

Simplified organizational mechanisms, more standardized and more peaceful accommodations, less festivity, and especially closer and more daily contact between athletes and directors, without any politicians or go-getters to divide them – such, I hope, is the sight that the Games of the Ninth Olympiad will show us.

In conclusion, I must express my gratitude for the insistence with which all countries have tried to keep me on as head of the International Committee. Such feelings do me honor. Please use those feelings on behalf of my successor, to make his task easier. I could not agree to stay on. It would be unwise to attempt to stay on much beyond this thirty-year period. Above all, I want to be able to use the time I have left to hasten an urgent undertaking, to the extent that I can: the advent of an educational philosophy that produces mental clarity and critical calm. In my opinion, the future of civilization does not rest now on political or economic foundations. It depends solely on the educational orientation that will be put in place. The social issue itself will not find any durable solution outside education. That is why the first nation or the first class that gives the signal will be guaranteed to lead the new Europe. The stakes are worth the effort.

It is our current educational philosophy that, in its obstinate error, has made the present generations stray into the impasse of excessive specialization, where they will find nothing but obscurity and disunity. They believe they are very powerful because they have great appetites, and they believe they are very wise because they have a great deal of scientific data. In reality, they are poorly prepared for the troubles ahead. Intelligence is smothered by knowledge, critical minds are debased by an overwhelming mass of facts, and adolescents are trained into the mentality of the anthill, surrounded by the artificial and the accepted, with categories and statistics, a fetish for numbers, an unhealthy search for detail and the exception. Truly let us beware that the exhausted and hallucinating European mind not end up becoming the source of some Asiatic reaction for which it is unprepared, and which it would not weather well.

Europe is rich in magnificent, slowly accumulated culture, but no longer does some guide wire lead those of a privileged social status through it, while access is simply forbidden to the non-privileged. The time has come to build an educational structure with architecture more suited to the needs of the day.

It would go beyond the limits imposed by the nature of this meeting to speak in greater detail on this matter. No doubt I have already surprised or even shocked some listeners in displaying revolutionary tendencies at a time when conservative instincts are more heavily accented. But I owed a frank explanation of my plans to my colleagues, to my faithful friends. I wanted to tell them, too, that I am taking on this new work in the athletic spirit that we have cultivated together, in other words in the spirit of effort, the taste for risk, and the pursuit of the impartial ideal.

In the same spirit, they will continue their ascent toward the mount where we hope to build the temple, while a great free-for-all will be held on the plain. The temple will last, and the free-for-all will pass. Fair or temple – sportsmen must make their choice; they cannot expect to frequent both one and the other ... let them choose!

Discours pononcé à l'ouverture des Congrès Olympiques
à l'Hôtel de Ville de Prague, le 29 mai 1925.
Special brochure. Prague, Government Printing Office, 1925.

5.1/12 TO THE YOUNG ATHLETES OF ALL NATIONS (1927)

In April 1927, Coubertin spent several weeks in Greece on the occasion of the unveiling of the column commemorating the restoration of the Olympic Games in Olympia. He was the guest of the Greek State, and had accepted the invitation only at the insistence of his friend and colleague in the U.P.U., Professor Chryssaphis[1]. Yielding to a sort of unhappy passion, Coubertin had not returned to Greece since the Olympic Games of 1896.

From Olympia on April 17, 1927, he issued the following text, "A la jeunesse sportive de toutes les nations" [To the Young Athletes of All Nations]. It is both an appeal for help and a farewell letter. Coubertin speaks directly to youths involved in sports throughout the world, and shows the possibilities of Olympism linked to the spread of athletics around the world.

During his stay in Greece, Coubertin gave two remarkable speeches. On March 31, 1927, he gave a speech about the work of the U.P.U. at the Parnassus Literary Society, where he had launched his appeal to the citizens of Athens in 1894 to hold the 1896 Games. On April 14, 1927, he gave a major address at the Academy of Athens. The focus of that speech was to present the meaning, from the historical perspective, of the subject-matter: "On the transformation and spread of historical studies[2]."

In his "Olympic Memoirs", Coubertin described his feelings at being back in Greece and at Olympia after thirty years had passed[3].

Olympia, April 17, 1927
(Year Four of the Eighth Olympiad)

To the Young Athletes of All Nations

Today, amid the illustrious ruins of Olympia, the monument commemorating the restoration of the Olympic Games, proclaimed thirty-three years ago, was unveiled. Through this gesture of the Greek government, the initiative that it has sought to honor has taken its place in history. Now it is up to you to maintain it. My friends and I have not worked to give you the Olympic Games so that they will be turned into a museum object or a subject for the movies, nor so that commercial or political interests should take them over. In restoring an institution that dates back twenty-five centuries, we wanted you to be able to become, once again, adepts of the worship of athletics as our great ancestors conceived it. In the modern world, full of powerful possibilities and yet also threatened by perilous decline, Olympism can become a school for moral nobility and purity as well as physical endurance and energy, but this can happen only if you continually raise your concept of athletic honor and impartiality to the level of your muscular ability. The future depends on you.

Pierre de Coubertin.

A la jeunesse sportive de toutes les nations.
Olympie, 17 avril 1927. Pamphlet, (1 page).

Olympie, 17 Avril 1927.
(An IV de la VIIIme Olympiade.)

A la Jeunesse sportive de toutes les nations

Aujourd'hui, au milieu des ruines illustres d'Olympie, a été inauguré le monument commémoratif du rétablissement des Jeux Olympiques, proclamé voici trente-trois ans. Par ce geste du gouvernement hellénique, l'initiative qu'il a bien voulu honorer a pris rang dans l'histoire. C'est à vous de l'y maintenir. Nous n'avons pas travaillé, mes amis et moi, à vous rendre les Jeux Olympiques pour en faire un objet de musée ou de cinéma, ni pour que des intérêts mercantiles ou électoraux s'en emparent. Nous avons voulu, rénovant une institution vingt-cinq fois séculaire, que vous puissiez redevenir des adeptes de la religion du sport telle que les grands ancêtres l'avaient conçue. Dans le monde moderne, plein de possibilités puissantes et que menacent en même temps de périlleuses déchéances, l'Olympisme peut constituer une école de noblesse et de pureté morales autant que d'endurance et d'énergie physiques, mais ce sera à la condition que vous éleviez sans cesse votre conception de l'honneur et du désintéressement sportifs à la hauteur de votre élan musculaire. L'avenir dépend de vous.

PIERRE DE COUBERTIN.

Special Print of Coubertin's message, "To the Young Athletes of All Nations", written in French, 1927 (N.Müller Collection)

1 Director of the Greek Academy of Athletics, Prof. Chryssaphis was one of the major Olympic leaders in Greece. Among other things, he wrote a *History of the Olympic Games*, and was one of the rare individuals who sought to carry out the work of the U.P.U. in specific ways.
See I. Chryssafis: *The International Olympic Games.* Athens, HOC, 1930. (In Greek)
Cf. Coubertin, "In memoriam [Frantz Reichel and Jean Chryssaphis]." in: *Bulletin du B.I.P.S.*, No. 10, Lausanne [1933], pp. 8-9.

2 See text 3.22 in this volume.

3 *Olympic Memoirs,* Chapter XXIII: "Olympia (1927)." Lausanne, IOC, 1997, pp. 224-229. See text 4.2.2/44. Because Coubertin writes: "This text has not always been faithfully reproduced and certain translations have misinterpreted one passage" we have chosen to use a new translation here.

5.1/13 THE ATHLETIC SPIRIT MUST DOMINATE ALL OTHER ISSUES

The impression that the 1928 Olympic Games made on Coubertin was such that, although he was unable to attend them, he expressed his ideas in a text in which he underscores the primordial importance to be given to the "Athletic Spirit", not to "technical organization."

Because I could not attend the Games of the Ninth Olympiad on account of illness, it is scarcely possible for me to evaluate them with full knowledge of the facts. I would know precious little about them if my only source of information on them were newspaper reports. The issue of the role of the press in the Olympic Games will ultimately have to be addressed. Since reporters are stirred up by the opportunity to travel, it happens that too many makeshift reporters attend the Games, ignorant of the sport and incapable of becoming interested in it. Their boredom gradually shows through in inaccurate reporting and recriminations about details, which cancels out the value of their involvement.

Through my friends and former colleagues, I am aware that the technical organization was remarkable, which came as no surprise to me, and that the athletic spirit of the competitors was excellent, as well. The second of these things is what really matters most to me. I always admire the fact that these young men, gathered from all the countries in the world for a competition enhanced in their eyes by its infrequency, historic example, and solemn setting, manage to find enough moral strength in themselves to handle a deeply-felt defeat, without any apparent bitterness, and to shake the winner's hand with heartfelt warmth. I have seen this happen a hundred times, and I have never grown tired of it. It fills me with delight. But one has to be in the company of athletes to have a sense of their manly beauty. If one goes over to the spectators' benches, one notes the ever-increasing lack of that same sporting spirit. More and more, modern crowds lack the chivalrous spirit that thrived in the Middle Ages among those attending tournaments and popular jousts. Education on this point, as on so many others, must be totally revised. I would like it if we were to treat today's spectators like great children, walking among them with enormous cards to teach them how to appreciate a splendid athletic feat, and how out of place on such occasions are those outbursts of crude nationalism that give our era a semi-barbaric stench.

L'esprit sportive doit dominer tout autre considération,
in: *La Revue Sportive Illustrée,*
Vol. 24, 1928, no. 3 [p. 24].

5.1/14 OLYMPIA. LECTURE GIVEN IN PARIS, IN THE FESTIVAL HALL OF THE 16TH ARRONDISSEMENT TOWN HALL

The topic of the lecture, "Olympia", presents a "difficult task, for this is one of the most wide-ranging names in history". Coubertin gave this lecture on March 6, 1929 in the presence of the Greek ambassador to France. The difficulty of which he speaks is more readily understood when one realizes that in this speech, Coubertin, in retrospect, links his vision of Hellenism to the restoration of the Olympic Games and various aspects of his doctrine, Olympism, which he calls here "a philosophical and religious doctrine".[1]

The comparison with ancient Greece shows how Coubertin evaluates modern sports. In outlining the Olympic movement since 1894, he takes into account the successes and misfortunes of his plan.

In agreeing – quite unwisely, I fear – to speak on a topic whose name is just four syllables and seven letters long, I have taken on a difficult task, because this is one of the most wide-ranging names in history.

Many among you, perhaps, do not realize that this is so. No doubt they expect me to give a general survey of ancient athletic practices, a quick summary of the artistic treasures unearthed through the meritorious efforts of the German school of archaeology, perhaps recalling the rudimentary blows of the pickax swung a hundred years ago by the French mission that accompanied the de Morée expedition. The discovery of Olympia is owed to that expedition, because for centuries all trace of it had been lost. The silt deposited by the Alphaeus and the Kladeos which merge at the feet of the ruins had finished the work begun by the convulsions of nature and the barbarianism of man. There was nothing left to mark the location where such great glory, passion, and energy had played out.

All this and many related subjects besides would be worth a series of lectures, and who knows! Perhaps some future Sorbonne will include a course on Olympism in its curriculum.

For an Olympism, a doctrine, does exist. I am sorry for those – and they are many – who have held me in contempt for adding this neologism to our common language, but it was quite necessary. Any philosophical and religious doctrine like this deserves a name that evokes and designates it.

So now my listeners know my plans, and are probably a bit disappointed. They were hoping for stories of festivities, anecdotes, an aviator's overview of the past that stretches back two and a half millennia. Yet here I am, inviting them to listen to a grim study of philosophy. I leave to others the task of detailing the sculptural and architectural splendors that adorned the monuments and sites at Olympia, and I refer you to the many papers that have been published for details of the competitions, although none of those works, certainly, is completely accurate or completely wrong. I want to focus on helping you understand how and why the place that bears that memorable name, which I wish to discuss, became

1 He coined the term "Olympism" for this doctrine. Since this text includes almost endless historical digressions, it might be classified with the historical writings, but that is not what the speech is about.

the cradle of an idea of life that is truly Hellenic in form, a place that gives the history of Hellenism its basic sense of depth.

Such a speech does not readily stay within the confines of such a setting as this, no matter how warmly it is welcomed. So I invite you to step outside with me, and to come take a seat on the wooded slopes of Mount Kronion at a time when the sun, rising from the other side of the Alphaeus, begins to fringe the rolling hills with gold, shining on the lush fields at their feet.

I have seen this sight on two occasions, thirty-three years apart. One morning in November 1894 at the sacred place, I became aware of the enormity of the work that I had taken on in proclaiming the restoration of the Olympic Games five months earlier after an interruption of fifteen hundred years. I caught a glimpse of all the hazards that lay ahead. One morning in April 1927, I was waiting in a sort of pious state of contemplation for the moment when the Minister of Public Instruction would drop the Greek and French flags covering the sparkling marble monument raised to mark the success of the venture. In the course of that ceremony, when I was called upon to respond to the praise of the representative of the Greek government, my first thought was to salute those who have never succeeded in life despite their best efforts, because fate had placed great pitfalls in their way. Mentioning this troubling procession of individuals teaches personal modesty and the vanity of what we call merit...

In the beautiful pine forest that scales Mount Kronion (a graceful and miniature version of the prestigious Pendelikon), we can easily imagine the long avenues of plane trees along which the athletes and pilgrims once came, with the embassies and the commercial goods, the traffic and the ambition, the appetites and the misplaced vanity of a civilization that was both complex and clearly-defined, more than any other since that time. The approaches to the temple, its steps and colonnades, and the multitude of buildings that surrounded it – the *ex-votos*, the oratories, the places for offerings and sacrifices – all this can be imagined. The sacred enclosure called the Altis was imposing as a religious and cultural center. Among this people and especially at that time, it is difficult to imagine a religion not based on a positive philosophical idea.

So let us look for the basis of that idea. If in fact there was a religion of athletics whose altars were subsequently raised, on several occasions, with greater or lesser grace and for longer or shorter periods of time, let us try to understand why it was in Greece that this religion took root, and whether the Greek ideal in this respect is still suitable for the rest of humanity. Depending on our answer, Olympia is either merely a splendid accident of history, or it is one of the most powerful sites of all human progress. As you can see, the alternatives are worth studying.

So what was an ancient athlete in comparison to the individual for whom we use the pretty, supple, elegant, but infinitely less profound term, a sportsman? Can the same definition not be used for both? Here is the definition that Professor Millioud of the University of Lausanne gave in 1913, at the first Congress on Sports Psychology held there. "Sports are a form of muscular activity that ranges from games to heroism, capable of filling all the levels in between". That, if I dare say so, is a philosophical definition. Here is a less eloquent, but more technical definition, the one that appears at the head of my little manual on athletic education.

View of the Temple of Zeus in the Altis, Olympia (Photo: N.Müller)

"Athletics is the *voluntary* and *habitual* practice of *intense* muscular exercise based on a desire for *progress* and extending as far as *risk*". So we have five ideas: initiative, perseverance, intensity, search for perfection, and scorn for potential danger. These five ideas are essential and fundamental.

I do not think that our great ancestors, if they were here with us this evening, would find anything to reword in these definitions. They would not make any changes whatsoever to the substance of the sentences I have just read, though certainly they would give them a more Hellenic form. Yet they would be astonished not to find any expression or suggestion of the religious idea of purification or sanctification.

Among the ancients, this idea went quite far. In the eleventh century AD, one could still see at Olympia a disk into which was carved the text of the agreement reached between Lycurgus and Iphitos, king of Elis, to establish the "sacred truce" during the Games. At that time, all armed conflicts and all combat among Hellenes had to cease. The territory of Olympia, declared neutral, was inviolable.

A competitor in the Games had to be of pure race, and not to have committed any crime, impiety, or sacrilege. Once "accepted" as a candidate, after an eighteen-month training period he had to spend thirty days at the gymnasium in Elis before being brought to the gymnasium at Olympia. All these ethnic, moral, social, and technical guarantees were framed in a clearly religious context.

"The gods are the friends of the Games" said Pindar, using that term in its most athletic sense. What is more, all this dates back a long way because the society described in the Iliad already appears highly athletic and religiously athletic. It was to honor the gods with their trained and well-balanced bodies that, for centuries on end, young Hellenes were urged to chisel their bodies through intense muscular exercise.

Here we are touching on the bedrock on which Hellenic society stood. Let me explain by citing this passage from volume two of my *World History*: "Above all, Hellenism is the *cult of humanity in its present life and in its state of equilibrium*. Let there be no mistake about it, this was a great novelty in the mentality of all people and of all time. In all other places, cults were based on aspirations for a better life, on the notion of recompense and on happiness in the beyond, as well as the fear of punishment for those who had offended the gods. But here, it was present-day existence that constitutes happiness. In the beyond, there is nothing but regret for being deprived of that existence. The beyond was merely survival in a diminished state. Thus there had to be "consolation for the dead", for those prisoners in the beyond, those "sons of earth and of the starry sky" in exile, far from flowers and the beautiful light. Lamartine's verse is well known: "Man is a fallen god who remembers heaven". Nietzsche speaks of "nature bemoaning its division into individuals". These two statements are vastly opposed in style and thought, but in them are reflected the bases of most individualistic or pantheistic religions. These concepts are as un-Greek as possible. Behold the Greek gods: magnificent men, but men and therefore imperfect. For the most part, they are wise, men of reason and of action. They gather together, they are sociable, athletic, highly individual, not much given to contemplation, even less to bookish learning. As Albert Thibaudet wrote, "Among the Egyptians, the Jews, the Persians, and the Muslims, religious life consists of learning scripture by heart, but Greek religion is a religion without books."

This, then, was paganism, with its highly-desired and fleeting companion, eurythmy. Our simplistic habit of cataloguing things leads us to define paganism as the adoration of idols, as if any religion, even the most materialistic, did not have its spiritual adherents and as though any religion, even the most mystical, did not have its adorers of idols, even if they merely adored the golden calf, stronger and more highly praised now than ever before. There is also the true paganism that humanity will never be rid of and which, to utter blasphemy, it is good that humanity cannot rid itself entirely. That paganism is the religion of the human body, mind and spirit, sense and will, instinct and conscience. The flesh, the senses, and the instinct have the upper hand at times, the will and the conscience at other times. These are the two despots fighting for primacy in us, a conflict that often tears us apart savagely. We must achieve balance. We do manage to do so, but we cannot hang on to it. The pendulum reaches the golden mean only when it is half-way from the two extremes between which it swings. Likewise, humanity – the individual or society – cannot stay midway in its race from one excess to another. When we do manage to restore the balance of an individual or a group, quite often the only way to achieve it is to aim for the opposite form of excess. How many are those who have unconsciously used this strategy to improve themselves, or merely to change themselves!

It was Hellenism's immortal glory to have conceived of the codification of the pursuit of balance, and to make of it a formula for social greatness. Here in Olympia we stand on the ruins of the first capital of the kingdom of eurythmy, for eurythmy is not applicable merely in the field of art. There is also eurythmy of life.

So we stand here meditating among the ruins of Olympia, ruins that are still alive, as the ceremony that I mentioned earlier suggests. From here, we can see the pagan and ascetic changeovers that form the framework of history, as it were, a framework left alone by historians because, in order to perceive it, one must seek it out under the events that cover it, and play more the archaeologist than the historian.

If you will, let us continue our reflection while the glory of the day replaces the caresses of dawn in this landscape whose infinite charm I have tried to evoke in feeble words. Sheep wearing their bells and shepherds from Arcadia are walking along the paths. There is nothing ornate about them, but they are very ancient. In the distance, a rising wisp of smoke makes us think of the thanksgiving offered by a recent victor, or the entreaty of a young man eager for future victory.

Olympia has now officially existed for eleven hundred sixty-eight years old, since the first recorded Olympiad dates from the year 776 BC and the Games were suppressed by edict of the Emperor Theodosius in 392 AD (in speaking to an audience such as this, I need not recall that an Olympiad is a calendar period, a four-year period the start of which is celebrated by holding the Games). This principle has been fully restored. The monument dedicated in 1927 in Olympia indicates that the First Olympiad of the modern era was held in Athens in 1896. The Amsterdam Games of 1928 were the Games of the Ninth Olympiad, just as those in Los Angeles in 1932 will be the Games of the Tenth Olympiad. In restoring the institution in its ancient spirit, and in keeping with the feeling of my day, I wanted to give the Games the global form that meets the hopes and needs of today. Therefore, it is grammatically and historically incorrect to equate the word "Olympiad" with the term "Olympic Games". When people say, as some commonly do, "the Olympiads of Amsterdam", their language is doubly barbaric and grating on the ears. This comment, which has been expressed before, is intended to pass over you to reach those people who have not reflected on the matter, and those hurried individuals who do not take the time to reflect.

So Olympia is alive after twelve centuries, but of course its life has not been without inequality and turbulence. We must admire the magnificent continuity of the celebration of the Games. Events of the most serious nature did not manage to interrupt them. Even during the time of the Persian threat, the Hellenes met on the banks of the Alphaeus for their quadrennial celebrations. Yet serious incidents did occur. The Eighth Olympiad was disturbed by disputes among the organizers. The One Hundred Fourth Olympiad, three centuries later, even saw the sacred truce violated. Of course the glory of the Games depended on the skill of the organizers, the amounts spent, and on the quality, quantity, enthusiasm, and preparation of the athletes. There were splendid festivals, stunning successes, unforgettable sights and, on other occasions, vulgarities, disarray, poorly run ceremonies, and ragged processions.

ΟΛΥΜΠΙΑ,
DAT IS
OLYMP-SPEELEN
DER
GRIEKEN,
nagebootſt van den ROMEINEN,
uit oude Griekſe en Romeinſe Schryvers opgehaalt
DOOR
THEODORUS ANTONIDES,
in zyn leven Prædikant te Weſterwytwert en Menkeweer.
Na zyn doot uitgegeven door deszelfs Zoon
MEINART ANTONIDES,
Prædikant te Onderwierum en Weſterdyxhorn.
Vermeerdert met eenige
KORTE AANMERKINGEN,
neffens de voorname Inhoud der Hoofdſtukken en wydlopige Regiſters, opgemaakt door een oud Medeleerling des Schryvers;
EN EEN
VOORREDEN
van eenig ligt door de Olymp-Jaaren en Olymp-Speelen aan het H. Woord toe te brengen
VAN
ALBERTUS VOGET,
Doctor en Profeſſor der Heilige Godgeleertheid, en Academie Prediker te Groningen.

Te GRONINGEN,
By de WED. J. COST, Boekverkoopſter aan de Markt. 1732.

Title page of the first comprehensive monograph on the ancient Olympic Games by Theodorus Antonides, published in Dutch in Groningen, 1732: "Olympia – They are the Olympic Games of Greeks". (N.Müller Collection)

We must recognize that our concept of antiquity is intentionally simplistic. Such sublime ruins would disappoint us if we could look upon them in their entirety in the early days. By contrast, how many modern monuments whose crowns and decoration truly offend us will influence our descendants who come to unearth their foundations or ruins. Without wishing to impede our lovely vision of antiquity, we must imagine that the dust, discordant noise, ill-arranged harmony, material wear, and bad taste of certain groupings is not a modern phenomenon. Thinking in this way gives us a certain capacity for indulgence with respect to modern artists, individuals dealt with at times rather unfairly by subsequent critics after being exalted beyond the limits of common sense by the initial critics (who are not necessarily disinterested parties).

To the end, Olympia kept its character as a sacred place, a center of pagan religion. It was Christianity in the end that extinguished the eternal flame of its altars. The suppression of the Games must be distinguished clearly from the destruction of the site. The sacrilegious edict of Theodosius II has nothing to do with the edict of Theodosius I thirty years earlier. In the interval, Alaric's hordes had come and gone. All the treasures had been pillaged, the wealth scattered, but the buildings still stood. Perhaps they were even more beautiful than ever, bearing the patina of time, semi-abandoned, alone, silent. Theodosius II ordered their destruction. The destruction was carried out only partially and doubtless with ill will, but the abandonment of the site continued apace. The dikes that protected the site were not maintained. The sudden floods of the Kladeos did their damage. Then in the sixth century two terrible earthquakes struck. The porticoes and colonnades collapsed. The shroud of oblivion covered the ruins, and knowledge of the site faded away.

This expression that I have just used deserves its own commentary, a lecture devoted to it alone. Olympia did not disappear merely from the face of the earth. It disappeared from people's minds. Asceticism became dominant. I do not mean to say that Europe was suddenly populated with ascetics. That is not how the term should be understood. But a belief took root, whether conscious or not, specific of not, but in any event recognized and respected by the very people who did not act in conformity with it. This belief was that the body is the enemy of the spirit, that the struggle between them is an inevitable and normal thing, and that no understanding should be sought out that would allow them to join together in governing the individual.

Was this return to asceticism (the word is a bad one, I agree, but it is the least bad of all those available) desirable for the general good? I do not hesitate to answer: Yes. I recall that I once saddened an athletic audience when I said that if metempsychosis does exist and if, as a result, I return to existence in a hundred years, you might see me using all my energy to destroy what I had worked to build up in my current existence. This is a paradox, but a sincere one. The reason is that Olympism, a doctrine of the fraternity of the body and the mind, and asceticism, a doctrine of the enmity between them, have never managed to understand each other and thereby respect each other. Since each contains the seeds of abuse that could degenerate into true evils, they are destined to clash, to hold power by turns like any absolute, violent political party. It is just that in this case, we are talking about evolution and change taking place over centuries. This successive series is useful, absent any better option. Moderation and the golden mean are utopias in all areas. The law of the pendulum applies to everything. The ancient world was much too taken with Olympism to be able to provide new harvests, just as the man of yesterday was far too deeply absorbed in the ascetic ideal to be open to being fruitful without first being freed of that yoke.

In the eyes of many, the Middle Ages were a period when ascetic tendencies predominated. That is more true of the pre-feudal era than of the feudal age itself. In any event, it was from the midst of feudal society that a clearly defined Olympic restoration proceeded: chivalry. For a long time, I hesitated to make this association. Of course, it is not immediately apparent and it was even less clear to the knights themselves. They had no inkling of it. Olympia did not exist for them. Yet once one studies their behavior, once one tries to examine their motives, their athletic passion is clear. Soon, it seems to flow in torrents. Then the Church appears and, in a strange twist, contributes to restoring what it had knocked down. You may hasten to say that it did so in another spirit. That is no doubt true, but by blessing the weapons of the knight, by providing a pious preamble to his enthronement, and by giving his exploits a generous purpose (for the church armed him for justice and right, and entrusted to him "the protection of the weak, and the defense of the widow and the orphan"), it sanctified his training and his physical violence, as pagan religions once did, and presents those acts to the knight as pleasing to God.

Christianized athletics did not stay within the bounds that the Church wished to impose on it. Athletic passion spread among the youth, uplifting it, and spreading across of all western Europe, from Germany to Spain, from Italy to England. France acted as a central crossroads for the movement. Rather quickly, the movement fell apart.

Shall we continue with the fiction of our encampment, in the place where we had come to contemplate the panorama of vanished ages? Let us imagine that we have picnicked at the site of the exhedra of Herod Atticus, and that the smoke from our cigarettes spiraled upward to join the clouds that scurry about in the sky, their transparent, shifting illusions standing out against the deep blue. The day is passing, and the atmosphere is growing somewhat listless. Though it is still far off, we sense the fatigue of nature as evening approaches. At one moment, one among us who was dozing, yielding to the sweet incentive of the earth and sky, thought he heard the shouts of joy of the young men in the gymnasium, and saw an attendant ascending the steps of the main sanctuary to place incense on the tripod standing at the feet of the image of Zeus, a work of the immortal Phidias. The traveler over there jotting down notes would be Pausanias, the benevolent author of a sort of *Guide Joanne* that would make it possible later – much later – to identify and find the Hermes by Praxiteles in the very spot where he said it stood...

Let us allow these illusions to fade away slowly like a dream when we awake, and let us return to reality to observe the birth of the third Olympia. It is far away, far away from all that. But what a strange thing: religion is involved, once again. A Church, the Anglican Church this time, presided over this rebirth. The two clergymen at the root of it, Kingsley and Thomas Arnold, were men of letters. They were thoroughly familiar with the classical age. Yet if they do mention it, it was only in passing, making no claim on its experiences. In a way, however, they went beyond it. Arnold makes the muscles the most thoroughly educated, meticulous, and constant servants in the formation of character. He set down the basic rules of athletic education, and very quickly, since his career was short. He had just fourteen years to transform Rugby when he was its headmaster. From Rugby, through the contagiousness of example, he changed other schools without resorting to thundering speeches or meddling indiscreetly. Soon, the cornerstone of the British empire had been laid. I am well aware that this is not yet the viewpoint of historians, nor even of the English themselves, but I am happy to have had this perspective approved by one of the greatest of those still alive from Arnold's day, Gladstone. When I asked him the question, worried at having made a mistake, he asked me for some time to think. After he had reflected, he said, "That is right. That is how things happened."

We reason in a simplistic fashion when the subject turns to England, as well. Yielding to the human tendency always to believe that the spectacle that surrounds us is permanent, whether it is a landscape or men, we identify the Englishman with that level-headed, well-balanced individual that we saw from the last third of the nineteenth century until the war. But that balance, which was at times more an appearance than a reality, was desired and learned, the result of discipline of the muscles, a relatively recent phenomenon.

The is no apparent link between Arnold's educational initiative and the restoration of the Olympic Games. Since the most wildly fantastic stories about the origins of the general rebirth of interest in sports have been published recently, and about the restoration of the Olympics in particular, you will certainly pardon me for taking this opportunity to make my explanation clear.

It is true that at one time I thought bringing Olympism back to life in a restored Olympia. This proved to be impossible from all perspectives. When the international university and athletic congress opened in the great amphitheater of the Sorbonne on June 16, 1894 – a congress called to support the project – it already looked exactly like what has been implemented so far, right down to the last detail. The year before in New York I had already contacted friends across the Atlantic who could help me in my work. Fourteen nationalities were represented when the principle of the project was put to a vote in Paris. The vote did not carry great conviction for many because the difficulties seemed insurmountable.

At the end of the nineteenth century, a century that was profoundly evolutionary but filled with illusory projects, continental Europe, and France in particular, needed educational reform urgently. Male youth lacked neither health nor courage, but it did lack drive and passion. Here in France, youth was living in grayness, if you will allow that expression. What it lacked was the garden to cultivate the will that organized sports provide. That opportunity was not available in the schools or afterwards. I have the feeling that once again I am touching on a subject that could take up a whole lecture of its own and that, since I cannot do that, I am leaving a large number of topics related to the one at hand in a sort of nebulousness. You are thoroughly entitled to bear me a grudge for touching on so many topics that I can barely point out in passing, as if I were leading some sort of Cook's tour. At the very least, I am making every effort not to have you lose the thread of my main argument. I would be glad if you retain the essential fact, which is that Olympia stood

Olympic education in the Altis of Olympia. Students of a Session of the International Olympic Academy studying Olympism in the ancient Gymnasium (Photo: R.Steeb)

for something that lived on after it, which is alive once again, and will continue to be reborn throughout history, alternately raised up and suppressed by our nature which is drawn by balance, a balance that we can achieve but not maintain.

This lack of capacity was greater in the modern era than it had ever been. Cosmopolitanism was on the rise in all quarters. The intoxication of speed was beginning to have its effects, and people were already repeating that clever and stupid expression, "Time is Money", which is now crushing us.

You are aware of the method I used to introduce athletics into French high schools: by breaking down the doors, or rather by having them be broken down from the inside, by the school children. My faithful companion Frantz-Reichel, who was one of those children, has told the story many times. He wrote, "How enthusiastically your appeal was heard by those who were exasperated by the countless bonds imposed by an outdated system! How can I express the surprise and wild joy that this appeal caused in all the young people in the Paris schools, provided that – and with the result that – we were able to implement what you were hoping for: the free establishment of the school athletic associations. Our capacity for initiative, freed and awakened by you, would serve passionately to found, direct, and manage them, even as we participated in their activities."

That all happened forty years ago. The previous year, the Académie de Médecine, while examining the issue of overworking which was beginning to attract attention, had suggested as a remedy that the recreation periods and weekly free time be increased. The Académie seemed surprised at our protests. We said, "Not on your life. Recreation periods and days off are put to abominable use. Not a shred of athletics takes place then. Let us begin by organizing how that time is used. Then we will be able to increase the length of time". Jules Simon had come out in favor of our proposal, which carried the day.

You might object, of course, that there were already gymnastics associations. Yes there were, it is true. But there were far fewer of them then, and those that existed were less competent than those that came later. At the time, these associations reached only a small, geographically limited number of people in the popular classes. Educational institutions closed their doors to them. The solution on the continent, as in England, was of course to establish free, independent school athletics associations. That was the unit of reform par excellence.

Following the eloquence of Jules Simon and the enthusiasm of the youths involved, fashion took a shine to us. Yet I have never been very fond of fashion. Given to excesses and caprice, fashion destroys its own future. What lasting undertaking can be founded on the basis of fashion? It was to buttress the fragile structure that I had just built that the restoration of the Olympic Games – this time on a completely international footing – seemed to me the only timely solution. The only way to ensure any relative long-term survival of the athletic renaissance then still in its infancy was to superimpose the immense prestige of antiquity on the passing fad of Anglomania, thereby undercutting, to some extent, any opposition from the students of classicism, and to impose on the world a system whose fame spread beyond all national borders. The rising tide of cosmopolitanism, which constituted a threat, had to be turned into a rampart and a safeguard.

To achieve these goals in our secular age, only one religion was open to us. The national flag, the symbol of modern patriotism being raised on the pole of victory to honor the winning athlete – that was what would keep the faith alive at the newly rekindled hearth.

We are still standing at the foot of Mount Kronion, but nightfall is coming. The glowing hues of the setting sun are fading away. In the deepening darkness, the first stars are beginning to shine, along with the lights of the small town nestled on the hillside where the museum stands, to the right. Let us cross the Kladeos and, on our way home, we pass in front of the new monument. The pale rays of moonlight that fall on the marble strike the last lines of the inscription in Greek and French carved into the monument. The inscription says, "Wherefore, having mentioned the restoration of the Games... Wherefore, the First Olympiad of the modern era was celebrated gloriously in the restored Stadium of Athens by all the people of the world in 1896, under the reign of George I, King of the Hellenes."

The restored Stadium of Athens! How I would love to show you a slide of the state the Stadium was back in November 1894 (I must be one of the few people to have that image, because it certainly did not tempt any buyers then. Only the embankments remained, worn down by wear and the weather), and then show you how it now stands, wearing its marble finery, filled with workers busily completing its stands, just as it was in the time of Pericles. It took only eighteen months to change the landscape. There were those who found fault with the project, with this resurrection, and those who said they missed the shapeless embankments. These are the same people who heap invective on the monument to Victor Emmanuel in Rome, calling those who do not share their opinions barbarians, certain that they are obtaining an invincible patent as artists by rising up the instant someone stands a fallen column back on its feet.

The historic scenes of 1896 took place in this restored enclosure. No one who was there will ever forget those events, which sent a thrill throughout all Greece. It was there that King George was first to intone the sacred words: "I proclaim the Games of the First Olympiad of the modern era open", as other sovereigns and heads of state have done every four years since then. It was there that we saw for the first time the prestigious procession of athletes, grouped by country, entering the stadium through the same arch where the last of the competitors, hounded out by decadence and cursed by the Church, had disappeared. Above all, that was also the place where the seventy thousand awaiting spectators saw the spectacle of the arrival of the first marathon runner, the shepherd Spiridion Louys. Having prepared himself through fasting and prayer before the icons, he easily surpassed his western and transatlantic rivals who had trained scientifically, reaching the finish line of this enormous trial without any unusual fatigue, winning the cup given by an illustrious member of the Institut de France, Mr. Michel Bréal. In his enthusiasm for the restoration of the Games, Bréal had told me, on the eve of the vote, "I will give a cup for the marathon race". Forty-two kilometers plus! I was a bit hesitant to agree to that distance, but history imposed it and fate legitimized this daring move. When Louys appeared at the entrance to the Stadium, thundering applause rose in tribute to the past and the present alike. To rescue him from the outpouring of emotion from the delirious crowd, the Crown Prince and his brother grasped the shepherd in their strong arms and carried him right to the marble steps where the king was standing...

Gradually, the restored Olympic Games took their place in the framework of the modern world, with the ancient spirit that was to breathe life into them. I took great pains not to move ahead too quickly. First, the basic rights of the International Olympic Committee had to be established and accepted by all countries. This was not an easy task, since its statutes stood in flagrant opposition to the ideas of the day. The statutes reject the principle of delegation which is so dear to our parliamentary democracies and which, after having rendered great service, seems to become less effective day by day. The members of the IOC are not in any way delegates within the Committee. They are even forbidden from accepting from their fellow countrymen any urgent mandate whatsoever, which could restrict their freedom. They must think of themselves as ambassadors of the Olympic idea in their respective countries. Their mandate is unlimited. Some have been in office for twenty, twenty-five, and even thirty years. Since they are not subsidized by anyone, their independence is complete... A high-level official once expressed regret that a similar organization could not be achieved at the League of Nations in Geneva.

The technical problems that had to be resolved through negotiation, mutual concession and, at times, through the imposition of legislation, were innumerable.

War did not destroy anything. The committee suspended its annual meetings, and started them up again once peace was restored. The Sixth Olympiad (1916) was not held. The Seventh Olympiad was held in Antwerp in 1920, with all the desired glory. In 1906, the arts and literature were called upon to take part. A conference held in the Foyer of the Comédie Française, whose deans, Madame Bartet and Mr. Mounet-Sully, sat at either side of Mr. Jules Claretie, approved the establishment of five competitions in painting, sculpture, architecture, music, and literature. After pouting a while, artists and writers began to show interest in the competitions, which are open to any previously unpublished work directly inspired by the idea of athletics.

From the very first time they were held, the opening and closing of the Games were as solemn as such occasions should be, but the ceremonies were not quite right until the athletes' oath, with its short and impressive wording, began to be sworn on the assembled flags of the competing countries. I did not turn day-to-day management of restored Olympism over to my successor until I felt that the renovation was complete to the last detail, in keeping with current needs while still in harmony with the memories and lessons of the past, with universal approval guaranteeing its long-term survival.

Nothing, or nearly nothing, remains of the initial hostility which was so widespread and often so violent. At first, the Catholic Church was, to say the least, distrustful. One day in 1905, I went to the Vatican to dispel the uneasiness. I was told that the holy Pope Pius X, quite busy with the salvation of souls, would not receive me. Yet that former patriarch of Venice had loved and encouraged the prowess of his gondoliers, and I was sure of his good will. His good will was great. After blessing the restoration, with its pagan overtones, the Pope told me that he would soon give me tangible proof of his support. In fact, the following year gymnasts met at the Vatican from the Catholic youth clubs of France, Belgium, Italy, and other countries. On the sumptuous dais built for the occasion, the sovereign Pontiff presided over their exercises in the courtyard of St. John of Damascus.

Despite all this one dispute continues to thrive, a dispute with which Ancient Olympia was quite familiar, one that will always come up everywhere. This dispute is physical education versus sports. It is tempting to imagine that men will manage to obtain the benefits of education without the competition of sports. In fact, the basic law remains: "For every hundred who engage in physical culture, fifty must engage in sports. For every fifty who engage in sports, twenty must specialize. For every twenty who specialize, five must be capable of astonishing feats". There is no way around this law. Everything is related and intertwined. Like doctors today in the name of health, in the past military leaders in the name of regimented training, as well as technical experts who start with the principle that level-headedness is a natural feature of man, have risen up to oppose this rule, which is imposed by our human nature.

Have there been deplorable excesses, and are there still some? Yes, clearly. Is this surprising? No one denies that it happens. The point is to determine whether these excesses can be avoided, and whether the benefits achieved through physical exercise practiced sportingly, i.e. with a tendency toward excess, can be achieved and maintained without such excess.

Essentially, this means asking the following question: *Can a religion survive without there being, among its adherents, those given to excess and those driven by passion to carry the crowd by its example, and to dominate it?* The answer is obvious.

So now we are brought back to the main idea that I have mentioned many times, and that I would like to leave in your minds in concluding this brief presentation. Like ancient athletics, modern athletics is a *religion*, a *belief*, a *passionate movement of the spirit* that can range from "games to heroism". Picture this basic principle, and you will come to see the athletes whose excesses you criticize and censure today as an elite who radiate energy, people who are far more idealistic (and, therefore, necessary for the public) than those who claim to stick to simple physical education to guarantee the future. These educators are people whose faith is flat, a faith that, left to its own, will have no followers in the near future, and no altars after that.

Thus Olympia is still alive. The Greek sanctuaries have all died out. No one will go to Epidaurus any more to take the cure, no one will be initiated at Eleusis. Madame Sikelianos has created an artistic life at Delphi, but the College of Priests will no longer run politics there. The Pythia has fallen silent, as has the oracle of Dodona...but Olympia lives on, for Olympism has spread throughout the world.

In this, we see a symbol of the durability of Greece. Your country, Mr. Minister, has upset the laws of history since it has contradicted what was held as a certainty, namely that nations necessarily had a youth, a mature period, and an old age, just like people. Humanity realized that this was utterly untrue through the example of Greece in the last century. Humanity saw that a people could stay buried in a tomb for three hundred years, and then come forth from it not just alive, but rejuvenated. Now, this is the supreme law of history: "Only those nations who want to die are killed". The outlook for human destiny has changed as a result.

People believed that Greece, once risen from the tomb, was a new Greece cut off from those that came before it. No one wanted to see the link between antiquity, what was called the Byzantine period, and the unexpected modern era that was dawning. But today, those on the forefront and the least well-informed alike are beginning to understand the power of Greek unity, and how the rising sap of present-day Hellenism is similar to that of former times. Europe and the world need that sap! May it rise, may it be fruitful, and may it be intoxicating! Zito Ellas!

Olympie,
in: *Le Sport Suisse*, Vol. 25,
July 10, 1929, p.1 (I); July 17, 1929, p. 1 (II); July 24, 1929, p. 1 (III); July 31, 1929, p. 1 (IV).
Offprint, Geneva 1929, 12 p.

5.1/15 MESSAGE TO AMERICAN YOUTH

This message to the American youth was sent through the Associated Press on the occasion of the celebration of the 40th anniversary of the revival of the Olympic Games. Coubertin stressed the importance of the 4 year rhythm of the Olympic Games, demanding a higher school education in all countries as basis for peace amongst the people.

MESSAGE TO AMERICAN YOUTH

SENT THROUGH THE ASSOCIATED PRESS

ON THE OCCASION OF THE CELEBRATION OF THE 40th ANNIVERSARY OF THE REVIVAL OF THE OLYMPIC GAMES

On this solemn occasion which probably closes the cycle of my public activities, I specially desire to send an appeal to American youth to take up and help to make fruitful the inheritance I pass on to them.

In doing so I evoke the memory of Theodore Roosevelt, of William M. Sloane, of many American friends who have worked willingly with me, understood me and sustained me throughout that long period in which I have had to struggle all over the world — and particularly in France, my own country — against the lack of understanding of public opinion, ill prepared to appreciate the value of the Olympic revival.

Whatever may be said, there is nothing excessive in the devotion of youth everywhere to muscular perfection. If it is pursued with passion, it is a healthy passion. But where there is exaggeration is in the increase of international competitions and championships. That is why sustained effort should be made to limit the number of these meetings. The quadriennal Olympic Games are necessary and adequate to maintain at the right level the spirit of emulation among nations.

A reform no less urgent is that of secondary education overloaded and obscured by special courses rightly belonging to the University curriculum. Secondary education in all countries should be a period of intellectual aviation *destined to fly over the domain of Knowledge so that each one may have at least the chance to perceive the vast panorama before landing on the particular points where he will make his productive effort.*

The relation between that question and peace between nations, and between individuals, is a close one. Too many people are as yet unwilling to recognize this. I am happy to have been able to lay down the bases of a reform which will end by forcing itself on everybody, to have drawn up the programs, to have summed up the aim and the methods.

Dear friends beyond the seas, I hope that you will work to strengthen what I have accomplisned and to complete what I will leave unfinished.

I thank you. I have the deepest faith in the desting of your great country which I stiil admire and love in the twilight as I did in the dawn of my life.

PIERRE DE COUBERTIN

Lausanne, June, 23. 1934,
(Ann. III-Olympiad Xth)

Message to American Youth, Special Print
published by the Associated Press
for the celebration of the 40th anniversary
of the restoration of the Olympic Games, 1934, 1 page.
(N.Müller Collection)

5.1/16 MESSAGE TO THE OLYMPIA-BERLIN RUNNERS

It was Coubertin who wanted the Olympic flame to burn (as was the practice in Ancient Olympia) in each Olympic stadium – a wish first realized in 1928. Carl Diem conceived the idea of having a relay of torch bearers cross Europe from Olympia to Berlin. This would provide a link between antiquity and modern times, as well as among the nations of the various countries through which the relay passed, nations that could take part in the celebration in this way. Coubertin welcomed the idea enthusiastically. He also agreed with Carl Diem's recommendation that excavation at Olympia continue, to unearth the ancient stadium[1]. Coubertin addressed the following message to the thousand participants in the torch race. He called this his final message, as though moved by a foreboding of his death, a feeling that had lain dormant in him since 1928 given his age.

In lighting the flame in Berlin, he called on the bearers of the torch to transmit his legacy to the youth gathered in that city, namely that, in keeping with his educational principles, youth should unite body and soul for the advancement and honor of humanity!

As the founder and honorary president of the modern Olympic Games, I am the first to address you, the athletes who will carry the symbolic torch in your eager hands from Olympia to Berlin, so I would like to tell you in what way my thoughts are with you, and what significance I attach to your efforts.

We are living in a grand age, for all around us we see the unexpected. As the shape of Europe and the new Asia begins to appear as though through a morning mist, it would seem that at long last, humanity will recognize that the crisis in which it finds itself is, above all, a crisis of education.

For me, fifty years have passed since that day in 1886 when, casting aside any concern of a personal nature, I vowed that my life's work would be to prepare for the reform of education, convinced as I was that from now on, no political or social stability can be achieved without educational reform first.

I am aware that I have completed my mission, but not fully.

Countless stadiums around the world now ring with the shouts of athletic joy, as they once rose from the gymnasiums of Greece. No nation, no class, no profession is excluded. The religion of restored athletics has done more than simply fortify public health. It provides a sort of joyful stoicism that can help the individual face the daily ups and downs of life.

Let us congratulate ourselves on what we have accomplished, yet remain aware that more remains to be done. The mind must be freed, too, from the bonds that excessive specialization has imposed on it. It must escape from the oppressive narrowness of exclusive professions.

The broad horizons available to our age must be shown to each person at the threshold of active life, no matter how fleeting that glimpse may be. The future belongs to those who will be the first to dare to change the instruction of the young adult.

It is that young adult, not the child, who holds and dictates fate.

This will bring about a vigorous and intentional peace well-suited to an age of athletics, ambition, and will.

Greek runner in national costume during the first Olympic torch run for the 1936 Olympic Games in Berlin (taken P. Wolff, Was ich bei den Olympischen Spielen sah. Berlin, Specht, 1936, no. 4)

I entrust my message to you, no doubt the last such message that I will give. May your route be happy. The German Committee has taken great pains in designing and organizing it, efforts deeply appreciated by all nations. The route begins, moreover, in the most illustrious of all places, under the sign of the eternal Hellenism that continues to shine on the path of the ages, whose ancient solutions still apply today to many a present-day problem.

On my behalf, ask the youth assembled in Berlin to accept the legacy of my work. Ask them to complete what I have begun, a task that pervasive routine and tedium prevented me from achieving completely. Let the union of the body and mind be sealed forever, for progress and for human dignity.

Aux coureurs d'Olympie-Berlin,
in: *Le Sport Suisse*,
Vol. 32, July 22, 1936, p. 1.

1 In tribute to the Berlin Games, the German Archaeological Institute continued the excavation of the sanctuary at Olympia, in 1937.

5.1/17 THE PHILOSOPHIC FOUNDATION OF MODERN OLYMPISM

In the introduction to this edition and to this chapter, the speech Coubertin gave in 1935 on "The Philosophic Foundation of Modern Olympism" was characterized as the most significant Olympic testimony that he gave in his final years. In it, Coubertin once again presents all the main characteristics of Olympism. The lecture given on August 4, 1935, recorded at the radio station in Geneva, was the first in a series of talks a year before the opening of the Games of the Eleventh Olympiad in Berlin. Coubertin was seventy-two. This was an opportunity that would never come again. Once again, Coubertin presented his thoughts to a vast audience. This speech completes the preceding lecture, "Olympia", which dates from 1929. In that speech, he established the link between antiquity and the historical development of the ideas that are the basis of Olympism. In this lecture, however, Coubertin analyzes the closed system of thought. It was in this speech that Coubertin entrusted his Olympic will and testament to future generations, a testament on the basis of which each of the partial values of Olympism is still evaluated today.

As the founder and honorary president of the Olympic Games, I was asked to present the first of the messages to be broadcast by radio that will explain the meaning of the Games. I was quick to accept this honor. I believe that the best way to go about this is to present my initial thoughts and the philosophical foundations on which I tried to base my work.

The primary, fundamental characteristic of ancient Olympism, and of modern Olympism as well, is that it is a *religion*. By chiseling his body through exercise as a sculptor does a statue, the ancient athlete "honored the gods". In doing likewise, the modern athlete honors his country, his race, and his flag. Therefore, I believe that I was right to restore, from the very beginning of modern Olympism, a religious sentiment transformed and expanded by the internationalism and democracy that are distinguishing features of our day. Yet this is the same religious sentiment that led the young Hellenes, eager for the victory of their muscles, to the foot of the altars of Zeus.

From this sentiment derive all the cultural expressions that constitute the ceremonies of the modern Games. I had to impose these ceremonies one after another on a public that was opposed to them for a long time, seeing them merely as theatrical displays, useless spectacles incompatible with the seriousness and dignity of international athletic competitions. The athletic religious concept, the *religio athletae*, took root slowly in the minds of competitors, many of whom still experience it only in an unconscious way. But they will come around, gradually.

It is not just internationalism and democracy, the foundations of the new human society now being constructed in civilized nations, but science as well that is involved in this sentiment. Through its constant progress, science has given man new ways to cultivate his body, to guide and straighten nature, and to snatch the body from the constraints of unbridled passions to which it had become subject in the name of individual freedom.

The second characteristic of Olympism is that it is an *aristocracy*, an *elite*. Of course, this aristocracy is completely egalitarian in origin since membership is determined solely by the physical superiority of the individual, by his muscular ability – improved to a certain extent by his willingness to train. Not all young men are destined to become athletes. Later, no doubt, through enhanced public and private hygiene and through astute measures intended to improve the race, it will be possible greatly to increase the number of individuals capable of handling intense athletic education. It is unlikely that we will ever reach more than about half, certainly no more than two thirds, of each generation. Currently we are far from that figure in all countries. Yet even if such a result were to be achieved, it would not necessarily follow that all these young athletes would be "Olympians", i.e. men capable of contesting world records. I have presented this idea before, in an axiom (now translated into various languages) unconsciously accepted by nearly everyone: "For every hundred who engage in physical culture, fifty must engage in sports. For every fifty who engage in sports, twenty must specialize. For every twenty who specialize, five must be capable of astonishing feats."

To try to make athletics conform to a system of mandatory moderation is to chase after an illusion. Athletes need the "freedom of excess". That is why their motto is *Citius, altius, fortius*: faster, higher, stronger, the motto of anyone who dares to try to beat a record!

Yet being an elite is not enough. This elite must also be a *knighthood*. Knights, above all else, are "brothers in arms", brave, energetic men united by a bond that is stronger than that of mere camaraderie, which is powerful enough in itself. In chivalry, the idea of competition, of effort opposing effort for the love of the effort itself, of courteous yet violent struggle, is superimposed on the notion of mutual assistance, the basis of camaraderie. In antiquity, that was the Olympic spirit in its purest form. It is easy to see the tremendous consequences that application of this principle can have when it comes to international competitions. Forty years ago, people thought that I was deluding myself with my plans to restore the impact of this principle in the Olympic Games. But it is becoming clear that not only can and should this principle exist in the solemn setting of the quadrennial Olympic Games, but that it is already being seen in less solemn circumstances. From country to country, its progress has been slow but steady. Now, its influence must reach the spectators themselves. This, too, has already taken place, in Paris, for example, at the football match last March 17. We must come to a point on such occasions, and especially at the Olympic Games, that the applause is expressed only in proportion to the feat accomplished, regardless of national sympathies. A truce must be called regarding exclusively nationalistic feelings, which must be put "on temporary leave", so to speak.

The idea of the *truce* is another element of Olympism. It is closely related to the notion of *rhythm*. The Olympic Games must be held on a strictly astronomical rhythm, because they are the quadrennial celebration of the human springtime, honoring the successive arrival of human generations. That is why we must adhere to this rhythm strictly. Today as in antiquity, an Olympiad may fail to be held if unforeseen circumstances present an insurmountable obstacle, but neither the order nor the number of the Olympiad may be changed.

The human springtime is neither childhood or adolescence. In our day, in many if not all countries we are making a serious mistake by placing too much significance on childhood, granting it a certain degree of autonomy and allowing it excessive and premature privileges. The theory is that we gain time this way, and increase the period of useful productivity. This approach comes from a mistaken interpretation of the

Coubertin in the Radio Suisse Romande studio, from where his famous speech on "The Philosophical Foundation of Modern Olympism" was broadcast on 4th August 1935. (IOC Archives)

expression "Time is money". This expression was not devised by a race or a specific form of civilization, but by a people – the American people – who were going through an exceptional and temporary period of productive opportunities at the time.

The human springtime is expressed in the *young adult male*, who can be compared to a superb machine in which all the gears have been set in place, ready for full operation. That is the person in whose honor the Olympic Games must be celebrated and their rhythm organized and maintained, because it is on him that the near future depends, as well as the harmonious passage from the past to the future.

How better to honor this than by proclaiming a temporary cessation of hostilities, disputes, and misunderstandings, at regular, set intervals for this express purpose? Men are not angels, and I do not believe that humanity would profit from having most men become angels. But the truly strong man is one whose will is powerful enough to make himself and his group stop pursuing its desire or passion for domination and possession, regardless of how legitimate such pursuits may be. I would welcome most warmly an interruption in hostilities in the midst of war between armed opponents, in order to celebrate athletic, fair, and courteous Games.

From what I have just said, one must conclude that the true Olympic hero is, in my view, the *individual adult male*. Should sports teams, therefore, be excluded? This is not absolutely essential, if one accepts another essential element in modern Olympism, as it was accepted in ancient Olympism: the existence of an *Altis*, or *sacred enclosure*. At Olympia, plenty of events took place outside the Altis. A whole community of life thrived all around it, even though that community did not enjoy the privilege of appearing inside the enclosure. The Altis itself was like a sanctuary reserved for the consecrated, purified athlete only, the athlete admitted to the main competitions and who became, in this way, a sort of priest, an officiating priest in the religion of the muscles. Similarly, I see modern Olympism as having at its core a sort of moral Altis, a sacred Fortress where the competitors in the manly sports par excellence are gathered to pit their strength against each other. The objectives of these sports are to defend man and to achieve self-mastery, to master danger, the elements, the animal, life. These athletes are gymnasts, runners, riders, swimmers and rowers, fencers and wrestlers – and then, around them, all the other types of athletic life one might want to include, such as football tournaments and other games, team exercises, etc. They will be honored in this way, as is fitting, but on a secondary level. Here, too, is where women could participate, if this is felt to be necessary. Personally, I do not approve of women's participation in public competitions, which does not mean that they should not engage in a great many sports, merely that they should not become the focus of a spectacle. At the Olympic Games, their role should be above all to crown the victors, as was the case in the ancient tournaments.

There is one final thing: *beauty*, the involvement of the arts and the mind in the Games. Indeed, can one celebrate the festival of the human springtime without inviting the mind to take part? But then we face the weighty issue of the reciprocal action of the muscles and the mind. What should their alliance, their cooperation, look like?

No doubt, the mind is the dominant figure. The muscles must remain the vassals of the mind, provided that we are focusing on the highest forms of artistic and literary creation, not the lower forms to which ever-increasing license has been given in our time to the great detriment of civilization, of human truth and dignity, and of international relations.

I know that in response to my request, the Games of the Eleventh Olympiad will open to the incomparable sounds of the last movement of Beethoven's Ninth Symphony, sung by powerful choral groups. Nothing could make me happier, because during my childhood this particular movement stirred and moved me deeply. The harmony of the piece seemed to communicate with the Divine. I hope that in the future choral music, which is so well-suited to translating the power of the hopes and joys of youth, will accompany their Olympic feats more and more. Similarly, I hope that history will hold a major place alongside poetry in intellectual exhibitions held along with the Games. This is only natural, since Olympism is part of history. To celebrate the Olympic Games is to lay claim to history.

History is also the best guarantee of peace. To ask people to love one another is merely a form of childishness. To ask them to respect each other is not utopian, but in order to respect each other they must first know each other. The only true basis for peace will come from taking into account the precise chronological and geographical outlines of World History as it can now be taught.

Now that I have come to the close of my days, I take advantage of the coming Games of the Eleventh Olympiad to express my best wishes to you, along with my thanks. At the same time, I express to you my unshakable faith in youth and in the future!

Les assises philosophiques de l'Olympisme moderne,
in: *Le Sport Suisse*, Vol. 31, August 7, 1935, p. 1;
and special print of the *Sport Suisse*, Geneva 1935, 4pp.

5.1/18 OLYMPISM AND POLITICS

In 1936, in his New Year's message printed in the Belgian *Revue Sportive Illustrée,* Coubertin unambiguously stated his position regarding political influences on sports. He rejected out of hand the boycott of the Olympics planned by the United States for 1936, and supported by France[1].

In Coubertin's view, Olympism must not be subject to the influence of temporary phenomena, and must remain independent of the chance conditions of politics[2].

In the "Statement" that he recently made upon his return from Germany (a trip undertaken to quiet concerns not all of which are spontaneous or sincere), Count de Baillet-Latour summarized strongly and logically, in excellent terms on all points, what we must think and say about the anti-Olympic campaign that originated across the Atlantic, a campaign that has been spread cleverly from one country to another in Europe. The Count rightly castigated the use of Olympic strengths in the service of electoral interests. True "Olympians" now know what to believe. Under the present circumstances, the unfair attack leveled against holding the Eleventh Olympiad in Berlin has been fended off. This attack will return in one form or another, no doubt, and it will fail once more. But should we be surprised that such steps are being taken?

I am too accustomed to living within the bosom of general history and to scrutinizing its meanderings to be unaware of the important concept of evolution. I am hardly surprised, and even less indignant, to find it everywhere. Every institution, every creation, no matter how vibrant it may be, evolves in keeping with the customs and passions of the moment. Today, politics is making its way into the heart of every issue. How can we expect athletics, the culture of the muscles, and Olympism itself to be immune?

Yet the ravages that this phenomenon can cause lie merely on the surface. In reality, there are almost always *two* forms of evolution in an institution: the evolution of appearances, and the evolution of the soul. The first tries to adapt to current trends, and changes according to the whims of fashion. The second remains as steadfast as the principles on which the institution is based. It evolves slowly and healthily, in conformity with the laws of humanity itself. Olympism falls within the second of these categories.

L'Olympisme et la politique,
in: *La Revue Sportive Illustrée,*
Vol. 32, 1936, special issue, [p. 38].

1 His position was exactly the same regarding the threat of an Olympic boycott in 1916, as indicated in his article, "La critique est aisée" ["It Is Easy To Criticize"] in *the Revue Olympique* (1912, no. 10, p. 151).

2 See also Coubertin's "Déclarations" ["Statements"] on August 27, 1936 in the daily paper *Le Journal,* reprinted in Chapter 4.2.2/49.

5.2 OLYMPIC PRINCIPLES AND SYMBOLS

Chapter 5.2 includes ten articles written by Coubertin regarding his fundamental statements on the Olympic movement. They complement his articles on Olympism. Today these articles provide extremely valuable insights into the most significant Olympic mottoes.

The most well-known motto is also the most ancient: "Citius, altius, fortius". The Dominican priest Henri Didon had made it the main topic of his speech during the opening of the first school sport event on March 7, 1891, before the athletic association of the École Albert-le-Grand, a school that he ran at Arcueil, near Paris. Coubertin was present on that occasion, and wrote a short report about it in the magazine *Les Sports Athlétiques*[1], of which he was editor-in-chief. He often used this motto thereafter, since it matched his educational conception of sports exactly[2].

At the founding congress in 1894, Coubertin made these three words the motto of the new Olympic movement[3].

In 1925 in his farewell speech, Coubertin said "Athletics [cannot be] united with moderation, nor made timid and cautious". He added, "The feat that glorifies the individual champion is necessary for maintaining general zeal and ambition[4]."

This motto must be viewed not only in its athletic and technical sense, but also from a moral and educational perspective. This is what Coubertin hopes to get across in the various texts included under "Olympism" (see the preceding chapter).

This concept is very well put in a quote from the famous Swiss Olympic champion, Paul Martin:

"Citius: fast not only in the race, but with a quick and vibrant mind, as well.

Altius: higher, not only toward a coveted goal, but also toward the uplifting of the individual.

Fortius: not only more courageous in the struggles on the field of play, but in life, also[5]."

The other texts in this chapter are also quite significant. They address the internationalism of the Olympic movement, and the equality of the sports of the Olympic Games. They underscore the independence of the IOC as far as a distinct "athletic geography" is concerned. They stress the chivalrous spirit and place greater significance on participation, rather than victory, in the Games.

Like the mottoes, the significance of protocol, which increased as the Olympic Games grew, lies in its symbolic value, this especially includes the Olympic rings.[6]

1 See Coubertin, "Championnats de l'A.A.A.G.", in: *Les Sports Athlétiques,* no 50, March 14, 1891, p. 4.

2 Initially the motto was "Citius, fortius, altius". The reasons that led Coubertin to invert the second and third words lies in the Latin wording.

3 It appears at the top of the first issue of the Bulletin of the IOC, published in July 1894. Note that initially the IOC was called the "International Committee of the Olympic Games". It was not until 1898 that the term "International Olympic Committee" was used.

4 Coubertin, *Speech Given at the Opening of the Olympic Congresses at the City Hall of Prague.* Special brochure, Government Printing Office, Prague, 1925, p. 5. See text 5.1/11 in this volume.

5 P. Martin, "La Psychologie de l'effort." [The Psychology of Effort], in: *Bulletin of the IOC,* 1953, no. 37, p. 28.

6 See N. Müller, "Henri Didon- Der Urheber der Olympischen Devise "Citius, altius, Fortius"." In: N.Müller/M.Messing (eds): *Auf der Suche nach der olympischen Idee.* Kassel, Agon, 1996, pp.49-62.

"The same rank", illustration underlining the equality of the various Olympic sports (taken from La Revue Sportive Illustrée, April 1906, no.1, p.5)

5.2/1 THE SAME RANK

In 1906, Coubertin found himself in the position of having to state – officially – the mutual equality of the various sports in the Olympic Games. The reason was the unequal importance attributed to some sports by the American press following the 1906 intermediate Olympic Games.

The appendix to the *Revue Olympique,* published monthly as of January 1906, served as the IOC Bulletin for such position statements.

People have been upset in France, and astonished in other countries, at certain articles published in newspapers on the other side of the Atlantic. According to these articles, first place in the Athens Olympic Games allegedly belonged to the American team, taking no account of the official ranking that the jury determined and made public. This news allegedly was sent to the United States by the American delegate himself. We are authorized to report that, given these circumstances, the head of state and the French ambassador have written from Washington to the President of the International Olympic Committee to seek information. The key to the puzzle came to light with the publication of an article on the Olympic Games in one of the major New York newspapers. That article presented the peculiar notion that modern Olympiads consist of two parts: the Olympic Games *strictly speaking,* i.e. the "athletic sports" (foot races and jumping), and then the "other sports" (fencing, shooting, swimming, rowing, etc.). Clearly, if one were to view things in this light, the Americans triumphed in the Olympic Games *strictly speaking*, but there are no grounds for anyone to make such distinctions among the competitions that are part of the Olympiad. All sports hold the same rank. It is difficult to see why gymnastics, the water sports and fencing should bow to foot races, and be deemed exercises of a lesser order. That runs counter to ancient tradition, which included boxing from the start and, later, equestrian sports. In any event, it is contrary to the regulations in force today. Therefore it is unacceptable, for any reason whatsoever, for anyone to set about changing the ranking determined by the jury at Athens, which remains the only lawful and accurate ranking.

Le même rang,
in: *Revue Olympique*,
August 1906, pp. 127-128.

The editor has determined that this text, though unsigned, was written by Coubertin.

5.2/2 THE TRUSTEES OF THE OLYMPIC IDEA

This speech, given at the reception held by the British government in honor of the guests of the Olympic Games in 1908, is one of the most often-quoted of Coubertin's statements.

Two comments in it are extremely important. In the first, Coubertin speaks of the lack of "fair play" that threatens the "Olympic idea". The second is even more important, but Coubertin is not its author, though it is attributed to him: "In these Olympiads, the important thing is not winning, but taking part."

The bishop of the Anglican Church of Central Pennsylvania, Ethelbert Talbot, had made that remark the dominant theme of the service held at St. Paul's Cathedral in London, in honor of the participants in the Olympic Games in London.

Coubertin took the comment and added: "The important thing in life is not victory, but struggle; the essential is not to conquer, but to fight well". That corresponds to his educational ideal.

Your Excellencies, My Lords, Gentlemen,

In the name of the International Olympic Committee, I would like to express my deep gratitude for the tribute that has just been paid to us. We shall remember it warmly, as we shall recall this Fourth Olympiad. Thanks to the zeal and the hard work of our English colleagues, a colossal effort has been made to ensure its technical excellence. As satisfying as these results may be, I hope that I am not being overly ambitious in saying that in the future, we hope that even more will be done, if such a thing is possible. We want to progress steadily. Anyone who does not progress is on the decline.

Gentlemen, the progress made by the Committee in whose name I am honored to speak has been considerable and fast, so far. When I think of the anonymous attacks of which it has been victim, and of the pitfalls and obstacles that improbable cabals and fanatical jealousies have thrown in its path over the past fourteen years, I cannot help but think that wrestling is a wonderful sport, even when, leaving aside the classic moves, your adversaries spring "catch as catch can" tactics on you. That is what the International Olympic Committee has faced since its inception, and it seems to have become strong and stalwart in the process.

The reason for these struggles? Good God! I'll tell you in just a few words. We are not elected. We are self-recruiting, and our terms of office are unlimited. Is there anything else that could irritate public opinion more? Increasingly the public is used to seeing the principle of elections expand, gradually placing all institutions under its yoke. In our case, we are infringing against the general rule, a difficult thing to tolerate, isn't it? Well we are delighted to take responsibility for this irregularity, and we are not in the least concerned about it.

I once learned a great many things in this country. Among them was that the best way to preserve freedom and to serve democracy is not always to abandon everything to elections, but rather to maintain islands in the great electoral ocean where the continuity of independent, stable effort can be guaranteed within certain narrowly-defined areas.

From this pulpit in St Paul's Cathedral in London, Bishop Ethelbert Talbot addressed the participants in the 1908 Olympics with these significant words: "In these Olympiads, the important thing is not winning, but taking part". (Photo: N.Müller)

Independence and stability. These, Gentlemen, are what has made it possible for us to accomplish great things. These are things that – too often, we must admit – groups today lack, athletic groups in particular. No doubt such independence would entail some inconvenience for us if we were to become involved in issuing strict regulations intended to become mandatory. But that is not our role. We do not tread on the privileges of the associations. We are not a technical police board. We are merely "trustees" of the Olympic idea.

In our view, the Olympic idea is the concept of strong physical culture based in part on the spirit of chivalry – what you here so pleasantly call "fair play" – and in part on the esthetic idea of the cult of what is beautiful and graceful. I will not say that the Ancients never failed to live up to this ideal. This morning I read about an incident that caused some excitement yesterday. In one of your major newspapers I read a statement of despair at the thought that some aspects of our modern-day athletic customs make it impossible for us to hope ever to attain the level of the classical period. Gentlemen, do you really believe that such incidents did not pepper the history of the Olympic, Pythian, and Nemean Games, and all the great athletic meetings in antiquity? It would be utterly naive to say so. Man has always been a creature of passions, and saints preserve us from a society devoid of excesses, where the expression of ardent feelings would be forever enclosed in the overly narrow confines of proprieties.

Yet it is also true that in our time, when the progress of material civilization – I would even say of mechanical civilization – has magnified everything, some problems threatening the Olympic idea are cause for concern. Yes, I do not wish to hide the fact, "fair play" is in danger. It is in danger particularly because of the chance that we have unwisely allowed to grow: the madness of gaming, the madness of the bet, of gambling. Well, if a crusade against gambling is what we need, we are ready to undertake it. I am sure that in this country, public opinion will support us – the opinion of those who love sports for sports' sake, for their educational value, for the human advancement in which they can be a most powerful factor. Last Sunday, at the ceremony held at the Cathedral of St. Paul in honor of the athletes, the Bishop of Pennsylvania recalled this in apt terms: "In these Olympiads, the important thing is not winning, but taking part."

Gentlemen, let us remember this strong statement. It applies to every endeavor, and can even be taken as the basis of a serene and healthy philosophy. What counts in life is not the victory, but the struggle; the essential thing is not to conquer, but to fight well. To spread these precepts is to help create a more valiant, stronger humanity, one that is also more scrupulous and more generous.

These are the ideas that prevail within our organization. We will continue to draw our inspiration from them. We will meet again in four years to celebrate the Fifth Olympiad. In the interim, of course, the Athens Games will be held once again. Once more, the world will turn its attention to the immortal land of Greece, the worship of which is inseparable from any ennobling aspiration.

In the name of my colleagues, allow me to salute your respective countries, first of all old England, mother of so many virtues, inspiration of so many efforts. Internationalism as we understand it consists of respect for countries and the noble sentiment that stirs the athlete's heart when he sees his nation's colors being raised on the mast of victory, the result of his efforts.

Gentlemen, to your countries, to the glory of your sovereigns, to the greatness of their reigns, to the prosperity of your government and of your fellow citizens.

Les "trustees" de l'idée olympique,
in: *Revue Olympique*, July 1908, pp. 108-110.

5.2/3 ATHLETIC GEOGRAPHY

In this letter to the editor addressed to Victor Silberer, editor of the *Allgemeine Sportzeitung* in Vienna, Coubertin spells out two essential Olympic principles with reference to the delicate problem raised by nationalities and flags during preparations for the 1912 Stockholm Games: "All games, all nations", and the definition of a "sporting geography."

All sports and all nations have the right to participate in the Olympic Games. In the view of Coubertin and the IOC, even such countries as Finland and Bohemia, which were not independent countries in 1912, had the right to appear on the list of participants.

Dear Sir,

I must note that the article published in your newspaper on February 26 may give rise to troublesome misunderstandings. The program for the Olympic Games in Stockholm is not nearly final yet, and it is not at all up to the Swedish Committee to "draw up the list of countries allowed to take part in the Olympic Games". The fundamental rule of the modern Olympiads is summarized in these terms: "All games, all nations". It is not even within the power of the International Olympic

"Athletic Geography": the Czechs arrived in Stockholm in 1912 as an independent team. It was agreed to use the name "Czech Austria" as a compromise and the flags of both Austria-Hungary and Bohemia (J.Kössl Collection)

Committee, the highest authority in this matter, to change this. I must add that a nation is not necessarily an independent State. There is an athletic geography that may differ at times from political geography. Long ago, the precedent was set by the European Office of Gymnastics Federations, directed by Mr. Cuperus of Antwerp. We believe that we have acted wisely in following this example.

As for your country, although no Austrian is on the list of members of the International Committee *for the time being*, we are not responsible for this gap. What is more, we are going to remedy this situation. I hope that our next meeting, to be held in Budapest in May at the invitation of the Hungarian government and under the patronage of His Imperial and Royal Apostolic Majesty, will not conclude without filling this void left among us. In any event, we are counting on there being many Austrian athletes involved in the Fifth Olympiad, something that is a source of happiness for us all.

Sincerely yours.

Pierre de Coubertin

Géographie sportive,
in: *Revue Olympique*,
April 1911, pp. 51-52.

5.2/4 NEW MOTTOES

It was not until 1911 that Coubertin mentioned the origins of the motto "Mens fervida in corpore lacertoso", ("An ardent mind in a well-trained body") in an article for the Revue Olympique[1]. He wanted to add to the medical aspects of the quote from the Roman author Juvenal, "Orandum est ut sit mens sana in corpore sano", in order to stir the ambition of youth. While the aim of the motto "Citius, altius, fortius" is athletic performance, the ideal of harmony between the body and the mind is invoked in "Mens fervida in corpore lacertoso". This motto is practically unknown even within the Olympic world.

The third quotation, "Athletae proprium est se ipsum noscere, ducere et vincere" (It is the athlete's duty and essence to know, to lead, and to conquer himself) underscores the transposition of physical strength to the level of spiritual and moral strengths, in keeping with the specific understanding of athletic education that Coubertin espoused. This motto, dating from 1923, did not become widely accepted, either. Its objective is explained in this passage.

One could long debate the origins of mottoes and their various wordings. They correspond to some need or instinct in humanity, because both barbarians and civilized peoples have used them with equal promptness. The modern world, being the heir of the ancient world, does not appear to be about to give up the practice.

Athletic associations, to some extent in all countries, have their mottoes. They write them at the top of their statutes, on the insignia worn by their members, on the programs of the festivals they hold, etc. It was inevitable that these mottoes should often become repetitious. The number of ideas that inspires them is very limited. The motto is always a call for effort, constancy, or balance. Among those in the last category, there is the well-known *mens sana in corpore sano* which so many speakers of little imagination have used. That saying has been overused so much that it is no exaggeration to say that it has become unbearably hackneyed.

CITIUS, ALTIUS, FORTIUS

Our era, which no longer studies Latin and believes that it can forget that language without any repercussions – no doubt a passing error – has nevertheless continued to turn to it for its mottoes, through its need for prestige and conciseness. Conciseness is the first of all a motto's necessary characteristics.

The oldest of the recent athletic mottoes dates back some thirty-five years. Its author was the famous Fr. Didon, of the Dominican order, then director of the school at Arcueil, near Paris. This great apostle with his manly energy soon saw the rebirth of athletics as a powerful educational tool, one that he did not hesitate to use. In a speech he gave while awarding the prizes at an interscholastic athletic meet held by the students, he suddenly used these three comparative adjectives. From that moment on, athletic records had found their glorification in the classic style. Their

1 Cf. Coubertin, "Mens fervida in corpore lacertoso." In: *Revue Olympique,* July 1911, no. 67, pp. 99-100. This text is reprinted in part I (text 3.15) of this edition.

essential characteristics were summed up in three succinct words. The fate of this new motto was broader and greater than its author ever imagined. Olympism adopted it as its own and spread it around the world. Today, this resounding appeal echoes over the youth of all countries. It is read, intertwined with the five symbolic rings, everywhere that athletics has taken hold in triumph. It is surrounded by successive records for speed, endurance, and strength, braving the vain protests of worried coaches but applauded by the crowd that feels that records are essential in athletic life, and that exceptional prowess is key for any general activity.

MENS FERVIDA IN CORPORE LACERTOSO

This motto was not the result of improvisation during a speech. It was well thought out and deliberate. The restorer of the Olympic Games worked out its wording with Mr. Morlet, a passionate Latinist, a great friend of sport, the former principal of the high schools of Marseilles, Troyes, and Vannes, near Paris. The *Revue Olympique* of July 1911 discussed its origins, and debated the value of the motto. The *Revue Olympique* returned to the topic later, because another eminent Latinist and member of the IOC was not fully satisfied with the use of the word *lacertosus*. Later on, it happened that as he evaluated the new expression during a conversation at the Vatican, Pope Pius XI expressed concern about the ideal *fervidus*. In both instances, the notion of excess was replacing the notion of balance. That is what its originator intended; his principles on this matter are well known. The modern educational system was creating a bold definition of itself: an ardent soul, a trained body, exuberance of the mind opposed to the exuberance of the muscles, or rather complementing it. This is the educational perspective of aviators, risk-takers, and the like. Circumstances, general evolution, and the passions of the day have made it so. Clearly there will always be those who protest, but who, these days, does not feel that the *mens sana* lacks prestige because it lacks truth? The particular condition that it advocates is magnificent, but it is a result, not a goal. If you want to reach a goal, as one educator has said, aim past it. Equilibrium within unavoidable modern commotion can be brought about only through combining or opposing excesses. One will not accomplish *enough* unless one strives for *too much*.

So the motto *Mens fervida in corpore lacertoso*, an ideal that seems intemperate, contains the seed of a most interesting historical and educational philosophical dispute, a dispute that is always of interest.

ATHLETAE PROPRIUM EST...

In 1923, under the auspices of the International Olympic Committee and thanks to the enlightened generosity of Mr. A. Bolanachi, a member of the IOC for Egypt, an "African medal" was established for the propagation of athletic activity among indigenous youth. This was a serious matter that created a storm in some centers of government, a topic to which we shall return. One side of the medal bears the image of a black man throwing a javelin. The other side shows a stand of bamboo, through which one can read an inscription. The question was what language should the inscription be in. There was no possibility of using African dialects, which are infinitely varied. In Africa, English, French, German, Italian, and Portuguese are regional languages, depending on the nature of local colonization. Why would we use one rather than another? Latin, if you will, is not understood by anyone in Africa, but the officers and missionaries know the language and can translate the inscription on the medal into whatever language their subordinates understand. Then there is the matter of the prestige of ancient example. There was no hesitation. We chose Latin and a whole system of education was carved into the exotic foliage, in just a few words. Here is the text: "*Athletae proprium est se ipsum noscere, ducere et vincere.* – It is the duty and the essence of the athlete to know, to lead and to conquer himself". Of course, in all the world's languages, it takes twice as many words as the original to express the idea. Yet these words encapsulate a whole lesson in manly athletic education, and that is the main thing. The transposition from the muscular to the moral sphere, the basis of athletic education, is indicated in terms that are superior in clarity and conciseness. We believe that, like the two others, this motto will spread throughout the world, and that in commenting on it and applying it, teachers will gain a more solid understanding of the fundamental principle of their instruction, and that students will gain deeper conviction about the value of that instruction.

Devises nouvelles,
in: *Bulletin du Bureau International de Pédagogie Sportive*,
Lausanne (1931), no. 4, pp. 12-14.

The editor has determined that this text, though unsigned, was written by Coubertin.

5.2/5 THE THOUGHTS OF ATHLETES

The quotations which follow are the ones included by Coubertin in the 1918 Olympic Almanac. The first clarifies the motto "citius, altius, fortius" for the second time. The Olympic champion becomes ideal. Coubertin sees in this a "law of the unconscious" which justifies competition sport and even makes it necessary.

The second quotation comes from 1899 under the pseudonym Georges Hohrod[1]. It is taken from *Roman d'un Rallié* published in the *Nouvelle Revue.* Here we find the same reasoning as in Coubertin's commentary on the quotation by the Bishop of Central Pennsylvania, Ethelbert Talbot[2]: "The important thing in life is not victory but struggle; the essential is not to have won but to have fought well."[3]

"For every hundred who engage in physical culture, fifty must engage in sports. For every fifty who engage in sports, twenty must specialize. For every twenty who specialize, five must be capable of astonishing feats. All this holds together and is interrelated. That is why theoreticians' campaigns against specialized athletes are puerile and without effect."

1 See Georges Hohrod [alias Pierre de Coubertin], *Le Roman d'un Rallié.* Auxerre, A. Lanier, 1902. It is under this pseudonym, to which he added that of Eschbach, that he wrote the "Ode to Sport", winning a gold medal in the literature competition at the Olympic Games in Stockholm.

2 See T. Widlund, "Ethelbert Talbot. His Life and Plays in Olympic History. Commentary by John Lucas." In: *Citius, Altius, Fortius. The Journal of the International Society of Olympic Historians,* Vol. 2, no. 2, Mai 1994, pp. 7-14.

3 See text 5.2/2 of this volume.

"Life is simple, because struggle is simple. A good fighter pulls back, but does not give up. He yields, but he never gives in. When faced with the impossible, he changes course and goes ahead. If his breath gives out, he rests and he waits. If he has been knocked out of the fight, he encourages his brothers with his words and his presence. Even when everything comes tumbling down around him, he never despairs."

Pensées d'athlètes,
in: *Almanach olympique pour 1918,*
Lausanne (1917), p. 15.

5.2/6 THE EMBLEM AND THE FLAG OF 1914

This is the first document to explain the creation and meaning of the "Olympic rings". Coubertin does not claim sole parenthood, but it is obvious from his correspondence that it was him who created the symbol. The Olympic rings were initially the emblem of the 1914 Congress of Paris, the major Olympic event aside from the Games since the foundation. The rings appear on the program, along with the Olympic motto "Citius, altius, fortius." The rings bear a certain resemblance to the symbol of the U.S.F.S.A., a symbol that Coubertin devised in 1890. It consists of two linking rings, along with the motto "Ludus pro Patria[1]".

There is a second significant statement in this text. Olympism is an event that is neither localized nor temporary; it is universal and timeless. As though he foresaw World War I, a year later, Coubertin said that no war would be able to stop the rise of Olympism, or make it turn back. As in antiquity, an Olympiad might not take place on account of war, but the Olympiad had to be counted as such.

The emblem selected to illustrate and represent the 1914 world congress which was to place the final seal on the restoration of the Olympics began to appear on various preliminary documents: five rings linked at regular intervals, their various colors – blue, yellow, black, green and red – standing out against the white of the paper. These five rings represent the five parts of the world now won over to Olympism, ready to accept its fruitful rivalries. In addition, the six colors combined in this way reproduce the colors of every country without exception. The blue and yellow of Sweden, the blue and white of Greece, the tricolor flags of France, England, the United States, Germany, Belgium, Italy and Hungary, and the yellow and red of Spain are included, as are the innovative flags of Brazil and Australia, and those of ancient Japan and modern China. This, truly, is an international emblem. It was made to be turned into a flag, and the look of the flag would be perfect. It is a light, appealing flag, a delight to see fluttering in the wind. Its meaning is largely symbolic. Its success is assured, to the point that after the Congress it can continue to be raised on solemn Olympic occasions. However this may turn out, the celebrations of 1914 now have the eurythmic messengers they needed to announce them. The great poster, the first copies of which have been given to the national Olympic Committees and which continues to be available to them, met with immediate general admiration. The

The Olympic rings with the Olympic motto "citius-altius-fortius", drawn in 1914 by Pierre de Coubertin himself (Navacelle Collection)

reduction to post card format is equally successful for that medium. The five rings and their various applications will also be deeply appreciated.

Are these five rings solidly riveted together? Will war some day shatter the Olympic framework? This is an issue we have been asked about before, and since the occasion presents itself, we are pleased to respond. Olympism did not reappear within the context of modern civilization in order to play a local or temporary role. The mission entrusted to it is universal and timeless. It is ambitious. It requires all space and all time. One must acknowledge that its initial steps immediately marked it out for that future. That being the case, war can merely delay, not stop, its advancement. As the preamble of the Regulations for the next Congress state, "an Olympiad may fail to be celebrated, but neither the order nor the interval may be changed". If, God forbid, the Seventh or Eighth Olympiads were unable to be celebrated, the Ninth Olympiad would be held. If bloody memories, still too fresh, made it impossible to hold the necessary celebrations in one part of the world, there will be people on the other side of the world ready to honor the eternal youth of humanity.

In addition, a more sporting conception of war – the word is not inappropriate – is becoming predominant. This will not make the heated exchange any less harsh, but it will make the aftermath somewhat more easily tolerated. People will learn a great lesson from the athlete: hatred without battle is not worthy of man, and insult without blows is utterly unbecoming.

Perhaps we have strayed from our topic. Let us return to it, repeating that war cannot influence the future of the Olympics. Once peace is restored, the International Committee will be at its post ready to continue its worldwide work. That is why the new emblem eloquently evokes both conquered terrain and guaranteed endurance.

L'emblème et le drapeau de 1914,
in: *Revue Olympique,*
August 1913, pp. 119-120.

The editor has determined that this text, though unsigned, was written by Coubertin.

1 As proven by Coubertin's grand-nephew, G. de Navacelle, Coubertin designed this symbol himself, and did so as a function of the meaning with which he intended to imbue it.

5.2/7 – 5.2/9 INTRODUCTION

According to Coubertin, a significant place must be reserved for ceremonies at the Olympics in the ideal plan for the "modern Olympia[1]", a plan previously mentioned several times. Most of these ideas were put into practice. They are just as valid today, even though no one refers to their creator any more. At the opening ceremony of the Olympic Games, the athletes' Olympic oath plays a very important role. In antiquity, participants had to stand before a statue of Zeus hurling thunderbolts and swear an oath to obey the rules.

Coubertin did not want to require participants in the modern Games to respect the rule by threatening them with sanctions (this relates particularly to the regulation on amateurs), but by recalling for them the commitment that they made when they swore the Olympic oath. In this letter, which he wrote in 1906 to Charles Simon, secretary general of the Fédération Gymnastique et Sportive des Patronages de France, Coubertin proposed introducing an Olympic oath for the first time.

It was not until the opening ceremonies of the 1920 Olympic Games in Antwerp that Victor Boin first swore the Olympic oath on behalf of all the athletes.

Twenty years later, Coubertin wrote a third report on the ceremonies of the Games. Its title clearly indicates that the emphasis is on the "educational value" of the Olympic ceremonies.

Coubertin noted that this protocol was intended only for the Olympic Games, that it symbolizes the basic religious idea that can be expressed only "at the great quadrennial celebration of the human springtime".

5.2/7 THE CEREMONIES

The issue of the "ceremonies" is understandably one of the most important to address. It is through them that the Olympiad is distinguished from a mere series of world championships. The Olympiad is a solemn occasion, and its ceremonies would not be appropriate without the prestige that its titles of nobility confer upon it.

Moreover, we must avoid the pitfalls of a vain parade, and be strictly bound by the limits of good taste and measure.

Looking back in history, the ancient Altis was crisscrossed during the Games by all types of processions, most of which were based on some religious pretext. Athletes, spectators, and functionaries offered sacrifice upon sacrifice to the symbolic deities whose images and altars were scattered about the sacred enclosure. It is quite difficult to determine what level of majesty and true beauty was achieved in these activities. In any event, they did take place with all desirable solemnity. The Ancients clearly had a *sense of collective evolution.* We have lost this sense, but it would be easy to regain. There is no reason to believe that the Ancients were innately superior in this regard. They acquired and developed this sense through habit. Clearly, the very human aspects of their religions made it easier for them to acquire and develop it. In our time, practically no public religion is possible anymore. In any event, the presentation of such a religion would not lend itself to anything of the sort. As for civilian festivals, no one has yet managed to give them a feeling of true nobility and eurythmy anywhere.

The experience of antiquity, nonetheless, can be of use to us. The "sacrifices" that we mentioned earlier were merely formulas for the expression of a two-fold sentiment of a high order. At Olympia, people gathered both to make a pilgrimage to the past and an act of faith in the future. This is certainly something that would be suitable for modern Olympiads, as well. It is their role and destiny to unite what was and what is to come in the fleeting moment. The Olympiads are, par excellence, celebrations of youth, beauty, and strength. Therefore we must try to discover the secret of the ceremonies to be inaugurated along these same lines.

There is one ceremony which did exist in the past that can be transposed nearly without modification: the oath. Before the opening of the Games, the athletes admitted to compete went to the temple of Zeus and swore to observe the law of the Games in all respects. They declared that they were without blemish and worthy to appear in the Stadium. With the image of the god replaced for each individual by the flag of his country, this ceremony would surely only increase in grandeur. Such "modernization" is so obviously appropriate that there is no need to dwell on the matter.

In recent Olympiads, the Games have been declared open in ceremonies that attempted to be suitably solemn. We say "attempted" because even the presence of sovereigns and heads of state saying these ritual words in 1896, 1904, and 1908 was not enough to make to these occasions as grand as they could be.

In Athens, admirable choruses and a releasing of doves accompanied the proclamation made by King George. In London, there was quite a rather parade of athletes, the "highlight of the day". In fact, parades seem better suited to the distribution of awards than to the opening of the Games. Until London, awards were distributed in a most common and unseemly manner. Winners appeared in street clothes, in no particular order, and without the slightest concern for esthetics. London introduced a few innovations. Most of the young athletes appeared in the dress appropriate for their particular sport, a simple thing which completely changed the look of the ceremony. But from one end to the other of the 1908 Games, music was omitted entirely. The only music at all was the brassy, tired old band melodies. Great choral groups alternating with far-away fanfares are the basis *par excellence* of Olympic symphonies that future musicians will certainly want to compose. They will need cooperation from architects, in a sense. The problems of acoustics are not solved by the simple fact of being outdoors. "Screens" play a major role in this. Besides, one must not overlook the fact that the invisibility of the performers was one of the innovative lessons of Wagnerian esthetics, a lesson that has attracted a following that is increasingly enthusiastic.

So ceremonies will be few but significant: the athletes' oath, the proclamation that the Games are open, the distribution of awards... these are the principal days, mandatory days. Add to them the possible distribution of Olympic diplomas, which are rarely awarded.

These festivals will include processions, the formation of groups in the *tableau vivant* style, speeches, and musical performances, as well.

Une Olympie moderne, Chapter VI: Les cérémonies,
in: *Revue Olympique*, March 1910, pp. 41-44.

The editor has determined that this text, though unsigned, was written by Coubertin.

1 Intended for entrants in the 1910 architecture competition sponsored by the IOC, entitled: "A Modern Olympia." See also text 4.1/3 of this volume.

Belgian fencer Victor Boin (1886-1974) was the first person to swear the Olympic Oath. "We swear that we are taking part in the Olympic Games as loyal competitors, observing the rules governing the Games, and anxious to show a spirit of chivalry for the honour of our countries and for the glory of sport" (taken from R.Renson, The VII Olympiad: Antwerp 1920. The Games Reborn. Antwerp/Ghent, Pandora/Snoeck-Ducaju, 1996, p.33)

5.2/8 THE ATHLETES' OATH (LETTER TO CHARLES SIMON)

Dear Mr. Secretary General,

I must tell you what a pleasure it was for me to respond to the kind invitation of Dr. Michaux, and to attend the wonderful festival held the other day by your recently-founded federation. I will be able to date the third stage of my work from that – I mean from being in your midst – and I am glad of that.

The nature of Olympiads in antiquity was threefold: they were periodic, artistic, and religious. In restoring them, first and foremost we re-established the regularity of the celebration of the Olympiads. Twelve years later, the arts and literature were invited to re-establish their bonds with sport, bonds that had long since been broken. That was the meaning of our recent efforts, and why the Comédie Française was an appropriate location. Now we must scale the third wall, the highest of them all, and perhaps the most inaccessible. But first, I must explain what I mean by the term "religion". It has a very special meaning in this context. The true religion of the ancient athlete did not consist of making solemn sacrifices at the altar of Zeus. That was merely a traditional gesture. Rather, it consisted of swearing an oath of loyalty and selflessness and, above all, in making every effort to adhere strictly to that oath. The individual who was to take part in the games had to be purified, in some sense, through professing and practicing these virtues. In this way, the moral beauty and the profound consequences of physical culture were revealed.

We must get back to something similar. We must do so, or else we will see the beginnings of decline in our modern sports, a decline that will become faster and faster, threatened in turn by these corrupting factors. There is no use denying it: these factors have already begun to do their nefarious work. Here in France we have seen one of the noblest sports, fencing, decline morally even as its technical worth was on the rise. The wonderful spirit of chivalry that reigned supreme in the sport a few years ago is becoming increasingly rare. A push-button hierarchy is forming before our very eyes. In other sports, cash prizes awarded directly, or works of art that can be sold are mixing up the various classifications, to the point that the terms "amateur" and "professional" are meaningless. If we allow things to go on as they are, repugnant snobbery, the habit of lying, and the spirit of gain will soon invade our athletic associations.

Therefore we must react. On the one hand, our reaction must be based on adopting a more intelligent, broader, and certainly narrower definition of an amateur. On the other hand, it will be based on restoring the oath sworn before competition. This will introduce into modern sports the spirit of joyful candor, the spirit of sincere altruism that will renew them, and will make of collective muscular exercise a true school for moral improvement.

Among the major federations that can help in pursuing such a goal, none is more appropriate than yours. I believe that it possesses the most generous will. In any case, it is the most perfectly democratic federation. I will say this clearly: democracy alone is capable of performing certain clean-up operations when they are necessary. Therefore let me appeal to your young people, and ask them to spread this program of moral purification, the program whose general principles I have presented to you today. I think that soon we shall be able to work out the details of methods for practical implementation of this plan.

Very sincerely yours,

Pierre de Coubertin

Le serment des athlètes. (Lettre à Charles Simon),
in: *Revue Olympique,*
July 1906, pp. 107-109.

5.2/9 THE EDUCATIONAL VALUE OF THE OLYMPIC CEREMONY

Despite unfavorable circumstances, methodical and determined preparations for the Games of the Tenth Olympiad are underway in Los Angeles. These Games are supported by well-organized advertising. It is likely that the scope of this advertising is increasing its effectiveness, not decreasing it. A recent letter from the advertising department was reproduced rather widely in Europe. It dealt with the opening ceremonies, and presented details of the successive events in those ceremonies. Several newspapers presented this description as being the result of resolutions adopted by the organizing committee, stating that it included interesting innovations. However, this is actually a changeless program, one that is the first act of "Olympic protocol". In 1924, the president of the French Olympic Committee explained the details of this protocol to Mr. A. Briand, then as now French Minister of Foreign Affairs. Mr. Briand replied, "I will follow this protocol gladly. As complicated as it may be, it must be less so than my own". In saying so, this statesman was alluding to diplomatic protocol. But the origins and nature of these two protocols differ greatly. Diplomatic protocol is the result of traditions of courtesy, and translates into an infinite gradation of precedence. Olympic protocol is essentially educational in nature, and it is in that regard that we shall consider it here.

As has often been said, the Olympic Games are not merely world championships dominated by the notion of achieving the best possible technical results. They are that, if one wants to see them that way. But they are something else again, and something more than that. They are the quadrennial and international celebration of youth, the "festival of the human springtime", uniting at the same time all forms of physical activity and all the nations of the world. Through them, each generation celebrates its coming of age, its joie de vivre, its faith in the future, its ambitions, and its desire to excel. That is why the arts and literature have been invited, as in the ancient world, to embellish so solemn a celebration through their own contributions.

Once the International Olympic Committee, the supreme and permanent guardian of the institution, has selected the city (and not the country) where the next Olympiad is to be held – a choice that is the Committee's primary and essential privilege – an Organizing Committee responsible for preparing the competitions, festivities, and ceremonies is given the authority it needs, either by the national government or the municipal authorities, or even by the Olympic Committee of the country in question. It doesn't matter much. Naturally, this committee is granted wide-ranging freedom. It is bound only by the fundamental provisions of the Olympic Charter, which specifies in particular the series of required sports: gymnastic and athletic sports, equestrian and water events, fencing competitions, winter sports, and art competitions. It is also bound by the ceremonials surrounding the solemn opening and closing of the Games, above all else.

The opening ceremonies include the procession of all the participants. They enter the Stadium by country, marching behind their respective national flags. They then stand in long lines facing the presidential dais where the head of state, the sovereign, or the president of the republic who has been called upon to declare the Olympiad open stands. So far, no head of state has failed to be present, except for President Loubet in 1900. The Kings of Greece, Sweden, and England, Presidents Roosevelt and Doumergue, and the King of the Belgians have repeated the short but prestigious opening formula at each successive Olympiad. It has been thirty-five years since George I was the first person to say: "I proclaim the Games of First Olympiad of the modern era open". At that point, doves are released (generally as many doves as there are participating countries, each bearing the colors of the respective countries), a cannon sounds, and choirs and bands burst forth, all saluting the great Olympic flag as it is raised on the central flag pole. The Olympic flag flies throughout the Games. Then those carrying the national flags join together in a semicircle at the foot of the stage, and an athlete from the host country swears the Olympic oath, which runs as follows: "We swear that we will take part in these Olympic Games in the true spirit of sportsmanship, and that we will respect and abide by the rules that govern them, for the glory of sport and the honor of our country."

Crown Prince Gustav Adolf of Sweden presenting the 2nd prize for the ladies' 400 m swimming relay race at the 1912 Stockholm Olympics (taken from E.Bergvall, The Official Report of the Olympic Games of Stockholm 1912, Stockholm, Wallström & Widstrand, 1913, p.784)

The Australian team marches into the stadium in Antwerp in 1920. (taken from Spalding's Athletic Library no.94R: Olympic Games Handbook, New York, ASP, 1922, p.60)

As everyone knows, the Olympic flag is white with five interlocking rings at the center. The rings are blue, yellow, black, green, and red, with the blue ring at the upper left nearest the pole. This design is symbolic, representing the five parts of the world united through Olympism. The six colors appearing on the flag reproduce the colors of all the national flags that fly anywhere in the world in our time. This flag does not date back to the beginning of the Games. It was inaugurated in Paris in June 1914, during the great celebrations of the Twentieth Anniversary of the restoration of the Olympic Games, which coincided with the first congress of the National Olympic Committees.

The closing ceremonies are no less impressive. After the medals are awarded (a simple medal has replaced the ancient crown of laurels, but its only true worth is its artistic value), the president of the International Committee pronounces the closing of the Games. After thanking the head of state and the host city as usual, he invites "youth from all countries in the world to meet again in four years" in the location selected for the celebration of the Games of the next Olympiad. He says, "May they take place in joy and peace, and in this way, may the Olympic torch continue its course through the ages for the good of a humanity that is ever more zealous, more courageous, and more pure. So be it!" Upon these words, the trumpets sound. The Olympic flag is lowered from the central flag pole and saluted with a five-gun salute as the choirs sing the final song.

Throughout the Games, gold-medal victories are saluted by raising the flag of the winner's country on a special flag pole, and by playing his national anthem. At the end of the Games, between the final competitions and the proclamation of the closing of the Games, three flags are raised, and three national anthems are sung. The countries are Greece, in tribute to the glories of ancient Olympism, the host country of the Games that are drawing to a close, and finally, the country where the city that will host the next Olympic Games is located. In Los Angeles, for example, homage will be paid to Greece, the United States, and Germany.

In this way, everything in the restored and modernized Olympism focuses on the ideas of mandatory continuity, interdependence, and solidarity. One must readily agree that such an arrangement is imbued with the greatest educational value, and is a powerful lesson in philosophy and history.

But what is suitable for the celebration of quadrennial Games would not be suitable for ordinary circumstances in daily athletic life. There is a tendency to overuse this prestigious ceremony for simple meets, matches that pit the athletes of only two or three nationalities against each other. This is an unjustifiable stretch. It diminishes the educational impact of the ceremonies.

La valeur pédagogique du cérémonial olympique,
in: *Bulletin du Bureau International de Pédagogie Sportive*,
no. 7, Lausanne (1931), pp. 3-5.

The editor has determined that this text, though unsigned, was written by Coubertin.

5.2/10 MESSAGE TO ALL ATHLETES AND PARTICIPANTS MEETING AT AMSTERDAM FOR THE NINTH OLYMPIAD

The message that Coubertin addressed to the representatives of the 1928 Olympic Games in Amsterdam sums up the most significant points which, in the eyes of its creator, must continue to be respected after his death. This text shows the major role that "symbolic signs" play in preparations for the Games. In 1937, the year of his death, Coubertin published the text a second time, changing almost nothing in his appeal. In so doing, he gave this message a particularly profound meaning[1].

It is with deep regret that I cannot be with you on account of my illness. When the Games of the Tenth Olympiad are held in Los Angeles in four years, no doubt I will be incapable of making the journey, so I bid you farewell now.

I would ask you to guard and maintain among you the flame of restored Olympism and to uphold the principles and institutions that are necessary for it. First, the equality of the major categories of individual sports: athletic and gymnastic sports, sports of combat, water sports, equestrian events, etc.

– then, the art competitions that link the works of the mind inspired by the idea of athletics to the wonderful activity of the muscles,

1 The origin of this second appeal is unknown, but there is a newspaper clipping in the archives of the IOC.

– the athletes' oath which, based on the feeling of honor, contains the seeds of the only effective solution to the problem of amateurism,

– the use of the Olympic flag, which includes the national colors of every country and symbolizes the five parts of the world united through sport,

– the ceremonies and formulas for the opening and closing of the Games, with the final salute to Hellenism, from which they come,

– finally, the authority of the International Committee; its independent recruitment guarantees that traditions will be upheld without any bothersome involvement in technical matters.

More and more, I believe that the major tournaments organized alongside the Games must be fully autonomous, and must not be confused with the Games themselves. The primary goal of the Games is the glorification of the individual athlete.

I hope that, as time goes on, the regular succession of Olympiads will help provide a rhythm for athletic life, to contain it and to protect it from its own excesses. To that end, it is very desirable that the prejudices that continue to separate gymnasts from other athletes disappear. They are two brothers who are unfamiliar with each other, too often through the fault of their managers.

Personally, I would like to see the modern pentathlon return to the directives that I set out when I created it. As for the participation of women in the Games, I continue to oppose such a move. It is against my wishes that they have been admitted to an increasing number of events.

Just as Olympism survived the world war intact, it will withstand social revolutions. In any case, Olympism has nothing to fear from current corporate trends. I have been delighted to see labor organizations embrace the Olympic ideal. No doubt students, too, will want to give this ideal a more clearly defined role in their university concerns. It is important that at every stage, from adolescence through maturity, men strive to spread the athletic spirit that consists of spontaneous loyalty and chivalrous selflessness.

Once again, I thank those who have followed and assisted me by turns in the task at which I have labored these forty years, through so many traps and against so much opposition.

Message à tous les athlètes et participants aux Jeux Olympiques d'Amsterdam,
in: *Le Gymnaste Suisse*, 2e année, 14 août 1928, p. 3.

5.3 THE CONTRIBUTION OF THE ARTS

In 1906, Coubertin guided the Olympic movement in the direction of his initial understanding of Olympism, creating a link between the Olympic Games and the arts.

This special relationship had been underscored from the start, but Coubertin wanted to move ahead gradually in this far-reaching undertaking[1]. After establishing the relationship with the sciences at the Olympic Congresses of Le Havre and Brussels, Coubertin determined that the next step was to create a link with the arts. Coubertin wrote about this idea quite enthusiastically in an article published in Le Figaro in 1904, before the assumed opening of the Olympiad in Rome:

"The time has come to take the next step, and to restore the Olympiad to its primal beauty. At the time of Olympia's splendor...the arts and literature in harmonious combination with sports made the Olympic Games great. The same must hold for the future[2]."

In the beginning, Coubertin hoped that the provisions of the IOC Charter which aimed at "making this celebration even more perfect" would guarantee that this relationship came about on its own[3]. The unexpected transfer to London of the Olympic Games planned for Rome brought a halt to any specific artistic initiative. This was Coubertin's reason for acting.

In a circular letter dated April 2, 1906, which we have included here, Coubertin invites the members of the IOC to an Advisory Conference, and requests that they send him the names of artists and of men of letters in their countries, in preparation for this Advisory Conference. That same month, he sent the official invitations (also included here), in which he defined the object of the deliberations of the conference: "To what extent and in what form the arts and literature can participate in the celebration of the modern Olympiads". Coubertin was inspired by Ancient Olympia in giving the world of the arts and literature a significant place in the Olympic Festival. Science and the arts, in harmony with sports, assured the greatness of the Olympic Games. In his often-quoted 1935 speech entitled "The Philosophic Foundation of Modern Olympism", Coubertin asked the following question: "Can one celebrate the human springtime without inviting the mind to take part?[4]"

Clearly not, because the reason for calling the 1906 Advisory Conference in Paris was "once again to reunite the muscles and the mind, formerly divorced, in the bonds of a legitimate marriage[5]."

The second half of the conference dealt with the potential for cooperation between art and athletics in the context of local athletic competitions. On the one hand, art should help "attenuate the unusual and technical nature of athletics"[6]. On the other hand, art should help present the quadrennial celebration of the human springtime in such a way that any form of youthful expression and any expression of art is given its proper value.

1 Cf. Coubertin, "Une Olympie moderne." [A Modern Olympia], in *Revue Olympique*, January 1910, p. 10.
2 Coubertin, "L'Olympiade romaine." [The Olympiad of Rome], in: Le Figaro, Vol. 50, no 218, August 4, 1904, p. 1.
3 The following point was included in the first statutes of the IOC, written by Coubertin, statutes that he caused to be adopted in 1894: "Goal 2: To make this celebration ever more perfect...."
4 See text 5.1/17 in this volume.
5 "Un Grand Mariage", [A Great Marriage] in *Revue Olympique*, June 1906, p. 83.
6 *Une Campagne de vingt-et-un ans* [A Twenty-One Year Campaign], p. 193.

Coubertin's understanding of eurythmics was heavily influenced by his aesthetic ideas: English philosopher John Ruskin (1819-1900) (Carl & Liselott Diem Archives, Cologne)

To achieve this on the technical level, Coubertin drew inspiration from the work of the Englishman John Ruskin (1819-1900), whose esthetic theory – faithful to ancient thought – defined external beauty as the reflection of inner beauty.

Ruskin planned to beautify modern civilization by creating garden cities, for example. Nature as a direct manifestation of God was considered as the guiding-principle of any artistic design. Ruskin's ethically grounded concept of history did not require any religious forms of organization.[7] Coubertin applied the idea to sports.[8]

The purpose of the union of sports and art to which Coubertin had aspired since 1904, a union born of the esthetic experience of the athlete during competition and athletic events, was to enable athlete and spectator to feel the perfect harmony that Coubertin called "eurythmy."

What does not appear in Coubertin's writings is his talent for the artistic organization of festivals. In every event Coubertin included special, solemn moments planned out in minute detail. The same concern for detail applied to invitations and programs. Most of the time, Coubertin himself designed and drew the models.

The texts published here on sports and art reflect only part of Coubertin's ideas, plans, and initiatives. Nevertheless the involvement of art, brought about in eurythmy, is clearly an important element in Coubertin's idea of what constitutes Olympism.

That is why all the other texts in this volume on Olympism have included fairly large examples of the significance of art in Coubertin's monumental and philosophical efforts.

7 See J.Paul, "Die Kunstanschauung John Ruskins" in: *Beiträge zur Theorie der Künste im 19.Jh.,* Vol.1, Frankfurt/M. 1971, p.287. See also K. Clark (ed.), *Ruskin Today,* New York, 1964, p.141.

8 See A. Krüger, "The masses are much more sensitive to the perfection of the whole than to any separate details: The Influence of John Ruskin's Political Economy on Pierre de Coubertin." In: *Olympika. The International Journal of Olympic Studies,* published by the International Centre for Olympic Studies. London/Ontario, Vol. V, 1996, pp. 25-43.

5.3/1 CIRCULAR LETTER TO THE IOC MEMBERS (MARCH 1906)

29 Mars 1906

10, Boulevard Flandrin,
PARIS.

Monsieur et Cher Collègue,

Vous trouverez ci-joint une invitation à assister aux Jeux d'Athènes que j'ai le plaisir de vous remettre de la part du Comité Athénien. Vous serez bien aimable de me dire s'il est dans vos intentions de vous rendre à Athènes; je ne pourrai malheureusement pas m'y rendre.

Je profite de l'occasion pour vous faire savoir que la remise solennelle du Diplôme Olympique à S. A. R. le Duc des Abruzzes et à Mr. le Commandant Lancrenon, ainsi que de la Coupe Olympique au Touring-Club de France aura lieu à Paris dans le grand amphithéâtre de la Sorbonne, le Samedi 26 Mai prochain. Je souhaite qu'il vous soit possible de prendre part à cette fête.

Elle coïncidera avec une Conférence consultative composée d'hommes de lettres et d'artistes (peintres, sculpteurs, architectes, musiciens, artistes dramatiques) à laquelle nous demanderons de vouloir bien étudier "dans quelle mesure et sous quelle forme les arts et les lettres pourraient être appelés à participer aux Olympiades modernes." Cette Conférence se tiendra les 23, 24 et 25 Mai au foyer de la Comédie Française mis gracieusement à notre disposition par Mr. Jules Claretie.

En prévision de sa réunion vous seriez bien aimable de m'envoyer le plus tôt possible les noms et adresses des dix personnalités littéraires et artistiques de votre pays que vous jugeriez utile d'y convier.

Veuillez agréer, Monsieur et Cher Collègue, l'expression de mes sentiments les plus distingués et dévoués.

Le Président du Comité,

Bn Pierre de Coubertin

**Circular from Coubertin to the IOC members concerning the Intermediate Olympic Games held in Athens in 1906. At the same time, he announces an Advisory Conference on the inclusion of art in modern Olympism and asks his IOC colleagues to name suitable artists from their respective countries.
(IOC Archives)**

You will find attached an invitation to attend the Games in Athens which I have pleasure in passing on to you on behalf of the Athens Committee. Please be so kind as to inform me if you intend to go to Athens; I shall unfortunately not be able to go.

Allow me to take this opportunity to inform you that the formal ceremony to award the Olympic Diploma to HRH the Duke of Abruzzi and Commandant Lancrenon, and the presentation of the Olympic Club to the Touring-Club de France, will take place in Paris, at the grand amphitheatre of the Sorbonne, on Saturday 26th May next. I hope that you will be able to attend this celebration.

It will coincide with an advisory conference comprising men of letters and artists (painters, sculptors, architects, musicians and dramatic artists), which will be asked to study "to what extent and in what form the arts and literature could be called upon to participate in the modern Olympic Games". This conference will be held on 23rd, 24th and 25th May in the foyer of the Comédie Française, which Mr Jules Claretie is graciously placing at our disposal.

In preparation for this meeting, please be kind enough to send me, as soon as possible, the names and addresses of the ten literary and artistic personalities of your country whom you feel it would be appropriate to invite.

Yours etc.

Lettre circulaire aux membres du CIO.
Paris, 29 mars 1906. Polycopie, 2 pages. (IOC Archives)

5.3/2 INVITATION TO THE ARTISTS (APRIL 1906)

On behalf of the International Olympic Committee, I have the honour to invite you to take part in the Advisory Conference being held at the Comédie Française (public foyer) on Wednesday 23rd, Thursday 24th and Friday 25th May 1906, under the honorary chairmanship of Mr Dujardin-Beaumetz, Under-Secretary of State for Fine Arts, and Mr Jules Claretie, Director of the Comédie Française, for the purpose of studying **to what extent and in what form the arts and literature could be called upon to participate in the modern Olympic Games and, in general, to be associated with the practice of sports in order to benefit from them and ennoble them.**

You will find attached the programme of the Conference, and we should be particularly pleased if you could contribute your valuable competence and authority to it.

Yours etc.

Conference Programme

ARCHITECTURE – Conditions and characteristics of the modern gymnasium – Architecture of outdoor and urban arenas, swimming pools, shooting ranges, riding centres, nautical clubs and drill halls – Sports halls and sports grounds – Architectural designs – Use of visible ironwork and ceramics – Expenses and estimates

PARIS, 10, Boulevard Flandrin

Avril 1906.

Monsieur

J'ai l'honneur de vous prier, au nom du Comité International Olympique, de bien vouloir prendre part à la Conférence consultative qui se réunira à la Comédie-Française (Foyer du public), les Mercredi 23, Jeudi 24 et Vendredi 25 Mai 1906, sous la présidence d'honneur de M. DUJARDIN-BEAUMETZ, Sous-Secrétaire d'Etat des Beaux-Arts et de M. Jules CLARETIE, Administrateur de la Comédie-Française, à l'effet d'étudier **dans quelle mesure et sous quelle forme les Arts et les Lettres pourraient participer à la célébration des Olympiades modernes et, en général, s'associer à la pratique des Sports pour en bénéficier et les ennoblir.**

Vous trouverez ci-joint le programme de cette Conférence à laquelle nous serons particulièrement heureux de vous voir apporter le précieux concours de votre compétence et de votre autorité.

Veuillez agréer, Monsieur, l'expression de nos sentiments les plus distingués.

Le Président du Comité International Olympique,

Bn Pierre de Coubertin

M..

T. S. V. P.

Invitation to artists to the 1906 Advisory Conference in Paris (IOC Archives)

DRAMATIC ART – Outdoor productions – Essential principles – Recent writings – Sports on stage

CHOREOGRAPHY – Processions, parades, group and coordinated movements – Dances

DECORATION – Stands and enclosures – Mats, badges, garlands, draperies, clusters – Night festivals: torchlit sports

LITERATURE – Possibility of setting up Olympic literary competitions; conditions for these competitions – Sporting emotion, source of inspiration for the man of letters.

MUSIC – Outdoor orchestras and choirs – Repertoire – Rhythms and alternation – Fanfares – Conditions for an Olympic music competition

Programme of the 1906 Advisory Conference in Paris (Special Print, IOC Archives)

Programme de la Conférence

ARCHITECTURE. — Les conditions et les caractéristiques du gymnase moderne. — Architecture des cercles de plein air et des cercles urbains, des piscines, stands, manèges, clubs nautiques, salles d'armes — Palais des sports et parcs des sports. — Motifs architecturaux. — Utilisation du fer apparent et de la céramique — Dépenses et devis.

ART DRAMATIQUE. — Représentations en plein air. — Principes essentiels. — Essais récents. — Les sports sur la scène.

CHORÉGRAPHIE. — Cortèges, défilés, mouvements groupés et coordonnés – Danses.

DÉCORATION. — Tribunes et enceintes. — Mâts, écussons, guirlandes, draperies, faisceaux. — Fêtes de nuit : les sports aux flambeaux.

LETTRES. — Possibilité d'établir des concours littéraires olympiques ; conditions de ces concours. — L'émotion sportive, source d'inspiration pour l'homme de lettres.

MUSIQUE. — Orchestres et chœurs de plein air. — Répertoire — Rythmes et alternances. — Fanfares. — Conditions d'un concours musical olympique.

PEINTURE. — Silhouettes individuelles et aspects d'ensemble. — Possibilité et conditions d'un concours de peinture olympique. — Aide apportée à l'artiste par la photographie instantanée.

SCULPTURE. — Attitudes et gestes athlétiques dans leurs rapports avec l'art. — Interprétation de l'effort. — Objets donnés en prix : statuettes et médailles.

Ordre des Séances

Le Mercredi 23 Mai, à 9 h. du matin et à 2 h. après-midi : Séances générales.
Le Jeudi 24 Mai : Séances de commissions.
Le Vendredi 25 Mai, à 9 h. du matin : Séances de commissions.
» » à 2 h. après-midi : Séance générale.

PAINTING - Individual silhouettes and general views - Possibility of and conditions for an Olympic painting competition - Photography as an aid to the artist

SCULPTURE - Athletic poses and movements and their relationship with art - Interpretation of effort - Objects given as prizes: statuettes and medals

Order of sessions

Wednesday 23rd May: 9 a.m. and 2 p.m.: General sessions
Thursday 24th May: Commission meetings
Friday 25th May: 9 a.m. Commission meetings
2 p.m. General session

5.3/3 SPEECH AT THE OPENING OF THE ADVISORY CONFERENCE ON THE ARTS, LITERATURE, AND SPORTS (MAY 23, 1906)

The opening speech of the Advisory Conference covers all the reasons that led Coubertin to undertake the risky initiative of linking the Olympic Games and art[1]. The conference was held in the Foyer of the Comédie-Française, indicating Coubertin's careful approach in laying the groundwork for the meeting. He had chosen the Sorbonne in 1894 to draw the sciences into his efforts to revive the Olympic Games. In approaching artists, he chose the most famous theater in Paris, the Comédie-Française.

Gentlemen, we have gathered in this unique place to hold a unique ceremony. Our purpose is this: to reunite the Muscles and the Mind, once divorced, in the bonds of a legitimate marriage. I would verge on being untruthful if I said that ardent desire compels them to renew their conjugal life today. Doubtless their cooperation was long and fruitful, but once separated by adverse circumstances, they had come to a point of complete mutual incomprehension. Absence had made them grow forgetful. Now their former home, Olympia, has been re-established, or rather renovated in a different form, a modern form imbued with a similar atmosphere. So now they can return to their shared abode. In the meantime, it is up to us to prepare for their return. That is why this Advisory Conference has been called, to study "the extent to which, and in what form, literature and the arts may participate in the celebration of modern Olympiads and, in general, be associated with the practice of sports, to benefit from them and to ennoble them". Therefore our purpose is twofold. On the one hand, we must organize the dynamic involvement of literature and the arts in the restored Olympic Games. On the other hand, we must work toward incorporating them modestly and within reasonable limits in day-to-day athletic events at the local level. Gentlemen, let us not doubt our success. Nor let us doubt that our task will require much time and patience.

We will ask for your opinions and advice regarding an initial item on our agenda, namely our plan to set up five competitions in architecture, sculpture, painting, music, and literature. These competitions, held every four years, are intended to honor previously unseen works inspired directly by the idea of athletics. In the beginning, perhaps, participation in these competitions may well seem small in quantity and poor in quality. The reason is that initially, no doubt, the competitions will appeal only to those artists and writers who are personally dedicated to the practice of sports. To interpret the muscular strain that effort causes in the athlete's body, should the sculptor not also have felt something similar in his own body? But what is this? Are we going to let ourselves be stopped by such baseless and outdated prejudice about the incompatibility of sports and certain professions? The power and universality that have been achieved in such a short time through the renaissance of athletics safeguard us against any such fear. The coming generation will see exceptional thinkers who are also athletes. Do we not already see this trend among fencers?

1 This speech was published for the first time in 1933, in a collection of texts entitled *Anthology*, published on the occasion of Coubertin's seventieth birthday. Aix-en-Provence, P. Roubaud, 1933, pp. 166-168.

The Foyer of the Comédie Française in Paris. Here the opening of the Advisory Conference on Arts took place (taken from 21 Years of Sports Campaingn, p.193)

Time is working with us and for us in this matter, but it would be unwise to expect too much from time alone with regard to the alliance that must be forged among athletes, artists, and spectators. This is a monumental task, because we have lost all sense of eurythmy. Today, the masses are incapable of linking the pleasures of various sorts of art together. They are used to scattering such pleasures into bits, lining them up in rows, and pigeonholing them. They do not find the ugliness and vulgarity of their surroundings offensive. Beautiful music stirs them, but it is a matter of indifference to them whether or not that music resonates within a noble architectural setting. Nothing in them seems to revolt at the miserably mundane decor, the ridiculous processions, the detestable cacophony, and the whole apparatus attendant upon what is called a "public festival" these days. One guest is always missing at these festivals: good taste.

Our meeting place is the very definition of good taste, and is acknowledged as such throughout the world. Nowhere else could we carve the cornerstone of the building we hope to construct with such success. In the name of the International Olympic Committee, I would like to thank Mr. Jules Claretie, director of the Comédie-Française, as well as Madame Bartet and Mr. Mounet-Sully, its illustrious deans, for having agreed to participate in the meeting. I would also like to extend a cordial welcome to the eminent individuals who have answered our call. I was criticized recently for keeping the guest list rather small. I believe earnestly that undertakings that begin small grow to become quite substantial. Let us be good guides. Let us place appropriate guideposts here and there. Public opinion will follow the direction we give it.

Discours d'ourverture (du 23 mai 1906) de la conférence consultative
des arts, lettres et sports,
in: *Anthologie*, Aix-en-Provence, P. Roubaud, 1933, pp. 166-168.

5.3/4 THE ARTS, LITERATURE, AND SPORTS

The 1906 Advisory Conference in Paris is a major focus in Coubertin's book entitled *Une Campagne de vingt-et-un ans* [A Twenty-One Year Campaign]. This autobiographical collection covers Coubertin's work from 1887 to 1908, at which time he felt his campaign had come to an end. This chapter describes in detail the steps leading up to the Paris conference, how the conference went, and the resolutions that were adopted[1].

Two days after the meeting held by the International Olympic Committee in London (June 1904), I wrote the following in *Le Figaro*: "The time has come to enter a new phase, and to restore the Olympiads to their original beauty. At the time of Olympia's splendor, and even later when Nero, the conqueror of Greece, made it his ambition to gather the ever-desired laurels along the banks of the Alphaeus, the arts and literature harmoniously joined with sports to ensure the greatness of the Olympic Games. This must also hold true in the future. The last thing on our minds, both when we began and for the future, is to undertake some childish, sacrilegious restoration of the magnificence of the past. But if the current age demands that in order to be vital and long-lasting, modern Olympiads must take on forms that their laws inspire, nothing should keep us from turning to the past to take what was human, i.e. immutable, in it. The importance of sport at the national level, its international role, the danger of allowing sports to become corrupt through an appetite for profits, and the need to link sports closely to other forms of activity are all certainties that have outlasted the destruction of Olympia and the temporary eclipse of the radiant ideal for which that astonishing city was built. From the start we wanted to restore this ideal completely, in a form and under conditions suited to the needs of the day. First however, a rejuvenated, viable form of athletics had to provide the requisite elements. Regular meetings had to be arranged among the nations, and a new series of Olympiads needed to point to way. Once this was accomplished, it became possible and desirable to bring muscles and thought together again in future festivals, as they had been in the festivals of antiquity. Some have, no doubt, noted that although poets came to read their new works in Ancient Olympia, and painters exhibited their recent paintings, publicity of this kind is no longer of any interest to either group. Yet publicity is not the issue. The point is to alleviate the unusually technical nature of modern athletics, in an effort to put sports back into general life. Besides, someday perhaps the artists of the pen and brush whom we have asked to help us will be grateful for rediscovering forgotten sources of majesty and beauty, eager as such artists are for new material."

This quotation explains how it happened that the International Olympic Committee called an advisory conference in May 1906, to study "to what extent and in what form literature and the arts might be involved in the celebration of the modern Olympiads and, in general, be associated with the practice of sports in

1 There is no need to refer to the article "Arts, Lettres et Sports" [The Arts, Literature and Sports] in the Chronique de France 1906 (Vol. 7, Paris 1907, pp. 191-204), because the statements contained in it are by and large the same as those in this chapter of the *Campagne de vingt-et-un ans.*

order to be of benefit to them, and to ennoble them". It also explains why the conference was held in Paris at the Comédie Française, under the guidance of Mr. Jules Claretie. Mr. Claretie, the delightful director of the Comédie Française, with Mr. Mounet-Sully and Mme. Bartet – the two senior members of the Comédie Française – beside him, opened and closed the conference by giving two charming speeches. Clearly he is well acquainted with the secrets of giving such speeches. The general sessions were held in the famous public foyer. For lack of suitable space, committee meetings were held in the Touring Club building, which was graciously made available to the International Committee.

The June 1906 *Revue Olympique* gave a detailed report of these meetings. In subsequent issues, it published full texts of the major papers presented by Messrs. Maurice Pottecher, Bourgault-Ducoudray, Frantz Jourdain, Emile Blémont, Max d'Ollone, Pierre Rocher, etc. Here, then, I will merely present the main conclusions that were adopted, as well as the devoted efforts of Mr. Truffier (of the Comédie Française) and of Mr. Pierre-Gaston Mayer, who served in the delicate position of secretary.

The task was twofold. On the one hand, preparations had to be made for the "dynamic involvement of literature and the arts in the restored Olympic Games". On the other hand, preparations were also necessary for "incorporating them modestly and within reasonable limits in day-to-day athletic events at the local level". With regard to the first point, the conference unanimously approved the idea of establishing five competitions, in architecture, sculpture, painting, literature, and music. These competitions were thenceforth to be annexed to the Olympiads, and would be part of the Olympiads on the same footing as the athletic competitions. Submitted works would have to be inspired by the idea of sports, or would have to relate directly to athletic matters. Works would be reviewed by international juries. To the extent possible, winning works would be exhibited, published, or implemented (depending on whether the works are pictorial, architectural, sculptural, or literary – or musical or dramatic) during the course of the Games.

The second point was the focus of lengthy debate. In architecture, two buildings must be considered: the gymnasium for exercises, and the stadium for competitions. Architecturally, the conference favored the ancient form of gymnasium preferred by utilitarian gymnastics. That is to say that the gymnasium will suggest a building that brings together all sports, insofar as possible. It will comprise outdoor spaces surrounded by optional shelters. The conference did not find the ancient stadium suitable for modern needs. It was decided that, from both the artistic and practical perspective, the lines and the shape of the ancient stadium should not be used as a model. A truly modern stadium would be an open field surrounded by greenery, with elegant and spacious stands decorated with flowers. As pleasing as it may be that the stadium in Athens could be brought back from ruins and rebuilt, it would nonetheless be regrettable to see newer cities try to build similar structures. Such modern structures would lack the historical glory and the special beauty of the unique landscape of Athens[2].

In terms of the dramatic arts, the conference brought to the attention of gymnastics and sports associations that suitable performances, especially in the open air, would be a wonderful accompaniment to festivals of the muscles. The conference recommended that the associations themselves cultivate the dramatic arts, especially comedy, in the form of an annual review that would feature the main points of interest to the members of the associations, in a fanciful way. This must be done, of course, on condition that such exercises are not allowed to overshadow physical exercise, which would direct the association away from its basic purpose.

The art of the dance has evolved in such a way that considerable efforts will have to be made to include it with sports once again. The attempts that have been made are laudable, but their uncertain and fragmentary nature makes it impossible to systematize the results so far. Processions, by contrast, have not fallen into disuse. Processions take place almost spontaneously in many settings in modern life, but with the exception of military parades, they are usually incoherent and lacking in harmony. A procession of athletes is the easiest of all to manage. The look of the procession and its reason for being are matters dealt with readily. All we need to do is imitate the gymnasts, who have retained the custom of processing in uniform. Fencers, boxers, ball players, and cyclists should appear in their exercise attire, holding or pulling their equipment, swords, racquets, or bicycles[3]. This would keep them in formation, as well. It goes without saying that athletes, better than other individuals, would understand how to give their movements and gait the appropriate martial elegance. As for the awarding of prizes, the most graceful ceremony seems to be the one used in the Middle Ages. The winner received his prize from a lady before whom he knelt. If the oath of loyalty once sworn by competitors before competition is restored, a scenario involving very simple movements and postures that would have a great impact would be easy to arrange.

In considering the matter of decoration, the conference was quick to rule out red satin, red velvet, gold crepe, painted fabric escutcheons, and, in general, the materials used routinely in most countries. The conference advocated the use of light-weight, light-colored fabrics, and a return to the trellis-work decorations favored at the time of Louis XV. Such decorations immediately emphasize even the smallest garland draped over them. Finally the conference recommended using displays of equipment during athletic festivals, similar to the displays set up during military festivals but using sports equipment rather than armor and shields. Oars, mallets, a bicycle wheel, balls, and racquets intertwined with garlands of leaves would lend themselves to the most picturesque designs. The large palm trees that today's rapid shipping has made available at reasonable cost without any loss of freshness, along with streamers and sashes, make for graceful designs, as well. Finally, flowers are not used enough. Flowers are a natural accompaniment for outdoor exercises. In earlier times, flowers were strewn over the winners, and in their eyes there was probably nothing to rival this poetic tribute. If asked to lend their support to solemn occasions of sport, florists' associations would certainly work hard to add to the stylishness of the occasion, providing new and harmonious decorations.

2 The "stadium" in London is not properly so called. Its elliptical shape is that of the ancient arenas. See the article on this topic in the *Revue Olympique*.
3 This resolution was taken into account partially at the close of the Olympics in London.

Then there are night-time festivities, to which modern fireworks skill has added unexpected new horizons. Sports by torch light is a new and quite attractive spectacle, one that is always easy to arrange. In fact, the play of the light interspersed with shadow covers up imperfections in the details, and spectators are most easily satisfied. The players are more isolated from the spectators, and are less preoccupied with being seen. All these elements combine to urge athletic associations in this direction, one very well-suited to attracting fans and winning friends.

Athletics may well provide the equipment for authors of dramatic works, but it does so all the more for the man of letters. The emotions of athletics derive from psychology as well as physiology. In order to interpret those emotions properly, however, one must have felt them personally. Writers who are involved in sports themselves are still a rarity. One need look no further to see why authors have hesitated to deal with topics whose riches are still unknown to them. This is true, too, of poets, who will find the athletic poem a cause of healthy renewal – but only when they themselves feel the powerful sensations that they will attempt to praise in verse.

Unlike literature, music can provide direct support for sports. The conference passed significant resolutions on this point, stating that the basis for this fruitful cooperation is outdoor choral music. The conference, therefore, asked the International Olympic Committee to invite all athletic associations, even the equestrian associations (in some Russian regiments, the soldiers sing on horseback), to form choral divisions. The value of singing in respiratory development has been rightly pointed out, which is very useful in most sports. Meanwhile, athletic and choral associations that coexist in the same place – and most often are quite unaware of each other's existence – will be invited to reach agreements on providing mutual assistance in the festivals that they organize. Finally, a Committee chaired by Mr. Bourgault-Ducoudray agreed to seek out ancient and modern pieces that could form a suitable repertory (for French associations) for such solemn occasions. An appeal will be made to composers, requesting that they work on writing odes and cantatas in honor of athletics and sports. The Conference did not deem it suitable to place any limits on the complete independence that artists must enjoy, by imposing any sort of requirements. However, it did point out to artists that it would be of benefit to them to study the main rhythms of athletics, the effects produced by alternating songs and military fanfares, and finally, the type of cantata used by that outstanding Greek composer, Samara, for his Olympic Anthem, consisting of unaccompanied choruses repeated *ad lib.*, and supported by one or more military bands.

Modern gymnasiums would provide both painters and sculptors with new models, as well as locations suitable for their works of art. In turn, these works of art would contribute to the education and eurythmic development of the young athletes. Here again, there is only one way to achieve this goal: artists must frequent athletic environments. Some recent examples have emphasized artists' inability to replace the living examples that only a real understanding of physical exercise in all its forms can convey, with secondhand information or hasty observation. The Conference was convinced that athletic movement (movement that apparently intimidated ancient sculptors often, since they show a marked tendency to depict the athlete at rest) could satisfy the twofold need today for movement and novelty, a constant torment for artists.

Self-portrait of Charles de Coubertin, a well-known painter in his time and father of Pierre. This painting, dating from 1878, bears the Coubertin coat of arms, six gold shells on a sky blue background (top left), (Navacelle Collection)

The conference heard a presentation on this matter, concerning on a project based on the genius of the great sculptor, Bartholdi. Two years earlier, I had had the idea of commemorating the restoration of gymnastics and sports through a suitable monument, and I had spoken of this plan to Bartholdi. He grew enthusiastic about the idea. After thinking about it, he wrote me a letter shortly before he died, in which he said, "I will place the *Meta* at the center, a fateful marker in the Stadium around which wrestling grew more daring and more fierce as it was revived, a marker where the superstitious fears of the Ancients installed an inferior, spiteful, and deceitful deity quick to cheat competitors of their victory. The throng of sports will rush to crowd the polished marble: fencing and football, skating and boxing, equestrian events and cycling, even a late-model automobile. The athletic storm changes aspect over time, but its soul remains the same, its expression similar – and, always, the *Meta* dominates. It is a simple, inexorable, and therefore captivating and understandable shape". Bartholdi wanted the *Meta* to be made of porphyry, tall and wide, with white images of youths and athletes winding around it. He wrote, "It would be a history lesson as well as a philosophy lesson – a reminder of eternal Greece, mother of all civilization, and a warning that the clash of effort and fate remains the supreme law of life."

Unfortunately, this project is too vast and too expensive to carry out just now, but I have not given up hope of seeing it through some day.

Such was the consultative conference of 1906. It ended with festivities in the great amphitheater of the Sorbonne for the solemn conferral of the Olympic Diploma on the Duke of Abruzzi and on Commander Lancrenon. The Olympic Cup was awarded to the Touring-Club de France then, as well. In that marvelous space, one after another, Madame Bartet, Mr. Mounet-Sully and Mr. Truffier recited from Victor Hugo; the Amateur Choral Society, under the direction of Mr. Griset, sang admirable ancient and modern refrains; Dr. Léon Petit gave a scientific lecture; and finally, the epées of Professors Dubois and Decanchy clashed in a classic match, while hunting horns rang out in the vestibule of the building. The eurythmy of this occasion, the first ever to reunite sports, science, literature, and the arts, left an unforgettable impression on those in attendance.

Shortly thereafter the Racing-Club de France abandoned its traditional band with commonplace brass instruments at its annual awards ceremony, replacing it with the School of Choral Song enthusiastically directed by Mr. Radiguer. The audience applauded the revolutionary-era pieces written by Gossec and Cherubini. These works were intended to be performed outdoors, and had not been sung for a hundred years. On this occasion the International Committee awarded the Olympic Medal to the Racing-Club de France in recognition of its great service to the cause of sports. The Olympic Medal was also awarded to the Comédie Française, and was placed into its archives by Mr. Jules Claretie.

At Bussang in August, Mr. Maurice Pottecher, who had taken an active role in the work of the Conference, incorporated an athletic program of fencing, foot races, etc. among the ever-popular events at his well-known "theater of the people". Finally, on October 4, the city of Tourcoing held an Olympic Festival under the direction of the Undersecretary of State for the Fine Arts, Mr. Dujardin-Beaumetz. This festival was held at the close of the Tourcoing fair, and came about through the tireless efforts of T. Vienne and generous support from the city. A cantata by Alexandre Georges, an exhibition of art work involving sports, and an exhibition of an ancient fight and Greek dances provided a magnificent setting for the athletic competitions.

This was how the reunion of the muscles and the mind, once divorced, was celebrated in the year of grace 1906.

Arts, lettres et sports,
in: *Une Campagne de vingt-et-un ans* [A Twenty-One Year Campaign]
Paris, Librairie Hachette, 1909, pp. 192-200 (Chapter XXI).

5.3/5 ADVISORY CONFERENCE. CIRCULAR LETTER (JULY 1906)

Berlin 15. OCT. 1906

MONSIEUR LE Président

La Conférence consultative convoquée par le Comité International Olympique à l'effet de rétablir l'union entre les Arts et les Sports et qui s'est tenue dernièrement à la Comédie Française à Paris sous la présidence d'honneur de M. Jules Claretie, a émis des vœux importants dont vous trouverez les détails dans la **Revue Olympique** de Juin.

Elle nous a surtout demandé d'intervenir auprès des principales universités, fédérations ou sociétés de sport de l'univers, à l'effet d'obtenir que, désormais, toutes grandes manifestations sportives puissent revêtir un caractère littéraire et artistique par l'adjonction de concours de poésies ou de représentations dramatiques appropriées, et surtout de musique chorale en plein air — insistant d'ailleurs sur les nombreux avantages qu'il y aurait pour les sociétés de sport à créer dans leur sein même des sections chorales.

J'ai l'honneur de vous communiquer l'expression de ce désir en vous priant de vouloir bien envisager la possibilité d'y donner satisfaction.

Veuillez agréer, Monsieur le Président, l'assurance de mes sentiments les plus distingués.

LE PRÉSIDENT DU COMITÉ INTERNATIONAL OLYMPIQUE.

Bn Pierre de Coubertin

Circular sent to heads of universities, sports federations and clubs, promoting literary and artistic elements in all major sporting events. Here: Letter to the German Olympic Committee/DRAFOS. (Carl & Liselott Diem Archives, Cologne)

The Advisory Conference convened by the International Olympic Committee with the aim of re-establishing the union between Art and Sport held recently at the Comédie Française in Paris, under the chairmanship of Mr Jules Claretie, gave rise to some important wishes, details of which you will find in the June edition of the **Olympic Review**.

In particular, it called upon us to approach the world's leading universities, federations or sports clubs with a view to ensuring that, in future, all major sports events include a literary or artistic component through the addition of poetry competitions or appropriate drama productions, and above all outdoor choral music - stressing, moreover, the numerous advantages that sports clubs would enjoy by creating choral sections within them.

I have the honour of communicating this desire to you and asking you to be kind enough to envisage the possibility of responding to it.

Yours etc.

Bulletin Officiel du CIO in: *Revue Olympique,* July 1906, p.112.

5.3/6 THE INCLUSION OF LITERATURE AND THE ARTS

Twenty-five years after the Advisory Conference, Coubertin's reflections in his Olympic Memoirs are of particular interest. Including the arts was not a resounding success, which is why Coubertin once again emphasizes their special role of making the Olympic Games into more than world championships.

It was not enough to bring "Muscle and Mind, ex-partners" together before the Justice of the Peace (in this instance, Mr. Jules Clarétie, who officiated at the ceremony in the historic foyer of the "Comédie Française", with Madame Bartet and Mr. Mounet-Sully on either side of him); it was equally important for the union to be fruitful. The fruit of this union was a long time in coming however, the first not appearing until 1926, some twenty years later. And among the early offspring, how many were imperfect or still-born! But in 1906, the important thing was merely to bring about a reconciliation between the two partners, who seemed to possess everything necessary to get on together but who, it must be confessed, really did not appear to care for each other at all. The important thing however was that the union should take place and above all that it should bear fruit.

I have already repeated – so often that I am a trifle ashamed of doing so once again, but so many people still do not seem to have understood – that the Olympic Games are not just ordinary world championships but a four-yearly festival of universal youth, "the spring of mankind", a festival of supreme efforts, multiple ambitions and all forms of youthful activity celebrated by each succeeding generation as it arrives on the threshold of life. It was no mere matter of chance that in ancient times, writers and artists gathered together at Olympia to celebrate the Games, thus creating the inestimable prestige the Games have enjoyed for so long. Wishing to revive not so much the form but the very principle of this millennial institution, because I felt it would give my country and mankind as a whole the educational stimulus they needed, I had to try and restore the powerful buttresses that had supported it in the past: the intellectual buttress, the moral buttress and, to a certain extent, the religious buttress. To which the modern world added two new forces: technical improvements and democratic internationalism.

In Athens, in 1896, the solemnity of this first contact of contemporary youth with Pericles' rebuilt stadium prevented the search for new artistic and literary works inspired by the idea of sport.

It would have been foolish. Moreover, it was not possible to do everything at once. Proceeding gradually by stages has always seemed to me the best way of going about any large-scale enterprise expected to last. In Paris, in 1900, apart from the unfavorable circumstances I have already described, the Universal Exhibition wallowed in a veritable plethora of new forms and ideas, far too abundant for there to be any point in trying to include an effort so detailed and of such a special nature... But right from the start Chicago showed an interest in this aspect of the Olympic question. The programs I mentioned above made allowances, a trifle awkwardly but nevertheless sincerely and enthusiastically, for art and thought. From this point of view, transferring the Games to St. Louis had been a misfortune. All efforts along these lines had to be postponed once more. Rome was now tending to fade away over the horizon. Wavering, a lessening of purpose and confidence began to become apparent, caused in fact by a regionalism that was still much too strong in spite of the appearance of unity... Another transfer was considered, this time to London. As time would then be very short, we should have to improvise a great deal and the artistic side of the Games would inevitably suffer...

The fear of seeing the launching of this idea delayed once again made me decide to summon a "Consultative Conference on Art, Letters and Sport" for the spring of 1906. At the same time, I would be able to use this as an excuse for not going to Athens, a journey I particularly wished to avoid. Even though we were now on very good terms with the Hellenic Committee, the reconciliation was a result more of a conscious effort on the part of both parties than of a serious alteration of our respective positions. Finally, what name should be given to these "additional" Games in 1906? How often should they be held? The idea of an intermediate four-year period, in which I had acquiesced without much conviction, was abandoned. In Athens, they were now thinking of a ten-year interval, which would make the two series coincide in 1916... All this was very uncertain; the situation would always be a trifle delicate. In any case, a great deal of friction and many difficulties were bound to arise during the contests. It was best for everyone and for everything that I should not be there. Count Brunetta d'Usseaux would take my place and would hedge whenever possible, saying the matter would have to be put to me, in this way delaying any awkward questions and avoiding hasty decisions.

I well remember the smile of delight on the face of André Beaunier – that sensitive, friendly writer who was carried off in the prime of life by a jealous fate – as I showed him, in his office at *Le Figaro,* the invitation to the Conference to be held at the Comédie Française. The invitation was to "come and study to what extent and in what way art and literature could be included in the celebration of the modern Olympiads and be associated with the practice of sport in general so as not only to benefit from it but at the same time ennoble it". "How beautifully put", he said, "and how well it goes with the setting chosen!" A rather unusual setting undoubtedly, and our request had certainly startled Jules Clarétie at first. But he had grown used to the idea and presided happily at the opening of a conference to which practically all artists and writers of note had been invited. Only about sixty actually came, but those who attended the first day returned for the discussions on the following days and helped draft the plans. Jean Richepin, Bourgault-Ducoudray, and Poilpot were enthusiastic about the whole idea. They had visions of processions, massed choirs, impressive tableaux, and triumphal odes. Others backed the scheme somewhat less enthusiastically or simply weighed the difficulties. The main stumbling block can be summed up in a few words: fear of the classical. The young artists, who considered 'classical' and 'stereotyped' as synonymous, were obviously those on whom the success of the scheme would depend. But this aversion of theirs turned them against the idea. In addition, in architecture no new needs had yet been expressed; in painting, sports scenes required more *line* than *color,* that is to say the opposite of the reigning trends, while in music, the public had completely lost all taste for open-air cantatas, and in literature writers – for the most part personally wholly unfamiliar with the joys of violent muscular effort – were incapable of describing them for a public that was not very familiar with them, either.

It would have been possible to remedy all this to a certain extent by calling on other countries to participate. This was a step I made the big mistake of not taking, limiting myself to sending out letters of invitation which were not fully understood and which brought us many telegrams of solidarity and encouragement, but no effective aid. Only the Royal Academy of arts in London showed itself really in favor of the idea, which was a good omen for the next Games (the choice of London becoming increasingly likely). At the opening session, Laffan had once again made one of his delightful speeches in French... and Madame Bartet, enchanted, reached over behind Clarétie and tugged me by the sleeve: "Who is he?" she asked with great curiosity mingled with admiration... "Who is he?".

The 1906 Conference none the less fulfilled its main purpose by proposing that the IOC should create "five contests of architecture, sculpture, music, painting, and literature for original works directly inspired by sport, such contests henceforth to become an integral part of the celebration of each Olympiad". The IOC would have made itself ridiculous if it had attempted to create contests of this kind right away, on its own. Invited to do so by a competent group composed of members of high repute, the IOC was well and truly supported in the eyes of the public.

In this respect, the Consultative Conference, which was brought to a fitting close with a very fine Festival of Sport and Art held at the Sorbonne, had not failed in its chief aim. The Charter of revived Olympism was now complete...

Or nearly so. The list of points drawn up by the original Congress in 1894 included a suggestion to the IOC (which had just been created) "to include within its regulations a clause authorizing it to exclude from the Games any person who, by his earlier deeds, might tarnish the reputation enjoyed by the Games". This wording was not likely to please André Beaunier! The idea was not only awkwardly put but not even very clear. However, the proposal had been made so as to keep the door open for some form of moral protection, thus gradually setting modern Olympism along the path towards the "purification" of the competitor that had been one of the fundamental tenets of ancient Olympism.

In what form though? I was not too sure, but since we could not get around the difficulties involved in the question of amateurism, it occurred to me that a start could be made by introducing the Olympic oath, which would be the occasion for a moving ceremony and would put the competitor on his honor while simplifying research into his status.

In sporting circles, in those days, no one was at all prepared for such a novelty and, my first overtures having brought forth nothing but smiles or protests, it was to the Fédération des Patronages that I made my first public proposal. At the time it had about fifty thousand members. It was continually persecuted, but it managed to survive even so and succeeded in obtaining playing fields without anyone really knowing how. At the end of the Federation's festivities in the spring of 1906, I wrote to its Secretary General, Charles Simon, who was a keen advocate as well as a remarkable organizer, a letter later published in the July number of the *Olympic Review*. In it, I recommended the introduction of the Olympic oath. The idea met with approval much more quickly than might have been expected and precisely in those lay circles which had been the most refractory up till then.

Olympic Memoirs, Chap. 8, Lausanne, IOC, 1997, pp. 88-93.

OLYMPIC COMPETITIONS IN PAINTING, SCULPTURE AND ARCHITECTURE FOR 1908

REGULATIONS

1. Competitions in Painting, Sculpture and Architecture will be held as an integral part of the Olympic Games of London, 1908.
2. The subjects selected are the following :-

I. PAINTING

CLASS A

Cartoons in black and white accompanied by a coloured sketch representing either-
(*a*) A triumphal procession; or
(*b*) The battle of the Greeks and Amazons;
either subject to be treated as a frieze 10 ft. long by. 4 ft. high.

The coloured sketch to be $\frac{1}{4}$ full size.

Prize : The Gold Olympic Medal.

CLASS B

Canvases representing either-
(*a*) (Modern Athletics) A Football Match : or
(*b*) (Classical Athletics) Discus throwers (not less than four, nor more than six, principal figures); or
(*c*) Hercules and Antaeus.
These subjects to be treated on canvases not more than 7 ft. 6 ins. and not less than 6 feet in the widest dimension.

Prize : The Gold Olympic Medal.

Announcement of the Olympic art competitions. Although scheduled for the 1908 London Games, these competitions did not take place due to a lack of preparation time. (taken from Revue Olympique, Oct.1907, pp.343-345)

5.3/7 OLYMPIC ARTS COMPETITIONS FOR 1908

These art competitions which were publicly announced in the Revue Olympique in October 1907 to take place at the Olympic Games in London in 1908 for the first time, represent such an important Olympic-historic document that it also has to be restored here.

As everybody knows the art competitions in 1908 could not be realised. In the introduction of this volume the short preparation time and the too strongly thematised inclusion were mentioned for being the reasons for the failure. In the Official Report of the British Olympic Committee for the 1908 Games it is noted that with future Olympic Games the announcement has to be made public at least three years in advance and the results should be shown at an exhibition during the Games.

An important resolution of the Conference in Paris in 1906 for Coubertin was, however, realised. The participants of the Games entered the stadium at the Opening Ceremony in their sports wear and in many cases their sports equipment.

II. SCULPTURE

CLASS A

A frieze in relief 10 ft. long by 4 ft. wide representing either-

(*a*) A triumphal procession; or

(*b*) The battle of the Greeks and Amazons.

Prize : The Gold Olympic Medal.

CLASS B. Open to all artists.

Any one of the following subjects to be treated either in the round or in relief-

(*a*) A Football Match.

(*b*) Discus throwers.

(*c*) Hercules and Antaeus.

The size of the reliefs to be not more than 7 ft. 6 ins. and not less than 6 feet in their widest dimension.

The figures in groups in the round to be not less than 4 ft. 6 in. high.

Prize : The Gold Olympic Medal.

III. ARCHITECTURE.

Open to all architects.

(*a*) A swimming bath 100 feet long by 83 feet wide surrounded by a colonnade and dressing rooms with a domed hall at one end and a vestibule at the other.

To include a plan, elevation and section on separate sheets to 1/8 th. in. scale, and a sheet of details to $\frac{1}{2}$ in. scale.

(*b*) A town house with front to a street 50 feet wide and provision for a fully fitted private gymnasium.

To include a plan, elevation and section on separate sheets to 1/8 th. in. scale and a sheet of details to $\frac{1}{2}$ in. scale.

(*c*) A Sports Club for a country town of 20.000 inhabitants. The building to stand in its own grounds of one acre, to include Fencing Hall, Gymnasium, Swimming Bath and Shooting Gallery and Fives Courts (2) and accommodation for as many other sports as possible, and to be capable of being constructed for £ 2.000.

To include a plan elevation and section on separate sheets to 1/8 th. in. scale and a sheet of details to $\frac{1}{2}$ in. scale.

Prize : The Gold Olympic Medal.

3. In addition to the Prizes each competitor will receive the Olympic Diploma and commemorative medal.

4. There is no limit to the number of entries in these competitions.

Revue Olympique,
Oct. 1907, pp. 343-345.

"A Modern Olympia"
Two Lausanne architects, Eugène Monod and Alphonse Laverrière, won the first prize in the International Architecture Competition organized by the IOC in 1910 and the gold medal for architecture in the inaugural Olympic art competition 1912 for their representation of a modern Olympia on the shores of Lake Leman.
(IOC Archives)

5.3/8 PROGRAM OF THE INTERNATIONAL ARCHITECTURE COMPETITION

The first definite result of the Conference of Paris was an architectural competition advertised by the IOC in 1910. The task was to build a model of a modern Olympia.

In May 1911, the competition was supervised by the College of Architecture in Paris, and was concluded by the public award of the prize to two architects from Lausanne, Eugène Monod and Alphonse Laverrière. For historic reasons the rendering of the original text of the announcement seems to be appropriate here.

Program of the International Architecture Competition
Paris 1910
Organized by the International Olympic Committee
Under the patronage of The President of the French Republic

I. THE PURPOSE OF THE COMPETITION IS TO DEVELOP PLANS FOR A MODERN OLYMPIA
including:

1. The buildings, porticos, arenas, tracks, etc. required for athletic and artistic events included in the program of the modern Olympic Games;
2. The structures required for spectators;
3. The building or spaces required for ceremonies associated with the Games;
4. The facilities for administration, athletes, etc.

The competitors must also determine the topographical requirements of the site selected or designed by them.

II. Competitors must send at least *four* and no more than *six* sketches measuring a total area of *two and a half meters by four meters*. One of these sketches must show the general layout of the City. Competitors may attach an explanatory report, not to exceed four thousand words.

III. All competitors will receive a *Commemorative Diploma*; their submissions will be exhibited to the public, and will be the subject of a *General Report* on the results of the Congress. This report will include a list of competitors. The *Olympic medal*, which has been awarded only seventeen times since 1894, will be awarded to the winner of the competition. The ruling will be made by a jury composed of five international experts representing the various points of view of art, technical considerations, and sports.

IV. Competitors are requested to register before May 1, 1910, if possible. The list of competitors will be closed on October 1, and submissions must reach Mr. Gaston Trélat, Director of the École Spéciale d'Architecture, General Commissioner of the Competition, 254, Boulevard Raspail, *Paris*, no later than November 15, 1910. Please send all correspondence regarding the competition to Mr. Trélat.

Une Olympiqe moderne. Special Print.
Auxerre, E. Juttefaux, 1910, pp.1-2.

5.3/9 – 5.3/10 INTRODUCTION

The organizers of the Fifth Olympic Games, which were to be held in 1912, drew lessons from the errors of 1908 for the five art competitions planned at the Stockholm Games. Very early on, in September 1911, the Olympic Review published the official English announcement of the competitions. This announcement is presented below (5.3/9). The upshot was that submitted works had to be previous unknown, and had to be inspired primarily by the athletic idea.

Coubertin comments on the running of the Games themselves in chapter 4.2.2/24, entitled "A Bird's Eye View of an Olympiad[1]". Nowhere does he mention his own victory in the Olympic competition for literature, which he entered under the pseudonyms Georges Hohrod/M. Eschbach. He won with a work entitled "Ode to Sport", which appeared in German and French[2]."

Coubertin's "Ode to Sport" as an example of his literary work is printed below.

Here is the jury's report on the "Ode to Sport". This report makes it possible for us to appreciate Coubertin's efforts, and to underscore the relationship of the texts on art included here:

"The great merit of the 'Ode to Sport,' which, in our view, was far and away the winner in the literature competition, was that it is the very model of what the competitions was looking for in terms of inspiration. In addition, it derives as directly as possible from the athletic idea. It praises athletics in a form that is both literate and athletic. It was compared, for a while, with a long and praiseworthy poem on aviation. Yet it was significantly better than that poem because of the sort of essence of athletic feeling that runs throughout every stanza. But there were other ways, as well, in which it was superior. Although its images are sober, the ideas it contains are varied. The ideas are arranged, classified, and expressed in a series that is flawless in logic and harmony. The only reproach that can and should be made against such a work is that when all is said and done, we do not know from what country or language it comes. The reader feels troubled by this double text in German and French. The reader would rather recognize right away that one language is simply a translation of the other. Rather, each seems to have been translated from the other. The thought seems of Latin origin, and the language is clearly Germanic in inspiration. Perhaps Messrs. Hohrod and Eschbach intended to show, in this way, that the mission of Olympic literature is to draw nations together in respect of beauty. This is all fine and good, but we believe that there is a danger in following this example. It is preferable for submitted works to bear the stamp of the genius of a specific nation, not seeking to straddle national borders.[3]"

1 *Revue Olympique*, 1912, pp. 115-119.

2 As confirmed by the general report of the Swedish organizing committee, the associations of artists in Sweden were loath to assume responsibility for these competitions. This lack of enthusiasm caused the IOC and the organizing committee in Stockholm to take full responsibility for the competitions themselves. See: The Swedish Olympic Committee (Ed.): *The Official Report of Stockholm*, 1912, Stockholm 1913, pp. 806-811.

3 "Report on the Artistic and Literary Competitions of the Fifth Olympiad." in *Revue Olympique*, July 1912, p. 103.

Emblem of the art competition in the Official Report of Stockholm 1912

5.3/9 RULES FOR THE LITERARY AND ARTISTIC COMPETITIONS OF 1912

Fifth Olympiad – Stockholm 1912
Rules for the Literary and Artistic Competitions of 1912.

1. The Vth Olympiad will include competitions in *Architecture, Sculpture, Painting, Music,* and *Literature.*

2. The Jury can only consider subjects which *have not been published or exhibited before and which have some direct connexion with sport.*

3. To the winner of each of the five competitions will be awarded the Prize medal of the Vth Fifth Olympiad. The exhibits selected will, so far as possible be exhibited, published or performed during the Olympic Games.

4. Competitors must notify their intension to enter for one or more of these competitions before January 15th 1912 and the exhibits themselves must be in the hands of the Jury before March 1st 1912.

5. No limitation of size or form are laid down for manuscripts, plans, drawings or canvasses. But sculptors are required to send in clay models not exceeding 80 centimetres in height, length and breadth.

6. For further information as for forms of entry, application should be made to M. le Président du Comité International Olympique, 20, rue Oudinot, Paris, or Olympiska Spelen, Stockholm.

Revue Olympique, September 1911, pp. 131-132.

5.3/10 ODE TO SPORT

I

O Sport, delight of the Gods, distillation of life!

In the grey dingle of modern existence, restless with barren toil, you suddenly appeared like the shining messenger of vanished ages, those ages when humanity could smile. And to the mountain tops came dawn's first glimmer, and sunbeams dappled the forest's gloomy floor.

II

O Sport, you are Beauty!

You – the architect of this house, the human body, which may become object or sublime according as to whether it is defiled by base passions or cherished with wholesome endeavour. There can be no beauty without poise and proportion, and you are the incornparable master of both, for you create harmony, you fill movement with rythm, you make strength gracious, and you lend power to supple things.

III

O Sport, you are Justice!

The perfect fairness which men seek in vain in their social institutions rises around you of its own accord. No man can surpass by one centimetre the height he can jump or the time for which he can run. His combined strength of body and mind alone set the bounds to his success.

IV

O Sport, you are Daring!

The whole meaning of muscular effort lies in one word – to dare. What good are muscles, what good is it to feel nimble and strong and to train one's nimbleness and strength if not to dare? But the daring you inspire is far from the rashness which impels the gambler to stake his all on a throw. It is a prudent and considered daring.

V

O Sport, you are Honour!

The titles you bestow are worthless save if won in absolute fairness and perfect unselfishness. Whoever succeeds in deceiving his fellows by some ignoble trick, suffers the shame of it in the depths of himself and dreads the dishonourable epithet which will be coupled with his name if the fraud from which he prospers should come to light.

VI

O Sport, you are Joy!

At your call the flesh makes holiday and the eyes smile; the blood flows free and strong in the arteries. Thought's horizon grows lighter and more clear. Even to the griefstricken you can bring a healing distraction from their sorrows, while you enable the happy to taste the joy of living to the full.

Road signs at the entrance to the Alsatian villages of Hohrod and Eschbach, not far from the family home of Coubertin's wife, Marie Rothan, in Luttenbach near Munster. He often spent his summer holidays here with his family until 1914. Pierre de Coubertin adopted these two names as a pseudonym when signing his "Ode to Sport". (Photo: N.Müller)

VII

O Sport, you are Fecundity!

You tend by straight and noble paths towards a more perfect race, blasting the seeds of sickness and righting the flaws which threaten its needful soundness. And you quicken within the athlete the wish to see growing about him brisk and sturdy sons to follow him in the arena and in their turn bear off joyous laurels.

VIII

O Sport, you are Progress!

To serve you well, man must better himself in body and in soul. You enjoin him to observe a loftier hygiene; you require him refrain from all excess. You teach him wise rules which will give his effort the maximum intensity without impairing the balance of his health.

IX

O Sport, you are Peace!

You forge happy bonds between the peoples by drawing them together in reverence for strength which is controlled, organised and selfdisciplined. Through you the young of all the world learn to respect one another, and thus the diversity of national traits becomes a source of generous and peaceful emulation.

Ode au Sport.
Georges Hohrod et M. Eschbach (Coubertin's pseudonym)
Special printing in German and French. Gand, van Dosselaere, 1912.
English version in: Coubertin, *The Olympic Idea.* Schorndorf 1967, pp. 39-40.

Pierre de Coubertin about 1907 with his family in the villa of his parents-in-law in Luttenbach near Munster in the Alsace. Coubertin holding his daughter Renée (1902-1968) on his knees, next to him his wife Marie (1861-1963) with son Jacques (1896-1952), next to them his mother-in-law Madame Rothan. (Navacelle Collection)

5.3/11 A GREAT MARRIAGE

We have placed this introduction to the report of the Advisory Conference, published in the June 1906 issue of the Revue Olympique, at the end of this group of texts relating to the Fine Arts. Its title, "A Great Marriage", is the symbol that was intended to accompany Olympism forever. Olympic arts competitions were still an official part of the program of the Olympic Games of London in 1948. In future Games, they were replaced by exhibitions and a requirement that art be combined with sports when the Olympic Games are held. They were definitely eliminated by the IOC in 1954.

The success that artistic events have had in the Games since then bolsters this arrangement, even if, in Coubertin's view, art competitions were of great value in his overall system. Happily, he did not live to see these competitions abolished.

"Gentlemen, we have gathered in this unique place, to hold a unique ceremony. Our purpose is this: to reunite the Muscles and the Mind, once divorced, in the bonds of a legitimate marriage". These words, repeated in the press throughout the world, were spoken at the opening of the Advisory Conference recently held at the Comédie Française. They reflect exactly what happened at the conference. We will provide a summary of its activities as we await publication of its principal documents. The Paris newspapers are fond of using the term "a great marriage" for ceremonies they describe in copious detail. But it has never been better used than on this occasion. The marriage at issue is far and away the greatest of them all, and it will also be the most fruitful.

Une "grand mariage",
in: *Revue Olympique*,
June 1906, p. 83.

5.3/12 OLYMPIC LETTER II: CONTRIBUTION BY THE ARTS, HUMANITIES AND SCIENCES TO RESTORING THE GREEK GYMNASIUM

In the second Olympic Letter to readers of the *Gazette de Lausanne* dated October 18, 1918, Coubertin offers a brief look back at the most important stages of the modern Olympic Movement. In addition to the revival of the Olympic Games in 1896 in Athens, the key points are also the invitation to men of letters and the arts, followed by scientists. With the idea of communal sports centers, he wanted to restore the unity of body and mind and in this balance give back urgently needed social peace to all people.

I am in the habit of disconcerting my friends. They are many, thank God; so are my enemies. In this world, the one doesn't go without the other. Enmity is the reverse side of friendship; a good cloth needs a lining – it preserves it. The same is true of friendship.

If, then, I have often disconcerted my friends it is by superimposing, or rather relating one to the other, ideas between which it did not seem that there could be any worthwhile connection. To remedy the overburdening of the schoolboy by introducing sport into the high school – this seemed, thirty years ago, to be a good idea. It was approved. There were recalcitrants, but they were few in number, and public opinion silenced them ... but why restore the Olympic Games? A strange ambition, manifestly colored by classical ideology! Victor Duruy and Jules Ferry, great partisans of the first initiative, were no longer there to support the second. Others hesitated to commit themselves. Jules Simon himself felt doubts. However the thing was done, the Olympiads resumed their course after the overthrow in Greece of the Tricoupis ministry, which was opposed to this restitution.

After several years, men of letters and artists were invited to gather around this renascent Olympism, not merely to enhance its prestige but to find fruitful inspiration in it. They seemed surprised that in the modern world anyone should dream of reassociating muscle and mind. The marriage of these once divorced partners was celebrated in the foyer of the Comédie Francaise. A gracious assembly. Mrs. Bartet and Mr. Mounet-Sully were witnesses. Mr. Clarétie officiated. Those present listened, smiling and amused.

Then came the turn of the scholars. We invited them to take up the study of the psychology of sport; the foundation of a new science, indeed. At first they held back skittishly. But the contributions of Marcel Prévost, Ferrero, and Roosevelt interested them. And the psychology of sport began to make some conquests among serious people.

The task now is to construct social peace by restoring the gymnasium of antiquity, the place where the philosophers preached ... And how can that be done, great Heavens! And furthermore what connection is there between all that and Olympism?

A close and intense connection, reader. These are merely different stages of a single undertaking, different aspects of the same problem. I will try to explain this next time.

Lettre Olympique II,
in: *La Gazette de Lausanne,* Vol. 286, October 18, 1918, p.1.

Congrès International Athlétique de Paris.

Voeux émis par le Congrès dans sa séance plénière du 23 Juin 1894.
après lecture du rapport de la Commission d'

Amateurisme.

Définition.

1er Est amateur en athlétisme
toute personne qui n'a jamais pris part à une course publique ouverte à tous venants, ni concouru pour un prix en espèces; ou pour une somme d'argent de quelque source qu'elle provienne, notamment des admissions sur le terrain; ou avec des professionnels, ou qui n'a jamais été à aucune période de sa vie, professeur ou moniteur salarié d'exercices physiques.

Très exceptionnellement, les Unions ou fédérations de Sociétés pourront autoriser la rencontre entre amateurs et professionnels, pourvu que les prix offerts ne soient pas des prix en espèces.

Toute infraction aux règles de l'amateurisme entraîne la disqualification d'amateur.

Amateur definition approved by the IOC Founding Congress in 1894 at the Plenary Session held on 23rd June 1894, after consideration of the Commission's report. (Translation in text 5.4/1) (IOC Archives)

5.4 THE ISSUE OF AMATEURISM

The next chapter, "Amateurism", comprises nine texts covering the entire period during which Coubertin was establishing the Olympic Games, even though he wrote in his *Olympic Memoirs,* "Personally, I wasn't particularly concerned[1]". This retrospective point of view too greatly diminishes the significance of what the matter held throughout Coubertin's life.

The amateur issue was the reason that the athletic associations of the entire world met in Paris in 1894. It was there that the decision to restore the Olympic Games was made. From the celebration of the first Games in 1896 to the Olympic Congress in Baden-Baden in 1981, the public, and the press in particular, has recognized the amateur rules of the Olympic Charter as the primary value of the Olympic movement. This reveals the critical role that amateurism played in the basic idea of Olympism.

For Coubertin, amateurism was first and foremost a matter of education. He believed, rightly, that far too often, the letter rather than the spirit of the rule was followed[2].

The search for the true Olympic amateur turned out to be a hopelessly idealistic goal, because no rules could be made to pin down what an amateur is. In every country, depending on the sport at issue, social and cultural circumstances create different types of Olympic participant. In other words, any change in the rules was only a partial solution. Coubertin acknowledged that, "To understand it [the notion of an amateur] has to go back to sporting life and customs in England fifty years ago[3]". In his Olympic Memoirs, published for the first time in 1931, Coubertin speaks ironically of his "honorable mummy", a reference to the endless debate about amateurism that defies the members of the IOC even more[4].

The problem of amateurism dogged Coubertin right up to his last day in office. As Coubertin said to the audience gathered to hear his farewell speech in Prague: "Fair or temple – sportsmen must make their choice; they cannot expect or frequent both one and the other ... let them choose! [5]"

5.4/1 THE CHARTER OF AMATEURISM (1902)

This text is critical for understanding the debate about amateurism within the Olympic movement, even if Coubertin's originality is scarcely expressed in it. In reproducing the resolutions regarding amateurism which were adopted at the Founding Congress in 1894, Coubertin intended to put in writing the status of the debate on this issue, as of that date, for his colleagues at the IOC and for certain other officials in the sports world. He assumed, rightly as it turned out, that they were readers of the Revue Olympique. The title "The Charter of Amateurism", which Coubertin chose, is intended to demonstrate the "immutable" nature of these principles.

Coubertin's remarks in this text reveal much about the history of sport, on certain topics in particular. This text tells us exactly who authored the various resolutions.

1 *Olympic Memoirs*, Lausanne 1997, p. 115.
2 Cf. Coubertin, *Une campagne de vingt-et-un ans*, p. 91.
3 Coubertin, *Olympic Memoirs*, Lausanne, 1997, p. 116. Coubertin is referring to England in the 1880s.
4 Cf. Coubertin, "Amateurism." *Olympic Memoirs,* Chapter XI, pp. 115-121.
5 Coubertin: *Speech Given at the Opening of the Olympic Congresses at the City Hall of Prague.* Special brochure, Government Printing Office, Prague, 1925, p. 7. See text 5.1/11 in this volume.

In our January 1901 issue, we summarized the work done over the past six years, since the founding of the International Olympic Committee. Of course, we included a long paragraph on the Paris Congress of 1894, which marked such a brilliant start to the restoration of the Olympics. For lack of space, however, we were unable to publish all the resolutions adopted by the Congress, resolutions that are, in a way, a Charter of Amateurism.

It is all the more useful to recall these resolutions today since the Congress of Brussels is scheduled to resume, modify, and complete the work begun at the Congress of Paris. Therefore, we feel that we are doing a service for everyone by reprinting the last part of the general report of 1894, as it appears in volume one of the Bulletin of the International Committee, dated July 1894.

"After reading the Reports submitted by Messrs. Mangeot and Borel, on Saturday, June 23 the Congress issued the following resolutions:

I. The following shall be considered an amateur athlete:

Any individual who has never participated in a competition open to all comers, nor competed for a cash prize, or for a prize of any amount of money regardless of its source, specifically from admissions to the field – or with professionals – and who has never been, at any time in his life, a teacher or paid instructor in physical exercise.

By and large, this is the definition that guides the major athletic federations throughout the world. The Victorian Rowing Association (Melbourne) had submitted a more complete text, but it was too long and too confusing. Yet the paragraph on the exclusion of any individual whose athletic successes have resulted in any pecuniary advantages whatsoever was drawn from that text.

By way of rare exception, Unions or Federations of Associations may authorize meets between amateurs and professionals, provided that the prizes offered are not cash prizes.

This proposal from the *Ligue Vélocipédique Belge* [Belgian Cycling League] was adopted after a heated debate. Mr. Roussel, vice president of the *Union Vélocipédique de France* [Cycling Union of France], recommended that meets between amateurs and professionals be permitted without restriction. While agreeing with him that encounters with professionals are useful in bringing about progress through imitation, Messrs. Gondinet, Todd, and Sloane dwelled on the dangers inherent in allowing young amateurs to be in regular and continuous contact with professionals. By contrast, it did seem that there was some advantage in allowing the barrier separating the two to be raised in certain cases.

Any infraction of the rules of amateurism shall result in disqualification of the amateur.

II. *Anyone who has been disqualified may not be requalified unless the Union, Federation, or Association of which he was most recently a member determines that the cause of the disqualification was error, ignorance, or good faith.*

(This wording was suggested by the National Cyclist's Union).

III. *Anyone who earns money through the prizes that he has won thereby loses his standing as an amateur.*

The value of art objects is not necessarily limited, but in general the value is not very high.

The New York Athletic Club had asked for a limit, as had the Australian associations, who suggested setting a maximum of three pounds (seventy-five francs). Mr. Todd proposed ten guineas (two hundred sixty francs). The Congress did not feel that it should follow this lead, while eagerly desiring that prizes should be merely "souvenirs", not compensation in and of themselves.

IV. *Money from admissions to the field may be shared as compensation for travel expenses among the participating associations, but never among the competitors themselves.*

No competitor may be allowed to travel alone in exchange for compensation paid by an opposing associations, unless this is handled and expressly desired by the association of which he is a member.

In no case may funds be paid directly to the competitor, but must be paid to the association to which he belongs.

This is probably the only way that the issue of "gate money" can be settled for the time being; agreement on this point was unanimous.

V. *Since public wagering is incompatible with amateurism, the associations shall forbid it or restrain it through any means at their disposal, specifically by opposing official wagering within the premises of the competitions.*

This resolution was deemed daring by some individuals. It will seem quite timid to our correspondents in America and Australia, who opted for absolute elimination of betting. The Australians even wanted a law that would make it possible to ticket anyone placing a bet on the spot, whether publicly or in private.

VI. *The tendency in all sports, without exception, is toward pure amateurism, since there is no permanent motive in any sport to legitimize cash prizes; for the time being, however, the general definition of the amateur will not apply to horse racing, shooting, and yachting.*

This item gave rise to a particularly lively debate. The Count de Villers, Mr. Todd, and many of their colleagues insisted that the argument that some sports incur higher costs was worthless. Why would wealthy individuals be excepted from observing on a large scale what those who are less well-off are required to observe on a smaller scale? The nature of amateurism does not change according to the fortunes of individuals, and to earn money while shooting clay pigeons is an infraction of its laws. Yet the Count de Pourtalès wisely noted that some sports had roots that are too deep, in France and in other countries, for it to be possible to change current regulations so completely overnight, no matter how imperfect those regulations may be.

Some then saw a way to avoid the problem by restricting the competence of the Congress to athletic sports as such. But the assembly determined that such a course of action would hardly be worthy of the Congress, and it courageously proclaimed that cash prizes are not indispensable anywhere.

VII. One cannot be an amateur in one sport and a professional in another.

La Charte de l'Amateurisme,
in: *Revue Olympique,*
January 1902, pp. 14-15.

The editor has determined that this text, though unsigned, was written by Coubertin.

5.4/2 THE SURVEY ON AMATEURISM

Given the IOC's experience at the London Olympic Games of 1908 in terms of the rules then in force regarding amateurism, there was a desire to achieve greater homogeneity at the next Olympic Games. This topic was discussed at the IOC Session in Berlin in 1909. The English magazine *Sporting Life* did a survey on the regulation concerning amateurism. Thus the matter was debated publicly. However, the IOC did not achieve any tangible results. They wanted to seek the opinion of the international federations first[1].

The news that the International Committee, in Berlin, was going to discuss a report by Count Albert de Bertier on the Sporting Life survey made the rounds of the English press, and seemed to meet with general satisfaction. *Sporting Life* praised the author of the report, recalling that his book on archery had become a classic. It also noted the mastery with which he oversaw the fate of one of the most handsome teams of horses in France, and his practice of a wide variety of sports, including wrestling, fencing, and rowing. The magazine concluded that few men are as well prepared for such an undertaking as this. In other settings, however, some concern was voiced here and there at the thought that the International Committee was on the verge of regulating, in a specific and definitive way, an issue that had been undecided for so long, and one about which it was no longer clear that complete agreement could ever be achieved. If the Committee wrote a definition of the amateur that was to be applied to the upcoming Olympiads, countries or federations that did not adhere to that definition entirely, or immediately, would find themselves in an unusual and decidedly disadvantaged position at the upcoming Olympiad. We cannot foresee what will happen in Berlin, and when all is said and done, we have insufficient information to form judgments about any decisions that may be made. Yet we would be quite surprised if the majority did not come out in favor of a slower, wiser, and more fruitful process. The first thing to be done is to gather the opinions that have been expressed during the inquiry, in order to get to the heart of the matter, so to speak, and to create a rather homogenous, clarified whole. Once that is done, the major players, namely the clubs and the federations, should be heard and given the opportunity to express their opinions on this issue. Currently, the worst of it is that *questions on this issue simply are not raised.* At least they are not raised in terms and in a manner that allows for resolution. Let there be no effort to resolve these questions before they are even raised. The greatest benefit of this survey will be, specifically, that it makes it possible to raise the question definitively and comprehensively. Once the various potential solutions have been studied, as is appropriate, agreement will no doubt be reached more easily than could be expected if the preliminary work had not been done.

L'enquête sur l'Amateurisme,
in: *Revue Olympique,*
May 1909, pp. 67-68.

The editor has determined that this text, though unsigned, was written by Coubertin.

1 See the questionnaire printed below. The results were published in the *Revue Olympique* of June 1910, in preparation for the Luxembourg Session; cf. "La question de l'amateurisme." [The Issue of Amateurism], in *Revue Olympique*, June 1910, pp. 89-95.

QUESTIONNAIRE ABOUT AMATEURISM

Sir

In accordance with the decision arrived at the Berlin meeting held under the patronage of H.S.H. the German Kronprinz, the International Olympic Committee now submits the undermentioned queries relating to the amateur question to the sporting societies and federations of the various countries:

1. Are you of the opinion that a man cannot be an amateur in sport and a professional in another?

2. Are you of the opinion that a professor can compete as an amateur in sports other than those he teaches?

3. Are you of the opinion that when an amateur becomes a professional he cannot recover his amateur status? Do you allow any exceptions to this rule? What are they?

4. Do you allow amateurs to receive their travelling and their hotel expenses? Up to what limit?

5. Are you agreed that a man loses his title to amateur by simply competing against a professional?

An answer is requested from your federation or society and will be deeply appreciated. Replies should be sent personally for the British Empire to Theodore A. Cook Esq. 54 Oakley Street, Chelsea, London and for the American Continent to Prof. W. M. Sloane, Columbia University, New York.

With anticipated thanks
Yours truly
Bon Pierre de Coubertin, president I.O.C., Cte Eug. Brunetta d'Usseaux (Italy) Hon. Sec., Bon Godefroy de Blonay (Switzerland) Hon. treas.

Questionnaire relativement à l'enquête sur l'Amateurisme,
in: *Revue Olympique*,
August 1909, p. 128.
English version: Manuscript, dated November 1909, (IOC Archives)

5.4/3 THE POSSIBLE UNIFICATION OF THE AMATEUR DEFINITION

The movement towards unification of the amateur definition has made much progress since the inquiry instituted by the "Sporting Life" a couple of years ago brought the subject within the bounds of practical politics. Earlier attempts to obtain data upon which a solution of this most difficult problem might be based had proved unsuccessful, but the remarkable dossier of evidence collected by that journal comprised expressions of opinion from representatives of sport all over the world, and when the International Olympic Committee took the matter in hand, they had before them a collection of opinions which could not but prove of the utmost value in enabling them to arrive at a conclusion on the subject. The exhaustive report prepared by Count de Bertier de Sauvigny, and submitted to the International Olympic Council in 1909, concluded with the suggestion that the Federations, Associations, & Societies principally interested should be called upon for their views on the subject, and five questions were submitted to them. Their replies given in the "Revue Olympique" form a further valuable contribution towards a settlement of the question, and while the progress towards a solution of the differences therein exposed that is somewhat slow, it need not be any the less correct. There is this to be said, that the varying shades of opinion upon the questions of expenses, of reinstatements, and disqualifications do not destroy the general, hue and cry principle that an amateur is the athlete who follows sport for sports sake, and not for any pecuniary inducement. That is the broad aspect of amateurism which has always been current where amateur sport prevails, and there is not the slightest indication that any of the bodies which have replied wish to deviate therefrom.

The replies from the American associations and universities are perhaps the most interesting of all the series because they exemplify the variations in point of detail which may accompany agreement in principle. The questions put by Professor Sloane are not identical with the five sent to the European associations, but they develop the same opinions. The preliminary question as to the desirability of a general definition of an amateur, and the advisability of restricting international sport by such a definition reveals a large majority in favor of the movement towards unification, while all are agreed that no athlete can derive profit directly in money or money's worth and remain an amateur. When, however, we arrive at the debateable ground of expenses, we find that while five universities agree on principle with the limitation of expenses, two universities and six associations do not. The United States, we may remember is a vast country, and the inherent difficulties concerning the development of amateur sport there have rendered some relaxation of the hard and fast limit necessary. But many suspensions have been made of athletes who have demanded unreasonable expense money, and it may be taken into consideration that the associations, while limiting expenses to the actual disbursements of the athlete, are not prepared to state any definite limit to the amount of expenses an athlete may incur, owing to the magnitude of the journeys which he may be compelled to take. Generally, in Europe the allowance of travelling and hotel expenses is recognised, but in several instances the wise precaution is recognised of making the reimbursements through a club, and not directly to a competitor.

The question of contact might have been resolved in a more satisfactory manner had it been divided under two headings: 1. individual competition 2. in the constitution of teams in such games as cricket, football, and baseball.

There is a marked difference between competition in games where team interests are at stake and where there is no offer of personal gain to the winning team, and competition in athletics, cycling, swimming, and the equivalent, where there are individual rewards for the winner. The superiority of the professional player over the average amateur does not in any way injure the general interests of football or cricket; but were the professional runner or cyclist allowed to compete freely against the amateur in those sports he would monopolise the awards, and the honours as well. The man who can devote all his time to training is bound, nine times out of ten, to beat the man who lacks that opportunity, and there would be many specious pretexts for the amateur to depart from the true principles of amateurism – were he to be threatened with the unfair competition of the man who made his living from athletic sport.

The question of the professor competing as an amateur in sports other than those he teaches is also complicated. There is, for instance, a vast difference between the school teacher who inculcates the knowledge of gymnastics or swimming, and the professional footballer or cricketer who makes his living by practising those sports. It may be said that the latter class might reasonably be regarded as amateurs in athletics or swimming, because it has no special facilities for practising those sports, but in the first place the professional has exceptional opportunities of acquiring physical fitness: in the second, having embraced the opportunity of gaining pecuniary advantage in one sport, it is not to be considered impossible that were similar opportunities offered in the other, he would despise them. The position of the school teacher is altogether different, and it is not unreasonable to regard him as a physician, having the development of the physical well-being of his scholars as his object, rather than his own advancement in the sport he is teaching.

As to the reinstatement of the professional into good standing as an amateur, there are a variety of opinions. The general view is that an act of professionalism does not altogether close the avenue to the amateur ranks, but that each case should be taken upon its merits. Some say that requalifications should not be authorised except by an International tribunal, but presumably this would only apply to such affecting International competition.

The lax views of certain English societies on this point do not find much support elsewhere, but it must be borne in mind that in many cases their reinstatements are not full time professionals, but of men whose offence lies in competing at meetings, or in events, not under their control, and this side of the subject, being purely domestic, is not raised in the discussion of an International definition. But the athlete who has embarked upon a professional career in full knowledge, should not be regarded as a desirable person in the amateur ranks even though he recants, and while the authorities of each sport in every country may reserve the right to reinstate under exceptional circumstances, the federations, if the question was presented to them would probably agree that a reinstated professional should not be allowed to compete in International sport; unless his reinstatement was confirmed by an International Committee at least twelve months before the entries for the games closed.

Returning from the side issues involved in the answers to the questions set by the International Olympic Committee to the whole subject of amateurism, we may note that the Committee has already prepared the way for a further forward movement by selecting two sports for special discussion – fencing, whereupon France is taking up the question of a definition, and track and field athletics, in regard to which the study of the subject is left to the United Kingdom representatives. The reason for selecting two sports so widely separated in their aspect may be questioned, but careful consideration suggests that in taking fencing, the most aristocratic of the Olympic sports, and athletics, the most democratic, the Committee has acted with great wisdom. If a formula can be found which will unite the extremes, dealing with the intermediate degrees of opinion will not be a great problem.

The pertinent enquiry which suggests itself, however, is: What course is to be adopted with regard to the 1912 Olympic Games ? From the report of Mr. Theodore Cook it appears that the intention is to adopt the amateur definition put forward by the country in which the Games are held for Stockholm in 1912, just as it was done for London in 1908. There is much wisdom in the reasoning of Mr. Cook that excessive rigidity on any attempt at unification will only result in friction. But it must be realised that unless, and until, a standardised definition is laid down, the position will be the same as in 1908 – that the country in which the Games are held, while holding its own athletes rigidly to its own definition, will have to accept entries from other countries on the basis of the amateur definition of those countries, and in the particular sports in each country, and that is the precise nature of the grievance which prompted the demand for unification.

Is it to be expected that because the British rules for athletes and cyclists deny the right of an amateur to ask for or accept expenses, countries which admit that right are to refrain from entering those of their men who have availed themselves of that permission ? Granted that the International Olympic Committee cannot issue definite orders to the federations of the various countries comprising it, there should not be any solid objection to the laying down of certain regulations governing the Olympic Games which it controls. It may be too late to enforce anything of this nature in 1912, but if the two delegations enquiring into the selected subjects should report in good time and it be found that there is substantial agreement between them, there could be no harm in negotiating with Sweden with a view to secure the adoption of the agreed formula for the Stockholm Games. Such a definition would have a force which the possibly varied pronouncements of the bodies governing each branch of sport would never possess.

Moreover in the event of any dispute the International jury would have something definite to go from, and, finally, the anomaly of athletes competing in one branch of sport who would not be eligible to take part in another would not exist, under the definition governing the Games. Needless to say any formula that is both acceptable and effective needs to be rather widely expressed, but it seems that effective progress would be best ensured by securing the acceptance of wide principles, rather than debating upon disputable points. The policy outlined above may at any rate be commended to the consideration of the International Olympic Committee, who will of a surety apply to it that earnest consideration which it has given to the whole question of the amateur definition.

In: *Revue Olympique*, September 1910, pp.138-142.

The editor has determined that this text, though unsigned, was written by Coubertin.

5.4/4 THE THORPE AFFAIR ONCE AGAIN

The Jim Thorpe affair was the first "amateur" scandal in Olympic history. America was upset by the fact that the American Olympic Committee and the Amateur Athletic Union had disqualified their greatest hero in Stockholm, the winner of the decathlon and the pentathlon, because in 1909-1910 he had played baseball in exchange for minor remuneration. The affair was debated in European publications, as well, all the more so since Thorpe was an American Indian and racism tinged the debate. The IOC had to make a decision on this case at its meeting in Lausanne in 1913. Coubertin found himself in the position of having to publish the correspondence on this affair, and of having to express his opinion on the matter in the following issue of the Revue Olympique, which came out in April. In that article, as was his custom, Coubertin did not merely give a clear description of the affair. Rather, he discussed the fundamental ideas that would apply to such cases in the future. He stressed the need to come up with new regulations on amateurism, regulations that were finally formulated in 1914 at the Olympic Congress in Paris. He focused on the idea that he had been following for years, that of introducing the Olympic oath. Seen in this light, one might say that the Jim Thorpe affair performed a great service for the Olympic movement.

In the end, the IOC went along with the decision of the American associations, and accepted the disqualification of Jim Thorpe.

The publication of documents related to the Thorpe affair in the latest issue of the *Revue Olympique* seems to have caused a stir among our readers. Several expressed their astonishment at seeing a man disqualified for a "peccadillo" who had provided such clear proof of his amateur spirit by turning down considerable offers. It is true that the entire letter sent by Mr. Thorpe to J. E. Sullivan is imbued with athletic feeling. The simplicity, even naïveté, with which he presents his case will win him over to the hearts of many a sportsman. He will also win favor for two places where he discusses – without rancor and in all fairness – his colleagues "who were earning money by ball playing during their vacations and who were regarded as amateurs at home", and apologizes for having done "what I knew several other college men had done except that they did not use their own names". With unintended but considerable irony, his letter is reminiscent of the fable of La Fontaine, "Les animaux malades de la peste".

However, if the indulgence that these considerations generate should win out over concern for strict application of the regulations, are we not opening the door to dangerous compromises of the law? Should these compromises, which are harmful in all instances, not be avoided especially where the Olympic Games are concerned? One need only recall the concern of the ancients that only athletes beyond reproach should participate in the Olympiads. Should it not be the same in the modern world?

It is not up to us to intervene in this matter. In this discussion of a few interesting assessments that have come to our attention, we are merely adding to the evidence for a hearing, if there is to be one. The only conclusion we will allow ourselves to draw is that there is a pressing need to revise the regulations on amateurism. No one will be surprised that we are dwelling on this matter that we have often said is close to our hearts. These regulations have become a network of weak links, and for some time now it has allowed avowed professionals to be called

Jim Thorpe, the great American athlete who won the decathlon at the 1912 Olympics in Stockholm. He was disqualified a year later at the USOC's instigation, because he had earned a few dollars as a baseball player some years previously (taken from E.Petersen/S.Hermlin, Dem Femte Olympiaden. Olympiska Spelen i Stockholm 1912 i bild och ord, Gothenburg, Ahlen & Akerlund, 1912, p.228)

amateurs, while holding back sportsmen whose amateur status is quite clear, labeling them professionals. If the Thorpe affair convinces everyone of the need for change, we must admit that it has done an invaluable service for sports.

Among the newspapers that have debated this case, some have alluded to the possibility of creating an athlete's oath. They recognize that this is a way of verifying an athlete's past, and it stands a fairly good chance of helping avoid such incidents as this. Ultimately we must adopt this solution, one that I have always advocated. Thorpe considered himself an amateur, and presented himself (or allowed himself to be presented) as such. How can one think even for an instant that if he had been called upon to swear on his country's flag that he had never committed any infraction of the regulations of amateurism, he would have run the risk of swearing a false oath? Not only would that have disqualified him as a sportsman, it would have remained a mark against his honor throughout his life. By asking the question, we give the answer. Beside its wonderful moral value, the athlete's oath is proving to be the only practical means to put an end to this intolerable state of affairs.

Encore l'affaire Thorpe, in: *Revue Olympique,* April 1913, pp. 58-59.

The editor has determined that this text, though unsigned, was written by Coubertin.

5.4/5 NEW ASPECTS OF THE PROBLEM

The Thorpe affair was a major turning point in the debate about amateurism. For Coubertin, the reasons were quite significant. In the following text, he puts himself in the position of the spectator, whom he qualifies as the worst enemy of amateurism. It is clear that Coubertin wanted to defend athletes, refusing to allow them to be accused without taking psychological factors into consideration.

It would certainly be unwise to believe that the various aspects of the problem of amateurism have become simpler since 1910. To do so would mean closing one's eyes to regrettable – but convincing – evidence. One fact dominates the situation, a fact that the recent efforts of the new International Amateur Federation have cast into sharp relief. Given the direction we have chosen, we cannot come to any agreement without complicating matters. The definition on which the directors of that organization managed to agree is striking for its great complexity. Yet the only solid and long-lasting agreements are those based on simplification.

Other events seem deceptive. "Athletic" sports are by nature involved in increasing difficulties. Professionals disguised as amateurs are flourishing in them in ever greater numbers, and swimming and boxing are facing a similar, immanent danger. Yet the gymnastics and rowing federations, which are far less fearful of professionals and even allow a certain amount of contact with them or with their principles, are experiencing far less rot. Logically the opposite should be happening, but it is not. The hidden reason for these anomalies is that the *spectator*, the great enemy of amateurism and the prime agent of the professional attitude, plays a less extensive and powerless role in those sports. The spectator attends their deeds of collective prowess which are infrequent and remote. The spectator is unaware of the individual's preparation, the details of his training, and his personality. A beneficial barrier stands between them. We can thus conclude that for the amateur, the danger is not external, but internal; that he must be kept not from contact with professionals but from contact with the demoralizing circumstances in which he pursues his own athletic activity. This is a serious observation, because it implies that the issue is not one of form, but of a state of mind, and that no external form will have any effect as long as the desirable state of mind has not been created and made more commonplace.

In addition, particularly since last year, Olympism evokes the specter of a new type of professionalism that one might call patriotic professionalism. Ancient Greece was familiar with it, and we do not really know if the Greeks managed to find a solution to it. All appearances tend to indicate, rather, that they reached an accommodation with it as a necessary evil. With the revival of Olympic enthusiasm, it is quite natural that athletes have called on the public authorities of their respective countries to provide generous subsidies making it possible to train better teams to send to the Olympiads. The term "prepare" is already in use. So far, this has been understood only in the sense of gathering and transporting athletes, but one can foresee that things will go much further. If athlete should end up being supported at the expense of the nation for the period of their training, does that not open the door to all sorts of excesses?

Perhaps, however, this would finally mean opening the door to a revolution that would utterly change the circumstances with which we began, and on which we still depend. One who wears a soldier's uniform is no longer either an amateur or a professional. He is a soldier and that is all. Is there not a similar unification underway for those who wear the uniform of the Olympic competitor, preparing to fight for the honor of the nation? However, in the final analysis, would such a state of affairs not harm true athleticism? Would nationalization not gradually break the springs of private initiative that remain indispensable to its progress?

Nouveau aspects du problème,
in: *Revue Olympique*, November 1913, pp. 178-179.

The editor has determined that this text, though unsigned, was written by Coubertin.

5.4/6 VARIOUS SOLUTIONS

After reading about new aspects of the problem of amateurism in the preceding article, one finds some solutions in the following text. The November 1913 issue of the Revue Olympique was devoted entirely to this topic. In addition to this text and the preceding one, the issue contained the 1909 IOC report on the situation of amateurism and the responses to the questionnaires sent out in 1910. In these comments, Coubertin tries to put an end to the debate for the time being. He wanted to state his point of view very clearly before the deliberations of the Olympic Congress of 1914, which was scheduled to be held in Paris.

His remarks include two proposals:

a) Introduce an "International License" that would be drawn up by an extraordinary and independent Olympic tribunal.

b) Have the amateur status of a participant in the Olympic games confirmed by individuals who live with him (a simple idea from an educational perspective, but an effective one for Coubertin).

In any event, we cannot foresee a development similar to the one now being debated. Other solutions must be sought out, temporary though they may be, but solutions that should not be considered temporary. Given current conditions in athletic life and organization throughout the world, only three such solutions seem worthy of serious consideration, especially from the Olympic perspective.

The first would be an International License, granted by a single, independent, and permanent tribunal. The establishment of such a license presupposes, no doubt, prior universal agreement on the basis for the definition of the amateur, but not necessarily absolutely uniform wording. The judges must take it as their mission to seek out the pure amateur, not merely by verifying dates or facts, but by evaluating, in their souls and consciences, whether a particular error should be pardoned or be considered unpardonable. Only then would the License take on its full value. Such a tribunal would be difficult to run, but not difficult to put together. Men of competence and honor can be found to take part in it. The administrative machinery, by contrast, would be expensive and slow.

We think that very quickly the judges themselves would have recourse to the athlete's oath. So, one might think, why not just begin using the oath right away, without incurring the costs of a tribunal? The oath would include drawing up a sort of table of laws that list the "commandments of the amateur". An athlete who swears on his country's flag that he has never broken those laws could be admitted to the Olympic Games, because a false oath sworn under such circumstances would cast dishonor on the competitor, a burden of infamy that he would bear throughout his life. In this way, the respect for honor that is so essential for sports would be placed, once again, at the heart of athletic institutions.

There is a third solution, a rather flat and vulgar one, but one that does have its advantages. In terms of the Olympics, however, it has the very serious problem that it facilitates, and even encourages, international disputes. This solution is the "to each his own" method, in other words admitting, without appeal, any amateur presented as such by his fellow citizens...

Solutions diverses,
in: *Revue Olympique,* November 1913, pp. 179-180.

The editor has determined that this text, though unsigned, was written by Coubertin.

5.4/7 THE MATTER OF MONEY

From the start, the Olympic movement experienced financial problems. In 1896, the Olympic Games took place only thanks to the generosity of wealthy Greeks living abroad. Early on, the press became interested in the expenses of the Olympic Games. In this article, published in the *Revue Olympique,* Coubertin found himself having to take a stand on the issue of financing the Games, and on the material assistance needed for preparing the participants. This topic remains current, even eighty years later.

The millions are flying around the Olympic Games, fanciful and real millions alike. Althoug` newspapers have sometimes exaggerated or inaccurately quoted the numbers that are circulating, their figures were based on accurate information, namely the enormous efforts that governments, cities, and athletic associations are prepared to make to see to it that the Olympiads are held. The poor advertising executive who cried out in his fury, following the Fourth Olympiad, "Let a wolf bite me if we see these Olympic Games in another four years..." must be pretty nervous for his hide. Happily, the wolf has forgotten him, or never cared about him in the first place. He will see the Olympic Games again in three years, and in seven years, and in thirteen years, too, if God lets him live. The question is not whether they will be held, but how they will be held, and at whose expense. The "small countries", which are often wealthier and more *comfortable* than larger ones, were a bit upset at the idea that it cost so much money to hold the modern Olympiads, or merely to prepare to participate in them. This did not dampen their enthusiasm. The only proof we need is one rather typical example. Of the three cities that competed to host the 1920 games, only one is a capital, and the capital of a moderate country at that. The two others are not capitals at all. Budapest, Amsterdam, and Antwerp rivaled each other in zeal and generosity in the plans they drew up for this occasion, as yet so far off. Yet in these countries, when they heard the French asking their government for 600,000 francs to "go to Berlin" and the English saying "We must pull together 1,200,000 francs, because otherwise we will accomplish nothing good at the Sixth Olympiad", they grew concerned. People are worried

This picture shows how the Stockholm organizers dealt with commerce. In 1912, thirty editions of the Official Organ of the Swedish Olympic Committees contained advertisements for mouthwash and toothpaste with direct reference to a whole range of Olympic sports and venues in Stockholm, e.g. the pole vault. (taken from Olympiska Spelens Tidning. The Olympic News. Official Organ of the Swedish Olympic Committees, Stockholm, 10th July 1912, p.7)

about the increases in the amount of money needed. People are also concerned about how athletes are "prepared" through financial support, a process that borders dangerously on the undeniably professional.

The president of the International Committee seized the opportunity offered to him the other day in London, at a banquet held in his honor by the British Olympic Council, to review the situation, and to recall that no matter how significant the issue of money may be, clearly it should not take precedence over the "issue of muscles" that people truly seem to forget from time to time. It is not through piling up bank notes that potential champions are created. The truth – and we have no reason to hide it; on the contrary, it is well worth stating plainly – the truth is that athletic associations have become gluttonously greedy, and that the occasion seemed a good enough one to them to obtain substantial subsidies.

The German Empire is rich and powerful. In many sports, it is still a novice. The movement taking shape there seems quite legitimate. Everyone understands that if an Olympiad is to be held in Berlin, it must be done in a splendid manner. The financial plan was put together very wisely. It calls for focusing the main effort on organizing the competitions and festivals. But it also provides for assistance – substantial, but far more modest than has been said – to be given to new associations that lack playing fields or training sites. Other countries do not have the same reasons for expenditure. To carry off the laurels at Berlin in 1916, countries that have been won over to athletics for a long time must go there armed with one commodity that cannot be bought: the desire to win. In cases where athletes making the trip would have to camp out alongside the imperial stadium, obviously it is desirable to ask governments to defray the expenses of the youths called upon to defend the flags of their respective countries under such circumstances. But it is difficult to see how those same governments could cover to the initial training of the athletes without turning them into sworn professionals.

When all is said and done, that is the delicate issue in this business, the one that raises suspicions about it. It gives off a faint whiff of professionalism, and forces us to recall that a whole swarm of false amateurs is involved in all sports. These amateurs are far less sporting than many a professional, whose sportsmanship is infinitely purer than theirs. People would like participation in the Olympic Games to be limited to young men motivated by the true spirit of sport, as it should be. How can this be accomplished?

If we look carefully at the origin of these conflicts, we find a single cause: the invasion of sports by those whom we have already had occasion to call the "resident aliens of sport", journalists on the hunt for copy, doctors looking for clients, hopefuls on the search for voters, loafers looking to be entertained, people of all kinds looking for fame. It is this vile population that has emphasized the "money question" out of all proportion to its role. Thanks to the uproar surrounding this issue, we are losing the only recipe for making an Olympic champion. To win at the Olympics, first you need muscles, then energy, and then perseverance. Then add the necessary money, but if you do not have the other three, the effort is useless.

La question d'argent,
in: *Revue Olympique*, December 1913, pp. 183-185.

The editor has determined that this text, though unsigned, was written by Coubertin.

5.4/8 AMATEURISM AT THE PRAGUE CONGRESS

The Olympic Congress of Paris in 1914 had rewritten the rules that made it possible to verify amateur status. Only those athletes subject to the "amateur" regulations of their international federation could participate in the Olympic Games. Olympic sports that did not have an international federation had to create one by June 30, 1915. In the future, the NOCs were to verify the amateur status of the athletes they sent to the Games.

A major responsibility had been shifted from the IOC to other organizations. World War I would inevitably interrupt the debate over amateurism for years. After the Antwerp Games of 1920, the problem faced the IOC once again.

The reflections that Coubertin presented to the Olympic Congress of Prague in 1925 summarize the issue of amateurism. This issue no longer had any real meaning for him. As he saw it, this was a problem that concerned the press, not the Olympic movement. At the same time, however, he remained intractable, protesting against payment or handling of bills for luxury hotels.

The Congress of Prague set the minimum conditions that the Olympic amateur had to meet. These conditions were written into the Olympic Charter. There was one new element: every participant had to sign a declaration on his honor stating that he fulfilled the conditions of Olympic amateurism.

The congresses that will meet in Prague next Pentecost (May 31, 1925) are unusual, in that they will make it possible to take full stock of the issue of athletics as it now stands throughout the world. The ramifications are many, in terms of both specialized technique and general educational principles. That is why there will be two congresses, meeting separately, though there will be some connection between them. The first will be the regular Olympic Congress that the International Committee has made a habit of calling during the year before an Olympiad is held. We are still very close to recent events, yet upsets and quarrels (if there were quarrels) have calmed, and the "objective" spirit has been restored in people's minds. By statute, the delegates to the Congress are: the members of the International Committee, some sixty-five individuals from forty-five different countries, the delegates of the National Olympic Committees, one committee per country and two delegates per country, and delegates from the international athletic federations, two delegates per federation. This is not an ideal assembly, but it comes reasonably close. Fair distribution of national interests and technical interests is apparent under the aegis of the representatives of the great Olympic idea, who attempt to stay above these two sets of interests through appropriate forms of internationalism and eclecticism.

The main problem that will be addressed in Prague at this congress will be that of amateurism. The reader has the right to smile. We have been hearing about this particular problem for nearly thirty years. The fact that we have seen it reappear periodically on the agendas of solemn meetings, and in the interim feed so many polemics in the press, is sufficient proof that no solution has ever been found.

And yet, it has. The issue is now clearly defined, and that is something that counts. Everyone knows that there are false amateurs, and that for the most part, these are wealthy athletes who think nothing of adding casual profits to their customary resources. When this "casual" aspect means a fairly long free stay at a first-class hotel for a tennis championship, one might well wonder what remains of "amateurism" in the person who benefits from such advantages. In contrast to such athletes, there are those who work hard to earn a living, and for whom any kind of travel may mean risking their pay or, as the saying goes, "a loss of earnings". For example, a football player often has a wife and children for whom even the shortest series of matches agreed to by his club is a burden. Should he, therefore, abstain?

Here, then, is the amateur problem raised to the level of the social question, no more, no less. It is one of the countless aspects of the struggle between the haves and the have-nots. One can deny this principle in well-meaning, lovely speeches, but the reality of the situation is the central mechanism where all activity comes, ends and begins again. Are athletes whose expenses are defrayed improperly and athletes who receive compensation for lost salary both amateurs, or is neither one an amateur? If only one of them is an amateur, which one is it?

In addition to this "socialization" of athletics, the issue takes on an unexpected but quite clear aspect of ethnic rivalry. The British concept and the "Latin" concept of athletics will always be at odds. We must recognize – and this is a curious paradox – that in the country where the great educator Thomas Arnold first sketched out the principles of athletic education, the educational role of athletics has been set aside. It is no longer of interest. The English in England and, in their footsteps, the English in the Dominions, sometimes stoop to deal with athletic education, but it bores them. In their view, a good sports club remains a club whose members are *gentlemen of the same station.* That was the fundamental condition. They cannot manage to detach themselves from it. That is why in rowing, for example, they once declared any manual laborer a professional. This was how the university rowers intended to maintain the rather aristocratic cachet of their sport. It took a long time to put an end, in theory, to legislation that was so medieval. In practice, one cannot say that it has disappeared entirely.

"Latin" sports are inspired by a different spirit. Above all else, this form of athletic endeavor tends to bring athletes together in view of the results to be achieved, the victory to be won. It tends to form a vast "athletic republic" with common interests. The competitions are certainly passionate, though at times the system does manage to overcome even the most zealous national passions. That is why I call it Latin. Of course, these are still merely nuances, but they are nuances that will become striking shades of color. This is the form of athletics that dominates nearly the entire continent, including the Germans and the Slavs. South America is beginning to provide significant support for it. It is clear that its influence is gradually increasing, rather rapidly. Now, we find ourselves at the threshold of an Anglo-Latin rivalry, where the numerical and moral strengths will be on the side of the Latins. On the British side there will be the strength of tradition, resulting from an established position and long-standing routine. European athletic opinion is beginning to become aware of this fatal opposition. From there to rebelling against British leadership in this matter is but a short step. That step is all the more sure to be taken if the British element continues to pride itself on dogmatic superiority in matters of athletic loyalty and the practice of fair play. Here as elsewhere, the actions of the United States will be essential, if not decisive. American athletes are readily disparaged. This is one of the general consequences of European ignorance and incomprehension of America. Of course they are not spotless lambs. But often they prove to be more deeply imbued with the athletic spirit than many of their attackers.

Such is the atmosphere in which, it appears, the discussions at the Congress of Prague will take place. The main pitfall of the congress will be the danger of getting lost in a maze of regulations and distinctions. If they expect to deal with and resolve all the "cases" presented to the wisdom of the delegates, they will risk failure. They must not hope to find a formula applicable to every situation, nor one that everyone can agree upon. Yet it would be a great contribution merely to establish some directives, to chart a course, and in this way to escape the quagmire in which we have been treading for so long. The charter of true amateurism can be written only after we truly agree on the principles that must inspire the wording.

In addition to the technical congress, a congress on education will meet at Prague. Each country will be asked by the Czechoslovakian government, in its own name and in the name of the International Olympic Committee, to appoint a certain number of delegates. There will also be free auditors. The congress on education will study nine questions submitted to it, regarding excesses in athletic exhibitions, boxing matches, restrictions during adolescence, the involvement of women in violent sports, the potential restoration of the "ancient gymnasium" at the municipal level, the advancement of fair play and of the chivalrous spirit, the cooperation of universities, the "sports cure", and the battle against sham athletes. Although they are narrowly phrased, these questions remain of great interest to a wide range of individuals: students, moralists, health scientists, feminists, etc. Each country will be entitled to send up to ten delegates, whose views will be carefully canvassed, resulting in useful reforms and fruitful initiatives.

L'amateurisme au Congrès de Prague,
in: *Bibliothèque Universelle et Revue de Genève*,
January 1925, pp. 106-110.

5.4/9 AMATEURISM

To Coubertin, the question of amateurism in the first decade of the 20th century was of such central importance that, when looking back, he devotes a whole chapter of his *Olympic Memoirs* to the issue. In that chapter, he lists the various stages and initiatives on the way to settling the question of amateur status at the Olympic Games, and explains why he regards the Olympic Oath as the only educationally meaningful solution.

Here it was again – the same old question! It was sixteen years now since we had rather naively thought that we had settled the whole matter, and here it was again, slipping and sliding out of your grasp like a cat, taunting you just out of reach. Personally, I was not particularly concerned. Today I can admit it; the question never really bothered me. It had served as a screen to convene the Congress designed to revive the Olympic Games. Realizing the importance attached to it in sports circles, I always showed the necessary enthusiasm, but it was an enthusiasm without real conviction. My own conception of sport has always been very different from that of a large number – perhaps the majority – of sportsmen. To me, sport was a religion with its church, dogmas, service... but above all a religious feeling, and it seemed to me as childish to make all this depend on whether an athlete had received a five franc coin as automatically to consider the parish verger an unbeliever because he receives a salary for looking after the church. Now that I have reached – and even passed – the age when one can practice one's heresies and even proclaim them freely, I no longer have any hesitation in owning to this point of view. However, for want of a better solution, I agreed that one had to accept certain rules, set up certain more or less fictitious barriers, and I did everything I could to help. The English, particularly, felt very strongly about the whole matter. It was a sign and a presage of strength for the IOC when they turned to it asking for help.

The questionnaire in three languages, sent out in 1902 to all clubs, had brought forth very few replies – and none of them particularly illuminating. After the London Games, *Sporting Life*, which enjoyed a certain prestige on the other side of the Channel, took the matter up very seriously and with great vigor carried out a new inquiry. Stating that the IOC alone, thanks to the independence it enjoyed as a result of its composition and its method of recruitment, was in a position to settle the matter, the English journal set about collecting the necessary information and opinions for it. A few months later, a huge file reached us, consisting of more than 150 documents. Having read it through carefully in the hope of finding something new, I was forced to admit that here too, even in this mass of material, everything had already been said before. I felt that the real trouble stemmed from the fact that the question had not been framed in terms and in a way that would enable it to be solved; everyone persisted in wanting to solve the problem before it was properly raised.

One of my French colleagues, Count Albert de Bertier, who was a great expert on all sporting matters – possessing above all, I would say, a great sporting spirit – agreed to present to the meeting in Berlin a report on which we worked together, at his home in Compiègne.

The definition of an amateur which had served as a model for most continental or transatlantic definitions was already quite out of date. It had come to us from England. It stipulated that an athlete ceased to be an amateur if he:

1. accepted a cash prize;
2. competed with a professional;
3. received a salary as a sports instructor or coach;
4. took part in "open" events, i.e. open to all comers.

What is particularly striking about these four points is their great disparity. The second is quite debatable for its absolutism. The third equates teacher or instructor with professional (which, for my part, I had never been able to accept), in such a way that the least one could say about it is that it is too superficial by far. The fourth has lost all meaning. What is an event "open to all comers"? To understand it, one has to go back to sporting life and customs in England some fifty years ago. In fact, it is a form of social protection, a relic of the class system.

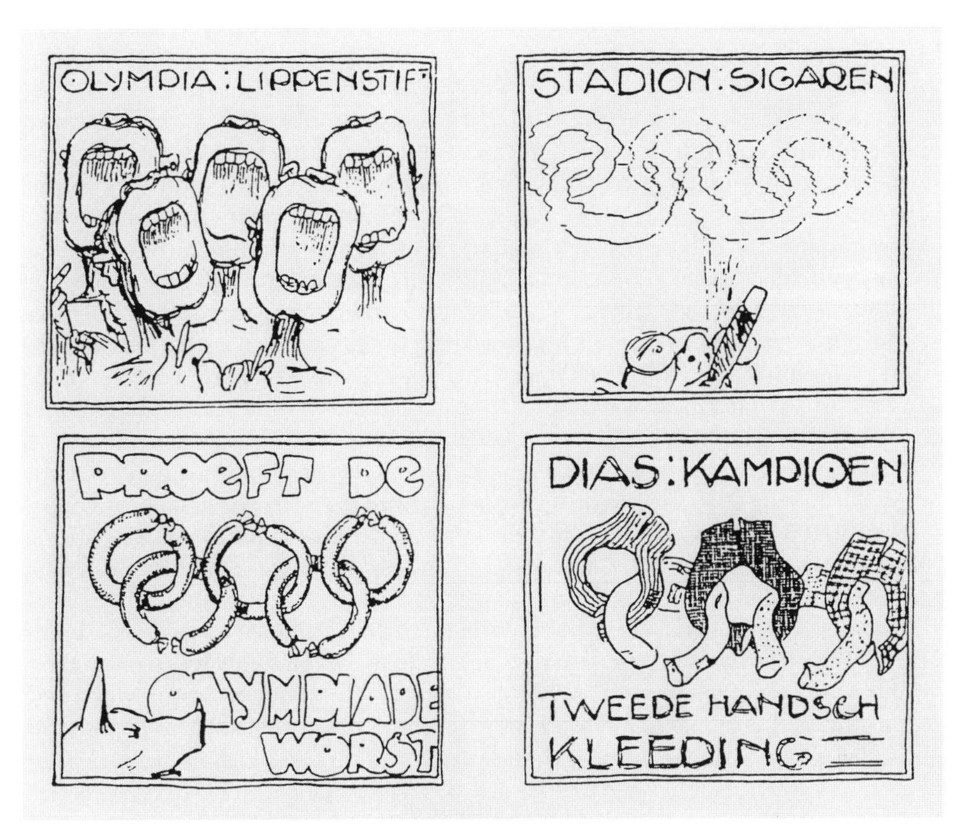

Dutch humour concerning the misuse of the Olympic rings. The Dutch Parliament refused to give financial support to the 1928 Olympic Games in Amsterdam, partly because of the obsession with individual performance which the Church thought unjustifiable. The Games therefore had to be privately funded, resulting in numerous examples of satire in the Netherlands (taken from Olympische Spiele 1928 in Amsterdam. Special Issue of the Review "Leibesübungen", 1928, p.523)

Even though the questionnaire was so outdated, it could nevertheless be used as a basis for a study of the question. It was necessary to consider in turn: money contacts – instructing or coaching – and the relations of the individual to the group.

The other day – a great many years later – I read through the 1909 report again overcoming all resistance. Its conclusions were straightforward and clear-cut. If they had been adopted, we would have avoided a great deal of trouble, fruitless disputes, and wasted time. Above all we could have, if not exactly smothered in the nest, at least greatly weakened the pernicious species of sham amateurs – who started to proliferate subsequently like the heresies of Byzantine times whose proliferation Tertullian likens to that of scorpions, in summer by the Nile. All sources of direct, continuous profit of considerable value were condemned; a great deal of indulgence was requested for minor infringements. The principle of re-qualification was allowed provided it was granted by a single independent court offering every possible guarantee: a sort of Court of The Hague for sport. The oath took on the force of custom; a detailed, written oath for ordinary events; an oral oath sworn on the athlete's national flag, for the Olympic Games. Expenses were allowed to be refunded in circumstances warranting it, provided the refund covered only travel and living expenses, not spending money.

We formally refused to allow an amateur to be deprived of his amateur status simply for having competed with a professional and even less for having competed with an athlete suspended by his federation or having taken part in a competition "not authorized" by the latter: a stupefying and absurd regulation that more than one federation had succeeded in imposing.

The status of a coach or an instructor was clearly distinguished from that of a professional. Regulations were suggested to serve as a basis for legislation based on all these revolutionary ideas which were nevertheless very sensible and well suited to the new democratic and cosmopolitan future that was just dawning and whose probable demands I took pleasure in drawing to the attention of my colleagues in the IOC. They were much less reluctant to agree to these new provisions than might have been expected and the most aristocratic among them were not the most reserved by any means.

On the other hand, several were apprehensive and, knowing full well the opinion of sports circles in their own country, were afraid of a head-on, violent clash.

They asked for modifications to be made, with regard to form at least, to several parts of the Report. The text, which was published in the Olympic Review for August 1909, is the revised, watered down version. I would very much like to have been able to consult again the original text as read to the IOC in Berlin. But it is not in its proper place in the archives and I have not been able to lay my hands on it.

The fears to which I have just referred made the Committee decide to take a small number of questions from the Report and submit them to the federations and associations concerned. Here is the questionnaire we sent out shortly afterwards:

1. Do you think that it is not possible to be a professional in one sport and an amateur in another?

2. Do you think that a coach or an instructor can on the contrary be an amateur in a sport he does not teach?

3. Do you think that an amateur who has once turned professional may never recover his amateur status? Do you allow exceptions to this rule? If so, which?

4. Do you agree that an amateur may have his travel and hotel expenses refunded? Up to what limit?

5. Do you agree that a sportsman may lose his amateur status by mere contact with a professional?[1]

The answers to these questions were to be returned, for the continent of Europe, to our Hungarian colleague Mr. J. de Muzsa; for the British Empire, to Mr. T. A. Cook; and for the American continent to Professor W. M. Sloane. This was the same division that I had inaugurated in 1894 and which seemed to work.

Plenty of time was allowed for studying the questions and replying in detail. There was nothing hurried about it. It was not until the following year, at our Session in Luxembourg (June 1910) that our colleagues were to return the documents they had received. Unfortunately, the answers were wildly contradictory. Neither in the same country from one sport to another, nor in different countries for the same sport, did there seem to be even the slightest agreement. Mere statements; no reasons. Pure fantasy; nothing concrete, nothing really well thought out. Noting this, I appreciated in retrospect the apprehensions of our colleagues who had been afraid to take the plunge. Perhaps they even saved us a great deal of trouble later on. But from that moment on I lost even the little interest I had had in the question of amateurism. I returned to my conviction that coach and professional must not be placed on the same footing, that an oath, not a mere public formality for show, but detailed and signed, is the only way of being sure about a man's sporting past because perjury in this instance disqualifies him for ever and in all fields, that class distinctions must play no role in sport, that the time is past when one can expect an athlete to pay his own travel and hotel expenses, that amateur status has nothing whatever to do with the administrative regulations of a sports association, etc., etc., etc., that there are not only a great many sham amateurs to be tracked down and condemned but a great many falsely attributed professionals for whom allowances must be made, etc., etc., etc.

What have I just written! Blasphemy! Like Alphonse Daudet's clergyman, stopping short in the middle of his drinking song, I feel I ought to say: "Mercy on me! If my parishioners could hear me now! "

Olympic Memoirs, Chap. 11, Lausanne, IOC, 1997, pp. 114-121.

1 In contrast to the English version of the questionnaire which Coubertin made in November, 1909, this is a new translation.

Pierre de Coubertin towards the end of his life, with his daughter Renée, with whom he worked regulary. (Navacelle Collection)

6. THE OLYMPIC MOVEMENT

Chapter 6 focuses primarily on issues of the structure and organization of the Olympic movement. In arranging them, we must recall that Coubertin never limited his thought to one particular point of view. Rather, he presented the broader educational perspective and then attempted to resolve individual issues.

The following selected texts show well, once again, that Coubertin, when presenting the theory of a particular problem, also thought of how it would apply in practice. The Olympic movement was able to flourish so readily only because, from the start, Coubertin was involved in great detail in decisions that had to be made regarding its structures and growth. He strongly opposed changes that he viewed as harmful. He did more than simply condemn mistakes; he suggested solutions, and even presented a detailed plan for organization and financing, as shown by the plan developed for the Fourth Olympic Games in Rome, in 1908.

In Coubertin's view, it was of the greatest significance that the IOC remain independent. Following the example of the Stewards of the Henley Regatta, he had founded the IOC as a "self-recruiting body". The significance of this step is explained in the comments in section 6.1, below.

The texts in section 6.2, on the development and spread of the Olympic movement, show the enormous difficulties that arose in setting up an "Olympic infrastructure."

The third section (6.3) shows Coubertin's concerns about the athletic program of the Olympic Games. The equality of the various sports seemed essential to him, an idea that we will see again in several of these reports[1].

Coubertin was only rarely concerned with the practical playing of the various sports, except for very specific reasons.

The writings included in this chapter complete the historical retrospective of section 4.2.1. We also find in them Coubertin's position on admitting women to the major sports in the Olympic Games.

The final section includes two of Coubertin's articles supporting Lausanne as the seat of the Olympic movement, a choice that would be confirmed on April 10, 1915 in a ceremony at the Town Hall of Lausanne.

1 See text 5.2/1 in this volume.

6.1 STRUCTURE AND ORGANIZATION

The following ten texts date from throughout the period from the establishment of the IOC to 1922. After that date, Coubertin almost never returned, in practice, to matters concerning the organization or structure of the Olympic movement, as we saw him do in the last chapter.

These texts were selected from among a large number of different documents. We took care to ensure that they are representative of similar events. In nearly every issue of the Revue Olympique, which Coubertin published from 1901 to 1914, and over the content of which Coubertin exercised great influence, we find many suggestions and ideas about the organization of the movement. Although these articles are not signed with his name, we recognize quite clearly the style of the president of the IOC. To expose his views to a large public, Coubertin used not only the supplement to the *Revue Olympique,* the "Bulletin of the IOC", which began with the January 1906 issue, but the "Reports and News" and the "Monthly Events" columns, as well. In addition, as we mentioned in the introduction to this volume, Coubertin also used the official circular letters to the members of the IOC.

Section 6.1 contains mainly texts that deal with the structure of the IOC, the NOCs, and the International Sports Federations. In addition, we have included a few representative pieces on organizational problems. The institution of the early Olympic decorations, the "Olympic Diploma" and the "Olympic Cup", is mentioned, as well.

6.1/1 CHRONICLE – THE CHARACTER OF OUR ENTERPRISE

In the second Bulletin of the International Committee of the Olympic Games, published in October 1894, Coubertin presented to a new circle of readers his ideas about the practical implementation of the decisions of the congress that founded the IOC, held in Paris, in June 1894. It is astonishing to see the extent to which Coubertin had already worked out specific ideas about its future growth, even at the start of the movement.

It is surprising to discover, so early on in this paper, a suggestion about founding national committees responsible for sending sports teams to the Olympic Games. For Coubertin, this was not a matter of setting up committees limited to the period of the respective Olympic Games, as at Athens in 1896. Rather, he was convinced that his project would live on, and that it would be necessary to set up a permanent infrastructure. We draw your attention to Coubertin's final comment concerning the financing of the IOC. He compared his work to that of a "veritable International Office of Athletics", which was true for his time.

We have been asked to specify the nature of our undertaking, and to indicate the means by which we plan to carry it out. Here is the answer, in a few short lines.

The Olympic Games will be International Competitions – true world championships, in which all sports and all physical exercises practiced in our time will be represented. They will take place in Athens in 1896, in Paris in 1900, and then

Comité International Olympique

Règlements

BUT.— Le Comité International Olympique auquel le congrès International de Paris a confié la mission de veiller au développement des Jeux Olympiques solennellement rétablis le 23 Juin 1894 se propose: 1°/ d'assurer la célébration régulière des Jeux – 2°/ de rendre cette célébration de plus en plus parfaite digne de son glorieux passé et conforme aux idées élevées dont s'inspirèrent ses rénovateurs – 3°/ de provoquer ou d'organiser toutes les manifestations et en général de prendre toutes les mesures propres à orienter l'athlétisme moderne dans les voies désirables.

Fundamental principles of the first Olympic Charter, handwritten by Pierre de Coubertin about 1899, first printed in 1908 (IOC Archives): "International Olympic Committee Statutes. Aim: The International Olympic Committee, to which the International Congress of Paris entrusted the task of overseeing the development of the Olympic Games, solemnly restored on June 23, 1894, is responsible for: 1. Ensuring the regular celebration of the Games; 2. Making that celebration increasingly perfect, worthy of their glorious history and in keeping with the high ideals that inspired those who restored it; and 3. Encouraging or organizing events of all kinds and, in general, taking all steps likely to guide modern athletics along desirable paths."

every four years after that in various world capitals. In keeping with the resolutions adopted by the Congress of Paris, these competitions will be open to adults only. Schools will not be represented at them. In order to participate, the athlete must be an amateur, that is, an individual who does not make any financial gain from his athletic success. No country will be allowed to be represented at the Games by anyone other than its own citizens. Finally, the Games will be held with the greatest possible solemnity. Wherever they take place, governments will be asked to give them their official support.

In reviving an institution that has been extinct for so many centuries, our thought is this: for the past thirty years, athleticism has taken on a significance that increases every year. Its role seems to have to be as large and as lasting in the modern world as it was in the ancient world. Moreover, it is reappearing with new characteristics. It is international, and democratic. Therefore it is well-suited to the ideas and needs of today. Yet now, as in the past, whether its effects will be beneficial or harmful depends on how it is handled, and the direction in which it is pointed. Athleticism can stir up the noblest as well as the basest of passions. It can foster selflessness and a sense of honor, or a love of gain. It can be chivalrous or corrupt, manly or bestial. Finally, it can be used to solidify peace or to prepare for war. Nobility of feelings, respect for selflessness and honor, the spirit of chivalry, manly energy, and peace are the primary needs of modern democracies, be they republican or monarchic.

Our intentions appear to have been understood aright. In the sports world, people have seen the broad scope of perspectives that came into play in setting up our programs. No form of physical exercise has been rejected, and no school, association, or country has been favored over any other. We appeal to all. It is our belief that issues of superiority between one system and another, between gymnastics and sports, exercises or games, should not be fought out around our Committee. Moreover, those who are more interested in the moral side of this undertaking have been generous in their encouragement. A certain degree of skepticism could have been expected from them. Rather, we have encountered only enthusiasm. The press has done more than merely pile on the praise; it has detailed our work carefully and faithfully. This was certainly the best way to help us, and to bring adherents to join us.

Nevertheless, these successes must not make us forget that only the preface has been written, and that what has been accomplished is nothing in comparison to what remains to be achieved.

Let us say a few words about our organization.

The Congress of Paris created an International Committee comprising individuals who agreed to head up the movement in their respective countries. In a way, these individuals are our representatives, our foreign correspondents. The administration is based in Paris, with the secretary general and the treasurer, but by statute the presidency belongs to the country in which the Olympic Games are to be held. Therefore, the presidency will be held by a Greek until 1896, by a Frenchman from 1896 to 1900, and by an American from 1900 to 1904 if the 1904 Games are held in the United States.

A National Committee must be set up in every country. Its purpose is to ensure the participation of that country in the Olympic Games every four years, until its turn comes to hold them "at home."

We think that, within the limits set by the Congress as summarized above, full and complete freedom must be given to the National Committees. It is not at all desirable for each Olympiad to see the same painting placed into different frames over and over again. The genius of each people, its manner of holding the festivals and of engaging in physical exercise, is what will give the modern Olympic Games their true character, and perhaps may make them superior to their ancient predecessors. It is obvious that Games held in Rome will not resemble in the slightest those that may be held in London or Stockholm.

There are two ways in which we can be helped:

First, we can be made more widely known through distribution of our *Bulletin* and through circulation of our program. Many people think that the Olympic Games are a new type of amusement, true Games imported from abroad, and that our intent is to update them and honor their national origins with this general title. Others see our project merely as a petty, awkward revival of the past, rather like tableaux vivants at the theater. We must disabuse all these people of such notions.

Secondly, our coffers will never be full enough. Any contributions or subscriptions sent to it will stay there but a little while. In fact, it is important for us to set up a real National Office of Athleticism. Such an organization entails considerable annual expense.

These are our plans and our needs. We appeal to all those who truly love sports, and to all those who wish to see the youth of all nations gather on that most peaceful of battlefields, the field of play.

Le caractère de notre entreprise,
in: *Bulletin du Comité International des Jeux Olympiques*,
Vol. 1, October 1894, no. 2, p. 1.

The editor has determined that this text, though unsigned, was written by Coubertin.

6.1/2 THE OLYMPIC ORGANIZATION

In this article, published in the *Revue Olympique* in 1903, Coubertin spells out his ideas on cooperation between the IOC and the national athletic federations. This text is remarkable because Coubertin underscores explicitly that in no case does the IOC claim the right to issue directives; rather, it would view such a position as incompatible with its own neutrality.

In addition, Coubertin defines the status of the members of the IOC in the various countries. As for the establishment of the National Olympic Committees, this article confirms the ideas that Coubertin had already expressed in 1894, while taking into account the experience gained in the interim.

The question has often been raised with the International Olympic Committee regarding the relationship that should exist between it and the national federations that govern sports in each country. Several parties have already expressed their desire for these relationships to be as close as possible, and for the Committee to take the place of a sort of higher council whose guiding actions would direct those federations liberally, but effectively.

We do not believe that this is desirable or possible. First, the internationalism of sports that is developing around us in a positive way is based on the meaning of rivalry and the spirit of competitiveness, not on the sort of cosmopolitanism and love of humanity that some politicians expect to see in the future. Under these circumstances, the more popular the meetings are, the more outside interference in the administration of national sports would quickly seem intolerable to those subject to it. This applies to the very principles of the institution, not to mention all the practically insurmountable obstacles that would stand in the way of implementing such a plan. In the future, there may well be some attempt to implement it. We are convinced that the outcome can be nothing but a resounding failure. The era that is dawning is much more an era of "trade agreements" applied to sports. It is up to the federations themselves to be in contact with each other, to come to agreements that will make encounters run more smoothly. Clauses in those agreements can be rejected or modified in due course, depending on the needs of the day. This, and the rational unification of the rules of play and of competition, is the goal we must pursue.

The International Olympic Committee, to whom people have turned in this regard, would be glad to help them achieve this beneficial unification. That is why it took the initiative of calling a congress that was first planned for 1903. With the permission of His Majesty King Leopold, its honorary president, the Congress has been rescheduled for 1905 to coincide with the Liege World's Fair, and to make it possible to use the experience gained at the 1904 Olympic Games in St. Louis. The Olympic Committee believes that it can take this course of action specifically because of its neutrality, and because it is careful to refuse any interference in its affairs by the various federations whose involvement is necessary to the success of such an undertaking. The Committee has refused, in advance, and will continue to refuse, any responsibility in the results that will be achieved, be they minimal or considerable.

In our view, then, nothing should be changed in the way things stand. The International Olympic Committee must continue to stay within the bounds that it wisely imposed on itself. But does this mean that outside of the Committee, nothing should be tried in order to complete and perfect the Olympic organization? This is far from our way of thinking. The members of the Committee have a considerable task, but it is up to each member to perform those tasks according to the capacities at his command, and the situation that he faces.

The members of the Committee are not delegates of their countries' athletic federations to the Olympic institution. To the contrary, they are representatives of that institution to the federations in their countries, its ambassadors in a sense. To choose the best possible candidates, the various federations of a particular country would have to agree on the selection of their single delegate. In most cases, it is fair to say that this would be nearly impossible. Many sports exist in isolation from the others, and are utterly unaware of what the others do. Some sports are jealous of each other and are involved in quarrels. Finally, one sport may be governed by several rival federations. How can so many forces be coordinated to create a single delegation? Moreover, it is far from certain that this reversal of roles is advantageous and enhances the chances of success of the Olympic Games. So far, it has seemed to us that the members of the International Committee will be better situated to help the work to prosper if they consider themselves representatives to the athletic federations, rather than placing themselves in the opposite position.

What are the duties imposed on them by such a mission? The first is to enter into and maintain frequent, close contact with the governing centers of the athletic movement in their own country. Precisely because they represent an institution that is not pledged to any clique, and that does not even advocate any form of athletics in preference to any other, it is easy for them to get along well with everyone, and to win over general sympathies for the common effort. To achieve this – and this is

Confidentielle. 8 Avril 1912.

Monsieur et cher Collègue,

Vous savez que, dans sa réunion de Budapest, le Comité International olympique a décidé de convoquer à Paris au printemps de 1914 à l'occasion du vingtième anniversaire du rétablissement des Jeux olympiques un congrès international des Comités olympiques nationaux en vue d'arrêter, conformément au voeu général, le programme obligatoire et définitif des Olympiades futures.

La Commission soussignée, désignée par le Comité International pour préparer le règlement dudit congrès, s'est assemblée ces jours-ci à Bâle et elle a pensé qu'il était opportun de vous rappeler l'urgence de constituer dans votre pays si ce n'est déjà fait - ou de rendre permanent s'il n'était que provisoire - un Comité olympique national dans lequel il est évidemment désirable que soient représentées, directement ou indirectement, les principales fédérations ou sociétés sportives du pays.

Nous saisissons donc cette occasion de vous recommander de travailler ainsi avec nous au succès du grand congrès de 1914 qui sera véritablement le couronnement de l'oeuvre accomplie depuis sa fondation par le Comité International.

Veuillez agréer, Monsieur et cher Collègue, l'expression de nos meilleurs sentiments.

Pierre de Coubertin, Eugène Brunetta d'Usseaux, Godefroy de Blonay, W. M. Sloane, R. C. de Courcy Laffan, F. W. de Tuyll, E. Callot, C. de Venningen

Circular from Coubertin to IOC members, calling for the establishment of permanent National Olympic Committees, 8th April 1912 (IOC Archives)

Confidential 8th April, 1912

Dear Sir and Colleague,

You are aware that, at its meeting in Budapest, the International Olympic Committee decided to convene in Paris in spring 1914, on the occasion of the twentieth anniversary of the revival of the Olympic Games, an international congress for National Olympic Committees. Its aim was to draw up the obligatory and definitive programme for future Olympiads, in accordance with the general wishes expressed.
The undersigned Commission, designated by the International Olympic Committee to prepare the rules of the said congress, recently met in Basle, where it decided that you should be reminded of the necessity of constituting a National Olympic Committee in your country, if you have not already done so, or to make permanent such committee if it is only temporary. It is clearly desirable that the country's main sporting federations or societies be represented directly or indirectly in such committee.
We would therefore like to take this opportunity to recommend that you work with us for the success of the great congress of 1914 which will indeed be the crowning of the work achieved since its foundation by the International Committee.

Yours sincerely,
Pierre de Coubertin, Eugène Brunetta d'Usseaux, Godefroy de Blonay, W.M. Sloane, R.C. de Courcy Laffan, F.W. de Tuyll, C. de Venningen

a second but no less serious duty – they must be fully imbued with the spirit of the work, of its goals and its purpose, which they see in the quadrennial Games, solemnly celebrated time and again in the major cities of the world. This is the logical and practical outcome of the great movement of physical rebirth that took place in the nineteenth century, and that will come to fruition and perfection in the twentieth. Thus the members of the International Committee can become skilled advocates of Olympism, listened to by all.

They can achieve more than this, as well. This is where the practical side of their mission comes in. In order for the Games to achieve the degree of technical perfection that they must attain, each country must acquire the habit of sending its best men. Travel can be long and costly, not only for Europeans when the competitions are held in St. Louis, but for everyone when they take place in Athens or Rome. The material and moral support of governments, the patronage of the authorities, subsidies from public institutions and, above all, interesting and serious elimination-round competitions, must be arranged in every country. We believe that the day will come when elimination rounds for the Olympiads will be the most important national competitions. Even now, it is desirable for these events to be held. They do not require any permanent agreement among the federations. In order to appoint their men, swimmers need not reach an agreement with runners, but they do have to agree among themselves, and they must prepare in due time. This implies a whole series of questions that are not vital, so to speak, but providing answers to them will contribute greatly to the success of the Games.

The members of the International Committee who have already begun to devote themselves to this task, in general, have felt the need for assistance from enthusiastic supporters. National Olympic committees have been set up in several countries. This is an excellent beginning, and meets all the criteria for present needs. But we believe that in order to do this work effectively, the national committees, like the International Committee, must not be an expression of the main athletic federations or associations of the country. Rather, as a rule they must stay above the intestine battles that exist more or less everywhere. Therefore, these committees must comprise competent individuals who are undisputed and not part of any clique.

It is quite advantageous for these committees to be permanent so that they can meet whenever it is useful to do so, even during the interval between Olympiads. However, these meetings need not be either long or frequent. One cannot stress too greatly the danger that would be posed in making a national Olympic committee the central, guiding machinery of the athletic activity of a country. Discord would necessarily follow because the federations would not look kindly on such an intrusion into their sphere of competence. The role of the national committee is to assist the federations, and to make it easier for their representatives to participate in the Olympic Games.

In truth, the entire work of the Olympics is based on concord. From the smallest to the greatest, working on its behalf means erasing the memories of old battles, or preventing new ones from cropping up. All forms of exercise are accepted in the Games. None must be privileged to the detriment of the others. If all those who take part in the Olympic organization are deeply imbued with the idea that, all in all, concord is the best way to reach the goal, their efforts will meet with swift success.

The Games cannot offend anyone. They must be an occasion for general emulation, a glorious sight for those ambitious for laurels.

In our view, these are the foundations on which it is desirable for the Olympic organization to be built, so that the modern Games may achieve the fame and value of which their illustrious past makes them worthy.

L'organisation olympique,
in: *Revue Olympique*,
July 1903, pp. 35-38.

The editor has determined that this text, though unsigned, was written by Coubertin.

6.1/3 ATHLETIC UNIONIZATION

This statement by Coubertin proves how greatly he opposed the unionization of athletes as soon as that phenomenon appeared, and how much he sought to ensure their independence with regard to organizations considered all-powerful.

The currency of this topic need not be underscored, but we must note that this text was published in January, 1907. It shows clearly the objectivity with which Coubertin considered this athletic organization that he helped to shape and sustain.

His interests as an educationist were always stronger than his interest in administration

This is the season of great football matches and automobile exhibitions. But everyone is talking about them and, rather than repeat what has already been said, we prefer to dedicate our review to a quick study of a unique phenomenon that is spreading throughout sports in several countries. We can use a highly appropriate term for this phenomenon, though it is one borrowed from political language: we could call it athletic unionization. In effect, the mania for unions is entering athletic life from political life.

Why is this happening? Is it from need or from analogy? It would be difficult to explain what need is addressed here. We must not forget that union politics is based, more or less, on class conflict, and that it is a life and death struggle. In the view of some economists, class conflict is an inescapable law. Others see it merely as a deplorable tactic. In any case, no one can deny its existence at present. That fact is obvious. Unionization was the inevitable result of class conflict. But what seeds of discord are there in sports? Where are the opposing interests? Why would one struggle? In truth, there has been no similar need, yet the trend toward unions is clear, and increasing. While small groups are seeking each other out as though an internal malaise were driving them to unite, to coalesce against an invisible threat, coalitions that have already formed are hurrying to tighten the bonds they have created. They build barricades of regulations and lay out mazes of interdictions. None of this is intended to make meetings any easier for sportsmen, or to smooth out the inevitable points of divergence. Far from it. This is intended above all to be an obstacle for those who are independent, to force them to join the coalition or disappear, clearing the way for the coalition. Consider, for example, the following enormity. One federation claims to encourage the practice of football, but has forbidden any match on fields it may have available to it indirectly, if the teams planning to play do not belong to federation-affiliated clubs. These are practices that would have struck people dumb ten years ago. They are tending to become commonplace in some large countries.

This goes hand in hand with another symptom of unionization, the development of a class of people whose career it is to "govern" or to "administer" athletic associations, doing so in such a way that one cannot see any other motivation to their actions than personal interest. These are not sportsmen. Often, their incompetence is complete, and they have neither a taste for nor the habit of exercise. In any event, the athletic spirit is completely foreign to them. They do not have it, and they do not understand it. Their sole intent is to increase their own importance, and to create ladders that they can then climb. All unionizers naturally turn their gaze to the public authorities, from whom they expect subsidies and, above all, awards, where any may be had.

Their strength comes from the repugnance that sportsmen feel at becoming bogged down in paperwork. The sportsman is glad to be replaced by an administrator who offers to hold the pen for him. Once that is done, sportsmen lack the energy to react against the increasing invasion by that individual. Thus the sportsman is swept away despite himself, heading in a disastrous direction. The sportsman may have the administrator in his employ, but ends up being in the employ of the administrator. Gradually, the administrator becomes an entrepreneur. He becomes the boss, and the sportsman is nothing more than the worker.

The worst consequence of this state of affairs is that gradually the sportsman loses his independence, not only the independence of his athletic expression, but that of the instinct that urges him to make that expression. There is something of the automaton in him. His effort is made, if not at the command, then at least at the suggestion of the administrator. Anything spontaneous, instinctive, or impulsive about athleticism is lost; nature flees in the face of calculation. What happens in schools eventually happens in the athletic club. How many teachers tend to focus their attentions only on the elite students – an understandable reaction, and one that can be excused to a certain extent – , neglecting the fat boy in the class. The best, those who are lucky enough to pass their exams, are the focus of all the teacher's attention. He fires them up, trains them for prizes, diplomas, placing well, honorable mentions, in short, for all sorts of distinctions that these young people can win. Deep down he takes absolutely no interest in the others. The unionized sports club is similar, in some ways. There are the potential champions and the future champions; the administrators are ready to make great sacrifices for them. For the others, their hearts are like stone, and they limit their actions to the strict minimum to keep them within the fold of the club, where they help beef up the numbers – and pay the dues.

In short, in clubs and federations alike, athletic unionization results in bringing together the largest possible number of inactive paying members around a small number of renowned athletes whose athletic activity is monopolized or the benefit of the club.

How can one fight against so harmful and un-sportsmanlike a state of affairs? The answer is quite simple: by chasing the money-changers out of the temple, or in this case, by dismissing from the club or the federation those who generate the paperwork, along with the paperwork itself. This is easier said than done, however. A moment ago, we noted how the sportsman, in his mental laziness, allowed himself easily to be dominated by the administrator to whom he left the care of handling the business aspects of the club or federation. One cannot count on the few exceptions that occur here and there, where former athletes, out of their sense of devotion, take on the task, and stick to it. In general, the invasion will continue as long as the cause persists. To settle the matter, paperwork would have to be scrapped. This is the only way to get rid of those who live off it, whose tendency and in whose interest it is, consequently, to cause it to multiply. Therefore regulations should be broadened, and many of them should be scrapped altogether. The rest should be designed in the most liberal manner. In any event, the independence of the athlete must be guaranteed with respect to the club, as well as that of the club with respect to the federation, in any circumstances where the issue may arise. The number of competitions must be strictly limited; the value of prizes must be decreased. In matters of amateurism and qualifications, the athlete's oath should replace the inquiry. Finally, and above all, as is already the case in England, judgments about disputes or the implementation of regulations should be handed down by absolutely independent committees comprising former athletes, committees that cannot be influenced by any form of camaraderie.

All this is necessary. Are we hoping for too much? Yet reform must take place, or sports will perish. They are too hardy to perish. On their own, some day sports will find the strength to wipe out the microbes that are consuming them. This unionizing threat is easily the most dangerous of them all. It may well have existed in antiquity, but it did not spread as it has in our time since there was no press, and communications were slow.

Le syndicalisme sportif,
in: *Revue Olympique,*
January 1907, pp. 202-205.

The editor has determined that this text, though unsigned, was written by Coubertin.

6.1/4 THE ROLE OF THE FEDERATIONS

After condemning "syndicalism" in sport, Coubertin explains in this text the role that federations should play as representatives of athletes and clubs. He proposes a structure which could correspond to this task. In his opinion, the administrative structure in place within the federations is too heavy, which restricts the freedom of the athletes.

The same thing has happened to a large number of sports federations as has happened to many governments. A shift has occurred in the conception of their role. In the same way that the notion of idol-state has in some places supplanted the notion of servant-state, the sports federation has evolved from utilitarianism to domination, from the role of secretary to that of policeman. It is concerned less with encouraging than with giving orders and imposing prohibitions. Throwing their weight around now seems to be the biggest concern of its leaders. In saying this, we are taking things to the extreme. There are degrees but, in many countries, federations are heading towards this unfortunate goal; some have almost reached it. England is the only country which has so far put up any serious resistance to this contagion.

The first and most vital of tasks which falls to a sports federation is to organize itself judicially. Indeed, it must be at once a council of state, a court of appeal and a jurisdiction court. Its job is to maintain rules, interpret them and give judgement at last instance; it has to ratify or overturn expulsions; it has to intervene between clubs and impose solutions to collective disputes. Now if there is one quality which a judicial apparatus must possess, it is of course independence. Independence in this case is achieved by the constitution within the federation of a judicial board whose members must not include anyone who is an active member of any of the groups whose interests are at issue. It will be composed of former sportsmen, and mature men of sufficient experience. The federation can either leave it up to them to recruit their membership, or undertake this itself, on condition that it appoints them for a specific term of office, at least three to five years. An organization resembling this exists in English-speaking countries; it is still very rare elsewhere. However, anyone who thinks about this will clearly see the vital need to adopt it, if one is concerned about rendering the most elementary form of justice. How can one accept having the delegates of clubs as both judge and party, being called upon to assess the fairness of measures directly involving their colleagues and clubs?

But who will create these rules, the strict and fair application of which the judicial board will have the duty to ensure? Will there be an administrative committee composed of representatives of a number of clubs? I say a number, as under integral law all of them would be represented, but how could this be achieved? If the seat of the federation is in the capital, the clubs established at the other end of the country would have great difficulty in being directly represented; so that they did not lose their vote, they would choose representatives of some kind, usually poorly informed about their affairs and more or less exposed to serving interests which, if not contrary, would at least be very different to their own. In some federations, we have seen dubious characters who, to get into the club, offered to "represent" clubs based far away which they known only through correspondence. This was rather reminiscent of the famous "rotten boroughs" of the former British parliamentary system. All of this has many disadvantages, and what is the use of it when one has available that admirable consultative instrument known as the referendum? Politics has not yet learned how to use it – even in Switzerland – because it obstinately continues to address the individual, instead of approaching the first-degree groups formed by such individuals. In sport, these groups are the clubs. It should be stipulated in the statutes that, when a certain number of clubs agree to propose an addition or change to the rules, a referendum must be held, and this referendum will be conducted by the secretary general of the federation, a salaried official, who knows the sporting environment but is not too involved himself. All the administrative part must rest with him; his is the key role and, if the paperwork is suitably reduced, he will be sufficient to do the work, monitored by between three and five commissioners appointed for one year, drawn by lots from a list produced by the clubs, and one of whom will be responsible for keeping the accounts.

The judicial board, referendum, secretary general and monitoring commissioners are all the machinery that a good sports federation needs. The rest is superfluous. But what about organizing championships, people will ask. Good Lord, we might reply, we will do nothing. There are enough inter-federal and international championships with sufficient justification and interest, and many purely federal championships seem difficult to prepare and produce inaccurate results, given the number of clubs which have to take part. In all cases, these are acceptable in countries of any size only if they are held in a different place each year. Consequently, there is no need to make provision for a standing committee with the task of looking after them: it is up to the clubs in the region chosen for the year in question to do so to the best of their means and in accordance with the rules of the federation. This is what already happens, in France particularly, for federal gymnastics festivals, and there is no question that this principle, the only rational and normal one, has played a large part in the homogeneous and regular development of French gymnastics clubs.

All that we are proposing here obviously applies to federations which one could call established, and only to these. There are others which might be called promotional; formed prematurely, rather with a view to assessing whether there is a movement in favour or sports in general or one sport in particular, they need a façade; they require protection and centralization. Members of honour and honorary members, a hierarchy of presidents and vice presidents, and at the same time a very coordinated and strong government will all help them to attract attention and create the solid mechanisms needed for their subsequent operation. But there is no need to concern ourselves with such cases, as these are totally transitory. One of two things will happen: either success will come and the federation will quickly have done with this delicate period; or it will stagnate, and in this case stagnation equates with failure. We should therefore not be looking at such promotional or initiating federations, rather at those which have their definitive machinery in place and are on the road to prosperity. And if these persist in retaining the institutions which perhaps suited their beginning, not their current status, there is every chance of seeing the emergence of that sports syndicalism which was justly attacked in a previous edition of this review. And the first consequence to appear is, rather than the free exchange which is a general law vital to groups truly steeped in the sporting spirit, a protectionist policy with its attendant panoply of rules, prohibitions and inquiries, and its characteristic meanness of ideas and bothersome procedures.

Le rôle des fédérations,
in: *Revue Olympique*, March 1907, pp. 231-234.

The editor has determined that this text, though unsigned, was written by Coubertin.

6.1/5 LETTER TO THE MEMBERS OF THE INTERNATIONAL OLYMPIC COMMITTEE (FEBRUARY, 1920)

The official circular letter from Coubertin to the members of the IOC show that in 1920, the situation did not seem clear to some individuals. Before and after the Olympic Games at Antwerp, as Coubertin tells in his memoirs, there was general agitation among the federations. Serious conflicts regarding spheres of competence grew up between the IOC and the international federations that had been founded recently.

That is why, in his circular letter of February, 1920, Coubertin discussed a new orientation of the Olympic movement, recommending for the first time the idea of regional eliminations, and the standardization of the structure of the National Olympic Committees.

Dear Colleague,

Our Committee will meet at Antwerp during the Games of the Seventh Olympiad. Its Sessions will be held at the City Hall, at the invitation of the Burgomaster and Deputy Burgomasters of that illustrious city. The meetings are likely to occur from August 17-27. We will confirm those dates as quickly as possible, but I wanted to bring your attention to the extreme importance of this Session now.

I

First, we must consider a number of topics related to the operation and improvement of the Olympic administrative machinery. Otherwise, we must also make a final decision regarding the site of the Eighth Olympiad (1924), or at least study and assess the merits of the various candidacies that have been offered. It may well be that a proposal will be made to link the World Championships permanently with the Olympic Games. The authorization that you gave to the Belgian Committee in that respect is temporary only. If those involved find the results of this trial favorable, we must, of course, be careful in hammering out the details of the agreement that is to be made between them and us.

In addition, the issue of elimination round competitions, which has always been of great concern to us though it falls within the competence of the National Committees, has produced an ingenious suggestion from America. The suggestion is to divide the world into "Olympic regions", such as: England, Belgium, and France; Denmark, Norway, and Sweden; Canada and the United States; Argentina, Brazil, Chili, Uruguay, etc. The Committees in these regions would reach an agreement to share the expenses for their respective elimination rounds, and would then work together to provide for the athletes' transportation. This would unarguably provide advantages. Since the cost of transportation has increased greatly (and, for the time being, there is no prospect of a return to previous prices), the principle of cooperation is going to be applied with positive results as far as the Olympics are concerned. It remains to be seen whether, technically, the details of this project would be difficult to coordinate. I do not know whether the promoters of this idea have thought of other perspectives than that of the savings to be realized. In any case, this advantage is worthy of our attention.

Any system would be welcome which enables the National Committees to become less dependent in the future on subsidies, which nearly all of them must now ask from their respective public authorities. These uncertain subsidies, which are granted unevenly and late, at times seem excessive in the light of public opinion, even when, in reality, they are inadequate. Non-athletes imagine that the principle of subsidies is incompatible with the regulations on amateurism, and draw the conclusion that holding an Olympiad involves excessive expense. These are misconceptions that we must not allow to spread.

We must also study the formation and operation of National Olympic Committees, as well as the nature of the bonds that unite them to the International Committee. Without imposing in the slightest on the independence of the National Committees, which must remain untouched, we might suggest to them some uniformity in the way they are organized. Although some of them are in keeping with logic and the practical spirit, there are others where sufficient account of cooperation among the various sports was not taken when they were being formed.

This brings us to the issue of the International Federations with which we hope to progress in perfect harmony. It is only right that the competitions in the Olympic Games be held under their regulations, and be judged, insofar as possible, by their representatives. But in order to do this, political excesses and momentary hatreds must not cause them to make unreasonable demands, as was recently the case for one of those federations.

II

Aside from these specific problems, there is another, more general issue that we must study. Modern Olympism, separated by so many centuries of athletic indifference from its glorious ancestor, is developing in a similar manner nonetheless, passing through the same stages.

As the great, periodic Games then grew in importance and brilliance, being in a way the foundations of athleticism, the local institutions intended to feed the flame grew alongside them. Everywhere, the mission of the town gymnasium was to make the training of youth easier, and to spread the principles of athletic education. There, in a setting that art embellished as best as the city's resources permitted, civic life was centered, in a way. In the gymnasium, thought joined forces with strength, and the efforts of the adolescent and the adult were encouraged by attentive elders. A true temple of the human springtime, the gymnasium was also one of the fundamental cells of athletic activity.

The restoration of the gymnasium did not seem useful when I began to advocate it nearly ten years ago. Events have made it an urgent necessity. From now on, it is no longer enough for benevolent municipalities to make a few existing sites or fields available to existing gymnastic or athletic associations. More is required. They must build buildings that are appropriate for implementing the program I presented to you last year, and that you welcomed so enthusiastically: all sports, all nations. It is no longer a question of physical education. Let us leave it up to school authorities to see to that.

Four Presidents of the IOC in front of the Casino de Montbenon at Lausanne.
From left to right: Siegfrid Edström (SWE), Pierre de Coubertin (FRA), the Count de Baillet-Latour (BEL), and the Baron de Blonay (SUI) (IOC Archives)

We are talking about the intense physical pleasure, essential for the balance of the adult and that only sports can provide to him in a healthy way. This is the cost of public health. This is the cost of victory over alcoholism. This is the cost of social peace.

The Olympic Institute at Lausanne has taken as its task to prepare the way for these reforms. Now it is up to the International Committee to give these reforms a strong boost.

III

In 1921, we will have an opportunity to advance the cause of these two types of issues: special, technical issues, and general, social issues. You have called a twofold Congress to study them in Lausanne then. While the representatives of the Council of State and of the High Council of Canton Vaud, and of the City of Lausanne, the rector of the University, and the presidents of the local associations met last December 22 at the Lausanne City Hall to discuss the first steps that should be taken, it will be up to us, at Antwerp, to write the program for the two Congresses, and to put out the call to those who should participate in them.

In these comments, you will note that I was correct in considering our 1920 Session as exceptionally significant. If there are other issues that you would like to see included on the agenda, please let the Office know as soon as possible. Let me take this opportunity to tell you that Councilor Jiri Guth (one of the four of us who has held the Olympic mandate for nearly twenty-six years) has agreed to succeed permanently our late friend, Eugène Brunetta d'Usseaux, as secretary of our Sessions.

Sincerely yours.

Pierre de Coubertin

Lettre no 3 à Messieurs les membres
du Comité International Olympique (février 1920),
Special print (Archives of the IOC)

6.1/6 FINANCIAL PLANNING FOR THE IVTH OLYMPIAD IN ROME

Among the organizational problems with which the Olympic Games confronted Coubertin, this text occupies a special place. Coubertin tries to identify the practical and financial problems associated with the holding of the Olympic Games. This is a memorandum which he drafted in late 1905 as an additional argument to overcome the reservations then being expressed in Rome regarding the celebration of the forthcoming Games of 1908. It was to allay the fears of the organizers in Rome. Coubertin envisaged a minimum of expenditure. The memorandum[1] was not published but merely distributed to those concerned. The schedule it contains, which is very accurate and not confined to the costs to be expected, demonstrates Coubertin's capacity to take the global view. The text also includes a retrospective account of the origins of these Rome Olympics, supplementing the historical aspects.[2]

As some hesitation and anxiety has been apparent on several occasions in Italian circles regarding the organization of the forthcoming Olympic Games, to be held in Rome in 1908, I thought I would try to assist the organizers of the celebration now eagerly anticipated by the entire world by drafting this Memorandum, in which my aim was to resolve the following problem: given the resources available to Rome, how can we arrange for the 1908 Games to be celebrated there under conditions which are both as advantageous as possible for the City and as satisfactory as possible for the Olympic Institution?

HISTORICAL BACKGROUND.

It was on 24 March 1903 that Senator Todaro, in his capacity as President of the Italian Gymnastics Federation, passed to me the official application drawn up by that Federation to the effect that Rome should be selected as the venue for the IVth Olympiad. The idea had been mooted, I believe, by the enthusiastic Secretary General of the Federation, Mr F. Ballerini, and at its meeting on 14 March 1903 the Council had adopted it and instructed its administrative office to take the necessary steps. There seemed to be great enthusiasm among Italian gymnasts at the thought of the 1908 celebrations, and these sentiments were reflected in Senator Todaro's letter. Subsequent reflection changed these attitudes: the fact is that it is not a matter for a single Federation, however powerful it may be, to undertake the organization of an Olympiad, since the Federation represents gymnasts alone, whereas competititions are to be held in all forms of sport. The Italian Gymnastic Federation took fright at the prospect of such a massive labour and the responsibilities that would derive from it, and withdrew on the pretext that the City Council of Rome had refused its support. That support has now been provided by César. The fact remains that the honour of this successful initiative rests with the Federation. In the event, a committee made up of the best qualified representatives of all Italy's major sporting associations was set up early in 1904 to follow up the project conceived by the Italian Gymnastics

1 It is virtually certain that this text has been translated back into French from an Italian text: the vocabulary, phraseology and style are not typical of Coubertin.

2 See texts 4.2.18 - 4.2.20 in this volume.

Federation. This committee held several meetings at the Grand Hotel in Rome and instructed Count E. Brunetta d'Usseaux to propose to the International Olympic Committee that it should select Rome as the venue for the IVth Olympiad in 1908, since other cities were entering the lists. Having been notified of these decisions by Count Brunetta d'Usseaux, and recalling that what had prompted Senator Todaro to withdraw the application made by him on behalf of the Italian Gymnastics Federation was the refusal of Rome's City Council to support the undertaking, I wrote to the Syndic of Rome to ask him whether the City Council's attitude was still the same, because if so it would have been difficult for us to accept the application by the Italian Committee. On 10 March 1904 I received a reply from Prince Colonna, then Syndic of Rome, to the effect that at its meeting of 27 February the City Council had "been delighted to accept the support of the City Authorities for the inspired and fertile initiative" with a view to organizing the celebration of the 1908 Games in Rome. Shortly after this, Prince Colonna accepted the Chair of the Italian Committee.

In June of that year, the International Olympic Committee met in London under the patronage of His Majesty the King of England. The meeting took place at the Mansion House, made available to the committee by the Lord Mayor. After a lengthy discussion, the Committee decided unanimously to accept the application made on behalf of the City of Rome, despite the advantages that Berlin would have offered in certain respects. At the last moment, the German delegates courteously withdrew their proposal in favour of Berlin, which had previously been approved by His Imperial Highness the Crown Prince, to make the choice of Rome unanimous. As soon as this result had been brought to the knowledge of His Excellency Cavaliere Pansa, Italian Ambassador to the Court of St James's, it was telegraphed by him to His Majesty King Victor Emmanuel, who graciously expressed his pleasure in a benevolent message sent to the President of the International Olympic Committee. The City Council of Rome, having been similarly advised, sent the Committee its thanks and best wishes.

Unfortunately, a great deal of time was subsequently wasted on barren debate; it even appeared that some groups were trying to block the organization of the Games; rivalries sprang up among those concerned. Happening to be in Rome last February, I nevertheless became doubly certain that the celebration of the IVth Olympiad enjoyed the support of public opinion across the political spectrum, and that the practicalities of organizing it would be much easier that in most other European cities.

Since an Executive Committee has been set up by the City Council to collaborate with the Grand Committee chaired by Prince Colonna on the dual task of organizing the 1908 Games and ensuring that they are sufficiently promoted outside Italy, it is to that Committee that I address the present study which I hope and believe will provide it with a useful starting point.

GENERAL PROGRAMME

In order to be complete and to comply with the decisions taken at the International Congress of Paris (1894) which proclaimed the rebirth of the Olympic Games, the Programme for an Olympiad must include the following disciplines: gymnastics – track and field events – games (football, lawn tennis, cricket and polo) – shooting – fencing

– boxing – wrestling – swimming – rowing – equestrianism – cycling – sailing – arts – motor racing – ballooning – archery – walking – mountaineering – hunting and fishing. There is no need for ice sports to be included. In the present case, the IVth Olympiad could include winter sports competitions which would act as a curtain-raiser and would be held, for example, in Turin; but since the foundation (1901) of the Nordic Games, which are genuine Northern Olympiads, it is generally felt that there is no longer any reason to try to include ice sports in the Programme of the Olympic Games. I will therefore review each of the disciplines referred to above, outlining the particular requirements they impose, the place where it seems to me they could best be organized and the sum of money I think could reasonably be allocated to them. I should make it clear here, once and for all, that these sums are overestimates rather than underestimates of those necessary. For my part, I have organized international competitions on many occasions without ever running up such high figures.

GYMNASTICS

Gymnastics is not supposed to play such an important part in the Olympic Games as it does in a Federal Festival; in particular, team gymnastics plays only an incidental part and could be dispensed with if necessary, though this would be regrettable and I would not advise it. However, I think it should be confined to a very simple programme of ensemble exercises suitable for all the schools; each team should be made up of not less than eight and not more than twelve gymnasts. The individual gymnastics would comprise weightlifting, fixed bar and climbing exercises, because jumping and vaulting appear in other parts of the programme. I know that this classification and these ideas will seem novel and therefore startling to many gymnasts, but it is necessary to accept the idea that gymnastics makes up only one-eighteenth of the modern Olympiad. The central part of the Piazza di Siena arena (Villa Borghese) is earmarked for gymnastics and field events, the grass track surrounding it being reserved for the track events. I suggest that 12 000 francs be allocated to making the necessary arrangements.

TRACK AND FIELD EVENTS

The track events should be run over the following distances: 100 metres, 400 metres, 800 metres, 1 500 metres, 110 metres hurdles and 400 metres hurdles – in other words four flat races and two hurdle races (though the word hurdle is not really appropriate since the obstacles used in all countries are lightweight bar-and-frame structures secured to the ground by spikes so as to be knocked over easily by a runner who strikes one). In addition, one race should be arranged over a course of from 12 to 16 kilometres; the start and finish of this race should be in the Piazza di Siena or alternatively in the Tor di Quinto area or that of the Appian Way. It is preferable to use metric distances – they are virtually the same as the British equivalents, and in any case the British are used to racing in France and Belgium over these distances.

The field events will comprise: the high jump – the long jump – the pole vault (all these jumping events will, of course, be performed without a springboard), the shot and the discus.

The sum of 8 000 francs is fully sufficient for the arrangements. Added to the 12 000 francs for the gymnastics, this makes a total of 20 000 francs for the works to be carried out at the Piazza di Siena.

GAMES

The games to be included in the Programme are football (Rugby Union and Association), cricket, lawn tennis and polo. There is no reason to expect many teams to enter for the football or cricket – four or five matches in all is the most that need be expected. I think it will be easy to find a venue for the games at Villa Borghese; otherwise, they can take place along with the polo in the New Hippodrome. I think 2 000 francs will be enough for the football and cricket and 3 000 for the polo, the latter also benefiting from the expenditure for the equestrian events (see below). As for the lawn tennis, it has a ready-made venue at the Club, outside the walls near the Porta del Popolo. There will be two lawn tennis events, singles for individual players and doubles for teams of two: 4 000 francs.

SHOOTING

The comments made with reference to gymnastics apply in exactly the same way to shooting, which also accounts for only one-eighteenth of the Olympiad. I am therefore ruling out any idea of a Federal Festival in the customary sense of the word. If a Federal Festival is attached to the Olympiad, this will be an ancillary organization with a separate budget that will have to be worked out. So we need only consider individual shooting, which should take two forms: target and clay-pigeon. The latter will replace pigeon shooting, which is too expensive and necessarily involves cash prizes. The target shooting championships can take place under ideal conditions at the Poligono di Tor di Quinto. It will be easy to organize the clay pigeon shooting in the same area. The idea should be to copy the very simple and very comprehensive installation at the Malden school of shooting, near London – nothing could be easier. This marvellous school is very little known outside England; we do know that the very inexpensive equipment used there make it possible to imitate the flight of a sequence of widely differing game birds. The sum of 15 000 francs should be earmarked for shooting.

FENCING

The fencing will comprise a collective épée championship for the "Horatii and Curiatii" Cup, founded by Mr W.H. Grenfell (see below). Each nation will have the right to be represented by a team of three. There will also be individual championships in épée, sabre, foil, singlestick and quarter-staff. The latter may attract only two or three entries, or better still none at all. The others, however, are guaranteed total success. The organization of this type of competition could hardly be easier. I have no hesitation in recommending that these events should take place at the Baths of Caracalla. No doubt there will be plenty of halls that might be suitable and could be used, for example, in the event of bad weather. But this seems to me a good time to bring about a change which has been recommended by so many successes on the health front and is beginning to be endorsed by public opinion – the conversion of fencing to an outdoor sport. I have also examined the Baths of Caracalla with the greatest care, having previously selected it in my mind, and I can say that no fencing competition has ever been held in better conditions, from both the aesthetic and the technical viewpoints. 6 000 francs will enable this project to go ahead.

BOXING AND WRESTLING

Boxing and wrestling will take place at the same venue, for an additional cost of 2 000 francs. There will be two boxing championships, in French boxing and English boxing. The wrestling will be divided into three, Greco-Roman, Swiss and jujitsu.

SWIMMING

There should be four swimming events: a sprint, a middle-distance race, a long-distance race and a diving competition. It is impossible to be absolutely accurate in advance about the distances over which these races should be swum, because the arrangements will have to take account of material circumstances – in this particular case, the configuration of the Tiber at the selected point, which I would think would be between the Ponte Molle and the Ponte Margherita. The sum of 3 000 francs should be set aside for these events.

ROWING

For the rowing events, the same course appears suitable, and there should naturally be four such events: the traditional races for single sculls, double sculls, fours and eights; additional events that could be added would be a canoe race, a kayak race and a gondola race. 6 000 francs would be necessary to arrange these races.

EQUESTRIANISM

This does not involve riding events, still less horse races in the traditional sense, but a genuine equestrian competition, in which only the skill of the rider will be judged and the horse will be considered only to the extent necessary to determine how his physique, gait and stubbornness have an unfavourable handicapping effect on his rider. There will also be a team championship: trick riding, showjumping, haute école and team championship for teamwork involving a team of at least four and at most eight riders. The best place for the equestrian events would seem to be the New Hippodrome or Tor di Quinto, and 18 000 francs would be more than adequate for the expenses.

CYCLING

The three cycle races – long-distance, sprint and road-race – are easy to organize and there is no need to dwell on them. The sum of 4 000 francs will be sufficient.

SAILING AND MOTOR RACING

I understand that the motor races will take place both in Milan and from Milan to Rome, and the sailing at Naples. The Automobile Club of Italy and the Italian Royal Yacht Club would take responsibility for organizing these events in their respective sports and arranging the financial programme. I suggest that the two societies should be given the appropriate grants of 18 000 francs for the sailing and 21 000 francs for the motor racing, which would help them to ensure that these events present all the appropriate spectacle.

ARCHERY

No competition is easier to organize, since it is merely necessary to buy targets and find a large enough field. On the other hand, it provides a very attractive spectacle and is sure to attract the British, French, Belgians and Swiss. The Villa Borghese is the venue of choice, and the sum to be allocated is 1 000 francs.

WALKING

Two walking races (for individuals, obviously), one over 1 000 metres and the other over 20 kilometres. Not more than 500 francs. It should particularly be noted that the new form of bending will be allowed.

MOUNTAINEERING

In accordance with the principle established by the 1894 Congress, the Olympic Mountaineering medal is to be awarded for the most notable climb achieved anywhere in the world since the previous Olympiad, meaning in the present case since 1 June 1904. Competitors should send their claims with supporting evidence to the International Jury which will be set up at the appropriate time.

HUNTING AND FISHING

We are proposing, similarly, that two Olympic medals should be awarded for hunting and fishing achievements performed since 1 June 1904 which are regarded as superior to all others.

ARTS

Five art competitions have been agreed upon and already announced: Painting, Sculpture, Music, Architecture and Literature. They will be open to works "directly inspired by the sporting idea" and will be opened on the occasion of the IVth Olympiad. We are setting aside the sum of 40 000 francs to print the book or play and, if possible, to perform the musical work and to show the prizewinning works of painting, sculpture and architecture. The international judges should be appointed as soon as possible.

TIMING AND DURATION

It is absolutely essential for the international success of the Olympiad that most of the competition should take place at Easter, during a period of 12 to 15 days. However, the car and ballooning races could take place before that date, and the sailing afterwards.

RULES

It is not necessary to draw up special rules for the Olympic Games. It is preferable to retain the systems adopted for the previous Olympiads, in other words to indicate in the conditions for each event the rules that will be followed. We recommend in particular: the rules of the Italian Rowing Club for rowing; those of the Italian Royal Yacht Club for sailing; those of the French Athletics Clubs Federation for track and field events; those of the All England Lawn Tennis Association, the Marylebone Cricket Club and the Rugby Union for the games; those of the French Aero Club for the ballooning, etc.

PRIZES

Since the Olympic competitions are championships, not handicaps, they involve only one prize per competition: there is never a second prize in a championship. On the other hand, for reasons which it would be unnecessary to stress, it is necessary not to allow anyone to go home empty-handed. I therefore suggest that three prizes be awarded: 1) a certificate, a copy of which will be given to each competitor showing the competition in which he took part and any successes achieved by him; 2) a cup for the team championships; and 3) a statuette for the individual championships. These three objets d'art will have to be ordered from genuine artists who will receive, respectively, the sums of 4,000, 1,500 and 500 francs for the cup, 4 000, 1 500 and

500 for the statuette and 3,000, 1,000 and 500 for the certificate. Each of the cups produced from the selected model will have an intrinsic value of about 300 francs. Similarly, each of the statuettes will be worth about 100 francs. After the Games, the printing plates and moulds must be destroyed, thus giving these articles a considerable artistic and historic value. This will comply with the wish expressed by the 1894 Congress regarding prizes, which are to be of low intrinsic value and preferably of uniform artistic value. It is as well to note, however, that Mr W.H. Grenfell, a member of the House of Commons and a personal friend of King Edward VII, founded a cup known as the "Horatii and Curatii" Cup for a team épée championship, and Mrs Montgomery has endowed a prize for the discus. The distribution of awards will take place at the Capitol after the Games, with all due solemnity.

DECORATIONS

The figures mentioned above for the arrangements generally include decorations; however, I am allowing an additional credit of 30 000 francs for this purpose; the places to be decorated are: the Piazza di Siena, the Tennis Club, the Poligono di Tor di Quinto, the Baths of Caracalla, the banks of the Tiber, the New Hippodrome, etc. In general, both the most graceful and least expensive form of decoration is that which excludes all forms of bunting and hoardings and is entirely restricted to garlands, foliage and the flags of all the nations, distributed in large numbers and artistically interwoven. This method allows for the most varied and novel combinations. It goes without saying that a place such as the Baths of Caracalla need no decoration other than masses of greenery.

The Lawn Tennis Club would fit in admirably with an antique-style decoration; here and at the Piazza di Siena an effort could be made to create a decorative environment that will not easily be forgotten. In no circumstances should modern-style tribunes be constructed there; there are magnificent natural tribunes in the Piazza di Siena and care should be taken not to diminish these. I would suggest launching a competition for these, with prizes of 1 000, 800 and 500 francs for the most attractive decorations.

OFFICE COSTS, INVITATIONS, ETC.

Office costs reached ridiculous levels at previous Olympiads. The sum of 10 000 francs allocated here is significantly more than is necessary. Personally, I would undertake to do everything necessary with 6 or 7 000 francs. Official invitations have to be sent to the Governments and the main Federations in each country through the Italian Embassies, Legations and Consulates from Easter 1907 onwards. In 1906, the preliminary Competition Programme will have to be sent to all the world's largest companies. This will mean sending out 8,000 copies; the Olympic Review can handle this for the sum of 2 500 francs.

APPOINTMENT OF A DIRECTOR GENERAL

I believe that considerable savings will be achieved, and at the same time better and faster results arrived at, if the general management of all works required for this programme is entrusted to a competent professional economist who has given proof of his abilities. The obvious person would be Mr Raymond, Secretary-General of Racing-Club de France. There is no one to match him anywhere in the world; but, without his consent, I cannot guarantee his acceptance in advance. I have entered a payment of 7 000 francs for the Director-General.

TRAVEL EXPENSES

Since the Olympic Games involves no cash prizes, it makes sense to earmark the sum of 30 000 francs for honorary "travelling expenses", and especially for equipment to assist expensive sports or those practised by more proletarian and less wealthy societies.

SUMMARY OF EXPENSES

The expenses envisaged by the present Memorandum can be summarized as follows:

Gymnastics	12 000 francs
Track and field events	8 000 francs
Games	9 000 francs
Shooting	15 000 francs
Fencing	15 000 francs
Boxing and wrestling	2 000 francs
Swimming	3 000 francs
Rowing	6 000 francs
Equestrianism	18 000 francs
Cycling	4 000 francs
Subsidies for sailing and motor racing	30 000 francs
Archery	1 000 francs
Walking	500 francs
Mountaineering, hunting and fishing	500 francs
Arts	40 000 francs
Total for arrangements:	155 000 francs
To which can be added:	
For prizes	28 000 francs
Additional credit for decorations	30 000 francs
Office costs	10 000 francs
Director-General	7 000 francs
Travel expenses	30 000 francs
GRAND TOTAL:	260 000 francs

THE ACCOMMODATION QUESTION

A special committee will have to concern itself with this very important question, though it is more easily solved in Rome than elsewhere. The Italian National Association for the Movement of Foreigners is a very obvious choice to deal with this question.

ASSESSMENT OF INCOME

There are two types of revenue: entry fees which will be payable for all competitions (minimum fee of 5 francs and maximum of 20 francs), plus revenue from spectator tickets which may amount to thirty or forty thousand francs, not more.

"Projet financier de la IVe Olympiade à Rome."
Polycopie, Paris 1905. (IOC Archives)
Reprinted in: *Textes choisis,* Vol. II, pp. 630-639.

6.1/7 A STANDARD ORGANISATION FOR THE OLYMPIADS

This essay was probably written against the background of Coubertin's personal difficulties with the Stockholm 1912 organizing committee. One issue was that, completely against his will, boxing and cycling could not be staged in 1912 in Sweden; another was that the introduction of modern pentathlon and art competitions was disputed for a long time on conceptual grounds. However, Coubertin sees the first staging of the equestrian Games as a large step forward. He calls for a standard program for the next Olympic Games in 1916, which was actually adopted at the 1914 Olympic Congress in Paris. He stresses that the IOC alone is competent to make decisions on this matter, while organizational responsibility lies exclusively with the organizing committee of the host country. Even now, in the second century of the modern Olympic Games, Coubertin's definition, which was exclusively published in English, is still highly relevant.

It had been thought possible that the Olympiad held in London in 1908 might become the standard, or type, by which the organisers of future Olympiads would be guided; but from what is at present known of the programme which has been drawn up for the games at Stockholm next year it is clear that this has not been the case. The outstanding difference between the Fourth (London) and the Fifth (Stockholm) Olympiads will be in the matter of equestrian events; for, thanks to the active cooperation of the Comte de Rosen, a skilled horseman who is an ideal organiser of such competitions, the series of important events which will be included promise to be a very imposing feature of the games. On the other hand, many of the contests which appeared on the London programme have been suppressed, the unsuitability of the ground, the climate, the conditions, being given as reasons for their decision not to include them by the Stockholm organisers.

It is a great pity that there is this lack of uniformity as regards the events at successive Olympiads; and, therefore, the announcement that the International Olympic Committee will shortly draw up a programme which shall serve as a standard for future Olympiads will be received with general satisfaction. This typical, or standard programme will be a guide for all future organisers the value of which cannot be over-estimated; for it will be a model to which all organising countries must henceforth adhere. In this, as in the other delicate matters of control, it is impossible not to admire the wisdom with which the International Olympic Committee introduced this important change. Slow and sure is the motto of the Committee; and, therefore, the work of progress is thoroughly done, whereas precipitancy would be fatal. During the experimental stages, while the Olympic Games were seedlings being acclimatised in strange lands, the greatest caution was necessary, and the organisers had to be allowed much latitude; but now that they have become firmly established (deeply-rooted, to continue the metaphor) it is right and necessary that certain hard and fast guiding rules should be laid down, for it is only in this way that the games can fulfil their ultimate high destiny.

The most important thing of all is to draw up a list of obligatory events, which no organising country shall be free to change – neither to cancel nor to increase. Secondly, this standardisation of distances is imperative, so that the anomaly of the present system may be banished; for now, owing to the difference between the various standards of measurements; uniformity is unobtainable, and races supposed to be over a standard distance differ in length considerably according to the place in which they are run. And, again, when once an event, such as boxing, has been admitted (as it should be) there is no reason why it should be eliminated from the programme of the following Olympiads. At the same time, it is clear that the independence of each organising country must be rigorously maintained and respected. The adoption of any other course would be little short of disastrous; for as it would choke national and individual enterprise, to which the games owe so much, it would deprive the celebrations of the originality and diversity which constitute one of their greatest charms. Also, it would be contrary to the ideal at which the organisers of the modern Olympiads aim: that each country shall impress its own celebration with its national individuality, so that each Olympiad may be stamped by the genius, thought, manners, and civilisation of the organising people.

So, it will be seen that, while laying down broad rules, the International Olympic Committee will not seek to interfere with any of the details of organisation. Indeed, such an attempt would be foredoomed to failure... and, if it could be enforced, it would be a most regrettable proceeding to exercise such authority. It is, therefore, a most delicate matter, requiring the exercise of fine diplomacy, to decide in how far rules shall be made and to what extent the organisers shall be left free to follow out their own ideas; and it is clear that the International Olympic Committee is the only body which is competent and powerful enough to perform such a task successfully. With the help and advice of the active and most useful National Committees, modelled and working on the same lines as the British Olympic Council, which have been formed in most of the countries where sports are practised, the Olympic organisation is very strong, and the International Committee can very well undertake the responsibility of devising what shall be accepted as a standard Olympiad. Indeed, satisfactory progress has already been made with the work; but although this has been rapidly done, owing to the fact that the National Committees are composed of men who are competent to form an opinion of the requirements of the countries they represent, as the delegates of associations and clubs, it is evident that the task cannot be completed soon enough for the „standard" to come into force before the Stockholm Olympiad takes place. And, therefore, not until the Sixth Olympiad is held, in 1916, will the games be modelled upon the standard programme. From that celebration onwards, however, it will be in force; and then the scope of the modern Olympiads will be clearly and finally defined, so that their aim and destiny, and their ever-increasing utility, may be more justly appreciated.

Revue Olympique, Mai 1911, pp. 67-69.

The editor has determined that this text, though unsigned, was written by Coubertin.

6.1/8 GOOD NEWS FROM BASLE

In his *Olympic Memoirs* Coubertin writes that once having received confirmation from the French Government that it accepted the patronage of the Olympic Congress in Paris 1914 he nominated a subcommission to deal with matters of procedures for the Congress and the program of future Olympic Games. This commission, headed by Coubertin, was composed as follows: Eugen Brunetta d'Usseaux (Italy), Godefroy de Blonay (Switzerland), Ernest Callot (France), Robert de Courcy Laffan (Great Britain), William Sloane (USA), Christiaan van Tuyll (Holland), Karl von Venningen-Ullner (Germany).

The Commission met in Basle March 27-28, 1912 and the results are described in the following article, which is exclusively published in English. The duty of the Commission was to prepare a report that could be presented at the IOC-Session in Stockholm in 1912.

The cordial tone which seems to have prevailed throughout the meeting of the 1914 sub-committee which assembled at Basle on Wednesday and Thursday the 27th and 28th of March 1912 cannot fail to have far-reaching effects. This meeting not only brought together the elements upon which the Olympic movement has always been able to count for support, but also those which in the past were, if not actually hostile, exceedingly unsympathetic. And as the change of attitude which was noticeable on this occasion is a fact to be chronicled with genuine pleasure, it is not the slightest exaggeration to say that the Basle meeting was an epoch-marking event in the history of the Olympic movement.

The American proposal, submitted by Professor W. M. Sloane, respecting the representation of the National Olympic Committees during the Paris Congress 1914, which was fully discussed and most carefully examined, was unanimously accepted. Concerning the details of this proposal, which dealt minutely with the number and nomination of delegates amongst other things, nothing can be said at present, as the matter must be referred to the International Olympic Committee for the final acceptance before publishing. But the importance and the value of the proposal is vouched by the reputation of its sponsor. Professor Sloane's influence in the United States is very great, and he is acting with the complete agreement of Messrs.

The participants of the 1914 Olympic Congress gathered around Pierre de Coubertin (IOC Archives)

Allison V. Armour and Evert J. Wendell, his two compatriot colleagues on the International Olympic Committee, and with the full approval and support of the American Olympic Committee, which is a very powerful body, full of vitality and entirely devoted to the Olympic work

This matter settled, the Committee discussed the most important question of the establishment of a standard Olympic programme, by which all future Olympiads should be regulated. The general conditions under which the Games take place and then the question of the establishment of a standard, on the lines suggested by the Rev. de Courcy Laffan, were examined. The difficulties in the way of a task, the drafting of a standard programme may well be imagined – indeed, they seem to be almost insurmountable – for there are so many people to please, and so many absolutely justifiable susceptibilities to be respected, that only a man of unusual tact and knowledge could possibly steer the happy mean course and evolve anything which would be acceptable to everybody alike. Luckily, the Rev. de Courcy Laffan is such a man: his profound knowledge of sports in general enables him to speak with the voice of authority. And the fact that, with Lord Desborough, he brought the London Olympiad of 1908 to a successful close, is the proof that he possesses more than the common share of tact.

The duty – by no means a light one – of preparing a report of the proceedings to be presented to the International Olympic Committee at Stockholm was delegated to Baron von Venningen, who enjoys the well-deserved reputation of being one of Germany's foremost all-round athletes. What the results will be, when this report is submitted to the International Olympic Committee, may be foreseen. Doubtless very important decisions will be decided upon, which will influence the trend of all the future Olympiads and Congresses; and the consequences will probably be to fully justify the assertion that the Basle meeting will rank as an epoch-marking event in the annals of the Olympic movement.

The three countries which form the foundation of the Olympic movement were very strongly represented. England, with its old traditions is the acknowledged cradle of sports, and was represented by the scheme prepared by the Rev. de Courcy

Laffan; the United States, with its enthusiasm and independence, was represented by the proposal of Professor Sloane; and Germany, with its status on the Continent, was represented by the choice of Baron von Venningen to prepare the report which is to be presented to the International Olympic Committee at Stockholm. These three countries have admittedly done more than any others to further the Olympic movement, to which it is no longer sufficient to refer as the Olympic Games, and from this combination it is justifiable to much hope; and the invitation to be presented at certain of the meetings which was extended to the Presidents of the French, Belgian, and Austrian Olympic Committees is not without significance. It shows that the International Olympic Committee is desirous in obtaining views, options, and information from all quarters and from all sources – from the ones who were once opponents as well as from the ones who have already been staunch supporters.

Again the harmonious tone of the meeting has to be mentioned. Nothing that could have happened would have been more welcome; and the signs, that differences are disappearing, that the sword – for in some cases it was almost war – is being sheathed, are most encouraging to all those who have the furtherance of the true aim of the Olympic movement at heart.

Let peace and progress remain the keynote of the future meetings: because only then the fullest amount of good derivable from the Olympic movement can be enjoyed. How true this conviction is, will be proved by the rally of British and American athletes which will be presented at the Olympiad of 1916; should it, what seems likely, be held in Berlin.

There is an old saying to the effect that the strength of a tree must be judged by the depth of its roots rather than by the length or height of its branches, which is specially applicable to the growth of the movement during the years since that memorable day on which the re-establishment of the Olympic Games was formally proclaimed at the Sorbonne, in Paris.

When that meeting took place on the 23rd of June, 1894, a lot of work had already been done, although up to then it was not made public. If I may retain the metaphor of the tree -which seems to be so applicable – the ground had been well dug and dressed, but the excellent seed which had been sown had scarcely begun to stir in the earth. Nevertheless, the prophetic eye of the originators of the movement had already foreseen what manner of plant would ultimately arise, and every effort was then concentrated towards the realisation of the ideal at which they aimed, as it has been ever since. Yet, greatly daring to hazard a conviction, I venture the option that not even the author of the idea foresaw the dimensions to which the little seed he planted a score years ago would grow, but I am equally convinced that his ideal has remained unchanged. All, that has altered, is that the scale of his ideas had to be changed, in order to cope with the unexpected demands which the wonderful extension of the movement has created. The seed was planted in a pot; but it has been necessary to transplant the fast-growing sapling into the open ground, in order that its far-reaching roots might push into every corner of the earth – unstopped by mountain ranges, wide rivers, or even by the ocean itself.

Revue Olympique, May 1912, pp. 67-70.

The editor has determined that this text, though unsigned, was written by Coubertin.

6.1/9 THE PRESENTATION OF OLYMPIC DIPLOMAS

In the *Revue Olympique* of june 1909, the following can be read: "In keeping with the program that had long been agreed upon while the late Count von der Asseburg was still alive, the Session opened in the Prussian House of Lords on Thursday, May 27, at 4:00 PM. The "reception hall" made available to the Committee occupied the center of the second story of that magnificent building. Its five windows, surrounded by tall columns, opened out on the facade of the palace that faced Leipziger Strasse. The large room was paneled in marble. The vaulted ceiling was decorated with somber gilt. Vast loggia-style balconies stood at either end of the room. At the center there was a portrait of Emperor Wilhelm II. Two large electric chandeliers provided light. For the occasion, enormous flower arrangements were placed in the corners. Between the windows hung the flags of Germany, Sweden, and France, in honor of the three laureates of the day. The Minister of Sweden, Mr. de Trolle, and the Baron de Berckheim, Chargé d'Affaires of France, were present, as were Their Excellencies the General von Schenck, aide-de-camp to His Imperial Highness the Crown Prince, representing the Prince, and Mr. Pecker, Vice-President of the House of Lords, representing that body. His Excellency Mr. von Studt, Minister of Culture, was there as well, as were the Vice-Presidents of the Deutscher Reichsausschuss für Olympische Spiele, Councilor von Oertzen and Baron von Hünefeld, Dr. Martin, its secretary, and several members of the Committee...".

Coubertin as President of the Committee spoke as follows, in awarding the Olympic Diplomas:

Your Excellencies, Ladies, and Gentlemen,

I do not think that any diploma is less widely distributed in all the world than our own. Since it was established in 1905, the Olympic Diploma has been awarded six times. Comparing the merit of the laureates who are receiving it today with those who began this illustrious series in Brussels, it is abundantly clear that the institution has not declined in the least. The intention of the International Committee was to create a diploma whose value would be linked to its rarity, a diploma that rewards not a specific deed or special feat, but rather a comprehensive set of athletic, physical, and moral qualities continually upheld throughout a man's life.

While President Roosevelt, Dr. Nansen, Mr. Santos-Dumont, W. H. Grenfell, the Duke of Abruzzi and Commander Lancrenon seemed to us to deserve such a diploma in the first instance, no one will disagree that Count Zeppelin is equally worthy of it. In the life of Count Zeppelin, more than one page has been devoted to his respect for energy. Certainly, though, that energy was never expressed more brilliantly than on the memorable day when nature inflicted an undeserved defeat on him even as he was conquering it, when pitiless flames devoured his work and seemed to deal a death blow to his hopes. No sooner was the fire out than the Count's face showed renewed determination struggling against unproductive sadness. As a poet has said, to well-born souls merit is not a matter of the passing years.

Olympic Diploma awarded to the Norwegian polar researcher Fridtjof Nansen, drawn by French painter André Slom. (IOC Archives)

At the time, it seemed that the passing years, in turn, was powerless against merit. This observation is far more significant, and far more beautiful, than the first.

Sir, we ask you to tell your illustrious father of the admiration that I now express in the name of my colleagues, which inspired the unanimous vote of the International Committee in awarding him the Olympic Diploma. Please express to him, with our congratulations, our best wishes *ad multos annos*.

Count Ferdinand Zeppelin, appointed by his uncle to represent him, came forward. After accepting the diploma, he thanked the International Committee graciously. He spoke of Count Zeppelin's regret at not being able to attend in person, since he held the honor that the Committee had done him in highest esteem. Mr. Coubertin then spoke again:

Sometimes our faults throw our good qualities into sharper relief. I say this with regard to Colonel Balck. For alas, he does have one great flaw, one that his colleagues hope that he will never correct. The flaw is that he belongs to our Committee, and in terms of awarding the Olympic Diploma, that was a major obstacle, indeed! In our decision to overlook that obstacle, we felt that the qualities of the laureate had to be so comparatively great that this fault I just mentioned appeared negligible. In a way, the axiom is justified. My dear Balck, you are the Gustavus Adolphus of physical exercise. You love battle, and, not content with waging war in the vicinity of your national borders, you carry the war far and wide. Neither triumph nor adversity hold you in their sway. It is your mission to go to all countries to shake up those who are lukewarm, and to stir up the will of people. Receive this diploma as a souvenir of the battles you have won for the glory and independence of sports.

In receiving the diploma, Colonel Balck expressed his heartfelt thanks to his colleagues for the exceptional favor that they had shown him, and assured them that, to the end of his days, the prosperity and honor of the International Committee would be close to his heart. Mr. Coubertin then closed with these words:

The most recent word we have received from Madame Jean Charcot concerning her husband and his companions dated from a far-off bay lost in the lonely sadness of the southern hemisphere. Norwegian whalers sailing in that deserted place carried the hero's letter back with them. Charcot, in sober and picturesque language, related that at the moment, even his chief of staff was growing tired of his painful labors, skiing across the snowy wastes. He, the leader, would love to have accompanied them, but he was kept at his little desk completing complex calculations. That small snapshot, gentlemen, is the picture of a soul. It enables us to grasp the inner balance of one of the most wonderful human beings that modern civilization has managed to produce. His is a character solidly based on these three noble things: feeling, effort, and duty. This was true even when, as a mere school boy, Jean Charcot set about fostering manly sports among his schoolmates; even then, his instinct was to use those sports as a training field. It is for that, Gentlemen, that we hope to reward him. I do not know what successes or disappointments await him at the South Pole, a name one cannot speak without hastening to add that of the valiant Englishman who came so close to it that all previous records were dashed at a single blow. Leaving to others the task of glorifying the explorer, we salute in Charcot the man who, resolutely and methodically, in an deliberate and on-going way, sought in athletics the total culture of the human being that we advocate. He loved and practiced our doctrines, as a true apostle. It is only fitting that we offer him as an example for the younger generations.

At the request of Madame Charcot, her husband's diploma was to be handed over to a representative of the Embassy of France. Baron de Berckheim, Chargé d'Affaires in the absence of the Ambassador, himself wished to represent his compatriot, and to express the laureate's gratitude.

Since the International Committee had resolved to award the Olympic Medal to the Prussian House of Lords, in commemoration of the 1909 Session, that ceremony took place next. The Reverend de Courcy Laffan, in an eloquent, improvised address given in the purest German, recalled that the Emperor Wilhelm II had been one of the first holders of the medal. He thanked them for the gracious hospitality offered to the International Committee. He expressed his hope that the fact that the House of Lords, so outstanding for the patriotism that it had demonstrated throughout history, was extending its hand to an undertaking that is, in essence, international, proves once again that, far from harming each other, love of country and love of humanity are made to complement and edify each other. Mr. Laffan ended by expressing his best wishes for the prosperity of the House of Lords and of the City of Berlin.

His Excellency, Mr. Pecker, Vice-President of the House of Lords, thanked him on behalf of that body, and said that the medal would be placed in its archives. He spoke of the beneficial role of sports, and expressed, in turn, his best wishes for the future of the International Committee.

The Session ended with the awarding of the Olympic Cup to the Turners Association. Baron Godefroy de Blonay, also speaking in German, presented it to its new owners, reminding them that it had been passed in succession from France to England to Sweden. He mentioned the conditions under which the Committee awards the Cup each year. He asked that the Turners see it as a tribute to their ancient heritage, and to the greatness of the services they have performed on behalf of the cause of physical education.

The Association was represented by Professor Reinhardt and Rechnungsrat Atzrott. Professor Reinhardt, after briefly presenting the growth of the Turners and of their powerful organization, expressed his colleagues gratitude, and stated that the German gymnasts would always be ready to answer the call of the International Committee, and to take part in the Olympic competitions held under its auspices.

La réunion du C.I.O. à Berlin: La séance inaugurale. [La remise des Diplômes olympiques],
in: *Revue Olympique*,
June 1909, pp. 83-88.

The editor has determined that this text, though unsigned, was written by Coubertin.

6.1/10 THE SESSION OF JULY 4, 1912 (SPEECH IN STOCKHOLM)

The following text complement Coubertin's previous statements about the structure of the IOC. It is the speech for the opening of the IOC Session in the Swedish Parliament at Stockholm on July 4, 1912, shortly before the Olympic Games were held. It is addressed to the King of Sweden, and attempts to make the advantages of the Olympic Charter understood and accepted.

Sir, We have lost count of all the signs of your benevolent – with Your Royal Highness' permission, I would even say amicable – sympathy. They are infinitely precious to us. By deigning to preside, today, over the opening of our Fourteenth Plenary Session, placed under the patronage of your august father, Your Royal Highness bears witness to the sensitive manner in which you take an interest in our work, a work in which you are so well versed.

Ours are not the labors of Hercules, since we are engaged in them together. But they do come close, perhaps, given the difficulties we have overcome. The other day, Your Majesty recalled a visit that I made to him here, thirteen years ago – Year Four of the First Olympiad, to use a calendar that has fallen out of use with everyone, a calendar that we are stylish enough to use with discretion, from time to time. That was a time of uncertainty and worry for our undertaking. Unjustified and strong opposition was coming at us from all sides. Things looked bad for the Second Olympiad, and some did not even dare think that there would be a third. The long series of roadblocks, so obstinately thrown in our path time and again, was just beginning. If one looks closely enough, even in our present circumstances, one will find traces of one last trench that belated hostility has tried to dig under our footsteps.

Yet we did not despair. For my part, all it took was to see the constellation of men smitten with sport and attentive to its needs growing in number from month to month. These men did me the honor of joining with me to revive Olympism by modernizing it. Now it is commonplace to praise our group's constitution. Two years ago, one prime minister delighted in sending us an astute commentary on the merits that he found in it. Everyone feels and agrees how much the total independence that this constitution ensures us has contributed to the success of our efforts. The sports communities, which our widely-known independence has offended so greatly and has made so combative, are the first to understand that under other circumstances, the Olympic Games would have perished in their infancy.

Yet there is another element to our success. It has been said that constitutions are made valid above all through those who implement them. The diplomatic qualities that my dear colleagues have, for the most part, managed to exemplify for the past twenty years, ensured a hard-fought victory. Our regulations forbid them from becoming delegates of anyone or anything, in any manner whatsoever. Our rules make them ambassadors; just look at the power of the Olympic idea, which dares to rely in this way on ambassadors who belong to the very nation to which they are accredited! How great the conflicts that would easily arise from the contacts that result from this unusual situation. Exceptional skill is absolutely necessary to serve the general interests of Olympism without doing disservice to the special interests of the countries or of the specializations whose support is indispensable for Olympism. The members of the International Committee have been excellent ambassadors. They have had patience, the political patience that was made easier for them by the permanence and stability

14th IOC Session, Budapest 1911: **IOC members and guests (IOC Archives)**

of the mandate entrusted to them; the social patience that came to them generally from their position in the world. They were in no hurry, while their opponents were, placing them at a great disadvantage. Yet they also had panache, and some of them swept away solid fortresses and well-defended encampments in the course of swift campaigns.

Sir, this manner of proceeding must be pleasing to you. It has been employed more than once in the history of this great kingdom whose scepter shall, one day, be in your hands: calm, headstrong patience, long periods of contemplation, followed by a sudden flurry of activity that astonished everyone. May Your Royal Highness not find anything to correct in my comparison. No doubt it is a pretentious one. Yet from the smallest to the greatest, in the annals of human history the same results are always achieved by the same means. This lesson is among those that youth cannot hear too often. Any occasion is good for reminding them of this recipe for success, a recipe that is far superior to any other: vigorous offensives nestled in among periods of great vigilance.

It was fitting that in these days of victory, we should acknowledge the merits of those who worked tirelessly on the strong foundation on which this Olympiad has been built. This is the Fifth Olympiad, one that is thoroughly Scandinavian in its originality, yet completely international, nonetheless. Sir, we shall not forget that we owe this Olympiad to Your Royal Highness and his assistants, among whom we are pleased to note the ever-youthful enthusiasm of Viktor Balck and the impetuous zeal of Clarence de Rosen, our cherished colleagues.

Sir, we ask that you accept the Olympic Medal, a modest thing made precious by the small number of those who hold it, and great by the deed and date that it evokes, the restoration of the Olympic Games. That restoration, proclaimed in Paris on June 23, 1894, will be solemnly commemorated here in two years' time.

Now, Sir, if Your Royal Highness pleases, let us get down to work.

La séance du 4 juillet 1912 (Discours à Stockholm),
in: *Revue Olympique,* August 1912, pp. 120-121.

6.2 GROWTH AND EXPANSION

This chapter contains 6 texts relating to the continuous growth of the Olympic movement throughout the world. Starting in the countries of Europe, which were the first to be confronted with Coubertin's Olympic idea, the Olympic movement gradually made its way to all countries and continents, mostly through Coubertin's initiative. The support of the YMCA concerning Regional Games must be emphasized.

This state of affairs is illustrated by the Olympic flag, whose five rings, conceived and designed by Coubertin himself, represent the five continents, with the colors representing, according to Coubertin, the basic elements of all national flags[1].

6.2/1 AN OLYMPIAD IN THE FAR EAST

In this article, entitled "An Olympiad in the Far East", Coubertin expresses his hopes of seeing the countries of the Far East join the Olympic movement, thus joining in the expansion of a modern athletic movement. By contrast, Coubertin criticizes "anthropological days" in this work, days when, within the framework of athletic exhibitions at the St. Louis World's Fair in 1904, Asians, among others, were called upon to give "demonstrations". All these demonstrations took place under the title "Olympic events", but they were not part of the real Olympic Games. Coubertin seized this opportunity to point out the universality of the Olympic movement, which is open to all races and all nations.

His hopes of seeing the countries of the Far East participate in large number at the 1916 Olympic Games in Berlin came to naught, since those Games were not held. It was to be a long time yet before the success of the Japanese team in 1932 in Los Angeles, which drew attention to sports in Asia.

We are now in possession of curious accounts of the beginnings of exotic athleticism. In truth, these really are not its beginnings. The festivities recently held in the capital of the Philippines did have a precedent. During the competitions of the Third Olympiad, held in St. Louis in 1904, one or more days were reserved for performances by Asians. The Americans clearly see themselves as athletic preceptors in the Far East. The day-long festivities in St. Louis were hardly flattering for the people in that part of the world. These descendants of such ancient and refined civilizations were called on to compete with the representatives of peoples scarcely refined out of their original barbarianism. This was a mistake. The International Committee, which is at times reproached for having too aristocratic a membership, is certainly more democratic in its procedures. It seeks to spread athleticism throughout the world without cataloguing races; it does not limit the recruitment of its members to Europe and America. Japan is represented on it. China and Siam will be represented soon, regardless of the fact that those countries are not very open to sports.

It is quite likely that they will open up to sports eventually. The American initiative in the Philippines has proved good in that regard. The Philippine Amateur

1 See text 5.2/6 in this volume.

Olympic sports in the Far East. Ten mile cycle race in Tokyo's Uyeno Park, 1906 (taken from Sport im Bild, no.29, 1906, p.735)

Athletic Federation, with headquarters in Manila, was founded in January 1911. Unless I am mistaken, it comprises some dozen clubs. The Governor General, W. C. Forbes, became its president, and made an immediate impression in the interest that he took in this undertaking, so clearly did he perceive its eminently civilizing aspect. The Office of Education, in other words the Department of Public Instruction, was quick to follow suit. Rather than being a simple union of athletic clubs gathered rather selfishly to protect their technical interests, the young federation upheld that characteristic so well-known of the American spirit outside that country: collective action for the public good.

A major "international" meet took place in Manila in February, 1912. Thirty-seven competitors came from China, while seventeen came from Japan. The Philippines supplied nearly seventy athletes of their own. The president of the international association set up for this occasion is Dr. Wu Ting Fang. The next championships are going to be held, apparently, at Shanghai. It must be noted that although the Filipinos, better trained by their Yankee educators, won first place in overall standings, the Japanese took top honors in the marathon and in baseball, while China won the decathlon. These are promising beginnings.

The organizers, rightfully proud of their success, contacted the International Committee to ask its approval of their undertaking. It is not easy to see under what form that approval could be given, but it is beyond any doubt that the IOC will observe these far-off expansions of its doctrines and influence with great interest.

For us, who are merely chroniclers of the event, there is nothing in this business that can disturb or surprise us. We have always believed that athletics would soon reach all parts of the Far East. We are convinced that sports will play a capital, decisive role there. We would be willing to bet that in twenty years, athletic associations will abound in that region. The "yellow men" seem to us to be admirably prepared to benefit from the athletic crusade that is taking shape. They are ready individually and collectively. They are ready individually because endurance, tenacity, patience, racial flexibility, the habit of self-mastery, of keeping silent, and of hiding pain and effort have shaped their bodies most effectively. They are ready collectively, because their young imperialism, which has not yet had its fill of domination, will impel them to taste the fresh joys of athletic victories, as well as the honor this brings to their national flags.

For a while still, clearly, athletic Asia will grow and become strong where it is. Yet it is quite probable that contacts with the West will be made and, at Berlin in 1916, the yellow teams will be able to show what they can do. If that comes as a "revelation", all those who have athleticism and its spread throughout the world close to their hearts must rejoice, with neither second thoughts nor hesitation.

Une Olympiade extrême orientale,
in: *Revue Olympique,*
May 1913, pp. 77-78.

The editor has determined that this text, though unsigned, was written by Coubertin.

6.2/2 ATHLETIC UNIFICATION

Australia and New Zealand, the fifth continent, were areas of interest to Coubertin from early on. The following article compares the efforts made in those countries to expand sports and to join the Olympic movement with the situation in Canada, Sweden, England, Germany, and Russia. Coubertin also provides a brief overview of the first twenty years of the Olympic movement.

The great movement toward athletic unification that Olympism has set in motion continues to progress day by day. The rapprochement in nearly all branches of sports, something utterly unexpected by the previous generation of athletes, has been perhaps the most striking feature of the year that is drawing to a close, particularly of the last few months of the year. The calling of the Congress of Paris has stepped up the pace of this movement even more, by setting a mandatory deadline. We see preparations underway on all sides in order to meet it.

So it is that the Lord Mayor of Sydney presided over a meeting the other day at the Town Hall of that great Australian metropolis, a meeting intended to set up an efficient organization of all sports. So it is, too, that next month delegates of the Australian and New Zealand Olympic Sub-Committees will meet in Melbourne to chose the Australian representatives to the Congress of Paris, and to agree on the instructions that they will be given. Similar meeting are taking place in Canada, while in Old Europe, athletic unification is constantly on the increase. In Sweden, the understanding reached during the Fifth Olympiad between the rival and, until then, mutually hostile schools, has stood the test of time. It has survived past the fleeting national interest that brought it about. The

Telephone 2865
Box 579, G.P.O.

R. COOMBES,
President.
c/o Referee Office, Castlereagh St., Sydney

E. S. MARKS,
Honorary Secretary.

STANLEY ROWLEY,
Honorary Treasurer.

The Amateur Athletic Union of Australasia.

HEADQUARTERS—Sydney, N.S. Wales.

Address:
c o N.S. WALES SPORTS CLUB, Ltd.,
10, 12 & 14 HUNTER STREET.

AFFILIATED ASSOCIATIONS.

N.S.W. Amateur Athletic Association.
W. B. Alexander, Hon. Sec., Box 579, G.P.O., Sydney.
New Zealand Amateur Athletic Association.
J. E. Green, Hon. Sec., Box 106, Christchurch, New Zealand.
Victorian Amateur Athletic Association.
H. D. Smith, c/o Amateur Sports Club, Collins Street, Melbourne, Vic.
Queensland Amateur Athletic Association.
G. Crawford, Hon. Sec., 530 Queen St., Petrie's Bight, Brisbane, Q.
Tasmanian Amateur Athletic Association.
E. H. Brooke, Hon. Sec. c/o A.M.P. Society, Hobart, Tasmania.
South Australian Amateur Athletic Association.
G. Elton Mayo, Hon. Sec. c/o J. H. Sherring & Co., Leigh St., Adelaide, S.A.
Western Australian Amateur Athletic Association.

Sydney, 12th Febry 1912

Objects:

a) The encouragement of systematic physical exercise and education in Australasia.

b) The improvement and promotion of athletic exercise amongst Amateurs.

c) The incorporation of all eligible Amateur Athletic Associations in the Union (with active membership and representation) so as to advance the cause of Amateur Athletics throughout the Australasian Colonies, and to promote and foster the interests of the several members.

d) The establishment and maintenance by allied membership or otherwise of alliances with other associations (governing kindred sport) devoted to physical culture or to some speciality in Amateur Athletics.

e) The establishment and maintenance throughout the Australasian Colonies of an uniform test of Amateur standing and uniform laws for the government of all athletic exercises within its jurisdiction.

f) The institution, regulation, and awarding of all amateur athletic championships of Australasia.

g) To deal with appeals of either complainant or defendant from the judgment of any member as to the amateur standing of any athlete, or on any agreed case submitted to it on voluntary appeal by or with the sanction of any member.

Kristian Hellstrom Esq.,
Secretary,
Fifth Olympiad, Stockholm.

Dear Sir,

I beg to acknowledge receipt of programmes and posters and have circulated same. It may interest you to know that Australasia will be represented in the following branches : Rowing, Swimming, Athletics, Lawn Tennis and most likely Rifle Shooting and Cycling.

Our representatives, totalling about 25, purpose leaving by the R.M.S."Osterley", due in London May 26th and I understand purpose going at once to Stockholm. The following well known men in Sport will most likely accompany the team :

Q.L.Deloitte, President N.S.Wales Rowing Association,
A.Thompson, Hon.Secretary N.S.Wales ,, ,,
W.B.Alexander, Hon.Secretary N.S.Wales Amateur Athletic Association
A.Watson, Hon.Secretary Manly Surf Club
G.E.Upward, late Captain Victorian Rowing Associatio[n]
C.Helsham, Member Committee N.S.Wales Rowing Assoc.
Dr.Newman, President New Zealand Amateur Athletic Association

and

Registration of the Australasian team for the 1912 Olympics. New Zealand and Australia formed a combined team. (National Archives, Stockholm) pessimists have gotten nothing in return for their gloomy predictions, and it is quite clear that on both sides, people are pleased with this rapprochement, and are prepared for effective cooperation in the future. In England, despite the concern apparent in people's minds about the value of athletic education (which was accepted before without debate), partisans of gymnastics are becoming, if not more numerous, at least much more enthusiastic and active in their efforts to win support. In Germany, everyone is working together in the same spirit for the success of the Sixth Olympiad. Now a kind of ministry of sports has been cr%ated in Russia. Its curious assignment will consist of spreading the practice of physical exercise throughout that vast empire, using any possible means to do so.

At the first call of renascent Olympism exactly twenty years ago, athletic unification, so critical for the success of the Olympiads, was taking its first baby steps. Hesitancy and resistance arose as soon as its strength began to wear down gradually. Three distinct periods took shape over the past twenty years. In the first period, there was mutual disdain among the sports disciplines, and condescension with respect to Olympic institutions. No one believed that they would survive, but people accepted the originality of these large meets, embellished as they were with ancient prestige. So people agreed to temporary cooperative agreements in light of such meets, agreements devoid of any technical significance. Then there came a second period, the period of quadrennial good will. The Olympiads took hold. It was agreed that in order to participate in them, the various sports had to reach an understanding and even, if need be, accept some mutual sacrifices. Yet once the Olympiad was over, everyone regained his freedom once again, and withdrew to his own corner without further consideration of the work accomplished together not long before. Finally, a third period began. The benefits of athletic cooperation were understood. A sort of instinct for mutual support replaced the scorn and envy of days past. Even those sports that are technically, and even socially, the furthest removed from one another, seem to seek each other out. There is no reason to think than another period of suspicion and distance will follow this period, by way of reaction. In addition, a phenomenon is occurring that we must take into account. In light of the vast size to which the Olympic Games have grown, the training of the participants can no longer be achieved in just a few months. This is quite clear in terms of the Sixth Olympiad which is preoccupying athletic opinion so strongly, three years in advance. So the understanding among sports can no longer be temporary. It must be permanent. This need is felt everywhere.

In this respect, 1913, with the Congress of Paris and the Berlin Games on the horizon, will have exerted decisive influence on the athletic mind set.

L'unification sportive,
in the "Monthly Events" column of the *Revue Olympique*,
December 1913, pp. 188-190.

The editor has determined that this text, though unsigned, was written by Coubertin.

6.2/3 – 6.2/4 INTRODUCTION

In his circular letter for the members of the IOC of September 15, 1921, Coubertin described the expansion of the Olympic movement. He had been planning to go on an extensive trip to South America, which, however, he finally did not. In his letter, Coubertin announced that the Executive Board would start work despite his absence. He was delighted in the success of the Fourth Far Eastern Games, and noted that he was working on bringing the "Continental Games" into the Olympic movement.

The "African Games" scheduled to be held in Algiers in 1925 did not take place. Coubertin appealed for the creation of a commemorative Medal for the next Games, to be held at Alexandria in 1927. What this appeal shows, essentially, is Coubertin's firm desire to expand sports in Africa. He went so far as to make this the most pressing task of the IOC, as shown by his opening speech at the IOC Session in Rome in 1923[1].

6.2/3 LETTER TO THE IOC MEMBERS (1921): "MY WORK IS DONE".

Dear Colleagues,

On October 1, the Executive Committee that you have appointed at my request to handle the operations of our Committee in my absence will begin its work. This Committee, which comprises Messrs. de Blonay, Guth-Jarkovsky, de Baillet-Latour, Edström, and Polignac, is as skilled as it is devoted. We can have every confidence that its work will be outstanding.

The situation of the Olympics is satisfactory from every perspective. The future of the Eighth Olympiad, and that of the Ninth, has been settled in the best interests of all, which should be the sole criterion for our decisions. The International Committee, which has fifty-two members from forty-one countries in Europe, Africa, America, and Asia, is truly "global". Its authority has never been more firmly founded nor more justified. Fruitful understanding exists among its members, the National Committees before which they represent us, and the International Federations.

Therefore, I can say that the goal has been reached, and my work is done. Yet in keeping with your wishes, I shall remain as your president until 1924 so that, together, we may celebrate in Paris the Thirtieth Anniversary of the restoration of the Olympic Games on the occasion of the Eighth Olympiad. Until then, according to my promise, I will work toward the advancement of the Regional Games. Held periodically under your patronage in various parts of the world, these Games will provide valuable human support for Olympism. Thus it was that the Fourth Far Eastern Games, recently held at Shanghai before a crowd of 150,000 spectators, achieved quite remarkable results in all respects.

While remaining as President of the Committee, however, I plan to exercise my freedom as of now, in the service of popular education. I firmly believe that modern society will not rise from the ruins accumulated through its ambitions and

ALFRED E. MARLING
CHAIRMAN

B. H. FANCHER
TREASURER

JOHN R. MOTT
GENERAL SECRETARY

The International Committee of Young Men's Christian Associations

347 Madison Avenue, New York.

FOREIGN DEPARTMENT

Paris, June 21st 1921

Baron Pierre de COUBERTIN
President International Olympic Committee
20 rue Oudinot
PARIS

My dear Baron de Coubertin,

You will remember that, after our last conference at Lausanne, I promised to send you a permanent form for your files, of my understanding of the action taken by your Committee, concerning the Young Men's Christian Association.

Herewith follows verbatim copy of the typewritten material which you and I went over in detail :

I. "The International Olympic Committee approves of and accepts the plan of promotion, by cooperation with the Young Men's Christian Association of (1) physical sports, athletics, play for everybody continuously; (2) annual competitive games where possible and necessary; (3) biennial regional development games where previously sanctioned by the I.O.C. all leading up to the quadrennial Olympic Games. The fundamental idea is to bring sports within the reach of every possible person in every possible country, the Olympic Games marking the logical and inevitable expression of this idea. The various National Olympic Committees will be asked by the I.O.C. to cooperate in the entire plan. The I.O.C. recognises its responsibility to accept paternal supervision over the whole program and is prepared to be consulted with, to advise and assist in any way possible."

II. "When, in the common opinion of the representatives of the International Olympic Committee in the countries concerned and of the Young Men's Christian Association physical directors, the time is propitious, additional regional development games to those previously approved and recognised (Far Eastern, South American, Indian Empire) should be organised; - namely Middle European Games (including Poland, Czechoslovakia, Roumania, Yugo Slavia, Hungary, Bulgaria) and Near Eastern Games comprising Greece Egypt, Turkey and Asia Minor."

Very sincerely yours,

Elwood S. Brown
Elwood S. BROWN
Secretary for Physical Education

An important part of the letter of understanding (June 21, 1921) concerning the cooperation between IOC and YMCA, especially with regards to Regional Games. The letter is signed by Elwood S. Brown (Secretary for Physical Education), friend and sports development counsellor of Pierre de Coubertin (1919-25). YMCA was awarded the Olympic Cup for 1929. (IOC Archives)

injustices. I believe that different forms of social existence will be needed before long. I see the only guarantee of general advancement in the prior spreading of culture, primarily the study of history.

Very sincerely yours,

Pierre de Coubertin

Circulaire aux membres du CIO (15 sept. 1921),
(Archives of the IOC).
Reprinted in: Textes choisis, Vol. II, p. 672.

1 Cf. Coubertin, "Discours d´ouverture de la Session de Rome (le 7 avril 1923)." In: *Textes choisis.* Vol. II, pp. 398-402.

6.2/4 ATHLETICS WANT TO CONQUER AFRICA. AN APPEAL FROM THE PRESIDENT OF THE IOC

COMITÉ
INTERNATIONAL
OLYMPIQUE

The time has come for sport to advance to the conquest of Africa, that vast continent which it has as yet hardly touched and to bring to its people the enjoyment of ordered and disciplined muscular effort, with all the benefits which flow from it.

With this object in view the International Olympic Committee has adopted two resolutions :

1° It has instituted the "**Games of Africa**" (to be in the main reserved for natives) which will be celebrated for the first time at Alexandria in Egypt, in 1927, and thereafter every two years in some town of the African coast;

2° It has resolved to institute a medal for the propaganda of sport in Africa. A large number of these medals will be distributed annually to native associations of sport as a recognition of their work and as a stimulus to effort. It as been thought well that this medal should be a gift presented to the youth of Africa by the Olympic representatives of the world assembled in Paris for the games of the VIIIth Olympiad

We appeal therefore to the athletes and all who take part in the Games to contribute their mite, however small it may be, to this work of drawing together the whole world into one brotherhood of sport and sympathy.

July 8th has been specially set apart for this subscription which the President of the French Republic has kindly consented to head.

Each separate nation should organize its own subscription list and kindly send the amount subscribed to Mr A.-C. BOLANACHI, commissioner general for the Games of Africa or pay it into his account at the Banque Imperiale Ottomane, 7, rue Meyerbeer, Paris, compte "Sports d'Afrique".

With my best thanks for your help.

Very cordially yours.

PIERRE DE COUBERTIN.
PRESIDENT OF THE INTERNATIONAL OLYMPIC COMMITTEE.

"All Sports – All Nations": in 1923, Coubertin began to call for the inclusion of Africa in the Olympic Movement through an Olympic Solidarity Campaign, which unfortunately was unsuccessful. Here, the IOC President appeals for a collection to be made for the African Games due to be held in Alexandria in 1927 (IOC Archives)

Le Sport veut conquérir l´Afrique. Appel du Président du CIO (1923), Off-print.
Reprinted in: Textes choisis, Vol. II, p. 675.

6.2/5 ATHLETIC COLONIZATION

In this article written for the Bulletin of the Bureau International de Pédagogie Sportive, Coubertin assesses the success of the Olympic movement in correlation with the spread of sports. The word "colonization" should not be taken, in any sense, as implying any "racist" position on Coubertin's part. On the contrary, Coubertin reaffirms, as he had said in 1912, that there cannot be any victory of one race over another[1].

Above all else, Coubertin sought the expansion of modern sports and of the Olympic movement. The fact that each race and nation has its own athletic culture and can engage in that culture is not his primary concern. Current works on "Olympic Solidarity" confirm the significance of this topic.

During the Session held in Rome at the Capitol under the patronage of the King of Italy in 1923, the International Committee decided to "conquer Africa", and established the African Games. These Games were to be held successively along the periphery of that vast continent, and were gradually to teach native populations the benefits of athletic activity. All those who, later on, will recall the dangers that weighed against Black life and will appreciate the value that such support would have provided for it, will be astonished at the reception given to this new undertaking. The Far East Games already existed. The educational influence of those Games in China, Japan and the Philippines was swift and profound. At other places around the globe, similar innovations were under way. There was talk in India of Hindu Games. This was the "Kindergarten" of Olympism, in which the IOC had expressed a special interest from the start. The *Revue Olympique* of January 1912 dealt with this topic. It denounced the false idea that "a victory by the dominated race over the dominating race might pose a threat, and could be exploited by local opinion as encouragement for rebellion". The Germans, in their colonies in Africa which are quite well equipped, had no fear of introducing sports among the natives. In India, the English did not oppose the movement, though they did little to encourage it. Italy accepted the idea with benevolence, without having had much time to think about it at length. It was France that objected. The honor of inaugurating the African Games had been given to Algiers. The Algerians, supported, if not urged, by continental France to do so, turned down the honor. Then the inaugural Games were pushed back two years, and awarded to the oldest of Africa's countries, Egypt. Alexandria built a magnificent stadium. The Organizing Committee that was headed up by Mr. A. Bolanachi worked wonders to see to it that everything was ready on time. In fact, everything was ready. All of a sudden, it was learned that the authorities, on a rather poor pretext, were side-stepping their agreement, and refused to make it easy for their colonial teams to attend. The Games did not take place. Since then, the Games have been waiting.

The inner workings of this affair are not our concern here. It is clear that at the base of the opposition, which was not distinguished for its frankness and fairness, there was the persistent notion of the prestige of the colonizing country being harmed by the successes of the colonies. How could one ever think that in the modern world, it would be possible to prevent the spread of athletics for very long,

1 Cf. Coubertin, "L'eugénie." [Eugenics]. In: *Revue Olympique*, November 1912, pp. 163-166.

and to limit progress to certain races and certain countries? It has been only three years, and yet the great colonial exhibition in Paris, planned in celebration of the centennial of French Africa, has been forced to dedicate considerable space to sports. Let there be no mistake, however. This does not mean that anything clear and definitive has been achieved. These are merely athletic displays. This does not mean, in any way, that native peoples will be encouraged to engage in manly exercises at home, or that such exercise will be made easier for them to learn. Nor does it mean that they will be brought to understand, in all its philosophical and educational depth, the motto that we quoted the other day, the motto engraved on the "African medal" established by the IOC in 1923 to encourage athletics. The motto on that medal reads: *athletae proprium est se ipsum noscere, ducere et vincere.*

Here, we are examining this matter only in relation to the fundamental precepts of athletic education. Are these precepts not applicable to native races, and to their existence, which is often primitive? Of course they are, even entirely so. For that is their beauty: they are so deeply human that they are fitting for the condition of man from his semi-savage to his ultra-civilized state.

Of course, some tempering is appropriate in applying those precepts. Gabon and Polynesia do not have the same systems of regulations. In general, it seems that athletic games, primarily football, will be predominant. These sports are simple in organization, and call for a large number of participants. Although we are at a point where we see excesses in team sports in some European countries, i.e. the limit at which the team begins to harm the individual – a limit that went unseen for a long time –, there is still no such state of affairs in the countries that have been colonized. Yet this does not mean that individual sports should be neglected by any means. Though the prejudice to which we alluded above may continue to exist for a while yet, a prejudice that led to the failure of the first "African Games", perhaps that prejudice will be less intense with regard to individual sports than to team sports, which always evokes some notion of battle, and of final victory won by a group that represents a country or a city. Foot races, all kinds of jumps, and gymnastics exercises on gymnastics equipment are a broad enough program, even if one excludes the various forms of fencing on principle, to provide for abundant colonial athletic activity.

In addition, there are certain forms of native athletics that should not be discouraged – far from it – , forms common to a region or even a single district. However, these activities will never be anything more than amusements, recreation. If one wishes to extend to natives in colonized countries what we will boldly call the benefits of "athletic civilization", they must be made to enter into the broad athletic system with codified regulations and comparative results, which is the necessary basis of that civilization.

More than one colonizing country balks at this decisive step. Yet we are going to have to reach a decision, or the natives will end up organizing on their own. After all, perhaps they would not be any the worse off that way, but perhaps so for those who direct them.

Colonisation sportive,
in: *Bulletin du Bureau International de Pédagogie Sportive*,
no 5, Lausanne [1931], pp. 12-14.

The editor has determined that this text, though unsigned, was written by Coubertin.

THE LAST MESSAGE OF BARON DE COUBERTIN

"The task of celebrating the XIIth Olympic Games will be the greatest ever given to a country, for it does not mean merely to pursue the Olympic Torch through the universe and to unite the whole of Asia with the modern Olympism in a most cordial manner, but also to combine Hellenism, the most precious civilization of ancient Europe, with the refined culture and art of Asia."

"It is a most enjoyable thought to me to be able to promote the rapprochement of world interest."

Pierre de Coubertin

Geneva, 29, July, 1937

Shortly before his death, Coubertin wrote this last message for a promotional brochure for the Organizing Committee of the 1940 Games, due to be held in Tokyo. (taken from the Organizing Committee of the XII Olympiad, Tokyo 1940 (ed.), Olympic Preparation for the Celebration of the XII Olympiad, Tokyo 1940. Tokyo, 1938, p.3)

6.2/6 THE NEXT GAMES WILL BE HELD IN TOKYO

In this short press release dated December 1936, Coubertin expresses his pleasure at the upcoming celebration of the Olympic Games in Tokyo in 1940, seeing in them a chance to expand Olympism to the furthest parts of the earth. Unfortunately, the Sino-Japanese war prevented the Tokyo Games from taking place. The Helsinki Games, which had been decided upon as a replacement, did not take place until 1952, on account of World War II.

At the close of this, the first year of the Eleventh Olympiad, I will respond to your appeal in a few words, but the importance of these words cannot be underscored enough. At this time, one fact dominates all other aspects of Olympism. Aside from that fact, all else pales, so great are the consequences. *Olympism is entering Asia*!

Plans are already underway for bringing the sacred flame kindled on the sacred soil of Greece to the Far East, when the time comes. This may not necessarily be indispensable. Perhaps the feat accomplished last July, with runners carrying the torch in relay from Olympia to Berlin, was enough to give this gesture it fullness, its definitive and permanent significance. From now on, whether the torch is carried in reality or symbolically, the meaning remains the same as the flame whose spiritual power it evokes. With Olympism restored, all Hellenism will fill the thoughts of the Japanese Empire for four years, sealing the contract between the purest of our European civilizations and one of the most illustrious among the Asian civilizations.

This is a profitable, peaceful date, one set in the destiny of humanity never to be forgotten.

Les prochains Jeux auront lieu à Tokio,
in: *La Revue Sportive Illustrée,*
Vol. 32, 1936, no. 3 [p. 17].

6.3 THE VARIOUS SPORTS IN THE OLYMPIC PROGRAM

It would have been quite surprising if Coubertin had not also dealt with the various sports in the Olympic program on several occasions in his copious published articles. For the most part, articles on this topic were written on the basis of specific examples, such as the inclusion or elimination of a sport at the Olympic Games. Sometimes he deals only with one aspect within a broader context. Coubertin was never involved in purely technical details. He viewed sports, rather, from a educational perspective.

The second group of texts deals with the situation of the various athletic disciplines within the Olympic program. Coubertin gladly pointed out on many occasions the equality of the various sports, which was rather revolutionary for his time.

Athletic sports had to share precedence with sports that were little known, if at all. It was in this respect that the Olympic movement greatly enhanced the spread of new forms of sports throughout the world.

This analysis of a permanent Olympic city, extensive portions of which are included in this volume (text 4.1/3), also takes into account Coubertin's thoughts about the Olympic program, the athletes who take part, and even the spectators. Coubertin's perspective in 1909 is a synthesis of tradition and progress.

6.3.1 THE PRINCIPLE OF EQUALITY

6.3.1/1 ALL SPORTS

Coubertin's reflections here focus on the basic principle of Olympism, which calls for the equality of rights of the various sports. The content of these remarks is quite significant. In this article, written in 1910, Coubertin returns to the meaning of this principle and its implementation from the beginnings of the Olympic movement. He underscores that this is one of the most important subjects in the rebirth of the Olympics.

It appears that in several countries, people are having difficulty in conceiving of the primordial and essential truth that the Olympic Games is a gathering of all sports. Yet that is how it was in the past and, even without being a great scholar, everyone generally knows that the horse races and boxing matches followed the foot races at Olympia. So no one was surprised that the basic charter of the restoration of the Olympiads should once again proclaim this logical and legitimate principle. From the very beginning, it was understood that the modern Games would include all forms of exercise practiced throughout the world today, to the greatest extent possible. Athens, Paris, St. Louis, and London provided experiences to take into consideration along with this theoretical stance. Yet even now – and the year of grace 1910 is proving to be no exception, given the deplorable upsurge in the number of similar initiatives – , simple foot races are being called "Olympic Games" by those who organize them. This approach is not always well

— 421 — OLYMPIQUES (JEUX)

JEUX OLYMPIQUES. — *Courses à pied :* 1. Départ ; 2. Cross-country ; 3. Arrivée ; 4. Courses de haies. — *Sauts :* 5. Saut en hauteur ; 6. Saut en longueur ; 7. Saut à la perche. — *Lancements :* 8. Du poids ; 9. Du marteau ; 10. Du disque. — *Levers :* 11. Du sac lourd ; 12. Des haltères. — *Tirs :* 13. Au javelot ; 14. A l'arc. — 15. *Lutte à la corde.* — *Football :* 16. Un dribbling ; 17. Une mêlée ; 18. Ballon de football (*rugby*) [le ballon de l'*association* est sphérique]. V. BOXE, CANNE, ESCRIME, ÉQUITATION, LUTTE, NATATION, SPORTS, TIR, VÉLODROME, etc.

The principle of equality of all Olympic sports in the Olympics was recognized in the Grand Larousse at the beginning of the 20th century. (N.Müller Collection)

received, as a major Belgian club found out recently. Because it insisted on using this inappropriate name, it lost the support of the World's Fair and of the Union belge des Sociétés de sports athlétiques [Belgian Union of Athletic Sports Associations]. The president of the Union, when called upon to act as honorary chairman of the meeting, refused because of the title they had chosen. As for the Brussels World's Fair, the government commission had given the International Committee its assurance beforehand that the use of the words "Olympic Games" would not be tolerated in competitions for which the administration was responsible. The International Committee has been quite sensitive about the name in many respects but, as is clear from the discussions in Luxembourg, it does not seem to be greatly moved by similar abuses. "Anyone can hold a race of asses and mules and call it Derby, because there is no way to prevent people from making asses of themselves", as one of our friends wrote to us commenting on such incidents. In fact, when one takes into account the prodigious efforts that went into organizing the four Olympiads of 1896, 1900, 1904, and 1908, one can only smile at the pretension of calling limited, specialized athletic events "Olympic."

Yet this is not the real issue. Again, these competitions are not a threat. Above all, we must look at the historical and technical error that occasions and inspires them. Since we must fight against any such error, we cannot possibly overwork ourselves in our efforts to uprooting it entirely. It is easy enough to see where the error comes from. We note that in the speeches customarily given when prizes are awarded, or at banquets, the sport for which these ceremonies or feasts are held is regularly dubbed "the best", and "the noblest" of them all. This old saw always goes hand-in-hand with commentary on the famous dictum "*mens sana in corpore sano*", which all humanists turn to whenever some hapless event requires them to praise athletic activity – an activity that, in most instances, they themselves have shunned. Sometimes it is fencing, at other times riding, sometimes rowing, other times skiing – all praised to the skies for their "beauty", their "nobility". These lofty accolades are awarded to them by their own enthusiastic practitioners. Not so long ago each sport remained completely ignorant, and disdainful, of every other sport. The restored Olympic Games have forced all sports to create unforeseen and fruitful contacts. This progress toward such valuable unification is one of the greatest aspects of the work of the Olympics. The passionate hostility that Olympism encountered among certain groups derives directly from the fact that the leaders of those groups, for entirely personal reasons, rejected the idea of unification. The vast majority of sportsmen, however, indicated that they were clearly in favor of such a move. But the principle has not been pushed as far as it can go, and clearly not all the logical consequences have been understood. Joint work has been done to ensure national participation in the Olympic Games. Yet secretly everyone continued to feel his own incontestable superiority over his neighbor, believing that the main focus of the Olympiads should be on his own sport, and that other sports deserved only secondary attention. Among the expert athletes, runners have always loudly expressed their views about their own exalted position. By dint of repetition, they have managed to persuade those who know nothing about it that runners are the only direct heirs of antiquity. Of course boxers could make the same claim, and rightly so, but they do not. Swimming is silent by nature. It was deemed of primordial importance, however, at a time when one had to know how "to read and swim" in order to count as a man. As for the equestrian sports, external forms have changed enormously, but the sports remains essentially the same at heart. Those who engage in them these days forget that equestrian sports were part of the Olympic program in antiquity.

These overlapping points of view – which are readily understood when all is said and done – help explain how it is that in the interval between modern Olympiads, one finds groups prepared to lay claim inappropriately to the title, in all good faith, calling a part by the name of the whole. Indeed in some group programs, we have even seen "Olympic Games" scheduled to take place *between* the fencing and swimming competitions. It is almost as though one were reading a list of various competitions: boxing – gymnastics – physical exercise – rowing. Have boxing, gymnastics, and rowing somehow become something other than physical exercise? When small town organizers stray into these misguided paths, the problem is not so great. The effect is harmful, however, when a major group is involved, like the one mentioned above. This group is taken seriously and is highly regarded for the high caliber of its members and the many services it has rendered to sports.

So it is impossible to overemphasize the fact that the word "Olympic" cannot and should not be used except for gatherings of a variety of sports. The term is in the public domain. If you are not afraid of looking ridiculous, and if your efforts are considerable enough to be compared to what goes into organizing a standard Olympiad, go ahead and use it. No one has the right to prevent you from doing so. But please, do not commit the heresy of applying it to a single category of sports, holding events suited for a small chapel and calling it a great cathedral. What is Olympic is universal. The Olympic Games are the temple of muscular activity in the most widely varied forms possible, though there is no need to assign degrees within some hierarchy of beauty and nobility. What is beautiful is noble, not one sport or another in and of itself, but the way in which it is played, the spirit that drives it, the soul that man brings to it. There can be nothing Olympic outside the contact and cooperation of the various branches of sports, united on a footing of total equality for the improvement of humanity.

Tous les sports,
in: *Revue Olympique,*
August 1910, pp. 115-118.

The editor has determined that this text, though unsigned, was written by Coubertin.

Women competed in Olympic swimming events for the first time in 1912. Here, the British team who won the 4 x 100 m relay. (taken from E.Petersen/ S.Hermlin, Dem Femte Olympiaden. Olympiska Spelen i Stockholm 1912 i bild och ord, Gothenburg, Ahlen & Akerlund, 1912, p.248)

The "divine" Suzanne Lenglen was the great star of the tennis courts. She won gold medals in the ladies' singles and mixed doubles in 1920. (IOC Archives)

6.3.1/2 THE WOMEN AT THE OLYMPIC GAMES

Coubertin's reservations regarding the participation of women in the Olympic Games is clear in many places in his writings. It reveals Coubertin's traditional approach based on his noble education, referring as he did primarily to the model of Antiquity and the Middle Ages.

In spite of his social-reformistic thoughts, particulary in the 1920s, he did not change his attitude any more. His only concern was the appearance of women at competitions in the Olympic stadium, not their activities in physical education.[1]

The question of allowing women to participate in the Olympic Games has not been settled. The answer cannot be negative merely on the grounds that that was the answer in antiquity; nor can it be affirmative solely because female competitors were admitted in swimming and tennis in 1908 and 1912. Not long ago, an application signed by a Neo-Amazon who intended to compete in the modern pentathlon was received. The Swedish Committee, which was free to take its own position, refused the agreement in the absence of any established legislation. So it is clear that the debate remains open.

It is good that too swift a decision has not been reached, and that this matter has dragged on. It will resolve itself quite naturally at the Congress of Paris, which will give the Olympiads their final form. Which way will it go? I am not a soothsayer, but for my own part I am not afraid of siding with the no vote. I feel that the Olympic Games must be reserved for men. First, in application of the well-known proverb depicted by Musset. A door must be either open or closed. Can we allow women access to *all* Olympic events? No? Then why should some sports be open to them while the rest are not? Above all, what basis can one use to place the barrier between the events that are permitted, and those that are not? There are not just women tennis players and swimmers. There are women fencers, women riders and, in America, women rowers. In the future, perhaps, will there be women runners or even women football players? Would such sports, played by women, constitute a sight to be recommended before the crowds that gather for an Olympiad? I do not think that any such claim can be made.

But there is another reason, a practical one. Would separate events be held for women, or would meets be held all together, without distinction as to sex, regardless of whether the competition is among individuals or teams? The second of these approaches would be logical, since the dogma of the equality of the sexes tends to expand. Yet this assumes the existence of coed clubs. There are hardly any such clubs now, with the exception of tennis and swimming. Even with coed clubs, ninety-five times out of a hundred, elimination rounds favor the men. Let us not forget that the Olympic Games are not parades of physical exercises, but aim to raise, or at least maintain, records. *Citius, altius, fortius*. Faster, higher, stronger. That is the motto of the International Committee, and the fundamental reason for the existence of any form of Olympism. Whatever the athletic ambitions of women

1 See also Coubertin: "La bataille continue [The battle continues]," in: *Bulletin du Bureau International de Pédagogie Sportive,* no 5, Lausanne 1931, pp. 5-7.

Women had been taking part in Olympic archery events since 1904. Here, the ladies' champion S.F.Queenie Newall (GBR) at the 1908 Games in London (taken from the BOA (ed.), The Fourth Olympiad. Official Report, London 1909, p.114)

may be, women cannot claim to outdo men in running, fencing, equestrian events, etc. To bring the principle of the theoretical equality of the sexes into play here would be to indulge in a pointless demonstration bereft of meaning or impact.

There remains the other possibility, that of adding women's competitions alongside men's competitions in the sports declared open to women, a little female Olympiad alongside the great male Olympiad. What is the appeal of that? Organizers are already overworked, deadlines are already too short, the problems posed by housing and ranking are already formidable, costs are already excessive, and all that would have to be doubled! Who would want to take all that on?

In our view, this feminine semi-Olympiad is impractical, uninteresting, ungainly, and, I do not hesitate to add, improper. It is not in keeping with my concept of the Olympic Games, in which I believe that we have tried, and must continue to try, to put the following expression into practice: the solemn and periodic exaltation of male athleticism, based on internationalism, by means of fairness, in an artistic setting, with the applause of women as a reward.

This combination of the ancient ideal and the traditions of chivalry is the only healthful and satisfactory one. It will impose itself on public opinion through its own strength.

Les femmes aux Jeux Olympiques,
in: *Revue Olympique,*
July 1912, pp. 109-111.

6.3.1/3 OLYMPIC RECORDS

The list of approved Olympic records drawn up in early 1920, before the Olympic Games in Antwerp, gives some idea of the level of performance at the time, and shows Coubertin's approval of this list of records in keeping with the motto "citius-altius-fortius[1]."

The Olympic records in running are as follows:

100 meters:	$10^{3/5}$ seconds
200 meters:	$21^{3/5}$ seconds
400 meters:	$48^{1/5}$ seconds
800 meters:	1 minute, 56 seconds
1,500 meters:	3 minutes, $56^{4/5}$ seconds
5,000 meters:	4 minutes, $36^{3/5}$ seconds
10,000 meters:	31 minutes, $20^{4/5}$ seconds
110 meter hurdles:	15 seconds.

1 See Chapter 5.2 in this volume.

Très Sport

QUELQUES CHAMPIONS OLYMPIQUES

A.-C. KRAENZLEIN
1er du saut en longueur aux Jeux de Paris en 1900 (7 m. 185).

L'AMERICAIN ORTON
1er du 2.500 mètres steeple, en 7 m. 34s. 2/5, aux Jeux de 1900.

En haut, Sheldon (Am.), 1er au poids (14 m. 10) en 1900. — En bas, P. O'Connor, Anglais, 1er au triple saut et 2e au saut en longueur, en 1906, aux Jeux hors série d'Athènes.

En haut, M.-W. Long (Amér.), 1er du 400 m. en 49s. 2/5 (1900). En bas, Kraenzlein (Am.), 1er du 60 m. du 110 m. haies, du 200 m. haies et du saut en longueur (1900).

En haut, Bauer (Hongrois), 1er au disque (36 m. 04), en 1900. — En bas, Baxter, (Am.), 1er en hauteur et à la perche, 2e en hauteur et en longueur et au triple saut sans élan (1900).

— 17 —

**Olympic Champions at the beginning of the 20th Century (taken from Très Sport, Edition spéciale sur les Jeux Olympiques de Paris 1924, p.17)
M. Long, 1900, 400m (49'4). G.W. Orton, 1900, 2500m steeple chase. R. Sheldon, 1900, shot put, (14,10m). P. O'Connor, 1906, triple jump, (14,075m). A. Kraenzlein, 1900, 60m (7'0), 110m hurdles (15'4), 200m hurdles (25'4), long jump (7,185m). R. Bauer, 1900, discus (36,04m). J.H. Baxter, 1900, high jump (1,90m), pole vault (3,30m).**

The Olympic records in jumping are as follows:

running high jump:	1 meter 93 cm
standing high jump:	1 meter 65 cm
running long jump:	7 meters 60 cm
standing long jump:	3 meters 48 cm
pole vault:	3 meters 95 cm

The records in shot put, discus, and javelin are:

shot put:	15 meters 34 cm
discus:	45 meters 21 cm
javelin:	61 meters

Nearly all these records are world records. However, we must point out that in pole vaulting, a record of 4 meters 3 cm has been achieved, and in javelin and discus, records of 62 meters 32 cm and 48 meters 27 cm, respectively, have also been set. In shot put, a record of 15 meters 64 has been set. Finally, the world record in the running long jump is 7 meters 61 cm. Two very interesting comments must be made about these records. First, in terms of dates, the Olympic records break down as follows: one dates from the Second Olympiad (1900); three from the Third Olympiad (1904), three from the Fourth Olympiad (1908), and eleven from the Fifth Olympiad (1912). What does the Seventh Olympiad hold in store for us? No doubt there will be a slight regression because athletes are not in as good a shape, but it will be interesting to see whether the upturn continues in 1924. Second, the Olympic records that have been beaten (we listed four above) were beaten in the years immediately following the Olympic Games, in 1901, 1909, and 1913. This is clear proof of the competitiveness engendered by Olympic events.

Les records olympiques,
in: *Almanach olympique pour 1920* [Olympic Almanac for 1920].
Lausanne (1919), pp. 6-8.
Excerpt from the article "Propos divers" ["Miscellaneous Items"], pp. 3-8.

The editor has determined that this text, though unsigned, was written by Coubertin.

6.3.2 CONSIDERATIONS RELATIVE TO CERTAIN OLYMPIC SPORTS

6.3.2/1 THE OLYMPIC GAMES AND GYMNASTICS

The standing of the sport of gymnastics was undisputed from the Olympic Games of 1896 onward. Yet quarrels arose because Austria, Germany, and Switzerland, which practiced gymnastics primarily, along with Sweden and the Nordic countries which engaged in the Swedish Gymnastics, were claiming a privileged position in the program of the Olympic Games. In this article, Coubertin repeats his unchanged position regarding gymnastics competitions, and defends himself against accusations of "Anglophilia."

One of the most recent issues of the official publication of the Union des Sociétés de Gymnastique de France [Union of French Gymnastics Associations] contains letters allegedly exchanged between the president of the International Gymnastics Federation and the president of the International Olympic Committee. This correspondence would lead one to think that so far, individual gymnastics competitions have been excluded from the program of the Olympic Games, and that they will be allowed at Los Angeles only temporarily by way of exception. They would be entering through the back door "like poor relations", in the words of one Swiss commentator, whose expression would be fully justified if the premises of his reasoning were correct. Yet that is not the case at all, and it seems to me to be time to restore the truth, not through some discreet correction as I have tried to do in the past, but in such a way that in the future, none but willful errors may be made on this point. Unfortunately, the possibility of such errors cannot be ruled out since frankness and fairness are not a clear sign of the present times.

The gymnastic sports, as I have called them from the start, include the horizontal bar, parallel bars, climbing rope, dumbbells, and barbells; to which I would like to add the rings, the flying trapeze, and the pommel horse. These gymnastic sports have been part of the mandatory, unchangeable program of the Olympic Games on the same footing as the so-called athletic sports, the water sports, the equestrian sports, and the sports of defense. This program, which was adopted unanimously at the Sorbonne in Paris on *June 23, 1894*, figured in the basic Charter of modern Olympism.

This was the starting point.

In drawing up this program, I remained faithful to the approach adopted from the start of the campaign on behalf of school sports in France.

The criticisms raised in 1888 regarding the French Gymnastics Associations may be brought up as objections, as well as a friendly but lively disagreement with a well-known gymnast and director at that time, Mr. Eugène Paz. Discipline was praised to no end in his circles; what they were after, in the final analysis, was military training.

My idea was that France was perishing from its devotion to discipline, that its entire educational system was infested with it, and that our Republic, then in its adolescence, could survive only if it managed to free youth from the shackles that bound it, preventing it from training for *self-government*. This was the source of my penchant for Anglo-Saxonism, for England and the United States. I was hardly the irrepressible admirer of those countries I have been made out to be. However, I did feel that at that point in its history, the education system of France should follow their lead, provided it did so with moderation.

The 1912 Stockholm Games included both Swedish and German gymnastics (taken from E.Petersen/ S.Hermlin, Dem Femte Olympiaden, p.127)

Later, when Edmond Demolins wanted to go further and set up actual English-style public schools in France, I did not support him. In my view, we needed to try to transform the methods used in French schools. We needed "to let air in" to those gloomy buildings, to humanize their administrations, to brighten up and liberate the lives of the "schoolkids" (a plan that was not followed in its entirety), but we needed no more than that...

To return to the matter of gymnastics, although the school associations that were proliferating at the time in the schools did bear the mark of Anglo-Saxon freedom, in the sense that I have just mentioned – Frantz Reichel remembers daily battles from that period which he loves to talk about – *gymnastic sports* were never excluded from them. For me, a gymnast who worked with gymnastic apparatus was an admirable sort of athlete. Hubert de la Rochefoucauld, who excelled at it, seemed to me to be a living advertisement for it and, in addition to him, so did our great fencers of that time, who were so elegant, and our French boxers, who were too few in number...

From that moment on, the group of *all sports* that were to serve as the basis for the restoration of the Olympic Games was indissolubly formed in my mind (I am speaking of a time more than forty years ago).

When the first interscholastic competitions in running, equestrian events, gymnastics, fencing, and swimming took place at the World's Fair of 1889, total equality was established among them. These competitions continued. The foot races became a regular championship of the young Union des Sports Athlétiques. Equestrian events went to the Société Hippique Française, which carried on the tradition. Gymnastics was entrusted to a Committee presided over by one of its elder statesmen, Mr. Sansboeuf...

Thus when the Olympic Games were restored, public opinion was prepared to see gymnasts take part in them on equal footing with the representatives of the other sports. In fact, they were outstanding at Athens, St. Louis, London, and Stockholm...

But who were these gymnasts?

They were gymnasts who worked with gymnastics equipment, and therefore they were individual gymnasts.

It was for these individuals that I wanted to restore Olympism.

The Olympic Games were established to exalt the individual male athlete, whose existence is necessary for the muscular activity of the group, and whose prowess is necessary to maintain the general competitiveness of all.

Now, however, we are being invaded – and would gladly become inundated – by team sports and by group events.

The gymnastics associations are encountering this problem among themselves. That is why it was difficult to keep the gymnastics program at the Olympic Games the same as it was from the beginning, as it should remain: a strictly individual program.

After long reflection, I suggested solutions to current technical problems, as well as moral and financial problems, when I drew up the Charter of Sports Reform submitted at Geneva last September. By now it has gone around the world, since it has been translated into so many languages and published in so many countries.

The individual gymnastic sports listed above must be considered (not just at the Olympic Games, but every day and everywhere) as the natural companions and the equals of the so-called athletic sports. It is not so much new legislation that must be worked out, but rather a state of mind, an attitude that must be created. Yet we must work toward this end with understanding and uprightness, but this has not been the case in some quarters... Sometimes it seems as though mental reservations about class and social prejudices are cropping up in these objections. Must there be a revolution here, too, to put an end to certain roadblocks in the way of progress?

In any event, Olympism remains unscathed by the accusation – thoughtlessly repeated here and there – that it has put and kept gymnastic sports at a lower level.

That accusation is now completely baseless, and any repetition of it is a deliberate lie.

Les Jeux Olympiques et la gymnastique,
in: *Le Sport Suisse*, Vol. 27,
Geneva, July 8, 1931, p. 1.

6.3.2/2 OLYMPIC LETTER IX: THE MODERN PENTATHLON

The modern pentathlon, a favorite idea of Coubertin, occupies a very special place in the history of modern Olympism. We saw its beginnings at the 1912 Olympic Games[1]. The disciplines of the pentathlon are connected with the idea that Coubertin endorsed starting in 1902 of "utilitarian gymnastics."[2]

This brief article, written in 1918, qualifies the competitor in the pentathlon as "the perfect athlete."

Someone wrote to ask me what I thought of the all-round athlete. Is he an "Olympian?" My dear correspondent, your all-round athlete is, in my view, notoriously incomplete. That, in fact, is what distinguishes him above all else. How can one use such a title to describe a young man who, perhaps, does not know how to handle a boat, ride a horse, hold a gun, or defend himself with his fists? All these are the basic underpinnings of athleticism. Just because in days past the English, in restoring running and jumping, called these exercises "athletic sports", it does not follow that the general term 'athleticism' should, in all languages, necessarily be limited to one meaning that is so specific, nor that the name of "athlete" should be denied to someone who engages in trick riding or rows with a racing team, for example. That person is an athlete in the best sense of the word. So before laying claim to Olympism, your "all-round athlete" should start by rounding himself out.

The individual who truly deserves that name "Olympian" is the competitor in the modern pentathlon, which began at the Fifth Olympiad, held in Stockholm in 1912. The following events were required of him: duel shooting at 25 meters, on visible targets, in three seconds; three hundred meters freestyle swimming; four kilometers on horseback over an obstacle course; a fencing event using the epée; and a 4,000-meter cross-country foot race.

Now that is real all-round athleticism, even though some significant events are not included.

The whole evolutionary movement toward athletic eclecticism is still in its early stages, but it is coming at a good time, since in this area as in so many others, we were becoming mired in particularly fruitless specialization, as far as manly improvement is concerned.

Lettre olympique IX: Le Pentathlon moderne,
in: *La Gazette de Lausanne,*
December 28, 1918, no. 355, p. 1.

1 See Text 4.2.2/25 "The Origins of the Modern Pentathlon".
2 See "La gymnastique utilitaire." in: *Textes choisis,* Vol. III, pp. 452 - 582.

6.4 LAUSANNE: OLYMPIC CITY

At the end of this volume we present three texts that underscore the Olympic tradition of Switzerland, and of the city of Lausanne in particular.

In 1913, a Session of the IOC and an Olympic Congress were held there. It is probable that Coubertin's liking for the city began then. In 1915, he moved the headquarters of the IOC from Paris to Lausanne. His speech at the opening ceremonies at Lausanne is reprinted here (6.4.1). In the first of his "Olympic Letters", of which there are about twenty, written to the *Gazette de Lausanne* newspaper, Coubertin described the various Olympic institutions in Lausanne.

The second text returns to the idea of a modern Olympia along the shore of Lake Geneva. In a small pamphlet published in 1918, Coubertin summarized his ideas on this issue, and presented Lausanne as the "metropolis of physical culture". Lausanne's current status as an "Olympic City" is in complete accord with Coubertin's intentions, even though he frequently went to Geneva in the last few years of his life. Coubertin died in Geneva on September 2, 1937.

The third text is a part of Coubertin's brochure "Le pays vaudois, son âme et son visage" which was written in 1919.

As well as a historical essay concerning the history of the town this essay ends with a declaration of love towards the city.[1]

6.4/1 THE CEREMONY AT LAUSANNE

In the number 2 IOC-Bulletin from 1915, this important event during World War I is described in the following unmemorial sentences: "Definitive installation of the headquarters of the International Olympic Committee at Lausanne took place the morning of Saturday, April 10, 1915. The ceremony was quite simple. In the meeting hall, beautifully decorated with flowers, the city, led by its Mayor, Professor Maillefer, welcomed the representatives of the International Committee, Baron Pierre de Coubertin, President, and Baron Godefroy de Blonay, Member of the Board, along with the members of the committee of the Congress of 1913. That Committee, when re-formed, was to be responsible for overseeing the archives and the Olympic Museum that plans called for creating soon, under the control of the board of the International Committee. Mr. Chuard, President of the Council of State, was detained by a meeting of that assembly, and sent his excuses."

Mr. Coubertin spoke as following:

Your Honor the Mayor,
Honorable Members of the City Council,

The groundwork for the deed being performed at this moment was laid long ago. Back in 1907, we planned for Switzerland to become the home base for our international activity. Since then, a Congress that brought together the friends of sport

1 Concerning Coubertin's relations to the City of Lausanne see C. Gilliéron, *Les relations de Lausanne et du Mouvement olympique à l'époque de Pierre de Coubertin (1894-1939)*. Lausanne, IOC, 1993.

45

28e du 10 avril 1915.

du dépôt du rapport de gestion de la Direction des Services Industriels pour 1914.

— Mesures concernant la situation. —

Secours militaires

La Direction de Police soumet la 83e série de secours militaires, soit 14 demandes pour un secours journalier de 37 frs et propose:

d'augmenter le secours accordé à Ernest Meyer;

de refuser le secours demandé par Aug. Monachon

La Municipalité adopte.

La séance (10h05 – 11h) est levée.

29e Séance du samedi 10 avril 1915.

Présidence de M. P. Maillefer, syndic

Assistent à la séance: MM. Gaillard, Rosset et Burnier, membres de la Municipalité. — M. Bersier, malade est excusé. Sont présents: MM. le Baron Pierre de Coubertin, président; Godefroy de Blonay, Dr Max Auckenthaler, Dr Reinbold, Maurice Millioud, Junod, rédacteur, les deux premiers membres du bureau du Comité international olympique, et les quatre suivants membres de la commission lausannoise.

M. Chuard, président du Conseil d'Etat, retenu par une séance de ce corps, se fait excuser.

Décision du Comité international olympique, d'élire domicile à Lausanne et d'y établir son siège social

La Municipalité prend acte de la récente décision du Comité international olympique déclarant élire domicile à Lausanne et y établir son siège social.

La déclaration officielle en est faite en ces termes: par M. le Baron de Coubertin, président du Comité:

"Monsieur le Syndic,

" Messieurs les membres du Conseil municipal,

" L'acte qui s'accomplit en ce moment était préparé depuis longtemps. Dès 1907, il avait été prévu que ce pays deviendrait le foyer central de notre activité internationale. Le Congrès qui depuis lors a, sous vos auspices, rassemblé à Lausanne les amis des sports et auquel les pouvoirs publics ont participé si efficacement, ne pouvait que fortifier une résolution que tout s'accorde à justifier. Cette belle cité, où la Grèce et la France comptent tant d'amis, n'est étrangère par ailleurs à aucune des formules diverses de la civilisation contemporaine. Son hospitalité est proverbiale, son renom universel. L'oeuvre d'équilibre et de beauté que le Comité International a entreprise et dirigée depuis 20 ans pourra s'y continuer fructueusement.

Minutes of the official meeting held at Lausanne Town Hall on 10th April 1915, documenting the establishment of the IOC headquarters in Lausanne (City of Lausanne Archives)

was held under your auspices. The public authorities took part in the work of the Congress to great effect. The outcome was that our resolve was strengthened, a resolve now fully justified by events. Indeed, this beautiful city where Greece and France alike have so many friends is well versed in the various expressions of contemporary civilization. Its hospitality is proverbial, its renown universal. The work of balance and beauty that the International Committee has started and directed these past twenty years will continue productively here. In the proud and independent atmosphere of Lausanne, Olympism will find guarantees of the freedom it must enjoy in order to move forward.

Our archives, which are already quite large, stood in need of faithful guardians. I am honored to introduce to you the members of the committee that will now help us to take good care of them. Memories of the recent Congress unite us, and their dedication to our work comes as no surprise.

Gentlemen, please accept our heartfelt gratitude for the welcome that the noble and illustrious city of Lausanne has shown the International Olympic Committee. In its name, I declare that from this day forward, the International Olympic Committee has chosen to reside here within your walls, and to make its headquarters here.

La cérémonie de Lausanne,
in: *Bulletin du Comité International Olympique*,
no. 2, Lausanne 1915, p. 2.

6.4/2 OLYMPIC LETTER I: OLYMPISM AT LAUSANNE

There are three aspects, three forms of Olympism in Lausanne. The International Olympic Committee is based there. The Committee was founded in 1894, and will celebrate its silver wedding anniversary next year. Its headquarters were established here in Lausanne by virtue of an agreement that was duly and solemnly recorded by the municipality in due course, with the approval of the federal government. It is the responsibility of the International Committee, the world center of the whole organization, to see to it that the quadrennial Olympiads are held in cooperation with the National Olympic Committees. These National Olympic Committees work with it, acting as links between the International Committee and the gymnastics and athletic federations in every country.

Alongside the International Committee, but in complete independence from it, there is the Olympic Institute of Lausanne, a much more recent establishment run by a smaller group, comprised almost exclusively of natives of Canton Vaud. Its goal is to revive the ancient gymnasium. Once that institution is modernized, it should become a focal point of civic spirit at the heart of the community, a factory of social peace. That was its role in ancient times. This point is readily forgotten because of all the classical institutions, it has been the least well studied and remains the least well known. Let us return to that institution. The disappearance of slavery does make it easier to restore it. The presence of the scourge of alcoholism makes such a restoration doubly desirable.

Finally, there is the Société Lausannoise des Amis de l'Olympisme [Lausanne Association of Friends of Olympism], founded last year. As its name indicates, its purpose is to support the Olympic movement in all its forms, and to see to it that Lausanne and Canton Vaud benefit as much as possible from it. It represents the individual efforts of each person, the contributions of citizens to the work as a whole.

These are the parts of the Olympic machine, and these are its fundamental ideas. I am not at all surprised at how slowly they are entering into public opinion. When it comes to new ideas, public opinion is like hard soil – drops of water seep into it bit by bit. In such circumstances, there is no substitute for the passage of time, provided that the drop of water is replaced every time it evaporates. I would like to thank the *Gazette* for giving me the opportunity to keep adding these drops. By giving me this opportunity, it is helping to further the work of this institution. I will take advantage of the opportunity afforded by these occasional letters to explain certain issues that have remained unclear. I will attempt to resolve any misunderstandings that may still remain about Olympism, its doctrine, the results achieved so far, and its hopes for the future.

Lettres Olympiques I: L'Olympisme à Lausanne,
in: *Gazette de Lausanne*,
Oct. 14, 1918, no. 282, p. 2.

6.4/3 LAUSANNE

The Capital of the Pays de Vaud has been in turn throughout the ages a Roman town and an episcopal town, a pleasure centre, an autonomous city and a captive one. Thus was formed its picturesque individuality- and the intense spirit of the place which permeates its atmosphere so perceptibly despite the modernity of its more recent transformations.

Antique Losonium, was situated lower down in the plain, at the branching of the roads leading from Vevey to Besancon and from Geneva to Avenches. It occupied thirty hectares surrounded by villas. In the Salle des Pas-Perdus of the Hotel de Ville one can see an inscription relating that the 'curateur' of those days, a certain Publius Clodius Primus of the tribe Cornelia implored the Sun and the Moon in the name of those he ruled for the 'good preservation,' as the Vaudois of today would call it, of the Emperor Marcus Aurelius.

Probably- having been pillaged and burned about the Vth century by the Barbarians whose repeated invasions laid waste the countryside, the inhabitants of Losonium abandoned a site which was too exposed and went to group themselves upon the nearby heights, oddly steep and relatively easy to defend. But it was not a war-like spirit which moved them. Christianity had made great progress in the surrounding country and soon there were formed around the first cathedral and its bodyguard of monasteries, an undisputed ecclesiastical power. To be exact, there were three distinct groups at first. On one side of the ravine at the left the Burgundians made a group; hence the name Bourg now one of the principal streets of present-day Lausanne. Beyond that on the right of the ravine another agglomeration was placed under the protection of St. Laurent. Between these summits there flowed at the bottom of the ravine two brooks toward which tended modest budding industries. The swampy junction

The Montbenon Casino in the centre of Lausanne was made available to the IOC in 1921 and 1922 for his office and an exhibition room. (IOC Archives)

Restitution of Coubertin's office in the first modest Olympic Museum (1926-70) in the Villa "Mon-Repos", site of the IOC, Lausanne (IOC Archives)

of the two streams little by little dried up and was called the Quartier de la Palud, where later was built the Hotel de Ville.

Episcopal Lausanne was never very densely populated; seven thousand inhabitants approximately, neither very rich nor poor, for when a long time afterwards in 1582 the revenues of the town were taken they amounted to only 47,877 francs. But the bishops themselves possessed considerable fortunes and the cathedral more and more sumptuous, dominated the network of little, narrow, ill-paved streets and the juxtaposition of small one- storied houses whose sole luxury was the tiny bit of garden attached to each.

Toward the year 1000, Rodolphe III, last king of Transjuran-Burgundy made a gift of the County of Vaud to the bishop of Lausanne, Henri de Lenzburg. It is noted that from 1125 the bishops were called Princes of the Empire and in fact governed as sovereigns though "in the name of the Blessed Virgin Mary", who was considered the real owner and whose administrator-delegates they claimed to be.

From that epoch also, the subjects began willy-nilly, to wrest franchises from their masters. In 1144, there was a 'Plaid General,' a sort of assembly of States, formed of deputies of the nobility, clergy and burghers.

These proxies met each year, the first three days of the month of May, in an inn in the rue de Bourg and, unprepossessing as was the setting, the support of this growing power was essential to the bishop for the making of laws and coining of money.

The bishop had a small army, but it was rather for show than action. This led to the dangerous expedient of arranging with some one of the feudal lords of the vicinity to purchase their protection. The Counts of Genevois, the Dukes of Zaehringen, the Sires de Faucigny and finally the Count de Savoy were in turn the interested protectors of Lausanne. Of these latter the more solid or more determined established their influence as a fixture, and were able to provoke and support in 1282 an insurrection of the people of Lausanne against the episcopal power: possibly fomented by the anti-clericals of the epoch whom this yoke humiliated. Nevertheless one must admit that the Lausanne folk of those days were relatively free and happy. Their town was visited by great personages who spent money lavishly. This was the case when on the 20th of October 1275 Pope Gregory X dedicated the reconstructed cathedral in the presence of Rodolphe of Habsbourg, who was therein consecrated Emperor, accompanied by thirty-seven arch-bishops, and a magnificent escort of nobles and abbots. Another joyous period, two centuries later, was when the Duke of Burgundy after the battle of Grandson, came to encamp his army near the town where the Duchess Yolande of Savoy was sojourning. For two months princes and diplomats poured in. The bishop of that time was none other than the future pope Julius II.

"Cité" and "Ville" were always separated despite their being surrounded and protected by- the same walls. A little municipal 'coup d'etat' welded them together finally- in 1481 and immediately the burghers in view of manifold favors obtained from the emperors, demanded the title and privilege of an imperial city ! The twilight of ecclesiastical power was falling. Moreover, for people who had remained so long under the jurisdiction of the mitre and crozier, the Lausannois had not become at all staid. They loved feasts and merry-making. The canons, themselves recruited from among the wealthy youths of the country, were as gay and aggressive as the rest of them to the despair of poor Saint Boniface who, for nine years bishop of Lausanne, went away comparing the town to Babylon.

Enlightened diplomacy might have been able to draw great profit from the close proximity of Savoy and Berne with between them that apple of discord: Geneva. Lausanne by opposing both of their jealous ambitions grew rich at their expense. But she threw herself into the lion's mouth when she signed in 1525 a deplorable alliance with Berne and Fribourg. This was the time when Vaudois gentlemen of Savoyard tendencies banded themselves together as "Knights of the Spoon", thus called because when they raised their spoons, they swore to "swallow" Geneva. It was Lausanne that was swallowed. Five years later upon pretext of succoring Geneva, the Bernese seized Lausanne and, establishing themselves there as despots imposed the Reformation upon her.

The resignation with which the inhabitants bent under this double yoke which weighed upon them showed that they lacked even then ardor, if not endurance. There was though at that time an "Abbaye", or club of young men which gave itself up to war-like exercises twice a week.

But unhappily it frequently finished in a saturnalia and these boys used to run through the town entirely naked singing shameless songs to a certain quarter of the town where the courtisans, recognizable by the braid sewed upon their sleeves lived herded together. Bernese rigidity finally got the better of this pagan effervescence. A dull and gloomy era began. The "Messieurs of Berne" reserved all remunerative services for themselves. The only ones left for the Lausannois were teaching and the ministry. Those who were able get away abroad went into business or led in battle. And more than one of them won to fortune and glory-sometimes both.

The arrival of the French refugees driven from their country by the Revocation of the Edict of Nantes was the signal for a general awakening. Commerce and agriculture were greatly benefited. Industries were established. Everywhere the spirit of initiative became manifest. But local patriotism continued dormant; the generous attempt of Major Davel (1723) to emancipate his fellow-citizens and his country, and for which he paid with his life, had no sequence. The thing was all the more surprising when the memory was still fresh in all minds of the fallacious promises made by the Bernese government during the 'Peasants War'. Five thousand Vaudois had naively lent a strong hand to their masters, and Lausanne had had none of the advantages agreed upon. Yet the people did not follow Davel. It needed an impulsion from outside from their neighbors of France to do this. It was not until the 24th of January 1798 that the green and white flag of the Republique Lemanique floated over Lausanne. The characteristics of modern Lausanne were already visible in the XVIII century. From all quarters of the globe people flocked to stay there. Young Englishmen and young Germans finished their education there.

The celebrated Dr. Tissot whose services were disputed by the King of Poland, the Elector of Hanover, the Duc de Choiseul, the Senate of Venice and the Emperor Joseph II, was overwhelmed with consultations to be given. Society became very learned and polished; at Mont-Repos, Voltaire had his "Zaire" played. Haller and Gibbon also contributed to the prestige of the town. There were few hotels aside from the famous Lion d'Or. But it was the fashion to lodge with the inhabitants.

**Lausanne:
The Olympic Capital
today (IOC Archives)**

A list of strangers staying at Lausanne in 1773 tells us of the presence at the house of Mr. De Chandieu of the reigning Duchess of Wurttemberg, while Mr. de Mezery sheltered the Prince d'Elbeut, Mme de Brionne and many milords'. The baron de Manteuffel and the Count de Wedel „with their tutors" were with Mr. d'Arnay, and at M. le Conseiller Polier's they were expecting the Prince de Carignan and his daughter. There were moreover the Duc de la Rochefoucauld, the Chevalier Brugton with 'Milady his spouse,' the Countess de Clermont-Tonnerre, the Bishop of Castres, the Count Razomovskv, a 'chanomesse' from Remiremont with many gentlemen, etc. Some years later Joseph II came himself, and the Chevalier de Boufflers, and Madame de Stael, and Benjamin Constant, and La Harpe, and Joseph de Maistre.

Then came the flood of emigres. At the Terror there were among the refugees an archbishop, two bishops, one hundred and sixty priests, two hundred nobles and as many merchants and artisans.

One day there were seen at the Hotel de Ville soup-kitchen "three duchesses eating from the same bowl". The sojourn of these ruined people was a source of prosperity. "Lausanne has become a commercial town", wrote Pastor Bugnion in 1797 to his nephew, a student at Leipzig,"Every day they are building new houses. It is nothing but money brokers, drafts, money at 8%, shipping of merchandise, fairs, offices, shops, movement of crowds who dream as they walk, holding in their hand a note to bearer or some letter of exchange. If this keeps on they will say we are like old Geneva where they make calculations and never laugh."

No! They will never say that. The banks, little and big did well to come and seat themselves in a ring around Place St. Francois, but laughter has not fled because they are there. Their quotations and balances have done nothing to silence the joyous chatter. The gayety which reigns in this Forum of Lausanne overflows from there in all directions. It invades the fine quarters of Ouchy as well as the steep streets by which one mounts to the assault of the old town. It climbs the antique stairways cut into the live rock, whose polished hand-rails bear the trace of centuries of wear and are yet solid; it curls about the august cathedral, the old castle with its rough walls where sits the Council of State, the ancient Academy where Sainte-Beuve loved to teach. It spreads toward Beauliela crowned by its barracks and toward Chailly sown with restful villas. One finds it everywhere, in the cafes and tea-rooms, along its tree-shaded avenues, in front of its alluring shop windows. And everywhere, it has the same turn of tranquil malice, of smiling philosophy, of full love of life.

Ask that workman and that student whose glances have just crossed on the Grand Pont, ask that advanced radical and that notorious reactionary who are conversing so amicably, ask that merchant and that dramatic author who are sauntering together down the slope of the Petit- Chene. They grumble a bit, just not to lose the habit and because it whets the appetite, but they are all agreed. "There is no place like Lausanne to live in. It is better than any where else in the world."

The Swiss Monthly, November 1925, pp. 34-39.
Extract from: "Le pays vaudois, son âme et son visage." Librairie Rouge, Lausanne, 1919, pp. 5-10

6.5 OLYMPIC RETROSPECTIVES

6.5.1 – 6.5.5 INTRODUCTION

Coubertin's articles grouped together in this section, "Olympic Retrospectives", relate to the growth of the Olympic movement at its various stages.

It was inevitable that when talking about Olympic events, given the passage of time until each of these articles was published, repetitions would arise. Yet not only does Coubertin change his style of writing, he changes his point of view as well. In this way, these articles provide important testimony about the historic development of the Olympic movement.

The first text, "L'œuvre du Comité International Olympique" [The Work of the International Olympic Committee], was published in the first volume of the *Revue Olympique* in 1901. Its purpose was to present right away to new readers what had been accomplished so far. These descriptions overlap in part with the corresponding chapters in *Une Campagne de vingt-et-un ans.* Since the founding of the IOC, time and again the IOC has been accused of having an antiquated and undemocratic structure. Throughout his life Coubertin continuously disputed this reproach.

In the second text, a reader's letter to the *London Times* dated July 13, 1908, he explains, the only way to guarantee the independence of the IOC and it's members is the structure he chose. He describes the IOC-members as "Ambassadors of the Committee".

As early as 1907 he expressed himself in the Olympic Revue[1]. He repeated the same conception in 1928 in his "Message to All Athletes and Participants Meeting at Amsterdam for the Ninth Olympiad", which is printed in this volume[2]. There he tells his successors that "the authority of the IOC, it's indebitent recruitment guarantee that traditions will be upheld".

The here mentioned reply of the Times Editor is of interest because Coubertin's part in the realization of the first Olympic Games 1896 is discussed.

The third text is a special kind of retrospective piece. In January 1919, Coubertin wrote to the members of the IOC, giving them guidelines on the activities of the IOC after the forced interruption due to World War I, and exhorting them to take part in its future activities.

The last Olympic retrospective published here is the lecture Coubertin gave for the fortieth anniversary of the founding of the IOC, celebrated at Lausanne in June 1934. The speech contains a host of facts, along with self-criticisms and recommendations. Here is Coubertin at 70, retracing the history of his Olympic movement, and taking stock of it.

1 See Coubertin, "Critiques et calomnies." in: *Revue Olympique* 1907, no 1, pp. 197-198.

2 See text 5.2/10.

6.5.1 THE WORK OF THE INTERNATIONAL OLYMPIC COMMITTEE

As we begin the year 1901, the International Olympic Committee is entering its seventh year. This would seem an opportune moment to recall the circumstances that led up to and accompanied the founding of the Committee, and to take stock of the work we have accomplished so far.

On November 25, 1892 a large audience gathered at the old Sorbonne in Paris to hear three lectures on athleticism in Antiquity, in the Middle Ages, and in the modern era, given by Georges Bourdon, Jusserand – French Ambassador to Denmark – , and Pierre de Coubertin. The conference was one of a series of festivals and meetings held by the Union des Sociétés Françaises des Sports Athlétiques to celebrate its fifth anniversary and the rapid progress it had achieved in so short a time. At the end of his lecture Mr. Coubertin stated that from that time on, while continuing to work with Union, he was going to devote himself to the second half of the task he had set out to accomplish: "to restore the Olympic Games on principles and conditions that are in keeping with the demands of modern life". As a result, shortly thereafter he proposed that the Board of the Union des Sports Athlétiques hold an International Athletic Congress. The Congress would meet in Paris on June 15, 1894, and in an eight-day session would try to bring the major Sports Associations of the world together, to coordinate their regulations (particularly with respect to the delicate issue of amateurism), and to make it possible to hold new Olympiads.

Three commissioners were responsible for handling preparations for the Congress: Mr. Coubertin, secretary general of the Union des Sports Athlétiques, for continental Europe; Mr. C. Herbert, secretary of the Amateur Athletic Association, for England and its colonies; and Professor W. M. Sloane, of Princeton University (United States), for the American continent. A preliminary meeting took place at the University Club in New York on November 27, 1893, and another at the Sports Club in London, on February 7, 1894.

THE CONGRESS OF PARIS

The Congress opened before an audience of two thousand on Saturday, June 16, 1894, in the large amphitheater of the new Sorbonne. Heading the long list of honorary members were His Majesty the King of the Belgians, Their Royal Highnesses the Prince of Wales, the Crown Prince of Sweden and Norway, and the Crown Prince of Greece, His Imperial Highness the Grand Duke Vladimir of Russia, Their Excellencies the Ministers of Public Instruction of Austria, Hungary, etc., the President of the Paris City Council, His Lordship the Duke of Aumale, etc. After a remarkable speech by Baron de Courcel, Senator and President of the Congress, and a lecture by the delightful poet Jean Aicard, the hymn to Apollo recently uncovered in the ruins of Delphi was sung by Madame Jeanne Remacle, and repeated by a choir of singers from the Opera accompanied by the harp. The effect was enthralling, worthy of the occasion and of the grandiose setting.

Other equally successful celebrations were held during the Congress. The one on Thursday evening, June 21, hosted by the Racing-Club de France at its site in the Bois de Boulogne, was a major success. The foot races and fencing bouts held on the illuminated lawns under the flames of the candelabras while an orchestra and hunting bands played alternately among the groves made for an unusual and quite appealing sight. Other meetings were held by the Paris Société de Longue Paume, the Société de Sport of the Island of Puteaux, and the Société d'Encouragement au Sport Nautique. Participants in the Congress were received at the City Hall of Paris by the President of the City Council, and at the Ministry of the Interior by Mr. Charles Dupuy, then President of the Council of Ministers. On Saturday evening, June 23, a closing banquet was held at the palmarium at the Jardin d'Acclimatation, followed by a torch-lit procession of cyclists.

This is not the forum to summarize the work of this Congress, whose participants, in addition to the members of the administration, included seventy-nine delegates from athletic or university associations representing a total of thirteen nationalities: French, Greek, Russian, Italian, Dutch, English, Australian, Swedish, Belgian, Spanish, Hungarian, Czech and American. In an upcoming issue we will print a list of the resolutions adopted by the Congress at the recommendation of its two commissions, one of which examined issues related to amateurism, while the other dealt with restoring the Olympic Games. The first commission was chaired by Mr. Gondinet, President of the Racing-Club de France, with Prof. W. M. Sloane, delegate from the New York Athletic Club and Princeton University, and R. Todd, delegate from the National Cyclist's Union of England, as vice-chairmen. The second commission was chaired by Mr. Bikelas, delegate from the Pan-Hellenic Gymnastics Association, with Baron de Carayon La Tour, delegate from the Société Hippique Française, as vice-chairman. The conclusions of these commissions, in terms of the breadth of the topics addressed and the competence of those who took part in the debate, amount to what is in all probability the most in-depth study ever attempted by an international meeting on sports. It is good for these conclusions to be brought to the attention of the sports world once again. They are a natural starting point for future efforts and improvements.

Before they went their separate ways, the delegates to the Congress appointed a permanent International Committee responsible for implementing the resolutions of the Congress concerning the Olympic Games, which were restored by unanimous vote. The members of that committee were Messrs. Coubertin and Callot for France; Bikelas for Greece; General de Boutovsky for Russia; Lord Ampthill and C. Herbert for England; Prof. W. Sloane for the United States; Commander Balck for Sweden; Count Lucchesi-Palli for Italy; Kemény for Hungary; Dr. Jiri Guth for Bohemia; L. A. Cuff for Australia; and Dr. Zubiaur for South America. Shortly thereafter, Dr. Gebhardt joined the committee to represent Germany, as did Count M. De Bousies for Belgium. Count Lucchesi-Palli resigned and was replaced by Dr. d'Andria Carafa. The committee's first task was to work on holding the 1896 Olympic Games, scheduled to take place in Athens.

THE OLYMPIC GAMES OF 1896

This was not an easy assignment. Despite the telegram in which His Majesty the King of the Hellenes had consented to support the work of the Congress of Paris, and despite the enthusiasm stirred up in Athens by the proclamation of the restoration of the Games, the Greek government, headed by Mr. Tricoupis, soon showed that it did not favor the plan. Under his influence, a letter was sent to Mr. Coubertin just as he was preparing to leave for Greece, suggesting that he not come and declining the honor that the Congress had paid to the Greek people. Mr. Coubertin, who had resolved to take no notice of these statements, arrived in Athens in October and immediately began work to awaken popular enthusiasm. Mr. Bikelas took over for Mr. Coubertin two months later, and completed this effort at overcoming resistance and smoothing out obstacles. Soon, an organizing committee chaired by His Royal Highness the Crown Prince of Greece began its work. On April 5, 1896, in the stadium at Athens restored by the generosity of Mr. Averof, a Greek patriot, King George solemnly opened the first Olympiad in the presence of the royal family, ministers, the diplomatic corps, and a huge crowd that grew in size over the next few days. In the end, an unexpected 70,000 spectators awaited the arrival of the runner from Marathon. The King of Serbia, the Grand Duke George of Russia and the Archduchess Maria Theresia of Austria honored the festivities with their presence. The fencing competitions were held in the rotunda of the Zappeion Exhibition Hall, the bicycle races in the Phaleron velodrome, the water sports in Zea Bay, and shooting and the other exercises in the marvelous setting of the Stadium. The illumination of the public monuments, the blaze of the Acropolis, and the night-time festival of the Piraeus alternated with glittering receptions held at the royal palace and at the legations. The Games closed with great ceremony on Wednesday, April 15.

This unforgettable week left such a stirring memory in the hearts of the Greek people that immediately a movement began to transform the Olympic Games restored by the Congress of Paris into a purely Greek institution permanently headquartered in Athens. The International Committee could not accept that idea, and while it did wish to see Pan-Hellenic Games take place in Greece, it considered that its duty, as well as the interests of the restoration the Olympic Games, commanded it to remain faithful to the program devised in 1894. This point of view was expressed in the letter of thanks sent by Mr. Coubertin to His Majesty the King of the Hellenes following the Athens Games. Mr. Coubertin expanded upon it in many communiqués sent to the international press.

THE CONGRESS OF LE HAVRE

The purpose of the Olympic Congress held at Le Havre from July 23 to August 1, 1897 was not to revise or to expand the work of the Congress of Paris, but rather to study issues of hygiene and education as related to physical exercise. It met at the City Hall of Le Havre, with the President of the French Republic as honorary president. The President received the participants in the Congress on two occasions. They took part in sea-going excursions and in a series of festivals, torch-lit gymnastics, a costume parade of cyclists, and an illumination of the cliffs at La Hève, among other things. Among the most warmly applauded speakers were the Rev. Didon, prior of the Collège d'Arcueil, Gabriel Bonvalot, the famous explorer, and the Rev. de Courcy-Laffan, headmaster of Cheltenham School and the delegate from the Conference of Headmasters of England. Much work and many heated debates resulted in a series of interesting resolutions, to which we shall refer as necessary. One might find fault with these resolutions for not being sufficiently general, because though many foreign delegates were present, the French point of view won out over the international perspective on one or two occasions. The prefect and sub-prefect of the Seine-Inférieure region, the city of Le Havre, and the representative of the Minister of Public Instruction participated in the 1897 Congress, whose deliberations were overseen by the president of the International Olympic Committee.

THE OLYMPIC GAMES OF 1900

Misunderstandings and an irritating lack of decisiveness nearly scuttled the great athletic exhibition that was to coincide with the Paris World's Fair. It is appropriate to recall here exactly what the role of the International Committee is, because errors have frequently been made on this subject. The mission of the International Committee is not to hold the Olympic Games, but to cause them to be held regularly, in conformity with the resolutions passed by the Congress of Paris. Of course, between Olympiads the Committee is authorized to sponsor special exhibitions that are clearly Olympic in nature, and to initiate meetings of the kind held in Le Havre in 1897. Once the national committee that will run the Games in the country chosen to host them has been formed and begins its work, the International Committee merely supports it as best it can, without otherwise becoming involved into the details of the operation. Since 1894, those who worked to restore the Games have insisted not only that it is appropriate to allow each country the greatest possible latitude in preparing for its Olympiad, but that the resulting diversity is a prerequisite for the success for each Olympic Games – and consequently for the long-term survival of the institution.

The office of the General Commissioner of the World's Fair focused serious attention on the athletic portion of the program as early as 1896. But as it became overwhelmed by more pressing concerns, its interest seemed to wane. As a result, by spring 1898 no preparations were underway, and well-justified fears were voiced on several occasions both in France and abroad concerning the success of the Paris Games. The rumor even spread that at the last minute, the World's Fair would refuse to hold the Games at all. That is when Mr. Coubertin called for the formation of an organizing committee comprising the most highly regarded sportsmen, under the chairmanship of the Viscount de La Rochefoucauld. The committee drew up and published a schedule for the Games, and decided to call upon the major athletic associations of Paris and the Compiègne Golf Association to assist in holding the Games. These associations agreed immediately to place their fields and equipment at the disposal of the organizers.

Pierre de Coubertin loved the mountains and often visited Haute Savoie in France. Here, near Combloux in 1934, he collects flowers, grasses and stones which he carefully arranged as a souvenir. (Navacelle Collection)

The office of the General Commissioner finally got around to doing its long-overdue duty, appointing a Committee headed up by the eminent and highly competent Mr. Mérillon, a former Representative and President of the Union Nationale des Sociétés de Tir [National Union of Shooting Associations]. This Committee used the same approach once it got down to work. The International Committee offered the same unselfish and immediate assistance to the official organizers that it would have provided to the private initiative. It was the members of the International Committee, Messrs. Sloane, Herbert, Jiri Guth, Keméný, Colonel Balck, Count Brunetta d'Usseaux, Dr. Gebhardt, Count Mercati, and Captain Holbeck, who guaranteed the participation of foreign athletes in these competitions. Most of these committee members accompanied their fellow countrymen to the competitions. In spring 1899, Mr. Coubertin had asked them to work hard to ensure that these athletes would take part, particularly because there was little time left for them to prepare to compete. For the same reason and at Mr. Mérillon's request, Coubertin himself traveled to Germany and the Scandinavian countries where two preparatory meetings were held, one in Stockholm, the other in Berlin under the leadership of the German imperial commissioner, Dr. Richter. At the latter meeting, Their Highnesses Prince Aribert von Anhalt and Lt. Gen. Prince von Salm-Horstmar were in attendance.

Whatever their flaws may have been, the competitions in 1900 were an impressive athletic display and their impact on athleticism was beneficial. May the 1904 Games advance the work of restoring the Olympic Games, winning over more and more youths around the world and enabling the Olympics to serve the cause of international peace and friendship better and better.

L'Œuvre du CIO,
in: *Revue Olympique*,
January 1901, pp. 5-11.

The editor has determined that this text, though unsigned, was written by Coubertin.

6.5.2 TO THE EDITOR OF THE TIMES: THE OLYMPIC GAMES (JULY 13, 1908)

The Olympic Games
To the Editor of the Times

Sir, it really seems a pity that the author of the article on the Modern Olympic Games should not have applied to the International Olympic Committee for information respecting their revival, for a great many mistakes which he has committed in reviewing this matter would thus have been avoided. For instance, I completely fail to see how my plans could have been in any way influenced by Mr. Averoff's decision to reconstruct the Athenian Stadium, since, when Mr. Averoff decided to undertake this reconstruction, the International Congress which I had called forth had already met at the Paris Sorbonne (1894) and the revival of the games had already been decicded by 79 representatives of many leading institutions and societies coming from 13 different European and American countries.

It was that same Paris Congress that chose Athens as the seat of the first Olympiad of 1896 a marble stadium did not seem at all necessary to make the games a success and Paris as the seat of the second 1900. Again , the Paris Congress of 1894 created the International Olympic Committee as a permanent body which has never since ceased to exist and work. People ask now and then why the members of the International Committee are not regular delegates nominated by the leading athletic organizations of each country. Indeed they are not. The privilege of the committee of nominating its own members is essential. They act in their respective countries rather as the "ambassadors" of the committee, and, if I may use such an expression, as "the trustees of the Olympic idea". Their independence and stability answer for the great work achieved by the committee between 1894 and 1908. No international organization could have succeeded unless standing above the petty quarrels and daily discussions of the athletic federations and clubs.

The International Committee never opposed the idea of holding Greek Olympiads apart from the original series; but it resisted any suggestion to give up the original plan and abandon the holding of its own international Olympiads. As to the connexion with exhibitions, it was merely accidential. Besides the connexion this time is more apparent than real, the games being under the complete control of the British Olympic Association, which was formed in 1904 after the International Olympic Committee had held its meeting of that year in London at the Mansionhouse under the patronage of his Majesty the King.

Allow me to direct your readers, if they care to know more respecting the history of modern Olympiads, to the articles published in the French periodical L'Education Physique (May 31, August 31, September 19 and 30, 1907; April 30, May 19 and 31, 1908), as well as to the article I published myself in the last number of the Fortnightly Review.

Believe me, Sir, yours very truly,

BARON PIERRE DE COUBERTIN,
President International Committee
Harrow on the Hill, July 9, 1908

Comment by the editor of the *Times*:

No one could or would wish to dispute to the eminent services which Baron Pierre de Coubertin has rendered to the cause of international athletics; but we may point out that his letter, which complains of "a great many mistakes", refers only in one single instance to any alleged error in the article which he criticizes. We did not say that his plans for reviving the Olympic Games were influenced by M. Averoff's decision to reconstruct the Athenian Stadium, or that M. Averoff's decision preceded the International Congress at which the revival was decided upon. We merely observed that it was a combination of M. de Coubertin's plans with M. Averoff's work which rendered the first Olympic Games at Athens a success. The remainder of his letter deals with matters of opinion.

The Times, London,
July 13, 1908, p.23.

6.5.3 LETTER TO THE MEMBERS OF THE INTERNATIONAL OLYMPIC COMMITTEE (JANUARY, 1919)

In resuming the presidency of the International Olympic Committee after a three-year interval, an office to which you have re-elected me for a third ten-year period, I must express my gratitude for this latest token of confidence and friendship. I must also thank our colleague and friend, Godefroy de Blonay, for the zeal and tact that he brought to the administration of our Committee from 1915 until now.

In a few weeks, we will celebrate the twenty-fifth anniversary of the founding of the Committee. Those who labored in the early days, back in 1894, are still represented among us. Four of them remain. In addition to me, there is General Balck (Sweden), Professor Sloane (United States), and Dr. Jiri Guth (Bohemia). We did not wait for recent events to recognize the athletic independence of the Czechs, and to defend that independence with respect to and against all nations.

This celebration will mean that we will receive expressions of support and gifts, once again; those of the Council of State of Canton Vaud and of the President of the French Republic have already been announced. It will also offer us an appropriate opportunity to review the work we have done during the past quarter century, and to assess the tasks that remain.

We are all well aware of the increasing excellence and success of the first five Olympiads of the modern era: Athens (1896), Paris (1900), St. Louis (1904), London (1908), and Stockholm (1912). The number of athletes, the quality of the events, and the pomp and circumstance of the ceremonies have all increased in a way that few institutions have managed to achieve to a similar degree in so short a period of time. All the people of the world had agreed to meet in Berlin in 1916, to celebrate the Sixth Olympiad worthily. But the German empire saw fit to unleash a terrible war, thus placing a bloody mark on the date set aside for the cult of Youth and Peace.

While these Games were taking place one after another, leaving behind such grand monuments as the stadiums at Athens and Stockholm, our Committee called a series of International Congresses at Le Havre (1897), Brussels (1905), Paris (1906), and Lausanne (1913), bringing together educators, technical experts, artists, and scholars. We asked them to join us in examining the interplay between athletic and moral education, the laws of athletic hygiene, the links that might once again tie Literature, the Arts, and Sports together, the role of sports psychology, etc. These congresses were attended by such men as Theodore Roosevelt, Rev. Didon, G. Ferrero, Marcel Prévost, and General Dodds, and produced a number of useful documents. Above all, they made it possible to create the athletic eclecticism that has been both the prerequisite for and the greatest benefit of restored Olympism. Until then, practitioners of the various sports had paid no attention to each other, or had been adversaries. They lived in isolation, believing that their preferred exercises were mutually exclusive, or mutually harmful. Olympism required them to work together. In this way, Olympism has done more than merely intensify the athletic movement. It has opened up new and fruitful paths for physical education.

This is not the place for me to retrace our work in detail. The Revue Olympique provides a summary of that history, in the more than one hundred issues that have been published since its founding as a monthly publication. Its articles, always anonymous, have been used widely for years by many authors who have drawn information and inspiration from them.

The Olympic Cup, that prodigious traveler, has continued its peregrinations. It was in America at the beginning of the war, when it was awarded to the Amateur Athletic Union of the United States. From there, it returned to England, to Rugby College, which had won it for 1915. Then you awarded it to the Confrérie St.-Michel of Ghent, the famous fencing association so well-known to all, followed by the Nederlandsche Voetbal Bond which has rendered such great service to the cause of sports in Holland. Finally, this year, you are giving it to the Institut Olympique of Lausanne. This is an institution dedicated to athletic education, my own work. In 1917, all of its activity was focused on the interned French and Belgian officers and soldiers, helping them to recover physically and mentally.

At the recommendation of the United States Olympic Committee, we have elected Judge Bartow S. Weeks, secretary general of the Amateur Athletic Union, to succeed our late colleague, Evert J. Wendell. Judge Weeks replaced James E. Sullivan in his position as secretary general. Mr. Bartow Weeks, a delegate to the Congress of Paris in 1914, was already a friend of the Committee, and we salute his arrival among us, as well as that of His Excellency Mr. Dorn y de Alsua, Ambassador of Equador, and of Mr. J. P. Matheu, Consul General of San Salvador, respectively the President and Secretary General of the "Latin American Olympic Propaganda Committee", founded under our auspices a year ago. The publications of that group, along with a pamphlet widely distributed by the Spanish Olympic Committee, have been effective in spreading the Olympic idea in Spanish-speaking countries. To the same end, the United States Committee has had a large number of Olympic flags made up, and has given them to universities and associations in the New World as a symbol of the perennial nature of Olympism, and of the upcoming resumption of these solemn celebrations.

Given these recent elections, our numbers have remained steady, with new countries added to our lists replacing those that are no longer represented.

So much for the past. Our attention, however, must be focused on the future. Recent events have resulted in entirely new circumstances. Sports are on the front lines of the forces that brought about victory. It is to sports that we owe the magnificent innovations that made it possible for England and the United States to transport unexpected armies to the theater of war. It is thanks to them that the valiant Sokols covered their homelands with laurels, even before the borders were set and freedom assured. It is through sports that France, as heroic as in 1870 but infinitely stronger, was able to raise a powerful rampart of muscle against the invasion. After helping train incomparable soldiers, athleticism also helped sustain their zeal and console them in their suffering. They played football, they fenced, and they boxed right up by the front lines and far from them, as well, in the sad prisoners' camps. Public opinion is aware of these things, and appreciates them. Well-deserved enthusiasm will guarantee the value of physical education, and proclaim the triumph of sports.

Yet with success comes risk, and the greater the success, the heavier the consequences. Excesses can provoke reactions that might compromise the results achieved. There is one matter that calls out for our immediate attention: excessive public competitions. This was a disturbing trend before the war. No one is asking that competitions be eliminated because the principle is essential to maintaining athletic activity. Yet the increasing number of competitions is a serious threat, because it is creating a large class of individuals who go to athletic events not to participate in them themselves, but to hang around with a small number of extremely talented athletes, drinking in the applause, placing bets, and turning a profit on their performances.

The lion's share of responsibility for this state of affairs lies no doubt with the federations. As they lose sight of their original educational role, too often they engage in sectarian trade unionism based on legislation that is, in turn, based on exclusion. In order to coerce associations and individuals to join ranks with them, some federations, linked to others through agreements, organized boycotts, forbidding their members to meet with independent players and even denying those who had sports fields the right to rent them to independents. Thus the practice of a sort of athletic excommunication spread, a practice that was even more ridiculous than it was loathsome. In addition, alleged professionals were disqualified on the pretext of upholding a doctrine of pure amateurism, even though their sporting spirit and selflessness were greater than those of many, duly qualified, sham amateurs. Hampered by difficulties in enforcing regulations that were neither logical nor clear, federation directors also failed to work toward streamlining athletic regulations to eliminate the grounds for technical conflicts. That would have made it easier to hold competitions, coordinate record keeping, etc. Efforts in that direction undertaken by the Olympic Committee in 1914 seem to have been followed up in France by a Commissioner of that Congress, Mr. Paul Rousseau, and we may hope to see it succeed some day.

Yet there is still no sign that the federations realize the need to adopt a broad, tolerant policy on the other matters. This new era demands such a change. For a long time, the renewed interest in athleticism during the nineteenth century was merely an occasional pastime for rich and semi-idle youth. Our Committee has fought more than anyone to make it a habitual pleasure of the youth of the lower middle class. Now it must be made fully accessible to proletarian adolescents. All sports for all people, that is the new goal to which we must devote our energies, a goal that is not in the least impracticable. The recent war was won by the Western powers thanks to a "sacred union", based on the conviction that the two-fold stakes of the fight were the political freedom of States, and the social equality of individuals. If we were to forget the second goal after achieving the first, civilization would run the risk of exploding like a boiler without a safety-valve.

Athleticism has a major role to play in bringing about social reforms. As I tried to demonstrate in my lecture to the Association des Hellènes Libéraux [Association of Liberal Hellenes] (February 1918), the athletic group is, in a way, the basic cell of democracy. The only inequality that continues to exist in that group derives from nature, whereas artificial inequality introduced by men is banished. Mutual assistance and competition, the two essential elements of any democratic society, necessary rub shoulders in this group, because sports – the leveler of class distinctions – , is also a powerful alternative to bad instincts, an antidote for alcoholism, a pursuer of tuberculosis, an unequaled agent for physical and moral health in our time. Finally, these groups sow the seeds of observation, critical thinking, self-control, calculated effort, expenditure of energy, and a practical philosophy in the face of failure. These are qualities that this generation needs desperately. If it does not acquire them, it is almost certain to fail in the tasks ahead.

One can readily understand that in the face of such boundless duties, the athletic world needs to renew itself, to expand its bases, and to transform its inner workings. "All sports for all people" cannot be accomplished through the efforts of existing groups only. Gymnastics and sports associations have furnished the best possible instrument for propaganda. They remain an essential – but not unique – factor for progress. The effectiveness of their actions will be directly linked to the liberalism of their regulations. Their present duty is to place themselves at the service of the masses without asking for anything in return, because those who must be reached now have neither money nor time to lose. Yet we must manage to arouse the need for sports in them. The physical and moral health of the nations of the world depends on it.

Once again, Sweden and the United States provide us with fruitful avenues to pursue. I will merely mention them here, because we will be inviting the parties involved to study this issue in depth soon. You are familiar with that Swedish institution that is a sort of athletic knighthood, with its three degrees of gold, silver and bronze insignia. Wearing of the insignia is governed by law. The athletic events are divided into five groups. The first covers gymnastics and swimming, the second jumping; the third, foot races; the fourth fencing and throwing. The fifth comprises long-distance events, ten to twenty kilometer races to be run on foot, on skis, and on bicycles, all within a given time limit. One must pass one test in each group. Anyone who does so receives the bronze insignia. If he does so for four years (consecutively or not), he gets the silver insignia; eight years and it's the gold. The gold insignia is won immediately if the candidate is more than thirty-two years old. The competition has everything it needs to generate intense popular propaganda. Such competitions, when made accessible to everyone without precondition or pointless inquiry, may change the hearts and minds of a whole generation.

No less intriguing is the way that the Amateur Athletic Union of the United States has celebrated the national July 4th holiday in New York since 1910. In previous years, there had been a number of accidents and deplorable excesses. People wanted a "Safe and Sane Fourth", and Sullivan swung into action. On July 4, 1912, forty-two meets in the public parks and gardens of New York and its suburbs brought together over thirty thousand competitors. They awarded 1,492 medals to winners of foot races, jumping competitions, throwing, etc. A thousand members of the gymnastics and athletics associations made sure that everything ran smoothly. We might add that in many cities in America, exercise fields already exist. There are tracks, gymnastics equipment, fences, etc., available free to the public. In Scandinavia, open-air spaces ingeniously designed for wrestling, with tarpaulins stretched over a bed of sand, are available to amateurs as well.

The time has come to make a firm commitment to the direction shown by these intriguing innovations. There is a magnificent career ahead of athleticism, provided that athleticism avoids overly-narrow structures, discards outdated distinctions, and above all condemns self-centered calculation and self-interested attention. Athleticism has already made its mark in education. Now it must lend effective support to the social transformation that the war has made inevitable, and that everyone must welcome with a loyal and joyful heart.

This expansion of the athletic horizon toward which we were already working comes at a time when our previous efforts have become highly prized. I have just been informed by the Ambassador of Greece to Switzerland that the Greek government is going to set up a stele in the ruins of Olympia to commemorate the restoration of the Olympic Games, and honoring the work to which I have been lucky enough to devote all my strength for the past twenty-five years. Relying on your continued warm and faithful support, I face the possibility of a resumption of certain hostilities without fear, for they are doomed to fail. We must not be surprised if our ideals still lie far beyond those of many people, nor if they run counter to the interests of many. Independent and united, we have faith in ourselves. For a long time now we have set our sights on the heights that restored Olympism can and must achieve.

Pierre de Coubertin

Lettre à Messieurs les membres du CIO.
Special printing: Lausanne, January 1919 (Archives of the IOC).
English version in: Coubertin, *The Olympic Idea,* Schorndorf 1967, pp. 67-72.

6.5.4 FORTY YEARS OF OLYMPISM, 1894-1934

Remarks delivered at the celebration of the fortieth anniversary of the restoration of the Olympic Games by Baron de Coubertin, Founder and Honorary President of the Olympic Games, Saturday, June 23, 1934, at the Aula of the University of Lausanne.

Your Excellency, the Member of the Council of State, Your Excellency Mr. Syndic, Mr. Pro-Rector, my dear Secretary General and friend, I am touched by your remarks. I thank you with my whole heart. Wrapped as they were in the warmth of true friendship, they are truly comforting.

Ladies and Gentlemen,

On this festive occasion, my thoughts turn to previous occasions on which the restoration of the Olympic Games has been commemorated at regular intervals.

In 1904, thirty years ago, we mentioned this anniversary only among ourselves. The restored institution was only ten years old at the time. Ten years! What is that in terms of an institution that lasted for thousands of years, and is hoping to do so once more? Yet that celebration was quite meaningful, through actions that bore every sign of succeeding. The International Committee met in London in 1904 under the patronage of King Edward, in the old palace of the Lord Mayor. We had six days of fruitful meetings enhanced by charming celebrations. Even then, the IOC was treated as a great international power, a fact attested to by the telegrams received from the King of Italy and from the Prince Colonna, Syndic of Rome, welcoming the decision that Italy's capital would be chosen as the site of the Games of the Fourth Olympiad. I have previously recounted why the Olympiad in Rome was delayed. Since then, it has remained on the horizon as something that is bound to happen.

Even as the IOC was holding this Session on the banks of the Thames, the Games of the Third Olympiad were being readied along the Mississippi. These Games were flawed in many respects, yet they did underscore that from the start the general, global nature of Neo-Olympism was beyond dispute. All games, all nations. In vain did subsequent acts of treachery attempt to spread the idea that this was an unstable venture, timidly making its way along as circumstances allowed. The truth is quite different. This time, Olympism was born fully equipped, like Athena! Its program was complete, and its geography intact. The whole planet would be its domain.

June, 1914. Ten years later. In the interim, the Games of the Fourth and Fifth Olympiads were held very successfully in London and Stockholm, with grandeur and eurythmia in their surroundings, enthusiasm in their crowds, and perfection in their details. It seems quite a simple thing, now, to praise Neo-Olympism. But the halo of its prestigious heritage was acknowledged in the blush of its twentieth anniversary. Representatives of the national committees already established in most countries were called to meet in Paris. Fourteen days of festivities made for a suitable setting for their meeting in that great metropolis. The public authorities competed with the ancient monarchic aristocracy in making their stay more pleasant, the hospitality more sumptuous. This was something never seen before, for such cooperation had never taken place under the Republican regime. Politically, the IOC had already shown its power by imposing athletic autonomy on Bohemia and Finland, which the Hapsburg and Romanov empires had initially refused to acknowledge. In addition, a special conference in 1906 established the program for the Art Competitions, that "Pentathlon of the Muses" which, from then on, would become an inseparable part of the quadrennial Games. The recently designed flag, with its five multicolored rings against a white background, fluttered in the wind and protocol fulfilled the prestigious formalities that marked the solemnity of the occasion.

A strange coincidence. Just after the Olympic Games were restored, President Carnot was assassinated. Then the festivities of 1914 celebrating its twentieth anniversary came to an end in the tragic light of upcoming catastrophes. No sooner had the participants gone their separate ways than Archduke Franz Ferdinand perished in that homicidal attack. But Olympism fears no tragedy and can stand up to any peril. That is why it survived four years of all-out war without a scratch. During those years, Olympism was honored during a special day "dedicated" to it, as is the American custom, at the World's Fair in San Francisco, a city where peace efforts had taken refuge. There has been no let up in applications to host future Olympiads. No sooner had peace been restored in fact, if not in law, than the IOC, meeting in Lausanne (which became its permanent headquarters in the intervening years), celebrated its twenty-fifth anniversary in the presence of Gustave Ador, President of the Swiss Confederation. Reprehensible plots were concocted in which alleged athletes – unaware of the fundamental fairness of frontal attacks in sports – tried to upset the order of the Olympiads and assume direction of them. Not a trace of these plots remains. General Pershing, with a single stroke of his honest pen, crossed out the term "Olympic" which they wanted to use to deck out allied military games. President Clemenceau, sending a squadron of planes to Lausanne, asked the IOC to see the gesture as an expression of his complete support.

In five years, restored Olympism would turn thirty (as would the Prince of Wales, who was born on the same day). These years were well spent. At Antwerp, the Seventh Olympiad picked up where the series had left off. The city was gleaming and peaceful, even though it had been liberated only recently. At the City Hall, King Albert presided over the first meeting of the Session of the IOC. He formally opened the Games in a stadium that was pretty much improvised out of sheer energy and the clever actions of the Count de Baillet. In 1921, a congress at Lausanne picked up where the 1914 congress had left off, this time with the addition of delegates from the international federations that had, at long last, completed their lengthy training period. The Winter Games were established. In 1923, the IOC held its Session at the Capitoline Hill in Rome, a Session opened by the King of Italy, and continuing the tradition of the magnificent meetings in London, The Hague, Stockholm, and Budapest.

1924. The celebration of the thirtieth anniversary, coinciding with the Games of the Eighth Olympiad, was as brilliant as Paris could possibly make it, though it did not equal the eurythmia of the celebrations in 1914 perhaps. This was the moment that the restorer of the Games chose to give up day-to-day management of the Olympics. In his view after thirty years in office, his work was done. In response to the extreme confidence of his colleagues, he traded in his former position for a lifetime honorary presidency. Yet to facilitate certain details, election of his successor was put off until 1925. Voting began that year in Prague. This is an appropriate time to congratulate and to thank the individual elected in 1925 (and already re-elected since then) for his profuse and wide-ranging efforts. His work is commendable, too, because nothing is more meritorious than knowing when to continue what is already in place, just seeing to it that operations run more and more smoothly all the time. One is so often tempted to knock down a cornice here or a wall there, to redo them and sign one's own name to the project, even if ultimately one has to restore them more or less to their original condition.

Nevertheless, there is never enough time to do everything. Drawn into a technical role that continued to expand, the IOC was unable to pursue the educational work that was the outcome of the 1897 congress, and for which the Revue Olympique was the official publication for eight years. It was important for Olympic intellectualism not to be interrupted. For that reason, and from a desire to safeguard certain rights obtained by Lausanne, the Bureau International de Pédagogie Sportive (B.I.P.S.) was founded. This is not the appropriate place to summarize its work. The final report which will be submitted to the City of Lausanne will soon provide a full account.

In this way, truly, this fourth Olympic decade (1924-1934) still belongs to the man speaking to you now. This is also true because he had assumed his own personal responsibility in having the 1924 Games awarded to his native city, Paris. Similarly, years in advance and contrary to wise and justifiable custom, he saw to it that the 1928 Games were awarded to Amsterdam, and the 1932 Games to Los Angeles. For various reasons in which the wandering paths of calculation and sentiment intersected, the Dutch Olympiad and the Californian Olympiad were close to his heart... What is more, this decade saw the publication of the history of the modern Olympic Games, in the form of a book entitled Mémoires, written by the only person who could do so. From the start, he collected private archives full of information not known to the public (at a time when typing had not yet conquered the world), and had access to the official archives. The Olympic Museum has also been opened in this decade. Recently there have also been educational efforts, whose principles may shed new light on all the "advanced courses", so often based on simplistic and naive understandings, within the narrow confines of programs for masters in physical education.

The decade ultimately produced those wonderful Greek festivals recently held in Athens and the Peloponnese, which closed at the foot of the monument raised in Olympia. There was a touching tribute from little school children in that region, who came with their teachers to place an ancient olive branch on the new marble. Among them, perhaps, stood some future Coroebus...

Pierre de Coubertin aged seventy (Navacelle Collection)

In conclusion, I must pay tribute to the modern athlete, because this is his festival, too, his day of renaissance dominated by the illustrious figure of his ancestor, the ancient athlete.

What else remains to be said against the modern athlete? I continue to consider him a victim of slander, and I hold his parents, teachers, politicians, the press, and the directors of federations responsible for his failings. I admire the fact that he has not stumbled more often.

Likewise, I continue to think that association with women's athleticism is bad, and that such athleticism should be excluded from the Olympic program – that the Olympiads were restored for the rare and solemn glorification of the individual male athlete. I believe that team sports are out of place in Olympiads, unless they compete in associated tournaments held outside the "Altis" (to use the ancient distinction), in other words, outside the sacred enclosure.

I continue to believe that the constitution of the IOC is excellent, based as it is on the principle that I will call "reverse delegation". This means that the mandate comes from the idea, which then attracts followers. A crowd of disjointed adherents does not come up with the idea. This principle could be applied in many fields, and would considerably reduce the evils of the age, if not save modern society. In the same way, the principle of intermittence provides the only certain way to alleviate the deplorable finances of modern society.

As you can see, my words as a septuagenarian remain full of impenitence... So let no one say that my work has been diverted, and that I am full of regret and alarmed at these alleged detours.

It has now been forty years since the restoration of the Olympic Games was formally proclaimed at the Sorbonne. Their destiny has been fully in keeping with my work and my wishes. I note this fact without pride, but with a simple need to reestablish the truth, which ignorance or calculation have betrayed.

Besides, let us not always be unfair to our age; let us respect it more.

At the celebration in 1919 that I mentioned a while ago, in my response to President Gustave Ador, I said, "Times are still hard. This dawn that is breaking is the dawn of the day after a storm; but toward noon, the sky will brighten and the rosy ears of grain will fill the arms of the harvesters once again."

It is not yet noon, Gentlemen. The days of history are long. Be patient, and let us remain confident.

Quarante années d'Olympisme,
in: *Le Sport Suisse,*
Vol. 30, July 4, 1934, p.1.

6.5.5 LEGENDS

The final text, Coubertin's end chapter of his *Olympic Memoirs* from 1930 is of extraordinary significance. Here he summarizes his feelings and thoughts in a kind of intellectual testament. In doing so he does not only speak about his Olympic lifework, but also about "Sport for All". The wording of the famous sentence is as follows: "Sport is the apanache of all races." This is the reason why Coubertin originally republished the "Charter for Sports Reform"[1] at the end of this text.

For Coubertin the Olympic idea remains firmly and solid on solid foundations facing a vast horizon. That is why the torch that is distinguished here- will be lit again elsewhere- the winds of the moment will be enough to blow the flame.

A number of legends were already growing up around the Olympic Games. The earlier ones were poetic inventions representing a graceful distortion of reality. Those of today are only too often merely the thoughtless repetition of erroneous assertions, which no one bothered to check before pronouncing them... and even less afterwards. They were uttered in the first place out of bigoted criticism or to satisfy some petty spirit of revenge; more often still because, quite simply, they represented a facile, over-hasty judgement offering an appearance of logic and convenient for subsequent development. It is in the last of these categories that the legend of my so-called "repentance" is to be included. How often have I not perceived here or there pitying or even slightly ironical allusions to my "disappointment", to my "disillusions", to the "distortion" of my original purpose, to the way in which events had "betrayed my hopes"!

Now this is all pure imagination. Furthermore, it is quite wrong to glorify ancient Olympism over and above the bounds of probability when one considers it from the aesthetic point of view and then to criticize it for its tendency to create "professionals", and similarly for neo-Olympism, by noticing only the international rivalry it arouses or the commercialism from which it is supposed to draw its funds exclusively. The terms "professional" and "amateur" applied to the ancient Games are devoid of all sense. What is similar between the two periods from the Olympic point of view is the same religious spirit, which in fact resurfaced for a while among young athletes during the Middle Ages. Religio athletae: the ancients had sensed the meaning of these words; the moderns have not yet grasped it. I feel however that they are beginning to. Novelists like Montherlant or Kessel, to mention but French writers, give me this impression.

For want of exact knowledge, mere common sense is sufficient to enable us to realize how the ancient Games were free neither from troublesome incidents, nor from periods of eclipse, nor from attacks led by relentless adversaries. Olympia experienced its moments of discord. Olympism survived them without going under. Neo-Olympism will evolve in the same way. The revived Games have the twofold advantage over their forerunners of being world-wide in character and being celebrated each time in a different place. They are thus more flexible and at the same time more solid. It was in the early days of their revival that they ran

1 As the "Charter for Sports Reform" appears as text 3.24 in this volume, we have decided not to repeat it here.

the greatest risks; at present, the sap flows too strongly for it ever to dry up. The 1914-1918 war did not shake them: the social revolution did not affect them either. It is interesting to note, moreover, that alongside the "capitalist" organization there is already a "proletarian" organization. "Workers' Olympiads" have been held at regular intervals and not without success. At the time of writing, a gigantic stadium is, I am told, being built in Moscow, where the next are to be held. They are even said to be going to take advantage of the occasion to change the name of this athletic meeting, which – if this were the case – would be infantile and only serve to emphasize an only too frequent failing of revolutionaries the world over: when so many institutions need radical renovation, they limit themselves merely to changing the name: what are needed deeds not words.

Anyway, this growing popularity of sport among manual workers is an undeniable guarantee for the survival of Olympism-whatever the outcome of the duel waged between two totally opposed social systems for the possession of power throughout the universe. It also implies recognition of the vital fact, strongly contested until quite recently, that sport is not a luxury pastime, an activity for the leisured few, nor merely a form of muscular compensation for brain work. For every man, woman and child, it offers an opportunity for self-improvement quite independent of profession or position in life. It is the prerogative of all, equally and to the same degree, and nothing can replace it.

The ethnic point of view is no different. Sport is the prerogative of all races. It is not so long since Asiatics were actually considered excluded by nature. Last year, in Geneva, one of the Japanese delegates at the League of Nations said to me, "It is impossible to imagine to what extent the revival of the Olympic Games has transformed my country. Since we have been taking part in the Games, our youth has taken on a fresh lease of life. I could quote similar statements by delegates from India and China.

It is a strange superiority for an institution that it can spread in this way both in social depth and international surface. What importance therefore do you expect me to attribute to the petty examples of shortsightedness that lie behind the predictions of gloom? During each Olympiad, I read that it will be the last because... Because, if you really want to know, the reporter (one has to see facts as they are) was poorly accommodated, was overcharged in a restaurant, or because the telegraph or telephone did not work as it should. This is only human. The organizers, therefore, should be more concerned about these three points, even though their connection with the ultimate destiny of Olympism appears distant and vague! Olympism remains firmly anchored on solid foundations facing vast horizons. That is why the torch that is extinguished here will be lit again elsewhere; the winds of the moment will be enough to blow the flame right around the earth.

It might be thought that these ideas are inspired by pride. But although I have a high opinion of and great pride in the work it has been given me to accomplish, I do not claim any personal merit; merit is only deserved when a person who is compelled to fight against himself or against tremendous odds wins victories over his own temperament and, as the saying goes, succeeds in "taming fortune". Favored in many respects by fate, kept continually at the task before me by a sort of inner compulsion that I have even at times tried to escape, I have no such victories to my credit.

This then is the spirit in which I have written these Memoirs, which are now drawing to a close. I had a choice of two methods: either to dress up the subject, interspersing it with anecdotes and brightening up the tale with entertaining tidbits at the risk of modifying, to a certain extent, the retrospective view of events, or to adhere strictly to the facts, respecting their proportional value and their correct natural sequence. This second method had the tiresome disadvantage of compelling me to multiply the I's and me's; but it was the only accurate method and the most sincere. In adopting it, moreover, I proposed not to leave out anything essential and especially not to forget any of my principal colleagues who gave so generously of their time and services and in whom I found such constant support. Being unable to mention all the others, the occasional helpers, I take the opportunity here of extending my sincere thanks to them all.

And now, if I say that I am perfectly satisfied with the evolution of neo-Olympism, does this mean that I am blind to its shortcomings? I can think of no better way of proving the contrary than by inserting here the text of one last document, the importance of which, to my mind, is vital. It is the "Charter of Sports Reform" made public on September 13, 1930 in Geneva during the course of a meeting presided over by Federal Councilor Motta. This Charter has been translated into many languages. Copies were printed on wall posters in French and German and met with great success at the last exhibition in Bern. It has been widely approved, but its articles demand too great a sacrifice and self-denial from those concerned for them to be willing to put the provisions into practice right away. This can only be done slowly, step by step.

As can be seen, this Charter proposes no reform of the Olympic Games. On the contrary, it shows a desire to clear the ground around the Games in order to give them greater emphasis, greater prominence, and greater grandeur. In fact, far from being a violation of the idea of championships, the Games are more likely to put a stop to any such violation. Far from encouraging the tendency to excess, they help to restrict it. But the idea of doing away completely with excess is a Utopia dreamed up by non-sportsmen.

"For one hundred to go in for physical education, fifty have to go in for sport. For fifty to go in for sport, twenty will have to specialize. For twenty to specialize, five will have to show themselves capable of astounding feats". It is impossible to get away from this basic truth. Everything is closely bound up with everything else. Thus the athletic record stands inescapably at the very summit of the sports edifice, like the "eternal axiom" referred to by the French writer Taine concerning Newton's law. You cannot hope to remove it without destroying everything else. Resign yourselves, therefore, you partisans of the unrealistic Utopia of moderation – which is quite against nature – to seeing us continue to put into practice the motto Father Didon used to quote to his students, and which has since become that of Olympism.

Olympic Memoirs, Chap. 24, Lausanne, IOC, 1997, pp.230-236.

On this shot taken shortly before his death, we can note his humourous facial expression. (Navacelle Collection)

APPENDIX

THE UNFINISHED SYMPHONY

The text following here is an "unfinished symphony" in a double sense. It is the only fragment we have of the incomplete final volume (vol.5) of Coubertin's memoirs[1]. He gives his reasons for choosing the title "The Unfinished Symphony", referring to examples from the world of music.

Coubertin describes Olympism as one half of his life's goals, the education reform connected to Olympism as the other half. Interpretation of this "Unfinished Symphony" shows that Coubertin did not give in to resignation at the end of his life, but looked ahead. He hands the yet unfinished part of his symphony of education over to posterity.[2]

The date is 1936. It is fifty years now since I took up the idea of educational reform to which I have devoted the better part of my life and the best of my efforts. Abandoning, once and for all, everything that had interested me in other careers, from then on I concentrated on this idea alone. But my work is far from completed. I am in my seventy-fourth year and, with the latter part of my life having been darkened with great worries and sorrows, I fear that my brain may lose some of its power. That is why, interrupting the regular course that I would have liked to follow in my memoirs, I am fitting in here the fifth and last of these small volumes, while the fourth and even the third are still only in the early stages of compilation. The first, entitled "Memories of childhood and youth" has been finished for a long time now, but is not yet printed. The second, "Olympic Memories", was published in 1932, while the Games of the 10th Olympiad were being celebrated in Los Angeles. The third is to be called "Politics, Experience and National Propaganda"; it deals with various subjects. Undoubtedly it is my friendship with Th. Delcassé that will give it its main interest, that is to say my friendship with a man whom I liked and admired greatly and with whom I enjoyed talking a great deal, without our necessarily being in agreement on all points because my views on Europe and the interests of France were quite different to his. Finally, the fourth volume, which I have called "Headless Victory", describes the war – and especially the peace that followed – as I saw them.

It will perhaps be thought that I have a partiality for fanciful names, choosing to call this last volume, "The Unfinished Symphony". I remember explaining this in a lecture I gave at the Polytechnicum in Zurich on 1st November 1935. Every human being, I said, belongs to the great orchestra of mankind. Most of us, it must be admitted, play a very minor role. Not everyone is able to fit in; some never succeed in finding their place. Very few are favoured by fate to the extent of being allowed

1 Only the *Olympic Memoirs* were published during Coubertin's lifetime. The other volumes of his memoirs were unfinished when he died and have never been published. Some chapters from Volume I have survived in the family archives. (Navacelle Collection). They can be found in: Y.-P. Boulongne, *La vie et l'œuvre pédagogique de Pierre de Coubertin* (1863-1937), Ottawa, Leméac, 1975, pp.455-451. They also exist in a German version, with two additional chapters, in: *Europäische Revue*, Vol.12, 1936, no.9, pp.703-710; no.10, pp.792-797 and no.12, pp.857-865.

2 This text, written after the 1936 Olympic Games, has supreme importance for sports history, as Coubertin now characterizes Adolf Hitler as "strange figure". See also introduction and texts 4.2.2/48 and 4.2.2/49.

Coubertin at one of his last public appearances, speaking at the Zurich Politechnikum on 1st November 1935, when he referred to his Unfinished Symphony. He explained that Olympism represented only one half of his life's work (IOC Archives)

to compose pieces themselves. Rarer still are those who are privileged to hear them performed during their lifetime. I know that people consider me to be among the latter because of Neo-Olympism, whose steady progress appears to have created so much surprise. People greeted it at first with smiles, then irony, then annoyance and even hostility. But nothing has been able to weaken it, not even four years of world war, which it survived without ill effects.

But Olympism is only part of my life's work, approximately half in fact. Consequently my educational "symphony" consists of a part that is complete and another that is still unfinished. Quite naturally, it is with the latter that I am going to deal in the pages that follow.

There will be grave flaws in the form and also, undoubtedly, in the substance. My time is too limited for me to be able to reflect sufficiently deeply and my brain will not be equal to the task of polishing the form as I would have liked. But what worries me most is the difficulty of finding those who will take over and continue the work I have started. To my mind, this is the most important point. Please forgive me therefore for the rambling nature of these notes with all their repetitions and reiterations. My main concern is that my meaning should be clear.

No, indeed, I would not have chosen to live in a period of history so full, so varied and so powerful as the one in which I have been a spectator, and even, to a certain extent, an actor. My earliest memory of public life dates back to Napoleon III and the 1867 Universal Exhibition in Paris; and now, on the eve of the eleventh of the modern Olympiads that I have revived, the strange figure of Adolf Hitler, one of the most curious and most unexpected that I have ever come across in my study of history, appears on the scene.

All through my life, universal history, of which I have been so fond – even from my schooldays – has remained closely linked with all my thoughts and reflections and I have always felt that it could not be ignored if one wanted to comprehend collective life in its entirety. For me, it has been not only a constant source of inspiration but also, in moments of sorrow and pain, a source of real consolation.

Those who have been kind enough to take a favourable interest in my work distinguish two distinct and successive entreprises – particularly as the methods I have used have been very different. Athletics – and especially its crowning glory, Olympism – has been the object, on my part of a somewhat noisy – and even, if you like, loud and insistent – development. It was the only way to achieve anything. The attempt to reform education, on the other hand, has been the object of slow, silent, gradual, and long thought-out study. Olympism has sailed serenely over the world like a gleaming airship, the reform of education has borrowed the method of moles, burrowing unseen a whole network of runs and raising veritable molehills here and there on the surface. But there is one thing they have in common: whether it was a matter of muscular training or improvement of the mind, the effort has, if I may say so, always been clearly defined and localised. The average Frenchman's infuriating sense of logic made my friends reproach me: you are working for the adolescent, for the boy ... what are you planning to do for the child, for the girl? ... Nothing at all, was my answer. They are not going to advance my cause. The reform that I am aiming at is not in the interests of grammar or hygiene. It is a social reform or rather it is a foundation of a new era that I can see coming and which will have no value or force unless it is firmly based on the principle of a completely new type of education.

It was pure instinct that made me feel this way half a century ago. 1886 was the year of my long sojourns as an observer in English universities. I watched, I listened, but spoke little. What did I care about statistics and documents ? Neither England nor France, at the time, gave much thought to the future. Nor did Germany. And Italy, even less. Towards the end of the 18th century all countries concentrated on the present pursued practical and particular aims, goals that were both shrewd and reasonable. No one was aware of any need for a "renovation" or any kind whatsoever. In religion alone, a few mystical and inspired groups thought about it, or perhaps the champions of social reform and a re-organisation of the intricate wheels of society, all of which, at the time, was still pure utopia.

That the day would come when such a utopia would become reality was however within realms of possibility. I was already taking great interest in noting the signs – even though few and far between – of an evolution that seemed as though it would eventually occur along these lines but extremely slowly. In any case, this evolution presupposed a prior reform of popular education, the creation of a neo-encyclopedism, wider programmes simplified methods ...

But no one wanted to give it a thought.

La symphonie inachevée. Manuscript (IOC Archives).
Reprinted in: *Revue Olympique,* no.99-100, 1976, pp.32-34.
English version "The Unfinished Symphony" in: *Olympic Review,* no.99-100, 1976, pp.32-34.

Coubertin, aged 40, at his desk. He left behind more than 15,000 printed pages, illustrating his tireless creativity, intellectual far-sightedness and great journalistic talent. (Navacelle Collection)

BIBLIOGRAPHY OF COUBERTIN'S WRITINGS

Compiled by Norbert Müller in collaboration with Otto Schantz

PREFACE

This bibliography, devoted to the writings of Pierre de Coubertin, is the result of twenty years extensive research. Its authors estimate that it covers about 95 percent of Coubertin's writings, or some 15,000 printed pages, reprints excluded.[1]

The first major bibliography of the works of Coubertin was published in Lausanne on the occasion of his seventieth birthday, under the direction of a group of Coubertin's friends in Lausanne, with the support of certain National Olympic Committees.[2]

A more complete and improved edition was published in 1966 by the Carl Diem Institute of Cologne, in the form of a supplement to a collection of essays and speeches by Coubertin.[3]

A short time later, a bibliography published by the IOC followed, which was quite similar to those referred to above.[4]

In 1971, Bernard Gillet (Paris) wrote and edited a bibliography which surpassed all others that existed. It proved to be of great practical value, thanks to the inclusion of references to the works of Coubertin preserved in the Bibliothèque Nationale in Paris.[5] Everyone who has done research on the writings of Coubertin has used it as an indispensable basis for their research.[6]

The bibliography presented here was compiled starting in 1981, based on the work of Bernard Gillet as revised and updated in 1971 by the Carl Diem Institute. The revised version contains twice the number of listed titles compared to the Gillet bibliography. This

1 The following bibliography is based on:
N. Müller, O.Schantz: *Bibliographie Pierre de Coubertin.* Lausanne, International Pierre de Coubertin Committee, 1991.
Former assumptions that Coubertin's printed works amount to over 60,000 printed pages - as stated in the bibliography of 1933 (cf. note 2) - are hereby refuted.

2 Cf. *Répertoire des Ecrits, Discours et Conférences de Pierre de Coubertin*, published on the occasion of his 70th birthday in homage by the Olympic Committees of Egypt, Greece, Latvia, Portugal, Sweden and Switzerland and the International Bureau for Sports Education. Aix-en-Provence, P. Roubaud, 1933. (14 pages).
The bibliography is divided into five chapters as follows:
- Technique et Pédagogie Sportive (pp.3-7),
- Pédagogie Générale et Réforme de l'Enseignement (pp.7-8),
- Études Historiques (pp.8-10),
- Politique et Sociologie (pp.10-12) and
- Variétés (pp.12-13).
This bibliography appeared in connection with the *Anthology*, published on the occasion of his 70th birthday, edited by A. Raymond and others, with a preface by Maurice Pottecher. Aix-en-Provence, P.Roubaud, 1933.

3 Carl Diem Institute (ed.): "Bibliography of the Works of Baron Pierre de Coubertin." In: *Pierre de Coubertin. The Olympic Idea. Discourses and Essays.* Schorndorf, Hofmann, 1967, pp.137-144. Off-print, Schorndorf, Hofmann, 1967, (8 pages).
This bibliography consists of a total of 226 titles and is based particularly on the bibliography cited in note 2 and a second in the work of A. Senay, R. Hervet: Monsieur de Coubertin. Paris, S.E.S., 1956, pp.177-189.

4 IOC (ed.): *Bibliography of the Works of Baron Pierre de Coubertin.* Lausanne, IOC, 1968. This bibliography consists of 278 titles.

5 B. Gillet: *Bibliographie des Œuvres de Pierre de Coubertin.* Special brochure, Paris 1971. This bibliography consists of a total of 625 titles.

6 This thought is also expressed in the book of Yves-Pierre Boulongne, who held this bibliography in high regard; cf. Y.P. Boulongne: *La vie et l'œuvre pédagogique de Pierre de Coubertin.* Ottawa, Léméac, 1975, pp.397-430.

expansion results from a systematic examination of periodicals found in the Bibliothèque Nationale in Paris, as well as those in Berne and Brussels, and the Bibliothèque Cantonale et Universitaire in Lausanne. All the entries figuring in the existing bibliographies were minutely examined, because often some precise detail was missing, such as a page number, the year or the place of publication, or even the indication of the missing numbers in a series of brochures or reviews, etc.

This patient work has resulted in significant corrections to about two-thirds of the references. Moreover, in the course of this research, hitherto unknown publications of Coubertin were discovered. Additionally, this bibliography was enhanced by the introduction of references to sports reviews published in Switzerland and Belgium.

One cannot pretend, however, that the work is perfect, even though it does add what was lacking in the preceding bibliographies. Earlier bibliographies were unable to take advantage of resources in Switzerland, inasmuch as the library and archives of the IOC were hardly accessible for a long time.

As we have said, this bibliography takes into account about 95 percent of the published writings of Coubertin. It is probable that other original texts, published in foreign languages particularly in England, Spain, and the United States, could be added to the bibliography.

Posthumous publications have been omitted, but the collection put together by the Carl Diem Institute with the approval of the IOC in 1966 entitled *The Olympic Idea* has been referenced, next to the French original version. It exists in several translations (German, English, Spanish, and Danish) and contains a number of Coubertin's previously unpublished circulars and lectures[7]. Also the 1986 IOC edition of Coubertin's writings in French was used as additional reference.

Finally, this bibliography mentions neither letters nor manuscripts, which would be out of place in this type of work. Hence the national libraries must at least make them available to the specialized public.

This bibliography is divided into several parts which permit a better understanding and facilitate its use:

a) book publications, b) brochures,
c) leaflets, posters, etc. d) articles.

The Coubertin bibliography lists all reprints found of a single contribution in chronological order, enabling the reader to find the original text and place of publication in case of later changes of text or title.

Frequently the publications bear no mention of the date or place where they were produced. Where we have been able to procure this information, it is indicated in parenthesis.

The spelling (usage of upper and lower case letters) of each title corresponds to the original. Titles originally printed in capitals only, however, have been changed to standard usage.

An asterisk (*) marks those writings which are not signed by Coubertin but which, after close study, can be considered as coming from him. This is the case especially of the reviews or annals that he published, such as *La Revue du Pays de Caux, La Revue pour les Français, La Revue Olympique, Le Bulletin du Bureau International de Pédagogie Sportive,* and others. In fact, a study of the content as well as the style made it possible to attribute authorship to Coubertin, even if the publications did not bear his signature.

Sometimes the discovery of a reprint of a doubtful text has helped to establish its authenticity. In the preface of the bibliography of 1933 (cf. note 2), Coubertin himself admits that he often did not sign his articles on purpose, in order to give his ideal a wider reception. However, computer analysis of text structure and vocabulary will probably enable us to decide these matters with some authority.

The experience gained from this sort of work has led the authors to believe that, beyond the publications, translations, and 500 reprints already discovered, numerous translations and additional copies must exist.

We wish to thank the Bibliothèque Nationale in Paris, which with goodwill over many years has encouraged our undertaking and has, by way of exception, placed at our disposal all the "out-of-use" documents which are being microfilmed. We would also like to thank the Musée National du Sport in Paris, the Bibliothèques Nationales in Berne and Brussels, as well as the University libraries of Bordeaux, Frankfurt, Graz, Lyons, Mainz, Mannheim, Strasbourg, Treves and Vienna.

We would also like to express our thanks to the British Museum, the Library of Congress in Washington, the Preussischer Kulturbesitz National Library in Berlin, the Deutsche Sporthochschule Library in Cologne, the Institut National du Sport et d'Éducation Physique in Paris, the Public Library of New York, the municipal libraries of Auxerre and Mainz, and the library of the International Olympic Academy at Olympia.

We wish to thank our colleagues of the Carl and Liselott Diem Archives, and those of the Olympic Museum in Lausanne.

7 French version edited by Carl Diem Institute at the Deutschen Sporthochschule Köln (ed.): *Pierre de Coubertin. L'Idée Olympique*. Discours et Essaais. Schorndorf, Hofmann, 1966. Short title of the French version in the following bibliography: *L'Idée Olympique.*
English version edited by the Carl Diem Institute (ed.): *Pierre de Coubertin. The Olympic Idea.* Discourses and Essays. Schorndorf, Hofmann, 1967.
Short title of the English version: *The Olympic Idea.*
German version edited by the Carl Diem Institute (ed.): *Pierre de Coubertin. Der Olympische Gedanke.* Reden und Aufsätze. Schorndorf, Hofmann, 1966.
Short title of the German version*: Der Olympische Gedanke.*
Spanish version edited by Delegacion Nacional de Educacion Fisica y Deportes (ed.): *Pierre de Coubertin. Ideario Olímpico.* Discoursos y Ensayos. Madrid, INEF, 1973.
Short title of the Spanish version: *Pierre de Coubertin. Ideario Olímpico.*
Danish version edited and introduced by C. Bøje, S.Riiskoer. Idroetsforsk, Frederiksberg, DET lille, 1996. The Danish version is not referenced in the following bibliography.

8 IOC/N.Müller (eds): *Pierre de Coubertin. Textes choisis.* [Selected writings of Pierre de Coubertin]. Coordinating editor and director of research: Norbert Müller. 3 volumes and an illustrated booklet. XXXVIII/2,252 pages.
Volume I: Revelation. General introduction and presentation by Georges Rioux, with a foreword by the President of the IOC, Juan Antonio Samaranch.
Volume II: Olympism. Introduction and presentation by Norbert Müller.
Volume III: Sport practice. Introduction and presentation by Norbert Müller and Otto Schantz. This volume contains a bibliography of the works of Pierre de Coubertin, compiled by Norbert Müller in collaboration with Otto Schantz.
The boxed set also contains: Pierre de Coubertin - Sa vie par l'image
An illustrated booklet on the life and work of Pierre de Coubertin by Geoffrey de Navacelle. 96 pages of texts, photographs and illustrations.
This edition is accessible in the world's major libraries. It contains about one-third of the texts of Pierre de Coubertin available to researchers. Citation of this edition in the following bibliography: "Coubertin: Textes choisis, vol. (1, 2 or 3)" or "Textes choisis, vol. (1, 2 or 3)".

Mr. Geoffrey de Navacelle de Coubertin, great-nephew of Pierre de Coubertin, and our colleagues of the Pierre de Coubertin International Committee, especially Dr Y.-P. Boulongne, have been of great assistance.

Above all, we express our gratitude to the IOC, who gave to the authors of this bibliography the basic elements for undertaking this immense work, in the context of the 1986 publication of the *Textes choisis de Pierre de Coubertin*[8], and the previous edition in English.

Mainz, January 2000

Norbert Müller

The titles of all Coubertin publications included in this book are underlined in the bibliography. The line is under the first word if the text is only partially reprinted.

Books

1888

L'Education en Angleterre. Collèges et Universités.
[Education in England. Secondary Schools and Universities]
Paris, Hachette, 1888 (327 pages).
Later reprinted, in excerpts (pp-.1-23, 63-85, 141-163, 286-326) in: Textes choisis, vol.I, pp.38-80.

1889

L'Education Anglaise en France.
[English Education in France.]
Paris, Hachette, 1889 (207 pages).
Later reprinted, in excerpts (pp.3-20, 91-107, 108-120, 199-202, 204-206) in: Textes choisis, vol.I, pp.81-112. (121-142) in: Textes choisis, vol.III, pp.210-221.

1890

Universités Transatlantiques.
[Transatlantic Universities.]
Paris, Hachette, 1890 (381 pages).
New edition: Saint-Jacques/Québec, Ed. du Pot de Fer, 1994.
Later reprinted, in excerpts (pp.27-29, 84-90, 94-98, 117-121, 133-136, 222-227, 231-233, 257-259, 266-267, 307-311, 361-379) in: Textes choisis, vol.I, pp.113-139.

1896

L'Evolution Française sous la Troisième République.
Paris, Plon-Nourrit, 1896 (432 pages).
[Series of articles, published in "Nouvelle Revue" 1896.]
English translation: **The Evolution of France under the Third Republic.** New York/Boston, Thomas Y. Crowell & Company, 1897 (Translation: Isabel F. Hapgood) ; 2nd edition: Londres, James Bowden, 1898 (430 pages).

1897

Souvenirs d'Amérique et de Grèce.
[Memories of America and Greece.]
Paris, Hachette, 1897 (183 pages).
[Articles of Reviews and Newspapers from 1894 to 1896.]
Later reprinted, in excerpts (pp.101-120, 139-159) in: Textes choisis, vol.II, pp.85-96, 148-162.

1900

France since 1814.
London, Chapman and Hall, 1900 (281 pages). [Series of articles published in "Fortnightly Review" de 1899.]

1900-1906

La Chronique de France. (I-VII).
[A Chronicle of France.]
Published under the direction of Pierre de Coubertin.
Auxerre, A. Lanier, 1900-1906 (7 volumes).

1901

Notes sur l'Education publique.
[Notes on Public Education.]
Paris, Hachette, 1901 (320 pages).
German translation: Schule - Sport - Erziehung. Gedanken zum öffentlichen Erziehungswesen. Published, translated, and with an introduction by E. Hojer in cooperation with R. Anselmet K. Ashtari. Schorndorf, Hofmann, 1972 (210 pages).
Later reprinted, in excerpts in: (pp.3-54, 152-173, 217-310) in: Textes choisis, vol.I, pp.195-273.
(pp.174-197) in: Textes choisis, vol.II, pp.147-157.
(pp.198-216) in: Textes choisis, vol.III, pp.375-383.

1902

Le Roman d'un Rallié.
Auxerre, A. Lanier, 1902 (322 pages). [Series of articles published in "Nouvelle Revue" 1899, signed with the pseudonym Georges Hohrod.]

1905

L'Education des Adolescents au XXe siècle.
[The Education of Adolescents in the XXth Century.]
I: L'Education physique: La Gymnastique utilitaire. Sauvetage - Défense - Locomotion. **[Physical Education: Life-Saving, Self-Defense, Locomotion.]** Paris, Alcan, 1905 (154 pages). 2nd edition: Paris, Alcan, 1906. Later reprinted in in: Textes choisis.Vol.III, pp.481-555.
3rd & 4th edition: Paris, Alcan, 1906.
Dutch translation: Praktische Lichaamsoefening. Naar het Fransch bezorgd, door den Nederllandschen Bond voor Lichamelijke Opvoeding. Baarn, J.F. van Ven, 1912 (100 pages).

1909

Une Campagne de vingt-et-un ans (1887-1908).
[A Twenty-One Year Campaign.]
Paris, Librairie de l'Education physique, 1909 (220 pages).
[Series of articles published in l' "Education physique" from December 1906 to October 1908.]
Chap.XX "La gymnastique utilitaire" later reprinted, in: Textes choisis, vol.III, pp.561-568.
Chap.XXI "Arts, lettres et sports" **[The Arts, Literature, and Sports]** later reprinted, in: Textes choisis, vol.II, pp.485-492.
Chap.XXII "La IVme Olympiade ... et après" later reprinted, in: Textes choisis, vol.II, pp.238-241.
German edition: Einundzwanzig Jahre Sportkampagne (1887-1908), published by the Carl-Diem-Institut, Cologne, under the direction of B. Wirkus. Translated by Wissenschaftlicher Sprachendienst G. Klitscher.

Pages d'Histoire contemporaine.
[Some Aspects of Contemporary History.]
Paris, Plon-Nourrit,1909 (306 pages).

1912
L'Analyse Universelle.
[The Universal Analysis.]
II: Education intellectuelle. **[Intellectual Education.]**
Analyse universelle. Paris, Alcan, 1912 (155 pages).
Later reprinted, in excerpts (pp.1-35, 96-155) in: Textes choisis, vol.I, pp.274-314.

1913
Essais de Psychologie sportive.
[Sports Psychology.]
Lausanne Paris, Payot, 1913 (266 pages).
[Contains most of the sport psychology articles published in the Revue Olympique from 1906 to 1913.]
New edition presented by Jean-Pierre Rioux. Grenoble, Editions Jérôme Millon, 1992.

1915
L'Education des Adolescents au XXe siècle.
[The Education of Adolescents in the XXth Century.]
III: Education morale. **[Moral Education.]** Le Respect mutuel. Paris, Alcan, 1915 (104 pages).
Later reprinted, in: Textes choisis, vol.I, pp.316-350.
German edition: Die gegenseitige Achtung. Published by the Carl-Diem-Institut, Cologne, under the direction of Hildegard Müller. St. Augustin, Academia, 1988.

1916
Leçons de Gymnastique utilitaire. Sauvetage - Défense - Locomotion. A l'usage des Instituteurs, Moniteurs, Instructeurs militaires, etc. Paris, Payot, 1916 (47 pages).
[Lessons in Useful Lifetime Sports.]
[Weekly chronicles "Excelsior" published from October 1914 to juillet 1915.]

1921
Leçons de Pédagogie sportive.
[Lessons in Athletic Education.]
Lausanne, La Concorde, 1921 (124 pages).
Other editions, published under the title: "Pédagogie Sportive":
1) Paris, G. Crès, 1922;
2) Lausanne, Bureau International de Pédagogie Sportive, 1934 (157 pages);
3) Paris, J. Vrin, 1972, avec une préface de Georges Rioux (157 pages). [Reprint of the 1934 edition.]
Later reprinted in excerpts (pp.127-154), in: Textes choisis, vol.I, 433-451;
(pp.56-58, 146-154), in: vol.II,669-670, 537-542;
(pp.24-63, 71-77, 77-84, 84-85, 87-90, 90-92, 92-94, 94-96, 96-99, 116-117) in: Textes choisis, vol.III, pp.27-51, 137-146; 158-162, 191-192, 206-209, 233-234, 248-249, 260-261, 272-273, 349-350.

German edition: Sportliche Erziehung, edited by A. Mallwitz, translated by Else Hoffmann, Stuttgart, Dieck, 1928 (91 pages).
Hungarian edition: Sportpedagógia. Budapest, Fordito Kiadàsa, 1931 (90 pages).

1926-1927
Histoire Universelle (I-IV).
[World History.]
Aix-en-Provence, Société de l'Histoire universelle, 1926- 1927.
Tome I: Les Empires d'Asie (92 pages); **[Asian Empires.]**
Tome II: Le Drame Méditerranéen (190 pages);
[The Mediterranean Drama.]
Tome III: Les Celtes, les Germains et les Slaves (157 pages); **[Celts, Ancient Germans, and Slavs.]**
Tome IV: La Formation et le Développement des Démocraties modernes (220 pages). **[Beginnings and Development of the Modern Democracies.]**
With a General Index in a special brochure (19 pages).
Forword of tome I later reprinted, in: Textes choisis, vol.I, pp.352-359.
La Confédération helvétique, later reprinted in excerpts, in:
1) Anthologie, Aix-en-Provence, P.Roubaud, 1933, pp.113-115.
2) Textes choisis, Vol.II, pp.724-725.

1930
Notre France.
[Our France.]
Aix-en-Provence, P. Roubaud, 1930 (206 pages).
[Reprint of the following four brochures published in 1916: Les grandes divisions de l'histoire de France; Cinq siècles et demi d'activité coloniale (1365 - 1915); La France à travers le XIXe siècle (1800 - 1900); L'évolution de la France républicaine (1870 - 1914).]
(Nouveau avant-propos: p.3; nouvelle postface p.206).

1932
Mémoires Olympiques.
[Olympic Memoirs.]
Lausanne, Bureau International de Pédagogie Sportive, 1932 (218 pages). [Series of articles published in the journal "L'Auto" in 25 chapters, from September 8, 1931 to March 27, 1932.]
2nd edition by the IOC with an introduction by G. de Navacelle. Lausanne, IOC, 1979 (140 pages).
3th edition by the IOC with an introduction by G. de Navacelle. Lausanne, IOC, 1996 (236 pages).

English translation:
Olympic Memoirs.
Edited by: IOC with introduction by G. de Navacelle.
Lausanne 1979 (141).
2nd edition: Lausanne 1997 (236 pages).

Spanish translation:
Memorias Olímpicas. Translated and introduced by José Maria Soler. Madrid 1965.
New edition by: IOC with introduction by G. de Navacelle.
Lausanne 1979 (140 pages).
2nd edition: Lausanne 1997 (236 pages).
German translations:
- Ein Leben für die Olympische Idee (extraits). traduit par Curt Riess. In: Die Woche, 34 année, 1932, pp.1013-1016(I), pp.1043-1046 (II), pp.1075-1078 (III), n° 37, pp. II-IV.
- Olympische Erinnerungen. Translation: Gertrud John. With a preface by Theodor Lewald, postface by Carl Diem. Berlin, W. Limpert, 1936 (242 pages). 2nd edition with a preface by Carl Diem, Frankfurt/Main, W. Limpert, 1959 (223 pages) ;
3rd edition Frankfurt/Main, W. Limpert, 1961. Reprint: Wiesbaden 1996.
- Olympische Erinnerungen, translation: Erhard Höhne. Annotations by Volker Kluge. Berlin, Sportverlag, 1987. 2nd edition: Frankfurt/M., Ullstein, 1996.
Czech translation:
Olympijské Paméti. Translation: Jirí Kroutil, Prague, Edition Olympia, 1977.
Japanes translation:
Orinpikku no Kaisou. Edited by Carl Diem. Prefaces by Carl Diem and Kenkichi Oshima. Translated by Kenkichi Oshima. Tokyo, Baseball Magazine Ed., 1962.

1933

Anthologie.
[**Anthology**.]
Aix-en-Provence, P. Roubaud, 1933 (184 pages).
Editors: A. Reymond, M. Bauer, J. Chryssafis, W. Hirschy, G.-L. Magnat, F. Messerli, M. Pottecher.
Edited on the occasion of the author's 70th birthday with a preface by Maurice Pottecher (pp.5-8).

Brochures

1889

L'Education athlétique.
[Athletic Education.]
Conférence faite le 26 janvier 1889 à l'Association pour l'Avancement des Sciences. Paris, Impr. Chaix, [Off-print, 23 pages, from: Association Française pour l'Avancement des Sciences. Compte rendu de la 18e session. Paris 1889, Masson, 1889,pp.15-25.]
Later reprinted, in: Textes choisis, vol.I, pp.159-173.

1898

Lettre aux Electeurs de l'arrondissement du Havre.
[Letter to the Citizens of the Le Havre District.]
Le Havre, Librairie Havraise, mars 1898 (9 pages).

La philosophie de l'histoire des Etats-Unis.
[The Philosophy of the History of the United States]
Ve Leçon donnée à l'Ecole des Sciences politiques à Paris, le mercredi 18 avril 1898. Texte réimprimé à l'occasion de la 70e année de l'auteur par ses amis d'Amérique, s.l. [1933] (16 pages).

1900

L'avenir de l'Europe.
[The Future of Europe.]
(Enquête entreprise à la demande du journal "L'Indépendance Belge".) Bruxelles, Impr. Deverver Deweuwe, 1900 (48 pages). [Series of articles published in "L'Indépendance Belge" in 1899.]

1904

L'Amérique française et le Centenaire de la Louisiane.
[French America and the Centenary of Louisiana.]
s.d., s.l. [Paris, 1904].

1905

Projet financier de la IVe Olympiade à Rome.
[Financial Planning for the IVth Olympiad in Rome.]
Polycopie, Paris, IOC, déc. 1909.
Later reprinted, in: Textes choisis, vol.II, pp.630-639.

1906

Traité d'escrime équestre.
[Fencing on Horseback.]
(In collaboration with Louis Pascaud.) Auxerre, A. Lanier, 1906.
Off-print from la Revue Olympique de 1906 (8 pages).
Later reprinted, in: Textes choisis, vol.III, pp.250-257.

1910

Nouveaux programmes d'enseignement secondaire.
[New Programmes for Secondary Education.]
Edited by l'Association pour la Réforme de l'Enseignement. Paris 1910 (Off-print 31 pages).
Later reprinted, in: L'Education des Adolescents au XIXe siècle. II. Education intellectuelle. Analyse universelle. Paris, Alcan, 1912, pp.39-93.

Une Olympie moderne.
[A Modern Olympia.]
Auxerre, Jattefaux, 1910 (24 pages).
Later reprinted, in:
1) L'Idée Olympique. Edited by: Carl-Diem-Institut, pp.20-35.
2) Textes choisis, vol.II, pp.54-71, pp. 464-465.
in English, in: The Olympic Idea, pp.22-36.
in Deutsch, in: Der Olympische Gedanke, pp24-43.
In Spanish, in: Ideario Olímpico, 1973, pp.42-66.

Les Sports à l'Hôtel.
[Sports at the Hotel.]
Edition de la Société des Sports Populaires, s. l. 1910 (8 pages).
[Published in the Revue Olympique of May and July 1910.]

1911

Décoration, Pyrotechnie, Harmonie, Cortèges.
[Decoration, Pyrotechnics, Harmonies, Processions.]
Essai de Ruskinianisme sportif à l'usage des Sociétés de Gymnastique et de Sport. Publication de la Société des Sports Populaires, s.l., s.d. [1911] (22 pages). [Series of articles published in the Revue Olympique of 1911.]

1912

Ode au Sport/Ode an den Sport.
[Ode to Sport.]
(Published under the double pseudonyme: Georges Hohrod and M.Eschbach.) Gand, Impr. Van Dosselaere, 1912 (12 pages). Edition in French/German.
French version is later reprinted, in: Textes choisis, vol.III, pp.665-667.
[Also published in the Revue Olympique of December 1912.]

Un collège modèle. **[A Model College.]**
Le Collège Léopold II. Projet rédigé pour S.M. le roi des Belges à l'occasion du Congrès d'Expansion mondiale de Mons. Gand/Paris, Van Dooselaere/E.Basset, 1912 (23 pages). [Published in the "Revue pour les Français" in 1906.]
Later reprinted, in: Textes choisis, Vol.I, pp.452-472.
German edition: Ein Kolleg-Modell. Das Kolleg Léopold II. Edited byle Carl-Diem-Institut, Cologne, sous la direction de B. Wirkus. Cologne, Barz & Beienburg, 1971.

1915

Amélioration et développement de l'éducation physique. Rapport présenté à S.E.M. le Ministre de l'Instruction publique. Lausanne, Impr. de la Société suisse de Publicité, mars 1915 (35 pages).

[Improvement and Development of Physical Education.]
Later reprinted, in: Textes choisis, vol.III, pp.405-427.

1916

Les grandes divisions de l'Histoire de France.
[Landmarks of French History.]
Petite Bibliothèque "Pour mieux comprendre la France", Brochure I (Redaction committee: P. de Coubertin, H. Didier, P. Géraldy, P. Rival). Paris, H. Didier, s.d. [1916].
Later reprinted, in:
Notre France. Aix-en-Provence, P. Roubaud, 1930, pp.5-52.

Cinq siècles et demi d'activité coloniale (1365-1915).
[Five and a Half Centuries of Colonial Activities.]
Petite Bibliothèque "Pour mieux comprendre la France", Brochure II (Redaction committee: P. de Coubertin, H. Didier, P. Géraldy, P. Rival). Paris, H. Didier, s.d. [1916].
Later reprinted, in:
1) Notre France. Aix-en-Provence, P. Roubaud, 1930, pp.53-110.
2) Cinq siècles et demi d'activité coloniale française. Aix-en-Provence, P. Roubaud, 1930. (Brochure, 68 pages.)

La France à travers le XIXe siècle (1800-1900).
[France in the XIXth Century.]
Petite Bibliothèque "Pour mieux comprendre la France", Brochure III (Redaction committee: P. de Coubertin, H. Didier, P. Géraldy, R. Rival). Paris, H. Didier, s.d. [1916].
Later reprinted, in: Notre France, Aix-en-Provence, P. Roubaud, 1930. pp.111-156.

L'évolution de la France républicaine (1870-1914).
[The Evolution of France as a Republic.]
Petite Bibliothèque "Pour mieux comprendre la France", Brochure III (Redaction committee: P. de Coubertin, H. Didier, P. Géraldy, R. Rival). Paris, H. Didier, s.d. [1916].
Later reprinted, in: Notre France. Aix-en-Provence, P. Roubaud, 1930, pp.157-206.

Les œuvres de la pensée française.
[French Thought.]
Petite Bibliothèque "Pour mieux comprendre la France", Brochure V (Redaction committee: P. de Coubertin, H. Didier, P. Géraldy, R. Rival). Paris, H. Didier, s.d. [1916].
Ier fasc.: Des orgines à la fin du XVIIe siècle. **[From the Beginnings to the End of the XVIIIth Century.]**
IIe fasc.: Du XVIIIe siècle à nos jours. **[From the XVIIIthe Century until Today.]**

Les grandes époques de l'art français.
[Great Eras of French Art.]
Petite Bibliothèque "Pour mieux comprendre la France", Broch. VI (Redaction committee: P. de Coubertin, H. Didier, P. Géraldy, R. Rival). Paris, H. Didier,
I[er]fasc.: Des origines à la fin du XVIe siècle. Oct. 1916 (60 pages). **[From the Beginnings to the End of the XVIth Century.]**
IIe fasc.: Du XVIIe siècle à nos jours. Nov. 1916 (46 pages). **[From the XVIIth Century until Today.]**
IIIe fasc.: La Musique et les Arts décoratifs. Déc. 1916 (64 pages). **[Music and the Decorative Arts.]**

A travers l'histoire sud-américaine.
[On South-American History.]
Offerte par la municipalité de Lyon en souvenir de la première semaine de l'Amérique latine, Lyon Décembre 1916. Paris, Plon-Nourrit, 1916 (24 pages).

1917

Qué es el Olimpismo ?
[What Is Olympism?]
Paris, Rirachowski, 1917 (30 pages).

Almanach Olympique pour 1918.
[Olympic Almanac for the Year 1918.]
Lausanne, Impr. Réunies, 1917.
[Edited by Pierre de Coubertin in the name of IOC and Institut Olympique de Lausanne.]

1918

Ce que nous pouvons maintenant demander au Sport... Conférence faite à l'Association des Hellènes Libéraux de Lausanne, le 24 février 1918.
[What We Can Now Ask of Sport. Address given to the Greek Liberal Club of Lausanne, February 24, 1918.]
Lausanne, Edition de l'Association des Hellènes Libéraux de Lausanne, 1918 (22 pages).
Later reprinted in French, in:
1) L'Idée Olympique, pp.42-51.
2) Textes choisis, Vol.III, pp.598-609.
Later reprinted
in English, in: The Olympic Idea, pp.43-51.
in German, in: Der Olympische Gedanke, pp.51-61.
in Spanish, in: Ideario Olímpico, 1973, pp.76-91.

A travers l'histoire grecque.
[On Greek History.]
Edition de l'Association des Hellènes Libéraux de Lausanne. Lausanne 1918 (14 pages).
[Published also in Revue Olympique, April 1906.]

Le projet d'Olympie moderne et l'avenir de Lausanne.
[Modern Olympics and the Future of Lausanne.]
Edité par la Société Lausannoise des amis de l'Olympisme. Lausanne, Impr.La Concorde, s.d. [1918] (3 pages).
Later reprinted, in: Textes choisis, vol.II, pp.738-741.

Almanach Olympique pour 1919.
[Olympic Almanac for the Year 1919.]
Lausanne, Impr. Réunies, 1918.
[Edited by Pierre de Coubertin in the name of the IOC and the Institut Olympique de Lausanne.]

1919

Le pays vaudois, son âme et son visage.
[The Vaud Region: Its Spirit and Its Character.]
Lausanne, Libr. Rouge, 1919 (31 pages).
Later reprinted: Vevey, Editions de l'Aire, 1995.

Les étapes de l'astronomie. **[Stages of Astronomy.]** - L'unité mécanique et l'unité chimique du monde. - La vie des astres. **[Mechanical and Chemical Unity of the World. – The Life of the Stars.]** Leçon d'ouverture de la IVe session de l'Institut Olympique de Lausanne, donnée à Lausanne le 8 octobre 1919. Lausanne, Impr. La Concorde, 1919 (27 pages).

Almanach Olympique pour 1920.
[The Olympic Almanac for the Year 1920.]
Lausanne, Imprimerie Réunies, 1919.
[Edited by Pierre de Coubertin in the name of IOC and the Institut Olympique de Lausanne.]

XXVe Anniversaire des Jeux Olympiques. Discours prononcé par le Président du IOC à la Cérémonie commémorative. Lausanne, avril 1919.
[XXVth Anniversary of the Olympic Games. Address delivered by the President of the International Olympic Committee at the Commemorative Ceremony, April 1919.]
Later reprinted, in French, in:
1) L'Idée Olympique. pp.72-74.
2) Textes choisis, vol.II, pp.388-390.
in English, in: The Olympic Idea, pp.73-75.
in German, in: Der Olympische Gedanke, pp.86-88.
in Spanish, in: Ideario Olímpico, pp.124-128.

1920

Autour de la VIIe Olympiade.
[The Seventh Olympic Games.]
Lausanne, Impr.La Concorde, 1920 (24 pages).
Later reprinted, in: Textes choisis, vol.II, pp.268-276.
Later reprinted in English, with modification in the last paragraph, in:
American Olympic Committee (ed.): Seventh Olympic Games Antwerp, Belgium 1920. Greenwich/Con.1921, pp.47-58.

Le sport est roi. Discours prononcé à la Séance d'Ouverture de la XVIIIme Session plénière du IOC tenue à l'Hôtel de Ville d'Anvers en présence de S.M. le Roi des Belges le mardi 17 août 1920. Anvers 1920. Off-print, s.d.s.l.[Anvers 1920]. (6 pages).
[Sport Is King. Address delivered at the Opening Meeting of the XVIIIth Plenary Session of the International Olympic Committee, Antwerp, August 1920.]
Later reprinted, in French, in:
1) L'Idée Olympique. pp.81-85.
2) Textes choisis, Vol.I, pp.622-626 et Vol.III, pp.611-616.
in English, in: The Olympic Idea, pp.82-85.
in German, in: Der Olympische Gedanke, pp.96-100.
in Spanish, in: Ideario Olímpico, pp.138-144.

1921

Les Universités Ouvrières.
[Labor Universities.] [Popular Universities.]
Lausanne, Impr. Populaire, 1921 (8 pages).
Later reprinted, in: Textes choisis, Vol.I, pp.519-527.
Published under the title: "Les Universités populaires", in: Pages de Critique et d'Histoire, V[e] fascicule, Lausanne 1919.

1923

Comité International Olympique (Ed.): Session de 1923 tenue au Capitole, à Rome. Discours prononcé par le président du Comité à la séance inaugurale en présence de S.M. le Roi d'Italie, le 7 avril 1923. Lausanne, Impr. La Concorde, 1923. (Off-print 7 pages).
[Address delivered by the President of the Committee at the Opening Session, April 1923.]
Later reprinted, in: Textes choisis, Vol II, pp.398-402.

Mémoire concernant l'instruction supérieure des travailleurs manuels et l'organisation des universités ouvrières, s.l. 1923 (11 pages).
[Report on the Higher Education of Manual Laborers and the Organization of the Labor Universities.]
Later reprinted, in: Textes choisis, Vol.I, pp.528-536.

Où va l'Europe ?
[Where to, Europe?]
Paris, Ed. G. Grès, 1923 (31 pages).
[Serie of articles in the "Tribune de Genève" 1918-1923.]

1924

Les responsabilités et la réforme de la presse.
[Responsibility and Press Reforms.]
Conférence donnée à la Ligue Française à Lausanne. Aix-en-Provence, P. Roubaud, 1924 (15 pages).

1925

Discours prononcé à l'ouverture des Congrès Olympiques à l'Hôtel de Ville de Prague le 29 mai 1925 par le Baron Pierre de Coubertin.
[Address delivered at the Opening of the Olympic Congresses, Prague, May 1925.]
Prague, Imprimerie d'Etat, 1925 (8 pages).
Later reprinted, in:
1) L'Idée Olympique, pp.95-99.
2) Textes choisis, Vol.II, pp.404-410.

1927

De la transformation et de la diffusion des études historiques: caractère et conséquences.
[On the Transformation and Spread of Historical Studies: Their Character and Consequences.]
Communication faite à l'Académie d'Athènes à la séance du jeudi 14 avril 1927, s.l. 1927 (8 pages).
Later reprinted, in: Textes choisis, Vol.I, pp.360-369.

1928

L'utilisation pédagogique de l'activité sportive.
[Educational Use of Sports Activities.]
Conférence donnée par M. le Baron Pierre de Coubertin à l'Aula de l'Université de Lausanne, Genève 1928 (8 pages).
[Excerpted from the columns of the "Sport Suisse" of novembre 1928].
Later reprinted, in: Textes choisis, Vol.I, pp.475-487.

La cure d'aviron.
[The Cure of Rowing.]
Ouchy, 1928 (15 pages).
[Published in"Praxis – Revue Suisse de Médecine", July 1928].
Later reprinted, in: Textes choisis, Vol.III, pp.226-231.

1929

Olympie. Conférence donné le 6 mars à la Mairie du XVIe Arrondissement, à Paris. Genève, Impr.Burgi, 1929 (12 pages).
[Olympia. Lecture Given in Paris, in the Festival Hall of the 16th Arrondissement Town Hall.]
[Published in"Le Sport Suisse", July 1929].
Later reprinted, in:
1) L'Idée Olympique, pp.106-119.
2) Textes choisis, Vol.II, pp.414-429.

1930

La Charte de la réforme sportive.
[The Charter for Sports Reform.]
Lausanne, Bureau International de Pédagogie Sportive, s.d. [1930], (7 pages). German, English, Spanish, French and Italien versions.
Later reprinted in French, in:
1) Bulletin du Bureau International de Pédagogie Sportive, n° 3, Lausanne [1930], pp.3-9.
2) Textes choisis, Vol.I, pp.636-637.

1932

Les Assises de la Cité prochaine.
[The City of the Future.]
Conférence donnée à Berne, le 19 avril 1932. Genève, Impr. Burgi, 1932 (8 pages).
Later reprinted, in:
Le Sport: Suisse, 28e année, 4-18 mai 1932.
Textes choisis, vol.I, pp.638-650.

Lettre à S.E. le Président du Conseil de la Société des Nations.
[Letter to the President of the League of Nations.]
(Lettre adressée par Pierre de Coubertin à M. Hymans, Président des Sociétés des Nations) s.l. [Genève], s.d. [1932], (7 pages).

Pour l'avenir de la civilisation.
[For the Future of Civilization.]
Publiée par l'Union Pédagogique Universelle (1925-1930), Commission de Propagande. Genève/Paris/Athènes/Lausanne/Aix-en-Provence, s.d. [1932], (3 pages).

1934

Quarante années d'Olympisme 1894 -1934.
[Forty Years of Olympism 1894-1934.]
Allocution prononcée lors de la célébration du 40e Anniversaire du Rétablissement des Jeux Olympiques par le baron de Coubertin le samedi 23 juin 1934 à l'Aula de l'Université de Lausanne. Genève, 1934.
Off-print (4 pages) of Sport Suisse, June 1934.
Later reprinted, in: Textes choisis, Vol.II, pp.346-351.

1935

Les Assises philosophiques de l'Olympisme moderne. Message radiodiffusé de Berlin le 4 août 1935. Genève 1935.
[The Philosophic Foundation of Modern Olympism.]
Off-print (4 pages) of Sport Suisse, August 1935.
Later reprinted, in French, in:
1) L'Idée Olympique, pp.129-133.
2) Textes choisis, Vol.II, pp.4435-439.
in English, in: The Olympic Idea, pp.130-134.
in German, in: Der Olympische Gedanke, pp.150-154.
in Spanish, in: Ideario Olímpico, pp.212-218.

1936

Note sur l'évolution du Philhellénisme.
[Note on the Evolution of Philhellenism.]
s.l., s.d. [1936], (4 pages).

Leaflets, posters, etc.

* The editor has determined that this text, though unsigned, was written by Pierre de Coubertin.

1894

Circulaire annonçant le Congrès International Athlétique. [Circular Letter (January 1894) Announcing the International Athletic Congress in Paris.]
Paris, 15 janvier 1894 (1 page).
[Archives of the Czech Olympic Committee Prague].

* Note pour la presse. **[A News Item.]**
Paris, 1894 (1 page).
Later reprinted, in: Textes choisis, vol.II, pp.107-108.

Congrès International de Paris. Programme Préparatoire. **[The International Congress of Paris. Preliminary Program (1894).]**
Paris, USFSA, janvier 1894 Off-print (1 page).
Later reprinted, in: Textes choisis, vol.II, pp.106-107.

Congrès International Athlétique de Paris. 16-24 Juin 1894 (Règlement, Programme).
[The International Athletic Congress of Paris (Regulations, Program).]
Paris, USFSA, mai 1894, Off-print (2 pages).
Later reprinted, in: Textes choisis, Vol.II, pp.109-110.

Congrès International de Paris pour le rétablissement des Jeux Olympiques.
[The International Congress of Paris (1894) for the Renovation of the Olympic Games.]
Paris, USFSA, juin 1894, Off-print (4 pages).
Later reprinted, in: Textes choisis, vol.II, pp.111-114.

1905

Chronologie de l'Histoire de France.
[A Chronology of French History.]
s.l., s.d. [1905.
Later reprinted, in: Textes choisis, vol.III, pp.554-555.

1906

Lettre circulaire aux membres du CIO (mars 1906).
[Cirular Letter to the IOC Members (March 1906).]
Paris, 29 mars 1906, Off-print (2 pages).
Later reprinted, in: Textes choisis, Vol.II, p.481.

Invitation aux artistes (avril 1906)
[Invitation to the Artists (April 1906).]
Paris, avril 1906, Off-print (one page).
Later reprinted, in: Textes choises, Vol.II, p.482.

Programme de la Conférence consultative à Paris.
[Program of the 1906 Advisory Conference in Paris.]
Paris, IOC, avril 1906, Off-print (one page).

Lettre Circulaire du Président du CIO aux universités, féderations et sociétés de sport de l'univers.
[Advisory Conference. Circular Letter (July 1906)]
Paris, juillet 1906, Off-print (one page).
Later reprinted, in: Textes choisis, Vol.II, p. 497.

Lettre au Président de l'Union des Sociétés Françaises de Sports Athlétiques.
[Open Letter to the President of the French Sports Associations.]
Paris, 11 déc. 1906, Off-print (one page).

1908

Gymnastique Utilitaire. **[Useful Sports.]**
s.l., s.d. [1908], (1 page A3).
Later reprinted, in: Textes choisis, vol.III, pp.554-555.

1912

Circulaire du président du CIO aux membres.
[Circular from the IOC President to the Members.]
Paris, 8 avril 1912, Polycopie (1 page).

Congrès de Lausanne. Psychologie et Physiologie Sportive. Lausanne, IOC, 1912 (4 pages).
[Program of the Lausanne Congress 1913. (Sports-Psychology and Physiology).]
Later reprinted, in: Textes choisis, Vol.II, pp.259-260.

1913

To the Editor of the Morning Post.
Gand, Van Dosselaere, 1913 (1 page).
Later reprinted,
in French, in: L'Idée Olympique, pp.40-41.
in English, in: The Olympic Idea, pp.39-40.
in German, in: Der Olympische Gedanke, p.49.
in Spanish, in: Ideario Olímpico, pp.73-74.

1915

Le Décalogue de 1915. **[The Decalogue of 1915.]**
s.l., s.d. [1915], (1 page A3).
[Published by Excelsior, January 1915; 1 page.]

La France depuis 1870. **[France after 1870.]**
Paris 1915, (2 pages A3).
Feuille 1: Ière Période (1870-1897).
Feuille 2: IIe Période (1897-1914).

1918

Notice sur l'Institut Olympique de Lausanne.
[The Institut Olympique (Olympic Institute) in Lausanne.]
Lausanne 1918 (2 pages).
Later reprinted, in: Textes choisis, vol.II, pp.734-737

1919

Feuille d'Information de la Société de l'Histoire universelle.
[Information Leaflet of the Society of World History.]
s.l., s.d. [1919], (1 page).

Lettre à Messieurs les membres du C.I.O.
[Letter to the Members of the International Olympic Committee.]
Off-print, [Lausanne, January,1919].
Later reprinted, in French, in:
1) L'Idée Olympique, pp.67-72.
2) Textes choisis, Vol.II, pp.340-345.
in English, in: The Olympic Idea, pp.67-72.
in German, in: Der Olympische Gedanke, pp.80-85,
in Spanish, in: Ideario Olímpico, pp.116-124.

Circulaire aux membres du C.I.O. (sept. 1919).
[Circular to the Members of the IOC.]
Off-print, Lausanne, Sept.1919 (2 pages).
Later reprinted, in: Textes choisis, vol.II, pp.709-710.

Circulaire aux membres du C.I.O. (Lausanne, 6 déc. 1919) [Boxing as olympic sport].
[Circular to the members of the IOC: Boxing as Olympic sport].

1921

Plan de Conférences Populaires.
[Plan for Popular Conferences.]
s.l., s.d. [1921], (1 page).

Circulaire aux membres du C.I.O. (15 sept.1921), (1 page).
[Letter to the Members of the IOC Members (1921): "My work is done".]
Lausanne, 15 sept.1921, Off-print (1 page).
Later reprinted, in: Textes choisis, vol.II, p.672.

1923

Le sport veut conquérir l'Afrique.
[Athletics Want to Conquer Africa. An Appeal from the President of the IOC.]
s.l. [Rome], s.d. [1923], (1 page).
Later reprinted, in: Textes choisis, vol.II, p.675.

1925

Message par radio transmis à l'occasion de l'inauguration des travaux de l'Union Pédagogique Universelle.
[Radio Broadcast Concerning the Inauguration of the Union Pédagogique Universelle (Universal Educational Union).]
Aix-en-Provence 1925 (1 page).
Later reprinted, in: Textes choisi, Vol.I, p.627.

1927

A la Jeunesse sportive de toutes les nations.
[To the Sporting Youth of All Nations.]
Olympie, 17 avril 1927 (1 page).
Later reprinted, in: Textes choisis, vol.II, p.412.

1928

Message à tous les athlètes et participants aux Jeux Olympiques, assemblés à Amsterdam pour la célébration de la IXe Olympiade.
[Message to All Athletes and Participants Meeting at Amsterdam for the Ninth Olympiad.]
s.l., s.d. (2 pages).
Later reprinted, in:
1) Bulletin Officiel du IOC, oct. 1928, p.31-32;
2) Textes choisis, vol.II, pp.476-477.

Note sur le but et le fonctionnement du Bureau International de Pédagogie Sportive.
[Goal and Function of the International Bureau of Sports Pedagogy.]
Lausanne, avril 1928 (4 pages).
Later reprinted, in:
1) Bulletin Officiel du CIO, mai 1929, p.13;
2) Textes choisis, Vol.I, pp.633-635.

1932

Lettre ouverte à Armand Massard,
[Open Letter to Armand Massard.]
La Croix (Var), 19 mai 1932 (1 page).

Lettre ouverte à S.E. Monsieur Hymans, Président de l'Assemblée de la Société des Nations
[Open Letter to S.E. Mr Hymans, President of the League of Nations.]
(1 page).

1934

A mes amis hellènes.
[To My Hellenic Friends. An Open Letter Dated April, 1934.]
s.l., avril 1934 (1 page).
Later reprinted, in: Textes choisis, Vol.II, p.73.

Message imprimé adressé par Pierre de Coubertin au Comité de l'Organisation de la Xe Olympiade.
[A Printed Message Addressed to the Organizing Committee of the Xth Olympiad, by Pierre de Coubertin.]
s.l., 29 janvier 1934.

Message to the American Youth sent through the Associated Press on the occasion of the celebration of the 40th Anniversary of the Revival of the Olympic Games.
Lausanne, 23 juin 1934 (1 page).
Later reprinted, in:
1) L'Idée Olympique, pp.123-124, and the French version pp.125-126.
2) Textes choisis, vol.I., pp.488-489.
in English, in:The Olympic Idea, pp.125-126.
in German, in: Der Olympische Gedanke, pp.144-145.
in Spanish, in: Ideario Olímpico, pp.204-205.

1935

Le devoir des Philhellènes.
[The Philhellene's Duty.]
A Monsieur le Docteur Fr.-M. Messerli, président des amitiés gréco-suisses. Lausanne, 25 mars 1935.
Later reprinted, in: Textes choisis, Vol.II, p.72.

1936

Aux coureurs d'Olympie - Berlin.
[To the Olympia - Berlin Runners.]
s.l., s.d. [juillet 1936].
Published in "Sport Suisse", July 1936 (1 page).
Later reprinted,
in French, in:
1) L'Idée Olympique, pp.133-134.
2) Textes choisis, Vol.II, pp.430-434.
in English, in: The Olympic Idea, pp.134-135.
in German, in: Der Olympische Gedanke, pp.154-155.
in Spanish, in: Ideario Olímpico, pp.218-220.

Discours du Baron de Coubertin pour la clôture des Jeux Olympiques de Berlin.
[Message at the Close of the Berlin Games.]
s.l., s.d. (1936).
Later reprinted, in French, in:
1) L'Idée Olympique, pp.134-135 (manuscrit).
2) Textes choisis, Vol.II, p.305.
in English, in: The Olympic Idea, pp.135-136.
in German, in: Der Olympische Gedanke, pp.155-156.
in Spanish, in: Ideario Olímpico, pp.220-221.

L'Olympisme pénètre en Asie.
[Olympism Seeps into Asia.]
s.l., 1er décembre 1936 (1 page).

Articles

* The editor has determined that this text, though unsigned, was written by Pierre de Coubertin.

1886

1er nov. Les collèges anglais, Harrow School.
[English Schools: Harrow.]
In: La Réforme Sociale, 6e année, 2e série, tome II, 1er novembre1886, pp.466-473.

1er déc. Les universités anglaises, Cambridge.
[English Universities: Cambridge.]
In: La Réforme Sociale, 6e année, 2e série, tome II, 1er décembre 1886, pp.593-604.

1887

15 fév. Courrier d'Irlande. Les difficultés de la situation.
[Ireland: The Difficulties of the Present Situation.]
In: La Réforme Sociale, 7e année, 2e série, tome III, 15 février 1887, pp.235-240.

10 mai Victorian Era 1837-1887.
In: Le Correspondant, nouvelle série, tome III, 3e livraison du 10 mai 1887, pp.405-424.

1er juin L'éducation anglaise.
[English Education.]
[Speech held in Paris on April 18, 1887, to the members of the Société d'Economie Sociale.]
In: La Réforme Sociale, 7e année, 2e série, tome III, 1er juin 1887, pp.633-648.
Later reprinted, in: Textes choisis, vol.I, pp.142-158.

25 août Souvenirs d'Oxford et de Cambridge.
[Memories of Oxford and Cambridge.]
In: Le Correspondant, nouvelle série, tome 112, 4e livraison du 25 août 1887, pp.705-727.
Reprinted, in the special brochure: Extraits du Correspondant, Paris, J. Gervais, 1887, pp.7-30.

30 août Le surmenage.
[Overworking.]
In: Le Français, 30 août 1887.
Later reprinted, in excerpts in: L'Education Physique, 5e année, 15 décembre 1906, n° 22, pp.591-595. And slightly modified in: L'Education en Angleterre, Paris 1888, pp.295-308.

1er sept. Toynbee Hall. Le patronage social à Londres et les étudiants anglais.
[Toynbee Hall. Charity in London and the English Students.]
In: La Réforme Sociale, 2e série, tome III, 1er sept. 1887, pp.227-233.
Reprinted with some editorial changes, in:
1) L'Education en Angleterre, Paris, Hachette, 1888, pp.265-285.
2) Textes choisis, vol.I, pp.500-506.

14 nov. Un Programme: Le Play.
[A Programme: Le Play.]
Conférence faite le 14 novembre1887 à la Société Nationale Française à Londres.
[The complete typed manuscript of this lecture is housed in the archives of the IOC]
Later reprinted, in excerpts, under the title: "Une Conférence à Londres", in:
1) La Réforme Sociale, 7e année, 2e série, tome IV, 15 décembre 1887, pp.621-622.
2)Textes choisis, vol.I, pp.543-559.

1888

1er juin Paysages Irlandais.
[The Irish Countryside.]
Vol. 52 de l'Anthologie Contemporaine des Ecrivains Français et Belges. Paris 1888, 5e série, n° 4, 12 pages.
Later reprinted, in excerpts, in: Revue Athlétique, 2e année, 25 mars 1891, n° 3, pp.161-171.

1er juin Statistiques irlandaises.
[Irish Statistics.]
(Enquête présentée à la Société d'Economie Sociale, séance du 9 avril 1888.) In: La Réforme Sociale, 8e année, 2e série, tome V, 1er juin 1888, pp.661-668.

1er juil. Visite du Lycée Lakanal.
[A Visit of the Lycée Lakanal.]
In: La Réforme Sociale, 8e année, 2e série, tome VI, 1er juillet 1888, pp.37-38.

15 août Lettre aux Présidents des Sociétés d'aviron de Paris et de la province.
[Letter to the Presidents of the Sociétés d'aviron (Rowing clubs) of Paris and the Provinces.]
In: L'Education Anglaise en France. Paris, Hachette, 1889, p.203.

1er sept. Le remède au surmenage et la transformation des lycées de Paris.
[The Cure for Overworking and the Transformation of the Schools of Paris.]
Conférence faite à la réunion annuelle le 29 mai 1888.
In: La Réforme Sociale, 8e année, 2e série, tome VI, 1er septembre 1888, pp.240-249.
Later reprinted, in:
1)L'Education Anglaise en France. Paris, Hachette, 1889, pp.3-20.
2)Off-print: Paris, Impr. de Chaix, 1888 (19 pages).
3)Textes choisis, vol.I, pp.82-91.

1er sept. Lettre aux membres de la Société d'Economie Sociale et des Unions.

[Letter to the Members of the Société d'Economie Sociale and the Unions.]
In: La Réforme Sociale, 8e année, 2e série, tome VI, 1er septembre 1888, pp.249-252.
Later reprinted under the title: "Lettre aux membres de la Société d'économie sociale et des Unions de la paix sociale, Paris 1er août 1888", in:
1) L'Education Anglaise en France. Paris, Hachette, 1889, pp.199-202.
2) Textes choisis, vol.I, pp.108-110.

1er oct. L'université catholique américaine.
[The American Catholic University.]
In: La Réforme Sociale, 8e année, 2e série, tome VI, 1er octobre 1888, pp.349-351.

27 oct. La Ligue Nationale de l'éducation physique.
[The National League of Physical Education.]
In: L'Education Anglaise en France. Paris, Hachette, 1889, pp.204-206.
Later reprinted, in: Textes choisis, vol.I, pp.111-112.

1889

26 janv. L'Education athlétique.
[Athletic Education.]
Conférence faite le 26 janvier 1889 à l'Association Française pour l'Avancement des Sciences. In: Association Française pour l'Avancement des Sciences. Compte rendu de la 18e session. Paris, Masson, 1889, pp.15-25.
Off-print: Paris, Impr. Chaix, 1889 (23 pages).
Later reprinted, in: Textes choisis, vol.I, pp.159-173.

mars Préface.
[Foreword.]
In: Manuel des Jeux Scolaires et des Exercices Athlétiques. Publié par le Comité pour la Propagation des Exercices Physiques dans l'Education. Paris, Delalain Frères, 1889, p.3.

5 juin Les exercices physiques.
[Physical Exercise.]
(Conférence faite le 19 mai au Prytanée de La Flèche.)
In: La Revue Prytanéenne.Organe des anciens élèves de La Flèche, 7e année, 5 juin 1889, n° 22, pp.1035-1038.
Later reprinted, in: Textes choisis, vol.I, pp.569-574

15 juin Les exercices physiques dans les écoles d'Angleterre, d'Amérique, d'Australie et dans les Colonies anglaises.
[Physical Exercise in Schools in England, America, Australia, and the English Colonies.]
In: Exposition Universelle de 1889. Congrès des Exercices Physiques. Compte rendu des séances et concours. Paris, Publications des Annales Economiques, 1889.

16 sept. L'éducation de la paix.
[The Education of Peace.]
In: La Réforme Sociale, 2e série, tome VII, 16 septembre 1889, pp.361-363.
Later reprinted, in: Textes choisis, vol.I, pp.174-177.

30 nov. Athletics and Gymnastics. Speech at the Physical Training Congress in Boston.
In: Barrows, Isabel (Ed.): Physical Training. A Full Report of the Papers and Discussions of the Conference held in Boston in novembre, 1889. Boston, Press of George H. Ellis, 1890, pp.112-115.

1890

Préface.
[Foreword.]
In: Charles, J-B.: Ma Méthode. Paris, Maison Quantin, 1890, pp.1-5.
Later reprinted, in: Textes choisis, vol.III, pp.181-182.

25 janv. Le Boniment.
[Marketing.]
In: La Revue Athlétique, 1ère année, 25 janvier 1890, n° 1, pp.1-5.

25 janv. Rapport. Présenté à l'Assemblée Générale du Comité de Propagation des Exercices physiques tenue à la Sorbonne le 15 janvier 1890.
[Report to the General Assembly of the Committee for the Propagation of Physical Exercise. Sorbonne, Paris, 15 January 1890.]
In: La Revue Athlétique, 1ère année, 25 janvier 1890, n° 1, 15 pp.43-47.

fév. A Monsieur Eusèbe Martincourt.
[To Eusèbe Martincourt.]
In: Revue Athlétique, 1ère année, 15 février 1890, n° 2, pp.81-82.

5 avr. Causerie d'Avril.
[April Small Talk.]
In: Les Sports Athlétiques, Paris, 1ère année, 5 avril 1890, n° 1, p. l.

25 avr. L'Université Cornell à Ithaca (Etat de New York).
[Cornell University at Ithaca (State of New York).]
In: La Revue Athlétique, 1ère année, 25 avril 1890, n° 4, pp.193-202.

25 mai L'Exposition Athlétique.
[Athletic Exposition.]
In: La Revue Atlétique, 1ère année, 25 mai 1890, n° 5, pp.259-264.

25 juil. Rapport du Secrétaire Général.
[Report of the Secretary General to the General Assembly of the USFSA.]
In: La Revue Athlétique, 1ère année, 25 juillet 1890, n° 7, pp.387-393.
Later reprinted, in: Textes choisis, vol.II, pp.545-550.

23 août Causerie.
[Small Talk.]
In: Les Sports Athlétiques, 1ère année, 23 août 1890, n° 21, p.3.

25 août Les Collèges d'Australie.
[Australian Colleges.]
Documents du Congrès des exercices physiques.
In: La Revue Athlétique, 1ère année, 25 août 1890, n° 8, pp.449-462.

6 sept. Aux bains de mer.
[At a Seaside Resort.]
In: Les Sports Athlétiques, 1ère année, 6 septembre 1890, n° 23, pp.3-4.

20 sept. Le Duel.
[The Duel.]
In: Les Sports Athlétiques, 1ère année, 20 septembre 1890, n° 25, p.3.

11 oct. Un peu de zèle, s.v.p.
[Some Zeal, If You Please!]
In: Les Sports Athlétiques, 1ère année, 11 octobre 1890, n° 28, pp.1,4.

25 oct. Louvain.
[Louvain/Leuven.]
In: La Revue Athlétique, 1ère année, 25 octobre 1890, n° 10, pp.577-589.

nov. Appel pour la création d'un enseignement universitaire ouvrier.
[Appeal for the Establishment of Worker Education.]
In: Anthologie, Aix-en-Provence, Impr. P. Roubaud, 1933, pp.165-166.
Later reprinted, in: Textes choisis, vol.I, pp.507-508.

9 nov. Equitation.
[Horse-Riding.]
In: Les Sports Athlétiques, 1ère année, 9 novembre1890, n° 32, pp.1,4.

22 nov. Changement de direction.
[A Change of Direction.]
In: Les Sports Athlétiques, 1ère année, 22 novembre1890, n° 32, pp.1-2.

25 nov. Un Athlète.
[An Athlete.]
In: La Revue Athlétique, 1ère année, 25 novembre1890, n° 11, pp.641-650. [Book Review.]

13 déc. Deux douches.
[Two Showers.]
In: Les Sports Athlétiques, 1ère année, 13 décembre 1890, n° 37, pp.5-6.

25 déc. Les Jeux Olympiques à Much Wenlock. Une page de l'histoire de l'athlétisme.
[The Olympic Games at Much Wenlock. A Page from the History of Athletics.]
In: La Revue Athlétique, 1ère année, 25 décembre 1890, n° 12, pp.705-713.
Later reprinted, in: Textes choisis, vol.II, pp.78-84.

27 déc. Mensonge. **[A Lie.]**
In: Les Sports Athlétiques, 1ère année, 27 décembre 1890, n° 39, p.4.

1891

8 janv. Le Conseil Supérieur de l'Education Physique.
[The Council for Physical Education.]
Rapport présenté à la troisième session annuelle du Comité de Propagation des Exercices Physiques, tenue à la Sorbonne le 8 janvier 1891.
In: La Revue Athlétique, 2e année, 25 janvier 1891, pp.24-31.There is an 8 pages off-print of this work.
Later reprinted, in: Textes choisis, vol.I, pp.575-580.

10 janv. Bonne année.
[Happy New Year.]
In: Les Sports Athlétiques, 2e année, 10 janvier 1891, n°41, p.3.

24 janv. Correspondance.
[Correspondence.]
In: Les Sports Athlétiques, 2e année, 24 janvier 1891, n° 43, p.6.

14 fév. Correspondance.
[Correspondence.]
In: Les Sports Athlétiques, 2e année, 14 février 1891, n° 46, p.9.

21 fév. Bons points. **[Some Good Points.]**
In: Les Sports Athlétiques, 2e année, 21 février 1891 n°51, pp.2-3.

25 fév. Au Prytanée de La Flèche.
[At the Prytanée de La Flèche College.]
In: La Revue Athlétique, 2e année, 25 février 1891, n° 2, pp.65-72.

7 mars- 14 mars Bons poings (I et II).
[Good Fists. (French Pun on "Good Points".)]
In: Les Sports Athlétiques,
1ère partie: 2e année, 7 mars 1891, n° 49, pp.2-3.
2e partie: 2e année, 14 mars 1891, n° 50, pp.3-4.
Later reprinted, in: Textes choisis, vol.III, pp.169-173.

21 mars La Ligue et l'Union.
[The League and the Union.]
In: Les Sports Athlétiques, 2e année, 21 mars 1891, n° 51, p.3.
Later reprinted, in: Textes choisis, vol.I, pp.581-582.

11 avr. L'Athlétisme, son rôle et son histoire.
[Athletism. Its Role and Its History.]
Conférence faite le 11 avril à l'Union Chrétienne de Jeunes Gens de Paris. In: La Revue Athlétique, 2e année, 25 avril 1891, n° 4, pp.193-207.
Later reprinted (slightly modified), in: L'Education Physique,
I: 9e année, 31 mars 1910, n° 6, pp.145-150.
II: 9e année, 15 avril 1910, n° 7, pp.159-172.

25 mai La vie scolaire au Cap.
Documents du Congrès des Exercices Physiques.
[School Life at the Cap. Documents of the Physical Exercises Congress (1889).]
In: La Revue Athlétique, 2e année, 25 mai 1891, n° 5, pp.257-265.

13 juin Attaques & Riposte.
[Attacks and Answers.]
In: Les Sports Athlétiques, 2e année, 13 juin 1891, n° 63, pp.2-3.

13 juin Correspondance.
[Correspondence.]
In: Les Sports Athlétiques, 2e année, 13 juin 1891, n° 63, p.8.

25 juin L'Egypte athlétique.
[Sports in Egypt.]
In: La Revue Athlétique, 2e année, 25 juin 1891, n°6, pp.368-370. [Regarding its authenticity, see Notes sur l'Education publique. Paris, Hachette, 1901, pp.128-130.]

25 juil. Assemblée Générale de l'Union des Sociétés Françaises de Sports Athlétiques. Rapport du Secrétaire Général.
[General Assembly of the USFSA. Report of the Secretary General.]
In: La Revue Athlétique, 2e année, 25 juillet 1891, n° 7, pp.385-388.
Later reprinted, in:
Les Sports Athlétiques, 2e année, 1er août 1891, n° 70, p.2, et 8 août 1891, n° 71, p.2.

25 juil. Un concours littéraire entre athlètes.
[A Literary Competition between Athletes.]
In: Les Sports Athlétiques, 2e année, 25 juillet 1891, n° 69, pp.2-3.
Later reprinted, in: Textes choisis, vol.I, pp.567-568.

5 sept. En bicyclette.
[Riding a Bike.]
In: Les Sports Athlétiques, 2e année, 5 septembre 1891, n° 75, pp.1-2.
Later reprinted, in: Textes choisis, vol.III, pp.262-263.

10 sept. La Renaissance universitaire.
[A University Renaissance.]
In: La Grande Revue, 5e année, 10 septembre 1891, pp.465-472.

10 oct. Un sport exotique.
[An Exotic Sport.]
In: Les Sports Athlétiques, 2e année, 10 octobre 1891, n° 80, p.2.
Later reprinted with slight editorial changes, under the title: "Le pêcheur de tortues". In:
1) Revue Olympique, 7e année, février 1907, pp.215-217.
2) Anthologie. Aix-en-Provence, Impr. P. Roubaud, 1933, pp.146-147.

25 oct. Les Ambitions du Docteur Lagrange.
[Doctor Lagrange's Ambitions.]
In: La Revue Athlétique, 2e année, 25 octobre 1891, n° 11, pp.577-584. [Book Review.]

25 nov. Dans la Hague. **[The Hague.]**
In: La Revue Athlétique, 2e année, 25 novembre1891, n° 11, pp.641-647.
Later reprinted, in: Revue du Pays de Caux, 1ère année, juillet 1902, n° 3, pp.113-115.

28 nov. Correspondance. (Lettre à Monsieur Stock.)
[Correspondence: Letter to Monsieur Stock.]
In: L'Aviron, 6e année, 28 novembre1891, p.79.

5 déc. Ceci tuera cela!
[This Will Kill That!]
In: Les Sports Athlétiques, 2e année, 5 décembre 1891, n° 88, pp.2-3.

10 déc. Dans les Universités transatlantiques. La Promotion de 1860 à Harvard. Un discours du Président Preston Johnston - Etudiants de Chicago.
[In Translatlantic Universities: Harvard, 1860. A Speech by President Preston Johnston. Students from Chicago.]
In: La Grande Revue, 5e année, 10 décembre 1891, pp.476-483.

26 déc. Union. Rapport de la Commission de Football. Présenté au Comité et adopté dans sa dernière séance.
[Report of the Commission de Football. Presented to the Committee and Accepted at Its Last Meeting.]
In: Les Sports Athlétiques, 2e année, 19 décembre 1891, n° 90, pp.2-3, et 26 décembre 1891, n° 91, p.2.

1892

2 janv. Aux Champs-Elysées.
[Olympics in the Netherworld.]
In: Les Sports Athlétiques, 3e année, 2 janvier 1892, n° 92, pp.10-11.
Later reprinted, in:
1) Revue Olympique, 7e année, avril 1907, pp.252-254.
2) L'Education physique, 10e année, 31 mai 1911, n° 10, pp.260-262.
3) Textes choisis, vol.III, pp.656-657.

9 jan.-27 fév.
* Caractères sportifs.
[Sportsmen.]
In: Les Sports Athlétiques, 3e année,
I: 9 janvier 1892, nº 93, pp.6-7;
II: 16 janvier 1892, nº 94, pp.4-5;
III: 30 janvier 1892, nº 96, pp.5-6;
IV: 6 février 1892, nº 97, pp.3-4;
V: 13 février 1892, nº 98, pp.3-4;
VI: 20 février 1892, nº 99, p.4;
VII: 27 février 1892, nº 100, p.5.

23 janv. Causerie du samedi.
[**Saturday Small Talk:** Union membership figures].
In: Les Sports Athlétiques, 3e année, 23 janvier 1892, nº 95, pp.4-5.

6 fév. Causerie du samedi.
[**Saturday Small Talk:** Believing and Acting]
In: Les Sports Athlétiques, 3e année, 6 février 1892, nº 97, pp.2-3.

13 fév. Correspondance.
[Correspondence.]
In: Les Sports Athlétiques, 3e année, 13 février 1892, nº 95, p.12.

20 fév. Causerie du samedi.
[**Saturday Small Talk:** The Philosophy of Football.]
In: Les Sports Athlétiques, 3e année, 20 février 1892, nº 99, p.3.
Later reprinted slightly modified in the article, in: "Les Associations Athlétiques. Organisation et fonctionnement dans les lycées et les collèges français (pp.523-525)". In: Revue Universitaire, 1ère année, tome 1, 15 mai 1892, pp.521-543.

12 mars Causeries du samedi.
[**Saturday Small Talk:** To Alphonse Daudet.]
In: Les Sports Athlétiques, 3e année, 12 mars 1892, nº 102, pp.2-3.

3 avr. Causerie du samedi.
[**Saturday Small Talk:** Voyage of Capt. Lancrenon. Sports Exhibition at Scheveningen.]
In: Les Sports Athlétiques, 3e année, 2 avril 1892, nº 105, pp.3-4.

15 mai Les Associations Athlétiques. Organisation et fonctionnement dans les lycées et les collèges français. (Rapport présenté à la séance du Comité de propagation des exercices physiques à la Sorbonne, le 7 mars 1892.)
[The Athletics Associations. Organization and Functionings in French Schools and Colleges. Report presented at the Meeting of the Committee for the Propagation of Physical Exercise at the Sorbonne.]
In: Revue Universitaire, 1ère année, tome 1, 15 mai 1892, pp.521-542.
Off-print Paris, Armand Colin, 1892 (24 pages).

28 mai Causerie du samedi.
[**Saturday Small Talk:** On an article published in the "Soleil".]
In: Les Sports Athlétiques, 3e année, 28 mai 1892, nº 113, pp.3-4.

10 juil. Union. Assemblée Générale. Rapport du Secrétaire Général.
[**General Assembly**. Report of the Secretary General.]
In: Les Sports Athlétiques, 3e année, 23 juillet 1892, nº 121, pp.1-3.

27 août Causerie du samedi.
[**Saturday Small Talk:** Excessive competitions.]
In: Les Sports Athlétiques, 3e année, 27 août 1892, nº 126, p.2.

10 sept. Causerie du samedi.
[**Saturday Small Talk:** Successes of the USFSA.]
In: Les Sports Athlétiques, 3e année, 10 sept. 1892, nº 128, pp.2-3.

19 sept. L'enseignement de la géographie.
[Teaching Geography.]
(Communication du congrès de l'Association Française pour l'Avancement des Sciences à Pau, le 19 septembre 1892.) In: Association Française pour l'Avancement des Sciences, Congrès de Pau, 1892. Paris 1892, pp.871-880. Later reprinted, in excerpts under the title "Géographie nouvelle", in: Anthologie. Aix-en-Provence, Impr. P. Roubaud, 1933, pp.11-12.

29 oct. Causerie du samedi.
[**Saturday Small Talk:** Letter of Mr. Brookes.]
In: Les Sports Athlétiques, 3e année, 29 octobre 1892 nº135, pp.2-3.

25 nov. Conférence faite à la Sorbonne, 25 novembre 1892, in: Pierre de Coubertin: Le Manifeste Olympique, introduit par François d'Amat, Lausanne, Les Editions du Grand Pont, 1994, pp.45-58.
Lecture given at the Sorbonne (November 1892)
[Physical Exercises in the Modern World.]
in: Pierre de Coubertin: Le Manifeste Olympique, ibidem, pp.66-79.

31 déc. Souhaits du Nouvel An.
[Good Wishes for the New Year.]
In: Les Sports Athlétiques, 3e année, 31 décembre 1892, nº 144, p.3.

1893

Californie d'autrefois.
[The California of the Past.]
In: Anthologie. Aix-en-Provence, P. Roubaud, 1933, pp.133-136.

1er avr. A travers l'Athlétisme.
[**On Athletism.** Introduction of Sports in France. International Role.]
In: Journal des Débats Politiques et Littéraires, 105e année, 1er avril 1893, pp.1-2.
Later reprinted, in: Textes choisis, vol.III, pp.264-266.

16 avr. Les petits Alpins.
In: Les Sports Athlétiques, 4e année, 16 avril 1893, n° 160, p.7.

6 mai A travers l'Athlétisme.
[**On Athletism.** Polo on horseback.]
In: Journal des Débats Politiques et Littéraires, 105e année, 6 mai 1893, p. l.
Later reprinted, in: Textes choisis, vol.III, pp.298-302.

6 juin A travers l'Athlétisme.
[**On Athletism.** Voyage of Capt. Lancrenon. Limits of modern sport.]
In: Journal des Débats Politiques et Littéraires, 105e année, 6 juin 1893, pp.1-2.

1er juil. La Politique de l'Union.
(Discours prononcé par le secrétaire de l'Union, le 25 juin 1893 à Chartres.)
[The Policies of the Union. Speech by the the Secretary of the Union. (Union of French Athletic Sports Associations/ USFSA).]
In: Les Sports Athlétiques, 4e année, 1er juillet 1893, n° 170, pp.3-5.

9 juil. A travers l'Athlétisme.
[**On Athletism.** At Henley. Gladstone.]
In: Journal des Débats Politiques et Littéraires, 105e année, 9 juillet 1893, p. l.

15 juil. Union. Assemblée Générale.
[Speech M. de Coubertin, July, 11, 1893.]
In: Les Sports Athlétiques, 4e année, 15 juillet 1893, n° 172, pp.2-4.
Later reprinted, in: Textes choisis, vol.II, pp.99-103.

15 juil. Correspondance.
[Correspondence.]
In: Les Sports Athlétiques, 4e année, 15 juillet 1893, n° 172, p.18.

7 août A travers l'Athlétisme.
[**On Athletism.** Cycling.]
In: Journal des Débats Politiques et Littéraires, 105e année, 7 août 1893, pp.1-2.
Later reprinted, in: Textes choisis, vol. III, pp.264-266.

8 sept. A travers l'Athlétisme.
[**On Athletism.** Tennis.]
In: Journal des Débats Politiques et Littéraires, 105e année, 8 septembre 1893, p.3.
Later reprinted, in: Textes choisis, vol.III, pp.275-278.

9 sept. Correspondance.
[Correspondence.]
In: Les Sports Athlétiques, 4e année, 9 septembre 1893, n° 180, pp.19-20.

16 sept. Correspondance.
[Correspondence.]
In: Les Sports Athlétiques, 4e année, 9 septembre 1893, n° 181, pp.1-2.

16 sept. Correspondance.
[Correspondence.]
In: Les Sports Athlétiques, 4e année, 16 septembre 1893, n° 181, pp.19-20.

14 oct. Lettre d'Amérique.
[Letter from America.]
In: Les Sports Athlétiques, 4e année, 2 octobre 1893, n° 185, pp.13-14.

28 oct. Chicago Chronique.
[A Chicago Chronicle.]
In: Les Sports Athlétiques, 4e année, 28 octobre 1893, n° 187, pp.3-4.

2 déc. Lettre d'Amérique.
[Letter from America.]
In: Les Sports Athlétiques, 4e année, 2 décembre 1893, n° 192, p.15.

1894

13 janv. Napoléon et le football.
[Napoleon and Football.]
In: Les Sports Athlétiques, 5e année, 13 janvier 1894, n° 198, pp.24-26.
Later reprinted, in: Textes choisis, vol.III, pp.283-286.

3 mars Lettre ouverte aux potaches de France.
[An Open Letter to the Students at French Schools.]
In: Les Sports Athlétiques, 5e année, 3 mars 1894, n° 205, pp.160-161.

14 avr. La Bataille de Caen.
[The Battle of Caen.]
In: Les Sports Athlétiques, 5e année, 14 avril, n° 211, p.291.

15 avr. Sur la côte de Californie.
[On the Californian Coast.]
In: La Revue de Paris, 15 avril 1894, pp.204-224.
Later reprinted, in: Souvenirs d'Amérique et de Grèce. Paris, Hachette, 1897, pp.33-59.

15 juin Le Rétablissement des Jeux Olympiques.
In: La Revue de Paris, 15 juin 1894, pp.170-184.
Later reprinted, in: Textes choisis, vol.II, pp.551-564.
English translation: The Reestablishment of the Olympic Games. In: The Chautauquan, A Monthly Magazine,

Vol. XIX, New Series, Volume X, April 1894, pp.696-700. [Partie I & III similar to the speech at the Sorbonne, november, 25, 1892.]

23 juin Lettre à M. A. Fleuret, président de la Fédération des Sociétés nautiques parisiennes.
[Letter to M.A. Fleuret, the President of the Nautical Societies of Paris.]
In: Les Sports Athlétiques, 5e année, 23 juin 1894, n° 221, p.520.

30 juin Congrès International de Paris. [Discours au Banquet de clôture.]
[Speech at the Closing Banquet of the Congress of Paris (1894).]
In: Les Sports Athlétiques, 5e année, 30 juin 1894, n° 222, p.537.
Later reprinted, in:
1) Bulletin du Comité International des Jeux Olympiques, 1ère année, juillet 1894, no 1,p.3.
2) Textes choisis, vol.II, pp.362-363.
3) L'Idée Olympique, pp.5-6.
in English, in: Olympic Idea, pp.6-7.
in German, in: Der Olympische Gedanke, pp.5-7.
in Spanish, in: Ideario Olímpico, pp.17-19.

juil. Le Congrès de Paris.
[The Congress of Paris.]
In: Bulletin du Comité International des Jeux Olympiques, 1ère année, juillet 1894, n° 1, p. l.
Later reprinted, in: Textes choisis, vol.II, pp.104-105.

14 juil. USFSA. Assemblée Générale. **[USFSA. General Assembly. Speech.]**
In: Les Sports Athlétiques, 5e année, 14 juillet 1894, n° 224, pp.572-573.

28 juil. Championnats "nationaux".
["National" Championships.]
In: Les Sports Athlétiques, 5e année, 28 juillet 1894, n° 226, pp.673-674.

11 août Exercices de sport.
[Exercises.]
In: Association Française pour l'Avancement des Sciences. Compte rendu de la 23e session. 1ère partie. Paris, Masson, 1894, pp.241-251.
[Speech at the Caen conference of the Association Française pour l'Avancement des Sciences, session of August 11, 1894.]
Later reprinted, in: Textes choisis, vol.III, pp.429-442.

11 août Un tennis dans les roses.
[Playing Tennis Surrounded by Roses.]
In: Les Sports Athlétiques, 5e année, 11 août 1894, n° 228, pp.711-712.

25 août Le bilan du Congrès de Caen.
[Summing up the Caen Congress.]
In: Les Sports Athlétiques, 5e année, 25 août 1894, n° 230, pp.752-753.
Later reprinted, in: Textes choisis, vol.I, pp.583-585.

oct. Chronique. [Le caractère de notre enterprise].
[Chronicle - The Character of Our Enterprise .]
In: Bulletin du Comité International des Jeux Olympiques, 1ère année, octobre 1894, n° 2, p. l.
Later reprinted, in: Textes choisis, vol.II, pp.593-595.

27 oct. Interpellation.
[Objection.]
In: Les Sports Athlétiques, 5e année, 27 octobre 1894, n° 239, pp.931-932.

16 nov. Le Néo-olympisme. Appel à l'opinion athénienne. Conférence faite à la société littéraire "Le Parnass" à Athènes.
[The Neo-Olympism. Appeal to the People of Athens (November 16, 1894). Lecture Given to the Parnassus Literary Society at Athens.]
In: Le Messager d'Athènes, Athènes/Paris, 1894, n° 39, pp.287-288, et 1894, n° 42, pp.306-309.
Later reprinted under the title "Jeux Olympiques. Discours à Athènes (16 nov.1894)", in:
1) Textes choisis, vol.II, pp.364-375.
Later reprinted in excerpts under the title: "L'Athlétisme dans le monde moderne et les Jeux Olympiques", in:
2) Bulletin du Comité International des Jeux Olympiques, 2e année, janvier 1895, n° 3, p.4.
3) L'Idée Olympique, pp.6-9.
Later reprinted,
in English, in: The Olympic Idea, pp.7-10.
in German, in: Der Olympische Gedanke, pp.7-10.
in Spanish, in: Ideario Olímpico, pp.19-24.

1895

Avant-propos. **[Foreword.]**
In: USFSA (Ed.): Manuel d'Hygiène athlétique. Paris, F. Alcan, 1895, pp.5-8.

1896

Il est d'ordinaire... [Les Jeux Olympiques modernes.]
[The Modern Olympic Games.]
In: Les Jeux Olympiques 776 av. J.-C. - 1896.Second part: Les Jeux Olympiques de 1896. Rapport officiel. Edition grecque-française: Athènes/Paris, Ch. Beck/H. Le Soudier, 1896, pp.1-7.
Edition allemande-anglaise: Athens/Leipzig/London, Ch. Beck/F.Volckmar/H.Grevel, 1897, pp.1-8.
Later reprinted, in:
1) L'Idée Olympique, pp.9-13.
2) Under the title: "Les Jeux Olympiques modernes", in: Textes choisis, vol.II, pp.124-128.
Later reprinted,
in English, in: The Olympic Idea, pp.10-14.
in German, in: Der Olympische Gedanke, pp.11-15.
in Spanish, in: Ideario Olímpico, pp.24-30.

15 fév.-15 mars L'évolution française sous la troisième république.
In: La Nouvelle Revue,
1ère partie, 18e année, tome 98, 15 février 1896, pp.705-723;
2e partie, 18e année, tome 99, 1er avril 1896, pp.52-69 ;
3e partie, 18e année, tome 99, 15 avril 1896, pp.265-284.
Reprinted, in book form: Paris, Plon & Cie, 1896.
English edition: The Evolution of France under the third Republic. New York, Boston, Th. Y. Crowell, 1897.

mars The Government of France and its Recent Changes.
In: The Review of Reviews, vol. XIII, mars 1896, pp.307-310.

avril La préface des Jeux Olympiques.
[Preface for the Olympic Games.]
In: Cosmopolis, vol. II, avril 1896, n° 4, pp.146-159.
Later reprinted, in:
1) Souvenirs d'Amérique et de Grèce. Paris, Hachette, 1897, pp.101-120.
2) Textes choisis, vol.II, pp.85-96.

6 avr. Au Jour Le Jour: Lettre Olympique (d'Athènes, le 26 mars 1896).
In: Journal des Débats, Politiques et Litteraires.
Paris, 6 avril 1896, p.1.
Later reprinted in: Souvenirs d'Amérique et de Grèce.
Paris, Hachette, 1897, pp.139-142.
in English: Olympic Letter from Athens (March 26, 1896),
in: Report of the Commissioner for the Year 1895-1896.
Washington D.C., Vol.1, pp.1329-1331.

8 avr. Au Jour le Jour: Lettre Olympique (d'Athènes, le 31 mars 1896).
In: Journal des Débats, Politiques et Litteraires.
Paris, 8 avril 1896, p.3.
Later reprinted, in English: Olympic Letter from Athens (March 31, 1896),
In: Report of the Commissioner for the Year 1895-1896.
Washington D.C., Vol.I, pp.1331-1332.

18 avr. Lettre à son Altesse Royale.
[Letter to His Royal Highness.]
Athènes, le 3/15 avril 1896.
In: Les Jeux Olympiques. Supplément n° 15 of the Messager d'Athènes, 18 avril 1896, n° 6, p.67.

18 avr. Protocole des décisions adoptées par le Comité.
[Protocol of the Decisions Taken by the Committee]
In: Les Jeux Olympiques. Supplément n° 15 du Messager d'Athènes, 18 avril 1896, n° 6, p.69.
Later reprinted, in: Textes choisis, vol.II, pp.596-597.

22 avr. Lettre Olympique (d'Athènes, le 12 avril 1896).
In: Journal des Débats, Politiques et Litteraires.
Paris, 22 avril 1896, p.3.
Later reprinted, in: Souvenirs d'Amérique et de Grèce.
Paris, Hachette, 1897, pp.149-152.
in English: Olympic Letter from Athens (April 12, 1896),
in: Report of the Commissioner for the Year 1895-1896.
Washington D.C., Vol.I, pp.1332-1334.

30 avr. To the Editor of the Times.
In: The Times, New York, 30 apvril, 1896, p.12.
Later reprinted, in: Textes choisis, vol.II, p.163.

juin The Franco-Russian Alliance.
In: The Review of Reviews, vol. XIII, juin 1896, pp.700-702.

13 juin Jules Simon.
In: Les Sports Athlétiques, 7e année, 13 juin 1896, n° 324, pp.443-444.

oct. Jules Simon.
In: The Review of Reviews, vol. XIV, octobre 1896, pp.450-454.

oct. Jules Simon intime.
In: Revue des Revues, vol.VIII, octobre 1896, p.261.

1er oct. La mission des va-nu-pieds.
[The Mission of the Barefoot Runners.]
In: La Nouvelle Revue, 18e année, tome 102, 1er octobre 1896, pp.364-370.
Later reprinted, in: Souvenirs d'Amérique et de Grèce.
Paris, Hachette, 1897, pp.89-98.

22 oct. Le mouvement universitaire aux Etats-Unis.
Au directeur du "Temps".
In: Le Temps, n° 12 927, 22 octobre, 1896, p. l.

nov. The Olympic Games of 1896.
In: The Century Illustrated Monthley Magazine, vol. LIII, nouvelle série, vol. XXXI, nov. 1896, pp.39-53.

15 déc. La formation des Etats-Unis: I. La vie coloniale.
[History of the United States I: Life in the Colonies.]
In: La Nouvelle Revue, 18e année, tome 103,
15 décembre 1896, pp.712-732.

1897

janv. A Typical Englishman: Dr. W.P. Brookes of Wenlock in Shropshire.
In: The Review of Reviews, vol. XV, janvier 1897, pp.62-65.

1er janv. La formation des Etats-Unis: II. Une guerre de cent ans.
[History of the United States II: A One-Hundred-Years War.]
In: La Nouvelle Revue, 19e année, tome 104, 1er janvier 1897, pp.55-79.

7 janv. Aux Associations Athlétiques Scolaires de l'USFSA.
[To the School Associations of the USFSA.]
In: Les Sports Athlétiques, 8e année, 7 janvier 1897, n° 553, pp.19-20.

15 janv. La formation des Etats-Unis: III. Depuis l'indépendance.
[History of the United States III: Independence.]
In: La Nouvelle Revue, 19e année, tome 104, 15 janvier 1897, pp.319-342.

1er fév. La formation des Etats-Unis: IV. Les influences étrangères et les ambitions nationales.
[History of the United States IV: Foreign Influences and National Ambitions.]
In: La Nouvelle Revue, 19e année, tome 104, 1er février 1897, pp.495-516.

mars L'Amérique universitaire.
[American Universities.]
In: Cosmopolis, vol. V, march 1897, n° XV, pp.780-794.

15 mars Un mensonge historique.
[A Historical Lie.]
In: La Nouvelle Revue, 19e année, tome 105, 15 mars 1897, pp.243-248.

29 mars Médecin, précepteur et homme politique.
[Sport: Physician, Teacher, and Politician.]
In: Tous les Sports, 8e année, 29 mars 1897, n° 409, p. l.

mai The Chancellor of the French Republic - Gabriel Hanotaux.
In: The Review of Reviews, vol. XV, mai 1897, pp.545-548.

juil. The Revival of the French Universities.
In: The Review of Reviews, vol. XVI, juillet 1897, pp.52-56.

1er juil. La formation des Etats-Unis: V. L'effervescence religieuse.
[History of the United States V: The Upsurge of Religion.]
In: La Nouvelle Revue, 19e année, tome 107, 1er juillet 1897, pp.459-481.

sept. Royalists and Republicans. Notes of a Parisian.
In: The Century Magazine, vol. LIV, septembre 1897, n° 5, pp.643-654

15 sept. Sigismond de Justh.
In: La Nouvelle Revue, 19e année, tome 108, 15 septembre 1897, pp.261-270.

1er déc. A French View of the British Empire.
In: The Fortnightly Review, vol. LXII, nouvelle série, 1er décembre 1897, n° 372, pp.803-816.

1898

L'Association Athlétique Alsacienne.
[The Athletic Association of the Ecole Alsacienne.]
In: 25e Anniversaire de l'Ecole Alsacienne (1873-1898). Paris, Camerot & Renouard, 1898, pp.149-150.

28 janv. La question des scolaires.
[School Matters.]
In: Tous les Sports, 9e année, 28 janv. 1898, n° 453, p. l.
Later reprinted, in: Bulletin Officiel de l'U.S.F.S.A., 9e année, 30 janvier 1898, n° 409, pp.33-34.

1er mars Contradictions of Modern France. The Military Paradox.
In: The Fortnightly Review, vol. LXIII, nouvelle série, 1er mars 1898, n° 375, pp.341-353.

avril Does Cosmopolitan Life Lead to International Friendliness ?
In: The Review of Reviews, vol. XVII, avril 1898, n° 4, pp.429-434.

mai Die Beziehungen zwischen Europa und den Vereinigten Staaten im 20. Jahrhundert.
[Relations between Europe and the United States in the Twentieth Century. (German Text)]
In: Deutsche Revue, 23e année, mai 1898, n° 5, pp.222-231.

juin Contradictions of Modern France. The Political Paradox. In: The Fortnightly Review, vol. LXIII, nouvelle série, juin 1898, pp.977-991.

4 juin La philosophie de l'histoire des Etats-Unis.
[The Philosophy of History of the United States.]
Ve leçon donnée à l'Ecole des Sciences Politiques à Paris, le mercredi 18 avril 1898.
In: Revue Bleue, 35e année, 4e série, tome IX, 4 juin 1898, n° 23, pp.708-715.
Reprinted in the form of a brochure, on the occasion of the author's 70th birthday, by his friends in America, s. l. 1933, (16 pages).

9 juil. Nos Lycéens.
[Our Students.]
In: La Revue Bleue.
I: 35e année, 4e série, tome IX, 25 juin 1898, n° 26, pp.801-810 ;
II: 35e année, 4e série, tome X, 2 juillet 1898, n° 1, pp.17-21 ;
III: 35e année, 4e série, tome X, 9 juillet 1898, n° 2, pp.47-52.

août The Present Problems and Politics of France.
In: The American Monthly Review of Review, vol. 18, août 1898, n° 2, pp.186-194.

sept. The Redemption of Athletics.
In: Monthly Building, vol. V, septembre 1988, pp.167-168.

nov. Building up a World's fair in France.
In: The Century Illustrated Monthly Magazine, vol. LVII, novembre1898, pp.114-126.

1899

fév.-déc. France since 1814.
In: Fortnightly Review, vol. LXV, nouvelle série, 1899, pp.186-211, 572-585, 817-834, 1026-1037; vol. LXVI, nouvelle série, 1899, pp.241-255, 843-855, 977-990.
Reprinted in book form. New York, Mac Millan, 1900, (281 pages).

15 fév.-15 avr.
Le Roman d'un Rallié.
In: La Nouvelle Revue,
I: 21e année, tome LXVI, 15 février, pp.577-601;
II: 21e année, tome LXVII, 1er mars, pp.44-68 ;
III: 21e année, tome LXVII, 15 mars, pp.222-247 ;
IV: 21e année, tome LXVII, 1er avril, pp.452-482 ;
V: 21e année, tome LXVII, 15 avril, pp.650-684 ;
[signed with the pseudonym Georges Hohrod].
Reprinted, in book form: Auxerre, A. Lanier, 1902.

mars Dépositions de M. de Coubertin.
[Contribution by Baron de Coubertin.]
In: Ribot, M: Enquête sur l'enseignement secondaire. Procès-verbaux des dépositions. Paris 1899, pp.433-435.

avril Some notes on the new French President.
In: The American Monthly Review of Reviews, vol. 19, avril 1899, pp.423-426.

1er avr. L'Urgente Réforme.
[An Urgent Reform.]
In: La Nouvelle Revue, tome 117, 1er avril 1899, pp.385-401.
Later reprinted, in: Textes choisis, vol.I, pp.178-193.

15 mai L'éducation en Hollande. Collégiens et étudiants.
In: La Revue des Deux Mondes, vol. 154, 4e période, 69e année, 15 mai 1899, pp.359-378.

juin Die religiöse Frage in den Vereinigten Staaten und in Europa.
[The Question of Religion in the United States and Europe. (German Text)]
In: Deutsche Revue, 24e année, juin 1899, n° 6, pp.287-296.

juil. Modern History and Historians in France.
In: The American Monthly Review of Reviews, vol. 20, juillet 1899, pp.43-50.

12 nov.-13 déc.
L'avenir de l'Europe.
[The Future of Europe.]
In: L'Indépendance Belge, 70e année,
12 nov. 1899, p.1: L'empire allemand (I) ;
[The German Empire.]
19 nov. 1899, p.1: L'imbroglio hongrois (II) ;
[Hungarian Chaos.]
22 nov. 1899, p.1: Le problème russe (III) ;
[The Russian Question.]
13 nov. 1899, p.1: Esprit public et nationalisme (IV) ;
[Public Spirit and Nationalism.]
Le monde anglo-saxon (V) ;
[The Anglo-Saxon World.]
Conclusion (VI).
[Conclusion.]
Brochure spéciale: Bruxelles, Impr. Deverver-Deweuwe, 1900 (48 pages). In excepts, In: Anthologie, Aix-en-Provence, P. Roubaud, 1933, pp.119-120.

1900

14 janv.-29 oct.
Lettres d'un indépendant I - XLII.
[Letters of an Independent.]
In: L'Indépendance Belge, 71e année, 1900.
14 janv. p.1: I [Peace];
24 janv. p.1: II [Stead and his pacifist movement];
26 janv. p.1: III [Austro-Hungary];
28 janv. p.1: IV [Kipling in the Transvaal];
1er fév. p.1: V [The French, arbiters of peace];
2 fév. p.1: VI [The French, arbiters of peace];
11 fév. p.1: VII [South Africa];
17 fév. p.1: VIII [Letter from Jordan, President of the University of Palo Alto, on democracy];
19 fév. p.1: IX [Sweden and Norway]
28 fév. p.1: X [A new Triplice];
4 mars pp.1-2: XI [Jacobinism];
14 mars p.1: XII [A letter from Sienkiewiez];
21 mars p.1: XIII [France and Italy];
26 mars p.1: XIV [The Episcopate];
3 avril p.1: XV [Arbitration];
11 avril p.1: XVI [Rev. Didon];
18 avril p.1: XVII [Queen Victoria in Ireland];
22 avril p.1: XVIII [Anglo-Saxonism];
1er mai p.1: XIX [Marchand, Colonel de Villebois, the Anglophobia of the French];
9 mai p.1: XX [India];
18 mai p.1: XXI [Contact between civilizations];
28 mai p.1: XXII [Boers and Hellenes];
12 juin p.1: XXIII [The English Government];
16 juin p.1: XXIV [The new French municipalities];
24 juin p.1: XXV [French democracy and monarchy];
29 juin p.1: XXVI [Mrs. Gladstone];
4 juil. p.1: XXVII [The regulation of marriage];
9 juil. p.1: XXVIII [Imbert de St-Amand];
18 juil. p.1: XXIV [The voyage of Li-Hung-Chang];
3 août p.1: XXX [South Africa];
5 août p.1: XXXI [China, France];
19 août p.1: XXXII [The anarchists];
23 août p.1: XXXIII [French novelists];
6 sept. p.1: XXXIV [England, France, and Asia];
9 sept. p.1: XXXV [The renewal of Greece]
10 sept. p.1: XXXVI [European diplomacy];

25 sept. p.1: XXXVII [The Priests' Conference and the Feminist Conference at the 1900 World's Fair];
9 oct. p.1: XXXVIII [Australia];
10 oct. p.1: XXXIX [The Balkans];
14 oct. p.1: XL [The state of mind of the French army and the risk of an Anglo-French conflict];
25 oct. p.1: XLI [The electoral fight of Bryan-Mac Kinley];
29 oct. p.1: XLII [Adrien Pauly and Paul Blanchet].

22 janv. Les Jeux Olympiques et le Congrès d'Education Physique de 1900.
[The Olympic Games and the Congress for Physical Education of 1900.]
In: L'Indépendance Belge, 71ᵉ année, 22 janv. 1900, p.2.
Later reprinted, in: Textes choisis, vol.II, pp.187-190.

fév. A French View of the German Empire.
In: The Review of Reviews, vol. XXI, février 1900, pp.177-183.

1er mai The Possibility of a War between England and France.
In: The Fortnightly Review, LXVII, nouvelle série, 1er mai 1900, n° 401, pp.719-729.

juin The Meeting of the Olympian Games.
In: The North American Review, vol. CLXX, juin 1900, pp.802-811.

1er juil. La Psychologie du Sport.
[Sports Psychology.]
In: La Revue des Deux Mondes, 70ᵉ année, 4ᵉ période, tome 160, 1er juillet 1900, pp.167-179.
Later reprintedavec quelques changements rédactionnels, In:
1) Notes sur l'Education Publique. Paris, Hachette, 1901, pp.152-173.
2) Essais de Psychologie Sportive. Lausanne/Paris, Payot, 1913, pp.9-16.
3) Textes choisis, vol. I, pp.221-230.

1901

janv. L'Œuvre du Comité International Olympique.
[The Work of the International Olympic Committee.]
In: Revue Olympique, 1ère année, janvier 1901, pp.5-11
Later reprinted, in: Textes choisis, vol.II, pp.325-330.

avr. Correspondance et faits divers.[Nordic Games. New IOC-members.Chicago 1904. IOC-Session 190].
In: Revue Olympique, 1ère année, avril 1901, pp.24-25.

avr. France on the Wrong Track.
In: The Review of Reviews, vol. XXIII, avril 1901, pp.447-450.

avr. Olympiades Boréales. Les Jeux du Nord à Stockholm.
[Boréales Olympics. The Nordic Games at Stockholm.]
In: Revue Olympique, 1ère année, avril 1901, pp.17-24.
Later reprinted, in: Textes choisis, vol.II, pp.311-317.

15 avr. Une Expérience Sportive.
[A Sports Experience.]
In: Revue Mensuelle du Touring-Club de France, 15 avril 1901, pp.148-149.

22 mai Everyday Training.
Not a Difficult Feat to Keep One's Muscles in Good Working Order. Baron Coubertin's Views. Describes His Remarkable Achievement of Six Hours' Continuous and Difficult Exercise.
In: The New York Herald, European Edition, Second Section, Paris, 26 mai 1901, p.2.

juin England and France.
The Conditions of Franco-British Peace.
In: The Fortnightly Review, vol. LXIX, nouvelle série, juin 1901, pp.1013-1021.

juil. * La réunion du Comité International Olympique.
[The Reunion of the International Olympic Committee.]
In: Revue Olympique, 1ère année, juillet 1901, pp.29-37.

oct. The Problem of Central Europe.
In: The Fortnightly Review, vol. LXX, nouvelle série, octobre 1901, pp.605-614.

oct. * Solidarité internationale.
[International Solidarity.]
In: Revue Olympique, 1ère année, octobre 1901, p.47.
Later reprinted, in: Textes choisis, vol.II, p.444.

oct. * Courrier de Chicago.
[News from Chicago.]
In: Revue Olympique, 1ère année, octobre 1901, pp.55-57.
Later reprinted, in: Textes choisis, vol.II, pp.192-194.

oct. * L'année sportive.
[Sports Throughout the Year.]
In: Revue Olympique, 1ère année, octobre 1901, p.47-54.
Later reprinted, in: Textes choisis, vol.III, pp.267-270.

1902

janv. * Le Congrès de Bruxelles.
[The Brussels Congress.]
In: Revue Olympique, 2ᵉ année, janvier 1902, pp.3-6.

janv. * Une Rectification nécessaire.
[A Necessary Correction.]
In: Revue Olympique, 2ᵉ année, janvier 1902, pp.10-12.
Later reprinted, in: Textes choisis, vol.II, pp.164-165.

janv. * La charte de l'amateurisme.
[The Charter of Amateurism (1902).]
In: Revue Olympique, 2ᵉ année, janvier 1902, pp.14-16.
Later reprinted, in: Textes choisis, vol.II, pp.565-567.

janv. M. Delcassé: A Character Sketch.
In: Fortnightly Review, vol. LXX, nouvelle série, janvier 1902, pp.71-80.

15 fév. La Force Nationale et le Sport.
[Sports and the Army.]
In: La Revue des Deux Mondes, 72e année, 15 février 1902, pp.916-924.

mars * Voir loin, parler franc, agir ferme.
[See Afar, Speak Openly, Act Firmly.]
In: Revue du Pays de Caux, 1ère année, mars 1902, n° 1, pp.3-4.

mars * Ce qui se passe dans le monde.
[Goings-on in the World.]
In: Revue du Pays de Caux, 1ère année, mars 1902, n° 1, pp.4-15.

mars * Questions pédagogiques.
[Educational Questions.]
In: Revue du Pays de Caux, 1ère année, mars 1902, n° 1, pp.16-21.

mars * Le problème de l'Europe Centrale.
[The Central Europe Question.]
In: Revue du Pays de Caux, 1ère année, mars 1902, n° 1, pp.21-29.

mars * La dernière gerbe de Victor Hugo.
[A Last Book by Victor Hugo.]
In: Revue du Pays de Caux, 1ère année, mars 1902, n° 1, pp.29-33.

mars * Hygiène et propreté.
[Hygiene.]
In: Revue du Pays de Caux, 1ère année, mars 1902, n° 1, pp.33-35.
Later reprinted, in: Textes choisis, vol.III, pp.625-627.

mars * La fille sauvage.
[The Savage Girl.]
In: Revue du Pays de Caux, 1ère année, mars 1902, n° 1, pp.36-39.

mars * Questions financières.
[Financial Questions.]
In: Revue du Pays de Caux, 1ère année, mars 1902, n° 1, pp.39-40.

20 mars Une Nouvelle Formule d'Education Physique.
[A New Formula for Physical Education.]
(Conférence faite à la Salle de la Société de Géographie le jeudi 20 mars 1902.)
In: Revue Mensuelle du Touring-Club de France, 20 mars 1902, pp.146-151.
Later reprinted, in:
1) Le Stand, 23e année,
12 juin 1902, n° 1049, p.181 ;
31 juillet 1902, n° 1055, p.237 ;
14 août 1902, n° 1056, p.246 ;
21/28 août 1902, n° 1058 et 1059, pp.255-256 ;
4 septembre 1902, n° 1060, p.265.
2) Le Sport Suisse, 26e année,
4 juin 1930, p.1, (I);
11 juin 1930, p.1, (II).
3) Textes choisis, vol.III, pp.453-463.

mai * Ni perdus ni sauvés.
[Neither Lost Nor Saved.]
In: Revue du Pays de Caux, 1ère année, mai 1902, n° 2, pp.43-44.

mai * Ce qui se passe dans le monde.
[Goings-on in the World.]
In: Revue du Pays de Caux, 1ère année, mai 1902, n° 2, pp.45-55.

mai * Un procès électoral aux Etats-Unis.
[Elections in the United States.]
In: Revue du Pays de Caux, 1ère année, mai 1902, n° 2, pp.56-57.

mai * Le drame sud-africain.
[The South-African Drama.]
In: Revue du Pays de Caux, 1ère année, mai 1902, n° 2, pp.57-70.

mai * Cecil Rhodes.
In: Revue du Pays de Caux, 1ère année, mai 1902, n° 2, pp.70-75.

mai * Les Français en Chine.
[The French in China.]
In: Revue du Pays de Caux, 1ère année, mai 1902, n° 2, pp.75-78.

mai * Questions financières.
[Financial Questions.]
In: Revue du Pays de Caux, 1ère année, mai 1902, n° 2, pp.78-79.

juil. * Echos et Nouvelles.[Prince Georges Bibesco. IOC News. Fondation of NOCs. Roosevelt and St.Louis. IOC and Physical Education].
In: Revue Olympique, 2e année, juillet 1902, pp.43-47.
Later reprinted, in: Textes choisis, vol.II, pp.655-666; pp.694-695.

juil. * Le coq et l'habit.
[The Cock and the New 20 Centimes Coin.]
In: Revue du Pays de Caux, 1ère année, juillet 1902, n° 3, pp.83-84.
Later reprinted, in: Revue pour les Français, 2e année, juin 1907, pp.683-685.

juil. * Ce qui se passe dans le monde.
[Goings-on in the World.]

In: Revue du Pays de Caux, 1ère année, juillet 1902, n° 3, pp.85-100.

juil. L'éducation physique de vos fils.
[Your Sons' Physical Education.]
In: Revue du Pays de Caux, 1ère année, juillet 1902, n° 3, pp.100-113.
Later reprinted, in:
1) L'Education Physique,
I: 7e année, 31 juillet 1908, n° 14, pp.390-391;
I: 7e année, 31 août 1908, n° 16, pp.447-448 ;
III: 7e année, 15 septembre 1908, n° 17, pp.474-476 ;
IV: 7e année, 31 décembre 1908, n° 24, pp.670-671 ;
V: 8e année, 15 janvier 1909, n° 1, pp.24-25.
2) Textes choisis, vol.III, pp.464-475.

14 juil. Le dilemme.
[The Dilemma.]
In: Le Figaro, 48e année, 14 juillet 1902, p.1.
Later reprinted, in: Pages d'Histoire contemporaine. Paris, Plon-Nourrit, 1909, pp.1-4.

25 juil. La politique extérieure des Etats-Unis.
[Foreign Policy of the United States.]
In: Le Figaro, 48e année, 25 juillet 1902, p.1.
Later reprinted, in: Pages d'Histoire contemporaine. Paris, Plon-Nourrit, 1909, pp.5-9.

16 août L'Education physique au XXe siècle: La débrouillardise.
[Physical Education in the XXth Century: Unraveling.]
In: Le Figaro, 48e année, 16 août 1902, p.3.
Later reprinted, in:
1) Le Stand, 23e année, 21 et 28 août 1902, n° 1058 et 1059, pp.254-255.
2) Textes choisis, vol.III, pp.476480.

21 août L'Education physique au XXe siècle: La mémoire des muscles.
[Physical Education in the XXth Century: The Memory of Muscles.]
In: Le Figaro, 4e année, 21 août 1902, pp.1-2.
Later reprinted, in: Textes choisis, vol.III, pp.335-338.

sept. * Le cadeau de la méchante fée.
[The Gift of the Bad Fairy.]
In: Revue du Pays de Caux, 1ère année, septembre 1902, n° 4, pp.123-124.

sept. * Ce qui se passe dans le monde.
[Goings-on in the World.]
In: Revue du Pays de Caux, 1ère année, septembre 1902 n°4, pp.124-135.

sept. * Que faut-il penser du socialisme ?
[What Should We Think of Socialism?]
In: Revue du Pays de Caux, 1ère année, septembre 1902, n°4, pp.136-146.

sept. * Un milliardaire américain - Andrew Carnegie.
[An Americain Billionaire: Andrew Carnegie.]
In: Revue du Pays de Caux, 1ère année, septembre 1902, pp.146-151.

1er sept. L'Espagne et ses filles.
[Spain and Her Daughters.]
In: Le Figaro, 48e année, 1er septembre 1902, p.1.
Later reprinted, in: Pages d'Histoire contemporaine. Paris, Plon-Nourrit, 1909, pp.10-14.

8 sept. L'Education physique au XXe siècle. Le raid et la gymkhana.
[Physical Education in the XXth Century: Endurance.]
In: Le Figaro, 48e année. 8 septembre 1982, pp.1-2.

23 sept. Les étapes d'une illusion.
[Stages of an Illusion.]
In: Le Figaro, 48e année, 23 septembre 1902, p. l.
Later reprinted, in: Pages d'Histoire contemporaine. Paris, Plon-Nourrit, 1909, pp.15-20.

oct. * Le tableau de l'éducation physique au XXe siècle.
[A Preview of Physical Education in the XXth Century.]
In: Revue Olympique, 2e année, octobre 1902, pp.51-65.
Later reprinted, in:
Textes choisis, vol.III, pp.384-396.
Last paragraphe "Les obstacles et les aides", in: Textes choisis, vol.II, pp.568-569.

15 oct. La résurrection des peuples.
[The Rebirth of Greek Democracy.]
In: Le Figaro, 48e année, 15 octobre 1902, p. l.
Later reprinted, in: Pages d'Histoire contemporaine. Paris, Plon-Nourrit, 1909, pp.21-25.

24 oct. Le Prestige français.
[French Prestige.]
In: Le Figaro, 48e année, 24 septembre 1902, p. l.
Later reprinted, in: Pages d'Histoire contemporaine. Paris, Plon-Nourrit, 1909, pp.26-31.

nov. * Mer ou continent.
[Sea or Continent.]
In: Revue du Pays de Caux, 1ère année, novembre 1902, n° 5, pp.163-165.

nov. * Ce qui se passe dans le monde.
[Goings-on in the World.]
In: Revue du Pays de Caux, 1ère année, novembre1902, n° 5, pp.165-185.

nov. * L'Indo-Chine française.
[French Indo-China.]
In: Revue du Pays de Caux, 1ère année, novembre1902, n° 5, pp.185-197.

6 nov. L'Education physique au XXe siècle: la peur et le sport.
[Physical Education in the XXth Century: Fear and Sports.]
In: Le Figaro, 6 novembre 1902, pp.1-2.
Later reprinted, in: Textes choisis, vol.I, pp.372-374.

14 déc. Notre épopée lointaine.
[Colonialism.]
In: Le Figaro, 48e année, 14 décembre 1902, p. l.
Later reprinted, in: Pages d'Histoire contemporaine. Paris, Plon-Nourrit, 1909, pp.32-36.

déc. Are the Public Schools a Failure ? A French View.
In: Fortnightly Review, vol. LXXI, décembre 1902, pp.979-986.

1903

janv. * Récapitulation.
[Summary.]
In: Revue du Pays de Caux, 2e année, janvier 1903, n° 1, pp.3-5.

janv. * Ce qui se passe dans le monde.
[Goings-on in the World.]
In: Revue du Pays de Caux, 2e année, janvier 1903, n° 1, pp.5-20.

janv. L'évolution de la démocratie.
[The Evolution of Democracy.]
In: Revue du Pays de Caux, 2e année, janvier 1903, n° 1, pp.21-29.
Later reprinted, in: Revue pour les Français, 2e année, novembre1907, pp.895-903.

janv. * Histoire d'un archipel brumeux (I et II).
[History of a Foggy Island.]
In: Revue du Pays de Caux,
I: 2e année, janvier 1903, n° 1, pp.29-39.
II: 2e année, mai 1903, n° 3, pp.112-118.

8 janv. Le Problème de l'Europe centrale.
[The Central Europe Question.]
In: Le Figaro, 49e année, 8 janvier 1903, p.1.
Later reprinted, in: Pages d'Histoire contemporaine. Paris, Plon-Nourrit, 1909, pp.37-41.

10 janv. L'Education physique au XXe siècle: le record.
[Physical Education in the 20th Century: Records.]
In: Le Figaro, 10 janvier 1903, pp.1-2.
Later reprinted, in: Textes choisis, vol.I, pp.375-377.

14 janv. Que ferons-nous ?
[What Are We Going to Do?]
In: Le Figaro, 49e année, 14 janvier 1903, p.1.
Later reprinted, in: Pages d'Histoire contemporaine. Paris, Plon-Nourrit, 1909, pp.42-46.

2 fév.-20 oct.
Lettres d'un indépendant (XLIV - LVIII)
[Letters of an Independent.]
In: L'Indépendance Belge, 74e année, 1903,
2 fév., p.1: XLIV [Théroigne de Méricourt];
9 fév., p.1: XLV [Naturalizations];
24 fév., p.1: XLVI [The Paris Congress of 1856];
9 mars, p.1: XLVII [The catechism of the Walloon, by Albert du Bois];
30 mars, p.1: XLVIII [Delcassé];
6 avr., p.1: XLIX [The chicken of the mousquetaires".];
4 mai, p.1: LII [On the resignation of Colonel de Coubertin];
19 mai, p.1: L [Bohemia];
4 juin, p.1: LI [The essays of Max Nordau];
8 juin, p.1: LIII [Shakespeare and Victor Hugo];
15 juin, p.1: LIV [Events in Serbia];
13 juil., p.2: LV [The sympathy of the English for France];
2 août, p.1: LVI [Pius IX and Leo XIII];
20 oct., p.1: LVIII [Travel].

fév. * Les Jeux du Nord à Kristiania.
[The Nordic Games in Kristiania.]
In: Revue Olympique, 3e année, février 1903, pp.13-14.
Later reprinted, in: Textes choisis, vol.II, pp.318-319.

13 fév. La Louisiane française.
[French Louisiana.]
In: Le Figaro, 49e année, 13 février 1903, p.1.
Later reprinted, in: Pages d'Histoire contemporaine. Paris, Plon-Nourrit, 1909, pp.47-50.

mars * Notre alliée.
[Our Ally.]
In: Revue du Pays de Caux, 2e année, mars 1903, n° 2, pp.43-45.

mars * Ce qui se passe dans le monde.
[Goings-on in the World.]
In: Revue du Pays de Caux, 2e année, mars 1903, n° 2, pp.45-58.

mars * Un passé compliqué.
[A Complicated Past.]
In: Revue du Pays de Caux, 2e année, mars 1903, n° 2, pp.59-69.

mars * L'impasse russe.
[The Russian Dead End.]
In: Revue du Pays de Caux, 2e année, mars 1903, n° 2, pp.69-77.

mars * Deux mots sur la Finlande.
[Some Remarks about Finland.]
In: Revue du Pays de Caux, 2e année, mars 1903, n° 2, pp.77-78.

13 mars Le Rêve de la Grèce.
[The Greek Dream.]

In: Le Figaro, 49e année, 13 mars 1903, p.1.
Later reprinted, in: Pages d'Histoire contemporaine. Paris, Plon-Nourrit, 1909, pp.51-55.

31 mars Le prochain pontificat
[The Next Pope.]
In: Le Figaro, 49e année, 31 mars 1903, p.1.
Later reprinted, in: Pages d'Histoire contemporaine. Paris, Plon-Nourrit, 1909, pp.60-64.

avril * Rome pour 1908.
[Rome for 1908.]
In: Revue Olympique, 3e année, avril 1903, pp.22-23.
Later reprinted, in: Textes choisis, vol.II, pp.218-219.

23 avril La Transformation de la Méditerranée.
[The Transformation of the Mediterranean.]
In: Le Figaro, 49e année, 23 avril 1903, p.1.
Later reprinted, in: Pages d'Histoire contemporaine. Paris, Plon-Nourrit, 1909, pp.56-59.

mai * Semailles et récoltes.
[Sowing and Reaping.]
In: Revue du Pays de Caux, 2e année, mai 1903, n° 3, pp.83-84.

mai * Ce qui se passe dans le monde.
[Goings-on in the World.]
In: Revue du Pays de Caux, 2e année, mai 1903, n° 3, pp.85-99.

mai * Le voyage présidentiel en Algérie et en Tunisie.
[The Journey of the French President to Algeria and Tunisia.]
In: Revue du Pays de Caux, 2e année, mai 1903, n° 3, pp.99-110.

mai * Sur les pentes du Pincio et du Parnasse.
[On the Hillsides of Pincio and Parnassos.]
In: Revue du Pays de Caux, 2e année, mai 1903, n° 3, pp.110-112.

13 juin Responsabilités nationales.
[National Responsibilities.]
In: Le Figaro, 49e année, 13 juin 1903, p.1.
Later reprinted, in: Pages d'Histoire contemporaine. Paris, Plon-Nourrit, 1909, pp.65-68.

juil. * L'organisation olympique.
[The Olympic Organization.]
In: Revue Olympique, 3e année, juillet 1903, pp.35-38.
Later reprinted, in: Textes choisis, vol.II, pp.598-601.

juil. * Le parapluie.
[The Umbrella.]
In: Revue du Pays de Caux, 2e année, juillet 1903, n° 4, pp.123-124.

juil. * Ce qui se passe dans le monde.
[Goings-on in the World.]
In: Revue du Pays de Caux, 2e année, juillet 1903, n° 4, pp.124-140.

juil. * Jules Simon.
In: Revue du Pays de Caux, 2e année, juillet 1903, n° 4, pp.141-151.
Later reprinted, in: Textes choisis, vol.I, pp.588-596.

juil. * La vie et la mort.
[Life and Death.]
Revue du Pays de Caux, 2e année, juillet 1903, n° 4, pp.151-153.

juil. * Le conclave.
[The Conclave.]
In: Revue du Pays de Caux, 2e année, juillet 1903, n° 4, pp.153-159.

2 juil. L'incertitude magyare.
[The Hungarian Kind of Independence.]
In: Le Figaro, 49e année, 2 juillet 1903, p.1.
Later reprinted, in: Pages d'Histoire contemporaine. Paris, Plon-Nourrit, 1909, pp.69-73.

23 juil. L'entente cordiale.
[The Entente Cordiale.]
In: Le Figaro, 49e année, 23 juillet 1903, p.1.
Later reprinted, in: Pages d'Histoire contemporaine. Paris, Plon-Nourrit, 1909, pp.74-78.

10 août Le redressement de l'axe.
[The French-Russian Axis.]
In: Le Figaro, 49e année, 10 août 1903, p.1.
Later reprinted, in: Pages d'Histoire contemporaine. Paris, Plon-Nourrit, 1909, pp.79-83.

31 août L'ère des vice-rois.
[The Era of Vice-Kings.]
In: Le Figaro, 49e année, 31 août 1903, p.1.
Later reprinted, in: Pages d'Histoire contemporaine. Paris, Plon-Nourrit, 1909, pp.84-87.

5 sept. Roosevelt et Tolstoï.
[Roosevelt and Tolstoy.]
In: Le Figaro, 49e année, 5 septembre 1903, p.1.
Later reprinted, in: Pages d'Histoire contemporaine. Paris, Plon-Nourrit, 1909, pp.88-92.

26 sept. La question nègre.
[The Negro Question.]
In: Le Figaro, 49e année, 26 septembre 1903, p.1.
Later reprinted, in: Pages d'Histoire contemporaine. Paris, Plon-Nourrit, 1909, pp.93-97.

oct. * Notes sportives. [Santos Dumont. Automobilism. Nordic Games. Pelota. Golf].
In: Revue Olympique, 3e année, oct. 1903, pp.58-63.

18 oct. Un empire latin.
[A Latin Empire.]
In: Le Figaro, 49e année, 18 octobre 1903, p.1.
Later reprinted, in: Pages d'Histoire contemporaine. Paris, Plon-Nourrit, 1909, pp.98-102.

nov. * Ce qui se passe dans le monde.
[Goings-on in the World.]
In: Revue du Pays de Caux, 2e année, novembre1903, n° 5, pp.163-177.

nov. * La France et l'Italie.
[France and Italy.]
In: Revue du Pays de Caux, 2e année, novembre1903, n° 5, pp.178-191.

nov. * La richesse italienne.
[Italian Wealth.]
In: Revue du Pays de Caux, 2e année, novembre1903, n° 5, pp.191-195.

nov. * L'union latine.
[The Latin Union.]
In: Revue du Pays de Caux, 2e année, novembre1903, n° 5, pp.195-198.

nov. * Changements prochains.
[Changes in the Near Future.]
In: Revue du Pays de Caux, 2e année, novembre1903, n° 5, pp.198-199.

12 nov. La revanche de Tammany.
[The Revenge of the Tammany.]
In: Le Figaro, 49e année, 12 novembre1903, p.1.
Later reprinted, in: Pages d'Histoire contemporaine. Paris, Plon-Nourrit, 1909, pp.103-107.

25 nov. La Campagne de l'Education physique.
[The Campaign for Physical Education.]
In: Le Correspondant, tome 177, nouvelle série, 4e livraison du 25 novembre1903, pp.701-717.

28 nov. Nos historiens.
[Our Historians.]
In: Le Figaro, 49e année, 28 novembre1903, p.1. Later reprinted, in: Pages d'Histoire contemporaine. Paris, Plon-Nourrit, 1909, pp.108-112.

23 déc. L'œuvre de paix.
[The Work of Peace.]
In: Le Figaro, 49e année, 23 décembre 1903, p.1.
Later reprinted, in: Pages d'Histoire contemporaine. Paris, Plon-Nourrit, 1909, pp.113-117.

1904

8 janv. La visite.
[The Visit.]
In: Le Figaro, 50e année, n° 8, 8 janvier 1904, p.1.
Later reprinted, in: Pages d'Histoire contemporaine. Paris, Plon-Nourrit, 1909, pp.118-121.

12 janv. Les bases de la pédagogie prochaine: I. Le retour de Dieu.
[The Foundations of the New Education I: The Return of God.]
In: Le Gaulois, 37, année, 12 janvier 1904, p.1.

18 janv. Le cercle de fer.
[The Ring of Iron.]
In: Le Figaro, 50e année, n° 18, 18 janvier 1904, p.1.
Later reprinted, in: Pages d'Histoire contemporaine. Paris, Plon-Nourrit, 1909, pp.122-126.

28 janv. Les bases de la pédagogie prochaine: . II. La paix armée.
[The Foundations of the New Education II: Peace in Arms.]
In: Le Gaulois, 37e année, 28 janvier 1904, p. I.

9 fév. Les bases de la pédagogie prochaine: III. La revanche des Anciens.
[The Foundations of the New Education III: The Revenge of Classical Antiquity.]
In: Le Gaulois, 37e année, 9 février 1904, p.1.

13 fév. L'entr'acte australien.
[Australian Interlude.]
In: Le Figaro, 50e année, n° 44, 13 février 1904, p.1.
Later reprinted, in: Pages d'Histoire contemporaine. Paris, Plon-Nourrit, 1909, pp.127-130.

24 fév. La marche arrière.
[Backward Movement.]
In: Le Figaro, 50e année, n° 55, 24 février 1904, p.1.
Later reprinted, in: Pages d'Histoire contemporaine. Paris, Plon-Nourrit, 1909, pp.131-134.

10 mars Le sens critique.
[The Critical Sense.]
In: Le Figaro, 50e année, n° 70, 10 mars 1904, p.1.
Later reprinted, in: Pages d'Histoire contemporaine. Paris, Plon-Nourrit, 1909, pp.135-138.

26 mars Renaissance navale.
[Nautical Renaissance.]
In: Le Figaro, 50e année, n° 86, 26 mars 1904, p.1.
Later reprinted, in: Pages d'Histoire contemporaine. Paris, Plon-Nourrit, 1909, pp.139-142.

6 avr. Grains de riz et rayons de gloire.
[Rice Grains and Halos.]
In: Le Figaro, 50e année, n° 97, 6 avril 1904, p.1.

Later reprinted, in: Pages d'Histoire contemporaine. Paris, Plon-Nourrit, 1909, pp.143-146.

15 avr. Regrets et espérances.
[Hopes and Regrets.]
In: Le Figaro, 50e année, n° 106, 15 avril 1904, p.1.
Later reprinted, in: Pages d'Histoire contemporaine. Paris, Plon-Nourrit, 1909, pp.147-151.

30 avr. La lumière du Nord.
[Northern Lights.]
In: Le Figaro, 50e année, n° 121, 30 avril 1904, p.1.
Later reprinted, in: Pages d'Histoire contemporaine. Paris, Plon-Nourrit, 1909, pp.152-156.

18 mai Les leçons d'un cortège.
[Lessons of a Parade.]
In: Le Figaro, 50e année, n° 139, 18 mai 1904, p.1.
Later reprinted, in: Pages d'Histoire contemporaine. Paris, Plon-Nourrit, 1909, pp.157-160.

27 mai Les Français en Océanie.
[The French in Oceania.]
In: Le Figaro, 50e année, n° 148, 27 mai 1904, p.1.
Later reprinted, in: Pages d'Histoire contemporaine. Paris, Plon-Nourrit, 1909, pp.161-165.

10 juin Donner sans retenir.
[Giving Without Holding Back.]
In: Le Figaro, 50e année, n° 162, 10 juin 1904, p.1.
Later reprinted, in: Pages d'Histoire contemporaine. Paris, Plon-Nourrit, 1909, pp.165-169.

28 juil. L'Angleterre nouvelle.
[The New England.]
In: Le Figaro, 50e année, n° 210, 28 juillet 1904, p.1.
Later reprinted, in: Pages d'Histoire contemporaine. Paris, Plon-Nourrit, 1909, pp.170-174.

4 août L'Olympiade romaine.
[The Roman Olympiad.]
In: Le Figaro, 50e année, n° 218, 4 août 1904, p.1.
Later reprinted, in:
1)Revue Olympique, 4eannée, août 1904, pp.75-78.
2)Textes choisis, vol.II, pp.220-222.

août * Notes sportives.[International activities].
In: Revue Olympique, 4e année, août 1904, pp.78-80.
Later reprinted, in: Textes choisis, vol.II, pp.657-659.

27 août Le carrefour néerlandais.
[Dutch Colonialism.]
In: Le Figaro, 50e année, n° 240, 27 août 1904, p.1.
Later reprinted, in: Pages d'Histoire contemporaine. Paris, Plon-Nourrit, 1909, pp.175-178.

22 sept. Chimères. **[Fantasies.]**
In: Le Figaro, 50e année, n° 266, 22 septembre 1904, p.1.
Later reprinted, in: Pages d'Histoire contemporaine. Paris, Plon-Nourrit, 1909, pp.179-182.

oct. The Statesmen of the Third Republic.
In: Fortnightly Review, vol. LXXVI, octobre 1904, pp.623-633.

5 oct. L'usine britannique.
[The British Factory.]
In: Le Figaro, 50e année, n° 280, 5 octobre 1904, p.1.
Later reprinted, in: Pages d'Histoire contemporaine. Paris, Plon-Nourrit, 1909, pp.183-186.

15 nov. La triple bataille de Bohême.
[The Threefold Fight of Bohemia.]
In: Le Figaro, 50e année, n° 320, 15 novembre1904, p.1.
Later reprinted, in: Pages d'Histoire contemporaine. Paris, Plon-Nourrit, 1909, pp.187-190.

30 nov. Les conditions du progrès scandinave.
[The Conditions of Scandinavian Progress.]
In: Le Figaro, 50e année, n° 335, 30 novembre 1904, p.1.
Later reprinted, in: Pages d'Histoire contemporaine. Paris, Plon-Nourrit, 1909, pp.191-194.

13 déc. Le flambeau à sept branches.
[The Seven-Branched Candelabrum.]
In: Le Figaro, 50e année, n° 348, 13 décembre 1904, p.1.
Later reprinted, in: Pages d'Histoire contemporaine. Paris, Plon-Nourrit, 1909, pp.195-198.

1905

Avant-propos. [The results of Brussels].
[Foreword.]
In: IOC (Ed.): Congrès International de Sport et d'Education physique. Auxerre, Lanier, 1905, pp.5-8.
Later reprinted, in: Textes choisis, vol.II, pp.214216.

Discours à la séance d'ouverture.
[Speech given at the opening session.]
In: IOC (Ed.): Congrès International de Sport et d'Education physique. Auxerre, Lanier, 1905, pp.15-16.

Séance solennelle pour la distribution des Diplômes Olympiques. (Laudationes)
[Ceremony at the Distribution of the Olympic Diplomas.]
In: IOC (Ed.): Congrès International de Sport et d'Education physique. Auxerre, Lanier, 1905, pp.237-246.

janv. * Programme du Congrès.
[Congress Programme.]
In: Revue Olympique, 5e année, janvier 1905, pp.9-15.

26 janv. L'homme des Nouvelles-Hébrides.
[The Man from the New Hebrides.]
In: Le Figaro, 51e année, 26 janvier 1905, p.1.

Later reprinted, in: Pages d'Histoire contemporaine. Paris, Plon-Nourrit, 1909, pp.199-202.

14 fév. Le partage nécessaire.
[The Necessary Division.]
In: Le Figaro, 51e année, 14 février 1905, p.1.
Later reprinted, in: Pages d'Histoire contemporaine. Paris, Plon-Nourrit, 1909, pp.203-207.

8 avr. L'ennemi.
[The Enemy.]
In: L'Auto, 51e année, 8 avril 1905, p.1.

10 avril L'hellénisme.
[Hellenism.]
In: Le Figaro, 51e année, 10 avril 1095, p.1.
Later reprinted, in: Pages d'Histoire contemporaine. Paris, Plon-Nourrit, 1909, pp.208-211.

17 avr. Un évangile germanique.
[A German Gospel.]
In: Le Figaro, 51e année, 17 avril 1905, p.1.
Later reprinted, in: Pages d'Histoire contemporaine. Paris, Plon-Nourrit, 1909, pp.212-215.

21 avr. France et Allemagne.
[France and Germany.]
In: Le Figaro, 51e année, 21 avril 1905, p.1.
Later reprinted, in: Pages d'Histoire contemporaine. Paris, Plon-Nourrit, 1909, pp.216-219.

24 mai 1453 et 1905.
[1453 and 1905.]
In: Le Figaro, 51e année, 24 mai 1905, p.1.
Later reprinted, in: Pages d'Histoire contemporaine. Paris, Plon-Nourrit, 1909, pp.220-223.

11 juin Der olympische Kongreß in Brüssel.
[The Olympic Congress of Brussels.] (German text)
In: Die Zeit, Wien, 11.6.1905, Nr. 978, p.29.

7 juil. Le Comité des missions.
[Church Missions.]
In: Le Figaro, 51e année, 7 juillet 1905, p.1.
Later reprinted, in: Pages d'Histoire contemporaine. Paris, Plon-Nourrit, 1909, pp.224-227.

25 juil. L'Afrique française.
[French Africa.]
In: Le Figaro, 51e année, 25 juillet 1905, p.1.
Later reprinted, in: Pages d'Histoire contemporaine. Paris, Plon-Nourrit, 1909, pp.228-231.

6 août La Fortune de l'Hellade.
[Greek Financial Circumstances.]
In: Le Figaro, 51e année, 6 août 1905, p.1.
Later reprinted, in: Pages d'Histoire contemporaine. Paris, Plon-Nourrit, 1909, pp.232-235.

5 sept. Le langage, la race et l'unité.
[Language, Race, and Unity.]
In: Le Figaro, 51e année, 5 septembre 1905, pp.1-2.
Later reprinted, in: Pages d'Histoire contemporaine. Paris, Plon-Nourrit, 1909, pp.236-239.

18 sept. La récompense. **[Reward.]**
In: Le Figaro, 51e année, 18 septembre 1905, p.1.
Later reprinted, in: Pages d'Histoire contemporaine. Paris, Plon-Nourrit, 1909, pp.240-243.

6 oct. Nos amis roumains.
[Our Romanian Friends.]
In: Le Figaro, 51e année, 6 octobre 1905, p.1.
Later reprinted, in: Pages d'Histoire contemporaine. Paris, Plon-Nourrit, 1909, pp.244-247.

18 oct. Victoires dédaignées.
[Spurned Victories.]
In: Le Figaro, 51e année, 18 octobre 1905, p.1.
Later reprinted, in: Pages d'Histoire contemporaine. Paris, Plon-Nourrit, 1909, pp.248-251.

1er nov. Toutes les Russies.
[All Russias.]
In: Le Figaro, 51e année, 1er novembre1905, p.1.
Later reprinted, in: Pages d'Histoire contemporaine. Paris, Plon-Nourrit, 1909, pp.252-255.

22 nov. L'erreur initiale.
[The Initial Mistake.]
In: Le Figaro, 51e année, 22 novembre1905, p.1.
Later reprinted, in: Pages d'Histoire contemporaine. Paris, Plon-Nourrit, 1909, pp.256-259.

26 nov. Les diplomates contre les consuls?
[Diplomats Against Consuls?]
In: Le Figaro, 51e année, 26 novembre1905, p.1.

déc. Circulaire aux membres du C.I.O. (déc.1905)
[Circular: Olympic Cup.]
Later reprinted, in: Textes choisis, vol.II, pp.648-649.

1er déc. Les Devoirs des Hellènes et des Philhellènes.
[The Duties of Hellenes and Philhellenes.]
In: L'Hellénisme, Paris, 2e année, 1er décembre 1905, n° 12, pp.1-2.

6 déc. Ni Rome ni Carthage?
[Neither Rome Nor Carthage?]
In: Le Figaro, 51e année, 6 décembre 1905, p.1.
Later reprinted, in: Pages d'Histoire contemporaine. Paris, Plon-Nourrit, 1909, pp.260-263.

18 déc. Maintenant... renouons.
[And Now ... Let's Take It Up Again.]
In: Le Figaro, 51e année, 18 décembre 1905, p.1.
Later reprinted, in: Pages d'Histoire contemporaine. Paris, Plon-Nourrit, 1909, pp.264-267.

1906

Le Play, réformateur et sociologue.
[Le Play: Reformer and Sociologist.]
In: La Chronique de France, 7e année, pp.158-173.
Later reprinted, in: Textes choisis, vol.I, pp.560-566.

janv. A propos du Jiu-Jitsu.
[About Jiu-Jitsu.]
In: Revue Olympique, 6e année, janvier 1906, pp.5-7.

janv. Le souci de l'hygiène est-il un signe de décadence?
[Are Hygienic Worries A Sign of Decadence?]
In: Revue Olympique, 6e année, janvier 1906, pp.7-9.

janv. Chronique du mois: La royauté du football. Prouesses nautiques et autres. Les Salons de l'Automobile. La revanche du fleuret.
[Chronicle of the Month: Football is King. Nautical Success and Others. Automobiles. Rapier Revenge.]
In: Revue Olympique, 6e année, janvier 1906, pp.9-14.

janv. Révolution mentale.
[Mental Revolution.]
In: Revue pour les Français, 1ère année, janvier 1906, pp.3-6.
Later reprinted, in:
1) Le Figaro, 52e année, 10 janvier 1906, p.1.
2) Pages d'Histoire contemporaine. Paris, Plon-Nourrit, 1909, pp.268-271.

janv. La Pologne inconnue.
[Unknown Poland.]
In: Revue pour les Français, 1ère année, janvier 1906, pp.14-25.

28 janv. Le contact de l'arme.
[Fighting for Peace.]
In: Le Figaro, 52e année, 28 janvier 1906, p.1.
Later reprinted, in: Pages d'Histoire contemporaine. Paris, Plon-Nourrit, 1909, pp.272-275.

fév. L'équitation populaire.
[Horse-Riding.]
In: Revue Olympique, 6e année, février 1906, pp.20-22.
Later reprinted, in:
1) L'Education physique, 7e année, 31 octobre 1908, n° 20, pp.554-557.
2) Textes choisis, vol.III, pp.194-196.

fév. Traité d'escrime équestre.
[Fencing on Horseback.]
Revised by Pierre de Coubertin et Louis Pascaud.
In: Revue Olympique, 6e année, février 1906, pp.27-32.
Off-print: Editions de la Revue Olympique. Auxerre, Lanier, 1906, 8 pages.
Later reprinted, in: Textes choisis, vol.III, pp.250-257.

fév. * La présidence de la République française.
[The Presidency of the French Republic.]
In: Revue pour les Français, 1ère année, février 1906, pp.43-46.

fév. Français et Romains en Afrique.
[The French and the Romans in Africa.]
In: Revue pour les Français, 1ère année, février 1906, pp.62-70.
Later reprinted, in: La Chronique de France, 6e année, 1905, pp.150-167.

fév. Paysages de Californie.
[Californian Landscapes.]
In: Revue pour les Français, 1ère année, février 1906, pp.74-78.
Later reprinted, in excerpts, under the title: "Californie d'autrefois", in: Anthologie. Aix-en-Provence, P. Roubaud, 1933, pp.133-135.

14 fév. Le balancier britannique.
[The British Pendulum.]
In: Le Figaro, 52e année, 14 février 1906, p.1.
Later reprinted, in: Pages d'Histoire contemporaine. Paris, Plon-Nourrit, 1909, pp.276-280.

mars La houle.
[The Swell.]
In: Revue pour les Français, 1ère année, mars 1906, pp.83-84.

mars La nudité dans les sports.
[Nudity and Sports.]
In: Revue Olympique, 6e année, mars 1906, n° 3, pp.35-38.
Later reprinted, in:
1) L'Education physique, 6e année, 15 octobre 1907, n° 19, pp.515-518.
2) Textes choisis, vol.III, pp.628-631.

mars Chronique du mois: Jeux artificiels. Ingérence inattendue. Encore ces prix en espèces. Entre boxeurs. Le train Renard.
[Chronicle of the Month: Artificial Games. Interference. Still Those Money Prizes. Among Boxers. The Train Renard.]
In: Revue Olympique, 6e année, mars 1906, pp.43-47.

mars Les premières épreuves de Gymnastique utilitaire.
[The First Tests for Useful Lifetime Sports.]
In: Revue Olympique, 6e année, mars 1906, pp.39-43.
Later reprinted, in: Textes choisis, vol.III, pp.556-560.

14 mars Faute d'un chemin de fer.
[A Railway in the Desert?]
In: Le Figaro, 52e année, 14 mars 1906, p.1.
Later reprinted, in: Pages d'Histoire contemporaine. Paris, Plon-Nourrit, 1909, pp.281-284.

avr. A travers l'histoire grecque.
[Greek History.]
In: Revue Olympique, 6ᵉ année, avril 1906. (Special edition on the occasion of the International Olympic Games of Athens), pp.51-57.
Later reprinted, in: Textes choisis, vol.II, pp.26-31.
Off-print: Auxerre, Lanier, 1906.

avr. * L'Hellénisme.
[Hellenism.]
In: Revue Olympique, 6ᵉ année, avril 1906. (Special edition on the occasion of the Intrnational Olympic Games of Athens), p.57.

avr. * Propos sur l'art grec.
[On Greek Art.]
In: Revue Olympique, 6ᵉ année, avril 1906. (Special edition on the occasion of the Intrnational Olympic Games of Athens), pp.57-58.
Later reprinted, in: Textes choisis, vol.II, p.53.

avr. * En fait d'athlétisme.
[Concerning Athletism.]
In: Revue Olympique, 6ᵉ année, avril 1906. (Special edition on the occasion of the Intrnational Olympic Games of Athens), pp.58-59.

avr. * Le devoir d'un Philhellène.
[The Philhellene's Duty.]
In: Revue Olympique, 6ᵉ année, avril 1906. (Special edition on the occasion of the Intrnational Olympic Games of Athens), p.64.
Later reprinted, in: Textes choisis, vol.II, p.47.

avr. * Programme électoral.
[Electoral Programme.]
In: Revue pour les Français, 1ère année, avril 1906, pp.123-125.

avr. * Olympie.
[Olympia.]
In: Revue pour les Français, 1ère année, avril 1906, pp.135-139.
Later reprinted, in: Textes choisis, vol.II, pp.41-45.

avr. * Les précurseurs de la puissance anglaise: I. Elisabeth.
[The Forerunners of English Power: I. Elizabeth.]
In: Revue pour les Français, 1ère année, avril 1906, pp.139-147.

avr. * A propos du sauvetage.
[Life-Saving.]
In: Revue pour les Français, 1ère année, avril 1906, pp.151-154.

10 avr. Terre de Californie.
[California.]
In: Le Figaro, 52ᵉ année, 10 avril 1906, p.1.
Later reprinted, in: Pages d'Histoire contemporaine. Paris, Plon-Nourrit, 1909, pp.285-288.

23 avr. La renaissance olympique.
[The Olympic Renaissance.]
In: L'Indépendance Belge, 77ᵉ année, 23 avril 1906, p.3.
Later reprinted, in:
1) Revue Olympique, 6ᵉ année, mai 1906, pp.68-75.
2) Textes choisis, vol.II, pp.331-337.

30 avr. France et Roumanie.
[France and Romania.]
In: Le Figaro, 52ᵉ année, 30 avril 1906, nº 120, p.1.

mai * Deuxième étape.
[The Next Step.]
In: Revue Olympique, 6ᵉ année, mai 1906, pp.67-68.

mai * Notre sœur roumaine.
[Our Romanian Sister.]
In: Revue pour les Français, 1ère année, mai 1906, pp.176-184.

mai Les précurseurs de la puissance anglaise: II. Cromwell, III. Guillaume.
[The Forerunners of English Power: II. Cromwell III. William.]
In: Revue pour les Français, 1ère année, mai 1906 pp.184-194.

23 mai Discours d'ouverture de la Conférence consultative des arts, lettres et sports prononcé au Foyer de la Comédie Française, à Paris le 23 mai 1906.
[Speech for the Opening of the Advisory Conference on the Arts, Literature, and Sports (May 23, 1906).]
In: Anthologie, Aix-en-Provence, P.Roubaud, 1933, pp.166-168.
Later reprinted in french, in:
1) L'Idée Olympique, pp.15-16.
2) In excerpts under the title: "Un grand mariage" In: Revue Olympique, 6ᵉ année, juin 1906, p.83. Later reprinted, in: Textes choisis, vol.II, p.543.
3) Textes choisis, vol.II, pp.483-484.
4) Cultures, vol. I, nº 2, off-print, UNESCO, Paris, 1982.
Later reprinted in
English, in: The Olympic Idea, pp.16-18.
German, in: Der Olympische Gedanke, pp.17-19.
Spanish, in: Ideario Olímpico, pp.33-36.

juin * Arts, Lettres et Sports.
[Arts, Letters, and Sports.]
In: Revue pour les Français, 1ère année, juin 1906, pp.211-215.
Later reprinted, in: Textes choisis, vol.II, pp.493-496.

juin Un "grand mariage".
[A Great Marriage.]
In: Revue Olympique, 6ᵉ année, juin 1906, p.83.

juin * L'Amérique aux Américains (I et II).
[America to the Americans.]
In: Revue pour les Français.
I: 1ère année, juin 1906, pp.215-220.
II: 1ère année, juillet 1906, pp.269-273.

juin * L'Ethiopie aujourd'hui.
[Ethiopia Today.]
In: Revue pour les Français, 1ère année, juin 1906, pp.222-235..

juin * Le Festival de la Sorbonne.
[The Sorbonne Festival.]
In: Revue Olympique, 6e année, juin 1906, pp.93-96.

3 juin Cosas de España.
[On Spain.]
In: Le Figaro, 52e année, 3 juin 1906, pp.1-2.
Later reprinted, in:
1) Pages d'Histoire contemporaine. Paris, Plon-Nourrit, 1909, pp.289-292.
2) Education physique, 5e année, 15 juin 1906, n° 10, pp.255-256.

15 juin Lois sociales. **[Social Law.]**
In: Le Figaro, 52e année, 15 juin 1906, p.1.
Later reprinted, in: Pages d'Histoire contemporaine. Paris, Plon-Nourrit, 1909, pp.293-296.

24 juin Maison de poupée...
[A Doll's House.]
In: Le Figaro, 52e année, 24 juin 1906, p.1.
Later reprinted, in: Pages d'Histoire contemporaine. Paris, Plon-Nourrit, 1909, pp.297-300.

juil. Le serment des athlètes. (Lettre à Monsieur Charles Simon).
[The Athletes' Oath. (Letter to Charles Simon).]
In: Revue Olympique, July 1906, pp.107- 109.
Later reprinted, in:
1) L'Idée Olympique, pp.13-14.
2) Textes choisis, vol.II, pp.466-468.
In English, in: The Olympic Idea, pp.15-16.
In Deutsch, in: Der Olympische Gedanke, pp.16-17.
In Spanish, in: Ideaio Olimpico,pp.31-32.

juil. La conférence consultative. (Circulaire du Président du C.I.O).
[Advisory Conference. Circular Letter of the President of the IOC.]
In: Bulletin Officiel du IOC, in: Revue Olympique, 6e année, juillet 1906, p.112.
Off-print, s.l., s.d. [1906], (1 page).

20 juil. La "La Course en section".
[One Step at a Time.]
In: Figaro, 52e année, 20 juillet 1906, p.1.
Later reprinted, in: Pages d'Histoire contemporaine. Paris, Plon-Nourrit, 1909, pp.301-304.

31 juil. Tournées d'Artistes.
In: Le Figaro, 52e année, 31 juillet 1906, p.1.

août * La cloison étanche.
[England Educates Gentlemen.]
In: Revue pour les Français, 1ère année, août 1906 pp.283-284.

août * L'Anglicanisme à son point d'arrivée.
[Anglicanism Reaching Its Goal.]
In: Revue pour les Français, 1ère année, août 1906, pp.292-298.

août * L'Ile Crète. **[Crete.]**
In: Revue pour les Français, 1ère année, août 1906, pp.298-302.

août * Henley Royal Regatta.
In: Revue Olympique, 6e année, août 1906, pp.115-116.

août L'équitation et la vie.
[Life and Horse-Riding.]
In: Revue Olympique, 6e année, août 1906, pp.125-126.
Later reprinted, in:
1) Essais de psychologie sportive. Lausanne/Paris, Payot, 1913, pp.21-22.
2) Anthologie, Aix-en-Provence, P. Roubaud, 1933 p.23 [in excerpts].
3) Textes choisis, vol.I, p.379.

août Bulletin officiel du Comité International Olympique. [Le même rang].
[The Same Rank.]
In: Revue Olympique, 6e année, août 1906, pp.127-128.
Later reprinted, in: Textes choisis, vol.II, p.445.

août Lauréats Olympiques.
[The Olympic Prizewinners.]
[Excerpts from speeches by Pierre de Coubertin given on May 26, 1906 on the occasion of the awarding of the Olympic Cup and the Olympic Diploma].
In: Revue Olympique, 6e année, août 1906, pp.122-125.

13 août A Bayreuth.
[In Bayreuth.]
In: Le Figaro, 52e année, 13 août 1906, n° 225, p.1.

sept. * Myopie.
[Myopia.]
In: Revue pour les Français, 1ère année, septembre 1906, pp.323-324.

sept. * Charlemagne et son empire.
[Charlemagne and His Empire.]
In: Revue pour les Français, 1ère année, septembre 1906, pp.332-343.

sept. La bastille mathématique.
[New Ways in Mathematics Teaching.]
In: Revue pour les Français, 1ère année, septembre 1906, pp.355-358.
Later reprinted, in excerpts, in: Anthologie, Aix-en-Provence, Impr. P. Roubaud, 1933, p.24.

sept. Le sabre à deux mains et l'infanterie montée.
[The Heavy Sword and the Riding Infantry.]
In: Revue Olympique, 6e année, septembre 1906, pp.132-135.

sept. Chronique du mois.
(Le triomphe de l'eau; Les regrets d'un baigneur ; l'Eglise et les sports; Me voilà, monsieur; Records aériens ; Les Fêtes d'Agram.)
[Chronicle of the Month: Regrets of a Swimmer. The Church and Sports. Here I am, Monsieur. Records in the Air. The Festival of Agram.]
In: Revue Olympique, 6e année, septembre 1906, pp.140-144.

sept. * A propos du festival de Berne.
[On the Berne Festival.]
In: Revue Olympique, 6e année, septembre 1906, pp.137-140.

oct. La chaise longue de l'athlète.
[Athletes Must Relax.]
In: Revue Olympique, 6e année, oct.1906, pp.147-150.
Later reprinted, in:
1) L'Education physique, 10e année, septembre 1911, n° 17, pp.456-459.
2) Essais de psychologie sportive, Lausanne/Paris, Payot, 1913, pp.23-31.
3) Textes choisis, vol.III, pp.329-332.

oct. Le vent, l'homme et la mer.
[The Wind, Man, and the Sea.]
In: Revue Olympique, 6e année, oct. 1906, pp.151-154.
Later reprinted, in: Textes choisis, vol.III, pp.325-327.

oct. Chronique du mois [La "Coupe de Paris", etc.].
[Chronicle of the Month: The "Coupe de Paris" etc.]
In: Revue Olympique, 6e année, oct. 1906, pp.154-157.

oct. La fête de Tourcoing.
[The Festival in Tourcoing.]
In: Revue Olympique, 6e année, oct. 1906, pp.157-160.

oct. Notre prochain numéro.
[Our Next Number.]
In: Revue pour les Français, 1ère année, oct. 1906, p.363.

oct. Les origines humaines.
[The Origins of Man.]
In: Revue pour les Français, 1ère année, octobre 1906, p.371-376.

oct. Foire normande. **[Norman Fair.]**
In: Revue pour les Français, 1ère année, octobre 1906, pp.376-379.

oct. Un Collège modèle.
[A Model College.]
In: Revue pour les Français, 1ère année, octobre 1906, pp.379-399.
Later reprinted in brochure form: Gand/Paris, Impr. Van Doosselaere / E. Basset, 1912.
Later reprinted, in: Textes choisis, vol.1, pp.452-472.

15 oct. Lettre du Baron Pierre de Coubertin à Monsieur Th. Vienne.
[Letter by Pierre de Coubertin to Th. Vienne.]
Luttenbach, 5 octobre 1906.
In: L'Education physique, 5e année, 15 octobre 1906, n° 18, p.484.

nov. La Suisse, reine des sports.
[Switzerland, Queen of Sports.]
In: Revue Olympique, 6e année, novembre1906, pp.163-165.

nov. A propos d'une émeute.
[On an Upheaval.]
In: Revue Olympique, 6e année, novembre1906, pp.165-168.

nov. Une société hippique modèle.
[A Modern Riding Society.]
In: Revue Olympique, 6e année, novembre1906, pp.170-172.

nov. Chronique du mois.
[**Chronicle of the Month**: The formation of a federation, etc.].
In: Revue Olympique, 6e année, novembre1906, pp.172- 174.

déc. * Arènes fin de siècle.
[Arenas of the End of the Century.]
In: Revue Olympique, 6e année, décembre 1906, p.179.

déc. * Une nouvelle étape.
[A New Step.]
In: Revue pour les Français, 1ère année, décembre 1906, pp.443-444.

déc. * Une guerre de cent ans (1689-1783), (I et II).
[A One-Hundred Years War.]
In: Revue pour les Français,
I: 1ère année, décembre 1906, pp.460-471.
II: 2e année, janvier 1907, pp.493-506.

déc. * La déclaration des devoirs.
[Declaration of Duties.]
In: Revue pour les Français, 1ère année, décembre 1906, pp.470-471.

déc. La presse française à l'étranger.
[The French Press Abroad.]
In: Revue pour les Français, 1ère année, décembre 1906, pp.472-473.

31 déc. La Campagne de l'Education physique: I. La pédagogie sportive.
[Campaign for Athletic Education: I. Sports Pedagogy.]
In: L'Education physique, 5e année, 31 décembre 1906, n° 23, pp.619-623.
Later reprinted, in:
1) Une Campagne de vingt-et-un ans (1887-1908). Paris, Librairie de l'Education physique, 1909, pp.1-7.
2) Textes choisis, vol.III, pp.52-58.

1907

Avant-propos.
[Foreword.]
In: Congrès d'Education physique sous le patronage de Monsieur le Ministre de la Guerre, Hôtel de Ville de Tourcoing. 5-6 octobre 1906. Lille, Bigot Frères, 1907, pp.7-8.

janv. L'œuvre du Touring-Club de France.
[The Achievements of the Touring Club of France.]
In: Revue Olympique, 7e année, janv. 1907, pp.195-197.

janv. Critiques et calomnies.[The Independency of the IOC].
In: Revue Olympique, 7e année, janv. 1907, pp.197-199.
Later reprinted, in: Textes choisis, vol.II, pp.602-603.

janv. La paix par la guerre.
[Peace Through War.]
In: Revue pour les Français, 2e année, janvier 1907, pp.483-484.

janv. La valeur morale du football.
[The Moral Values of Football.]
In: Revue pour les Français, 2e année, janvier 1907, pp.506-510.
Later reprinted, in: Textes choisis, vol.III, pp.289-292.

janv. * La réforme de l'enseignement.
[School Reform.]
In: Revue pour les Français, 2e année, janvier 1907, pp.510-516.

janv. * La déchéance d'un mets national.
[Die Dismissal of a National Dish.]
In: Revue pour les Français, 2e année, janvier 1907, pp.516-517.

janv. The Conditions of Franco-German Peace. (Translation by Helen Chisholm.)
In: Fortnightly Review, vol. LXXXI, nouvelle série, pp.223-229.

janv. La renaissance athlétique aux Etats-Unis.
[The Athletic Renaissance in the United States.]
In: Revue Olympique, 7e année, janv. 1907, pp.199-202.
Later reprinted, in: L'Education physique, 10e année, 15 janvier 1911, n° 1, pp.6-9.

janv. Chronique du mois: Le syndicalisme sportif.
[Chronicle of the Month: Athletic Unionization.]
In: Revue Olympique, 7e année, janvier 1907, pp.202- 205.
Later reprinted, in: Textes choisis, vol.II, pp.612-615; also in:Vol.III, pp.351-354.

janv. * Le comité français pour 1908.
[The French Committee for 1908.]
In: Revue Olympique, 7e année, janv. 1907, pp.206-208.

15 janv. La Campagne d'Education physique: II. L'état des choses en France.
[Campaign for Athletic Education: II: The State of Things in France.]
In: L'Education physique, 6e année, 15 janvier 1907, n° 1, pp.1-5.
Later reprinted, in:
1) Une Campagne de vingt-et-un ans (1887-1908). Paris, Librairie de l'Education physique, 1909, pp.8-14.
2) Textes choisis, vol.III, pp.59-64.

31 janv. La Campagne d'Education physique: III. Les Précurseurs.
[Campaign for Athletic Education: III: The Forerunners.]
In: L'Education physique, 6e année, 31 janvier 1907, n° 2, pp.29-33.
Later reprinted under the title: "Quvriers de la première heure", in:
1) Une Campagne de vingt-et-un ans (1887-1908). Paris, Librairie de l'Education physique, l909, pp.15-22.
2) Textes choisis, vol.III, pp.65-70.

fév. Le retour à la vie grecque.
[Back to a Greek Lifestyle.]
In: Revue Olympique, 7e année, fév. 1907, pp.211-215.
Later reprinted, in:
1) L'Education physique, 9e année, 31 juillet 1910, n° 14, pp.384-388.
2) Sports populaires, 4e année, 28 sept. 1910, n° 92, p.1.
3) Essais de psychologie sportive, Lausanne/Paris, Payot, 1913, pp.32-41.
4) Textes choisis, vol.I, pp.380-384 and vol.II, pp.48-52.

fév. Questions d'amateurisme.
[Questions of Amateurism.]
In: Revue Olympique, 7e année, fév. 1907, pp.217-219.
Later reprinted, in: Textes choisis, vol.II, pp.570-572.

fév. Chronique du mois: Sports de glace. Endurance italienne. En Espagne. Les deux boxes. A l'occasion d'un centenaire.
[Chronicle of the Month: Ice-Sports. Italian Endurance. In Spain. Two Kinds of Boxing. A Centenary.]
In: Revue Olympique, 7e année, fév. 1907, pp.220-223.

fév. Le tunnel sous la Manche.
[The Channel Tunnel.]
In: Revue pour les Français, 2e année, février 1907, pp.547-550.

15 fév. La Campagne d'Education physique: IV. La fondation du Comité.
[Campaign for Athletic Education: IV: Founding the Committee.]
In: L'Education physique, 6e année, 15 février 1907, n° 3, pp.57-63.
Later reprinted under the title: "La fondation du Comité et l'accueil de l'opinion", in:
1)Une Campagne de vingt-et-un ans (1887-1908). Paris, Librairie de l'Education physique, 1909, pp.23-32.
2) Textes choisis, vol.III, pp.71-77.

28 fév. La Campagne d'Education physique: V. Le Congrès de 1889.
[Campaign for Athletic Education: V: The Congress of 1889.]
In: L'Education physique, 6e année, 28 février 1907, n° 4, pp.85-91.
Later reprinted under the title: "Le congrès et les concours de 1889", in:
1) Une Campagne de vingt-et-un ans (1887-1908). Paris, Librairie de l'Education physique, 1909, pp.33-42.
2) Textes choisis, vol.III, pp.78-85.

mars Automatisme, obéissance et initiative répétée. Les classifications sportives.
[Automatism, Reaction, and Repetition. Classifications of Sports.]
In: Revue Olympique, 7e année, mars 1907, pp.227-231.
Later reprinted, in:
1) L'Education physique, 9e année, 31 octobre 1910, n° 20, pp.553-556.
2) Sports populaires, 4e année, 21 décembre 1910, n° 98, p.1.
3) Essais de psychologie sportive, Lausanne/Paris, Payot, 1913, pp.43-52.
4) Textes choisis, vol.III, pp.127-130.

mars * Le rôle des fédérations.
[The Role of the Federations.]
In: Revue Olympique, 7e année, mars 1907, pp.231-234.
Later reprinted, in: Textes choisis, vol.III, pp-355-357.

mars * Chronique du mois
[Chronicle of the Month: Nature. Air. Nutrition].
In: Revue Olympique, 7e année, mars 1907, pp.234-238.

mars * A propos de rallyes.
[About Rallyes.]
In: Revue Olympique, 7e année, mars 1907, pp.238-240.
Later reprinted, in: Textes choisis, vol.III, pp.333-334.

mars * Nécrologie.
[Obituary.]
In: Revue Olympique, 7e année, mars 1907, p.240.

mars * Ce qui restera du socialisme.
[What Will Remain of Socialism.]
In: Revue pour les Français, 2e année, mars 1907, pp.580-586.

15 mars La Campagne d'Education physique: VI. Le Comité, l'Union et la Ligue.
[Campaign for Athletic Education: VI. The Committee, the Union, and the League.]
In: L'Education physique, 6e année, 15 mars 1907, n° 5, pp.113-120.
Later reprinted under the title "Le Comité, la Ligue et l'Union", in:
1) Une Campagne de vingt-et-un ans (1887-1908). Paris, Librairie de l'Education physique, 1909, pp.43-53.
2) Textes choisis, vol.III, pp.86-94.

31 mars La Campagne d'Education physique: VII. Tous les sports.
[Campaign for Athletic Education: VII. All Sports.]
In: L'Education physique, 6e année, 31 mars 1907, n° 6, pp.141-148.
Later reprinted, in:
1) Une Campagne de vingt-et-un ans (1887-1908). Paris, Librairie de l'Education physique, 1909, pp.54-64.
2) Textes choisis, vol.III, pp.95-102.

avr. * Pacifisme et nationalisme.
[Pacifism and Nationalism.]
In: Revue pour les Français, 2e année, avril 1907, pp.603-604.

avr. L'hellénisation de Rome.
[The Hellenisation of Rome.]
In: Revue pour les Français, 2e année, avril 1907, pp.611-617.

avr. Les sanatoriums pour bien-portants.
[Sanatoriums for the Healthy.]
In: Revue Olympique, 7e année, avril 1907, pp.243-248.
Later reprinted, in:
1) L'Education physique, 9e année, 30 septembre 1910, n° 18, pp.498-503.
2) Sports populaires, 5e année, 15 mars 1911, n° 104, pp.1-2.
3) Essais de psychologie sportive, Lausanne/Paris, Payot, 1913, pp.53-65.
4) Anthologie, Aix-en-Provence, P. Roubaud, 1933, pp.28-32.
5) Textes choisis, vol.III, pp.638-643.

avr. * Mauvais exemples.
[Bad Examples.]
In: Revue Olympique, 7e année, avril 1907, pp.248-251.

avr. * Architecture sportive.
[Sports Architecture.]
In: Revue Olympique, 7e année, avril 1907, pp.251-252.

avr. * Chronique du mois: Le foot-ball en Amérique. Le foot-ball en Europe.
[Chronicle of the Month: Football in America. Football in Europe.]
In: Revue Olympique, 7e année, avril 1907, pp.254-256.

15 avr. La Campagne d'Education physique: VIII. Une année prospère.
[Campaign for Athletic Education: VIII. A Successful Year.]
In: L'Education physique, 6e année, 15 avril 1907, n° 7,pp.169-176.
Later reprinted, in:
1) Une Campagne de vingt-et-un ans (1887-1908). Paris, Librairie de l'Education physique, 1909, pp.65-76.
2) Textes choisis, vol.III, pp-103-111.

30 avr. La Campagne d'Education physique: IX. D'Andrésy à Henley.
[Campaign for Athletic Education: IX. From Andrésy to Henley.]
In: L'Education physique, 6e année, 30 avril 1907, n° 8, pp.197-204.
Later reprinted, in:
1) Une Campagne de vingt-et-un ans (1887-1908). Paris, Librairie de l'Education physique, 1909, pp.77-88.
2) Textes choisis, vol.III, pp.112-119.

mai * L'art arabe.
[Arab Art.]
In: Revue pour les Français, 2e année, mai 1907, pp.661- 667.

mai * La France aux Indes après Dupleix
[France in India after Dupleix.]
(1754-1782).
In: Revue pour les Français, 2e année, mai 1907, pp.672- 677.

mai Renaissance choréographique.
[A Choreography Renaissance.]
In: Revue Olympique, 7e année, mai 1907, pp.259-263.
Later reprinted, in:
1) L'Education physique, 12e année, 31 mai 1913, pp.158-161.
2) Textes choisis, vol.III, pp.309-314.

mai Trop de concours.
[Too much Competition.]
In: Revue Olympique, 7e année, mai 1907, pp.264-267.
Later reprinted, in:
1) L'Education physique, 10e année, 15 juillet 1911, n° 13, pp.357-359.
2) Sports populaires, 5e année, 19 juillet 1911, n° 113, p.1.

mai * Les origines de la gymnastique allemande.
[The Origins of German Gymnastics.]
In: Revue Olympique, 7e année, mai 1907, pp.267-270.

31 mai La Campagne d'Education physique: X. Le Congrès de la Sorbonne.
[Campaign for Athletic Education: X. The Congress of the Sorbonne.]
In: L'Education physique, 6e année, 31 mai 1907, n° 10, pp.281-287.
Later reprinted, in:
1) Une Campagne de vingt-et-un ans (1887-1908). Paris, Librairie de l'Education physique, 1909, pp.89-98.
2) Textes choisis, vol.II, pp.115-123.

juin * L'impôt global dans l'antiquité.
[Taxes in Classical Antiquity.]
In: Revue pour les Français, 2e année, juin 1907, pp.711-715.
Later reprinted, in: Pages de Critique et d'Histoire, 1er fascicule, 1918, pp.5-8.

juin * L'Achilleïon de Corfou.
[The Achilleion at Corfu.]
In: Revue pour les Français, 2e année, juin 1907, pp.715- 717.

La réunion de la Haye (1907): Les règlements de Londres.
[The Meeting of La Haye: The Rules for London.]
In: Revue Olympique, 7ème année, juin 1907, pp.279-281.
Later reprinted, in: Textes choisis, vol.II, pp.696-698.

juin * Le bain d'air et la convalescence.
[Fresh Air and Convalescence.]
In: Revue Olympique, 7e année, juin 1907, pp.282-284.

juin * Chronique du mois
[Chronicle of the Month: Expositions. Sports, etc.].
In: Revue Olymique, 7e année, juin 1907, pp.285-287.

15 juin La Campagne d'Education physique: XI. La Bataille de Caen.
[Campaign for Athletic Education: XI: The Battle of Caen.]
In: L'Education physique, 6e année, 15 juin 1907, n° 11, pp.281-287.
Later reprinted, in:
1) Une Campagne de vingt-et-un ans (1887-1908). Paris, Librairie de l'Education physique, 1909, pp.99-107.
2) Textes choisis, vol.III, pp.120-125.

30 juin La fête de la Sorbonne. (Speech).
[The Sorbonne Festival.]
In: L'Education physique, 6e année, 30 juin 1907, n° 3, pp.338-340.
Later reprinted under the title:"La philosophie du débrouillard" dans:
1) Une Campagne de vingt-et-un ans (1887-1908). Paris, Librairie de l'Education physique, 1909, pp.216-220.
2) Textes choisis, vol.III, pp.569-573.

juil. * Fausse honte.
[False Modesty.]
In: Revue pour les Français, 2e année, juillet 1907, pp.734-737.

juil. * La question de la Chambre des Lords.
[The House of Lords.]
In: Revue pour les Français, 2e année, juillet 1907, pp.755-758.

juil. * Une relique.
[A Relic.]
In: Revue Olympique, 7e année, juillet 1907, pp.291-292.

juil. * L'homme qui boxe.
[The Boxing Man.]
In: Revue Olympique, 7e année, juillet 1907, pp.292-293.

juil. * Les frontières sportives de l'aviation.
[The Limits of the Aviatory Sports.]
In: Revue Olympique, 7e année, juillet 1907, pp.293-298.
Later reprinted, in: Textes choisis, vol.III, pp.318-321.

juil. Chronique du mois. Autour des Sokols - Les régates de Kiel - Circuits automobiles - Paris-Pékin - Les débrouillards à la Sorbonne.
[Chronicle of the Month: The Sokols. Regattas at Kiel. Motor Racing. Paris-Peking. The Smart Lads at the Sorbonne.]
In: Revue Olympique, 7e année, juillet 1907, pp.298-302.

août Festivités transatlantiques: La cérémonie du Richmond, la folie du pétard.
[Transatlantic Festivities: The Ceremony of Richmond.]
In: Revue pour les Français, 2e, août 1907, pp.773-779.

août * Coup d'œil sur l'histoire chilienne.
[A Look at Chilean History.]
In: Revue pour les Français, 2e, août 1907, pp.794-800.
Later reprinted, in: Pages de Critique et d'Histoire, 2e fascicule, 1918, pp.4-8.

août Les sports en Camargue.
[Sports in the Camargue.]
In: Revue Olympique, 7e année, août 1907, pp.307-308.
Later reprinted, in:
1) L'Education physique, 9e année, 30 novembre1910, n°22, pp.594-596.
2) Sports populaires, 5e année, 10 mai 1911, n°108, p.1.

août Votre chambre de Gymnastique.
[Your Home Gymnasium.]
In: Revue Olympique, 7e année, pp.309-312.
Later reprinted, in:
1) L'Education physique, 9e année, 15 novembre1910, n°21, pp.565-568.
2) Sports Populaires, 5e année, 15 mars 1911, n°104, pp.1-2.

août * La question des prix.
[The Trouble With Prizes.]
In: Revue Olympique, 7e année, août 1907, pp.312-315.
Later reprinted, in: Textes choisis, vol.II, pp.573-575.

août Les Sokols.
[The Sokols.]
In: Revue Olympique, 7e année, août 1907, pp.315-518.

31 août La Campagne d'Education physique. XII. La résistance de la Grèce.
[Campaign for Athletic Education: XII: Greek Resistance.]
In: L'Education physique, 6e année, 31 août 1907, n°16, pp.421-427.
Later reprinted, in:
1) Une Campagne de vingt-et-un ans (1887-1908). Paris, Librairie de L'Education physique, 1909, pp.108-117.
Textes choisis, vol.II, pp.131138.

sept. Bains de mer en toute saison.
[Bathing in the Sea Throughout the Year.]
In: Revue Olympique, 7e année, septembre 1907, pp.335-336.
Later reprinted, in: L'Education physique, 10e année, 15 octobre 1911, n° 19, pp.524-525.

sept. Les caractéristiques de l'esprit américain.
[Characteristics of the American Spirit.]
In: Revue pour les Français, 2e année, septembre 1907, pp.818-826.

sept. La Bulgarie contemporaine.
[Contemporary Bulgaria.]
In: Revue pour les Français, 2e année, septembre 1907, pp.826-839.

15 sept. La Campagne d'Education physique: XIII. La première Olympiade.
[Campaign for Athletic Education: XIII. The First Olympiad.]
In: L'Education physique, 6e année, 15 septembre 1907, n° 17, pp.451-458.
Later reprinted, in:
1) Une Campagne de vingt-et-un ans (1887-1908). Paris, Librairie de l'Education physique, 1909, pp.118-128.
2)Textes choisis, vol.II, pp.139-147.

30 sept. La Campagne d'Education physique:
XIV. Le Congrès du Havre.
[Campaign for Athletic Education: XVI: The Congress of Le Havre.]
In: L'Education physique, 6e année, 30 septembre 1907, n° 18, pp.482-485.
Later reprinted, in:
1) Une Campagne de vingt-et-un ans (1887-1908). Paris, Librairie de l'Education physique, 1909, pp.129-135.
2)Textes choisis, vol.II, pp.166-172.

oct. * L'exposition franco-anglaise de 1908.
[The Anglo-French Exposition of 1908.]
In: Revue pour les Français, 2e année, octobre 1907, pp.916-917.

oct. Le camping scolaire aux Etats-Unis.
[School Camps in the United States.]
In: Revue Olympique, 7e année, octobre 1907, pp.346-348.
Later reprinted, in: L'Education physique, 11e année, 30 juin 1912, n° 13, pp.347-349.

oct. * La question du Cervin.
[The Matterhorn Question.]
In: Revue Olympique, 7e année, octobre 1907, pp.349-350.

oct. * Cavaliers pêcheurs.
[Gentleman Fishers.]
In: Revue Olympique, 7e année, octobre 1907, pp.351-352.

nov. * Art sportif. **[Sports Art.]**
In: Revue Olympique, 7e année, novembre1907, pp.355-357.
Later reprinted, in: Textes choisis, vol.II, pp.498-500.

déc. * Opium et alcool.
[Opium and Alcohol.]
In: Revue pour les Français, 2e année, décembre 1907, pp.942-944.

déc. Sa Majesté la neige.
[Majestic Snow.]
In: Revue Olympique, 7e année, décembre 1907, pp.371-373.
Later reprinted, in: L'Education physique, 7e année, 15 décembre 1908, n° 23, pp.625-627.

déc. * Les progrès de la locomotion.
[The Progress of Locomotion.]
In: Revue Olympique, 7e année, décembre 1907, pp.374-376.

déc. * Chronique du mois.
[Chronicle of the Month: Aeronautic, etc.]
In: Revue Olympique, 7e année, décembre 1907, pp.376-379.

1908

janv. * Récapitulation.
[Summary.]
In: Revue Olympique, 8e année, janvier 1908, pp.3-5.

janv. * Les excès du syndicalisme.
[Athletic Associations Behaving Like Unions.]
In: Revue Olympique, 8e année, janvier 1908, pp.5-8.
Later reprinted, in: Textes choisis, vol.III, pp.358-361.

janv. Les sports de neige:
I. Luges, toboggans, bobsleighs.
[Winter Sports: I. Luge, Toboggan, Bobsleigh.]
In: Revue Olympique, 8e année, janvier 1908, pp.9-14.
Later reprinted, in:
1) L'Education physique, 11e année, 31 décembre 1912, n° 24, pp 658-664.
2) Textes choisis, vol.III, pp.235-240.

25 janv. La réforme de l'enseignement secondaire (I and II).
[The Reform of Secondary Education.]
In: Revue pour les Français, 3 année,
I: 25 janvier 1908, pp.35-40;
II: 25 avril 1908, pp.211-216.

fév. A propos du Pentathlon.
[On Pentathlon.]
In: Revue Olympique, 8e année, février 1908, pp.19-22.
Later reprinted, in: L'Education physique, 7e année, 15 mars 1908, n° 5, pp.133-135.

fév. * Simplicité princière.
[Lavish Simplicity.]
In: Revue Olympique, 8e année, février, 1908, pp.22-23.

fév. Les sports de neige: II. Le ski.
[Winter Sports: Skiing.]
In: Revue Olympique, 8e année, février 1908, pp.23-28.
Later reprinted, in:
1) L'Education physique, 12e année, 15 janvier, 1913, n° 1, pp.12-20.
2) Textes choisis, vol.III, pp.240-245.

fév. * Chronique du mois: Le knock-out.
[Chronicle of the Month: Knock-Out.]
In: Revue Olympique, 8e année, février 1908, pp.28-30.
Later reprinted, in: Textes choisis, vol.III, pp.174-176.

mars * L'automobile aux Etats-Unis.
[The Car in the United States.]
In: Revue Olympique, 8e année, mars 1908, pp.35-38.

mars * Groupements sportifs.
[Free Sports Groups.]
In: Revue Olympique, 8e année, mars 1908, pp.38-41.

mars * Chronique du mois: Un sport éternel - Le pigeon olympique - Entêtement comique.
[Chronicle of the Month: An Eternal Sport. The Olympic Pigeon. Funny Stubbornness.]
In: Revue Olympique, 8e année, mars 1908, pp.44-47.
The chapter "Un sport éternel" was later reprinted under the title "La chasse" in: L'Education physique, 12e année, 15 janvier 1913, n° 1, pp.11-12.

mars * Les préliminaires du Jiu-Jitsu.
[Jiu-Jitsu Preliminaries.]
In: Revue olympique, 8e année, mars 1908, pp.41-44.

avr. * Sir Howard Vincent.
In: Revue Olympique, 8e année, avril 1908, pp.51-53.

avr. * Un gymnase... presque olympique.
[A Near-Olympic Gymnasium.]
In: Revue Olympique, 8e année, avril 1908, pp.53-55.

avr. * Vers la Chevalerie.
[Towards Chivalry.]
In: Revue Olympique, 8e année, avril 1908, pp.55-60.
Later reprinted, in: L'Education physique, 12e année, 30 novembre 1913, n° 22, pp.605-610.

avr. Chronique du mois: L'aviron.
[Chronicle of the Month: Rowing.]
In: Revue Olympique, 8e année, avril 1908, pp.60-63.
Later reprinted, in: Textes choisis, vol.III, pp.222-224.

30 avr. La Campagne d'Education physique: XV. Les apprêts de la IIe Olympiade.
[Campaign for Athletic Education: XV: Preparations for the Second Olympiad.]
In: L'Education physique, 7e année, 30 avril 1908, n° 8, pp.197-203.
Later reprinted, in:
1) Une Campagne de vingt-et-un ans (1887-1908). Paris, Librairie de l'Education physique, 1909, pp.136-145.
2) Textes choisis, vol.II, pp.174-181.

mai L'éperon.
[Spurs.]
In: Revue Olympique, 8e année, mai 1908, pp.67-68.
Later reprinted, in:
1) Essais de psychologie sportive. Lausanne/Paris, Payot, 1913, pp.66-70.
2) Textes choisis, vol.I, pp.385-386.

mai Une lettre de M. Ch. Diehl.
[A Letter from C. Diehl.]
In: Revue Olympique, 8e année, mai 1908, pp.74-75.

mai * Les sports et l'armée.
[Sports and the Army.]
In: Revue Olympique, 8e année, mai 1908, pp.70-74.

mai * Chronique du mois.
[Chronicle of the Month: International events. Cecil Rhodes. Aviation].
In: Revue Olympique, 8e année, mai 1908, pp.76-78.

15 mai La Campagne d'Education physique: XVI. Sports officiels.
[Campaign for Athletic Education: XVI: Official Sports.]
In: L'Education physique, 7e année, 15 mai 1908, n° 9, pp.225-230.
Later reprinted, in:
1) Une Campagne de vingt-et-un ans (1887-1908). Paris, Librairie de l'Education physique, 1909, pp.146-152.
2) Textes choisis, vol.II, pp.182-186.

31 mai La Campagne d'Education physique: XVII. Chicago ou Saint Louis.
[Campaign for Athletic Education: XVII: Chicago or Saint Louis?]
In: L'Education physique, 7e année, 31 mai 1908, n° 10, pp.253-260.
Later reprinted, in:
1) Une Campagne de vingt-et-un ans (1887-1908). Paris, Librairie de l'Education physique, 1909, pp.153-161.
2) Textes choisis, vol.II, pp.196-202.

juin Anarchasis à Olympie.
[Anarchasis at Olympia.]
In: Revue Olympique, 8e année, juin 1908, pp.83-85.
Later reprinted, in: L'Education physique, 12e année, 15 mai 1913, pp.120-122.

juin La nouvelle pierre philosophale et le néo-empirisme.
[The New Philosophers' Stone and Neo-Empirism.]
In: Revue Olympique, 8e année, juin 1908, pp.85-88.
Later reprinted, in:
1) Essais de Psychologie sportive, Lausanne/Paris, Payot, 1913, pp.71-72.
2) Textes choisis, vol.III, pp.397-400.

juin * Dumferline.
In: Revue Olympique, 8e année, juin 1908, pp.89-91.

juin * Appareils de natation.
[Swimming Aids.]
In: Revue Olympique, 8e année, juin 1908, pp.91-93.

juin * Chronique du mois.
[Chronicle of the Month.]
In: Revue Olympique, 8e année, juin 1908, pp.93-95.

juil. * L'ouverture de la IVe Olympiade.
[The Opening of the IVth Olympiad.]
In: Revue Olympique, 8e année, juillet 1908, pp.99-102.

juil. * La réunion du Comité International Olympique.
[The IOC Session.]
In: Revue Olympique, 8e année, juillet 1908, pp.103-105.

juil. * Autour des Jeux Olympiques.
[Around the Olympic Games.]
In: Revue Olympique, 8e année, juil. 1908, pp.105-107.

juil. Les "Trustees" de l'idée olympique.
[The Trustees of the Olympic Idea.]
In: Revue Olympique, 8e année, juillet 1908, pp.108-110.
Later reprinted, in:
1) L'Education physique, 7e année, 31 août 1908, n° 16, pp.440-441.
2) L'Idée olympique, pp.17-19.
3) Textes choisis, vol.II, pp.448-450.
Later reprinted,
in English, in: The Olympic Idea, pp.18-20.
in German, in: Der Olympische Gedanke, pp.20-22.
in Spanish, in: Ideario Olímpico, pp.36-39.

juil. * La distribution des récompenses.
[Prize-Giving.]
In: Revue Olympique, 8e année, juillet 1908, pp.111-112.

juil. Why I Revived the Olympic Games.
In: Fortnightly Review, vol. LXXXIV, nouvelle série, juillet 1908, pp.110-115.

13 juil. To the Editor of the Times: The Olympic Games.
In: The Times, London, July 13, 1908, p.23.

28 juil. Autour des Olympiades. Déclarations du Baron Pierre de Coubertin. [Interview]
[About the Olympiads.]
In: La Presse, 28 juillet 1908.

août * La chronique des Jeux de 1908.
[The Chronicle of the 1908 Games.]
In: Revue Olympique, 8e année, août 1908, pp.115-118.
Later reprinted, in: Textes choisis, vol.II, pp.233-237.

août * L'Olympiade nautique. **[Water Olympics.]**
In: Revue Olympique, 8e année, août 1908, pp.123-125.

août * En l'air. **[In the Air.]**
In: Revue Olympique, 8e année, août 1908, pp.125-127.

sept. * Demetrius Bikelas.
In: Revue Olympique, 8e année, septembre 1908, pp.131-132.
Later reprinted, in: Textes choisis, vol.II, pp.356-357.

sept. * Paroles sages et paroles folles.
[Wise Words, Foolish Words.]
In: Revue Olympique, 8e année, septembre 1908, pp.132-134.

sept. * Le lancement du javelot.
[Throwing the Javelin.]
In: Revue Olympique, 8e année, septembre 1908, pp.138-140.
Later reprinted, in: Textes choisis, vol.III, pp.142-144.

sept. * Chronique du mois.
[Chronicle of the Month: Strasbourg. C.V.Peel. Aviation School. Alphonse XIII.]
In: Revue Olympique, 8e année, septembre 1908, pp.141-144.

30 sept. La Campagne d'Education physique: XVIII. Londres et Bruxelles.
[Campaign for Athletic Educatin: XVIII. London and Brussels.]
In: L'Education physique, 7e année, 30 septembre 1908, n° 18, pp.477-483.
Later reprinted, in:
1) Une Campagne de vingt-et-un ans (1887-1908). Paris, Librairie de l'Education physique, 1909, pp.162-171.
2) Textes choisis, vol.II, pp.204-212.

oct. * Statistiques à méditer.
[Statistics to Contemplate.]
In: Revue Olympique, 8e année, oct. 1908, pp.147-148.

oct. * La lutte islandaise. **[The Icelandic Wrestling.]**
In: Revue Olympique, 8e année, oct. 1908, pp.148-152.
Later reprinted, in: L'Education physique, 7e année, 30 novembre1908, n° 22, pp.604-608.

oct. A travers les vieux livres.
[In Old Books.]
In: Revue Olympique, 8e année, oct. 1908, pp.152-154.
Later reprinted, in: L'Education physique, 12e année, 31 janvier 1913, pp.47-48.

oct. En voulez-vous, des Marathons ?
[Do You Want Marathons?]
In: Revue Olympique, 8e année, octobre 1908, pp.154- 155.

oct. Chronique du mois: Sports pontificaux - Paris - Francfort - En Suisse - Athlétisme Ottoman.
[Chronicle of the Month: Sportsmen Performing for the Pope. Paris. Frankfurt. In Switzerland. Ottoman Athletics.]
In: Revue Olympique, 8e année, oct. 1908, pp.156-159.
Later reprinted, in excerpts, in: Textes choisis, vol.I, pp.597-598.

15 oct. La Campagne d'Education physique: XIX. Au pied du Capitole.
[Campaign for Athletic Education: XIX: At the Capitol.]
In: L'Education physique, 7e année, 15 octobre 1908, n° 19, pp.505-512.
Later reprinted, in:
1) Une Campagne de vingt-et-un ans (1887-1908). Paris, Librairie de l'Education physique, 1909, pp.172-181.
2) Textes choisis, vol.II, pp.223-230.

25 oct. Rien de changé en Angleterre.
[Nothing New in England.]
In: Revue pour les Français, 3e année, 25 octobre 1908, pp.596-604.

nov. Les Wintergames. [**The Winter Games.**]
In: Revue Olympique, 8e année, novembre1908, pp.163-166.

nov. * Les droits du baigneur.
[**The Swimmer's Rights.**]
In: Revue Olympique, 8e année, novembre1908, pp.171-173.

nov. Chronique du mois
[**Chronicle of the Month:** Outstanding achievements of celebreties].
In: Revue Olympique, 8e année, novembre1908, pp.173-175.

déc. * American ambitions.
In: Revue Olympique, 8e année, décembre 1908, pp.179-181.

déc. * La route. [**The Course.**]
In: Revue Olympique, 8e année, décembre 1908, pp.181-184.

déc. 1908-fév. 1909
Autour des costumes de sport (I, II, III).
[**Sportswear.**]
I. Costume général et costumes spéciaux.
In: Revue Olympique, 8e année, décembre 1908, pp.184-187.
II. Le point de vue hygiénique.
In: Revue Olympique, 9e année, janvier 1909, pp.8-10.
III. La psychologie du costume sportif.
In: Revue Olympique, 9e année, février 1909, pp.26-29.
Part III later reprinted, in:
1) Essais de psychologie sportive. Lausanne/Paris, Payot, 1913, pp.80-88.
2) Textes choisis, vol.I, pp.387-389.

déc. * Chronique du mois
[**Chronicle of the Month:** J.P Müller].
In: Revue Olympique, 8e année, décembre 1908, pp.187-188.

1909

janv. * Une Souveraine.
[**A Sovereign.**]
In: Revue Olympique, 9e année, janvier 1909, p.3.

janv. * L'Ecole de Springfield.
[**Springfield College.**]
In: Revue Olympique, 9e année, janvier 1909, pp.3-7.
Later reprinted, in: L'Education physique, 10e année, 30 septembre 1911, n° 18, pp.487-492.

janv. * L'oiseau artificiel.
[**The Artificial Bird.**]
In: Revue Olympique, 9e année, janvier 1909, pp.10-13.
Later reprinted, in: Textes choisis, vol.III, pp.322-324.

7 janv. Dopo le Olimpiadi di Londra. [Interview]
[**After the London Olympiad. (Italian Text.)**]
In: Gli Sports, Roma, 2e année, 7 janvier 1909, n° 3, p.1.

fév. * La conquête du Rouvenzori (I et II).
[**The Conquest of Ruvenzori.**]
In: Revue Olympique, 9e année, février 1909, pp.19-24 (I), et mars 1909, pp.36-42 (II).

fév. * Chronique du mois: Le ski en Europe - Bains d'hiver - Une formule sans reproche.
[**Chronicle of the Month: Skiing in Europe. Winter Bathing. A Perfect Formula.**]
In: Revue Olympique, 9e année, février 1909, pp.29-32.

15 fév. * Fernand Lagrange.
In: L'Education physique, 8e année, 15 février 1909, n° 3, pp.57-58.

mars * Le cyclisme aux Jeux Olympiques.
[**Cycling and the Olympic Games.**]
In: Revue Olympique, 9e année, mars 1909, pp.35-36.
Later reprinted, in: Textes choisis, vol.II, pp.718-719.

mars * De la danse à la philosophie.
[**From Dancing to Philosophy.**]
In: Revue Olympique, 9e année, mars 1909, pp.43-45.
Later reprinted, in: Textes choisis, vol.III, pp.315-317.

mars Patineurs, jouez au hockey.
[**Ice-Skaters, Play Hockey!**]
In: Revue Olympique, 8e année, mars 1909, pp.45-47.
Later reprinted, in:
1) L'Education physique, 12e année, 31 janvier 1913, n° 2, pp.35-38.
2) Textes choisis, vol.III, pp.295-297.

mars * Chronique du mois
[**Chronicle of the Month:** President Taft].
In: Revue Olympique, 9e année, mars 1909, pp.47-48.

avr. * Le général von der Asseburg.
[**General von der Asseburg.**]
In: Revue Olympique, 9e année, avril 1909, pp.51-52.

avr. * Le préjugé des saisons.
[**Seasonal Prejudices.**]
In: Revue Olympique, 9e année, avril 1909, pp.52-53.

avr. L'homme et l'animal.
[**Men and Animals.**]
In: Revue Olympique, 9e année, avril 1909, pp.53-56.
Later reprinted, in:
1) Essais de psychologie sportive. Lausanne/Paris, Payot, 1913, pp.87-93.
2) Textes choisis, vol.I, pp.390-392.

avr. * Extravaganza.
In: Revue Olympique, 9e année, avril 1909, pp.56-59.

avr. * Chronique du mois: Autour d'un vélodrome. Lignes aériennes. La névrose administrative. Point de vue culinaire.
[Chronicle of the Month: A Velodrome. Overhead Cables. Administrative Neurosis. From the Culinary Point of View.]
In: Revue Olympique, 9e année, avril 1909, pp.59-62.

25 avr. A propos des démocraties antiques.
[On Classical Democracy.]
In: Revue pour les Français, 4e année, 25 avril 1909, pp.292- 296.

mai * L'enquête sur l'amateurisme.
[The Survey on Amateurism.]
In: Revue Olympique, 9e année, mai 1909, pp.67-68.
Later reprinted, in: Textes choisis, vol.II, pp.576-577.

mai Un plaidoyer pour le jeu.
[A Plea for Games.]
In: Revue Olympique, 9e année, mai 1909, pp.68-72.
Later reprinted, in: L'Education physique, 10e année, 30 novembre 1911, n° 22, pp.608-614.

mai * Mere bigness.
In: Revue Olympique, 9e année, mai 1909, pp.72-73.

mai La philosophie de la culture physique.
[Philosophy of Physical Culture.]
In: Revue Olympique, 9e année, mai 1909, pp.73-76.
Later reprinted, in:
1) Essais de psychologie sportive. Lausanne/Paris, Payot, 1913, pp.94-102.
2) Textes choisis, vol.I, pp.393-396.

mai * Chronique du mois: La pelota.
[Chronicle of the Month: Pelota.]
In: Revue Olympique, 9e année, mai 1909, pp.77-79.
Later reprinted, in: Textes choisis, vol.III, pp.303-305.

juin La réunion du IOC à Berlin. La séance inaugurale. Remise des diplômes olympiques.
[The IOC Meeting in Berlin. Opening Session. The Presentation of Olympic Diplomas.]
In: Revue Olympique, 9e année, juin 1909, pp.83-88.
Later reprinted, in: Textes choisis, vol.II, pp.650-653.

juil. * Une brochure et un livre.
[A Booklet and a Book.]
In: Revue Olympique, 9e année, juillet 1909, pp.99-102.

juil. * Die Entwicklung der Olympischen Spiele. Die schwedisch-germanische Periode.
[Development of the Olympic Games: The Swedish-German Era.]
In: Revue Olympique, 9e année, juillet 1909, pp.102- 105.

juil. Savoir dételer. **[How to Relax.]**
In: Revue Olympique, 9e année, juillet 1909, pp.105-108.
Later reprinted, in:
1) L'Education physique, 9e année, 15 juin 1910, n° 11, pp.292-294.
2) Sports populaires, 4e année, 28 sept. 1910, n° 92, p.2.
3) Essais de psychologie sportive, Lausanne/Paris, Payot, 1910, pp.103-110.

juil. * Votre gymnase de plein air.
[Your Open-Air Gymnasium.]
In: Revue Olympique, 9e année, juillet 1909, pp.108-110.

août Les sports à Monaco.
[Sports in Monaco.]
In: Revue Olympique, 9e année, août 1909, pp.122-124.

août Sportsmen malgré eux.
[Reluctant Sportsmen.]
In: Revue Olympique, 9e année, août 1909, pp.125-126.
Later reprinted, in:
1) Essais de psychologie sportive, Lausanne/Paris, Payot, 1913, pp.111-113.
2) L'Education physique, 8e année, 15 octobre 1909, n° 19, pp.523-524.

août * Chronique du mois
[Chronicle of the Month: Louis Blériot, etc.].
In: Revue Olympique, 9e année, août 1909, pp.126-128.

août Questionaire sur l'amateurisme.
[Questionnaire Concerning Amateurism.]
In: Revue Olympique, 8e année, août 1909, p.128.
Later reprinted, in: Textes choisis, vol.II, p.577.

sept. L'architecture sportive en Allemagne.
[Sports Architecture in Germany.]
In: Revue Olympique, 9e année, septembre 1909, pp.131-135.
Later reprinted, in:
1) L'Education physique, 9e année, 31 janvier 1910, n° 2, pp.39-42.
2) Sports populaires, 4e année, 2 mars 1910, n° 70, pp.1- 2.

sept. Le rythme et la vitesse.
[Rhythm and Speed.]
In: Revue Olympique, 9e année, septembre 1909, pp.135-137.
Later reprinted, in: Essais de psychologie sportive. Lausanne/Paris, Payot, 1913, pp.114-118.

sept. * The grammar of rowing.
In: Revue Olympique, 9e année, septembre 1909, pp.137-141.

sept. * Chronique du mois. Armée anglaise: le sport préparateur - Armée française: le sport réparateur.
[Chronicle of the Month: The English Army: Sports as Preparation. The French Army: Sports as Repair.]
In: Revue Olympique, 9e année, septembre 1909, pp.141-144.

oct. * En vue du concours international d'architecture.
[Regarding the International Architecture Competition.]
In: Revue Olympique, 9e année, oct. 1909, pp.147-148.
Later reprinted, in: Textes choisis, vol.II, pp.503-504.

oct. * Les gammes musculaires quotidiennes.
[Training All Muscles.]
In: Revue Olympique, 9e année, oct. 1909, pp.148-153.
Later reprinted, in:
1) L'Education physique, 8e année, 15 novembre1909, no 21, pp.581-585.
2) Textes choisis, vol.III, pp.547-578.

oct. 1909 - mars 1910
Une Olympie moderne (I-VI).
[A Modern Olympia.]
In: Revue Olympique,
I: 9e année, octobre 1909, pp.153-156 ;
(Le cadre), [The Setting.]
II: 9e année, novembre1909, pp.167-170 ;
(L'Administration), [Administration.]
III: 9e année, décembre 1909, pp.184-187 ;
(Le Programme des Jeux), [The Program of the Games.]
IV: 10e année, janvier 1910, pp.9-13 ;
(Les Qualifiés), [Qualified Individuals.]
V: 10e année, février 1910, pp.26-28 ;
(Les Spectateurs), [The Spectators.]
VI: 10e année, mars 1910, pp.41-44.
(Les Cérémonies), [The Ceremonies.]
Later reprinted in French, in:
1) In brochure form: Auxerre, E. Jattefaux, 1910 (24 pages);
2) L'Idée olympique, pp.20-35.
3) Textes choisis, vol.II, pp.54-71; pp.683-691.
Later reprinted,
in English, in: The Olympic Idea, pp.22-36.
in German, in: Der Olympische Gedanke, pp.24-43.
in Spanish, in: Ideario Olímpico, pp.42-66.

oct. * Chronique du mois: A propos du pôle.
[Monthly Chronicle: On the Pole.]
In: Revue Olympique, 9e année, octobre 1909, pp.158-160.

25 oct. Tout est changé en Allemagne.
[Everything Has Changed in Germany.]
In: Revue pour les Français, 4e année, 25 octobre 1909, pp.812-817.

nov. Les trois âges.
[The Three Ages.]
In: Revue Olympique, 9e année, novembre1909, pp.163-164.
Later reprinted, in:
1) Sports populaires, 4e année, 16 mars 1910, no 78, p.1.
2) Essais de psychologie sportive, Lausanne/Paris, Payot, 1913, pp.119-122.
3) Textes choisis, vol.I, pp.397-398.

nov. La limite du record.
[The Limits of Records.]
In: Revue Olympique, 9e année, novembre1909, pp.164-166.
Later reprinted, in:
1) L'Education physique, 9e année, 15 mars 1910, no 5, pp.115-118.
2) Sports populaires, 4e année, 30 mars 1910, no 79, p.1.
3) Essais de psychologie sportive, Lausanne/Paris, Payot, 1913, pp.123-128.

nov. * Chronique du mois. Une église sans fidèles: tous pontifes!
[Chronicle of the Month: A Church Without Church-Goers: All of Them Priests!]
In: Revue Olympique, 9e année, novembre1909, pp.174-176.
Later reprinted, in: Textes choisis, vol.III, pp.362-363.

1910

janv. * Hier et demain.
[Today and Tomorrow.]
In: Revue Olympique, 10e année, janvier 1910, pp.4-6.

janv. * Chronique du mois: De Los Angeles à Héliopolis.
[Chronicle of the Month: From Los Angeles to Heliopolis.]
In: Revue Olympique, 10e année, janvier 1910, pp.13- 15.

5 janv. La S.S.P. en 1910.
[The Société des Sports Populaires.]
In: Sports populaires, 4e année, no 73, 5 janvier 1910, p.1.

fév. Le sport et la morale.
[Sport and Ethics.]
In: Revue Olympique, 10e année, février 1910, pp.19-22. Later reprinted, in
1) L'Education physique, 9e année, 30 avril 1910, no 8, pp.202-204.
2) Essais de Psychologie sportive, Lausanne/Paris, Payot, 1913, pp.129-137.
3) Textes choisis, vol.I, pp.399-402.

fév. * Une page de littérature sportive.
[A Page in Sports Literature.]
In: Revue Olympique, 10e année, février 1910, pp.22-25.

fév. * Les perfectionnements du Bob.
[Improving the Bob.]
In: Revue Olympique, 10e année, février 1910, pp.25-26.
Later reprinted, in: L'Education physique, 11e année, 29 février 1912, no 4, pp.94-96.

fév. * Chronique du mois: A propos des inondations. L'unique rescapé.
[Chronicle of the Month: On Floods. A Unique Survivor.]
In: Revue Olympique, 10e année, février 1910, pp.29-31.

2 fév. La croisade des partageux.
[A Crusade: Sports for Everyone.]
In: Sports populaires, 4e année, 2 février 1910, n° 75, p.1.
Later reprinted, in:
1) L'Education physique, 9e année, 15 mars, n° 5. pp.132-134.
2) Textes choisis, vol.III, pp.584-565.

mars * La revanche du bon sens.
[The Revenge of Common Sense.]
In: Revue Olympique, 10e année, mars 1910, pp.35-36.

mars * La carte cynégétique du globe.
[A Hunter's Map of the World.]
In: Revue Olympique, 10e année, mars 1910, pp.36-41.

mars * Chronique du mois
[Chronicle of the Month: Sports. Spitzberg. Jean Charcot].
In: Revue Olympique, 10e année, mars 1910, pp.46-47.

2 mars Le délégué-éponge.
[A Sponge Delegate.]
In: Sports populaires, 4e année, 2 mars 1910, n° 77, p.1.

avr. Méfiance et confiance.
[Trust and Mistrust.]
In: Revue Olympique, 10e année, avril 1910, pp.51-54.
Later reprinted, in:
1) L'Education physique, 9e année, 15 juillet 1910, n° 13, pp.351-358.
2) Sports populaires, 4e année, 23 novembre1910, pp.1-2.
3) Textes choisis, vol.I, pp.403-405.

avr. Les Vikings.
[The Vikings.]
In: Revue Olympique, 10e année, avril 1910, pp.54-56.
Later reprinted, in:
1) Sports populaires, 4e année, 20 juillet 1910, n° 87, pp.1-2.
2) L'Education physique, 9e année, 15 août 1910, n° 15, pp.418-419.

avr. * Stades anciens et modernes.
[Ancient and Modern Stadiums.]
In: Revue Olympique, 10e année, avril 1910, pp.56-60.

avr. * Un remède sportif: le dermatol.
[A Sports Remedy: Dermatol.]
In: Revue Olympique, 10e année, avril 1910, pp.60-61.

avr. Chronique du mois: Le triomphe du sport. Contre le duel.
[Chronicle of the Month: The Triumph of Sport. Against Duelling.]
In: Revue Olympique, 10e année, avril 1910, pp.61-64.

25 avr. L'évolution française vue du dehors. Un programme d'action nationale.
[The Development of France Seen from Abroad. A Programme for National Action.]
In: La Revue pour les Français, 5e année, 25 avril 1910, pp.279-291.

mai Le faux sportsman. (D'après Labruyère).
[The False Sportsman. Adapted from Labruyère.]
In: Revue Olympique, 10e année, mai 1910, pp.67-70.
Later reprinted, in:
1) L'Education physique, 9e année, 15 septembre 1910, n° 17, pp.461-464.
2) Sports populaires, 4e année, 12 octobre 1910, n° 93, p.1.
3) Textes choisis, vol.III, pp.658-661.

mai * Lutteurs à cheval.
[Fighters on Horseback.]
In: Revue Olympique, 10e année, mai 1910, pp.70-71.
Later reprinted, in: Sports populaires, 4e année, 16 mars 1910, n° 78, p.2.

mai La Face.
[The Bourgeois Society.]
In: Revue Olympique, 10e année, mai 1910, pp.72-74.
Later reprinted, in:
1) L'Education physique, 10e année, 15 août 1911, n° 15, pp.397-400.
2) Essais de Psychologie sportive, Lausanne/Paris, Payot, 1913, pp.146-153.

mai-juil. Les Sports à l'Hôtel (I et II).
[Sports at the Hotel.]
In: Revue Olympique, 10e année.
I: mai 1910, pp.76-78.
II: juillet 1910, pp.105-108.
Later reprinted, in:
1) L'Education physique, 11e année, 15 août 1912, n° 15, pp.404-405 et 408.
II: 31 août 1912, n° 16, pp.430-433.
2) Edition spéciale de la Société des Sports populaires, s.l., 1910 (8 pages).

mai * Chronique du mois.
[Chronicle of the Month: Hunting. **Edward VII**. Baden Powell. The Dresden Hygiene Exposition].
In: Revue Olympique, 10e année, mai 1910, pp.78-80.

juin * La question de l'amateurisme.
[On Amateurism.]
In: Revue Olympique, 10e année, juin 1910, pp.89-95.

22 juin Fête artistique et sportive au gymnase Christmann. [Excerpts of a speech].
[Arts and Sports Festival at the Christmann Gymnasium.]
In: Sports populaires, 4e année, 7 décembre 1910, n° 85, p.1.

juil. Le comte d'Artois, sportsman.
[The Count of Artois, a Sportsman.]
In: Revue Olympique, 10e année, juillet 1910, pp.99-101.
Later reprinted, in: L'Education physique, 11e année, 15 janvier, n° 1, pp.4-5.

juil. Psychologie, internationalisme, démocratie.
[Psychology, Internationalism, Democracy.]
(Extraits d'une conférence faite à l'Exposition de Bruxelles).
In: Revue Olympique, 10e année, juillet 1910, pp.101-104.
Later reprinted under the title: "L'avenir des sports", in:
1) L'Education physique, 9e année, 30 septembre 1910, n° 18, pp.486-489.
2) Sports populaires, 4e année, 26 oct. 1910, n° 94, p.1.
3) Textes choisis, vol.I, pp.423-426.

juil. * Chronique du mois: Duel de races - Le mépris de la mort - Défense aux femmes - Palais des sports - Le prix d'un athlète.
[Chronicle of the Month: Duel. Despising Death. Against Women Participation. Palais des sports. The Price of an Athlete.]
In: Revue Olympique, 10e année, juillet 1910, pp.108-111.

20 juil. * Deux morts.
[Two Deaths.]
In: Sports populaires, 4e année, 20 juillet 1910, n° 87, p.1.

août Tous les sports.
[All Sports.]
In: Revue Olympique, 10e année, août 1910, pp.115- 118.
Later reprinted, in:
1) L'Education physique, 11e année, 30 mars 1912, n° 8, pp.216-218.
2) Textes choisis, vol.II, pp.699-701.

août L'apôtre des harmonies viriles.
[The Apostle of Virile Harmony.]
In: Revue Olympique, 10e année, août 1910, pp.118- 120.

août Le jeu de"Pallone".
[The Game of "Pallone".]
In: Revue Olympique, 10e année, août 1910, pp.120- 122.
Later reprinted, in:
1) L'Education physique, 10e année, 31 janvier 1911, n° 2, pp.39-41.
2) Textes choisis, vol.III, pp.306-307.

août La question des parfums.
[A Matter of Smell.]
In: Revue Olympique, 10e année, août 1910, pp.123- 125.
Later reprinted, in: L'Education physique, 11e année, 15 mai 1912, n° 9, pp.369-372.

août * Chronique du mois: Un sujet scabreux... et oiseux.
[Chronicle of the Month: A Tricky and Superfluous Subject.]
In: Revue Olympique, 10e année, août 1910, pp.125-128.

3 août Non ! Non ! Pas ça !
[No! No! Not That!]
In: Sports populaires, 4e année, 3 août 1910, n° 88, p.1.
Later reprinted, in: L'Education physique, 9e année, 30 septembre 1910, n° 18, pp.477-478.

sept. * Trop d'argent. **[Too Much Money.]**
In: Revue Olympique, 10e année, septembre 1910, pp.131-132.

sept. La Rhompaïa.
[A Weapon from Byzantium.]
In: Revue Olympique, 10e année, septembre 1910, pp.132-134.
Later reprinted, in: L'Education physique, 11e année, 30 avril 1912, n° 8, pp.302-303.

sept. Notes sur le lawn-tennis.
[On Lawn Tennis.]
In: Revue Olympique, 10e année, septembre 1910, pp.134-138.
Later reprinted, in:
L'Education physique, 10e année, 15 mars 1911, n° 5, pp.122-128.
Textes choisis, vol.III, pp.279-282.

sept. * The possible unification of the amateur definition.
In: Revue Olympique, 10e année, septembre 1910, pp.138-142.

sept. * Chronique du mois: L'aviron et le Pactole - Le fisc rapace.
[Chronicle of the Month: Rowing. The Greedy Government.]
In: Revue Olympique, 10e année, septembre 1910, pp.143-144.

oct. * Le cheval à bascule.
[The Rocking-Horse.]
In: Revue Olympique, 10e année, octobre 1910, pp.147-149.

oct. Le sport peut-il enrayer la névrose universelle ?
[Can Sports Stop Neurosis?]
In: Revue Olympique, 10e année, octobre 1910, pp.149-156.
Later reprinted, in:
1) L'Education physique, 10e année, 15 février 1911, n° 3, pp.68-73.
2) Sports populaires, 5e année, 12 avril 1911, n° 106, p.1.
3) Essais de Psychologie sportive. Lausanne/Paris, Payot, 1913, pp.154-171.

oct. * La conduite d'un haras de pur-sang.
[A Stud-Farm.]
In: Revue Olympique, 10e année, octobre 1910, pp.156-158.

oct. * Chronique du mois: Un drame dans les airs.
[Chronicle of the Month: Dramatic Goings-On in the Air.]
In: Revue Olympique, 10e année, novembre1910, pp.158-160.

nov. * Une piscine dans une cave.
[A Swimming-Pool in the Basement.]
In: Revue Olympique, 10e année, novembre 1910, pp.163-164.

nov. * Gibt es ein französisches System der körperlichen Erziehung ?
[Is There a French System of Physical Education?]
In: Revue Olympique, 10e année, novembre 1910, pp.164-168.

nov. Nouveaux programmes d'enseignement.
[New Teaching Programmes.]
In: Revue Olympique, 10e année, novembre 1910, pp.168-172.
Later reprinted, in: L'Education physique, 10e année, 15 juin 1911, n° 11, pp.285-288.

nov. * Le sport du piano.
[Piano Sports.]
In: Revue Olympique, 10e année, novembre 1910, pp.172-173.

nov. * Chronique du mois: En Amériques - En Hollande.
[Chronicle of the Month: In the Americas. In the Netherlands.]
In: Revue Olympique, 10e année, nov. 1910, n° 95, p.173-175.

9 nov. L'Amiral de Maigret.
[The Admiral Maigret.]
In: Sports populaires, 4e année, 9 novembre1910, n° 95, p.1.

23 nov. Le Comte de Cossé Brissac.
[The Count de Cossé Brissac.]
In: Sports populaires, 4e année, 23 nov. 1910, n° 96, p.1.

déc. Le concours olympique d'architecture.
[The Olympic Architecture Competition.]
In: Revue Olympique, 10e année, décembre 1910, pp.179-180.

déc. Les deux skieurs. Conte de Noël.
[The Two Skiers. A Christmas Carol.]
In: Revue Olympique, 10e année, décembre 1910, pp.181-183.
Later reprinted, in: L'Education physique, 10e année, 31 décembre 1911, n° 24, pp.651-654.

déc. In memoriam.
[Obituaries: Léon de Janzé. Maurice de Cossé-Brissac. Angelo Mosso.Octave Chanute. Leo N.Tolstoï].
In: Revue Olympique, 10e année, décembre 1910, pp.183-186.
Later reprinted, in:
1) L'Education physique, 9e année, 31 décembre 1910, n° 24, pp.660-662.
2) Sports populaires, 5e année, 4 janvier 1911, n° 98, p.2.

déc. * Chronique du mois: L'odyssée de deux prix.
[Chronicle of the Month: The Odyssey of Two Prizes.]
In: Revue Olympique, 10e année, décembre 1910, pp.186-188.

7 déc. Toile d'Araignée.
[Spiderweb.]
In: Sports populaires, 4e année, 7 décembre 1910, n° 97, p.1.

1911

janv. * La campagne contre les Jeux Olympiques.
[The Campaign Against the Olympic Games.]
In: Revue Olympique, 11e année, janvier 1911, pp.3-5.
Later reprinted, in: Textes choisis, vol.II, pp.616-618.

janv. Réflexions dans un gymnase.
[Thoughts in a Gymnasium.]
In: Revue Olympique, 11e année, janvier 1911, pp.5-9.
Later reprinted, in:
1) L'Education physique, 11e année, 31 janvier 1911, n° 2, pp.34-37.
2) Essais de Psychologie sportive, Lausanne/Paris, Payot, 1913, pp.172-181.
3) Textes choisis, vol.I, pp.406-409.

janv. Le reflet de l'athlétisme dans les œuvres d'Horace.
[Athletism in Horace's Works.]
In: Revue Olympique, 11e année, janvier 1911, pp.9-13.
Later reprinted, in: L'Education physique, 10e année, 15 avril 1911, n° 7, pp.173-177.

janv. Ce que nous souhaitons à nos lecteurs.
[What We Wish Our Readers.]
In: Revue Olympique, 11e année, janvier 1911, pp.13-14.
Later reprinted, in:
1) L'Education physique, 11e année, 31 janvier 1911, n° 2, pp.28-29.
2) Sports populaires, 5e année, 8 février 1911, n° 102, p.1.

janv. * Chronique du mois
[Chronicle of the Month: Mayor. Berthelot. Flammarion].
In: Revue Olympique, 11e année, janvier 1911, pp.14-16.

25 janv. Ce qu'il y a de changé aux Etats-Unis.
[What Has Changed in the United States.]
In: La Revue des Français, 1ère année, 25 janvier 1911.

fév. La rapière.
[The Rapier.]
In: Revue Olympique, 11e année, février 1911, pp.19-20.
Later reprinted, in:
1) L'Education physique, 11e année, 28 février 1911, n° 4, pp.120-122.
2) Essais de Psychologie sportive, Lausanne/Paris, Payot, 1913, pp.182-186.

fév. Croquis d'hiver sur la montagne.
[A Winter Sketch of the Mountains.]
In: Revue Olympique, 11e année, février 1911, pp.21-26.
Later reprinted, in:
1) L'Education physique, 10e année, 15 mars 1911, n° 5, pp.122-128.
2) Sports populaires, 5e année, 22 mars 1911, n° 105, pp.1-2.
Under the title: "En hiver dans le pays d'En-Haut", in: Le pays vaudois, son âme et son visage, Lausanne, 1919, pp.23-27.
Textes choisis, vol.III, pp.668-671.

fév. * Chronique du mois: Un point d'histoire à propos d'un match de football.
[Chronicle of the Month: Historical Remarks Triggered Off By a Football Match.]
In: Revue Olympique, 11e année, février 1911, pp.29-31.
25 fév. Sir Charles Dilke.
In: Revue des Français, 6e année, tome X, 25 février 1911, pp.132-135.

mars * Les concours d'art de 1912: suggestions aux concurrents.
[The 1912 Art Competition: Suggestions for the Competitors.]
In: Revue Olympique, 11e année, mars 1911, pp.35-38.
Later reprinted, in: Textes choisis, vol.II, pp.508-511.

mars La Haute-Ecole.
[Haute Ecole.]
In: Revue Olympique, 11e année, mars 1911, n° 63, pp.38-4l.
Later reprinted, in:
1) L'Education physique, 10e année, 30 juin 1911, n° 12, pp.520-523.
2) Essais de Psychologie sportive, Lausanne/Paris, Payot, 1913, pp.187-192.
3) Textes choisis, vol.I, pp.410-412.

mars * Encouragement au pillage.
[Encouragement to Theft.]
In: Revue Olympique, 11e année, mars 1911, pp.41-42.

mars * La crise évitable.
[The Avoidable Crisis.]
In: Revue Olympique, 11e année, mars 1911, pp.42-44.

mars * Chronique du mois: Assez d'accidents - Prouesses de skieurs - La défense de l'Alpe.
[Chronicle of the Month: Accidents. Triumphant Skiers. Defence for the Alpe.]
In: Revue Olympique, 11e année, mars 1911, pp.45-47.

avr. * Géographie sportive.
[Athletic Geography.]
In: Revue Olympique, 11e année, avril 1911, pp.51-52.
Later reprinted, in: Textes choisis, vol.II, p.452.

avr. * L'Exposition de Dresde.
[The Dresden Exhibition.]
In: Revue Olympique, 11e année, avril 1911, pp.52-54.

avr.-oct. Décoration, Pyrotechnie, Harmonies, Cortèges. Essai de ruskinianisme sportif (I - V).
[Decoration, Pyrotechnics, Harmonies, Processions: Essay on Athletic Ruskinianism.]
In: Revue Olympique, 11e année,
I: avril 1911, pp.54-59 ;
II: mai 1911, pp.71-76 ;
III: juillet 1911, pp.106-110 ;
IV: août 1911, pp.122-124 ;
V: octobre 1911, pp.149-153.
Reprinted, in bochure form by the Société des Sports populaires, s.l., s.d. [1912] (22 pages).
Later reprinted, in: Textes choisis, vol.II, pp.517-535.

avr. Pour l'Honneur !
[For the Honour of It!]
[The speech was held by P.de Coubertin in Amsterdam, march 29, 1911.] In: Revue Olympique, 11e année, avril 1911, pp.59-62.
Later reprinted, in:
1) L'Education physique, 11e année, 15 mai 1911, n° 9, pp.232-234.
2) Sports populaires, 5e année, 24 mai 1911, n° 109, pp.1-2.
3) Textes choisis, vol.II, pp.391-394.

mai * A standard organisation for the Olympiads.
In: Revue Olympique, 11e année, mai 1911, pp.67-69.

mai La bicyclette et l'hésitation.
[Hesitation and the Bike.]
In: Revue Olympique, 11e année, mai 1911, pp.69-71.
Later reprinted, in:
1) L'Education physique, 10e année, 31 octobre 1911, n° 20, pp.538-541.
2) Essais de Psychologie sportive, Lausanne/Paris, Payot, 1913, pp.199-204.
3) Textes choisis, vol.I, pp.413-414.

mai * Les étapes de la compréhension.
[Stages of Understanding.]
In: Revue Olympique, 11e année, mai 1911, pp.76-78.
Later reprinted, in: Textes choisis, vol.I, pp.415-416.

mai * Chronique du mois: L'escrime et les femmes.
[Chronicle of the Month: Women and Fencing.]
In: Revue Olympique, 11e année, mai 1911, pp.78-80.

juin * La fête olympique de la Sorbonne.
[The Sorbonne Olympic Festival.]
In: Revue Olympique, 11e année, mai 1911, pp.83-85.

juin La XIIIe réunion plénière du Comité International Olympique.
[The XIIIth General Meeting (Session) of the IOC.]
In: Revue Olympique, 11e année, juin 1911, pp.85-92.

juin * Le vingtième anniversaire des Jeux Olympiques.
[The Twentieth Anniversary of the Olympic Games.]
In: Revue Olympique, 11e année, juin 1911, pp.93-94.

juil. Mens fervida in corpore lacertoso.
In: Revue Olympique, 11e année, juillet 1911, pp.99- 100.
Later reprinted, in: Textes choisis, vol.I, pp.603-604.

juil. Fauchez donc vos prés.
[Mow Your Lawns.]
In: Revue Olympique, 10e année, juillet 1911, pp.104-105.
Later reprinted, in:
1) L'Education physique, 10e année, 15 septembre 1911, nº 17, pp.467-469.
2) Essais de Psychologie sportive, Lausanne/Paris, Payot, 1913, pp.211-215.

15 juil. M. A. Fringnet.
In: L'Education physique, 10e année, 15 juillet 1911, nº 13, p.338.

août * La chasse et l'alpinisme aux Jeux Olympiques.
[Hunting and Alpinism at the Olympic Games.]
In: Revue Olympique, 11e année, août 1911, pp.115-116.

août * Chronique du mois
[Chronicle of the Month: Holland. Independence Day in New York. Women and Ballooning].
In: Revue Olympique, 11e année, août 1911, pp.125- 127.

25 août Y a-t-il quelque chose de changé en Autriche-Hongrie?
[Any Changes in the Austro-Hungarian Empire?]
In: Revue des Français, 1ère année, 25 août 1911, pp.297- 302.

sept. Où en est l'aviron ?
[What About Rowing?]
In: Revue Olympique, 11e année, septembre 1911,pp.139-142.
Later reprinted, in: L'Education physique, 11e année, 15 avril 1911, nº 7, pp.174-178.

sept. Chronique du mois: Sports et pouvoirs publics.
[Chronicle of the Month: Sports and the Authorities.]
In: Revue Olympique, 11e année, septembre 1911, pp.142-144.

oct. Chronique du mois.
[Chronicle of the Month: Crossing the Channel].
In: Revue Olympique, 11e année, oct. 1911, pp.156-158.

oct. L'initiative du Comité Olympique français.
[Suggestion from the French Olympic Committee.]
In: Revue Olympique, 11e année, octobre 1911, pp.147-148.
Later reprinted, in: Textes choisis, vol.II, pp.707-708.

oct. Communication du Président du C.I.O.
[From the President of the IOC: The Stadiums].
In: Bulletin du C.I.O. Annexe de la Revue Olympique, 11e année, octobre 1911, pp.158-160.
Later reprinted, in: Textes choisis, vol.II, pp.641-642.

25 oct. L'éducation des adolescents au XXe siècle.
[Educating the Youth in the Twentieth Century.]
In: Revue des Français, 1ère année, 25 octobre 1911, pp.297-302.

28 oct. Coubertin Scores English. President of International Olympic Committee Makes Statements.
In: The New York Times, 27 octobre 1912, p.4.

nov. * Le Pentathlon moderne.
[Modern Pentathlon.]
In: Revue Olympique, 11e année, novembre1911, pp.163-165.

nov. * Philosophie de sportsman.
[A Sportsman's Philosophy.]
In: Revue Olympique, 11e année, novembre1911, pp.165-166.

nov. Les bienfaits et les méfaits de l'automobilisme.
[Good and Bad Effects the Car Has on Our Lives.]
In: Revue Olympique, 11e année, novembre1911, nº 71, pp.166-169.
Later reprinted, in:
1) L'Education physique, 11e année, février 1912, nº 3, pp.62-65.
2) Textes choisis, vol.I, pp.417-419 and vol.III, pp.339-341.

nov. * Journées de chasse en Floride (1 et Il).
[Hunting in Florida.]
In: Revue Olympique, 11e année.
I: novembre1911, pp.169-174;
II: décembre 1911, pp.180-184.

nov. * La semaine d'un original.
[An Odd Person's Week.]
In: Revue Olympique, 11e année, novembre1911, pp.174-175.

déc. * Les réflexions du bonhomme Noël.
[Santa's Thoughts.]
In: Revue Olympique, 11e année, décembre 1911, pp.184-186.
Later reprinted, in: Textes choisis, vol.III, pp.662-664.

déc. * Chronique du mois.
[**Chronicle of the Month:** The Fencing Federations].
In: Revue Olympique, 11e année, décembre 1911, pp.186-188.
Later reprinted, in: Textes choisis, vol.III, pp.364-365.

1912

Die Arbeit des Internationalen Olympischen Komitees.
In:Wagner, J. (Ed.): Olympische Spiele Stockholm 1912, Zurich et Munich, Verlag von Julius Wagner, 1912, pp.4-5.
In English: Swedish Olympic Committee (Ed.): Olympic Games, Stockholm 1912 (June 29th - juillet 22nd). Stockholm, Centraltryckeriet, 1912, pp.5-7
In French: Swedish Olympic Committee (Ed.): Jeux Olympiques. Stockholm 1912. Stockholm, Centraltryckeriet, 1912, pp.5-7.

janv. * Un inventaire. **[An Inventory.]**
In: Revue Olympique, 12e année, janvier 1912, pp.3-6.

janv. * Concertation latine.
[Interpreting the Meaning of "Mens fervida..."]
In: Revue Olympique, 12e année, janvier 1912, pp.6-7.

janv. Les sports et la colonisation.
[Sports and Colonialisation.]
In: Revue Olympique, 12e année, janvier 1912, pp.7-10.
Later reprinted, in: L'Education physique, 11e année, 31 mars 1912, n° 6, pp.145-147.

janv. * Le judo (I et II). **[Judo.]**
In: Revue Olympique, 12e année,
I: janvier 1912, pp.11-13;
II: février 1912, pp.24-27.

janv. * Chronique du mois: Une nouvelle formule de récompenses musculaires.
[Chronicle of the Month: A New Formula for Muscular Rewards.]
In: Revue Olympique, 12e année, janvier 1912, pp.13-15.

fév. * De la condition des sports en Suisse.
[Sports in Switzerland.]
In: Revue Olympique, 12e année, février 1912, pp.19-21.

fév. Remèdes sportifs pour les neurasthéniques.
[Sports as a Remedy for Neurasthenics.]
In: Revue Olympique, 12e année, février 1912, pp.27-30.
Later reprinted, in:
1) L'Education physique, 11e année, 31 mai 1912, n° 10, pp.275-279.
2) Essais de Psychologie sportive, Lausanne/Paris, Payot, 1913, pp.242-250.
3) Textes choisis, vol.III, pp.644-647.

fév. * Chronique du mois.
[**Chronicle of the Month:** The English and Continental snow].
In: Revue Olympique, 12e année, février 1912, pp.30-31.

mars L'escrime est-elle énervante ou pacifiante ?
[Does Fencing Trigger Off Or Quench Aggression?]
In: Revue Olympique, 12e année, mars 1912, pp.37-40.
Later reprinted, in:
1) Psychologie sportive, Lausanne/Paris, Payot, 1913, pp.251-257.
2) Textes choisis, vol.I, pp.420-422.

mars * La classification des sports.
[Classification of Sports.]
In: Revue Olympique, 12e année, mars 1912, pp.40-42.
Later reprinted, in: Textes choisis, vol.II, pp.702-704.

mars Hydrothérapie et aérothérapie (I et II).
[Hydrotherapeutics and Aerotherapeutics.]
In: Revue Olympique, 12e année,
I: mars 1912, pp.42-45;
II: avril 1912, pp.61-63.
Later reprinted, in:
1) L'Education physique, 13e année,
I: 15 mai 1914, n° 9, pp.232-236 ;
II: (under the title: "Aérothérapie et Hydrothérapie"), 31 mai 1914, n° 10, pp.257-259.
2) Textes choisis, vol.III, pp.632-637

mars * Chronique du mois.
[**Chronicle of the Month:** Ski, Mouillard].
In: Revue Olympique, 12e année, mars 1912, pp.45-47.

avr. Congrès de psychologie et de physiologie sportives.
[Sports Psychology and Physiology.]
In: Revue Olympique, 12e année, avril 1912, pp.51-56.

avr. * Une vocation. Conte de Pâques.
[A Vocation. An Easter Story.]
In: Revue Olympique, 12e année, avril 1912, pp.56-58.

avr. Le sport et la guerre.
[Sports and War.]
In: Revue Olympique, 12e année, avril 1912, pp.58-61.
Later reprinted, in:
1) L'Education physique, 11e année, 30 novembre1912, n° 22, pp.612-614.
2) Essais de Psychologie sportive, Lausanne/Paris, Payot, 1913, pp.258-264.

mai * Good News from Basle.
In: Revue Olympique, 12e année, mai 1912, pp.67-70.

mai Educations de princes.
[Princely Education.]
In: Revue Olympique, 12e année, mai 1912, pp.70-74.
Later reprinted, in: L'Education physique, 11e année, 15 octobre 1912, n° 19, pp.526-529.

mai L'art de la canne.
[A Special French Fencing Style: "La Canne".]
In: Revue Olympique, 12e année, mai 1912, pp.74-76.
Later reprinted, in:
1) L'Education physique, 11e année, 30 juin 1912, n° 12, pp.328-330.
2) Textes choisis, vol.III, pp.183-185.

mai * Chronique du mois.
[Chronicle of the Month: Sports and strikes, etc.].
In: Revue Olympique, 12e année, mai 1912, pp.76-78.

mai Lettre à Monsieur le Maire de Prague.
[Letter to the Mayor of Prague.]
In: Revue Olympique, 12e année, mai 1912, pp.79-80.

juin * Le rôle éducatif des Olympiades.
[The Educational Role of the Olympiads.]
In: Revue Olympique, 12e année, juin 1912, pp.83-84.
Later reprinted, in: Textes choisis, vol.II, pp.376-377.

juin * A travers l'histoire suédoise.
[On Swedish History.]
In: Revue Olympique, 12e année, juin 1912, pp.86-90.

juin * Upsal. **[Uppsala.]**
In: Revue Olympique, 12e année, juin 1912, pp.90-92.

juin * L'organisation sportive en Suède.
[Sports Organisation in Sweden.]
In: Revue Olympique, 12e année, juin 1912, pp.92-95.

juil. * Les femmes aux Jeux Olympiques.
[The Women at the Olympic Games.]
In: Revue Olympique, 12e année, juillet 1912, pp.109-111.
Later reprinted, in: Textes choisis, vol.II, pp.705-706.

août * Une Olympiade à vol d'oiseau.
[A Bird's Eye View of an Olympiad.]
In: Revue Olympique, 12e année, août 1912, pp.115- 119.
Later reprinted, in: Textes choisis, vol.II, pp.244-248.

août La séance du 4 juillet 1912.
[The Session of July 4, 1912 (Speech in Stockholm).]
[Speech at Stockholm, in the Swedish Parliament, July 4, 1912]
In: Revue Olympique, 12e année, août 1912, pp.119-122.
Later reprinted in French, in:
1) L'Idée Olympique. pp.35-37.
2) Textes choisis, vol.II, pp.605-607.
Later reprinted,
in English, in: The Olympic Idea, pp.36-38.
in German, in: Der Olympische Gedanke, pp.43-45.
in Spanish, in: Ideario Olímpico, pp.66-69.

sept. Histoire à retenir.
[History to Keep.]
In: Revue Olympique, 12e année, septembre 1912, pp.140-142.
Later reprinted, in: L'Education physique, 11e année, 15 septembre 1912, n° 17, pp.458-459.

sept. Paroles de clôture.
[Closing Words (Stockholm 1912).]
In: Revue Olympique, 12e année, septembre 1912, pp.142-143.
Later reprinted, in:
1) L'Idée Olympique, pp.38-39.
2) Textes choisis, vol.II, pp.252-253.
Later reprinted,
in English, in: The Olympic Idea, pp.38-39.
in German, in: Der Olympische Gedanke, pp.45-46.
in Spanish, in: Ideario Olímpico, pp.69-70.

oct. * La critique est aisée...
[On a Speech.]
In: Revue Olympique, 12e année, octobre 1912, pp.147-151.
Later reprinted, in: Textes choisis, vol.II, p.451.

oct. * Les débuts du Pentathlon moderne.
[The Origins of the Modern Pentathlon.]
In: Revue Olympique, 12e année, octobre 1912, pp.151-154.
Later reprinted, in: Textes choisis, vol.II, pp.249251.

oct. * L'Art à l'Olympiade.
[Fine Arts at the Olympics.]
In: Revue Olympique, 12e année, octobre 1912, pp.154-157.
Later reprinted, in: Textes choisis, vol.II, pp.513-515.

oct. Sport et diplomatie.
[Sports and Diplomacy.]
In: Revue Olympique, 12e année, octobre 1912, pp.157-159.
Later reprinted, in: L'Education physique, 11e année, 15 juin, n° 11, pp.294-297.

23 nov. Discours de M. de Coubertin.
[Speech by Pierre de Coubertin at the Award of the Olympic Cup to the Union des Sociétés de Gymnastique.]
In: Le Gymnaste, 23 novembre 1912, pp.905-907.
Later reprinted, in excerpts under the title: "Vers le gymnase antique", in:
1) Revue Olympique, 12e année, décembre 1912, pp.184-186.
2) Also under the title: "Le rétablissement du Gymnase municipal de l' antiquité", in: Le Gymnaste Suisse, 5e année, 10 septembre 1926, n° 7, p.2.
3) Textes choisis, vol.III, pp.586-589.

nov. * L'Eugénie. **[Eugenics.]**
In: Revue Olympique, 12e année, novembre1912, pp.163-166.
Later reprinted, in: Textes choisis, vol.I, pp.599-602.

nov.-janv. 1913
* L'équitation populaire: but, conditions, moyens (I, II and III).
[Horse-Riding as a Popular Sport: Goal, Conditions, Devices.]
In: Revue Olympique,
I: 12e année, novembre1912, pp.170-173;
II: 12e année, décembre 1912, pp.181-184;
III: 13e année, janvier 1913, pp.8-11.
Later reprinted, in: Textes choisis, vol.III, pp.197-205.

nov. * Chronique du mois: Découvertes successives.
[Chronicle of the Month: Successive Discoveries.]
In: Revue Olympique, 12e année, novembre1912, pp.173-175.

déc. Ode au Sport.
[Ode to Sport.]
[Under the double pseudonym of Georges Hohrod and M. Eschbach. Gold medal in the literature competition of the Olympic Games in Stockholm].
In: Revue Olympique, 12e année, décembre 1912, pp.179-181.
Brochure form in French and German: Impr. Gand, Van Dooselaere, 1912.
Later reprinted in French, in:
1) L'Education physique, 12e année, 15 janvier 1913, n° 1, pp.22-24.
2) L'Idée Olympique, pp.38-39.
3) Textes choisis, vol.III, pp.665-667.
Later reprinted,
in English, in: The Olympic Idea, pp.39-40.
in German,
under the Title: " Ode an den Sport. 1. Literaturpreis der Stockholm Olympischen Spiele", in: Athletik-Jahrbuch 1914, Berlin 1915, pp.47-48.
Der Olympische Gedanke, pp.47-48.
in Spanish, in: Ideario Olímpico, pp.70-73.

déc. * Chronique du mois.
[Chronicle of the Month: Youth and Sports].
In: Revue Olympique, 12e année, décembre 1912, pp.186-187.

20 déc. La crise de l'Histoire de France et l'initiative de la Ligue d'Education Nationale.
[The Crisis of French History and the Initiative of the National League of Education.]
In: Revue des Français, 7e année, 20 décembre 1912, pp.329-331.

1913

janv. * Ernest Callot.
In: Revue Olympique, 13e année, janvier 1913, p.3.

janv. * Le docteur Morax.
[Doctor Morax.]
In: Revue Olympique, 13e année, janvier 1913, p.4.

janv. * Les métèques du sport.
[Foreign Sportsmen.]
In: Revue Olympique, 13e année, janvier 1913, pp.6-8.

janv. * Chronique du mois.
[Chronicle of the Month: The Sports Year 1912].
In: Revue Olympique, 13e année, janvier 1913, pp.11-15.
Later reprinted, in: Textes choisis, vol.II, pp.663-666.

fév. Les Congrès olympiques.
[The Olympic Congresses.]
In: Revue Olympique, 13e année, février 1913, pp.19-20.
Later reprinted, in: Textes choisis, vol.II, pp.257-258.

fév. * La psychologie sportive.
[Sports Psychology.]
In: Revue Olympique, 13e année, février 1913, pp.20-23.
Later reprinted, in: Textes choisis, vol. I, pp.427-429.

fév. Lausanne.
In: Revue Olympique, 13e année, février 1913, pp.24-29.
Later reprinted, in: Le Pays Vaudois, son âme et son visage, Lausanne, F. Rouge, 1919, pp.5-10.

mars * Règlement pour une coupe de sabre à cheval.
[Rules for Fencing on Horseback.]
In: Revue Olympique, 13e année, mars 1913, pp.40-42.

mars * A l'hippodrome de Byzance.
[The Hippodrome at Byzantium.]
In: Revue Olympique, 13e année, mars 1913, pp.42-44.

mars De la volupté sportive.
[Enjoyment of Sports.]
In: Revue Olympique, 13e année, mars 1913, pp.44-46.
Later reprinted, in: L'Education physique, 12e année, 15 septembre 1913, n° 17, pp.474-475.

avr. * Le roi des Hellènes.
[The King of the Hellenes.]
In: Revue Olympique, 13e année, avril 1913, pp.51-52.

avr. * L'organisation olympique en Allemagne.
[The Olympic Organisation in Germany.]
In: Revue Olympique, 13e année, avril 1913, pp.52-55.

avr. Les méfaits de l'accoutumance.
[Consequences of Sticking to One's Habits.]
In: Revue Olympique, 13e année, avril 1913, pp.55-58.
Later reprinted, in:
1) Education physique, 13e année, 15 avril 1914, n° 7, pp.169-172.
2) Textes choisis, vol.III, pp.339-341.

avr. * Encore l'affaire Thorpe.
[The Thorpe Affair Once Again.]
In: Revue Olympique, 13e année, avril 1913, pp.58-59.
Later reprinted, in: Textes choisis, vol.II, pp.578-579.

avr. * Chronique du mois.
[**Chronicle of the Month:** Advances in Physical Education, etc.].
In: Revue Olympique, 13e année, avril 1913, pp.60-62.

mai * A la veille du Congrès de Lausanne.
[Before the Lausanne Congress.]
In: Revue Olympique, 13e année, mai 1913, pp.67-68.

mai Olympisme et utilitarisme.
[Olympism and Utilitarianism.]
In: Revue Olympique, 13e année, mai 1913, pp.68-73.
Later reprinted, in:
1) L'Education physique, 12e année, 31 août 1913, n° 16, pp.438-441.
2) Textes choisis, vol.II, pp.378-382.

mai * Récits d'escrime. **[Fencing Stories.]**
In: Revue Olympique, 13e année, mai 1913, pp.73-76.
Later reprinted, in:
L'Education physique, 13e année, 31 mars 1914, n° 6, pp.165-168.

mai * Chronique du mois: Une Olympiade extrême-orientale.
[Chronicle of the Month: An Olympiad in the Far East.]
In: Revue Olympique, 13e année, mai 1913, pp.77-78.
Later reprinted, in: Textes choisis, vol.II, pp.660-662.

juil. Les journées de Lausanne.
[The Days of Lausanne.]
In: Revue Olympique, 13e année, juillet 1913, pp.103-112 (Coubertin's speech: pp.106-109).

juil. * Une campagne contre l'athlète spécialisé.
[A Campaign Against Specialized Athletes.]
In: Revue Olympique, 13e année, juillet 1913, pp.114-115.
Later reprinted, in: Textes choisis, vol.III, pp.590-591.

août L'emblème et le drapeau de 1914.
[The Emblem and the Flag of 1914.]
In: Revue Olympique, 13e année, août 1913, pp.119-120.
Later reprinted, in: Textes choisis, vol.II, pp.460-461.

août * Le sport et la question sociale.
[Sports and the Social Issue.]
In: Revue Olympique, 13e année, août 1913, pp.120- 123.
Later reprinted, in: Textes choisis, vol.I, pp.607-609.

août * Le handicapage de l'idée de retour.
[The Problem of Returning.]
In: Revue Olympique, 13e année, août 1913, pp.126- 128.
Later reprinted, in: Textes choisis, vol.I, pp.430-432.

août * Chronique du mois: Le record de l'heure - Des envolées merveilleuses - Variante pour le Pentathlon - Opinions d'Australie.
[Chronicle of the Month: Records. Fantastic Thoughts. Pentathlon Variations. Australian Opinions.]
In: Revue Olympique, 13e année, août 1913, pp.128-131.

sept. L'œuvre Olympique et ses rouages.
[How the Olympics Work.]
(Rapport au Congrès mondial des Associations internationales tenu à Gand et Bruxelles du 15e au 18 juin 1913.)
In: Revue Olympique, 13e année, septembre 1913, pp.136-140.
Later reprinted, in: Textes choisis, vol.II, pp.608-611.

sept. * Les échelons d'une éducation sportive.
[Echelons of Sports Education.]
In: Revue Olympique, 13e année, septembre 1913, pp.142-145.
Later reprinted, in:
1) L'Education physique, 13e année, 15 mai 1913, n° 9, pp.242-246.
2) Textes choisis, vol.III, pp.443-446.

sept. * Chronique du mois
[**Chronicle of the Month:** A likable European...].
In: Revue Olympique, 13e année, septembre 1913, pp.146-147.

oct. * En vue du Congrès de Paris.
[Looking Ahead to the Paris Congress.]
In: Revue Olympique, 13e année, octobre 1913, pp.151.

oct. * Le sport, passeport de vertus.
[Sport, Virtue's Passport.]
In: Revue Olympique, 13e année, octobre 1913, pp.151-152.
Later reprinted, in: Textes choisis, vol.I, pp.605-606.

oct. * Sports carolingiens.
[Carolingian Sports.]
In: Revue Olympique, 13e année, octobre 1913, pp.158-160.

oct. * Chronique du mois.
[**Chronicle of the Month:** International shooting competition, etc.].
In: Revue Olympique, 13e année, octobre 1913, pp.160-162.

nov. * Nouveaux aspects du problème.
[New Aspects of the Problem (Thorpe)]
In: Revue Olympique, 13e année, novembre1913, pp.178-179.
Later reprinted, in: Textes choisis, vol.II, pp.580-581.

nov. * Solutions diverses.
[Various Solutions.]
In: Revue Olympique, 13e année, novembre 1913,pp.179-180.
Later reprinted, in: Textes choisis, vol.II, pp.582-583.

30 nov. Gymnastique équestre préparatoire à l'équitation.
[**Acrobatics on Horseback as a Preparation for Horse-Riding.**]
In: L'Education physique, 12e année, 30 novembre1913, n° 22, pp.611-613.

déc. * La question d'argent.
[The Matter of Money.]
In: Revue Olympique, 13e année, décembre 1913,pp.183-185.
Later reprinted, in: Textes choisis, vol.II, pp.584-586..

déc. * La requête des haltérophiles.
[**The Weight-Lifters' Request.**]
In: Revue Olympique, 13e année, décembre 1913, pp.185-186.
Later reprinted, in: Textes choisis, vol.II, pp.720-721.

déc. Le sport et l'art de vieillir.
[**Sports and the Art of Aging.**]
In: Revue Olympique, 13e année, décembre 1913, pp.187-188.
Later reprinted,
in French, in: Textes choisis, vol.I., pp.473-474,
in German, in: Rheinisch-Westfälische Sportzeitung, 3e année, 30 juin 1914, n° 27, pp.12-13.

déc. Chronique du mois. [L'unification sportive].
[Chronicle of the Month: Athletic Unification.]
In: Revue Olympique, 13e année, décembre 1913, pp.188-190.
Later reprinted, in: Textes choisis, vol.II, pp.667-668.

1914

janv. * Un congrès oublié.
[**A Forgotten Congress.**]
In: Revue Olympique, 14e année, janvier 1914, pp.4-8.

janv. * Philosophe, sportsman et neurasthénique.
[**Philosopher, Sportsman, and Neurasthenic.**]
In: Revue Olympique, 14e année, janvier 1914, pp.8-10.

janv.- avr. Critique du Congrès de Lausanne (I - IV).
[**Critique of the Lausanne Congress.**]
In: Revue Olympique, 14e année,
I: janvier 1914, pp.10-12 ;
II: février 1914, pp.28-29 ;
III: mars 1914, pp.42-45;
IV: avril 1914, pp.54-58.

janv. * Chronique du mois
[**Chronicle of the Month:** The Athens Interim Games, etc.].
In: Revue Olympique, 14e année, janvier 1914, pp.12-15.

fév. * Amoros et Arnold.
[**Amoros and Arnold.**]
In: Revue Olympique, 14e année, fév. 1914, pp.25-27.

fév. * Chronique du mois
[**Chronicle of the Month:** A Minister of Sports].
In: Revue Olympique, 14e année, février 1914, pp.30-31.

mars * La leçon et l'assaut en boxe et en escrime.
[**Lessons and Attacking in Boxing and Fencing.**]
In: Revue Olympique, 14e année, mars 1914, pp.35-39.
Later reprinted, in: Textes choisis, vol.III, pp.177-180.

mars * La décadence des sports d'hiver.
[**The Decline of Winter Sports.**]
In: Revue Olympique, 14e année, mars 1914, pp.39-40.
Later reprinted, in: Textes choisis, vol.III, pp.246-247.

mars * Hydrothérapie japonaise.
[**Japanese Hydrotherapeutics.**]
In: Revue Olympique, 14e année, mars 1914, pp.41-42.

mars * Chronique du mois: Le jargon sportif.
[**Chronicle of the Month: Sports Jargon.**]
In: Revue Olympique, 14e année, mars 1914, pp.45-46.

avr. * Le Collège d'athlètes de Reims.
[**The Athletes' College at Reims.**]
In: Revue Olympique, 14e année, avril 1914, pp.52-54.

avr. * Statistique sportive.
[**Sports Statistics.**]
In: Revue Olympique, 14e année, avril 1914, pp.58-59.

avr. * Chronique du mois
[**Chronicle of the Month:** Dueling].
In: Revue Olympique, 14e année, avril 1914, pp.59-61.

mai * Les pourvoyeurs du royaume d'utopie.
[**A Utopian Kingdom.**]
In: Revue Olympique, 14e année, mai 1914, pp.75-77.
Later reprinted, in: Textes choisis, vol.I, pp.610-611.

juin Pour bien comprendre la France.
[Understanding France.]
In: Notes sur la France d'aujourd'hui. (Brochure offerte aux délégués des Comités Olympiques Nationaux à l'occasion des fêtes du XXe anniversaire du rétablissement des Jeux Olympiques.) Paris, juin 1914, pp.7-9.
Also published, in: Revue des Français, 9e année, 20 juin 1914, pp.435-438.

juin * Le vaisseau de Lutèce.
[The Boat from Lutetia.]
In: Revue Olympique, 14e année, juin 1914, pp.83-84.

juin * Dix-neuf cents ans d'histoire.
[Nineteen Hundred Years of History.]
In: Revue Olympique, 14e année, juin 1914, pp.84-89.

juin * A la mode de Paris.
[Following Paris Fashions.]
In: Revue Olympique, 14e année, juin 1914, pp.89-90.

juin * Paris invisible.
[Invisible Paris.]
In: Revue Olympique, 14e année, juin 1914, pp.90-91.

juin * Le Congrès Olympique à travers Paris.
[The Olympic Congress in Paris.]
In: Revue Olympique, 14e année, juin 1914, pp.91-95.

20 juin Le Sport et la Société moderne.
[Sports and Modern Society.]
(Discours prononcé en Sorbonne, en présence de Raymond Poincaré, Président de la République, à l'occasion du XXe anniversaire du rétablissement des Jeux Olympiques.)
In: La Revue Hebdomadaire, 23e année, 20 juin 1914, pp.376-386.
Later reprinted, in: Textes choisis, vol.I, pp.612-619.

juil. * Les fêtes et le congrès de 1914.
[The 1914 Festival and Congress.]
In: Revue Olympique, 14e année, juillet 1914, p.99.

juil. * Les fêtes olympiques de Paris.
[The Olympic Festival in Paris.]
In: Revue Olympique, 14e année, juil. 1914, pp.100-110.

juil. * Les fêtes olympiques de Reims.
[The Olympic Festival in Reims.]
In: Revue Olympique, 14e année, juil. 1914, pp.110-111.

8 oct. 1870-1914.
In: La Petite Gironde, 35e année, 8 octobre 1914, p.1.

26 oct. Appel à tous.
[Appeal to Everyone.]
In: Excelsior, 5e année, 26 octobre 1914, n° 1441, p.2.

2 nov. L'esprit nouveau.
[The New Spirit.]
In: Excelsior, 5e année, 2 novembre1914, n° 1448, p.2.

9 nov. Un exemple en chair et en os.
[A Model in Flesh and Blood.]
In: Excelsior, 5e année, 9 novembre1914, n° 1455, p.3.

16 nov. L'air et l'eau.
[Air and Water.]
In: Excelsior, 5e année, 16 novembre1914, n° 1462, p.3.
Later reprinted, in: Leçons de gymnastique utilitaire. Paris, Payot, 1916, pp.36-38.

23 nov. Une sanction.
[A Sanction.]
In: Excelsior, 5e année, 23 novembre1914, n° 1469, p.3.

30 nov. Un ton plus haut s.v.p.
[Louder, Please!]
In: Excelsior, 5e année, 30 novembre1914, n° 1476, p.3.

7 déc. Du jeu à l'héroïsme.
[From Play to Heroism.]
In: Excelsior, 5e année, 7 décembre 1914, n° 1483, p.3.

11 déc. Chronique pour après: Crise salutaire.
[A Chronicle for the Future: A Healthy Crisis.]
In: La Petite Gironde, 35e année, 11 décembre 1914, p.1.

14 déc. Juste hommage.
[A Just Tribute.]
In: Excelsior, 5e année, 14 décembre 1914, n° 1490, p.3.

17 déc. Chronique pour après: Nos pacifistes.
[A Chronicle for the Future: Our Pacifists.]
In: La Petite Gironde, 35e année, 17 décembre 1914, p.1.

21 déc. Au pied des remparts de Carcassonne.
[At Carcassonne.]
In: Excelsior, 5e année, 21 décembre 1914, n° 1497, p.3.

28 déc. Equilibre et combat.
[Balance and Fight.]
In: Excelsior, 5e année, 28 décembre 1914, n° 1504, p.3.
Later reprinted, in: Textes choisis, vol.III, pp.131-132.

30 déc. Chronique pour après: Acquérir pour donner.
[A Chronicle for the Future: Gathering for Giving.]
In: La Petite Gironde, 35e année, 30 décembre 1914, p.1.

1915

4 janv. Le Décalogue de 1915. Aux jeunes Français.
[A 1915 Decalogue: To the Youth of France.]
In: Excelsior, 6e année, 4 janvier 1915, n° 1511, p.3.
Later reprinted, in: Le Gymnaste Vaudois, 2e année, 25 janvier 1915, n° 22, pp.173-174.
Also published in poster form by Excelsior, january 1915.

11 janv. De quelques détails et précisions nécessaires.
[Some Necessary Details.]
In: Excelsior, 6e année, 11 janvier 1915, nº 1518, p.3.
Later reprinted, in: Textes choisis, vol.III, pp.594-596.

14 janv. Chronique pour après: Notre philosophie.
[A Chronicle for the Future: Our Philosophy.]
In: La Petite Gironde, 36e année, 14 janvier 1915, p.1.

15 janv. Un intervista col Presidente del Comitato Olimpico internazionale.
[Interview given to Gustavo Verona, director of the "Stampa Sportiva". **(Italian Text.)**]
In: Rivista degli sports, 15 janvier 1915, pp.7-8.

18 janv. Qu'est-ce qu'un collège d'athlètes ?
[What Is an Athletes' College?]
In: Excelsior, 6e année, 18 janvier 1915, nº 1525, p.3.
Later reprinted, in: Textes choisis, vol.III, pp.366-367.

22 janv. Chronique pour après: Nos journalistes.
[Chronicle for the Future: Our Journalists.]
In: La Petite Gironde, 36e année, 22 janvier 1915, p.1.

25 janv. Pourquoi donc, cette manie de nudité ?
[Why Is There a Nudomania?]
In: Excelsior, 6e année, 25 janvier 1915, nº 1532, p.3.
Later reprinted, in: Leçons de gymnastique utilitaire. Paris, Payot, 1916, pp.40-42.

1er fév. La marche.
[Walking.]
In: Excelsior, 6e année, 1er février 1915, nº 1539, p.3.
Later reprinted, in:
1) Leçons de gymnastique utilitaire. Paris, Payot, 1916, pp.23-25.
2) Le Gymnaste Vaudois, 5e année, 25 avril 1917, nº 8, pp.63-64.

3 fév. Chronique pour après: Nos diplomates.
[Chronicle for the Future: Our Diplomats.]
In: La Petite Gironde, 36e année, 3 février 1915, p.1.

8 fév. La course.
[Running.]
In: Excelsior, 6e année, 8 février 1915, nº 1546, p.3.
Later reprinted, in: Leçons de gymnastique utilitaire. Paris, Payot, 1916, pp.5-6.

12 fév. Chronique pour après: Plus de dénigreurs.
[Chronicle for the Future: No More Liars.]
In: La Petite Gironde, 36e année, 12 février 1915, p.1.

15 fév. Le saut. **[Jumping.]**
In: Excelsior, 6e année, 15 février 1915, nº 1553, p.3.
Later reprinted, in:
1) Leçons de gymnastique utilitaire. Paris, Payot, 1916, pp.6-8.
2) Le Gymnaste Suisse, 2e année, 6 avril 1923, nº 8, pp.1-2.

22 fév. L'escalade.
[Mountain-Climbing.]
In: Excelsior, 6e année, 22 février 1915, nº 1560, p.3.
Later reprinted, in:
1) Le Gymnaste Vaudois, 3e année, 25 avril 1915, nº 4, pp.43-44.
2) Leçons de gymnastique utilitaire. Paris, Payot, 1916, pp.8-10.
3) Le Gymnaste Suisse, 2e année, 5 janvier 1923, nº 1, pp.1-2.

1er mars Le lancer.
[Throwing.]
In: Excelsior, 6e année, 1er mars 1915, nº 1567, p.3.
Later reprinted, in: Leçons de gymnastique utilitaire. Paris, Payot, 1916, pp.11-12.

4 mars Chronique pour après: Nos gens de lettres.
[Chronicle for the Future: Our Writers.]
In: La Petite Gironde, 36e année, 4 mars 1915, p.1.

8 mars Porter.
[Carrying.]
In: Excelsior, 6e année, 8 mars 1915, nº 1574, p.3.
Later reprinted, in: Leçons de gymnastique utilitaire. Paris, Payot, 1916, pp.13-14.

15 mars Ramper.
[Crawling.]
In: Excelsior, 6e année, 15 mars 1915, nº 1581, p.3.
Later reprinted, in: Leçons de gymnastique utilitaire. Paris, Payot, 1916, pp.14-16.

22 mars Dans l'eau.
[In the Water.]
In: Excelsior, 6e année, 22 mars 1915, nº 1588, p.3.
Later reprinted, in: Leçons de gymnastique utilitaire. Paris, Payot, 1916, pp.16-18.

29 mars A l'arme blanche.
[Call to Arms.]
In: Excelsior, 6e année, 29 mars 1915, nº 1595, p.3.
Later reprinted, in: Leçons de gymnastique utilitaire. Paris, Payot, 1916, pp.18-20.

5 avr. A poings nus.
[With Naked Fists.]
In: Excelsior, 6e année, 5 avril 1915, nº 1602, p.3.
Later reprinted, in: Leçons de gymnastique utilitaire. Paris, Payot, 1916, pp.20-22.

10 avr. La cérémonie de Lausanne. (Speech, April 10, 1915.)
[The Ceremony at Lausanne.]
In: Bulletin du Comité International Olympique, 1915, nº 2, p.2.
Later reprinted, in French, in:
1) L'Idée Olympique, pp.41-42.
2) Textes choisis, vol.II, 731-732.

Later reprinted, in
English, in: The Olympic Idea, pp.41-43.
German, in: Der Olympische Gedanke, pp.49-51.
Spanish, in: Ideario Olímpico, pp.74-76.

12 avr. Le tir.
[Shooting.]
In: Excelsior, 6e année, 12 avril 1915, n° 1609, p.3.
Later reprinted, in: Leçons de gymnastique utilitaire. Paris, Payot, 1916, pp.22-23.

19 avr. L'équitation populaire.
[Horse-Riding as a Popular Sport.]
In: Excelsior, 6e année, 19 avril 1915, n° 1616, p.3.
Later reprinted, in:
1) Leçons de gymnastique utilitaire. Paris, Payot, 1916, pp.25-27.
2) Le Gymnaste Suisse, 2e année, 20 avril 1923, n° 16, p.1.

3 mai A cheval.
[On Horseback.]
In: Excelsior, 6e année, 3 mai 1915, n° 1630, p.3.
Later reprinted, in: Leçons de gymnastique utilitaire. Paris, Payot, 1916, pp.29-31.

10 mai L'aviron.
[Rowing.]
In: Excelsior, 6e année, 10 mai 1915, n° 1637, p.3.
Later reprinted, in: Leçons de gymnastique utilitaire. Paris, Payot, 1916, pp.31-33.

24 mai Vélo, auto, ski, etc.
[Bike, Car, Ski, etc.]
In: Excelsior, 6e année, 25 mai 1915, n° 1644, p.3.
Later reprinted, in: Leçons de gymnastique utilitaire. Paris, Payot, 1916, pp.33-34.

31 mai Travaux manuels.
[Handicraft.]
In: Excelsior, 6e année, 31 mai 1915, n° 1651, p.3.
Later reprinted, in: Leçons de gymnastique utilitaire. Paris, Payot, 1916, pp.35-36.

7 juin La supériorité du football.
[The Superiority of Football.]
In: Excelsior, 6e année, 7 juin 1915, n° 1658, p.3.
Later reprinted, in:
1) Leçons de gymnastique utilitaire. Paris, Payot, 1916, pp.42-43.
2) Textes choisis, vol.III, pp.293-294.

14 juin Dans votre chambre.
[In Your Room.]
In: Excelsior, 6e année, 14 juin 1915, n° 1665, p.3.
Later reprinted, in: Leçons de gymnastique utilitaire. Paris, Payot, 1916, pp.38-40.

21 juin Comment se servir du record ?
[What Can We Do With a Record?]
In: Excelsior, 6e année, 21 juin 1915, n° 1672, p.3.
Later reprinted, in: Leçons de gymnastique utilitaire. Paris, Payot, 1916, pp.44-45.

28 juin N'oubliez pas!
[Don't Forget!]
In: Excelsior, 6e année, 28 juin 1915, n° 1679, p.3.
Later reprinted, in: Leçons de gymnastique utilitaire. Paris, Payot, 1916, pp.45-46.

5 juil. La restauration du Gymnase antique.
[The Restoration of the Classical Gymnasium.]
In: Excelsior, 6e année, 5 juillet 1915, n° 1686, p.3.
Later reprinted, in: Textes choisis, vol.III, pp.592-593.

12 juil. Le Gymnase "Excelsior".
[The"Excelsior" High School – A Fictitious Institution of Adult Education.]
In: Excelsior, 6e année, 12 juillet 1915, n° 1693 p.2.

juil. Les néo-encyclopédistes et la guerre.
[The Neo-Encyclopedians and the War.]
In: Bibliothèque universelle et Revue suisse, tome LXXIX, juillet 1915, pp.49-59.

19 juil.-27 déc.
Leçons dans le Gymnase d' "Excelsior".
[Lessons at the "Excelsior" High School.]
In: Excelsior, 6e année,
19 juillet 1915, n° 1700, p.2: I. Notre France; **[Our France.]**
26 juillet 1915, n° 1707, p.2: II. Vous n'êtes qu'une pierre du mur... ; **[You're Just a Brick in the Wall.]**
2 août 1915, n° 1714, p.2: III. Cérémonies désirables ; **[Desirable Ceremonies.]**
9 août 1915, n° 1721, p.2: IV. Des origines du sport ; **[The Origins of Sport.]**
16 août 1915, n° 1728, p.2: V. Des origines du sport (fin) ; **[The Origins of Sport II.]**
Later reprinted, in: Textes choisis, vol.III, pp.25-26.
23 août 1915, n° 1735, p.2: VI. Connais-toi toi-même ; **[Know Yourself.]**
Later reprinted, in: Textes choisis, vol.I, pp.620-621.
30 août 1915, n° 1742, p.2: VII. Sur la côte de Californie ; **[At the Californian Coast.]**
6 septembre 1915, n° 1749, p.2: VIII. L'histoire se répète...; **[History Repeats Itself.]**
13 septembre 1915, n° 1756, p.2: IX. Le triomphe africain ; **[The African Triumph.]**
20 septembre 1915, n° 1763, p.2: X. Encore de l'histoire ; **[More History.]**
27 septembre 1915, n° 1770, p.2: XI. Erreurs concernant la Pologne ; **[False Impressions of Poland.]**
4 octobre 1915, n° 1777, p.2:. XII [sic]. Pourquoi donc tant d'histoire ? ; **[Why So Much History?]**
11 octobre 1915, n° 1784, p.2: XIII. Pour la santé publique ; **[For Public Health.]**

18 octobre 1915, n° 1791, p.2: XIV. Le chapitre de la propreté; **[Hygiene.]**
25 octobre 1915, n° 1798, p.2: XV. Ceux à qui je m'adresse ; **[Those I Am Talking to.]**
2 novembre1915, n° 1805, p.2: XVII [sic]. L'équilibre ; **[Balance.]**
8 novembre1915, n° 1812, p.2: XVIII. L'esprit du corps ; **[Esprit de Corps.]**
15 novembre1915, n° 1819, p.2: XIX. Le silence ; **[Silence.]**
22 novembre1915, n° 1826, p.2: XX. L'arrivisme ; **[Over-Ambition.]**
29 novembre1915, n° 1833, p.2: XX [sic]. L'esprit critique ; **[Criticizing.]**
6 décembre 1915, n° 1840, p.2: XXII. Du calme ; **[Calmness.]**
13 décembre 1915, n° 1847, p.2: XXIII. L'eurythmie ; **[Eurhythmics.]**
20 décembre 1915, n° 1854, p.2.: XXIV. La logique ; **[Logic.]**
27 décembre 1915, n° 1861, p.2: XXV. La délation. **[Denunciation.]**

déc. Extracts from a letter received from Baron Pierre de Coubertin.
In: American Physical Education Review, vol. XX, décembre 1915, pp.568-569.

1916

3 janv. Leçons dans le gymnase d' "Excelsior". Un bon système nerveux.
[Lessons at the "Excelsior" High School: A Stable Nervous System.]
In: Excelsior, 7e année, 3 janvier 1916, n° 1868, p.9.

25 nov. A travers l'histoire sud-américaine.
[On South-American History.]
In: La Revue Hebdomadaire, 25e année, 25 novembre1916, n° 48, pp.451-473.
Later reprinted, in brochure form: Paris, Plon-Nourrit, 1916. (Brochure spéciale de 27 pages éditée à l'occasion de la première semaine de l'Amérique latine, Lyon - décembre 1916.)

1917

* Calendrier olympique.
[Olympic Calendar.]
In: Almanach olympique pour 1918. Lausanne, Impr. Réunies, 1917, pp.1-4.
Later reprinted, in: Textes choisis, vol.II, pp.339-340.

* Les Jardins de l'Effort.
[The Gardens of Effort.]
In: Almanach olympique pour 1918. Lausanne, Impr. Réunies, 1917, pp.4-7.
Later reprinted, in: Textes choisis, vol.II, p.446.

* L'histoire se répète...
[History Repeats Itself.]
In: Almanach olympique pour 1918. Lausanne, Impr. Réunies, 1917, pp.9-14.

Pensées d'athlètes.
[The Thoughts of Athletes.]
In: Almanach olympique pour 1918. Lausanne, Impr. Réunies, 1917, pp.14-16. [Coubertin quotes excerpted from books and articles.]
Later reprinted, in: Textes choisis, vol.II, p.458.

Pour avoir chaud cet hiver.
[How to Keep Warm This Winter.]
In: Almanach olympique pour 1918. Lausanne, Impr. Réunies, 1917, pp.16-19.
Later reprinted, in: Le Gymnaste Vaudois, 8e année, 10 novembre1920, n° 21, p.188.

* Le chant choral.
[Hymns.]
In: Almanach olympique pour 1918. Lausanne, Impr. Réunies, 1917, pp.19-20.
Later reprinted, in: Textes choisis, vol.II, p.536.

* Regards rétrospectifs.
[Looking Back.]
In: Almanach olympique pour 1918. Lausanne, Impr. Réunies, 1917, pp.20-24.

Proclamation de Hugues Capet (1er juin 987).
[Proclamation of Hugo Capet.]
In: Anniversaires historiques à célébrer entre bons Français. Paris, Delagrave, 1917, pp.45-56.

1er mars Ceci tuera cela !
[This Will Kill That!]
In: La Revue, vol. LXVII, 28e année, 1er mars 1917, VIIIe série, n° 5-6, pp.513-518.

mai L'Institut Olympique de Lausanne.
[The Olympic Institute at Lausanne.]
In: Bibliothèque universelle et Revue suisse, tome LXXXV, mai 1917, n° 257, pp.185-202.
Off-print, entitled " A l'Institut Olympique de Lausanne": Lausanne, Bibliothèque universelle et Revue suisse, 1917 (20 pages).

juin La troisième République et la politique capétienne.
[The Third Republic and Capetian Politics.]
In: Bibliothèque universelle et Revue suisse, tome LXXXVI, juin 1917, n° 258, pp.363-375 (published under the pseudonym Georges Hohrod).

1918

* Les étapes de l'Olympisme: le nouvel échelon.
[Stages of Olympism: The New Echelon.]
In: Almanach olympique pour 1919. Lausanne, Impr. Réunies, 1918, pp.1-6.
Later reprinted, in: Textes choisis, vol.II, pp.395-397.

* Springfield.
In: Almanach olympique pour 1919. Lausanne, Impr. Réunies, 1918, pp.6-8.

* Les découvertes de l'année.
[Discoveries of the Year.]
In: Almanach olympique pour 1919. Lausanne, Impr. Réunies, 1918, pp.8-12.

* Dialogue vaudois.
[A Dialogue in the Vaude Region.]
In: Almanach olympique pour 1919. Lausanne, Impr. Réunies, 1918, pp.13-14.

La gamme du sauvetage.
[Aspects of Life-Saving.]
In: Almanach olympique pour 1919. Lausanne, Impr. Réunies, 1918, pp.14-20.
Later reprinted, in: Le Gymnaste Vaudois, 9e année, 10 janvier 1921, n° 3, pp.18-19.

* La chevalerie du sport.
[Chivalry of Sports.]
In: Almanach olympique pour 1919. Lausanne, Impr. Réunies, 1918, pp.20-24.

* L'évolution de la boxe.
[The Evolution of Boxing.]
In: Pages de Critique et d'Histoire, 2e fascicule, s.d. [1918], pp.2-4.
Later reprinted, in: Textes choisis, vol.III, pp.165-168.

Ouvrez les portes du temple.
[Open the Doors of the Temple.]
In: Pages de Critique et d'Histoire, 3e fascicule, s.d. [1918], pp.1-2.
Later reprinted, in:
1) Anthologie. Aix-en-Provence, P. Roubaud, 1933, pp.120-122.
2) Textes choisis, vol.I, pp.509-510.

L'individualisme sportif.
[Sport and Individualism.]
In: Pages de Critique et d'Histoire, 3e fascicule, s.d. [1918], pp.2-3.
Later reprinted, in:
1) Le Gymnaste Suisse, 3e année, 5 septembre 1924, n° 36, p.1.
2) Textes choisis, vol.III, pp.342-343.

* Cataclysmes sidéraux.
[A Siderian Catastrophe.]
In: Pages de Critique et d'Histoire, 3e fascicule, s.d. [1918], pp.4-5.

* La courbe de l'histoire de France.
[The Change in French History.]
In: Pages de Critique et d'Histoire, 3e fascicule, s.d. [1918], pp.5-8.

14 juin Bonaparte, président de la République italienne.
[Bonaparte, President of the Republic of Italy.]
In: Tribune de Genève, 40e année, 14 juin 1918, n° 141, p.4.

13 juil. A propos des Tchécoslovaques.
[About the Chekhoslovakians.]
In: Gazette de Lausanne, 121e année, 13 juillet 1918, n° 190, p.1.

24 août La Belgique devant l'histoire.
[Belgium and History.]
In: Tribune de Genève, 40e année, 24 août 1918, p.2.

7 sept. Un nouveau chapitre de l'histoire d'Angleterre.
[A New Chapter in English History.]
In: Tribune de Genève, 40e année, 7 septembre 1918, p.2.

14 oct.-28 déc.
Lettres olympiques (I - IX).
[Olympic Letters.]
In: Gazette de Lausanne, 121e année,
14 octobre 1918, n° 282, p.2: I. [Olympism at Lausanne];
18 octobre 1918, n° 286, p.1: II. [Contribution by the Arts, Humanities and Sciences in Restoring the Greek Gymnasium];
26 octobre 1918, n° 294, p.1: III. [Olympism and Education]; Later reprinted, in: Textes choisis, vol.II, p.384.
22 novembre 1918, n° 319, p.1: IV. [Olympism as a State of Mind]; Later reprinted, in: Textes choisis, vol.II, p.319.
28 novembre 1918, n° 325, pp.1-2: V. [Olympic Pedagogy];
4 décembre 1918, n° 331, p.3: VI. [Panem et circenses];
11 décembre 1918, n° 338, p.1: VII. [The Recipe for "Becoming Olympic"]; Later reprinted, in: Textes choisis, vol.II, p.386.
14 décembre 1918, n° 341, pp.1-2: VIII. [The Formation of Character];
28 décembre 1918, n° 355, p.1: IX. [The Complete Athlete and the Modern Pentathlon].
All these Olympic Letters were later reprinted
in French, in: L'Idée Olympique, pp.51-58.
in English, in: The Olympic Idea, pp.52-59.
in German, in: Der Olympische Gedanke, pp.62-70.
in Spanish, in: Ideario Olímpico, pp.91-102.
Letters I, III, IV, VII, IX were later reprinted in French,

in: Textes choisis, vol.II, p.733 (I), p.384 (III), p. 385 (IV), p.386 (VII), pp.716-717 (IX). Letter Olympic IX were later also reprinted, in: Textes choisis, vol.III, p.258.

23 nov. L'épopée coloniale française.
[The French Colonial Epic.]
In: Tribune de Genève, 40e année, 23 novembre1918, p.4.

29 déc.-30 déc.
Idéalisme dans l'histoire des Etats-Unis.
[Idealism in the History of the United States.]
In: Tribune de Genève, 40e année, 29 et 30 décembre 1918, n° 309, p.3.

1919

* Les noces d'argent de l'Olympisme.
[The Silver Wedding Anniversary of Olympism.]
In: Pages de Critique et d'Histoire, 4e fascicule, s.d. [1919], pp.1-3.

* Un discours sur l'histoire universelle.
[On World History.]
In: Pages de Critique et d'Histoire, 4e fascicule, s.d. [1919], pp.5-6.

* La cure de sport.
[The Cure of Sports.]
In: Pages de Critique et d'Histoire, 4e fascicule, s.d. [1919], pp.7-8.
Later reprinted, in: Textes choisis, vol. III, pp.648-649.

Les universités populaires.
[Popular Universities.]
In: Pages de Critique et d'Histoire, 5e fascicule, s.d. [1919], pp.1-8.
Later reprinted,
1) in brochure form, under the title: "Les Universités Ouvrières", Lausanne, Imprimerie populaire, 1921.
2) in: Textes choisis, vol.I, pp.519-527.

La VIIe Olympiade.
[The VIIth Olympiad.]
In: Almanach olympique pour 1920. Lausanne, Impr. Réunies, 1919, pp.1-3.
Later reprinted, in: Textes choisis, vol.II, pp.263-264.

* Propos divers. [Jeux Olympiques. Le football. Records olympiques]
[Miscellany: Olympics. The ball. Olympic Records.]
In: Almanach olympique pour 1920. Lausanne, Impr. Réunies, 1919, pp.3-8.
Later reprinted, in: Textes choisis, vol.II, p.459; p.711; Vol.III, p.274.

* Leçons du passé.
[Lessons of the Past.]
In: Almanach olympique pour 1920. Lausanne, Impr. Réunies, 1919, pp.8-12.

* L'avenir de l'agriculture.
[The Future of Agriculture.]
In: Almanach olympique pour 1920. Lausanne, Impr. Réunies, 1919, pp.13-18.

* Art sportif. **[Arts and Sports.]**
In: Almanach olympique pour 1920. Lausanne, Impr. Réunies, 1919, pp.18-20.

* La cure de sport. **[The Cure of Sports.]**
In: Almanach olympique pour 1920. Lausanne, Impr. Réunies, 1919, pp.20-24.

janv. Lettre à Messieurs les membres du IOC
[Letter to the Honourable Members of the IOC.]
(janv. 1919), off-print, Lausanne, janv. 1919. (2 pages).
Later reprinted, in:
1) L'Idée Olympique, pp.67-72.
2) Textes choisis, vol. II, pp.340-345.
in English, in: The Olympic Idea, pp.67-72.
in German, in: Der Olympische Gedanke, pp.80-85.
in Spanish, in: Ideario Olímpico, pp.116-124.

Lettre No 2 à Messieurs les membres du CIO (avr. 1919)
[Letter No 2 to the Honourable Members of the IOC.]
Off-print, Lausanne, avril 1919. (4 pages)

5 janv.-17 mai
Lettres Olympiques (X-XXI).
[Olympic Letters.]
In: Gazette de Lausanne, 122e année,
5 janvier 1919, n° 4, p.1: X. [Sport in the Universities];
13 janvier 1919, n° 12, p.1: XI. [Sporting Spirit of Students];
26 janvier 1919, n° 25, p.1: XII. [Theodore Roosevelt];
1er février 1919, n° 31, p.1: XIII. [The Periodicity of the Olympic Games];
11 février 1919, n° 41, p.1: XIV. [The Value of Boxing I];
22 février 1919, n° 52, p.1: XV. [The Value of Boxing II: The English and French Method];
3 mars 1919, n° 61, p.1: XVI. [Horse Riding];
6 mars 1919, n° 64, p.1: XVII. [Physical exercise and Constraint];
20 mars 1919, n° 76, p.1: XVIII. [Apparatus];
17 avril 1919, n° 104, p.1: XIX. [Sporting pleasure];
29 avril 1919, n° 116, p.1: XX. [Reason for the citizens of Lausanne to Engage in Rowing];
17 mai 1919, n° 134, p.1: XXI. [The Pershing Olympiad]
Olympic Letters X to XX were later reprinted, in: L'Idée Olympique. Edited by: Carl-Diem-Institut, pp.59-67.
Olympic Letters XI, XV, XX were later reprinted, in: Textes choisis, vol.III, p.610 (XI), pp.163-164 (XV), p.225 (XX).
Olympic Letter XVIII was later reprinted, in: Le Gymnaste Vaudois, 7e année, 10 avril 1919, no 7, p.52.
Olympic Latters I – XX were later reprinted
in English, in: The Olympic Idea, pp.59-66.
in German, in: Der Olympische Gedanke, pp.70-79.
in Spanish, in: Ideario Olímpico, pp.102-116.

avr. XXVe anniversaire des Jeux Olympiques. Discours prononcé par le Président du Comité International Olympique à la cérémonie commémorative.
[The XXVth Anniversary of the Proclamation of the Olympic Games. Address Delivered by the President of the IOC at the Commemorative Ceremony.]
Off-print: Lausanne, avril 1918.
Later reprinted,
in French, in: L'Idée Olympique, pp.72-74.
in English, in: The Olympic Idea, pp.73-75.
in German, in: Der Olympische Gedanke, pp.86-88.
in Spanish, in: Ideario Olímpico, pp.124-128.

6 oct. Les bases de l'Education populaire.
[The Basis of Education for Everyone.]
In: Gazette de Lausanne, 122e année, 5 et 6 octobre 1919, n° 272, p.1.
Off-print: Lausanne, octobre 1919 (1 page).

8 déc. Le dilemme.
[The Dilemma.]
In: Tribune de Genève, 41e année, 8 décembre 1919, p.1.
Off-print: Lausanne, décembre 1919 (3 pages).
Later reprinted, in: Textes choisis, vol.I, pp.537-540.

11 déc.-28 déc.
Correspondance de Monsieur le Baron de Coubertin et Monsieur G. Chaudet.
[Correspondence by Baron de Coubertin and Monsieur G. Chaudet.]
in: L'Idée Olympique, pp.75-77.
Later reprinted,
in English, in: The Olympic Idea, pp.75-77.
in German, in: Der Olympische Gedanke, pp.88-90.
in Spanish, in: Ideario Olímpico, pp.128-131.

1920

La Suisse, reine des sports.
[Switzerland, Queen of Sports.]
In: Barthou, Louis M. (Ed.): La Suisse et les Français, Paris, Editions G. Grès, 1920, pp.383-393.
Later reprinted, in: Textes choisis, vol.II, pp.726-730.

7 janv. Les conférences de M. de Coubertin. (Compte rendu des conférences sur la Troisième République française.)
[Lectures by Monsieur de Coubertin, Regarding the Third French Republic.]
In: Feuille d'avis de Lausanne, 159e année, 7 janvier 1920, n° 5, p.3.

fév. Lettre No 3 à Messieurs les membres du C.I.O.
[Letter No 3 to the Members of the International Olympic Committee (February, 1920).]
Off-print: Lausanne, Impr.La Concorde, février 1920. (4 pages)
Later reprinted, in:
1) L'Idée Olympique, pp.77-79.
2) Textes choisis, vol.II, pp.620-623.
in English, in: The Olympic Idea, pp.77-80.
in German, in: Der Olympische Gedanke, pp.91-93.
in Spanish, in: Ideario Olímpico. Edited, pp.131-135.

déc. Lettre No 4 à Messieurs les membres du C.I.O.
[Letter No. 4 to the Members of the IOC.] Off-print. Lausanne, décembre 1920. (4 pages)
Later reprinted, in: Textes choisis, vol.II, pp.624-629.

juin Le rôle des Jeux Olympiques.
[The Role of the Olympic Games.]
In: Revue des Sports, Bruxelles, 1ère année, juin 1920, n° 15, pp.197-198.
Later reprinted, in: Textes choisis, vol.II, pp.473-475.

juil. La victoire de l'Olympisme.
[The Victory of Olympism.]
In: La Revue sportive illustrée, 16e année, juillet 1920, n° 2, p.2.
Later reprinted, in:
1) L'Idée Olympique, pp.80-81.
2) Textes choisis, vol.II, pp.277-278.
in English, in: The Olympic Idea, pp.80-81.
in German, in: Der Olympische Gedanke, pp.94-95.
in Spanish, in: Ideario Olímpico, pp.135-138.

sept. L'apport de la VIIe Olympiade.
[The Contribution of the Seventh Olympiad.]
In: Le Revue sportive illustrée, 16e année, septembre 1920, n° 3, p.1.
Later reprinted, in:
1) L'Idée Olympique, pp.85-86.
2) Textes choisis, vol.II, pp.265-267.
in English, in: The Olympic Idea, pp.86-87.
in German, in: Der Olympische Gedanke, pp.100-102.
in Spanish, in: Ideario Olímpico, pp.144-146

oct. Quelle fut la performance la plus extraordinaire réalisée au cours de la VIIe Olympiade ?
[What Was the Most Remarkable Performance at the VIIth Olympiad?]
In: La Revue sportive illustrée, 16e année, octobre 1920, n° 3, p.20.

1921

31 juil. Les chances de l'Allemagne.
[Germany's Chances.]
In: Journal de Genève, 92e année, 30 juillet 1921, n° 208, p.1.

1922

20 janv. Entre deux batailles.
De l'Olympisme à l'université ouvrière.
[Between Two Battles: From Olympism to the Popular University.]
In: La Revue de la Semaine, 3e année, 20 janvier 1922, n° 1, pp.299-310.
Reprinted as 12-pages off-print.
Later reprinted, in: Textes choisis, vol.I, pp.511-518.

5 mai La cité olympique.
[The Olympic Capital.]
(Lettre de Pierre de Coubertin au directeur du journal.)
In: La feuille d'avis de Lausanne, 16e année, 5 mai 1922.

15 nov. Le sport et l'intelligence.
[Sport and Intelligence.]
(Enquête de la Revue Mondiale.)
In: La Revue Mondiale, 33e année, 15 novembre1922, n° 22, pp.146-148.

22 déc. Correspondance.
(Lettre à J.-O. Frischknecht, président de la société fédérale de gymnastique, 15 décembre 1922.)
[Letter to J.-O. Frischknecht.]
In: Le Gymnaste Suisse, 1ère année, n° 51, 22 décembre 1922, p.1.

1923

31 mai Discours. **[Speech.]**
In: Cérémonie Commémorative du 35e Anniversaire de la Fondation du Comité Jules Simon à la Salle de la Société de Géographie à Paris. Paris, 1923, pp.24-27.

1er juin Une campagne de trente-cinq ans.
[A Thirty-Five Years Campaign.]
In: La Revue de Paris, 30e année, 1er juin 1923, n° 11, pp.688-694.

3 oct. Pour l'instruction des prolétaires.
[Educating the Working Class.]
In: Le Droit du peuple, 15e année, n° 231, 3 octobre 1923, p.1.
Part of: Mémoire concernant l'instruction supérieure des travailleurs manuels et l'organisation des Universités Ouvrières, s. 1. 1923.

3 déc. A propos des Olympiades.
[On Olympiads.]
In: La Suisse, 3 décembre 1923.

1924

Discours de Monsieur le Baron Pierre de Coubertin.
(Discours à l'Hôtel de Ville de Paris, le 24 juin 1924.)
[Address by Baron de Coubertin in the City Hall of Paris.]
In: Rapport officiel. VIIIe Olympiade. Paris, Librairie de France, 1924, p.637.
Later reprinted
in French, in: 1) L'Idée Olympique, p.89.
2) Textes choisis, vol.II, p.403.
in English, in: The Olympic Idea, p.91.
in German, in: Der Olympische Gedanke, pp.107-108.
in Spanish, in: Ideario Olímpico, pp.150-151.

Mens fervida in corpore lacertoso.
In: Rapport officiel. VIIIe Olympiade. Paris, Librairie de France, 1924, p.4.
Later reprinted, in:
1) L'Idée Olympique, p.60.
2) Textes choisis, vol.II, p.403.
in English, in: The Olympic Idea, p.92.
in German, in: Der Olympische Gedanke, p.106.
in Spanish, in: Ideario Olímpico, pp.151-153.

Je pense que...
(Discours prononcé au Stade de glace de Chamonix avant la clôture des Jeux, mardi 5 février 1924.)
[Speech at the Closing Ceremony of the Winter Games (Chamonix, February 5, 1924).]
In: Rapport officiel, VIIe Olympiade. Paris, Librairie de France, 1924, p.721.
Later reprinted, in: Textes choisis, vol.II, pp.320-321.

Per orbem terrarum.
In: Wagner, J./Eicherberger, G. (Ed.): Die Olympischen Spiele Paris 1924. Erinnerungswerk. Zürich/ München, Verlag J. Wagner, 1924, p.2.

Réponse du Baron Pierre de Coubertin.
[Response by Baron de Coubertin.]
(Réponse au discours du Mgr le Prince de Galles, lors du banquet de la British Olympic Association, le 7 juillet 1924.)
In: VIIIe Olympiade (Paris, 1924). Banquet de la British Olympic Association présidé par S.A.R. le Prince de Galles (7 juillet 1924), s.l., s.d. (1924) (pp.3-4).

28 avr. Avant les Jeux Olympiques. La formule d'une organisation.
[Before the Olympic Games: The Formula of an Organisation.]
In: Le Gaulois, 28 avril 1924, pp.1-2.
Later reprinted, in: Textes choisis, vol.II, pp.673-674.

9 mai Correspondance. (Lettre au Gymnaste Suisse.)
[Correspondence: Letter to the Editor of Le Gymnaste Suisse.]
In: Le Gymnaste Suisse, 3e année, n° 19, 9 mai 1924, p.3.

2 juil. Een onderhoud met Baron de Coubertin I.
[An Interview with Baron de Coubertin I. (Dutch Text)]
In: De Olympiade, 2 juillet 1924, p.2.

9 juil. Een onderhoud met Baron de Coubertin II.
[An Interview with Baron de Coubertin II. (Dutch Text)]
In: De Olympiade, 9 juillet 1924, p.2.

5 sept. Autour des Jeux de la VIIIe Olympiade.
[On the VIIIth Olympiad.]
In: La Revue de Genève, 5e année, 5 septembre 1924, n° 51, pp.262-269.
Later reprinted, in: Textes choisis, vol.II, pp.281-288.

1925

Vorwort **[Preface.** (German text).]
In: Scharroo, P.W. Wils, J.: Gebäude und Gelände für Gymnastik, Spiel und Sport. Berlin, O. Baumgärtel, 1925, pp.VII-VIII.

janv. L'amateurisme au Congrès de Prague.
[Amateurism at the Prague Congress.]
In: Bibliothèque Universelle et Revue de Genève, 130e année, janvier 1925, pp.106-110.
Later reprinted, in:
1) L'Idée Olympique, pp.90-93.
2) Textes choisis, vol.II, pp.587-590.
in English, in: The Olympic Idea, pp.93-95.
in German, in: Der Olympische Gedanke, pp.108-111.
in Spanish, in: Ideario Olímpico, pp.153-157.

16 janv. La France et les "Jeux " d'hiver en 1928.
[France and the 1928 Winter Olympic Games.]
Lettre à la rédaction de "L'Auto".
In: L'Auto, 26e année, 16 janvier 1925, p.1.
Later reprinted, in: Textes choisis, vol.II, p.322.

21 fév. Le dualisme français. **[French Dualism.]**
In: Gazette de Lausanne, 128e année, 21 février 1925, p.1.

mai Les sanatoriums pour bien-portants.
[Sanatoriums for the Healthy.]
In: Bibliothèque Universelle et Revue de Genève, 130e année, mai 1925, pp.633-636.
Later reprinted, in: Textes choisis, vol.III, pp.639-643.

29 mai Discours prononcé à l'ouverture des Congrès olympiques à l'hôtel de ville de Prague le 29 mai 1925.
[Speech Given at the Opening of the Olympic Congresses at the City Hall of Prague, May 29, 1925.]
Prague, Imprimerie de l'Etat, 1925.
Later reprinted, in:
1) L'Idée Olympique, pp.93-98.
2) Textes choisis, vol.II, pp.404-410.
3) De Olympiade, supplément, Amsterdam 30 déc. 1925, p.1.
in English, in: The Olympic Idea, pp.95-99.
in German, in: 1) Jahrbuch der Leibesübungen, Berlin 1926, pp.9-17. 2) Der Olympische Gedanke, pp.111-115.
in Spanish, in: Ideario Olímpico, pp.157-164.

21 août On ne peut être à la fois sportif et fêtard.
[You Cannot Be a Sportsman *and* a Playboy.]
In: Le Gymnaste Suisse, 4e année, 21 août 1925, n° 34, p.1.
Publié en néerlandais, en français, en anglais et en allemand, in: De Olympiade, supplément, Amsterdam, 30 septembre 1925, p.1.

28 août Le domaine des "sports gymniques".
[The Variability of Gymnastics.]
In: Le Gymnaste Suisse, 4e année, 28 août 1925, n° 35, p.1.
Later reprinted, in: Textes choisis, vol.III, pp.133-135.

25 sept. Ne troublons pas l'équilibre des saisons...
[Let's Not Upset the Balance of the Seasons.]
In: Le Gymnaste Suisse, 4e année, 25 septembre 1925, n° 39, p.1.
Later reprinted, in: Textes choisis, vol.III, pp.447-448.

nov. Lausanne.
In: The Swiss Monthly, novembre 1925, pp.34-39.
Translation from: Le pays vaudois, son âme et son visage. Lausanne, Libr.Rouge, 1919, pp.5-10.

1926

Message par radio transmis à l'occasion de l'inauguration des travaux de l'Union Pédagogique Universelle.
[Radio Broadcast Concerning the Inauguration of the Union Pédagogique Universelle (Universal Educational Union).]
(Aix-en-Provence., 15 novembre1925.)
In: Union Pédagogique Universelle I, année 1925-1926, p.5.
Later reprinted, in:
Anthologie. Aix-en-Provence, P. Roubaud, 1933, pp.172-173.

1er janv. Les annales méditerranéennes.
(Le drame méditerranéen - La crise de l'hellénisme - Les Jeux Olympiques.)
[Mediterranean Annals: The Mediterranean Drama. The Crisis of Hellenism. The Olympic Games.]
In: Le Feu, 20e année, 1er janvier 1926, pp.3-6.

29 déc. Jeux Olympiques d'hiver.
[Olympic Winter Games.]
In: De Olympiade, supplément, 29 décembre 1926, p.1.
(In French, English, German, and Dutch.)

1927

Rapport annuel. Présenté au conseil d'administration et au comité de perfectionnement de l'Union Pédagogique Universelle.
[Annual Report to the Administrative Council and the Committee of the Union Pédagogique.]
In: Union Pédagogique Universelle II, année 1926-1927, p.5.

Les résultats de la conférence de Lausanne.
[Results of the Lausanne Meeting.]
(Letter to the president of the Union Internationale des Villes, signed by P. de Coubertin and G.E. Magnat.)
In: Union Pédagogique Universelle III, années 1926-1927, pp.6-7.

23 janv. La Fête de l'Empire espagnol.
[Spanish Festival.]
In: Le Figaro, 73e année, 23 janvier 1927 p.1.

5 avr. L'œuvre de l'Union Pédagogique Universelle. La renaissance du gymnase hellénique. La conférence de M. de Coubertin au Parnassos (jeudi, 31 mars 1927).
[The Work of the Union Pédagogique Universelle (Universal Educational Union): The Renaissance of the Hellenic Gymnasium. Lecture by Coubertin at the Parnassos.]
In: Le Messager d'Athènes, 5 avril 1927, p.3.
Later reprinted, in: Textes choisis, vol.I, pp.628-632.

22 avr. La peur. **[Fear.]**
In: Le Gymnaste Suisse, 6 année, 22 avril 1927, n° 17, p.1.
Extrait de: L'Education des Adolescents au XXe siècle. I. L'Education physique. La Gymnastique utilitaire, Paris, Alcan, 1905, pp.78-83.

juin A la jeunesse sportive de toutes les nations. Olympie, 17 avril 1927.
[To the Young Athletes of All Nations.]
Off-print, s.d.s.l. (1 page).
Later reprinted, in:
1) De Olympiade, 11 juin 1927, p.3. Published in French, English, and Dutch under the title: "Een brief van Baron Pierre de Coubertin aan de jeugd van alle landen".
2) Bulletin Officiel du IOC, juin 1927, p.5.
3) Le Gymnaste Suisse, 6e année, 3 juin 1927, n° 23, p.2.
4) Anthologie. Aix-en-Provence, P. Roubaud, 1933, p.176.
5) L'Idée Olympique, p.98.
6) Textes choisis, vol.II, p.412.
Later reprinted, in English, in:
The Olympic Idea, p.100,
under the title "To the Sporting Youth of All Nations", in: British Olympic Journal, vol. 1, autumn 1927, n°7, p.127.
in German, in: Der Olympische Gedanke, p.116.
in Spanish, in: Ideario Olímpico, pp.164-165.

8 juil. La vérité sportive. Les idées de Pierre de Coubertin. (An Open Letter to Frantz-Reichel, juin 1927.)
[The Truth about Sport. The Ideas of Pierre de Coubertin. (An Open Letter to Frantz-Reichel).]
In: Le Figaro, 73e année, 8 juillet 1927, p.2.
Later reprinted,
in French, in: L'Idée Olympique, pp.98-100.
in English, in: The Olympic Idea, pp.100-102.
in German, in: Der Olympische Gedanke, pp.116-118.
in Spanish, in: Ideario Olímpico, pp.165-168.

22 juil. La vie est un match...
[Life Is a Game.]
In: Le Gymnaste Suisse, 6e année, 22 juillet 1927, n° 30, p.1.

27 août A propos d'une "Histoire Universelle".
[Concerning a "World History."]
(Lettre au directeur de la Gazette de Lausanne.)
In: Gazette de Lausanne, 130e année, 27 août 1927, p.2.

sept. Les nouvelles Panathénées.
[The New Panathenean Games.]
In: Bulletin Officiel du Comité International Olympique, septembre 1927, pp.5-6.
Published under the title "The New Panathenaea", in: De Olympiade, 19 oct. 1927, p.4.
Later reprinted,
in French, in: L'Idée Olympique, pp.102-103.
in English, in: The Olympic Idea, pp.104-105.
in German, in: Der Olympische Gedanke, pp.120-122.
in Spanish, in: Ideario Olímpico, pp.170-173.

31 déc.-1er janv.
Paterne, Pierrefeu, Hellenus et moi, (I et II).
[Paterne, Pierrefeu, Hellenus, and I.]
In: L'Auto,
I: 28e année, 31 décembre 1927, p.1;
II: 29e année, 1er janvier 1928, p.1.
Later reprinted, in: Textes choisis, vol.III, pp.672-680.

1928

Hommage à Chavez.
[Tribute to Chavez.]
In: Anthologie. Aix-en-Provence, P. Roubaud, 1933, p.177.

L'Esprit sportif doit dominer toute autre considération.
[The Athletic Spirit Must Dominate All Other Issues.]
In: La Revue Sportive Illustrée, 24e année, n° 3, 1928 [p.24].
Later reprinted, in: Textes choisis, vol.II, p.413.

"La Cure de Sport la Santé à ceux qui la suivent".
[The Cure of Sports: From Sports to Health.]
In: La Revue Sportive Illustrée, 24e année, 1928, numéro spécial [p.41].

La chevalerie moderne.
[Modern Chivalry.]
In: 1) Officieel Feestnummer. Olympische Spelen te Amsterdam 1928. Textes recueillis par J. Feith/J. Hoven/ W.J.M. Linden-Gouda 1928 [p.8].
Later reprinted, in:
2) L'Idée Olympique, pp.100-102.
3) Textes choisis, vol.II, pp.290-291.
Later reprinted,
in English, in: The Olympic Idea, pp.102-103.
in German, in: Der Olympische Gedanke, pp.118-120.
in Spanish, in: Ideario Olímpico, pp.168-170.

18 janv. De Toekomst der Olympische Spelen.
[The Future of the Olympic Games. (Dutch Text)]
In: De Olympiade, 4e année, no 29, 18 janvier 1928, p.1.

18 janv. La confédération helvétique.
[Confederatio Helvetica.]
In: Le Gymnaste Suisse, 7e année, 18 janv. 1928, n° 30, p.2.

24 janv. La médecine sportive et le "cas morbide".
[Sports as a Medicine and the "Sick Case".]
In: Praxis - Revue Suisse de Médecine, 17e année, n° 4, 24 janv. 1928, pp.1-2.
Later reprinted, in: Textes choisis, vol.III, pp.650-653.

3 avr. La création du BIPS.
[The Founding of the Bureau International de Pédagogie Sportive. (International Bureau of Sports Pedagogy.]
In: Sport Suisse, 24e année, 3 avril 1928, p.1.

3 juil. La cure d'aviron.
[The Cure of Rowing.]
In: Praxis - Revue Suisse de Médecine, 17e année, n° 27, 3 juillet 1928, p.1-2.
Later reprinted, in
1) Off-print, Ouchy 1928, (15 pages).
2) Le Gymnaste Suisse, 8e année, 14 juin 1929, n° 24, p.1.
3) Textes choisis, vol.III, pp.226-231.

15 juil. Internationale Bedeutung der Olympischen Spiele.
[International Relevance of the Olympic Games. (German Text)]
In: Prager Presse, 15 juillet 1928, p.4.

18 juil. Olympische Gedachte.
[Olympic Ideas.]
In: De Telegraaf, 36e année, Amsterdam, 18 juillet 1928, s.p. .

27 août A la rédaction de Pro Sport, Lausanne. (Letter)
[Letter to the Editor of Pro Sport, Lausanne.]
In: Pro Sport, 5e année, 27 octobre 1928, n° 36, p.1.

oct. Message à tous les athlètes et participants aux Jeux Olympiques d'Amsterdam.
[Message to All Athletes and Participants Meeting at Amsterdam for the Ninth Olympiad.]
In: Le Gymnaste Suisse, 2e année, 14 août 1928, p.3.
Later reprinted, in:
1) Bulletin Officiel du Comité International Olympique, octobre 1928, pp.31-32.
2) Off-print (one page).
3) Comité Olympique Hollandais (Ed.): Rapport officiel des Jeux de la IXe Olympiade Amsterdam 1928. Amsterdam 1928, pp.11-12.
4) L'Idée Olympique, pp.103-104.
5) Textes choisis, vol.II, pp.476-477.
Published in German under the title: Das Olympische Testament, in: Mainzer Journal, 81e année, 3 août 1928, n° 180, p.6.
Published in English under the title "Farewell Message from Baron Coubertin", in: British Olympic Journal, vol. 1, décembre 1928, n° 11, p.210.
Later reprinted,
in English, in: The Olympic Idea, pp.105-106.
in German, in: Der Olympische Gedanke, pp.122-123.
in Spanish, in: Ideario Olímpico, pp.173-174.

21 nov.-28 nov.
L'utilisation pédagogique de l'activité sportive (I et II).
[Educational Uses of Athletic Activity.]
In: Le Sport Suisse, 24e année,
I: 21 novembre1928, n° 1074, p.1;
II: 28 novembre1928, n° 1075, p.1.
Off-print, 7 pages: Genève, Sport Suisse, 1928.
Later reprinted, in: Textes choisis, vol.I, pp.475-487.

déc. Die Schweiz und die Olympische Bewegung.
[Switzerland and the Olympic Movement.]
In: Wagner, J./Klipstein, F./Messerli, Fr. (Ed.): Die Olympischen Spiele 1928 St. Moritz-Amsterdam. Zürich/Stuttgart, Verlag Julius Wagner, 1928, p.6.

20 déc. Silhouettes disparues.
[**The Dear Departed:** Viktor Balck. William M.Sloane. Courcy Laffan].
In: La Gazette de Lausanne, 31e année, 20 décembre 1928, p.1.
Later reprinted, in: Textes choisis, vol.II, pp.352-355.

1929

* Religio athletae.
In: Bulletin du Bureau International de Pédagogie Sportive, Lausanne, s.d. [1929], n° 1, pp.5-6.

* Le domaine de l'activité musculaire.
[Muscular Activity.]
In: Bulletin du Bureau International de Pédagogie Sportive, Lausanne, s.d. [1929], n° 1, pp.3-4.

* La reprise des travaux du Congrès de Lausanne.
[Resumption of the Work of the Lausanne Congress.]
In: Bulletin du Bureau International de Pédagogie Sportive, Lausanne, s.d. [1929], n° 1, pp.6-14.
Later reprinted, in: Textes choisis, vol.III, pp.449-451.

mai Note sur le but et le fonctionnement du Bureau International de Pédagogie Sportive.
[Goal and Function of the Bureau International de Pédagogie Sportive. (International Bureau of Sports Pedagogy.]
In: Bulletin Officiel du Comité International Olympique, 4e année, mai 1929, n° 13, pp.13-14 et en allemand pp.31-32.
(Signed by Pierre de Coubertin, Paul Rosset, Col. Div. Guisan and Jean Rubattel.)
Off-print, (4 pages), Lausanne, avril 1928.
Later reprinted, in: Textes choisis, vol. I, pp.633-635.

mai Propagation des exercices physiques.
[Propagation of Physical Execises.]
In: Excelsior, 20e année, mai 1929.

juin Le principe de l'intermittence appliqué à la pédagogie sportive.
[The Principle of Variety in Physical Education. Summary of a lecture.]
In: Congrès national d'Education physique et d'Education morale de l'Athlète. Lausanne, 1929, pp.61-62.

10 juil.-31 juil.
Olympie. (Conférence donnée le 6 mars à la mairie du XVIe arrondissement, à Paris.)
[Olympia. Lecture Given in Paris, in the Festival Hall of the 16th Arrondissment Town Hall.]
In: Le Sport Suisse, 25e année,
I: 10 juillet 1929, n° 1112, p.1 ;
II: 17 juillet 1929, n° 1113, p.1
III: 24 juillet 1929, n° 1114, p.1 ;
IV: 31 juillet 1929, n° 1115, p.1.
Off-print, 12 pages, Genève, Imprimerie Burgi, 1929.
Later reprinted,
in French, in: 1) L'Idée Olympique, pp.98-100. 2) Textes choisis, vol.II, pp.414-429.
in English, in: The Olympic Idea, pp.106-119.
in German, in: Der Olympische Gedanke, pp.123-137.
in Spanish, in: Ideario Olímpico, pp.175-195.

18 août Monsieur le Ministre, ... [Lettre à Henry Pathé].
[To the Minister, Henry Pathé.]
In: Eyquem, M.-T.: Pierre de Coubertin. Paris, Calmann-Lévy, 1966, p.284.

nov. Union Pédagogique Universelle IV.
[Universal Education Union IV.]
Rapport général et conclusions. Lausanne, novembre1929 (22 pages).

1930

"L'or du Rhin". Quelques souvenirs du temps passé...
[Rhinegold.]
In: La Revue Sportive Illustrée, 26e année, 1930, numéro spécial [p.44].

Erkenne Dich selbst.
[Know Yourself. (German Text)]
In: Internationale Lehrfilmschau, Roma, 2e année, 1930, n° 7, pp.745-747.
Later reprinted, in French under the title "Le Sportif et le cinéma", in: Bulletin du Bureau International de Pédagogie sportive, Lausanne, s.d. [1932], n° 8, pp.7-9.
Later reprinted, in: Textes choisis, vol.III, pp.344-347.

* Les remèdes. I. La question des stades.
[Remedies: I. Stadiums.]
In: Bulletin du Bureau International de Pédagogie Sportive, Lausanne, s.d. [1930], n° 2, pp.3-6.
Later reprinted, in: Textes choisis, vol.II, pp.643-646.

Croquis sportifs.
[Sports Sketches.]
In: Bulletin du Bureau International de Pédagogie Sportive Lausanne, s.d. [1930], n° 2, pp.9-12.

* Angst und Sport.
[Sports and Fear.]
In: Bulletin du Bureau International de Pédagogie Sportive, Lausanne, s.d. [1930], n° 2, pp.12-14.

La charte de la réforme sportive.
[Charter of Sports Reform.]
In: Bulletin du Bureau International de Pédagogie Sportive, Lausanne, s.d. [1930], n° 3, pp.3-9.
Later reprinted, in:
1) Off-print, 7 pages: Lausanne, Bureau International de Pédagogie Sportive, s.d. [1930].
2) Le Sport Suisse, 26e année, 17 septembre 1930, p.1.
3) Le Gymnaste Suisse, 9e année, 3 octobre 1930, n° 40, pp.1-2.
4) Textes choisis, vol. I, pp.636-637.

* La gamme gymnique.
[The Scale of Physical Exercises.]
In: Bulletin du Bureau International de Pédagogie Sportive, Lausanne, s.d. [1930], n° 3, pp.10-12.
Later reprinted, in Spamish under the title "La gama gimnastica", in: Bulletin du Bureau International de Pédagogie Sportive, Lausanne, s.d. [1932], n° 8, pp.9- 12.
Later reprinted, in: Textes choisis, vol.III, pp.579-582.

Le sport peut-il enrayer la névrose universelle ?
[Can Sport Stop Neurosis?]
In: Bulletin du Bureau International de Pédagogie Sportive, Lausanne, s.d. [1930], n° 3, p.14.

10 janv. Je ne veux pas tarder...
[I Don't Want to Delay Things...]
(Billet de Pierre de Coubertin au Gymnaste Suisse.)
In: Le Gymnaste Suisse, 9e année, n° 2, 10 janvier 1930, p.3.

15 févr. Une lettre du Baron Pierre de Coubertin.
[A Letter by Baron de Coubertin.]
In: Le Sport Nautique. 1 année, no 23, 15 février 1930, pp.706-707.

26 fév. Olympisme.
[Olympism.]
In: Le Sport Suisse, 26e année, n° 1145, 26 février 1930, p.1. [Excerpt from a message sent to the President of the Hellenic Committee, Mr. Georges Averoff.]

26 mars Vers l'unité sportive.
[Towards a Unity of Sports.]
In: Le Sport Suisse, 26e année, 26 mars, n° 1151, p.1.

1931

* Une première victoire.
[First Victory.]
In: Bulletin du Bureau International de Pédagogie Sportive, Lausanne, s.d. [1931], n° 4, p.3.

* Athlète complet.
[The Complete Athlete.]
In: Bulletin du Bureau International de Pédagogie Sportive, Lausanne, s.d. [1931], n° 4, pp.3-5.

* Zorn und Sport.
[Anger and Sport.]
In: Bulletin du Bureau International de Pédagogie Sportive, Lausanne, s.d. [1931], n° 4, pp.6-9.

* Les remèdes. II. La réforme des parents et des maîtres.
[Remedies: II. The Reform of Parents and Teachers.]
In: Bulletin du Bureau International de Pédagogie Sportive, Lausanne, s.d. [1931], n° 4, pp.9-11.

* Is it true ?
In: Bulletin du Bureau International de Pédagogie Sportive, Lausanne, s.d. [1931], n° 4, pp.11-12.

* Devises nouvelles.
[New Mottoes.]
In: Bulletin du Bureau International de Pédagogie Sportive, Lausanne, s.d. [1931], n° 4, pp.12-14.
Later reprinted, in: Textes choisis, vol.II, pp.453-456.

* España en la cultura fisica y los deportes. **[Spanish]**
In: Bulletin du Bureau International de Pédagogie Sportive, Lausanne, s.d. [1931], n° 5, pp.3-5.

* La bataille continue.
[The Battle Continues.]
In: Bulletin du Bureau International de Pédagogie Sportive, Lausanne, s.d. [1931], n° 5, pp.5-7.
Later reprinted, in: Textes choisis, vol.II, pp.292-294.

* Les remèdes. III. Les institutions.
[Remedies: III. The Institutions.]
In: Bulletin du Bureau International de Pédagogie Sportive, Lausanne, s.d. [1931], n° 5, pp.7-12.
Later reprinted, in: Textes choisis, vol.III, pp.368-372.

* Colonisation sportive.
[Athletic Colonization.]
In: Bulletin du Bureau International de Pédagogie Sportive, Lausanne, s.d. [1931], n° 5, pp.12-14.
Later reprinted, in: Textes choisis, vol.II, pp.676-678.

* Heart disease.
In: Bulletin du Bureau International de Pédagogie Sportive, Lausanne, s.d. [1931], n° 5, p.14.

* L'école psycho-physiologique.
[The Psycho-Physiological School.]
In: Bulletin du Bureau International de Pédagogie Sportive, Lausanne, s.d. [1931], n° 6, pp.3-5.
Later reprinted, in: Textes choisis, vol.III, pp.401-404.

* Delphi und Olympia.
[Delphi and Olympia.]
In: Bulletin du Bureau International de Pédagogie Sportive, Lausanne, s.d. [1931], n° 6, pp.5-7.

* Les fléaux du jour affectent-ils la vie sportive et comment ? (I et II).
[Do the Scourges of Today Affect Sports?]
In: Bulletin du Bureau International de Pédagogie Sportive, Lausanne, s.d. [1931], n° 6, pp.7-11, n° 7, pp.7-10.

* La valeur pédagogique du cérémonial olympique.
[The Educational Value of the Olympic Ceremony.]
In: Bulletin du Bureau International de Pédagogie Sportive, Lausanne, s.d. [1931], n° 7, pp.3-5.
Later reprinted, in: Textes choisis, vol.II, pp.469-472.

* A forgotten side of the question.
In: Bulletin du Bureau International de Pédagogie Sportive, Lausanne, s.d. [1931], n° 7, pp.5-7.

* Archéologie intellectuelle.
[Intellectual Archaelogy.]
In: Bulletin du Bureau International de Pédagogie Sportive, Lausanne, s.d. [1931], n° 7, pp.10-11.

* Les trois carrières obligatoires.
[Three Ages.]
In: Bulletin du Bureau International de Pédagogie Sportive, Lausanne, s.d. [1931], n° 7, pp.11-12.

23 avr. La mission d'un Journal sportif.
Lettre de M. le Baron Pierre de Coubertin.
[The Mission of a Sports Newspaper.Letter by Baron Pierre de Coubertin.]
In: La Suisse Sportive, 35e année, 23 avril 1931, n° 1, p.5.

8 juil. Les Jeux Olympiques et la Gymnastique.
[The Olympic Games and Gymnastics.]
In: Le Sport Suisse, 27e année, 8 juillet 1931, n° 1239, p.1.
Later reprinted in French, in:
1) Le Gymnaste Suisse, 10e année, 24 juillet 1931, n° 30, pp.300-301.
2) Textes choisis, vol.II, pp.712-715.
3) L'Idée Olympique, pp.117-119.
in English, in: The Olympic Idea, pp.119-122.
in German, in: Der Olympische Gedanke, pp.138-140.
in Spanish, in: Ideario Olímpico, pp.195-198.

20 juil. Gedanken über die Erziehung zur individuellen Höchstleistung.
[Thoughts about an Education Leading to an Individual Supreme Performance. (German text)]
In: Neue Züricher Zeitung, 20 juillet 1931.

24 juil. Die Tendenz der modernen Sportbewegung.
[Tendencies in the Modern Sports Movement. (German text)]
In: Neue Züricher Zeitung, 24 juillet 1931, p.3.

8 déc.-27 mars 1932
Mémoires Olympiques. [Chapitres 1-25.]
[Olympic Memoirs.]
In: L'Auto,
1 - 32e année, 8 décembre 1931, n° 11315, p.1 ; [The Paris Congress and the Revival of the Olympic Games I]
2 - 32e année, 12 décembre 1931, n° 11319, p.2 ; [The Paris Congress and the Revival of the Olympic Games II]
3 - 32e année, 18 décembre 1931, n° 11325, p.2 ;
[The Conquest of Greece]
4 - 32e année, 23 décembre 1931, n° 11330, p.2 ;
[The First Olympiad: Athens 1896]
5 - 32e année, 29 décembre 1931, n° 11336, p.2 ;
[The Olympic Congress at Le Havre 1897. The Second Olympiad: Paris 1900]
6 - 33e année, 1er janvier 1932, n° 11339, p.2 ;
[The Second Olympiad: Paris 1900]
7 - 33e année, 5 janvier 1932, n° 11343, p.2 ;
[The Third Olympiad in the United States and the IOC Meeting in London]
8 - 33e année, 8 janvier 1932, n° 11346, p.2 ;
[A Succesful Congress and a Few Real Achievements]
9 - 33e année, 14 janvier 1932, n° 11352, p 2 ;
[The Inclusion of Literature and the Arts.The Fourth Olympiad: London 1908 I]
10 - 33e année, 19 janvier 1932, n° 11357, p.2 ;
[The Fourth Olympiad: London 1908 II]
11 - 33e année, 24 janvier 1932, n° 11362, p.2 ;
[The IOC in Berlin 1909]
12 - 33e année, 29 janvier 1932, n° 11367, p.2 ;
[Amateurism. Budapest 1911 I]
13 - 33e année, 2 février 1932, n° 11371, p.2 ;
[Budapest 1911 II.The Fifth Olympiad : Stockholm 1912 I] 33e année, 6 février 1932, n° 11375, p.2 ;
[The Fifth Olympiad : Stockholm 1912 II]
15 - 33e année, 10 février 1932, n° 11379, p.2 ;
[The Sports Psychologie Congress: Lausanne 1913]
16 - 33e année, 14 février 1932, n° 11383, p.2 ; [The 20th Anniversary of the Olympic Games : Paris 1914]
17 - 33e année, 20 février 1932, n° 11389, p.2 ;
[The Four War Years: 1914-1918]
18 - 33e année, 24 février 1932, n° 11393, p.2 ;
[The Seventh Olympiad : Antwerp 1920]
19 - 33e année, 28 février 1932, n° 11397, p.2 ;
[The 1921 Maneuver]
20 - 33e année, 2 mars 1932, n° 11400, p.2 ;
[Six Government Departments For One Stadium]
21 - 3e année, 6 mars 1932, n° 11404, p.2 ;
[The Capitol in Rome 1923]
22 - 33e année, 10 mars 1932, n° 11408, p.2 ;
[The Eighth Olympiad: Paris 1924]
23 - 33e année, 13 mars 1932, n° 11411, p.2 ;
[Prague 1925]
24 - 33e année, 20 mars 1932, n° 11418, p.2 ;
[Olympia 1927]
25 - 33e année, 27 mars,1932, n° 11425, p.2. [Legends]

Published in book form by the B.I.P.S. :
Mémoires Olympiques, Lausanne, B.I.P.S., 1932.
[Imprimé chez P. Roubaud, Aix-en-Provence.]
German translation by Gertraud John: Olympische Erinnerungen, Berlin, Limpert, 1936.
German translation in excepts by Curt Riess: Ein Leben für die Olympische Idee.
In: Die Woche, 34e année, 1932, pp.1013-1016 (I), pp.1043-1046 (II), pp.1075-1078 (III), n° 37, pp. II-IV.

1932

L'apothéose de l'Olympisme. Le magnifique succès des Jeux de la Xe Olympiade.
[The Apotheosis of Olympism.]
In: La Revue Sportive Illustrée, 28e année, 1932, n° 3, [p.26].
Later reprinted, in:
1) L'Idée Olympique, pp.121-123.
2) Textes choisis, vol.II, pp.298-299.
in English, in: The Olympic Idea, pp.124-125.
in German, in: Der Olympische Gedanke, pp.142-144.
in Spanish, in: Ideario Olímpico, pp.201-204.

* Le "Gymnase antique" rénové.
[Restoration of the Ancient Gymnasium.]
In: Bulletin du Bureau International de Pédagogie Sportive, Lausanne, s.d. [1932], n° 8, pp.3-4.
Later reprinted, in: Textes choisis, vol.III, pp.617-619.

Introduction.
[Introduction.]
In: Souvenir photographique officiel de la Xe Olympiade, 1932, p.11.

Préface.
[Foreword.]
In: Pescatore, M.: Chasses et voyages au Congo. Paris, Ed. de la Revue Mondiale, 1932, pp.5-9.

Discours de Monsieur le Baron de Coubertin prononcé au cours de la cérémonie en l'honneur de Monsieur le Baron de Coubertin à l'occasion de son 70e anniversaire.
[Address by Baron de Coubertin, Delivered at the Ceremony of His 70th Anniversary.]
In: 70e Anniversaire de Pierre de Coubertin, Publication du Comité Olympique Suisse et du Bureau International de Pédagogie Sportive, Lausanne 1932. Off-print.
Later reprinted,
in French, in: l'Idée Olympique. pp.120-121.

in English, in: The Olympic Idea, pp.122-123.
in German, in: Der Olympische Gedanke, pp.140-142.
in Spanish, in: Ideario Olímpico, pp.199-201.

4 mai-18 mai
Les assises de la cité prochaine.
[Conférence faite à Berne.]
[City of the Future.]
In: Le Sport Suisse, 28 année, 4 mai 1932, p 1 (I), 11 mai 1932, p.1 (II, III), 18 mai 1932, p.1, (IV).
Also published in brochure form.
Later reprinted, in: Textes choisis, vol.I, pp.638-650.

5 août Après la Fête fédérale, n'oubliez pas les bonnes fées...
[Don't Forget the Good Fairies after the Festival Is over.]
In: Le Gymnaste Suisse, 11e année, 5 août 1932, n° 32, p.365.

9 nov. La vérité sur la composition et le fonctionnement du Comité international olympique.
[The Truth about the Composition and the Functioning of the IOC.]
In: Sport Suisse, 28e année, 9 novembre1932, p.1.
(Excerpted from the " Mémoires Olympiques" published at the request of Pierre de Coubertin.)

23 nov. Le rôle du corps.
[The Role of the Body.]
In: Sport Suisse, 28e année, 23 novembre1932, p.1

30 nov. Le Sport soutien ou péril pour l'esprit.
[Sports: Support of or Danger for the Spirit.]
In: Sport Suisse, 28e année, 30 novembre1932, p.1

7 déc. Sports et divertissements.
[Sports and Diversion.]
In: Le Sport Suisse, 28e année, 7 décembre 1932, p.1

14 déc. La modération dans les Sports.
[Sports and Moderation.]
In: Sport Suisse, 28e année, 30 novembre1932, p.1.

1933

* Aarau, Prague, Los Angeles.
In: Bulletin du Bureau International de Pédagogie Sportive, Lausanne, s.d. [1933], n° 9, pp.3-7.
Later reprinted, in: Textes choisis, vol.II, pp.296-297.

* Le jiu-jitsu est-il un sport ?
[Is Jiu-Jitsu Sport?]
In: Bulletin du Bureau International de Pédagogie Sportive, Lausanne, s.d. [1933], n° 9, pp.11-13.
Later reprinted, in: Textes choisis, vol.III, pp.186-189.

* Bibliographie. **[Bibliography.]**
In: Bulletin du Bureau International de Pédagogie Sportive, Lausanne, s.d. [1933], n° 9, pp.13-14.

* L'hostilité européenne.
[European Hostility.]
In: Bulletin du Bureau International de Pédagogie Sportive, Lausanne, s.d. [1933], n° 10, pp.5-8.
Later reprinted, in: Textes choisis, vol.II, pp.300-303.

* In Memoriam.
[Obituary.]
In: Bulletin du Bureau International de Pédagogie Sportive, Lausanne, s.d. [1933], n° 10, pp.8-9.

* Sports équestres antiques.
[Horse-Riding in Classical Antiquity.]
In: Bulletin du Bureau International de Pédagogie Sportive, Lausanne, s.d. [1933], n° 10, pp.11-14.

An Expression.
In: Xth Olympiad Committee (Ed.): The Games of the Xth Olympiad. Official Report. Los Angeles 1933, p.11.

1934

J'ai été bien touché...
[I was moved...]
(Lettre à M. le Dr Messerli, président des Amitiés Gréco-Suisses, Lausanne, le 7 juillet 1934.)
In: Célébration du 40e Anniversaire du Rétablissement des Jeux Olympiques.
Publication de l'Association des Amitiés Gréco-Suisses et du Bureau International de Pédagogie Sportive, s.l. [1934], p.19.

L'Olympisme à l'école. Il faut l'encourager.
[Olympism at School: It Must Be Encouraged!]
In: La Revue Sportive Illustrée, 30e année, 1934, numéro exceptionnel, [p.36].
Later reprinted, in: Textes choisis, vol.II, pp.679-680.

Le XLe anniversaire de la rénovation des Jeux Olympiques.
[The XLth Anniversary of the Modern Olympic Games.]
In: La Revue Sportive Illustrée, 30e année, 1934, n° 2, [p.28].

31 janv. Le Bureau International de Pédagogie Sportive. Son but et sa doctrine.
[The Bureau International de Pédagogie Sportive. (International Bureau of Sports Pedagogy).]
In: Le Sport Suisse, 30e année, 31 janvier, n° 1371, p.1.

14 fév.-23 mai
Chronique du B.I.P.S. (II-IX).
[Chronicle of the Bureau International de Pédagogie Sportive. (International Bureau of Sports Pedagogy).]
In: Le Sport Suisse, 30e année,
14 février 1934, n° 1373, p.1: II. Réforme du vocabulaire ; **[Reform of the Terminology.]**
28 février 1934, n° 1375, p.1: III. Le sport et la politique ; **[Sports and Politics.]**

14 mars 1934, n° 1377, p.1: IV. [sic] L'enfant contre l'adulte ; [**The Grown-Up – the Child.**]
23 mars 1934, n° 1379, p.1: VI. Pierre angulaire ; [**Corner-Stone.**]
18 avril 1934, n° 1383, p.1: VII. La science contre le progrès ; [**Science against Progress.**]
2 mai 1934, n° 1385, p.1: VIII. Impolitesse et jargons ; [**Impoliteness and Jargon.**]
23ᵉ mai 1934, n° 1388, p.1-2: IX. Le B.I.P.S. et l'Olympisme. [**The International Bureau and Olympism.**]

4 juil. Quarante années d'Olympisme 1894-1934. (Allocution prononcée lors de la célébration du 40ᵉ anniversaire du rétablissement des Jeux Olympiques par le baron de Coubertin, le samedi 23 juin 1934 à l'aula de l'université de Lausanne.)
[Forty Years of Olympism, 1894-1934.]
In: Le Sport Suisse, 30ᵉ année, 4 juillet 1934, n° 1394, p.1.
Off-print: Genève, Le Sport Suisse, 1934 (3 pages).
Later reprinted, in:
1) Célébration du 40ᵉ anniversaire du Rétablissement des Jeux Olympiques. Publication de l'Association des Amitiés Gréco-Suisses et du Bureau International de Pédagogie Sportive, s.l. [1934], pp.15-18.
2) Bulletin Officiel du Comité International Olympique, 9ᵉ année, déc. 1934, n° 27, pp.7-9.
3) Textes choisis, vol.II, pp.346-351.
4) In French, in: l'Idée Olympique. pp.125-129.
In English, in: The Olympic Idea, pp.126-130.
In German, in: Der Olympische Gedanke, pp.145-149.
In Spanish, in: Ideario Olímpico, pp.205-212.

1935

Le sport est pacificateur... [Sport Is a Peacemaker.]
In: La Revue Sportive Illustrée, 31ᵉ année, 1935, numéro spécial [p.44].
Later reprinted, in excerpts, in:
1) L'Echo du Littoral et du Var, 24 février 1935.
2) Textes choisis, vol.I, pp.651-652.

Ver sacrum...
(Lettre du 29 janvier 1934.)
In: Diem, C.: Das Olympiade-Buch. Leipzig, Reclam, 1935, p.6.

5 août Pax olympica.
In: Pro Sport, 5 août 1935, p.1.

7 août Les Assises philosophiques de l'Olympisme moderne.
(Message radiodiffusé de Berlin, le 4 août 1935.)
[The Philosophical Foundation of Modern Olympism.]
In: Le Sport Suisse, 31ᵉ année, 7 août 1935, p.1.
Off-print: Genève, Le Sport Suisse, 1935 (4 pages).
Later reprinted, in:
1) Organisationskomitee für die XI. Olympiade Berlin 1936 (Ed.): Pax Olympica. Off-print, Berlin 1935, pp.8-16 (in French); pp.17-26 (in German).
2) Pro Sport, 13ᵉ année, 5 août 1935, n° 31, p.1. (In excerpts, under the title: "Pax Olympica".)
3) L'Idée Olympique, pp.129-132.
4) Olympische Rundschau, 3ᵉ année, juillet 1940, n° 10, p.1-3. [Excerpts published in German under the title: "Olympische Gedanken"].
5) Textes choisis, vol.II, pp.435-439.
6) In English, in: The Olympic Idea, pp.130-134.
In German, in: Der Olympische Gedanke, pp.150-154.
In Spanish, in: Ideario Olímpico, pp.212-218.

8 août Moralische und Soziale Wirkung des Sports. [**The Ethical and Social Impact of Sports.**]
In: Neue Freie Presse, Vienne 8 août 1935, n° 25469, p.7.

déc. L'Olympisme et la Politique.
[Olympism and Politics.]
In: La Revue Sportive Illustrée, 31ᵉ année, décembre 1935 [p.14]. Later reprinted, in:
1) La Revue Sportive Illustrée, 32ᵉ année, 1936, numéro spécial [p.38].
2) Textes choisis, vol.II, pp.440-441.

1936

La symphonie inachevée.
[The Unfinished Symphony.]
Mémoires, Vol.V. (Manuscrit, Navacelle Collection).
Later reprinted, in :
1) Y.P.Boulongne, La vie et l'œuvre pédagogique de Pierre de Coubertin. Ottawa, Leméac, 1975, pp.462-464.
2) Revue Olympique, no 99-100, 1976, pp.32-34.
Later reprinted in English, in: Olympic Review, no 99-100, 1976, pp.32-34.

Les prochains Jeux auront lieu à Tokio.
[The Next Games Will Be Held in Tokyo.]
In: La Revue Sportive Illustrée, 32ᵉ année, 1936, n° 3 [p.17].
Later reprinted, in: Textes choisis, vol.II, p.681.

mars Pourquoi j'ai retabli les Jeux Olympiques.
[**Why I Revived the Olympic Games.**]
In: Olympische Spiele 1936. Off. Organ der XI. Olympischen Spiele Berlin 1936 und der IV. Olympischen Winterspiele Garmisch-Partenkirchen, Berlin, März 1936, n° 10, p.27. [Facsimile of a letter dated 1913-14.]

24 juin Quellen und Grenzen sportlichen Aufstiegs (I-IV).
[The Origins and Limits of Athletic Progress. **(German text)**]
In: BZ am Mittag [Sportteil],
23 juin 1936, n° 150, (I) ;
24 juin 1936, n° 151, p.11, (II) ;
25 juin 1936, n° 152, (III) ;
26 juin 1936, n° 153, (IV).
Later reprinted in French under the title: "Les sources et les limites du progrès sportif", In:

1) Olympische Rundschau, 1ère année, 1938, n° 1, pp.1-2 (I) ; n° 3, pp.1-2 (II) ; n° 4, pp.1-2 (III) ; n° 5, pp.1-2 (IV).
2) Textes choisis, vol.I, pp.490-498.
3) Textes choisis, vol.II, pp.74-76. (chap.IV)

juil. Gespräch mit Baron Pierre de Coubertin. (Interview given to Otto Kriegk.)
[An Interview with Baron de Coubertin. (German text)]
In: Europäische Revue, 12e année, juillet 1936, n° 7, pp.609-614.

22 juil. Le Message du Rénovateur des Jeux Olympiques aux coureurs d'Olympie-Berlin.
[To the Olympia-Berlin Runners.]
In: Le Sport Suisse, 32e année, 22 juillet 1936, p.1.
Off-print: Genève, Le Sport Suisse, 1936 (1 page).
Later reprinted, in:
1) Pro Sport, 14e année, 3 août 1936, p.1.
2) L'Idée Olympique, Schorndorf, Hofmann, 1966, n° 56, pp.133-134.
3) Textes choisis, vol.II, pp.430-434.

août Message du Baron de Coubertin pour la clôture des Jeux Olympiques de Berlin.
[Message at the Close of the Berlin Games.] Manuscrit (IOC Archives).
Later reprinted in :
1) L'Idée Olympique, pp.134-135.
2) Textes choisis, vol.II, p.305.
in English, in : The Olympic Idea, pp.135-136.
in German, in: Der Olympische Gedanke, pp.155-156.
in Spanish, in: Ideario Olímpico, pp.220-221.

27 août Les Jeux à Tokio en 1940 ?... Déclarations de M. Pierre de Coubertin recueillies par André Lang.
[The Games in Tokyo in 1940? Comments by Mr. Pierre de Coubertin, Recorded by André Lang.]
In: Le Journal, 27 août 1936, n° 16019, p.1.
Later reprinted, in: Textes choisis, vol.II, pp.306-308.

4 et 5 sept.
Comment M. de Coubertin conçoit ses Jeux Olympiques. (Interview accordée à Fernand Lomazzi.)
[How Monsieur de Coubertin Understands His Olympic Games.Interview Recorded by Fernand Lomazzi.]
In: L'Auto, 4 sept. 1936, p.1 (I); 5 sept. 1936, p.1 (II).
Later reprinted in: Le Gymnaste Suisse, 15e année,
I: 11 septembre 1936, n° 37, pp.398-399 ;
II: 9 octobre 1936, n° 41, pp.437-439.

15 sept. Une lettre du Baron Pierre de Coubertin,
[A Letter of Baron Pierre de Coubertin.]
in: Le Temps, 15 sept. 1936.

sept.-nov.
Erinnerungen (I-III).
[Memoirs.]
In: Europäische Revue, 12e année 1936,
n° 9, septembre 1936, pp.703-710 : I. Erste Begegnung mit Deutschland / Innere und äußere Politik / Nationale Propaganda / Mein Programm / Aufbruch ;
[A First Impression of Germany. Home and Foreign Policies. National Propaganda. My Programme. Awakening. (German texts)]
n° 10, octobre 1936, pp.792-797 : II. Die Gewinnung Amerikas; **[America.]**
n° 42. novembre1936, pp.857-865 : III. Frankreich und Deutschland. **[France and Germany.]**

déc. Les universités, le sport et le devoir social.
[Unviersities, Sports, and Social Duties.]
In: Schweizer Hochschulzeitung, Zurich, décembre 1936, pp.45-47.
Later reprinted, in: Textes choisis, vol.III, pp.620-622.

1937

Discours de P. de Coubertin.
[Speech by Baron Pierre de Coubertin.]
In: Bulletin de l'Association des Anciens Elèves de l'Externat de la Rue de Madrid, n° 2, 7 juillet 1937.

1938

Die letzte Botschaft Baron de Coubertins.
In: Olympische Vorbereitungen für die Feier der XII. Olympiade in Tokyo 1940. Edité par: The Organizing Committee of the XIIth Olympiad Tokyo 1940. Tokyo 1938, p.3.
In English: Olympic Préparation for the Celebrations of the XIIth Olympiad Tokyo 1940. Tokyo 1938, p.3.
In French: Les préparations pour la célébration de la XIIe Olympiade, Tokyo 1940. Tokyo 1938, p.2.

INDEX OF NAMES

Bibliography of Coubertin's writings on pp. 759-827 not included

INDEX OF TOPICS

Bibliography of Coubertin's writings on pp. 759-827 not included

GEOGRAPHICAL INDEX

Bibliography of Coubertin's writings on pp. 759-827 not included

Coubertin's stele on the IOA grounds in Ancient Olympia, where his heart is buried in accordance with his will. (Photo: H.Lieb)

Printed in June 2000
by Imprimeries Réunies Lausanne SA, Renens

Printed in Switzerland

Le Congrès
de

Un soir de Novembre 1892...
grand amphithéatre de l'anc
teinté, si j'ai bonne mémoire
niches carrées d'où saillai
prélats qui devaient être Bo
maussade j'avais passé l
cherché quelque chose à dire
Mais les potaches présents
1892 pensaient à toute a
contemplaient, au centre, l
de coupe impeccable du plu
:dains d'alors le vicomte
peu avant, élu président de
sachant fort bien qu'il n'
:dain mais un homme de
:tère sûr. À ses cotés, se ten
Mr. Octave Gréard et le p
la cour du Grand Duc Wla
de patronner ce « jubilé »
au Bois de Boulogne le sur